THE PHYSICS PROBLEM SOLVER®

REGISTERED TRADEMARK

THE PHYSICS PROBLEM SOLVER®

REGISTERED TRADEMARK

Staff of Research and Education Association,

Dr. M. Fogiel, Chief Editor

Research and Education Association
505 Eighth Avenue
New York, N. Y. 10018

THE PHYSICS PROBLEM SOLVER®

Printed in the United States of America

Library of Congress Catalog Card Number 76-332

International Standard Book Number 0-87891-507-9

Revised Printing, 1984

PROBLEM SOLVER is a registered trademark of
Research and Education Association, New York, N. Y. 10018

WHAT THIS BOOK IS FOR

For as long as physics has been taught in schools, students have found this subject difficult to understand and learn. Despite the publication of hundreds of textbooks in this field, each one intended to provide an improvement over previous textbooks, students continue to remain perplexed, and the subject is often taken in class only to meet school/departmental requirements for a selected course of study.

In a study of the problem, REA found the following basic reasons underlying students' difficulties with physics taught in schools:

(a) No systematic rules of analysis have been developed which students may follow in a step-by-step manner to solve the usual problems encountered. This results from the fact that the numerous different conditions and principles which may be involved in a problem, lead to many possible different methods of solution. To prescribe a set of rules to be followed for each of the possible variations, would involve an enormous number of rules and steps to be searched through by students, and this task would perhaps be more burdensome than solving the problem directly with some accompanying trial and error to find the correct solution route.

(b) Textbooks currently available will usually explain a given principle in a few pages written by a professional who has an insight in the subject matter that is not shared by students. The explanations are often written in an abstract manner which leaves the students confused as to the application of the principle. The explanations given are not sufficiently detailed and extensive to make the student aware of the wide range of applications and different aspects of the principle being studied. The numerous possible variations of principles and their applications are usually not discussed, and it is left for the students to discover these for themselves while doing exercises. Accordingly, the average student is expected to rediscover that which has been long known and practiced, but not published or explained extensively.

(c) The examples usually following the explanation of a topic are too few in number and too simple to enable the student to obtain a thorough grasp of the principles involved. The explanations do not provide sufficient basis to enable a student to solve problems that may be subsequently assigned for homework or given on examinations.

The examples are presented in abbreviated form which leaves out much material between steps, and requires that students derive the omitted material themselves. As a result, students find the examples difficult to understand--contrary to the purpose of the examples.

Examples are, furthermore, often worded in a confusing manner. They do not state the problem and then present the solution. Instead, they pass through a general discussion, never revealing what is to be solved for.

Examples, also, do not always include diagrams/graphs, wherever appropriate, and students do not obtain the training to draw diagrams or graphs to simplify and organize their thinking.

(d) Students can learn the subject only by doing the exercises themselves and reviewing them in class, to obtain experience in applying the principles with their different ramifications.

In doing the exercises by themselves, students find that they are required to devote considerably more time to physics than to other subjects of comparable credits, because they are uncertain with regard to the selection and application of the theorems and principles involved. It is also often necessary for students to discover those "tricks" not revealed in their texts (or review books), that make it possible to solve problems easily. Students must usually resort to methods of trial-and-error to discover these "tricks", and as a result they find that they may sometimes spend several hours to solve a single problem.

(e) When reviewing the exercises in classrooms, instructors

usually request students to take turns in writing solutions on the boards and explaining them to the class. Students often find it difficult to explain in a manner that holds the interest of the class, and enables the remaining students to follow the material written on the boards. The remaining students seated in the class are, furthermore, too occupied with copying the material from the boards, to listen to the oral explanations and concentrate on the methods of solution.

This book is intended to aid students in physics to overcome the difficulties described, by supplying detailed illustrations of the solution methods which are usually not apparent to students. The solution methods are illustrated by problems selected from those that are most often assigned for class work and given on examinations. The problems are arranged in order of complexity to enable students to learn and understand a particular topic by reviewing the problems in sequence. The problems are illustrated with detailed step-by-step explanations, to save the students the large amount of time that is often needed to fill in the gaps that are usually found between steps of illustrations in textbooks or review/outline books.

The staff of REA considers physics a subject that is best learned by allowing students to view the methods of analysis and solution techniques themselves. This approach to learning the subject matter is similar to that practiced in various scientific laboratories, particularly in the medical fields.

In using this book, students may review and study the illustrated problems at their own pace; they are not limited to the time allowed for explaining problems on the board in class.

When students want to look up a particular type of problem and solution, they can readily locate it in the book by referring to the index which has been extensively prepared. It is also possible to locate a particular type of problem by glancing at just the material within the boxed portions. To facilitate rapid scanning of the problems, each problem has a heavy border around it. Furthermore, each problem is identified with a number immediately above the problem at the right-hand margin.

To obtain maximum benefit from the book, students should familiarize themselves with the section, "How To Use This Book," located in the front pages.

To meet the objectives of this book, staff members of REA have selected problems usually encountered in assignments and examinations, and have solved each problem meticulously to illustrate the steps which are usually difficult for students to comprehend. Gratitude for their patient work in this area is due to Michael Abrams, Philip Druck, Metin Durgut, Steven Landovitz, Rae Mendelson, and Daniel Wyschogrod. Anthony Longhitano deserves special praise for his contributions and conscientious efforts.

Gratitude is also expressed to the many persons involved in the difficult task of typing the manuscript with its endless changes, and to the REA art staff who prepared the numerous detailed illustrations together with the layout and physical features of the book.

Finally, special thanks are due to Helen Kaufmann for her unique talents to render those difficult border-line decisions and constructive suggestions related to the design and organization of the book.

Max Fogiel, Ph.D.
Program Director

HOW TO USE THIS BOOK

This book can be an invaluable aid to students in physics as a supplement to their textbooks. The book is subdivided into 37 chapters, each dealing with a separate topic. The subject matter is developed beginning with fundamental concepts of vector quantities and extending through all major fields currently studied in physics. For students in science and engineering, advanced problems and solution techniques have been included.

TO LEARN AND UNDERSTAND A TOPIC THOROUGHLY

1. Refer to your class text and read there the section pertaining to the topic. You should become acquainted with the principles dicussed there. These principles, however, may not be clear to you at that time.

2. Then locate the topic you are looking for by referring to the "Table of Contents" in the front of this book, "The Physics Problem Solver."

3. Turn to the page where the topic begins and review the problems under each topic, in the order given. For each topic, the problems are arranged in order of complexity, from the simplest to the most difficult. Some problems may appear similar to others, but each problem has been selected to illustrate a different point or solution method.

To learn and understand a topic thorougly and retain its contents, it will be generally necessary for students to review the problems several times. Repeated review is essential in order to gain experience in recognizing the principles that should be applied, and to select the best solution technique.

TO FIND A PARTICULAR PROBLEM

To locate one or more problems related to a particular

subject matter, refer to the index. In using the index, be certain to note that the numbers given there refer to problem numbers, not to page numbers. This arrangement of the index is intended to facilitate finding a problem more rapidly, since two or more problems may appear on a page.

If a particular type of problem cannot be found readily, it is recommended that the student refer to the "Table of Contents" in the front pages, and then turn to the chapter which is applicable to the problem being sought. By scanning or glancing at the material that is boxed, it will generally be possible to find problems related to the one being sought, without consuming considerable time. After the problems have been located, the solutions can be reviewed and studied in detail. For this purpose of locating problems rapidly, students should acquaint themselves with the organization of the books as found in the "Table of Contents."

In preparing for an exam, it is useful to find the topics to be covered in the exam from the Table of Contents, and then review the problems under those topics several times. This should equip the student with what might be needed for the exam.

CONTENTS

Chapter No. **Page No.**

1 VECTORS 1

Vector Fundamentals 1
Displacement Vectors 5
Velocity Vectors 13

2 STATICS 19

Force Systems in Equilibrium 19
Equilibrium Conditions for Forces and Moments 25
Static and Kinetic Friction 43

3 KINEMATICS 55

Fundamentals of Velocity and Acceleration, Free Fall 55
Vector Components of Velocity and Acceleration 75

4 DYNAMICS 88

Rectilinear 88
Gravitational Forces 120
Curvilinear Dynamics 137
Moments of Inertia 156
Rotation of Rigid Bodies About Fixed Axes 165
Rolling Bodies 181
Frames of Reference 201

5 ENERGY/POWER 210

Potential Energy 210
Kinetic Energy 214
Work and Energy Conversion 238
Power 265
Efficiency 271

6 IMPULSE/MOMENTUM 276

Linear 276
Angular Momentum 323

7 GYROSCOPIC MOTION 330

8 ELASTIC DEFORMATION 334

9 HARMONIC MOTION 343

10 **HYDROSTATICS/AEROSTATICS** 392
Density, Specific Gravity, Pressure 392
Buoyancy Effects 395
Fluid Forces 405
Capillary Action 418

11 **HYDRODYNAMICS/AERODYNAMICS** 424

12 **TEMPERATURE, THERMOMETRY, THERMAL EXPANSION** 439

13 **HEAT/CALORIMETRY** 452
Thermal Energy 452
Heat of Fusion 458
Calorimetry 462

14 **GASES** 472
Atomic/Molecular Characteristics of Gases 472
Gas Laws 486

15 **THERMODYNAMICS** 506
Entropy 506
Work/Heat Cycles 510

16 **HEAT TRANSFER** 525
Thermal Conductivity 525
Heat Radiation 535

17 **ELECTROSTATICS-FUNDAMENTALS** 540

18 **ELECTROSTATIC INTERACTIONS AMONG PARTICLES AND BODIES** 567
Electrostatic Instruments 567
Capacitance 591

19 **ELECTRODYNAMICS** 608

20 **ELECTRIC CIRCUITS** 631
D.C. Circuit Elements and Instruments 631
Resistance-Temperature Characteristics 642
Resistor Networks 647
Capacitor and Inductor Networks 668

21 **MAGNETICS** 683
Magnetic Fields, Flux, Intensity, Permeability 683
Magnetic Forces 702
Magnetic Circuits 712

22 **MAGNETIC INDUCTION** 721

23 ALTERNATING CURRENTS/CIRCUITS 746

24 ELECTRIC POWER 761

25 WAVE MOTION 775
- Traveling and Standing Waves 775
- Electromagnetic Waves, Polarization 781
- Vibrating Rods and Strings 787

26 ACOUSTICS 795

27 GEOMETRICAL OPTICS 812
- Reflection 812
- Refraction 821
- Prisms 834

28 LENSES AND OPTICAL INSTRUMENTS 839
- Photometry 849

29 OPTICAL INTERFERENCE 853

30 OPTICAL DIFFRACTION/SPECTRA/COLOR 864

31 ATOMIC/MOLECULAR STRUCTURE 874

32 RELATIVISTIC EFFECTS 888

33 QUANTUM MECHANICS 915

34 RADIATION 974

35 X-RAYS 996

36 NUCLEAR ENERGY/REACTIONS 1006

37 SPECIAL ADVANCED PROBLEMS AND APPLICATIONS 1028
- Basic Kinetics and Kinematics 1028
- Energy Methods 1033
- Angular Momentum 1037
- Electromagnetics 1054
- Optical Diffraction and Interference 1060
- Doppler Effect 1068
- Traveling and Standing Waves 1070
- Polarization 1073
- Resistive Circuits 1078
- Basic Circuit Analysis 1081
- RL and RC Circuits 1086

INDEX 1093

CHAPTER 1

VECTORS

VECTOR FUNDAMENTALS

• PROBLEM 1

Find the resultant of the vectors $\vec{S}_1$ and $\vec{S}_2$ specified in the figure.

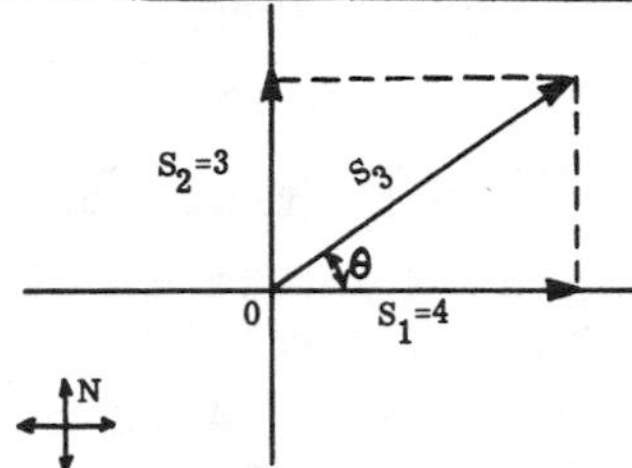

Solution. From the Pythagorean theorem, $S_1^2 + S_2^2 = S_3^2$, or $4^2 + 3^2 = S_3^2$, and $S_3 = 5$ units. The direction of S_3 may be specified by the angle θ which it makes with S_1.

$$\sin\theta = \frac{S_2}{S_3} = 0.60 \quad \text{gives } \theta = 37°.$$

Resultant $\vec{S}_3$ therefore represents a displacement of 5 ft from O in the direction 37° north of east.

• PROBLEM 2

Three forces acting at a point are $\vec{F}_1 = 2\hat{i} - \hat{j} + 3\hat{k}$, $\vec{F}_2 = -\hat{i} + 3\hat{j} + 2\hat{k}$, and $\vec{F}_3 = -\hat{i} + 2\hat{j} - \hat{k}$. Find the directions and magnitudes of $\vec{F}_1 + \vec{F}_2 + \vec{F}_3$, $\vec{F}_1 - \vec{F}_2 + \vec{F}_3$, and $\vec{F}_1 + \vec{F}_2 - \vec{F}_3$.

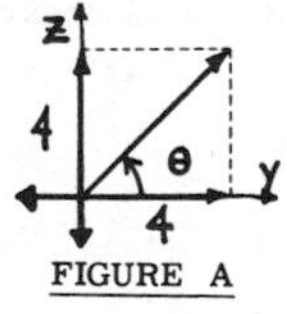

FIGURE A

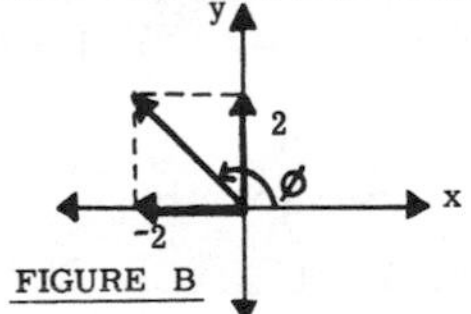

FIGURE B

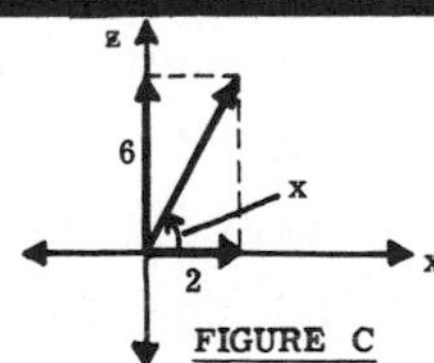

FIGURE C

Solution: When vectors are added (or subtracted), their components in the directions of the unit vectors add (or subtract) algebraically. Thus since

$$\vec{F}_1 = 2\hat{i} - \hat{j} + 3\hat{k},\ \vec{F}_2 = -\hat{i} + 3\hat{j} + 2\hat{k},\ \vec{F}_3 = -\hat{i} + 2\hat{j} - \hat{k},$$

then it follows that

$$\vec{F}_1 + \vec{F}_2 + \vec{F}_3 = (2 - 1 - 1)\hat{\imath} + (-1 + 3 + 2)\hat{\jmath}$$

$$+ (3 + 2 - 1)\hat{k}$$

$$= 0\hat{\imath} + 4\hat{\jmath} + 4\hat{k}.$$

Similarly,

$$\vec{F_1} - \vec{F_2} + \vec{F_3} = \left[2 - (-1) - 1\right]\hat{\imath} + \left[-1 - (3) + 2\right]\hat{\jmath} + \left[3 - (2) - 1\right]\hat{k}$$

$$= 2\hat{\imath} - 2\hat{\jmath} + 0\hat{k}$$

and $\vec{F_1} + \vec{F_2} - \vec{F_3} = \left[2 - 1 - (-1)\right]\hat{\imath} + \left[-1 + 3 - (2)\right]\hat{\jmath} + \left[3 + 2 - (-1)\right]\hat{k}$

$$= 2\hat{\imath} + 0\hat{\jmath} + 6\hat{k}$$

The vector $\vec{F_1} + \vec{F_2} + \vec{F_3}$ thus has no component in the x-direction, one of 4 units in the y-direction, and one of 4 units in the z-direction. It therefore has a magnitude of $\sqrt{4^2 + 4^2}$ units = $4\sqrt{2}$ units = 5.66 units, and lies in the y- z plane, making an angle θ with the y - axis, as shown in figure (a), where $\tan\theta = 4/4 = 1$. Thus $\theta = 45°$.

Similarly, $\vec{F_1} - \vec{F_2} + \vec{F_3}$ has a magnitude of $2\sqrt{2}$ units = 2.82 units, and lies in the x - y plane, making an angle ϕ with the x-axis, as shown in figure (b), where $\tan\phi = -2/2 = -1$. Thus $\phi = 135°$.

Also, $\vec{F_1} + \vec{F_2} - \vec{F_3}$ has a magnitude of $\sqrt{2^2 + 6^2}$ units = $2\sqrt{10}$ units = 6.32 units, and lies in the x - z plane at an angle χ to the x-axis, as shown in figure (c), where $\tan\chi = 6/2 = 3$. Thus $\chi = 71°34'$.

• PROBLEM 3

We consider the vector

$$\vec{A} = 3\hat{x} + \hat{y} + 2\hat{z}$$

(a) Find the length of $\vec{A}$.
(b) What is the length of the projection of $\vec{A}$ on the xy plane?
(c) Construct a vector in the xy plane and perpendicular to $\vec{A}$.
(d) Construct the unit vector $\hat{B}$.
(e) Find the scalar product with $\vec{A}$ of the vector $\vec{C} = 2\hat{x}$.
(f) Find the form of $\vec{A}$ and $\vec{C}$ in a reference frame obtained from the old reference frame by a rotation of $\pi/2$ clockwise looking along the positive z axis.
(g) Find the scalar product $\vec{A} \cdot \vec{C}$ in the primed coordinate system.
(h) Find the vector product $\vec{A} \times \vec{C}$.
(i) Form the vector $\vec{A} - \vec{C}$.

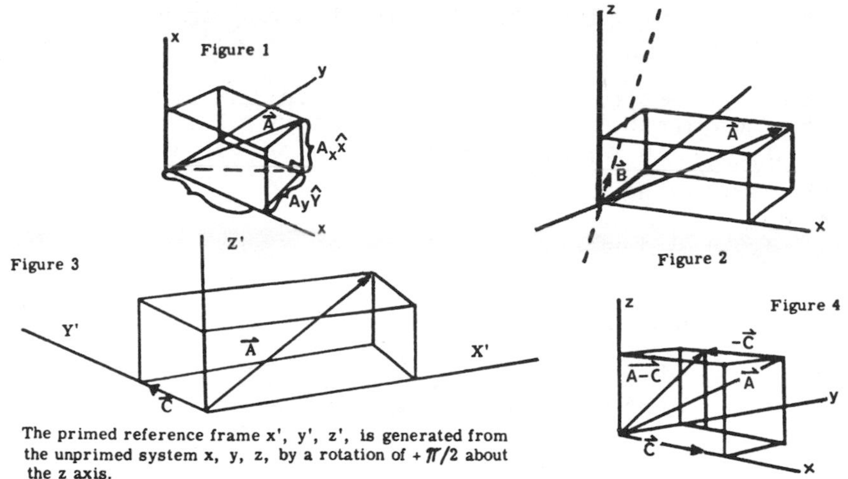

The primed reference frame x', y', z', is generated from the unprimed system x, y, z, by a rotation of $+\pi/2$ about the z axis.

Solution: (a) When a vector is given in the form $A_x\hat{x} + A_y\hat{y} + A_z\hat{z}$, its length is given by $\sqrt{A_x^2 + A_y^2 + A_z^2}$. This can be seen from diagram 1. Vector $\vec{A}$ has components in the x, y and z directions. The x and y components form the legs of a right triangle. By the Pythagorean theorem the length of the hypotenuse of this triangle is $\sqrt{A_x^2 + A_y^2}$. But this line segment whose length is $\sqrt{A_x^2 + A_y^2}$ is one leg in a right triangle whose other leg is $A_z\hat{z}$ and whose hypotenuse is vector $\vec{A}$. Applying the Pythagorean theorem again, we find that the length of $\vec{A}$ is $\sqrt{A_x^2 + A_y^2 + A_z^2}$. Substituting our values we have $\sqrt{3^2 + 1^2 + 2^2} = \sqrt{14}$.

(b) We refer again to diagram 1. The projection of $\vec{A}$ on the xy plane is simply the dotted line which is the vector $A_x\hat{x} + A_y\hat{y}$. Its length is $\sqrt{A_x^2 + A_y^2}$ by the Pythagorean theorem. In our problem, the length is $\sqrt{3^2 + 1^2} = \sqrt{10}$.

(c) Construct a vector in the xy plane and perpendicular to A. We want a vector of the form

$$B = B_x\hat{x} + B_y\hat{y}$$

with the property $A \cdot B = 0$ (since $\vec{A} \cdot \vec{B} = |\vec{A}||\vec{B}| \cos \phi$ where ϕ is the angle between $\vec{A}$ and $\vec{B}$). Hence

$$(3\hat{x} + \hat{y} + 2\hat{z}) \cdot \left(B_x\hat{x} + B_y\hat{y}\right) = 0.$$

On taking the scalar product we find

$$3B_x + B_y = 0,$$

or

$$\frac{B_y}{B_x} = -3.$$

The length of the vector B is not determined by the specification of the problem. We have therefore determined just the slope of vector B, not its magnitude. See diagram 2.

(d) The unit vector B is the vector in the B direction but with the magnitude 1. It lies in the xy plane, and its slope $\left(B_y/B_x\right)$ is equal to - 3. Therefore, $\hat{B}$ must satisfy the following two equations:

$$\hat{B}_x^{\,2} + \hat{B}_y^{\,2} = 1$$

$$\frac{\hat{B}_y}{\hat{B}_x} = -3$$

Solving simultaneously we have: $\hat{B}_x^{\,2} + \left(-3\hat{B}_x\right)^2 = 1$ or $\hat{B}_x = 1/\sqrt{10}$ and $\hat{B}_y = -3/\sqrt{10}$.

The vector B is then:

$$\hat{B} = (1/\sqrt{10})\hat{x} - (3/\sqrt{10})\hat{y}$$

(e) Converting the vectors into coordinate form and computing the dot product (scalar product):

$$(3\hat{x} + \hat{y} + 2\hat{z}) \cdot (2\hat{x} + 0\hat{y} + 0\hat{z}) =$$

$$6 + 0 + 0 = 6$$

(f) Find the form of $\vec{A}$ and $\vec{C}$ in a reference frame obtained from the old reference frame by a rotation of $\pi/2$ clockwise looking along the positive z axis. The new unit vectors $\hat{x}'$, $\hat{y}'$, $\hat{z}'$ are related to the old $\hat{x}$, $\hat{y}$, $\hat{z}$ by (see fig. 3)

$$\hat{x}' = \hat{y}; \quad \hat{y}' = -\hat{x}; \quad \hat{z}' = \hat{z}.$$

Where $\hat{x}$ appeared we now have $-\hat{y}'$; where $\hat{y}$ appeared, we now have $\hat{x}'$, so that

$$A = \hat{x}' - 3\hat{y}' + 2\hat{z}'; \qquad C = -2\hat{y}'.$$

(g) Using the results of part (f), we convert the vectors $\vec{A}$ and $\vec{C}$ into coordinate form in the primed coordinate system, giving us the following dot product:

$$\vec{A} \cdot \vec{C} = (\hat{x}' - 3\hat{y}' + 2\hat{z}') \cdot (0\hat{x}' - 2\hat{y}' + 0\hat{z}') =$$

$$0 + 6 + 0 = 6$$

This is exactly the result obtained in the unprimed system.

(h) Find the vector product $\vec{A} \times \vec{C}$. In the unprimed system $\vec{A} \times \vec{C}$ is defined as

$$\begin{vmatrix} \hat{x} & \hat{y} & \hat{z} \\ 3 & 1 & 2 \\ 2 & 0 & 0 \end{vmatrix} = 4\hat{y} - 2\hat{z}.$$

(i) Form the vector $\vec{A} - \vec{C}$. We have

$$\vec{A} - \vec{C} = (3 - 2)\hat{x} + \hat{y} + 2\hat{z} = \hat{x} + \hat{y} + 2\hat{z}.$$

• **PROBLEM 4**

Show that the area of a parallelogram, whose sides are formed by the vectors $\vec{B}$ and $\vec{C}$ (see figure) is given by

$$\text{Area} = |\vec{B} \times \vec{C}|.$$

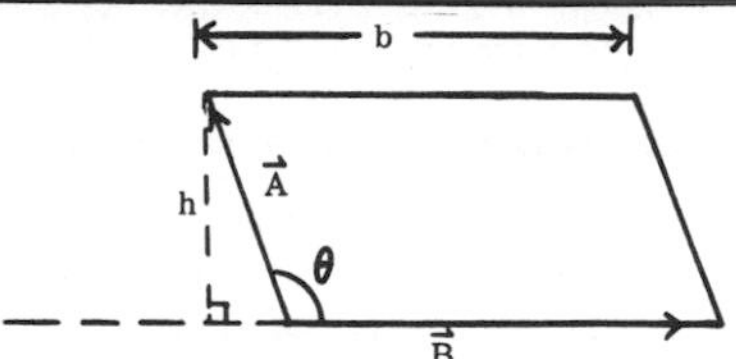

Solution: The area of the parallelogram shown in the figure is

$$\text{Area} = bh$$

But $h = |\vec{A}| \sin\theta$ and $b = |\vec{B}|$

$$\text{Area} = |\vec{A}||\vec{B}| \sin\theta \qquad (1)$$

The left side of (1) is the magnitude of $\vec{A} \times \vec{B}$, hence

$$\text{Area} = |\vec{A} \times \vec{B}| = |\vec{A}||\vec{B}| \sin\theta$$

If we are interested in obtaining a vector area, we may write

$$\vec{\text{Area}} = \vec{A} \times \vec{B}$$

where the direction of the area is the direction of $\vec{A} \times \vec{B}$. Such vector areas are useful in defining certain surface integrals used in physics.

DISPLACEMENT VECTORS

• **PROBLEM 5**

Two hikers set off in an eastward direction. Hiker 1 travels 3 km while hiker 2 travels 6 times the distance covered by hiker 1. What is the displacement of hiker 2?

Solution: From the information given the displacement vector is directed east. The magnitude of the displacement vector for hiker 2 is 6 times the magnitude of the displacement vector for hiker 1. Therefore, its magnitude is

$$6 \times (3 \text{ km}) = 18 \text{ km}$$

• **PROBLEM 6**

Two wires are attached to a corner fence post with the wires making an angle of 90° with each other. If each wire pulls on the post with a force of 50 pounds, what is the resultant force acting on the post? See Figure.

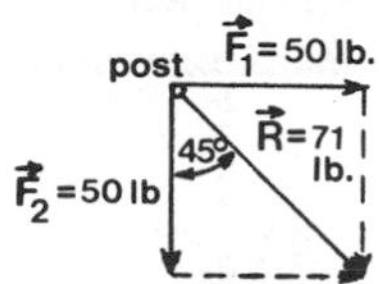

Solution: As shown in the figure, we complete the parallelogram. If we measure R and scale it, we find it is equal to about 71 pounds. The angle of the resultant is 45° from either of the component vectors.

If we use the fact that the component vectors are at right angles to each other, we can write

$$R^2 = 50^2 + 50^2$$

whence

$$R = 71 \text{ pounds approximately at } 45° \text{ to each wire.}$$

• PROBLEM 7

If a person walks 1 km north, 5 km west, 3 km south, and 7 km east, find the resultant displacement vector.

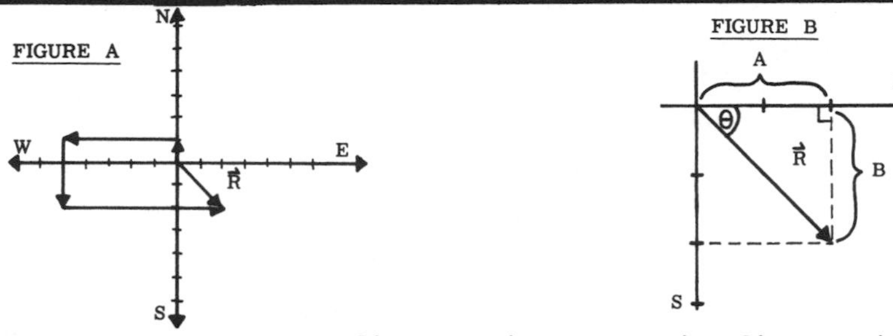

Solution: The vector diagram is shown in figure (a). The resultant displacement vector is labelled $\vec{R}$. The magnitude of this vector is 2.8 km. The direction, as measured with a protractor, is 45° south of east, or the tangent may be used to find the direction, since a right triangle is formed.

We shall also compute the solution analytically.

In figure (b) a closeup of the resultant vector $\vec{R}$ is shown. We can see from the graph that side A and side B each equal 2 km. Thus, by the Pythagorean theorem:

$$R^2 = A^2 + B^2 = (2 \text{ km})^2 + (2 \text{ km})^2 = 8 \text{ km}^2$$

$$R = 2\sqrt{2} \text{ km} = 2(1.4)\text{km} = 2.8 \text{ km}$$

$$\tan\theta = \frac{2 \text{ km}}{2 \text{ km}} = 1, \qquad \theta = 45°$$

$$\vec{R} = 2.8 \text{ km, } 45° \text{ south of east.}$$

• PROBLEM 8

An army recruit on a training exercise is instructed to walk due west for 5 mi, then in a northeasterly direction for 4 mi, and finally due north for 3 mi. When he completes his exercise, what is his resultant displacement $\vec{R}$? How far will he be from where he started?

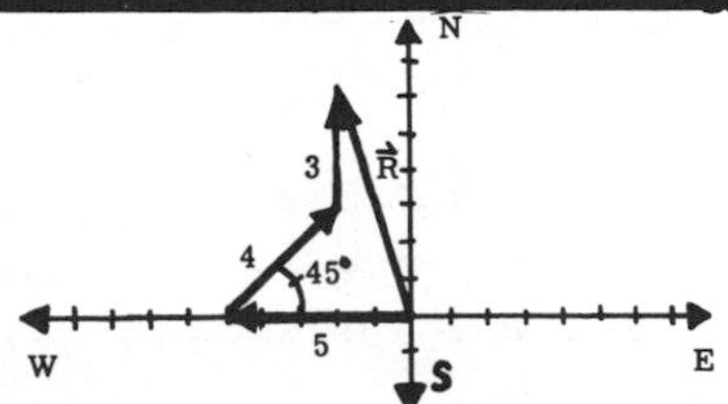

Solution: The recruit's path is shown in the figure, where each division on the graph represents one mile.

We find $\vec{R}$ by first adding the components of his individual displacements which we regard as vectors. We will let $\vec{E}$ and $\vec{N}$, representing east and north, be our unit vectors, regarding western and southern displacements as being negative eastern and negative northern displacements, respectively. Assume north & east are given equal weights. Then $\vec{NE}$ is as shown in the diagram. Thus, the sum of the components is:

$\vec{E}$	$\vec{N}$
-5 mi	0 mi
$4\cos 45°$ mi	$4\sin 45°$ mi
0 mi	3 mi
$(4\cos 45° - 5)$mi	$(4\cos 45° + 3)$mi

$$\vec{R} = \left[4\left(\frac{1}{\sqrt{2}}\right) - 5\right]\text{mi}\ \vec{E} + \left[4\left(\frac{1}{\sqrt{2}}\right) + 3\right]\vec{N}$$

$$= (2.8 - 5)\text{mi}\ \vec{E} + (2.8 + 3)\text{mi}\ \vec{N}$$

$$= -2.2\ \text{mi}\ \vec{E} + 5.8\ \text{mi}\ \vec{N}$$

The recruit's final distance from the starting point will be the magnitude of $\vec{R}$:

$$R = \sqrt{(-2.2\ \text{mi})^2 + (5.8\ \text{mi})^2} = 6.20\ \text{mi}$$

• PROBLEM 9

One of the holes on a golf course runs due west. When playing on it recently, a golfer sliced his tee shot badly and landed in thick rough 120 yd. WNW of the tee. The ball was in such a bad lie that he was forced to blast it SSW onto the fairway, where it came to rest 75 yd. from him. A chip shot onto the green, which carried 64 yd., took the ball to a point 6 ft. past the hole on a direct line from hole to tee. He sank the putt. What is the length of this hole? (Assume the golf course to be flat.)

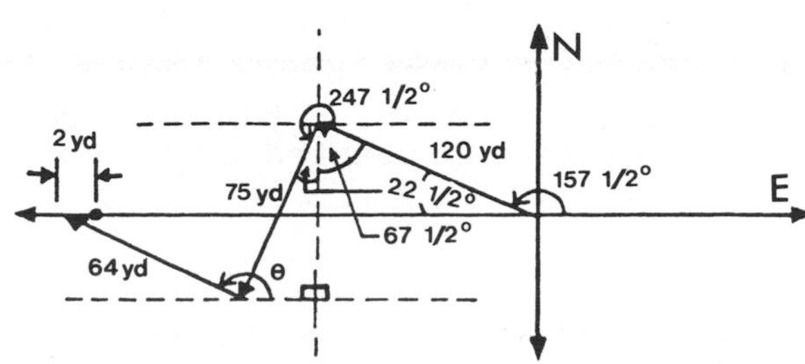

Solution: Since the course is flat, all displacements are in the one horizontal plane. Since we know that the hole is due west of the tee, we only need to calculate its easterly component which is the sum of the easterly components of the ball's displacements (see figure). We take east to be the positive abscissa of the axes shown, and the direction angles ϕ of all displacement vectors will be measured counter-clockwise from the positive east-axis.

Since we know that WNW means $22\frac{1}{2}°$ west of north-west, or $\phi = 157\frac{1}{2}°$, and that SSW means $22\frac{1}{2}°$ south of southwest, or $\phi = 247\frac{1}{2}°$;

$$\begin{aligned}\Sigma \text{ easterly components} &= 120 \cos 157\tfrac{1}{2}° \text{ yd} + 75 \cos 247\tfrac{1}{2}° \text{ yd} \\ &\quad + 64 \cos \theta \text{ yd} + 2 \text{ yd} \\ &= -\ 110.9 \text{ yd} - 28.7 \text{ yd} + 64 \cos \theta \text{ yd} \\ &\quad + 2 \text{ yd} \\ &= -\ 137.6 \text{ yd} + 64 \cos \theta \text{ yd}\end{aligned}$$

We can solve for θ by noting that the sum of the northerly components of displacement must equal zero:

$$\begin{aligned}\Sigma \text{ northerly components} &= 120 \sin 157\tfrac{1}{2}° \text{ yd} + 75 \sin 247\tfrac{1}{2}° \text{ yd} \\ &\quad + 64 \sin \theta \text{ yd} = 0\end{aligned}$$

$$\sin \theta = \frac{-\ 120 \sin 157\frac{1}{2}° - 75 \sin 247\frac{1}{2}°}{64} = \frac{-\ 45.9 + 69.3}{64}$$

$$= \frac{23.4}{64}$$

Thus:

$$\theta = 158.6°$$

$$\cos \theta = -\ 0.93125$$

Finally, inserting this into the equation for the sum of the easterly components:

$$\begin{aligned}\Sigma \text{ easterly components} &= -\ 137.6 \text{ yd} + 64(-\ 0.93125)\text{yd} \\ &= -\ 137.6 \text{ yd} - 59.6 \text{ yd} \\ &= -\ 197.2 \text{ yd}\end{aligned}$$

Thus, the hole is 197.2 yd due west of the tee.

• PROBLEM 10

Consider an airplane trip which takes place in four stages. Each stage is represented by a vector as follows (see figure).

A to B	AB = 120 mi	$\phi_1 = 30°$
B to C	BC = 50 mi	$\phi_2 = 60°$
C to D	CD = 700 mi	$\phi_3 = 210°$

D to E DE = 400 mi $\phi_4 = 90°$

The angle describing these vectors is with respect to the positive x-axis. Find the resultant displacement vector.

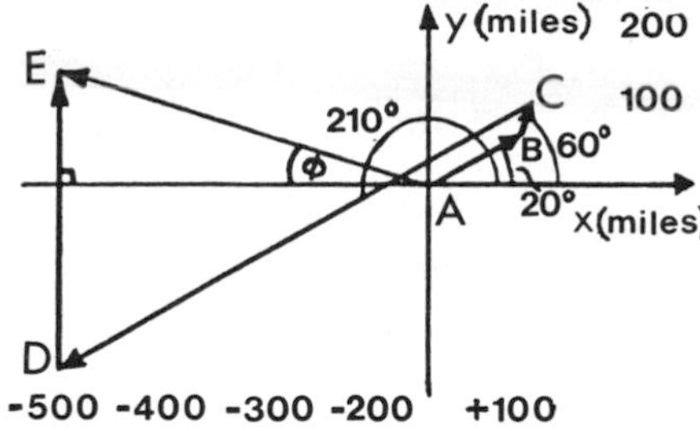

Solution: First we can calculate the x- and y-components.

$(AB)_x = AB \cos \phi_1$ $(AB)_y = AB \sin \phi_1$

$= 120 \cos 30 = 60\sqrt{3}$ mi $= 120 \sin 30 = 60$ mi

$(BC)_x = BC \cos \phi_2$ $(BC)_y = BC \sin \phi_2$

$= 50 \cos 60 = 25$ mi $= 50 \sin 60$

$= 25\sqrt{3}$ mi

$(CD)_x = CD \cos \phi_3$ $(CD)_y = CD \sin \phi_3$

$= 700 \cos 210$ $= 700 \sin 210$

$= -350\sqrt{3}$ mi $= -350$ mi

$(DE)_x = DE \cos \phi_4$ $(DE)_y = DE \sin \phi_4$

$= 400 \cos 90 = 0$ $= 400 \sin 90$

$= 400$ mi

These components are summed to find the x and y components of the resultant.

	x-component	y-component
AB	104 mi	60 mi
BC	25 mi	43 mi
CD	- 606 mi	- 350 mi
DE	0 mi	400 mi
Resultant AE	- 477 mi	153 mi

The magnitude of the resultant is therefore, by the Pythagorean theorem:

$$AE^2 = (-477)^2 + (153)^2$$

$$AE = 501 \text{ mi}$$

and its direction is given by the angle ϕ where

$$\sin \phi = \frac{153}{501} = 0.305$$

$$\cos \phi = \frac{-477}{501} = -0.952$$

$$\phi = 17.8°$$

The same thing can be found by making a graph (see figure). The resultant vector, AE, is drawn from the starting point A to the end point E of the trip.

• PROBLEM 11

A ship leaving its port sails due north for 30 miles and then 50 miles in a direction 60° east of north. See the Figure. At the end of this time where is the ship relative to its port?

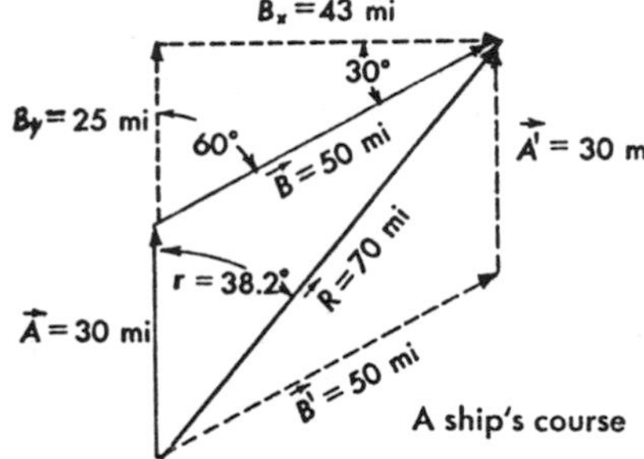

A ship's course

Solution by Parallelogram Method:

The figure shows the parallelogram completed by the dashed vectors $\vec{A}'$ and $\vec{B}'$. Also shown is the resultant $\vec{R}$ which is found to represent about 70 miles. Angle r is found to be about 38.2° east of north.

Solution by Component Method:

The figure also shows the vector $\vec{B}$ resolved into the components $\vec{B}_x$ and $\vec{B}_y$, which are found to be 43 miles and 25 miles, respectively. (By trigonometry

$\vec{B}_x$ = 50 miles × cos 30° = 43 miles, and

$\vec{B}_y$ = 50 miles × sin 30° = 25 miles).Since $\vec{A}$ and $\vec{B}$ lie along the same direction in this problem, we add them directly to get 30 miles + 25 miles, or 55 miles. We then have a right triangle with one side equal to 55 miles and the other side equal to 43 miles. From these data we find the resultant R according to the equation:

$$R^2 = 55^2 + 43^2$$

whence

$$R = \text{about } 70 \text{ miles}$$

Solution by the Cosine Law:

In solving this problem by means of the cosine law, we write

$$R^2 = A^2 + B^2 + 2\ AB \cos \theta$$

$$R^2 = 30^2 + 50^2 + 2 \times 30 \times 50 \times 0.5000$$

$$= 4900$$

whence the magnitude of R is

$$R = 70 \text{ miles}$$

$$\tan r = \frac{B \sin \theta}{A + B \cos \theta} = \frac{50 \times 0.866}{30 + 50 \times 0.500}$$

$$= 0.788$$

whence

$$r = 38.2° \text{ approximately.}$$

• PROBLEM 12

The crew of a spacecraft, which is out in space with the rocket motors switched off, experience no weight and can therefore glide through the air inside the craft.

The cabin of such a spaceship is a cube of side 15 ft. An astronaut working in one corner requires a tool which is in a cupboard in the diametrically opposite corner of the cabin. What is the minimum distance which he has to glide and at what angle to the floor must he launch himself?

If he decided instead to put on boots with magnetic soles which allow him to remain fixed to the metal of the cabin, and thus enable him to walk along the floor and, in the absence of gravitational effects, up the walls and across the ceiling, what is the minimum distance he needs to get to the cupboard?

Solution: Figure (a) shows the cabin. Axes have been set up with the x, y and z directions coinciding with the length, breadth, and height of the room. The astronaut must get from point A to point B. The vector $\vec{A}$ going from the origin 0 to point A is

$$\vec{A} = (15 \text{ ft}, 0, 0)$$

The vector from 0 to point B is:

$$\vec{B} = (0, 15 \text{ ft}, 15 \text{ ft})$$

The vector going from A to B is then:

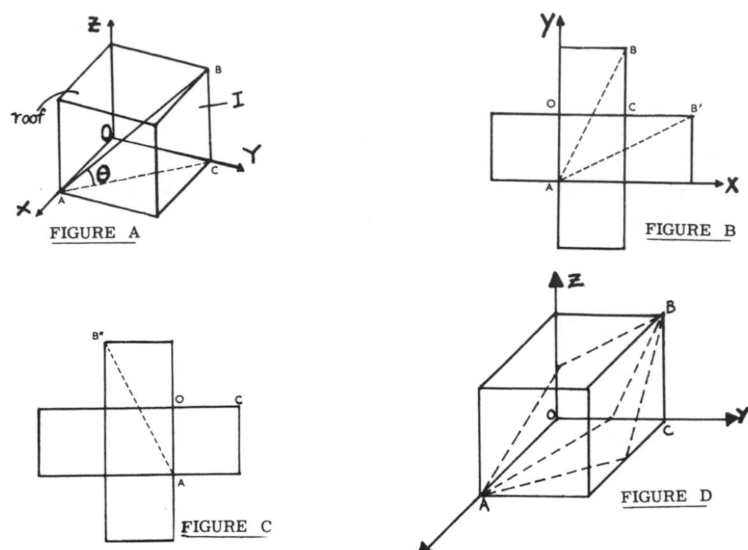

$\vec{B} - \vec{A} = (0,\ 15\ \text{ft},\ 15\ \text{ft}) - (15\ \text{ft},\ 0,\ 0)$

$= (-\ 15\ \text{ft},\ 15\ \text{ft},\ 15\ \text{ft})$

Its length is:

$|\vec{B} - \vec{A}| = \sqrt{(-\ 15\text{ft})^2 + (15\ \text{ft}^2) + (15\ \text{ft})} = 15\sqrt{3}\ \text{ft}$
$= 26\ \text{ft}$

This is the distance the astronaut must glide.

The angle to the floor at which he launches himself is θ, where tan θ = BC/AC. Point C has coordinates (0, 15 ft, 0). Thus BC has length 15 ft and AC has length $\sqrt{15^2 + 15^2}$ ft = 15 $\sqrt{2}$ ft = 21.2 ft.

$$\therefore \quad \tan\theta = \frac{15\ \text{ft}}{15\ \sqrt{2}\ \text{ft}} = \frac{1}{\sqrt{2}} = 0.707 \quad \text{or} \quad \theta = 35.25°.$$

Figure (b) shows the cabin minus the roof in an exploded diagram; points A, B, and C are again marked in. For convenience a new set of coordinate axes has been chosen. The astronaut walks the same distance along the walls from A to B by any particular route whether the walls are upright or flat as in the exploded diagram. But in the diagram it is much easier to see that the minimum distance from A to B is the straight-line path between the two points. The vector $\vec{B} - \vec{A}$ has components 15 ft in the x-direction and 30 ft in the y-direction. Distance $|\vec{B} - \vec{A}|$ therefore equals $\sqrt{15^2 + 30^2}$ ft = 33 ft 6½ in.

Note that B' is the same point as B in the exploded diagram; AB' is thus an alternative route. There is a further alternative route AB" which can be seen most clearly in figure (c) in which the wall marked I in figure (a) has been removed and the cabin exploded in a different way.

In figure (d), figure (a) is redrawn showing the routes the astronaut takes in figures (b) and (c) instead of his direct flight across the cabin.

In the first route, the astronaut crosses the floor and climbs a "breadth" wall; in the second, he crosses the floor and climbs a "length" wall; and in the third he crosses neither floor nor ceiling, but climbs two different walls. In this particular problem, since the cabin is cubical, all these routes are of the same length. In a problem in which the length ℓ, breadth b, and height h are all different, the three routes correspond to vectors having components $(\ell; b + h)$, $(b; \ell + h)$, and $(h; \ell + b)$. The shortest of these will be the one in which the x-component is the longest dimension and the y-component the sum of the other two.

VELOCITY VECTORS

• PROBLEM 13

An aircraft is climbing with a steady speed of 200 m/sec at an angle of 20° to the horizontal (see figure). What are the horizontal and vertical components of its velocity?

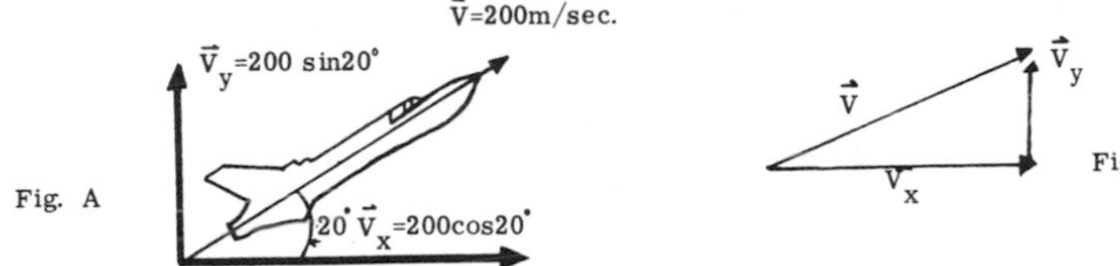

Solution: Using trigonometric relations for right triangles, the velocity can be broken down into two components perpendicular to each other.

Horizontal component = 200 cos 20°

Vertical component = 200 sin 20°.

Trigonometric tables tell us that

cos 20° = 0.9397 and sin 20° = 0.3420

Therefore, horizontal component = 200 × 0.9397
= 187.94 m/sec

Vertical component = 200 × 0.3420
= 68.40 m/sec.

Notice that the sum of 187.94 and 68.40 is not 200, but you can check that $(187.94)^2 + (68.40)^2 = (200)^2$. This occurs because the horizontal and vertical components, $\vec{V}_x$ and $\vec{V}_y$, of the velocity are vectors and must be added accordingly. Since they are pernependicular to each other, forming a right triangle with $\vec{V}$ as the hypotenuse,

$$V_x^2 + V_y^2 = V^2$$

• PROBLEM 14

An automobile driver, A, traveling relative to the earth at 65 mi/hr on a straight, level road, is ahead of motorcycle officer B, traveling in the same direction at 80 mi/hr. What is the velocity of B relative to A? Find the same quantity if B is ahead of A.

Solution: The velocity of B relative to A is equal to the velocity of B relative to the earth minus the velocity of A relative to the earth, or

$$V_{BA} = V_{BE} - V_{AE} = 80 \text{ mi/hr} - 65 \text{ mi/hr}$$

$$= 15 \text{ mi/hr}$$

If B is ahead of A, the velocity of B relative to A is still the velocity of B relative to the earth minus the velocity of A relative to the earth or 15 mi/hr.

In the first case, B is overtaking A, and, in the second, B is pulling ahead of A.

• PROBLEM 15

At $t_1 = 0$ an automobile is moving eastward with a velocity of 30 mi/hr. At $t_2 = 1$ min the automobile is moving northward at the same velocity. What average acceleration has the automobile experienced?

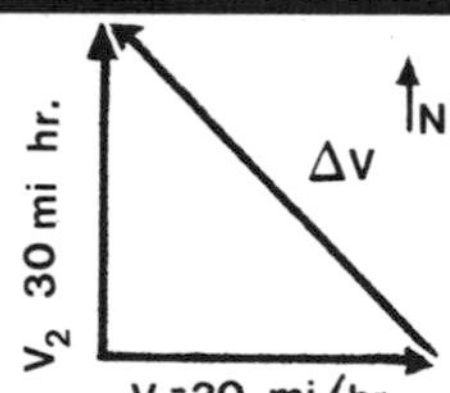

Solution: Since velocity is a vector quantity, vector addition must be used to solve this problem. Geometrically, when two vectors are added, the tail of the second vector is placed at the head of the first and the resultant vector is drawn from the tail of the first to the head of the second. To find the difference between the two velocities, we write

$$\vec{v}_2 - \vec{v}_1 = \Delta\vec{v}$$

Changing the expression above into one including only addition:

$$\vec{v}_2 = \Delta\vec{v} + \vec{v}_1$$

This is shown in the accompanying vector diagram.

The magnitude of Δv is (refer to the figure and use the Pythagorean theorem)

$$\Delta v = \sqrt{(30 \text{ mi/hr})^2 + (30 \text{ mi/hr})^2}$$

$$= \sqrt{1800 \text{ (mi/hr)}^2}$$

$$= 42.4 \text{ mi/hr}$$

The magnitude of the average acceleration is

$$\bar{a} = \frac{\Delta v}{\Delta t}$$

$$= \frac{42.4 \text{ mi/hr}}{60 \text{ sec}}$$

$$= 0.71 \text{ (mi/hr)/sec}$$

The direction of Δv, and hence the direction of a is, from the figure, in the direction northwest.

• PROBLEM 16

City A is 100 miles north and 200 miles west of city B. An airplane flies in a direct line between the cities in a time of one hour. What are the vectors that describe the distance of A from B, and the velocity of the airplane?

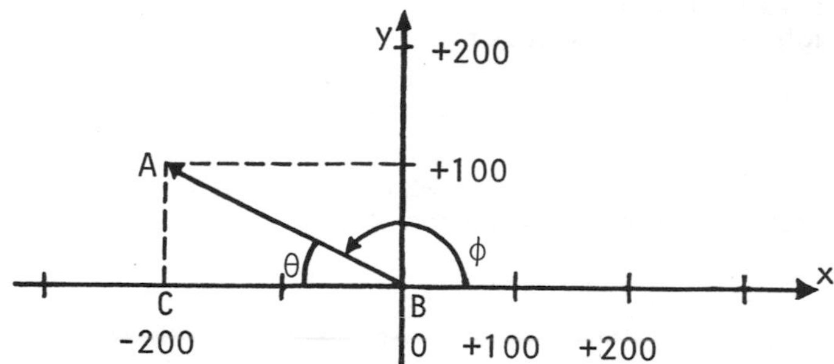

Solution: We will define first a coordinate system with B at the origin (see the figure below). The x-direction is east and the y-direction is north. The vector BA is specified by its coordinates

$$x = -200 \text{ mi}$$
$$y = 100 \text{ mi}$$

or by its magnitude and direction

$$(BA)^2 = x^2 + y^2$$

$$= \left((200)^2 + (100)^2\right)\text{mi}^2$$

$$BA = 100\sqrt{5} \text{ mi}$$

$$\sin\theta = \frac{CA}{BA} = \frac{100}{100}\sqrt{5} \doteq \frac{1}{\sqrt{5}}$$

$$\theta = 26.5^\circ$$

$$\phi = 180^\circ - \theta = 153.5^\circ$$

The velocities are given in a similar way. Since they are constant

$$V_x = \frac{x}{1 \text{ hr}} = \frac{-200 \text{ mi}}{1 \text{ hr}} = -200 \text{ mi/hr}$$

$$V_y = \frac{y}{1 \text{ hr}} = \frac{100 \text{ mi}}{1 \text{ hr}} = 100 \text{ mi/hr}$$

$$V^2 = V_x^2 + V_y^2 = \left((-200)^2 + (100)^2\right)\text{mi}^2/\text{hr}^2$$

$$V = 100\sqrt{5} \text{ mi/hr}$$

$$\phi = 153.5^\circ$$

• **PROBLEM 17**

A certain boat can move at a speed of 10 mi/hr in still water. The helmsman steers straight across a river in which the current is 4 mi/hr. What is the velocity of the boat?

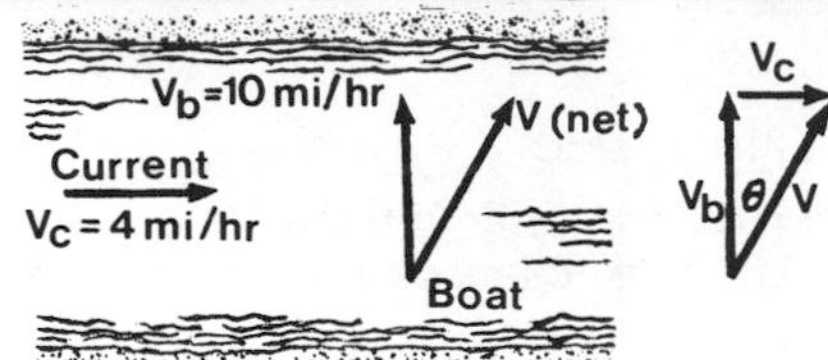

Solution: The boat has a speed of $v_b = 10$ mi/hr perpendicular to the river due to the power of the boat. The current gives it a speed of $v_c = 4$ mi/hr in the direction of flow of the river. The boat's resultant velocity (having both magnitude and direction) can be found through vector addition.

$$\vec{v} = \vec{v}_b + \vec{v}_c$$

The magnitude of the velocity which is the speed of the boat is found using the Pythagorean theorem (see figure).

$$v = \sqrt{v_b^2 + v_c^2}$$

$$= \sqrt{(10)^2 + (4)^2} = \sqrt{116}$$

$$= 10.8 \text{ mi/hr.}$$

The angle θ, which determines the direction of the velocity is,

$$\theta = \tan^{-1}\left(\frac{v_c}{v_b}\right)$$

$$= \tan^{-1}\left(\frac{4}{10}\right)$$

$$= 22°$$

• **PROBLEM 18**

A boy can throw a baseball horizontally with a speed of 20 m/sec. If he performs this feat in a convertible that is moving at 30 m/sec in a direction perpendicular to the direction in which he is throwing (see figure), what will be the actual speed and direction of motion of the baseball?

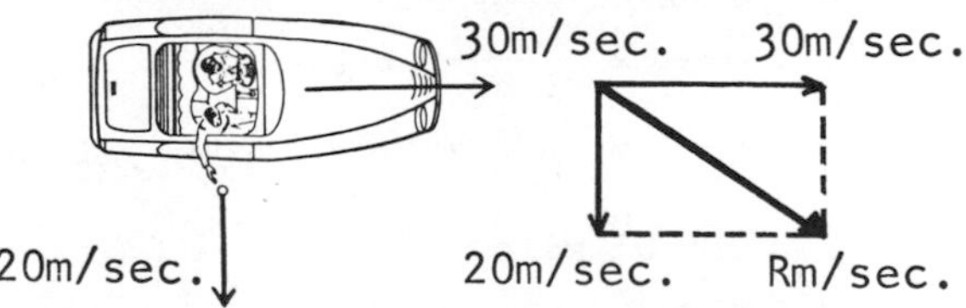

Solution: Since the baseball is originally travelling with the convertible, it has the speed of 30 m/sec in the direction the car is travelling. When the boy throws the ball perpendicular to the car's path, he imparts an additional velocity of 20 m/sec in that direction. The ball's velocity is then 30 m/sec in the direction the convertible is moving and 20 m/sec perpendicular to this movement. Its resultant velocity can be found through adding vectors as shown in the diagram.

If the resultant velocity is R m/sec at an angle θ to the direction in which the convertible is moving, then

$$R^2 = (20)^2 + (30)^2 = 1300$$
$$R = \sqrt{1300} = 36.06 \text{ m/sec}$$

Also, $\tan\theta = \frac{20}{30} = 0.666$

From tables of tangents, θ = 33.69°. Therefore, the ball has a speed of 36.06 m/sec in a direction at an angle of 33.69° to the direction in which the convertible is travelling.

• PROBLEM 19

An airplane, whose ground speed in still air is 200 mi/hr, is flying with its nose pointed due north. If there is a cross wind of 50 mi/hr in an easterly direction, what is the ground speed of the airplane?

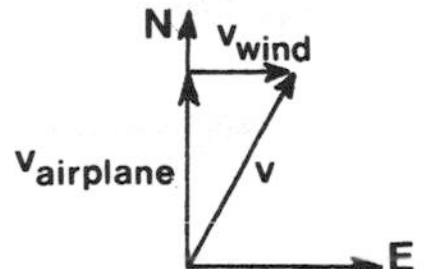

Solution: The cross wind causes the plane to travel 50 mi/hr to the east in addition to its speed of 200 mi/hr to the north. To find its speed with respect to ground, use vector addition. Vectors are quantities that have both magnitude and direction; and velocity fits this specification. Using the Pythagorean theorem, we can find the magnitude of the resultant velocity v. This magnitude is the plane's speed. Speed does not have direction (note that speed is not a vector).

$$v = \sqrt{v^2_{airplane} + v^2_{wind}}$$
$$= \sqrt{(200)^2 + (50)^2}$$
$$= \sqrt{42{,}500}$$
$$= 206 \text{ mi/hr.}$$

• PROBLEM 20

The compass of an aircraft indicates that it is headed due north, and its airspeed indicator shows that it is moving through the air at 120 mi/hr. If there is a wind of 50 mi/hr from west to east, what is the velocity of the aircraft relative to the earth?

Solution: Let subscript A refer to the aircraft, and subscript F to the moving air. Subscript E refers to the earth. We have given

$$v_{AF} = 120 \text{ mi/hr, due north}$$

$$\vec{v}_{FE} = 50 \text{ mi/hr, due east,}$$

and we wish to find the magnitude and direction of $\vec{v}_{AE}$. By the law of addition of velocities

$$\vec{v}_{AE} = \vec{v}_{AF} + \vec{v}_{FE}.$$

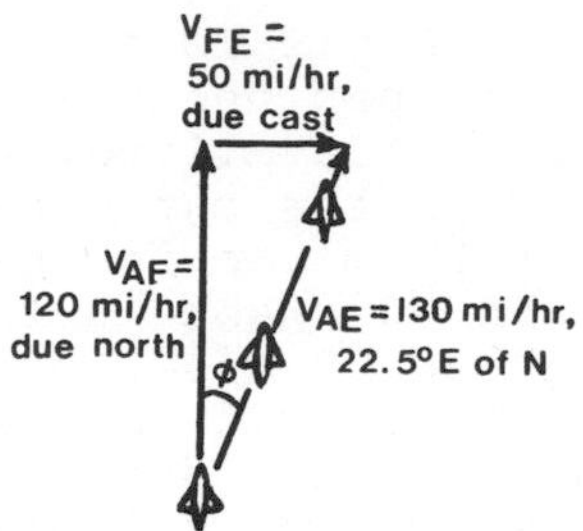

The three relative velocities are shown in the figure. It follows from this diagram that

$$|\vec{v}_{AE}| = 130 \text{ mi/hr}.$$

Furthermore,

$$\tan \varphi = \frac{50 \text{ mi/hr}}{120 \text{ mi/hr}}$$

and

$$\tan \varphi = .4167$$

$$\varphi = 22.5^{\circ}$$

The airplane travels at a speed of 130 mi/hr at an angle of 22.5° east of due north.

• PROBLEM 21

A plane has an airspeed of 120 mi/hr. What should be the plane's heading if it is to travel due north, relative to the earth, in a wind blowing with a velocity of 50 mi/hr in an easterly direction?

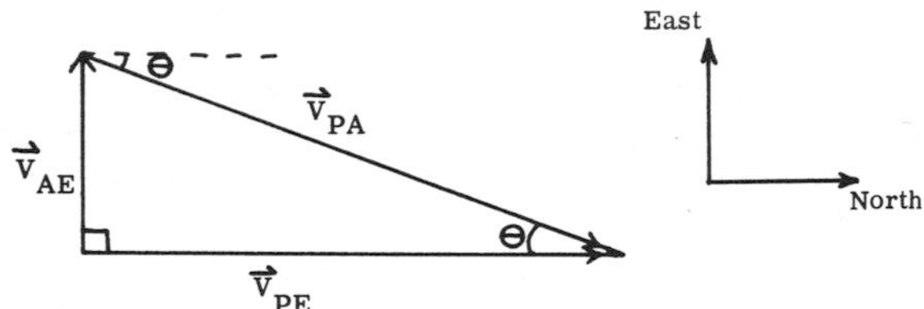

Solution: The figure shows the situation. The plane has a velocity relative to the air, $\vec{V}_{PA}$, of 120 mi/hr in a direction of θ degrees west of north. The air has a velocity relative to the earth of $\vec{V}_{AE}$ (50 mi/hr east). We require the plane to travel with speed v_{pa} due north. From the figure

$$\tan \theta = \frac{|\vec{V}_{AE}|}{|\vec{V}_{PE}|} = \frac{V_{AE}}{\left(V_{PA}{}^2 - V_{AE}{}^2\right)^{\frac{1}{2}}}$$

Here, we have used the Pythagorean theorem.

$$\tan \theta = \frac{50 \text{ mi/hr}}{\left((120 \text{ mi/hr})^2 - (50 \text{ mi/hr})^2\right)^{\frac{1}{2}}}$$

$$= \frac{50 \text{ mi/hr}}{109.09 \text{ mi/hr}}$$

$$= \tan^{-1} (.4584) \approx 24°38'.$$

CHAPTER 2

STATICS

FORCE SYSTEMS IN EQUILIBRIUM

• PROBLEM 22

A block hangs at rest from the ceiling by a vertical cord. Find the forces acting on the block and on the cord.

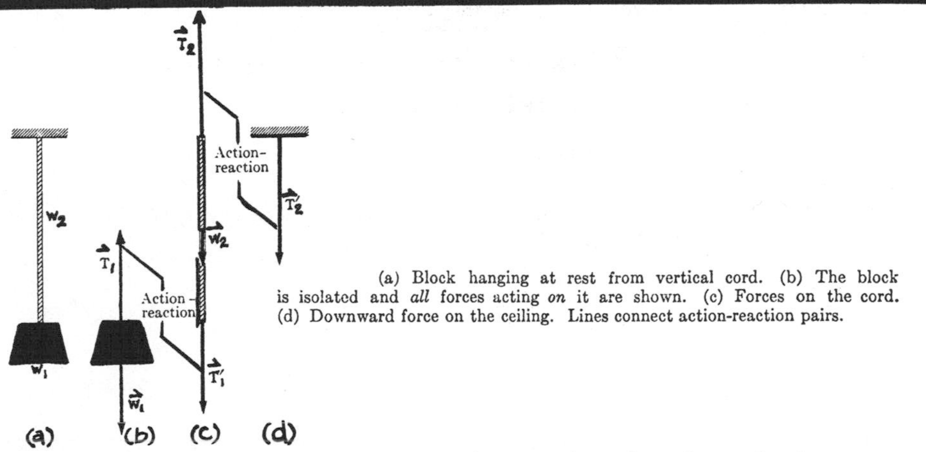

(a) Block hanging at rest from vertical cord. (b) The block is isolated and *all* forces acting *on* it are shown. (c) Forces on the cord. (d) Downward force on the ceiling. Lines connect action-reaction pairs.

Solution: Part (b) of the figure is the free-body diagram for the body. The forces on it are its weight $\vec{w}_1$ and the upward force $\vec{T}_1$ exerted on it by the cord. If we take the x-axis horizontal and the y-axis vertical, there are no x-components of force, and the y-components are the forces $\vec{w}_1$ and $\vec{T}_1$. Then, from the condition that $\Sigma F_y = 0$, we have

$$\Sigma F_y = T_1 - w_1 = 0, \qquad T_1 = w_1$$

from Newton's first law.

In order that both forces have the same line of action, the center of gravity of the body must lie vertically below the point of attachment of the cord.

Let us emphasize again that the forces $\vec{w}_1$ and $\vec{T}_1$ are not an action-reaction pair, although they are equal in magnitude, opposite in direction, and have the same line of action. The weight $\vec{w}_1$ is a force of attraction exerted on the body by the earth. Its reaction is an equal and opposite force of attraction exerted on the earth by the body. The reaction is one of the set of forces acting on the earth, and therefore it does not appear in the free-body diagram of the suspended block.

The reaction to the force $\vec{T}_1$ is an equal downward force, $\vec{T}'_1$, exerted on the cord by the suspended body.

$T_1 = T'_1$ (from Newton's third law).

The force $\vec{T}'_1$ is shown in part (c), which is the free-body diagram of the cord. The other forces on the cord are its own weight $\vec{w}_2$ and the upward force $\vec{T}_2$ exerted on its upper end by the ceiling. Since the cord is also in equilibrium,

$$\Sigma F_y = T_2 - w_2 - T'_1 = 0$$

$$T_2 = w_2 + T'_1 . \qquad \text{(1st law)}$$

The reaction to $\vec{T}_2$ is the downward force $\vec{T}'_2$ in part (d), exerted on the ceiling by the cord.

$$T_2 = T'_2 \qquad \text{(3rd law)}$$

As a numerical example, let the body weight 20 lb and the cord weigh 1 lb. Then

$$T_1 = w_1 = 20 \text{ lb},$$

$$T'_1 = T_1 = 20 \text{ lb},$$

$$T_2 = w_2 + T'_1 = 1 \text{ lb} + 20 \text{ lb} = 21 \text{ lb},$$

$$T'_2 = T_2 = 21 \text{ lb}.$$

• PROBLEM 23

Three forces acting on a particle and keeping it in equilibrium must be coplanar and concurrent. Show that the vectors representing the forces, when added in order, form a closed triangle; and further show that the magnitude of any force divided by the sine of the angle between the lines of action of the other two is a constant quantity.

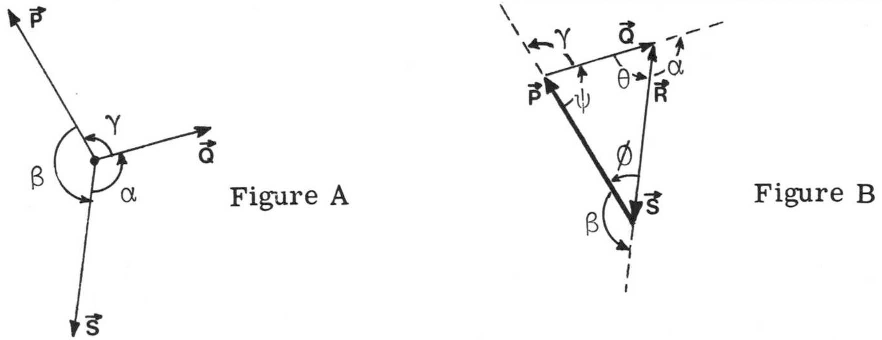

Solution: Let the three forces be $\vec{P}$, $\vec{Q}$, and $\vec{S}$, at angles α, β, and γ to one another as shown in figure (a). In order that the three forces shall be in equilibrium, the resultant $\vec{R}$ of $\vec{P}$ and $\vec{Q}$ must be equal and opposite to $\vec{S}$. The vectors $\vec{P}$, $\vec{Q}$, and $\vec{S}$ are concurrent and, since the vector $\vec{R}$ is in the same plane as $\vec{P}$ and $\vec{Q}$, they are coplanar.

But the resultant of $\vec{P}$ and $\vec{Q}$ is obtained by vector addition, as in figure (b). That is, $\vec{R}$ is the third side of the triangle formed by placing the tail of $\vec{Q}$ at the head of $\vec{P}$. The force $\vec{S}$ is equal and opposite to $\vec{R}$ and thus will occupy the same space as $\vec{R}$, the third side of the triangle, but will be opposite in direction to $\vec{R}$. Thus $\vec{P} + \vec{Q} + \vec{S}$ taken in order, form a closed triangle and their sum is of necessity zero. Applying the law of sines to the triangle of figure (b)

$$\frac{P}{\sin\theta} = \frac{Q}{\sin\phi} = \frac{S}{\sin\psi}$$

$$\therefore \frac{P}{\sin(180 - \alpha)} = \frac{Q}{\sin(180 - \beta)} = \frac{S}{\sin(180 - \gamma)}$$

$$\therefore \frac{P}{\sin\alpha} = \frac{Q}{\sin\beta} = \frac{S}{\sin\gamma} = \text{const.}$$

• PROBLEM 24

A 200 lb man hangs from the middle of a tightly stretched rope so that the angle between the rope and the horizontal direction is 5°, as shown in Figure A. Calculate the tension in the rope. (Figure B).

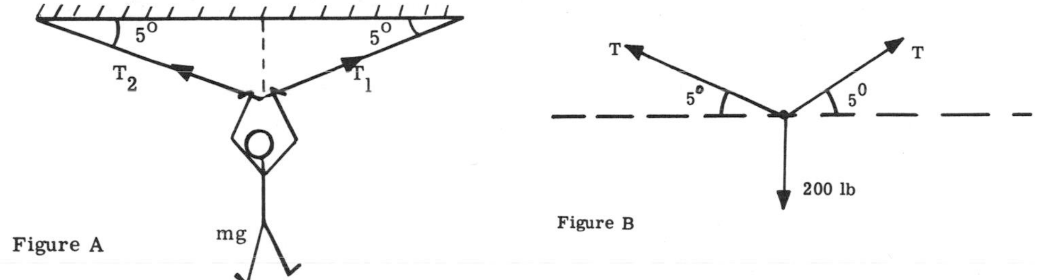

Solution: Since the two sections of the rope are symmetrical with respect to the man, the tensions in them must have the same magnitude, (Fig. B.) This can be arrived at by summing the forces in the horizontal direction and setting them equal to zero since the system is in equilibrium. Then

$$\Sigma F_x = T_1 \cos 5^\circ - T_2 \cos 5^\circ = 0$$

and

$$T_1 = T_2 = T$$

Considering the forces in the vertical direction,

$$\Sigma F_y = T \sin 5^\circ + T \sin 5^\circ - 200 \text{ lb} = 0$$

$$200 \text{ lb} = 2T \sin 5^\circ = 2T(0.0871)$$

$$T = \frac{(200)}{(2)(0.0871)} = 1150 \text{ lbs.}$$

Note the significant force that can be exerted on objects at either end of the rope by this arrangement. The tension in the rope is over five times the weight of the man. Had the angle been as small as 1°, the tension would have been

$$T = \frac{200}{2 \sin 1^\circ} = \frac{200}{(2)(0.0174)} = 5730 \text{ lbs.}$$

This technique for exerting a large force would only be useful to move something a very small distance, since any motion of one end of the rope would change the small angle considerably and the tension would decrease accordingly.

• PROBLEM 25

Find the tension in the cable shown in Figure A. Neglect the weight of the wooden boom.

Figure A

Figure B: Force Diagram

Solution: Take the directions of the tensions in the cable and the boom to be as shown in the force diagram(fig.B). We assume at this point, that the given directions are correct. However, the forces may turn out to point in the opposite direction. If this is the case, our solutions for the tensions will be negative. We can thus correct ourselves at the end of the problem. The first condition of equilibrium yields

$$\Sigma F_x = T_2 \cos 60^\circ - T_1 \cos 30^\circ = 0 \qquad (1)$$

$$\Sigma F_y = T_2 \sin 60^\circ - T_1 \sin 30^\circ - 2000 = 0 \qquad (2)$$

We wish to find T_1, the tension in the cable. Solving for T_2 in terms of T_1 in equation (1) gives

$$T_2 = \frac{T_1 \cos 30^\circ}{\cos 60^\circ}$$

Substituting this in equation (2),

$$\left(\frac{T_1 \cos 30^\circ}{\cos 60^\circ}\right) \sin 60^\circ - T_1 \sin 30^\circ = 2000$$

Solving for T_1:

$$T_1(\cos 30^\circ \tan 60^\circ - \sin 30^\circ) = 2000$$

$$T_1 = \frac{2000}{\cos 30^\circ \tan 60^\circ - \sin 30^\circ} = \frac{2000}{(0.8660)(1.7321) - (0.5000)}$$

$$= \frac{2000}{1.5 - 0.5} = 2000 \text{ lb}$$

Since our answer is positive, the force acts in the direction assumed in the beginning.

• PROBLEM 26

In figure A, a block of weight w hangs from a cord which is knotted at O to two other cords fastened to the ceiling. Find the tensions in these three cords. Let w = 50 lb, $\theta_2 = 30°$, and $\theta_3 = 60°$. The weights of the cords are negligible.

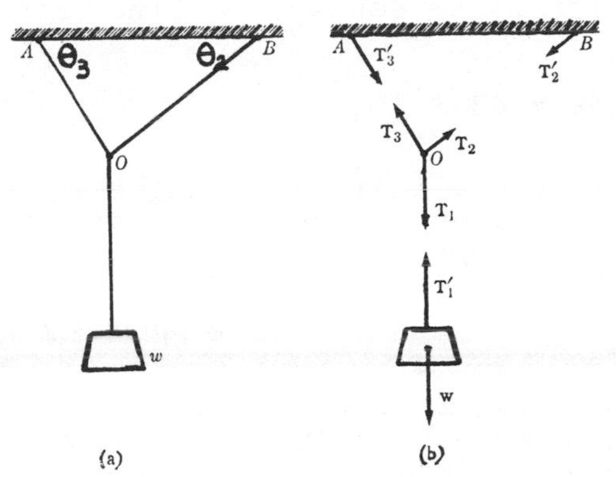

(a) A block hanging in equilibrium. (b) Forces acting on the block, on the knot, and on the ceiling.

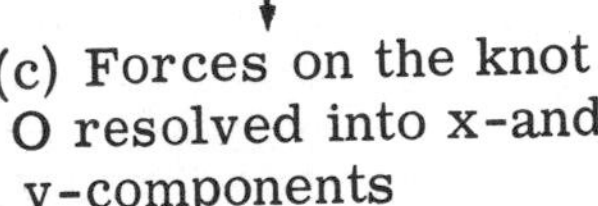

(c) Forces on the knot O resolved into x-and y-components

Solution: In order to use the conditions of equilibrium to compute an unknown force, we must consider some body which is in equilibrium and on which the desired force acts. The hanging block is one such body and the tension in the vertical cord supporting the block is equal to the weight of the block. The inclined cords do not exert forces on the block, but they do act on the knot at O. Hence, we consider the knot as a small body in equilibrium, whose own weight is negligible.

The free body diagrams for the block and the knot are shown in figure B, where $\vec{T_1}$, $\vec{T_2}$, and $\vec{T_3}$ represent the forces exerted on the knot by the three cords and $\vec{T_1'}$, $\vec{T_2'}$, and $\vec{T_3'}$ are the reactions to these forces.

Consider first the hanging block. Since it is in equilibrium,

$$T_1' = w = 50 \text{ lb}$$

Since $\vec{T_1}$ and $\vec{T_1'}$ form an action-reaction pair,

$$T_1' = T_1$$

Hence $T_1 = 50$ lb.

To find the forces $\vec{T_2}$ and $\vec{T_3}$, we resolve these forces (see fig. C) into rectangular components. Then, from Newton's second law,

$$\Sigma F_x = T_2 \cos\theta_2 - T_3 \cos\theta_3 = 0,$$

$$\Sigma F_y = T_2 \sin\theta_2 + T_3 \sin\theta_3 - T_1 = 0$$

We have $T_2 \cos 30^\circ - T_3 \cos 60^\circ = 0$

$$T_2 \sin 30^\circ + T_3 \sin 60^\circ = 50$$

or $0.866\, T_2 - 0.500\, T_3 = 0$

$$0.500\, T_2 + 0.866\, T_3 = 0$$

Solving these equations simultaneously, we find the tensions to be

$$T_2 = 25 \text{ lb}, \qquad T_3 = 43.3 \text{ lb}.$$

Finally, we know from Newton's third law that the inclined cords exert on the ceiling the forces $\vec{T}_2'$ and $\vec{T}_3'$, equal and opposite to $\vec{T}_2$ and $\vec{T}_3$, respectively.

• PROBLEM 27

A yule log is being dragged along an icy horizontal path by two horses. The owner keeps the log on the path by using a guide rope attached to the log at the same point as the traces from the horses. Someone in the adjacent woods fires a shotgun, which causes the horses to bolt to opposite sides of the path. One horse now exerts a pull at an angle of 45°, and the other an equal pull at an angle of 30°, relative to the original direction. What is the minimum force the man has to exert on the rope in order to keep the log moving along the path?

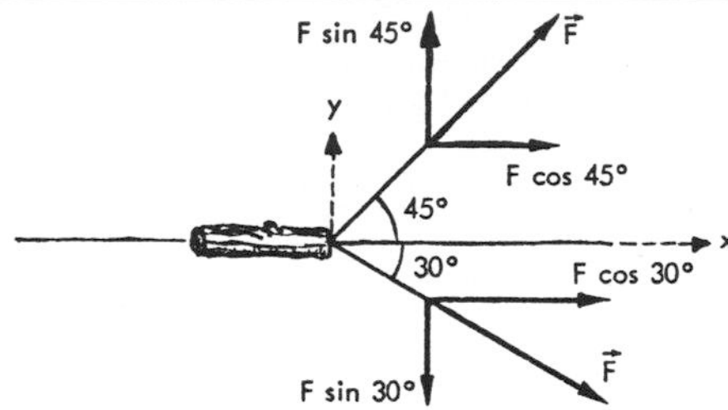

<u>Solution:</u> The figure shows the forces exerted on the log by the horses at the moment they bolt. These forces can be resolved into components along the path and at right angles to the path. Thus the total forces in the x- and y-directions are

$$\Sigma \vec{F}_x = F \cos 45° \hat{\imath} + F \cos 30° \hat{\imath}$$

and $$\Sigma \vec{F}_y = F \sin 45° \hat{\jmath} - F \sin 30° \hat{\imath}$$

where F is the magnitude of the force that each horse exerts.

To keep the log on the path the man must counteract the unbalanced force in the y-direction, $\Sigma \vec{F}_y$, by an equal and opposite force $- \Sigma \vec{F}_y$. We can see that any force he may have exerted to keep the log moving along the path, exerted in other than the y-direction of the figure, would not have been the minimum force possible. Any otherwise directed force would have an x-component as well as $- \Sigma \vec{F}_y$. But the latter alone could keep the log moving along the path. The magnitude of the resultant force would then have a greater magnitude than $- \Sigma \vec{F}_y$. Hence the minimum force he must exert has magnitude

$$P_y = F(\sin 45° - \sin 30°) = F\left(\frac{1}{\sqrt{2}} - \frac{1}{2}\right)$$

$$= 0.207\ F,$$

and must be directed in the negative y-direction, i.e., at right angles to the path.

In the above analysis, frictional forces have been ignored. The frictional force acting along the path does not affect the solution. The frictional force trying to prevent motion at right angles to the line of the path reduces the magnitude of the force the man need apply. It is, however, assumed that on an icy path this frictional force is small in comparison with F, and its effect is therefore ignored.

EQUILIBRIUM CONDITIONS FOR FORCES AND MOMENTS

• PROBLEM 28

A light horizontal bar is 4.0 ft long. A 3.0-lb force acts vertically upward on it 1.0 ft from the right-hand end. Find the torque about each end.

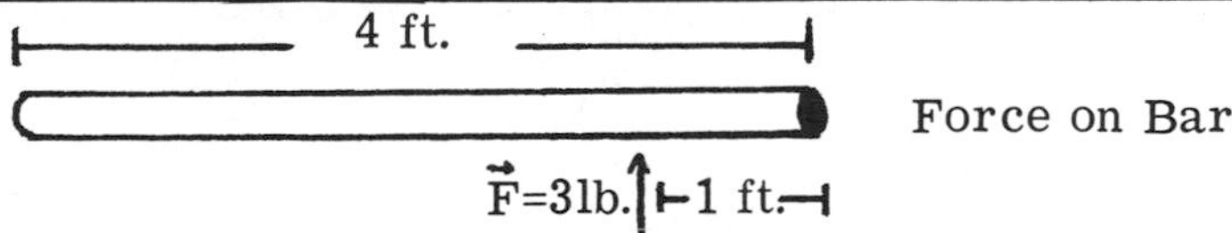

Solution: Since the force is perpendicular to the bar, the moment arms are measured along the bar.

About the right-hand end

$$L_r = 3.0 \text{ lb} \times 1.0 \text{ ft} = 3.0 \text{ lb-ft} \quad \text{clockwise}$$

About the left-hand end

$$L_1 = 3.0 \text{ lb} \times 3.0 \text{ ft} = 9.0 \text{ lb-ft counterclockwise}$$

The torques produced by this single force about the two axes differ in both magnitude and direction. This causes the bar to twist through an angle θ which is proportional to the torque.

• PROBLEM 29

A rigid rod whose own weight is negligible (see figure) is pivoted at point O and carries a body of weight w_1 at end A. Find the weight w_2 of a second body which must be attached at end B if the rod is to be in equilibrium, and find the force exerted on the rod by the pivot at O.

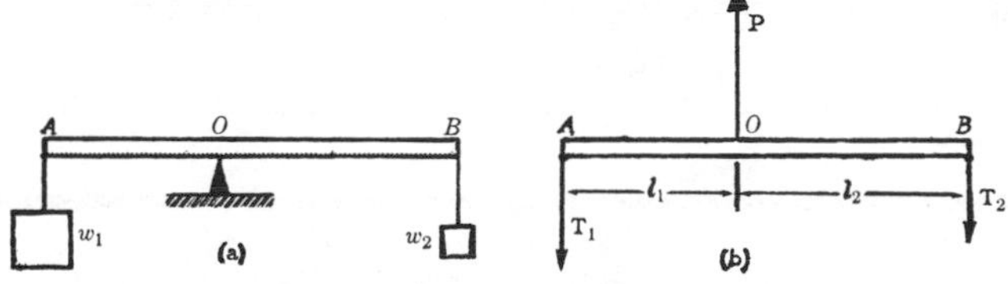

Solution: The question states that the rod is in equilibrium. In this case, the net force on the rod must be zero, and the net torque on the rod about the pivot must also be zero.

The forces on the rod are $\vec{T}_1$ and $\vec{T}_2$, the weights of masses 1 and 2, respectively, and $\vec{P}$, the force of the pivot on the rod. Hence

$$T_1 + T_2 - P = 0$$

or
$$T_1 + T_2 = P \qquad (1)$$

The torque about a point O is

$$\vec{\tau} = \vec{r} \times \vec{F}$$

where $\vec{r}$ is the vector from O locating the point of application of $\vec{F}$. The net torque about O is

$$T_2 \ell_2 - T_1 \ell_1 = 0$$

since the torque due to T_2 is opposite in direction to the torque due to T_1. Then

$$T_2 \ell_2 = T_1 \ell_1 \qquad (2)$$

Substituting (2) in (1)

$$T_1 + \frac{T_1 \ell_1}{\ell_2} = P$$

$$P = T_1 \left(1 + \frac{\ell_1}{\ell_2} \right)$$

But $T_1 = w_1$, and

$$P = w_1 \left(1 + \frac{\ell_1}{\ell_2} \right)$$

If $\ell_1 = 3$ ft, $\ell_2 = 4$ ft and $w_1 = 4$ lb

$$P = 4 \text{ lb} \left(1 + \frac{3}{4} \right) = 7 \text{ lb}$$

Furthermore, $T_2 = \dfrac{T_1 \ell_1}{\ell_2}$.

Since $T_2 = w_2$, and $T_1 = w_1$

$$w_2 = \frac{w_1 \ell_1}{\ell_2} = (4 \text{ lb}) \left(\frac{3}{4} \right) = 3 \text{ lb}$$

• PROBLEM 30

What scale readings would you predict when a uniform 120-lb plank 6.0 ft long is placed on two balances as shown in the figure, with 1.0 ft extending beyond the left support and 2.0 ft extending beyond the right support?

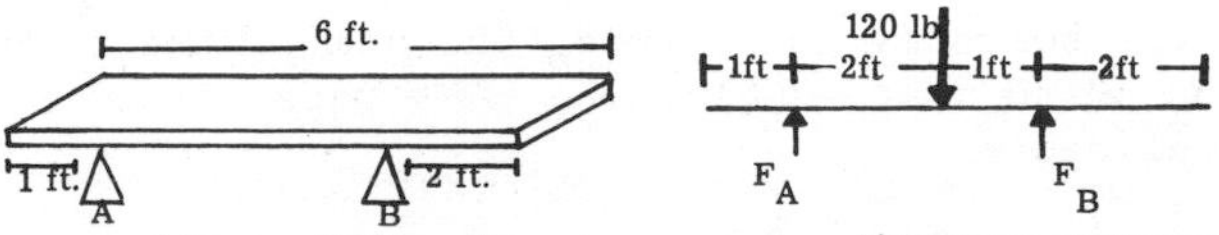

a) Beam with Supports b) Diagram of Forces

Solution: From the first condition for equilibrium, the forces upward must equal the forces downward,

$$F_A + F_B - 120 \text{ lb} = 0$$

The plank is uniform, meaning that the center of mass is at the center of the beam, three feet from each end. This is the point at which the 120 lb gravitational force can be considered to act.

Torque about a point is defined as the tendency of a force to cause rotation about the point. The magnitude of the torque is given by the product of the magnitude of the force and the perpendicular distance of the line of action of the force (the line along which the force acts) from the point of rotation. The direction of the torque can be found using the right hand rule. Place the fingers of the right hand in the direction of the distance vector. Rotate the distance vector into the direction of the force vector. If this rotation is in the clockwise direction, the torque is negative. For counterclockwise rotation, the torque is positive. For equilibrium, the sum of all the torques about any point in the body must equal zero.

To apply this second condition for equilibrium, we may choose to write torques about an axis through A, noting that the center of mass of the plank is 2.0 ft from A.

$$- 120 \text{ lb} \times 2.0 \text{ ft} + F_B(3.0 \text{ ft}) = 0 \text{ or } F_B = 80 \text{ lb}$$

Substitution of 80 lb for F_B in the first equation gives F_A = 40 lb. Alternatively, we may write a second torque equation, this time about an axis through B.

$$+ 120 \text{ lb} \times 1.0 \text{ ft} - F_A(3.0 \text{ ft}) = 0 \quad \text{or } F_A = 40 \text{ lb.}$$

• PROBLEM 31

(a) At what point should a uniform board 100 cm long be supported so that it balances a 10 gram mass placed at one end, a 60 gram mass on the other end, and a 40 gram mass 30 cm from the 10 gram mass (see figure). (b) What is the magnitude of the supporting force $\vec{F}$?

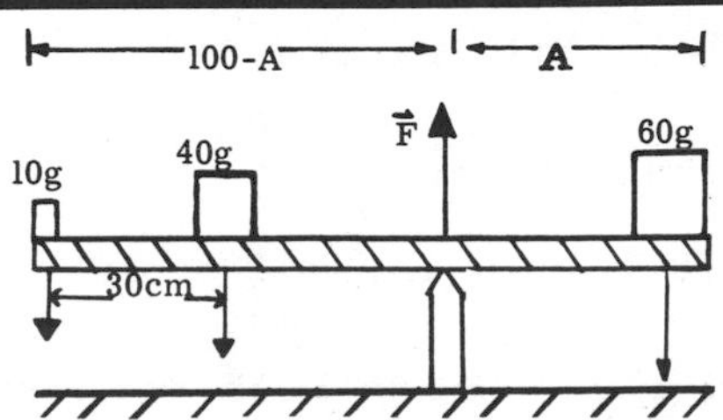

Solution: If the board is to balance, the sum of the moment about any point along the board must equal zero. A torque τ with respect to the point is defined as

$$\vec{\tau} = \vec{r} \times \vec{F}$$

where the direction of the torque is given by the right hand rule for the vector product of two vectors. For a two dimensional problem, such as this one, we note whether each torque produced is clockwise or counterclockwise; with clockwise torques taken as negative. This is done by noting the direction in which the fingers of the right hand must curl in order to swing $\vec{r}$ into $\vec{F}$ through the smaller angle θ between them. The magnitude of the torque is given by

$$\tau = rF \sin\theta .$$

For this problem, $\vec{r}$ and $\vec{F}$ are perpendicular so that the magnitudes of the torques are just rF. Since the force $\vec{F}$ produced at the support is unknown, we take moments about this point. In this case, $\vec{F}$ does not contribute to the net torque since its displacement vector is zero. We have

$$(10)(g)(100-A) + (40)(g)(100-A-30) - (60)(g)(A) = 0$$

where g is the acceleration due to gravity. We solve for A, the distance of point of support from the 60gm mass:

$$1000 - 10A + 4000 - 40A - 1200 - 60A = 0$$

$$110A = 3800$$
$$A = 34.5 \text{ cm}$$

(b) The force $\vec{F}$ can be found by applying the first condition of equilibrium in the vertical direction.

$$\Sigma F_y = 0 = F - (10)(g) - (40)(g) - (60)(g)$$

$$F = (110)(g) = (110 \text{ gm})(980 \text{ cm/sec}^2) = 1.078 \times 10^5 \text{ dynes} = 1.078 \text{ Newtons}$$

• PROBLEM 32

Locate the center of mass of the machine part in the figure consisting of a disk 2 in. in diameter and 1 in. long, and a rod 1 in. in diameter and 6 in. long, constructed of a homogeneous material.

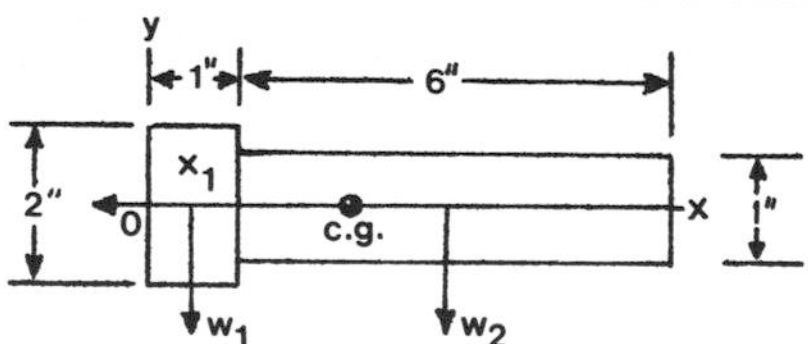

Solution: By symmetry, the center of mass lies on the axis and the center of mass of each part is midway between its ends.

The volume of the disk is:

$$v_d = \pi r^2 h = \pi(1 \text{ in})^2(1 \text{ in}) = \pi \text{ in}^3.$$

The volume of the rod is:

$$v_r = \pi r^2 h = \pi(\tfrac{1}{2} \text{ in})^2(6 \text{ in}) = \frac{3}{2}\pi \text{ in}^3$$

Since the disk and the rod are both constructed of the

same homogeneous material, the ratio of their masses will equal the ratio of their volumes:

$$\frac{\text{mass of disk}}{\text{mass of rod}} = \frac{m_d}{m_r} = \frac{\rho v_d}{\rho v_r} = \frac{\pi \text{ in}^3}{\frac{3}{2}\pi \text{ in}^3} = \frac{2}{3}$$

where ρ is their common density.

The formula for the distance of the center of mass from a given origin 0 is:

$$\bar{x} = \frac{m_d x_d + m_r x_r}{m_d + m_r}$$

where x_d and x_r are the distances of the centers of mass of m_d and m_r respectively from 0.

Take the origin 0 at the left face of the disk, on the axis. Then $x_d = \frac{1}{2}$ in., and $x_r = 4$ in. Since $m_d = 2/3\ m_r$

$$\bar{x} = \frac{\frac{2}{3} m_r (\frac{1}{2} \text{ in}) + m_r (4 \text{ in})}{\frac{2}{3} m_r + m_r} = 2.6 \text{ in.}$$

The center of gravity is on the axis, 2.6 in. to the right of 0.

• PROBLEM 33

A uniform eccentric drive wheel is circular and of radius 4 in. It has a circular hole cut in it, of radius ½ in., for the drive shaft. The center of the hole is ½ in. from the center of the wheel. What is the location of the center of gravity of the drive wheel?

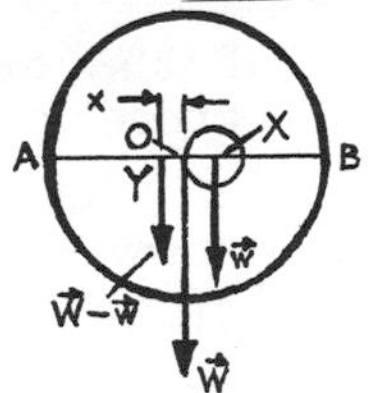

Solution: By symmetry the center of gravity must lie on the diameter AB which passes through O and X, the centers of the circular wheel and circular hole. Set AB horizontal and let Y, which is a distance x from O, be the location of the center of gravity of the drive wheel. Weights acting vertically are now at right angles to AB.

If the circular piece removed to form the hole were replaced, the resultant of the weight $\vec{W} - \vec{w}$ of the drive wheel plus the weight $\vec{w}$ of the piece replaced would have to be the weight $\vec{W}$ of the whole circle which acts at O. But the moment of the resultant weight about any point in the plane of the wheel must be equal to the sum of the moments about the same point of the individual forces making up the resultant. For simplicity let this point chosen be O.

The weight of the circle replaced must act at X (see figure).

The moment of the resultant weight about O is zero. Hence $(W - w)x - w \times \frac{1}{2}$ in. $= 0$.

$$\therefore \quad x = \tfrac{1}{2} \text{ in.} \times \frac{w}{W - w} \qquad (1)$$

But $\quad w = mg$

$$W - w = (M - m)g$$

where m is the mass of the piece originally occupying the space of the hole, and M - m is the mass of the drive wheel minus the hole. Then

$$x = \tfrac{1}{2} \text{ in.} \times \frac{m}{M - m} \qquad (2)$$

If σ is the surface density of the material of which the drive wheel is composed

$$m = \sigma\pi\ (\tfrac{1}{2} \text{ in.})^2$$

$$M - m = \sigma\pi\ \left((4 \text{ in.})^2 - (\tfrac{1}{2} \text{ in.})^2\right)$$

Using this in (2)

$$x = \tfrac{1}{2} \text{ in.} \times \frac{\sigma\ \pi\ (\tfrac{1}{4} \text{ in.}^2)}{\sigma\ \pi\ (16 - \tfrac{1}{4}) \text{in.}^2}$$

$$x = \tfrac{1}{2} \text{ in.} \times \frac{1/4}{63/4} = \frac{1}{126} \text{ in.}$$

The center of gravity of the drive-wheel is thus (4 - 1/126)in. = 3.992 in. from point A in the figure.

• PROBLEM 34

Two men lift the ends of a 20 ft beam weighing 200 lb onto their shoulders. Both men are of the same height so that the beam is carried horizontally, but one is much the stronger of the two and wishes to bear 50% more of the weight than his mate. How far from the end of the beam should he put his shoulder?

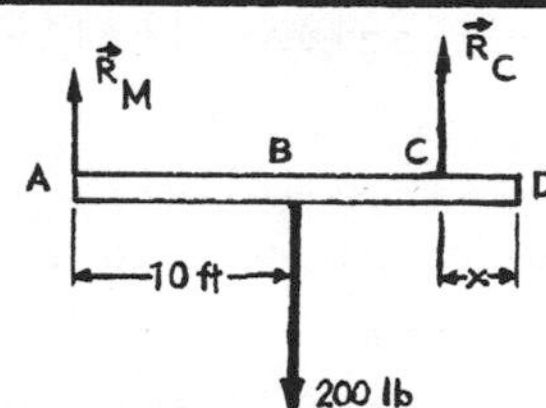

Solution: The beam exerts downward forces on the shoulders of the 2 men. This total downward force is just the weight of the beam and, since the beam is uniform, the weight acts through it's center (see figure). The 2 men exert upward forces $\vec{R}_c$ and $\vec{R}_m$, the former at distance x from one end and the latter at the other end. The beam is in equilibrium vertically since it experiences no motion in that direction. Therefore we can apply the first condition of equilibrium in the vertical direction.

$$\sum F_y = R_m + R_c - 200 \text{ lb} = 0$$

$$R_m + R_c = 200 \text{ lb}. \tag{1}$$

But we were given in the problem that one man, (the one on the right end) carries 50% more of the weight than his mate. Therefore

$$R_c = \frac{150}{100} R_m$$

$$\text{or} \quad R_m = \frac{2}{3} R_c \tag{2}$$

Substituting equation (2) in (1), we find

$$\frac{2}{3} R_c + R_c = 200 \text{ lb}$$

$$\frac{5}{3} R_c = 200 \text{ lb}$$

$$R_c = 120 \text{ lb}$$

Note that we solved for $\vec{R}_c$ since it is this force's distance from end D that we wish to know. Since the beam is in equilibrium rotationally, the second condition of equilibrium can be applied. Taking moments about end **A**, the magnitude of the force $\vec{R}_m$ is not needed. We have

$$\sum T_A = \left(R_m\right)(0) + R_c\ (20 \text{ ft} - x) - (200 \text{ lb})(10 \text{ ft}) = 0$$

$$20 \text{ ft} - x = \frac{2000 \text{ ft-lb}}{R_c} = \frac{2000 \text{ ft-lb}}{120 \text{ lb}} = 16\ \frac{2}{3} \text{ ft}.$$

$$x = 20 \text{ ft} - 16\ \frac{2}{3} \text{ ft} = 3\ \frac{1}{3} \text{ ft}$$

• PROBLEM 35

A uniform wooden beam, of length 20 ft and weight 200 lb, is lying on a horizontal floor. A carpenter raises one end of it until the beam is inclined at 30° to the horizontal. He maintains it in this position by exerting a force at right angles to the beam while he waits for his mate to arrive to lift the other end. What is the magnitude of the force he exerts?

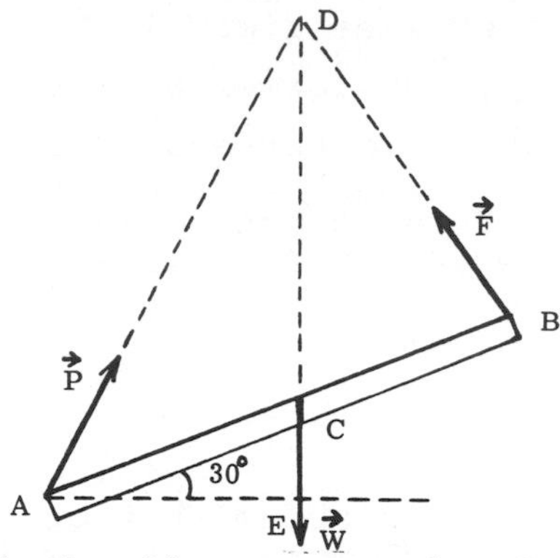

Solution: Consult the diagram: AB is the beam and C its midpoint. The weight W acts through C, since the beam is uniform and the two other forces acting on the beam are the force $\vec{F}$ exerted by the carpenter at B at right angles to AB and a total force $\vec{P}$ exerted by the floor at A in an unspecified direction.

Since the beam is acted on by three forces which maintain it in equilibrium, the lines of action of the three forces must be concurrent. Thus, the direction of force $\vec{P}$ is from A to the point D at which $\vec{F}$ and $\vec{W}$ meet.

Since the board is not in motion, the second condition of equilibrium can be applied. Taking moments about point A, we have

$$\sum T_A = P \times 0 + F \times AB - W \times AE = 0$$

$$F = W \frac{AE}{AB} = W \frac{AC \cos 30}{AB} = \frac{1}{2} W \cos 30 = \frac{\sqrt{3}}{4} W.$$

$\therefore$ F = 86.6 lb.

• PROBLEM 36

A rope C helps to support a uniform 200-lb beam, 20 ft long, one end of which is hinged at the wall and the other end of which supports a 1.0-ton load. The rope makes an angle of 30° with the beam, which is horizontal. (a) Determine the tension in the rope. (b) Find the force $\vec{F}$ at the hinge.

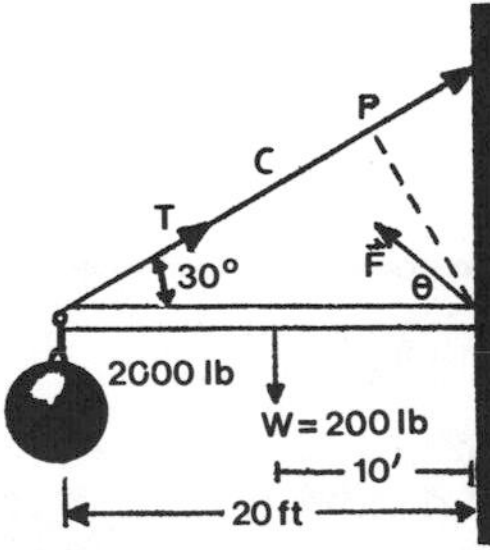

Solution: Since all the known forces act on the 20-ft beam, let us consider it as the object in equilibrium. In addition to the 200- and 2000-lb forces straight down, there are the pull of the rope on the beam and the force F which the hinge exerts on the beam at the wall. Let us not make the mistake of assuming that the force at the hinge is straight up or straight along the beam. A little thought will convince us that the hinge must be pushing both up and out on the beam. The exact direction of this force, as well as its magnitude, is unknown. The second condition for equilibrium is an excellent tool to employ in such a situation for if we use an axis through the point O as the axis about which to take torques, the unknown force at the hinge has zero moment arm and therefore, causes zero torque. The remarkable result is that we can determine the tension T in the rope without knowing either the magnitude or the direction of the force at O.

(a) The torques about an axis through O are

$$(200 \text{ lb})(10 \text{ ft}) = 2000 \text{ lb-ft} \quad \text{counterclockwise}$$

$$(2000 \text{ lb})(20 \text{ ft}) = 40{,}000 \text{ lb-ft} \quad \text{counterclockwise}$$

The moment arm of T is OP = (20 ft)(sin 30°) = 10 ft. Thus we have

$$T\,(20 \text{ ft}) \sin 30° = T(10 \text{ ft}) \quad \text{clockwise}$$

Since the beam is in equilibrium, the torque about any point of the beam is zero. We can then say

$$-\,T(10 \text{ ft}) + 2000 \text{ lb-ft} + 40{,}000 \text{ lb-ft} + F(0 \text{ ft}) = 0$$

or $$T = 4200 \text{ lb} = 2.1 \text{ tons}$$

The trick just used in removing the unknown force from the problem by taking torques about the hinge as an axis is a standard device in statics. The student should always be on the lookout for the opportunity to sidestep (temporarily) a troublesome unknown force by selecting an axis of torques that lies on the line of action of the unknown force he wishes to avoid.

(b) Using the first condition for equlibrium,

$$\Sigma F_x = 0 = T \cos 30° - F \cos \theta$$

$$\Sigma F_y = 0 = T \sin 30° + F \sin \theta + W - 2000 \text{ lb}$$

The above two equations can be solved simultaneously, since there are two unknowns. Substituting numerical values,

$$F \cos \theta = T \cos 30° = (4200 \text{ lb})(0.866) = 3640 \text{ lb}$$

$$F \sin \theta = -W + 2000 \text{ lb} - T \sin 30°$$

$$= 200 \text{ lb} + 2000 \text{ lb} - (4200 \text{ lb})(0.500) = 100 \text{ lb}$$

Dividing the first equation by the second,

$$\frac{F \cos \theta}{F \sin \theta} = \cot \theta = \frac{3640}{100} = 36.4$$

$$\theta \approx 1.5°$$

Since θ is almost zero, we have from the first equation

$$F \cos 1.5° \approx F \cos 0° = F = 3640 \text{ lb.}$$

• PROBLEM 37

The quadrilateral ABCD is a square of side 1 ft which can rotate about the fixed point 0, which is the midpoint of the diagonals. Forces 2, 3, 2, and 1 lb act along sides AB, BC, CD, and DA, respectively. Find the magnitude and line of action of a single force which would produce the same effect as these four forces.

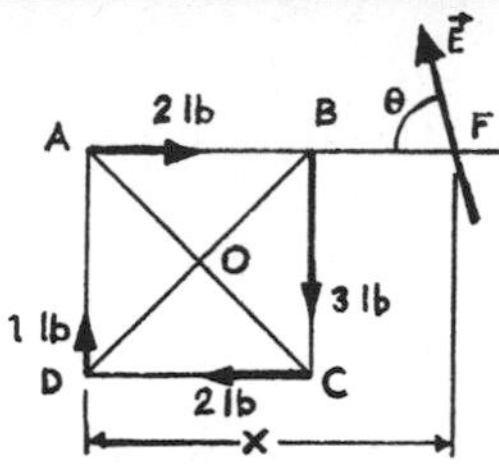

Solution: At first sight this may not appear to be a problem in equilibrium, but the easiest method of solution is obtained when it is changed into one.

Add a fifth force $\vec{E}$, the force necessary to produce equlibrium. This force is just sufficient to negate the translational and rotational effects of the resultant force. $\vec{E}$ (see diagram) acts at the angle θ to AB, at a distance of x from A. The resultant required in the problem must be equal and opposite to $\vec{E}$, since the single force equivalent to the four given forces must, with $\vec{E}$, produce equilibrium.

Resolve the five forces parallel to AB and at right angles to AB. Since the forces are in equilibrium,

$$2 \text{ lb} - 2 \text{ lb} - E \cos \theta = 0$$

and $1 \text{ lb} - 3 \text{ lb} + E \sin \theta = 0.$

$$E \cos \theta = 0 \qquad \text{and} \qquad E \sin \theta = 2 \text{ lb.}$$

$$\theta = 90° \qquad \text{and} \qquad E = 2 \text{ lb.}$$

Taking moments about 0 and using the condition for equilibrium, one obtains

$$-2 \text{ lb} \times \tfrac{1}{2} \text{ ft} - 3 \text{ lb} \times \tfrac{1}{2} \text{ ft} - 2 \text{ lb} \times \tfrac{1}{2} \text{ ft} - \text{lb} \times \tfrac{1}{2} \text{ ft}$$

$$+ E(x - \tfrac{1}{2} \text{ ft}) = 0$$

$$E(x - \tfrac{1}{2} \text{ ft}) = 4 \text{ ft} \cdot \text{lb}$$

$$x - \tfrac{1}{2} \text{ ft} = \frac{4 \text{ ft} \cdot \text{lb}}{2 \text{ lb}} = 2 \text{ ft} \quad \text{or } x = 2\tfrac{1}{2} \text{ ft.}$$

Thus, the equilibrant has a magnitude of 2 lb and acts at right angles to AB in a direction away from 0, along a line passing through a point at a distance of 2½ ft from A. The resultant required has thus the same magnitude and position but acts at right angles to AB toward 0.

A 1000 lb weight is suspended from the wooden boom (see the figures) which has a weight of 200 lb. Calculate the tension in the supporting cable, and the compression in the boom. This compression is the force exerted by the boom on the wall and the force exerted by the boom at the point of connection of the two cables.

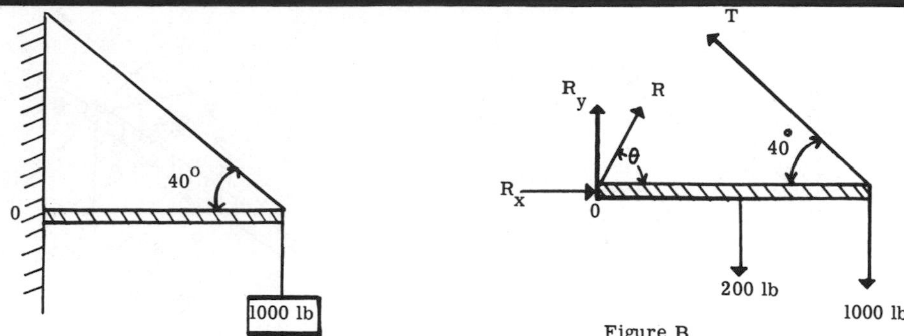

Figure A

Figure B

Solution: Figure (B) shows all the forces acting on the boom. Note that the force $\vec{R}$ exerted on the boom by the wall cannot be assumed to act along the boom if the weight of the boom is not neglected. This force $\vec{R}$ has been broken up into x and y components, as shown. Since $\vec{R}$ is unknown, we find the tension $\vec{T}$ in the cable by taking moments about point 0 at the left end of the boom. About this point, $\vec{R}$ does not contribute to the net torque. Though the length of the boom is not given, all distances can be expressed as some fraction of this length L, so that L appears on both sides of the moment equation and cancels.

The second condition of equilibrium, applied about 0, yields

$$(200)\left(\frac{L}{2}\right) + 1000L = T(\sin 40^\circ)L = (0.6428T)L$$

$$1100 = 0.6428T$$

$$T = 1711 \text{ lbs.}$$

The horizontal component of $\vec{R}$ can be obtained using the first condition of equilibrium.

$$\Sigma F_x = 0 = R_x - T\cos 40^\circ$$

$$R_x = T\cos 40^\circ = (1711)(0.7660)$$

$$R_x = 1311 \text{ lbs.}$$

For the vertical component of $\vec{R}$, $\Sigma F_y = 0 = R_y + T\sin 40^\circ - 1000 - 200$

$$R_y = 1000 + 200 - T\sin 40^\circ = 1200 - (1711)(0.6428)$$

$$R_y = 1200 - 1100 = 100 \text{ lbs.}$$

From vector summation, we know

$$R = \sqrt{R_x^2 + R_y^2} = \sqrt{(1311)^2 + (100)^2} = 1314 \text{ lbs.}$$

The angle is found from

$$\tan\theta = \frac{R_y}{R_x} = \frac{100}{1311} = 0.0763$$

$$\theta = 4.33^\circ$$

Figure A shows a strut AB, of length ℓ, pivoted at end A, attached to a wall by a cable, and carrying a load w at end B. The weights of the strut and of the cable are negligible. Suppose the weight w, and the angles θ_1 and θ_2 are known. What is the direction of $\vec{C}$?

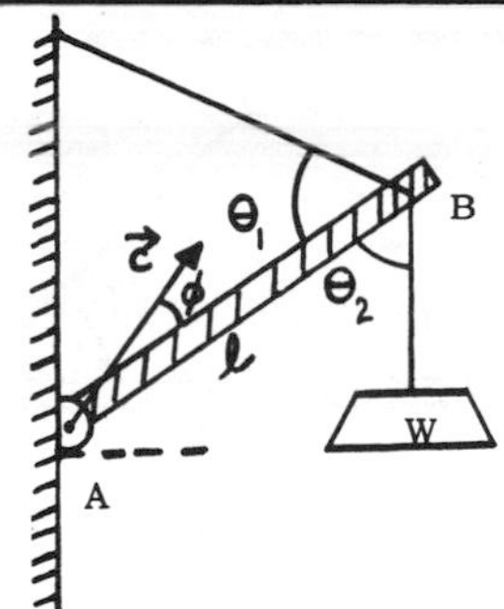

Figure A

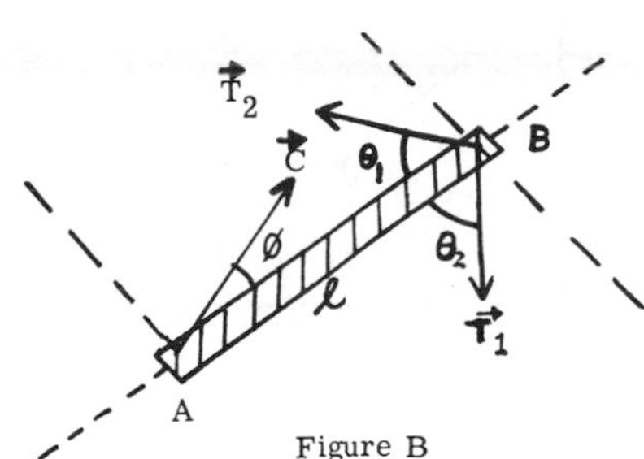

Figure B

Solution: The system shown in figure A is in equilibrium. Hence, the net external force on the system must be zero. Also, the net external torque acting on the system about any point must be zero. Then, using figures (a) and (b)

$$\vec{T}_1 + \vec{T}_2 + \vec{C} = 0 \tag{1}$$

and, taking torques about point A

$$\ell(T_2 \sin \theta_1) - \ell(T_1 \sin \theta_2) = 0 \tag{2}$$

Changing (1) into 2 scalar equations using figure B,

$$C \sin \varphi + T_2 \sin \theta_1 = T_1 \sin \theta_2 \tag{3}$$

$$C \cos \varphi = T_2 \cos \theta_1 + T_1 \cos \theta_2$$

To find the direction of $\vec{C}$, we must solve for φ. Using (3)

$$C \sin \varphi = T_1 \sin \theta_2 - T_2 \sin \theta_1$$
$$C \cos \varphi = T_1 \cos \theta_2 + T_2 \cos \theta_1$$

Dividing these last 2 equations

$$\tan \varphi = \frac{T_1 \sin \theta_2 - T_2 \sin \theta_1}{T_1 \cos \theta_2 + T_2 \cos \theta_1} \tag{4}$$

Solving (2) for T_1

$$T_1 = \frac{T_2 \sin \theta_1}{\sin \theta_2}$$

Substituting this equation in (4)

$$\tan \varphi = \frac{\left(\frac{T_2 \sin \theta_1}{\sin \theta_2}\right) \sin \theta_2 - T_2 \sin \theta_1}{\left(\frac{T_2 \sin \theta_1}{\sin \theta_2}\right) \cos \theta_2 + T_2 \cos \theta_1}$$

$$\tan \varphi = 0$$

and

$$\varphi = 0^\circ$$

Hence, $\vec{C}$ is directed along the strut AB.

A uniform drawbridge has a weight W of 3600 lb and is 20 ft long. It is hinged at one end and a chain is attached to the center of the other end. The drawbridge is lowered by letting out the chain over a pulley which is located in the castle wall 34.6 ft above the hinge. When the drawbridge is horizontal but has not yet touched the ground, what is the force $\vec{F}$ acting on it at the hinge?

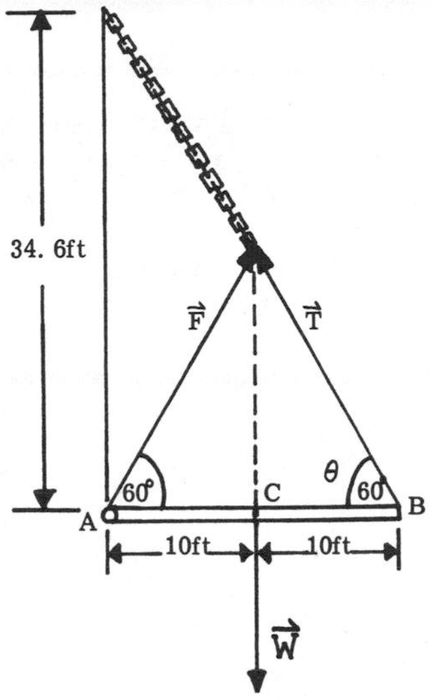

Solution: In the position stated in the problem, three forces are acting on the drawbridge: the weight acting downward, the tension in the chain, and the reaction at the hinge. The direction of $\vec{W}$ is as shown in the figure, and must act through the center point of the drawbridge, since the drawbridge is uniform. The tension $\vec{T}$ acts along the chain which makes an angle θ with the drawbridge, where tan θ is the height of the chain's pulley above the hinge divided by the length of the drawbridge:

$$\tan\theta = \frac{34.6\text{ ft}}{20\text{ ft}} = 1.73$$

Thus: $\theta = 60°$

Since the three forces are in equilibrium, the horizontal component of $\vec{F}$ must be equal and opposite to that of $\vec{T}$ (since $\vec{W}$ has no horizontal component) and the sum of the vertical components of $\vec{T}$ and $\vec{F}$ must equal $\vec{W}$. The latter bit of information alone doesn't help us to solve for the vertical component of $\vec{F}$. However, we know that the moments about any point in the drawbridge must cancel. Taking moments about point C, we note that the vertical components of $\vec{T}$ and $\vec{F}$ both act over moment arms of the same length (10 ft). This being the case we know that the vertical components of $\vec{T}$ and $\vec{F}$ must be equal. Since both the horizontal and vertical components

of $\vec{F}$ are equal in magnitude to those of $\vec{T}$, $\vec{F}$ must also make an angle $\theta = 60°$ with the drawbridge.
Thus, since we know that the vertical component of $\vec{F}$ equals half the weight of the drawbridge:

$$F \sin\theta = \tfrac{1}{2} W$$

$$F = \frac{W}{2 \sin\theta} = \frac{3{,}600 \text{ lb}}{2 \sin 60°} = \frac{3{,}600 \text{ lb}}{2 \frac{\sqrt{3}}{2}} = 2{,}079 \text{ lb.}$$

• PROBLEM 41

A non-uniform bar of weight $\vec{W}$ is suspended at rest in a horizontal position by two light ropes as shown in the figure. One rope makes an angle of 30° with the vertical and the other an angle of 60°. If the length ℓ of the bar is 10 m compute: (a) the tension in each rope and (b) the distance X from the left-hand end of the bar to the center of gravity.

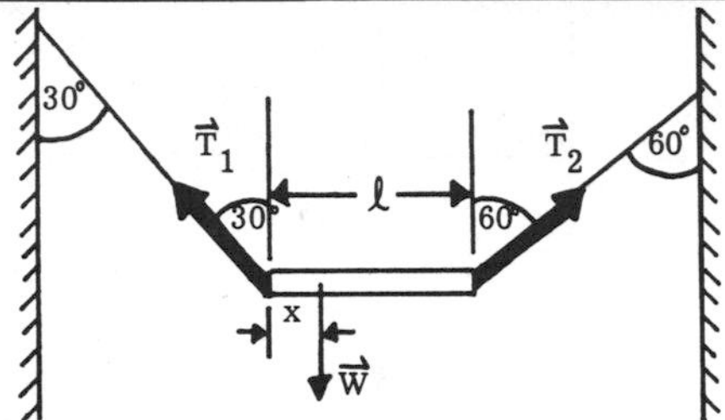

Solution: For the bar to be in equilibrium the sum of the forces that act on it and the sum of the torques must equal zero.

(a) We will treat the forces in terms of their horizontal and vertical components. The sum of the components in these directions must equal zero. The sum of the components in the horizontal direction is:

$T_2 \sin 60° - T_1 \sin 30° = 0$ $\sin 60° = \sqrt{3}/2$ and $\sin 30° = \tfrac{1}{2}$. Then

$$\frac{\sqrt{3}}{2} T_2 = \tfrac{1}{2} T_1$$

$$T_1 = \sqrt{3}\, T_2$$

where T_1 is the tension of the wire making an angle of 30° with the verticle and T_2 is the tension of the other wire. Forces pointing to the right are taken as positive and those pointing to the left as negative.

The sum of the components in the vertical direction is:

$$T_2 \cos 60° + T_1 \cos 30° - W = 0$$

$$W = \frac{\sqrt{3}}{2} T_1 + \tfrac{1}{2} T_2 = \frac{\sqrt{3}}{2} \left(\sqrt{3}\, T_2\right) + \tfrac{1}{2} T_2$$

$$= \frac{3}{2} T_2 + \tfrac{1}{2} T_2 = 2 T_2$$

$$T_2 = \tfrac{1}{2} W$$

$$T_1 = \sqrt{3} \left(\tfrac{1}{2} W\right) = \frac{\sqrt{3}}{2} W$$

where forces pointing upward are taken as positive and those pointing downward as negative.

(b) To calculate X, we set the sum of the torques equal to zero. Torque is defined as:

$$\vec{\tau} = \vec{r} \times \vec{F}$$

$$\tau = r F \sin \theta$$

where r is the distance of the point of action of the force F from an arbitrary reference point. The sum of the magnitudes of the torques about the point of application of the force W is:

$$T_2 (\ell - X) \sin 150° - T_1 X \sin 120° = 0$$

$\sin 150° = \sqrt{3}/2$, $\sin 120° = \tfrac{1}{2}$. Then

$$\frac{\sqrt{3}}{2} T_2 (\ell - X) = \tfrac{1}{2} T_1 X$$

$$\frac{\sqrt{3}}{2} \left(\tfrac{1}{2} W\right)(10 \text{ m}) - \frac{\sqrt{3}}{2} \left(\tfrac{1}{2} W\right) X = \tfrac{1}{2} \left(\frac{\sqrt{3}}{2} W\right) X$$

$$\frac{\sqrt{3}}{2} WX = \frac{5\sqrt{3}}{2} Wm, \qquad X = 1 \text{ m}.$$

• PROBLEM 42

In the figure, a ladder 20 ft. long leans against a vertical frictionless wall and makes an angle of 53° with the horizontal, which is a rough surface. The ladder is in equilibrium. Its weight is 80 lb. and its center of gravity is in the center of the ladder. Find the magnitudes and directions of the forces $\vec{F}_1$ and $\vec{F}_2$.

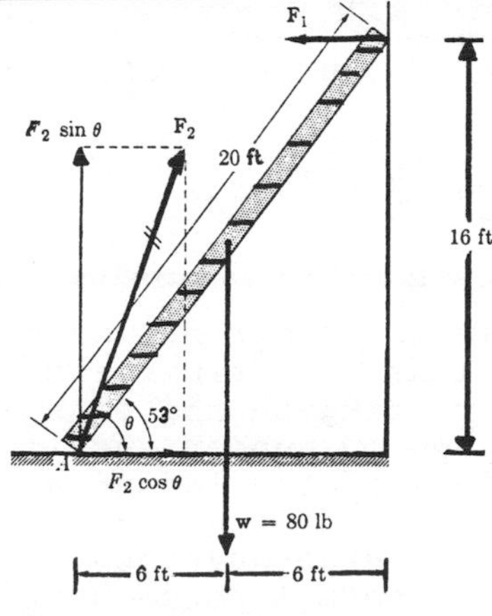

Solution: If the wall is frictionless, $\vec{F}_1$ is horizontal.

The direction $\vec{F}_2$ is unknown (except in special cases, its direction does not lie along the ladder). Instead of considering its magnitude and direction as unknowns, it is simpler to resolve the force $\vec{F}_2$ into x- and y-components and solve for these. The magnitude and direction of $\vec{F}_2$ may then be computed. The first condition of equilibrium states that the net horizontal component of force on an object is zero. Similarly for the net vertical component. Hence, from the figure,

$$\sum F_x = F_2 \cos\theta - F_1 = 0,$$

$$\sum F_y = F_2 \sin\theta - 80 \text{ lb.} = 0. \qquad \text{(1st condition)}$$

The second condition of equilibrium states that the net torque acting on a body is zero. If the body is in translational equilibrium $\left(\vec{F}_{net} = 0\right)$ we may compute the torques about any axis. (Torques coming out of the plane of the figure will be considered positive) The resulting equation is simplest if one selects a point through which two or more forces pass, since these forces then do not appear in the equation. Let us therefore take moments about an axis through point A.

$$\sum \tau_A = F_1 \times 16 \text{ ft.} - 80 \text{ lb.} \times 6 \text{ ft.} = 0.$$

(2nd condition)

From the second equation, $F_2 \sin\theta = 80$ lb., and from the third,

$$F_1 = \frac{480 \text{ lb}\cdot\text{ft}}{16 \text{ ft}} = 30 \text{ lb.}$$

Then from the first equation,

$$F_2 \cos\theta = 30 \text{ lb.}$$

Hence,

$$F_2 = \sqrt{(80 \text{ lb})^2 + (30 \text{ lb})^2} = 85.5 \text{ lb.}$$

$$\theta = \tan^{-1} \frac{80 \text{ lb}}{30 \text{ lb}} = 69.5°.$$

• PROBLEM 43

A man is using a uniform ladder of weight W = 75 lb, one end of which is leaning against a smooth vertical wall, the other end resting on the sidewalk. It is prevented from slipping by rubber suction pads rigidly attached to the feet of the ladder and stuck firmly to the concrete. If the man of weight w = 150 lb is standing symmetrically three-quarters of the way up the ladder, and if the normal force $\vec{N}$ exerted by the wall on each leg of the ladder is 43.3 lb, what is the force exerted on the ladder by each suction pad?

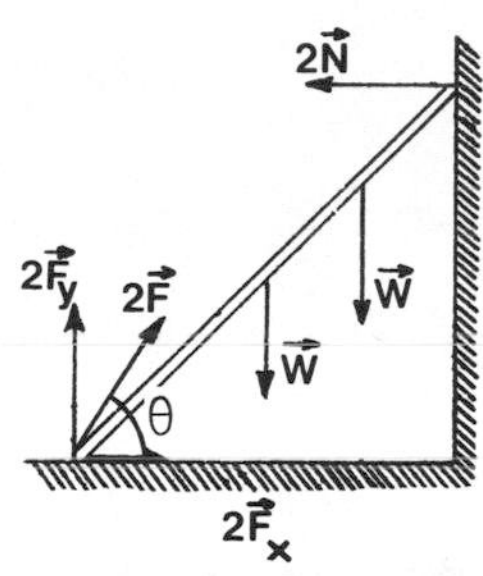

Solution: The ladder is uniform and thus its weight acts as its center. The man is symmetrically placed on the ladder. Hence, by symmetry, the normal forces exerted by the wall on the two legs of the ladder are equal, as are the forces exerted by the two suction pads.

Let the force exerted by either suction pad on the ladder be resolved into component forces F_x and F_y along the sidewalk and normal to it, respectively. The complete force system acting on the ladder is as shown in the figure, the man exerting a force equal to his weight on the ladder. The ladder, of course, exerts an equal and opposite force on him, since he is in equilibrium.

The whole system is in equilibrium. It follows from Newtons Second Law that

$$2F_x = 2N, \quad F_x = N = 43.3 \text{ lb}$$

and $2F_y = W + w, \quad F_y = \frac{W + w}{2} = \frac{75 \text{ lb} + 150 \text{ lb}}{2} = 112.5 \text{ lb}$

The total force exerted by each suction pad on the ladder thus has magnitude

$$F = \sqrt{F_x^2 + F_y^2} = \sqrt{(43.3 \text{ lb})^2 + (112.5 \text{ lb})^2} = 120.6 \text{ lb}$$

and it acts at an angle θ to the horizontal, where

$$\tan\theta = \frac{F_y}{F_x} = \frac{112.5 \text{ lb}}{43.3 \text{ lb}} = 2.60, \qquad \theta = 69°.$$

• PROBLEM 44

In figure (a), block A of weight w_1 rests on a frictionless inclined plane of slope angle θ. The center of gravity of the block is at its center. A flexible cord is attached to the center of the right face of the block, passes over a frictionless pulley, and is attached to a second block B of weight w_2. The weight of the cord and friction in the pulley are negligible. If w_1 and θ are given, find the weight w_2 for which the system is in equilibrium, that is, for which it remains at rest or moves in either direction at constant speed.

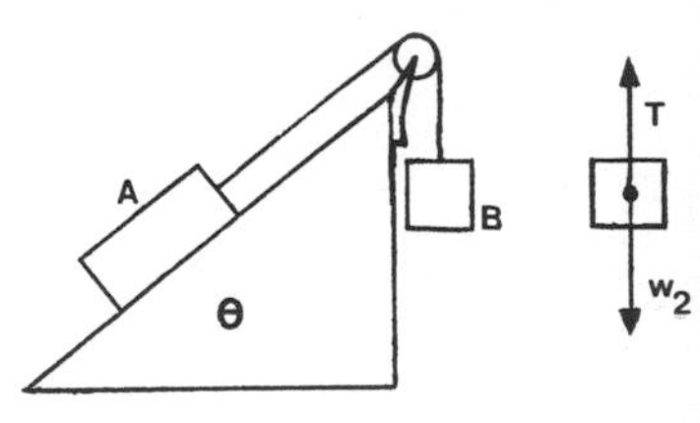

FIGURE A

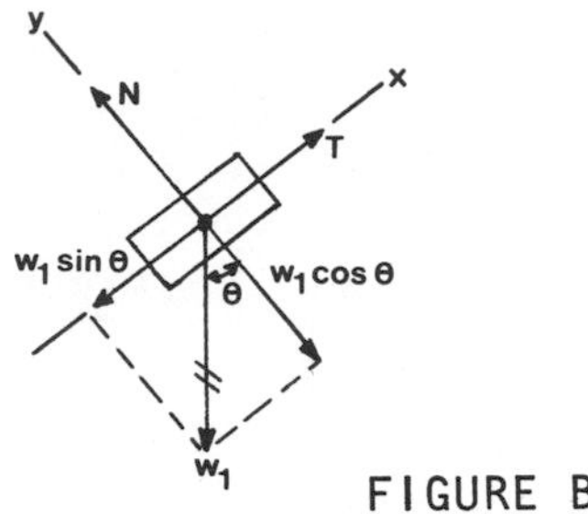

FIGURE B

<u>Solution:</u> The free-body diagrams for the two blocks are shown in figure (b) and to the right of fig. (a). The forces on block B are its weight $\vec{w}_2$ and the force $\vec{T}$ exerted on it by the cord. Since it is in equilibrium, the block has no acceleration and

$$T - w_2 = 0$$

by Newton's Second Law.

Block A is acted on by its weight $\vec{w}_1$, the force $\vec{T}$ exerted on it by the cord and the force $\vec{N}$ exerted on it by the plane. We can use the same symbol ($\vec{T}$) for the force exerted on each block by the cord, because these forces are equivalent to an action-reaction pair and have the same magnitude. The force $\vec{N}$, if there is no friction, is perpendicular or normal to the surface of the plane. Since the lines of action of $\vec{w}_1$ and $\vec{T}$ intersect at the center of gravity of the block, the line of action of $\vec{N}$ passes through this point also. It is simplest to choose x- and y-axes parallel and perpendicular to the surface of the plane, because then only the weight $\vec{w}_1$ needs to be resolved into components. The conditions of equilibrium for block A give, since it isn't accelerated,

$$\left.\begin{aligned} \Sigma F_x &= T - w_1 \sin\theta = 0 \\ \Sigma F_y &= N - w_1 \cos\theta = 0. \end{aligned}\right\}$$

Thus, if $w_1 = 100$ lb and $\theta = 30°$, we have from the first equation above

$$w_2 = T = w_1 \sin\theta = 100 \text{ lb} \times 0.500 = 50 \text{ lb},$$

and from the second equation above

$$N = w_1 \cos\theta = 100 \text{ lb} \times 0.866 = 86.6 \text{ lb}.$$

Note carefully that in the absence of friction the same weight w_2 of 50 lb is required whether the system remains at rest or moves with constant speed in either direction. This is not the case when friction is present.

• PROBLEM 45

For the block and tackle shown in the figure (a) find the displacement ratio. (b) What force, F, must be exerted on the free end of the rope to lift a 200 lb load?

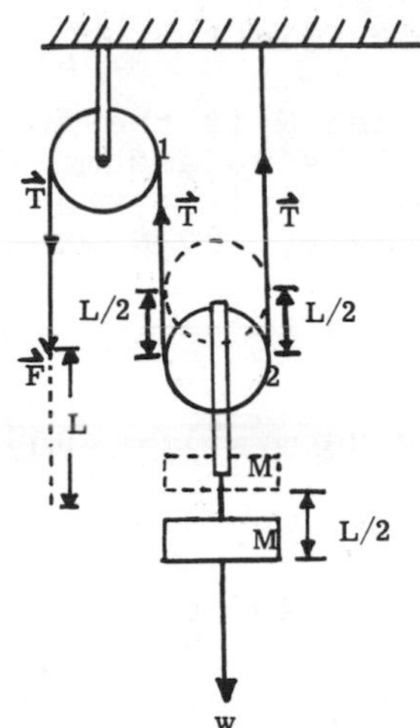

Solution: (a) When $\vec{F}$ pulls down the rope by an amount L, pulley 2 moves up by ½L (as shown in the figure) since the shortening of the rope is shared by the two segments of rope that hold the pulley. Therefore, the ratio of the displacement of load to the displacement of the rope is

$$\frac{\frac{1}{2}L}{L} = \frac{1}{2} .$$

(b) From the figure, we see that the load is held up by a force $2\vec{T}$ where $\vec{T}$ is the tension in the rope. Hence, in order to lift the load, the minimum tension should satisfy

$$W = 2T$$

or $T = \frac{1}{2}W$

where W is the weight of the load.

$\vec{F}$ is equal to $\vec{T}$ as long as the rope does not break since the stress in the rope is caused by the action of $\vec{F}$. We have

$$F = T = \frac{W}{2}$$

$$= \frac{200 \text{ lb}}{2} = 100 \text{ lb}.$$

STATIC & KINETIC FRICTION

• PROBLEM 46

The force required to start a mass of 50 kilograms moving over a rough surface is 343 Nt. What is the coefficient of starting friction?

Solution: The coefficient of starting friction is given by the relation

$$F = \mu_{st} N$$

where F is the force of friction, μ_{st} is the coefficient of starting friction, and N is the force normal to the direction of travel. Since we assume the object is travelling on a horizontal plane, the normal force is simply the force of gravity, by Newton's Second Law. This force is

$$N = mg$$

$$N = 50 \text{ kg}(9.80 \text{ m/s}^2) = 490 \text{ Newton}$$

Therefore

$$343 \text{ nt} = \mu_{st} \times 490 \text{ nt}$$

$$\mu_{st} = 0.70.$$

• PROBLEM 47

A box is dragged up and down a concrete slope of 15° to the horizontal. To get the box started up the slope, it is necessary to exert six times the force needed to get it started down the slope. If the force is always parallel to the slope, what is the coefficient of static friction between the box and the concrete?

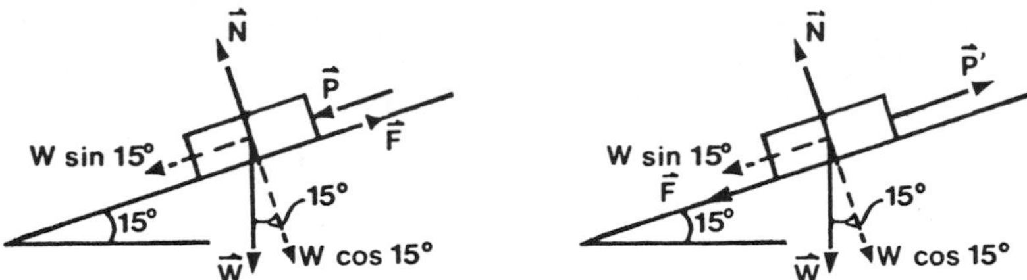

FIGURE A FIGURE B

Solution: When the box is about to slide down the slope, the forces acting on it are as shown in (figure (a)). The weight of the box W acts vertically downward, the frictional force which attempts to prevent the motion acts up the slope, and the concrete exerts a normal force at right angles to the slope. When the box is just on the point of moving, $F = \mu_s N$, where μ_s is the coefficient of static friction required.

Let us resolve the force $\vec{W}$ into its components along, and at right angles to, the slope. Since the angle between the slope and the horizontal is 15°, this is also the angle between the normal to the slope and the normal to the horizontal (i.e., the vertical). Thus $\vec{W}$ has components W cos 15° at right angles to the plane and W sin 15° down the plane.

The box is just in equilibrium. From the conditions for equilibrium, we know that

$$N = W \cos 15°.$$

and $$P + W \sin 15° = F = \mu_s N = \mu_s W \cos 15°.$$

$$\therefore \quad P = \mu_s W \cos 15 - W \sin 15°.$$

Figure (b) shows that, when the box is about to slide up the slope, the situation is very similar. The box is in equilibrium once more, so that

$$N = W \cos 15°$$

and $\quad P' = W \sin 15° + F = W \sin 15° + \mu_s N$

$$= W \sin 15° + \mu_s W \cos 15°.$$

But we know that the force $P' = 6P$.

$$\therefore \quad W \sin 15° + \mu_s W \cos 15° = 6\left(\mu_s W \cos 15° - W \sin 15°\right).$$

$$\therefore \quad 5\mu_s W \cos 15° = 7\, W \sin 15°.$$

$$\therefore \quad \mu_s = \frac{7}{5} \tan 15° = \frac{7}{5} \times 0.268 = 0.375.$$

• PROBLEM 48

A man hangs from the midpoint of a rope 1 m long, the ends of which are tied to two light rings which are free to move on a horizontal rod (see the figure). What is the maximum possible separation d of the rings when the man is hanging in equilibrium, if the relevant coefficient of static friction is 0.35?

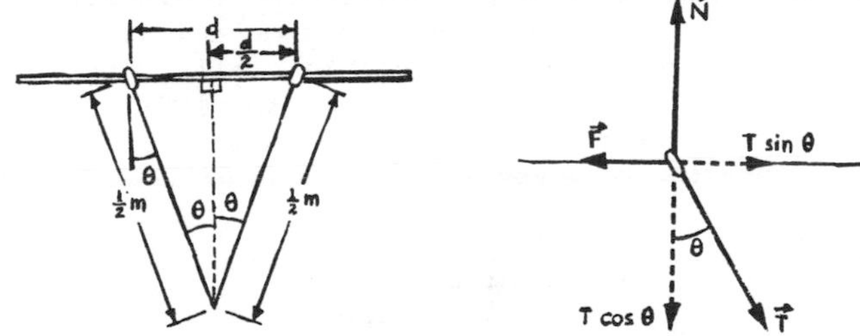

Solution: Since the man hangs from the midpoint of the rope, by symmetry the tensions in the two portions of the rope must be equal and have magnitude T, and each portion will be inclined at the same angle θ to the vertical. Thus the system of forces acting on each ring will be the same.

Now consider one of the rings. Three forces are acting on it: the tensional pull on the ring due to the rope, the normal force exerted upward by the rod, and the frictional force attempting to prevent motion of the ring toward its fellow. Since the ring is light, its weight may be ignored. If the ring is too far out, slipping will occur. At the maximum distance apart, each ring is just on the point of slipping. Hence $F = \mu_s N$.

When we resolve $\vec{T}$ into its horizontal and vertical components, the equations for equilibrium become

Σ perpendicular forces = N - T cos θ = 0

Σ parallel forces = T sin θ - F = 0

where we take the positive perpendicular direction as pointing upward and the positive parallel direction as pointing to the right. Then:

$$N = T \cos\theta \qquad \text{and} \qquad F = \mu_s N = T \sin\theta .$$

$$\mu_s = \frac{\mu_s N}{N} = \frac{T \sin\theta}{T \cos\theta} = \tan\theta = 0.35$$

or $\theta = 19.6°$

Finally, we solve for d:

$$\sin\theta = \sin 19.6° = \frac{d/2}{\frac{1}{2}\text{ m}} = d \text{ m}^{-1}$$

$$0.33 = d \text{ m}^{-1}$$

$$d = 0.33 \text{ m}$$

which is the maximum separation permissible.

Note that θ and d do not depend on T and therefore the ring separation is not dependent on what it is that is hanging from the midpoint of the rope.

• PROBLEM 49

In the figure, suppose that the block weighs 20 lb., that the tension T can be increased to 8 lb. before the block starts to slide, and that a force of 4 lb. will keep the block moving at constant speed once it has been set in motion. (a) Find the coefficients of static and kinetic friction. (b) What is the frictional force if the block is at rest on the surface and a horizontal force of 5 lb. is exerted on it?

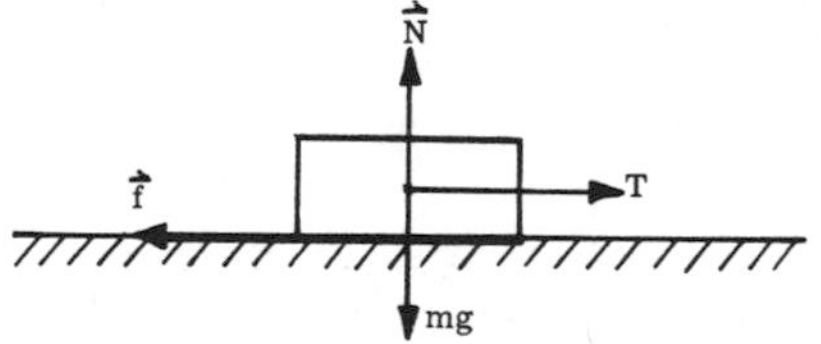

<u>Solution:</u> a) There are 2 forces of friction which can act on a body. These are the forces of kinetic and static friction. If a body, such as that in the figure, is initially at rest and we begin pulling on it with a variable force T, the block will remain at rest. This means that no matter what force T we apply to the body, the frictional force f always balances it. However, at some value of T, the frictional force no longer balances it, and the block begins translating. We may describe this static frictional force by

$$f_s \le \mu_s N \qquad (1)$$

where μ_s is the coefficient of static friction and N is the normal force of the table on the block. (The equality holds when the block begins translating). Once the block begins translating, the static frictional force stops acting and the kinetic frictional force takes over. This force is

$$f_k = \mu_k N \qquad (2)$$

It is also found that $f_k < f_{s\,max}$, and that once the block starts moving, we may reduce T and the block will still move. Applying the Second Law to the block of mass m

$$N - mg = ma_y$$

$$T - f = ma_x$$

Here a_x and a_y are the x and y components of the block's acceleration. Because the block coesn't leave the surface of the table, $a_y = 0$. Hence

$$N = mg \qquad (3)$$

$$T - f = ma_x \qquad (4)$$

The block is initially at rest, and just begins to slip when T = 8 lb. If we examine the block just before it moves, $a_x = 0$, and f is the maximum force of static friction. Then, using (1)

$$T - f_{s\,max} = 0$$

$$T = \mu_s N$$

$$8\text{ lb} = \mu_s N$$

Using (3)

$$\mu_s = \frac{8\text{ lb}}{mg} = \frac{8\text{ lb}}{20\text{ lb}} = .4$$

Once translation at constant velocity begins, T = 4 lb, $a_x = 0$ and f in (4) is $f_k = \mu_k N$. Hence

$$T - f_k = 0$$

$$T = \mu_k N$$

$$\mu_k = \frac{4\text{ lb}}{20\text{ lb}} = .20$$

b) Note that, if the block is initially at rest, a force of 8 lb is needed to start the motion of the block. Hence, if we pull the block with a force of 5 lb., $a_x = 0$ and, the force of static friction is acting. Then, from (4)

$$T - f_s = 0$$

$$T = f_s = 5\text{ lb.}$$

• PROBLEM 50

(a) What force T, at an angle of 30° above the horizontal is required to drag a block of weight w = 20 lb to the right at constant speed along a level surface if the coefficient of sliding friction between block and surface is 0.20? (b) Determine the line of action of the normal force $\vec{N}$ exerted on the block by the surface. The block is 1 ft high, 2 ft long, and its center of gravity is at its center.

Solution: (a) There can be no net vertical force because there is no accelerated motion upwards; similarly, there is no net horizontal force because the block moves with constant velocity. If T is the rope tension, N, the normal force, and f_k the force of friction, we have

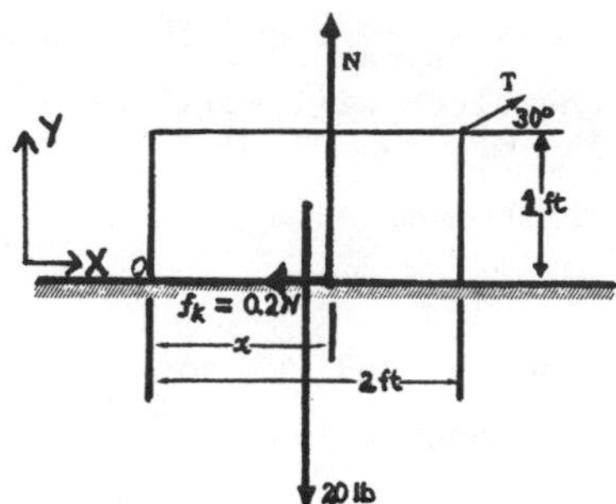

using Newton's Second Law,

$$\left.\begin{aligned}\Sigma F_x &= T\cos 30° - f_k = 0,\\ \Sigma F_y &= T\sin 30° + N - 20\text{ lb} = 0.\end{aligned}\right\} \qquad (1)$$

A body may experience translational equilibrium without experiencing rotational equilibrium. The general condition for rotational equilibrium is that the sum of torques taken about the center of mass of the body be zero. However, if no net external force acts, this condition is less stringent. The condition in this case is that the sum of torques taken about any point (i.e. C) be zero.

Let x represent the distance from point 0 (see diagram) to the line of action of $\vec{N}$, and take moments about an axis through 0. Then, from the condition of rotational equilibrium, the net torque about 0 must be zero, or

$$T\sin 30° \times 2\text{ ft} - T\cos 30° \times 1\text{ ft} + N \times x$$

$$- 20\text{ lb} \times 1\text{ ft} = 0. \qquad (2)$$

We may now solve for N. From (1) and (2)

$$T\sin 30° = 20\text{ lb} - N \qquad (3)$$

$$T\cos 30° = f_k \qquad (4)$$

$$(2\text{ ft})(T\sin 30°) - (1\text{ ft})(T\cos 30°) + (x)(N)$$

$$= 20\text{ ft}\cdot\text{lb} \qquad (5)$$

But $f_k = \mu_k N$, where μ_k is the coefficient of static friction. Hence

$$T\cos 30° = \mu_k N = .2\,N \qquad (5)$$

Dividing (3) by (5)

$$\tan 30° = \frac{20\text{ lb} - N}{.2\,N}$$

$$\frac{\sqrt{3}}{3} = \frac{20\text{ lb} - N}{.2\,N}$$

$$\left(\frac{.2\sqrt{3}}{3}\right) N + N = 20\text{ lb}$$

$$N = \frac{20 \text{ lb}}{\frac{.2\sqrt{3}}{3} + 1} = 17.9 \text{ lb} \qquad (6)$$

Substituting (6) into (5), we obtain

$$T \frac{\sqrt{3}}{2} = .2(17.9 \text{ lb})$$

or $$T = \frac{.4}{\sqrt{3}} (17.9 \text{ lb}) = 4.15 \text{ lb} \qquad (7)$$

Using (6) and (7) in (5)

$$(2 \text{ ft})(4.15 \text{ lb})(\tfrac{1}{2}) - (1 \text{ ft})(4.15 \text{ lb})(\sqrt{3}/2) + x(17.9 \text{ lb}) = 20 \text{ ft}\cdot\text{lb}$$

$$x(17.9 \text{ lb}) = (20 \text{ ft} \cdot \text{lb}) - (4.15 \text{ ft} \cdot \text{lb}) + (3.6 \text{ ft} \cdot \text{lb})$$

$$x = \frac{(20 \text{ ft} \cdot \text{lb} - 4.15 \text{ ft} \cdot \text{lb} + 3.6 \text{ ft} \cdot \text{lb})}{(17.9 \text{ lb})}$$

$$x = 1.08 \text{ ft}$$

Therefore, the line of action of N must be .08 ft to the right of the center of mass if the block is to maintain its rotational equilibrium.

• PROBLEM 51

If the coefficient of sliding friction for steel on ice is 0.05, what force is required to keep a man weighing 150 pounds moving at constant speed along the ice?

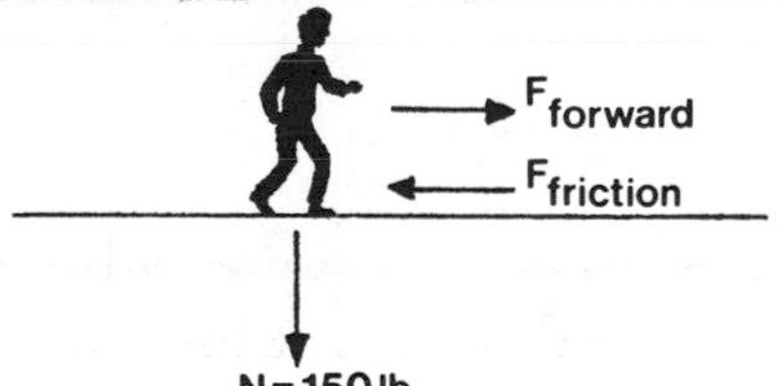

Solution: To keep the man moving at constant velocity, we must oppose the force of friction tending to retard his motion with an equal but opposite force (see diagram).

The force of friction is given by:

$$F = \mu_{kinetic} N$$

By Newton's Third Law

$$F_{forward} = F_{friction}$$

Therefore

$$F_{forward} = \mu_{kinetic} N$$

$$F_{forward} = (.05)(150 \text{ lb}) = 7.5 \text{ lb.}$$

• **PROBLEM 52**

A 1200-lb sled is pulled along a horizontal surface at uniform speed by means of a rope that makes an angle of 30° above the horizontal (see figure (a)). If the tension in the rope is 100 lb, what is the coefficient of friction?

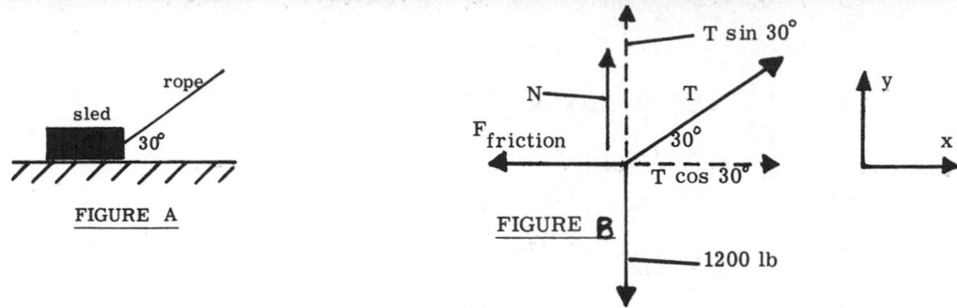

Solution. Since the sled is being pulled at constant velocity, there are no unbalanced forces. We break up the tension in the rope into components parallel and perpendicular to the horizontal (see figure (a)). By Newton's second law

$$\sum F_x = 0 \text{ therefore } F_{friction} = \mu N = T \cos 30° \tag{1}$$

$$\sum F_y = 0 \text{ therefore } N + T \sin 30° = 1200$$

$$N = 1200 \text{ lb} - T \sin 30° \tag{2}$$

From (1), $\mu = \dfrac{T \cos 30°}{N}$

Substituting (2) into this expression,

$$\mu = \frac{T \cos 30°}{1200 \text{ lb} - T \sin 30°} = \frac{(100 \text{ lb})(.866)}{1200 \text{ lb} - (100)\left(\frac{1}{2}\right)\text{lb}}$$

$$= \frac{86.6}{1150} = 0.0753.$$

• **PROBLEM 53**

Suppose the coefficient of friction between a horizontal surface and a moving body is μ. With what speed must a body of mass m be projected parallel to the surface to travel a distance D before stopping?

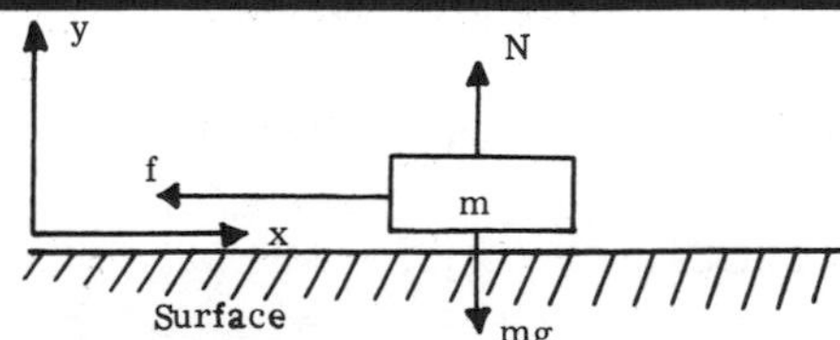

Solution: In this problem, we actually want to describe the motion of m, for we want it to travel a distance D before stopping. Our task is to determine the initial velocity which the mass must have in order for this to be possible.

We are seeking to describe the properties of the motion of m, such as its acceleration. Therefore, we apply Newton's Second Law, $F = ma$, to both the vertical and horizontal directions for the mass m (see the free-body diagram). In the horizontal direction, Newton's Law becomes

$$F_x = ma_x \tag{1}$$

where F_x represents the sum of all forces acting horizontally on m, and a_x represents the resulting acceleration in the x direction due to these forces. From the figure, we see that f, the force of friction, is the only horizontal force acting on m. Therefore, substituting into equation (1) we find

$$-f = ma_x \tag{2}$$

where the minus sign appears because f acts in the negative x direction. (We are taking a_x to be positive in the positive x direction). Writing Newton's Second Law for the vertical direction, we find

$$F_y = ma_y \tag{3}$$

where F_y is the sum of all forces acting on m in the y direction, and a_y is the resulting acceleration of m in the y direction. The only forces which act on m in the vertical direction are N, the normal force of the surface which pushes on m, and mg, the weight of the mass, which points downward. Substituting into equation (3), we obtain

$$N - mg = ma_y \tag{4}$$

where the minus sign indicates that the two forces point in opposite directions. Furthermore, note that a_y must be zero since the mass never rises off the surface on which it slides. Substituting this into equation (4), we have

$$N = mg \tag{5}$$

Now, the frictional force law is given by

$$f = \mu N \tag{6}$$

where μ is the coefficient of sliding friction between m and the surface, and N is the magnitude of the normal force. Substituting equation (5) into equation (6), we obtain

$$f = \mu mg \tag{7}$$

Inserting this into equation (2),

$$-\mu mg = ma_x \tag{8}$$

Solving for a_x

$$a_x = -\mu g \tag{9}$$

Note that because μ and g are constants, a_x is also constant. Hence we may use the kinematical equations for constant acceleration to describe the position of the mass. The equation needed is

$$v_f^2 - v_o^2 = 2a_x\left(x_f - x_o\right) \tag{10}$$

where x_o and v_o are the initial positiion and velocity of m, respectively, and x_f, v_f are the final position and velocity of m, respectively. For this problem:

$$x_o = 0 \qquad x_f = D$$
$$v_o = ? \qquad v_f = 0 \tag{11}$$

v_f is 0 because the mass is at rest after travelling to its final position, which is D. Substituting these values into equation (10),

$$0 - v_o^2 = 2a_x\left(D - 0\right) \tag{12}$$

or

$$-v_o^2 = 2a_x D \tag{13}$$

Then, substituting equation (9) into equation (13), we obtain

$$v_o^2 = 2\mu g\ D$$

or

$$v_o = \sqrt{2\mu g D} \tag{14}$$

for the initial velocity of m needed so that it may travel a distance D before stopping.

• PROBLEM 54

In the figure, a block has been placed on an inclined plane and the slope angle θ of the plane has been adjusted until the block slides down the plane at constant speed, once it has been set in motion. Find the angle θ.

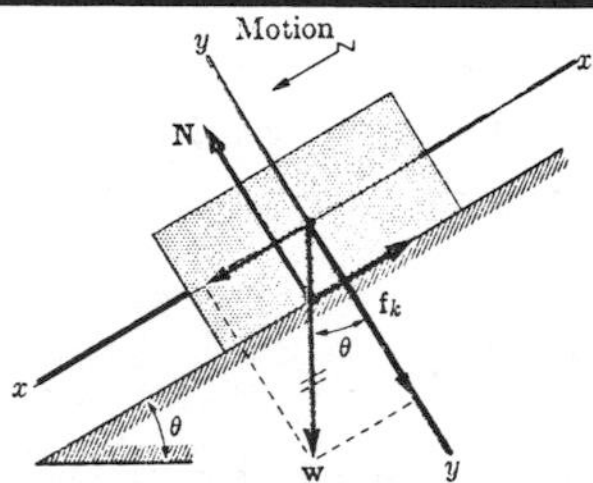

Solution: The forces on the block are its weight w and the normal and frictional components of the force exerted by the plane. The angle θ of the inclined plane is adjusted until the block slides down the plane. Since motion exists, the friction force is $f_k = \mu_k N$. Take axes perpendicular and parallel to the surface of the plane. Then, applying Newton's Second Law to the x and y components of the block's motion, we obtain (see figure)

$$\Sigma F_x = \mu_k N - w \sin\theta = 0$$

$$\Sigma F_y = N - w \cos\theta = 0 .$$

where ΣF_x and ΣF_y are the x and y components of the net force on the block. Both of these equations are equal to zero because the block accelerates neither parallel nor perpendicular to the plane. Hence

$$\mu_k N = w \sin\theta ,$$

$$N = w \cos\theta .$$

Dividing the former by the latter, we get

$$\mu_k = \tan\theta .$$

It follows that a block, regardless of its weight, slides down an inclined plane with constant speed if the tangent of the slope angle of the plane equals the coefficient of kinetic friction. Measurement of this angle then provides a simple experimental method of determining the coefficient of kinetic friction.

• PROBLEM 55

A boy is sledding on a snowy slope and looks very weary as he drags his sled up again after each run down. A helpful physics student who is passing by, and who knows that the coefficient of kinetic friction between a sled and snow is around 0.10, points out to the boy that he is exerting pull on the tow rope at an incorrect angle to the ground for minimum effort. At what angle to the slope should the pull be exerted?

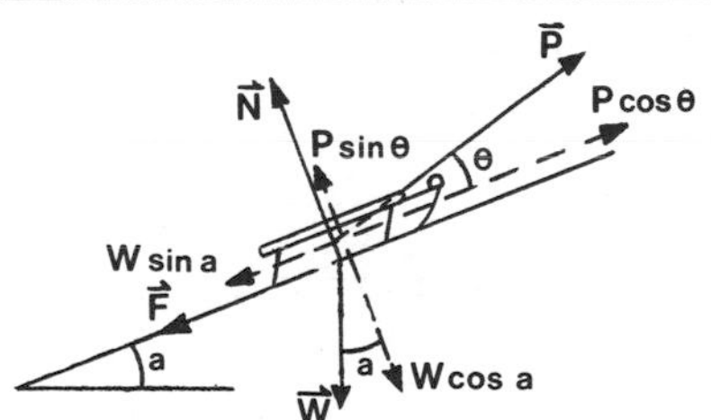

Solution: There are four forces acting on the sled, as shown in the diagram; the weight $\vec{W}$, the normal force $\vec{N}$ exerted by the slope, the frictional force $\vec{F}_f$ exerted by the snow down the slope opposing the motion, and the upward pull $\vec{P}$ exerted by the boy at an angle θ to the slope. The sled is moving with uniform velocity up the hill and thus the forces are in equilibrium, and $F_f = \mu_k N$, where μ_k is the coefficient of kinetic friction.

Let us now resolve all the forces into components parallel and perpendicular to the surface of the slope. We will take forces going up the slope as positive in the parallel direction, and forces pointing upward out of the slope as positive in the perpendicular direction. Imposing the conditions of equilibrium, we have:

$$\Sigma F_{\parallel} = P \cos\theta - W \sin\alpha - \mu_k N = 0 \qquad (1)$$

$$\Sigma F_{\perp} = N + P \sin\theta - W \cos\alpha = 0 \qquad (2)$$

where α is the angle of the slope's incline. We can thus solve for P.

From equation (2)

$$N = W \cos\alpha - P \sin\theta$$

From equation (1)

$$P \cos\theta = W \sin\alpha + \mu_k N$$

$$= W \sin\alpha + \mu_k (W \cos\alpha - P \sin\theta)$$

$$P\left(\cos\theta + \mu_k \sin\theta\right) = W \sin\alpha + \mu_k W \cos\alpha$$

$$P = \frac{W \sin\alpha + \mu_k W \cos\alpha}{\cos\theta + \mu_k \sin\theta}$$

We see now that P is a function of θ alone since W, α, and μ_k are constants. Thus, to find the angle θ at which the boy must exert the minimum force, we use the calculus to find the value of θ at which a minimum occurs for P. These minima occur when the derivative of P with respect to θ is zero. Since the numerator is constant with respect to θ:

$$\frac{dP}{d\theta} = -\frac{W \sin\alpha + \mu_k W \cos\alpha}{\left(\cos\theta + \mu_k \sin\theta\right)^2}\left(-\sin\theta + \mu_k \cos\theta\right) = 0$$

or $$\sin\theta = \mu_k \cos\theta$$

$$\tan\theta = \mu_k = 0.10$$

$$\theta = 5.7°$$

Thus the boy should drag his sled up in such a way that the rope makes an angle of 5.7° with the slope.

It might have seemed at first sight that a force parallel to the slope would be most efficient. It is now clear that this is not so. Any component of the pull $\vec{P}$ at right angles to the slope decreases the normal force $\vec{N}$ and thus the frictional force $\vec{F}$. The best compromise between maximum forward force and least frictional force is achieved at the angle 5.7°.

CHAPTER 3

KINEMATICS

FUNDAMENTALS OF VELOCITY & ACCELERATION, FREE FALL

• PROBLEM 56

A car covers a distance of 30 miles in ½ hour. What is its speed in miles per hour and in feet per second?

Solution:

$$v_{average} = \frac{s}{t} = \frac{30 \text{ mi}}{\frac{1}{2} \text{ hr}} = 60 \text{ mi per hr}$$

$$= \frac{60 \text{ mi}}{\text{hr}} \times \frac{5280 \text{ ft}}{\text{mi}} \times \frac{1 \text{ hr}}{3600 \text{ sec}}$$

$$= 88 \text{ ft per sec}$$

This useful relation, that 60 miles per hour equals 88 feet per second, is one you should commit to memory.

• PROBLEM 57

An eastbound car travels a distance of 40 mi in 5 s. Determine the speed of the car.

Solution: The observables of distance, d = 40 m, and time interval, t = 5 s, are given. We know that, since the velocity v of the car is constant,

$$v = \frac{d}{t} = \frac{40 \text{ m}}{5 \text{ s}} = 8 \frac{\text{m}}{\text{s}}$$

Here, d is the distance travelled in time t. The speed of the car is 8 m/s.

• PROBLEM 58

A car starts from rest and reaches a speed of 30 miles per hour in 8 seconds. What is its acceleration?

Solution: $v = at$ for constant acceleration. We shall convert the velocity in miles per hour into feet per second. A useful conversion factor to remember is that 60 mph is about 88 ft. per second. Therefore, 30 mph is about 44 ft. per second. Substituting we have:

$$a = \frac{v_{final}}{t} = \frac{44 \text{ ft}}{\text{sec} \times 8 \text{ sec}}$$

$$= 5.5 \text{ ft per sec per sec.}$$

• PROBLEM 59

A car starts from rest and reaches a speed of 88 feet per second in 16 seconds. How far does it travel during this time?

Solution 1: In this problem we assume constant acceleration.

The acceleration of the car is

$$a = \frac{88 \text{ ft}}{16 \text{ sec} \times \text{sec}} = 5.5 \text{ ft per sec}^2$$

Then

$$s = \frac{1}{2} at^2 = \frac{1}{2} \times 5.5 \frac{\text{ft}}{\text{sec}^2} \times (16 \text{ sec})^2 = 704 \text{ ft.}$$

Solution 2:

The average velocity of the car is

$$v_{average} = \frac{v_{final} - v_{initial}}{2}$$

$$= \frac{88 \text{ ft/sec} - 0 \text{ ft/sec}}{2} = 44 \text{ ft per sec.}$$

Then

$$s = v_{average} \times \text{time} = 44 \text{ ft per sec} \times 16 \text{ sec}$$

$$= 704 \text{ ft}$$

• PROBLEM 60

An object, starting from rest, is given an acceleration of 16 feet per second^2 for 3 seconds. What is its speed at the end of 3 seconds?

Solution: Since the acceleration is constant, we have

$$a = \frac{v_{final} - v_{initial}}{t}$$

or $v_{final} = v_{initial} + at$

But $v_{initial} = 0$ for the object started from rest. Therefore

$$v_{final} = a \times t = \frac{16 \text{ ft}}{\text{sec}^2} \times 3 \text{ sec} = 48 \text{ ft per sec.}$$

• PROBLEM 61

Suppose that the first half of the distance between two points is covered at a speed $v_1 = 10$ mi/hr and, that during the second half, the speed is $v_2 = 40$ mi/hr. What is the average speed for the entire trip?

Solution: The average speed is the total distance traveled divided by the total traveling time. The average speed is not

$$\bar{v} = \frac{10 \text{ mi/hr} + 40 \text{ mi/hr}}{2} = 25 \text{ mi/hr.}$$

Let 2x be the total distance traveled and let t_1 and t_2 denote the times necessary for the two parts of the trip. Then,

$$\bar{v} = \frac{2x}{t_1 + t_2}$$

Since only the velocities are known, the average velocity must be expressed in terms of these variables. In order to eliminate unknown variables, we see that

$$t_1 = \frac{x}{v_1};\ t_2 = \frac{x}{v_2}.$$

$$t_1 + t_2 = \frac{x}{v_1} + \frac{x}{v_2} = \frac{x(v_1 + v_2)}{v_1 v_2}.$$

Therefore,

$$\bar{v} = \frac{2x}{\frac{x(v_1 + v_2)}{v_1 v_2}} = \frac{2v_1 v_2}{v_1 + v_2}$$

$$= \frac{2(10\ \text{mi/hr})(40\ \text{mi/hr})}{10\ \text{mi/hr} + 40\ \text{mi/hr}} = \frac{800}{50}\ \text{mi/hr}$$

$$= 16\ \text{mi/hr}.$$

• PROBLEM 62

A car travels at the constant speed of 30 mph for 20 miles, at a speed of 40 mph for the next 20 miles, and then travels the final 20 miles at 50 mph. What was the average speed for the trip?

Solution: For situations in which the speed is variable, the rate at which distance d is traveled as a function of time, t, can be described by the average speed. The average speed $\bar{v}$ is equal to that constant speed which would be required for an object to travel the same distance d in the same time t. Therefore

$$\bar{v} = \frac{d}{t}.$$

The total time the car travels is the sum of the times for each segment of the trip.

$$t = t_1 + t_2 + t_3 = \frac{d_1}{v_1} + \frac{d_2}{v_2} + \frac{d_3}{v_3}$$

$$t = \frac{20\ \text{mi}}{30\ \text{mph}} + \frac{20\ \text{mi}}{40\ \text{mph}} + \frac{20\ \text{mi}}{50\ \text{mph}} = (0.67 + 0.50 + 0.40)\text{hr} = 1.57\ \text{hr}$$

The total distance is

$$d = d_1 + d_2 + d_3 = (20 + 20 + 20)\text{mi} = 60\ \text{mi}$$

Therefore, the average speed is

$$\bar{v} = \frac{d}{t} = \frac{60\ \text{mi}}{1.57\ \text{hr}} = 38.2\ \text{mph}$$

• PROBLEM 63

An automobile accelerates at a constant rate from 15 mi/hr to 45 mi/hr in 10 sec while traveling in a straight line. What is the average acceleration?

Solution. The magnitude of the average acceleration, or the rate of change of speed in this case, is the change in speed divided by the time in which it took place, or

$$\bar{a} = \frac{45\text{ mi/hr} - 15\text{ mi/hr}}{10\text{ sec} - 0} = \frac{30\text{ mi/hr}}{10\text{ sec}}.$$

Changing units so as to be consistent,

$$\bar{a} = \frac{\left(\frac{30\text{ mi}}{\text{hr}}\right) \times \left(\frac{5280\text{ ft}}{\text{mi}}\right) \times \left(\frac{\text{hr}}{3600\text{ sec}}\right)}{10\text{ sec}} = \frac{44\text{ ft/sec}}{10\text{ sec}} = 4.4\text{ ft/sec}^2$$

This statement means simply that the speed increases 4.4 ft/sec during each second, or 4.4 ft/sec^2.

• PROBLEM 64

An automobile traveling at a speed of 30 mi/hr accelerates uniformly to a speed of 60 mi/hr in 10 sec. How far does the automobile travel during the time of acceleration?

Solution. Converting to ft-sec units,

$$30\frac{\text{mi}}{\text{hr}} = 30\frac{\text{mi}}{\text{hr}} \times \frac{5280\text{ ft}}{1\text{ mi}} \times \frac{1\text{ hr}}{3600\text{ sec}} = 44\text{ ft/sec}$$

$$60\frac{\text{mi}}{\text{hr}} = 88\text{ ft/sec}.$$

Uniform acceleration can be found from the change in velocity divided by the time elapsed during the change.

$$a = \frac{\Delta v}{\Delta t} = \frac{88\text{ ft/sec} - 44\text{ ft/sec}}{10\text{ sec}} = 4.4\text{ ft/sec}^2$$

$$x = v_0 t + \frac{1}{2}at^2$$

$$= (44\text{ ft/sec}) \times (10\text{ sec}) + \frac{1}{2} \times (4.4\text{ ft/sec}^2) \times (10\text{ sec})^2$$

$$= 440\text{ ft} + 220\text{ ft}$$

$$= 660\text{ ft}.$$

Suppose next that the automobile, traveling at 60 mi/hr, slows to 20 mi/hr in a period of 20 sec. What was the acceleration?

$$a = \frac{v_2 - v_1}{\Delta t} = \frac{20\text{ mi/hr} - 60\text{ mi/hr}}{20\text{ sec}}$$

$$= -2\text{(mi/hr)/sec}.$$

The automobile was slowing down during this period so the acceleration is negative.

• PROBLEM 65

The graph shows a displacement-time curve for a motion along a straight line. What are the average velocities from A to B and from A to C?

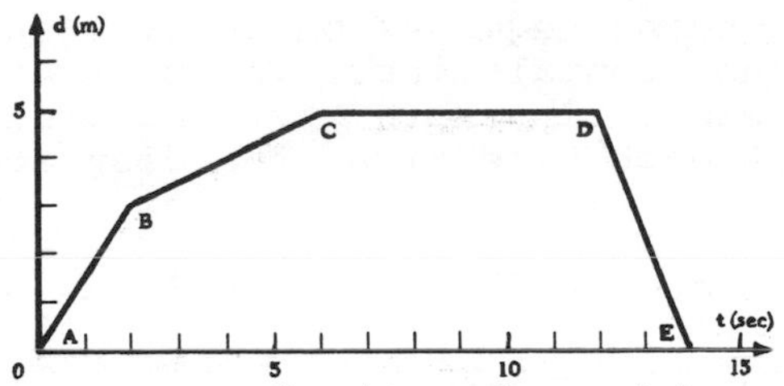

Solution: The average velocity of an object in motion is the distance d it travels divided by the time t it takes in transit.

$$v_{av} = \frac{d}{t}$$

Looking at the figure:

from A to B $\quad v_{av} = \frac{d_{AB}}{t_{AB}} = \frac{3\ m}{2\ s} = 1.5\ m/sec$

from A to C $\quad v_{av} = \frac{d_{AC}}{t_{AC}} = \frac{5\ m}{6\ s} = 0.83\ m/sec.$

• PROBLEM 66

Using the given d-t curve calculate the velocity-time curve.

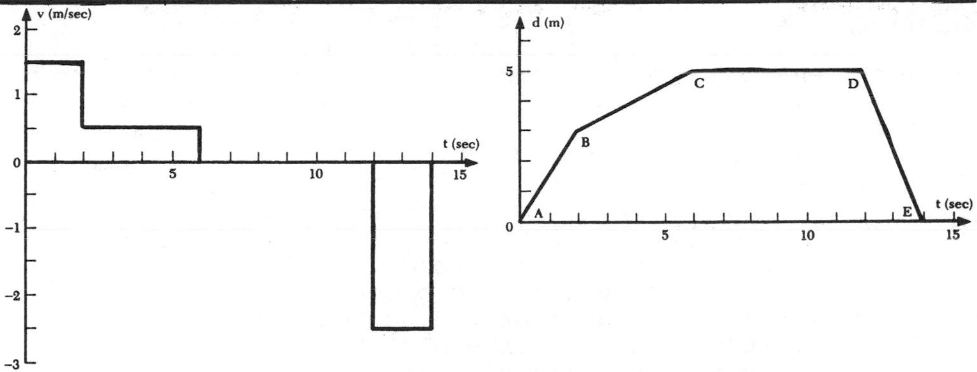

Solution: A velocity-time curve is found from a displacement-time curve by plotting the slope of the d-t curve versus time. Our task in this particular case is made easier by the fact that the velocity in each segment of the trip is constant.

From A to B $\quad v_{AB} = \frac{d_{AB}}{t_{AB}}$

$$= \frac{(3 - 0)m}{(2 - 0)\ sec} = 1.5\ m/sec$$

From B to C $\quad v_{DE} = \frac{d_{DE}}{t_{DE}}$

$$= \frac{(0 - 5)\ m}{(14 - 12)\ sec} = -\ 2.5\ m/sec.$$

The corresponding segments on the v-t curve are represented by horizontal lines. The rest of the curve is found similarly. Note that the area under the v-t curve at each time gives the displacement. That is,

$$\text{at } t = 6 \text{ sec,} \quad \text{area} = (1.5 \times 2 + 0.5 \times 4)\text{m}$$
$$= 5 \text{ m}$$
$$\text{at } t = 14 \text{ sec,} \quad \text{area} = (1.5 \times 2 + 0.5 \times 4 - 2.5 \times 2)\text{m}$$
$$= 0 \text{ m}$$

• PROBLEM 67

A motion, starting from rest, has the acceleration-time graph shown in figure (a). Draw the **v**-t graph and calculate the net displacement.

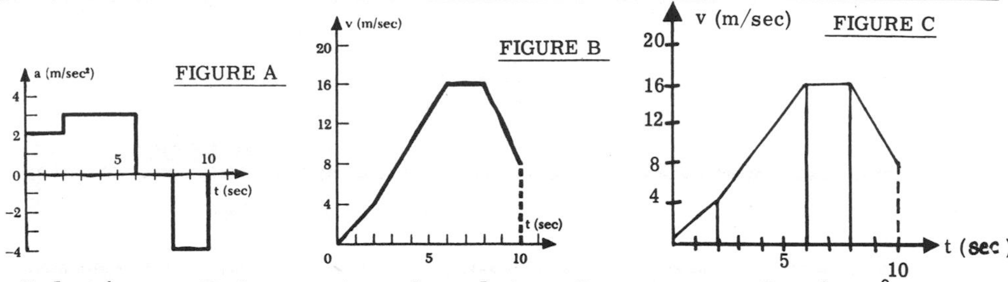

Solution: Between t = 0 and t = 2 sec, a = 2 m/sec^2. Thus $\Delta \mathbf{v} = a\Delta t = 4$ m/sec. Thus at t = 2, **v** = 4 m/sec. Between t = 2 and t = 6, a = 3 m/sec^2; thus $\Delta \mathbf{v} = 3 \times (6 - 2) = 12$ m/sec $= \mathbf{v} - 4$. At t = 6, **v** = 16 m/sec and so forth.

Having found the velocities at various times and plotting the points as in figure (b), we can connect them with straight lines, since, as we can see from the acceleration-time graph, all accelerations are constant (therefore velocity is a linear function of t).

Since displacement equals the product of velocity and time, the net displacement can be found by calculating the area under the **v**-t curve until t = 10 sec. In figure (c), we break the area under the **v**-t curve into triangles and trapezoids. The total area under the curve is equal to the sum of the areas of these figures:

$$d = \text{area} = \tfrac{1}{2}(4 \times 2) + \tfrac{1}{2}(4 + 16) \times 4 + 16 \times 2 + \tfrac{1}{2}(16 + 8) \times 2$$
$$= 4 + 40 + 32 + 24$$
$$= 100 \text{ m}$$

• PROBLEM 68

Suppose the motion of a particle traveling along the x-axis is described by the equation

$$x = a + bt^2$$

where a = 20 cm and b = 4 cm/sec^2.

(a) Find the displacement of the particle in the time interval between $t_1 = 2$ sec and $t_2 = 5$ sec. (b) Find the average velocity in this time interval. (c) Find the instantaneous velocity at time $t_1 = 2$ sec.

Solution: (a) The displacement of a particle moving from position $\vec{r}_1$ to position $\vec{r}_2$ is

$$\Delta\vec{r} = \vec{r}_2 - \vec{r}_1 \ .$$

In this problem, the motion of the particle is one-dimensional and we may neglect the vector nature of the displacement. Hence,

$$\Delta x = x(t_2) - x(t_1)$$

$$\Delta x = \left(a + bt_2^2\right) - \left(a + bt_1^2\right)$$

$$\Delta x = b\left(t_2^2 - t_1^2\right)$$

$$\Delta x = \left(4 \frac{cm}{sec^2}\right)\left(25 - 4\right)sec^2$$

$$\Delta x = 84 \text{ cm}$$

The displacement is positive, so the particles position has increased in the positive direction along the x-axis. $\left(x_2 > x_1\right)$

(b) Average velocity is given by the relation

$$\vec{V}_{avg} = \frac{\Delta\vec{r}}{\Delta t} = \frac{\vec{r}_2 - \vec{r}_1}{t_2 - t_1}$$

where $\vec{r}_2$ and $\vec{r}_1$ are the positions of the particle at times t_2 and t_1 respectively. This is a one-dimensional problem, hence

$$V_{avg} = \frac{\Delta x}{\Delta t} = \frac{84 \text{ cm}}{3 \text{ sec}} = 28 \text{ cm/sec}$$

and it points in the positive x direction since $\Delta x > 0$.

(c) The instantaneous velocity is

$$\vec{V} = \frac{d\vec{r}}{dt}$$

Again, since we have a one-dimensional problem

$$V = \frac{dx}{dt} = \frac{d}{dt}\left(a + b^2\right) = 2bt$$

$$V(2 \text{ sec}) = (2)\left(4 \text{ cm/sec}^2\right)(2 \text{ sec})$$
$$= 16 \text{ cm/sec}$$

• PROBLEM 69

Suppose the velocity of the particle in the diagram is given by the equation

$$\vec{v} = \left(m + nt^2\right)\hat{\imath}$$

where $m = 10$ cm/s and $n = 2$ cm/s^3. (a) Find the change in velocity of the particle in the time interval between $t_1 = 2$ sec and $t_2 = 5$ sec. (b) Find the average acceleration in this time interval. (c) Find the instantaneous acceleration at $t_1 = 2$ sec.

Solution: (a) At time $t_1 = 2$ sec

$$\vec{v}_1 = \left(10\frac{cm}{s} + \left(\frac{2cm}{s^3}\right)(2s)^2\right)\hat{\imath}$$

$$\vec{v}_1 = 18\frac{cm}{s}\ \hat{\imath}$$

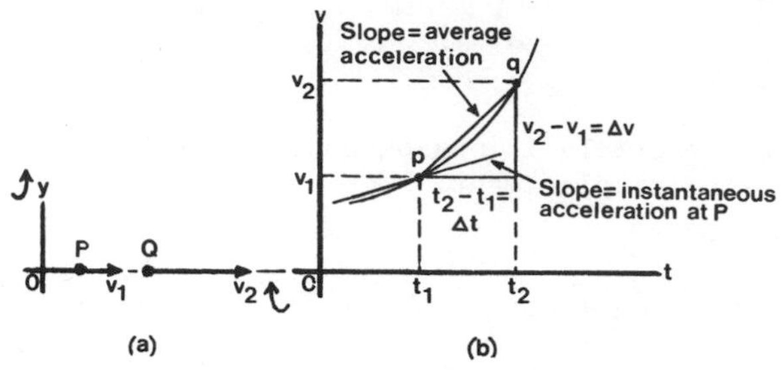

(a) Particle moving on the x-axis. (b) Velocity-time graph of the motion. The average acceleration between t_1 and t_2 equals the slope of the chord pq. The instantaneous acceleration at p equals the slope of the tangent at p.

where $\hat{\imath}$ is a unit vector in the positive x direction.

At time $t_2 = 5$ sec

$$\vec{v}_2 = \left(10\frac{\text{cm}}{\text{s}} + \left(\frac{2\text{cm}}{\text{s}^3}\right)(5\text{s})^2\right)\hat{\imath}$$

$$\vec{v}_2 = \frac{60\ \text{cm}}{\text{s}}\ \hat{\imath}$$

The change in velocity is therefore

$$\vec{v}_2 - \vec{v}_1 = \frac{60\text{cm}}{\text{s}}\hat{\imath} - \frac{18\text{cm}}{\text{s}}\hat{\imath} = \frac{42\text{cm}}{\text{s}}\hat{\imath}$$

(b) The average acceleration is defined as

$$\vec{a}_{avg} = \frac{\vec{v}_2 - \vec{v}_1}{t_2 - t_1}$$

where $\vec{v}_2$ and $\vec{v}_1$ are the velocities at t_2 and t_1, respectively. Hence, in the given interval

$$\vec{a}_{avg} = \frac{\left(60\frac{\text{cm}}{\text{s}} - 18\frac{\text{cm}}{\text{s}}\right)\hat{\imath}}{(5\text{s} - 2\text{s})} = 14\frac{\text{cm}}{\text{s}^2}\ \hat{\imath}$$

This corresponds to the slope of the chord pq in the diagram.

(c) The instantaneous acceleration is

$$\vec{a} = \frac{d\vec{v}}{dt} = 2nt\hat{\imath}$$

At $t_1 = 2$ sec,

$$\bar{a} = (2)\left(\frac{2\text{cm}}{\text{s}^3}\right)(2\text{s}) = 8\ \text{cm/s}^2$$

This corresponds to the slope of the tangent at point P in the figure.

• PROBLEM 70

Two motorcycles are at rest and separated by 24.5 ft. They start at the same time in the same direction, the one in the back having an acceleration of 3 ft/sec^2, the one in the front going slower at an acceleration of 2 ft/sec^2. (a) How long does it take for the faster cycle to overtake the slower. (b) How far does the faster machine go before it catches up? (c) How fast is each cycle going at this time?

Solution: (a) Both cycles travel for the same length of time t. At the instant the two machines pass each other, the faster one has traveled exactly 24.5 ft more than the slower one. With the subscripts 1 and 2 representing the faster and slower cycles respectively, we have

$$d_1 = v_{01}t + \tfrac{1}{2}a_1t^2 = \tfrac{1}{2}a_1t^2$$

$$d_2 = v_{02}t + \tfrac{1}{2}a_2t^2 = \tfrac{1}{2}a_2t^2$$

since the initial velocities v_{01} and v_{02} are both zero. Now

$$d_1 = d_2 + 24.5 \text{ ft.}$$

or

$$\tfrac{1}{2}a_1t^2 = \tfrac{1}{2}a_2t^2 + 24.5 \text{ ft.}$$

Substituting values, we find the time t at which the two cycles pass each other.

$$\tfrac{1}{2}(3 \text{ ft/sec}^2)(t^2) = \tfrac{1}{2}(2 \text{ ft/sec}^2)(t^2) + 24.5 \text{ ft}$$

$$t^2 = 49 \text{ sec}^2$$

$$t = 7 \text{ sec}$$

(b) The distance d_1 traveled by the faster cycle when it passes the slower one is

$$d_1 = \tfrac{1}{2}a_1t^2 = \tfrac{1}{2}(3 \text{ ft/sec})(7 \text{ sec})^2 = 73.5 \text{ ft.}$$

(c) The velocities of the two cycles can be found from

$$v = v_0 + at$$

Then, as they pass each other, their velocities are

$$v_1 = a_1t = (3 \text{ ft/sec}^2)(7 \text{ sec}) = 21 \text{ ft/sec}$$

$$v_2 = a_2t = (2 \text{ ft/sec}^2)(7 \text{ sec}) = 14 \text{ ft/sec} .$$

• PROBLEM 71

A skier is filmed by a motion-picture photographer who notices him traveling down a ski run. The skier travels 36 ft during the fourth second of the filming and 48 ft during the sixth second. What distance did he cover in the eight seconds of filming? Assume that the acceleration is uniform throughout.

Solution: The fact that the acceleration is uniform gives us a big advantage since, in this case, the instantaneous acceleration is equivalent to the average acceleration:

$$\vec{a} = \frac{\Delta \vec{v}}{\Delta t} = \frac{\vec{v}_f - \vec{v}_0}{t_f - t_0}$$

where $\vec{v}_f$ and $\vec{v}_0$ are the velocities at times t_f and t_0 respectively. To solve for $\vec{a}$ we use the kinematic equation

$$s = v_0t + \tfrac{1}{2}at^2$$

where s is the distance covered in time t.

$$36 = v_0(1) + \tfrac{1}{2}a(1) = v_0 + \tfrac{1}{2}a$$

$$48 = v_f(1) + \frac{1}{2}a(1) = v_f + \frac{1}{2}a$$

where v_0 and v_f are the velocities at the beginning of the fourth and sixth seconds respectively, and both time intervals are one second long.

$$\frac{1}{2}a = 36 - v_0 = 48 - v_f$$

$$v_f = v_0 + 12$$

Since there is a two second interval between the times when the skier has velocities v_0 and v_f:

$$a = \frac{v_f - v_0}{\Delta t} = \frac{(v_0 + 12) - v_0}{2} = \frac{12}{2} = 6 \text{ ft/sec}^2$$

Knowing the acceleration, we can now solve for the skier's velocity v_0 at the beginning of the 4th second:

$$36 = v_0(1) + \frac{1}{2}(6)(1)$$

$$v_0 = 36 - 3 = 33 \text{ ft/sec}$$

Now, we may solve for v_0', the velocity at the beginning of the filming

$$v_0 = v_0' + at, \qquad v_0' = v_0 - at$$

$$v_0' = 33 - (6)(3) = 15 \text{ ft/sec}$$

Thus the distance covered in the eigth seconds of filming is:

$$s = v_0't + \frac{1}{2}at^2$$

$$= (15 \text{ ft/sec})(8 \text{ sec}) + \frac{1}{2}\left(6 \text{ ft/sec}^2\right)(8 \text{ sec})^2$$

$$= 312 \text{ ft.}$$

• PROBLEM 72

During the takeoff roll, a Boeing 747 jumbo jet is accelerating at 4 m/sec^2. If it requires 40 sec to reach takeoff speed, determine the takeoff speed and how far the jet travels on the ground.

Solution: The initial speed, $v_0 = 0$, the acceleration $a = 4$ m/sec^2, and the time interval of the takeoff, $t = 40$ sec are given. The unknown observables are the final speed, v, and the distance the plane traveled, d. From the laws of kinematics for constant acceleration

$v_f = v_0 + at$, $v_0 = 0$ and v_f is the plane's final velocity.

Therefore, $v_f = at = (4 \text{ m/sec}^2)(40 \text{ sec}) = 160$ m/sec

The plane's takeoff velocity is 160 m/sec in the same direction as the acceleration.

The distance s an object with constant acceleration travels in time t is:

$$s = v_0 t + \tfrac{1}{2} at^2, \qquad v_0 = 0$$

Hence, $s = \tfrac{1}{2}(4\ \text{m/sec}^2)(40\ \text{sec})^2 = 3{,}200\ \text{m}$

The plane travels a distance of 3.2 km during the takeoff.

• PROBLEM 73

The turntable of a record player is accelerated from rest to a speed of 33.3 rpm in 2 sec. What is the angular acceleration?

Solution: The angular kinematics equation for constant acceleration

$$\omega = \omega_0 + \alpha t$$

can be used. The initial velocity ω_0 is zero. The final angular velocity after t = 2 sec is

$$\omega = 2\pi f = 2\pi \times \frac{33.3\ \text{rev/min}}{60\ \text{sec/min}}$$
$$= 2\pi \times 0.556\ \text{sec}^{-1} = 3.48\ \text{sec}^{-1}$$

The angular acceleration is then

$$\alpha = \frac{\omega - \omega_0}{t} = \frac{3.48\ \text{sec}^{-1} - 0\ \text{sec}^{-1}}{2\ \text{sec}}$$
$$= 1.74\ \text{sec}^{-2}$$

• PROBLEM 74

Use the definite integral to find the velocity and coordinate, at any time t of a body moving on the x-axis with constant acceleration. The initial velocity is v_0 and the initial coordinate is zero.

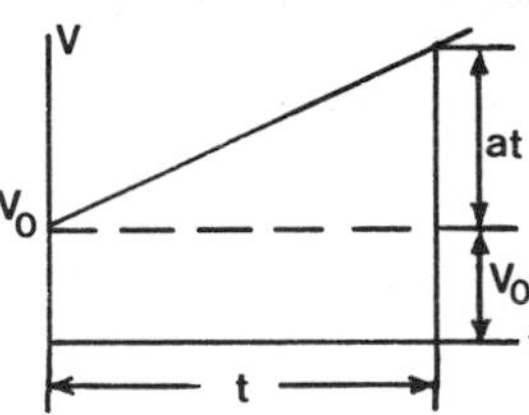

Solution: Acceleration is defined as the time rate of change of velocity. Since we are concerned with motion along the x-axis, we may neglect the vector nature of acceleration ($\vec{a}$), velocity ($\vec{v}$) and position ($\vec{r}$) and write

$$a = dv/dt$$

$$dv = adt$$

Because a is constant

$$\int_{v_1}^{v_2} dv = a \int_{t_1}^{t_2} dt$$

As the limits of integration, we take $v_1 = v_0$ at $t_1 = 0$, and $v_2 = v$ at $t_2 = t$. Then

$$\int_{v_0}^{v} dv = a \int_0^t dt$$

$$v - v_0 = at$$

$$v = v_0 + at$$

But

$$v = dx/dt = v_0 + at$$

where x is the position of the body along the x-axis. Then

$$dx = v_0 dt + at\ dt$$

$$\int_{x_1}^{x_2} dx = v_0 \int_{t_1}^{t_2} dt + a \int_{t_1}^{t_2} t\ dt \qquad (1)$$

We take $x_1 = x_0$ at $t_1 = 0$, and $x_2 = x$ at $t_2 = t$, whence

$$\int_{x_0}^{x} dx = v_0 \int_0^t dt + a \int_0^t t\ dt$$

$$x - x_0 = v_0 t + \frac{at^2}{2}$$

$$x = x_0 + v_0 t + \tfrac{1}{2} at^2$$

We can also obtain this result by noting that evaluating the integral in (1) is equivalent to finding the area under the velocity vs. time curve shown in the figure.

• PROBLEM 75

In a drag race, a dragster reaches the quarter-mile (402 m) marker with a speed of 80 m/s. What is his acceleration and how long did the run take?

Solution: The initial velocity, $v_0 = 0$, the final velocity, $v = 80$ m/s, and the distance traveled, $d = 402$ m, are given. The acceleration a and the time interval t are the unknown observables.

From the kinematics equations,

$$a = \frac{v^2 - v_0^2}{2d} = \frac{(80\ m/s)^2 - (0)}{(2)(402\ m)} = 7.96\ m/s^2$$

$$t = \frac{v - v_0}{a} = \frac{(80\ m/s) - (0)}{7.96\ m/s^2} = 10.1\ s$$

• PROBLEM 76

A ball is released from rest at a certain height. What is its velocity after falling 256 ft?

Solution: Since the initial velocity is zero, we use

$$y = v_0 t + \tfrac{1}{2}at^2 = \tfrac{1}{2} gt^2$$

taking "down" as the positive y-direction.

Solving for the time to fall 256 ft, we have

$$t = \sqrt{\frac{2y}{g}}$$

$$= \sqrt{\frac{2 \times 256 \text{ ft}}{(32 \text{ ft/sec}^2)}} = \sqrt{16 \text{ sec}^2} = 4 \text{ sec}$$

The velocity after 4 sec fall is

$$v = v_0 + at = gt = (32 \text{ ft/sec}^2) \times (4 \text{ sec})$$

$$= 128 \text{ ft/sec.}$$

• PROBLEM 77

On a long straight road a car accelerates uniformly from rest, reaching a speed of 45 mph in 11 s. It has to maintain that speed for 1½ mi behind a truck until a suitable opportunity for passing the truck arises. The car then accelerates uniformly to 75 mph in a further 11 s. After maintaining that speed for 3 min, the car is brought to a halt by a uniform deceleration of 11 ft/s^2.

Illustrate the motion on a suitable diagram, and calculate (a) the total distance traveled, (b) the total time taken, (c) the average speed, and (d) the average acceleration in the first 142 s.

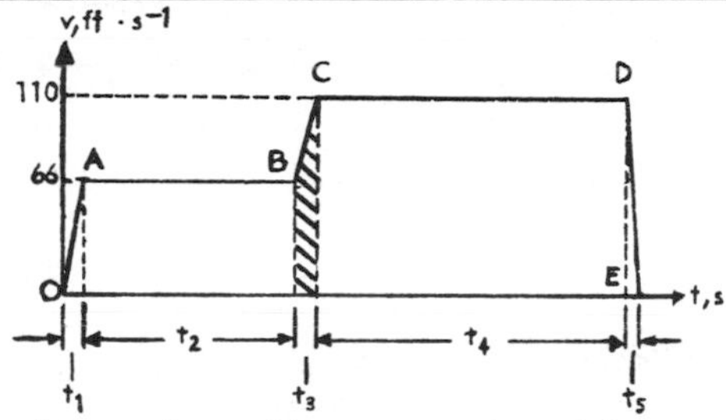

Solution: A velocity-time diagram should be drawn. During the first 11 s the car accelerates uniformly to a speed of 45 mph = 66 ft/s. This part of the diagram is therefore a straight line OA inclined to the t-axis at an angle whose tangent is 66/11. The distance traveled, s_1, is the area under this portion of the graph. Thus

$$s_1 = \tfrac{1}{2} \times 11 \text{ s} \times 66 \text{ ft/s} = 363 \text{ ft.}$$

In the second portion of the motion, the car travels for 1 ½ mi at a constant speed of 45 mph. This part of the graph, AB, is a straight line parallel to the t-axis, its length being

$$t_2 = \frac{1\tfrac{1}{2} \text{ mi}}{45 \text{ mi/hr}} \times 60 \text{ min/hr} \times 60 \text{ s/min} = 120 \text{ s.}$$

In the third portion of the motion, the car increases its speed by 30 mph = 44 ft · s^{-1} at uniform acceleration in 11 s. This part of the graph is thus a straight line BC of slope 44/11. The distance traveled in this 11 s, s_3, is the area under this part of the graph, i.e., the shaded portion.

$$s_3 = \tfrac{1}{2} \times 11 \text{ s} \times 44 \text{ ft/s} + 11 \text{ s} \times 66 \text{ ft/s} = 968 \text{ ft}.$$

The next portion of the graph is again a straight line parallel to the t-axis. The time t_4 is 3 min = 180 s, and thus

$$s_4 = 75 \text{ mi/hr} \times \frac{3}{60} \text{ hr} = 3.75 \text{ mi}.$$

In the final part of the motion, the car is brought to rest from a speed of 110 ft $\cdot$ s^{-1} by a uniform deceleration of 11 ft/s^2. This portion of the graph, DE, is thus a straight line with a negative slope of 110/11. The time taken to come to rest, t_5, and the distance traversed, s_5, are

$$t_5 = \frac{110 \text{ ft/s}}{11 \text{ ft/s}} = 10 \text{ s} \quad \text{and} \quad s_5 = \tfrac{1}{2} \times 10\text{s} \times 110 \text{ ft/s}$$

$$= 550 \text{ ft}.$$

(a) The total distance traveled is

$$s = s_1 + s_2 + s_3 + s_4 + s_5$$

$$= 363 \text{ ft} + 1\tfrac{1}{2} \text{ mi} + 968 \text{ ft} + 3\,\frac{3}{4} \text{ mi} + 550 \text{ ft}$$

$$= 5\tfrac{1}{4} \text{ mi} + 1881 \text{ ft} = 5 \text{ mi } 3201 \text{ ft} = 5 \text{ mi } 1067 \text{ yd}.$$

(b) The total time taken is

$$t = t_1 + t_2 + t_3 + t_4 + t_5$$

$$= (11 + 120 + 11 + 180 + 10)\text{s} = 332 \text{ s} = 5 \text{ min } 32 \text{ s}.$$

(c) The average speed, $\bar{v}$, is the total distance traveled divided by the total time taken. Thus

$$\bar{v} = \frac{5 \text{ mi } 1067 \text{ yd}}{332 \text{ s}} = \frac{29{,}601}{332} \text{ ft/s}$$

$$= 89.16 \text{ ft/s} \times \frac{60 \text{ mph}}{88 \text{ ft/s}} = 60.8 \text{ mph}.$$

(d) The average acceleration in the first 142 s, $\bar{a}$, is the final speed achieved divided by the total time taken. Thus

$$\bar{a} = \frac{110 \text{ ft/s}}{142 \text{ s}} = 0.78 \text{ ft/s}^2.$$

• PROBLEM 78

A body is released from rest and falls freely. Compute its position and velocity after 1, 2, 3, and 4 seconds. Take the origin O at the elevation of the starting point, the y-axis vertical, and the upward direction as positive.

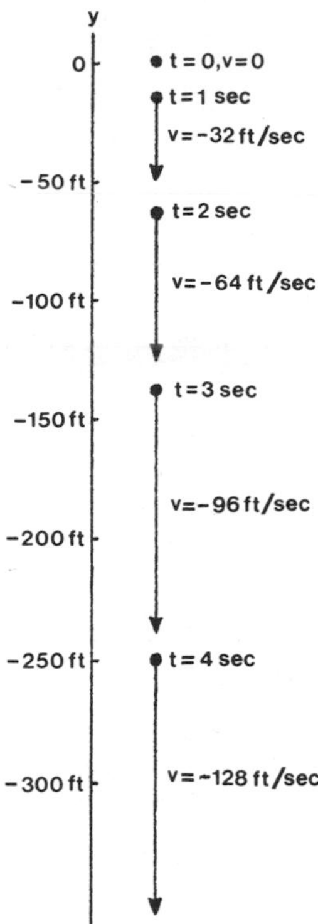

Solution: The initial coordinate y_0 and the initial velocity v_0 are both zero (see figure). The acceleration is downward, in the negative y-direction, so $a = -g = - 32\ \text{ft/sec}^2$.

Since the acceleration is constant, we may use the kinematical equations for constant acceleration, or

$$y = v_0 t + \frac{1}{2}at^2 = 0 - \frac{1}{2}gt^2 = -16\frac{\text{ft}}{\text{sec}^2} \times t^2,$$

$$v = v_0 + at = 0 - gt = -32\frac{\text{ft}}{\text{sec}^2} \times t.$$

When t = 1 sec,

$$y_1 = -16\frac{\text{ft}}{\text{sec}^2} \times 1\ \text{sec}^2 = -16\ \text{ft},$$

$$v_1 = -32\frac{\text{ft}}{\text{sec}^2} \times 1\ \text{sec} = -32\frac{\text{ft}}{\text{sec}}.$$

The body is therefore 16 ft below the origin (y is negative) and has a downward velocity (v is negative) of magnitude 32 ft/sec.

The position and velocity at 2, 3, and 4 sec are found in the same way.

$$y_2 = -16\frac{\text{ft}}{\text{sec}^2} \times (2\ \text{sec})^2 = -16\frac{\text{ft}}{\text{sec}^2} \times 4\ \text{sec}^2 = -64\ \text{ft}$$

$$v_2 = -32\frac{\text{ft}}{\text{sec}^2} \times 2\ \text{sec} = -64\ \text{ft/sec}$$

$$y_3 = -16\frac{ft}{sec^2} \times (3\ sec)^2 = -16\frac{ft}{sec^2} \times 9\ sec^2 = -144\ ft$$

$$v_3 = -32\frac{ft}{sec^2} \times 3\ sec = -96\ ft/sec$$

$$y_4 = -16\frac{ft}{sec^2} \times (4\ sec)^2 = -16\frac{ft}{sec^2} \times 16\ sec^2 = -256\ ft$$

$$v_4 = -32\frac{ft}{sec^2} \times 4\ sec = -128\ ft/sec$$

The results are illustrated in the diagram.

• PROBLEM 79

A ball is thrown upward with an initial speed of 80 ft/sec. How high does it go? What is its speed at the end of 3.0 sec? How high is it at that time?

Solution. Since both upward and downward quantities are involved, upward will be called positive. At the highest point the ball stops, and hence at that point $v_1 = 0$. The only force acting on the ball is the gravitational force which gives a constant acceleration of $g = -32\ ft/sec^2$. For constant acceleration and unidirectional motion,

$$2as = v_1^2 - v_0^2$$

$$2(-32\ ft/sec^2)s_1 = 0 - (80\ ft/sec)^2$$

$$s_1 = \frac{-(80\ ft/sec)^2}{2(-32\ ft/sec^2)} \approx 100\ ft.$$

s_1 is the highest point the ball reaches. To find the speed of the ball after 3 seconds,

$$v_2 = v_0 + at$$

$$= 80\ ft/sec + (-32\ ft/sec^2)(3.0\ sec)$$

$$= 80\ ft/sec - 96\ ft/sec = -16\ ft/sec.$$

After 3 seconds, the speed of the ball is $v_2 = 16$ ft/sec downward. The height of the ball after 3 seconds can be found from

$$s_2 = v_0t + \tfrac{1}{2}at^2$$

$$= (80\ ft/sec)(3.0\ sec) + \tfrac{1}{2}(-32\ ft/sec^2)(3.0\ sec)^2$$

$$= 240\ ft - 144\ ft = 96\ ft.$$

As a check, s_2 can also be found by using

$$s_2 = \bar{v}t = \left(\frac{v_2 + v_0}{2}\right)t = \frac{-16 \text{ ft/sec} + 80 \text{ ft/sec}}{2} \times 3.0 \text{ sec}$$

$$= 96 \text{ ft}$$

where $\bar{v}$ is the average velocity.

Note that s is the magnitude of the displacement, not the total distance traveled. If the ball returns to the starting point or goes on past it, s will be zero or negative, respectively.

• PROBLEM 80

A man standing on the roof of a building 30 meters high throws a ball vertically downward with an initial velocity of 500 cm sec^{-1} as it leaves his hand (see the figure). The acceleration due to gravity is 9.8 m sec^{-2}. (a) What is the velocity of the ball after it has been falling for 0.5 second? (b) Where is the ball after 1.5 second? (c) What is the velocity of the ball as it strikes the ground?

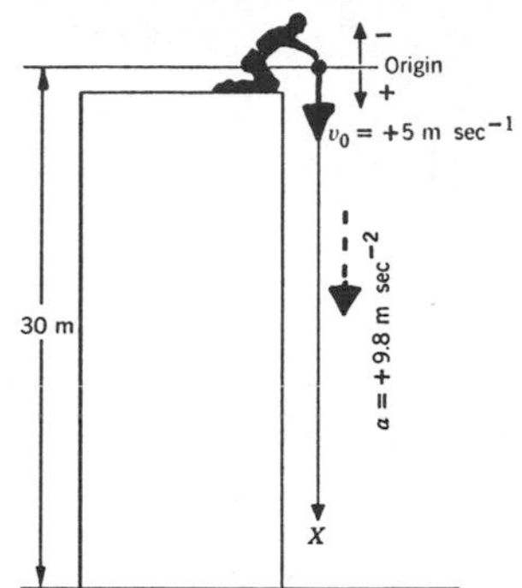

Solution: We will use the MKS system of units because most of the given quantities are expressed in these units. Then the initial velocity must be expressed as 5 meters per second since 1 cm/s = .01 m/s. Place the origin at the top of the building. Then x = 0 when t = 0. Let the positive direction of x be downward. The initial velocity is downward and therefore positive, so v_o = +5 m sec^{-1}. The acceleration is downward and therefore positive, so a = +9.8 m sec^{-2}.

(a) In this part of the problem one is given v_0, a, and t, and must deduce v. Since the acceleration is constant, we may use the kinetmatics equations for constant acceleration, or

$$v = v_0 + at = \left(+5 \frac{m}{sec}\right) + \left(+9.8 \frac{m}{sec^2}\right)(+0.5 \text{ sec})$$

$$= 5 \frac{m}{sec} + 4.9 \frac{m}{sec} = +9.9 \frac{m}{sec}.$$

After 0.5 second the velocity is 9.9 m sec^{-1} downward.

(b) In this part of the problem one is given v_0, a, and t, and must calculate x. By definition of velocity,

$$v = \frac{dx}{dt}.$$

Therefore, $\int_{x_0}^{x} dx = \int_{t=0}^{t} v\,dt$ where x_0 is the initial position of the ball. Using the formula for v given in the previous part, we have

$$x - x_0 = \int_0^t (v_0 + at)dt$$

or $x = x_0 + v_0t + \frac{1}{2}at^2$. Because $x_0 = 0$

$$x = v_0t + \frac{1}{2}at^2$$

$$= \left(+5 \frac{m}{sec}\right)(+1.5 \text{ sec}) + \frac{1}{2}\left(+9.8 \frac{m}{sec^2}\right)(+1.5 \text{ sec})^2$$

$$= 7.5 \text{ m} + \left(4.9 \frac{m}{sec^2}\right)\left(2.25 \text{ sec}^2\right)$$

$$= 7.5\text{m} + 11.025 \text{ m}$$

$$= 18.525 \text{ m}.$$

After 1.5 second the ball is 18.525 meters below the roof or 11.475 meters above the ground.

(c) When the body strikes the ground x = +30 m. So one is given v_0, a, and x, and asked to calculate v. The correct equation, then, should not contain t as a variable. The equation to be used is, since a = constant,

$$v^2 = v_0^2 + 2ax$$

$$= \left(+5 \frac{m}{sec}\right)^2 + 2\left(+9.8 \frac{m}{sec^2}\right)(+30\text{m})$$

$$= 25 \frac{m^2}{sec^2} + 588 \frac{m^2}{sec^2}$$

$$v^2 = 613 \frac{m^2}{sec^2}$$

$$v = 24.76 \frac{m}{sec}.$$

When it strikes the ground, the ball has a velocity of 24.76 m sec^{-1}.

• PROBLEM 81

A ball is thrown upward with an initial velocity of 32 ft/sec from the top of a building. Calculate the velocity and the position as functions of the time.

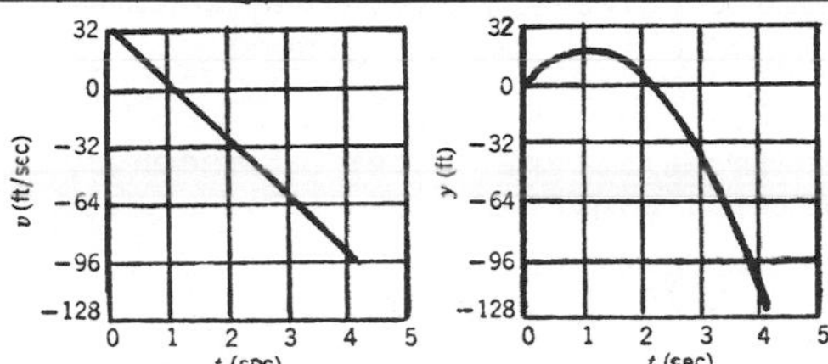

Solution: The only force acting on the ball is the gravitational force, which is directed downward. Throughout its motion, therefore, the ball will be accelerated downward, at $a = -g = 132$ ft / sec^2. We have chosen the positive direction to be up. We have two directions of motion to consider: first, the upward motion to the maximum height and then the downward motion toward the ground. Therefore, we must be careful to use the proper signs in our equations. We choose the origin for distance ($y = 0$) at the point from which the ball is thrown. The initial velocity of the ball is $v_0 = + 32$ ft /sec. The ball gradually loses velocity until it reaches its maximum height. Then it falls down towards the ground. The equations for velocity and distance therefore become

$$v = v_0 + at = (32 \text{ ft/sec}) - (32 \text{ ft/sec}^2) \times t$$

$$y = v_0 t + 1/2\, at^2 = (32 \text{ ft/sec}) \times t - (16 \text{ ft/sec}^2) \times t^2$$

From these equations we find,

t(sec)	v(ft/sec)	y(ft)
0	32	0
1	0	16
2	-32	0
3	-64	-48
4	-96	-128

After 1 sec, the velocity of the ball has become zero; that is, the maximum height has been reached (16 ft) and the subsequent motion is downward. All velocities for $t > 1$ sec are therefore negative. At $t = 2$ sec, the ball has returned to its starting point ($y = 0$) and for all subsequent times, y is negative. The diagrams below show the velocity and the distance as functions of the time.

• PROBLEM 82

(a) With what speed must a ball be thrown directly upward so that it remains in the air for 10 seconds? (b) What will be its speed when it hits the ground? (c) How high does the ball rise?

Solution: Near the surface of the earth, all objects fall towards its center with a constant acceleration $g = 32$ ft/sec^2. Therefore, when the ball is thrown, its speed must decrease by 32 ft/sec each second until it reaches its maximum height. Then it starts to fall, gaining speed at the rate of 32 ft/sec^2, and retraces its path, hitting the ground with the same speed at which it started the trip upward. This is so because the acceleration is constant and the distance traveled is the same during the rising and falling portions of the motion of the ball. Thus, the average velocity must have the same magnitude in each case and the time required to reach the maximum height must equal the time required to fall back to the ground.

(a) Let the upward direction be positive. Then v_0 is positive and the acceleration a is negative. After 10 seconds, v must equal $-v_0$. From the kinematics equation

$$v = v_0 + at$$

we have for the instant before it hits the ground,

$$-v_0 = v_0 - gt$$

$$-2v_0 = -gt$$

and

$$v_0 = \frac{gt}{2} = \frac{(32\ \text{ft/sec}^2)(10\ \text{sec})}{2} = 160\ \text{ft/sec}$$

(b) The speed of the ball when it hits the ground is $-v_0$ or -160 ft/sec.

(c) The height reached by the ball can be obtained by realizing that the rise of the ball must take half the total time the ball is in the air, or 5 seconds. The average velocity for this part of the motion must be

$$\bar{v} = \frac{v_i + v_f}{2} = \frac{(160\ \text{ft/sec} + 0\ \text{ft/sec})}{2} = 80\ \text{ft/sec}.$$

The height the ball rises is then

$$d = \bar{v}t = (80\ \text{ft/sec})(5\ \text{sec}) = 400\ \text{ft}.$$

This result can also be obtained using the kinematics equation

$$d = v_0 t + \tfrac{1}{2} at^2$$

Substituting values,

$$d = (160\ \text{ft/sec})(5\ \text{sec}) + \tfrac{1}{2}(-32\ \text{ft/sec}^2)(5\ \text{sec})^2$$

$$= 800\ \text{ft} - 400\ \text{ft} = 400\ \text{ft}.$$

• PROBLEM 83

A racing car passes one end of the grandstand at a speed of 50 ft/sec. It slows down at a constant acceleration $\vec{a}$, such that its speed as it passes the other end of the grandstand is 10 ft/sec. **(a)** If this process takes 20 seconds, calculate the acceleration $\vec{a}$ and (b) the length of the grandstand .

Solution: (a) For constant acceleration, we have

$$a = \frac{\text{change in velocity}}{\text{time elapsed}} = \frac{\Delta v}{\Delta t}$$

Therefore

$$a = \frac{v_f - v_i}{\Delta t} = \frac{10\ \text{ft/sec} - 50\ \text{ft/sec}}{20\ \text{seconds}} = -2\ \text{ft/sec}^2$$

where v_f and v_i are the final and initial velocities, respectively.

(b) The length of the grandstand is equal to the distance d the car travels during the 20 seconds. This distance is equal to its final position x_f minus its initial position x_i and can be found from the kinematics equation

$$x_f = x_i + v_i t + \frac{1}{2}at^2 .$$

Hence,

$$d = x_f - x_i = v_i t + \frac{1}{2}at^2$$

$$= (50 \text{ ft/sec})(20 \text{ sec}) + \frac{1}{2}(-2 \text{ ft/sec}^2)(20 \text{ sec})^2$$

$$= 1000 \text{ ft} - 400 \text{ ft} = 600 \text{ ft}$$

The length d can also be found using $d = \bar{v}t$ where $\bar{v}$ is the average velocity. For constant acceleration, $\bar{v}$ is given by

$$\bar{v} = \frac{v_i + v_f}{2} = \frac{50 \text{ ft/sec} + 10 \text{ ft/sec}}{2} = 30 \text{ ft/sec}.$$

Then,

$$d = \bar{v}t = (30 \text{ ft/sec})(20 \text{ sec}) = 600 \text{ ft}.$$

which agrees with the first answer.

VECTOR COMPONENTS OF VELOCITY & ACCELERATION

• PROBLEM 84

The pilot of an airplane flying on a straight course knows from his instruments that his **airspeed** is 300 mph. He also knows that a 60-mph gale is blowing at an angle of 60° to his course. How can he calculate his velocity relative to the ground?

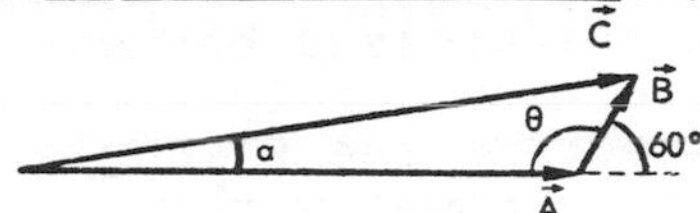

Solution: Relative to an observer on the ground, the airplane has two velocities, one of 300 mph relative to the air and the other of 60 mph at an angle of 60° to the course, due to the fact that it is carried along by the moving air mass.

To obtain the resultant velocity, it is therefore necessary to add the two components by vector addition. In the diagram, $\vec{A}$ represents the velocity of the aircraft relative to the air, and $\vec{B}$ the velocity of the air relative to the ground. When they are added in the normal manner of vector addition, $\vec{C}$ is their resultant. The magnitude of $\vec{C}$ is given by the trigonometric formula known as the law of cosines (see figure).

$$C^2 = A^2 + B^2 - 2AB \cos \theta .$$

But $A = 300$ mph, $B = 60$ mph, and $\theta = (180° - 60°) = 120°$. Therefore

$$C^2 = (300 \text{ mph})^2 + (60 \text{ mph})^2 - 2 \times 300 \text{ mph} \times 60 \text{ mph} \left(-\frac{1}{2}\right) = 111{,}600 \text{ (mph)}^2;$$

$$\therefore \qquad C = 334 \text{ mph}.$$

Also, from the addition formula for vectors, we have

$$\sin \alpha = \frac{B}{C} \sin \theta = \frac{60 \text{ mph}}{334 \text{ mph}} \times \frac{\sqrt{3}}{2} = 0.156.$$

$$\therefore \qquad \alpha = 9°.$$

A motor boat can move with a maximum speed of 10 m/sec, relative to the water. A river 400 m wide flowing at 5 m/sec must be crossed in the shortest possible time to reach a point on the other bank directly opposite the starting point. In which direction must the boat be pointed and how long will it take to cross?

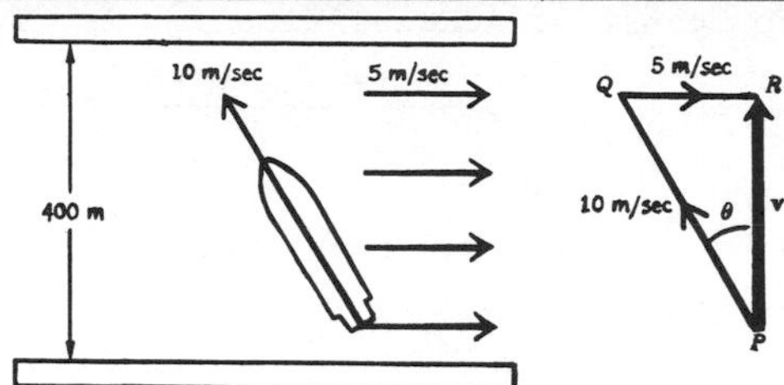

Solution: If the boat were pointed directly at the opposite bank, then during the crossing it would drift downstream and it would not reach the other bank at a point directly opposite the starting point. It must therefore be pointed in a direction tilted in the upstream direction as shown in the figure. As illustrated in the vector diagram PQR, the result of adding the velocity of the boat relative to the water to the velocity of the water must be a resultant velocity $\vec{v}$ pointing directly toward the opposite bank. We cannot draw this triangle of vectors immediately because we do not know the angle θ between the direction of motion and the direction straight across the stream. However, inspecting the triangle PQR and remembering that in trigonometry the sine of the angle θ is defined as

$$\sin\theta = \frac{QR}{PQ}$$

$$= \frac{5}{10} = 0.5$$

we refer to table of sines and find that the angle whose sine is 0.5 is 30°. The boat must therefore be pointed upstream at an angle of 30° from the direction perpendicular to the bank.

Applying Pythagoras' theorem to the triangle PQR

$$PQ^2 = QR^2 + PR^2$$

or $PR^2 = PQ^2 - QR^2$

that is; $v^2 = 10^2 - 5^2 = 75$

$$v = \sqrt{75} = 8.66 \text{ m/sec}$$

The boat therefore crosses the river at a speed of 8.66 m/sec. Since the distance across the river is 400 m, the time taken is, since v = constant,

$$t = \frac{d}{v} = \frac{400 \text{ m}}{8.66 \text{ m/sec}}$$

$$t = 46.2 \text{ sec.}$$

• PROBLEM 86

A plane can travel 100 miles per hour (mph) without any wind. Its fuel supply is 3 hours. (This means that it can fly 300 miles without a wind). The pilot now proposes to fly east with a tail wind of 10 mph and to return with, of course, a head wind of 10 mph. How far out can he fly and return without running out of fuel?

(The student should first reflect on whether or not the answer is the same as it is without a wind, namely, 150 miles.)

Solution: Our basic equation is

(time out) + (time back) = 3 hours

We now use the fact that time = $\frac{\text{(distance)}}{\text{(speed)}}$ so that if d represents the distance out (= distance back) in miles we have

$$\frac{d}{110 \text{ miles/hr}} + \frac{d}{90 \text{ miles/hr}} = 3 \text{ hours}$$

since the speed out is (100 + 10)and the speed back is (100 - 10)mph. Thus:

$$\frac{90\ d + 110\ d}{9900 \text{ miles/hr}} = \frac{200\ d}{9900 \text{ miles/hr}} = 3 \text{ hours}$$

$d = 148.5$ miles.

• PROBLEM 87

A boy leaning over a railway bridge 49 ft high sees a train approaching with uniform speed and attempts to drop a stone down the funnel. He releases the stone when the engine is 80 ft away from the bridge and sees the stone hit the ground 3 ft in front of the engine. What is the speed of the train?

Solution: Applying the equation applicable to uniform acceleration, $x - x_0 = v_0 t + \frac{1}{2}at^2$, to the dropping of the stone 49 ft from rest under the action of gravity, we can find the time t the stone is in motion. The initial velocity of the stone v_0 is zero. The distance the stone travels, $x - x_0 = 49$ ft. Therefore,

$$49 \text{ ft} = 0 + (\tfrac{1}{2})\left(32 \text{ ft/sec}^2\right)\left(t^2\right)$$

$$\therefore\ t = \sqrt{\frac{2 \times 49 \text{ ft}}{32 \text{ ft/s}^2}} = \frac{7}{4} \text{ s.}$$

In the time of 7/4 s it takes the stone to drop, the engine has moved with uniform speed u a distance of (80 - 3) ft.

$$\therefore\ u = \frac{d}{t} = \frac{77 \text{ ft}}{7/4 \text{ sec}} = 44 \text{ ft/sec} = 30 \text{ mph.}$$

• PROBLEM 88

An airplane lands on a carrier deck at 150 mi/hr and is brought to a stop uniformly, by an arresting device, in 500 ft. Find the acceleration and the time required to stop.

Solution. Converting units to ft-sec,

$$v_0 = (150\ \text{mi/hr}) \times \left(\frac{5280\ \text{ft/mi}}{3600\ \text{sec/hr}}\right) = 220\ \text{ft/sec.}$$

Since there is a constant deceleration,

$$2as = v_1^2 - v_0^2$$

$$2a(500\ \text{ft}) = 0 - (220\ \text{ft/sec})^2$$

$$a = \frac{-(220\ \text{ft/sec})^2}{2(500\ \text{ft})} = -48.4\ \text{ft/sec}^2.$$

Solving for t in the following formula,

$$v_1 = v_0 + at$$

$$t = \frac{v_1 - v_0}{a} = \frac{0 - 220\ \text{ft/sec}}{-48.4\ \text{ft/sec}^2} = 4.55\ \text{sec.}$$

• PROBLEM 89

A ball is projected horizontally with a velocity v_0 of 8 ft/sec. Find its position and velocity after $\frac{1}{4}$ sec (see the figure).

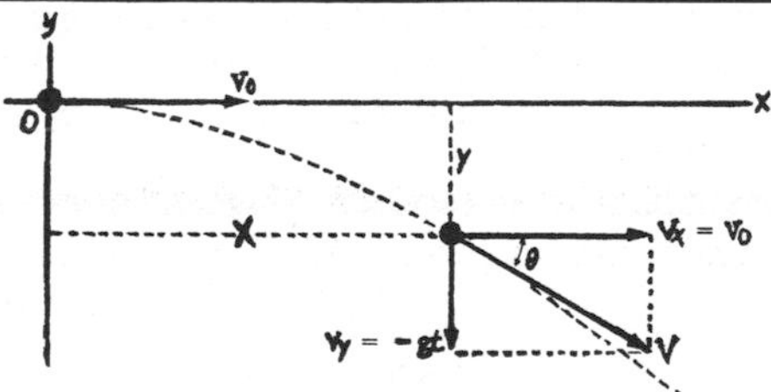

Solution: Since the acceleration of gravity, g, is constant, we may use the equations for constant acceleration to find the velocity $\left(v_y\right)$ and position (y) of a particle undergoing free fall motion

$$v_y = v_{0_y} - gt$$

$$y = y_0 + v_{0_y} - \tfrac{1}{2}gt^2$$

Here, y_0 and v_{0_y} are the initial y position and velocity of the particle. In this case, the departure angle is zero. The initial vertical velocity component is therefore zero. The horizontal velocity component equals the initial velocity and is constant. Since no horizontal force acts on the flying object, it is not accelerated in the horizontal direction. Therefore,

$$v_y = -gt \qquad y = -\tfrac{1}{2}gt^2$$

$$v_x = v_{0_x} \qquad x = v_{0_x} t$$

and, at $t = \frac{1}{4}$ sec,

$$y = \left(-\tfrac{1}{2}\right)\left(32 \text{ ft/sec}^2\right)\left(\tfrac{1}{16} \text{ sec}^2\right) = -1 \text{ ft.}$$

$$v_y = \left(-32 \text{ ft/sec}^2\right)\left(\tfrac{1}{4} \text{ sec}\right) \qquad x = (8 \text{ ft/sec})\left(\tfrac{1}{4} \text{ sec}\right) = 2 \text{ ft.}$$

$$= -8 \text{ ft/sec}$$

$$v_x = 8 \text{ ft/sec}$$

• PROBLEM 90

A ball is thrown with an initial velocity, v_0, of 160 ft/sec, directed at an angle, θ_o, of 53° with the ground.
(a) Find the x- and y-components of v_0.
(b) Find the position of the ball and the magnitude and direction of its velocity when $t = 2$ sec.
(c) At the highest point of the ball's path, what is the ball's altitude (h) and how much time has elapsed?
(d) What is the ball's range d? (See figure).

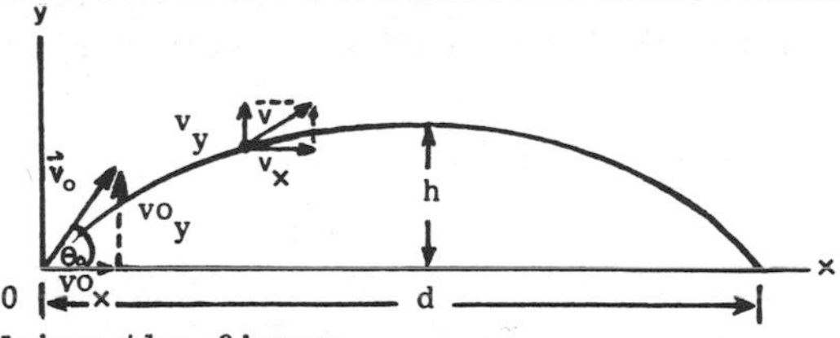

Solution: (a) Using the figure

$$v_{0_x} = v_0 \cos \theta_0; \; v_{0_y} = v_0 \sin \theta_0$$

Hence,

$$v_{0_x} = 160 \text{ ft/sec} \cdot \cos 53^\circ = 160 \text{ ft/sec } (3/5) = 96 \text{ ft/sec}$$

$$v_{0_y} = 160 \text{ ft/sec} \cdot \sin 53^\circ = 160 \text{ ft/sec } (4/5)$$

$$= 128 \text{ ft/sec}$$

(b) The acceleration due to gravity is constant. Furthermore, there is no force acting on the projectile in the x-direction, and its acceleration in the x-direction is therefore zero. Hence

$$a_x(t) = 0 \qquad a_y(t) = -g$$

$$v_x(t) = v_{0_x} \qquad v_y(t) = v_{0_y} - gt$$

$$x(t) = x_0 + v_{0_x} t \qquad y(t) = y_0 t \; v_{0_y} t - \tfrac{1}{2}gt^2$$

Here, x_0, y_0 are the initial coordinates of the projectile, and v_{0_x}, v_{0_y} are the initial x and y components of the ball's velocity. Taking the origin (0) as shown in the figure, we have, at $t = 2$ sec

$$v_x = 96 \text{ ft/sec}$$

$$x = (96 \text{ ft/sec})(2 \text{ sec}) = 192 \text{ ft.}$$

$$v_y = 128 \text{ ft/sec} - \left(32 \text{ ft/sec}^2\right)(2 \text{ sec}) = 64 \text{ ft/sec}$$

$$y = (128\ \text{ft/sec})(2\ \text{sec}) - \left(\tfrac{1}{2}\right)\left(32\ \text{ft/sec}^2\right)\left(4\ \text{sec}^2\right)$$

$$y = 256\ \text{ft} - 64\ \text{ft} = 192\ \text{ft}.$$

The magnitude of the ball's velocity is

$$v = \left(v_x^2 + v_y^2\right)^{\frac{1}{2}}$$

$$v = \left((64\ \text{ft/sec})^2 + (96\ \text{ft/sec})^2\right)^{\frac{1}{2}}$$

$$v = 115.4\ \text{ft/sec}.$$

The direction of the velocity relative to the x-axis is

$$\tan\theta = \frac{v_y}{v_x} = \frac{64}{96} = 2/3$$

$$\theta = 34^\circ$$

(c) At the highest point of the path, the ball has no vertical velocity. Then, by our kinematics equations,

$$v_y = 0 = v_0 - gt$$

$$t = \frac{v_{0_y} - 0}{g} = \frac{128\ \text{ft/sec}}{32\ \text{ft/sec}^2} = 4\ \text{sec}\ .$$

It takes 4 sec. for the ball to reach its maximum height. It has traveled a vertical distance,

$$y_{max} = v_{0_y} t - \tfrac{1}{2} gt^2$$

$$= (128\ \text{ft/sec})(4\ \text{sec}) - \tfrac{1}{2}\left(32\ \text{ft/sec}^2\right)(4\ \text{sec})^2$$

$$= 512\ \text{ft} - 256\ \text{ft} = 256\ \text{ft}.$$

(d) It takes the ball as much time to fall as it does to rise. Hence, the entire trajectory requires 8 sec. By the kinematics equations, we find its horizontal position at the end of its trajectory,

$$x(t) = v_{0_x} t = 96\ \text{ft/sec} \cdot 8\ \text{sec} = 768\ \text{ft}.$$

This is the range of the ball.

• PROBLEM 91

The total speed of a projectile at its greatest height, v_1, is $\sqrt{\frac{6}{7}}$ of its total speed when it is at half its greatest height, v_2. Show that the angle of projection is 30°.

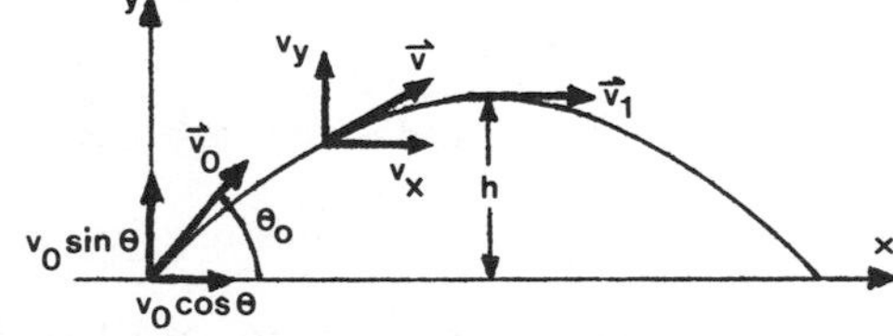

Solution: When a particle is projected as shown in the figure, the component of the velocity in the x-direction stays at all times the same, $v_x = v_0 \cos\theta_0$, since there is no acceleration in that direction, owing to the fact that there is no horizontal component of force acting on the projectile.

In the y-direction, the upward velocity is initially $v_0 \sin \theta_0$ and gradually decreases, due to the acceleration g acting downward. At its greatest height h, the upward velocity is reduced to zero. The kinematic relation for constant acceleration which does not involve time is used to find the greatest height of the trajectory. It is

$$v_f^2 = v_i^2 + 2as \quad (1)$$

In this case $v_f = 0$, v_i, the initial velocity, is $v_0 \sin \theta_0$, $a = -g$ and $s = h$. Then

$$0 = (v_0 \sin \theta_0)^2 - 2\,gh \quad \text{or } h = \frac{(v_0 \sin \theta_0)^2}{2g} .$$

The total velocity at the highest point is thus the x-component only. That is, $v_1 = v_0 \cos \theta_0$. At half the greatest height, $h/2 = (v_0 \sin \theta_0)^2/4g$, the velocity in the y-direction, v_y, is obtained from the equation (1) with $v_f = v_y$, $v_i = v_0 \sin \theta_0$, $a = -g$, and $s = h/2$.

$$v_{y2}^2 = (v_0 \sin \theta_0)^2 - 2g\,\frac{h}{2}$$

$$= (v_0 \sin \theta_0)^2 - \tfrac{1}{2}(v_0 \sin \theta_0)^2$$

$$= \tfrac{1}{2}(v_0 \sin \theta_0)^2 . \quad (2)$$

In addition, there is also the ever-present x-component of the velocity $v_0 \cos \theta_0$. Hence the total velocity at this point is obtained by the Pythagorean theorem,

$$v_2^2 = v_x^2 + v_{y2}^2 = (v_0 \cos \theta_0)^2 + \tfrac{1}{2}(v_0 \sin \theta_0)^2$$

$$= (v_0 \cos \theta_0)^2 + \tfrac{1}{2}v_0^2(1 - \cos^2 \theta_0)$$

$$= \tfrac{1}{2}v_0^2 + \tfrac{1}{2}(v_0 \cos \theta_0)^2 . \quad (3)$$

Here we used the trigonometric identity $\sin^2 \theta + \cos^2 \theta = 1$. However, we are given that

$$v_1 = \sqrt{\frac{6}{7}}\, v_2 \quad \text{or} \quad \frac{v_1^2}{v_2^2} = \frac{6}{7} .$$

Therefore,

$$\frac{(v_0 \cos \theta_0)^2}{\tfrac{1}{2}v_0^2 + \tfrac{1}{2}(v_0 \cos \theta_0)^2} = \frac{6}{7} ;$$

or $\quad 7(v_0 \cos \theta_0)^2 = 3v_0^2 + 3(v_0 \cos \theta_0)^2$,

or $\quad 4 \cos^2 \theta_0 = 3$. One can therefore say that

$$\cos \theta_0 = \frac{\sqrt{3}}{2} \qquad \text{or} \qquad \theta_0 = 30° .$$

An army captain wants to fire an artillery shell deep into the enemy's flank. However, he knows that there are strong winds blowing above at height H that would blow his shells off course. If his artillery fires shells with muzzle velocity v_0, what is the farthest that he can fire them without their going off course?

Solution: The equations of motion for such a projectile are the kinematical equations for constant acceleration, with $v_{0_x} = v_0 \cos\theta$ and $v_{0_y} = v_0 \sin\theta$. (Here, v_0 is the initial velocity).

$$x = (v_0 \cos\theta)t$$

$$y = (v_0 \sin\theta)t - \tfrac{1}{2}gt^2$$

where we take the +x-direction as pointing toward the enemy, the +y-direction as going straight up, - g is the acceleration of gravity and θ is the angle the shell makes with the horizontal axis as it is fired. We can solve for the time t' at which the shell is at its maximum height since at that point the shell's velocity in the y-direction is zero:

$$v_y = \frac{dy}{dt} = v_0 \sin\theta - gt = 0; \quad t' = \frac{v_0 \sin\theta}{g}$$

The maximum height that the shell reaches is:

$$y_{max} = (v_0 \sin\theta)t' - \tfrac{1}{2}gt'^2$$

$$= (v_0 \sin\theta)\left(\frac{v_0 \sin\theta}{g}\right) - \tfrac{1}{2}g\left(\frac{v_0 \sin\theta}{g}\right)^2$$

$$= \frac{v_0^2 \sin^2\theta}{g} - \frac{v_0^2 \sin^2\theta}{2g} = \frac{v_0^2 \sin^2\theta}{2g}$$

But we know that the captain must aim his artillery at an angle θ such that $y_{max} = H$, so that the shells just pass under the wind that would blow them off course. Thus we can solve for θ:

$$y_{max} = \frac{v_0^2 \sin^2\theta}{2g} = H$$

$$\sin\theta = \frac{\sqrt{2gH}}{v_0}$$

Since the shell follows a parabolic path through the air, at time t', when it reaches its maximum height, it has traveled half of its maximum horizontal distance or range. Thus we can solve for its range R:

$$\tfrac{1}{2}R = (v_0 \cos\theta)t'$$

$$R = 2(v_0 \cos\theta)\left(\frac{v_0 \sin\theta}{g}\right) = \frac{2\,v_0^2 \sin\theta \cos\theta}{g}$$

Before we can calculate R we must determine cos θ (see figure (b)).

To find cos θ, we must find the value of side x in the right triangle, since $\cos\theta = x/v_0$. From the Pythagorean theorem:

$$x^2 + 2gH = v_0^2$$

$$x = \sqrt{v_0^2 - 2gH}$$

$$\cos\theta = \frac{\sqrt{v_0^2 - 2gH}}{v_0}$$

Finally,

$$R = \frac{2\,v_0^2\left(\frac{\sqrt{2gH}}{v_0}\right)\left(\frac{\sqrt{v_0^2 - 2gH}}{v_0}\right)}{g}$$

$$= \frac{2\sqrt{2gH(v_0^2 - 2gH)}}{g}$$

• PROBLEM 93

A workman sitting on top of the roof of a house drops his hammer. The roof is smooth and slopes at an angle of 30° to the horizontal. It is 32 ft long and its lowest point is 32 ft from the ground. How far from the house wall is the hammer when it hits the ground?

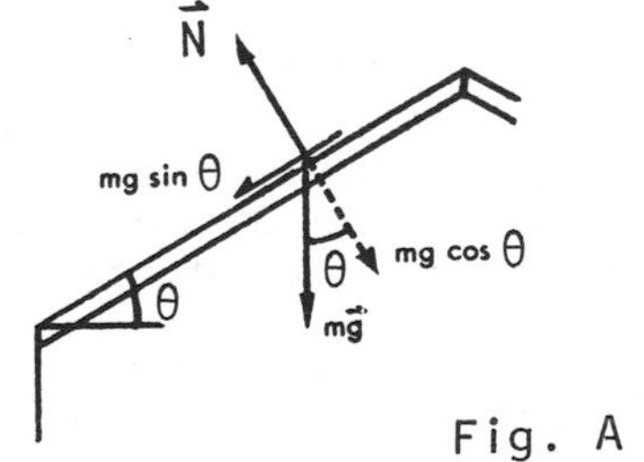

Fig. A

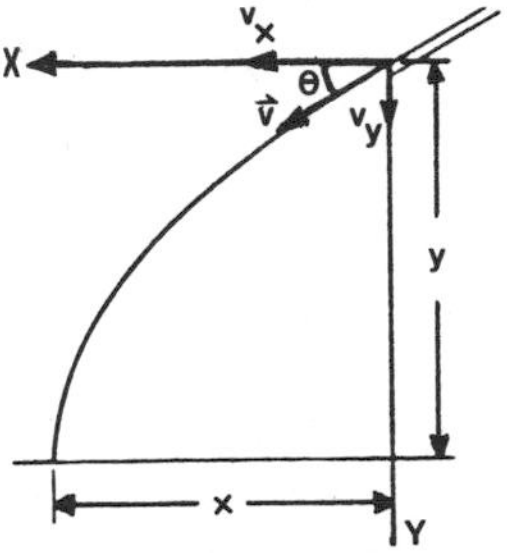

Fig. B

Solution: Figure A illustrates the first part of the motion. Two forces are acting on the hammer as it slides down the roof; the weight $m\vec{g}$ acting downward, one component of which, mg cos θ, balances the second force, the normal force exerted by the roof. At the same time, the component parallel to the roof, mg sin θ, is unbalanced and produces the acceleration on the hammer.

Apply Newton's second law to the unbalanced force to obtain mg sin θ = ma. Thus the hammer accelerates down the roof with acceleration a = g sin θ. In this case sin θ = sin 30° = ½. The kinematic relation for constant acceleration which does not involve time is used to find the velocity with which the hammer leaves the roof. It is $v^2 = v_0^2 + 2as$, where v_0, the initial velocity, is 0 and s is the distance the hammer moves on the roof (= 25 ft). Hence, v is obtained from

$$v^2 = 2 \times \frac{32}{2} \text{ ft/sec}^2 \times 32 \text{ ft; that is,}$$

$$v = 32 \text{ ft/sec.}$$

In the second stage of the fall, the hammer undergoes projectile motion. It drops 32 ft in time t while traveling a distance x horizontally. Let the positive direction of y be taken as downward, and resolve v into its vertical and its horizontal components: v sin θ and v cos θ, respectively (see fig. B). θ is the same as the angle of the slope of the roof. Since there is no horizontal component of force acting on the hammer when it leaves the roof, there is then no horizontal acceleration. The kinematic equation for constant velocity is then x = (v cos θ)t. The vertical acceleration is the constant acceleration of gravity g. Therefore $y = (v \sin \theta)t + \frac{1}{2} gt^2$ **where t = x/v cos θ.**

$$y = v \sin \theta \frac{x}{v \cos \theta} + \frac{g}{2} \times \frac{x^2}{v^2 \cos^2 \theta} .$$

$$\frac{x^2 \times 32 \text{ ft/sec}^2}{2 \times (32 \text{ ft/sec})^2 \times \frac{3}{4}} + \frac{x}{\sqrt{3}} - 32 \text{ ft} = 0$$

or $$x^2 + 16\sqrt{3}\, x \text{ ft} - 1536 \text{ ft}^2 = 0$$

$$(x + 32\sqrt{3} \text{ ft})(x - 16\sqrt{3} \text{ ft}) = 0$$

$$x = -32\sqrt{3} \text{ ft} \qquad \text{or} \qquad +16\sqrt{3} \text{ ft.}$$

The negative answer is clearly inadmissible. It is the answer that would result if the direction of projection were reversed. Hence the correct answer is

$$x = 16\sqrt{3} \text{ ft} = 27.7 \text{ ft from the house.}$$

• PROBLEM 94

The moon revolves about the earth in a circle (very nearly) of radius R = 239,000 mi or 12.6 X 10^8 ft, and requires 27.3 days or 23.4 X 10^5 sec to make a complete revolution. (a) What is the acceleration of the moon toward the earth?

(b) If the gravitational force exerted on a body by the earth

is inversely proportional to the square of the distance from the earth's center, the acceleration produced by this force should vary in the same way. Therefore, if the acceleration of the moon is caused by the gravitational attraction of the earth, the ratio of the moon's acceleration to that of a falling body at the earth's surface should equal the ratio of the square of the earth's radius (3950 mi or 2.09×10^6 ft) to the square of the radius of the moon's orbit. Is this true?

Solution: (a) The velocity of the moon is

$$v = \frac{\text{distance}}{\text{time}} = \frac{\text{circumference}}{\text{time for one orbit}} = \frac{2\pi R}{T} = \frac{2\pi \times 12.6 \times 10^8 \text{ft}}{23.4 \times 10^5 \text{ sec}}$$

$$= 3360 \frac{\text{ft}}{\text{sec}} .$$

Its radial acceleration is therefore

$$a = \frac{v^2}{R} = \frac{(3360 \text{ ft/sec})^2}{12.6 \times 10^8 \text{ft}} = 0.00896 \frac{\text{ft}}{\text{sec}^2} = 8.96 \times 10^{-3} \frac{\text{ft}}{\text{sec}^2}$$

(b) The ratio of the moon's acceleration to the acceleration of a falling body at the earth's surface is:

$$\frac{a}{g} = \frac{8.96 \times 10^{-3} \text{ ft/sec}^2}{32.2 \text{ ft/sec}^2} = 2.78 \times 10^{-4}$$

The ratio of the square of the earth's radius to the square of the moon's orbit is:

$$\frac{(2.09 \times 10^6 \text{ ft})^2}{(12.6 \times 10^8 \text{ ft})^2} = 2.75 \times 10^{-4}$$

The agreement is very close, although not exact because we have used average values.

• PROBLEM 95

An airplane is traveling horizontally at 480 mph at a height of 6400 ft. The airplane drops a bomb aimed at a stationary target on the ground. To an observer on the aircraft, what angle must the target make with the vertical, when the bomb is dropped, if the bomb is to hit the target? (See the figure.)

Suppose that the target is a ship which is steaming at 20 mph away from the aircraft along its line of flight. What alterations would need to be made to the previous calculations?

Solution: At the moment of release of the bomb, time $t = 0$, the airplane is at the point which is taken as the origin of the coordinate system, traveling in the positive x-direction with a speed u of 480 mph.

$$480 \text{ mph} = 480 \frac{\text{mile}}{\text{hr}} \times \frac{5280 \text{ ft}}{\text{mile}} \times \frac{1 \text{ hr}}{60 \text{ min}} \times \frac{1 \text{ min}}{60 \text{ sec}}$$

$$= 704 \text{ ft/sec.}$$

The bomb has the same initial speed.

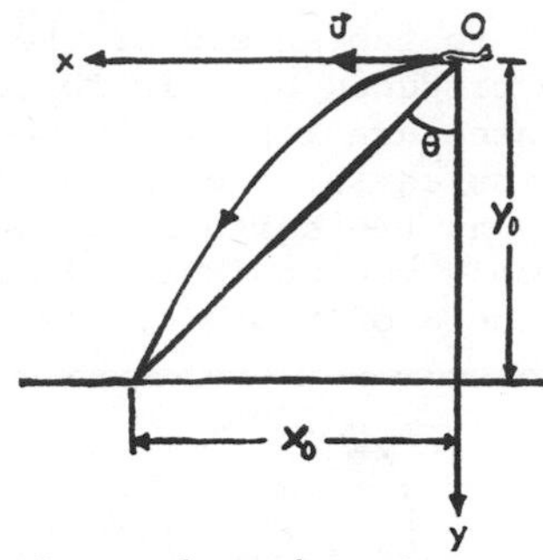

There is no acceleration in the x-direction, for no horizontal force acts on the system. Hence, after time t, when the bomb strikes the target, the distance traveled by the bomb in this direction is given by the kinematic equation for constant velocity, $x_0 = ut$.

The airplane and bomb have no initial speed in the y-direction, but the acceleration g acts in this direction. After time t, the downward distance traveled by the released bomb will be, using the kinematic equation for constant acceleration

Since $v_{o_y} = 0$, this becomes $y_o = 1/2gt^2$. $y_o = v_{o_y}t + 1/2\ gt^2$.

But $y_0 = 6400$ ft in this problem, and the time it takes the object to fall this distance is therefore

$$t = \sqrt{\frac{2y_0}{g}} = \sqrt{\frac{2 \times 6400 \text{ ft}}{32 \text{ ft}\cdot\text{s}^{-2}}} = 20 \text{ s}.$$

Thus, in the same time, the object moves a horizontal distance

$$x_0 = ut = 704 \text{ ft}\cdot\text{s}^{-1} \times 20 \text{ s} = 14{,}080 \text{ ft}$$

and $$\tan\theta = \frac{x_0}{y_0} = \frac{14{,}080 \text{ ft}}{6400 \text{ ft}} = 2.2 \quad \text{or} \quad \theta = 65.5°.$$

The bomb should be released when the target is seen at an angle of 65.5° to the vertical.

If the target is moving, the relative velocity between plane and ship is the important velocity. For, relative to the ship, the bomb has an initial velocity $\vec{v}_{BS} = \vec{v}_{BW} + \vec{v}_{WS}$, where $\vec{v}_{BW}$ is the initial velocity of the bomb relative to the water, and $\vec{v}_{WS}$ the velocity of the water relative to the ship. Since the velocity of the ship relative to water $(\vec{v}_{SW})$ is given as 20 mph, the $\vec{v}_{WS} = -\ 20$ mph. Thus

$$\begin{aligned} v_{BS} &= (480 - 20)\text{mph} = 460 \text{ mph} \\ &= 460\ \frac{\text{mile}}{\text{hr}} \times \frac{5280 \text{ ft}}{\text{mile}} \times \frac{1 \text{ hr}}{60 \text{ min}} \times \frac{1 \text{ min}}{60 \text{ sec}} \\ &= 674.6 \text{ ft/sec} \end{aligned}$$

The foregoing analysis can thus be carried out once more, with v_{BS} in place of u. Thus

$$x_0 = v_{B_S} t = 674.6 \text{ ft/sec} \times 20 \text{ sec} = 13,492 \text{ ft}$$

$$\tan \theta' = \frac{13,492 \text{ ft}}{6400 \text{ ft}} = 2.1$$

and the bomb should now be released when the target is seen at an angle $\theta' = 64.5°$ to the vertical.

CHAPTER 4

DYNAMICS

RECTILINEAR

• **PROBLEM 96**

What is the resultant force on a body of mass 48 kg when its acceleration is 6 m/sec^2?

Solution: The relationship between a body's acceleration and the net force on it is given by Newton's Second Law. The mass of the body is given, hence the net force on the body is

$$\Sigma F = ma = 48 \text{ kg} \times 6 \frac{m}{sec^2} = 288 \text{ newtons.}$$

• **PROBLEM 97**

A force of 2000 dynes produced an acceleration of 500 centimeters per $second^2$. What was the mass of the object accelerated?

Solution: Here, we can apply Newton's Second Law, F = ma.

In this case F = 2000 dynes and a = 500 cm/sec^2. Then

$$2000 \text{ dynes} = M \times 500 \text{ cm/sec}^2$$

whence

$$M = 4 \text{ gm}$$

• **PROBLEM 98**

A force of 0.20 newton acts on a mass of 100 grams. What is the acceleration?

Solution: From Newton's Second Law we have

$$F = ma$$

$$a = \frac{F}{m}$$

Also, 100 grams = 0.10 kg. Therefore

$$a = \frac{0.20 \text{ nt}}{0.10 \text{ kg}} = \frac{0.20 \text{ kg-m/g}^2}{0.10 \text{ kg}}$$

$$= 2.0 \text{ m/sec}^2.$$

• **PROBLEM 99**

What is the resultant force on a body weighing 48 lb when its acceleration is 6 ft/sec^2?

Solution: We find the resultant force by using Newton's Second Law, F = ma. Here, F is the net force on a body of mass m having a net acceleration a. In order to use this law, we must first find the mass of the body. Since the weight of a body is defined as the gravitational force of attraction on it, we have

$$w = mg$$

where g is the acceleration due to gravity. Hence

$$m = \frac{w}{g}$$

and

$$F = \frac{w}{g}\, a = \frac{(48\ \text{lb})(6\ \text{ft/s}^2)}{(32\ \text{ft/s}^2)}$$

$$F = 9\ \text{lb}.$$

• PROBLEM 100

A 65-lb horizontal force is sufficient to draw a 1200-lb sled on level, well-packed snow at uniform speed. What is the value of the coefficient of friction?

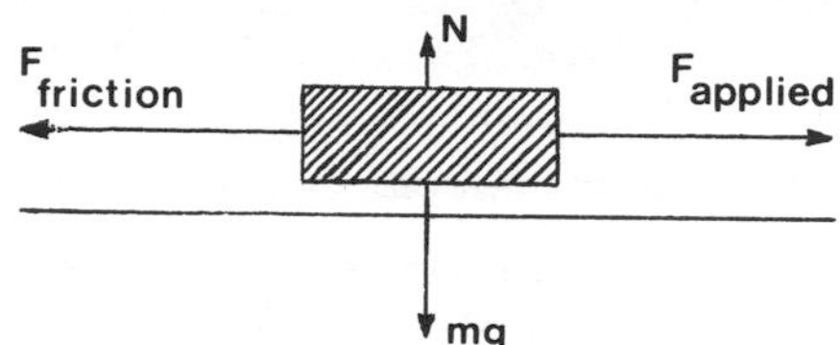

Solution: If the sled moves at constant velocity, it experiences no net force. Therefore, the applied force must be equal to the frictional force.

$$F_{applied} = 65\ \text{lb} = F_{friction}$$

Since the frictional force is proportional to the normal force

$$F_{friction} = \mu_k N$$

Applying Newton's Second Law, F = ma, to the vertical forces acting on the block, we find

$$N - mg = ma_y$$

where a_y is the vertical acceleration. In this problem, $a_y = 0$ because the sled doesn't rise off the surface upon which it slides. Hence

$$N = mg$$

and $F_{friction} = \mu_k N = \mu_k mg$

But $F_{friction} = 65\ \text{lb}$

Therefore $(65\ \text{lb}) = \mu_k\ (mg)$

$$\mu_k = \frac{65\ \text{lb}}{1200\ \text{lb}} = .054$$

• **PROBLEM 101**

What is the gravitational force on a person whose mass is 70 kg when he is sitting in an automobile that accelerates at 4 m/s^2?

Solution: The mass, m = 70 kg, and the acceleration, g = 9.8 m/s^2, are the known observables. The gravitational force on the person is given by Newton's Second Law,

$$F = mg$$

where g is the acceleration due to gravity.

$$F = mg = (70\ kg)\left(9.8\ m/s^2\right) = 6.86 \times 10^2 N.$$

Although the person will experience the force causing the acceleration, 4 m/s^2, his weight is unaffected by the car's motion. This occurs since the acceleration of the automobile is perpendicular to that caused by gravity and has no effect upon the person in the downward direction.

• **PROBLEM 102**

An object of mass 100 g is at rest. A net force of 2000 dynes is applied for 10 sec. What is the final velocity? How far will the object have moved in the 10-sec interval?

Solution. Since the force is constant, the acceleration is also. To find a, apply Newton's second law of motion.

$$a = \frac{F}{m}$$

$$= \frac{2000\ dynes}{100\ g} = 20\ cm/sec^2.$$

The kinematics equations for constant acceleration can be used to find the final velocity. The initial velocity is zero in this problem, since the object is initially at rest.

$$v = v_0 + at$$

$$v = at$$

$$= \left(20\ cm/sec^2\right) \times (10\ sec)$$

$$= 200\ cm/sec.$$

To find the distance traveled in 10 seconds, use $s = v_0 t + \frac{1}{2}at^2$, and since $v_0 = 0$

$$s = \frac{1}{2}\ at^2$$

$$= \frac{1}{2}\left(20\ cm/sec^2\right) \times (10\ sec)^2$$

$$= 1000\ cm = 10\ m.$$

• **PROBLEM 103**

In what distance can a 3000-lb automobile be stopped from a speed of 30 mi/hr (44 ft/sec) if the coefficient of friction between tires and roadway is 0.70?

Solution: The retarding force furnished by the roadway can be no greater than

$$F_s = \mu N = (0.70)(3000 \text{ lb}) = 2100 \text{ lb}.$$

Since the work done by this force is equal to the kinetic energy of the car, the stopping distance can be found from

$$W = Fs = 1/2mv^2.$$

We must divide the weight by the acceleration due to gravity, g, to obtain the mass

$$m = \frac{W}{g} = \frac{3000 \text{ lb}}{32 \text{ ft/sec}^2} = 94 \text{ slugs}$$

$$s = \frac{1/2mv^2}{F} = \frac{94 \text{ slugs } (44 \text{ ft/sec})^2}{2 \times 2100 \text{ lb}} = 43 \text{ ft.}$$

• **PROBLEM 104**

A drag racer achieves an acceleration of 32 (mi/hr)/sec. Compare this value with g.

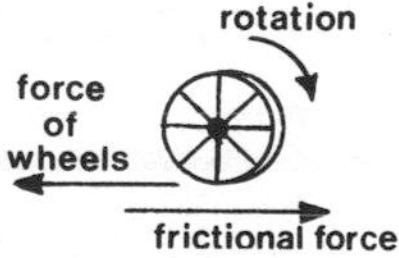

Solution: To remain consistent with the units in which g is given, we convert to m/sec^2.

$$a = 32 \frac{\text{mi}}{\text{hr-sec}}$$

$$= 32 \frac{\text{mi}}{\text{hr}} \times \frac{1}{\text{sec}} \times \frac{5280 \text{ ft}}{1 \text{ mi}} \times \frac{1 \text{ hr}}{3600 \text{ sec}}$$

$$= 32 \times \frac{5280}{3600} \frac{\text{ft}}{\text{sec}^2}$$

$$= 1.46 \times 32 \text{ ft/sec}^2$$

$$= 1.46 \text{ g}$$

This acceleration is about the maximum that can be achieved by a vehicle that travels on wheels and depends on the friction between the wheels and the road for its thrust. A vehicle moves according to Newton's third law of motion: Every action has an equal but opposite reaction. The wheels of a car exert a force on the road in the backward direction. The reaction force is the force which acts in the direction opposite to the friction on the wheels, pushing the car forward. There is a maximum reaction force that the road can exert on the wheels, limited by the coefficient of friction which depends on the smoothness of the road, and by the weight of the car. This maximum thrust which the frictional force can exert on the car, limits its maximum acceleration. Attempts to surpass this maximum value by using a more powerful engine will result merely in spinning tires. (Rocket-powered cars and sleds can, of course, achieve much greater accelerations.)

• PROBLEM 105

A 1000-gram mass slides down an inclined plane 81 centimeters long in 0.60 seconds, starting from rest. What is the force acting on the 1000 grams?

Solution: Given the mass of an object, we must know its acceleration in order to calculate the force acting upon it. For an object starting at rest

$$\tfrac{1}{2}at^2 = d$$

where d is the distance travelled. In our case:

$$\tfrac{1}{2}a(0.60s)^2 = 81\text{ cm}$$

$$a = 450\text{ cm/s}^2$$

Therefore

$$F = ma$$

$$1000\text{ gm} \times 450\text{ cm/s}^2 = 450{,}000\text{ dynes.}$$

• PROBLEM 106

A baseball pitcher throws a ball weighing 1/3 pound with an acceleration of 480 feet per second^2. How much force does he apply to the ball?

Solution: Newton's Second Law tells us that F = ma. However, we do not have the mass of the ball, but its weight which has the units of force. Since

$$W = mg$$

$$m = \frac{W}{g}$$

where W is weight, m is mass, and g is the acceleration due to gravity. Therefore,

$$m = \frac{\frac{1}{3}\text{ lb}}{32\text{ ft/sec}^2} = \frac{32}{3}\text{ slugs}$$

Since the pitcher accelerates an object of mass $\frac{32}{3}$ slugs with an acceleration of 480 ft/s^2, the force is

$$F = \frac{32}{3} \frac{lb - s^2}{32\ ft} \times 480 \frac{ft}{s^2} = 5 \text{ lbs. of force.}$$

• PROBLEM 107

A man holds a ball of weight $w = \frac{1}{4}$ lb at rest in his hand. He then throws the ball vertically upward. In this process, his hand moves up 2 ft and the ball leaves his hand with an upward velocity of 48 ft/sec. Find the force $\vec{P}$ with which the man pushes on the ball.

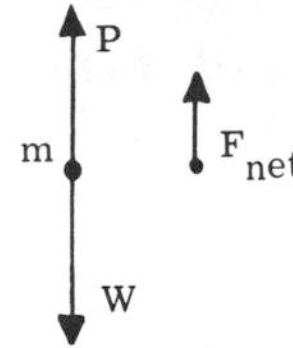

Solution: During the action of throwing the ball, it experiences a net force (see figure) equal to the force of the hand, P, less the gravitational force of the earth on the ball, or mg. Hence,

$$F_{net} = P - mg$$

By Newton's Second Law, F = ma, the ball's acceleration, a, is given by

$$a = \frac{F_{net}}{m} = \frac{P - mg}{m}$$

This acceleration is delivered to the ball over a distance s = 2 ft, and accelerates the ball from rest ($v_0 = 0$) to $v_f = 48$ ft/sec. Hence, by our kinematics equations (a = constant if P is constant)

$$v_f^2 - v_0^2 = 2as$$

$$v_f^2 = 2\left(\frac{P - mg}{m}\right) s = \frac{2Ps}{m} - \frac{2mgs}{m}$$

$$v_f^2 + 2gs = \frac{2Ps}{m}$$

$$P = \frac{m}{2s}\left(v_f^2 + 2gs\right)$$

$$P = \frac{mv_f^2}{2s} + mg$$

To calculate the mass of the ball from its weight, w, note that

$$w = mg$$

and $$m = \frac{w}{g}$$

Therefore $$P = \frac{wv_f^2}{2gs} + w = w\left(\frac{v_f^2}{2gs} + 1\right)$$

$$P = (\tfrac{1}{4}\ lb)\left[\frac{(48\ f/s)^2}{(2)\left(32\ f/s^2\right)(2\ f)} + 1\right]$$

$$P = (\tfrac{1}{4}\ lb)(18 + 1) = 4.75\ lb.$$

A 3200-lb car is slowed down uniformly from 60 mph to 15 mph along a level road by a force of 1100 lb. How far does it travel while being slowed down?

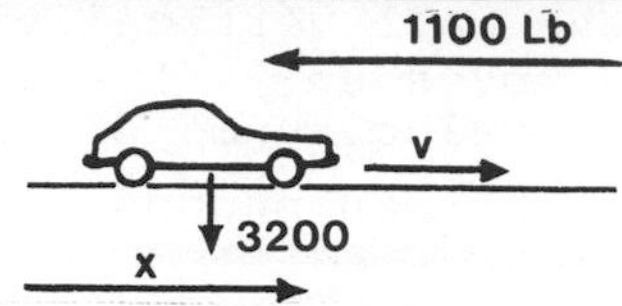

Solution: A diagram should first be drawn so that our sign conventions are consistent (see diagram).

We are given the change in velocity of the car in the positive x direction, the force acting against it in the negative x direction, and the weight of the car. We can calculate the deceleration of the car, and from this we can calculate the time the car is decelerated by its change in velocity.

First, we must find the mass of the car, given its weight. $W = mg$

$$3200 \text{ lb} = m\ 32 \text{ ft/s}^2$$

$$m = 100 \text{ lb-s}^2/\text{ft[slugs]}$$

From this we can calculate the deceleration of the car. Remember that the force acts in the negative x direction. $F = ma$

$$-\ 1100 \text{ lb} = 100 \text{ lb-s}^2/\text{ft}\ a$$

$$a = -\ 11 \text{ ft/s}^2$$

Assuming constant deceleration:

$$a = \frac{\Delta v}{\Delta t}$$

where $\Delta v = 15 \text{ mph} - 60 \text{ mph} = -\ 45 \text{ mph}$.

A useful conversion factor to remember is 60 mph = 88 ft/s, so that - 45 mph = - 66 ft/s. Hence,

$$-\ 11 \text{ ft/s}^2 = -\ \frac{66 \text{ ft/s}}{\Delta t}$$

$$\Delta t = 6\text{s}$$

Distance is given by the formula

$$\tfrac{1}{2}\, at^2 + v_i t + d_i = d$$

where v_i is initial velocity, and d_i is the initial position (which we will here set equal to 0). Therefore

$$d = \frac{1}{2}\left(-\ 11 \text{ ft/s}^2\right)(6\text{s})^2 + 88 \text{ ft/s}^2\ (6\text{s}) + 0$$

$$d = 330 \text{ ft.}$$

In a car which is accelerating, a plumb line hanging from the roof maintains a constant angle of 30 with the vertical. What is the acceleration value?

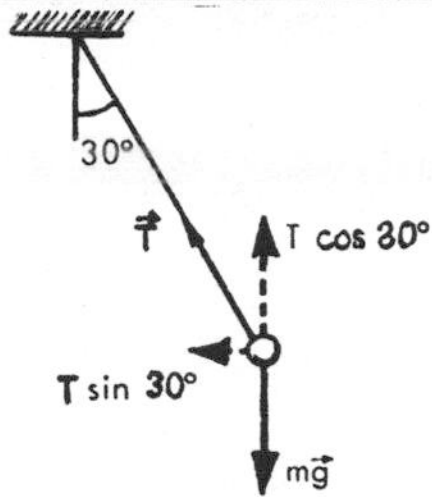

Solution: Since the plumb line maintains a constant angle, the acceleration of the car must be constant.

There are only two forces acting on the bob of the plumb line, the weight $\vec{W} = mg$ acting downward, and the tension $\vec{T}$ in the string. Splitting $\vec{T}$ into its vertical and horizontal components (see figure) one obtains for the vertical direction

$$T \cos 30° = mg, \tag{1}$$

This results because the bob does not move in the vertical direction, hence the vertical forces must balance.

By Newton's second law,

$$T \sin 30° = ma, \tag{2}$$

since the horizontal force must produce acceleration a to match the motion of the car. Dividing equation (2) by equation (1)

$$\frac{T \sin 30°}{T \cos 30°} = \tan 30° = \frac{a}{g}$$

Thus $a = g \tan 30° = g\left(\frac{1}{\sqrt{3}}\right) = \dfrac{32 \text{ ft/sec}^2}{1.732}$

$= 18.47 \text{ ft/sec}^2$.

• PROBLEM 110

An elevator is accelerated upward at 2 ft/sec^2. If the elevator weighs 500 lb, what is the tension in the supporting cable?

Solution: The net force acting on the elevator is

$$\Sigma F = T - mg$$

where T is the cable tension, and mg is the elevator's weight. (Note that the positive direction is taken as upward). By Newton's Second Law, this must equal the product of the elevator's mass and acceleration, whence

$$T - mg = ma$$

Solving for T

$$T = m(g + a) \qquad (1)$$

We don't know the mass, m, of the elevator, but we do know its weight W. Since

$$W = mg$$

(1) becomes

$$T = \frac{W}{g}(g + a)$$

Using the data provided

$$T = \left(\frac{500 \text{ lb}}{32 \text{ ft/s}^2}\right)(32 \text{ ft/s}^2 + 2 \text{ ft/s}^2)$$

$$T = \left(\frac{34}{32}\right) 500 \text{ lb}$$

$$T = 531.2 \text{ lb.}$$

• PROBLEM 111

A 500-kg ore bucket is raised and lowered in a vertical mine shaft using a cable. Determine the upward force exerted by the cable when (a) the upward acceleration is 4 m/s^2 and (b) the bucket is moving upward with a constant velocity.

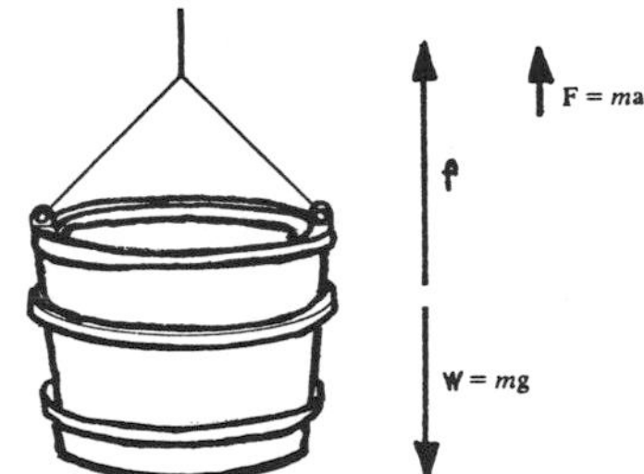

Solution: (a) The known quantities are the mass of the ore bucket, $m = 5 \times 10^2$ kg, and the acceleration, $a = 4 \text{ m/s}^2$. The two forces acting on the bucket are the weight and the tension of the cable, as illustrated in the figure. To accelerate the bucket upward, the tension, f, must be larger than the weight of the bucket. This is a consequence of Newton's first law. Newton's first law states that an object will maintain a constant velocity (or remain at rest) when no net force acts on the object. If the object accelerates, a net force must be acting on it. By vector addition, the resultant upward force, F, is equal to f + w, where w = mg. Since f and w are oppositely directed, the magnitude of their vector sum is equal to the difference of their magnitudes.

$$F = f - w.$$

Using Newton's second law,

$$f - w = ma \qquad (1)$$

$$f = ma + w$$

The weight of the bucket is

$$w = mg$$

and

$$f = ma + mg.$$

Substituting the known observables,

$$f = \left(5 \times 10^2 \text{ kg}\right)\left(4 \text{ m/s}^2\right) + \left(5 \times 10^2 \text{ kg}\right)\left(9.8 \text{ m/s}^2\right)$$

$$= 6.9 \times 10^3 \text{ N}.$$

(b) If the bucket moves upward with constant velocity (uniform motion), the acceleration is zero. (This follows from Newton's first law). Equation (1) becomes

$$f = w.$$

The upward force (tension) exerted by the cable equals the weight of the bucket, 4.9×10^3 N.

• PROBLEM 112

An automobile of mass 50 slugs is traveling at 30 ft/sec. The driver applies the brakes in such a way that the velocity decreases to zero according to the relation

$$v = v_0 - kt^2,$$

where $v_0 = 30$ ft/sec, $k = 0.30$ ft/sec^3, and t is the time in seconds after the brakes are applied. Find the resultant force decelerating the automobile, 5 sec after the brakes are applied.

Solution: With constant force, (and, hence, constant acceleration), the velocity can be expressed as $v = v_0 + at$. In this problem, velocity is proportional to the time squared. We can find the force at any instant by finding the acceleration at that instant and, then using Newton's Second Law, F = ma, to relate acceleration to force. Hence

$$a = \frac{dv}{dt} = \frac{d}{dt}\left(v_0 - kt^2\right) = -2kt.$$

Hence when t = 5 sec,

$$a = -2 \times 0.30\frac{\text{ft}}{\text{sec}^3} \times 5 \text{ sec} = -3\frac{\text{ft}}{\text{sec}^2}.$$

Therefore, at this instant

$$\Sigma F = ma = 50 \text{ slugs} \times \left(-3\frac{\text{ft}}{\text{sec}^2}\right) = -150 \text{ lb}.$$

The negative sign indicates the force opposes the motion of the car and therefore acts to decelerate it.

A cycle and rider together weigh 186 lb. When moving at 10 mi/hr on a level road, the rider ceases to pedal and observes that he comes to a stop after traveling 200 yd. What was the average frictional force resisting his motion?

Solution. Once the acceleration of the rider as he is stopping is known, the frictional force can be found from F = ma, since it is the only force acting on the rider during the deceleration process. Knowing the initial velocity, distance traveled, and final velocity of zero, the acceleration can be found using the kinematics equation:

$$v_f^2 = 2as + v^2.$$

Since $v_f = 0$, $-v^2 = 2as$.

Substituting and converting units to ft-lb-sec,

$$a = \frac{-v^2}{2s} = \frac{-\left[\left(10\frac{mi}{hr}\right) \times \left(\frac{5280\ ft}{1\ mi}\right) \times \left(\frac{1\ hr}{3600\ sec}\right)\right]^2}{2 \times (200\ yd) \times \left(\frac{3\ ft}{1\ yd}\right)}$$

$$= \frac{-(14.7\ ft/sec)^2}{1200\ ft} = -0.18\ ft/sec^2.$$

$$m = \frac{W}{g} = \frac{186\ lb}{32\ ft/sec^2} = 5.8\ slugs$$

$$F = ma = (5.8\ slugs)\left(-0.18\ ft/sec^2\right) = -1.0\ lb.$$

The frictional force is negative since it opposes the direction of motion.

• PROBLEM 114

A ball bearing is released from rest and drops through a viscous medium. The retarding force acting on the ball bearing has magnitude kv, where k is a constant depending on the radius of the ball and the viscosity of the medium, and v is the bearing's velocity. Find the terminal velocity acquired by the ball bearing and the time it takes to reach a speed of half the terminal velocity.

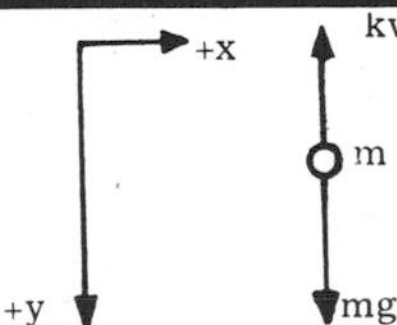

Solution: As the ball falls through the medium, it is accelerated by gravity and the viscous force. To find the acceleration of the bearing, we use Newton's Second Law to relate the net force on the ball to its acceleration. Taking the positive direction downward (see figure).

$$mg - kv = ma,$$

where a is the acceleration produced at any time. The initial value of a is g, since at the moment of release v = 0. As the value of v increases, the acceleration decreases until, when $v = v_0$, the terminal velocity, a = 0. Thus $mg - kv_0 = 0$. Therefore

$$v_0 = (m/k)g.$$

In order to find out at what time $v = v_0$, we must calculate v as a function of t (or vice versa).

At any time t, it will be found that $mg - kv = ma = m(dv/dt)$.
or

$$(mg - kv)dt = mdv$$

$$dt = \frac{mdv}{mg-kv} = \frac{mdv}{m(g-(k/m)v)}$$

$$dt = \frac{dv}{g-(k/m)v} \quad ; \quad \text{and} \quad \int_0^t dt = \int_0^v \frac{dv}{g-(k/m)v} \ .$$

where, in the integration limits, v = 0 at t = 0 and v = v at t = t. Hence

$$t = \int_0^v \frac{dv}{g-(k/m)v}$$

Letting $u = g - (k/m)v$

$$du = -k/m \ dv$$

To find the new integration limits, we realize that when v = 0, u = g and when v = v, $u = g-(k/m)v$, whence

$$t = \int_g^{g-(k/m)v} \frac{-m/k \ du}{u} = \frac{-m}{k} \ \ell n\left(|u|\right) \Big|_g^{g-(k/m)v}$$

$$t = \frac{-m}{k} \{\ell n\left(|g-(k/m)v|\right) - \ell n(g)\}$$

$$t = -\frac{m}{k} \ \ell n\left(\left|\frac{g-(k/m)v}{g}\right|\right)$$

$$t = -m/k \ \ell n|1 - (k/mg)v| \qquad (1)$$

The time to acquire half the terminal velocity, T, is thus found by inserting $v = v_0/2$ in (1)

$$T = -\frac{m}{k} \ell n\left|1 - \frac{k}{mg} \cdot \frac{mg}{2k}\right| = -\frac{m}{k} \ell n\left|\frac{1}{2}\right| = +\frac{m}{k} \ell n|2| = 0.69 \frac{m}{k} \ .$$

• PROBLEM 115

Two bodies having masses m_1 = 30 gm and m_2 = 40 gm are attached to the ends of a string of negligible mass and suspended from a light frictionless pulley as shown in the diagram. Find the accelerations of the bodies and the tension in the string.

Solution: In order to find the acceleration of the masses, we use Newton's Second Law (F = ma) to relate the external forces applied to each mass to the acceleration of each mass.

Consider the body of mass m_1. Two external forces act on it, the weight $m_1 g$ downward and the upward pull T of the string. The resultant force on this body is T

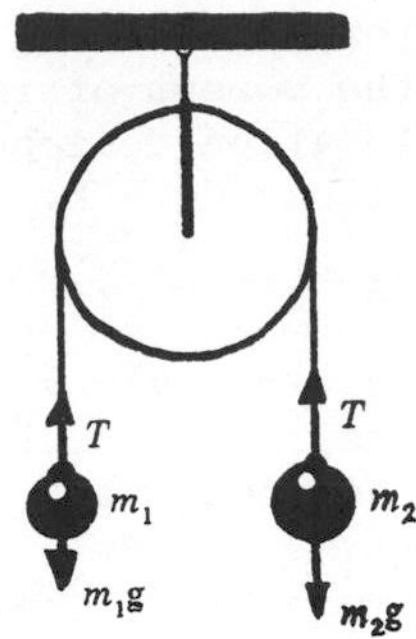

$- m_1g$ upward. Using the Second Law

$$T - m_1g = m_1a \qquad (1)$$

where the negative sign implies that T and m_1g are in opposite directions, and a is the upward acceleration of this body.

Now consider the body of mass m_2. The forces acting on this body are its weight m_2g downward and the tension T upward. The resultant force is $m_2g - T$ downward and

$$m_2g - T = m_2a \qquad (2)$$

where a is the downward acceleration of this body. Since the two bodies move together, the accelerations are equal in magnitude but they are opposite in direction.

To find the acceleration of the string and two masses, we add (1) and (2) and solve for a:

$$m_2g - m_1g = m_1a + m_2a = (m_1 + m_2)a$$

or
$$a = \frac{m_2g - m_1g}{m_1 + m_2} = \frac{(m_2 - m_1)g}{m_1 + m_2}$$

$$\frac{(.04 \text{ kg} - .03 \text{ kg})(9.8 \text{ m/s}^2)}{.04 \text{ kg} + .03 \text{ kg}}$$

$$= \frac{(.01 \text{ kg})(9.8 \text{ m/s}^2)}{.07 \text{ kg}} = \frac{.098 \text{ Nt}}{.07 \text{ kg}} = 1.4 \text{ m/s}^2 \qquad (3)$$

We can substitute this value for a in either of the original equations ((1) or (2)) to obtain the value for T, the string tension. Substituting (3) in (1):

$$T - m_1g = m_1a$$

$$T = m_1g + m_1a = m_1(g + a)$$

$$= .03 \text{ kg } (9.8 \text{ m/s}^2 + 1.4 \text{ m/s}^2)$$

$$= .03 \text{ kg } (11.2 \text{ m/s}^2) = .336 \text{ Nt.}$$

• **PROBLEM 116**

Starting from rest, an engine at full throttle pulls a freight train of mass 4200 slugs along a level track. After 5 min, the train reaches a speed of 5 mph. After it has picked up more freight cars, it takes 10 min to acquire a speed of 7 mph. What was the mass of the added freight cars? Assume that no slipping occurs and that frictional forces are the same in both cases.

Solution: In the first case the train acquires a speed of 5 mph in 5 min = 1/12 hr. When one applies the formula $v_1 = v_0 + a_1 t_1$, for constant acceleration a_1, where $v_0 = 0$, then

$$a_1 = 5 \text{ mph}/1/12 \text{ hr} = 60 \text{ mi/hr}^2.$$

In the second case the train acquires a speed of 7 mph in 10 min = 1/6 hr. When one applies the formula $v_2 = v_0 + a_2 t_2$, then $a_2 = 7 \text{ mph}/1/6 \text{ hr} = 42 \text{ mi/hr}^2$.

In both cases the engine is at full throttle and is thus applying the same net force F to the train: In the first case it is applying it to a mass of 4200 slugs and in the second case to a mass of M + 4200 slugs. Thus

$$F = 4200 \text{ slugs} \times a_1 = (4200 \text{ slugs} + M) \times a_2.$$

$$M = 4200 \left(\frac{a_1}{a_2} - 1\right) \text{ slugs} = 4200 \left(\frac{60 \text{ mi/hr}^2}{42 \text{ mi/hr}^2} - 1\right) \text{slugs}$$

$$= 4200 \times \frac{3}{7} \text{ slugs} = 1800 \text{ slugs}.$$

Note that although it is not normal to measure acceleration in mi/hr^2, it is a mistake to convert to more familiar units unless and until it is found to be necessary. In this case the units of acceleration cancel out and no conversion is ever necessary.

• **PROBLEM 117**

A 60.0-lb block rests on a smooth plane inclined at an angle of 20° with the horizontal. The block is pulled up the plane with a force of 30.0 lb parallel to the plane. What is its acceleration?

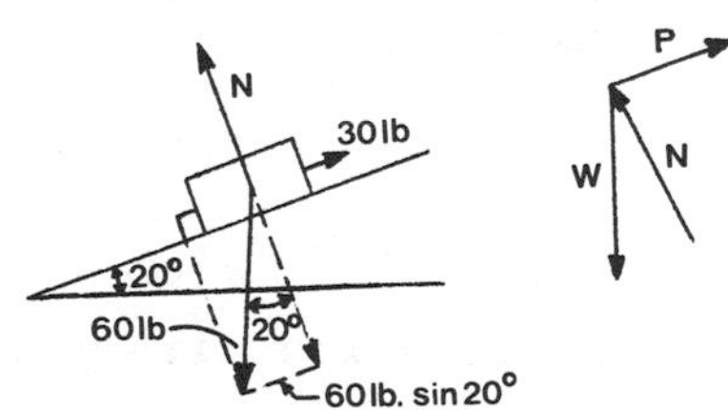

Solution. Here three forces are acting on the block. Its weight W is 60 lb downward. The force of the plane on the block is a thrust N normal to the plane. There is a pull P parallel to the plane. The force acting on the block can be resolved into forces acting normal and parallel to the plane.

The weight of the block may be resolved into components of 60.0 lb × cos 20° normal to the plane and 60.0 lb × sin 20° parallel to the plane.

Since there is no motion in the direction perpendicular to the plane, forces in that direction cancel each other. Therefore, the normal component of the weight is balanced by the force N. Parallel to the plane, taking the direction of P as positive, the sum of the forces is

$$F = 30.0 \text{ lb} - 60.0 \text{ lb} \times \sin 20°$$

$$= 30.0 \text{ lb} - (60.0 \times 0.342)\text{lb} = 9.5 \text{ lb}$$

$$m = \frac{W}{g} = \frac{60.0 \text{ lb}}{32 \text{ ft/sec}^2} = 1.87 \text{ slugs}$$

From F = ma,

$$a = \frac{F}{m} = \frac{9.5 \text{ lb}}{1.87 \text{ slugs}} = 5.1 \text{ ft/sec}^2.$$

Note that if the angle were 30°, the component of the weight down the plane would be equal to the force up the plane and there would be no unbalanced force acting on the block. Hence it would not be accelerated. If the angle were greater than 30°, the block would be accelerated down the plane.

• PROBLEM 118

As shown in the figure, a block of mass .5 slugs moves on a level frictionless surface, connected by a light flexible cord passing over a small frictionless pulley to a second hanging block of mass .25 slugs. What is the acceleration of the system, and what is the tension in the cord connecting the two blocks?

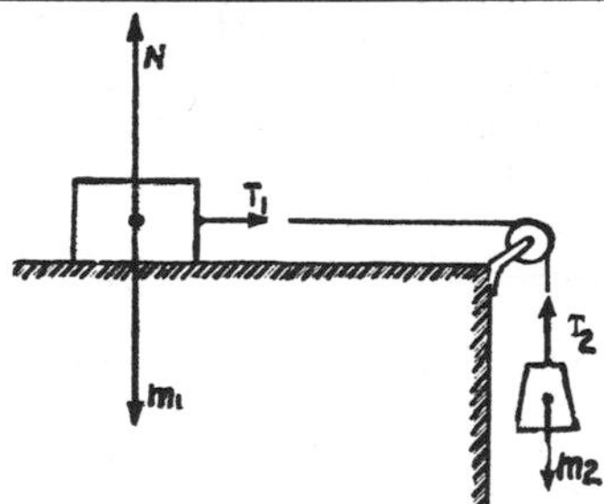

Solution: In order to find the system's acceleration, we must relate the net force on the system to the acceleration via Newton's Second Law. First we isolate the rope, and calculate its acceleration. By the second law,

$$T_1 - T_2 = m_{rope}a$$

where T_1 and T_2 are in opposite directions. In this problem, we assume $m_{rope} = 0$, and

$$T_1 = T_2$$

Hence, the rope acts only to transmit the force of tension to the block.

Applying Newton's Second Law to the horizontal (x) and vertical (y) directions of motion of the block on the table, we obtain

$$T = m_1 a_{x_1}$$

$$N - w_1 = a_{y_1}$$

where m_1 is the mass of the block on the table, and a_{x_1} is its horizontal acceleration. Noting that $a_{y_1} = 0$, since the block doesn't accelerate vertically, we find

$$T = m_1 a_{x_1} \qquad (1)$$

$$N = w_1 \qquad (2)$$

We next apply the third law to the hanging block of mass m_2, and

$$m_2 g - T = m_2 a_{y_2} \qquad (3)$$

where a_{y_2} is the vertical acceleration of block 2. Now, since the 2-block system moves as a unit, $a_{x_1} = a_{y_2} = a$, and, using (1), (2) and (3)

$$T = m_1 a \qquad (4)$$

$$N = w_1 \qquad (5)$$

$$m_2 g - T = m_2 a \qquad (6)$$

Substituting (4) in (6), and solving for a

$$m_2 g - m_1 a = m_2 a$$

$$a = \frac{m_2 g}{m_1 + m_2}$$

From (4),

$$T = \frac{m_1 m_2 g}{m_1 + m_2}$$

Substituting the given data in these equations

$$a = \frac{(.25\ \text{sl})\left(32\ \text{f/s}^2\right)}{(.75\ \text{sl})} = 10.7\ \text{f/s}^2$$

$$T = \frac{m_1 m_2 g}{m_1 + m_2} = m_1 a = (.50\ \text{sl})\left(10.7\ \text{f/s}^2\right)$$

$$T = 5.4\ \text{lb}$$

• PROBLEM 119

A Martian performs an experiment to determine the Martian g with the local type of Atwood's machine (see figure). He hangs two equal weights of mass 0.02 slug over a frictionless pulley and adds a rider of mass 0.002 slug to one side. When the heavier side has descended 2 ft the rider is removed and the system travels 4 ft in the next 3.5s. What value does he obtain for g?

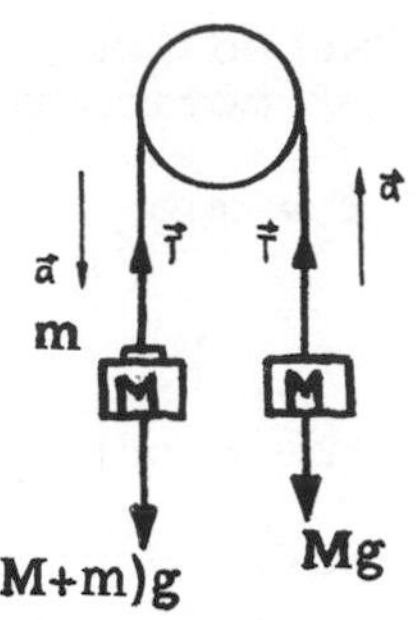

Solution: Initially, there are equal masses on both sides of the Atwood's machine (see figure). The apparatus is then in equilibrium. When we add the rider mass (m), the system is no longer in equilibrium, and each mass accelerates, as shown in the figure. After the heavier side drops 2 ft., the system is moving with a velocity $\vec{v}$, and then we remove the rider. By Newton's First Law, the left side must continue to move with a velocity $\vec{v}$, since the system is no longer accelerating. As will be shown below, the acceleration of the system is related to the Martian value of g. If we know the velocity attained by the left hand mass at the instant the rider is removed, we can find a numerical value for g.

To find the acceleration of the system, we apply Newton's Second Law to each separate mass shown in the figure. Therefore, taking the acceleration of the left hand mass as positive downward, we obtain

$$(M+m)g - T = (M+m)a_1$$

where a_1 is the acceleration of the left hand mass. Similarly, taking the acceleration (a_2) of the right hand mass as positive upward, we find

$$T - Mg = Ma_2$$

But $a_1 = a_2$, since the 2 masses are connected by a string, and, therefore accelerate as a unit, whence

$$(M+m)g - T = a(M+m) \quad (1)$$

$$T - Mg = Ma \quad (2)$$

To find a, we eliminate T by adding (1) and (2)

$$mg = (2M+m)a$$

whence

$$a = \frac{mg}{2M+m} \quad (3)$$

Since a is constant, we know that a is related to the position (y) and velocity (v) of the left hand mass by

$$v^2 = v_0^2 + 2a\left(y-y_0\right)$$

where y_0 and v_0 are the initial position and velocity of this mass. Since the left hand mass is initially at rest, $v_0 = 0$.

$$v^2 = 2a\left(y-y_0\right)$$

Using (3)

$$v^2 = \left(\frac{2mg}{m+2M}\right)\left(y-y_0\right)$$

Hence

$$\frac{(m+2M)v^2}{2m\left(y-y_0\right)} = g$$

and, to find g, we must know v. Note that $y-y_0$ is the distance traversed during acceleration. But, we observe that the left side must move with constant velocity after the rider is removed (m = 0) since, by (3), a = 0. Since this mass moves 4 ft in 3.5s after the rider is removed, and its velocity is constant, we may write

$$v = \frac{4\text{ ft}}{3.5\text{s}} = \frac{8}{7}\frac{\text{ft}}{\text{s}}$$

Therefore,

$$g = \frac{(.042\text{ sl})\left(64/49\text{ ft}^2/\text{s}^2\right)}{(2)(.002\text{ sl})(2\text{ ft})}$$

$$g = 6.86\text{ ft/s}^2$$

• PROBLEM 120

(a) Calculate the acceleration experienced by the two weights, shown in the figure, if the coefficient of friction between the 32 lb. weight and the plane is 0.2. (b) Calculate also the tension in the cable, whose weight we assume to be negligible.

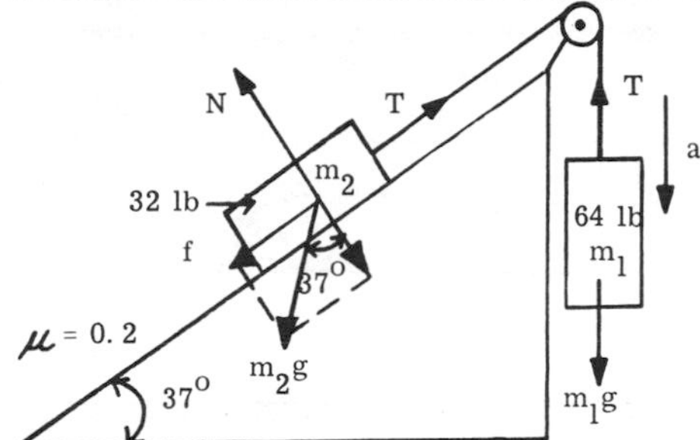

Solution: Consider the two weights as a system. This implies that the cable does not stretch and no internal forces have to be considered, since they consist of action-reaction forces and therefore cancel. The external forces acting on the system are the frictional force on the 32 lb block and the gravitational force on both weights. Since the frictional force F_f is proportional to the normal force, we first find N. The 32 lb block has no movement perpendicular to the plane. Setting the sum of the forces in this direction equal to zero, we get from the diagram,

$$N - mg\cos 37^\circ = 0$$

Therefore

$$N = 32\cos 37^\circ$$

and

$$F_f = \mu N = (0.2)(32\cos 37^\circ)$$

with direction down the plane, since it opposes the motion. All the cable does is change the direction of forces which are applied to each weight and which are in line with the cable. In the same direction as the 64 lb. force on m_1 (the cable makes it so), the 32lb. weight experiences the frictional force and the component of the gravitational force parallel to the cable or 32 sin 37°. Applying Newton's second law to the system, we have

$$\Sigma F = (m_1 + m_2)a$$

since both weights experience the same acceleration. Then

$$64 - 32\sin 37^\circ - (0.2)(32\cos 37^\circ) = \left(\frac{64}{32} + \frac{32}{32}\right)a$$

$$64 - 19.2 - 5.1 = 3a$$

$$39.7 = 3a$$

$$a = 13.2 \text{ ft/sec}^2 \qquad \text{(a)}$$

The tension is obtained by isolating the 64 lb weight and noting that the only two forces acting on it are T and the force of gravity. Calling the downward direction positive, we obtain from Newton's second law,

$$64 - T = m_1 a = \left(\frac{64}{32}\right)(13.2) = 26.4$$

$$T = 64 - 26.4 + 37.6 \text{ lbs.} \qquad \text{(b)}$$

• PROBLEM 121

An Eskimo is about to push along a horizontal snowfield a sled weighing 57.6 lbs carrying a baby seal weighing 70 lbs which he has killed while hunting. The coefficient of static friction between sled and seal is 0.8 and the coefficient of kinetic friction between sled and snow is 0.1. Show that the maximum horizontal force that the Eskimo can apply to the sled without losing the seal is 114.8 lbs. Calculate the acceleration of the sled when this maximum horizontal force is applied.

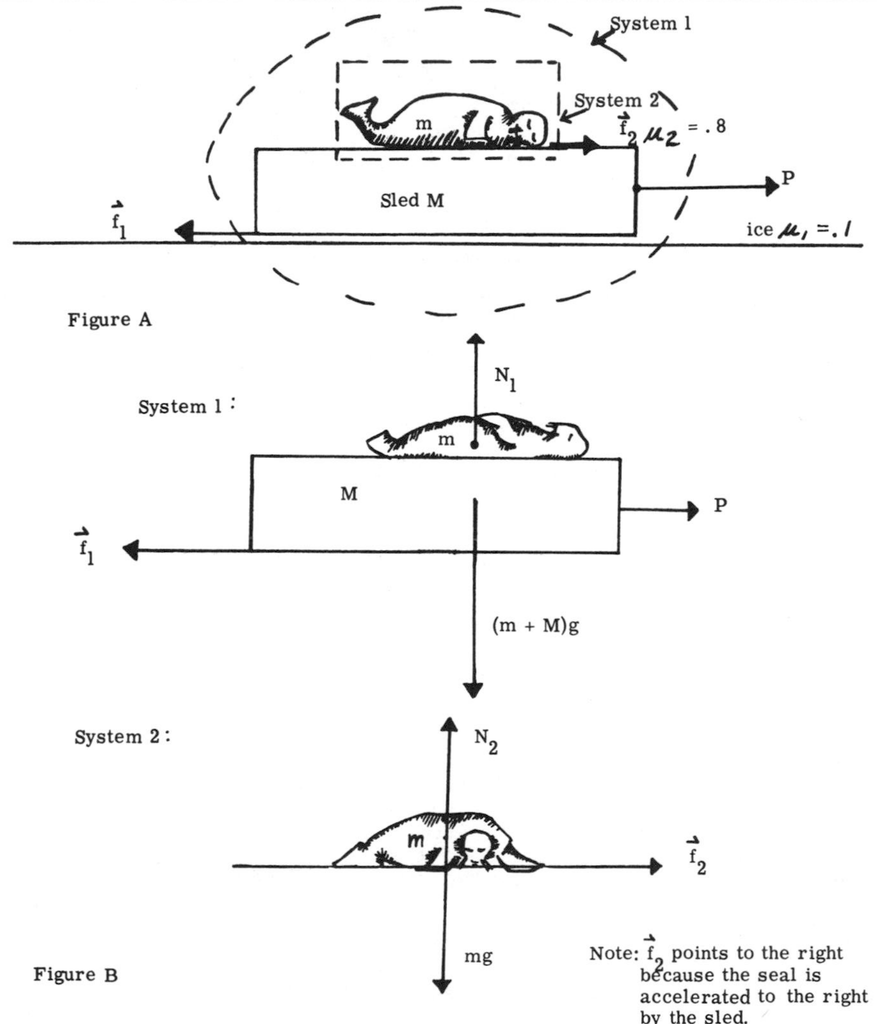

Solution: The seal will slide off the sled when the acceleration provided by $\vec{P}$ is greater than the maximum acceleration which $\vec{f}_2$ can provide to the seal. (See figure (A)). The acceleration of the seal is the same as the acceleration of the seal-sled system. (See figure (B)). Using Newton's Second Law to calculate the latter, we obtain

$$P - f_1 = (m + M)a \tag{1}$$

where a is the acceleration of the system, taken as positive in the direction of P. The frictional force law is

$$f_1 = u_1 N_1 \tag{2}$$

where u_1 is the coefficient of kinetic friction between sled and ice, and N_1 is the normal force of the ice on the sled-seal system. Substituting (2) in (1)

$$P - u_1 N_1 = (m + M)a$$

Since the system is in vertical equilibrium

$$N_1 = (m + M)g$$

and

$$P - u_1(M + m)g = (M + m)a$$

Finally,

$$a = \frac{P - u_1(m + M)g}{(m + M)} \tag{3}$$

is the acceleration of the sled-seal system.

Now, applying the Second Law to the system consisting of seal alone, (see figure (B)) we obtain

$$f_2 = ma \tag{4}$$

where a is the acceleration in (3). But, since we require the seal to remain at rest on the sled,

$$f_2 \le u_2 N_2 \tag{5}$$

where u_2 is the coefficient of static friction between sled and seal, and N_2 is the normal force of the sled on the seal. Inserting (5) in (4)

$$ma \le u_2 N_2 \tag{6}$$

Substituting (3) in (6)

$$m\left(\frac{P - u_1(m + M)g}{(m + M)}\right) \le u_2 N_2$$

Since the seal is in equilibrium vertically,

$$N_2 = mg$$

and

$$m\left(\frac{P - u_1(m + M)g}{(m + M)}\right) \le u_2 mg$$

Solving for P

$$P - u_1(m + M)g \le u_2(m + M)g$$

$$P \le (u_1 + u_2)(m + M)g$$

$$P \le (.9)(57.6 + 70)\text{lbs.}$$

$$P \le 114.8 \text{ lbs.}$$

The maximum value of P is 114.8 lbs.

What is the acceleration of a block on a frictionless plane inclined at an angle θ with the horizontal?

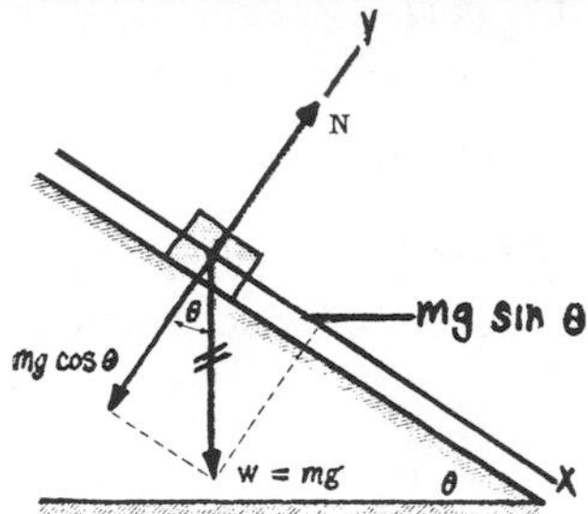

Solution: In order to find the acceleration, a, of the block, we must calculate the net force, F, on the block, and relate this to its acceleration via Newton's Second Law, F = ma. (Here m is the mass of the block).

The only forces acting on the block are its weight mg and the normal force N exerted by the plane (see figure). Take axes parallel and perpendicular to the surface of the plane and resolve the weight into x- and y-components. Then

$$\Sigma F_y = N - mg\cos\theta\ ,$$

$$\Sigma F_x = mg\sin\theta\ .$$

But we know that the acceleration in the y direction, $a_y = 0$, since the block doesn't accelerate off the surface of the inclined plane. From the equation $\Sigma F_y = ma_y$ we find that $N = mg\cos\theta$. From the equation $\Sigma F_x = ma_x$, where a_x is the acceleration of the block in the x direction, we have

$$mg\sin\theta = ma_x\ ,$$

$$a_x = g\sin\theta .$$

The mass does not appear in the final result, which means that any block, regardless of its mass, will slide on a frictionless inclined plane with an acceleration down the plane of $g\sin\theta$. (Note that the velocity is not necessarily down the plane).

• PROBLEM 123

Two rough planes A and B, inclined, respectively, at 30° and 60° to the horizontal and of the same vertical height, are placed back to back. A smooth pulley is fixed to the top of the planes and a string passed over it connecting two masses, the first of 0.2 slug resting on plane A and the other of mass 0.6 slug resting on plane B. The coefficient of kinetic friction on both planes is $1/\sqrt{3}$. Find the acceleration of the system.

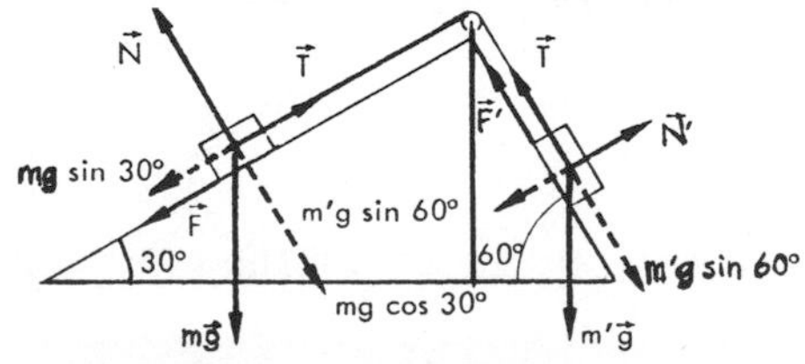

Solution: There are four forces acting on each of the two masses: the weight acting downward, the normal force exerted by the plane at right angles to the plane, and the two forces acting along the plane, the tension in the string, and the retarding force due to kinetic friction.

In each case, resolve the weight into components along the plane and at right angles to it, as shown in the figure. Since there is no tendency for either mass to rise from the plane, the normal force and the component of the weight at right angles to the plane must be equal and opposite. Further, if μ is the coefficient of kinetic friction between mass and plane, the frictional force in each case is μ times the normal force (μN).

The larger mass on the steeper plane will descend. The frictional force is opposite to the motion, i.e., up the plane, and therefore, by Newton's second law $\left(F_{net} = m'a\right)$

$$m'g \sin 60° - T - F'$$

$$= m'g \sin 60° - T - \mu\, m'g \cos 60° = m'a.$$

where a is the acceleration of m', and $N = m'g \cos 60°$.

Since the pulley is smooth, the tension is the same at all points in the string. For the other mass, motion is up the plane and thus the frictional force acts down the plane. Thus

$$T - mg \sin 30° - F = T - mg \sin 30° - \mu\, mg \cos 30°$$

$$= ma.$$

Adding the two equations obtained, one has

$$m'g \sin 60° - mg \sin 30° - \mu(m'g \cos 60° + mg \cos 30°)$$

$$= (m + m')a.$$

Therefore one can write, for the acceleration of the system,

$$a = \frac{m'g \sin 60° - mg \sin 30° - \mu(m'g \cos 60° + mg \cos 30°)}{m + m'}$$

$$\sin 60° = \frac{\sqrt{3}}{2} \qquad \sin 30° = \tfrac{1}{2}$$

$$\cos 60° = \tfrac{1}{2} \qquad \cos 30° = \frac{\sqrt{3}}{2}$$

Then

$$a = \frac{[0.6 \text{ slug} \times (\sqrt{3}/2) - 0.2 \text{ slug} \times \frac{1}{2}] - (1/\sqrt{3})[0.6 \text{ slug} \times \frac{1}{2} + 0.2 \text{ slug} \times (\sqrt{3}/2)]}{0.8 \text{ slug}}\, g$$

$$= \frac{(2\sqrt{3}/10) - 0.2}{0.8} \times 32 \text{ ft/sec}^2 = 5.9 \text{ ft/sec}^2.$$

Had we guessed that mass m would descend, the above analysis would have lead to a negative acceleration indicating that m ascends.

• PROBLEM 124

A 0.96-lb ball A and a 1.28-lb ball B are connected by a stretched spring of negligible mass as shown in the diagram. When the two balls are released simultaneously, the initial acceleration of B is 5.0 ft/sec² westward. What is the initial acceleration of A?

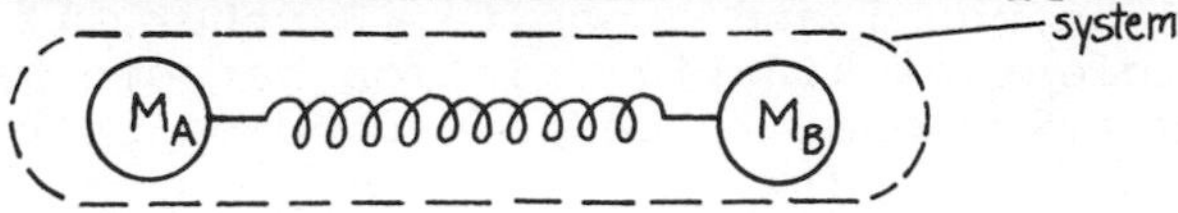

Solution: If we take the balls and spring as our system, as shown in the figure, no external forces act. The only forces acting are then internal, and consist of the force of m_A on m_B, and the force of m_B on m_A, $\left(\vec{f}_{AB} \text{ and } \vec{f}_{BA}, \text{ respectively}\right)$. But by Newton's Third Law,

$$\vec{f}_{AB} = - \vec{f}_{BA} \tag{1}$$

at each instant of time.

By Newton's Second Law,

$$\begin{aligned} \vec{f}_{AB} &= m_B \vec{a}_B \\ \vec{f}_{BA} &= m_A \vec{a}_A \end{aligned} \tag{2}$$

since $\vec{f}_{AB}$ is the only force on m_B, and similarly for $\vec{f}_{BA}$ and m_A. Using (2) in (1)

$$m_B \vec{a}_B = - m_A \vec{a}_A$$

or $$m_B g \vec{a}_B = - m_A g \vec{a}_A \tag{3}$$

But $m_B g = W_B$

$$m_A g = W_A$$

where W_A and W_B are the weights of A and B. Hence, (3) yields

$$W_B \vec{a}_B = - W_A \vec{a}_A$$

Solving for $\vec{a}_A$,

$$\vec{a}_A = - \frac{W_B}{W_A} \vec{a}_B \tag{4}$$

To find $\vec{a}_A$ at t = 0, we use the value of $\vec{a}_B$ at t =

0 in (4), giving

$$\vec{a}_A(t = 0) = -\left(\frac{1.28 \text{ lb}}{.96 \text{ lb}}\right)(5 \text{ ft/s}^2 \text{ westward})$$

$$\vec{a}_A(t = 0) = -6.7 \text{ ft/s}^2 \quad \text{westward}$$

$$\vec{a}_A(t = 0) = 6.7 \text{ ft/s}^2 \text{ eastward}$$

since eastward is the opposite of westward.

• PROBLEM 125

An elevator and its load weigh a total of 1600 lb. Find the tension T in the supporting cable when the elevator, originally moving downward at 20 ft/sec, is brought to rest with constant acceleration in a distance of 50 ft. (See fig.)

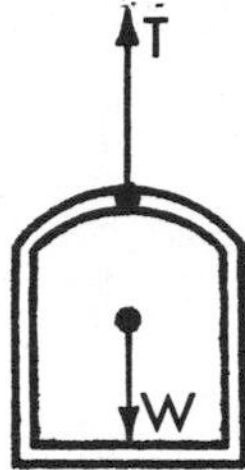

Solution: The mass of the elevator is

$$m = \frac{w}{g} = \frac{1600 \text{ lb}}{32 \text{ ft/sec}^2} = 50 \text{ slugs}$$

where w is the weight of the elevator and its load. From the equations of motion with constant acceleration,

$$v^2 = v_0^2 + 2ay, \quad a = \frac{v^2 - v_0^2}{2y}.$$

Let the upward direction be positive and the origin (y = 0) be at the point where the deceleration begins. Then the initial velocity v_0 is -20 ft/sec, the final velocity v is zero, and its displacement during this interval is y = -50 ft. Therefore

$$a = \frac{0 - (-20 \text{ ft/sec})^2}{-2 \times 50 \text{ ft}} = 4 \frac{\text{ft}}{\text{sec}^2}.$$

The acceleration is therefore positive (upward). From the free-body diagram (Fig.) the resultant force is

$$\sum F = T - w = T - 1600 \text{ lb}.$$

Hence, from Newton's second law,

$$\sum F = ma,$$

$$T - 1600 \text{ lb} = 50 \text{ slugs} \times 4 \frac{\text{ft}}{\text{sec}^2} = 200 \text{ lb},$$

$$T = 1800 \text{ lb}.$$

• PROBLEM 126

A swimmer whose mass is 60 kg dives from a 3-m high platform. What is the acceleration of the earth as the swimmer falls toward the water? The earth's mass is approximately 6×10^{24} kg.

Solution: The diver's mass, $m_d = 60$ kg, the acceleration of the diver, $a_d = 9.8\ m/s^2$, and the mass of the earth, $m_e = 6 \times 10^{24}$ kg, are the known observables. The earth's acceleration can be determined using the fact the force on the earth on the diver is equal in magnitude and opposite in direction to the force of the diver on the earth. Letting the subscripts d and e refer to the diver and earth, respectively, we obtain

$$m_d \vec{a}_d = - m_e \vec{a}_e$$

Considering just the magnitude of the two vectors, we find

$$(60\ kg)\left(9.8\ m/s^2\right) = \left(6 \times 10^{24} kg\right) a_e$$

$$a_e = \frac{(60\ kg)\left(9.8\ m/s^2\right)}{6 \times 10^{24} kg} = 9.8 \times 10^{-23}\ m/s^2$$

Since the diver is accelerated downward, the earth is accelerated upward, toward the falling diver.

• PROBLEM 127

With what force will the feet of a passenger press downward on the elevator floor when the elevator has an acceleration of 4 ft/sec^2 upward if the passenger weighs 160 lb?

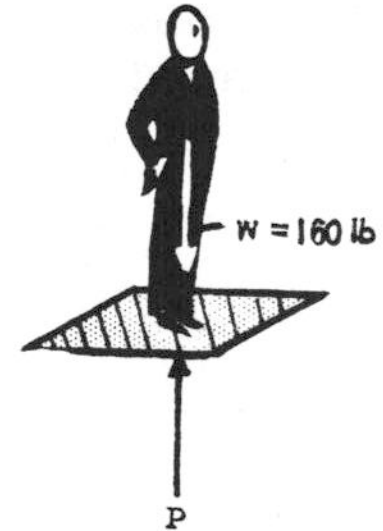

Solution: This example illustrates a problem that is frequently encountered, in which it is necessary to find a desired force by first computing the force that is the reaction to the one desired, and then using Newton's third law. That is, we first calculate the force with which the elevator floor pushes upward on the passenger P; the force desired is the reaction to this. The figure shows the forces acting on the passenger. We may use Newton's Second Law, F = ma, to relate the net force on the man to his acceleration. The resultant force is $P - \omega$. The mass m of the passenger is his weight, mg, divided by

$32\ f/s^2$, or 5 slugs, and his acceleration is the same as that of the elevator,

$$\Sigma F = ma$$

$$P - 160\ lb = 5\ slugs \times 4\ \frac{ft}{sec^2} = 20\ lb,$$

$$.P = 180\ lb.$$

The passenger exerts an equal and opposite force downward on the elevator floor.

• PROBLEM 128

A curling stone of mass 1 slug is sent off along the ice and comes to rest after 100 ft. If the force of kinetic friction between stone and ice is ½ lb, with what velocity did the stone start, and how long did it take to come to rest?

Solution: The force decelerating the stone is ½ lb and the stone has a mass of 1 slug. Using the equation F = ma, the deceleration is $a = -\frac{1}{2}\ ft/s^2$.

Apply the equation of uniform motion, $v_0^2 + 2a(x - x_0) = v$, where v_0 is the stone's initial velocity and $x - x_0$ is the distance it travels. We obtain

$$v_0^2 = 2 \times \tfrac{1}{2}\ ft/s^2 \times 100\ ft$$

$$\therefore \quad v_0 = 10\ ft/s,$$

which is the initial velocity of the stone.

If we now apply the further equation $v = v_0 + at$, the time of motion is

$$t = -\frac{v_0}{a} = \frac{10\ ft/s}{\frac{1}{2}\ ft/s^2} = 20\ s.$$

• PROBLEM 129

A mass m hangs at the end of a rope which is attached to a support fixed on a trolley (as shown in the figures). Find the angle α it makes with the vertical, and its tension T when the trolley 1) moves with a uniform speed on horizontal tracks, 2) moves with a constant acceleration on horizontal tracks.

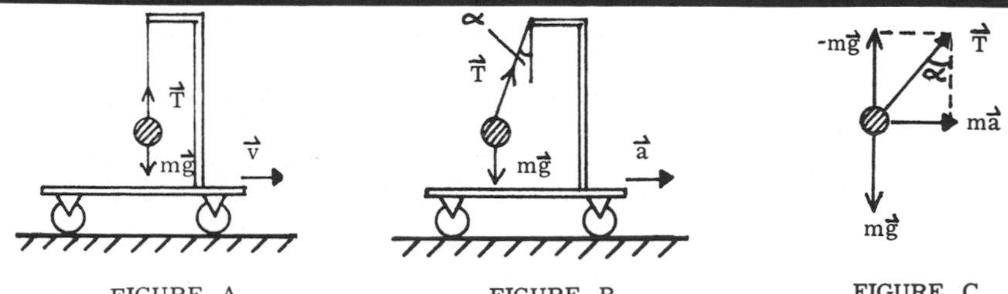

FIGURE A FIGURE B FIGURE C

Solution. 1) When the trolley moves with a uniform speed, the only external force acting on m is the gravitational force $m\vec{g}$. It is balanced by the tension $\vec{T}$ in the rope, since m is in equilibrium (Fig. a). Hence $\alpha = 0$. 2) When the trolley has acceleration a, the effect of the acceleration is transmitted to the mass through the rope. We see (Fig. b), that the magnitudes of the gravitational and horizontal accelerations determine the magnitude of the angle α. The tension in the rope provides the upward force $-m\vec{g}$ to hold the mass (since m is in vertical equilibrium) as well as the external force ma acting on the mass as a result of the motion of the trolley, (Fig. c). Hence,

$$T \sin \alpha = ma \tag{1}$$

$$T \cos \alpha = mg \tag{2}$$

Dividing (1) by (2), we get

$$\frac{T \sin \alpha}{T \cos \alpha} = \frac{ma}{mg}$$

$$\tan \alpha = \frac{a}{g}$$

Therefore, α is given by

$$\alpha = \tan^{-1} \frac{a}{g}.$$

• PROBLEM 130

A hunter enters a lion's den and stands on the end of a concealed uniform trapdoor of weight 50 lb freely pivoted at a distance x from the other end. Given that the hunter's weight is 150 lb, what fraction of the total length must x be in order that he and the end of the trapdoor shall start dropping into the depths with acceleration g when the trapdoor is released?

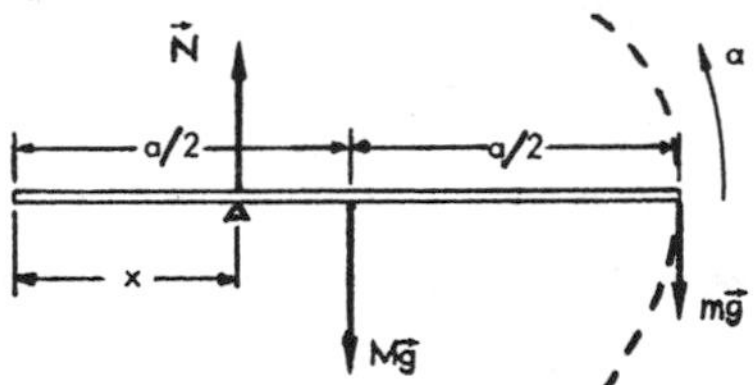

Solution: The forces acting on the trapdoor of length a are its weight Mg acting downward at the center, since it is uniform, the hunter's weight mg acting downward at the end, and the normal force N exerted by the pivot upward (see the figure). When we take moments about the pivot, counterclockwise moments being taken as positive, the moments causing rotational acceleration are

$-Mg\left(\frac{a}{2} - x\right) - mg(a - x)$, and thus using the rigid body analog of Newton's second law, if T is the resultant torque acting on the rigid bar, I_T, the moment of inertia of the man-bar system about the pivot, and α its angular acceleration, then $T = I_T\alpha$ or

$$-Mg\left(\frac{a}{2} - x\right) - mg(a - x) = I_T\alpha$$

The moment of inertia of the trapdoor about a horizontal line parallel to the pivot and passing through the center of gravity is $\frac{1}{12}Ma^2$. By the parallel-axis theorem, if I_{cm} is the moment of inertia of the bar (or any rigid body) about its center of gravity and I_b is its moment of inertia about any axis, where h is the distance separating the two axes, then $I_b = I_{cm} + Mh^2$. Thus, I_b about the pivot is $\frac{1}{12}Ma^2 + M\left[(a/2) - x\right]^2$. The moment of inertia of the hunter about the pivot is $I_m = m(a - x)^2$. Hence

$$T = \left(I_b + I_m\right)\alpha \quad \text{for } I_T = I_b + I_m$$

$$-Mg\left(\frac{a}{2} - x\right) - mg(a - x) = \alpha\left[\frac{1}{12}Ma^2 + M\left(\frac{a}{2} - x\right)^2 + m(a - x)^2\right]. \tag{1}$$

If the hunter and the end of the trapdoor are to have a linear acceleration g downward, then $-g = (a - x)\alpha$. Where $(a - x)$ is the radius of the circular arc path the man follows about the pivot (see the figure). Therefore, upon division of both sides of equation (1) by α and using the above relation between g and α,

$$M\left(\frac{a}{2} - x\right)(a - x) + m(a - x)^2 = \frac{1}{12}Ma^2 + M\left(\frac{a}{2} - x\right)^2 + m(a - x)^2.$$

$$\not{M}\left(\frac{a}{2} - x\right)(a - x) = \frac{1}{12}\not{M}a^2 + \not{M}\left(\frac{a}{2} - x\right)^2$$

$$\frac{a^2}{2} - ax - \frac{ax}{2} + x^2 = \frac{1}{12}a^2 + \frac{a^2}{4} - ax + x^2$$

$$\left(\frac{a^2}{2} - \frac{a^2}{4}\right) - \frac{3}{2}ax + ax = \frac{1}{12}a^2$$

$$\frac{a^2}{4} - \frac{ax}{2} = \frac{1}{12}a^2$$

$$\therefore\ \frac{a}{2}\left(\frac{a}{2} - x\right) = \frac{1}{12}a^2 \qquad \therefore\ 3a^2 - 6ax = a^2 \qquad \therefore\ x = \frac{1}{3}a$$

The pivot must be located one-third of the length of the trapdoor from the end.

• PROBLEM 131

An automobile of mass 50 slugs accelerates from rest. During the first 10 sec, the resultant force acting on it is given by $\Sigma F = F_0 - kt$, where $F_0 = 200$ lb, $k = 10$ lb/sec, and t is the time in seconds after the start. Find the velocity at the end of 10 sec, and the distance covered in this time.

Solution: The resultant force decreases with time, since

$$F(t) = F_0 - kt$$

where t is the elapsed time in seconds. Newton's Second Law tells us that at any time F = ma, where F is the net force on a mass m, and a is its acceleration. Hence

$$F(t) = m\,a(t); \quad a(t) = \frac{F(t)}{m} = \frac{F_0 - kt}{m}$$

We integrate to find v(t), the instantaneous velocity at time t.

$$v(t) = \int a(t)dt = \int\left(\frac{F_0}{m} - \frac{kt}{m}\right)dt = \left(\frac{F_0}{m}\right)t - \frac{k}{m}\frac{t^2}{2} + C_1$$

To evaluate the constant of integration, C_1, we use our knowledge that the car accelerates from rest. Hence, $v(0) = 0$

$$v(0) = \left(\frac{F_0}{m}\right)(0) - \left(\frac{k}{2m}\right)(0)^2 + C_1 = 0$$

$$\therefore \; C_1 = 0.$$

The velocity function is therefore

$$v(t) = \left(\frac{F_0}{m}\right)t - \left(\frac{k}{2m}\right)t^2$$

and, at t = 10s, $v = \left(\frac{200 \text{ lb}}{50 \text{ sl}}\right)(10 \text{ s}) - \left(\frac{10 \text{ lb/s}}{100 \text{ sl}}\right)\left(100 \text{ s}^2\right) =$
$= 30 \text{ f/s}$

Again, we integrate v(t) to find s(t), the instantaneous position at time t.

$$s(t) = \int v(t)dt = \int\left(\frac{F_0}{m}\right)t - \left(\frac{k}{2m}\right)t^2 = \left(\frac{F_0}{2m}\right)t^2 - \left(\frac{k}{6m}\right)t^3 + C_2$$

We assume that the car starts at position s(0) = 0.
Evaluating C_2,

$$s(0) = \left(\frac{F_0}{2m}\right)(0)^2 - \left(\frac{k}{6m}\right)(0)^3 + C_2 = 0$$

$$\therefore \; C_2 = 0$$

The position (and displacement) function is given by

$$s(t) = \left(\frac{F_0}{2m}\right)t^2 - \left(\frac{k}{6m}\right)t^3$$

At t = 10, the displacement from the origin is

$$s(10s) = \left(\frac{200 \text{ lb}}{100 \text{ sl}}\right)\left(100 \text{ s}^2\right) - \left(\frac{10 \text{ lb/s}}{300 \text{ sl}}\right)\left(1000 \text{ s}^3\right)$$

$$s(10 \text{ s}) = 200 \text{ f} - 33\frac{1}{3} \text{ f} = 166\frac{2}{3} \text{ f}$$

• PROBLEM 132

A rocket, when unloaded, has a mass of 2000 kg, carries a fuel load of 12,000 kg, and has a constant exhaust velocity of 5000 km · hr^{-1}. What are the maximum rate of fuel consumption, the shortest time taken to reach the final velocity, and the value of the final velocity? The greatest permissible acceleration is 7g. The rocket starts from rest at the earth's surface, and air resistance and variations in g are to be neglected.

Solution: The problem can be approached using Newton's second law for a system of variable mass.

$$m\frac{d\vec{v}}{dt} = \vec{F}_{ext} + \vec{v}_{rel}\frac{dm}{dt} \qquad (1)$$

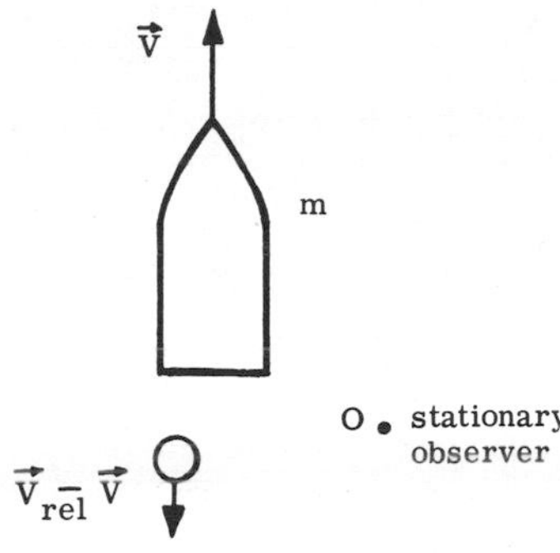

$\vec{F}_{ext}$ is the external force acting on the rocket of mass M. In this case, it is the attractive gravitational force due to the earth (i.e. the weight of the rocket Mg). $\vec{v}$ is the velocity of the rocket relative to a stationary observer O and $\vec{v}_{rel}$ is the relative velocity of the ejected mass with respect to the rocket. The last term is the rate at which momentum is being transferred out of the system by the mass that the system has ejected.

$\vec{F}_{ext}$ = -mg, the negative sign indicating that the force acts downward. Also $v_{rel} = -v_r$ where v_r is the velocity of the rocket relative to that of the material ejected, i.e., the reverse of the exhaust velocity. Regarding dm as a very small bit of material ejected in a time dt, and the resulting small increase in velocity of the rocket by dv, then equation (1) becomes

$$m\frac{dv}{dt} = -v_r \frac{dm}{dt} - mg$$

Upon division of both sides of this equation by m, and multiplication of both sides by dt,

$$dv = -v_r \frac{dm}{m} - gdt \qquad (2)$$

Therefore the acceleration at any time is

$$a = \frac{dv}{dt} = -\frac{v_r}{m}\frac{dm}{dt} - g.$$

The velocity v_r is constant and dm/dt must be constant also (for any change in the rate at which mass is ejected would necessarily lead to a change in the velocity of the mass ejected), so that a varies only with m. The smallest value of m gives the greatest value of a; but a cannot exceed 7g. Therefore

$$7g = -\left(\frac{5 \times 10^6 m - hr^{-1}}{60 min - hr^{-1} \times 60 s - min^{-1}}\right) \times \frac{1}{2 \times 10^3 kg}\frac{dm}{dt} - g$$

$$\therefore \frac{dm}{dt} = -\frac{8g \times 72 \times 10^5 kg}{5 \times 10^6 m \cdot s^{-1}} = -\frac{8 \times 9.8 m \cdot s^{-2} \times 72 \times 10^5 kg}{5 \times 10^6 m \cdot s^{-1}}$$

$$= -112.9\ kg \cdot s^{-1},$$

where -dm/dt is the maximum rate of fuel consumption. This rate of consumption then equals the total fuel load divided by the time taken to reach the final velocity (T).

Thus

$$T = \frac{12 \times 10^3 kg}{112.9 kg \cdot s^{-1}} = 106.3\ s = 1.77\ min.$$

Integrating equation (2) one has $v = -v_r \ln m - gt + C$. But if m_0 is the total load at time $t = 0$, when $v = 0$, then

$0 = -v_r \ln m_0 + C$.

$C = v_r \ln m_0$ and $v = -v_r \ln m - gt + v_r \ln m_0$

$$\therefore\ v = v_r \ln\frac{m_0}{m} - gt.$$

for $\ln\frac{m_0}{m} = \ln m_0 - \ln m$

The final velocity is thus

$$v = \frac{5 \times 10^6 m \cdot hr^{-1}}{60 \times 60\ s \cdot hr^{-1}} \ln\frac{14,000\ kg}{2000\ kg} - 9.8\ m \cdot s^{-2} \times 106.3\ s$$

$$= (2703 - 1042) m \cdot s^{-1} = 1661\ m \cdot s^{-1} = 5980\ km \cdot hr^{-1}.$$

• PROBLEM 133

What is the radius of gyration of a slender rod of mass m and length L about an axis perpendicular to its length and passing through the center?

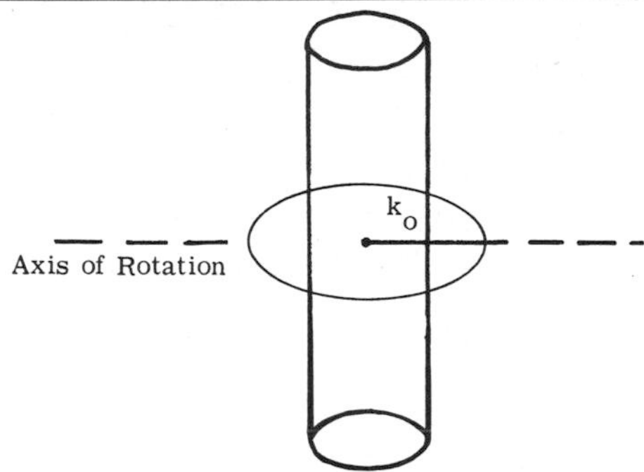

Solution: The radius of gyration is the distance from the axis of rotation to the radius at which we may consider all the object's mass to be concentrated in a thin hoop, as the diagram shows. For a thin hoop of radius k_0, the moment of inertia, I_0, is mk_0^2, where m is the mass of the hoop. To find k_0, we set I of the object equal to I_0 the moment of inertia of the equivalent hoop

$$I = I_0$$

or

$$\frac{1}{12} ml^2 = mk_0^2$$

Hence

$$k_0 = \frac{\sqrt{\frac{1}{12} mL^2}}{m} = \frac{L}{2\sqrt{3}} = 0.289\ L.$$

The radius of gyration, like the moment of inertia, depends on the location of the axis.

Note carefully that, in general, the mass of a body can not be considered as concentrated at its center of gravity for the purpose of computing its moment of inertia. For example, when a rod is pivoted about its center, the distance from the axis to the center of gravity is zero, although the radius of gyration is $L/2\sqrt{3}$.

• PROBLEM 134

> A skier whose mass is 70 kg, takes off from a ski jump with a velocity of 50 m/sec at an unknown angle to the horizontal and lands at a point whose vertical distance below the point of take-off is 100 m. (as shown in the figure). What is his speed just before landing, if the friction of the air can be ignored?

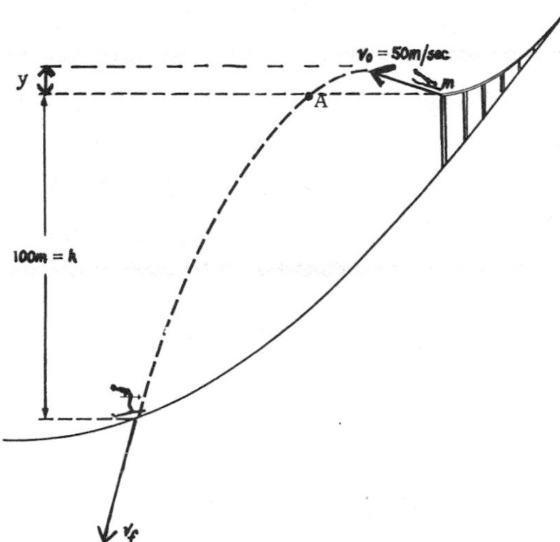

Solution: In the absence of friction the law of conservation of energy demands that the sum of the kinetic energy and the potential energy remain constant. At take-off the kinetic energy of the skier is

$$E_k = \frac{1}{2} m v_0^2$$

where $v_0 = 50$ m/sec is the skier's speed as he leaves the ramp. During the skier's flight he rises to a maximum height of $(h + y)$ meters above the ground and then falls to the ground. However, the skier's net loss of potential energy during his flight is mgh and not $mg(h + y)$. From our study of projectile motion, all of the skier's original kinetic energy is converted to potential energy when he reaches his maximum height, but this added potential energy is converted back to kinetic energy when the skier falls back to the height at which he started (point A in the diagram). At point A, the skier has total energy equal to that at the beginning of his flight. Therefore, the skier's loss of potential energy between point A and the landing point, is equal to his net loss of potential energy over the entire flight. The net amount of potential energy he loses and gains as kinetic energy is given by:

$$E_p = mgh$$

Thus, the skier's final kinetic energy is equal to the sum of his original kinetic energy and his net loss in potential energy:

$$\frac{1}{2} mv_f^2 = \frac{1}{2} mv_0^2 + mgh$$

where, v_f is the skier's speed as he hits the ground

$$v_f = \sqrt{v_0^2 + 2gh} = \sqrt{(50\ m/sec)^2 + 2(9.8\ m/sec^2)(100m)} = \sqrt{4,460\ (m/sec)^2}$$

$$= 66.8\ m/sec$$

Just before landing the skier has a speed of 66.8 m/sec.

The power of the law of conservation of energy lies in the fact that we can derive this result without knowing the angle of take-off, the horizontal distance traveled, or the exact nature of the curved trajectory. We also note that our result is independent of the mass of the skier.

GRAVITATIONAL FORCES

• PROBLEM 135

Calculate the value of the universal gravitational constant, G, assuming that the earth's radius is 6.4×10^6 m the earth has an average density of $5.5 \quad 10^3\ kg/m^3$. The volume V of a sphere is $V = \frac{4}{3}\pi r^3$, where r is the radius of the sphere.

Solution: Begin by computing the volume of the earth:

$$V = \frac{4}{3}\pi r^3 = \left(\frac{4}{3}\pi\right)\left(6.4 \times 10^6\ m\right)^3 = 1.1 \times 10^{21}\ m^3.$$

Since Density $= \frac{\text{Mass}}{\text{Volume}}$, we have

$$\text{Mass} = \text{Density} \times \text{Volume}$$

or, the total mass of the earth,

$$m_2 = \left(1.1 \times 10^{21}\ \cancel{m^3}\right)\left(5.5 \times 10^3\ kg/\cancel{m^3}\right) = 6.0 \times 10^{24}\ kg.$$

If an object of mass m_1 is placed on the Earth's surface, the gravitational force of attraction (W) between it and the Earth (i.e., its weight) is found by use of Newton's second law.

$$W = m_1 g$$

where g is the acceleration of the object due to the gravitational force (i.e., acceleration of gravity). According to the Universal Law of Gravitation, however, the gravitat tional force of attraction between m_1 and m_2 is

$$W = \frac{Gm_1m_2}{d^2}$$

where d is the radius of the Earth. Then

$$\frac{G\cancel{m_1}m_2}{d^2} = \cancel{m_1}g$$

After rearranging,

$$G = \frac{gd^2}{m_2} = \frac{(9.8\ m/s^2)(6.4 \times 10^6\ m)^2}{6.0 \times 10^{24}\ kg} = 6.7 \times 10^{-11}\ N\ m^2/kg^2$$

Since the value of the earth's radius is more accurately known today, Newton's estimate of G differed from this calculated value.

• PROBLEM 136

With what force does the Earth attract the moon?

Solution: By the Universal Law of Gravitation, we have

$$F_G = G\frac{m_m m_E}{r_m^2}$$

where r_m is the distance between the earth and moon, and m_m and m_e are the masses of the moon and the earth respectively.

$$G = 6.67 \times 10^{-8}\ \frac{dyne - cm^2}{g^2}$$

$$r_m = 3.84 \times 10^{10}\ cm$$

$$m_m = 7.35 \times 10^{25}\ g$$

$$m_e = 5.98 \times 10^{27}\ g$$

$$F_G = \left(6.67 \times 10^{-8}\ dyne\text{-}cm^2/g^2\right) \times \frac{\left(7.35 \times 10^{25}\ g\right) \times \left(5.98 \times 10^{27}\ g\right)}{\left(3.84 \times 10^{10}\ cm\right)^2}$$

$$= 2.0 \times 10^{25}\ dynes\ .$$

• PROBLEM 137

Discuss the motion of a freely falling body of mass m taking into account the variation of the gravitational force on the body with its distance from the earth's center. Neglect air resistance.

Solution: The gravitational force on the body at a distance r from the earth's center is $-Gmm_E/r^2$. From Newton's second law its acceleration is

$$a = \frac{F}{m} = -\frac{Gm_E}{r^2}, \qquad (1)$$

where the positive direction is upward

But
$$a = \frac{dv}{dt} = \frac{dv}{dr}\frac{dr}{dt}$$

$$a = v\frac{dv}{dr}$$

Then, from (1)

$$v\frac{dv}{dr} = -\frac{Gm_E}{r^2},$$

$$\int_{v_1}^{v_2} v\,dv = -Gm_E \int_{r_1}^{r_2} \frac{dr}{r^2}$$

where v_1 and v_2 are the velocities at the radial distances r_1 and r_2. It follows that

$$\frac{1}{2}(v_2^2 - v_1^2) = -Gm_E \left[-\frac{1}{r}\right]_{r_1}^{r_2}$$

$$\frac{1}{2}(v_2^2 - v_1^2) = Gm_E \left(\frac{1}{r_2} - \frac{1}{r_1}\right)$$

$$v_2^2 - v_1^2 = 2Gm_E\left(\frac{1}{r_2} - \frac{1}{r_1}\right)$$

• PROBLEM 138

Compute the force of gravitational attraction between the large and small spheres of a Cavendish balance, if $m = 1$ gm, $m' = 500$ gm, $r = 5$ cm.

Solution: Two uniform spheres attract each other as if the mass of each were concentrated at its center. By Newton's Law of Universal Gravitation, the force of attraction between 2 masses m and m' separated by a distance r is

$$F = \frac{Gmm'}{r^2} = \frac{\left(6.67 \times 10^{-8}\,\text{dyne}\cdot\text{cm}^2/\text{gm}^2\right) \times (1\text{ gm}) \times (500\text{ gm})}{(5\text{ cm})^2}$$

$$= 1.33 \times 10^{-6}\,\text{dyne},$$

or about one-millionth of a dyne.

• PROBLEM 139

(1) Two lead balls whose masses are 5.20 kg and .250 kg are placed with their centers 50.0 cm apart. With what force do they attract each other?

(2) At the surface of the earth $g = 9.806\text{ m/s}^2$. Assuming the earth to be a sphere of radius 6.371×10^6 m, compute the mass of the earth.

Solution: (1). The force of gravitational attraction between two bodies with masses m_1 and m_2 separated by a distance s is

$$F = \frac{G\,m_1 m_2}{s^2}$$

$$= \left(6.67 \times 10^{-11}\,\frac{\text{nt}-\text{m}^2}{\text{kg}^2}\right)\left(\frac{5.20\text{ kg} \times .250\text{ kg}}{(.500\text{ m})^2}\right)$$

$$= 3.46 \times 10^{-10}\text{ nt}$$

(2). The only force acting on a body of mass m near the surface of the earth is the gravitational force. Hence, using Newton's Second Law

$$F = ma = \frac{G\,m\,m_e}{r^2}$$

where r is the distance of m from the earth's center. At the surface of the earth, a = g and $r = R_e$

$$mg = \frac{Gmm_e}{R_e^2}$$

whence

$$m_e = \frac{gR_e^2}{G}$$

$$= \frac{(9.806\ m/s^2)(6.371 \times 10^6\ m)^2}{6.670 \times 10^{-11}\ nt \cdot m^2/kg^2}$$

$$= 5.967 \times 10^{24}\ kg$$

• PROBLEM 140

A newly discovered planet has twice the density of the earth, but the acceleration due to gravity on its surface is exactly the same as on the surface of the earth. What is its radius?

Solution: This problem must be approached carefully. We must express the acceleration due to gravity in terms of the density and the radius of the planet. If the radius is R and the mass of the planet M, then the acceleration due to gravity on its surface is found from Newton's Second Law, F = ma. Consider an object of mass m on the surface of the planet. Then the only force on m is the gravitational force F, and

$$F = \frac{GMm}{R^2}$$

But a is the acceleration of m due to the planet's gravitational field, or g_p. Then

$$g_v = \frac{GM}{R^2}$$

Assuming the planet is spherical, its volume is the volume of a sphere of radius R:

$$V = \frac{4}{3}\pi R^3$$

Since Mass = Volume × Density.

$$M = \frac{4\pi R^3 \rho}{3}$$

where ρ (the Greek letter rho) is the density of the planet. Therefore

$$g_v = \frac{G\frac{4}{3}\pi R^3 \rho}{R^2}$$

$$= \frac{4\pi}{3} GR\rho$$

Similarly, the acceleration due to gravity on the surface of the earth is

$$g = \frac{4}{3}\pi G R_e \rho_e$$

where ρ_e is the density of the earth, and R_e is its radius. If

$$g_v = g$$

Then

$$\frac{4}{3}\pi GR\rho = \frac{4}{3}\pi GR_e\rho_e$$

Canceling $\frac{4}{3}\pi G$ on both sides

$$R\rho = R_e\rho_e$$

If the density of the planet is twice that of the earth,

$$\rho = 2\rho_e$$

So $$R2\rho_e = R_e\rho_e$$

Whence $$R = \tfrac{1}{2} R_e$$

$$= \tfrac{1}{2} \times 6.38 \times 10^6 \text{ m}$$

$$= 3.19 \times 10^6 \text{ m}$$

The radius of the planet is one half of the radius of the earth, or 3.19×10^6 meters.

• PROBLEM 141

At what point between moon and earth do the gravitational fields of these two bodies cancel? The earth's mass is 5.98×10^{24} kg, and the moon's is 7.35×10^{22} kg. The distance between the centers of the earth and the moon is 3.85×10^7 m.

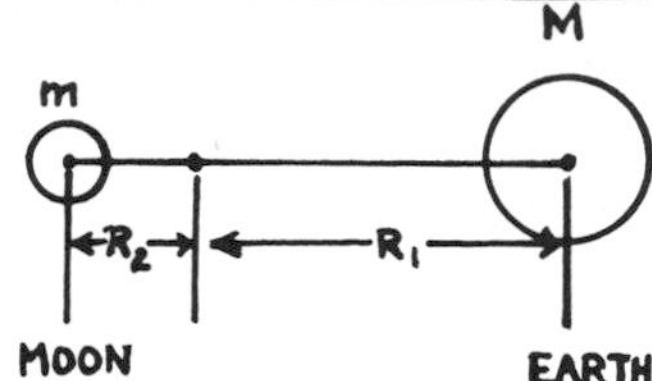

Solution: Let the point where the gravitational fields cancel be at a distance R_1 from the earth's center, R_2 from the moon's center. The attraction of the earth at this point will equal that of the moon's:

$$G = \frac{M\mu}{R_1{}^2} = G\,\frac{m\mu}{R_2{}^2}$$

where G is the gravitational constant, M the mass of the earth, and m that of the moon, or

$$G = \frac{M}{R_1{}^2} = G\,\frac{m}{R_2{}^2}\ .$$

The term on the left side of the equation is called the earth's gravitational field, the term on the right is the moon's. The gravitational field at a point in space is the gravitational force experienced by a unit mass at that point. (It is similar to the electric field, which is the electrostatic force per unit charge experienced due to a particular charged body). Gravitational fields are vector fields and the resultant gravitational field due to two or more masses is calculated by adding the field vectors from all sources at every point in space.

The only point in space where the gravitational fields of the earth and the moon cancel, must be collinear to the centers of both bodies since no two vectors cancel if they are not oppositely directed. From the equation above, we get

$$\left(\frac{R_1}{R_2}\right)^2 = \frac{M}{m}\ ,$$

$$\frac{R_1}{R_2} = \left(\frac{M}{m}\right)^{\frac{1}{2}} = \left(\frac{5.98 \times 10^{24} \text{ kg}}{7.35 \times 10^{22} \text{ kg}}\right)^{\frac{1}{2}} = 9.$$

Since the point in question is collinear to both the earth and moon's centers, the distance between the centers must equal $R_1 + R_2$ (see diagram), thus:

$$R_1 + R_2 = 3.85 \times 10^7 \text{ m}$$

$$R_1 = 3.85 \times 10^7 \text{ m} - R_2$$

$$\frac{R_1}{R_2} = \frac{3.85 \times 10^7 \text{ m} - R_2}{R_2} = \frac{3.85 \times 10^7 \text{ m}}{R_2} - 1 = 9$$

$$R_2 = 3.85 \times 10^6 \text{ m}$$

$$R_1 = 9R_2 = 9\left(3.85 \times 10^6 \text{ m}\right) = 34.7 \times 10^6 \text{ m.}$$

• PROBLEM 142

A parachutist, after bailing out, falls 50 meters without friction. When the parachute opens, he decelerates downward 2.0 meters/sec^2. He reaches the ground with a speed of 3.0 meters/sec. (a) How long is the parachutist in the air? (b) At what height did he bail out?

Solution: (a) The parachutist, starting at rest, falls 50 m at an acceleration equal to g, the acceleration of gravity. Since this is constant

$s = v_0 t + \frac{1}{2}at^2$, where v_0 is the initial velocity.

Here $v_0 = 0$ and

$$50 = \tfrac{1}{2} gt^2, \quad t = \sqrt{100/g} = 10/g^{\frac{1}{2}} = 10(3.13) = 3.2 \text{ sec}$$

He then decelerates at 2.0 m/sec^2 until he reaches a final velocity, v_f of 3 m/sec^2. When he begins his deceleration he has reached a speed:

$$v_f = v_0 + at, \qquad v_0 = 0$$

$$= gt = 9.8(3.2)$$

$$= 31.3 \text{ m/sec}$$

Thus: $v_f' = v_0' + a't'$

$$3 = 31.3 - 2t'; \quad 2t' = 31.3 - 3; \quad t' = 14.2$$

total time of flight $= t + t' = 3.2 \text{ sec} + 14.2 \text{ sec}$
$= 17.4 \text{ sec.}$

(b) We know that the parachutist falls 50 meters before the parachute opens. Thus, the problem reduces to one in which we must find the distance s the parachutist travels until he is decelerated to a speed of 3.0 m/sec, having started at velocity $v = 31.3$ m/sec.
We know that:

$s = vt' + \frac{1}{2} at'^2$

$s = (31.3 \text{ m/sec})(14.2 \text{ sec}) + \frac{1}{2}(-2.0 \text{ m/sec}^2)(14.2 \text{ sec})^2$

$= 444.5 - 201.6 = 242.9$ meters.

Hence the parachutist bailed out from a height of 50 + 242.9 = 292.9 meters.

• PROBLEM 143

(a) What is the acceleration of gravity on the moon's surface, g_m (as compared to the acceleration of gravity on the earth surface, g_e) if the diameter of the moon is one-quarter that of the earth's and its density is two-thirds that of the earth? (b) An astronaut, in his space suit and fully equipped, can jump 2 ft vertically on earth using maximum effort. How high can he jump on the moon?

Solution: (a) On the earth's surface; G is the Universal Gravitational Constant, M_e is the earth's mass and R_e is the radius of the earth. The volume of the earth is

$$V_e = \frac{4}{3} \pi R_e^3$$

If ρ_e is the earth's density, then, by definition of density

$$M_e = \rho_e V_e = \frac{4}{3} \pi R_e^3 \rho_e$$

Hence, by Newton's Law of Universal Gravitation

$$g_e = \frac{GM_e}{R_e^2} = \frac{4\pi}{3} \frac{G R_e^3 \rho_e}{R_e^2} = \frac{4}{3} \pi \rho_e G R_e \qquad (1)$$

On the surface of the moon, we have a similar relation for the acceleration of gravity

$$g_m = \frac{GM_m}{R_m^2} = \frac{4}{3} \pi \rho_m G R_m \qquad (2)$$

Therefore, upon division of equation (1) by equation (2),

$$\frac{g_e}{g_m} = \frac{\rho_e R_e}{\rho_m R_m} = \frac{3}{2} \times \frac{4}{1} = 6; \qquad \text{that is,} \quad g_m = \frac{1}{6} g_e.$$

Here, use was made of the given ratios ρ_e/ρ_m and D_e/D_m (D_e and D_m are the diameters of the earth and the moon, respectively).

(b) When he jumps at maximum effort, the astronaut can launch himself upward with an initial velocity v_0. On earth, when $v_{final} = 0$, then, using the kinematic relation for constant acceleration,

$$v_{final}^2 = v_0^2 + 2as$$

$$0 = v_0^2 - 2g_e \times 2 \text{ ft}$$

where the negative sign for g_e indicates that it is in the downward direction.

$$\therefore \quad v_0^2 = 2g_e \times 2 \text{ ft} = 12\, g_m \times 2 \text{ ft}.$$

Similarly, on the moon, when he starts with the same initial velocity, he jumps the distance y vertically, where $0 = v_0^2 - 2g_m \times y$.

$$\therefore \quad y = \frac{v_0^2}{2g_m} = \frac{24g_m}{2g_m} \text{ ft} = 12 \text{ ft}.$$

• PROBLEM 144

Consider a satellite in a circular orbit concentric and coplanar with the equator of the earth. At what radius r of the orbit will the satellite appear to remain stationary when viewed by observers fixed on the earth? We suppose the sense of rotation of the orbit is the same as that of the earth.

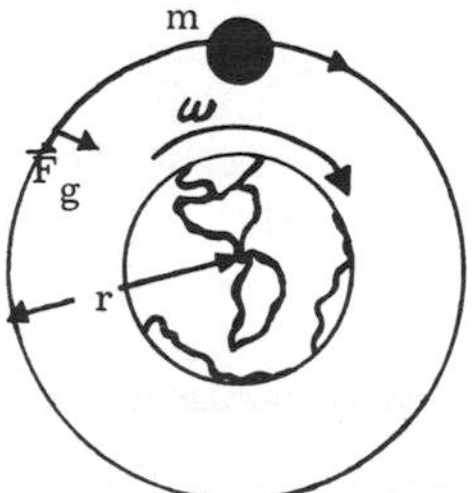

Solution: The satellite is being pulled towards the earth by a gravitational force $\vec{F}_g$. By Newton's second law, this force equals ma where m is the mass of the satellite and a is the linear acceleration along the direction parallel to the force $\vec{F}_g$ (which acts as the centripetal force in this case since the motion is circular). Therefore

$$F_g = ma$$

Furthermore, we know that in circular motion, linear acceleration is given by $a = \omega^2 r$ where ω is the angular velocity of m. The force of gravity (F_g) is given by GmM/r^2 where G is the gravitational constant and M is the mass of the earth. Substituting in the equation above we have

$$\frac{GmM}{r^2} = m\omega^2 r$$

Solving for r we have

$$r^3 = \frac{GM}{\omega^2}$$

In this equation we note that G is a constant as is M (the mass of the earth). Therefore, r varies as a function of ω (or vice versa). If we fix ω, we necessarily fix r. For the satellite to appear to remain stationary when viewed by observers fixed on the earth, the satellite must have the same angular velocity as the earth. The angular velocity of the earth ($\omega_e = \Delta\theta/\Delta t$, or change of angle per unit time) is

$$\frac{2\pi}{1 \text{ day}} = \frac{2\pi}{(60 \text{ sec/min})(60 \text{ min/hr})(24 \text{ hr/day})}$$

$$= \frac{2\pi}{8.64 \times 10^4 \text{ sec}^{-1}} = 7.3 \times 10^{-5} \text{ sec}^{-1}$$

Substituting in the above equation we have:

$$r^3 = \frac{(6.67 \times 10^{-11} \text{ N} \cdot \text{m}^2/\text{kg}^2)(5.98 \times 10^{24} \text{ kg})}{(7.3 \times 10^{-5} \text{ sec}^{-1})^2}$$

$$r^3 \simeq 7.49 \times 10^{22} \text{ m}^3$$

$$r \simeq 4.2 \times 10^7 \text{ m}$$

$$r \simeq 4.2 \times 10^9 \text{ cm}$$

The radius of the earth is 6.38×10^8 cm. The distance calculated is roughly one-tenth of the distance to the moon.

• PROBLEM 145

Find the period of a communications satellite in a circular orbit 22,300 mi above the earth's surface, given that the radius of the earth is 4000 mi, that the period of the moon is 27.3 days, and that the orbit of the moon is almost circular with a radius of 239,000 mi.

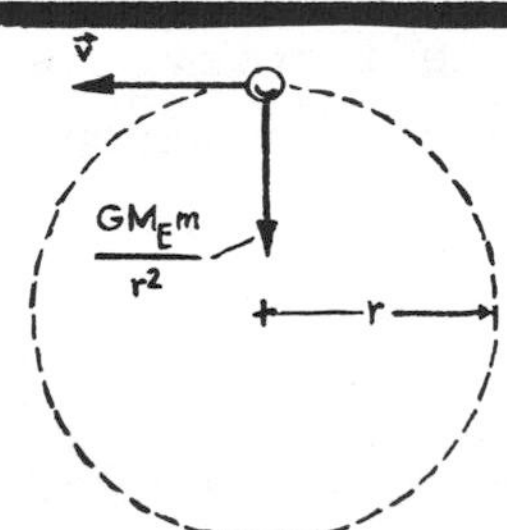

Solution: In a circular orbit of radius r an earth satellite of mass m has a velocity v. The distance, d, the satellite moves in one revolution equals $2\pi r$. Its period T is the time it takes for the satellite to make one revolution. Therefore

$$T = \frac{d}{v} = \frac{2\pi r}{v} \qquad (1)$$

The centripetal force necessary to keep the satellite moving in a circle is supplied by the gravitational force exerted by the earth. By Newton's Second Law,

$$G\,\frac{M_E m}{r^2} = \frac{mv^2}{r}$$

where G is the gravitational constant and M_E is the mass of the earth. From equation (1),

$$\frac{V^2}{r^2} = \left(\frac{2\pi}{T}\right)^2 = \frac{4\pi^2}{T^2}$$

and $$G\,\frac{M_E m}{r^2} = \frac{4\pi^2\,mr}{T^2} \qquad (2)$$

The same arguments apply to the moon of mass M_M which moves in a circle of radius R with period T_M.

$$G\,\frac{M_E M_M}{R^2} = \frac{4\pi^2\,M_M R}{T_M^2}\,; \qquad (3)$$

Solving for GM_E in equations (2) and (3), we have respectively

$$GM_E = \frac{4\pi^2\,r^3}{T^2}$$

$$GM_E = \frac{4\pi^2\,R^3}{T_M^2}$$

Equating the above two expressions,

$$\frac{4\pi^2\,r^3}{T^2} = \frac{4\pi^2\,R^3}{T_M{}^2}$$

or $$\frac{T^2}{T_M^2} = \frac{r^3}{R^3}$$

Therefore, the period of the satellite can be found by substitution of the numerical values given. Using

$$r = 22{,}300\text{ mi} + R_E = 22{,}300\text{ mi} + 4000\text{ mi} = 26{,}300\text{ mi}$$

the period is

$$T = T_M\sqrt{\frac{r^3}{R^3}} = 27.3 \text{ days } \sqrt{\frac{(2.63 \times 10^4)^3 \text{ mi}^3}{(2.39 \times 10^5)^3 \text{ mi}^3}}$$

$$= 1.00 \text{ day.}$$

Such a satellite therefore rotates about the center of the earth with the same period as the earth rotates about its axis. In other words, if it is rotating in the equatorial plane, it is always vertically above the same point on the earth's surface.

• PROBLEM 146

What would be the period of rotation of the earth about its axis if its rotation speed increased until an object at the equator became weightless?

Solution: The two forces acting on a body at the equator are the force exerted on it due to the gravitational attraction of the earth, $m\vec{g}_0$, where $\vec{g}_0$ is the free-fall acceleration at the equator and acts toward the center, and the normal force exerted by the surface of the earth on the body, $\vec{N}$. This latter force acts upward. On a non-rotating earth, or at the poles (which by definition do not rotate), these forces are equal since a body would be in equilibrium. At the equator, where a body does experience rotation and therefore a centripetal acceleration, the forces are unequal so that their resultant provides the centripetal force necessary to keep the body traveling in a circle. Therefore, Newton's Second Law yields:

$$mg_0 - N = \frac{mv^2}{R}$$

where v is the speed of the body and R is the radius of the earth. But the distance traveled in one period of rotation, T, is $2\pi R$. Therefore $T = 2\pi R/v$, and $v^2 = 4\pi^2R^2/T^2$. Substituting this into the first expression, we get

$$N = mg_0 - \frac{mv^2}{R} = mg_0 - \frac{4\pi^2 mR}{T^2} = m\left(g_0 - \frac{4\pi^2 R}{T^2}\right) = mg,$$

where g is the acceleration as measured at the earth's surface, and N is a measure of the apparent weight of the body, which is thus less than the gravitational force exerted on the body by the earth. If the speed of revolution of the earth increases, the body becomes weightless when the normal force exerted on it by the surface becomes zero. Thus weightlessness occurs when

$$N = 0 = m\left(g_0 - \frac{4\pi^2 R}{T^2}\right)$$

$$g_0 = \frac{4\pi^2 R}{T^2}$$

or when the period of rotation is

$$T = 2\pi \sqrt{\frac{R}{g_0}} = 2\pi \sqrt{\frac{4 \times 10^3 \text{ mi} \times 5280 \text{ ft/mi}}{32.4 \text{ ft/s}^2}}$$

$$= \frac{2\pi}{3600 \text{ s/hr}} \times \sqrt{\frac{4 \times 5280 \times 10^3}{32.4}} \text{ s} = 1.41 \text{ hr.}$$

• PROBLEM 147

Find the speed and period of an earth satellite traveling at an altitude h = 135 mi above the surface of the earth where g´ = 30 ft/sec. Take the radius of the earth R = 3960 mi.

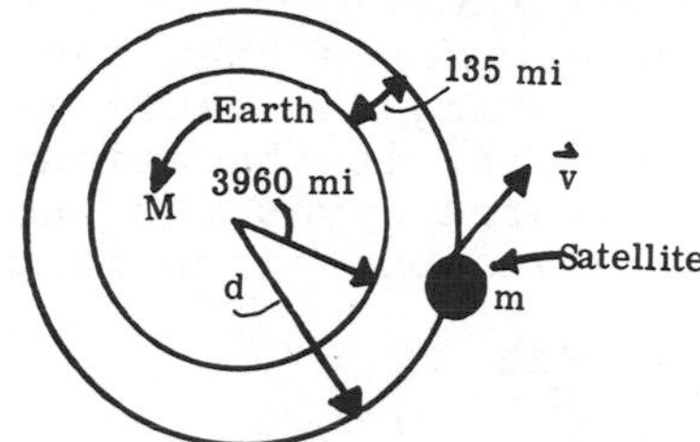

Solution: The satellite experiences a force in the radial direction, towards the center of the earth. This force, the gravitational force on the satellite, provides the centripetal force that will keep the satellite in its circular orbit. Using Newton's Second Law, F = ma, we may write $ma = mg'$

where g' is the acceleration due to gravity at a height of 135 miles above the earth's surface. Because the satellite is in a circular orbit, $a = v^2/d$ (see figure). Then

$$\frac{mv^2}{d} = mg'$$

and $$v = \sqrt{g'd}$$

$$v = \sqrt{(30 \text{ f/s}^2)(3960 \text{ mi} + 135 \text{ mi})}$$

But 1 mi = 5280 ft

$$v = \sqrt{(30 \text{ f/s}^2)(4095)(5280 \text{ f})}$$

$$v = \sqrt{6.49 \times 10^8 \text{ f}^2/\text{s}^2} = 2.55 \times 10^4 \text{ f/s}$$

To find the period of the satellite, we note that its speed is constant. Hence

$$v = \frac{2\pi d}{T}$$

where $2\pi d$ is the distance travelled by the satellite in 1 revolution and T is the time required for this traversal.

$$T = \frac{2\pi d}{v} = \frac{(2)(\pi)(4095 \text{ mi})(5280 \text{ f/mi})}{(2.55 \times 10^4 \text{ f/s})}$$

$$= \frac{1.36 \times 10^8 \text{ f}}{2.55 \times 10^4 \text{ f/s}}$$

$$= 5.33 \times 10^3 \text{ s}$$

A 2.0-ton elevator is supported by a cable that can safely support 6400 lb. What is the shortest distance in which the elevator can be brought to a stop when it is descending with a speed of 4.0 ft/sec?

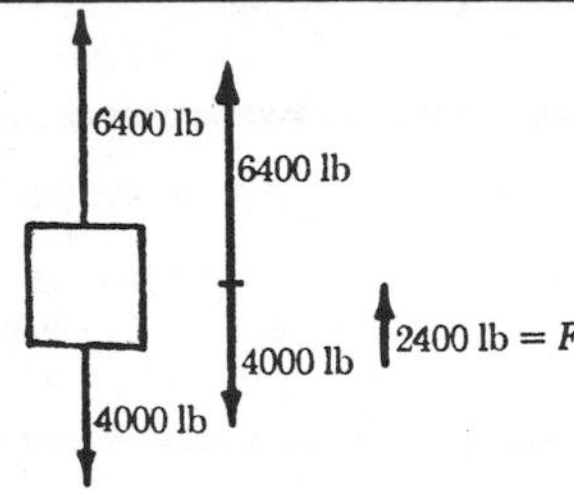

Solution. The maximum force that can be used to stop the elevator without breaking the cable is 6400 lb - 4000 lb = 2400 lb upward (4000 lb. is the weight of the elevator).

This maximum force gives the shortest distance in which the elevator can be stopped since it provides a maximum deceleration $a_{max} = \frac{F_{max}}{m}$.

$$m = \frac{W}{g} = \frac{4000 \text{ lb}}{32 \text{ ft/sec}^2} = 125 \text{ slugs}$$

$$a = \frac{F}{m} = \frac{2400 \text{ lb}}{125 \text{ slugs}} = 19.2 \text{ ft/sec}^2.$$

With $v_{final} = 0$ and taking up as positive, the minimum stopping distance can be found using the kinematics equation

$$v_f^2 = 2as + v^2$$

$$s = \frac{-v^2}{2a} = \frac{-(-4.0 \text{ ft/sec})^2}{2 \times 19.2 \text{ ft/sec}^2} = -0.42 \text{ ft.}$$

• PROBLEM 149

At what distance from the center of the earth does the acceleration due to gravity have one half of the value that it has on the surface of the earth?

Solution: Newton's Second Law implies that W = mg. W is the weight of an object of mass m (that is, the gravitational force of attraction between the earth and the object), and g is the acceleration due to gravity. Then, by Newton's Law of universal gravitation,

$$W = \frac{GM_e m}{R^2} = mg$$

where R is the distance of the object of mass m from the center of the earth, and M_e is the mass of the earth. Therefore.

$$g(R) = \frac{GM_e}{R^2}$$

At the surface of the earth,

$$g(R_e) = \frac{GM_e}{R_e^2}$$

But we want $g(R) = \frac{1}{2}g(R_e)$. Therefore,

$$\frac{GM_e}{R^2} = \frac{1}{2}\frac{GM_e}{R_e^2}$$

$$R^2 = 2R_e^2$$

$$R = \sqrt{2}\, R_e$$

$$= 1{,}414 \times 6.38 \times 10^6 \text{ m} = 9.02 \times 10^6 \text{ m}$$

The acceleration due to gravity is reduced to one half of its usual value at a distance of 9.02×10^6 meters from the center of the earth. This is equivalent to a height of 2.64×10^6 meters or 1640 miles above the surface of the earth.

• PROBLEM 150

A spaceship from earth enters a circular orbit 22,000 km above the surface of Mars at the equator, which allows it to rotate at the same speed as Mars and thus to stay always above the same point on the planet's surface. The Martians set up a guided missile directly beneath it and fire it vertically upward in an attempt to destroy the intruder. With what minimum velocity must the missile leave the surface in order to succeed in its mission? Mars is a sphere of radius 3400 km and of mean density 4120 $kg \cdot m^{-3}$.

Solution: The missile will just reach the spaceship if its velocity at the latter's position is zero. We must therefore calculate the missile's velocity as a function of position. Using Newton's Second Law, we obtain

$$F = ma \qquad (1)$$

where m is the missile's mass, a is its acceleration and F is the net force acting on it. Note that

$$F = \frac{-GmM_m}{r^2} \qquad (2)$$

where M_m is the mass of Mars and r is the radial distance of the missile from the center of Mars. Assuming that the missile travels in a radial direction, we may write

$$a = \frac{dv}{dt} = \frac{dv}{dr}\frac{dr}{dt} = v\frac{dv}{dr}$$

Substituting (2) and (3) in (1)

$$\frac{-GmM_m}{r^2} = mv\frac{dv}{dr}$$

or

$$v\frac{dv}{dr} = \frac{-GM_m}{r^2}$$

$$v\,dv = -GM_m \frac{dr}{r^2}$$

$$\int_{v_0}^{v} v dv = -GM_m \int_{R_0}^{R} \frac{dr}{r^2}$$

where $v = v$ at $r = R$, and $v = v_0$ at $r = R_0$. (R_0 is the position of the surface of Mars relative to its center).

$$\frac{V^2 - V_0^2}{2} = GM_m\left(\frac{1}{R} - \frac{1}{R_0}\right)$$

$$V_0^2 = V^2 + 2GM_m\left(\frac{1}{R_0} - \frac{1}{R}\right)$$

The minimum value of v_0 is found by requiring that the missle's velocity at the spaceship's position be zero ($v = 0$). Hence

$$V_{0\ min}^2 = 2GM_m\left(\frac{1}{R_0} - \frac{1}{R}\right) \qquad (3)$$

The mass of Mars is its volume times its density (ρ_m).

$$M_m = \frac{4}{3}\pi R_m^3 \times \rho_m = \frac{4}{3}\pi \times \left(3.4 \times 10^6 m\right)^3 \times 4120 kg\cdot m^{-3} = 0.678 \times 10^{24} kg.$$

or

$$V^2 = 2 \times 6.67 \times 10^{-11} N\cdot m^2\cdot kg^{-2} \times 0.678 \times 10^{24} kg\left(\frac{1}{3.4 \times 10^6 m} - \frac{1}{25.4 \times 10^6 m}\right)$$

$$= 2.30 \times 10^7\ m^2\cdot s^{-2}.$$

Therefore

$$V = 4.8\ km\cdot s^{-1}.$$

Note that R in (3) is the position of the spaceship from the center of Mars, or

$$R = R_0 + 2.2 \times 10^6\ m$$

$$R = 25.4 \times 10^6\ m$$

• PROBLEM 151

The earth acts on any body with a gravitational force inversely proportional to the square of the distance of the body from the center of the earth. Calculate the escape velocity from the earth, i.e., the speed with which a vertically moving body must leave the earth's surface in order to coast along without being pulled back to the earth. Also find the time it takes for a rocket projected upward with this escape velocity to attain a height above the earth's surface equal to its radius. In both cases ignore the effect of any other heavenly bodies and take the earth's radius as 6.38×10^6 m.

Solution: Assuming that the body moves along a radial trajectory after leaving the earth, it continually experiences a gravitational force

$$F = -\frac{Gmm_e}{r^2}$$

where m and m_e are the mass of the body and the earth,

respectively. By Newton's Second Law, F = ma, and the acceleration of m is then

$$a = -\frac{Gm_e}{r^2}$$

But, being that the trajectory is radial,

$$a = \frac{dv}{dr}\frac{dr}{dt} = v\frac{dv}{dr} = -\frac{Gm_e}{r^2}$$

where v is the object's velocity.

$$v\,dv = -G\,m_e\frac{dr}{r^2} \qquad (1)$$

Now, we want a projectile to leave the earth ($r = R_e$) with a velocity v_e and to reach a destination at which it no longer feels the effect of the earth's gravitational force. If it reaches this point , the body can have no velocity and yet still not be accelerated towards the earth.

Since the gravitational force is zero at ∞, we require that v = 0 at $r = \infty$. Hence

$$\int_{v_e}^{0} v\,dv = -G\,me_e\int_{R_e}^{\infty}\frac{dr}{r^2}$$

$$-\frac{v_e^2}{2} = Gm_e\left(\frac{1}{r}\right)_{R_e}^{\infty}$$

$$v_e^2 = \frac{2Gm_e}{R_e} \qquad (2)$$

At the surface of the earth

$$\frac{Gm_e}{R_e^2} = g$$

and $\quad v_e^2 = 2gR_e$

$$v_e = \sqrt{2gR_e} = \sqrt{2\times 9.81\text{ m}\cdot\text{s}^2\times 6.38\times 10^6\text{ m}}$$

$$v_e = 11.2\times 10^3\text{ m/s}^2$$

The second part of the problem asks us to find out how long it takes for an object to reach a distance r = $2R_e$ from the center of the earth if its initial velocity is v_e. In order to do this, we must find r as a function of t. Going back to (1)

$$v\,dv = -\,Gm_e \frac{dr}{r^2}$$

But, now, $v = v$ at $r = r$, and $v = v_e$ at $r = R_e$ and

$$\int_{v_e}^{v} v\,dv = -\,G\,m_e \int_{R_e}^{r} \frac{dr}{r^2}$$

$$\frac{v^2 - v_e^2}{2} = Gm_e \left(\frac{1}{r} - \frac{1}{R_e}\right)$$

$$v^2 = v_e^2 + \frac{2Gm_e}{r} - \frac{2Gm_e}{R_e} \qquad (3)$$

However, from (2)

$$v_e^2 = \frac{2Gm_e}{R_e}$$

Therefore, from (3)

$$v^2 = \frac{2Gm_e}{r}$$

$$v = \frac{\sqrt{2Gm_e}}{r^{\frac{1}{2}}}$$

To find v as a function of t, note that

$$v = \frac{dr}{dt}$$

Therefore, $$\frac{\sqrt{2Gm_e}}{r^{\frac{1}{2}}} = \frac{dr}{dt}$$

$$r^{\frac{1}{2}}\,dr = \sqrt{2Gm_e}\,dt$$

Since $r = R_e$ when $t = 0$, and $r = 2R_e$ when $t = t$,

$$\int_{Re}^{2R_e} r^{\frac{1}{2}}\,dr = \sqrt{2Gm_e} \int_0^t dt$$

$$\frac{2}{3}\,r^{3/2} \Bigg|_{R_e}^{2R_e} = \sqrt{2Gm_e}\;t$$

$$(2R_e)^{3/2} - (R_e)^{3/2} = \frac{3}{2}\sqrt{2Gm_e}\;t$$

or $t = \dfrac{2[(2R_e)^{3/2} - (R_e)^{3/2}]}{3\sqrt{2Gm_e}} = \dfrac{2R_e^{3/2}[(2)^{3/2} - 1]}{3\sqrt{2Gm_e}}$

$$t = \frac{2(6.38 \times 10^6 \text{ m})^{3/2}[(2)^{3/2} - 1]}{3\sqrt{(2)(6.67\times10^{-11} \text{ N}\cdot\text{m}^2/\text{kg}^2)(5.98\times10^{24} \text{ kg})}}$$

$$t = \frac{2(1.61 \times 10^{10} \text{ m}^{3/2})(1.83)}{3(2.82 \times 10^7 \text{ N}^{\frac{1}{2}} \cdot \text{m/kg}^{\frac{1}{2}})}$$

$t = 696.53$ s $= 11.61$ minutes

This is the time required for the object to reach $r = 2R_e$.

CURVILINEAR DYNAMICS

• PROBLEM 152

What is the rotational inertia of a 50-lb cylindrical flywheel whose diameter is 16 in.?

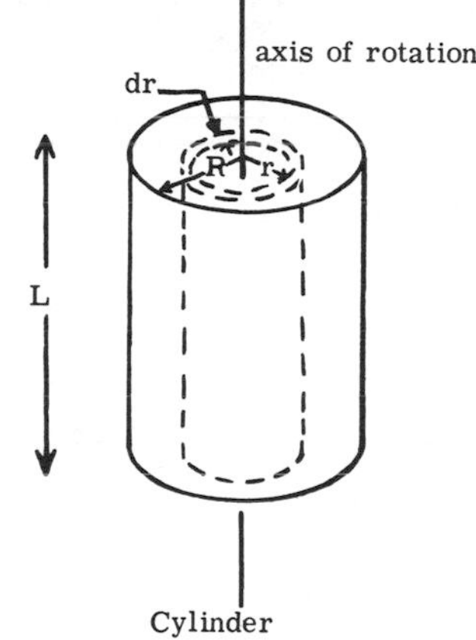

Cylinder

Solution: To find the rotational inertia of the flywheel, consider a mass element consisting of a thin cylindrical shell of radius r, thickness dr, and length L, as shown in the figure. Then

$$dV = (2\pi r)(dr)(L)$$

density, $\rho = \dfrac{m}{V} = \dfrac{m}{\pi R^2 L}$

and $dm = \rho dV = \dfrac{m}{\pi R^2 L}(2\pi r \, dr \, L) = \dfrac{2m}{R^2} r \, dr$

The moment of inertia is given by

$$I = \int r^2 \, dm = \int (r^2)\left(\frac{2m}{R^2} r \, dr\right)$$

$$= \frac{2m}{R^2}\int_{r=0}^{R} r^3\,dr = \frac{2m}{R^2}\frac{r^4}{4}\Bigg]_{r=0}^{R} = \tfrac{1}{2}\,mR^2$$

For the given cylindrical flywheel,

$$m = \frac{w}{g} = \frac{50\text{ lb}}{32\text{ ft/sec}^2} = 1.6\text{ slugs}$$

$$R = 8.0\text{ in} = 2/3\text{ ft}$$

$$I = \tfrac{1}{2}\,mR^2 = \tfrac{1}{2}(1.6\text{ slugs})(2/3\text{ ft})^2$$

$$= 0.35\text{ slug-ft}^2$$

• PROBLEM 153

The distance between the sun and earth is 1.5×10^{11} m and the earth's orbital speed is 3×10^4 m/s. Use this information to calculate the mass of the sun.

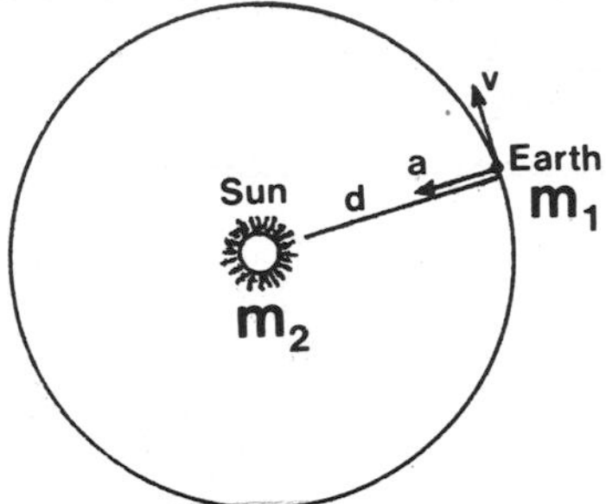

Solution: Since the earth's orbit around the sun is very nearly circular, it is assumed that it is exactly circular. The radius of the circle is equal to the distance d between the earth and sun. The centripetal acceleration of the earth is then

$$a = \frac{v^2}{d}$$

Newton's second law, F = ma, may then be written as

$$F = \frac{m_1 v^2}{d}$$

where m_1 is the mass of the earth.

F is the force acting on the earth and is responsible for its centripetal acceleration. This force is also the gravitational force of attraction between the two objects. It is described by the law of universal gravitation,

$$F = \frac{Gm_1 m_2}{d^2}$$

where m_2 is the mass of the sun.

Equating these two expressions

$$\frac{Gm_1 m_2}{d^2} = \frac{m_1 v^2}{\not{d}}$$ Upon

rearranging and substituting the known quantities, the mass of the sun is

$$m_2 = \frac{v^2 d}{G} = \frac{(3 \times 10^4 \text{ m/s})^2 (1.5 \times 10^{11} \text{ m})}{6.67 \times 10^{-11} \text{N m}\not{^2}/\text{kg}^2} =$$

$$= 2.02 \times 10^{30} \text{ kg}$$

The mass of the sun is more than 300,000 times as large as the mass of the earth.

• PROBLEM 154

What is the acceleration of a point on the rim of a flywheel 0.90 m in diameter, turning at the rate of 1200 rev/min?

Solution: For uniform circular motion, the acceleration of a particle at distance r from the axis of rotation is given by

$$a = \frac{v^2}{r} \qquad (1)$$

and is directed towards the center of the circle. Linear velocity, v, is related to angular velocity, ω, by the relationship

$$v = \omega r \qquad (2)$$

Substitution of (2) into the equation for linear acceleration gives

$$a = \frac{(\omega r)^2}{r} = \omega^2 r$$

where ω is expressed in radians/second. For the point on the rim of the flywheel

$$\omega = 1200 \text{ rev/min} = 20 \text{ rev/sec}$$

$$= 20 \times 2\pi \text{ rad/sec}$$

$$r = 0.45 \text{ m}$$

$$a = \omega^2 r = (20 \times 2\pi \text{ rad/sec})^2 (0.45 \text{ m})$$

$$= 7100 \text{ m/sec}^2$$

• PROBLEM 155

Consider the tire on a car wheel, outer radius R = 0.36 m, as the car accelerates uniformly from rest to a maximum speed of 27 m/sec in a time of 30 sec. Calculate the acceleration of the car as well as the angular velocity and angular acceleration of the tire.

Solution: Since the acceleration is constant,

$$a_c = \frac{V_{Final} - V_{Initial}}{\Delta t} = \frac{27 \frac{m}{sec} - 0}{30 \text{ sec}} = 0.9 \frac{m}{sec^2}$$

The angular velocity vector ω, which is constant for uniform motion, is perpendicular to the plane of the circle.

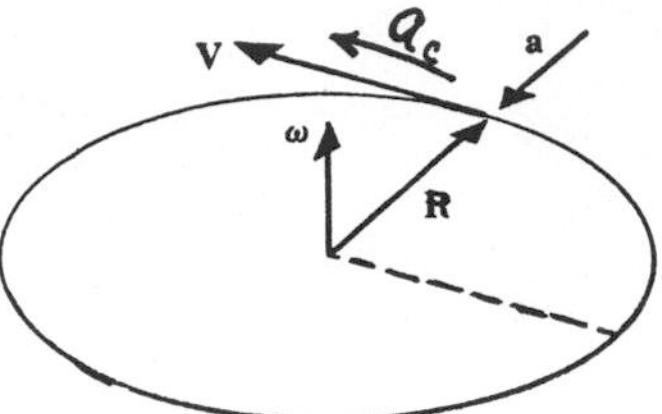

This will be the linear acceleration of the axle on which the wheel is supported. Imagine that you are sitting on the axle. You will observe the road moving by with velocity V and the tire spinning with a velocity such that, at the maximum speed, the angular velocity

$$\omega = \frac{V}{R} = \frac{27 \frac{m}{sec}}{0.36 \ m} = 75 \ sec^{-1}$$

when the acceleration is constant, the angular acceleration is given by

$$\alpha = \frac{\omega_{Final} - \omega_{Initial}}{\Delta t} = \frac{75 \ sec^{-1} - 0}{30 \ sec} = 2.5 \ sec^{-2}$$

and we can see that $a_c = \alpha R$.

A point on the circumference of the wheel experiences an acceleration, directed toward the axle, of magnitude

$$a = \frac{V^2}{R} = \omega^2 R = \left(75 \ sec^{-1}\right)^2 (0.36 \ m) = 2.0 \times 10^3 \ \frac{m}{sec^2}$$

since this point is travelling in a circular path.

• **PROBLEM 156**

Ignoring the motion of the earth around the sun and the motion of the sun through space, calculate (a) the angular velocity, (b) the velocity, and (c) the acceleration of a body resting on the ground at the equator.

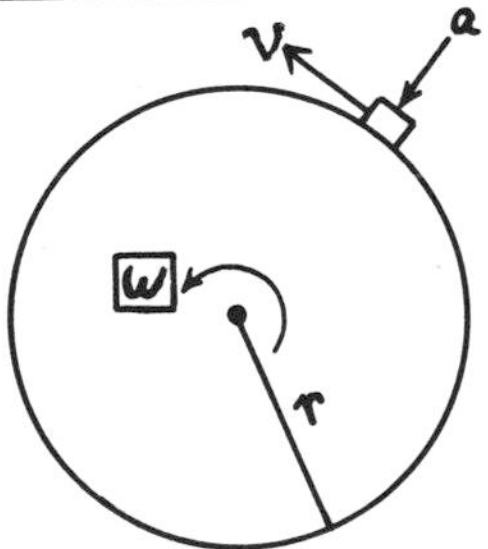

View from the North Pole.

Solution: Because of the rotation of the earth the body at the equator moves in a circle whose radius is equal to the radius of the earth (see figure).

$$r = \text{radius of earth}$$
$$= 6.37 \times 10^6 \text{ meters}$$

We are going to use the MKS System of units. One revolution, which is 2π radians, takes 1 day or

$$\frac{24 \ hr}{1 \ day} \times \frac{60 \ min}{1 \ hr} \times \frac{60 \ sec}{1 \ min} = 24 \times 60 \times 60 \ \frac{secs}{day}$$

(a) Since the frequency of revolution is $f = \frac{1}{T}$, where T is the period (the time for one revolution), then

$$2\pi f = \omega = \frac{2\pi}{T} \quad .$$

This equals the number of radians traveled per unit time, or the angular velocity ω .

$$\omega = \frac{2\pi}{24 \times 60 \times 60}$$
$$= 7.27 \times 10^{-5} \text{ radians per second}$$

(b) The linear velocity is, by definition

$$v = \omega r$$
$$= \left(7.27 \times 10^{-5}\right) \times \left(6.37 \times 10^{6}\right) \frac{\text{rad}}{\text{s}} \cdot \text{m}$$
$$= 4.64 \times 10^{2} \text{ m/sec} \; .$$

Since 1 mph = 0.447 m/sec

$$v = \left(4.64 \times 10^{2} \; \frac{\text{m}}{\text{sec}}\right)\left(\frac{1}{.447} \; \frac{\text{sec}}{\text{m}}\right)$$
$$= 1040 \text{ mph}$$

(c) The acceleration toward the center of the earth is, since the motion is circular,

$$a = \frac{v^2}{r}$$
$$= \frac{\left(4.64 \times 10^{2} \text{ m/sec}\right)^2}{(6.38 \times 10^{6} \text{ m})}$$
$$= 3.37 \times 10^{-2} \text{ m/sec}^2$$

• PROBLEM 157

A stone of mass 100 grams is whirled in a horizontal circle at the end of a cord 100 cm long. If the tension in the cord is 2.5 newtons, what is the speed of the stone?

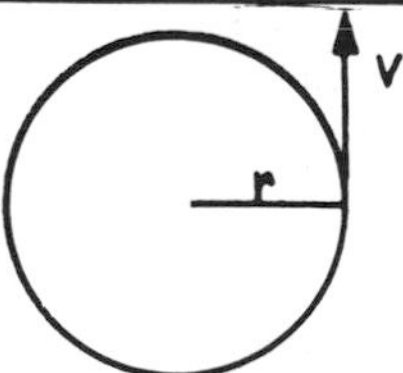

Solution: First, we shall calculate the acceleration of the object, and from that we may calculate its velocity. Firstly,

$$F = mg$$

$$2.5 \text{ newtons} = 100 \text{ gm} \times a$$

Newtons have the units $\frac{\text{kg - m}}{\text{s}^2}$, and 100 gm = 0.100 kg, so that

$$2.5 \; \frac{\text{kg-m}}{\text{s}^2} = 0.100 \text{ kg} \times a$$

$$a = 25 \text{ m/s}^2$$

Also $\quad a = \frac{v^2}{r}$ for uniform circular motion, where a is the linear acceleration and v is the linear velocity of the object. Therefore,

$$25 \frac{m}{s^2} = \frac{v^2}{1\ m}$$

$$v = 5 \frac{m}{s} .$$

• PROBLEM 158

What is the centripetal force required to cause a 3200-pound car to go around a curve of 880-ft radius at a speed of 60 mph?

Solution: When a body travels in uniform circular motion, it experiences an acceleration towards the center of the circle. Since the object has a mass, a force towards the center of the circle is produced.

In circular motion, the acceleration of the body is given by

$$a = \frac{v^2}{r}$$

where v is the linear velocity of the object and r is the radius of the circle. In our case (using 60 mph = 88 ft/sec):

$$a = \frac{(88\ \text{ft/sec})^2}{880\ \text{ft}} = 8.8\ \text{ft/sec}^2$$

The mass of the car is

$$m = \frac{Wt}{a} = \frac{3200\ \text{lb}}{32\ \text{ft/sec}^2} = 100\ \frac{\text{lb - sec}^2}{\text{ft}} \quad [\text{slugs}]$$

And $\quad F = ma$

$$F = 100\ \frac{\text{lb - sec}^2}{\text{ft}} \times 8.8\ \frac{\text{ft}}{\text{sec}^2}$$

$$= 880\ \text{lb}.$$

• PROBLEM 159

A racing car traveling in a circular path maintains a constant speed of 120 miles per hour. If the radius of the circular track is 1000 ft, what if any acceleration does the center of gravity of the car exhibit?

Solution: Since the car is traveling a circular path at constant speed, v, its acceleration is radial, and given by

$$a = \frac{v^2}{R}$$

Here, R is the radius of the circular path. Using the given data

$$a = \frac{(120\ \text{miles/hr})^2}{(1000\ \text{ft})} = \frac{14400\ \text{miles}^2}{1000\ \text{ft}\cdot\text{hr}^2}$$

$$a = 14.4 \text{ miles}^2/\text{ft}\cdot\text{hr}^2$$

In order to keep units consistent, note that

$$1 \text{ hr} = 3600 \text{ s}$$

and 1 mile = 5280 ft

Then $$a = \frac{14.4(5280 \text{ ft})^2}{(1 \text{ ft})(3600 \text{ s})^2}$$

$$a = 30.98 \text{ ft/s}^2$$

• PROBLEM 160

A body is whirled in a vertical circle by means of a cord attached at the center of the circle. At what minimum speed must it travel at the top of the path in order to keep the cord barely taut, i.e., just on the verge of collapse? Assume radius of circle to be 3 ft.

Solution: At the top of the circle, the net force on the body of mass m is

$$\Sigma F = mg + T$$

where the positive direction is taken downward, and T is the cord tension. Since the motion is circular, the net force is centripetal and

$$\Sigma F = \frac{mv^2}{R}$$

where v is the body's velocity and R is the circle's radius. Hence

$$mg + T = \frac{mv^2}{R}$$

and $$T = \frac{mv^2}{R} - mg$$

If the cord is just on the verge of collapse, T = 0 and

$$\frac{mv^2}{R} - mg = 0$$

whence $$v = \sqrt{gR}$$

Using the given data

$$v = \sqrt{(32 \text{ ft/s}^2)(3 \text{ ft})} = \sqrt{96 \text{ ft}^2/\text{s}^2}$$

$$v = 9.8 \text{ ft/s}$$

• PROBLEM 161

A 3200-lb car traveling with a speed of 60 mi/hr rounds a curve whose radius is 484 ft. Find the necessary centripetal force.

Solution: A centripetal force is a force which results when a particle executes circular motion with constant speed. It is called centripetal because it points to the center of the circle. Note that although the speed of the particle is constant, its velocity is not, because the latter is continually changing in direction. As a result, the centripetal force is responsible for changing the velocity of the particle.

Using Newton's Second Law, we may write

$$F = ma \qquad (1)$$

where F is the net force acting on the mass, m.

Because this is uniform circular motion, $a = \frac{v^2}{R}$, where v is the speed of the particle in a circular orbit of radius R. Inserting this result in (1),

$$F = \frac{mv^2}{R} \qquad (2)$$

Equation (2) gives the centripetal force needed to accelerate m. In order to use this formula, we must transform the weight, mg, given in the question as 3200 lb., into a mass by dividing by 32 ft/sec.^{2} . Then, using (2)

$$F = \left(\frac{3200}{32}\ \text{sl}\right)\frac{(88\ \text{f/s})^2}{(484\ \text{ft})} = 1600\ \text{lb.}$$

• PROBLEM 162

Consider a molecule suspended in a liquid in the test chamber of an ultracentrifuge. Suppose that the molecule lies 10 cm from the axis of rotation and that the ultracentrifuge rotates at 1000 revolutions per second (60,000 rpm). What is the magnitude of the acceleration associated with the circular motion?

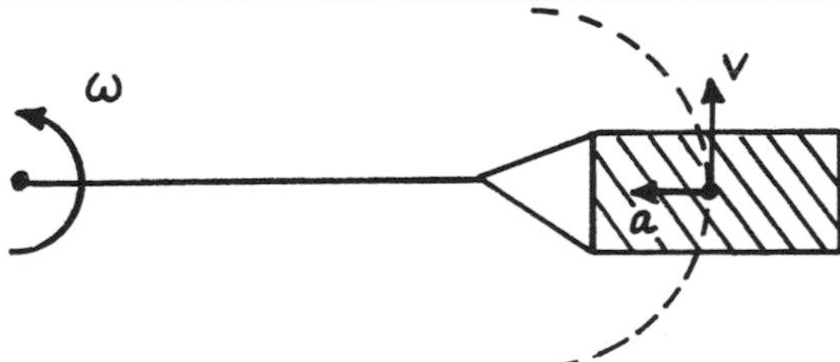

Solution: The angular velocity of the molecule is $\omega = 2\pi n$ where n is the number of revolutions per second that the molecule is executing. Or,

$$\omega = 2\pi \times 1 \times 10^3\ \frac{\text{rev}}{\text{sec}} \cong 6 \times 10^3\ \frac{\text{rad}}{\text{sec}}$$

The linear velocity is

$$v = \omega r \cong \left(6 \times 10^3\ \frac{\text{rad}}{\text{sec}}\right)(10\ \text{cm}) \cong 6 \times 10^4\ \frac{\text{cm}}{\text{sec}}$$

The magnitude of the acceleration associated with circular motion is

$a = \frac{v^2}{r} = \omega^2 r$ since the particle is going around in a circle.

$$a \cong \left(6 \times 10^3 \frac{rad}{sec}\right)^2 (10\ cm) \cong 4 \times 10^8 \frac{cm}{sec^2}$$

Now the acceleration g due to gravity is only 980 cm/s^2 at the surface of the earth , so that the ratio of the rotational acceleration to the gravitational acceleration is

$$\frac{a}{g} \approx \frac{4 \times 10^8}{10^3} \approx 4 \times 10^5$$

• PROBLEM 163

A 2-ft-long string which can just support a weight of 16 lb is fixed at one end to a peg on a smooth horizontal surface. The other end is fixed to a mass of ½ slug. With what maximum constant speed can the mass rotate about the peg? (See figure).

Top View

Solution: If the tension in the string exceeds 16 lb, the string will break. Thus the maximum centripetal force that can be exerted on the mass is 16 lb. But if the mass is circling the peg with a velocity v, the centripetal force necessary to keep it in the circle is mv^2/R, where m is ½ slug and R is the length of the string, 2 ft. Thus

$$16\ lb = T_{max} = \frac{mv^2_{max}}{R} = \frac{\frac{1}{2}\ slug \times v^2_{max}}{2\ ft}$$

therefore

$$v^2_{max} = 64\ ft\cdot lb\cdot slug^{-1} = 64\ ft^2\cdot s^{-2}$$

or

$$v_{max} = 8\ ft\cdot s^{-1}\ .$$

• PROBLEM 164

A train whose speed is 60 mi/hr rounds a curve whose radius of curvature is 484 ft. What is its acceleration?

Solution: For uniform circular motion, we have an acceleration directed towards the center of curvature of magnitude

$$a = \frac{v^2}{R}$$

where v is the speed of the object, and R is the radius of the circle. To keep the units consistent, we have to convert the speed from mi/hr to ft/sec, since R is in feet.

$$v = \left(60\ \frac{mi}{hr}\right)\left(\frac{5280\ ft/mi}{3600\ sec/hr}\right) = 88\ ft/sec.$$

Substituting the appropriate values, we find the acceleration to be

$$a = \frac{v^2}{R} = \frac{(88\ ft/sec)^2}{484\ ft} = 16\ ft/sec^2.$$

• **PROBLEM 165**

At the National Air Races in Reno, Nevada, the planes fly a course around a series of pylons. In a turn around a pylon, the maximum centripetal acceleration that the pilot can withstand is about 6g. For a plane traveling at 150 m/s, what is the turning radius for an acceleration of 6g?

Solution: The speed is $v = 1.5 \times 10^2$ m/s, and the acceleration $a = 6g = (6)\left(9.8\ \text{m/s}^2\right) = 5.88 \times 10^1\ \text{m/s}^2$.

$$R = \frac{v^2}{a} = \frac{\left(1.5 \times 10^2\ \text{m/s}\right)^2}{5.88 \times 10^1\ \text{m/s}^2} = 3.83 \times 10^2\ \text{m}.$$

This is the minimum turning radius.

• **PROBLEM 166**

The outside curve on a highway forms an arc whose radius is 150 ft. If the roadbed is 30 ft. wide and its outer edge is 4 ft. higher than the inner edge, for what speed is it ideally banked?

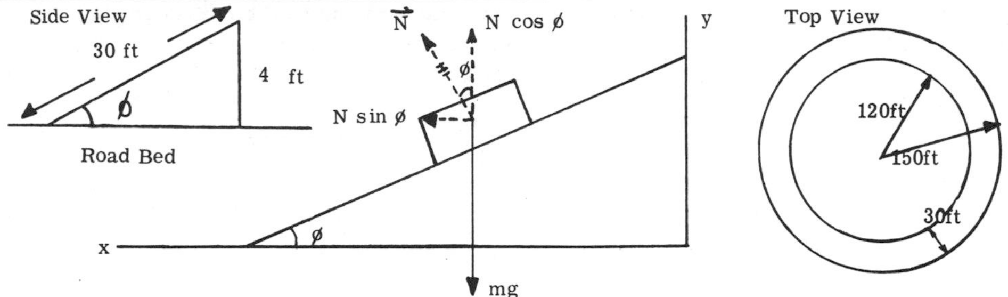

Solution: We wish to relate the velocity of the car to ϕ, the banking angle. Note that the car is undergoing circular motion, hence its acceleration in the x-direction is $a = \frac{v^2}{R}$, where R is its distance from the center of the circle (see figure). Applying Newton's Second Law, F=ma, to the x component of motion,

$$ma = N \sin \phi$$

But $a = v^2/R$ and

$$\frac{mv^2}{R} = N \sin \phi \qquad (1)$$

The acceleration of the car in the y-direction is zero, since it remains on the road. Applying the Second Law to this component of motion,

$$N \cos \phi = mg \qquad (2)$$

Dividing (1) by (2),

$$\frac{\frac{mv^2}{R}}{mg} = \frac{N \sin \phi}{N \cos \phi} = \tan \phi$$

$$\tan \phi = \frac{v^2}{Rg}$$

Hence $$v = \sqrt{Rg \tan \phi}$$

Now, note that the width of the road bed is much smaller than the inner radius of the road. Hence, we may approximate R as the inner radius.

$$R \simeq 150 \text{ ft}$$

$$v = \sqrt{(150 \text{ ft})(32 \text{ ft/s}^2) \tan\phi}$$

From the figure,

$$\sin\phi = 4/30$$

$$\cos^2\phi = 1 - \sin^2\phi = \frac{900}{900} - \frac{16}{900} = \frac{884}{900}$$

Hence $$\cos\phi = \frac{\sqrt{884}}{30}$$

and $$\tan\phi = \frac{\frac{4}{30}}{\frac{\sqrt{884}}{30}} = \frac{4}{\sqrt{884}} = .1345$$

Therefore $$v = \sqrt{(150 \text{ ft})(32 \text{ ft/s}^2)(.1345)}$$

$$v = \sqrt{645.6 \text{ ft}^2/\text{s}^2}$$

$$v = 25.41 \text{ ft/s}$$

• PROBLEM 167

An unbanked curve has a radius of 80.0 m. What is the maximum speed at which a car can make the turn if the coefficient of friction μ_s is 0.81?

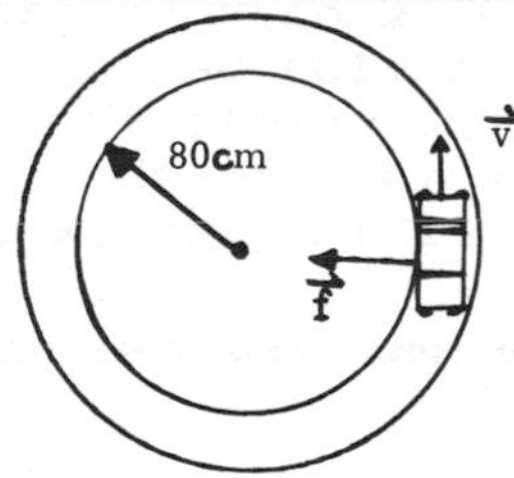

Figure A

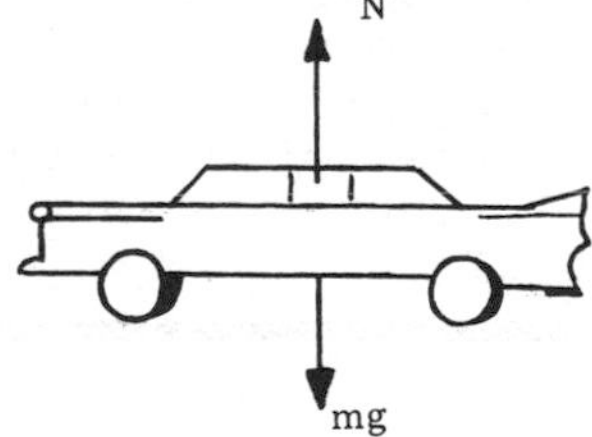

Figure B

Solution: We assume that the car is travelling in a circular path (see fig.(a)) at a constant speed. However, its velocity is constantly changing in direction. Hence, the car is accelerating, and, therefore, a force must be acting on the car. This force accelerates the car towards the center of the circular path and is therefore centripetal. Applying Newton's Second Law, F = ma, to the car, we obtain

$$f = ma \qquad (1)$$

where f is the frictional force and a is the acceleration of the car. But, in uniform circular motion

$$a = \frac{v^2}{R} \qquad (2)$$

where v is the speed of the car and R is the radius of the circle. Furthermore, the frictional force f is

$$f \leq \mu_s N \qquad (3)$$

where N is the normal force exerted by the road on the car. (Note that if $f = \mu_s N$, the car will begin to slip relative to the road.) Combining (1), (2) and (3)

$$\frac{mv^2}{R} = f \leq \mu_s N$$

$$\frac{mv^2}{R} \leq \mu_s N \qquad (4)$$

Applying Newton's Second Law to the vertical direction of motion (see fig. (b)), we obtain

$$N - mg = 0$$

because there is no acceleration of the car in this direction. Using this in (4)

$$\frac{mv^2}{R} \leq \mu_s mg$$

Solving for v

$$v \leq \sqrt{\mu_s g R}$$

$$v_{max} = \sqrt{\mu_s g R}$$

$$v_{max} = \sqrt{(.81)(9.8 \text{ m/s}^2)(80 \text{ m})}$$

$$v_{max} = 25 \text{ m/s}$$

• PROBLEM 168

What is the maximum speed at which a car can safely round a circular curve of radius 160 ft on a horizontal road if the coefficient of static friction between tires and road is 0.8? The width between the wheels is 5 ft and the center of gravity of the car is 2 ft above the road. Will the car overturn or skid if it just exceeds this speed?

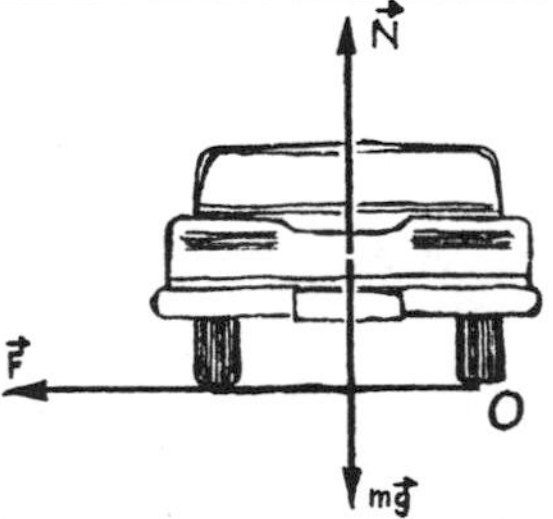

Solution: The magnitude of the maximum frictional force that can be brought into play between tires and road is $F = \mu N$, where $\vec{N}$ is the normal force exerted by the road on the car and μ is the coefficient of static friction. But, since there is no upward movement of the car, $\vec{N}$ just balances the third force acting on the car, the weight $m\vec{g}$. Hence $F = \mu mg$.

This must provide the centripetal force necessary

to keep the car in the curve of radius r when it is moving with the maximum permissible speed v. Hence,

$$\mu mg = \frac{mv^2}{r}$$

$$v = \sqrt{\mu rg} = \sqrt{0.8 \times 160 \text{ ft} \times 32 \text{ ft}\cdot\text{s}^{-2}}$$

$$v = 64 \text{ ft}\cdot\text{s}^{-1}.$$

The frictional force $\vec{F}$ acts in the plane of the road surface and not through the center of mass of the car. In addition to providing the centripetal force necessary to keep the car in the curve, the frictional force must therefore produce a rotational motion about the center of mass.

The only point of contact between car and road will then be at O in the diagram. Therefore, $\vec{N}$ must act through this point; but the weight of the car of magnitude mg = N still acts through the center of gravity. These two parallel but displaced forces form a couple of positive moment, tending to restore all car wheels to the road and to prevent the overturning.

The moment of the frictional force is $-\mu N = -mv^2/r$ multiplied by the height of the center of mass above the road. Thus $M_1 = -\mu N \times 2$ ft $= -\mu mg \times 2$ ft.

Assuming that the center of gravity of the car is centrally located, the moment of normal force is N = mg, multiplied by **half the** width between the wheels. Thus $M_2 = mg \times 2.5$ ft.

$$\therefore \quad M_2 + M_1 = mg \times 2.5 \text{ ft} - 0.8 \times mg \times 2 \text{ ft}$$

$$= mg \times 0.9 \text{ ft}.$$

Since this is positive, $|M_2| > |M_1|$.

The restoring moment is therefore greater than the overturning moment at the maximum speed. If this speed is just exceeded, the car does not overturn. It skids, since the centripetal force is not now great enough to provide the acceleration necessary to keep it going round the curve, and the overturning moment is less than the restoring moment.

• PROBLEM 169

We know that if we drop an object of mass m while giving it a horizontal velocity component, the object will fall toward the surface of the Earth with the horizontal velocity remaining constant. With what velocity must an object be projected so that the curvature of its path is just equal to the curvature of the Earth?

Solution: In such a situation, the object would fall toward the Earth at the same rate that the surface of the Earth curves away from the instantaneous velocity vector; that is, the object would fall around the Earth. The height of the object above the surface of the Earth would therefore never decrease and the object would become a satellite of the Earth.

Suppose that we start with the object at a distance h above the surface of the Earth. The radius of the Earth is R so that the radius of the desired circular path of the object is R + h.

The centripetal force required to maintain the circular motion is

$$F = ma_c = \frac{mv^2}{r} = \frac{mv^2}{R + h}$$

The centripetal acceleration is furnished by gravity, so we can substitute g $(= GM_e/(R + h)^2)$ for a_c where G is the gravitational constant and M_e is the mass of the Earth. Thus,

$$m\left(\frac{v^2}{R + h}\right) = m\left(\frac{GM_e}{(R + h)^2}\right), \quad \text{hence} \quad v = \sqrt{\frac{GM_e}{R + h}}$$

The period of the motion is

$$\tau = \frac{2\pi}{\omega} = \frac{2\pi r}{v}$$

$$\text{for } v = \frac{\text{length of one orbit}}{\text{time to make one orbit}} = \frac{\text{circumference}}{\text{period}}$$

• PROBLEM 170

An astronaut is to be put into a circular orbit a distance of 1.6×10^5 m (about 100 miles) above the surface of the earth. The earth has a radius of 6.37×10^6 m. and mass of 5.98×10^{24} kg. What is the orbital speed?

Solution: The force between the astronaut and the earth is:

$$F = G\frac{mM}{R^2} = ma$$

where G is the gravitational constant, m the mass of the astronaut and his ship, M the mass of the earth, and the letter a the centripetal acceleration of the ship. The term on the far right of the equation is just a statement of Newton's second law.

We know that centripetal acceleration a, is equal to $\frac{V_2}{R}$ where V is the instantaneous linear velocity of the orbiting body at any time, thus:

$$G\frac{mM}{R^2} = m\frac{V^2}{R}$$

$$V = \left(G\frac{M}{R}\right)^{1/2}$$

$$= \left((6.67 \times 10^{-11}\ \text{N-m}^2/\text{kg}^2)\frac{5.98 \times 10^{24}\ \text{kg}}{6.37 \times 10^6\ \text{m}}\right)^{1/2}$$

$$= 7.91 \times 10^3 \text{ m/sec}$$

$$\left(\text{Note } 1\text{N} = 1 \frac{\text{kg - m}}{\text{sec}^2}\right).$$

• PROBLEM 171

> The string of a conical pendulum is 10 ft long and the bob has a mass of ½ slug. The pendulum is rotating at ½ rev·s^{-1}. Find the angle the string makes with the vertical, and also the tension in the string.

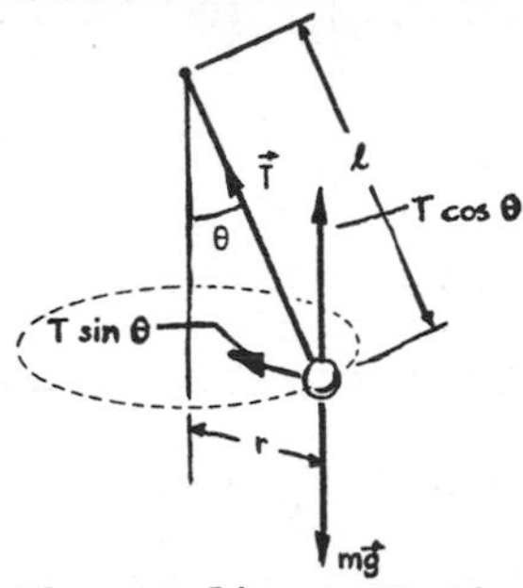

Solution: Let r be the radius of the horizontal circle traversed by the bob of mass m, ℓ be the length of the string, and $\vec{T}$ be the tension which the string exerts on the mass. The forces acting on the bob are the weight $\vec{mg}$ downward and the tension $\vec{T}$ at an angle θ to the vertical. Resolve $\vec{T}$ into horizontal and vertical components. Applying Newton's Second Law to the horizontal direction of motion

$$F_{net} = ma$$

where a is the horizontal acceleration of m, and F_{net} is the net horizontal force on m. Since m is in uniform circular motion, T sin θ provides the centripetal force necessary to keep the bob in the circle. Thus T sin θ = mv^2/r, where v is the velocity of the bob. But v is the distance traveled in 1 s. That is, $v = n \times 2\pi r = 2\pi rn$, where n is the angular speed in rev·s^{-1}. Also, from the figure, $\sin\theta = r/\ell$.

$$\therefore\ T = \frac{4\pi^2\ rmn^2}{r/\ell} = 4\pi^2 m\ell n^2 =$$

$$= 4\pi^2 \times \tfrac{1}{2}\text{ slug} \times 10\text{ ft} \times \left(\tfrac{1}{2}\text{ s}^{-1}\right)^2$$

$$= 49\text{ lb.}$$

The bob stays in the same horizontal plane, so that the vertical forces must balance. Thus, from Newton's Second Law, T cos θ = mg.

$$\therefore\quad \cos\theta = \frac{mg}{4\pi^2 m\ell n^2}$$

$$= \frac{32}{4\pi^2 \times 10\text{ ft} \times \left(\tfrac{1}{2}\text{ s}^{-1}\right)^2} = 0.327;$$

$$\therefore\quad \theta = 71°.$$

The angular velocity of a body is 4 rad/sec at time t = 0, and its angular acceleration is constant and equal to 2 rad/sec^2. A line OP in the body is horizontal $\left(\theta_0 = 0\right)$ at time t = 0. (a) What angle does this line make with the horizontal at time t = 3 sec? (b) What is the angular velocity at this time?

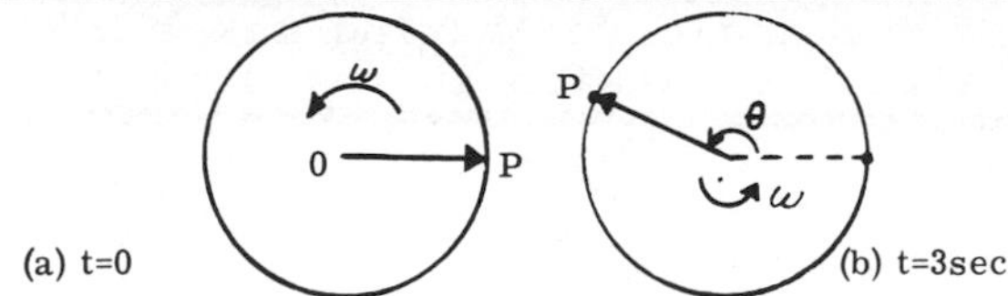

Solution: The angular kinematics equations for constant angular acceleration are identical in form to the linear kinematic equations with α corresponding to a, ω to v, and θ to x.

(a) Comparable to $x = x_0 + \omega_0 t + \frac{1}{2}\alpha t^2$, we have $\theta = \theta_0 + \omega_0 t + \frac{1}{2}\alpha t^2$ where θ_0, ω_0 are the initial angular position and velocity of the body.

Since $\theta_0 = 0$, we have

$$\theta = \omega_0 t + \frac{1}{2}\alpha t^2$$

$$= 4\,\frac{\text{rad}}{\text{sec}} \times 3\text{ sec} + \frac{1}{2} \times 2\,\frac{\text{rad}}{\text{sec}^2} \times (3\text{ sec})^2$$

$$= 21\text{ radians}$$

$$= 21\text{ radians}\ \frac{1\text{ revolution}}{2\pi\text{ radians}}$$

$$= 3.34\text{ revolutions.}$$

The angle θ is then

$$\theta = 0.34 \times \text{one revolution} = 0.34 \times 360° \simeq 122°.$$

(b) $\omega = \omega_0 + \alpha t$

$$= 4\,\frac{\text{rad}}{\text{sec}} + 2\,\frac{\text{rad}}{\text{sec}^2} \times 3\text{ sec} = 10\,\frac{\text{rad}}{\text{sec}}.$$

Alternatively,

$$\omega^2 = \omega_0^2 + 2\alpha\theta$$

$$= 4\left(\frac{\text{rad}}{\text{sec}}\right)^2 + 2 \times 2\,\frac{\text{rad}}{\text{sec}^2} \times 21\text{ rad}$$

$$= 100\,\frac{\text{rad}^2}{\text{sec}^2}, \qquad \omega = 10\,\frac{\text{rad}}{\text{sec}}.$$

• PROBLEM 173

The owner of a car and a helpful passer-by attempt to pull the former's car from the field into which it has skidded. They attach two ropes to the front of the chassis symmetrically, each rope being 1 ft from the center point, C, and exert pulls of 200 lb and 150 lb in parallel directions, both at an angle of 30° to the horizontal (see the figure). To what point of the chassis must a tractor be attached and what horizontal force must it exert to produce an equivalent effect?

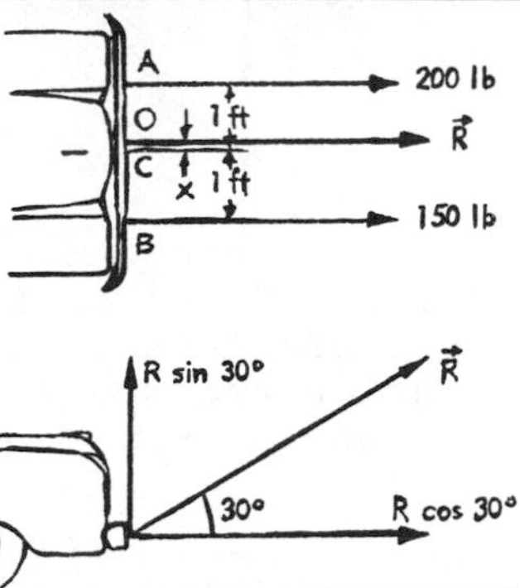

Solution: The resultant force of the two pulls exerted by the men must be $\vec{R}$ of magnitude (200 + 150) lb = 350 lb, in the same direction as either of the forces, i.e., at 30° to the horizontal. Only the horizontal component of this force is doing useful work in pulling the car from the field. This component has magnitude R cos 30 = 350 lb $\times\sqrt{3}/2$ = 303.1 lb. This is the force that the tractor must exert.

The point of attachment of the tractor must be the point O at which the line of action of the resultant $\vec{R}$ cuts the front of the chassis. The forces that the two men exert on the chassis produce a net torque τ about the center point C. The point of action O of $\vec{R}$ must lie at a distance from C, along the front of the chassis, such that $\vec{R}$ produces a net torque equal to τ:

$$\tau = (150 \text{ lb})(1 \text{ ft}) - (200 \text{ lb})(1 \text{ ft}) = (350 \text{ lb})x$$

$$x = \frac{-50 \text{ ft-lb}}{350 \text{ lb}} = -\frac{1}{7} \text{ ft}$$

where x is the distance of O from C. All counterclockwise torques are taken as positive. Since x is negative, we see that R produces a clockwise torque about C. This tells us that O must be to the left of C (above C in the figure).

Thus the point of attachment of the tractor is 6/7 ft from A, that is, 1/7 ft from the center point of the front of the chassis.

• PROBLEM 174

A car on a country road in **Maryland** passes over an old-fashioned hump-backed bridge. The center of gravity of the car follows the arc of a circle of radius 88 ft. Assuming that the car has a weight of 2 tons, find the force exerted by the car on the road at the highest point of the bridge if the car is traveling at 30 mph. At what speed will the car lose contact with the road?

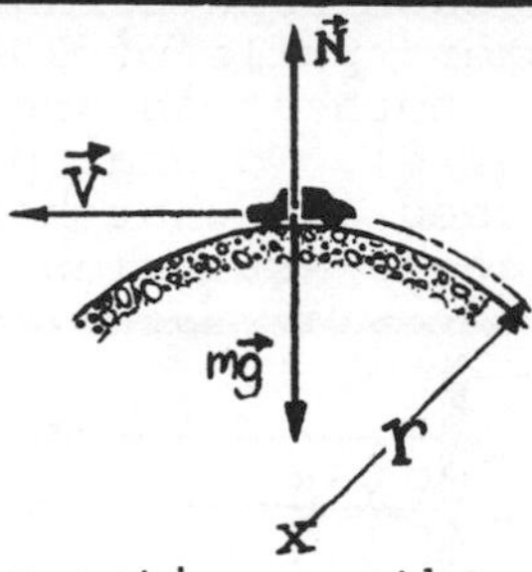

Solution: The forces acting on the car at the highest point of the bridge are its weight $\vec{W} = m\vec{g}$ downward and the normal force $\vec{N}$ exerted by the bridge upward. These cannot be equal, since there must be a net downward force to provide the acceleration necessary to keep the car traveling in a circle. Thus $mg - N = mv^2/r$, by Newton's Second Law.

$$N = m\left(g - \frac{v^2}{r}\right) = \frac{W}{g}\left(g - \frac{v^2}{r}\right) = W\left(1 - \frac{v^2}{rg}\right) .$$

where W is the weight of the car.

Here v = 30 mph = 44 ft/s.

$$\therefore \quad N = 2 \text{ tons}\left(1 - \frac{44^2 \text{ ft}^2/\text{s}^2}{88 \times 32 \text{ ft/s}^2}\right)$$

$$= 2\left(1 - \frac{11}{16}\right) \text{ ton} = \frac{5}{8} \text{ ton.}$$

But action and reaction are equal and opposite. Thus, if the road exerts a force of 5/8 ton on the car, the car exerts the same force on the road.

The car loses contact with the road when N = 0, that is, when $v^2 = rg$. Thus the speed required is

$$v = \sqrt{rg} = \sqrt{88 \text{ ft} \times 32 \text{ ft/s}^2} = 16\sqrt{11} \text{ ft/s}$$

$$= 53.1 \text{ ft/s} = 36 \text{ mph.}$$

• PROBLEM 175

Suppose that a satellite is placed in a circular orbit 100 miles above the earth's surface. Determine the orbital speed v and the time t required for one complete revolution of the satellite.

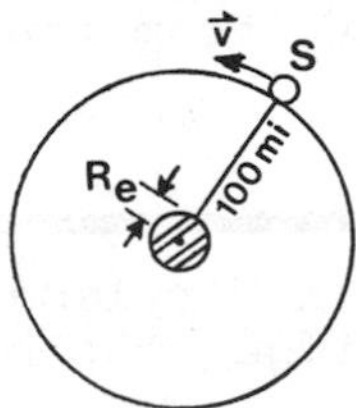

Solution: The radius R of the circular path is determined as follows (see the figure).

$R = R_e + 100$ miles where R_e, the earth's radius, is 6.378×10^6m; a distance of 1 mile is equal to 1,609m; therefore, 100 miles = 1.61×10^5m

$R = 6.378 \times 10^6\text{m} + 1.61 \times 10^5\text{m} = 6.539 \times 10^6\text{m}$.

For our purposes, it is sufficient to retain only the first two digits:

$$R = 6.5 \times 10^6\text{m}$$

The gravitational pull on the satellite is

$$F_g = mg \ .$$

This pull provides the centripetal force for the circular motion, therefore

$$F_{centr} = \frac{mv^2}{R} = mg$$

or

$$v^2 = gR = \left(9.8\text{m/s}^2\right)\left(6.5 \times 10^6\text{m}\right)$$
$$= 63.7 \times 10^6\text{m}^2/\text{s}^2 \approx 64 \times 10^6\text{m}^2/\text{s}^2$$
$$v = 8 \times 10^3\text{m/s}$$

This orbital speed is only approximately correct because it has been assumed that the effect of gravity 100 miles above the earth is the same as at the earth's surface. The gravitational "pull" weakens as one recedes from the earth's surface, but at 100 miles above the earth it is only slightly different from the value g, so the calculation above is reasonably accurate. To determine the time interval required for one revolution of the satellite, the distance the satellite travels in one revolution must be calculated. This is just the circumference C of a circle of radius R:

$$C = 2\pi R = (2)(3.14)\left(6.5 \times 10^6\text{m}\right) = 4.1 \times 10^7\text{m}$$

The period of the motion is

$$t = \frac{C}{v} = \frac{4.1 \times 10^7 \not{\text{m}}}{8 \times 10^3 \not{\text{m}}/\text{s}} = 5.1 \times 10^3\text{s}$$

$$t = \frac{5.1 \times 10^3 \not{\text{s}}}{60 \not{\text{s}}/\text{min}} = 85 \text{ min}$$

The time required for one complete revolution of the satellite is about 85 min.

• PROBLEM 176

A cylinder rests on a horizontal rotating disc, as shown in the figures. Find at what angular velocity, ω, the cylinder falls off the disc, if the distance between the axes of the disc and cylinder is R, and the coefficient of friction $\mu > \frac{D}{h}$, where D is the diameter of the cylinder and h is its height.

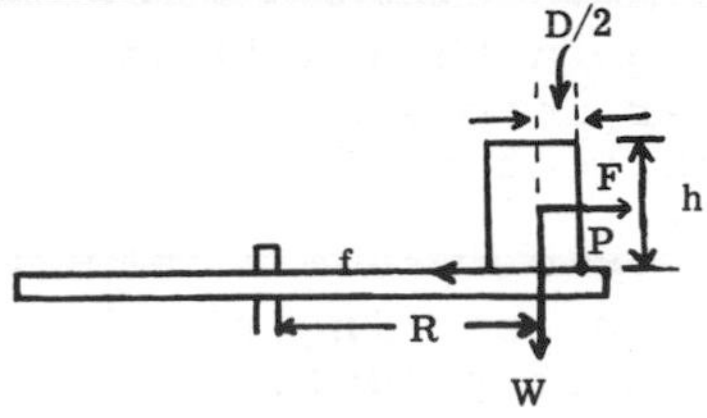

Figure A

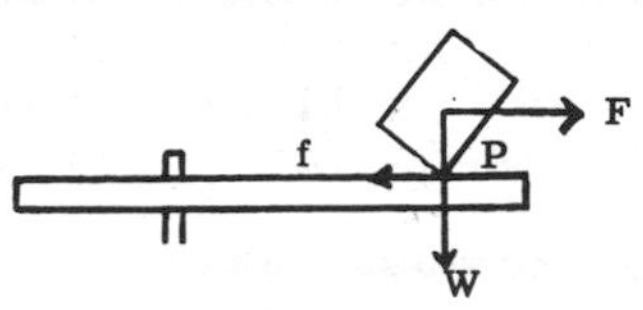

Figure B

Solution: The centripetal force that keeps the cylinder at rest on the disc is the frictional force f. According to Newton's third law of motion, the cylinder reacts with an equal and opposite force, F, which sometimes is referred to as the **centrifugal force,**

$$F = M\omega^2 R$$

where M is the mass of the cylinder. The cylinder can fall off either by slipping away (Fig. A) or by tilting about point P (Fig. B), depending on whichever takes place first. The critical angular speed, ω_1, for slipping occurs when F equals f;

$$F = f$$

$$M\omega_1^2 R = \mu g M$$

where g is the gravitational acceleration. Hence

$$\omega_1 = \sqrt{\frac{\mu g}{R}}\,.$$

F tries to rotate the cylinder about P, but the weight W opposes it. The rotation becomes possible, when the torque created by F is large enough to take over the opposing torque caused by W;

$$F\frac{h}{2} = W\frac{D}{2}$$

$$F = W\frac{D}{h}$$

$$M\omega_2^2 R = Mg\frac{D}{h}$$

giving $\omega_2 = \sqrt{\frac{D}{hR}}$

Since we are given that $\mu > \frac{D}{h}$, we see that

$$\omega_1 > \omega_2$$

and the cylinder falls off by rolling over at $\omega = \omega_2$.

MOMENTS OF INERTIA

• PROBLEM 177

Evaluate the inertial coefficients for a thin uniform spherical shell of mass density σ per unit area and thickness d, for an axis through the center of the sphere.

Solution: The angular momentum $\vec{L}$ of a rotating rigid body of mass M is related to its angular **velocity** $\vec{\omega}$ by:

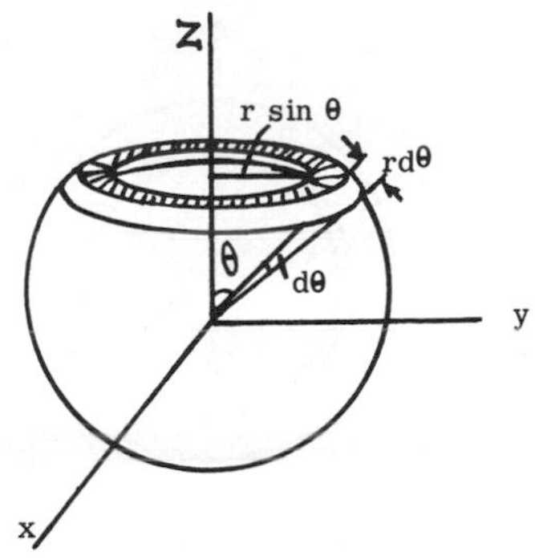

$$\begin{pmatrix} L_x \\ L_y \\ L_z \end{pmatrix} \quad \begin{pmatrix} I_{xx} & I_{xy} & I_{xz} \\ I_{yx} & I_{yy} & I_{yz} \\ I_{zx} & I_{zy} & I_{zz} \end{pmatrix} \quad \begin{pmatrix} \omega_x \\ \omega_y \\ \omega_z \end{pmatrix}$$

where 'I's are the inertial coefficients given by

$$I_{xy} = \int dm\ xy$$

$$I_{xx} = \int dm\ (y^2 + z^2), \text{ etc.}$$

The off diagonal elements are zero for the spherical shell as a result of its symmetry. This follows, because for every contribution xy to the integral for I_{xy}, there is an equal but opposite contribution $(-x)y$ on the sphere. Hence, the integral of xy over a sphere is zero.

The diagonal elements are equal since the three axes are equivalent as far as the geometry of the shell is concerned. The ring shown in the figure has a mass

$$dm = \sigma(2\pi\ r \sin\theta)(r\ d\theta)$$

hence $$I_{zz} = \int dm(y^2+x^2) = 2\pi\ \sigma\ r^2 \int_0^{\pi} d\theta \sin\theta\ (r^2 \sin^2\theta)$$

$$= 2\pi\ \sigma\ r^4 \int_{-1}^{1} d(\cos\theta)[1 - \cos^2\theta]$$

$$= 2\pi\ \sigma\ r^4 \left(\frac{4}{3}\right) = \frac{8}{3}\pi\sigma r^4$$

$$= (4\pi\ r^2\ \sigma)\ \frac{2}{3}\ r^2 = \frac{2}{3}\ Mr^2$$

Therefore, $I_{xx} = I_{yy} = I_{zz} = \frac{2}{3}\ Mr^2$.

• PROBLEM 178

Evaluate I for a sphere of uniform density ρ, for an axis through the center of the sphere.

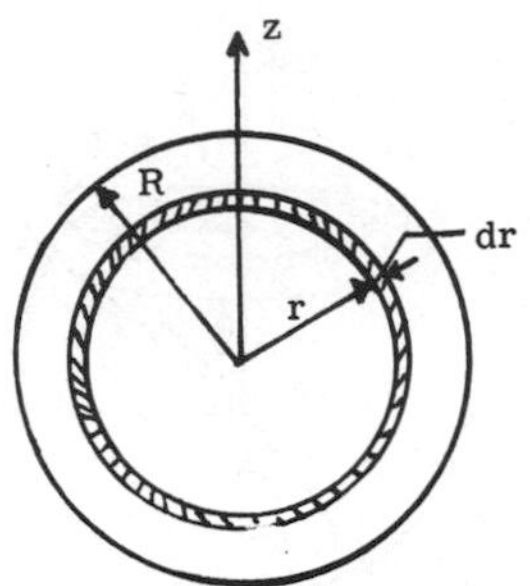

Solution: We may assemble the sphere from spherical shells of thickness dr and having mass density $\sigma = \rho\, dr$ per unit area as shown in the figure.

The moment of inertia, dI, of the thin spherical shell of mass dm shown in the figure, about a radius, is

$$dI = \frac{2}{3} r^2\, dM = \frac{2}{3} r^2 \, (4\pi r^2 \rho\, dr)$$

$$= \frac{8}{3} \pi r^4 \rho\, dr$$

The total moment of inertia of the solid sphere therefore becomes

$$I = \int dI = \int_0^R \frac{8}{3} \pi r^4 \rho\, dr = \frac{8}{15} \pi \rho R^5$$

$$= \frac{2}{5} \left(\frac{4}{3} \pi \rho R^3\right) R^2$$

$$= \frac{2}{5} MR^2,$$

where M is the mass of the sphere.

• PROBLEM 179

A solid cylinder of radius R rolls on a flat surface. Find the moment of inertia I_s of the cylinder about its line of contact with the surface.

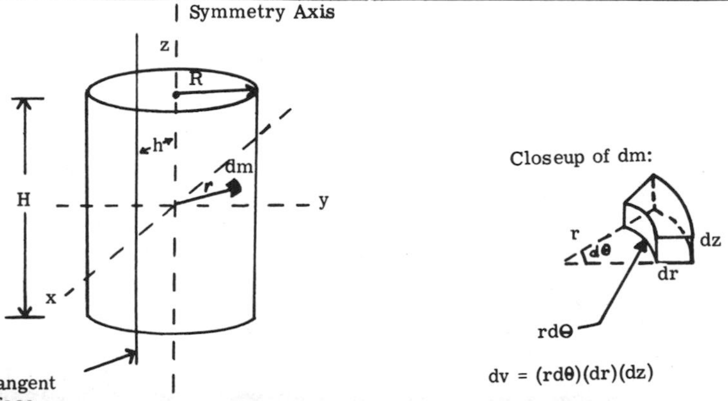

Solution: The definition of moment of inertia for a continuous mass distribution is dependent upon which axis we wish to calculate the moment of inertia about. In this case, we want to calculate I_s, the moment of inertia about an axis parallel to the symmetry axis of the cylinder, but tangent to the surface of the cylinder. To simplify the required integrations, we may equivalently calculate the moment of inertia, I_o, of the cylinder about its symmetry axis, and then employ the parallel axis theorem to find I_s.

The moment of inertia I_o is (with reference to the figure) defined as:

$$I_o = \int r^2 \, dm \tag{1}$$

where r is the perpendicular distance between the symmetry axis of the cylinder and the mass element dm. Also note that dm, the mass contained in a differential volume dv, is the mass per volume contained in the cylinder times the volume dv, or

$$dm = \left(\frac{M}{\pi R^2 H}\right) r \, dr \, d\theta \, dz \tag{2}$$

where M is the total mass of the cylinder, and $\pi R^2 H$ is the volume of the cylinder. Combining (2) and (1), we obtain

$$I_o = \int \left(\frac{M}{\pi R^2 H}\right) r^3 \, dr \, d\theta \, dz \tag{3}$$

where the integral is over the volume of the cylinder. Performing the integral:

$$I_o = \left(\frac{M}{\pi R^2 H}\right) \int_{-\frac{H}{2}}^{\frac{H}{2}} \int_0^{2\pi} \int_0^R r^3 \, dr \, d\theta \, dz$$

$$I_o = \left(\frac{M}{\pi R^2 H}\right) \left(\frac{R^4}{4}\right) \int_{-\frac{H}{2}}^{\frac{H}{2}} \int_0^{2\pi} d\theta \, dz$$

$$I_o = \left(\frac{M}{\pi R^2 H}\right) \left(\frac{R^4}{4}\right) (2\pi) \int_{-\frac{H}{2}}^{\frac{H}{2}} dz$$

$$I_o = \left(\frac{M}{\pi R^2 H}\right) \left(\frac{R^4}{4}\right) (2\pi) (H)$$

$$I_o = \frac{1}{2} M R^2 \tag{4}$$

This is the moment of inertia about the symmetry axis. To find the moment of inertia about the axis tangent to the surface of the cylinder, use the parallel axis theorem. Mathematically, (see the diagram)

$$I_s = I_o + M\eta^2 \tag{5}$$

where η is the separation of the 2 axes. Rewriting this using (4), and noting that $\eta = R$, we have

$$I_s = \frac{1}{2} MR^2 + MR^2$$

or $$I_s = \frac{3}{2} MR^2$$

• PROBLEM 180

Two masses of 200 gm and 300 gm are separated by a light rod 50 cm in length. The center of mass of the system serves as the origin of a Cartesian coordinate system. The rod lies in the xy plane and makes an angle of 20° with the y axis. Find the inertial coefficients I_{xx} and I_{xy} with respect to the center of mass.

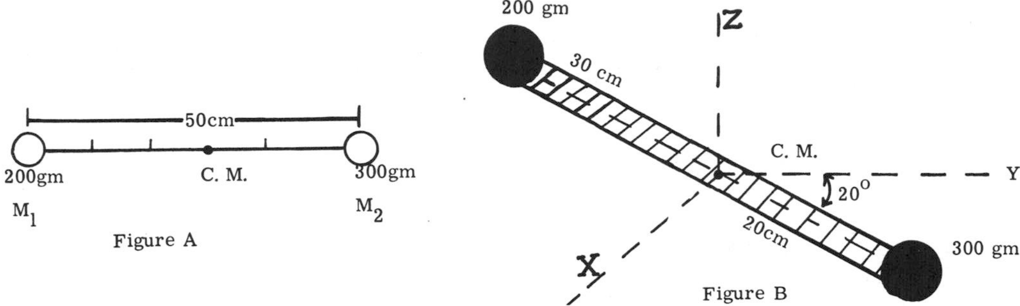

Figure A

Figure B

Solution: Since we must calculate the moment of inertia of the rod about an axis through the center of mass, we must first locate the center of mass. Let us find the distance of the center of mass from the 200-gm mass. By definition of center of mass

$$R_{c.m.} = \frac{M_1 x_1 + M_2 x_2}{M_1 + M_2}$$

where x_1, x_2 are the distances of M_1 and M_2 from the origin (in our case, the 200 gm. mass). Hence, using figure (A),

$$R_{c.m.} = \frac{(200 \text{ gm})(0) + (300 \text{ gm})(50 \text{ cm})}{500\text{gm}}$$

$$R_{c.m.} = 30 \text{ cm}$$

Looking at figure (B), the Cartesian coordinates of the 200 gm mass (denoted as M_1) are referred to the center of mass as origin,

$$x_1 = (30 \text{ cm}) \sin 20^\circ = (30 \text{ cm})(.342) \approx 10.3 \text{ cm}$$

$$y_1 = (30 \text{ cm}) \cos 20^\circ = (30 \text{ cm})(.940) \approx 28.2 \text{ cm} \tag{1}$$

$$z_1 = 0$$

The Cartesian coordinates of the 300 gm mass (denoted as M_2) are

$$x_2 = (-20 \text{ cm}) \sin 20^\circ \approx -6.8 \text{ cm}$$

$$y_2 = (-20\text{ cm})\cos 20^\circ \approx -18.8\text{ cm} \qquad (2)$$

$$z_2 = 0$$

Using these values of the coordinates, we proceed to evaluate the inertial coefficients defined by the equations

$$I_{xx} = \sum_i m_i(y_i^2 + z_i^2)$$

$$I_{xy} = -\sum_i m_i\, x_i\, y_i$$

For our problem, these reduce to

$$I_{xx} = M_1(y_1^2 + z_1^2) + M_2(y_2^2 + z_2^2)$$

$$I_{xy} = -M_1x_1y_1 - M_2x_2y_2$$

From (1) and (2)

$$I_{xx} = (200\text{ gm})\left[(28.2\text{ cm})^2 + 0\right] + (300\text{ gm})\left[(-18.8\text{cm})^2+0\right]$$

$$I_{xx} = 265080\text{ gm-cm}^2 = 2.65 \times 10^5\text{ gm}\cdot\text{cm}^2$$

$$I_{xy} = -(200\text{ gm})(10.3\text{ cm})(28.2\text{ cm}) - (300\text{ gm})(-6.8\text{cm})(-18.8\text{cm})$$

$$I_{xy} = -96444\text{ gm-cm}^2 = -.96 \times 10^5\text{ gm-cm}^2$$

Now suppose that the rod rotates about the x axis with angular velocity ω. Find the components of J. In general,

$$\begin{pmatrix} J_x \\ J_y \\ J_z \end{pmatrix} = \begin{pmatrix} I_{xx} & I_{xy} & I_{xz} \\ I_{yx} & I_{yy} & I_{yz} \\ I_{zx} & I_{zy} & I_{zz} \end{pmatrix} \begin{pmatrix} \omega_x \\ \omega_y \\ \omega_z \end{pmatrix}$$

where J_x, J_y, J_z are the vector components of $\vec{J}$, and $\omega_x, \omega_y, \omega_z$ are the components of $\vec{\omega}$. The quantities I_{xx}, I_{xy}, etc., are the products and moments of inertia of the system we are studying.

In our problem, $\omega_z = \omega_y = 0$ and $I_{zx} = 0$, and

$$\begin{pmatrix} J_x \\ J_y \\ J_z \end{pmatrix} = \begin{pmatrix} I_{xx} & I_{xy} & I_{xz} \\ I_{yx} & I_{yy} & I_{yz} \\ 0 & I_{zy} & I_{zz} \end{pmatrix} \begin{pmatrix} \omega_x \\ 0 \\ 0 \end{pmatrix}$$

Therefore, by the definition of matrix multiplication

$$\begin{pmatrix} J_x \\ J_y \\ J_z \end{pmatrix} = \begin{pmatrix} I_{xx}\,\omega_x & 0 & 0 \\ I_{yx}\,\omega_x & 0 & 0 \\ 0 & 0 & 0 \end{pmatrix}$$

and

$$J_x = I_{xx}\,\omega_x$$

$$J_y = I_{yx}\,\omega_x$$

$$J_z = 0\,.$$

Then

$$\frac{J_y}{J_x} = \frac{I_{yx}}{I_{xx}} = \frac{-.96 \times 10^5}{2.65 \times 10^5} = -.363$$

• PROBLEM 181

Show that if k is the radius of gyration of a body, then

$$k = \sqrt{\frac{I}{m}}$$

where I is the body's rotational inertia about a given axis.

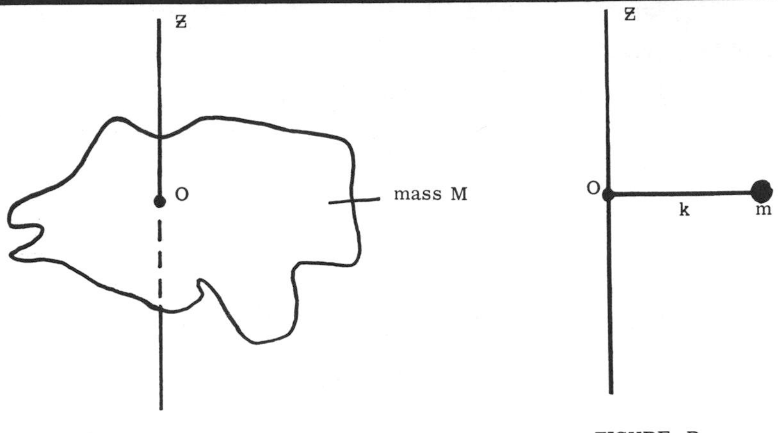

FIGURE A

FIGURE B

Solution: The radius of gyration of a rigid body is defined as the radial distance from a given axis at which the entire mass of the body can be concentrated, without altering the object's moment of inertia about the axis.

The definition implies 2 equivalent configurations (see figure), either of which may be used to calculate the body's moment of inertia about axis Z. From the discussion above, the moment of inertia of the body of mass m about axis Z in figure (a) is equivalent to the moment of inertia, about Z, of a mass particle m at a radial distance k from Z. (See figure (b)). Hence

$$mk^2 = I$$

or $$k = \sqrt{\frac{I}{m}}$$

• PROBLEM 182

Show that the moment of inertia of a body about any axis is equal to the moment of inertia about a parallel axis through the center of mass plus the product of the mass of the body and the square of the distance between the axes. This is called the parallel-axes theorem.

Prove also that the moment of inertia of a thin plate about an axis at right angles to its plane is equal to the sum of the moments of inertia about two mutually perpendicular axes concurrent with the first and lying in the plane of the thin plate. This is called the perpendicular-axes theorem.

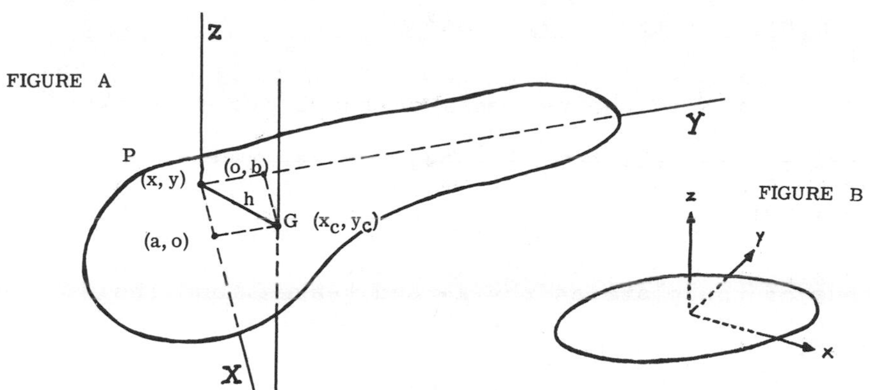

Solution: Let I be the moment of inertia of the body about an arbitrary axis and I_G the moment of inertia about the parallel axis through the center of mass G, the two axes being distance h apart. (See fig. (A)).

By definition of the center of mass of a body relative to an arbitrary axis through a point P, we obtain

$$I = \sum_i m_i r_i^2 = \sum_i m_i \left(x_i^{\,2} + y_i^{\,2}\right)$$

$$= \sum_i m_i x_i^{\,2} + \sum_i m_i y_i^{\,2}$$

where the sum is carried out over all mass particles m_i of the body, and $r_i^{\,2}$ is the distance from P to m_i. Now,

$$x_i = x_i' + a$$

$$y_i = y_i' + b$$

as shown in figure (A). Here, $\left(x_i', y_i'\right)$ locates m_i relative to G, the center of mass. Then

$$I = \sum_i m_i \left(x_i' + a\right)^2 + \sum_i m_i \left(y_i' + b\right)^2$$

$$I = \sum_i m_i \left(x_i'^{\,2} + y_i'^{\,2}\right) + \sum_i m_i \left(a^2 + b^2\right) + 2a \sum_i m_i x_i'$$

$$+ 2b \sum_i m_i y_i'$$

But $x_i'^{\,2} + y_i'^{\,2} = r_i'^{\,2}$ and $a^2 + b^2 = h^2$, whence

$$I = \sum_i m_i r_i'^{\,2} + \sum_i m_i h^2 + 2a \sum_i m_i x_i' + 2b \sum_i m_i y_i'$$

By definition of the center of mass, however,

$$\sum_i m_i x_i' = \sum_i m_i y_i' = 0, \qquad \text{and}$$

$$I = \sum_i m_i r_i'^2 + \sum_i m_i h^2 = I_G + Mh^2$$

where $M \left(= \sum_i m_i \right)$ is the net mass of the body. This is the parallel-axes theorem. Although we derived this theorem in 2 dimensions, it is equally applicable in three dimensions.

Take, in the case of the thin plate, the axes in the plane of the plate as the x- and y-axes, and the axis at right angles to the plane as the z-axis (see fig. (B)).

Then the moment of inertia of the plate about an axis perpendicular to the plate (the z-axis) is

$$I_z = \sum_i m_i r_i^2$$

where r_i locates m_i relative to O. But

$$r_i^2 = x_i^2 + y_i^2$$

where x_i and y_i are the x and y coordinates of m_i.

Then

$$I_z = \sum_i m_i x_i^2 + \sum_i m_i y_i^2$$

But $\sum_i m_i x_i^2 = I_y$ and $\sum_i m_i y_i^2 = I_x$, whence

$$I_z = I_x + I_y$$

This is the perpendicular axes theorem.

• PROBLEM 183

Internal torques:—The interaction which may be present between particles themselves give rise to internal torques. Show that the sum of all internal torques is zero.

Solution: The total torque is defined as

$$N = \sum_{n=1}^{N} r_n \times F_n ,$$

$\vec{r}_n$ is the position vector of the particle and $\vec{F}_n$ is the force acting upon it.

For internal forces

$$F_i = \sum_{j=1}^{N}{}' \; F_{ij} ,$$

the sum of the forces on particle i from all other particles j. (The prime on the summation sign means that the term j = i is excluded.) Thus the internal torque is

$$N_{int} = \sum_i r_i \times F_i = \sum_i \sum_j{}' r_i \times F_{ij} ,$$

Here we simply substitute $\sum\limits_{j=1}^{N}{}' \vec{F}_{ij}$ for $\vec{F}_i$.

but by relabeling the dummy indices i and j, we have

$$\sum_i \sum_j{}' r_i \times F_{ij} \equiv \sum_j \sum_i{}' r_j \times F_{ji} ,$$

so that

$$N_{int} = \frac{1}{2} \sum_i \sum_j{}' \left(r_i \times F_{ij} + r_j \times F_{ji}\right) .$$

We now assume that the forces are Newtonian, which means we assume $F_{ji} = - F_{ij}$. Substituting we have:

$$N_{int} = \frac{1}{2} \sum_i \sum_j{}' \left[\vec{r}_i \times \vec{F}_{ij} + \vec{r}_j \times \left(- \vec{F}_{ij}\right)\right]$$

Factoring and rearranging we have:

$$N_{int} = \frac{1}{2} \sum_i \sum_j{}' \left(r_i - r_j\right) \quad F_{ij} .$$

Now, $\vec{r}_i - \vec{r}_j$ is a vector between particle i and particle j. Since the $\vec{F}_{ij}$ are central forces (that is, they act along the line joining particles i and j) they are parallel to $\vec{r}_i - \vec{r}_j$. Therefore, $\left(r_i - r_j\right) \times F_{ij} = 0$, and thus

$$N_{int} = 0.$$

ROTATION OF RIGID BODIES ABOUT FIXED AXES

• PROBLEM 184

If a disk is rotating at 1200 rev/min, what torque is required to stop it in 3.0 min?

Solution: If the disk is to decelerate from 1200 rev/min to 0 rev/min uniformly, then the angular acceleration (α) will be constant. Hence

$$\alpha = \text{constant}.$$

But $\alpha = \frac{d\omega}{dt}$ where ω is the angular velocity of rotation.

Therefore,

$$\alpha = \frac{d\omega}{dt}$$

or $$d\omega = \alpha dt$$

$$\int_{\omega_0}^{\omega} d\omega \quad \int_{t=0}^{t=t} \alpha dt$$

$$\omega - \omega_0 = \alpha t \tag{1}$$

where $\omega = \omega$ at $t = t$ and ω_0 is the initial angular velocity of rotation.

$$\omega_0 = 1200 \text{ rev/min.}$$

Since 1 rev/min = $\frac{1}{60}$ rev/sec

$$\omega_0 = 20 \text{ rev/sec.}$$

But 1 rev = 2π radians and

$$\omega_0 = 40\pi \text{ rad/sec.}$$

$$t = 3.0 \text{ min} = 180 \text{ sec}$$

Substituting in (1)

$$0 - 40\pi \text{ rad/sec} = \alpha(180 \text{ sec})$$

$$\alpha = \frac{-40\pi}{180} \text{ rad/sec}^2.$$

This is the acceleration which must be applied to the disk if it is to come to rest in the required time. Because the disk is rotating about a fixed axis, the torque L is the product of the angular acceleration of the disk and the moment of inertia of the disk about the axis of rotation.

$$L = I\alpha$$

$$= \left(38 \text{ slug-ft}^2\right)\left(-\frac{40\pi}{180} \text{ rad/sec}^2\right)$$

$$= -26 \text{ lb-ft.}$$

Hence, a torque of -26 lb-ft must act on the disk in order to bring it to rest in 3 minutes from a velocity of 1200 rev/min. The negative sign is consistent with a retarding torque.

• PROBLEM 185

A force F = 10 newtons in the +y-direction is applied to a wrench which extends in the +x-direction and grasps a bolt. What is the resulting torque about the bolt if the point of application of the force is 30 cm = 0.3 m away from the bolt?

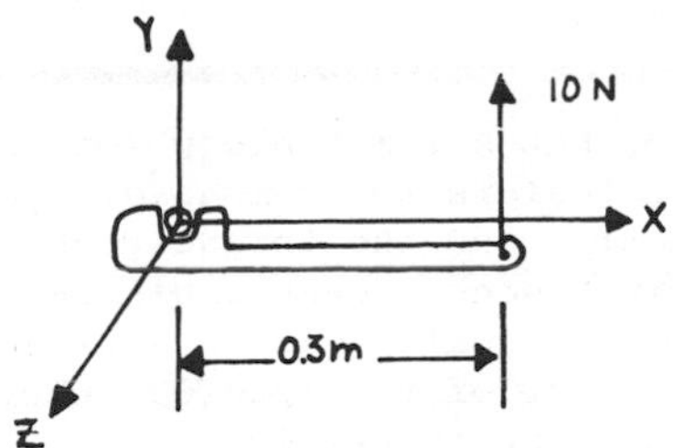

Solution: Torque is calculated from the relation:

$$\vec{\tau} = \vec{r} \times \vec{F}$$

where τ stands for torque, F stands for the force, and r denotes the distance from the origin, about which the torque is calculated, of the point of application of the force. In this problem we use the bolt as our origin about which we calculate the torque (see the Figure above). Then,

$$\vec{\tau} = 0.3 \text{ m } \hat{\imath} \times 10\text{N}\hat{\jmath} = 3 \text{ N·m } (\hat{\imath} \times \hat{\jmath}) = 3 \text{ N·m } \hat{k}$$

where $\hat{\imath}$, $\hat{\jmath}$, and $\hat{k}$ are the unit vectors in the +x, +y, and +z directions respectively.

• PROBLEM 186

The motor driving a grindstone is switched off when the latter has a rotational speed of 240 rev·min^{-1}. After 10 s the speed is 180 rev·min^{-1}. If the angular retardation remains constant, how many additional revolutions does it make before coming to rest?

Solution: The initial speed ω_0 is 240 rev·min^{-1} and the later speed ω is 180 rev·min^{-1}. Thus since the angular acceleration, α, is constant, we may write $\omega = \omega_0 + \alpha t$. Here, t is the time it takes for the grindstone's angular velocity to go from ω_0 to ω. Solving for α,

$$\alpha = \frac{\omega - \omega_0}{t} = \frac{180 \text{ rev·min}^{-1} - 240 \text{ rev·min}^{-1}}{10 \text{ s}}$$

Noting that 1 min^{-1} = 1/60 s^{-1}, we find

$$\alpha = -\frac{60 \text{ rev·s}^{-1}}{60 \times 100 \text{ s}} = -.1 \text{ rev·s}^{-2}$$

Considering the subsequent slowing-down period, the final speed is zero and the grindstone traverses an angular distance θ. Hence, using the equation

$$\omega^2 = \omega_0^2 + 2\alpha\theta$$

with $\omega = 0$ and $\omega_0 = 180$ rev·min^{-1} = 3 rev·s^{-1}, we find

$$0 = 9 \text{ rev}^2\text{·s}^{-2} + 2(-.1 \text{ rev·s}^{-2})\theta$$

or $\theta = \dfrac{9 \text{ rev}}{.2} = 45$ rev.

A record player, has a turntable which is a flat plate of radius 12cm and mass 0.25 kg.Calculate the moment of inertia of the turntable about its axis of symmetry, and the torque required to accelerate the turntable to 33.3 rpm in 2 sec. Because his records are warped, the owner of the record player usually places a brass cylinder (radius 4 cm and mass 3 kg) on the center of the record. What torque would then be required to accelerate the turntable?

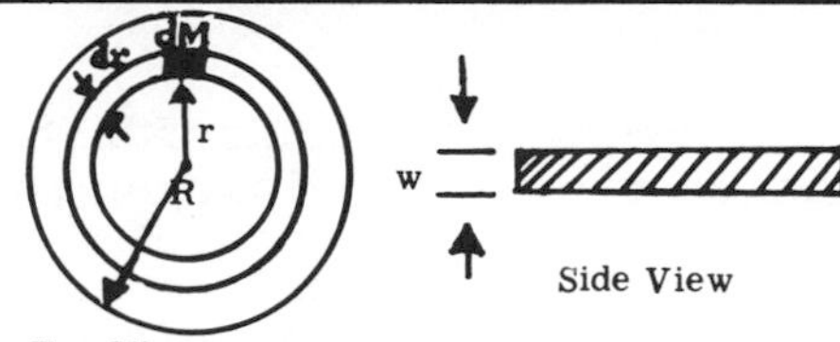

Solution: Torque and angular acceleration are related by $\tau = I\alpha$ where τ, I, and α are the torque, moment of inertia, and angular acceleration respectively.

First we must calculate the moment of inertia of a cylinder of uniform density ρ (see diagram):

The volume of the mass element dM is given by:

$$dV = 2\pi\, rw\, dr$$

and since the mass contained in dM is given by $dM = \rho dV$:

$$dM = 2\pi\, \rho rw\, dr$$

Since:

$$I = \int r^2\, dM$$

where r is the radial distance from the axis about which we calculate I, we have for the disk:

$$I = \int_0^R r^2(2\pi\rho rw dr) = 2\pi\rho w \int_0^R r^3 dr = 2\pi\rho w \left.\frac{r^4}{4}\right|_0^R = \frac{1}{2}\pi\rho w R^4 = \frac{1}{2}(\rho\pi R^2 w)R^2 = \frac{1}{2}MR^2$$

We note that the volume of the disk is given by its surface area multiplied by its thickness:

$$V = \pi R^2 w$$

and since $M = \rho V$:

$$M = \rho\, \pi R^2 w$$

where M is the mass of the disk.

Thus for the turntable:

$$I_+ = \frac{1}{2}(0.25\text{ kg})(0.12\text{m})^2 = 1.8 \times 10^{-3}\text{ kg-m}^2$$

The moment of inertia of the brass cylinder is:

$$I_c = \frac{1}{2}(3\text{ kg})(0.04\text{m})^2 = 2.4 \times 10^{-3}\text{ kg-m}^2$$

To calculate the angular acceleration, we must first convert 33.3 rpm to rad/sec.

$$\frac{3.33\text{ revolutions}}{\text{min.}} = \frac{33.3(2\pi\text{ rad})}{60\text{ sec.}} = 3.49\text{ rad/sec}$$

$$\alpha = \frac{3.49\text{ rad/sec}}{2\text{ sec}} = 1.74\text{ rad/sec}^2$$

where α is the angular acceleration

The torque that must be applied to the turntable to produce α is:

$$\tau = I_t\alpha = \left(1.8 \times 10^{-3} \text{kg-m}^2\right)\left(1.74 \text{ rad/sec}^2\right) = 3.13 \times 10^{-3} \frac{\text{kg-m}}{\text{sec}^2} - \text{m}$$

$$= 3.13 \times 10^{-3} \text{ N-m}$$

The torque required to accelerate the turntable plus the cylindrical weight is:

$$\tau = (I_t + I_c)\alpha = \left(1.8 \times 10^{-3} \text{kg-m}^2 + 2.4 \times 10^{-3} \text{kg-m}^2\right)\left(1.74 \text{ rad/sec}^2\right)$$

$$= \left(4.2 \times 10^{-3} \text{kg-m}^2\right)\left(1.74 \text{ rad/sec}^2\right) = 7.31 \times 10^{-3} \text{N-m}$$

• PROBLEM 188

A man stands at the center of a turntable, holding his arms extended horizontally with a 10-lb weight in each hand. He is set rotating about a vertical axis with an angular velocity of one revolution in 2 sec. Find his new angular velocity if he drops his hands to his sides. The moment of inertia of the man may be assumed constant and equal to 4 slug-ft^2. The original distance of the weights from the axis is 3 ft, and their final distance is 6 in.

Solution: If friction in the turntable is neglected, no external torques act about a vertical axis and the angular momentum about this axis is constant. That is,

$$I\omega = (I\omega)_0 = I_0\omega_0,$$

where I and ω are the final moment of inertia and angular velocity, and I_0 and ω_0 are the initial values of these quantities.

$$I = I_{man} + I_{weights}$$

The moment of inertia of a weight at a distance r from the axis of rotation is given by

$$I = mr^2$$

Therefore

$$I = 4 + 2 \left(\frac{10}{32}\right)\left(\frac{1}{2}\right)^2 = 4.16 \text{ slug}\cdot\text{ft}^2,$$

$$I_0 = 4 + 2 \left(\frac{10}{32}\right)(3)^2 = 9.63 \text{ slug}\cdot\text{ft}^2,$$

$$\omega_0 = 2\pi f_0 = (2\pi)(\tfrac{1}{2} \text{ rev/sec}) = \pi \text{ rad/sec}$$

where f_0 is the original frequency of rotation

$$\omega = \omega_0 \frac{I_0}{I} = 2.31\pi \text{ rad/sec}.$$

That is, the angular velocity is more than doubled.

• PROBLEM 189

A satellite of mass M_s is placed in a stable circular orbit of radius R around the earth. What is its angular momentum about an axis through the earth perpendicular to the plane of its orbit? Assume that R > > radius of satellite.

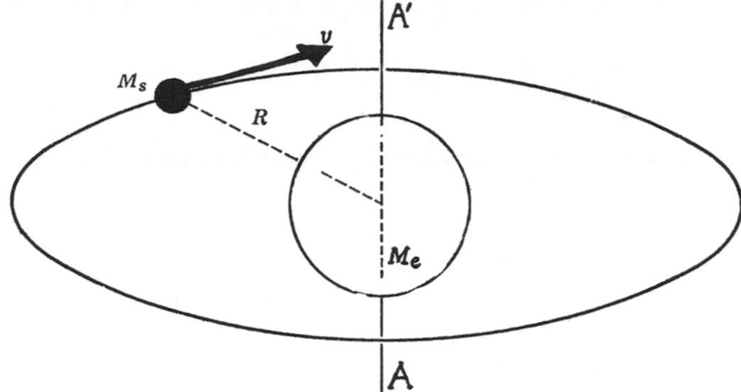

Solution: In the figure, the earth's gravitational pull on the satellite accounts for the satellite's centripetal acceleration:

$$\frac{M_s v^2}{R} = \frac{G M_s M_e}{R^2}$$

where M_e is the mass of the earth.

Thus:
$$v = \sqrt{\frac{GM_e}{R}}$$

Its angular velocity is therefore:

$$\omega = \frac{v}{R} = \sqrt{\frac{GM_e}{R^3}}$$

Since R > > radius of satellite, when calculating the satellite's moment of inertia, with respect to the axis A-A', we can take all of its mass to be at a distance R from the axis.

This reduces to the case of finding the moment of inertia of a point mass with respect to an axis. This is:

$$I = M_s R^2$$

The angular momentum L of the satellite is therefore:

$$L = I\omega = M_s R^2 \sqrt{\frac{GM_e}{R^3}} = M_s \sqrt{GM_e R}$$

• PROBLEM 190

A flywheel, in the form of a uniform disk 4.0 ft in diameter, weighs 600 lb. What will be its angular acceleration if it is acted upon by a net torque of 225 lb-ft? (The rotational inertia of a wheel is $I = \frac{1}{2}mR^2$, where m is the wheel's mass and R is its radius.)

Solution: The flywheel is a massive wheel whose use is the "storing" of kinetic energy. The problem is one of applying the formula $\vec{T} = I\vec{\alpha}$ (analogous to $\vec{F} = m\vec{a}$), in which $\vec{T}$ is applied torque, and $\vec{\alpha}$ is the resulting angular acceleration. We are given $\vec{\tau}$, we can determine I, and solve for $\vec{\alpha}$. Since the weight (W) of any object is

$$W = mg$$

where m is its mass and g is the acceleration due to gravity, we can find m

$$m = \frac{W}{g} = \frac{600 \text{ lb}}{32 \text{ ft/sec}^2} = 18.8 \text{ slugs}$$

$$I = \tfrac{1}{2}mR^2 = \tfrac{1}{2}(18.8 \text{ slugs})(2.0 \text{ ft})^2$$

$$= 38 \text{ slug-ft}^2$$

Therefore, substituting into $\tau = I\alpha$,

$$225 \text{ lb-ft} = \left(38 \text{ slug-ft}^2\right)\alpha$$

$$\alpha = 5.9 \text{ rad/sec}^2$$

In radian measure the angle is a ratio of two lengths and hence is a pure number. The unit "radian" therefore does not always appear in the algebraic handling of units.

• PROBLEM 191

The flywheel of a cutting machine has a mass of 62.5 slugs and a radius of gyration of 3 ft. At the beginning of the cutting stroke it has a rotational speed of $120 \text{ rev}\cdot\text{min}^{-1}$, and at the end a speed of $90 \text{ rev}\cdot\text{min}^{-1}$. If it cuts in a 6-in. stroke, what is the average cutting force exerted?

Solution: The energy lost during the stroke is the difference between the rotational kinetic energies of the flywheel at the beginning and at the end of the operation. If $I = Mk^2$ is the moment of inertia of the flywheel where k is its radius of gyration, and ω_0 and ω the initial and final rotational speeds, then the energy lost is $\tfrac{1}{2}I\left(\omega_0^2 - \omega^2\right) = \tfrac{1}{2} Mk^2\left(\omega_0^2 - \omega^2\right)$. This energy is lost in producing the cutting stroke. If $\vec{F}$ is the average cutting force exerted over the distance $\vec{d}$, by the work energy theorem, the work done by $\vec{F}$ equals the change in kinetic energy of the flywheel. Hence

$$\vec{F} \cdot \vec{d} = Fd = \tfrac{1}{2}Mk^2\left(\omega_0^2 - \omega^2\right) \qquad \text{or}$$

$$F = \frac{\tfrac{1}{2}Mk^2\left(\omega_0^2 - \omega^2\right)}{d}$$

$$= \frac{(\tfrac{1}{2})(62.5 \text{ sl})\left(9 \text{ ft}^2\right)(14400 - 8100) \text{ rev}^2\cdot\text{min}^{-2}}{\tfrac{1}{2} \text{ ft}}$$

In order to obtain F in conventional units, note that

$$1 \text{ rev}\cdot\text{min}^{-1} = \frac{2\pi}{60} \text{ rad}\cdot\text{s}^{-1}$$

Hence

$$F = \frac{(\tfrac{1}{2})(62.5 \text{ sl})\left(9 \text{ ft}^2\right)(6300)\left(4\pi^2/3600 \text{ rad}^2\cdot\text{s}^{-2}\right)}{(\tfrac{1}{2} \text{ ft})}$$

$$F \simeq 38861.6 \text{ lb.}$$

Two men, each of whom weighs 150 lb, stand opposite each other on the rim of a small uniform circular platform which weighs 900 lb. Each man simultaneously walks clockwise and at a fixed speed once around the rim. The platform is free to rotate about a vertical axis through its center. Find the angle in space through which each man has turned. (The platform's moment of inertia is $I = \frac{1}{2}MR^2$, where M is its mass).

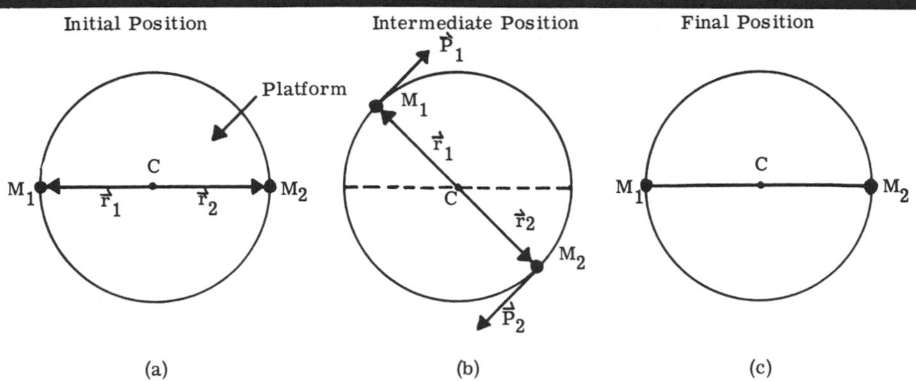

Solution: The figure (parts (a) through (c)) illustrates various positions of the 2 men, and the platform, relative to an observer on the ground. Our ultimate goal is to find an equation, for each man, describing his angular position, θ, as a function of time, relative to his initial position (figure (a)). It is equally acceptable to find an equation for the angular velocity $\vec{\omega}$ of each man, since this may be integrated to find θ. Rather than jumping right into a dynamic analysis of this problem, it might be worth our while to see if we can use any conservation relations in solving this problem.

Note that the angular momentum of the system consisting of the 2 men and platform is constant in time, since no external torques (i.e., friction) act on the system. Furthermore, using angular momentum as our conserved quantity will give us a relation between the angular kinematical variables (α, ω, θ) at 2 times during the motion of the system. We take these 2 times to be as illustrated in figures (a) and (b). The initial angular momentum of the system, L_0, is zero, since figure (a) shows the system at rest. The final angular momentum, $\vec{L}_f$, is due to the angular momentum of each man $\left(\vec{L}_1, \vec{L}_2\right)$ plus the platform's angular momentum, $\vec{L}_p$. Hence,

$$\vec{L}_f = \vec{L}_1 + \vec{L}_2 + \vec{L}_p \tag{1}$$

But, by the definition of the angular momentum of a particle about point C,

$$\vec{L}_1 = \vec{r}_1 \times \vec{p}_1$$

$$\vec{L}_2 = \vec{r}_2 \times \vec{p}_2$$

where $\vec{p}_1$ and $\vec{p}_2$ are the linear momentum of each man, and $\vec{r}_1$ and $\vec{r}_2$ are as illustrated in figure (a). Also, from figure (b)

$$\vec{r}_1 = -\vec{r}_2$$

$$\vec{p}_1 = -\vec{p}_2$$

since each man walks with the same velocity. Then

$$\vec{L}_1 = \vec{r}_1 \times \vec{p}_1$$

and (2)

$$\vec{L}_2 = \vec{r}_1 \times \vec{p}_1$$

Furthermore, the angular momentum of the platform is

$$\vec{L}_p = I\,\vec{\omega} \qquad (3)$$

where $\vec{\omega}$ and I are its angular velocity and moment of inertia relative to C. (See figure (a)). Using (2) and (3) in (1)

$$\vec{L}_f = 2\vec{r}_1 \times \vec{p}_1 + I\,\vec{\omega} \qquad (4)$$

But, the momentum of particle 1$\left(\vec{p}_1\right)$ is related to its angular velocity $\left(\vec{\omega}_1\right)$ relative to an external observer by

$$\vec{p}_1 = m_1\vec{\omega}_1 \times \vec{r}_1$$

Therefore,

$$\vec{r}_1 \times \vec{p}_1 = m_1\vec{r}_1 \times \left(\vec{\omega}_1 \times \vec{r}_1\right) \qquad (5)$$

Since, for any vectors $\vec{A}$, $\vec{B}$ and $\vec{C}$

$$\vec{A} \times (\vec{B} \times \vec{C}) = (\vec{A}\cdot\vec{C})\vec{B} - (\vec{A}\cdot\vec{B})\vec{C}$$

we obtain, using (5)

$$\vec{r}_1 \times \vec{p}_1 = m_1\vec{r}_1 \times \left(\vec{\omega}_1 \times \vec{r}_1\right) = m_1 r_1^2\left(\vec{\omega}_1\right) - m_1\left(\vec{r}_1\cdot\vec{\omega}_1\right)\vec{r}_1 \qquad (6)$$

Now $\vec{\omega}_1$ is perpendicular to the plane of the platform, which contains $\vec{r}_1$. Then

$$\vec{\omega}_1 \cdot \vec{r}_1 = 0$$

and (6) becomes

$$\vec{r}_1 \times \vec{p}_1 = m_1\vec{r}_1 \times \left(\vec{\omega}_1 \times \vec{r}_1\right) = m_1 r_1^2\,\vec{\omega}_1 \qquad (7)$$

Using (7) in (4)

$$\vec{L}_f = 2m_1 r_1^2\,\vec{\omega}_1 + I\,\vec{\omega} \qquad (8)$$

By the principle of conservation of angular momentum

$$\vec{L}_f = \vec{L}_0 = 0$$

and (8) yields

$$2m_1 r_1^2\,\vec{\omega}_1 + I\,\vec{\omega} = 0$$

or

$$\vec{\omega}_1 = \left(\frac{-I}{2m_1 r_1^2}\right)\vec{\omega} \qquad (9)$$

Since each man travels with the same speed,

$$\vec{\omega}_1 = \vec{\omega}_2 = \vec{\omega}' \qquad (10)$$

Also, the masses of the 2 men are equal, and

$$m_1 = m_2 = m\,. \qquad (11)$$

Noting that r_1 equals r_2, and that each equals the platform's radius, R, we obtain

$$r_1 = r_2 = R\,. \qquad (12)$$

Using (10) through (12) in (9)

$$\vec{\omega}' = \left(\frac{-I}{2mR^2}\right)\vec{\omega} \qquad (11)$$

Now

$$\omega = \frac{d\theta}{dt} \quad \text{and} \quad \omega' = \frac{d\theta'}{dt}$$

by definition, where θ and θ' are the angular positions of the platform and either man relative to an outside observer. Then

$$\frac{d\theta'}{dt} = \frac{-I}{2mR^2}\frac{d\theta}{dt}$$

or

$$\int_{\theta'_0}^{\theta'} d\theta' = \frac{-I}{2mR^2}\int_{\theta_0}^{\theta} d\theta$$

where $\theta' = \theta'_0$ and $\theta = \theta_0$ at $t = 0$. (figure (a)). Finally

$$\theta' - \theta'_0 = \frac{-I}{2mR^2}\left(\theta - \theta_0\right)$$

This relates the net angle traversed by each man (relative to an observer on the ground) to the net angle which the platform rotates through. Using the given data

$$\theta' - \theta'_0 = -\frac{\frac{1}{2}MR^2}{2mR^2}\left(\theta - \theta_0\right) = \frac{-M}{4m}\left(\theta - \theta_0\right)$$

$$\theta' - \theta'_0 = \frac{-Mg}{4mg}\left(\theta - \theta_0\right) = \frac{-900\text{ lb}}{600\text{ lb}}\left(\theta - \theta_0\right)$$

$$\theta' - \theta'_0 = -\frac{3}{2}\left(\theta - \theta_0\right) \qquad (12)$$

Each man makes 1 revolution (or traverses 2π radians) relative to the disc. (See figure (c)). Then, relative to an outside observer, the man traverses an angle $\left(\theta' - \theta'_0\right)$ equal to 2π, plus the angle the disc turns through relative to him $\left(\theta - \theta_0\right)$. Hence,

$$\left(\theta' - \theta'_0\right) = \left(\theta - \theta_0\right) + 2\pi \qquad (13)$$

Using (12) in (13)

$$\left(\theta' - \theta'_0\right) = -\frac{2}{3}\left(\theta' - \theta'_0\right) + 2\pi$$

$$\frac{5}{3}\left(\theta' - \theta'_0\right) = 2\pi$$

$$\theta' - \theta'_0 = \frac{6\pi}{5} = 216^\circ$$

Then

$$\theta - \theta_0 = -\frac{2}{3}\left(\theta' - \theta'_0\right) = -144^\circ$$

The negative sign indicates that the men move in a direction opposite to the direction of motion of the disc.

• PROBLEM 193

A thin rigid rod of weight W is supported horizontally by two props as shown in Figure A. Find the force F on the remaining support immediately after one of the supports is kicked out.

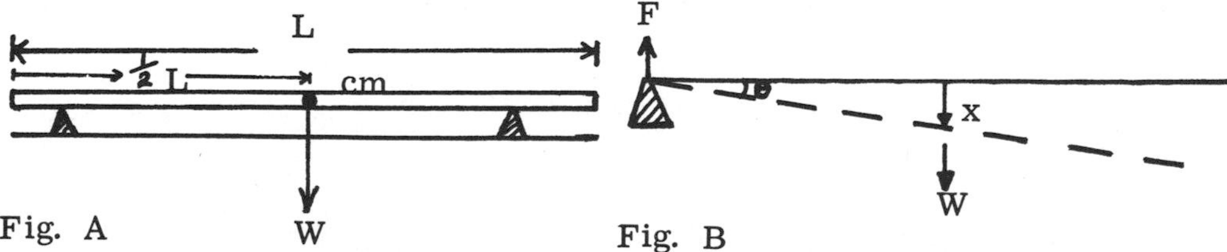

Fig. A Fig. B

Solution: The moment the support is kicked out, the rod starts rotating about the other support as the free end of the support falls (Figure B).

Let x be the displacement of the center of mass of the rod. Immediately after the kicking of the support, x is very small and is vertical. In this case, $\frac{d^2x}{dt^2}$ becomes the downward acceleration of the center of mass:

$$m \frac{d^2x}{dt^2} = W - F \qquad (1)$$

where m is the mass.

The torque on the rod about the remaining support is

$$\tau = W \frac{L}{2} = I \frac{d^2\theta}{dt^2}$$

where I is the moment of inertia with respect to the axis of rotation. The moment of inertia of a thin rod with respect to an end is known to be $\frac{1}{3} mL^2$, hence

$$\frac{1}{2} WL = \frac{1}{3} mL^2 \frac{d^2\theta}{dt^2}$$

or

$$\frac{d^2\theta}{dt^2} = \frac{3}{2} \frac{W}{mL}$$

For small x,

$$x \simeq \frac{L}{2} \theta$$

or

$$\frac{d^2x}{dt^2} \simeq \frac{L}{2} \frac{d^2\theta}{dt^2} .$$

From (1) and (2),

$$m \frac{L}{2} \frac{d^2\theta}{dt^2} = m \frac{L}{2} \frac{3W}{2mL} = W - F$$

$$\frac{3}{4} W = W - F$$

giving $\quad F = W - \frac{3}{4} W = \frac{1}{4} W .$

• PROBLEM 194

A turntable of mass M and radius $\vec{R}$ is rotating with angular velocity $\vec{\omega}_a$ on frictionless bearings. A spider of mass $\vec{m}$ falls vertically on to the rim of the turntable. What is the new angular velocity $\vec{\omega}_b$? The spider then slowly walks in toward the center of the turntable. What is the angular velocity $\vec{\omega}_c$ when the spider is at a distance $\vec{r}$ from the center? Assume that, apart from a negligibly small inward velocity along the radius, the spider has no velocity relative to the turntable.

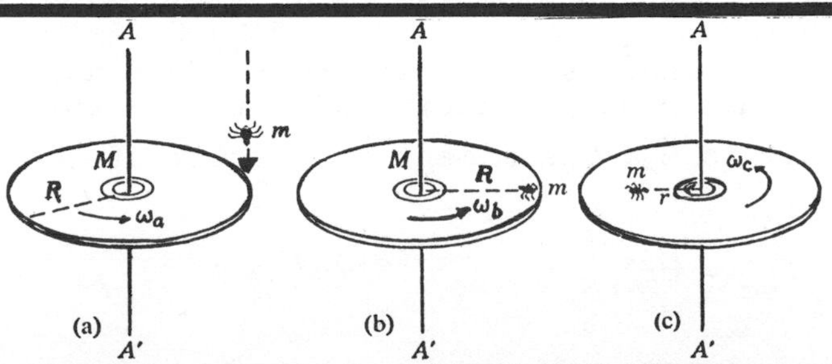

Solution: Consider the system which includes the turntable and the spider. Since the bearing is frictionless and the resistance of the air is to be ignored, no external couple acts on this system and its angular momentum must always remain the same. Just before the spider lands on the rim (figure a) the spider has no angular motion about the axis $\vec{A}A'$ and the angular momentum is contained entirely in the turntable. The turntable is a disc whose moment of inertia about its axis of symmetry is:

$$I_t = \tfrac{1}{2}MR^2$$

The angular momentum is therefore

$$L = I_t\omega_a$$

$$= \tfrac{1}{2} MR^2\omega_a$$

When the spider is standing on the rim (figure b) he takes up the motion of the turntable and both have an angular velocity $\vec{\omega}_b$. The moment of inertia of the spider is

$$I_{sb} = mR^2$$

since all of the spider's mass is at a distance $\vec{R}$ from the center of the turntable. The total moment of inertia of the system is

$$I_b = I_t + I_{sb}$$

$$= \tfrac{1}{2}MR^2 + mR^2$$

$$= \tfrac{1}{2}(M + 2m)R^2$$

The angular momentum is

$$L = I_b\omega_b$$

$$= \tfrac{1}{2}(M + 2m)R^2\omega_b.$$

Applying the law of conservation of angular momentum and equating the angular momenta before and after the spider lands,

$$\tfrac{1}{2}(M + 2m)R^2\omega_b = \tfrac{1}{2}MR^2\omega_a$$

$$\omega_b = \frac{M}{M + 2m}\,\omega_a$$

When the spider is at a distance $\vec{r}$ from the center (figure c), the angular velocity of both the spider and the turntable is $\vec{\omega}_c$. The moment of inertia of the spider is then

$$I_{sc} = mr^2$$

The total moment of inertia is

$$I_c = I_t + I_{sc}$$

$$= \tfrac{1}{2}MR^2 + mr^2$$

The angular momentum is

$$L = I_c\omega_c$$

$$= \left(\tfrac{1}{2}MR^2 + mr^2\right)\omega_c$$

Applying the law of conservation of angular momentum

$$\left(\tfrac{1}{2}MR^2 + mr^2\right)\omega_c = \tfrac{1}{2}MR^2\omega_a$$

$$\omega_c = \frac{\tfrac{1}{2}MR^2}{\left(\tfrac{1}{2}MR^2 + mr^2\right)}\omega_a$$

$$= \frac{\omega_a}{\left(1 + \dfrac{2mr^2}{MR^2}\right)}$$

Check that this agrees with the equation for $\vec{\omega}_b$ when $\vec{r} = \vec{R}$. As the spider walks inward and $\vec{r}$ decreases, the angular velocity increases since angular momentum must remain constant. When the spider reaches the center and $\vec{r} = 0$

$$\omega_c = \omega_a \quad \text{when } \vec{r} = 0.$$

• PROBLEM 195

A uniform rod of mass m and length 2a stands vertically on a rough horizontal floor and is allowed to fall. Assuming that slipping has not occurred, show that, when the rod makes an angle θ with the vertical,

$$\omega^2 = (3g/2a)(1 - \cos\theta)$$

where ω is the rod's angular velocity.

Also find the normal force exerted by the floor on the rod in this position, and the coefficient of static friction involved if slipping occurs when $\theta = 30°$.

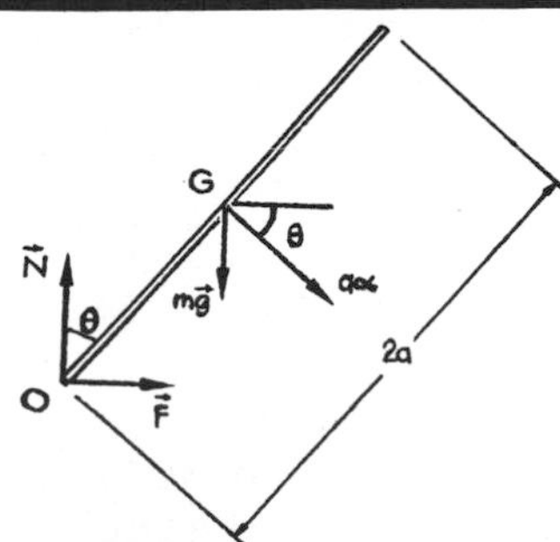

Solution: The forces acting on the rod are the weight $\vec{mg}$ acting downward and the normal force $\vec{N}$ and the frictional force $\vec{F}$ of magnitude μN exerted by the floor at the end O in contact with the floor. In order to find ω, we relate the net torque τ on the rod to the rod's angular acceleration α by using

$$\tau = I\alpha$$

Here, I is the rod's moment of inertia. We will then be able to solve for ω.

When one takes moments about 0, the only force producing rotation about O is the weight of the rod. Hence

$$\tau = mga \sin \theta = I_0 \alpha = \frac{4}{3} ma^2 \alpha$$

Here, I_O is the rod's moment of inertia about 0. Now,

$$\alpha = \frac{d\omega}{dt} = \frac{d\omega}{d\theta} \times \frac{d\theta}{dt} = \omega \frac{d\omega}{d\theta} = \frac{3}{4} \frac{g}{a} \sin \theta.$$

$$\int_0^\omega \omega \, d\omega = \int_0^\theta \frac{3}{4} \frac{g}{a} \sin \theta \, d\theta.$$

$$[\tfrac{1}{2} \omega^2]_0^\omega = \left[-\frac{3}{4} \frac{g}{a} \cos \theta \right]_0^\theta \text{ or } \omega^2 = \frac{3g}{2a} (1 - \cos \theta).$$

The center of gravity G has an angular acceleration α about O, and thus a linear acceleration $a\alpha$ at right angles to the direction of the rod. This linear acceleration can be split into two components, $a\alpha \cos \theta$ horizontally and $a\alpha \sin \theta$ vertically downward. The horizontal acceleration of the center of gravity is due to the force μN and the vertical acceleration is due to the net effect of the forces mg and N. Thus, using Newton's Second Law, and taking the positive direction downward,

$$mg - N = ma\alpha \sin \theta = \frac{3}{4} mg \sin^2 \theta \qquad (1)$$

$$\text{and} \quad F_{max} = \mu N = ma\alpha \cos \theta = \frac{3}{4} mg \sin \theta \cos \theta. \qquad (2)$$

From (1)

$$N = mg - \frac{3}{4} mg \sin^2 \theta = \frac{mg}{4} \left(4 - 3 \sin^2 \theta\right).$$

But when $\theta = 30°$, slipping just commences. At this angle F has its limiting, maximum value of F_{max}.

We have

$$\mu_s = \frac{F_{max}}{N} = \frac{\frac{3}{4} mg \sin \theta \cos \theta}{\frac{mg}{4} \left(4 - 3 \sin^2 \theta\right)} = \frac{3 \sin \theta \cos \theta}{\left(4 - 3 \sin^2 \theta\right)}$$

$$= \frac{3 \times \frac{1}{2} \times (\sqrt{3}/2)}{4 - \frac{3}{4}} = \frac{3\sqrt{3}}{13} = 0.400.$$

A missile is fired radially from the surface of the earth (of radius 3.4×10^6 m) at a satellite orbiting the earth. The satellite appears stationary at the point where the missile is launched. Its distance from the center of the earth is 25.4×10^6 m. Will the missile actually hit the satellite?

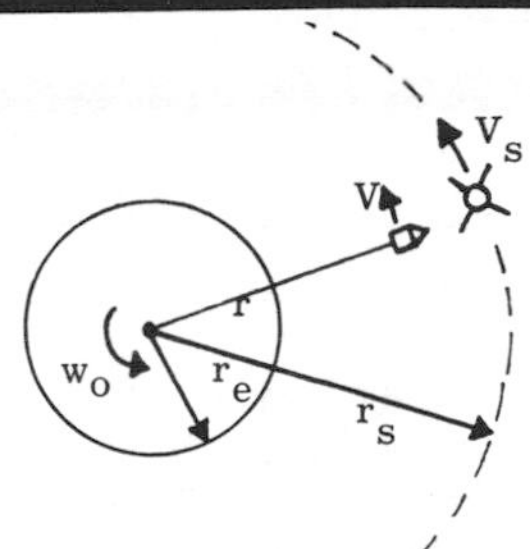

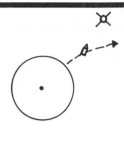

FIGURE A: View of outside observer

FIGURE B: View from earth

Solution: To an observer outside the planet (see fig. A), the earth and the missile (of mass m) on the surface are rotating about the axis of the planet with angular velocity ω_0. When the missile is fired radially from the surface, its distance from the center of the earth increases and thus its moment of inertia ($I = mr^2$) about the rotation axis increases also. There are no forces with a moment about the rotation axis acting on the missile (the gravitational force of attraction acting on it is exerted along the rotational axis and has no moment). The net torque Γ acting on the missile is then zero. According to the rigid body analogue of Newton's second law, if L is the magnitude of the angular momentum of the missile, then

$$\Gamma = \frac{dL}{dt}$$

but $\Gamma = 0$ and $$0 = \frac{dL}{dt}$$

or L = constant at all times. But $L = mvr$ where v is the tangential velocity of the missile. Since $v = \omega r$ where ω is the angular velocity of the missile, then $L = m\omega r^2 = I\omega$. Thus since L and m are constant at all times, as the missile moves farther away from the earth and closer to the satellite (i.e., r increases) then ω must decrease.

We are given that the satellite appears stationary at the point where the missile is fired. Thus the radius vector passing through the launching pad and the satellite continues to rotate with angular velocity ω_0. The missile has an angular velocity ω which drops more and more from the value ω_0 as the missile rises. At the height of the satellite, the moment of inertia of the rocket about the axis of rotation is

$$I_1 = mr_s^2 = m \times (25.4 \times 10^6 \text{ m})^2, \qquad \text{whereas,}$$

at the launching pad, its moment of inertia is only

$I_2 = mr_e^2 = m \times (3.4 \times 10^6 \text{ m})^2$. Thus, finally, if ω is the satellite's angular velocity at height r_s, and ω_0 its angular velocity at launching (equal to that of the earth) then

$$I_1\omega = L = I_2\,\omega_0$$

$$\frac{\omega}{\omega_0} = \frac{I_2}{I_1} = \frac{\not{m}r_e^2}{\not{m}r_s^2} = \frac{(3.4 \times 10^6 \text{ m})^2}{(25.4 \times 10^6 \text{ m})^2} = 0.018.$$

The missile thus moves further and further from the vertical as it rises and will miss the satellite (unless the missile is fitted with a homing device).

To an observer on the planet, the departure of the missile from the vertical is, of course, also observed and is explained in terms of the Coriolis force associated with a rotating frame of reference.

• PROBLEM 197

A satellite of mass m moves around the Earth as shown (actually, the path is an ellipse). Which instantaneous velocity is greater, v_P (at point P) or v_A (at point A)?

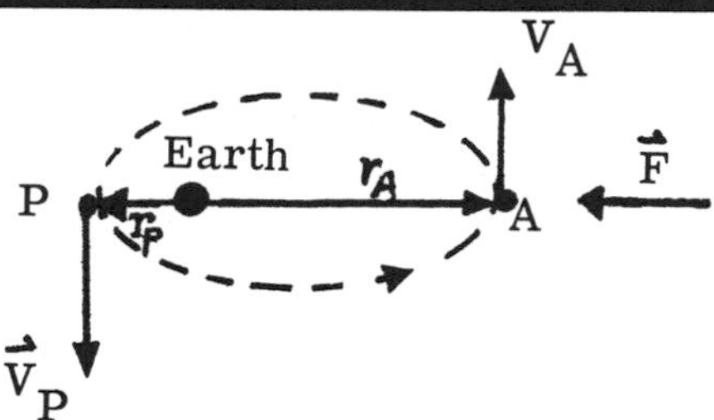

Solution: Consider the Earth as a fixed object and neglect the influence of the Sun and other planets.

The angular momentum of the satellite around the earth L, is given by

$$\vec{L} = \vec{r} \times m\vec{v}$$

where $\vec{r}$ is the vector from the earth to the satellite, and $\vec{v}$ is the velocity of the satellite. Since $\vec{v}$ and $\vec{r}$ are perpendicular

$$L = mvr$$

However,

$$T = \frac{dL}{dt} \qquad (1)$$

where the torque T is defined as

$$\vec{T} = \vec{r} \times \vec{F}$$

$\vec{F}$ is the gravitational force on the satellite keeping it in its orbit. (It is due to the mass of the Earth). Since the angle between $\vec{F}$ and the radius vector $\vec{r}$ is 0° we have

$$T = Fr \sin 0^\circ = 0$$

Therefore, by equation (1), L of the satellite is constant in time. At time t_1 the particle is at A and at time t_2 it is at P. Hence, the angular momentum at the two points must be the same. Or

$$L = mv_A r_A = mv_P r_P$$

Since $r_P < r_A$ we must then have $v_P > v_A$.

The velocity is greatest when the satellite is nearest the Earth; this point is called the perigee (labeled P in the diagram). The velocity is least at the farthest point from the Earth - the apogee (A) of the orbit.

ROLLING BODIES

• PROBLEM 198

An automobile changes its speed from 0 to 30 m/sec (about 63 mph) in 12 sec and continues to accelerate at this rate. A tire of the auto has a radius of R=0.4 m. Calculate the angular acceleration of the tire, assuming no slipping, and plot the angular velocity, tangential velocity at the circumference, and centripetal acceleration at the circumference as a function of time.

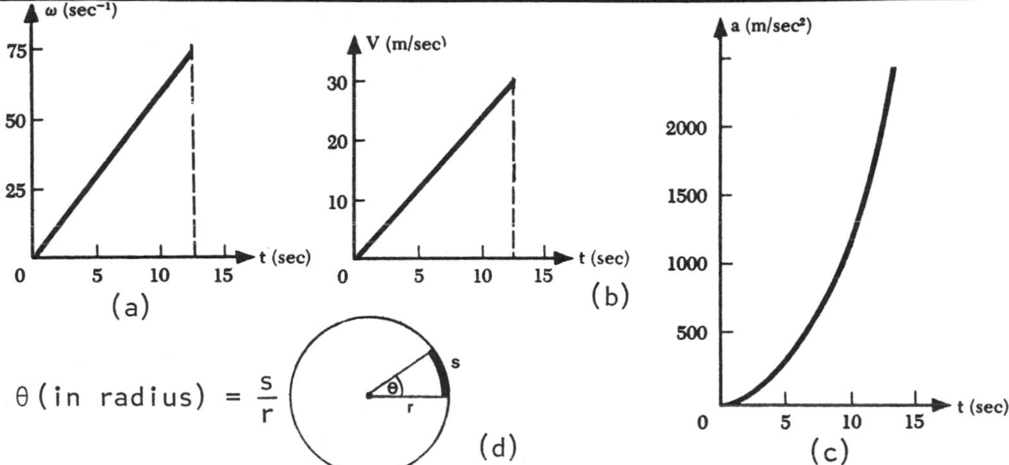

Solution: Linear and angular velocity are related by the equation:

$$v = \omega R$$

where v is linear velocity, ω the angular velocity, and R the radius of the wheel.

We will assume, in this problem, that the velocity increases uniformly since nothing to the contrary has been stated. By definition:

$$a = \frac{\Delta v}{\Delta t} \qquad \alpha = \frac{\Delta w}{\Delta t}$$

where a and α are the linear and angular accelerations respectively. However:

$$a = \frac{\Delta v}{\Delta t} = \frac{\Delta \omega}{\Delta t} R = \alpha R$$

We thus have a relationship between a and α.

$$a = \frac{30 \text{ m/sec} - 0 \text{ m/sec}}{12 \text{ sec}} = 2.5 \text{ m/sec}^2$$

Therefore: $\alpha = \dfrac{a}{R} = \dfrac{2.5 \text{ m/sec}^2}{0.4 \text{ m}} = 6.25 \text{ rad./sec.}^2$

Note that although by dimensional analysis the units in α should reduce to $\dfrac{1}{\text{sec.}^2}$, we express angular acceleration in terms of rad./sec.^{2}. This is done because of the physical considerations of the problem. We consider the wheel as rotating through a discrete angle measured in radians, in a certain amount of time. However, our rigorous dimensional analysis has not really been violated since radians are dimensionless.

As we know, radians are defined using a central angle of a circle. The magnitude of this angle in radians is calculated by dividing the length of the arc that the central angle subtends, by the length of the circle's radius. (See diagram.)

$$\theta \text{ (in radians)} = \frac{s}{r}$$

Both s and r are measured in units of length which cancel in the ratio. We see, therefore, that radians are dimensionless.

To calculate the angular velocity, we must remember the formula:

$$\omega = \omega_o + \alpha t$$

where ω_o is the initial angular velocity, and t is time.

$$w = 0 + (6.25 \text{ rad./sec.}^2)(t \text{ sec.})$$
$$= 6.25 \text{ t rad./sec.}$$

The tangential velocity is:

$$v = \omega R = (6.25 \text{ t rad./sec.})(0.4 \text{ m}) = 2.5 \text{ t m/sec.}$$

Note that we may now drop the radians from our units.

To calculate the centripetal acceleration at the circumference we must remember the formula:

$$a_c = \frac{v^2}{R} = \frac{\omega^2 R^2}{R} = w^2 R$$
$$= (6.25 \text{ t rad./sec.})^2 (0.4 \text{ m}) = 15.6 \text{ t}^2 \text{ m/sec.}^2$$

w, v, and α are plotted against time in figures 1, 2 and 3.

• PROBLEM 199

A solid cylinder 30 cm in diameter at the top of an incline 2.0 m high is released and rolls down the incline without loss of energy due to friction. Find the linear and angular speeds at the bottom.

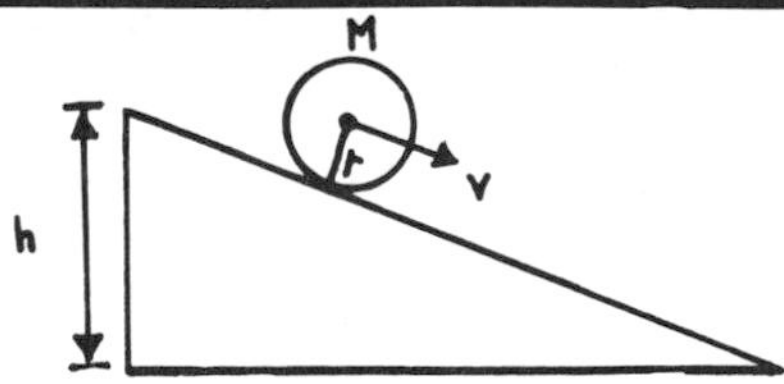

Solution: This problem can be solved using the conservation of energy principle. The cylinder initially at rest at the top of the incline has only gravitational (potential) energy. Taking the bottom of the incline as the zero level of the potential energy (see the figure above), we get

$$E_p = mgh$$

where m is the mass of the cylinder, g is the acceleration of gravity, and h = 2.0 m is its height above ground level. When the cylinder reaches the bottom of the incline, all of its energy will be kinetic:

$$E_k = \frac{1}{2} mv^2 + \frac{1}{2} I\omega^2$$

where v is the cylinder's linear velocity, I its moment of inertia about the central axis, and ω its angular momentum. ($I = \frac{1}{2} mR^2$ for cylinders, where R is the radius.)

In the process of rolling down the incline the cylinder's potential energy turns to kinetic, the total change in each being equal to:

$$\Delta E_p = \Delta E_k$$

$$mgh = \frac{1}{2} mv^2 + \frac{1}{2} I\omega^2$$

$$= \frac{1}{2} mv^2 + \frac{1}{2} \left|\frac{1}{2} mR^2\right| \left(\frac{v}{R}\right)^2$$

$$= \frac{1}{2} mv^2 + \frac{1}{4} mv^2 = \frac{3}{4} mv^2$$

using $\omega = \frac{v}{R}$

Thus, $gh = \frac{3}{4} v^2$

$$v = \frac{2\sqrt{3}}{3} (gh)^{\frac{1}{2}} = 1.15 \left[(9.8 \text{ m/sec}^2)(2.0 \text{ m}) \right]^{\frac{1}{2}}$$

$$= 5.09 \text{ m/sec.}$$

Note that the linear speed does not depend upon the size or mass of the cylinder.

To find ω, we use the formula:

$$w = \frac{v}{R} = \frac{5.09 \text{ m/sec}}{0.15 \text{ m}} = 34 \text{ rad/sec.}$$

• PROBLEM 200

A string is wrapped around a uniform homogeneous 3 lb cylinder with a 6 in. radius. The free end is attached to the ceiling from which the cylinder is then allowed to fall (as in **the Figure**), starting from rest. As the string unwraps, the cylinder revolves. (a) What is the linear acceleration of the center of mass? (b) What is the linear velocity, and (c) how fast is the cylinder revolving after a drop of 6 ft? (d) What is the tension in the cord?

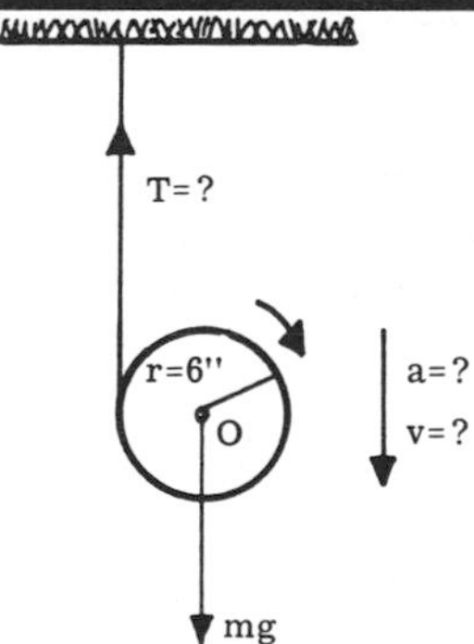

Solution: (a) Isolate the cylinder, and indicate forces acting on it.

There is no need to tabulate x- and y-components since they are all up or down forces.

Set $\Sigma F = ma$

where ΣF is the net force acting on the cylinder, a is the acceleration of the cylinder's center of mass, and m is its mass. (Note that in problems such as this one, it is convenient to take the direction of motion as positive.)

$$mg - T = ma \qquad \therefore\ a = g - \frac{T}{m} \qquad (1)$$

Now, consider rotation.

Consider torques about the center of mass 0, and set $\Sigma L = I\alpha$, where ΣL is the net torque about 0, I is the moment of inertia at the cylinder about 0, and α is its angular acceleration. Hence

$$\Sigma L = rT = I\alpha$$

$$\therefore\ T = I\,\frac{\alpha}{r}$$

(Clockwise rotation corresponds to downward motion, already assumed to have the positive direction.)

But I for a cylinder = $\frac{1}{2}\,mr^2$, where r is the cylinder radius.

In this problem $\qquad a = r\alpha$

$$T = \frac{1}{2}\,\frac{mr^2}{r}\,\frac{a}{r} = \frac{ma}{2}$$

whereupon, using (1),

$$a = \frac{-ma}{2m} + g = \frac{-a}{2} + g$$

$$\therefore\quad 3a = 2g$$

$$a = \frac{2}{3}\,g = 21.3\ \text{ft/sec}^2 \qquad \text{(downward)}$$

(b) Now since a = constant (2/3 g), the linear motion is uniformly accelerated, such that the velocity of the center of mass is

$v^2 = v_0^2 + 2as$, where s becomes the drop, h,

that the cylinder experiences, and v_0 is its initial velocity.

$$v^2 = 0 + (2)\left(21.3\ \text{ft/sec}^2\right)(6\ \text{ft})$$

$$v^2 = (12)\left(21.3\ \text{ft}^2/\text{sec}^2\right)$$

$$\therefore\ v = \sqrt{256} = 16\ \text{ft/sec}$$

(c) The angular velocity $\omega = \dfrac{v}{r}$

$$= \frac{16\ \text{ft/sec}}{\frac{1}{2}\ \text{ft}} = 32\ \text{rad/sec}$$

(d) From (1)

$$T = m(g - a) = m\left(g - \frac{2}{3} g\right)$$

$$T = \frac{1}{3} mg = \left(\frac{1}{3}\right) (3 \text{ lb}) = 1 \text{ lb}$$

• PROBLEM 201

A yo-yo rests on a level surface. A gentle horizontal pull (see the figure) is exerted on the cord so that the yo-yo rolls without slipping. Which way does it move and why?

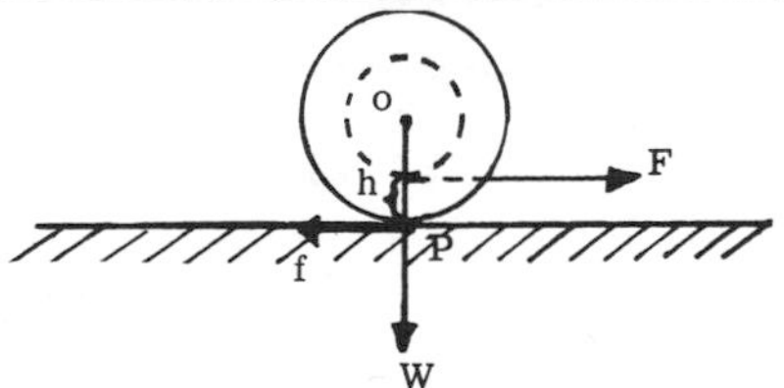

Solution: The forces acting on the yo-yo are the horizontal pull F and the frictional force f

$$f = \mu W$$

where μ is the coefficient of friction.

Instantaneous rotation takes place about an axis through the point of contact P (not about the center of the yo-yo, although it might appear so) since the instantaneous velocity of the contact point is zero. Therefore, the yo-yo rolls in the direction of the pull and its rotation is determined by the torque about P,

$$\tau = Fh.$$

It should be observed that the frictional force does not contribute to this torque, since f is acting at P.

• PROBLEM 202

Two circular cylinders have the same mass and dimensions, but one is solid while the other is a thin hollow shell. If they are released together to roll without slipping down a plane inclined at 30° to the horizontal, how far apart will they be after 10 s?

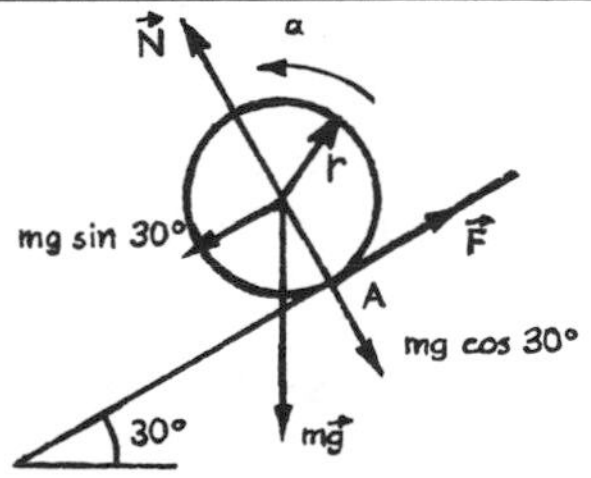

Solution: In either case the forces acting on the cylinder are as shown in the diagram. The weight $\vec{mg}$ acting downward is split up into its components parallel to and perpendicular to the plane. The other two forces acting on the cylinder are the normal force $\vec{N}$ exerted by the plane and the frictional force attempting to prevent motion, $\vec{F}$, which has magnitude μN.

Since the cylinder does not lift from the plane,

$$N = mg \cos 30°.$$

Further, by Newton's second law,

$$mg \sin 30° - \mu N = mg(\sin 30 - \mu \cos 30) = ma,$$

where m is the mass of the cylinder and a the acceleration produced. Rotation about the center of the cylinder also takes place. Since we are dealing with rotations of distributed masses, a relation involving the moment of inertia must be used. That relation is the rigid body analogue of Newton's second law, F = ma, or

$$\Gamma = I\alpha$$

where the torque Γ corresponds to F, the moment of inertia I corresponds to m, and the angular acceleration α of the cylinder corresponds to a. If an axis is taken about the center of the sphere, then the only torque acting on the sphere is μNr due to the frictional force μN. Then

$$\mu Nr = \mu r\, mg \cos 30° = I\alpha,$$

Since no slipping takes place, the point A is instantaneously at rest. Hence $a = r\alpha$, and

$$mg(\sin 30° - \mu \cos 30°) = ma, \qquad (1)$$

$$\mu r\, mg \cos 30° = \frac{Ia}{r}. \qquad (2)$$

or, multiplying (1) by r^2, and (2) by r

$$mgr^2 \sin 30 - \mu mgr^2 \cos 30 = mar^2 \qquad (3)$$

and

$$\mu r^2 mg \cos 30 = Ia \qquad (4)$$

Substituting (4) in (3)

$$mg\, r^2 \sin\theta - Ia = mar^2 \quad \text{or } a = \frac{mgr^2 \sin\theta}{I + mr^2}$$

For the solid cylinder, $I = 1/2mr^2$

$$a_1 = \frac{mgr^2 \sin\theta}{1/2mr^2 + mr^2} = \frac{2}{3} g \sin\theta,$$

and for the hollow cylinder, $I = mr^2$

$$a_2 = \frac{mgr^2 \sin\theta}{mr^2 + mr^2} = \frac{1}{2} g \sin\theta.$$

The distances traveled in 10 s from rest are, found by using the kinematic equations for constant acceleration. If the top of the inclined plane is taken as the initial position, then $s_0 = 0$. Also the initial velocity $v_0 = 0$. Then $S = s_0 + v_0 t + \frac{1}{2}at^2$. Hence

$$S_1 = 0 + \frac{1}{2}a_1 t^2 = \frac{1}{2} \times \frac{2}{3} \times 32 \text{ ft}\cdot\text{s}^{-2} \times \frac{1}{2} \times 100 \text{ s}^2 =$$

$$= \frac{1600}{3} \text{ ft}$$

and

$$S_2 = \frac{1}{2}a_2t^2 = \frac{1}{2} \times \frac{1}{2} \times 32\ \text{ft}\cdot\text{s}^{-2} \times \frac{1}{2} \times 100\ \text{s}^2 =$$

$$= 400\ \text{ft.}$$

$$\therefore\ S_1 - S_2 = (533.3 - 400)\text{ft} = 133.3\ \text{ft.}$$

• PROBLEM 203

A billiard ball is struck by a cue as in figure (a). The line of action of the applied impulse is horizontal and passes through the center of the ball. The initial velocity $\vec{v}_0$ of the ball after impact, its radius R, its mass M, and the coefficient of friction μ between the ball and the table are all known.

(a) How far will the ball move before it ceases to slip on the table and starts to roll?

(b) What will its angular velocity be at this point?

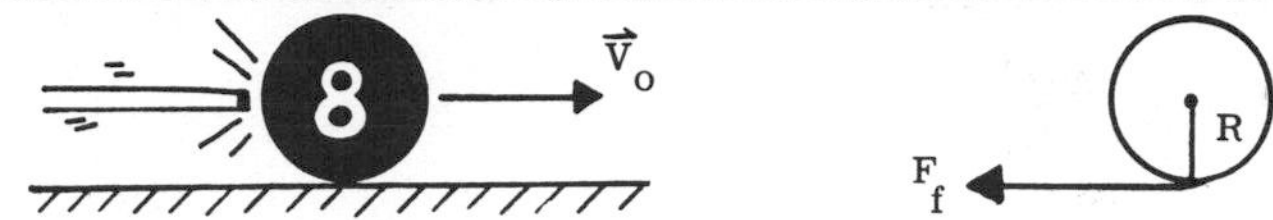

FIGURE A FIGURE B

Solution: (a) Between the time the ball is struck by the cue, and the time it begins pure rolling, friction with the table decelerates it linearly, but simultaneously exerts a torque upon it about its center of mass. This causes the ball to undergo an angular acceleration. The ball begins pure rolling when its linear velocity and its angular velocity have been decreased and increased respectively to the point at which the relation

$$v = R\omega$$

holds. We recognize this as the definition of linear velocity with respect to angular velocity for pure rolling. The force of friction on the ball is by definition:

$$F_f = \mu N = \mu mg$$

where N = mg is the normal force between the ball and the table. The negative sign indicates that F_f is directed opposite to v_0.

The ball's linear acceleration is:

$$a = \frac{F_f}{M} = -\ \mu g$$

Thus, its linear velocity at time t is given by:

$$v(t) = v_0 + at = v_0 - \mu gt$$

The torque on the ball is (see figure (b)):

$$\tau = F_f R = \mu MgR$$

Since we know that the moment of inertia of a solid sphere about an axis passing through the center is $I = 2/5\ MR^2$, we can calculate its angular acceleration:

$$\tau = I\alpha, \qquad \alpha = \frac{\tau}{I} = \frac{\mu\, MgR}{\frac{2}{5}\, MR^2} = \frac{5}{2}\, \frac{\mu g}{R}$$

The ball's angular velocity at time t is given by:

$$\omega(t) = \omega_0 + \alpha t, \qquad \omega_0 = 0$$

$$\omega(t) = \alpha t = \frac{5}{2}\, \frac{\mu g}{R}\, t$$

To calculate the distance the ball will move before it begins pure rolling, we must first calculate how long it is after the ball has been struck that this occurs. Rolling begins when

$$v(t) = R\omega(t)$$

$$v_0 - \mu g t = R\left(\frac{5}{2}\, \frac{\mu g}{R}\right) t = \frac{5}{2}\, \mu g t$$

$$\frac{7}{2}\, \mu g t = v_0, \qquad t = \frac{2}{7}\, \frac{v_0}{\mu g}$$

The distance the ball travels is therefore, since the acceleration is constant,

$$s = v_0 t + \tfrac{1}{2}\, a t^2 = v_0 t - \tfrac{1}{2}\, \mu g t^2$$

$$s = v_0\left(\frac{2}{7}\, \frac{v_0}{\mu g}\right) - \tfrac{1}{2}\, \mu g \left(\frac{2}{7}\, \frac{v_0}{\mu g}\right)^2 = \frac{2}{7}\, \frac{{v_0}^2}{\mu g} - \frac{2}{49}\, \frac{v_0^2}{\mu g}$$

$$= \frac{12}{49}\, \frac{v_0^2}{\mu g}$$

Here v_0 is the ball's initial velocity.

(b) Its angular velocity at this point is:

$$\omega(t) = \omega_0 + \alpha t$$

$$\omega(t) = \alpha t = \frac{5}{2}\, \frac{\mu g}{R}\left(\frac{2}{7}\, \frac{v_0}{\mu g}\right) = \frac{5}{7}\, \frac{v_0}{R}$$

since the ball's initial angular velocity $\omega_0 = 0$.

• PROBLEM 204

A cable drum of inner and outer radii r and R is lying on rough ground, the cable being wound round the inner cylinder and being pulled off from the bottom at an angle θ to the horizontal. An inquiring student strolling by notes that when the cable is pulled by a workman, with θ a small angle, the drum rolls without slipping toward the workman. Whereas if θ is large, the drum rolls without slipping in the opposite direction. He works out a value for the critical angle θ_0 which separates the two types of motion. What is the value of θ_0?

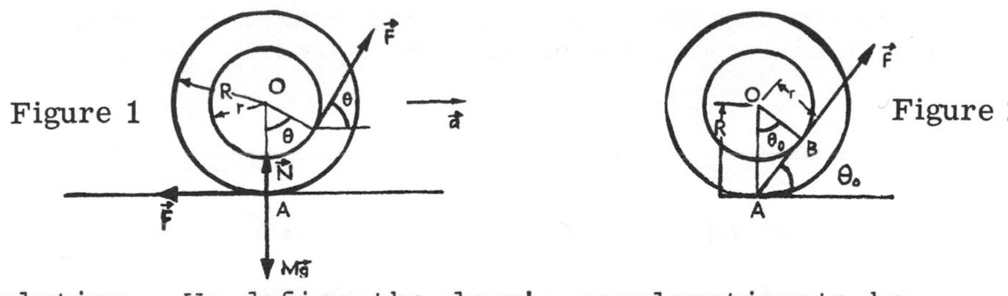

Solution: We define the drum's acceleration to be positive when the drum moves toward the workman. Hence the mathematical condition that the drum roll toward or away from the worker is that a (the acceleration) be positive or negative, respectively. The critical condition distinguishing the 2 types of motion is that a = 0. Therefore, to find the critical angle θ_0, we find a as a function of θ, set it equal to zero, and solve for θ.

We can use Newton's Second Law to relate the net force on the drum to its acceleration. (We do this for the vertical and horizontal directions separately.)

Figure (1) shows the drum with the forces acting on it. The force applied by the workman acts tangentially to the inner cylinder at such a position that the angle between this tangent and the horizontal is θ. It follows that the angle between the corresponding radius and the vertical is θ also, and that this radius is at right angles to the tangential force $\vec{F}$.

The other forces acting are the weight $\vec{Mg}$ of the cable drum, the normal forces exerted by the ground on the drum at the two points of contact, which combine into a resultant $\vec{N}$ passing through the center of gravity, and the frictional forces at the same points of contact which combine to form a single resultant force $\vec{f}$.

There is no movement in the vertical direction. Hence

$$N = Mg - F \sin \theta. \qquad (1)$$

The forces in the horizontal direction produce an acceleration a. Thus

$$F \cos \theta - f = Ma. \qquad (2)$$

Further, the moments of the forces about the center of mass O produce a rotational acceleration about that point. The only forces whose lines of action do not pass through the center of gravity are F and f. Hence

$$Fr - fR = I\alpha \qquad (3)$$

where I is the moment of inertia of the drum about its center of mass.

At the points at which the drum touches the ground no slipping occurs. Therefore instantaneously these points are at rest. But all points of the drum have an acceleration a forward and in addition the points of contact, due to the rotation about the center of mass, have a further linear acceleration $R\alpha$ forward. Thus

$$a + \alpha R = 0$$

or
$$\alpha = - a/R \tag{4}$$

We wish to eliminate f from (2). Solving (3) for f

$$\frac{Fr - I\alpha}{R} = f \tag{5}$$

Substituting (4) in (5)

$$f = \frac{Fr + Ia/R}{R}$$

$$f = \frac{Fr}{R} + \frac{Ia}{R^2} \tag{6}$$

Inserting (6) in (2)

$$F \cos \theta - \frac{Fr}{R} - \frac{Ia}{R^2} = Ma$$

Solving for a

$$\frac{F \cos \theta - \frac{Fr}{R}}{M + \frac{I}{R^2}} = a$$

or
$$a = \frac{F(\cos \theta - r/R)}{M + \frac{I}{R^2}} \tag{7}$$

Since we do not know F, we solve (1) for F and insert this in (7)

$$F = \frac{Mg - N}{\sin \theta}$$

and
$$a = \frac{\left(\frac{Mg - N}{\sin \theta}\right)\left(\cos \theta - \frac{r}{R}\right)}{M + \frac{I}{R^2}} \tag{8}$$

The critical value of θ, (θ_0), is found by setting (8) equal to 0, whence

$$a = 0$$

$$\cos \theta_0 - \frac{r}{R} = 0$$

$$\cos \theta_0 = \frac{r}{R} \tag{9}$$

If $\cos \theta > r/R$, the drum rolls towards the workman, and vice versa.

This result could be obtained more easily by considering rotation about A, the line of the drum instantaneously at rest. The only force that does not pass through A is $\vec{F}$, the applied force. If the line of action of $\vec{F}$ cuts the ground to the left of A, the moment of $\vec{F}$ about A causes the drum to roll to the right. If the line of action of $\vec{F}$ cuts the ground to the right of A, the moment of $\vec{F}$ about A causes the drum to move to the left. If the line of action of $\vec{F}$ passes through A, the drum is stationary and θ has the critical value θ_0.

Figure (2) shows this situation. Since the line of action of $\vec{F}$ is tangential to the inner cylinder, OB and AB are at right angles and $\angle$ AOB is θ_0.

$$\therefore \cos\theta_0 = \frac{r}{R}.$$

• PROBLEM 205

A cylinder is rolled up an incline by a tape arranged as shown. What minimum force T is required if the angle $\theta = 30^\circ$? The weight of the cylinder is 2 lb and the elevation h = 2 ft.

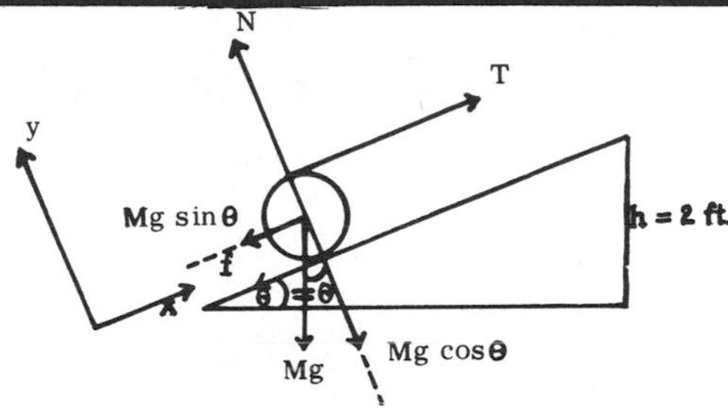

Solution: The force, T, needed to pull the cylinder up the incline can be found by applying Newton's Second Law, F = ma, to the x and y directions of the cylinder's motion. Hence, using the figure,

$$T - f - Mg\sin\theta = ma_x \tag{1}$$

$$N - Mg\cos\theta = ma_y \tag{2}$$

where f is the frictional force, N is the normal force of the plane, and a_x and a_y are the x and y directed accelerations of the cylinder. Since the cylinder does not leave the incline, $a_y = 0$, and, from (2)

$$N = Mg\cos\theta \tag{3}$$

Now, f is an unknown in (1) since we do not know the coefficient of rolling friction for the plane. In order to eliminate this unknown, we calculate the net torque, $\vec{\tau}$, on the cylinder. By definition,

$$\vec{\tau} = \vec{r} \times \vec{F}$$

$$\tau = |\vec{\tau}| = rF\sin\theta$$

where θ is the angle between $\vec{r}$ and $\vec{F}$, and $\vec{r}$ is a vector locating the point of application of $\vec{F}$. In our case, taking torques about the center of mass

$$\tau = Rf + RT$$

But

$$\tau = I\alpha$$

where I and α are the cylinder's moment of inertia and angular acceleration, respectively. Then

$$I\alpha = fR + TR \qquad (4)$$

Because the cylinder rotates without slipping

$$v = wR \qquad (5)$$

where v is the velocity of the cylinder's center of amss, and w is its angular velocity. Hence, differentiating (5)

$$\frac{dv}{dt} = \left(\frac{dw}{dt}\right)R$$

$$a = \alpha R$$

Since v is directed along the x-axis, a is also, and $a = a_x$, whence

$$a_x = \alpha R \qquad (6)$$

Substituting (6) in (4)

$$I\,\frac{a_x}{R} = (f + T)R$$

$$f = \frac{Ia_x}{R^2} - T \qquad (7)$$

Inserting (7) in (1)

$$T - \frac{Ia_x}{R^2} + T - Mg \sin\theta = ma_x$$

$$2T - Mg \sin\theta = \left(m + \frac{I}{R^2}\right) a_x$$

$$a_x = \frac{2T - Mg \sin\theta}{m + \frac{I}{R^2}} \qquad (8)$$

The minimum applied force T will not accelerate the cylinder, but move it with constant velocity ($a_x = 0$). Hence, from (8)

$$2T = Mg \sin\theta$$

$$T = \frac{(2\ \text{lb})(\frac{1}{2})}{2} = \tfrac{1}{2}\ \text{lb.}$$

• PROBLEM 206

A string is wrapped around a cylinder of mass M and radius R (see figure (a)). The string is pulled vertically upward to prevent the center of mass from falling as the cylinder unwinds the string. (a) What is the tension in the string? (b) How much work has been done on the cylinder once it has reached an angular speed w? (c) What is the length of string unwound in this time?

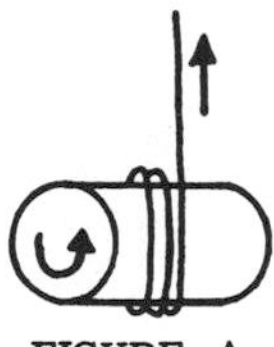

FIGURE A

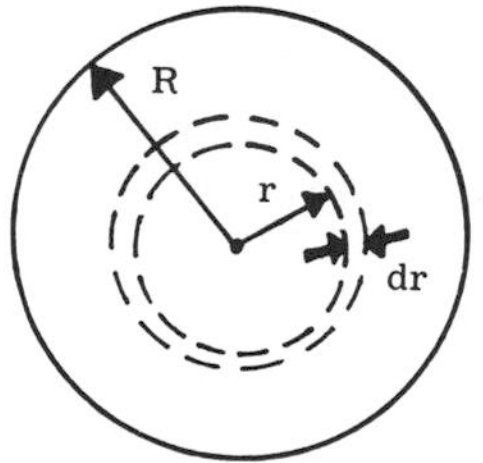

FIGURE B

Solution: We must first find the moment of inertia I of a cylinder of mass M and radius R. To start, we first calculate the moment of inertia of a disk of mass density ρ and radius R, whose thickness is negligible (see figure (b)).

The differential mass element dm, shown as the dotted ring in the figure, has area $2\pi r\, dr$. Thus:

$$dm = 2\pi\rho r\, dr$$

Therefore:

$$I = \int r^2\, dm = \int r^2\, (2\pi\rho r\, dr) = 2\pi\rho \int_0^R r\, dr$$

$$= 2\pi\rho \left.\frac{r^4}{4}\right]_0^R = \frac{\pi\rho R^4}{2} = \tfrac{1}{2}\left(\pi R^2\rho\right) R^2 = \tfrac{1}{2}\, mR^2$$

We have used the fact that $\pi R^2\rho$ is the mass m of the disk, since ρ is the mass density, and πR^2 is the total area.

We can think of a cylinder as many disks squeezed together, and we know that the total moment of inertia about a common axis, of many objects, is the sum of the individual moments of inertia:

$$I_t = I_1 + I_2 + I_3 + \ldots$$

In the case of a cylinder:

$$I = \tfrac{1}{2}\, m_1 R^2 + \tfrac{1}{2}\, m_2 R^2 + \tfrac{1}{2}\, m_3 R^2 + \ldots = \tfrac{1}{2}\, MR^2$$

where $M = m_1 + m_2 + m_3 + \ldots$

(a) The tension T of the string must exactly balance the cylinder's weight if the cylinder is not allowed to fall. Thus:

$$T = Mg$$

(b) The amount of work done on the cylinder equals its gain in (rotational) kinetic energy. Since the initial angular velocity is assumed to be zero:

$$W = KE_r = \tfrac{1}{2}\, I\, \omega^2 = \tfrac{1}{2}\left(\tfrac{1}{2}\, MR^2\right)\omega^2$$

$$\tfrac{1}{4}\, MR^2\omega^2$$

(c) To calculate the length of string unwound we place ourselves in the reference frame in which the string is at rest. In this frame, the cylinder rolls forward at a linear acceleration:

$$a = R\alpha$$

leaving a trail of string behind.

Here α is the angular acceleration of the rotating cylinder. From the laws of rotational dynamics:

$$\tau = I\alpha, \qquad \alpha = \frac{\tau}{I}$$

where $\tau = MgR$ is the torque that the string exerts about the cylinder's center of mass. The length of string, S, that the cylinder unwinds after time t equals the distance it travels in this reference frame:

$$S = v_0 t + \tfrac{1}{2} at^2, \qquad v_0 = \text{initial velocity} = 0$$

$$S = \tfrac{1}{2} at^2 = \tfrac{1}{2} \alpha R t^2 = \tfrac{1}{2} \frac{\tau}{I} Rt^2 = \tfrac{1}{2} \frac{MgR}{\tfrac{1}{2} MR^2} Rt^2$$

$$= gt^2$$

(These are the kinematics equations for constant acceleration.)

We know that the time t it takes for the cylinder's angular velocity to reach w is given by the angular kinematics equations for constant α:

$$w = w_0 + \alpha t, \qquad w_0 = \text{initial velocity} = 0$$

$$w = \alpha t$$

$$t = \frac{w}{\alpha} = \frac{w}{MgR/\tfrac{1}{2} MR^2} = \frac{wR}{2g}$$

Thus: $$S = g\left(\frac{wR}{2g}\right)^2 = \frac{w^2 R^2}{4g}$$

• PROBLEM 207

Starting from rest at the top, a small sphere rolls without slipping off a large fixed sphere. At what point will the small sphere leave the surface of the big sphere? (See figure).

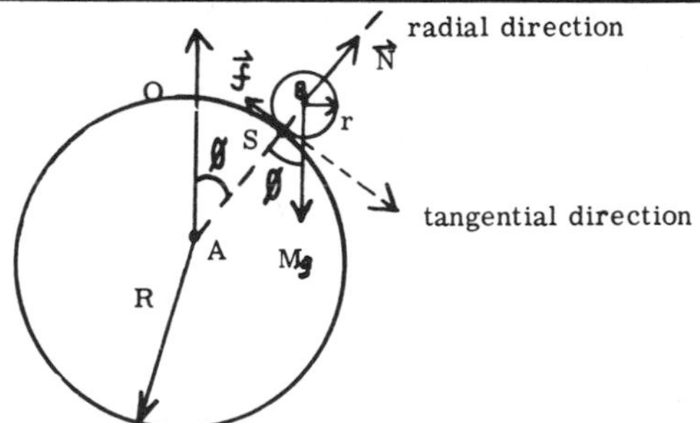

Solution: The small sphere will leave the surface of the large sphere when the normal force ($\vec{N}$) of the latter on the former is zero, for this means that contact has ceased. Applying Newton's Second Law to the tangential and radial components of motion of the small sphere (see figure), we obtain

$$F_{radial} = Ma_{radial} = Mg \cos \varphi - N$$

$$F_{tangential} = Ma_{tangential} = mg \sin \varphi$$

where a_{radial} is positive in the direction of $\vec{BA}$, and $a_{tangential}$ is positive in the direction of motion of the sphere. Furthermore, $a_{radial} = v^2/R+r$, since the small sphere is traveling along a circular arc. (Here, v is the latter's speed.) Then

$$\frac{Mv^2}{R+r} = Mg \cos \varphi - N$$

or

$$N = Mg \cos \varphi - \frac{Mv^2}{R+r}$$

We require $N = 0$, or

$$Mg \cos \varphi = \frac{Mv^2}{R+r}$$

Therefore

$$\cos \varphi = \frac{v^2}{(R+r)g} \tag{1}$$

We are not yet finished, since we don't know v in (1). In order to find it, we may use the principle of conservation of energy to relate the energy of the small sphere at points O and S. Since the sphere starts from rest at O, it has only potential energy. Measuring potential energy from A, the energy at O is

$$E = Mg(R+r) \tag{2}$$

At S, the sphere has potential and kinetic energy equal in amount to the energy at O. Hence

$$E = \tfrac{1}{2} Mv^2 + \tfrac{1}{2} Iw^2 + Mg(R+r) \cos \varphi \tag{3}$$

where the first and second terms are the translational and rotational kinetic energies of the sphere respectively. Equating (2) and (3)

$$\tfrac{1}{2} Mv^2 + \tfrac{1}{2} Iw^2 + Mg(R+r) \cos \varphi = Mg(R+r) \tag{4}$$

Since the small sphere rolls without slipping $v = wr$, whence, using (4)

$$\tfrac{1}{2} Mv^2 + \tfrac{1}{2} I \frac{v^2}{r^2} = Mg(R+r)(1 - \cos \varphi)$$

The moment of inertia of a sphere about its center is

$$I = \frac{2}{5} Mr^2$$

Then

$$\tfrac{1}{2} Mv^2 + \tfrac{1}{2} \frac{2}{5}(Mr^2) \frac{v^2}{r^2} = Mg(R+r)(1 - \cos \varphi)$$

$$\tfrac{1}{2} Mv^2 + \frac{1}{5} Mv^2 = Mg(R+r)(1 - \cos \varphi)$$

$$\frac{7}{10} v^2 = g(R+r)(1 - \cos \varphi)$$

$$v^2 = \frac{10}{7} g(R+r)(1 - \cos \varphi) \tag{5}$$

Utilizing (5) in (1),

$$\cos \varphi = \frac{10g(R+r)(1 - \cos \varphi)}{7(R+r)g}$$

$$\cos \varphi = \frac{10}{7}(1 - \cos \varphi)$$

Solving for φ

$$\frac{10}{7} \cos \varphi + \cos \varphi = \frac{10}{7}$$

$$\cos \varphi\left(\frac{17}{7}\right) = \frac{10}{7}$$

$$\cos \varphi = \frac{10}{17}$$

and

$$\varphi = \cos^{-1}\left(\frac{10}{17}\right) \approx 54^\circ$$

• PROBLEM 208

A uniform cylinder rolls from rest down the side of a trough whose vertical dimension y is given by the equation $y = Kx^2$. The cylinder does not slip from A to B, but the surface of the trough is frictionless from B on toward C. (See figure). How far will the cylinder ascend toward C? Under the same conditions, will a uniform sphere of the same radius go farther or less far toward C than the cylinder?

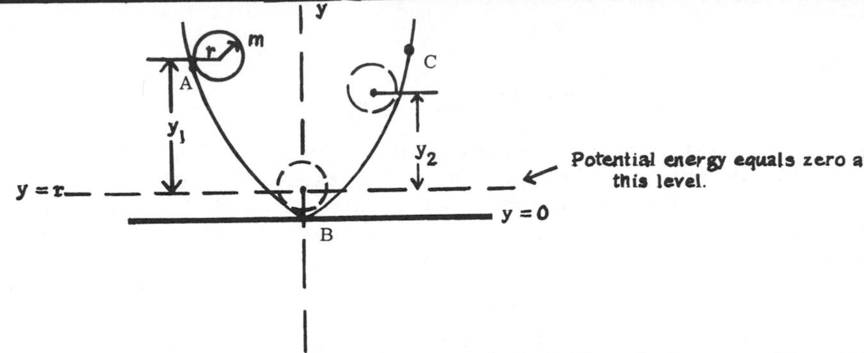

Solution: Since we do not know the actual frictional force acting on the cylinder, we cannot use dynamical methods to solve for the final position of the cylinder. Our only other recourse is to use the principle of conservation of energy to relate the energy of the cylinder at point A to its energy at point C. By doing this, we will find an expression for the final position of the cylinder, and the problem will be solved.

Since friction acts along path AB, but not along path BC, we apply the principle of energy conservation in 2 steps. First, we relate the cylinder's energy at points A and B. Then, using the data obtained from the first step, we relate the cylinder's energy at points B and C.

The cylinder begins from rest at point A, and therefore has only potential energy. Taking the reference level for potential energy at y = r (see figure), we obtain

$$E_A = mgy_1 \tag{1}$$

for the cylinder's energy at A.

In traveling from A to B, friction is present. However, this force does no work because we are given the fact that the cylinder is not slipping. By definition, this means that the velocity of the contact point of cylinder and surface is zero. Under these conditions the velocity of the cylinder's center of mass, v, is related to the angular velocity by

$$v = \omega r \tag{2}$$

where r is the cylinder radius. Hence, the energy of the cylinder at B is

$$E_B = \tfrac{1}{2}\, mv^2 + \tfrac{1}{2}\, I\omega^2 \tag{3}$$

where I is the cylinder's moment of inertia. The first term represents the cylinder's translational motion, and the last term represents its rotational motion.

Now, in going from B to C, no friction acts. As a result, the cylinder cannot roll, and the rotational motion it had at B is preserved throughout the trip to C. At C, the cylinder's center of mass has no velocity, but it is still spinning, with angular velocity ω, about its center of mass. The energy at C is then

$$E_C = mgy_2 + \tfrac{1}{2}\, I\omega^2 \tag{4}$$

By the principle of conservation of energy

$$E_A = E_B$$

and

$$E_B = E_C .$$

Therefore, using (1), (3) and (4)

$$mgy_1 = \frac{1}{2} mv^2 + \frac{1}{2} I\omega^2 \tag{5}$$

$$mgy_2 + \frac{1}{2} I\omega^2 = \frac{1}{2} mv^2 + \frac{1}{2} I\omega^2 \tag{6}$$

From (2)

$$\omega = v/r$$

Substituting this in (5)

$$mgy_1 = \frac{1}{2} mv^2 + \frac{1}{2} I \frac{v^2}{r^2} \tag{7}$$

Solving for v^2

$$mgy_1 = \frac{v^2}{2}\left(m + \frac{I}{r^2}\right)$$

or

$$v^2 = \frac{2mgy_1}{(m + I/r^2)} \tag{8}$$

From (6)

$$mgy_2 = \frac{1}{2} mv^2 \tag{9}$$

We may eliminate v^2 from (9) by substituting (8) in (9), whence

$$mgy_2 = \frac{1}{2} m\left\{\frac{2mgy_1}{(m + I/r^2)}\right\}$$

then

$$y_2 = \frac{my_1}{(m + I/r^2)}$$

For a cylinder, $I = \frac{1}{2}mr^2$ and

$$y_2 = \frac{my_1}{m + \frac{1}{2}mr^2/r^2} = \frac{my_1}{\frac{3}{2} m}$$

$$y_2 = \frac{2}{3} y_1 .$$

For a sphere, the above analysis still holds. Since $I = 2/5\ mr^2$

$$y_2 = \frac{my_1}{m + \frac{2}{5} mr^2/r^2} = \frac{my_1}{\frac{7}{5} m}$$

$$y_2 = \frac{5}{7} y_1 .$$

Hence, the sphere travels further.

• PROBLEM 209

A uniform, spherical bowling ball is projected without initial rotation along a horizontal bowling alley. How far will the ball skid along the alley before it begins to roll without slipping? Assume that the ball does not bounce. (See figure).

Solution: The ball is projected along the alley at point A. When it hits the alley at point B, the ball will roll and slip. At point C, the ball has begun to roll without slipping. In order to find the distance at which skidding (or slipping) stops, we must find the acceleration of the ball, and then solve for its position.

Applying Newton's Second Law to the horizontal direction of motion of the ball, we obtain

$$ma_x = -f \tag{1}$$

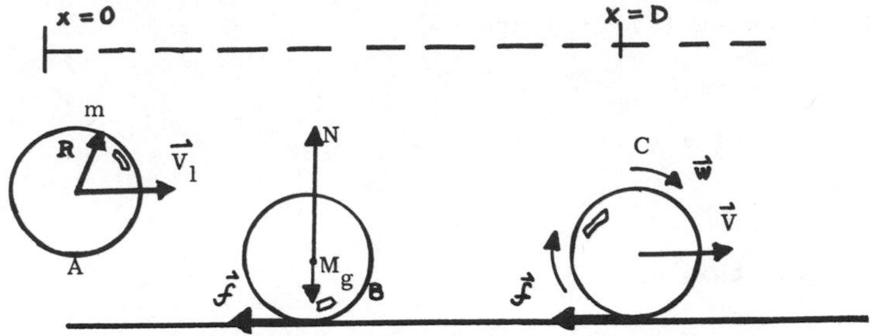

where a_x is the horizontal acceleration of the ball of mass m. Note that we take a_x to be positive in the positive x-direction. Applying the Second Law to the vertical direction

$$ma_y = N - mg$$

But a_y, the y acceleration of the ball, is zero since the ball doesn't bounce. Therefore

$$N = mg \tag{2}$$

In order to calculate torques, $\vec{\tau}$, about 0, we use

$$\vec{\tau} = I\vec{\alpha} \tag{3}$$

where $\vec{\alpha}$ is the angular acceleration of the ball. But, the only torque acting on the ball is due to f. Hence

$$\vec{\tau} = \vec{r} \times \vec{f}$$

where $\vec{r}$ is the location of the point of application of $\vec{f}$. Since $\vec{r}$ and $\vec{f}$ are perpendicular (see figure),

$$\tau = Rf$$

From (3)

$$Rf = I\alpha \tag{4}$$

where α is positive in a direction pointing into the plane of the figure. Now, if f is constant, (1) tells us that a_x is constant, since

$$a_x = \frac{-f}{m}$$

Hence, we may use the kinematics equations for constant acceleration to find

$$v_x = v_{x_0} \frac{-f}{m} t \tag{5}$$

$$x = x_0 + v_{x_0} t \frac{-f}{2m} t^2 \tag{6}$$

where x_0 and v_{x_0} are the initial position and velocity of the ball.

Similarly, we use (4) to solve for the angular velocity of the ball.

$$\alpha = \frac{Rf}{I}$$

But $\alpha = \frac{d\omega}{dt}$ where ω is the angular velocity of the ball. Therefore

$$\frac{d\omega}{dt} = \frac{Rf}{I}$$

$$\int_{\omega_0}^{\omega} d\omega = \frac{Rf}{I} \int_0^t dt$$

where ω_0 is the angular velocity at $t = 0$.

$$\omega = \omega_0 + \frac{Rf}{I} t \tag{7}$$

While the ball is skidding, (7) and (5) are completely independent relations. However, when the ball starts rolling without slipping, they are related by

$$v_x = \omega R \tag{8}$$

Substituting (7) and (5) in (8)

$$v_{x_0} - \frac{f}{m}t' = \omega_0 R + \frac{R^2 f}{I}t'$$

But $\omega_0 = 0$. Solving for t'

$$v_{x_0} = t'\left(\frac{R^2 f}{I} + \frac{f}{m}\right)$$

$$t' = \frac{v_{x_0}}{\frac{R^2 f}{I} + \frac{f}{m}} \tag{9}$$

At $t = t'$, slipping stops. To find the position of the ball when slipping stops, we substitute (9) in (6)

$$x = x_0 - v_{x_0}\left[\frac{v_{x_0}}{\frac{R^2 f}{I} + \frac{f}{m}}\right] - \frac{f}{2m}\left[\frac{v_{x_0}^2}{\left(\frac{R^2 f}{I} + \frac{f}{m}\right)}\right]$$

Furthermore, $x_0 = 0$ (see figure), and

$$x = \frac{v_{x_0}^2}{f\left(\frac{R^2}{I} + \frac{1}{m}\right)} - \frac{-f\,v_{x_0}^2}{2mf^2\left(\frac{R^2}{I} + \frac{1}{m}\right)^2} \tag{10}$$

The frictional force law is

$$f = u_k N \tag{11}$$

where N is the normal force of the alley on the ball, and u_k is the coefficient of kinetic friction. (We use the coefficient of kinetic friction because the ball skids from $t = 0$ to $t = t'$.) Substituting (2) in (11)

$$f = u_k mg$$

Substituting this in (10),

$$x = \frac{v_{x_0}^2}{u_k mg\left(\frac{R^2}{I} + \frac{1}{m}\right)} - \frac{v_{x_0}^2}{2u_k m^2 g\left(\frac{R^2}{I} + \frac{1}{m}\right)^2}$$

$$x = \frac{v_{x_0}^2}{u_k mg\left(\frac{R^2}{I} + \frac{1}{m}\right)}\left\{1 - \frac{1}{2m\left(\frac{R^2}{I} + \frac{1}{m}\right)}\right\}$$

For a sphere $I = 2/5\ mR^2$ and $R^2/I = R^2/(2/5\ mR^2) = 5/2m$ then

$$x = \frac{v_{x_0}^2}{u_k mg\left(\frac{5}{2m} + \frac{1}{m}\right)}\left\{1 - \frac{1}{2m\left(\frac{5}{2m} + \frac{1}{m}\right)}\right\}$$

$$x = \frac{2v_{x_0}^2}{7u_k g} \left\{ 1 - \frac{1}{7} \right\} = \frac{12v_{x_0}^2}{49\, u_k g}$$

This is the position at which slipping stops.

• PROBLEM 210

A circus clown whose mass is 1×10^2kg steps onto the outer edge of a large disk with a radius of 2.0×10^1m and a mass of 2×10^3kg. Assume that the disk is mounted on a frictionless bearing with a vertical axis of rotation and is initially at rest. If the clown now runs clockwise around the edge of the disk at a speed of 2m/s, how fast does the disk turn and what is the angular momentum?

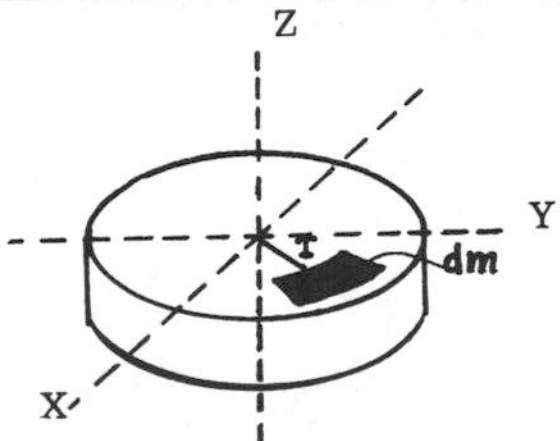

Solution: Since no external torques are acting on the clown-disk system, we may apply the principle of conservation of angular momentum to this system. The angular momentum of the system before the clown stepped on the disk was zero. Therefore, after the clown steps on the disk, the angular momentum of the disk-clown system must remain zero, or

$$\vec{J}_{system} = 0$$

But

$$\vec{J}_{system} = \vec{J}_{disk} + \vec{J}_{clown} = 0$$

and

$$\vec{J}_{disk} = - \vec{J}_{clown}$$

This last equation states that the magnitude of $\vec{J}_{disk}$ and $\vec{J}_{clown}$ are the same, but that $\vec{J}_{disk}$ and $\vec{J}_{clown}$ are opposite in direction. Hence, because the clown is running clockwise, the disk travels counter-clockwise. If it is assumed that the clown can be represented as a particle, the orbital angular momentum of the clown, is

$$\vec{J} = \vec{r} \times \vec{p}$$

where $\vec{p}$ is the linear momentum of the clown, and $\vec{r}$ is a vector from the axis of rotation to the clown. Because the clown is running in a circle $\vec{r}$ is perpendicular to $\vec{p}$ and

$$|\vec{J}_{clown}| = rp_{clown} = mrv_{clown}$$

$$= (1 \times 10^2 \text{kg})(2 \text{ m/s})(2 \times 10^1 \text{m}) = 4 \times 10^3 \text{J} \cdot \text{s}$$

which is also the magnitude of the disk's angular momentum. Now,

$$|\vec{J}_{disk}| = I_{disk}\, \omega_{disk}$$

where I_{disk} is the moment of inertia of the disk about its axis of rotation. Therefore, since $|\vec{J}_{disk}| = |\vec{J}_{clown}|$,

$$\omega_{disk} = \frac{|\vec{J}_{clown}|}{I_{disk}} \qquad (1)$$

The only variable we don't know in (1) is I_{disk}. This we now calculate.

By definition,

$$I_{disk} = \int r^2\, dm$$

where r is the distance of a mass element dm from the axis about which we calculate I_{disk} (see figure), and the integral is taken over the mass of the disk. Now,

$$\rho = \frac{dm}{dv}$$

where ρ is the density of the disk and dv is a volume element. Whence

$$I_{disk} = \int r^2 \rho\, dv$$

If we consider the disk to be very thin, $dv = ds$, an element of area of the disk, and

$$ds = r\, dr\, d\theta$$

$$I_{disk} = \int_0^{2\pi}\int_0^R \rho r^3\, dr\, d\theta$$

$$I_{disk} = \int_0^{2\pi} \rho(R^4/4)\, d\theta$$

$$I_{disk} = \frac{\pi\rho R^4}{2}$$

where R is the disk radius. But $\rho = M/\pi R^2$, M being the disk's mass.

$$I_{disk} = (\pi R^4/2)(M/\pi R^2) = MR^2/2$$

Using (1),

$$\omega_{disk} = \frac{|\vec{J}_{clown}|}{MR^2/2} = \frac{4 \times 10^3 J\cdot s}{(2\times10^3 kg/2)(4\times10^2 m^2)}$$

$$\omega_{disk} = \frac{4 \times 10^3 J\cdot s}{4 \times 10^5 m^2\cdot kg} = 10^{-2}\ N\cdot m\cdot s/kg\cdot m^2$$

$$\omega_{disk} = 10^{-2}\ \frac{kg\cdot m^2/s^2\cdot s}{kg\cdot m^2} = 10^{-2}\ s^{-1}$$

Furthermore, $v_{disk} = \omega_{disk} R$ is the velocity of a point on the rim of the disk.

$$v_{disk} = (10^{-2} s^{-1})(2 \times 10 m) = 0.2\ m/s$$

The disk rotates much slower than the clown runs around the edge.

FRAMES OF REFERENCE

• PROBLEM 211

An elevator is descending with an acceleration of $5\ ft\cdot s^{-2}$. The shade on the ceiling light falls to the floor of the elevator, 9 ft below. At the instant that it falls, one of the passengers sees it, and realizes that the shade will hit his foot. How long does he have to get his foot out of the way?

Solution: At the instant that the light shade becomes detached, it has a downward speed of v_0, and it will drop freely under the action of gravity. Suppose that there is an observer outside the elevator. By the time the shade strikes the (moving) floor of the elevator, it will have been seen by the observer to have dropped a distance s in a time t. This distance is given by the free fall equation

$$s = v_0 t + \tfrac{1}{2}gt^2.$$

In the same time t, the elevator floor will have traveled s - 9 ft (9 ft less than the shade, since the elevator floor doesn't have to traverse the length of the elevator) with the acceleration of 5 ft $\cdot$ s^{-2}, having started with the same downward speed v_0.

$$\therefore \quad s - 9\text{ ft} = v_0 t + \tfrac{1}{2} \times 5\text{ ft}\cdot s^{-2} \times t^2.$$

Subtract one equation from the other. Thus

$$9\text{ ft} = \tfrac{1}{2}(g - 5\text{ ft}\cdot s^{-2})t^2 = \tfrac{1}{2} \times 27\text{ ft}\cdot s^{-2} \times t^2.$$

This equation could have been obtained more easily by considering the motion of the shade relative to the elevator in an accelerated frame of reference. For, relative to the elevator, the light shade starts off with zero velocity and has an acceleration of g - 5 ft$\cdot s^{-2}$. Thus, applying the same equation of motion as before, we find that the shade drops 9 ft relative to the elevator in a time t, and

$$9\text{ ft} = 0 \times t + \tfrac{1}{2}(g - 5\text{ ft}\cdot s^{-2})t^2.$$

$$t = \sqrt{\frac{2 \times 9\text{ ft}}{27\text{ ft}\cdot s^{-2}}} = \sqrt{\frac{2\ s^2}{3}} = 0.82\text{ s}.$$

The passenger has therefore less than 1 s to get his foot out of the way, and must react rapidly.

• PROBLEM 212

A boat travels directly upstream in a river, moving with constant but unknown speed v with respect to the water. At the start of this trip upstream, a bottle is dropped over the side. After 15 minutes the boat turns around and heads downstream. It catches up with the bottle when the bottle has drifted one mile downstream from the point at which it was dropped into the water. What is the current in the stream?

Solution: Consider a coordinate system at rest with respect to the water. Then the water is at rest and it is the banks which appear to move upstream. The bottle is at rest with respect to the water. From the point of view of this coordinate system, it is just as though the boat were moving at speed v in a perfectly still pond.

We can see that the return trip downstream must also take 15 minutes. Once it is known that the round trip takes half an hour, we can see that the current in the river must be 2 miles per hour since the bottle moves one mile in a half hour.

• PROBLEM 213

Suppose the force applied to a mass M by a spring stretched in the x direction is $F_x = - Cx$, where C is a constant. Consider a noninertial frame with the acceleration $\vec{a}_o = a_o\hat{x}$ in the x direction. Derive a relation between the displacement of the spring (x) and the acceleration of the noninertial frame (a_o) relative to the earth.

Solution: If we wish to analyze this problem from the point of view of an observer in a non-inertial reference frame, we cannot use Newton's Laws in their usual form. (A non-inertial frame is one which accelerates with respect to the fixed stars.) However, if we modify these laws, we may apply them in accelerated frames. The modified form of Newton's Second Law is

$$\vec{F} - \vec{F}' = M\vec{a}'' \qquad (1)$$

where $\vec{a}''$ is the acceleration of the system as examined with respect to the non-inertial frame,
$\vec{F}$ is the sum of all real forces acting on the mass M,
and $-\vec{F}'$ is the sum of all fictitious forces acting. (Real forces are gravitational, elastic, etc., while fictitious forces arise only because we insist upon doing the problem in an accelerated frame. Examples of the latter are Coriolis forces, centrifugal forces, etc.)

In our case, M is at rest in the accelerated frame, so that $\vec{a}'' = 0$. $\vec{F}$ is the real force acting on M and is supplied by the spring. Hence,

$$F = - Cx \qquad (2)$$

The minus sign indicates that F is a restoring force. No matter how we displace the mass, the spring tends to restore M to its initial position. $- F'$, the fictitious force, is defined as $- \vec{F}' = - M\vec{a}'$, where $\vec{a}'$ is the acceleration of the non-inertial frame with respect to the earth $\left(a_o\hat{x}\text{ in this problem}\right)$. Therefore,

$$- F' = - Ma_o \qquad (3)$$

Inserting (3) and (2) in (1) we find

$$- Cx - Ma_o = 0 \qquad (4)$$

Solving (4) for a_o, we obtain

$$a_o = - \frac{Cx}{M} \qquad (5)$$

which is the desired relation.

The noninertial frame might be an aircraft or an automobile. We see that Eq. (5) describes the operation of an accelerometer in which a mass M is attached to a spring and constrained to move in the direction of the acceleration. The displacement x of the mass measures the acceleration a_o of the noninertial reference frame.

• PROBLEM 214

Let the acceleration of a noninertial frame, a freely falling elevator, be

$$\vec{a}_o = - g\hat{y}$$

where $\hat{y}$ is measured upward from the surface of the earth and g is the acceleration of gravity. Under these conditions, what is the net force acting on a mass M at rest in the elevator?

Solution: Note that in this problem, we are doing an experiment in a noninertial reference frame. It is very important to realize that Newton's Laws only hold in inertial frames. If we want to analyze this experiment from the point of view of an observer in a noninertial frame, we must use a modified form of Newton's Second Law,

$$M\vec{a}'' = \vec{F} - \vec{F}' \qquad (1)$$

where $\vec{a}''$ is the acceleration of M as observed in the noninertial frame (the elevator), $\vec{F}$ is the sum of all real forces acting on M (i.e., tensions, gravity, etc.) and $-\vec{F}'$ is the sum of all fictitious forces. These latter forces arise because we are doing our experiment in a non-inertial frame. (Fictitious forces include Coriolis forces, centrifugal forces, etc.) In this particular problem, $\vec{a}'' = 0$ because the mass M is at rest in the elevator. $\vec{F}$, the sum of the real forces acting on M, includes Mg, the weight of M, and N, the normal force exerted by the floor of the elevator on the mass. Hence,

$$F = N - Mg \qquad (2)$$

where the minus sign appears because N and Mg are in opposite directions. We may now substitute equation (2) into equation (1) and solve the latter for $\vec{F}'$:

$$0 = F - F'$$
$$F' = F$$
$$F' = N - Mg \qquad (3)$$

Now, $-F'$, the fictitious force, is defined as $-M\vec{a}'$, where $\vec{a}'$ is the acceleration of the noninertial frame with respect to the earth ($-g\hat{y}$ in our case). Hence,

$$-F' = Mg \tag{4}$$

Inserting this in (3), we find

$$-Mg = N - Mg \tag{5}$$

$$N = 0 \tag{6}$$

Hence, the floor exerts no force on M. If this is the case, then M must be floating inside the elevator, i.e., M is weightless.

• PROBLEM 215

Consider a point mass M at rest in a noninertial frame, so that in this frame a = 0. The noninertial frame rotates uniformly about an axis fixed with respect to an inertial frame. What is the acceleration of M with respect to an inertial reference frame? What is the fictitious force acting on M?

Inertial Frame:

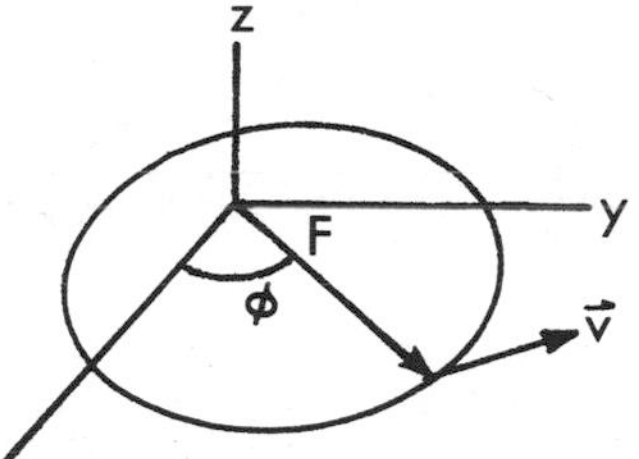

Non-Inertial Frame:

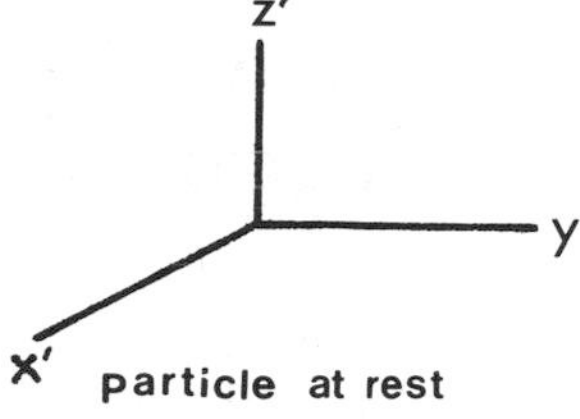

Solution: Viewed from an inertial reference frame, M seems to be travelling in a circular path with constant speed. This is so because the noninertial frame, in which M is at rest, is rotating uniformly with respect to the inertial frame. Hence, to restate the first part of the problem, we are looking for the acceleration of a particle undergoing circular motion with constant speed.

Now, acceleration is defined as

$$\vec{a} = \frac{d^2\vec{r}}{dt^2} \tag{1}$$

where $\vec{r}$ is the vector from the origin to the particle. We may write $\vec{r}$ in terms of its x and y components as

$$\vec{r} = x\hat{\imath} + y\hat{\jmath} \tag{2}$$

where $\hat{\imath}$ and $\hat{\jmath}$ are unit vectors (vectors of magnitude 1) in the positive x and y directions, respectively. We may also write

$$\begin{aligned} x &= r\cos\phi \\ y &= r\sin\phi \end{aligned} \tag{3}$$

where r is the radius of the circle in which M travels. Substituting (3) in (2) we obtain:

$$\vec{r} = r\ (\hat{\imath} \cos \phi + \hat{\jmath} \sin \phi)$$

Noting that r, $\hat{\imath}$, and $\hat{\jmath}$ are constant, and differentiating twice with respect to time, we obtain:

$$\frac{d\vec{r}}{dt} = r(- \hat{\imath} \sin \phi + \hat{\jmath} \cos \phi) \frac{d\phi}{dt}$$

$$\frac{d^2\vec{r}}{dt^2} = r\ (- \hat{\imath} \cos \phi - \hat{\jmath} \sin \phi)\left(\frac{d\phi}{dt}\right)^2$$

$$\frac{d^2\vec{r}}{dt^2} = - \vec{r} \left(\frac{d\phi}{dt}\right)^2 \qquad (4)$$

We now define $\frac{d\phi}{dt}$ to be equal to ω, the angular velocity of the particle. (Physically, this is the number of radians the particle traces out per second.) Then, from (4) and (1)

$$\vec{a} = \frac{d^2\vec{r}}{dt^2} = -\omega^2\ \vec{r} \qquad (5)$$

This acceleration, which always points in the $-\vec{r}$ direction (towards the center of the circular path), is called the centripetal acceleration.

If we now choose to analyze the forces acting on M from the point of view of an observer sitting in the noninertial frame, we must use a modified form of Newton's Second Law, because the usual form ($\vec{F} = m\vec{a}$) only holds in inertial reference frames. The new form of the Second Law is

$$\vec{F} - \vec{F}' = M\vec{a}'' \qquad (6)$$

where $\vec{a}''$ is the acceleration of the system being examined as recorded in the noninertial frame, $\vec{F}$ is the sum of all "real" forces acting on the system (i.e., tensions, gravity), $-\vec{F}'$ is the sum of all "fictitious" forces acting on the system (Coriolis forces, centrifugal forces, etc.), and M is the mass of the system. In our example, since M is at rest in the noninertial system, $\vec{a}'' = 0$. Substituting this in equation (6), we find:

$$\vec{F} = \vec{F}' \qquad (7)$$

Now, of course, we must obtain the same value for $\vec{F}$ no matter which frame we examine the mass M from, whether it be the rotating frame or the non-rotating frame, because $\vec{F}$ represents all real forces acting on M. Since we know nothing about $-\vec{F}'$, let us find $\vec{F}$ in the inertial frame, and substitute this $\vec{F}$ into (7). In this way, we will be using our knowledge of dynamics in non-rotating frames to foster our knowledge of dynamics in rotating frames, and we will obtain $-\vec{F}'$.

In the inertial frame, we may use the standard form of the Second Law, and obtain:

$$\vec{F} = M\vec{a} \tag{8}$$

From the first part of this solution we known that $\vec{a} = -\omega^2\vec{r}$. Substituting in (8), we find

$$\vec{F} = -M\omega^2\vec{r} \tag{9}$$

Now, using (7), we obtain

$$\vec{F} = \vec{F}' = -M\omega^2\vec{r}$$

But, $-\vec{F} = M\omega^2\vec{r}$, and this is just the fictitious force acting on M. Note that it points away from the axis of rotation, and, hence, is called a centrifugal force.

• PROBLEM 216

A river flows due north. Which side of the bank should be the most worn?

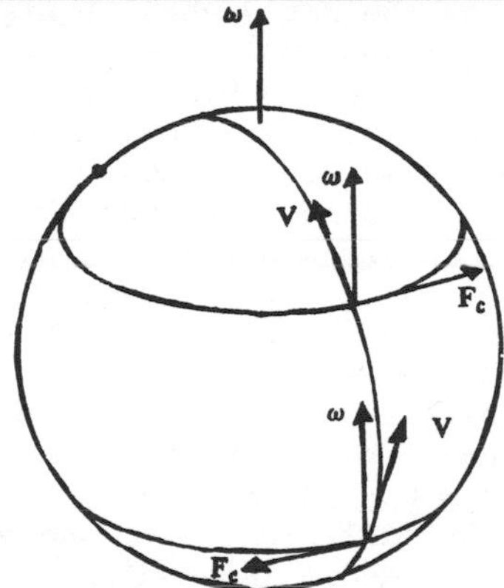

Solution: This will depend on the hemisphere in which the river exists. The force which presses the river against the bank is the Coriolis force:

$$\vec{F}_c = 2\, m\vec{v} \times \vec{\omega}$$

In the **northern** hemisphere, we see from the diagram that $\vec{v} \times \vec{\omega}$ is to the east, whereas in the southern hemisphere $\vec{v} \times \vec{\omega}$ is to the west. Thus the river will tend to wear down its right bank in the northern hemisphere and left bank in the southern hemisphere.

• PROBLEM 217

Three coordinate systems S, S', and S" have a common x-axis. With respect to S, S' moves in the direction of the x-axis with a speed v, and S" accelerates along the x-axis with acceleration a. At time $t = 0$, the origins of all three coordinate systems coincide and S" has zero velocity with respect to S. At that instant, a man starts out running from the origin along the x-axis and an observer in S measures his speed as constant and of magnitude $u(u > v)$. How do observers in S' and S" describe his motion, using Galilean relativity?

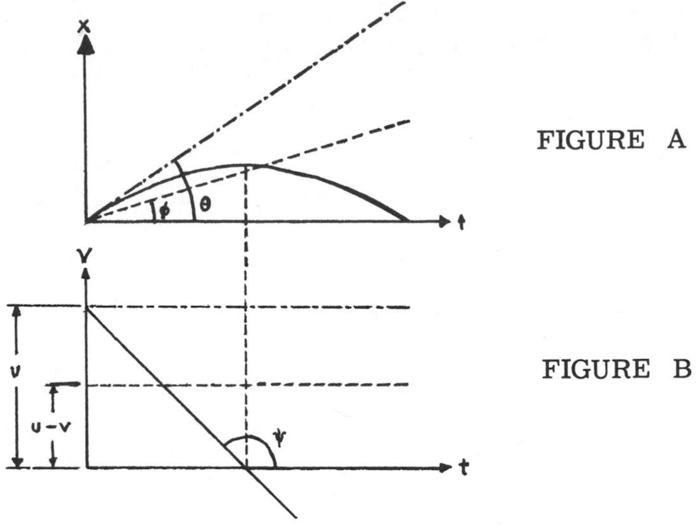

Solution: The observer in S sees the man running along the x-axis with constant speed u. The motion is thus observed as one in which the x-displacement increases linearly with time. On a displacement-time diagram, the motion appears as the dot-dashed straight line at an angle θ to the t-axis, where $\tan\theta = x/t = u$; and on a velocity-time diagram it appears as the dot-dashed straight line parallel to the t-axis. (See figs. (a) and (b)).

To an observer in S', the man has only the speed $(u - v)$, the relative speed between the two. But the man is still seen as moving with constant speed and his motion is shown in the diagrams by the dashed straight lines. The angle ϕ is such that $\tan\phi = u - v$.

An observer in S'', who is accelerating along the x-axis with acceleration a relative to S and therefore to the running man, considers himself at rest and therefore attributes to the runner an acceleration of $-a$. The runner appears to start off with velocity u but to decelerate gradually to rest and then go backward. His velocity at any time is seen to be, using the kinematics equations for constant acceleration, $V = u - at$, and on the velocity-time diagram this is represented by the full line at an angle ψ to the t-axis, where $\tan\psi = -a$. Also his x-displacement relative to the origin of S'' is given by the constant acceleration kinematics equation $x = ut - \frac{1}{2}at^2$, which is represented by a parabola in the displacement-time diagram, tangent to the dot-dashed line at the origin and having its highest point at the time t where the corresponding velocity-time graph cuts the t-axis.

• PROBLEM 218

In an inertial frame a body moves freely with a trajectory given by

$$x_I = v_0 t; \qquad y_I = 0; \quad z_I = 0.$$

What is the trajectory in a frame rotating with constant angular velocity ω counterclockwise about the z_I axis?

Solution: In the figure the particle is travelling at velocity v_0 in the inertial coordinate system. After time t, the body has traveled a distance $v_0 t$ along the x-axis. Now, we consider a coordinate system which rotates with angular velocity ω about the z_I axis. Therefore the z-

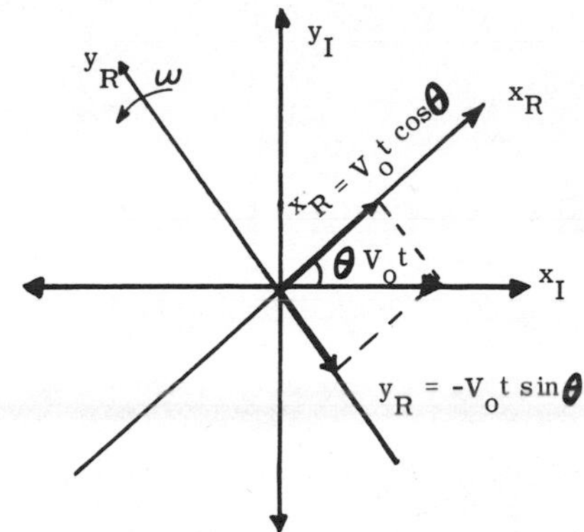

axis of the new system coincides with the inertial z_I axis and the angle between the rotating (x_R, y_R) axes and the inertial (x_I, y_I) axes is by definition of ω, $\theta = \omega t$.

The coordinates of the position of the particle in the rotating frame in terms of the coordinates of the particle in the inertial frame can be read off the figure as

$$x_R = v_0 t \cos \omega t$$

$$y_R = - v_0 t \sin \omega t$$

$$z_R = 0.$$

CHAPTER 5

ENERGY/POWER

POTENTIAL ENERGY

• PROBLEM 219

What is the potential energy of a 1-pound weight that has been raised 16 feet?

Solution: Potential energy is given by mgs, where mg is the weight of the object that has been raised. But mg is also the net force acting on this object, hence, via Newton's Second Law, we obtain

$$F = mg$$

Therefore

$$P.E. = mgs = Fs$$

Substituting the given data into this relation, we find

$$P.E. = Fs = 1 \times 16 = 16 \text{ ft-lb.}$$

• PROBLEM 220

Spring-Heel Jack was a legendary English criminal who was never captured because of his ability to jump over high walls and other obstacles which his pursuers were unable to scale. It is believed that he had a powerful spring attached to each shoe for this purpose. Assuming that he weighed 150 lb and that his springs were compressed by 1 in. when he stood on them, by how much did he need to keep his springs compressed on one of his operations in order to be ready to clear a 10-ft wall in the event of an emergency?

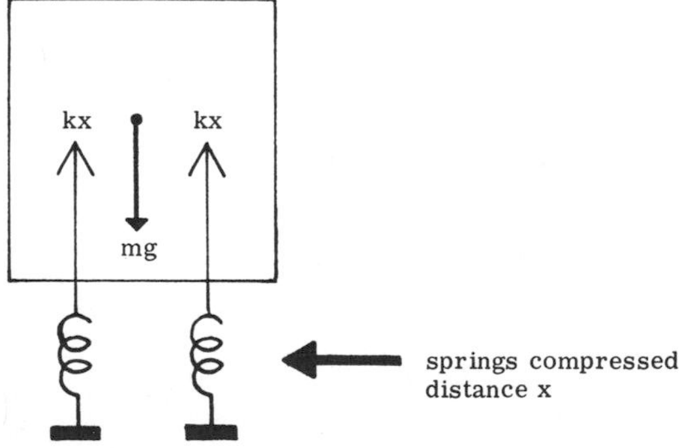

Solution: The figure shows an idealized drawing of Spring-Heel Jack. When Jack stands up, the springs are compressed a distance x. When in equilibrium, the net force on Jack is zero. Hence,

$$2kx = mg$$

or $$k = \frac{mg}{2x}$$

where m is his mass and k is the spring constant. Thus

$$k = \frac{(150 \text{ lb})}{(2)(1 \text{ in})} = \frac{75 \text{ lb}}{\frac{1}{12} \text{ ft}} = 900 \text{ lb/ft}.$$

If Jack wishes to clear a height h while remaining erect, the potential energy stored in the springs must have been sufficient to raise his 150-lb weight through a vertical distance h. But if x was the compression of each spring, then by conservation of energy

$$\tfrac{1}{2} kx^2 + \tfrac{1}{2} kx^2 = mgh$$

$$x^2 = mgh/k$$

$$\therefore \quad x^2 = \frac{150 \times 10 \text{ ft} \cdot \text{lb}}{900 \text{ lb} \cdot \text{ft}^{-1}} = \frac{20}{12} \text{ ft}^2.$$

$$x = \sqrt{1.67} \text{ ft} = 1.29 \text{ ft}.$$

• PROBLEM 221

A boy drops a rubber ball from a height of 4 feet and lets it bounce. If the ball loses 10% of its energy, due to friction of compression on each bounce, how many bounces will it take before the ball will only rise 2 feet above the ground?

Solution: When the boy first lets go of the ball, its energy is purely potential and is given by $E_p = mgh$ where h is the ball's original height above the ground. (In this problem h = 4 feet). When the ball hits the ground its energy is purely kinetic. This is also the case when the ball just leaves the ground and begins its upward flight. As it rises its energy gradually changes from kinetic to potential. We note from the above equation that the potential energy is directly proportional to the height the ball rises. Thus, each time the ball bounces and loses 10% of its energy, it rises to 9/10 of its previous height. After the first bounce the ball rises (9/10) 4 feet, then after 2 bounces it rises

$$\left(\frac{9}{10}\right)\left(\frac{9}{10}\right)4 \text{ feet} = \left(\frac{9}{10}\right)^2 4 \text{ feet}.$$

We can see that after n bounces:

$$\text{maximum height of ball} = \left(\frac{9}{10}\right)^n 4 \text{ feet}$$

Thus, we set the expression for maximum height equal to 2 feet and solve for n:

$$\left(\frac{9}{10}\right)^n 4 \text{ feet} = 2 \text{ feet}$$

$$\left(\frac{9}{10}\right)^n = \tfrac{1}{2}$$

$$n \log \frac{9}{10} = \log \tfrac{1}{2}$$

$$n[\log 9 - \log 10] = -\log 2$$

$$n[0.9542 - 1.0000] = -0.3010$$

$$-0.0458n = -0.3010$$

$$n = 6.55$$

We must round this off to 7 since physically we cannot have a fraction of a bounce.

A block of mass m, initially at rest, is dropped from a height h onto a spring whose force constant is k. Find the maximum distance y that the spring will be compressed. See figure.

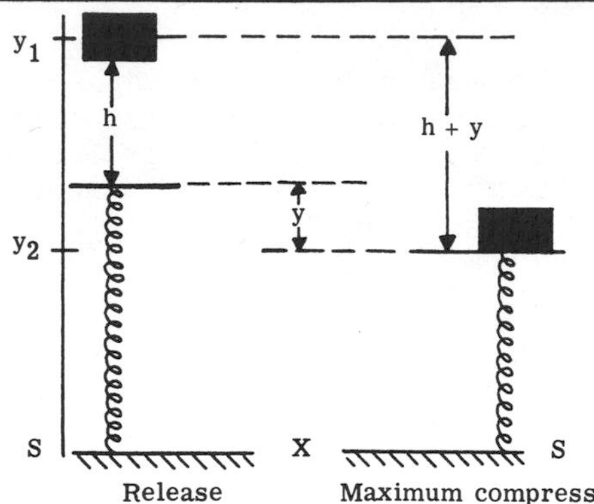

The total fall of the block is h + y.

Solution: The general procedure used in solving any problem in mechanics is to calculate all the forces acting on the system and then derive the equation of motion of the system.

An easier way to do mechanics problems involves the use of conservation principles. These laws are not applicable to all problems, but when they are, they simplify the calculation of the solution tremendously.

In this problem, we may use the principle of conservation of energy. We relate the energy of the block before it was released to the block's energy at the point of maximum compression (see figure). At the moment of release, the kinetic energy is zero. At the moment when maximum compression occurs, there is also no kinetic energy.

As shown in the figure, the reference level for gravitational potential energy is the surface S. The initial gravitational potential energy of m is mgy_1.

At the point of maximum compression, the potential energy of m is mgy_2. However, at this point, the spring is compressed a distance y and also has elastic potential energy $\frac{1}{2}ky^2$. Hence, equating the energy at the point of release to the energy at the point of maximum compression,

$$mgy_1 = mgy_2 + \tfrac{1}{2}ky^2$$

$$mg(y_1 - y_2) = \tfrac{1}{2}ky^2$$

But $y_1 - y_2 = h + y$ and

$$mg(h + y) = \tfrac{1}{2}ky^2$$

$$y^2 = \frac{2\,mg}{k}(h + y)$$

$$y^2 - \left(\frac{2\,mg}{k}\right)y - \frac{2\,mgh}{k} = 0$$

Therefore, using the quadratic formula to solve for y,

$$y = \frac{1}{2}\left(\frac{2mg}{k} \pm \sqrt{(2mg/k)^2 + (8mgh/k)}\right) .$$

• PROBLEM 223

A 40-lb stone is pushed, on a 30° incline, to the top of a building 100 feet tall. By how much does its potential energy increase?

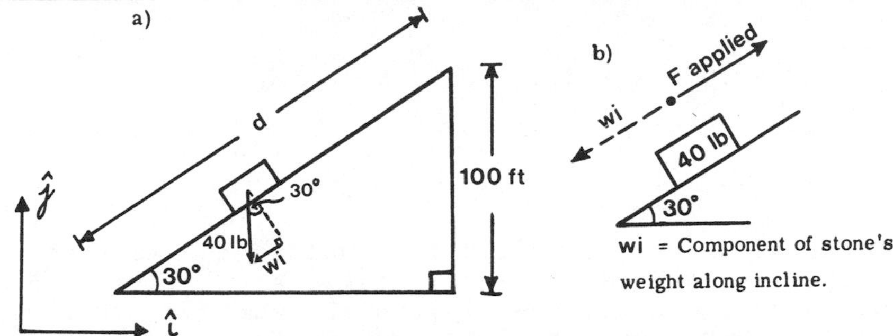

Solution: The change in a body's gravitational potential energy is the negative of the work done by gravity on the object in displacing it. By definition, this is

$$W = -\int \vec{F}_g \cdot d\vec{r}$$

where $\vec{F}_g$, the force of gravity, is

$$\vec{F}_g = -mg\hat{j} \qquad (1)$$

The symbol $\hat{j}$ is a unit vector in the positive y direction (see figure). Now

$$d\vec{r} = dx\hat{i} + dy\hat{j}$$

where $\hat{i}$ is a unit vector in the positive x direction. Then

$$\vec{F}_g \cdot d\vec{r} = -mg\hat{j} \cdot (dx\hat{i} + dy\hat{j}) = -mgdy$$

and

$$W = -\int -mgdy \qquad (2)$$

We evaluate (2) over the path of motion of the block. If we take the origin of our coordinate system at the foot of the plane, y varies from 0 to 100 ft. Therefore

$$W = mg\int_0^{100\text{ ft}} dy = mg(100\text{ ft})$$

$$W = (40\text{ lb})(100\text{ ft}) = 4000\text{ ft. lb.}$$

• PROBLEM 224

A 200-kg satellite is lifted to an orbit of 2.20×10^4 mi radius. How much additional potential energy does it acquire relative to the surface of the earth?

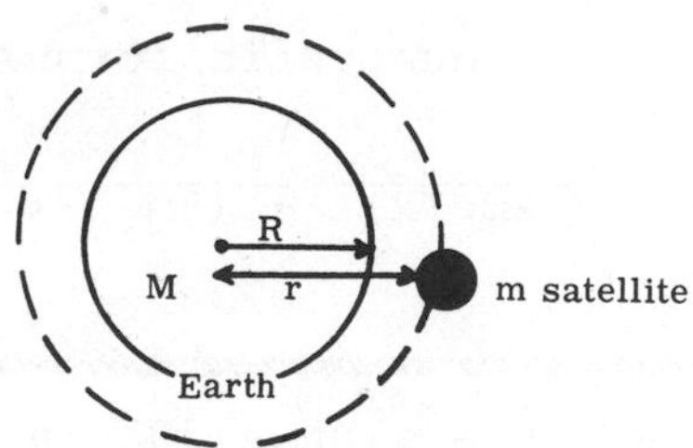

Solution: As in the diagram, R is the earth's radius, M is the earth's mass, m is the satellite mass, and r is the distance between the earth's center and the satellite.

$$R = 6.37 \times 10^6 \text{ m}$$

$$r = 2.20 \times 10^4 \text{ mi} = 3.54 \times 10^7 \text{ m}$$

$$M = 5.98 \times 10^{24} \text{ kg}$$

$$m = 200 \text{ kg}$$

The additional potential energy is equal to the work done against the earth's gravitational field. At a distance R from the earth's center, that is, on the earth's surface, the satellite has a potential energy, $U_{surface}$

$$U_{surface} = -\frac{GMm}{R}$$

In orbit of radius r the potential is $U_{orbit} = -\frac{GMm}{r}$

Then the additional potential energy involved in launching the rocket to its orbit, ΔU, is given by

$$\Delta U = U_{orbit} - U_{surface} = -\frac{GMm}{r} - \left(-\frac{GMm}{R}\right) = GMm\left(\frac{1}{R} - \frac{1}{r}\right)$$

$$= (6.67 \times 10^{-11} \text{ nt} - \text{m}^2/\text{kg}^2)(5.98 \times 10^{24} \text{ kg})(200\text{kg})$$

$$\times \left(\frac{1}{6.37 \times 10^6 \text{ m}} - \frac{1}{3.54 \times 10^7 \text{ m}}\right)$$

$$= 1.03 \times 10^{10} \text{ joules}$$

This is about equal to the work needed to lift an object weighing 3800 tons to a height of 1000 ft above the earth.
Note that the change in potential energy of the satellite cannot be found by using U = mgh. This formula applies only to objects near the earth's surface, where g is approximately constant.

KINETIC ENERGY

• PROBLEM 225

The mass of a bullet is 2 grams and its velocity is 30,000 centimeters per second (approximately true for a .22 caliber bullet). What is its kinetic energy?

Solution: $K.E. = \frac{1}{2} Mv^2$

$$= \frac{2\ \text{gm} \times (30{,}000\ \text{cm/sec})^2}{2}$$

$$= (30{,}000)^2 \text{ergs.}$$

• PROBLEM 226

Air consists of a mixture of gas molecules which are constantly moving. Compute the kinetic energy K of a molecule that is moving with a speed of 500 m/s. Assume that the mass of this particle is 4.6×10^{-26} kg.

Solution: The mass of the gas molecule, $m = 4.6 \times 10^{-26}$ kg, and its speed $v = 5 \times 10^2$ m/s, are the known observables. Using the equation:

$$K = \tfrac{1}{2} mv^2$$

$$K = (\tfrac{1}{2})\left(4.6 \times 10^{-26}\ \text{kg}\right)\left(5.0 \times 10^2\ \text{m/s}\right)^2$$

$$= 5.75 \times 10^{-21}\ \text{J}.$$

• PROBLEM 227

A pitcher can throw a baseball weighing 5 ounces so that it will have a velocity of 96 feet per second. What is its kinetic energy?

Solution: $5\ \text{oz} = \frac{5}{16}\ \text{lb}$

Therefore, since

$$\text{K. E.} = \frac{1}{2} mv^2 = \frac{1}{2}\left(\frac{W}{g}\right)v^2$$

where W is the weight of the ball. This is equal to

$$\frac{5\ \text{lb} \times (96\ \text{ft/sec})^2}{2 \times 16 \times (32\ \text{ft/sec}^2)} = 45\ \text{ft-lb}.$$

• PROBLEM 228

If we project a body upward with speed 1000 cm/s, how high will it rise?

Solution: We use the principle of energy conservation to find the height h. Assume that the level of projection is the position of zero potential energy. Then at the point of projection the total energy is purely kinetic

$$E = 0 + \tfrac{1}{2}Mv^2 = \tfrac{1}{2}M \times \left(10^6\ \text{cm}^2/\text{s}^2\right)$$

At maximum height v = 0, and the total energy is now purely potential, hence E = Mgh

By equating the two expressions for E, we have

$$Mgh = \tfrac{1}{2} M \times \left(10^6\ \text{cm}^2/\text{s}^2\right)$$

$$h = \frac{\frac{1}{2} \times 10^6 \text{ cm}^2/\text{s}^2}{g} = \frac{10^6 \text{ cm}^2/\text{s}^2}{2(980 \text{ cm/s}^2)}$$

$$h = .51 \times 10^3 \text{ cm}$$

$$h = 510 \text{ cm.}$$

• PROBLEM 229

A free particle, which has a mass of 20 grams is initially at rest. If a force of 100 dynes is applied for a period of 10 sec, what kinetic energy is acquired by the particle?

Solution: In order to calculate the kinetic energy we must compute the final velocity acquired by the particle: $v = at + v_o$ where v_o is the initial velocity. Since we are told that initially the particle is at rest, the expression for velocity becomes $v = at$. Now, from Newton's Laws we know that $a = \frac{F}{m}$. Substituting this for a yields

$$v = \left(\frac{F}{m}\right)t$$

$$= \left(\frac{100 \text{ dynes}}{20 \text{ g}}\right) \times (10 \text{ sec}) = 50 \text{ cm/sec}$$

Then,

$$KE = \frac{1}{2} mv^2$$

$$= \frac{1}{2} \times (20 \text{ g}) \times (50 \text{ cm/sec})^2 = 25{,}000 \text{ ergs}$$

How much work was done by the applied force? The distance moved is

$$s = \frac{1}{2} at^2 = \frac{1}{2}\left(\frac{F}{m}\right)t^2$$

$$= \frac{1}{2} \times \left(\frac{100 \text{ dynes}}{20 \text{ g}}\right) \times (10 \text{ sec})^2 = 250 \text{ cm}$$

so that the work done is $W = Fs$ since the force and displacement are in the same direction.

$$W = (100 \text{ dynes}) \times (250 \text{ cm}) = 25{,}000 \text{ ergs}$$

Thus, the work done is transformed entirely into the kinetic energy of the particle.

• PROBLEM 230

A 1-kg block slides down a rough inclined plane whose height is 1 m. At the bottom, the block has a velocity of 4 m/sec. Is energy conserved?

Solution: Energy will be conserved if the kinetic energy gained by the block is equal to the potential energy lost.

At top: $$PE = mgh$$
$$= (1\ \text{kg}) \times \left(9.8\ \text{m/sec}^2\right) \times (1\ \text{m})$$
$$= 9.8\ \text{J}.$$

At bottom: $$KE = \frac{1}{2}mv^2$$
$$= \frac{1}{2} \times (1\ \text{kg}) \times (4\ \text{m/sec})^2$$
$$= 8\ \text{J}.$$

Apparently, energy is not conserved. But we know that friction is present between the block and the rough plane. A certain amount of energy (1.8 J) has evidently been expended in overcoming this friction. This amount of energy appears as thermal energy and could be detected by measuring the temperature rise in the block and the plane after the slide is completed.

• PROBLEM 231

What is the kinetic energy of a 1-pound weight that has fallen 16 feet?

Solution: Kinetic energy is the energy of an object due to its motion, and it is given by $\frac{1}{2}mv^2$. The mass of a 1 lb object is

$$F = mg$$

$$m = \frac{F}{g}$$

$$m = \frac{1\ \text{lb}}{32\ \text{ft/s}^2} = \frac{1}{32}\ \text{slug}$$

We now calculate the velocity of the object after falling 16 feet:

$\frac{1}{2}gt^2 = d$ and $gt = v$ so $v = \sqrt{2gd}$,

Substituting in this equation we have:

$$v = \sqrt{2(32\ \text{ft/s}^2)(16\ \text{ft})} = 32\ \text{ft/s}$$

The kinetic energy is

$$\text{K.E.} = \frac{1}{2}mv^2$$

$$\text{K.E.} = \frac{1}{2}\,\frac{1}{32}\ \text{slug}\ (32\ \text{ft/s})^2 = 16\ \text{ft-lb}.$$

• PROBLEM 232

What is the kinetic energy of a 3.0-kg ball whose diameter is 15 cm if it rolls across a level surface with a speed of 2.0 m/sec? (Assume that I for the ball is equal to $2/5\ mR^2$, where R is the radius of the ball and m its mass.)

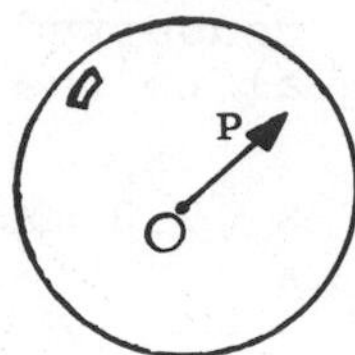

Solution: Consider a point P of the ball, as shown in the figure. Since the ball is rolling and translating, P has rotational kinetic energy and translational kinetic energy. This is true for every point of the ball. Hence, we may represent the total kinetic energy of the ball as

$$E_k = \tfrac{1}{2} mv^2 + \tfrac{1}{2}I\omega^2$$

where m is the mass of the ball, v is its velocity, ω its angular velocity, and I is its moment of inertia about its axis of rotation, O.

By definition

$$\omega = \frac{v}{R} = \frac{2.0 \text{ m/sec}}{0.075 \text{ m}} = 27 \text{ rad/sec}$$

$$I = \frac{2}{5} mR^2 = \frac{2}{5} (3.0 \text{ kg})(0.075 \text{ m})^2$$

$$= 6.8 \times 10^{-3} \text{ kg-m}^2$$

$$E_k = \tfrac{1}{2}(3.0 \text{ kg})(2.0 \text{ m/sec})^2 + \tfrac{1}{2}\left(6.8 \times 10^{-3} \text{ kg-m}^2\right)$$

$$(27 \text{ rad/sec})^2 = 2.5 \text{ joules}$$

• PROBLEM 233

A car coasts down a long hill and then up a smaller one onto a level surface, where it has a speed of 32 ft/sec. If the car started 200 ft above the lowest point on the track, how far above this lowest point is the level surface? Ignore friction.

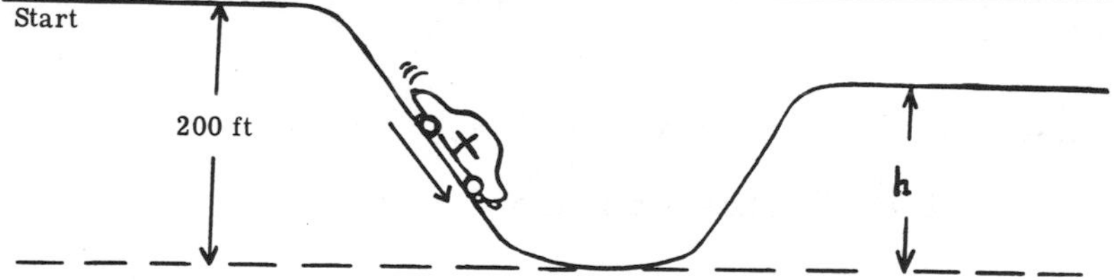

Solution: The initial velocity of the car is zero. Since there is no friction, the change in potential energy of the car equals its increase in kinetic energy. On the smaller hill of height h, the change in potential energy with respect to the starting point is

$$PE = mg(200 - h)$$

Its kinetic energy is given as

$$kE = \tfrac{1}{2}mv^2 = \tfrac{1}{2}m(32)^2$$

Equating the two,

$$mg(200 - h) = \tfrac{1}{2}m(32)^2$$

$$g(200 - h) = 32(200 - h) = \tfrac{1}{2}(32)^2$$

$$200 - h = \tfrac{1}{2}(32)$$

$$h = 200 - 16 = 184 \text{ ft.}$$

Therefore in order for the car to have speed 32 ft/sec, the lower hill must be at a height of 184 ft above the lowest point on the track.

• PROBLEM 234

Use the principle of conservation of mechanical energy to find the velocity with which a body must be projected vertically upward, in the absence of air resistance, to rise to a height above the earth's surface equal to the earth's radius, R.

Solution: Let the center of the earth be the origin. Then the initial distance of the body is $r_1 = R$ and its final position is $r_2 = 2R$. Let v_1 be the initial velocity. v_2, the final velocity, of the body of mass m is zero since 2R is the maximum height the body rises. Using conservation of energy, we have

$$KE_1 + PE_1 = KE_2 + PE_2$$

$$\frac{1}{2}mv_1^2 - G\frac{mm_E}{r_1} = \frac{1}{2}mv_2^2 - G\frac{mm_E}{r_2}$$

where m_E is the earth's mass.

Note that potential energy is negative. Substitution yields

$$\frac{1}{2}mv_1^2 - G\frac{mm_E}{R} = 0 - G\frac{mm_E}{2R},$$

$$v_1^2 = \frac{Gm_E}{R}.$$

• PROBLEM 235

A roller coaster starts from rest at the highest point of the track 30 m above the ground. What speed will it have at ground level if the effect of friction is neglected?

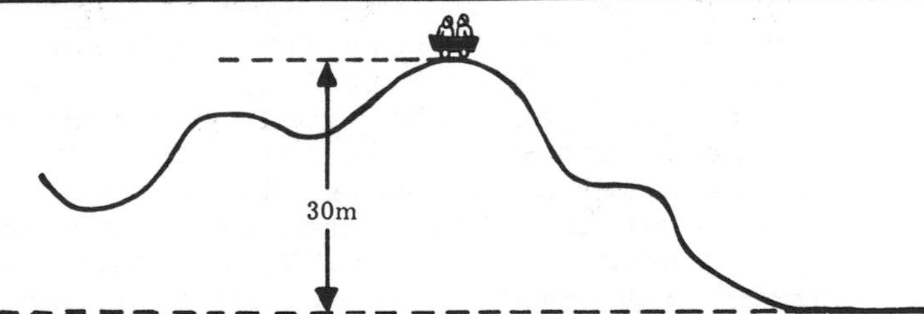

Solution: The given observables are $v_0 = 0$ m/s, $h_0 = 30$ m, and $h_f = 0$ m. When the cart is at the top of the track, the total energy is all potential energy.

$$E_0 = mgh_0$$

When the car is moving with speed v at the bottom, the total energy is

$$E_T = \frac{1}{2} mv^2 + mgh_f = \frac{1}{2}mv^2 \qquad \text{since } h_f = 0$$

Since the total energy is constant, we have, by the principle of conservation of energy,

$$\cancel{m}gh_0 = \frac{1}{2}\cancel{m}v^2$$

$$v^2 = 2gh_0 = (2)\left(9.8 \text{ m/s}^2\right)\left(3 \times 10^1 \text{ m}\right)$$

$$= 5.88 \times 10^2 \text{ m}^2/\text{s}^2$$

$$v = 2.4 \times 10^1 \text{ m/s}$$

Notice that the mass of the roller coaster was not required to solve the problem.

• PROBLEM 236

An athlete in his run-up for a pole vault can achieve a speed of 30 ft/s. What is the maximum possible record for the pole vault likely to be?

Solution: At the end of the run with a velocity of 30 ft/s, the athlete possesses kinetic energy of amount

$$E_k = \frac{1}{2} \times m \times 30^2 \text{ ft}^2/\text{s}^2,$$

where m is his mass. By causing rotation about the end of his pole he transforms this kinetic energy into potential energy. The mass of the pole is negligible in comparison with that of the man and need not be considered. Further, the pole must not be made of a material which can boost the athlete's energy by its elastic springiness.

The most favorable case occurs when the athlete plans his jump in such a way that, as he clears the bar, he has negligible kinetic energy left. Thus if h is the height by which the athlete's center of gravity alters in the jump, we have, by conservation of energy,

$$\frac{1}{2}m \times 30^2 \text{ ft}^2/\text{s}^2 = mgh. \therefore h = \frac{30^2 \text{ ft}^2/\text{s}^2}{2g} = 14 \text{ ft } \frac{3}{4} \text{ in.}$$

But if the athlete is very tall, his center of gravity may be as much as 3 ft 9 in. from the ground during his run-up. Hence the final height of his center of gravity above the ground is maximally 17 ft 9 3/4 in. His center of gravity is located inside his body and the bar must be lower than his center of gravity by roughly half the thickness of his body. If we assume a reasonably thin athlete, a minimum of 4½ in. must be subtracted from the height previously mentioned to allow for clearance. The maximum possible record for the pole vault would appear to be 17 ft 5¼ in. (as measured by the height of the bar). The present world record is 17 ft 4 in. (It should be noted that fiber-glass poles do not meet the conditions about elasticity stated above.)

If a particle of mass 100 g initially had speed 1×10^2 cm/s, what would be its kinetic energy and velocity at the end of its 10-cm fall?

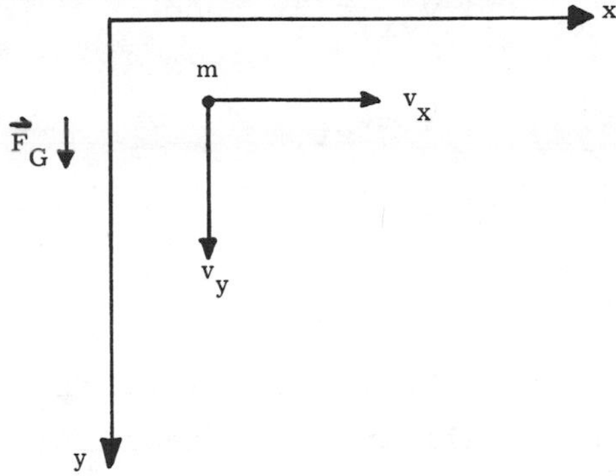

Solution: The initial kinetic energy is

$$E_i = \tfrac{1}{2} mv_i^2 = (\tfrac{1}{2})(100\ g)(10^4\ cm^2/s^2) = 5 \times 10^5\ ergs$$

During the fall, the particle moves as a result of the gravitational force $\vec{F}_G$ acting on it. The work done by $\vec{F}_G$ as the particle falls through the height h is, since $\vec{F}_G$ is constant and in the same direction as the displacement,

$$W = F_G \times h = (100\ g)(980\ cm/s^2)(10\ cm)$$

$$= 9.8 \times 10^5\ \ ergs$$

W is the change in kinetic energy as the particle moves in the direction of the gravitational force.

Therefore, the final kinetic energy at the end of the fall is

$$E_f = E_i + W \simeq 15 \times 10^5\ ergs \qquad \text{or}$$

$$\tfrac{1}{2} mv_f^2 \simeq 15 \times 10^5\ ergs$$

$$v_f^2 \simeq \frac{30 \times 10^5\ ergs}{100\ g}$$

$$v_f^2 \simeq 3 \times 10^4\ cm^2/s^2$$

$$v_f \simeq 1.73 \times 10^2\ cm/s$$

This result agrees with what we would calculate from $\vec{F} = \vec{M}a$, but note that we have not specified above the direction of the initial speed 1×10^2 cm/s. If it were in horizontal x direction (see the Fig.) it would remain constant and from

$$E_f - E_i = W, \qquad \text{we would have}$$

$$\tfrac{1}{2} m\left(v_{xf}^2 + v_{yf}^2\right) - \tfrac{1}{2} m\left(v_{xi}^2 + v_{yi}^2\right) = W$$

But $v_{xf} = v_{xi}$ and $v_{yi} = 0$, hence

$$\tfrac{1}{2} m\left(v_{xf}^2 + v_{yf}^2\right)^2 - \tfrac{1}{2} mv_{xi}^2 = W \quad \text{or} \quad \tfrac{1}{2} mv_{yf}^2 = W$$

and $v_{yf} = \sqrt{2W/m} = \sqrt{(2)(9.8 \times 10^5 \text{ erg})/100\text{g}}$

$$v_{yf} = 139 \text{ cm/s.}$$

Or if $\vec{v}_y$ were initially downward in the negative $\vec{y}$ direction, we could call upon the familiar relationships for falling bodies:

$$y = y_i + v_{yi}t + \tfrac{1}{2} gt^2$$

$$v_{yf} = v_{yi} + gt$$

where x_i, v_{yi} are the initial y position and y velocity of the particle. Hence

$$h = y - y_i = v_{yi}t + \tfrac{1}{2} gt^2 \qquad (1)$$

$$v_{yf} = v_{yi} + gt \qquad (2)$$

where $y - y_i$ is the distance the particle falls through (h). To eliminate t in equation (1), solve (2) for t and substitute in (1).

$$\frac{v_{yf} - v_{yi}}{g} = t$$

$$h = v_{yi}\left(\frac{v_{yf} - v_{yi}}{g}\right) + \frac{g}{2}\left(\frac{v_{yf} - v_{yi}}{g}\right)^2 \qquad \text{or}$$

$$h = 2v_{yi}\left(\frac{v_{yf} - v_{yi}}{2g}\right) + \frac{\left(v_{yf} - v_{yi}\right)^2}{2g}$$

• PROBLEM 238

(a) Compute the maximum height attained by a projectile launched with velocity of magnitude v_0 directed at an angle θ_0 to the horizontal, using the principle of conservation of energy.

(b) What is the magnitude of the projectile's velocity $\vec{u}$, when it has reached half its greatest height?

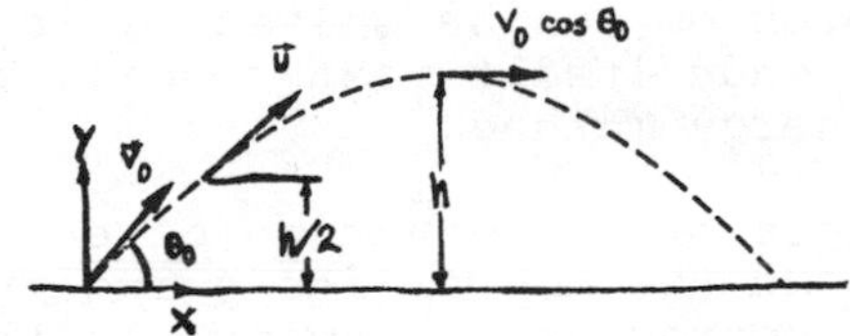

Solution: (a) At the start of the motion, the projectile possesses kinetic energy of amount $\frac{1}{2} mv_0^2$. At its greatest height, h, it possesses kinetic energy due to the component of its velocity in the x-direction $(v_0 \cos \theta)$ only, $\frac{1}{2} m(v_0 \cos \theta_0)^2$ and also potential energy due to its increased height, mgh. By the principle of conservation of energy,

$$\frac{1}{2}mv_0^2 = \frac{1}{2}mv_0^2 \cos^2 \theta_0 + mgh$$

$$\therefore \quad h = \frac{v_0^2(1 - \cos^2 \theta_0)}{2g} = \frac{v_0^2 \sin^2 \theta_0}{2g}$$

(b) By the principle of conservation of energy, the sum of the projectile's potential and kinetic energies at half its greatest height must equal its initial kinetic energy at the time of launching. (The potential energy at the point of launching is also zero.) At half the greatest height, the potential energy possessed by the projectile is

$$mg\frac{h}{2} = mg\frac{v_0^2 \sin^2 \theta_0}{4g} = \frac{1}{4} mv_0^2 \sin^2 \theta_0 \ .$$

and its kinetic energy is $\frac{1}{2}mu^2$. Thus:

$$\frac{1}{2} mv_0^2 = \frac{1}{2} mu^2 + \frac{1}{4} mv_0^2 \sin^2 \theta_0$$

$$u = \sqrt{v_0^2 - \frac{1}{2} v_0^2 \sin^2 \theta_0}$$

• PROBLEM 239

A simple pendulum consists of a small object (a so-called bob) hanging from a relatively long cord whose weight is negligible with respect to the bob. The to-and-fro motion of this bob in a vertical plane is called pendulum motion. If the cord is 3 ft long and the suspended bob is drawn back so as to allow the cord to make an angle of 10° with the vertical before being released, calculate the speed of the bob as it passes through its lowest position.

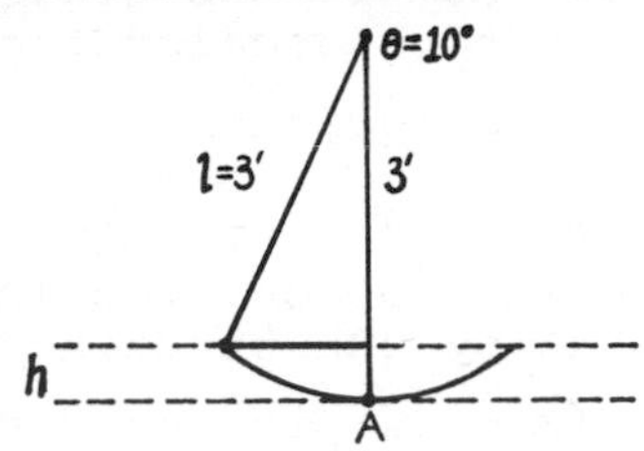

Solution: This problem can be solved by force analysis, but it lends itself most readily to a solution by the energy method.

By the principle of conservation of energy, the energy of the bob at the top of its swing must equal its energy at the bottom of its swing. At the top of its swing, the bob is momentarily at rest and it has only potential energy. Taking point A as the reference level for potential energy (see figure), and letting h be the height of the bob at the top of its swing, we may write

$$E_{top} = mgh$$

At the bottom of its swing (that is, point A), the bob has only kinetic energy. Hence

$$E_{bottom} = \frac{1}{2} mv^2$$

where v is the bob's speed at A. But

$$E_{top} = E_{bottom}$$

or $\quad mgh = \frac{1}{2} mv^2$

whence $\quad v = \sqrt{2gh}$

To determine h, use the figure and note that it is $\ell - \ell \cos \theta$

$$= 3 - 3 \cos 10° = 3 - 3(.985)$$

$$= 3 - 2.96 = .04 \text{ ft.}$$

whence $\quad v = \sqrt{2(32 \text{ ft/s}^2)(.04 \text{ ft})}$

$$v = \sqrt{2.56 \text{ ft}^2/\text{s}^2}$$

$$v = 1.6 \text{ ft/s}$$

• PROBLEM 240

A bricklayer is supplied with bricks by his mate who is 10 ft below him, the mate tossing the bricks vertically upward. If the bricks have a speed of 6 ft/s when they reach the bricklayer, what percentage of the energy used up by the mate serves no useful purpose?

Solution: Once the bricks leave the mate's hands, the only force which acts on them is the gravitational force. Since this produces a constant acceleration $\left(a = -g = -32 \text{ ft/s}^2\right)$, the kinematics equation

$$v^2 = v_0^2 - 2a\left(x - x_0\right)$$

can be used to describe its motion. The initial velocity v_0 of the bricks is found by substituting known values in the above equation. $\left(x - x_0\right.$ is the distance travelled by the bricks$\left.\right)$

$$v_0^2 = v^2 + 2g(x - x_0) = 36 ft^2/s^2 + 2 \times 32\ ft/s^2 \times 10\ ft$$

$$= 676\ ft^2/s^2 \quad . \quad \therefore \quad v_0 = 26\ ft/s\ .$$

The kinetic energy given each brick, and supplied by the bricklayer's mate, is

$$E_1 = \tfrac{1}{2} mv_0^2 = m \times 338\ ft^2/s^2$$

If the bricklayer's mate supplied only just enough energy to the bricks for them to reach the required level and no more, the initial velocity being u, they would have zero velocity at the level of the bricklayer. Hence

$$u^2 = 0 + 2g(x - x_0) = 2 \times 32\ ft/s^2 \times 10\ ft.$$

$\therefore$ $u = 8\sqrt{10}$ ft/s.

The kinetic energy supplied by the mate in this case is

$$E_2 = \tfrac{1}{2} mu^2 = m \times 320\ ft^2/s^2.$$

The mate supplies an energy equal to E_1, when he only needs to expend energy equal to E_2. Therefore he wastes an amount of energy $E_1 - E_2$. The percentage of energy wasted is

$$\frac{E_1 - E_2}{E_1} \times 100 = \frac{338 - 320}{338} \times 100 = \frac{18}{338} \times 100 = 5.3\%.$$

• PROBLEM 241

A pendulum with a bob of mass M is raised to height H and released. At the bottom of its swing, it picks up a piece of putty whose mass is m. To what height h will the combination (M + m) rise?

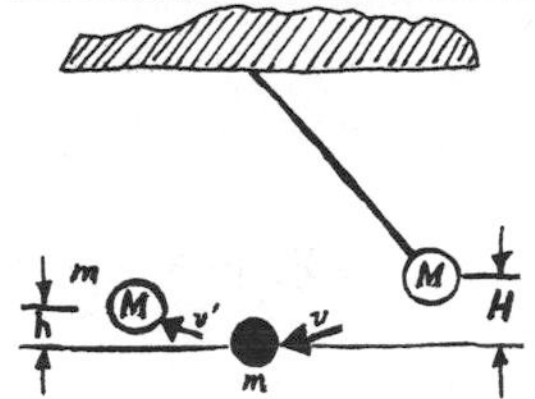

Solution: There are three phases to the problem—the fall of M, the collision of M and m, and the rise of M + m. The first and last phases involve energy conservation and the second phase involves momentum conservation.

(1) Fall: $(PE)_{initial} = (KE)_{final}$

$$MgH = \frac{1}{2} Mv^2$$

from which

$$v = \sqrt{2gH}$$

(2) Collision: $p_{initial} = p_{final}$

$$Mv = (M + m)v'$$

(3) Rise: $(KE)_{initial} = (PE)_{final}$

$$\frac{1}{2}(M + m)v'^2 = (M + m)gh$$

from which

$$v' = \sqrt{2gh}$$

Substituting Eqs. 1 and 3 into Eq. 2 gives

$$M\sqrt{2gH} = (M + m)\sqrt{2gh}$$

Canceling $\sqrt{2g}$ and squaring, we have

$$M^2H = (m + M)^2h$$

so that the final height is

$$h = \left(\frac{M}{m + M}\right)^2 H$$

• PROBLEM 242

A small block of mass m slides along the frictionless loop-the-loop track shown in the figure. (a) If it starts from rest at P, what is the resultant force acting on it at Q? (b) At what height above the bottom of the loop should the block be released so that the force it exerts against the track at the top of the loop equals its weight?

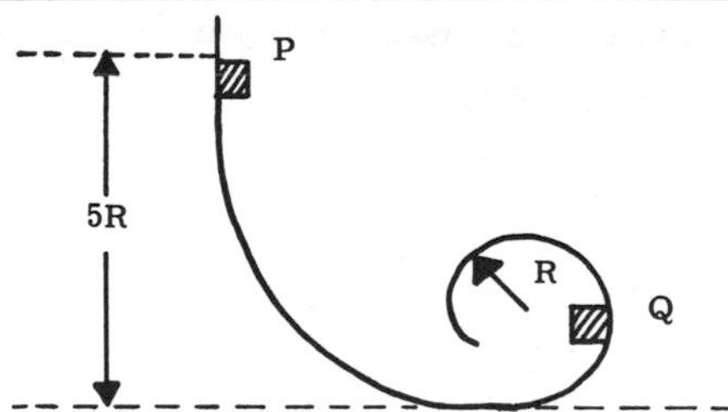

Solution: (a) Point Q is at a height R above the ground. Thus, the difference in height between points P and Q is 4R, and the difference in gravitational potential energy of the block between these two points is:

$$mgh_2 - mgh_1 = mg(h_2 - h_1) = mg(4R)$$
$$= 4\ mgR$$

Since the block starts from rest at P, its kinetic energy at Q is equal to its change in potential energy, 4 mgR; by the principle of conservation of energy

$$\tfrac{1}{2}\, mv^2 = 4\, mgR$$

$$v^2 = 8\, gR$$

At Q, the only forces acting on the block are its weight, mg, acting downward, and the force N of the track on the block, acting in the radial direction. Since the block is moving in a circular path

$$N = \frac{mv^2}{R} = \frac{8\, mgR}{R} = 8\, mg$$

The loop must exert a force on the block equal to eight times the block's weight.

(b) For the block to exert a force equal to its weight against the track at the top of the loop:

$$\frac{mv'^2}{R} = 2\, mg, \qquad v'^2 = 2gR$$

This is the case because gravity exerts a downward force mg on the block. Thus, in order to keep the block moving in a circular path, the rest of the force (= mg) must be exerted by the loop-the-loop. Therefore:

$$mgh = \tfrac{1}{2}\, mv'^2$$

$$h = \frac{v'^2}{2g} = \frac{2gR}{2g} = R$$

The block must be released at a height R, above the top of the loop or 3R above the bottom of the loop.

• PROBLEM 243

A block of mass m slides down a plane inclined at an angle θ, the surface of which has coefficient of sliding friction μ. The mass collides with a spring, having force constant k, after it has slid a distance d from rest. The spring will then reduce the speed of the block, which, will come to a momentary halt, when the spring has been compressed a distance X. The block will then be pushed back up the incline and begin a frictionally damped harmonic oscillation. Calculate X.

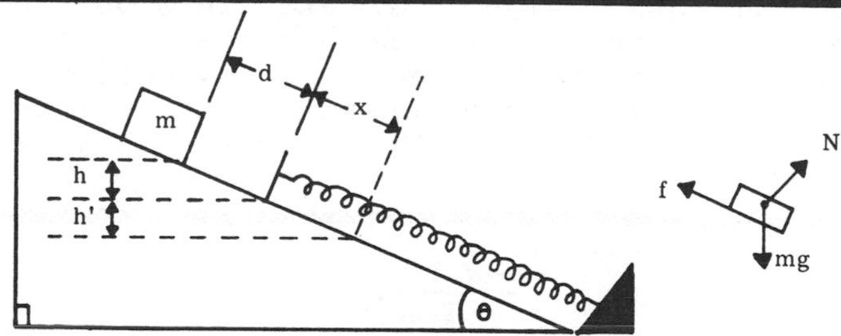

Solution: We will use the law of energy conservation. The kinetic energy of the block at the moment it collides with the spring is equal to the sum of its loss of gravitational potential energy and the work done on it by friction. Since the frictional force, f, acts in a direction opposite to the motion, the work due to friction is negative. Then

$$\frac{1}{2} mv^2 = mgh - \mu Nd$$

where $f = \mu N$, and $h = d \sin\theta$ is the vertical height through which the block falls, (see figure). $N = mg\cos\theta$ is the force the plane exerts, normal to its surface, on the block to cancel the component of the block's weight perpendicular to the plane. Thus:

$$\frac{1}{2} mv^2 = mg\, d \sin\theta - \mu\, mg\, d \cos\theta = mg\, d(\sin\theta - \mu\cos\theta)$$

Once the spring has brought the block to rest, the spring's potential energy is equal to the sum of the block's kinetic energy, the further gravitational potential energy the block loses as it falls through height $h' = X \sin\theta$, and the additional (negative) work done by friction on the block (see figure).

$$\frac{1}{2} kX^2 = \frac{1}{2} mv^2 + mgh' - \mu NX$$

$$\frac{1}{2} kX^2 = mgd(\sin\theta - \mu\cos\theta) + (mg\sin\theta)X - (\mu\, mg\cos\theta)X$$

$$\frac{1}{2} kX^2 - mg(\sin\theta - \mu\cos\theta)X - mgd(\sin\theta - \mu\cos\theta) = 0$$

From the quadratic formula: $x = \dfrac{-b \pm \sqrt{b^2 - 4ac}}{2a}$

with $a = \frac{1}{2}k$, $b = -mg(\sin\theta - \mu\cos\theta)$, and $c = -mg\,d(\sin\theta - \mu\cos\theta)$

$$X = \frac{mg(\sin\theta - \mu\cos\theta) \pm \sqrt{m^2g^2(\sin\theta-\mu\cos\theta)^2 - 4(\frac{1}{2}k)\left[-mgd(\sin\theta - \mu\cos\theta)\right]}}{2(\frac{1}{2}k)}$$

$$X = \frac{mg(\sin\theta-\mu\cos\theta) \pm \sqrt{m^2g^2(\sin\theta-\mu\cos\theta)^2 + 2mgdK(\sin\theta-\mu\cos\theta)}}{k}$$

This yields two answers for X. If we had been given numerical values for m, d, μ, θ, and k, we would find that one of the solutions for X would be negative and unacceptable. The other solution would be correct for the problem at hand.

• PROBLEM 244

A small body of mass 1 slug is rotated in a vertical circle at the end of a string 2 ft. long. If the tension in the string just vanishes at the top of the circle, what is the velocity of the body and the tension in the string (a) when the string is horizontal, and (b) when the body is at its lowest point?

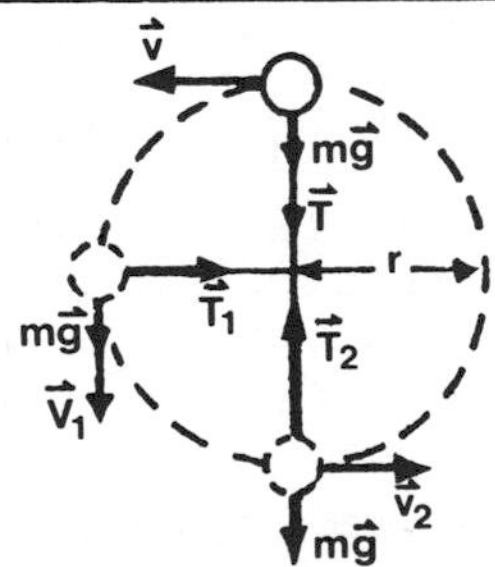

Solution: At each of the positions of the body in its rotation, only two forces act on it, the weight $m\vec{g}$ acting downward and the tension of the string, $\vec{T}$, acting toward the center of the circle.

At the top of the swing, the two forces act in the same direction and together provide the centripetal force necessary to keep the body in its circular path. Thus (see figure) by Newton's Second Law,

$$mg + T = \frac{mv^2}{r} .$$

When T is just zero at the top,

$$v^2 = rg = 2\ \text{ft} \times 32\ \text{ft/s}^2 = 64\ \text{ft}^2/\text{s}^2.$$

$$\therefore v = 8\ \text{ft} \cdot \text{s}^{-1}.$$

(a) When the string is horizontal, the body has lost potential energy and gained a corresponding quantity of kinetic energy. If we refer to the diagram we have from the principle of conservation of energy.

$$\tfrac{1}{2}\ mv_1^2 = \tfrac{1}{2}\ mv^2 + mg \times r \quad \text{or } v_1^2 = v^2 + 2gr = 3\ gr.$$

$$\therefore v_1 = 8\ \sqrt{3}\text{ft/s} = 13.86\ \text{ft/s}.$$

Here, the potential energy is taken to be zero at the height of the center of the circle.

Further, $\vec{T}_1$ is the only force acting radially. Hence

$$T_1 = \frac{mv_1^2}{r} = 3\ mg = 3 \times 1\ \text{slug} \times 32\ \text{ft} \cdot \text{s}^{-2} = 96\ \text{lb}.$$

(b) When the body is at its lowest point, similar arguments about gain of kinetic energy and loss of potential energy apply. Thus $\tfrac{1}{2}\ mv_2^2 - mgr = \tfrac{1}{2}\ mv^2 + mgr$

$$\therefore \quad v_2^2 = v^2 + 4gr = 5gr. \quad \therefore v_2 = 8\sqrt{5}\ \text{ft/s} = 17.9\ \text{ft/s}$$

Although $\vec{T}_2$ still acts radially, it is now opposed by the gravitational force which equals the weight of the body. The resultant force provides the necessary centripetal force, and, by Newton's Second Law

$$T_2 - mg = \frac{mv_2^2}{r}$$

Then $$T_2 = \frac{mv_2^2}{r} + mg = 5mg + mg = 6mg =$$

$$= 6 \times 1\ \text{slug} \times 32\ \text{ft/s}^2 = 192\ \text{lb}.$$

• PROBLEM 245

(a) From what height above the bottom of the loop must the car in the figure start in order to just make it around the loop? (b) What is the velocity of the car at point A and at point B?

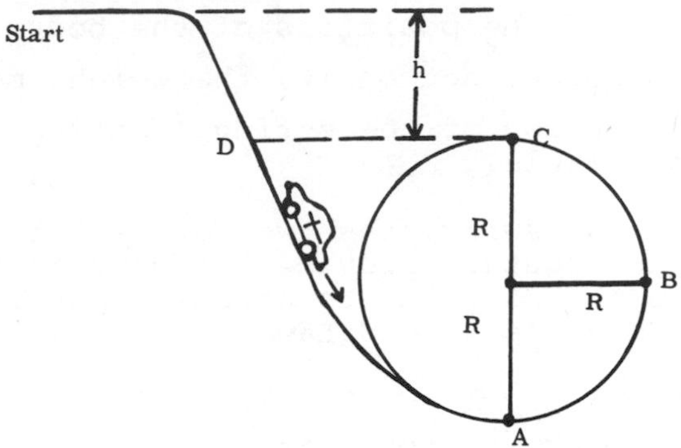

Solution: (a) For the car to just make it around the loop, its speed at the highest point of the loop must be such that the force of gravity on it is sufficient to provide the centripetal force needed to keep it in a circular path. For this to be the case,

$$F_{centripetal} = \frac{mv_C^2}{R} = mg$$

or the velocity must be given by

$$v_C = \sqrt{Rg} \qquad (1)$$

at point C. Neglecting friction, we use conservation of energy and note that the velocity of the car at point D must be the same as at point c, since both correspond to the same net change in potential energy relative to the starting point. The change in potential energy equals the change in kinetic energy and is proportional to the square of the velocity. The change in potential energy from the starting point to point D equated to the corresponding change in kinetic energy yields.

$$mgh = \tfrac{1}{2}m(v_D - v_0)^2 = \tfrac{1}{2}mv_D^2$$

$$v_D = \sqrt{2gh} \qquad (2)$$

where h is the vertical height of the starting point above points C and D (as shown in figure), and v_0 is the initial velocity of the car, which is zero at the starting point. Equating equations (1) and (2),

$$\sqrt{Rg} = \sqrt{2gh}$$

we have

$$h = R/2 \ .$$

This indicates that the starting point must be $2R + R/2 = (5/2)R$ above the bottom of the loop in order for the car to have just enough energy to make it around the loop.

(b) Equating the change in potential energy to the kinetic energy of the car at the point in question, as we did in part (a), we find for point A

$$mg(h + 2R) = \tfrac{1}{2}mv_A^2$$

$$\frac{5}{2}Rg = \tfrac{1}{2}v_A^2$$

$$v_A = \sqrt{5\ gR}$$

For point B,

$$mg(h + R) = \tfrac{1}{2}mv_B^2$$

$$\frac{3}{2}gR = \tfrac{1}{2}v_B^2$$

$$v_B = \sqrt{3gR}$$

A block starting from rest slides a distance of 5 meters down an inclined plane which makes an angle of 37° with the horizontal. The coefficient of friction between block and plane is 0.2. (a) What is the velocity of the block after sliding 5 meters? (b) What would the velocity be if the coefficient of friction were negligible?

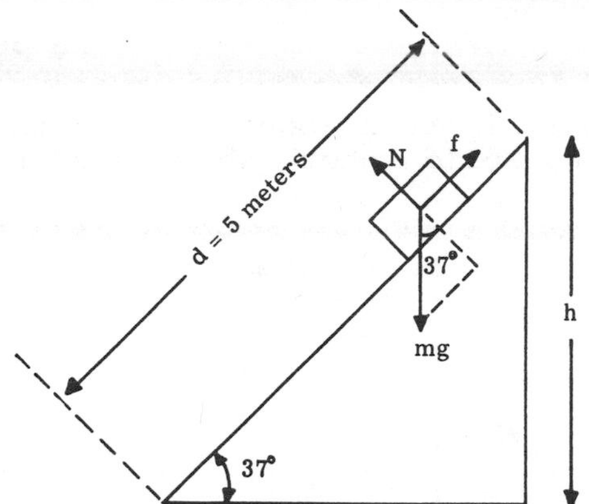

Solution: The change in potential energy of the block is

$$\Delta PE = mgh$$

where h is the height of the block and equals 5 sin 37°. Some of this energy goes into doing work against the frictional force f. The frictional force is proportional to the normal force N. The block is in equilibrium in the direction perpendicular to the inclined plane. Therefore, the sum of the forces in that direction must equal zero.

$$N - mg \cos 37^\circ = 0$$

thus

$$N = mg \cos 37^\circ$$

Then the frictional force is

$$F_f = \mu N = 0.2\ mg \cos 37^\circ$$

where μ is the coefficient of friction. The energy expended in combating this force equals the work done against it. The work equals the product of the frictional force and the distance over which it acts.

$$W = F_f d = (0.2\ mg \cos 37^\circ)(5) = mg \cos 37^\circ$$

From the conservation of energy principle, the change in potential energy of an object equals its change in kinetic energy plus the work it does.

$$\Delta PE = W + \Delta KE = W + \tfrac{1}{2}m(v^2 - v_0^2)$$

Since the initial velocity v_0 of the block is zero, and its height h is d sin 37° = 5 sin 37°,

$$\Delta PE = mgh = mg \cos 37^\circ + \tfrac{1}{2}mv^2$$

$$\tfrac{1}{2}v^2 = g(h - \cos 37^\circ) = g(5 \sin 37^\circ - \cos 37^\circ)$$

$$v = \sqrt{2g(5 \sin 37^\circ - \cos 37^\circ)}$$

$$= \sqrt{2(9.8)[(5)(0.602) - (0.799)]}$$

$$= \sqrt{43.3} \approx 6.57 \text{ m/sec}$$

where v is the final velocity of the block.

(b) If friction can be neglected, then we have

$$\Delta PE = \Delta KE$$

or

$$mgh = \frac{1}{2}mv^2$$

$$g(5 \sin 37^\circ) = \frac{1}{2}v^2$$

$$v = \sqrt{(2)(g)(5 \sin 37^\circ)}$$

$$= \sqrt{(2)(9.8)(5)(0.602)}$$

$$= \sqrt{59} \approx 7.68 \text{ m/sec}$$

• PROBLEM 247

What is the rotational inertia about an axis through the center of a 25-kg solid sphere whose diameter is 0.30 m?

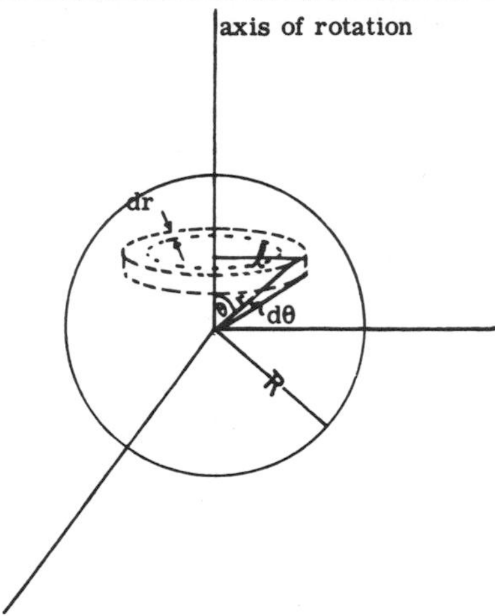

Solution: For a rigid body rotating with angular speed ω about a fixed axis, the kinetic energy is $K = \frac{1}{2} mv^2 = \frac{1}{2} m(\omega r)^2$. Each particle of this body can be considered as contributing to the total kinetic energy. The angular velocity, ω, of all the particles is the same, but their distance r from the axis of rotation varies. Therefore, the total kinetic energy can be written as

$$K = \frac{1}{2}\left(m_1 r_1^2 + m_2 r_2^2 + \ldots\right)\omega^2 = \frac{1}{2}\Sigma\left(m_i r_i^2\right)\omega^2$$

where the summation is taken over all the particles in the rigid body. The rotational inertia, I, is defined as

$$I = \Sigma m_i r_i^2 .$$

As can be seen from the above equations, the rotational energy of a body, for a given angular speed ω, depends on the mass of the body and the way that mass is distributed around the axis of rotation. Since most rigid bodies are not composed of discrete point masses but are continuous distributions of matter, the summation for I in the above equation becomes an integration. Let the body be divided into infinitesimal elements of mass dm at a distance r from the axis of rotation. Then the rotational inertia is

$$I = \int r^2 \, dm$$

where the integral is taken over the whole body.

For a solid sphere of radius R,

$$dm = \rho \, dV$$

where ρ is the density of the sphere and dV is an infinitesimal volume. For dV, take a circle of radius ℓ and of thickness $r\,d\theta$, where ℓ is the distance from the axis of rotation. We have

$$dV = (2\pi\ell)(dr)(rd\theta) = 2\pi\,(r \sin\theta)\, r\, drd\theta$$

$$= 2\pi\, r^2 \sin\theta \, dr\, d\theta$$

$$\rho = \frac{m}{V} = \frac{m}{\frac{4}{3}\pi R^3}$$

Then

$$I = \int \ell^2 \, dm = \int (r \sin\theta)^2 \rho dV$$

$$= \int_{\theta=0}^{\pi} \int_{r=0}^{R} (r^2 \sin^2\theta) \left(\frac{m}{\frac{4}{3}\pi R^3}\right) (2\pi\, r^2 \sin\theta\, dr\, d\theta)$$

$$= \int_{\theta=0}^{\pi} \int_{r=0}^{R} \frac{3m}{2\,R^3} r^4 \sin^3\theta \, dr\, d\theta$$

$$= \int_{\theta=0}^{\pi} \left\{ \frac{3m}{2\,R^3} \frac{r^5}{5} \sin^3\theta \Big]_{r=0}^{R} \right\} d\theta$$

$$= \frac{3}{10} m\, R^2 \int_{\theta=0}^{\pi} \sin^3\theta \, d\theta$$

$$= \frac{3}{10} m\, R^2 \int_{\theta=0}^{\pi} \sin\theta\,(1 - \cos^2\theta) d\theta$$

Let $x = -\cos\theta$ and $dx = \sin\theta\, d\theta$. Then

$$I = \frac{3}{10} m\, R^2 \int_{x=-\cos 0°}^{x=-\cos\pi} (1 - x^2) dx$$

$$= \frac{3}{10} m\, R^2 \left(x - \frac{x^3}{3}\right)\Big]_{-1}^{1}$$

$$= \frac{3}{10} m\, R^2 \left(1 - \frac{1}{3} + 1 - \frac{1}{3}\right) = \left(\frac{3}{10} m\, R^2\right)\left(\frac{4}{3}\right) = \frac{2}{5} mR^2$$

For the given sphere, the mass is 25 kg and the radius is 0.30 m/2 = 0.15 m. Its rotational inertia is then

$$I = \frac{2}{5} mR^2 = \frac{2}{5} (25 \text{ kg})(0.15 \text{ m})^2 = 0.22 \text{ kg-m}^2.$$

• PROBLEM 248

A flywheel has a mass of 30 kg and a radius of gyration of 2 m. If it turns at a rate of 2.4 rev/sec, what is its rotational kinetic energy?

Solution: The rotational kinetic energy of a body about a given axis is

$$T = \tfrac{1}{2} I \omega^2 \qquad (1)$$

where I and ω are the rotational inertia and angular velocity of the body about the given axis. By definition of the radius of gyration, ρ, we may write

$$m\rho^2 = I \qquad (2)$$

where m is the body's mass. Using (2) in (1)

$$T = \tfrac{1}{2} m \rho^2 \omega^2$$

Using the given data

$$T = (\tfrac{1}{2})(30 \text{ kg})(4 \text{ m}^2)(2.4 \text{ rev/s})^2$$

$$T = 345.6 \text{ kg}\cdot\text{m}^2\cdot\text{rev}^2/\text{s}^2$$

To put this answer in conventional energy units, note that

$$1 \text{ rev/s} = 2\pi \text{ rad/s}$$

whence $T = 1382.4\pi^2$ Joules

$$T = 13643.74 \text{ Joules}$$

• PROBLEM 249

A flywheel of mass 12 kg and radius of gyration 20 cm is mounted on a light horizontal axle of radius 5 cm which rotates on frictionless bearings. A string wound round the axle has attached to its free end a hanging mass of 4 kg, and the system is allowed to start from rest. If the string leaves the axle after the mass has descended 3 m, what torque must be applied to the flywheel to bring it to rest in 5 revs?

Solution: Consider the hanging mass. It has two forces acting on it, its weight, $m\vec{g}$, downward and the tension in the string, $\vec{T}$, upward. Since the mass descends with acceleration $\vec{a}$, by Newton's second law

$$mg - T = ma$$

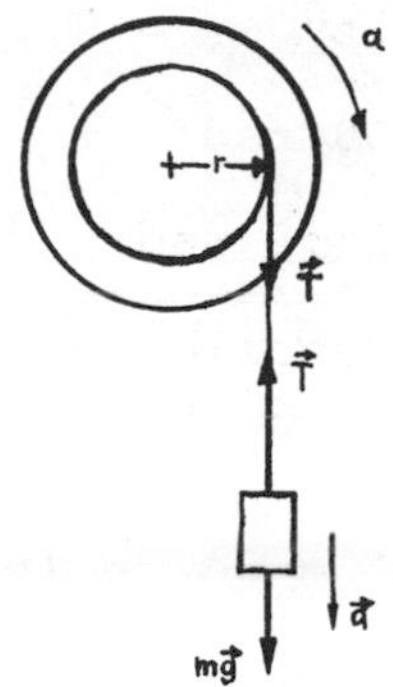

But, if the flywheel rotates with angular acceleration α, then the tangential acceleration

$$a = r\alpha, \qquad \text{and thus} \qquad mg - T = mr\alpha \qquad (1)$$

The tension $\vec{T}$ acts at distance r from the axis of the flywheel of mass M and radius of gyration k. Therefore the torque is $\Gamma = Tr$. Using the rigid body analogue of Newton's second law, where torque takes the place of force, moment of inertia, I, takes the place of m, and angular acceleration α takes the place of linear acceleration, $\Gamma = Tr = I\alpha$. Since $I = Mk^2$, $Tr = Mk^2\alpha$. Also, upon multiplication of both sides of equation (1) by r, $mgr - Tr = mra = mr^2\alpha$.

$$\therefore \qquad mgr = \alpha(mr^2 + Mk^2).$$

$$\alpha = \frac{mgr}{mr^2 + Mk^2}$$

$$= \frac{4\ \text{kg} \times 9.8\ \text{m}\cdot\text{s}^{-2} \times 0.05\ \text{m}}{4\ \text{kg} \times (0.05)^2\text{m}^2 + 12\ \text{kg} \times (0.2)^2\ \text{m}^2}$$

$$= \frac{1.96}{0.49}\ \text{s}^{-2} = 4\ \text{rad}\cdot\text{s}^{-2}.$$

The flywheel starts from rest and accelerates as long as the string is exerting a couple on it. In that time the mass descends 3 m. But in 1 rev, the string unwraps a length equal to its circumference, $2\pi r$, and the mass descends by this distance. Thus the angular distance the flywheel turns during the period of acceleration is

$$\frac{3\ \text{m}}{2\pi \times 0.05\ \text{m/rev}} = \frac{3}{0.05} \times \frac{1\ \text{rev}}{2\pi} \times \frac{2\pi\ \text{rad}}{1\ \text{rev}}$$

$$= \frac{3}{.05}\ \text{rad} = 60\ \text{rad}$$

The angular speed when the string leaves the axle can be found by using the rigid body analogue of the kinematic equations for constant acceleration. If ω is the analogue of linear velocity, v, α the analogue of linear acceleration, a, and θ the analogue of linear displacement, s, then the kinematic equation not involving the time variable is

$$\omega^2 = \omega_0^2 + 2\alpha\theta.$$

The initial angular velocity $\omega_0 = 0$ and

$$\omega^2 = 2 \times 4 \text{ rad}\cdot\text{s}^{-2} \times 60 \text{ rad} \qquad \text{or}$$

$$\omega = 4\times\sqrt{30} \text{ rad}\cdot\text{s}^{-1} = 21.9 \text{ rad}\cdot\text{s}^{-1}.$$

If a torque Γ' is now applied to the wheel, it produces a constant deceleration α', and since the flywheel is being brought to rest,

$$\omega_{final} = 0 \text{ or } \quad 0^2 = \omega^2 + 2\alpha' \times 10\pi \text{ rad}.$$

$$\therefore \quad \alpha' = \frac{-\omega^2}{20\pi \text{ rad}} = -\frac{480 \text{ rad}^2\cdot\text{s}^{-2}}{20\pi \text{ rad}} = -\frac{24}{\pi} \text{ rad}\cdot\text{s}^{-2}.$$

But $\quad \Gamma' = I\alpha' = Mk^2\alpha'$

$$= -12 \text{ kg} \times 0.04 \text{ m}^2 \times \frac{24}{\pi} \text{ rad}\cdot\text{s}^{-2} = -3.67 \text{ N}\cdot\text{m}.$$

Thus a torque of 3.67 N·m applied against the direction of rotation is necessary.

Note that the result is more easily obtained from a consideration of energy of the mass-flywheel system. The mass m descends a height h. In so doing it loses potential energy, which reappears in the form of kinetic energy of the mass and of the flywheel. Thus, if the bottom of the fall is taken as the reference level, then

$$mgh = \tfrac{1}{2}mv^2 + \tfrac{1}{2}I\omega^2 = \tfrac{1}{2}mr^2\omega^2 + \tfrac{1}{2}Mk^2\omega^2$$

$$\therefore \quad \omega^2 = \frac{2mgh}{mr^2 + Mk^2} = 480 \text{ rad}^2\cdot\text{s}^{-2}.$$

In the final stage, the work done by the retarding torque in the 5 rev= 10π radians must equal the kinetic energy possessed by the flywheel before the couple is applied. Thus

$$-10\pi\Gamma = \tfrac{1}{2} I\omega^2 = \tfrac{1}{2}Mk^2\omega^2.$$

$$\therefore \quad \Gamma = -\frac{Mk^2\omega^2}{20\pi} = -3.67 \text{ N}\cdot\text{m}.$$

• PROBLEM 250

Delivery trucks which operate by making use of the energy stored in a rotating flywheel have been in use for some time in Germany. The trucks are "charged up" before leaving by using an electric motor to get the flywheel up to its top speed of 6000 rev·min^{-1}. If one such flywheel is a solid homogeneous cylinder of weight 1120 lb and diameter 6 ft, how long can the truck operate before returning to its base for "recharging", if its average power requirement is 10 hp?

Solution: The angular speed of the flywheel is

$$\omega = 6000 \text{ rev}\cdot\text{min}^{-1} \times 2\pi \text{ rad}\cdot\text{rev}^{-1} \times \frac{1}{60} \text{ min}\cdot\text{s}^{-1}$$

$$= 200\pi \text{ rad}\cdot\text{s}^{-1}$$

The kinetic energy stored in the flywheel is given by

$$E_k = \tfrac{1}{2} I\omega^2$$

where I is the moment of inertia. For a disc of radius r and mass M, $I = \frac{1}{2} Mr^2$. Therefore,

$$E_k = \tfrac{1}{2} \times \tfrac{1}{2} Mr^2 \times \omega^2$$

$$= \tfrac{1}{4} Mr^2\omega^2 = \tfrac{1}{4} \times \frac{1120}{32} \text{ slugs} \times 9 \text{ ft}^2 \times 4\pi^2 \times 10^4 \text{ s}^{-2}$$

$$= \frac{63\pi^2}{2} \times 10^5 \text{ ft}\cdot\text{lb}.$$

The truck consumes this energy at a rate of

$$P = 10 \text{ hp} = 10 \times 550 \text{ ft}\cdot\text{lb}\cdot\text{s}^{-1},$$

Thus, assuming that the frictional losses are negligible, the truck can work for

$$t = \frac{E_k}{P}$$

$$= \frac{63\pi^2 \times 10^5 \text{ ft}\cdot\text{lb}}{2 \times 5500 \text{ ft}\cdot\text{lb}\cdot\text{s}^{-1}} = \frac{63\pi^2 \times 10^5}{2 \times 5500 \times 60} \text{ min}$$

$$= 94.2 \text{ min}.$$

The flywheel must therefore be "recharged" before this time has elapsed.

• PROBLEM 251

What velocity must a rocket be given so that it escapes the gravitational field of the earth?

Solution. In order to escape the earth's gravitational field, the rocket must travel an infinite distance from the earth. The change in potential energy, ΔV, of the rocket as it goes from the earth's surface to infinity is

$$\Delta V = G\, M_E m_R \left(\frac{1}{R_E} - \frac{1}{r}\right)$$

$$= G\, M_E m_R \left(\frac{1}{R_E} - \frac{1}{\infty}\right) = \frac{G\, M_E m_R}{R_E}.$$

The gravitational acceleration at the surface of the earth is written as

$$g = \frac{G\, M_E}{R_E^2} = 9.8 \text{ m/sec}^2.$$

Rewriting ΔV so that g appears in the expression, we have

$$\Delta V = \frac{G\ M_E}{R_E^2} \times R_E\ m_R = g\ R_E m_R.$$

This is the potential energy that the rocket must acquire if it is to escape the earth's pull. This energy comes from the conversion of kinetic energy to potential energy. Therefore the initial kinetic energy given to the rocket must at least equal this change in potential energy. Equating the two energy expressions, with $R_E = 6.36 \times 10^6$ meters,

$$\Delta V = g\ R_E m_R = \frac{1}{2}\ m_R v^2$$

$$v^2 = 2g\ R_E = 2 \times 9.8 \times 6.36 \times 10^6$$

$$v = 1.12 \times 10^4 \text{ m/sec.}$$

This minimum velocity needed to escape the earth's gravitational field is known as the escape velocity.

WORK & ENERGY CONVERSION

• PROBLEM 252

How much work is done in joules when a mass of 5 kilograms is raised a height of 2 meters?

Solution: Mechanical work is given by the product of the force applied to a body, and the distance for which it is applied (W = Fs when force is constant and force and line of travel are in the same direction). The force of gravity on the 5 kilogram weight is equal to the force exerted against gravity (by Newton's Third Law) and is given by:

$$F = mg$$

$$F = 5 \text{ kg}\ (9.80 \text{ m/sec}^2) = 49.0\ \frac{\text{k-m}}{\text{sec}^2}\ \text{(newtons)}$$

and the work is given by

$$W = 49.0 \text{ newtons}\,(2\text{m}) = 98 \text{ joules.}$$

• PROBLEM 253

How much work is required to raise a 100-g block to a height of 200 cm and simultaneously give it a velocity of 300 cm/sec?

Solution: The work done is the sum of the potential energy, PE = mgh, and the kinetic energy, $KE = \frac{1}{2}\ mv^2$:

$$PE = mgh$$

$$= (100 \text{ g}) \times \left(980 \text{ cm/sec}^2\right) \times (200 \text{ cm})$$
$$= 1.96 \times 10^7 \text{ g-cm}^2/\text{sec}^2$$
$$= 1.96 \times 10^7 \text{ ergs}$$

$$KE = \frac{1}{2} mv^2$$
$$= \frac{1}{2} \times (100 \text{ g}) \times (300 \text{ cm/sec})^2$$
$$= 4.5 \times 10^6 \text{ g-cm}^2/\text{sec}^2$$

$$W = PE + KE$$
$$= 1.96 \times 10^7 \text{ ergs} + 0.45 \times 10^7 \text{ ergs}$$
$$= 2.41 \times 10^7 \text{ ergs}$$
$$= 2.41 \text{ J}$$

• PROBLEM 254

If a 50 g bullet traveling at 40,000 cm/sec is stopped by a steel plate, how much heat is generated, on the assumption that the energy is completely converted into heat?

Solution: We are told that all of the bullet's energy is converted into heat, Q. Since the bullet has only kinetic energy

$$Q = \tfrac{1}{2} mv^2$$

where m is the bullet's mass, and v is its speed. Hence, the amount of heat energy produced is

$$Q = (\tfrac{1}{2})(50 \text{ g})\left(4 \times 10^4 \text{ cm/s}\right)^2$$

$$Q = 25 \times 16 \times 10^8 \text{ ergs}$$

$$Q = 4 \times 10^{10} \text{ ergs}$$

• PROBLEM 255

A suitcase is dragged 30 m along a floor by a force F = 10 newtons inclined at an angle 30° to the floor. How much work is done on the suitcase?

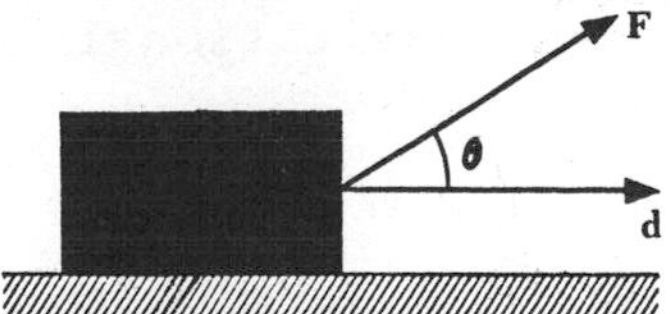

Solution: Work is defined as the scalar product of the force acting on an object, and the distance through which the object moves while the force is being applied.

$$W = \vec{F} \cdot \vec{d}$$

where $\vec{F}$ is the force and $\vec{d}$ is the distance. (See the figure above.) Note that the force and distance are vectors while work is a scalar, hence the "scalar product" nomenclature for the dot.

$$W = \vec{F} \cdot \vec{d} = Fd \cos \theta = Fd \cos 30°$$

$$= (10N)(30\ m)\left(\frac{\sqrt{3}}{2}\right) = 150\sqrt{3}\ N\text{-}m$$

• PROBLEM 256

A horizontal force of 5 N is required to maintain a velocity of 2 m/sec for a box of mass 10 kg sliding over a certain rough surface. How much work is done by the force in 1 min?

Solution: First, we must calculate the distance traveled:

$$s = vt$$
$$= (2\ m/sec) \times (60\ sec)$$
$$= 120\ m.$$

Then, $W = Fs \cos \theta$, where θ is the angle between the force and the distance. In this case $\theta = 0°$ so we can write,

$$W = Fs$$
$$= (5\ N) \times (120\ m)$$
$$= 600\ N\text{-}m = 600\ J$$

• PROBLEM 257

A boy bailing a boat lifts 2.0 kg of water to a height of 1.2 m above the bilge as he pours the water over the side. (a) How much work does he perform? (b) How much work is done by the force of gravity?

Solution: (a) The boy does work against gravity. Therefore, the force he must exert on the water is just equal to its weight mg. Work equals the product of force and the distance the force acts over.

$$W = Fs = 2.0\ kg\ \frac{9.8\ nt}{kg} \times 1.2\ m = 23.5\ joules$$

The boy's work is converted to potential energy, which is then converted to the kinetic energy of the falling water.

(b) If the direction of the upward displacement is called positive, then the gravitational force is in the negative direction, and

$$W = Fs = (-\ 19.6\ nt)(1.2\ m) = -\ 23.5\ joules$$

The negative sign means that work was done against gravity.

• PROBLEM 258

How much work in joules is done when a mass of 150 kilograms is dragged a distance of 10 meters if the coefficient of sliding friction is 0.30?

Solution: Work is given by $F \cdot s$ when the force is

constant and is applied in the direction of travel (F being force and s being distance). To calculate the force needed to move the object at constant velocity against the force of friction, we use

$$F = \mu_{kinetic} \cdot N$$

where N is the normal force which in this case is the weight of the object:

$$N = mg$$

$$N = 150 \text{ kg } 9\cdot 80 \text{ m/s}^2 = 1470 \text{ nt}$$

and the force of friction is:

$$F = 0.30 \cdot (1470 \text{ nt}) = 441 \text{ nt}$$

The work done

$$= W = Fs = 441 \text{ nt} \times 10 \text{ m} = 4410 \text{ joules.}$$

• PROBLEM 259

A 40-lb stone is carried up a ramp, along a path making a 30° angle to the horizontal, to the top of a building 100 ft high. How much work is done? (Neglect friction.)

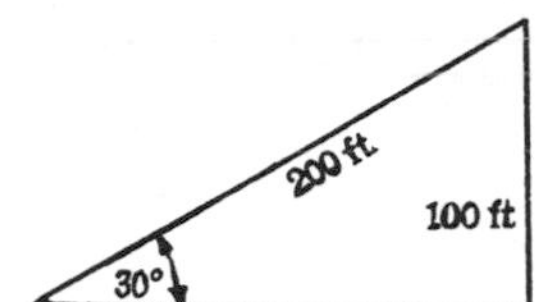

FIGURE A

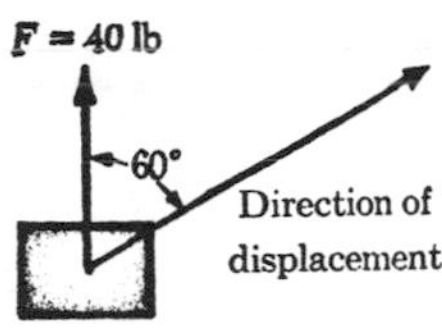

FIGURE B

Solution: Work is defined as the component of the force in the direction of the displacement multiplied by the displacement, for constant forces. In mathematical terms,

$$W = \vec{F} \cdot \vec{S} = FS \cos \theta$$

where θ is the angle between the force and the displacement. We may compute the length of the ramp because from the figure (part a),

$$\sin 30° = \frac{1}{2} = \frac{100}{\text{length of ramp}}$$

Therefore, length of ramp = 200 ft. Since the stone is being carried up the ramp the force is upwards and we see that the angle θ is 60° (see figure (b)). Hence the work is

$$W = (40 \text{ lb})(200 \text{ ft})\cos 60° = (40)(200)\left(\frac{1}{2}\right)\text{ft-lbs}$$
$$= 4000 \text{ ft-lbs.}$$

As a check we can use the fact that this work done must equal the change in the potential energy of the stone.

$$\Delta PE = (\text{weight})(\Delta \text{ height}) = (40 \text{ lb})(100 \text{ ft}) = 4000 \text{ ft-lbs.}$$

A 5 -kg block slides down a frictionless plane inclined at an angle of 30° with the horizontal as shown in figure (a). Calculate the amount of work W done by the force of gravity for a displacement of 8 m along the plane.

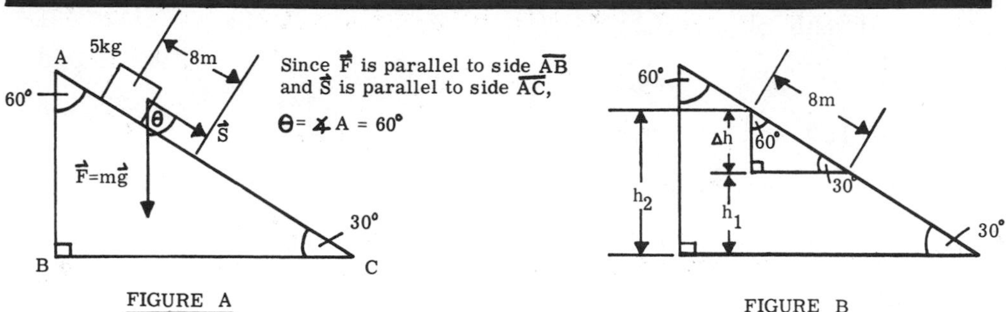

FIGURE A

FIGURE B

Solution: We will solve this problem first by the dynamics method and then by the energy method.

The formula for calculating work is:

$$W = \vec{F} \cdot \vec{s}$$

$$= F\ s \cos\theta$$

where θ is the angle between the force $\vec{F}$ and the displacement $\vec{s}$ of the mass in question. We see from figure (a) that the angle between $\vec{F}$ and $\vec{s}$ is 60°:

$$W = Fs \cos 60° = \tfrac{1}{2}\ mgs$$

$$= \tfrac{1}{2}(5\ \text{kg})(9.8\ \text{m/sec}^2)(8\ \text{m}) = 196\ \text{kg-m}^2/\text{sec}^2$$

$$= 196\ \text{Joules}$$

Another way to solve this problem is to calculate the difference in gravitational potential energy that the block goes through as it slides 8 m down the incline.

We know that this equals the amount of work that gravity does on the block.

As the block slides 8 m down the incline it falls through a vertical height Δh (see figure (b)):

$$\Delta h = 8(\sin 30°)\text{m} = 4\text{m}$$

The gravitational potential energy difference that the block experiences is:

$$W = \Delta E_p = mgh_2 - mgh_1 = mg(h_2 - h_1) = mg\Delta h$$

$$= (5\ \text{kg})(9.8\ \text{m/sec}^2)(4\ \text{m}) = 196\ \text{Joules}$$

• PROBLEM 261

(a) Find the displacement ratio of a screw jack (Fig.) whose threads have a pitch p and whose handle has a length R. (b) If p = 0.15 in, R = 18 ft, and the jack has an efficiency of 30 percent, find the force needed to lift a load of 3300 lb.

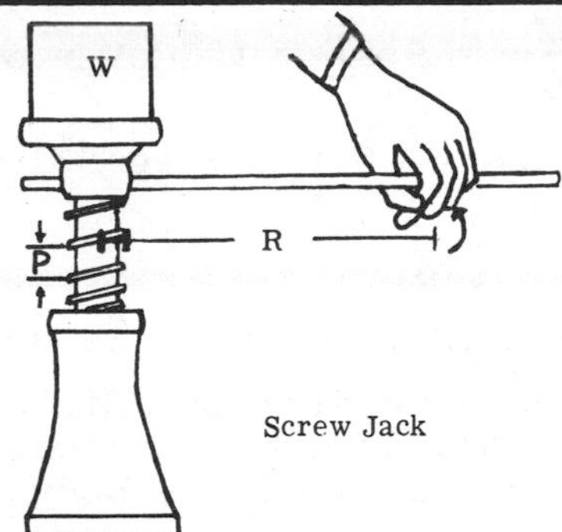

Screw Jack

Solution: (a) A screw is a cylinder with an inclined plane wrapped around it. The distance between two adjacent threads is called the pitch (p) of the screw, as shown in the figure. As the handle is turned through one complete revolution, the weight moves through distance p. At the same time, the man's hand moves a distance $2\pi R$. The displacement ratio DR, is the distance the man's hand moves divided by the resultant displacement of the screw:

$$DR = \frac{2\pi R}{p} = \frac{(2\pi)(1.8\text{ ft})(12\text{ in/ft})}{(0.15\text{ in})} = 144$$

(b) The efficiency is defined as the ratio of work output to work input. The work output for the screwjack is equal to the product of the weight W and the distance it is moved. The work input is the force F the man exerts multiplied by the distance $(2\pi R)$ through which he moves the handle. For a displacement p of the weight, the efficiency is

$$e = \frac{Wp}{F(2\pi R)}$$

Substituting the known values, we find the force the man exerts to be

$$F = \frac{Wp}{e(2\pi R)} = \frac{(3300\text{ lb})(0.15\text{ in})}{(0.30)(2\pi)(1.8\text{ ft})(12\text{ in/ft})}$$

$$= 77\text{ lb.}$$

• PROBLEM 262

What is the energy equivalent in MeV of a particle whose mass is 1 amu?

Solution: The energy equivalent is given by the Einstein

relation $E = mc^2$. In M.K.S. units, a mass of 1 amu is 1.66×10^{-27} kg. Hence its equivalent energy is

$$E = mc^2 = (1.66 \times 10^{-27}\text{ kg})(3 \times 10^8\text{ m/s})^2 = 1.49 \times 10^{-10}\text{J}$$

Since 1 eV = 1.6×10^{-19} J, this energy can be expressed in eV:

$$E = \frac{1.49 \times 10^{-10}\ \not{J}}{1.6 \times 10^{-19}\ \not{J}/\text{eV}} = 9.31 \times 10^8\text{ eV} = 931\text{ MeV}$$

Thus the energy equivalent of 1 amu is 931 MeV.

• PROBLEM 263

A single body of mass M in free space is acted on by a constant force $\vec{F}$ in the same direction in which it is moving. Show that the work done by the force is equal to the increase in kinetic energy of the body.

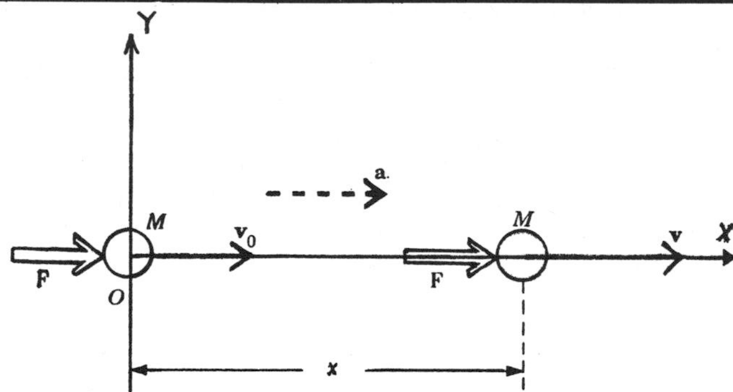

Solution: This is a case of motion in a straight line with constant acceleration. In the figure suppose that at the zero of time the body is at the origin and is moving with a velocity $\vec{v}_0$. Suppose that at time t it has moved through a distance $\vec{x}$ and its velocity has changed to $\vec{v}$. If $\vec{a}$ is the constant acceleration, then we can derive an equation relating v to x.

From the equations

$$v = v_0 + at \qquad \text{and } x = v_0 t + \tfrac{1}{2}at^2$$

we must eliminate t. Since

$$t = \frac{v - v_0}{a}, \qquad \text{then}$$

$$x = v_0\left(\frac{v - v_0}{a}\right) + \frac{1}{2}a\left(\frac{v - v_0}{a}\right)^2 = \frac{v^2 - v_0^2}{2a}$$

The work done by the force $\vec{F}$ in moving the body from the origin through a distance $\vec{x}$ is

$$\text{Work Done} = Fx = \frac{F(v^2 - v_0^2)}{2a}$$

But from Newton's second law $F = Ma$. So work done

$$= \frac{Ma\left(v^2 - v_0^2\right)}{2a}$$

$$= \tfrac{1}{2}M\left(v^2 - v_0^2\right)$$

$$= \tfrac{1}{2}\,Mv^2 - \tfrac{1}{2}Mv_0^2$$

Work done = Final kinetic energy - initial kinetic energy.

• PROBLEM 264

(a) If the x direction is normal to the surface of the earth and directed upward, the gravitational force is $F_G = -\,Mg\,\hat{x}$, where g is the acceleration of gravity and has the approximate value 980 cm/sec^2. Calculate the work done by gravity when a mass of 100 gm falls through 10 cm. (b) If the particle in (a) was initially at rest, what is its kinetic energy and its velocity at the end of its 10-cm fall?

Solution:

(a) Work done by a force $\vec{F}$ is calculated by $\int \vec{F} \cdot d\vec{s}$.

Here $\vec{F} = mg\hat{x}$ which is a constant, and since the object falls in a straight line, the work is given by

$$W = mgx$$

This is a scalar quantity since we are taking the dot product of $\vec{F} \cdot d\vec{s}$. Since $\vec{F}$ and $\vec{s}$ are parallel, we take the simple arithmetic product:

$$W = (100 \text{ gm})\ (980 \text{ cm/s})(10 \text{ cm}) = 980{,}000 \text{ ergs}$$

(b) The initial value K_A of the kinetic energy is zero; the terminal value K_B is equal to the work done by gravity on the particle, so that

$$K_B = W \simeq 10^6 \text{ ergs} = \tfrac{1}{2}\, m\nu_B^2,$$

whence $\nu_B^2 \simeq 2\left(10^6 \text{ ergs}\right)/\left(100 \text{ gm}\right) \simeq 2 \times 10^4 \text{ cm}^2/\text{sec}^2$.

Therefore, $v_B \cong 1.41 \times 10^2$ cm/sec

We may obtain the same result from the equations of motion. We have $v = gt$ and $h = \tfrac{1}{2}\,gt^2$. (These equations are adaptations of the more complete equations of motion, $d = \tfrac{1}{2}\,at^2 + v_0t + d_0$ and $v = at + v_0$, to the initial conditions of our problem where $v_0 = 0$, d_0 is assumed to be 0, and $a = g$.) Eliminating t, we have $v^2 = 2gh$. Therefore,

$$v^2 = 2(980\ cm/s^2)(10\ cm)$$

$$v^2 \cong 2 \times 10^4\ cm^2/s^2$$

$$v \cong 1.41 \times 10^2\ cm/sec.$$

• PROBLEM 265

A man stands at rest on frictionless roller skates on a level surface, facing a brick wall. He sets himself in motion (backward) by pushing against the wall. Discuss the problem from the work-energy standpoint.

Fig. A) Man pushes against wall with force $\vec{F}$; Wall exerts equal and opposite force $\vec{R}$. (B) Free-body diagram of forces acting on the man, including his weight $\vec{W}$ and the normal force $\vec{N}$ of the ground on the man.

Solution: The external forces on the man are his weight, the upward force exerted by the surface, and the horizontal force exerted by the wall. (The latter is the reaction to the force with which the man pushes against the wall.) The definition of the work done by a force $\vec{F}$ is

$$W = \int \vec{F} \cdot d\vec{s}$$

where $d\vec{s}$ is an element of the path traversed by the object acted on by $\vec{F}$. No work is done by the first two forces because they are at right angles to the motion. No work is done by the third force because there is no motion of its point of application. The external work is therefore zero and the internal work (of the man's muscular forces) equals the change in his kinetic energy.

• PROBLEM 266

A small object of weight $\vec{w}$ hangs from a string of length ℓ, as shown in the figure. A variable horizontal force $\vec{P}$, which starts at zero and gradually increases, is used to pull the object very slowly (so that equilibrium exists at all times) until the string makes an angle θ with the vertical. Calculate the work of the force $\vec{P}$.

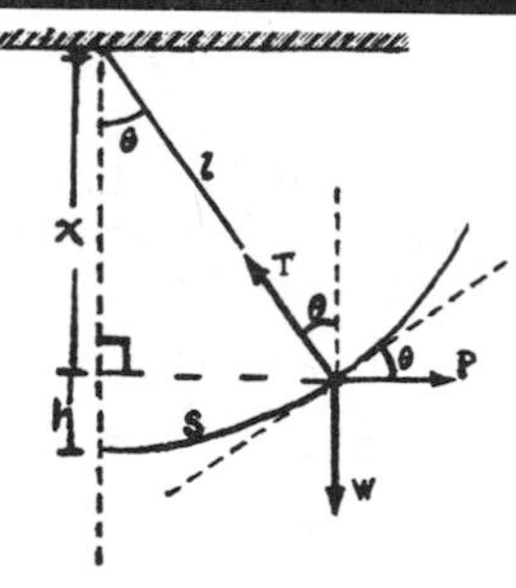

Solution: The object is in equilibrium, meaning that its acceleration is zero and the net force acting on the weight is zero. Consider the forces acting on the object, as shown in the diagram. We can say

$$\Sigma F_x = 0 = P - T \sin \theta \qquad (1)$$

$$P = T \sin \theta \qquad (2)$$

and $$\Sigma F_y = 0 = T \cos \theta - W \qquad (3)$$

$$W = T \cos \theta \qquad (4)$$

Dividing eq. (2) by eq. (4), we get $P = W \tan \theta$

Since P is variable, the work done by it must be found through integration. Recall that work is the integral of the dot product of the force $\vec{F}$ and the displacement vector $d\vec{x}$:

$$W = \int_{x_1}^{x_2} \vec{F} \cdot d\vec{x} = \int_{x_1}^{x_2} F \cos \gamma \, dx$$

where γ is the angle between $\vec{F}$ and $d\vec{x}$. In this case, the force is P, the differential displacement is $\ell d\theta$ and the angle between the two is θ. Substituting these expressions, we have

$$W = \int_0^\theta \vec{P} \cdot \ell d\vec{\theta} = \int_0^\theta (\omega \tan \theta)(\cos \theta)(\ell) d\theta$$

$$= \omega\ell \int_0^\theta \sin \theta \, d\theta = - \omega\ell \cos \theta \Big|_0^\theta = \omega\ell(1 - \cos \theta)$$

This result can also be derived using conservation of energy. Since the object's initial and final velocity is zero, kinetic energy is not involved. The change in the object's potential energy must be due completely to the work done on the weight by the force $\vec{P}$. This change in potential energy, ΔPE, is

$$\Delta PE = Wh = W(\ell - x)$$

But $x = \ell \cos \theta$

Therefore, we have

$$\Delta PE = \omega(\ell - \ell \cos \theta) = \omega\ell(1 - \cos \theta)$$

This is equal to the work:

$$W = \omega\ell(1 - \cos \theta)$$

• PROBLEM 267

A force of 100 nt is required to stretch a steel wire 2.0 mm^2 in cross-sectional area and 2.0 m long a distance of 0.50 mm. How much work is done?

Solution. In this problem we will make use of Hooke's Law which states that the force needed to stretch a material a distance y is proportional to this distance; i.e., $F = ky$, where k is called the spring constant. Therefore, to find k, we divide the force by the distance y,

$$k = \frac{100 \text{ nt}}{5.0 \times 10^{-4} \text{ m}} = 20 \times 10^4 \text{ nt/m}$$

The work done is given by,

$$W = \int \vec{F} \cdot \vec{dy} \tag{1}$$

Since the force and the displacement are in the same direction, (1) may be simplified to

$$W = \int F dy \tag{2}$$

but $F = ky$ so (2) becomes

$$W = \int kydy = \frac{1}{2}ky^2$$

$$= \frac{1}{2}(20 \times 10^4 \text{ nt/m})(5.0 \times 10^{-4} \text{ m})^2$$

$$= 0.025 \text{ nt - m.}$$

• PROBLEM 268

The figure shows a box being dragged along a horizontal surface by a constant force $\vec{P}$ making a constant angle θ with the direction of motion. The other forces on the box are its weight $\vec{W} = m\vec{g}$, the normal upward force $\vec{N}$ exerted by the surface, and the friction force $\vec{f}$. What is the work done by each force when the box moves a distance s along the surface to the right?

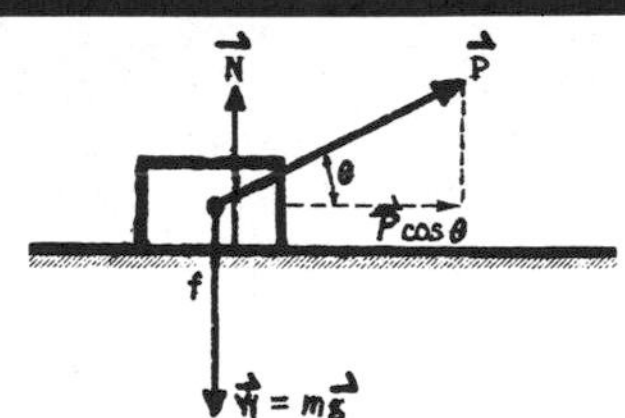

Solution: The component of $\vec{P}$ in the direction of motion is $P \cos \theta$. The work of the force $\vec{P}$ is by definition

$$W_P = \int \vec{P} \cdot \vec{ds} = P \cos \theta \int ds = P(\cos \theta)(s)$$

for $\vec{P}$ is a constant force. $\vec{ds}$ is a vector in the direction of horizontal motion.

The forces $\vec{w}$ and $\vec{N}$ are both at right angles to the displacement. Hence

$$W_w = \int \vec{w} \cdot \vec{ds} = ws \cos 90^\circ = 0 \text{ (}\vec{W} \text{ is constant.}$$

Therefore it may be taken out of the integral).

$$W_N = \int \vec{W} \cdot \vec{ds} = Ns \cos 90^\circ = 0 \text{ } (\vec{N} \text{ is constant.}$$

Therefore it was taken out of the integral).

The friction force $\vec{f}$ is opposite to the displacement, so the work of the friction force is

$$W_F = \int \vec{f} \cdot \vec{ds} = fs \cos 180^\circ = -fs$$

Since work is a scalar quantity, the total work W of all forces on the body is the algebraic (not the vector) sum of the individual works.

$$\begin{aligned} W &= W_p + W_w + W_N + W_f \\ &= (P \cos \theta) \cdot s + 0 + 0 - f \cdot s \\ &= (P \cos \theta - f)s. \end{aligned}$$

But $(P \cos \theta - f)$ is the resultant force on the body. The sum of the forces in the vertical direction, acting on the body is zero, for the object moves only in the horizontal direction. Hence the total work of all forces is equal to the work of the resultant force.

Suppose that $w = 100$ lb, $P = 50$ lb, $f = 15$ lb, $\theta = 37^\circ$, and $s = 20$ ft. Then

$$W_P = (P \cos \theta) \cdot s = 50 \times 0.8 \times 20 = 800 \text{ ft.lb},$$

$$W_f = -fs = -15 \times 20 = -300 \text{ ft.lb},$$

$$\begin{aligned} W &= W_P + W_w + W_N + W_f \\ &= 800 \text{ ft}\cdot\text{lb} + 0 + 0 - 300 \text{ ft}\cdot\text{lb} \\ &= 500 \text{ ft}\cdot\text{lb} \end{aligned}$$

• PROBLEM 269

What average force is necessary to stop a bullet of mass 20 gm and speed 250 m/sec as it penetrates wood to a distance of 12 cm?

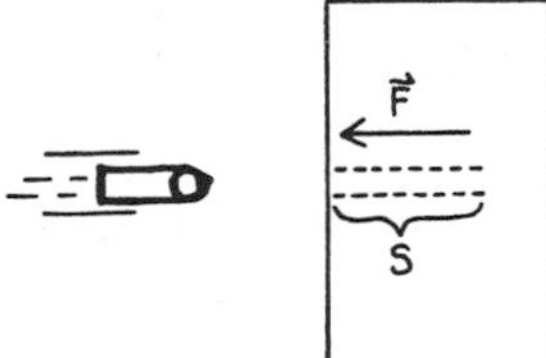

Solution: As it travels through the block, the bullet experiences an average force, $\vec{F}_{avg}$, which retards its motion. By the work-energy theorem, the work done by the net force on an object equals the change in kinetic energy of the object. Hence

$$\int \vec{F} \cdot \vec{ds} = \tfrac{1}{2}mv_f^2 - \tfrac{1}{2}mv_0^2$$

But we only know $\vec{F}$ as an average value. Hence

$$\int \vec{F} \cdot \vec{ds} \simeq \vec{F}_{avg} \cdot \Delta\vec{s} = \tfrac{1}{2}mv_f^2 - \tfrac{1}{2}mv_0^2$$

By definition

$$\vec{F}_{avg} \cdot \Delta\vec{s} = |\vec{F}_{avg}||\Delta\vec{s}| \cos\theta = \tfrac{1}{2} mv_f^2 - \tfrac{1}{2} mv_0^2$$

where θ is the angle between $\vec{F}_{avg}$ and Δs, 180° in this problem. Whence

$$-|\vec{F}_{avg}||\Delta\vec{s}| = \tfrac{1}{2} mv_f^2 - \tfrac{1}{2} mv_0^2$$

$$|\vec{F}_{avg}| = \frac{\tfrac{1}{2} mv_0^2 - \tfrac{1}{2} mv_f^2}{|\Delta\vec{s}|}$$

Hence, $$|\vec{F}_{avg}| = \frac{\tfrac{1}{2}(.02\text{kg})(250\ \text{m/s})^2 - 0}{.12\ \text{m}}$$

$$= 5.2 \times 10^3\ \text{nt}$$

This force is nearly 30,000 times the weight of the bullet.

The initial kinetic energy, $\tfrac{1}{2} mv^2 = 620$ joules, is largely wasted in heat and in work done in deforming the bullet.

• PROBLEM 270

Suppose a body of mass 0.5 kg slides down a track of radius $\vec{R} = 1$ m, like that in **the fig,** but its speed at the bottom is only 3 m/sec. What was the work of the frictional force acting on the body?

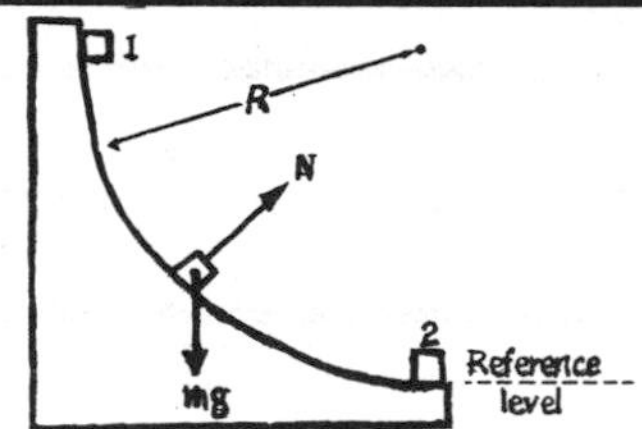

Solution: Note that we cannot calculate the work done by friction from the definition of work because

$$W_{friction} = \int \vec{F}_{friction} \cdot d\vec{s}$$

and we do not know the functional form of $\vec{F}_{friction}$.

Since work is a form of energy, our next thought may be to try to calculate the work done by the frictional force by using the principle of conservation of energy.

At position 1, the mass is at rest, and its energy is equal to its potential energy

$$E = mgR \qquad (1)$$

In sliding down the track, some of this energy will be dissipated by friction and be transferred into heat energy Q and some will be transformed into the kinetic energy of the mass. Hence, at position 2,

$$E = Q + \tfrac{1}{2}mv^2 \qquad (2)$$

Note that the potential energy of the mass at position 2 is zero, since this is our reference position for potential energy. Combining equations (1) and (2)

$$mgR = Q + \tfrac{1}{2}mv^2$$

and
$$mgR - \tfrac{1}{2}mv^2 = Q$$

or
$$(.5\ \text{kg})\left(9.8\ \text{m/s}^2\right)(1\ \text{m}) - \tfrac{1}{2}(.5\ \text{kg})\left(9\ \text{m}^2/\text{s}^2\right) = Q$$

$$4.9\ \text{kg} \cdot \frac{\text{m}^2}{\text{s}^2} - 2.25\ \text{kg} \cdot \frac{\text{m}^2}{\text{s}^2} = Q$$

$$Q = 2.65\ \text{Joules}$$

This is the heat energy produced by friction, and it is positive because heat energy has been gained by the system. Therefore, the work done by friction must be negative because this energy was lost to heat. Hence

$$W_f = -Q = -2.65\ \text{Joules}$$

• PROBLEM 271

A 3000-lb automobile at rest at the top of an incline 30 ft high and 300 ft long is released and rolls down the hill. What is its speed at the bottom of the incline if the average retarding force is 200 lb?

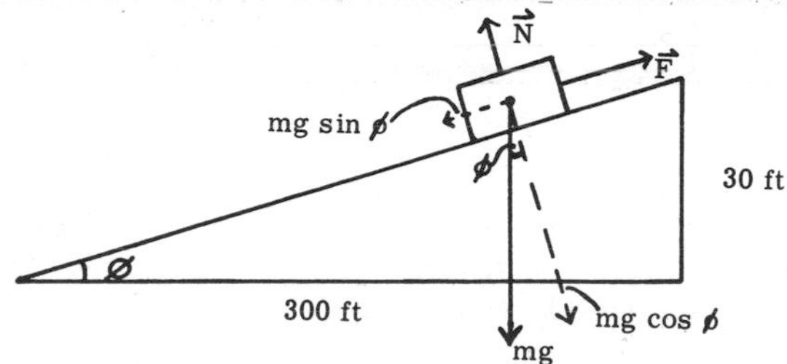

Solution: The potential energy at the top of the hill is available to do work against the retarding force $\vec{F}$ and to supply kinetic energy. The work done by the retarding force $\vec{F}$ is

$$W = \int \vec{F} \cdot d\vec{s}$$

where the integral is evaluated over the path of motion of the auto. If $\vec{F}$ is constant,

$$W = \vec{F} \cdot \int d\vec{s} = \vec{F} \cdot \vec{s}$$

$\vec{s}$ being the vector displacement of the auto. Hence, by the principle of energy conservation,

$$mgh = \vec{F} \cdot \vec{s} + \tfrac{1}{2}\ mv^2$$

where v is the velocity at the bottom of the incline. Since $\vec{F}$ and $\vec{s}$ are parallel and in the same direction, we may write
$$Wh = Fs + \tfrac{1}{2}\ mv^2 \qquad (1)$$

Since the height of the incline is much less than the length of the base, we may use 300 feet as an approximation to the length of the hypotenuse (see figure). Then, substituting into (1)

$$3000 \text{ lb} \times 30 \text{ ft} = 200 \text{ lb} \times 300 \text{ ft} + \tfrac{1}{2} \times 94 \text{ slugs} \times v^2$$

$$9.0 \times 10^4 \text{ ft-lb} - 6.0 \times 10^4 \text{ ft-lb} = \tfrac{1}{2} \times 94 \text{ slugs} \times v^2$$

$$v^2 = \frac{3.0 \times 10^4 \text{ ft-lb}}{47 \text{ slugs}} = 640 \text{ ft}^2/\text{sec}^2$$

$$v = 25 \text{ ft/sec.}$$

• PROBLEM 272

(1) Calculate the work done by gravity when a mass of 100 g moves from the origin to $\vec{r} = (50\hat{i} + 50\hat{j})$ cm. (2) What is the change in potential energy in this displacement? (3) If a particle of mass M is projected from the origin with speed v_0 at angle θ with the horizontal, how high will it rise?

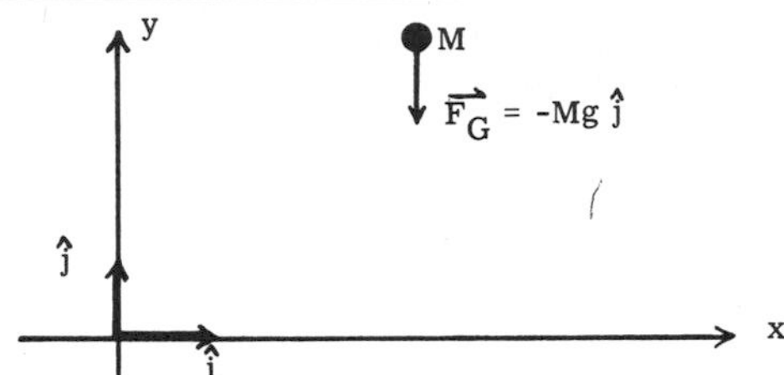

Solution:

(1) Let $(\hat{i},\hat{j})$ be the unit vectors along the horizontal and vertical directions respectively, as shown in the figure. The gravitational force is

$$\vec{F}_G = -Mg\,\hat{j}$$

The work W done by $\vec{F}_G$ is

$$W = \int_{(0,0)\text{ cm}}^{(50,50)\text{cm}} \vec{F}_G \cdot d\vec{r} = -Mg \int_0^{50 \text{ cm}} dy \qquad (1)$$

$$W = -Mg\ (50 \text{ cm})$$

$$W = -(100 \text{ g})(980 \text{ cm/s}^2)(50 \text{ cm})$$

$$W = -4.9 \times 10^6 \text{ ergs} \qquad (2)$$

The gravitational force does a negative amount of work. The reason for this is that $\vec{F}_G$ opposes the upward motion of M from the origin.

(2) The definition of potential difference is

$$V_{(50,50)} - V_{(0,0)} = -\int_{(0,0)}^{(50,50)} \vec{F}_G \cdot d\vec{r}$$

From (1) and (2)

$$V_{(50,50)} - V_{(0,0)} = 4.9 \times 10^6 \text{ ergs}$$

(3) In order to find the maximum height h that the particle attains, we relate the energy at the point of projection (x = 0, y = 0) to the energy at y = h. This may be done using the principle of energy conservation. Hence,

$$E_f = E_i$$

$$\tfrac{1}{2} Mv_f^2 + V_f = \tfrac{1}{2} Mv_0^2 + V_0$$

We may arbitrarily set V = 0 at y = 0. Hence, $V_0 = 0$.

$$\tfrac{1}{2} Mv_f^2 + Mgh = \tfrac{1}{2} Mv_0^2 \qquad (3)$$

But $$v_f^2 = v_{xf}^2 + v_{yf}^2 \qquad (4)$$

$$v_0^2 = v_{x0}^2 + v_{y0}^2 \qquad (5)$$

Because there is no x-component of acceleration, $v_{x0} = v_{xf}$. Also, at y = h, $v_y = 0$, hence $v_{yf} = 0$. Substituting this data in (4) and (5)

$$v_f^2 = v_{x0}^2$$

$$v_0^2 = v_{x0}^2 + v_{y0}^2$$

Substituting this in (3)

$$\tfrac{1}{2} Mv_{x0}^2 + Mgh = \tfrac{1}{2} M(v_{x0}^2 + v_{y0}^2)$$

or $$Mgh = \tfrac{1}{2} M v_{y0}^2$$

or $$h = \frac{v_{y0}^2}{2g}$$

But $v_{y0} = v_0 \sin\theta$, and

$$h = \frac{v_0^2 \sin^2\theta}{2g}$$

• PROBLEM 273

A stone of mass 5 kg drops through a distance of 15 m under the influence of gravity. Dráw graphs of the work done by the stone and the power of the stone as a function of time.

Solution. This is a case of constant acceleration with $a = g = 9.8 \text{ m/sec}^2$. The equation $d = v_0 t + \frac{1}{2}at^2$ can be used to find the total time the stone is in motion.

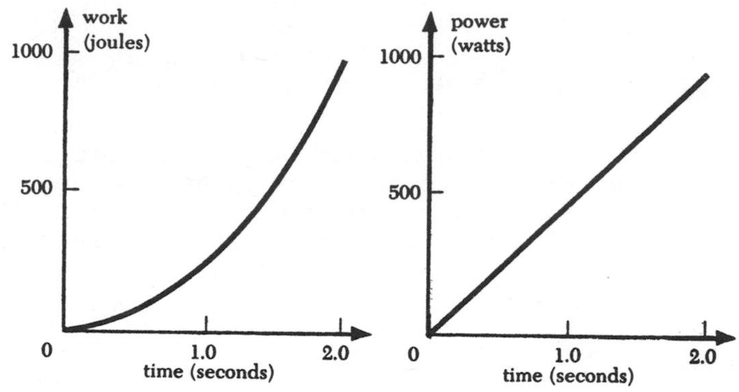

The initial velocity is zero, thus $d = \frac{1}{2}gt^2$ where $d = 15$ m. The time required for the stone to fall through 15 m is

$$t^2 = \frac{2 \times 15}{9.8} = 3.06$$

$$t = 1.75 \text{ sec.}$$

The force acting on the stone is constant at

$$F = mg = 5 \text{ kg} \times 9.8 \text{ m/sec}^2 = 49 \text{ newtons.}$$

The work done by the stone is equal to $W = Fd$.

To find the power of the stone, note that $P = Fv$. The velocity can be found from $v = v_0 + at = gt$. Below are the calculated values of d, v, W, and P for intervals of 0.25 seconds and the graphs requested.

t	$v = gt$	$d = \frac{1}{2}gt^2$	$W = Fd$	$P = Fv$
0	0 m/sec	0 m	0 J	0 W
0.25	2.45	0.31	15.2	120
0.5	4.9	1.23	60	240
0.75	7.35	2.76	135	360
1.0	9.8	4.90	240	480
1.25	12.3	7.66	376	600
1.50	14.7	11.0	540	720
1.75	17.2	15.0	735	840

• PROBLEM 274

A delicate machine weighing 350 lb is lowered gently at constant speed down planks 8 ft long from the tailboard of a truck 4 ft above the ground. The relevant coefficient of sliding friction is 0.5. Must the machine be pulled down or held back? If the required force is applied parallel to the planks, what is its magnitude?

The machine is reloaded in the same manner, a force of 330 lb being applied. With what velocity does it reach the tailboard? What kinetic energy and what potential energy has it then acquired and how much work has been performed in overcoming friction? What relationship exists between these quantities?

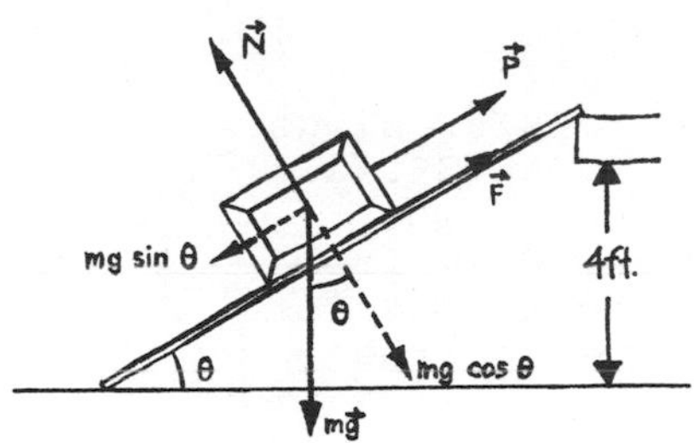

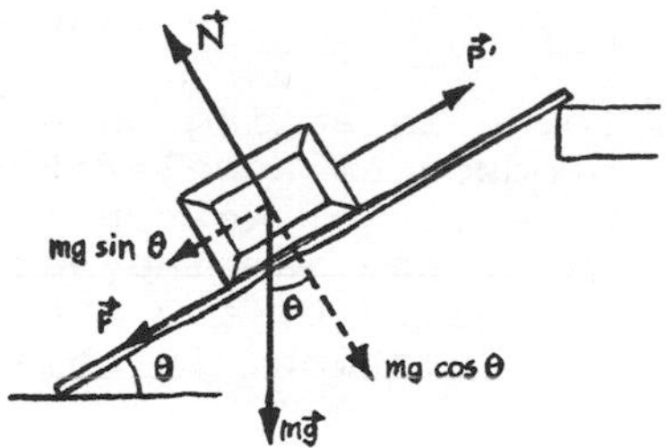

FIGURE A　　　　　　　　FIGURE B

Solution: The forces acting on the machine are four in number. (1) The weight, $\overrightarrow{mg}$, acting vertically downward. (2) The normal force exerted by the plane, $\vec{N}$. (3) The frictional force $\vec{F}$, acting up the plane opposing the motion down it. If μ is the coefficient of sliding friction, this force has magnitude μN. (4) The force $\vec{P}$ necessary to keep the machine moving with constant speed. In the diagram this is drawn acting up the plane. If the machine has to be pulled down, $\vec{P}$ will be negative.

Resolve the force $\overrightarrow{mg}$ into its components along the plane and at right angles to the plane. The forces are in equilibrium since there is no acceleration taking place. Hence, by Newton's Second Law,

$$N = mg \cos \theta \quad \text{and}$$

$$mg \sin \theta = P + \mu N = P + \mu \, mg \cos \theta.$$

$$P = mg (\sin \theta - \mu \cos \theta).$$

Therefore $P = mg(\sin \theta - \mu \cos \theta)$. But $\sin \theta = 4/8 = \frac{1}{2}$, as shown in figure (a)

$$\therefore \quad \theta = 30°.$$

$$\therefore \; P = 350 \text{ lb} \left(\frac{1}{2} - 0.5 \frac{\sqrt{3}}{2}\right) = 350 \times 0.067 \text{ lb}$$

$$= 23.45 \text{ lb}.$$

The machine must be held back with a force of this magnitude.

During the loading process, the forces acting are those shown in figure (b). Compared with the previous case, (1) and (2) are the same as before, (3) is of the same magnitude but, since it still acts against the motion, its direction is now reversed; (4) is replaced by the force $\vec{P}'$ supplied by the loaders.

There is no tendency to move at right angles to the plane. Thus $N = mg \cos \theta$. The net force up the plane is

$$P' - mg \sin \theta - \mu N = P' - mg(\sin \theta + \mu \cos \theta)$$

$$= 330 \text{ lb} - 350 \left(\frac{1}{2} + 0.5 \frac{\sqrt{3}}{2}\right) \text{ lb}$$

$= (330 - 326.55)\text{lb} = 3.45 \text{ lb}.$

This force is acting on a mass of 350/32 slugs, and will produce an acceleration $a = 3.45/(350/32)$ ft/s^2 as a result of Newton's Second Law. The velocity after the machine has traveled 8 ft. from rest is thus given by the kinematics equations for constant acceleration. In this case, we use the equation

$$v^2 = v_0^2 + 2a(x - x_0)$$

where $x - x_0$ is the distance travelled along the plane, a is the machine's acceleration parallel to the plane, and v_0 is its initial velocity. Since $v_0 = 0$,

$$v^2 = 2 \times \frac{32 \times 3.45 \text{ ft/s}^2}{350} \times 8 \text{ ft}$$

or $v = 2.25$ ft/s.

The kinetic energy at that time is

$$\tfrac{1}{2} mv^2 = \tfrac{1}{2} \times \frac{350}{32} \text{ slugs} \times 2 \times \frac{32 \times 3.45}{350} \times 8 \text{ ft}^2/\text{s}^2$$

$$= 27.6 \text{ ft-lb}.$$

Or, alternatively, the work-energy theorem tells us the kinetic energy is the net force up the plane times 8 ft = 3.45 lb × 8 ft = 27.6 ft·lb.

The potential energy is Wh = 350 lb × 4 ft = 1400 ft-lb.

The work done in overcoming friction is $\vec{F} \cdot \vec{s} = \mu N \times 8 \text{ ft} = 8 \text{ ft} \times \mu mg \cos\theta = 1212.4$ ft-lb.

The work done by the applied force P' is $\vec{P}' \cdot \vec{s} =$ 330 lb × 8 ft = 2640 ft-lb.

But 27.6 + 1400 + 1212.4 = 2640. Thus the work done by the applied force equals the kinetic energy plus the potential energy gained by the machine added to the work done to overcome friction. This is merely a statement of the conservation of energy applied to this problem.

• PROBLEM 275

A neutron traveling at a speed of 2×10^3 m/s collides with a nucleus and rebounds with a speed of 3×10^2 m/s. (a) Determine the work done by the force of interaction between the nucleus and neutron and (b) estimate the strength of the force if the distance over which the collision occurred is 2×10^{-15} m. The mass of a neutron is 1.67×10^{-27} kg.

Solution: The mass of the neutron, $m = 1.67 \times 10^{-27}$ kg, its initial speed $v_0 = 2 \times 10^3$ m/s, its final speed, v = 3 × 10^2 m/s, and the distance over which the particles interacted, d = 2 × 10^{-15} m, are the known observables. The work done by the force of the interaction of the particle, W, and the force F are the unknown observables.

(a) Assume that the nucleus experiences no change in velocity due to the collision with the neutron. Then the total change in energy of the system is due only to the change in the kinetic energy of the neutron. This change in energy is equal to the work W.

$$W = \Delta KE = \tfrac{1}{2} m(v^2 - v_0^2)$$

$$W = (\tfrac{1}{2})(1.67 \times 10^{-27} \text{ kg})(3 \times 10^2 \text{ m/s})^2$$

$$- (\tfrac{1}{2})(1.67 \times 10^{-27} \text{ kg})(2 \times 10^3 \text{ m/s})^2$$

$$= 7.5 \times 10^{-23} \text{ J} - 3.34 \times 10^{-21} \text{ J}$$

$$= - 3.27 \times 10^{-21} \text{ J}$$

The minus sign indicates that the work done by the force decreased the kinetic energy of the neutron.

(b) Although it is not stated that the force is constant during the collision, assume that it is and also assume that it is parallel to the displacement vector. Using these assumptions, the force can be determined from

$$F = \frac{W}{d} = \frac{-3.27 \times 10^{-21} \text{ N}\not{m}}{2 \times 10^{-15} \not{m}} = -1.64 \times 10^{-6} \text{ N}$$

• PROBLEM 276

Let us estimate the gravitational energy of the Galaxy. We omit from the calculation the gravitational self-energy of the individual stars.

Solution: The gravitational energy of an arbitrary system of N particles consists of the sum of the mutual potential energies of each pair of particles. Hence,

$$U = \tfrac{1}{2}\Big\{\left(U_{12} + U_{13} + U_{14} + \dots U_{1N}\right) + \left(U_{21} + U_{23} + U_{24} + \dots + U_{2N}\right)$$
$$+ \left(U_{31} + U_{32} + U_{34} + \dots + U_{3N}\right)$$
$$+ \dots + \left(U_{N1} + U_{N2} + U_{N3} + \dots + U_{NN-1}\right)\Big\} \qquad (1)$$

The terms U_{12}, etc., represent the mutual potential energy of particles 1 and 2. By including sets of terms such as U_{12} and U_{21} we have double counted, because these represent the mutual potential energies of particles 1 and 2, and particles 2 and 1, respectively. However, these 2 terms are the same. Hence, the factor ½ must be included in (1) to negate the process of double counting. Furthermore, terms such as U_{11} are omitted because they represent the mutual potential energy of particle 1 with particle 1, i.e., they are self energies.

We approximate the gross composition of the Galaxy by N stars, each of mass M, and with each pair of stars at a mutual separation of the order of R.

From the definition of potential energy

$$U_{ij} = \frac{-Gm_i m_j}{r_{ij}}$$

where m_i and m_j are the masses of particles i and j, respectively, $G = 6.67 \times 10^{-11}\ N\cdot m^2/kg^2$, is their mutual separation. For our case

$$r_{ij} = R$$

and

$$m_i = m_j = M$$

for all pairs of particles. Then

$$U_{ij} = \frac{-GM^2}{R} \qquad (2)$$

for any 2 particles.

Notice that in equation (1), the first parenthesis has N-1 terms of the type (2), the second parenthesis has N-1 terms of this type, and similarly for all N **parenthesises.** Altogether, there are N(N-1) terms of type (2) in (1). Therefore,

$$U = \tfrac{1}{2}(N)(N-1)\left(\frac{-GM^2}{R}\right)$$

$$U = -\tfrac{1}{2}\,\frac{N(N-1)GM^2}{R}$$

If $N \approx 1.6 \times 10^{11}$, $R \approx 10^{21}$m, and $M \approx 2 \times 10^{30}$ kg, then

$$U \approx \frac{-\tfrac{1}{2}(1.6 \times 10^{11})(1.6 \times 10^{11}-1)(6.67 \times 10^{-11} N\cdot m^2/kg^2)(2 \times 10^{30} kg)^2}{10^{21}\ m}$$

$$U \approx \frac{-34.15 \times 10^{71}}{10^{21}}\ J = -34.15 \times 10^{50}\ J$$

$$U \approx -3.42 \times 10^{51}\ J$$

• PROBLEM 277

Estimate the average temperature of the interior of the sun. The gravitational self-energy, U_s, of a uniform star of mass M_s and radius R_s is

$$U_s = -\frac{3GM_s^2}{5R_s}$$

Solution: The average kinetic energy of a single atom in a star is proportional to the absolute temperature T:

$$\langle \text{K.E. of a particle} \rangle = \frac{3}{2}kT,$$

with the constant k (the Boltzmann constant) given by:

$$k = 1.38 \times 10^{-16} \text{ erg/deg Kelvin}.$$

Here, the brackets < > denote an average value.

The total kinetic energy in the star is 3/2 kNT_{av}, where T_{av} is an appropriate average temperature over the interior of the star, and N is the number of atoms in the star. Then, the virial theorem gives:

$$\langle \text{K.E. of all atoms} \rangle = -\tfrac{1}{2} \langle \text{P.E. of sun} \rangle$$

where P.E. is potential energy. Hence,

$$\frac{3}{2} NkT_{av} = \frac{3GM_s^2}{10R_s}$$

Thus, we have

$$T_{av} = \frac{GM_s^2}{5R_s Nk} = \frac{GM_s M}{5R_s k} \qquad (1)$$

where $M = M_s/N$ is the average mass of an atom in the star. (Most of the atoms in a star are generally hydrogen or helium.)

The mass of the sun, M_s, approximately equals 2×10^{33} gm, and its radius R_s is approximately 7×10^{10}cm. Let us take M as 3×10^{-24} gm, about twice the proton mass. Then (1) becomes

$$T_{av} \approx \frac{(7 \times 10^{-8}\ \text{dynes}\cdot\text{cm}^2/\text{gm}^2)(2 \times 10^{33}\ \text{gm})(3 \times 10^{-24}\ \text{gm})}{5(7 \times 10^{10}\ \text{cm})(1 \times 10^{-16}\ \text{erg}/^\circ\text{K})}$$

$$T_{av} \approx 10^7\ ^\circ\text{K}$$

We have performed what is known as an order of magnitude calculation for T_{av}.

• PROBLEM 278

A particle of mass M is attached to a string (see the figure) and constrained to move in a horizontal plane (the plane of the dashed line). The particle rotates with velocity v_0 when the length of the string is r_0. How much work is done in shortening the string to r?

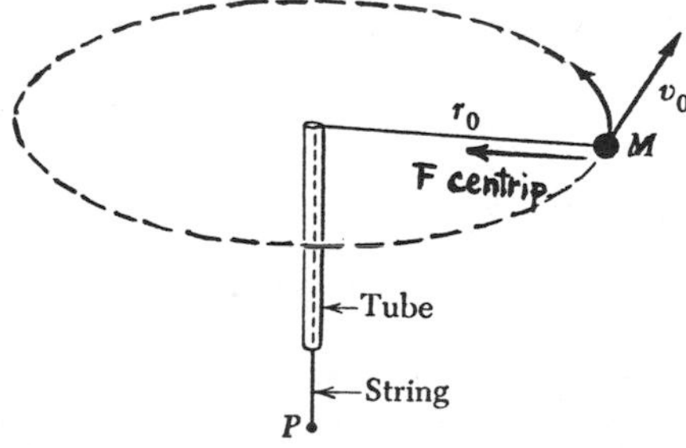

Solution: The string is stretched under the action of the radial centripetal force which keeps the mass M on its circular path. When we pull in the string we shorten r_0 by increasing the radial force $\vec{F}_{centrip}$ on M. As we know, a force can only produce a torque about the axis of rotation if it has a component perpendicular to the radius which locates the mass M. A purely radial force like $\vec{F}_{centrip}$ has no such component, therefore the angular momentum must remain constant as the string is shortened.

$$Mv_0r_0 = Mvr \tag{1}$$

The kinetic energy at r_0 is $\frac{1}{2} Mv_0{}^2$; at r it has been increased to

$$\frac{1}{2} Mv^2 = \frac{1}{2} Mv_0{}^2 \left(\frac{r_0}{r}\right)^2$$

because $v = v_0r_0/r$ from above. It follows that the work W done from outside in shortening the string from r_0 to r is

$$W = \frac{1}{2} Mv^2 - \frac{1}{2} Mv_0{}^2 = \frac{1}{2} Mv_0{}^2 \left[\left(\frac{r_0}{r}\right)^2 - 1\right] \tag{2}$$

This can also be calculated directly as the work done by $\vec{F}_{centrip}$ along the distance $r_0 - r$;

$$W= \int_{r_0}^{r} \vec{F}_{centrip} \cdot d\vec{r} = - \int_{r_0}^{r} F_{centrip}\, dr$$

$$W = - \int_{r_0}^{r} dr\, \frac{Mv^2}{r} = - \int_{r_0}^{r} dr\, \frac{M}{r} \frac{v_0{}^2r_0{}^2}{r^2}$$

where we have used (1). Hence

$$W = - Mv_0{}^2r_0{}^2 \int_{r_0}^{r} \frac{dr}{r^3}$$

$$W = \left.\frac{Mv_0{}^2r_0{}^2}{2r^2}\right|_{r_0}^{r} = \frac{Mv_0{}^2r_0{}^2}{2} \left(\frac{1}{r^2} - \frac{1}{r_0{}^2}\right)$$

$$W = \frac{1}{2} Mv_0{}^2 \left[\left(\frac{r_0}{r}\right)^2 - 1\right]$$

which is (2).

We see that the angular momentum acts on the radial motion as an effective repulsive force. We have to do extra work on the particle on bringing it from large distances to small distances if we require that the angular momentum be conserved in the process.

What is the relation between the total energy and the angular momentum for a 2-body system, each body executing a circular orbit about the system center of mass?

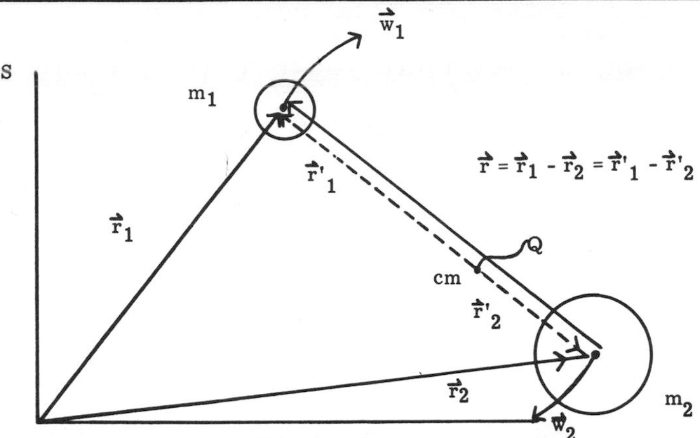

Solution: In order to solve this problem we must transform the given 2-body problem to an equivalent one-body problem. To do this, we find the equation of motion of each mass shown in the figure. Using Newton's Second Law and his Law of Universal Gravitation, we obtain:

$$\vec{F}_{12} = m_2\ddot{\vec{r}}_2 = \frac{Gm_1m_2(\vec{r}_1 - \vec{r}_2)}{|\vec{r}_1 - \vec{r}_2|^3} \tag{1}$$

$$\vec{F}_{21} = m_1\ddot{\vec{r}}_1 = -\frac{Gm_1m_2(\vec{r}_1 - \vec{r}_2)}{|\vec{r}_1 - \vec{r}_2|^3} \tag{2}$$

where $\vec{F}_{12}$ is the force exerted on 2 by 1, and similarly for $\vec{F}_{21}$. Rewriting (1) and (2)

$$\ddot{\vec{r}}_2 = \frac{1}{m_2}\frac{Gm_1m_2(\vec{r}_1 - \vec{r}_2)}{|\vec{r}_1 - \vec{r}_2|^3} \tag{3}$$

$$\ddot{\vec{r}}_1 = -\frac{1}{m_1}\frac{Gm_1m_2(\vec{r}_1 - \vec{r}_2)}{|\vec{r}_1 - \vec{r}_2|^3} \tag{4}$$

Subtracting (3) from (4), and using the figure to realize that $\vec{r}_1 - \vec{r}_2 = \vec{r}$, we obtain

$$\ddot{\vec{r}}_1 - \ddot{\vec{r}}_2 = \ddot{\vec{r}} = -\frac{1}{m_1}\frac{Gm_1m_2\vec{r}}{r^3} - \frac{1}{m_2}\frac{Gm_1m_2\vec{r}}{r^3}$$

or $$\ddot{\vec{r}} = -\frac{Gm_1m_2\vec{r}}{r^3}\left(\frac{1}{m_1} + \frac{1}{m_2}\right)$$

Defining the reduced mass μ as

$$\frac{1}{\mu} = \frac{1}{m_1} + \frac{1}{m_2} \tag{5}$$

we find $\mu\ddot{\vec{r}} = -\dfrac{Gm_1m_2\vec{r}}{r^3}$ (6)

This equation is a one body equation describing the motion of a particle of mass μ under the influence of a gravitational force.

Now, to further reduce the problem, assume that each mass shown in the figure rotates in a circular orbit with the given angular velocitites about Q, the center of mass. Using Newton's Second Law for each mass,

$$\frac{m_1v_1'^2}{r_2'} = \frac{Gm_1m_2}{r^2} \qquad (7)$$

$$\frac{m_2v_2'^2}{r_2'} = \frac{Gm_1m_2}{r^2} \qquad (8)$$

where the primed variables are measured with respect to the point Q. By definition of the center of mass

$$m_1\vec{r}_1' + m_2\vec{r}_2' = 0$$

or $$\vec{r}_1' = -\frac{m_2\vec{r}_2'}{m_1} \qquad (9)$$

Furthermore, $\vec{r} = \vec{r}_1' - \vec{r}_2'$

or $$\vec{r}_2' = \vec{r}_1' - \vec{r} \qquad (10)$$

Inserting (10) in (9), and solving for $\vec{r}_1'$

$$\vec{r}_1' = -\frac{m_2}{m_1}\vec{r}_2' = -\frac{m_2}{m_1}(\vec{r}_1' - \vec{r})$$

$$\vec{r}_1'\left(1 + \frac{m_2}{m_1}\right) = \frac{m_2}{m_1}\vec{r}$$

$$\vec{r}_1' = \frac{m_2/m_1\ \vec{r}}{1 + m_2/m_1} = \frac{m_2\vec{r}}{m_1 + m_2} \qquad (11)$$

But using (5)

$$\mu = \frac{m_1m_2}{m_1 + m_2}$$

Hence, (9) becomes $\vec{r}_1' = \dfrac{\mu}{m_1}\vec{r}$ (12)

Similarly, $\vec{r}_2' = -\dfrac{\mu}{m_2}\vec{r}$ (13)

Hence $r_1' = \dfrac{\mu}{m_1} r$

(14)

$r_2' = \dfrac{\mu}{m_2} r$

Using (14) in (7) and (8)

$$\frac{m_1^2 v_1'^2}{\mu r} = \frac{G m_1 m_2}{r^2}$$

$$\frac{m_2^2 v_2'^2}{\mu r} = \frac{G m_1 m_2}{r^2}$$

or

$$\frac{m_1 v_1'^2}{2} = \frac{\mu\, G m_2}{2r}$$

$$\frac{m_2 v_2'^2}{2} = \frac{\mu\, G m_1}{2r}$$

Therefore, the net kinetic energy of the system relative to the center of the mass is

$$T = \tfrac{1}{2}\, m_1 v_1'^2 + \tfrac{1}{2}\, m_2 v_2'^2 = \frac{\mu G}{2r}\,(m_1 + m_2) \tag{15}$$

$$T = \frac{G m_1 m_2}{2r} \tag{16}$$

by definition of μ. The total energy is

$$E = T + V = \frac{G m_1 m_2}{2r} - \frac{G m_1 m_2}{r}$$

$$E = -\frac{G m_1 m_2}{2r} \tag{17}$$

To remove the variable r, we replace it with the angular momentum $\vec{J}$ as follows. The total system angular momentum is (relative to Q)

$$\vec{J} = \vec{r}_1' \times m_1 \vec{v}_1' + \vec{r}_2' \times m_1 \vec{v}_2'$$

Since $\vec{r}_1'$ and $\vec{v}_1'$ are perpendicular, and similarly for $\vec{r}_2'$ and $\vec{v}_2'$, we obtain

$$J = m_1 r_1' v_1' + m_2 r_2' v_2' \tag{18}$$

From (12) and (13)

$$\vec{v}_1' = \frac{\mu}{m_1}\,\vec{v} \qquad \vec{r}_1' = \frac{\mu}{m_1}\,\vec{r}$$

$$\vec{v}_2' = -\frac{\mu}{m_2}\,\vec{v} \qquad \vec{r}_2' = -\frac{\mu}{m_2}\,\vec{r}$$

or

$$v_1' = \frac{\mu}{m_1}\, v \qquad r_1' = \frac{\mu}{m_1}\, r$$

$$v_2' = \frac{\mu}{m_2}\, v \qquad r_2' = \frac{\mu}{m_2}\, r \tag{19}$$

Using (19) in (18)

$$J = (m_1)\left(\frac{\mu}{m_1} r\right)\left(\frac{\mu}{m_1} v\right) + (m_2)\left(\frac{\mu}{m_2} r\right)\left(\frac{\mu}{m_2} v\right)$$

$$J = \frac{\mu^2}{m_1} vr + \frac{\mu^2}{m_2} vr = \mu^2 vr \left[\frac{1}{m_1} + \frac{1}{m_2}\right]$$

By definition of μ

$$J = \mu vr \qquad (20)$$

We now eliminate v in (20) so that we may substitute (20) in place of r in (17). We know, from (15) that

$$T = \tfrac{1}{2} m_1 v_1'^2 + \tfrac{1}{2} m_2 v_2'^2 = \frac{\mu G}{2r} (m_1 + m_2) \qquad (15)$$

Substituting for v_1', v_2' from (19) in (15),

$$T = \tfrac{1}{2} m_1 \left(\frac{\mu^2}{m_1^2} v^2\right) + \tfrac{1}{2} m_2 \left(\frac{\mu^2}{m_2^2} v^2\right) = \frac{\mu G}{2r} (m_1 + m_2)$$

$$T = \frac{\mu^2 v^2}{2m_1} + \frac{\mu^2 v^2}{2m_2} = \frac{\mu G}{2r} (m_1 + m_2)$$

$$T = \frac{\mu^2 v^2}{2} \left(\frac{1}{m_1} + \frac{1}{m_2}\right) = \frac{\mu G}{2r} (m_1 + m_2)$$

By definition of μ

$$T = \frac{\mu v^2}{2} = \frac{\mu G}{2r} (m_1 + m_2) \qquad (21)$$

Hence $$v^2 = \frac{G}{r} (m_1 + m_2) \qquad (22)$$

Using (22) in (20)

$$J = \mu r \sqrt{\frac{G(m_1 + m_2)}{r}}$$

or $J^2 = \mu^2 r G(m_1 + m_2)$

Therefore $$r = \frac{J^2}{\mu^2 G(m_1 + m_2)} \qquad (23)$$

Inserting (23) in (17)

$$E = -\frac{Gm_1 m_2}{2} \left(\frac{\mu^2 G(m_1 + m_2)}{J^2}\right)$$

$$E = -\frac{G^2 m_1 m_2 (m_1 + m_2)\mu^2}{2 J^2}$$

Finally,

$$m_1 m_2 (m_1 + m_2)\mu^2 = m_1 m_2 (m_1 + m_2)\left(\frac{m_1 m_2}{m_1 + m_2}\right) \mu$$

or $$m_1 m_2 (m_1 + m_2)\mu^2 = m_1^2 m_2^2 \mu$$

Then $$E = -\frac{G^2 \mu m_1^2 m_2^2}{2 J^2}$$

POWER

• PROBLEM 280

A constant horizontal force of 10 N is required to drag an object across a rough surface at a constant speed of 5 m/sec. What power is being expended? How much work would be done in 30 min?

Solution: Power is the rate of doing work,

$$P = \frac{\Delta W}{\Delta t} = \frac{F\Delta s}{\Delta t}\ .$$

(Note that in this problem the work reduces to the force multiplied by the distance the object is moved.) But $\frac{\Delta s}{\Delta t}$ is just the velocity. Therefore,

$$\begin{aligned} P &= Fv \\ &= (10\ N) \times (5\ m/sec) \\ &= 50\ J/sec \\ &= 50\ W \end{aligned}$$

$$\begin{aligned} W &= Pt \\ &= (50\ W) \times \left(\frac{1}{2}\ hr\right) \\ &= 25\ W\text{-}hr. \end{aligned}$$

The work, of course, is done against the force of sliding friction.

• PROBLEM 281

The engine of a jet aircraft develops a thrust of 3000 lb. What horsepower does it develop at a velocity of 600 mi/hr = 880 ft/sec?

Solution: $$\text{Power} = \frac{\text{Work}}{\text{Time}} = \frac{Fs}{T} \qquad (1)$$

where F is the force acting on a body and s is the displacement of the object in the direction of F in time t. By definition of velocity

$$v = \frac{s}{t} \qquad (2)$$

Therefore, combining equations (1) and (2)

$$P = Fv$$

In this example,

$$P = Fv = 3000 \text{ lb} \times 880 \frac{\text{ft}}{\text{sec}} = 2,640,000 \frac{\text{ft}\cdot\text{lb}}{\text{sec}}$$

Since $1 \text{ hp} = 550 \frac{\text{ft}\cdot\text{lb}}{\text{sec}}$

$$= \frac{2.64 \times 10^6 \text{ft}\cdot\text{lb/sec}}{550(\text{ft}\cdot\text{lb/sec})/\text{hp}} = 4800 \text{ hp}.$$

• PROBLEM 282

A string of freight cars weighs 200 tons. The coefficient of rolling friction is 0.005. How fast can a freight engine of 400 hp pull the string of cars along?

Solution: Power is defined as Work divided by time.

$$P = \frac{W}{t}$$

and W = Fs (where F and s are in the same direction and are force and distance respectively). Then,

$$P = \frac{Fs}{t} \quad \text{and since} \quad \frac{s}{t} = v$$

$$p = Fv$$

The force of friction can be calculated from $F = \mu N$, where μ is the coefficient of rolling friction and N is the normal force:

$$F = 0.005 \times (200 \text{ ton} \times 2000 \text{ lb/ton}) = 2000 \text{ lb}$$

Using P = Fv from above and the conversion factor $\left(\frac{550 \text{ ft-lb/sec}}{1 \text{ hp}}\right)$ to convert 400 hp to power in units $\frac{\text{ft-lb}}{\text{sec}}$:

$$400 \text{ hp } (550 \text{ ft-lb/sec/hp}) = 2000 \text{ lb} \times v$$

$$v = 110 \text{ ft/sec} = 75 \text{ mi/hr}.$$

• PROBLEM 283

A car engine working at the rate of 33 horsepower is moving the car at a rate of 45 mi/hr. What force is the engine exerting?

Solution: Force can be calculated from the expression for power: P = Fv. Converting horsepower to ft-lb/sec we have

$$P = 33 \text{ hp} \times 550 \frac{\text{ft-lb/sec}}{\text{hp}} = 18150 \text{ ft-lb/sec}$$

Since 60 mph = 88ft/sec, 45 mph = 66 ft/sec

Then

$$P = Fv$$

$$18150 \text{ ft-lb/s} = F \ 66 \text{ ft/s}$$

$$F = 275 \text{ lbs.}$$

• PROBLEM 284

A mass of 100 kilograms is pushed along the floor at a constant rate of 2 m/sec. If the coefficient of sliding friction is 0.25, at what rate is work being done in watts, in horsepower?

Solution: The weight of the mass is

$$100 \text{ kg} \times 9.8 \text{ m/sec}^2 = 980 \text{ nt} = N$$

$$\text{The force of friction} = F = \mu \times N = 0.25 \times 980 \text{ nt} = 245 \text{ nt}$$

$$\text{Power} = Fv = 245 \text{ nt} \times 2 \text{ m/sec} = 490 \text{ watts}$$

$$= \frac{490 \text{ watts}}{746 \text{ watts/hp}} = 0.66 \text{ hp}$$

• PROBLEM 285

A water pump motor has a horsepower rating of 11.3 hp. If it is to pump water from a well at the rate of 1 ft^3/sec (water has a weight density of 62.4 lbs/ft^3), what is the maximum depth the well may have? Neglect friction in your calculations.

Solution: The performance of a motor can be measured by the rate at which it does work. This rate is called the power P and is defined as

$$P = \frac{\Delta W}{\Delta t}$$

where ΔW is the work done in the time interval Δt. One unit of power is the horsepower, and is defined as 550 ft-lbs/sec. Therefore, the maximum power the motor can provide is

$$P_{max} = (11.3 \text{ hp})\left(\frac{550 \text{ ft-lbs/sec}}{\text{hp}}\right) = 6215 \text{ ft-lbs/sec}$$

The work the pump must do is just equal to the water's change in potential energy, which is due only to gravity. It is equal to

$$\Delta W = mgh$$

where h is the height through which the water is raised and is equal to the well's depth. In one second, the pump lifts one ft^3 of water or 62.4 lbs. Then

$$\frac{\Delta W}{\Delta t} = \frac{(62.4)h \text{ lbs}}{1 \text{ sec}}$$

and the maximum depth is found from

$$P_{max} = 6215 \frac{\text{ft-lbs}}{\text{sec}} = 62.4 \ h_{max} \frac{\text{lbs}}{\text{sec}}$$

$$h_{max} = \frac{6215}{62.4} \text{ ft} \approx 100 \text{ ft.}$$

• PROBLEM 286

The drive shaft of an automobile rotates at 3600 rev/min and transmits 80 hp from the engine to the rear wheels. Compute the torque developed by the engine.

Solution: By definition, the infinitesimal amount of work done by the torque Γ (provided by the drive shaft) in turning the wheel through an infinitesimal angular displacement Δθ is

$$\Delta W = \Gamma \ \Delta\theta$$

Dividing both sides by Δt

$$\frac{\Delta W}{\Delta t} = \Gamma \ \frac{\Delta\theta}{\Delta t}$$

Taking the limit as $\Delta t \to 0$

$$\frac{dW}{dt} = \Gamma \ \omega$$

where ω is the angular velocity of the wheel. But power P is defined as

$$P = \frac{dW}{dt} = \Gamma \ \omega$$

Hence $$\Gamma = \frac{P}{\omega} = \frac{80 \text{ hp}}{3600 \text{ rev/min}}$$

But $1 \text{ hp} = 550 \dfrac{\text{ft} \cdot \text{lb}}{\text{s}}$ and $\dfrac{1 \text{ rev}}{\text{min}} = \dfrac{2\pi \ \text{rad}}{60 \text{ s}}$

and $$\Gamma = \frac{(8)\ (550)\text{ft} \cdot \text{lb/s}}{\dfrac{(3600)\,(2\pi)\text{rad}}{60 \text{ s}}} = 117 \text{ lb} \cdot \text{ft}$$

$$\Gamma = \frac{P}{\omega} = \frac{44{,}000 \text{ ft} \cdot \text{lb/sec}}{120\pi \text{ rad/sec}} = 117 \text{ lb} \cdot \text{ft}.$$

• PROBLEM 287

A bicycle and its rider together weigh 200 lb. If the cyclist free-wheels down a slope of 1 in 100, he has a constant speed of 10 mph, and if he free-wheels down a slope of 1 in 40, he has a constant speed of 20 mph. Suppose that he free-wheels on the level while holding on to the back of a moving truck. Find the power expended by the truck in maintaining his speed at 15 mph. Assume that air resistance varies as the square of his speed, while frictional forces remain constant at all times.

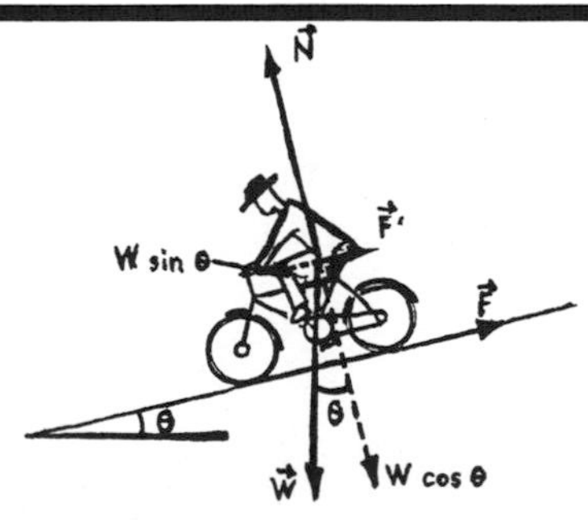

Solution: Let the frictional force be $\vec{F}$ and the force of air resistance $\vec{F}'$ with magnitude kv^2, where k is a constant and v is the speed of the bicycle.

On a slope, the forces acting on the bicycle and rider are the weight $\vec{W}$ acting downward, which can be resolved into components parallel to and perpendicular to the slope, the normal force exerted by the slope $\vec{N}$, and the forces of friction and air resistance acting up the slope opposing the motion. The forces perpendicular to the slope are equal and opposite and are of no further interest. Since the bicycle is moving with constant speed, the forces parallel to the slope must also cancel out. Hence

$$W \sin \theta = F + F' = F + kv^2.$$

For the two cases given, values can be inserted. Thus

$$200 \text{ lb} \times \frac{1}{100} = F + k \times 10^2 \text{ mi}^2 \cdot \text{hr}^{-2} \qquad \text{and}$$

$$200 \text{ lb} \times \frac{1}{40} = F + k \times 20^2 \text{ mi}^2 \cdot \text{hr}^{-2}.$$

$$\therefore\ 2 \text{ lb} = F + 100k \text{ mi}^2 \cdot \text{hr}^{-2} \qquad \text{and}$$

$$5 \text{ lb} = F + 400k \text{ mi}^2 \cdot \text{hr}^{-2}.$$

$$\therefore\ 300k \text{ mi}^2 \cdot \text{hr}^{-2} = 3 \text{ lb} \qquad \text{or}$$

$$k = \frac{1}{100} \text{ lb} \cdot (\text{mph})^{-2} \qquad \text{and} \qquad F = 1 \text{ lb}.$$

For the case of the bicycle traveling on a level surface, a force $\vec{P}$ must be supplied to overcome the forces of friction and air resistance and keep the bicycle moving with constant speed. Since there is no acceleration, $\vec{P}$ must just balance $\vec{F}$ and $\vec{F}'$, or

$$P = F + kv^2 = \text{lb} + \frac{1}{100} \text{ lb} \cdot (\text{mph})^{-2} \times 225 \ (\text{mph})^2$$

$$= 3.25 \text{ lb}.$$

The rate of working (the mechanical power) is $\vec{P} \cdot \vec{v}$ and $v = 15 \text{ mph} = 22 \text{ ft} \cdot \text{s}^{-1}$.

$$\therefore\ P \times v = 3.25 \text{ lb} \times 22 \text{ ft} \cdot \text{s}^{-1}.$$

But $1 \text{ hp} = 550 \text{ ft} \cdot \text{lb} \cdot \text{s}^{-1}$. Therefore:

$$\text{The rate of working} = \frac{3.25 \times 22 \text{ ft} \cdot \text{lb} \cdot \text{s}^{-1}}{550 \text{ ft} \cdot \text{lb} \cdot \text{s}^{-1}/\text{hp}}$$

$$= \frac{3.25 \times 22}{550} \text{ hp} = 0.13 \text{ hp}.$$

What power is needed to move a 3000-lb car up an 8.0° incline with a constant speed of 50 mi/hr against a frictional force of 80 lb?

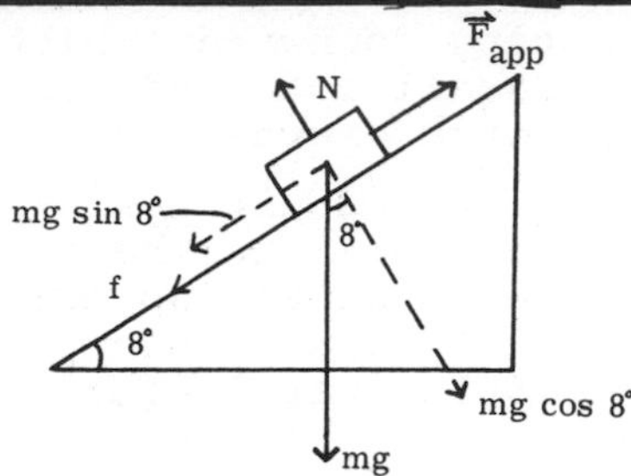

Solution: In order to just be able to move the car up the incline at constant velocity, there must be no net force on the car. Looking at the figure, we see that the net force on the car, acting down the plane, is

$$F_{net} = mg \sin 8° + f.$$

If there is to be no resultant force on the car, we must act on it with a force equal in magnitude to F_{net}, but acting up the plane. Therefore,

$$\begin{aligned} F_{app} &= mg \sin 8° + f \\ &= (3000 \text{ lb})(.149) + 80 \text{ lb} \\ &= 510 \text{ lb} \end{aligned}$$

Now, the power expended in moving an object equals the time rate of change of the work done on the object. Hence,

$$P = \frac{dW}{dt}$$

But $$W = \int \vec{F}_{app} \cdot d\vec{s}$$

$$P = \frac{d}{dt}\left(\int \vec{F}_{app} \cdot d\vec{s}\right)$$

In our case, $\vec{F}_{app}$ is constant, and

$$P = \frac{d}{dt}\vec{F}_{app} \cdot \int d\vec{s} = \frac{d}{dt}\vec{F}_{app} \cdot \vec{s}$$

Since $\vec{F}_{app}$ is constant in time also, we obtain

$$P = \vec{F}_{app} \cdot \frac{d\vec{s}}{dt} = \vec{F}_{app} \cdot \vec{v}$$

since $d\vec{s}/dt$ is defined as the velocity of the object we're moving. In this problem, $\vec{F}_{app}$ and $\vec{v}$ are parallel and in the same direction and

$$P = \vec{F}_{app} \cdot \vec{v} = F_{app} v = (510 \text{ lb})(50 \text{ mi/hr})$$

But 1 mi/hr = 1.48 ft/sec

and $\quad P = (510 \text{ lb})(50)(1.48 \text{ ft/sec})$

$\quad\quad = 3.7 \times 10^4 \text{ ft} \cdot \text{lb/sec}$

EFFICIENCY

• PROBLEM 289

An inclined plane 5 meters long has its upper end 1 meter above the ground. A load of 100 newtons is pushed up the plane against a force of friction of 5 newtons. What is the effort, the work input, the work output, the AMA, the IMA, and the efficiency?

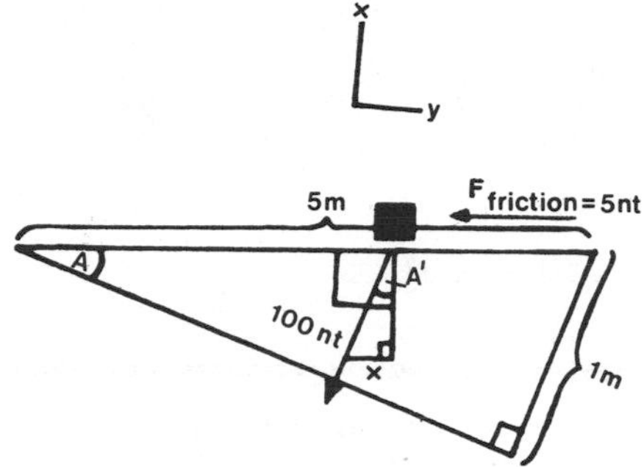

Solution: We first construct a diagram (see diagram). A vector is drawn vertically downward representing the force of gravity. Orienting our axes so that the y-axis coincides with the inclined plane, we resolve the gravitational force into its x and y components. This gives us a right triangle in which angle A' is equal to angle A, which the inclined plane forms with the ground, since they both are complements of the same angle. Therefore, since both large and small right triangles have equal angles, they are similar, so that we can write a proportion:

$$\frac{1 \text{ m}}{5 \text{ m}} = \frac{x}{100 \text{ nt}}$$

$$x = 20 \text{ nt}$$

Therefore, the force that the load exerts parallel to the inclined plane is 20 nt. This, plus the frictional force, is the effort. Hence,

Effort = Gravitational force along plane + frictional force

$$E = 20 \text{ nt} + 5 \text{ nt} = 25 \text{ nt}$$

Work is force × distance when the force is in the direction of the distance. Therefore, the work input (W_i) is:

$$W_i = 25 \text{ nt} \times 5 \text{ m} = 125 \text{ joules}$$

AMA (actual mechanical advantage) is:

$$AMA = \frac{R}{E}$$

where R is resistance (load), and E is effort. Then,

$$AMA = \frac{100 \text{ nt}}{25 \text{ nt}} = 4$$

The IMA (imaginary mechanical advantage) is the ratio of the length of the plane to its height:

$$IMA = \frac{5 \text{ m}}{1 \text{ m}} = 5$$

Efficiency is output work over input work.

$$\text{Efficiency} = \frac{W_o}{W_i} = \frac{100 \text{ joules}}{125 \text{ joules}} = \frac{AMA}{IMA} = \frac{4}{5}$$

$$= 0.80 = 80\%$$

• PROBLEM 290

A box weighing 100 pounds is pushed up an inclined plane 10 feet long with its upper end 4 feet above the ground. If the plane is 80% efficient, what is the force of friction?

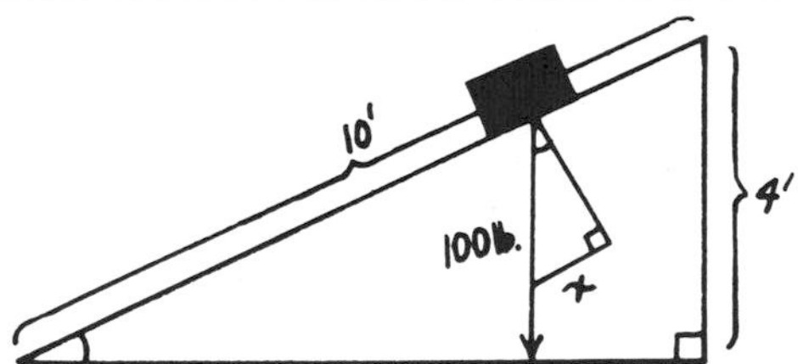

Solution: In approaching this problem, a careful plan of attack must be laid out. We are asked to find the force of friction in an inclined plane, given the dimensions and efficiency of the plane. Reasoning backwards, we begin by noticing that the effort consists of the force gravity exerts down the plane, plus the friction. The force exerted down the plane by gravity is calculable from the dimensions of the inclined plane and the weight of the box by constructing a proportion between the force triangle and the inclined plane (see diagram).

$$\frac{4'}{10'} = \frac{x}{100 \text{ lb}}$$

$$x = 40 \text{ lb}$$

Efficiency is calculated from AMA over IMA. IMA is calculated from the dimensions of the inclined plane (length over height, in this case 10 ft/4 ft = 2.5). The AMA is resistance over effort. The resistance is simply the weight of the box. We are only left with one unknown - the frictional force, which we now solve for

$$\text{efficiency} = \frac{AMA}{IMA} = \frac{\text{resistance/effort}}{2.5}$$

$$= \frac{\text{resistance}/\left(x + F_{friction}\right)}{2.5}$$

$$= \frac{100\ \text{lb}/\left(40\ \text{lb} + F_{friction}\right)}{2.5} = 80\%$$

$$= .80$$

Hence, $F_{friction} = 10$ lb.

• PROBLEM 291

> A pulley system consisting of two fixed and two movable pulleys (making four supporting strands) is used to lift a weight. If the system has an efficiency of 60%, how much weight can be lifted by an applied effort of 50 pounds?

Solution: With four supporting strands the IMA = 4.

IMA = imaginary mechanical advantage

AMA = actual mechanical advantage

E = effort

R = resistance (weight of load)

Since $\text{efficiency} = \frac{AMA}{IMA}$, $0.60 = \frac{AMA}{4}$,

whence AMA = 2.4.

Since $AMA = \frac{R}{E}$, $2.4 = \frac{R}{50\ \text{lb}}$,

whence R = 120 lb.

• PROBLEM 292

> A differential hoist is used to lift a load of 450 pounds. If the larger wheel of the hoist has 9 slots and the smaller wheel 8 slots and if the efficiency of the hoist is $33\frac{1}{3}$ %, what is the effort required to raise the load?

Solution: The IMA = 2 × 9 = 18.

This is to since there are 9 strands supporting the load.

Since $\text{efficiency} = \frac{AMA}{IMA}$, $0.33\frac{1}{3} = \frac{AMA}{18}$,

whence AMA = 6.

Since $AMA = \frac{R}{E}$, $6 = \frac{450\ \text{pounds}}{E}$, whence

E = 75 pounds.

• PROBLEM 293

A hoist raises a load of 330 pounds a distance of 15 feet in 5 seconds. At what rate in horsepower is the hoist working?

Solution: Power is equivalent to work per unit of time. In 5 seconds, the hoist does

$$W = Fs = 330 \text{ lbs} \times 15 \text{ ft} = 4950 \text{ ft-lbs}$$

of work. The rate at which work is done (the power) is:

$$\frac{4950 \text{ ft-lb}}{5 \text{ sec}} = 990 \frac{\text{ft-lbs}}{\text{sec}}$$

Since there are 550 ft-lb/sec per horsepower,

$$\frac{990 \frac{\text{ft-lbs}}{\text{sec}}}{550 \frac{\text{ft-lbs}}{\text{sec-hp}}} = 1.8 \text{ hp}$$

• PROBLEM 294

An engine used to pump water out of a mine shaft raises the water 150 ft and discharges it on the surface with a speed of 20 mph. It removes 2 slugs per second from the mine. One-fifth of the work it does is used in overcoming frictional forces. What is the horsepower of the engine?

Solution: During the process of removal from the mine, the water gains both potential and kinetic energy. The potential energy acquired per second is the weight of water ejected per second times the height raised. Thus

$$E_p = mgh = 2 \text{ slugs/s} \times 32 \text{ ft/s}^2 \times 150 \text{ ft} = 9600 \text{ ft}\cdot\text{lb/s}$$

The water also acquires kinetic energy, the final speed of ejection being 20 mph = 88/3 ft/s . The kinetic energy acquired per second is thus

$$E_k = \tfrac{1}{2} mv^2 = \tfrac{1}{2} \times 2 \text{ slugs/s} \times \left(\frac{88}{3}\right)^2 \text{ ft}^2/\text{s}^2$$

$$= 860\,\frac{4}{9} \text{ ft} \cdot \text{lb/s} .$$

The total energy acquired by the water is thus

$$E = E_p + E_k = 10{,}460\,\frac{4}{9} \text{ ft} \cdot \text{lb/s}.$$

The work done by the engine, including the quantity used in overcoming friction is, if the given conditions are to be maintained,

$$W = \frac{5}{4} E = \frac{5}{4} \times 10{,}460\,\frac{4}{9} \text{ ft} \cdot \text{lb/s}$$

and its rate of working is

$$P = \frac{\frac{5}{4} \times 10{,}460\,\frac{4}{9}\ \text{ft} \cdot \text{lb/s}}{550\ \text{ft} \cdot \text{lb/s} \cdot (\text{hp})^{-1}} = 23.8\ \text{hp}.$$

Here, we have used the fact that

$$1\ \text{hp} = 550\ \text{ft} \cdot \text{lb/s}.$$

• PROBLEM 295

In the casualty department of a hospital, it is necessary to raise or lower the examination table without disturbing the patient. This is accomplished by mounting the table on a screw jack which has a pitch of ½ in. The raising of the table is accomplished by applying a force of 12.5 lb tangentially at the end of a lever 12 in. long and rotating the lever in a circle. Find the efficiency of this machine if patient and table together have a weight of 480 lb.

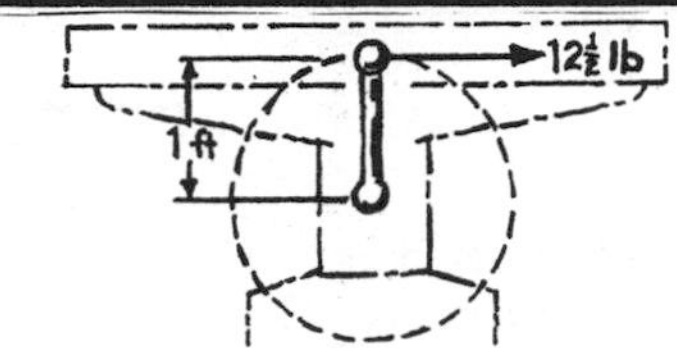

Solution: When the lever is rotated through one complete circle, the table is raised by one pitch of the screw. The work done on the machine by the operator is the force applied times the distance traveled in the direction of the force. Thus $W_1 = F \times 2\pi R$, where R is the radius of the circle swept out by the lever.

$$W_1 = 12\tfrac{1}{2}\ \text{lb} \times 2\pi \times 1\ \text{ft} = 25\pi\ \text{ft} \cdot \text{lb}.$$

The table and patient acquire additional potential energy, since their height above the ground is increased. The additional energy is their combined weight times the extra height. Thus

$$W_2 = 480\ \text{lb} \times \frac{1}{24}\ \text{ft} = 20\ \text{ft} \cdot \text{lb}.$$

The efficiency of the machine is the energy gained by the table divided by the energy supplied. Thus the efficiency is

$$E = \frac{W_2}{W_1} = \frac{20\ \text{ft} \cdot \text{lb}}{25\pi\ \text{ft} \cdot \text{lb}} = 0.255 \quad \text{or} \quad E = 25.5\%.$$

CHAPTER 6

IMPULSE/MOMENTUM

LINEAR

• PROBLEM 296

A cue ball traveling at a speed of 3 m/s collides with a stationary billiard ball and imparts a speed of 1.8 m/s to the billiard ball. If the billiard ball moves in the same direction as the oncoming cue ball, what is the velocity of the cue ball after the collision? Assume that both balls have the same mass.

Solution: Linear momentum must be conserved in this isolated, two particle system. Thus, the initial momentum of the system must equal the system's final momentum. Since the collision is 1-dimensional, we may drop the vector nature of momentum and write

$$P_f = P_i$$

$$mv + m(1.8\ m/sec) = m\ (3\ m/sec) + m(0\ m/sec)$$

$$m(v + 1.8\ m/sec) = m(3\ m/sec)$$

$$v + 1.8\ m/sec = 3\ m/sec$$

$$v = 1.2\ m/sec.$$

• PROBLEM 297

A 100-gram marble strikes a 25-gram marble lying on a smooth horizontal surface squarely. In the impact, the speed of the larger marble is reduced from 100 cm/sec to 60 cm/sec. What is the speed of the smaller marble immediately after impact?

Solution: The law of conservation of momentum is applicable here, as it is in all collision problems. Therefore, Momentum after impact = Momentum before impact.

$$\text{Momentum before impact} = M_{B1} \times V_{B1}$$

$$= 100\ gm \times 100\ cm/sec$$

$$= 10,000\ gm\text{-}cm/sec$$

$$\text{Momentum after impact} = M_{A1} \times V_{A1} + M_{A2} \times V_{A2}$$

$$= 100\ gm \times 60\ cm/sec$$

$$+ 25 \text{ gm} \times V_{A2} \text{ cm/sec}$$

Then

$$10{,}000 \text{ gm-cm/sec} = 6000 \text{ gm-cm/sec} + 25 \text{ g} \times V_{A2}$$

whence $V_{A2} = 160$ cm/sec.

• PROBLEM 298

A 4.0-gm bullet is fired from a 5.0-kg gun with a speed of 600 m/sec. What is the speed of recoil of the gun?

Solution: Originally, the momentum of the system consisting of the gun and the bullet is zero. Even if external forces act on the system, the principle of momentum conservation can be applied if the time interval of "collision" is small enough. Therefore we can say that after the bullet has been fired from the gun, the total momentum of the system remains zero. Letting m_1 be the mass of the gun and m_2 the mass of the bullet, with v_1 and v_2 their respective final velocities, we have

$$m_1 v_1 + m_2 v_2 = 0$$

$$v_1 = -\frac{m_2}{m_1} v_2$$

$$v_1 = -\frac{0.0040 \text{ kg}}{5.0 \text{ kg}} (600 \text{ m/s})$$

$$= -0.48 \text{ m/sec}$$

where the minus sign indicates that the gun moves in a direction opposite to that of the bullet.

• PROBLEM 299

Two particles of equal mass move initially on paths parallel to the x axis and collide. After the collision one of the particles is observed to have a particular value $v_y(1)$ of the y component of the velocity. What is the y component of the velocity of the other particle after the collision? (Recall that each component x, y, or z of the total linear momentum is conserved separately).

Solution: As shown in the figure, before the collision the particles were moving along the x axis, so that the total y component of the momentum is zero. By momentum conservation the total y component of momentum must also be zero after the collision, so that

$$M\left[v_y(1) + v_y(2)\right] = 0$$

where M is the mass of the particles, whence

$$v_y(2) = -v_y(1)$$

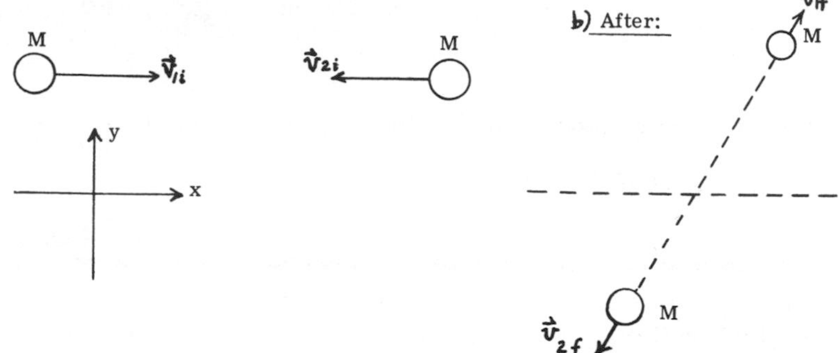

The Velocities (a) Before and (b) after collision.

We cannot calculate $v_y(1)$ itself without specifying the initial trajectories and the details of the forces during the collision process.

• PROBLEM 300

A cart of mass 5 kg moves horizontally across a frictionless table with a speed of 1 m/sec. When a brick of mass 5 kg is dropped on the cart, what is the change in velocity of the cart?

Solution: Assume that the brick has no horizontal velocity when it is dropped on the cart. Its initial horizontal momentum is therefore zero. Since no external horizontal forces act on the system of cart and brick, horizontal momentum must be conserved. We can say, for the horizontal direction,

$$m_c v_{ci} + m_b v_{bi} = m_c v_{cf} + m_b v_{bf}$$

Since the final velocities of the brick and cart are the same,

$$m_c v_{ci} = (m_c + m_b) v_f$$

Substituting values,

$$v_f = \frac{m_c v_{ci}}{m_c + m_b} = \frac{(5 \text{ kg})(1 \text{ m/sec})}{(5 \text{ kg} + 5 \text{ kg})} = .5 \text{ m/sec}$$

The change in velocity of the cart is

$$v_f - v_{ci} = (0.5 - 1.0)\text{m/sec} = - 0.5 \text{ m/sec.}$$

• PROBLEM 301

Suppose a 15-g bullet is fired into a 10-kg wooden block that is mounted on wheels and the time required for the block to travel a distance of 45cm is measured. This can easily be accomplished with a pair of photocells and an electronic clock. If the measured time is 1 sec, what is the muzzle velocity of the bullet?

Solution: In this example, the bullet comes to rest in the block and imparts its momentum to the block. Since the block travels 45 cm in one second, the recoil velocity

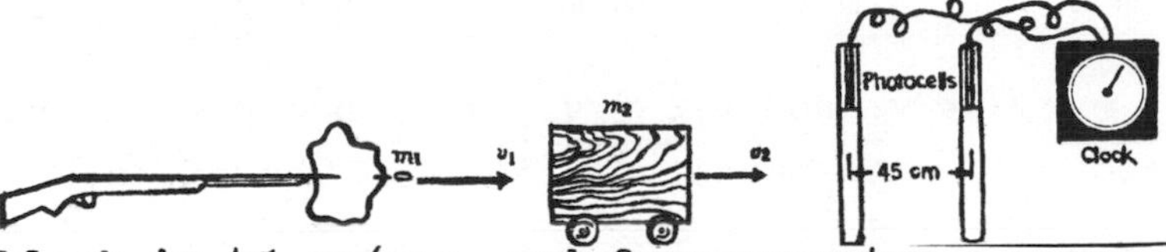

of the block is 45 cm/sec, and from momentum conservation we have

$$m_1 v_1 = m_2 v_2$$

(Here, we do not have a negative sign because both velocities are in the same direction. Also, we take m_2 to be 10 kg, that is, we neglect the mass of the bullet embedded in the block.) Then,

$$v_1 = \frac{m_2 v_2}{m_1}$$

$$= \frac{(10^4 g) \times (45 \text{ cm/sec})}{15 \text{ g}}$$

$$= 3 \times 10^4 \text{ cm/sec}$$

$$= 300 \text{ m/sec}$$

$$\cong 985 \text{ ft/sec}$$

• PROBLEM 302

Two particles of equal mass and equal but opposite velocities $\pm v_i$ collide. What are the velocities after the collision?

Solution: Since no external forces act on the 2 particle system, we may use the principle of conservation of momentum. This principle will relate the velocities of the particles after the collision to their velocities before the collision. Therefore,

$$m \vec{v}_{1_i} + m \vec{v}_{2_i} = m \vec{v}_{1f} + m \vec{v}_{2f} \qquad (1)$$

where the subscript $\vec{v}_{1_i}$ defines the initial velocity of particle 1, and similarly for $\vec{v}_{2_i}$, $\vec{v}_{1f}$, and $\vec{v}_{2f}$. Substituting $\vec{v}_{1_i} = \vec{v}_i$ and $\vec{v}_{2_i} = -\vec{v}_i$, into (1), we obtain

$$m \vec{v}_i - m \vec{v}_i = m \vec{v}_{1f} + m \vec{v}_{2f} = 0$$

Hence $\qquad \vec{v}_{1f} = -\vec{v}_{2f}$.

If the collision is elastic, then kinetic energy is conserved in the collision, and

$$\frac{1}{2} m v_{1_i}^2 + \frac{1}{2} m v_{2_i}^2 = \frac{1}{2} m v_{1_f}^2 + \frac{1}{2} m v_{2_f}^2 \qquad (2)$$

But $v_{1_i} = v_{2_i} = v_i$ and $v_{1_f} = v_{2_f} = v_f$ because we are concerned only with magnitudes in (2). Therefore,

$$\frac{1}{2} m v_i^2 + \frac{1}{2} m v_i^2 = \frac{1}{2} m v_f^2 + \frac{1}{2} m v_f^2$$

or
$$v_i^2 = v_f^2$$

and the conservation of energy demands that the final speed v_f equal the initial speed v_i. If one or both particles are excited internally by the collision, then $v_f < v_i$ because some of the initial energy must go into the excitation energy. Hence, the final energy < initial energy. If one or both particles initially are in excited states of internal motion and on collision they give up their excitation energy into kinetic energy, then v_f can be larger than v_i.

• PROBLEM 303

A ball of mass 100 gm is thrown against a brick wall. When it strikes the wall it is moving horizontally to the left at 3000 cm/sec, and it rebounds horizontally to the right at 2000 cm/sec. Find the impulse of the force exerted on the ball by the wall.

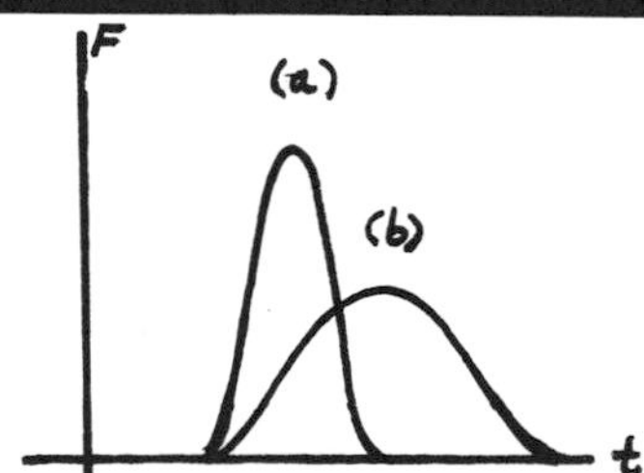

Solution: The impulse of a force on an object is defined as the change in momentum of the object during the time that the force acts.

The initial momentum of the ball is equal to the product of its mass and initial velocity, or

$$100 \text{ gm} \times -3000 \text{ cm/sec} = -30 \times 10^4 \text{ gm·cm/sec}.$$

The final momentum is equal to the product of the ball's mass and final velocity, or

$$+20 \times 10^4 \text{ gm·cm/sec}.$$

Note that the final and initial momenta are in opposite directions. We have defined the final direction of travel of the ball to be the positive direction. The change in momentum is then

$$mv_f - mv_i = 20 \times 10^4 \text{gm·cm/sec} - \left(-30 \times 10^4 \text{gm·cm/sec}\right)$$
$$= 50 \times 10^4 \text{ gm·cm/sec}.$$

Hence the impulse of the force exerted on the ball was 50×10^4 dyne·sec. Since the impulse is positive, the force is toward the right.

Note that the force exerted on the ball cannot be found without further information regarding the collision. The general nature of the force-time graph is shown by one of the curves in the figure. The force is zero before impact, rises to a maximum, and decreases to zero when the ball leaves the wall. If the ball is relatively rigid, like a baseball, the time of collision is small and the maximum force is large, as in curve (a). If the ball is more yielding, like a tennis ball, the collision time is larger and the maximum force is less, as in curve (b). In any event, the area under the force-time graph must equal 50×10^4 dyne·sec.

• PROBLEM 304

A high-powered rifle whose mass is 5 kg fires a 15-g bullet with a muzzle velocity of 3×10^4 cm/sec. What is the recoil velocity of the rifle?

$m_1 = 5$ kg, $m_2 = 15$ g, $v_1 = ?$, $v_2 = 3 \times 10^4$ cm/sec

Solution: The momentum of the system after the gun has fired must equal the momentum before the gun went off. Originally, the momentum of the bullet and rifle is zero since they are at rest. Using the conservation of momentum equation:

$$(m_1 + m_2)v_0 = m_1v_1 + m_2v_2 = 0$$

$$m_1v_1 = -m_2v_2$$

$$v_1 = -\frac{m_2v_2}{m_1}$$

$$= -\frac{(15g) \times (3 \times 10^4 \text{ cm/sec})}{5 \times 10^3 \text{ g}}$$

$$= -90 \text{ cm/sec.}$$

This is a sizable recoil velocity and if the rifle is not held firmly against the shoulder, the shooter will receive a substantial "kick". However, if he does hold the rifle firmly against his shoulder, the shooter's body as a whole absorbs the momentum. That is, we must use for m_1 the mass of the rifle plus the mass of the shooter. If his mass is 100 kg, then the recoil velocity (now of the rifle plus shooter) is

$$v_1 = -\frac{(15g) \times (3 \times 10^4 \text{ cm/sec})}{5 \times 10^3 \text{ g} + 10^5 \text{ g}}$$

$$\cong -4.5 \text{ cm/sec.}$$

This magnitude of recoil is quite tolerable.

• PROBLEM 305

A ball of mass $m_1 = 100$ g traveling with a velocity $v_1 = 50$ cm/sec collides "head on" with a ball of mass $m_2 = 200$ g which is initially at rest. Calculate the final velocities, v_1' and v_2', in the event that the collision is elastic.

Solution. In any collision there is conservation of momen-

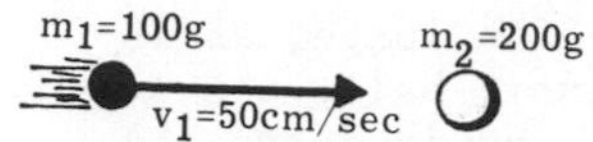

tum and since this is an elastic collision, kinetic energy is also conserved.

First, we use momentum conservation to write

$$p(\text{before}) = p(\text{after})$$

$$m_1v_1 + m_2v_2 = m_1v_1' + m_2v_2'.$$

In order to prevent the equations from becoming too clumsy, we suppress the units (which are CGS throughout); then we have

$$100 \times 50 + 0 = 100v_1' + 200v_2'.$$

Dividing through by 100 gives

$$50 = v_1' + 2v_2' \qquad (1)$$

From energy conservation, we have (since there is no PE involved and since the collision is elastic)

$$\text{KE}(\text{before}) = \text{KE}(\text{after})$$

$$\frac{1}{2}m_1v_1^2 + \frac{1}{2}m_2v_2^2 = \frac{1}{2}m_1v_1'^2 + \frac{1}{2}m_2v_2'^2$$

$$\frac{1}{2} \times 100 \times (50)^2 + 0 = \frac{1}{2} \times 100\ v_1'^2 + \frac{1}{2} \times 200\ v_2'^2.$$

Dividing through by 100/2 = 50 gives

$$2500 = v_1'^2 + 2v_2'^2. \qquad (2)$$

We now have two equations, (1) and (2), each of which contains both of the unknowns, v_1' and v_2'. We can obtain a solution by solving Eq. 1 for v_1',

$$v_1' = 50 - 2v_2' \qquad (3)$$

and substituting this expression into Eq. 2:

$$2500 = \left(50 - 2v_2'\right)^2 + 2v_2'^2 \qquad \text{or,}$$

$$2500 = 2500 - 200v_2' + 4v_2'^2 + 2v_2'^2.$$

From this equation we find

$$6v_2'^2 = 200v_2'$$

so that

$$v_2' = \frac{200}{6} = 33\frac{1}{3} \text{ cm/sec.}$$

Substituting this value into Eq. 3 we find

$$v_1' = 50 - 2 \times 33\frac{1}{3}$$

$$= -16\frac{2}{3} \text{ cm/sec.}$$

The negative sign means that after the collision, m_1 moves in the direction opposite to its initial direction (see figure).

• PROBLEM 306

A 2.0-kg ball traveling with a speed of 22 m/sec overtakes a 4.0-kg ball traveling in the same direction as the first, with a speed of 10 m/sec. If after the collision the balls separate with a relative speed of 9.6 m/sec, find the speed of each ball.

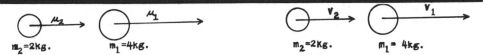

a) Before Collision   b) After Collision

Solution: No external forces act on the system. Since this is a collision problem, the principle of conservation of momentum can be used. Letting u_1 and u_2 be the initial velocities and v_1 and v_2 the final velocities of the two masses m_1 = 40 kg and m_2 = 2.0 kg, we find

$$m_1u_1 + m_2u_2 = m_1v_1 + m_2v_2 \qquad (1)$$

$$(4.0 \text{ kg})(10 \text{ m/sec}) + (2.0\text{kg})(22 \text{ m/sec}) = (4.0 \text{ kg})v_1 + (2.0 \text{ kg})v_2$$

$$(2.0 \text{ kg})v_1 + (1.0 \text{ kg})v_2 = 42 \text{ kg-m/sec}$$

or

$$2.0\, v_1 + v_2 = 42 \text{ m/sec} \qquad (2)$$

The difference in speed of the two masses after collision is given as 9.6 m/sec. Since the two masses initially move along the same axis, they must continue to do so after the collision, assuming their center of mass lies along this axis of motion. Since, physically, the 2.0 kg ball cannot pass through the 4.0 kg ball, the 4.0 kg ball continues to have greater velocity in the initial direction of motion. Taking this initial direction as positive,

$$v_1 - v_2 = 9.6 \text{ m/sec}$$

Substituting $v_2 = v_1 + 9.6$ m/sec in equation (2), we find the final velocities to be

$$v_1 = 17.2 \text{ m/sec}$$

$v_2 = 7.6$ m/sec

Both balls continue to move in the initial direction but with their speeds changed.

• PROBLEM 307

A proton (mass 1.67×10^{-27} kg) collides with a neutron (mass almost identical to the proton) to form a deuteron. What will be the velocity of the deuteron if it is formed from a proton moving with velocity 7.0×10^6 m/sec to the left and a neutron moving with velocity 4.0×10^6 m/sec to the right? (Figure A)

4.0×10^6 m/sec -7.0×10^6 m/sec -1.5×10^6 m/sec

n p d

Fig. A: Before collision Fig. B: After collision

Solution: According to the conservation of momentum we write:

$$m_d v_d = m_p u_p + m_n v_n$$

where m_d, m_p, and m_n are the masses of the deuteron, proton, and neutron respectively. Since the masses of the proton and neutron are almost identical:

$$m_p = m_n = \tfrac{1}{2} m_d$$

Inserting this into the momentum conservation equation (we adopt the convention that velocities to the right are positive):

$$2m_p v_d = m_p v_p + m_p v_n$$

$$v_d = \frac{v_p + v_n}{2} = \frac{-7.0 \times 10^6 \text{m/sec} + 4.0 \times 10^6 \text{m/sec}}{2} = -1.5 \times 10^6 \text{m/sec (figure B)}.$$

Thus the neutron moves to the left with speed 1.5×10^6 m/sec. In the actual collision a photon is produced and carries off some of the momentum, therefore the velocity calculated above is somewhat too large.

• PROBLEM 308

A heavy particle of mass M collides elastically with a light particle of mass m (see the figure below). The light particle is initially at rest. The initial velocity of the heavy particle is $\vec{v}_h = \upsilon_h \hat{i}$; the final velocity is $\vec{w}_h$. If the particular collision is such that the light particle goes off in the forward $(+\hat{i})$ direction, what is its velocity $\vec{w}_l$? What fraction of the energy of the heavy particle is lost in this collision?

Solution: This problem can be solved using the principle of conservation of linear momentum. The linear momentum before collision must equal the linear momentum after collision. The initial momentum p_i of the system is:

$$p_i = Mv_h + mv_l = Mv_h$$

since the smaller mass m is initially at rest. The final momentum p_f of the system is:

$$p_f = Mw_h + mw_l$$

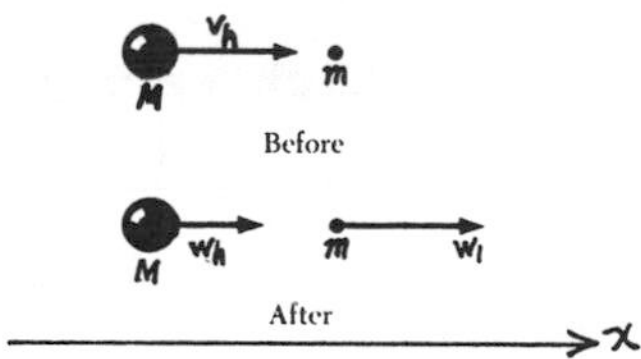

By the conservation of linear momentum, $p_i = p_f$:

$Mv_h = Mw_h + mw_l$

Thus: $mw_l = Mw_h - Mw_h$

$$w_l = \frac{M}{m}\left(v_h - w_h\right)$$

The energy of the heavy particle before the collision is $\frac{1}{2}Mv_h{}^2$.

After the collision the kinetic energy is $\frac{1}{2}Mw_h{}^2$.

The fraction of its original kinetic energy that the heavy mass M retains after the collision is:

$$\frac{E_f}{E_i} = \frac{\frac{1}{2}Mv_h{}^2}{\frac{1}{2}Mw_h{}^2} = \left(\frac{v_h}{w_h}\right)^2$$

where E_i and E_f are the initial and final kinetic energies respectively.

The fraction of the energy of the heavy particle that is lost in the collision is

$$\text{Fractional energy loss} = \frac{E_i - E_f}{E_i}$$

$$= 1 - \frac{E_f}{E_i} = 1 - \left(\frac{v_h}{w_h}\right)^2$$

• PROBLEM 309

A bag of candies is emptied onto the pan of a spring scale which was originally reading zero. Each piece of candy weighs 1 oz. and drops from a height of 4 ft. at the rate of 6 per second. What is the scale reading at the end of 10 sec. if all collisions are perfectly inelastic?

Solution. Each piece of mass m_0 loses $\Delta E_p = m_0gh$ amount of potential energy while falling through a height h, g being the gravitational acceleration. This loss of potential energy is compensated for by an increase ΔE_k in the kinetic energy since the total energy of each piece remains constant during the fall.

$$\Delta E_k = \Delta E_p$$

$$\frac{1}{2}m_0 v^2 = m_0 gh$$

where v is the speed with which each piece strikes the pan. We have

$$v^2 = 2gh = 2 \times 32 \text{ ft/s}^2 \times 4 \text{ ft}$$

$$= 256 \text{ ft}^2/\text{s}^2$$

$$v = 16 \text{ ft/s}.$$

Since the collision is perfectly inelastic, each time a piece hits the pan, it loses all its momentum and stays on the pan. The mass m striking the pan will exert a force $\vec{F}$ on it as a result of the change in its momentum such that the impulse created by the impact equals the momentum change,

$$\vec{F}t = m\vec{v},$$

$$\vec{F} = \vec{v}\,\frac{m}{t}.$$

Here $\vec{F}$ is the force acting on the candies due to the pan, and t is the duration of the impact. But, the candy pieces are constantly striking the pan and there is a continuous flux of candies incident on the pan. Hence, if $\frac{m}{t} = \frac{w}{gt}$ is the mass of candies striking the pan per second,

$$F = (16 \text{ ft/s}) \times (6 \text{ pieces/s}) \times \left(1 \text{ oz/piece} \times \frac{1}{16 \text{ oz/lb}} \times \frac{1}{32 \text{ ft/s}^2}\right)$$

$$= \frac{6}{32} \text{ lb} = 3 \text{ oz}.$$

The candies must provide an equal and opposite force F on the pan. After 10 seconds, the force acting on the scale is the continuous force F due to the constant impact plus the weight of the candies already in the pan. The scale reading

$$= 3 \text{ oz.} + (6 \text{ pieces/s}) \times (1 \text{ oz/piece}) \times 10\text{s}$$

$$= 3 \text{ oz.} + 60 \text{ oz.} = 63 \text{ oz.}$$

$$= 3 \text{ lb. } 15 \text{ oz.}$$

• PROBLEM 310

(a) A moving particle makes a perfectly elastic collision with a second particle, initially at rest, along their line of centers. Find the ratio of the masses which makes the kinetic energy transferred to the second particle a maximum.

(b) If the ratio of the masses is not that calculated above, show that the amount of energy transferred can be increased by inserting a third particle between the first two. For optimal transfer, the mass of the third particle is the geometric mean of the other two.

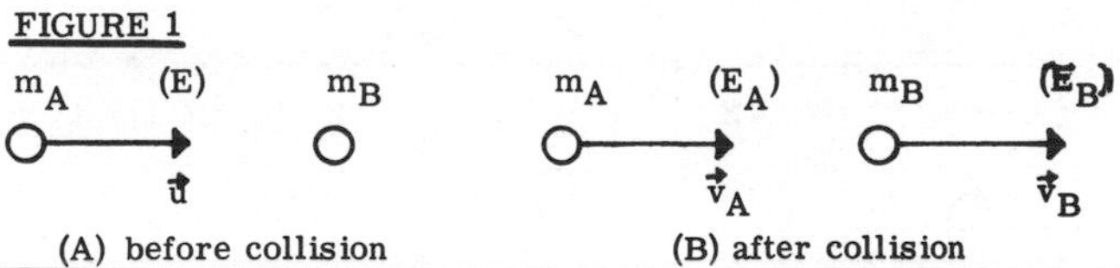

m_A (E) m_C m_B — $\vec{u}$

(A) before collision

m_A (E_A) m_C (E_C) m_B — $\vec{v}_A$ $\vec{u}_C$

(B) after collision of m_A with m_C

m_A (EA) m_C (E_C) m_B (E_B) — $\vec{v}_A$ $\vec{v}_C$ $\vec{v}_B$

(C) after collision of m_C with m_B

FIGURE 2

Solution: (a) Let the energy of the incoming particle be E, and refer to figure (1) for the system of notation. Since the collision is perfectly elastic, both energy and momentum are conserved. Therefore

$$E = E_A + E_B \qquad \text{and} \qquad m_A u = m_A v_A + m_B v_B.$$

But $E = \frac{1}{2} m_A u^2 = \dfrac{m_A^2 u^2}{2m_A}$ or $m_A u = \sqrt{2m_A E}$,

and similarly for the other kinetic energies. The second equation is therefore

$$\sqrt{2m_A E} = \sqrt{2m_A E_A} + \sqrt{2m_B E_B} \qquad \text{or} \qquad \sqrt{E} = \sqrt{E_A} + \sqrt{xE_B},$$

where $x = m_B/m_A$. Then

$$E = \left(\sqrt{E_A} + \sqrt{xE_B}\right)^2 = E_A + xE_B + 2\sqrt{xE_A E_B}$$

$$\therefore \quad E_A + E_B = E = E_A + xE_B + 2\sqrt{xE_A E_B}$$

Transposing,

$$E_A + E_B - E_A - xE_B = 2\sqrt{xE_A E_B}$$

$$(1 - x)\, E_B = 2\sqrt{xE_A E_B}$$

Squaring both sides and using $E_A = E - E_B$,

$$(1 - x)^2 E_B = 4xE_A = 4x(E - E_B).$$

$$\therefore \quad \frac{E_B}{E - E_B} = \frac{4x}{(1 - x)^2}$$

Inverting, $\dfrac{E - E_B}{E_B} = \dfrac{E}{E_B} - 1 = \dfrac{(1 - x)^2}{4x}$

$$\frac{E}{E_B} = \frac{(1 - x)^2}{4x} + 1 = \frac{(1 - x)^2}{4x} + \frac{4x}{4x} = \frac{(1 - x)^2 + 4x}{4x}$$

Inverting once more so as to get the needed ratio of E_B to E,

$$\frac{E_B}{E} = \frac{4x}{(1 - x)^2 + 4x} = \frac{4x}{1 + x^2 - 2x + 4x} = \frac{4x}{1 + 2x + x^2}$$

$$= \frac{4x}{(1 + x)^2}$$

For maximum energy transfer, E_B should be as large a proportion of E as possible and $(d/dx)\left(E_B/E\right)$ should be zero. Thus, for maximum energy transfer,

$$\frac{d}{dx}\left(\frac{E_B}{E}\right) = \frac{4}{(1 + x)^2} - \frac{8x}{(1 + x)^3} = 0$$

or $4(1 + x) = 8x$. $\therefore\ x = 1$, $\left(\text{i.e. } \frac{m_B}{m_A} = 1\right)$

Thus, the two masses should be equal when all the energy is transferred to the second particle.

(b) If x has a fixed value not equal to 1, insert a further mass m_c between m_A and m_B. Then in the first collision, we have from part (a),

$$\frac{E_c}{E} = \frac{4y}{(1 + y)^2} \quad ,$$

where $y = m_c/m_A$ (see Fig. (2)). Now m_c collides with m_B and

$$\frac{E_B}{E_c} = \frac{4z}{(1 + z)^2} \quad ,$$

where $z = m_B/m_c$. But $yz = x$, and therefore

$$\frac{E_B}{E_c} = \frac{4(x/y)}{\left[1 + (x/y)\right]^2} \quad .$$

$$\frac{E_B}{E} = \frac{E_B}{E_c} \cdot \frac{E_c}{E} = \frac{16x}{(1 + y)^2\left[1 + (x/y)\right]^2} \quad .$$

$$\frac{d}{dy}\left(\frac{E_B}{E}\right) = -\frac{32x}{(1 + y)^3\left[1 + (x/y)\right]^2} + \frac{32x^2/y^2}{(1 + y)^2\left[1 + (x/y)\right]^3}$$

For maximum energy transfer to the final mass, this quantity must be zero, and so

$$32x\left(1 + \frac{x}{y}\right) = \frac{32x^2}{y^2}(1 + y).$$

Multiplying by y^2 and cancelling the term 32x,

$$y^2 + xy = x + xy \qquad \text{or} \qquad y^2 = x.$$

$$\therefore \frac{m_C^2}{m_A^2} = \frac{m_B}{m_A} \qquad \text{or} \qquad m_C = \sqrt{m_A m_B}\,.$$

For maximum energy transfer the intermediate particle must have a mass which is the geometrical mean of the other two.

But the first term in the final inequality is the maximum transfer of energy when three particles are involed, using the necessary relation $y^2 = x$. The second term is the energy transfer when only two particles are involved. Therefore, not only is maximum energy transferred in the three-particle case when $m_C = \sqrt{m_A m_B}$, but the energy acquired by the particle of mass m_B is greater than it is when only two particles are involved.

• PROBLEM 311

Two masses $m_1 = 5$ kg and $m_2 = 10$ kg have velocities $\vec{u}_1 = 2$m/sec in the +x direction and $\vec{u}_2 = 4$ m/sec in the +y direction. They collide and stick together. What is their final velocity after collision?

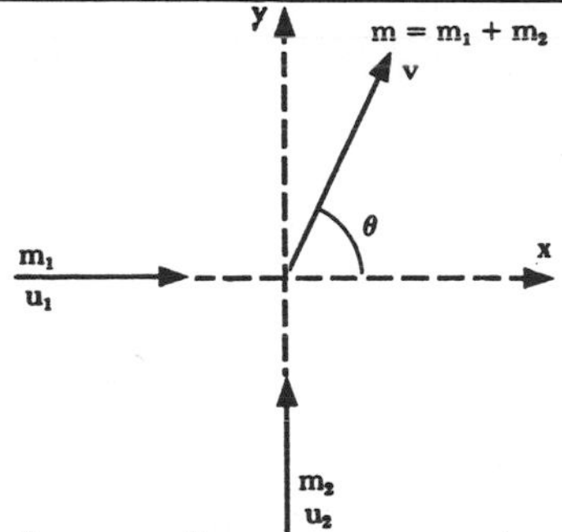

Solution: The total x and y components of linear momentum must be conserved after the collision. The mass of the body resulting after the collision is

$$m = m_1 + m_2$$

and the velocity $\vec{v}$ is inclined at angle θ to the x axis. We know that the total momentum vector is unchanged, and we can write down the x and y components of momentum.

	INITIAL MOMENTUM	FINAL MOMENTUM
x component	m_1u_1	$(m_1 + m_2)\upsilon \cos\theta$
y component	m_2u_2	$(m_1 + m_2)\upsilon \sin\theta$

Thus $\qquad m_1u_1 = (m_1 + m_2)\upsilon \cos\theta$

$$m_2u_2 = (m_1 + m_2)\upsilon \sin\theta$$

or $$\tan\theta = \frac{m_2u_2}{m_1u_1}$$

$$= \frac{4 \times 10}{5 \times 2} = 4$$

$$\theta = 75.97°$$

From the first momentum equation above:

$$\upsilon = \frac{m_1u_1}{(m_1 + m_2)\cos\theta}$$

$$= \frac{2 \times 5}{15 \times 0.2424}$$

$$= 2.750 \text{ m/sec.}$$

• PROBLEM 312

Coal drops at the rate of 25 slugs per second from a hopper onto a horizontal moving belt which transports it to the screening and washing plant. If the belt travels at the rate of 10 ft per second, what is the horsepower of the motor driving the belt? Assume that 5% of the energy available is used in overcoming friction in the pulleys. (See figure.)

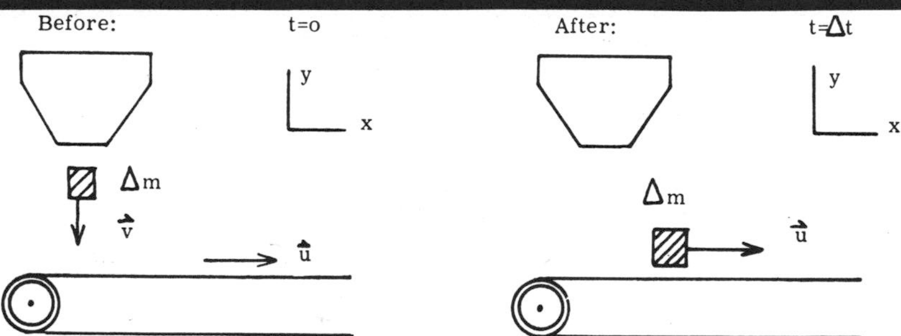

Solution: We take the belt and hopper as our system. By using the principle of conservation of momentum, we can relate the net external force on the system (provided by the motor) to the time rate of change of the system momentum $\vec{P}$, or

$$\frac{d\vec{P}}{dt} = \vec{F}_{ext} \tag{1}$$

We examine a small element of mass, Δm, leaving the hopper and falling on the belt. (See figure.) At $t = 0$, the momentum of Δm in the x direction is

$$\vec{P}_0 = (\Delta m)(0)$$

and, at $t = \Delta t$, it is

$$\vec{P}_f = \Delta m\,\vec{u}$$

Hence $\Delta\vec{P} = \vec{P}_f - \vec{P}_0 = \Delta m\,\vec{u}$

or $$\frac{\Delta \vec{P}}{\Delta t} = \vec{u}\ \frac{\Delta m}{\Delta t}$$

Taking the limit as $\Delta t \to 0$,

$$\frac{d\vec{P}}{dt} = \vec{u}\ \frac{dm}{dt} \tag{2}$$

Comparing (2) with (1)

$$\vec{F}_{ext} = \vec{u}\ \frac{dm}{dt}$$

The power provided by the motor must be the time rate of change of the work, W, done on the belt by the motor. Hence,

$$P = \frac{dW}{dt} = \frac{d}{dt}\left(\int \vec{F}_{ext} \cdot d\vec{s}\right)$$

where $d\vec{s}$ is an element of path traversed by the belt. Assuming $\vec{F}_{ext}$ = constant, and noting that $d\vec{s}/dt = \vec{u}$, we obtain

$$P = \frac{d}{dt}\left(\vec{F}_{ext} \cdot \int d\vec{s}\right) = \frac{d}{dt}\left(\vec{F}_{ext} \cdot \vec{s}\right)$$

$$P = \vec{F}_{ext} \cdot \frac{d\vec{s}}{dt} = \vec{F}_{ext} \cdot \vec{u}$$

Since $\vec{F}_{ext}$ and $\vec{u}$ are parallel, we find, using (2)

$$P = \left(F_{ext}\right)(u) = u^2\ \frac{dm}{dt}$$

$$P = (10\ \text{ft/s})^2(25\ \text{s}^1/\text{s}) = 2500\ \text{lb} \cdot \text{ft/s} \tag{3}$$

This power must be supplied by the motor to keep the belt moving at a uniform rate, assuming that none of it is dissipated in friction. Now, if 5% of the power supplied by the motor is used in overcoming friction, only 95% remains to power the belt. Since the power needed to move the belt is given by (3), we obtain,

$$P = 95\%\ P'$$

or $$P' = \frac{100}{95}\ P = \left(\frac{100}{95}\right)(2500\ \text{lb} \cdot \text{ft/s})$$

$$P' = 2631.6\ \text{ft} \cdot \text{lb/s}$$

Since $1\ \text{hp} = 550\ \text{ft} \cdot \text{lb/s}$

$$P' = 4.8\ \text{hp}$$

Taking friction into account, the rate of working of the motor is 4.8hp.

A railway gun whose mass is 70,000 kg fires a 500-kg artillery shell at an angle of 45° and with a muzzle velocity of 200 m/sec. Calculate the recoil velocity of the gun.

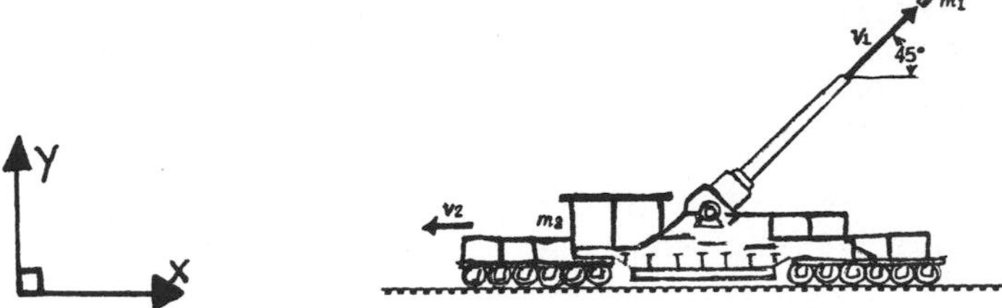

Solution: In this problem momentum must be conserved in both the horizontal and vertical directions. Let us refer to the bullet by using the subscript 1, and the gun by the subscript 2. We can state this conservation of momentum in the horizontal direction as follows:

$$p_{1x} = p_{2x}$$

or

$$m_1 v_{1x} = m_2 v_{2x}$$

but

$$v_{1x} = v_1 \cos 45°$$

Therefore, we may express p_{1x} as,

$$p_{1x} = m_1 v_1 \cos 45°$$

$$= (500 \text{ kg}) \times (200 \text{ m/sec}) \times 0.707$$

$$= 7.07 \times 10^4 \text{ kg-m/sec}$$

This must equal (except for the sign) the recoil momentum of the gun which moves only horizontally:

$$p_2 = m_2 v_2 = -7.07 \times 10^4 \text{ kg-m/sec}$$

Therefore,

$$v_2 = -\frac{7.07 \times (10^4 \text{ kg-m/sec})}{7 \times 10^4 \text{ kg}}$$

$$\cong -1 \text{ m/sec}$$

or, approximately 2 mi/rh. What has happened to the vertical component of the recoil momentum, $p_{1y} = 7.07 \times 10^4$ kg-m/sec? Since the railway platform is in contact with the Earth, the Earth absorbs the vertical momentum. The Earth does recoil, but because of the extremely large value of the Earth's mass compared to that of the railway gun, the recoil velocity cannot be measured.

A rubber ball bounces off a brick wall. It's incident velocity makes a 45° angle with the normal to the wall at the point of contact. If the collision is inelastic and the ball loses 20% of its kinetic energy during collision what will be its final momentum? Assume there is no gravity or sliding friction between the ball and the wall.

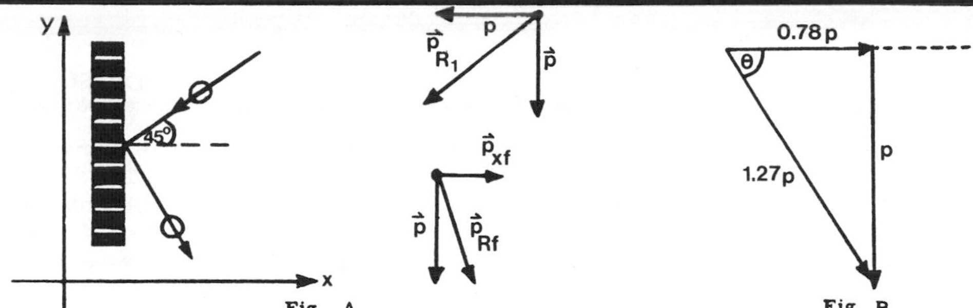

Fig. A Fig. B

Solution: As can be seen in figure A, before the ball strikes the wall it has components of linear momentum, in the - x and -y-directions, of equal magnitude p. In this problem we assume that the ball touches the wall for an infinitesimal time, so that there is no sliding friction between the ball and the wall resulting from the y-component of the ball's momentum. Thus, only the x-component of the balls' momentum is affected by the energy loss.

When the ball leaves the wall, its x-component of momentum must be reduced by an amount that will cause the kinetic energy to be reduced by 20%. Kinetic energy and momentum are related by:

$$E_k = \tfrac{1}{2}mv^2 = \frac{(mv)^2}{2m} = \frac{p_R^2}{2m}$$

where p_R is the magnitude of the resultant momentum,

kinetic energy after collision = 80% kinetic energy before collision

$$\frac{p_{xf}^2 + p^2}{2m} = 0.8\,\frac{p^2 + p^2}{2m} = \frac{0.8\,p^2}{m}$$

$$0.5\ p_{xf} = 0.3\ p^2$$

$$p_{xf}^2 = \frac{3}{5}\,p^2$$

$$p_{xf} = 0.78\ p$$

where p_{xf} is the ball's momentum in the x-direction after collision and $p_{xf}^2 + p^2$ is the square of the magnitude of the final resultant momentum.

We now find the balls' final resultant momentum.

magnitude of final momentum = $\sqrt{p_{xf}^2 + p^2}$

$$= \sqrt{\frac{3}{5} p^2 + p^2} = \sqrt{\frac{8}{5} p^2} = 1.27 p$$

To find the final momentum's orientation with respect to the normal, we use the laws of geometry (see diagram b).

$$\sin \theta = \frac{p}{1.27 p} = 0.7873$$

$$\theta \cong 52°.$$

• PROBLEM 315

In a cloud-chamber photograph, a proton is seen to have undergone an elastic collision, its track being deviated by 60°. The struck particle makes a track at an angle of 30° with the incident proton direction. What mass does this particle possess? (See figure).

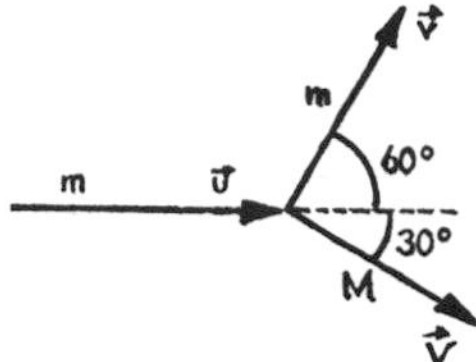

Solution: Let the incident proton have mass m and velocity $\vec{u}$, the velocity becoming $\vec{v}$ after scatter. Let the struck particle of mass M acquire velocity $\vec{V}$ after the collision. Then, by the principle of conservation of energy, $\frac{1}{2}mu^2 = \frac{1}{2}mv^2 + \frac{1}{2}MV^2$, and since momentum is conserved both parallel and perpendicular to the original direction of travel of the proton $mu = mv \cos 60° + MV \cos 30°$ and $mv \sin 60° = MV \sin 30°$. Thus

$$V = \frac{m}{M} v \frac{\sin 60°}{\sin 30°} = \sqrt{3} \frac{m}{M} v .$$

Substituting into the other two equations gives

$$\frac{1}{2} mu^2 = \frac{1}{2} mv^2 + \frac{3}{2} \frac{m^2}{M} v^2$$

and

$$mu = \frac{1}{2}mv + \frac{3}{2} mv .$$

$$u^2 = v^2 + 3 \frac{m}{M} v^2 = v^2\left(1 + \frac{3m}{M}\right) \qquad (1)$$

$$u = \frac{1}{2}v + \frac{3}{2}v = v\left(\frac{1}{2} + \frac{3}{2}\right)$$

or

$$u^2 = v^2\left(\frac{1}{2} + \frac{3}{2}\right)^2 \qquad (2)$$

Equating (1) and (2)

$$v^2\left(\frac{1}{2} + \frac{3}{2}\right)^2 = v^2\left(1 + \frac{3m}{M}\right)$$

or

$$\frac{1}{4} + \frac{9}{4} + \frac{3}{2} = 1 + \frac{3m}{M}$$

$$\frac{m}{M} = 1$$

and the struck particle must have been a hydrogen nucleus (a proton).

• **PROBLEM 316**

The forces shown in the force-time diagram are applied to a body of mass 5 kg. What is the impulse after 6 sec, and after 12 sec? What are the velocities at these times?

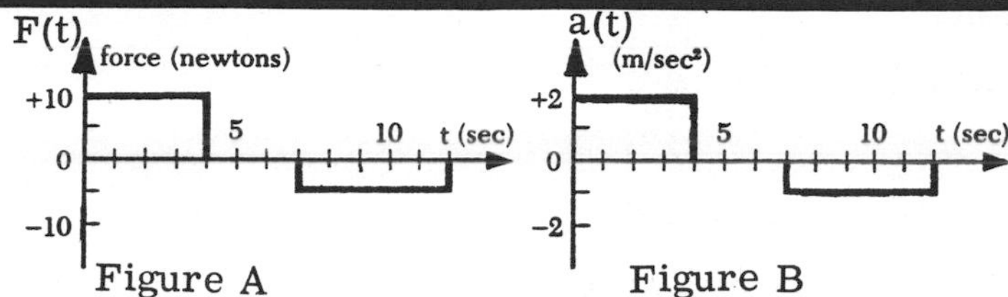

Figure A Figure B

Solution: We know that when a force $\vec{F}$ acts on a system, for a time interval dt, the impulse resulting is given as

$$\int \vec{F}\, dt.$$

One can interpret impulse as the area under the force-time curve, as shown in Fig. 1. In the case of a constant force, the impulse is simply the product of the force acting on the system and the time interval over which it acts. Thus at t = 6 sec, the area is $+ 10 \times 4 = 40$ newton-sec. After t = 7 sec the impulse becomes negative. The total area at t = 12 sec is $+ 10 \times 4 - 5 \times 5 = +15$ newton-sec.

From the force-time curve we can drawn an acceleration-time curve by dividing each value of F(t) by the mass of the body 5 kg. This follows since, by Newton's Second Law,

$$a = \frac{F}{m}.$$

The area under the acceleration-time curve gives the change in velocity between the indicated times, since $\Delta v = a\Delta t$, by definition for a constant force. Thus at t = 6 sec, $v = 2 \times 4 = 8$ m/sec. At t = 12 sec, $v = 2 \times 4 - 1 \times 5 = 3$ m/sec.

• **PROBLEM 317**

A sports car weighing 1200 lb and traveling at 60 mph fails to stop at an intersection and crashes into a 4000-lb delivery truck traveling at 45 mph in a direction at right angles to it. The wreckage becomes locked and travels 54.7 ft before coming to rest. Find the magnitude and direction of the constant force that has produced this deceleration.

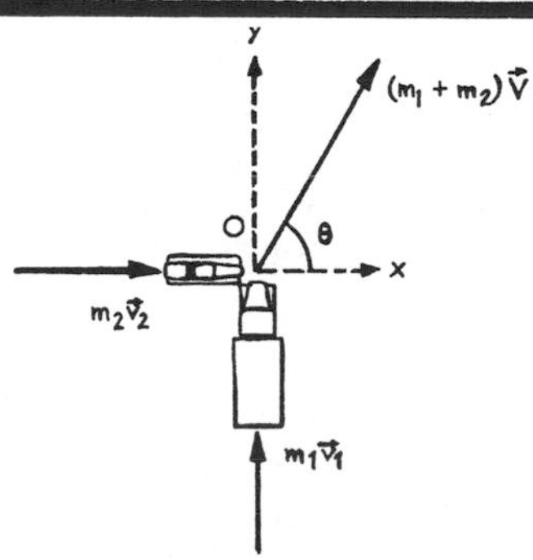

Solution: Let the sports car be traveling in the positive x-direction and the truck in the positive y-direction. After the collision at the origin, the combined mass travels in a direction inclined at $\theta°$ to the positive x-axis with a velocity $\vec{V}$. Momentum must be conserved in both the x- and y-directions. Therefore, referring to the diagram,

$$m_1 v_1 = (m_1 + m_2) V \sin\theta \tag{1}$$

and $$m_2 v_2 = (m_1 + m_2) V \cos\theta \tag{2}$$

Dividing equation (1) by (2),

$$\frac{(m_1 + m_2)\ V \sin\theta}{(m_1 + m_2)\ V \cos\theta} = \frac{m_1 v_1}{m_2 v_2}$$

$$\tan\theta = \frac{m_1 v_1}{m_2 v_2} = \frac{m_1 g v_1}{m_2 g v_2} = \frac{4000 \text{ lb} \times 45 \text{ mph}}{1200 \text{ lb} \times 60 \text{ mph}} = 2.5$$

$$\therefore\ \theta = 68.2°.$$

Squaring equations (1) and (2) and then adding them, we get

$$(m_1 + m_2)^2\ V^2 \sin^2\theta + (m_1 + m_2)^2\ V^2 \cos^2\theta$$

$$= m_1^2 v_1^2 + m_2^2 v_2^2$$

$$V^2 (\sin^2\theta + \cos^2\theta) = V^2 = \frac{m_1^2 v_1^2 + m_2^2 v_2^2}{(m_1 + m_2)^2}$$

$$= \frac{m_1^2 g^2 v_1^2 + m_2^2 g^2 v_2^2}{(m_1 g + m_2 g)^2}$$

$$= \frac{(4000 \text{ lb})^2 \times (45 \text{ mph})^2 + (1200 \text{ lb})^2 \times (60 \text{ mph})^2}{(4000 \text{ lb} + 1200 \text{ lb})^2}$$

$$= 1389.9\ (\text{mph})^2.$$

$$\therefore\quad V = 37.3 \text{ mph} = 54.7 \text{ ft/s},$$

which is the velocity of the combined mass immediately after impact.

The wreckage comes to rest in 54.7 ft. Apply the equation for constant acceleration, $v^2 = v_0^2 + 2as$. Here v_0 is the initial velocity of the locked mass, s is the distance it travels, and a is the applied acceleration. Hence, when $v = 0$, $s = 54.7$ ft and

$$0 = (54.7 \text{ ft/s})^2 + 2a \times 54.7 \text{ ft}.$$

$$\therefore\ a = -\ 27.35 \text{ ft/s}^2.$$

The deceleration due to friction is thus 27.35 ft/s^2, and since the mass affected is (1200 + 4000)/32 slugs, the magnitude of the frictional force is

$$F = \frac{5200}{32} \text{ slugs} \times 27.35 \text{ ft/s}^2 = 4443 \text{ lb.}$$

This decelerating force must act in a direction opposite to that in which the wreckage is traveling in order to bring it to rest. Thus it is a force of 4443 lb acting at an angle of 68.2° to the negative x-axis. Note that momentum is conserved only during the collision, for, at that time, the collision forces are much greater than the external forces acting (friction), and the latter may be neglected.

• PROBLEM 318

A 100-kg man jumps into a swimming pool from a height of 5 m. It takes 0.4 sec for the water to reduce his velocity to zero. What average force did the water exert on the man?

Solution: The man's initial velocity (before jumping) is zero. Therefore, as he strikes the water, his velocity v is $v^2 = v_0^2 + 2gh$, which reduces to $v^2 = 2gh$

$$\begin{aligned} v &= \sqrt{2gh} \\ &= \sqrt{2 \times (9.8 \text{ m/sec}^2) \times (5 \text{ m})} \\ &= 10 \text{ m/sec} \end{aligned}$$

Therefore, the man's momentum on striking the water was

$$\begin{aligned} p_1 &= mv \\ &= (100 \text{ kg}) \times (10 \text{ m/sc}) \\ &= 1000 \text{ kg-m/sec} \end{aligned}$$

The final momentum was $p_2 = 0$, so that the average force was

$$\begin{aligned} \overline{F} &= \frac{\Delta p}{\Delta t} = \frac{p_2 - p_1}{\Delta t} \\ &= \frac{0 - 1000 \text{ kg-m/sec}^2}{0.4 \text{ sec}} \\ &= -2500 \text{ N} \end{aligned}$$

The negative sign means that the retarding force was directed opposite to the downward velocity of the man.

• PROBLEM 319

Consider the changes in momentum produced by the following forces: (a) A body moving on the x-axis is acted on for 2 sec by a constant force of 10 n toward the right. (b) The body is acted on for 2 sec by a constant force of 10 n toward the right and then for 2 sec by a constant force of 20 n toward the left. (c) The body is acted on for 2 sec by a constant force of 10 n toward the right and then for 1 sec by a constant force of 20 n toward the left.

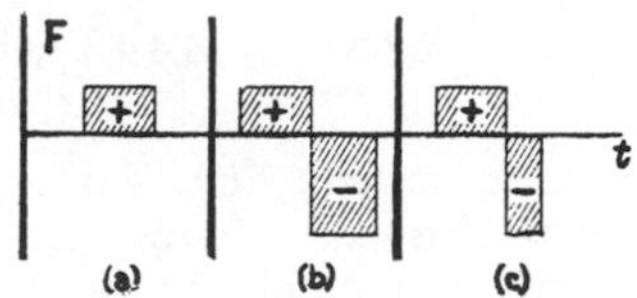

Solution: If the mass of a system (i.e. a group of particles) is constant, we may write

$$\vec{F}_{ext} = \frac{d\vec{P}}{dt} \qquad (1)$$

where $\vec{F}_{ext}$ is the net external force on the system and $\vec{P}$ is the total momentum of the system. (Note that if $\vec{F}_{ext} = 0$, we obtain the law of conservation of momentum).

From (1), we find

$$d\vec{P} = \vec{F}_{ext}\ dt$$

or $$\int_{\vec{P}_0}^{\vec{P}_f} d\vec{P} = \int_{t=t_0}^{t=t_f} \vec{F}_{ext}\ dt$$

$$\Delta\vec{P} = \vec{P}_f - \vec{P}_0 = \int_{t=t_0}^{t=t_f} \vec{F}_{ext}\ dt \qquad (2)$$

The left side of equation (2) is the change of momentum of the system due to $\vec{F}_{ext}$, and the right side is called the impulse. If $\vec{F}_{ext}$ is time independent, we may write

$$\Delta\vec{P} = \vec{F}_{ext}\ \Delta t \qquad (3)$$

(a) The impulse of the force is + 20 n × 2 sec = + 20 n · sec. Hence the momentum of any body on which the force acts increases by 20 kg · m/sec. This change is the same whatever the mass of the body and whatever the magnitude and direction of its initial velocity.

Suppose the mass of the body is 2 kg and that it is initially at rest. Its final momentum then equals its change in momentum and its final velocity is 10 m/sec toward the right.

Had the body been initially moving toward the right at 5 m/sec, its initial momentum would have been 10 kg · m/sec, its final momentum 30 kg · m/sec, and its final velocity 15 m/sec toward the right.

Had the body been moving initially toward the left at 5 m/sec, its initial momentum would have been - 10 kg · m/sec, its final momentum + 10 kg · m/sec,

since $\vec{P}_f - \vec{P}_0 = 20$ kg · m/s

$$\vec{P}_f = -10 \text{ kg·m/s} + 20 \text{ kg·m/s}$$

$$= 10 \text{ kg·m/s}$$

Hence its final velocity is 5 m/sec toward the right. That is, the constant force of 10 n toward the right would first have brought the body to rest and then given it a velocity in the direction opposite to its initial velocity.

(b) The impulse of this force is (+ 10 n × 2 sec - 20 n × 2 sec) = - 20 n·sec. The momentum of any body on which it acts is decreased by 20 kg· m/sec.

(c) The impulse of this force is (+ 10 n × 2 sec - 20 n × 1 sec) = 0. Hence the momentum of any body on which it acts is not changed. Of course, the momentum of the body is increased during the first two seconds but it is decreased by an equal amount in the next second.

• PROBLEM 320

A 3000-lb car traveling with a speed of 30 mi/hr strikes an obstruction and is brought to rest in 0.10 sec. What is the average force on the car?

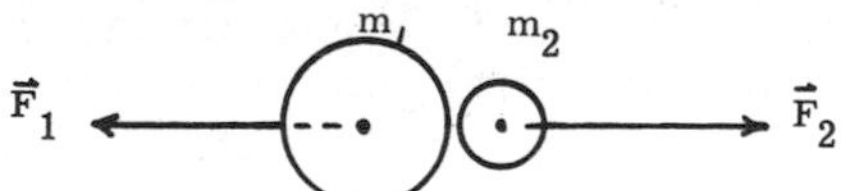

Solution: The momentum of a body is defined as p = mv. Since

$$\vec{F} = m\vec{a} = m\frac{d\vec{v}}{dt}$$

and $\quad d\vec{p} = d(m\vec{v}) = md\vec{v}$

we have $\vec{F}\,dt = d\vec{p}$.

Consider a collision between two masses m_1 and m_2, as shown in the figure. During the collision, the two objects exert forces on each other where F_1 is the force on m_1 due to m_2, and F_2 is the force on m_2 due to m_1. By Newton's third law, these forces at any instant are equal in magnitude but opposite in direction. The change in momentum of m_1 resulting from the collision is

$$\Delta\vec{p}_1 = \int_{t_0}^{t_1} \vec{F}_1\,dt = \overline{F}_1\Delta t = mv_1 - mv_0$$

where $\overline{F}_1$ is the average value of the force $\vec{F}_1$ during the time interval of the collision $\Delta t = t_1 - t_0$.

For the car colliding with an obstruction, we can say

$$\overline{F}\Delta t = mv_1 - mv_0$$

$$m = \frac{W}{g} = \frac{3000 \text{ lb}}{32 \text{ ft/sec}^2} = 94 \text{ slugs}$$

$$v_0 = 30 \text{ mi/hr} = 44 \text{ ft/sec}$$

$$\overline{F} = \frac{m(v_1 - v_0)}{\Delta t} = \frac{94 \text{ slugs } (0 - 44 \text{ ft/sec})}{0.10 \text{ sec}}$$

$$= -4.1 \times 10^4 \text{ lb.}$$

• PROBLEM 321

Suppose the collision in the figure is completely inelastic and that the masses and velocities have the values shown. What is the velocity of the 2 mass system after the collision? What is the kinetic energy before and after the collision?

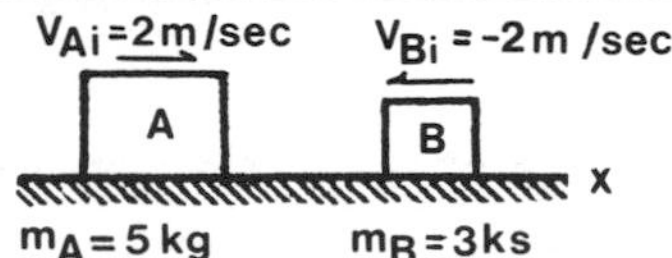

Solution: Since we wish to relate the final velocity of the system to its initial velocity, we will use conservation of momentum The total momentum before the collision is equal to the total momentum after the collision, if no forces external to the system act. Hence

$$m_A\vec{v}_{Ai} + m_B\vec{v}_{Bi} = (m_A + m_B)\vec{v}$$

where $\vec{v}_{Ai}$, $\vec{v}_{Bi}$ are the initial velocities of m_A and m_B, and $\vec{v}$ is the final velocity of the combined masses. Solving for $\vec{v}$,

$$\vec{v} = \frac{m_A\vec{v}_{Ai} + m_B\vec{v}_{Bi}}{m_A + m_B}$$

Changing the vectors to magnitudes, and noting that $\vec{v}_{Ai}$ and $\vec{v}_{Bi}$ are in the opposite directions

$$v = \frac{m_A v_{Ai} - m_B v_{Bi}}{m_A + m_B}$$

where v_{Ai} is in the positive x direction. Therefore,

$$v = \frac{(5 \text{ kg})(2 \text{ m/s}) - (3 \text{ kg})(2 \text{ m/s})}{8 \text{ kg}}$$

$$v = .5 \text{ m/s}$$

Since v_2 is positive, the system moves to the right after the collision. The kinetic energy of body A before the collision is

$$\tfrac{1}{2} m_A v_{Ai}^2 = (\tfrac{1}{2})(5 \text{ kg})(4 \text{ m}^2/\text{s}^2) = 10 \text{ joules}$$

and that of body B is

$$\tfrac{1}{2}\, m_B v_{Bi}^2 = (\tfrac{1}{2})(3 \text{ kg})(4 \text{ m}^2/\text{s}^2) = 6 \text{ joules}$$

The total kinetic energy before collision is therefore 16 joules.

Note that the kinetic energy of body B is positive, although its velocity v_{Bi} and its momentum mv_{Bi} are both negative.

The kinetic energy after the collision is

$$\tfrac{1}{2}(m_A + m_B)v^2 = \tfrac{1}{2}(8 \text{ kg})(.25 \text{ m}^2/\text{s}^2) = 1 \text{ joule}$$

Hence, far from remaining constant, the final kinetic energy is only 1/16 of the original, and 15/16 is "lost" in the collision. If the bodies couple together like two freight cars, most of this energy is converted to heat through the production of elastic waves which are eventually absorbed.

If there is a spring between the bodies and the bodies are locked together when their velocities become equal, the energy is trapped as potential energy in the compressed spring. If all these forms of energy are taken into account, the total energy of the system is concerved although its kinetic energy is not. However, momentum is always conserved in a collision, whether or not the collision is elastic.

• PROBLEM 322

A lump of clay of mass 30 gm traveling with a velocity of 25 cm/sec collides head on with another lump of clay of mass 50 gm traveling with a velocity of 40 cm/sec in exactly the opposite direction. If the two lumps coalesce (a) what is the velocity of the combined lump after the collision, assuming that no external forces act on the system? (See figure.) (b) What is the energy lost due to collision?

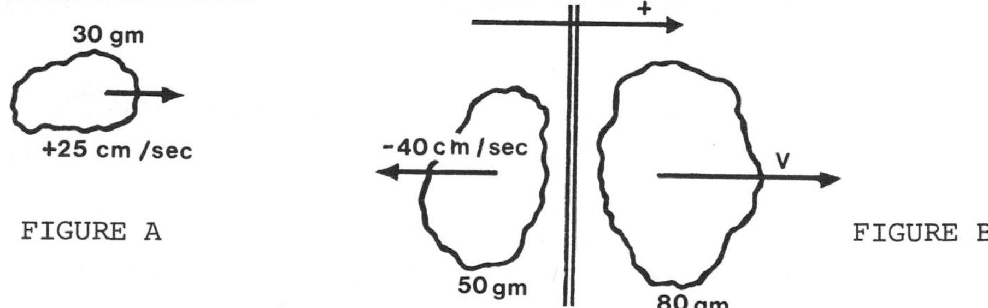

FIGURE A

FIGURE B

Solution: (a) Although all the velocities are in the same straight line, it is important to remember that momentum is really a vector and to distinguish carefully between positive and negative directions. Choose the positive direction to be to the right, in the same direction as the initial velocity of the 30 gm lump of clay. Then,

Initial momentum of 30 gm lump = (30 gm)(25 cm/sec)

$= 750$ gm - cm/sec

Initial momentum of 50 gm lump = (50 gm)(- 40 cm/sec)

= - 2,000 gm-cm/sec

Therefore, total initial momentum = 750 gm-cm/sec - 2,000 gm-cm/sec

= - 1250 gm-cm/sec.

If V is the velocity of the combined 80 gm lump after the collision,

Momentum after collision = (80 gm)V

The law of conservation of linear momentum assures that the total momentum of the system before collision is equal to the system's momentum after collision.

Equating the total momentum before to the total momentum after the collision,

$$-1250 \text{ gm-cm/sec} = (80 \text{ gm})V$$

$$V = -15.6 \text{ cm/sec.}$$

The negative sign indicates that the combined lump is really traveling to the left in the diagram. Therefore, after the collision the combined lump has a velocity of 15.6 cm/sec in the same direction as the initial velocity of the 50 gm lump.

(b) The energy lost in the collision is just the difference between the kinetic energy before collision and the kinetic energy after collision:

$$\Delta E = E_i - E_f = \left[\tfrac{1}{2}(30 \text{ gm})(25 \text{ cm/sec})^2 + \tfrac{1}{2}(50 \text{ gm})(-40 \text{ cm/sec})^2\right] - \tfrac{1}{2}(80 \text{ gm})(-15.6 \text{ cm/sec})^2$$

$$= 49{,}375 \text{ ergs} - 9{,}734 \text{ ergs} = 39{,}641 \text{ ergs}$$

• PROBLEM 323

Show that momentum is conserved in a chemical reaction in which the atoms of the reactants are rearranged or exchanged while conserving the total mass. We assume that there are no external forces (see Figs. A,B).

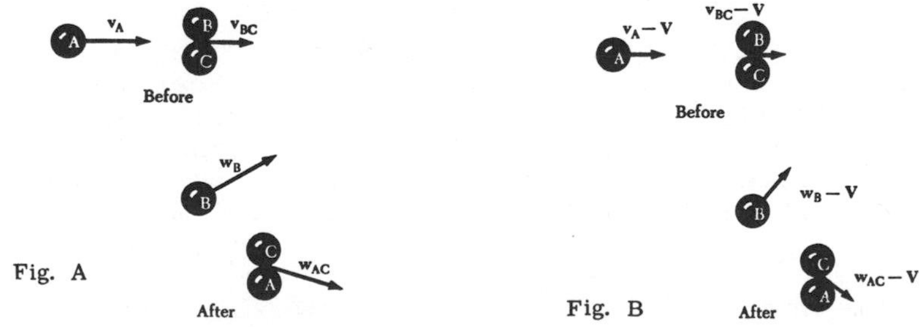

Fig. A

Fig. B

Solution: Let the reaction be represented by

$$A + BC \rightarrow B + AC$$

where BC means a molecule consisting of atoms B and C. In the reaction, atom C attaches itself to atom A to form AC. In the inertial frame of Figure.A , let us write the equation of conservation of energy before and after the collision (here, the final total energy should also include the energy lost during collision)

$$E_i = E_f \qquad \text{or}$$

$$\tfrac{1}{2}M_A v_A^2 + \tfrac{1}{2}\left(M_B + M_C\right) v_{BC}^2$$

$$= \tfrac{1}{2}M_B w_B^2 + \tfrac{1}{2}\left(M_A + M_C\right) w_{AC}^2 + \Delta\varepsilon$$

Here $\Delta\varepsilon$ represents changes in the binding energy of the molecules taking part in the reaction. In a second inertial frame moving with velocity V with respect to the first the new velocities of the particles will be their velocities in the old frame minus the velocity of the old frame relative to the new one. With this replacement of $\vec{v}_A$ by $\vec{v}_A - \vec{V}$, etc. the law of conservation of energy in the new frame is (Fig.B).

$$\tfrac{1}{2}M_A\left(v_A - V\right)^2 + \tfrac{1}{2}\left(M_B + M_C\right)\left(v_{BC} - V\right)^2$$

$$= \tfrac{1}{2}M_B\left(w_B - V\right)^2 + \tfrac{1}{2}\left(M_A + M_C\right)\left(w_{AC} - V\right)^2 + \Delta\varepsilon$$

On writing out the squares of the quantities in parantheses and comparing this equation with the previous one, we see that the two equations are consistent if

$$M_A v_A + \left(M_B + M_C\right) v_{BC} = M_B w_B + \left(M_A + M_C\right) w_{AC}$$

which is exactly a statement of the law of conservation of linear momentum.

• PROBLEM 324

Suppose a particle of mass m, initially travelling with velocity $\vec{v}$, collides elastically with a particle of mass m initially at rest. Prove that the angle between the velocity vectors of the two particles after the collision is 90°.

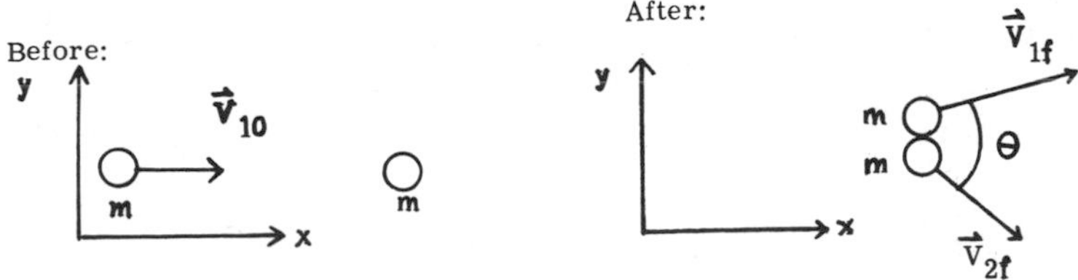

Solution: Whenever we are confronted with a collision problem, we may apply the law of conservation of momentum if no external forces act on the system. External forces are forces which act upon the system being considered (in our case, the system consists of the 2 masses) that are due to the environment external to the system. (i.e. friction). Because no external forces are acting in this problem, we may use this conservation law, ,which is written mathematically as

$$\vec{p}_{10} + \vec{p}_{20} = \vec{p}_{1_f} + \vec{p}_{2_f} \tag{1}$$

In this equation, $\vec{p}_{10}$ and $\vec{p}_{20}$ are the initial momenta of particles 1 and 2, respectively, and $\vec{p}_{1_f}$ and $\vec{p}_{2_f}$ are the final momenta of particles 1 and 2, respectively. Note two things: first, momentum is defined as the product of the mass of a particle and its velocity (i.e. $\vec{p} = m\vec{v}$) and, secondly, because $\vec{v}$ is a vector (i.e. it has direction and magnitude, as in 50 mph EAST), $\vec{p}$ is also a vector.

Applying equation (1), and noting that $\vec{v}_{20}$ is 0 because particle 2 is initially at rest, we may write

$$\vec{p}_{10} = \vec{p}_{1_f} + \vec{p}_{2_f} \tag{2}$$

Now, we have still not used one last bit of information. The collision is elastic, and, whenever this is the case, kinetic energy is conserved. The law of kinetic energy conservation may be written mathematically as

$$\frac{1}{2} m_1 v_{10}^2 + \frac{1}{2} m_2 v_{20}^2 = \frac{1}{2} m_1 v_{1_f}^2 + \frac{1}{2} m_2 v_{2_f}^2 \tag{3}$$

where v_{10}, v_{1_f}, v_{20}, v_{2_f} have the same meaning as previously. Using this equation, we obtain

$$\frac{1}{2} m_1 v_{10}^2 = \frac{1}{2} m_1 v_{1_f}^2 + \frac{1}{2} m_2 v_{2_f}^2 \tag{4}$$

But $m_1 = m_2 = m$, hence

$$\frac{1}{2} m v_{10}^2 = \frac{1}{2} m v_{1_f}^2 + \frac{1}{2} m v_{2_f}^2 \tag{5}$$

$$v_{10}^2 = v_{1_f}^2 + v_{2_f}^2 \tag{6}$$

Rewriting equation (2), we find

$$m \vec{v}_{10} = m \vec{v}_{1_f} + m \vec{v}_{2_f} \tag{7}$$

Dividing both sides of (7) by m,

$$\vec{v}_{10} = \vec{v}_{1_f} + \vec{v}_{2_f} \tag{8}$$

We now want to express equation (8) in terms of magnitudes. To find the magnitude of a vector, we multiply it by itself, using the dot product, and take the square root. The dot product of 2 vectors is defined as

$$\vec{A} \cdot \vec{B} = AB \cos \theta$$

where A is the magnitude of $\vec{A}$, B is the magnitude of $\vec{B}$, and θ is the angle between $\vec{A}$ and $\vec{B}$. Note that

$$\vec{A} \cdot \vec{A} = (A)(A) = A^2$$

because, in this case, $\theta = 0°$ and $\cos 0° = 1$.

Now, dotting each side of equation (8) into itself, we find

$$\vec{v}_{10} \cdot \vec{v}_{10} = \left(\vec{v}_{1_f} + \vec{v}_{2_f}\right) \cdot \left(\vec{v}_{1_f} + \vec{v}_{2_f}\right) \qquad (9)$$

$$\vec{v}_{10} \cdot \vec{v}_{10} = \vec{v}_{1_f} \cdot \vec{v}_{1_f} + 2\vec{v}_{1_f} \cdot \vec{v}_{2_f} + \vec{v}_{2_f} \cdot \vec{v}_{2_f}$$

or $$v_{10}^2 = v_{1_f}^2 + v_{2_f}^2 + 2\vec{v}_{1_f} \cdot \vec{v}_{2_f} \qquad (10)$$

Subtracting equation (6) from (10)

$$\begin{array}{rl} v_{10}^2 & = v_{1_f}^2 + v_{2_f}^2 + 2\vec{v}_{1_f} \cdot \vec{v}_{2_f} \\ - \; v_{10}^2 & = v_{1_f}^2 + v_{2_f}^2 \\ \hline 0 & = 2\vec{v}_{1_f} \cdot \vec{v}_{2_f} \end{array}$$

or $$\vec{v}_{1_f} \cdot \vec{v}_{2_f} = 0 \qquad (11)$$

$$v_{1_f} v_{2_f} \cos \theta = 0 \qquad (12)$$

But because $v_{1_f}, v_{2_f} \neq 0$, this means that $\cos\theta = 0$ or $\theta = 90°$, as was to be shown.

• PROBLEM 325

A space probe explodes in flight into three equal portions. One portion continues along the original line of flight. The other two go off in directions each inclined at 60° to the original path. The energy released in the explosion is twice as great as the kinetic energy possessed by the probe at the time of the explosion. Determine the kinetic energy of each fragment immediately after the explosion.

Solution: Take the direction in which the probe is moving immediately prior to the explosion as the positive x-direction and the point at which the explosion takes place as the origin of coordinates. Let M be the mass of

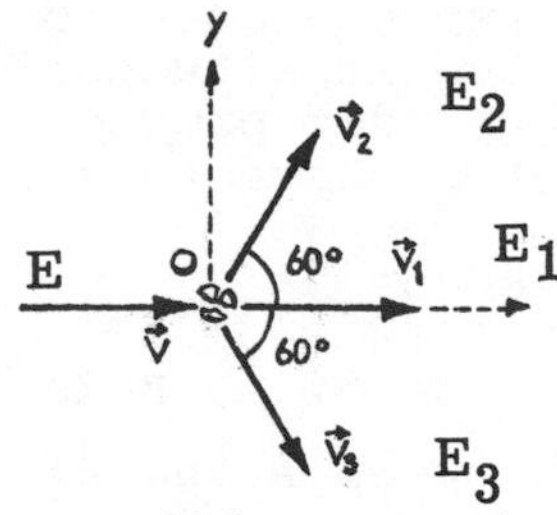

the probe and let the quantities applicable to the probe and its fragments be given subscripts as in the diagram.

Momentum must be conserved in the x-direction, the y-direction, and the z-direction independently. It follows that $\vec{V}_1$, $\vec{V}_2$, $\vec{V}_3$, and $\vec{V}$ must be coplanar and that

$$MV = \frac{1}{3} MV_1 + \frac{1}{3} MV_2 \cos 60° + \frac{1}{3} MV_3 \cos 60° \qquad \text{and}$$

$$\frac{1}{3} MV_2 \sin 60° = \frac{1}{3} MV_3 \sin 60°.$$

From the second of these equations $V_3 = V_2$, and thus the first equation becomes

$$MV = \frac{1}{3} MV_1 + \frac{1}{3} MV_2 \cos 60° + \frac{1}{3} MV_2 \cos 60°$$

$$= \frac{1}{3} MV_1 + \frac{2}{3} MV_2 \cos 60°$$

$$= \frac{1}{3} MV_1 + \frac{2}{3} MV_2 (\tfrac{1}{2}) = \frac{1}{3} MV_1 + \frac{1}{3} MV_2$$

But $E = \frac{1}{2} MV^2 = \dfrac{M^2V^2}{2M}$ or $MV = \sqrt{2ME}$.

Similarly,

$$E_1 = \frac{1}{2}\left(\frac{1}{3}M\right)V_1^2 = \frac{M^2V_1^2}{(3)(2M)} = \left(\frac{3\ M^2V_1^2}{2M}\right)\left(\frac{1}{9}\right) \qquad \text{or}$$

$$\frac{1}{3} MV_1 = \sqrt{\frac{2}{3} ME_1}$$

and $\dfrac{1}{3} MV_2 = \sqrt{\dfrac{2}{3} ME_2}$

The first equation thus becomes

$$\sqrt{2ME} = \sqrt{\frac{2}{3}ME_1} + \sqrt{\frac{2}{3} ME_2} \text{ or } \sqrt{3E} = \sqrt{E_1} + \sqrt{E_2}.$$

$$\therefore \quad 3E = E_1 + E_2 + 2\sqrt{E_1E_2} .$$

The original kinetic energy of the probe plus the energy released by the explosion must equal the sum of the kinetic energies of the fragments, since no energy can be lost in the process. (That is, we assume an elastic "collision" occurs.) Hence

$$E + 2E = 3E = E_1 + E_2 + E_3 = E_1 + 2E_2.$$

$$\therefore \quad E_1 + 2E_2 = E_1 + E_2 + 2\sqrt{E_1E_3} \qquad \text{or } E_2 = 2\sqrt{E_1E_2}.$$

$$\therefore \quad E_2^2 = 4E_1E_2 \qquad \text{or } E_2 = 4E_1.$$

Thus, $\quad 3E = E_1 + 2E_2 = E_1 + 8E_1 \qquad \text{or} \qquad E_1 = \frac{1}{3}E.$

$$\therefore \quad E_2 = \frac{4}{3}E.$$

Thus the fragment that continues in the line of flight has one-third of the original kinetic energy. The other fragments each have four-thirds of the original kinetic energy. The sum of these kinetic energies is three times the original kinetic energy, as required by the conservation principle.

• PROBLEM 326

The ballistic pendulum (see figure) is a device for measuring the velocity of a bullet. The bullet is allowed to make a completely inelastic collision with a body of much greater mass. Find the bullet's velocity before the collision.

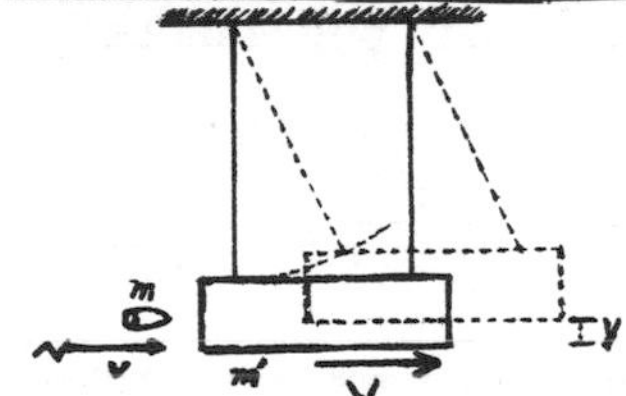

Solution: The momentum of the bullet-block system immediately after the collision equals the original momentum of the bullet since the block is initially at rest. Although the ballistic pendulum has now been superseded by other devices, it is still an important laboratory experiment for illustrating the concepts of momentum and energy.

In the figure, the pendulum, consisting perhaps of a large wooden block of mass m', hangs vertically by two cords. A bullet of mass m traveling with a velocity v, strikes the pendulum and remains embedded in it. If the collision time is very small compared with the time of swing of the pendulum, the supporting cords remain practically vertical during this time. Hence no external horizontal forces act on the system during the collision, and the horizontal momentum is conserved. Then, if V represents the velocity of bullet and block immediately after the collision,

$$mv = (m + m')V,$$

by the principle of conservation of momentum. Hence

$$V = \frac{mv}{m + m'} \qquad (1)$$

The kinetic energy of the system, immediately after the collision, is

$$E_k = \frac{1}{2}(m + m')V^2.$$

The pendulum now swings to the right and upward until all of its kinetic energy is converted to gravitational potential energy. (Small frictional effects can be neglected.)

Hence

$$\frac{1}{2}(m + m')V^2 = (m + m')gy,$$

$$V^2 = 2gy$$

By (1)

$$\frac{m^2v^2}{(m + m')^2} = 2gy$$

$$v^2 = \frac{2gy(m + m')^2}{m^2}$$

$$v = \frac{(m + m')}{m}\sqrt{2gy}.$$

By measuring m, m', and y, the original velocity v of the bullet can be computed.

It is important to remember that kinetic energy is not conserved in the collision. The ratio of the kinetic energy of bullet and pendulum, after the collision, to the original kinetic energy of the bullet, is

$$\frac{\frac{1}{2}(m + m')V^2}{\frac{1}{2}mv^2} = \frac{m}{m + m'} .$$

Thus if m' = 1000 gm and m = 1 gm, only about one-tenth of one percent of the original energy remains as kinetic energy; 99.9% is converted to heat.

• PROBLEM 327

A bullet weighing 4 g is fired at a speed of 600 m/s into a ballistic pendulum of weight 1 kg and thickness 25 cm. The bullet passes through the pendulum and emerges with a speed of 100 m/s. Calculate the constant retarding force acting on the bullet in its passage through the block, and the height to which the pendulum rises.

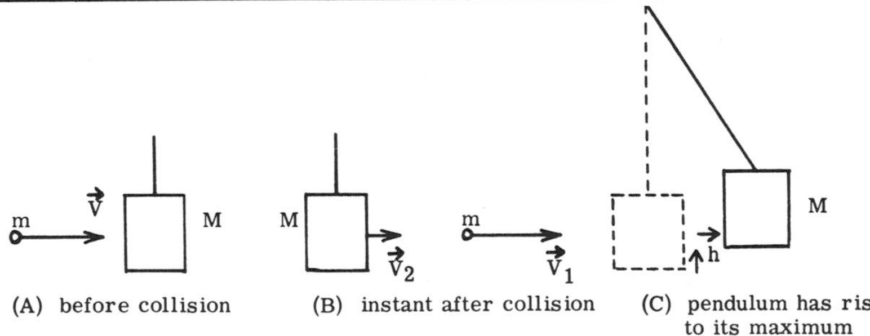

(A) before collision (B) instant after collision (C) pendulum has risen to its maximum height h

Solution: The ballistic pendulum is used to measure bullet speeds. The three stages of the motion of the system are as shown in the diagram. In the first stage, the bullet of mass m approaches with velocity $\vec{V}$ the ballistic pendulum of mass M. In the second, the bullet, having passed through the pendulum, is moving off with velocity $\vec{v}_1$, leaving the pendulum just starting to move with velocity $\vec{v}_2$. Since momentum must be conserved, $m\vec{V} = m\vec{v}_1 + M\vec{v}_2$.

$$\therefore \quad v_2 = \frac{mg(V - v_1)}{Mg}$$

$$= \frac{4 \times 10^{-3}\ \text{kg}\ (600 - 100)\text{m/s}}{1\ \text{kg}} = 2\ \text{m/s}.$$

In the third stage, the pendulum, which has acquired kinetic energy $\frac{1}{2} Mv_2^2$, swings through a certain angle such that the bob loses all its kinetic energy but gains an equivalent quantity of potential energy in rising a height h, in accordance with the principle of conservation of energy. But $= Mgh = \frac{1}{2}Mv_2^2$. Therefore $h = \sqrt{v_2^2/2g} = 0.45$ m = 45 cm. The loss of kinetic energy as the bullet passes through the pendulum is

$$\frac{1}{2} mV^2 - \frac{1}{2} mv_1^2 - \frac{1}{2} Mv_2^2$$

$$= \frac{4 \times 10^{-3}\ \text{kg}}{2} \left(600^2 - 100^2\right)\ \text{m}^2/\text{s}^2$$

$$- \frac{1\ \text{kg}}{2} \times 4\ \text{m}^2/\text{s}^2 = 698\ \text{J}.$$

By the principle of conservation of energy, this quantity of energy must represent the work done against the retarding force, $\vec{F}$, as the bullet pushes its way through the pendulum. Thus,

$$W = \vec{F} \cdot \vec{s} = F \times 0.25\ \text{m} = 698\ \text{J or}$$

$$F = 4\ \text{m}^{-1} \times 698\ \text{J} = 2792\ \text{N}.$$

• PROBLEM 328

A star of mass 2×10^{30} kg moving with a velocity of 2×10^4 m/sec collides with a second star of mass 5×10^{30} kg moving with a velocity of 3×10^4 m/sec in a direction at right angles to the first star. If the two join together, what is their common velocity?

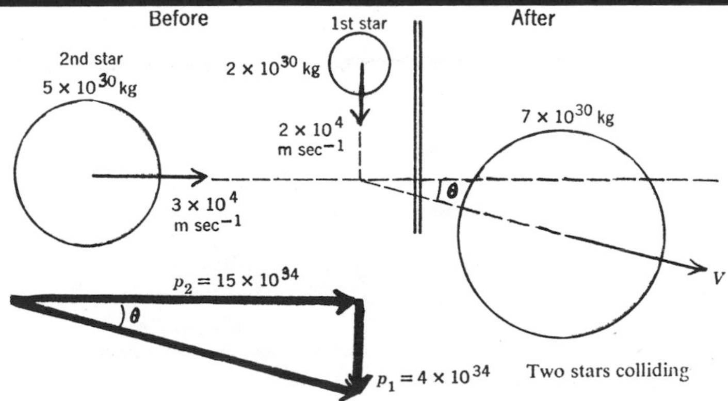

Two stars colliding

Solution: The figure shows the situation before and after the collision. The momentum of the first star is

$$p_1 = m_1v_1 = (2 \times 10^{30} \text{ kg})(2 \times 10^4 \text{ m/sec})$$

$$= 4 \times 10^{34} \text{ kg-m/sec}$$

and is depicted in a vertical direction. The momentum of the second star is

$$p_2 = m_2v_2 = (5 \times 10^{30} \text{ kg})(3 \times 10^4 \text{ m/sec})$$

$$= 15 \times 10^{34} \text{ kg-m/sec}$$

and is depicted in a horizontal direction. The vector diagram shows how to add the initial momenta of the two stars. The total momentum of the system of the two stars before the collision is represented by the resultant in the triangle of vectors. According to the law of conservation of momentum this also represents the momentum of the single star resulting from the coalescence.

Applying Pythagoras' theorem to the triangle of vectors, the magnitude of the total momentum is

$$\left(\sqrt{4^2 + 15^2}\right) \times 10^{34} = 15.52 \times 10^{34} \text{ kg-m/sec.}$$

Since the combined mass is 7×10^{30} kg, the velocity after coalescence is

$$\frac{15.52 \times 10^{34}}{7 \times 10^{30}} = 2.22 \times 10^4 \text{ m/sec.}$$

To obtain the angle θ, notice that

$$\tan\theta = \frac{4 \times 10^{34}}{15 \times 10^{34}}$$

$$= 0.2667$$

Whence $\theta = 14.93°$.

Therefore, the single star resulting from the coalescence moves with a velocity of 2.22×10^4 m/sec in a direction making an angle of 14.93° with the direction in which the second star was initially moving.

• PROBLEM 329

A nail of mass M is driven into a board against a constant resistive force F by a hammer of mass m which is allowed to fall freely at each stroke through a height h. The hammer does not rebound after striking the nail. Find the distance the nail is driven in at each blow.

Show that the total energy expended in raising the hammer during the operation of driving the nail fully in to a depth d is independent of the value of h, and can be decreased by making the hammer more massive.

Solution: The hammer falls through a height h, losing potential energy and gaining kinetic energy. By the principle of conservation of energy, $mgh = \frac{1}{2} mv^2$, and that the hammer strikes the nail with a velocity v, where

$v = \sqrt{2gh}$. An inelastic collision takes place and momentum is conserved, so that $mv = (m + M)V$. Therefore the kinetic energy of hammer and nail together, after the impact, is

$$\tfrac{1}{2}(m + M)V^2 = \tfrac{1}{2}\,\frac{m^2}{(m + M)}\,v^2 .$$

When the hammer hits the nail, we assume it loses all its kinetic energy. This energy is converted into the work necessary to drive the nail a distance x against the resistive force F. If the hammer drives the nail this distance x at each stroke, then we have from the work-energy theorem,

$$W = \vec{F} \cdot \vec{x} = -\,Fx \qquad 0 \;-\; \tfrac{1}{2}\,\frac{m^2}{m + M}\,v^2$$

since the final kinetic energy is zero and F opposes the nail's displacement. Solving for x and substituting $v = \sqrt{2gh}$, we have

$$x = \frac{m^2v^2}{2F(m + M)} = \frac{ghm^2}{F(m + M)} .$$

If it requires n strokes to drive the nail fully home a distance d, then

$$d = nx = \frac{nghm^2}{F(m + M)} . \qquad (1)$$

But the energy E supplied to the system is that energy required to raise the hammer n times through a height h. Thus

$$E = nmgh$$

In equation (1), solve for nmgh. Then

$$E = \frac{Fd(m + M)}{m} = Fd + Fd\,\frac{M}{m} .$$

Thus the energy does not depend on h and will be decreased if m is made larger.

• PROBLEM 330

A rifle weighing 7 pounds shoots a bullet weighing 1 ounce, giving the bullet a speed of 1120 feet per second.

(a) If the rifle is free to move, what is its recoil speed?

(b) If the rifle is held tight against the shoulder of a man weighing 133 pounds and if he were free to move, what would be the recoil speed of the rifle and man?

(c) If the bullet imbeds itself in a block of wood weighing 3 pounds and 7 ounces and if the block were free to move, what would be the speed of the block plus bullet?

Solution: The law of conservation of momentum may be applied in an isolated system where no external forces are applied.

(a) The momentum of the gun plus bullet before firing is zero, and it is therefore also zero after firing. The momentum after firing is

$$M_{bullet} \times v_{bullet} + M_{gun} \times v_{gun} = 0 \qquad (1)$$

Since the law of conservation of momentum involves mass and not weight, we must convert weight into mass by dividing by the acceleration of gravity

$\left(M = \frac{Wt}{g}\right)$. Therefore

$$M_{bullet} = \frac{\frac{1}{16}\text{ lb}}{32\text{ ft/s}^2} = 2\text{ slugs and}$$

$$M_{gun} = \frac{7\text{ lb}}{32\text{ ft/s}^2} = \frac{7}{32}\text{ slugs}$$

Equation (1) then becomes

$$2\text{ slugs} \times 1120\text{ ft/sec} + 7/32\text{ slugs} \times v_{gun} = 0$$

whence

$$v_{gun} = -\ 10\text{ ft/sec, or 10 ft/sec backwards}$$

(b) The momentum after firing is

$$M_{bullet} \times v_{bullet} + M_{gun + man} \times v_{gun + man} = 0 \quad \text{or}$$

$$2\text{ slugs} \times 1120\text{ ft/sec} + \left(\frac{133}{32}\text{ slugs} + \frac{7}{32}\text{ slugs}\right) \times v_{gun + man} = 0$$

whence

$$v_{gun + man} = -\ 0.5\text{ ft/sec, or 0.5 ft/sec backwards}$$

(c) The momentum of the bullet before the collision with the block is

$$M_{bullet} \times v_{bullet} = 2\text{ slugs} \times 1120\text{ ft/sec} = 70\text{ lb-ft/sec}$$

The momentum after collision is the same, 70 lb-ft/sec. Then

$$70\text{ lb-ft/sec} = \left(M_{bullet + block}\right) \times \left(v_{bullet + block}\right)$$

$$= \left(\frac{3}{32}\text{ slugs} + \frac{7}{2}\text{ slugs} + 2\text{ slugs}\right) \times \left(v_{bullet+block}\right)$$

whence

$$\left(v_{bullet + block}\right) = 20\text{ ft/sec forwards.}$$

• PROBLEM 331

When a block of wood of mass 1 kg is held in a vise, a bullet of mass 10 g fired into it penetrates to a depth of 10 cm. If the block is now suspended so that it can move freely and a second bullet is fired into it, to what depth will the bullet penetrate? (The retarding force in both cases is assumed constant.)

Solution: The wood exerts a constant retarding force $\vec{F}$ on the bullet. The work this force does on the bullet is equal to its change in kinetic energy in accordance with the work-energy theorem. This work is given by

$$W = \vec{F} \cdot \vec{s} \qquad (1)$$

where $\vec{s}$ is the distance the bullet penetrates the block. Since the force acts in a direction opposite to the path of motion of the bullet, equation (1) reduces to

$$W = - Fs$$

In the first case, all of the bullet's kinetic energy is converted to heat due to the work done on it by the retarding force. If the distance the bullet penetrates the block is d_1, then the work done on it is

$$W_1 = - Fd_1 = \tfrac{1}{2} mv_1^2 - \tfrac{1}{2}mv^2 = 0 - \tfrac{1}{2} mv^2 = - \tfrac{1}{2}mv^2$$

$$Fd_1 = \tfrac{1}{2} mv^2 \qquad (2)$$

where v is the bullet's initial velocity and v_1 is the bullet's final velocity, which equals zero since the bullet comes to rest in the block.

In the second case, the bullet's final velocity, v_2, is not zero. Even after it stops inside the block, it has a speed since the block is now free to move and the bullet moves with it. Since there are no external forces acting on the system, the principle of conservation of momentum can be applied. This is an inelastic collision where the block and bullet move together with the same final velocity, v_2. If the bullet's mass is represented by m and that of the block by M, then we have

$$mv = (m + M)v_2 \qquad (3)$$

where v has the same significance as before.

Further, the work done by the retarding force in stopping the bullet over a distance d_2, must equal the total change in kinetic energy of the system.

$$W_2 = - Fd_2 = \tfrac{1}{2}(m + M)v_2^2 - \tfrac{1}{2} mv^2 \qquad (4)$$

Solving for v_2 in equation (3) and substituting into equation (4)

$$- Fd_2 = \tfrac{1}{2}(m + M)\left(\frac{mv}{m + M}\right)^2 - \tfrac{1}{2} mv^2$$

$$Fd_2 = \tfrac{1}{2} mv^2 - \tfrac{1}{2} \frac{m^2}{m + M} v^2 \qquad (5)$$

Dividing equation (5) by (2), we obtain

$$\frac{Fd_2}{Fd_1} = \frac{\tfrac{1}{2} mv^2 - \tfrac{1}{2} \frac{m^2}{m + M} v^2}{\tfrac{1}{2} mv^2}$$

$$\frac{d_2}{d_1} = \frac{m - \frac{m^2}{m + M}}{m} = \frac{\frac{m^2 + mM - m^2}{m + M}}{m} = \frac{M}{m + M}$$

Substituting the known values, we have for the distance d_2 that the second bullet penetrates

$$d_2 = \frac{M\,d_1}{m + M} = \frac{(1\text{ kg})(0.1\text{ m})}{(0.01\text{ kg} + 1\text{ kg})} = \frac{0.1}{1.01}\text{ m}$$

$$= 0.099\text{ m} = 9.9\text{ cm}$$

• PROBLEM 332

Consider the collision of 2 particles of mass M_1 and M_2, that stick together after colliding. Let M_2 be at rest initially, and let $\vec{v}_1$ be the velocity of M_1 before the collision. (1) Describe the motion of $M = M_1 + M_2$ after the collision. (2) What is the ratio of the final kinetic energy to the initial kinetic energy? (3) What is the motion of the center of mass of this system before and after collision? (4) Describe the motion before and after the collision in the reference frame in which the center of mass is at rest.

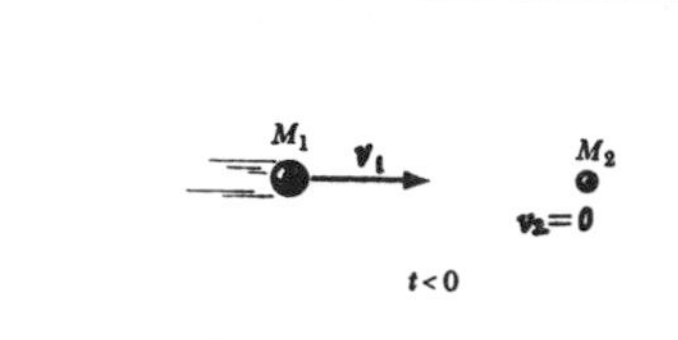

Fig. 1 Before Collision

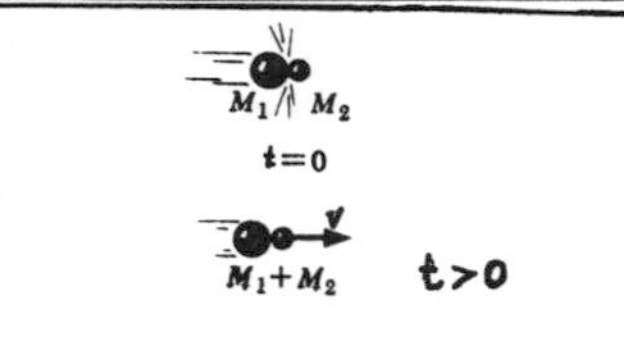

Fig. 2 During and After Collision

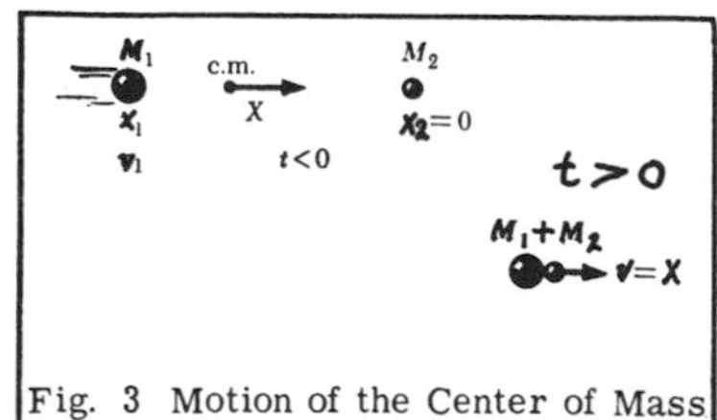

Fig. 3 Motion of the Center of Mass

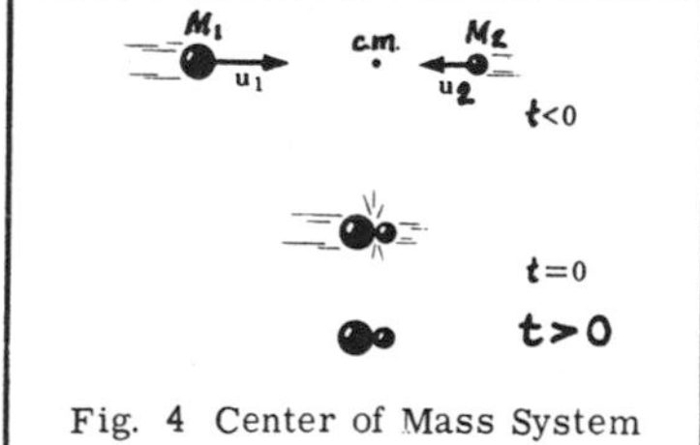

Fig. 4 Center of Mass System

Solution: The basic principle used in solving a collision problem is the law of conservation of total momentum. This principle may be applied to any collision, so long as there are no external forces (forces due to the outside environment) acting on the system.

From figures (1) and (2), we see that the initial momentum is $M_1\vec{v}_1$, and the final momentum is $(M_1 + M_2)\vec{v}$, and we obtain

$$M_1\vec{v}_1 = (M_1 + M_2)\,\vec{v}$$

$$\vec{v} = \frac{M_1}{M_1 + M_2}\,\vec{v}_1$$

Hence, $(M_1 + M_2)$ moves with velocity $\vec{v}$, parallel to $\vec{v}_1$.

(2) The kinetic energy k_f after the collision is

$$k_f = \tfrac{1}{2}(M_1 + M_2)v^2 = \tfrac{1}{2}(M_1 + M_2)\frac{M_1^2 v_1^2}{(M_1 + M_2)^2}$$

$$k_f = \frac{M_1^2 v_1^2}{2(M_1 + M_2)}$$

The initial kinetic energy, k_i is $\tfrac{1}{2} M_1 v_1^2$, hence

$$\frac{k_f}{k_i} = \frac{M_1^2 v_1^2}{2(M_1 + M_2)} \cdot \frac{1}{\tfrac{1}{2} M_1 v_1^2} = \frac{M_1}{M_1 + M_2}$$

$$\frac{k_f}{k_i} = 1 - \frac{M_2}{M_1 + M_2}$$

The difference, $k_i - k_f$, is lost to increased internal motion in the $(M_1 + M_2)$ system (i.e. internal excitations and heat). When a meteorite (M_1) strikes and sticks to the earth (M_2), essentially all the kinetic energy of the meteorite will be lost to heat in the earth. This follows from the fact that if $M_2 >> M_1$,

$$\frac{k_f}{k_i} = \frac{M_1}{M_1 + M_2} = \frac{1}{1 + \frac{M_2}{M_1}} \simeq 0$$

Hence, $k_f \simeq 0$ and all the initial kinetic energy is transformed into heat.

(3) The center of mass of a system of particles is a fictitious point whose motion is supposed to describe the trajectory of an imaginary bag which contains all the particles in that system. As the particles move around, the shape and the volume of this bag changes but not its momentum. The interactions of particles among themselves cannot result in a net-resultant force or change in momentum of the bag as a result of the action-reaction principle (for each force exerted on one particle by the others, there is an equal and opposite force exerted by this particle on the others). Furthermore, the collisions of particles with each other conserve the momentum of the colliding particles in each collision and cannot change the total momentum of the bag. In this way, we can view the motion of the center of mass as representing the net effect of only the external forces on the system. If there are no external forces, then the center of mass will not change its velocity, irrespective of the final velocities of the particles.

The position of the center of mass is given by

$$\vec{R}_{cm} = \frac{\text{Sum of all } m_i\vec{v}_i}{M_t}$$

where m_i and $\vec{r}_i$ are the masses and the positions of individual particles, M_t is the total mass. In our problem, let the collision take place at the origin of our coordinate system and at time t = 0. After the collision, the center of mass will just coincide with the mass $(M_1 + M_2)$ and we have

$$\vec{R}_{cm} = \vec{v}t = \frac{M_1}{M_1 + M_2} \vec{v}_1 t$$

The center of mass velocity is

$$\vec{v}_{cm} = \frac{\text{Sum of all } \vec{p}_i}{M_t}$$

where $\vec{p}_i$ are the individual momenta. For our problem

$$\vec{v}_{cm} = \vec{v} = \frac{M_1}{M_1 + M_2} \vec{v}_1$$

This expression for the velocity of center of mass will be true for all times, i.e. also before the collision (for which $t < 0$).

(4) In this reference frame $\vec{v}'_{cm} = 0$. (This reference frame is attached to the center of mass of the system.)

The new velocity of M_1 with respect to this observer will be the velocity of M_1 in the old frame minus the velocity of the c.m. frame with respect to the old frame or

$$\vec{u}_1 = \vec{v}_1 - \vec{v}_{cm} = \frac{M_2}{M_1 + M_2} \vec{v}_1$$

and, for M_2

$$\vec{u}_2 = \vec{v}_2 - \vec{v}_{cm} = -\vec{v}_{cm} = -\frac{M_1}{M_1 + M_2} \vec{v}_2$$

This result for $\vec{u}_2$ could be guessed right away. When the observer was in the old frame, M_2 was stationary. As the observer moves with $\vec{v}_{cm}$ with respect to the old frame, then with respect to this observer M_2 will appear to move in the opposite direction with equal speed:

$$\vec{u}_2 = -\vec{v}_{cm}.$$

The total momentum $\vec{p}_{total}$ in this system should add up to zero since $\vec{v}'_{cm}$ is zero; indeed we have

$$\vec{p}'_{total} = M_1\vec{u}_1 + M_2\vec{u}_2$$

$$= \frac{M_1 M_2}{M_1 + M_2} \vec{v}_1 - \frac{M_1 M_2}{M_1 + M_2} \vec{v}_1 = 0$$

The advantage of the center of mass frame is that the total momentum in it is zero.

A 3.60×10^4 -kg rocket rises vertically from rest. It ejects gas at an exhaust velocity of 1800 m/sec at a mass rate of 580 kg/sec for 40 sec before the fuel is expended. Determine the upward acceleration of the rocket at times t = 0,20, and 40 sec.

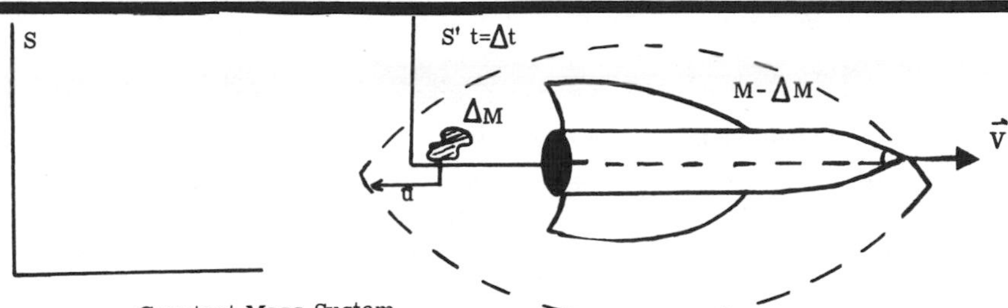

Constant Mass System

Solution: Suppose a rocket is travelling with a velocity $\vec{v}$ relative to a stationary cooordinate system (S), and emits fuel at velocity $\vec{u}$ with respect to the rocket (S') (see figure). The exhaust velocity with respect to S, $\vec{w}$, is the exhaust velocity with respect to S' plus the velocity of S' with respect to S or

$$\vec{w} = \vec{u} + \vec{v}.$$

Now that we know all the velocities with respect to a stationary frame, we may use the law of conservation of momentum in this frame to find the velocity of the rocket after a mass Δm has been emitted.

At t = 0, no fuel has been emitted and the initial momentum of the fuel-rocket system is

$$\vec{P}_0 = M\vec{v}.$$

At $t = \Delta t$, a mass ΔM (where $\Delta M > 0$) of fuel has been emitted and travels with velocity $\vec{w}$. The rocket now has mass $M - \Delta M$ and travels with a velocity $\vec{v} + \Delta\vec{v}$. The momentum is then

$$\vec{P}_f = (M - \Delta M)(\vec{v} + \Delta\vec{v}) + \Delta M(\vec{w})$$

or $$\vec{P}_f = (M - \Delta M)(\vec{v} + \Delta\vec{v}) + \Delta M(\vec{u} + \vec{v})$$

Hence, the change in momentum is

$$\Delta\vec{P} = \vec{P}_f - \vec{P}_0 = (M - \Delta M)(\vec{v} + \Delta\vec{v}) + \Delta M(\vec{u} + \vec{v}) - M\vec{v}$$

$$= M\vec{v} - \Delta M\vec{v} + M\Delta\vec{v} - \Delta M\Delta\vec{v} + \vec{u}\Delta M + \vec{v}\Delta M - M\vec{v}$$

$$= M\Delta\vec{v} + \vec{u}\,\Delta M - \Delta M\Delta\vec{v}$$

Then $$\frac{\Delta\vec{P}}{\Delta t} = M\frac{\Delta\vec{v}}{\Delta t} + \vec{u}\frac{\Delta M}{\Delta t} - \frac{\Delta M\Delta\vec{v}}{\Delta t}$$

Taking the limit as $\Delta t \to 0$

$$\frac{d\vec{P}}{dt} = \lim_{\Delta t \to 0}\frac{\Delta\vec{P}}{\Delta t} = M\frac{d\vec{v}}{dt} + \vec{u}\frac{dM}{dt}$$

because $\frac{\Delta M\Delta\vec{v}}{\Delta t} \to 0$ as $\Delta t \to 0$, whence

$$\frac{d\vec{P}}{dt} = M\frac{d\vec{v}}{dt} + \vec{u}\frac{dM}{dt}$$

But, for a constant mass system, which our's is, (see figure) the time rate of change of momentum of the system equals the net external force on the system and

$$M\frac{d\vec{v}}{dt} + \vec{u}\frac{dM}{dt} = \vec{F}_{ext} \qquad (1)$$

In this equation, $d\vec{v}/dt$ is the rocket's acceleration, M is the instantaneous mass of the rocket, $\vec{F}_{ext}$ is the net force on the fuel-rocket system, and dM/dt is the rate of change of the rocket's mass. Note that in (1), dM/dt > 0 due to our derivation. Hence, we may replace dM/dt by - dM/dt if we redefine dM/dt to be less than zero. Then

$$M\frac{d\vec{v}}{dt} - \vec{u}\frac{dM}{dt} = \vec{F}_{ext}$$

$$\text{or} \quad M\frac{d\vec{v}}{dt} = \vec{F}_{ext} + \vec{u}\frac{dM}{dt} \qquad (2)$$

We define $\vec{u}\frac{dM}{dt}$ as the rocket's thrust. Solving for $\frac{d\vec{v}}{dt}$

$$\frac{d\vec{v}}{dt} = \frac{\vec{F}_{ext}}{M} + \frac{\vec{u}}{M}\frac{dM}{dt} \qquad (3)$$

For our problem, $\vec{F}_{ext} = -Mg\hat{j}$, where $\hat{j}$ is a unit vector in the positive y direction. Furthermore, if the rocket is propelled straight up, $\vec{u} = -u\hat{j}$. Hence,

$$\frac{d\vec{v}}{dt} = -g\hat{j} - \frac{u}{M}\hat{j}\frac{dM}{dt} = -\hat{j}\left(g + \frac{u}{M}\frac{dM}{dt}\right) \qquad (4)$$

Note that since M is a function of time, $d\vec{v}/dt$ will also be time dependent.

At t = 0, $M = 3.60 \times 10^4$ kg

$$\text{and} \quad \frac{d\vec{v}}{dt} = -\hat{j}\left(\frac{9.8m}{S^2} + \frac{(1800\ m/s)}{(3.6\times 10^4\ kg)}\left(-\frac{580\ kg}{S}\right)\right)$$

$$\frac{d\vec{v}}{dt} = -\hat{j}\,(9.8\ m/s^2 - 29\ m/s^2)$$

$$\frac{d\vec{v}}{dt} = 19.2\ m/s^2\ \hat{j}$$

At t = 20 secs, $M = 3.6\times 10^4$ kg - (580 kg/s)(20s)

$$= 3.6\times 10^3\ kg - 11.6\times 10^3\ kg$$

$$= 24.4\times 10^3\ kg$$

$$\text{and} \quad \frac{d\vec{v}}{dt} = -\hat{j}\left(\frac{9.8\ m}{S^2} + \frac{(1800\ m/s)}{(2.44\times 10^4\ kg)}\left(-\frac{580\ kg}{S}\right)\right)$$

$$\frac{d\vec{v}}{dt} = -\hat{j}\,(9.8\ m/s^2 - 42.79\ m/s^2) = 32.99\ m/s^2\ \hat{j}$$

At t = 40 secs, $M = 3.6 \times 10^4$ kg - (580 kg/s)(40s)

$$= 3.6 \times 10^4 \text{ kg} - 2.32 \times 10^4 \text{ kg}$$

$$= 1.28 \times 10^4 \text{ kg}$$

and $$\frac{d\vec{v}}{dt} = -\hat{\jmath}\left[\frac{9.8 \text{ m}}{S^2} + \frac{(1800 \text{ m/s})}{(1.28 \times 10^4 \text{ kg})}\left(-\frac{580 \text{ kg}}{S}\right)\right]$$

$$\frac{d\vec{v}}{dt} = -\hat{\jmath}\,(9.8 \text{ m/s}^2 - 81.56 \text{ m/s}^2)$$

$$\frac{d\vec{v}}{dt} = 71.76 \text{ m/s}^2\ \hat{\jmath}$$

In this example we have neglected air friction and the variation of $\vec{g}$ with altitude.

• PROBLEM 334

In the first second of its flight, a rocket ejects 1/60 of its mass with velocity of 6800 ft/sec. What is the acceleration of the rocket?

Solution: The acceleration of the rocket at any time is

$$\frac{d\vec{v}}{dt} = \frac{\vec{F}_{ext}}{M} + \frac{\vec{u}}{M}\frac{dM}{dt} \qquad (1)$$

where M is the instantaneous mass of the rocket, $\vec{F}_{ext}$ is the net external force on the rocket-fuel system, $\vec{u}$ is the exhaust velocity of the fuel, and dM/dt is the time rate of change of the mass of the rocket.

In our case, $\vec{F}_{ext} = -Mg\hat{\jmath}$ where $\hat{\jmath}$ is a unit vector pointing up from the surface of the earth. Also $\vec{u} = -u\hat{\jmath}$. Then

$$\frac{d\vec{v}}{dt} = -\frac{Mg}{M}\hat{\jmath} - \frac{u}{M}\hat{\jmath}\frac{dM}{dt} = -\hat{\jmath}\left(g + \frac{u}{M}\frac{dM}{dt}\right)$$

Now, after the first second of flight,

$$M = M_0 - \frac{M_0}{60} = \frac{59}{60}M_0$$

where M_0 is the mass of the rocket at t = 0. Also,

$$\frac{dM}{dt} = -\frac{1/60\ M_0}{1 \text{ sec}} \doteq -\frac{M_0}{60 \text{ sec}}$$

where the negative sign accounts for the fact that M is decreasing as time increases. Hence,

$$\frac{d\vec{v}}{dt} = -\hat{\jmath}\left[\frac{32\text{f}}{s^2} + \left(\frac{6800 \text{ f/s}}{\frac{59}{60}M_0}\right)\left(-\frac{M_0}{60 \text{ sec}}\right)\right]$$

$$= -\hat{\jmath}\left(32 \text{ f/s}^2 - 115.2 \text{ f/s}^2\right)$$

$$= 83.2 \text{ f/s}^2\ \hat{\jmath}$$

• PROBLEM 335

In an experiment, a block of beryllium is bombarded with α-particles. A nearby block of paraffin, shielded from the α-particles, is observed to be emitting protons and nitrogen nuclei in separate events. The ratio of the velocity of the proton to that of the nitrogen nucleus is measured to be 7.5. It is suspected that this is a result of a chargeless particle being emitted by the beryllium and absorbed by the paraffin. What is the mass of this particle?

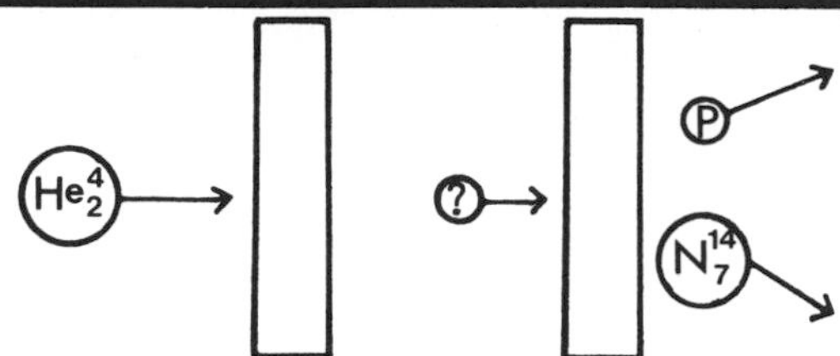

Solution: Let the mass of the unknown particle be m and its velocity υ.

Paraffin contains many hydrogen atoms (for it is a hydrocarbon). Hence we assume that protons are emitted after a head-on collision with one of the hydrogen atoms, (initially at rest). The momentum of the unknown "particle-hydrogen" system, before the collision, must equal the total momentum of the system after the collision, by the law conservation of momentum.

$$m\upsilon = m_p \upsilon_p' + m\upsilon' \qquad (1)$$

where υ_p' and υ' are the new velocities of the emitted proton and of the unknown particle, respectively. By conservation of energy, the sum of the kinetic energies of the particles before the collision must be equal to the total kinetic energy after the collision or

$$\frac{1}{2} m\upsilon^2 = \frac{1}{2}\left(m_p \upsilon_p'\right)^2 + \frac{1}{2} m\upsilon'^2 \qquad (2)$$

Equation (1) is rewritten as

$$\upsilon - \upsilon' = \frac{m_p}{m} \upsilon_p' \qquad (3)$$

and (2) as

$$\upsilon^2 - \upsilon'^2 = \frac{m_p}{m} \upsilon_p'^2 \qquad (4)$$

Dividing (4) by (3) gives

$$\upsilon + \upsilon' = \upsilon_p' \qquad (5)$$

Then combining (3) and (5) we obtain

$$\upsilon = \frac{m_p + m}{2m} \upsilon_p' \qquad (6)$$

Similarly for the collision with the nitrogen atom we obtain

$$\upsilon = \frac{m_N + m}{2m} \upsilon'_N \qquad (7)$$

Thus from (6) and (7)

$$\frac{\upsilon'_p}{\upsilon'_N} = \frac{m_N + m}{m_p + m}$$

This ratio equals 7.5 so that

$$7.5 = \frac{m_N + m}{m_p + m}$$

$$7.5\ m_p + 7.5\ m = m_N + m$$

$$7.5\ m_p - m_N = -\ 6.5\ m$$

$$\frac{m_N - 7.5\ m_p}{6.5} = m$$

But $\quad m_N = 14.008$ amu

$\quad m_p = 1.008$ amu

Hence, $\quad m = \dfrac{6.458}{6.5}$ amu $= .99$ amu

$$m = \frac{m_N - 7.5\ m_p}{6.5}$$

In other words the unknown particle has a mass almost identical to that of the proton. The particle is called a neutron, and actually has a mass larger than the proton by about 0.18 per cent.

• PROBLEM 336

Show that the principle of conservation of momentum results from the principle of conservation of kinetic energy and the Galilean transformation.

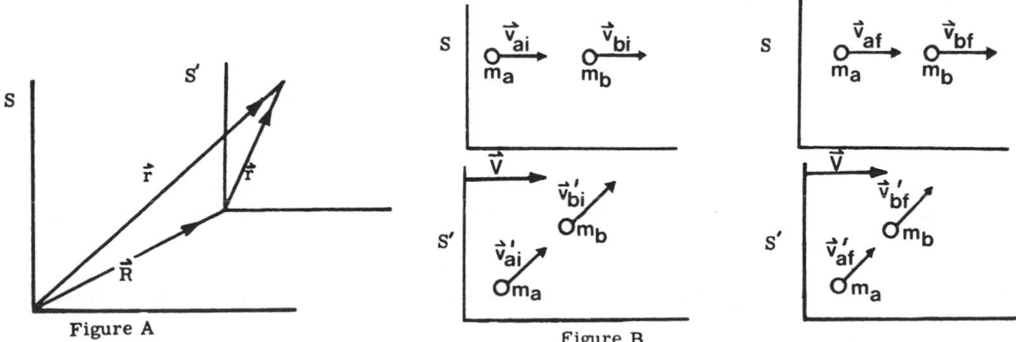

Figure A

Figure B

Solution: Suppose we observe a collision from two separate frames of reference, S and S', moving with a relative velocity $\vec{V}$ see figure (B) .

The position of a particle relative to S is related to its position relative to S' by see figure (A) .

$$\vec{r} = \vec{r}' + \vec{R} \tag{1}$$

Differentiating (1) with respect to time,

$$\vec{v} = \vec{v}' + \vec{V} \tag{2}$$

where $\vec{v}'$ and $\vec{v}$ are the velocity of the particle relative to S' and S respectively. Equations (1) and (2) constitute the Galilean transformation.

We apply the principle of conservation of kinetic energy in frame S see figure (B) , or

$$\tfrac{1}{2} M_a \vec{V}_{ai} \cdot \vec{V}_{ai} + \tfrac{1}{2} M_b \vec{V}_{bi} \cdot \vec{V}_{bi} = \tfrac{1}{2} M_a \vec{V}_{af} \cdot \vec{V}_{af} + \tfrac{1}{2} M_b \vec{V}_{bf} \cdot \vec{V}_{bf} \tag{3}$$

But, from (2)

$$\vec{v}_{ai} = \vec{v}'_{ai} + \vec{V} \qquad \vec{v}_{af} = \vec{v}'_{af} + \vec{V}$$
$$\vec{v}_{bi} = \vec{v}'_{bi} + \vec{V} \qquad \vec{v}_{bf} = \vec{v}'_{bf} + \vec{V} \tag{4}$$

Substituting (4) in (3)

$$\tfrac{1}{2} M_a(\vec{v}'_{ai} + \vec{V}) \cdot (\vec{v}'_{ai} + \vec{V}) + \tfrac{1}{2} M_b(\vec{v}'_{bi} + \vec{V}) \cdot (\vec{v}'_{bi} + \vec{V}) = \tfrac{1}{2} M_a(\vec{v}'_{af} + \vec{V}) \cdot (\vec{v}'_{af} + \vec{V})$$
$$+ \tfrac{1}{2} M_b(\vec{v}'_{bf} + \vec{V}) \cdot (\vec{v}'_{bf} + \vec{V})$$

or

$$\tfrac{1}{2} M_a \vec{v}'_{ai} \cdot \vec{v}'_{ai} + \tfrac{1}{2} M_b \vec{v}'_{bi} \cdot \vec{v}'_{bi} + \tfrac{1}{2}(M_a + M_b)(\vec{V} \cdot \vec{V}) + M_a \vec{v}'_{ai} \cdot \vec{V}$$
$$+ M_b \vec{v}'_{bi} \cdot \vec{V}$$
$$= \tfrac{1}{2} M_a \vec{v}'_{af} \cdot \vec{v}'_{af} + \tfrac{1}{2} M_b \vec{v}'_{bf} \cdot \vec{v}'_{bf} + \tfrac{1}{2}(M_a + M_b)(\vec{V} \cdot \vec{V})$$
$$+ M_a \vec{v}'_{af} \cdot \vec{V} + M_b \vec{v}'_{bf} \cdot \vec{V}$$

Rewriting this last equation:

$$\tfrac{1}{2} M_a \vec{v}'_{ai} \cdot \vec{v}'_{ai} + \tfrac{1}{2} M_b \vec{v}'_{bi} \cdot \vec{v}'_{bi} + (M_a \vec{v}'_{ai} + M_b \vec{v}'_{bi}) \cdot \vec{V} =$$
$$\tfrac{1}{2} M_a \vec{v}'_{af} \cdot \vec{v}'_{af} + \tfrac{1}{2} M_b \vec{v}'_{bf} \cdot \vec{v}'_{bf} + (M_a \vec{v}'_{af} + M_b \vec{v}'_{bf}) \cdot \vec{V} \tag{5}$$

Now, if conservation of kinetic energy holds

$$\tfrac{1}{2} M_a \vec{v}'_{ai} \cdot \vec{v}'_{ai} + \tfrac{1}{2} M_b \vec{v}'_{bi} \cdot \vec{v}'_{bi} = \tfrac{1}{2} M_a \vec{v}'_{af} \cdot \vec{v}'_{af} + \tfrac{1}{2} M_b \vec{v}'_{bf} \cdot \vec{v}'_{bf}$$

and (5) becomes

$$(M_a \vec{v}'_{ai} + M_b \vec{v}'_{bi}) \cdot \vec{V} = (M_a \vec{v}'_{af} + M_b \vec{v}'_{bf}) \cdot \vec{V} \tag{6}$$

But, since $\vec{V}$ is an arbitrary vector (6) holds for all $\vec{V}$ and we obtain the principle of conservation of momentum in frame S'

$$M_a \vec{v}'_{ai} + M_b \vec{v}'_{bi} = M_a \vec{v}'_{af} + M_b \vec{v}'_{bf} \tag{7}$$

Note also that S' is an arbitrary frame, and, therefore, (7) holds in all frames.

• PROBLEM 337

What is the angular deflection of a light beam or photon which passes by the sun at its edge?

Solution: This problem involves a photon moving with the velocity of light in a gravitational field. We do not get the correct answer without doing a careful

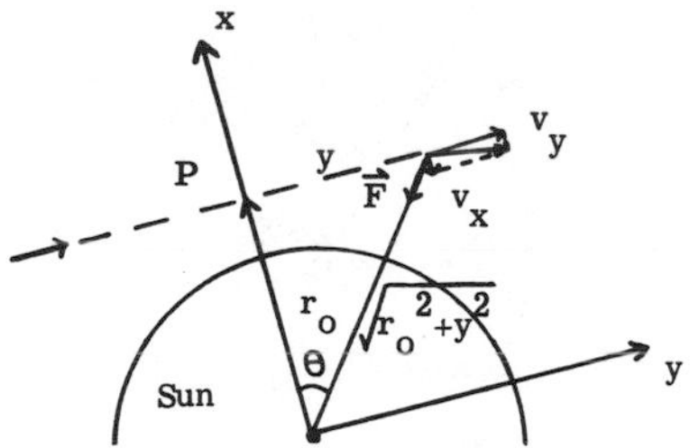

calculation using special relativity, but we can get the order of magnitude of the correct answer by a naive calculation.

Suppose that the photon has an effective mass M_L; it will turn out that M_L drops out of the calculation of the deflection and thus we do not have to know what it is. Let the light beam pass the sun at a distance of closest approach, r_0, as measured from the center of the sun. We suppose that the deflection will turn out to be very small, so that r_0 is essentially the same as if the light beam were not deflected. The force F on the photon at the position (r_0, y) is

$$F = -\frac{G M_s M_L}{(r_0^2 + y^2)}$$

The transverse component, F_x, is

$$F_x = -\frac{GM_s M_L}{(r_0^2 + y^2)} \cos\theta = -\frac{GM_s M_L}{(r_0^2 + y^2)} \frac{r}{(r_0^2 + y^2)^{\frac{1}{2}}}$$

$$= -GM_s M_L \frac{r_0}{(r_0^2 + y^2)^{3/2}}$$

where y is measured from the point P, as in the figure.

The final value of the transverse velocity component v_x of the photon has the value given by

$$M_L v_x = \int F_x\, dt = \int F_x \frac{dy}{v_y} \cong \frac{1}{c} \int F_x\, dy$$

so that

$$v_x \cong -\frac{2GM_s r_0}{c} \int_0^\infty \frac{dy}{(r_0^2 + y^2)^{3/2}} \cong -\frac{2GM_s}{cr_0}$$

ANGULAR MOMENTUM

• PROBLEM 338

A satellite of mass 3×10^3 kg moves with a speed of 8×10^3 m/s in an orbit of radius 7×10^6 m. What is the angular momentum of the satellite as it revolves about the earth?

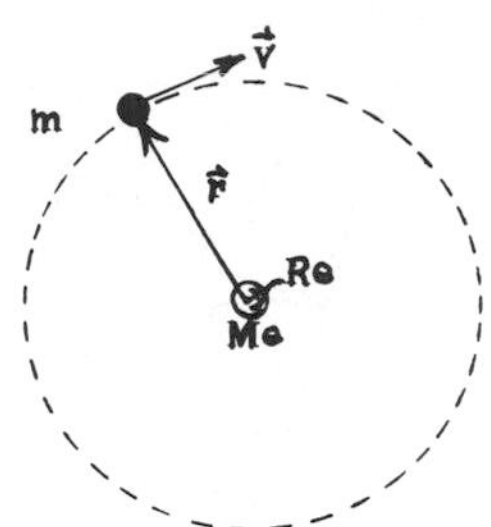

Solution: The angular momentum of an object about a point 0 is defined as

$$\vec{L} = \vec{r} \times \vec{p}$$

where $\vec{p}$ is the linear momentum of the object and $\vec{r}$ is the distance vector from 0 to the object. In this problem, $\vec{r}$ and $\vec{p}$ are perpendicular, hence the magnitude of $\vec{L}$ is

$$L = rp = r(mv) = mvr.$$

The known observables are mass, $m = 3 \times 10^3$ kg; speed $v = 8 \times 10^3$ m/s; and orbit radius, $r = 7 \times 10^6$ m; therefore,

$$L = mvr = \left(3 \times 10^3 \text{ kg}\right)\left(8 \times 10^3 \text{ m/s}\right)\left(7 \times 10^6 \text{ m}\right) =$$

$$= 1.68 \times 10^{14} \text{ Js.}$$

• PROBLEM 339

In the Bohr-atom model an electron of mass 9.11×10^{-31} kg revolves in a circular orbit about the nucleus. It completes an orbit of radius 0.53×10^{-10} m in 1.51×10^{-16} sec. What is the angular momentum H of the electron in this orbit?

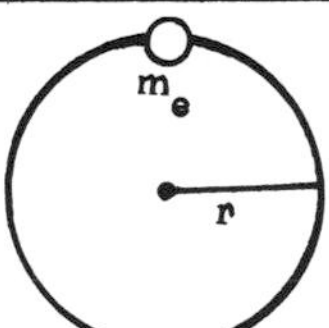

Solution: $\vec{H} = \vec{r} \times \vec{p}$ where $\vec{p}$ is the linear momentum of the electron, and $\vec{r}$ is the vector from the proton to the electron. Because the orbit of the electron is circular, $\vec{r}$ is perpendicular to $\vec{p}$. Hence

$$|\vec{H}| = H = rp = mrv$$

But $v = \omega r$, where ω is the angular velocity of the electron.

The frequency of revolution is $f = \frac{1}{T}$, where T is the period, or the time it takes for the electron to make one revolution in its orbit. In T units of time, then, the electron goes through an angle of 2π radians. Hence

$$\omega = \frac{2\pi}{T}$$

Therefore,

$$H = mr^2\omega = (m)\left(\frac{2\pi}{T}\right)\left(r^2\right) =$$

$$H = \left(9.11 \times 10^{-31} \text{ kg}\right) \frac{2\pi \text{ rad}}{1.51 \times 10^{-6} \text{ sec}} \left(0.53 \times 10^{-10} \text{ m}\right)^2$$

$= 1.06 \times 10^{-34}$ kg-m^2/sec .

• PROBLEM 340

A rod of negligible mass with length 2 meters has a small 2kg mass mounted on each end.
(a) Calculate the moment of inertia of this rod about an axis perpendicular to the rod and through its center.
(b) Find its angular momentum if the rod rotates about this axis with an angular velocity of 10 radians per second.

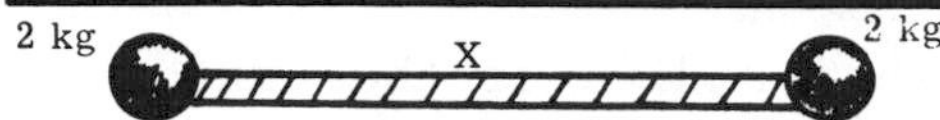

Rotational axis is perpendicular to page and passes through x.

Solution: (a) Rotational inertia I of a system is defined as the sum of the products of the masses m of the particles in the system and the squares of their respective distances r from the rotational axis. Then

$$I = \sum_i m_i r_i^2$$

For the system shown in the figure, we have

$$I = (2\text{kg})(1\text{m})^2 + (2\text{kg})(1\text{m})^2 = 4 \text{ kg-m}^2 \; .$$

(b) The angular momentum is defined as the product of the rotational inertia and the angular velocity ω. Therefore the angular momentum L in this problem is

$$L = I\omega = (4 \text{ kg-m}^2)(10 \text{ rad/sec}) = 40 \text{ kg-m}^2/\text{sec} \; .$$

Note that angular momentum is analogous to linear momentum which equals the product of inertial mass m and linear velocity v.

• PROBLEM 341

If the radius of the earth were to decrease by ½ percent what would be the change in the length of the day?
Consider the earth to be a uniform sphere whose moment of inertia is $I = 2/5\, mR^2$.

Solution: A dancer's technique of increasing her angular velocity by pulling her arms in to her side conveys the idea of conservation of angular momentum. The dancer is initially rotating at angular velocity ω_0, and she has a moment of inertia I_0. After she pulls her arms in, she has decreased her moment of inertia to I_f. We observe that she has an increased angular velocity, ω_f, and we may therefore write

$$I_0\omega_0 = I_f\omega_f$$

Since $I\omega$ is angular momentum, we have motivated the principle of conservation of angular momentum

$$L_0 = L_f$$

where L_0 and L_f are the initial and final angular momenta. This general principle holds whenever no external torques act on the system which we are observing.

In the present case, we may apply this principle to find the final angular velocity of the earth. We then relate this to the period of the earth's rotation, and, hence, the length of the day.

$$L_0 = L_f$$

$$I_0\omega_0 = I_f\omega_f$$

$$\left(\frac{2}{5}\,mR_0^2\right)\omega_0 = \left(\frac{2}{5}\,mR_f^2\right)\,\omega_f$$

$$R_0^2\omega_0 = R_f^2\omega_f$$

$$\omega_f = \frac{\omega_0 R_0^2}{R_f 2}$$

But $R_f = R_0 - .005R_0$ since the final radius of the earth is .5% less than its initial radius.

$$\omega_f = \frac{\omega_0 R_0}{(R_0 - .005R_0)^2}$$

$$\omega_f = \frac{\omega_0 R_0^2}{R_0^2(1 - .005)^2}$$

$$\omega_f = \frac{\omega_0}{(.995)^2} = 1.01\ \omega_0 \qquad (1)$$

But angular velocity is defined as

$$\omega = \frac{2\pi}{T}$$

where it takes a body T secs to traverse 2π radians of angular distance. Hence

$$\frac{\omega_f}{\omega_0} = \left(\frac{2\pi}{T_f}\right)\left(\frac{T_0}{2\pi}\right) = \frac{T_0}{T_f} \qquad (2)$$

Combining (1) and (2)

$$\frac{T_0}{T_f} = 1.01$$

or $$T_f = \frac{T_0}{1.01}$$

But T_0 is the time it took the earth to sweep out 2π radians originally, before its radius decreased. This time is 1 day, and

$$T_f = \frac{1\ \text{day}}{1.01} = \frac{86400\ \text{secs}}{1.01} = 85544.55\ \text{secs}$$

Hence, the change in the length of a day, is

$$T_f - T_0 = (86400 - 85544.55)\text{secs} = 855.45\ \text{secs}$$

$$T_f - T_0 = 14.28\ \text{minutes.}$$

• PROBLEM 342

A man of mass 80 kg is standing on the rim of a stationary uniform circular platform, of mass 140 kg and diameter 8 m, which is free to rotate about its center. The man throws to a companion on the ground in a direction tangential to the rim a package of mass 1 kg at a speed of 20 $m \cdot s^{-1}$ relative to the ground. What angular velocity of the man and platform is produced in consequence?

The man then walks so as to bring him to a position halfway between the rim and the center of the platform. What is the new angular velocity of the system?

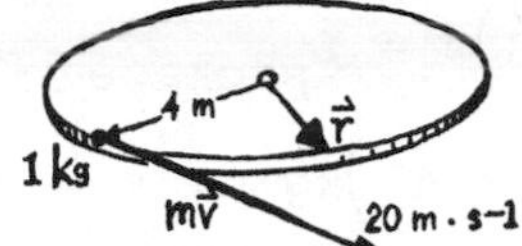

Solution: The package is thrown tangentially at a speed of 20 $m \cdot s^{-1}$ relative to the ground and consequently has an initial angular momentum about the center of the platform given by

$$|\vec{L}| = |\vec{r} \times m\vec{v}| = |mvr\sin\theta| = mvr = 1\text{ kg} \times 20\text{ m}\cdot\text{s}^{-1} \times 4\text{m}$$
$$= 80\text{ kg}\cdot\text{m}^2\cdot\text{s}^{-1}.$$

where θ (=90°) is the angle between $\vec{r}$ and $\vec{v}$.

Since the platform is free to rotate about its center, there are no external (e.g. in the form of friction) forces acting on the man-package-platform system. There are no external torques acting on this system, but

$$\vec{\Gamma} = \frac{d\vec{L}}{dt}$$

where $\vec{\Gamma}$ is the sum of the external torques acting on the system. Thus

$$0 = \frac{d\vec{L}}{dt}$$
$$\vec{L} = \text{constant}$$

That is, the angular momentum of the system remains the same at all instances of time when no external force acts on the system. This is the principle of conservation of angular momentum. Since the man-package-platform system was initially at rest, $\vec{L} = 0$. After the package is thrown, $\vec{L}$ must still be zero, thus the man-platform must acquire a momentum equal and opposite to the momentum of the package, to satisfy the condition that the $\vec{L} = 0$ for the man-platform-package system at all times. The platform is a distributed mass, as opposed to the localized masses of the man and package (which to a very good approximation may be treated as point masses). The following expression involving the moment of inertia I of the platform must then be used. (The moment of inertia accounts for this mass distribution).

$$I\omega = L \qquad (1)$$

where I is the angular velocity of the platform due to the throwing of the package. (This is the rigid body analogue of linear momentum mv = p, where I corresponds to m, v corresponds to ω and L corresponds to P.) I for the uniform circular platform is

$$I_1 = \frac{1}{2}m_1R^2$$

where m_1 is the mass of the platform and R is its radius. For the man, the definition of moment of inertia for a discrete particle gives $I_2 = m_2R^2$, where m_2 is the man's mass. Then, since the man also revolves about the center with angular velocity ω, equation (1) becomes

$$(I_1 + I_2)\omega = L_1 + L_2 = L_{package}$$

$$\left(m_2R^2 + \frac{1}{2}m_1R^2\right)\omega = L_{package}$$

$$\left(80 \times 4^2 + \frac{1}{2} \times 140 \times 4^2\right)\text{kg}\cdot\text{m}^2 \times \omega = 80\ \text{kg}\cdot\text{m}^2\cdot\text{s}^{-1},$$

$$\omega = \frac{80\ \text{s}^{-1}}{80 \times 16 + 70 \times 16} = \frac{1}{30}\ \text{rad}\cdot\text{s}^{-1}.$$

If the man walks toward the center, his moment of inertia about the center decreases. At the halfway position, his moment of inertia is $m_2\left(\frac{R}{2}\right)^2 = (80 \times 2^2)\text{kg}\cdot\text{m}^2$. But the angular momentum must stay the same, and so the angular velocity must increase to ω', and $(m_2R^2)\omega = L = \left[m_2\left(\frac{R}{2}\right)^2\right]\omega'$

$$\left(80 \times 4^2 + \frac{1}{2} \times 140 \times 4^2\right)\text{kg}\cdot\text{m}^2 \times \omega = \left(80 \times 2^2 + \frac{1}{2} \times 140 \times 4^2\right)\text{kg}\cdot\text{m}^2 \times \omega'.$$

$$\therefore\ \omega' = \frac{150}{90}\omega = \frac{1}{18}\ \text{rad}\cdot\text{s}^{-1}.$$

• PROBLEM 343

What is the angular momentum of a long thin rod that rotates as shown in the figure if it makes three revolutions per second? Assume that the mass of the rod is 2 kg and its length is 6 m.

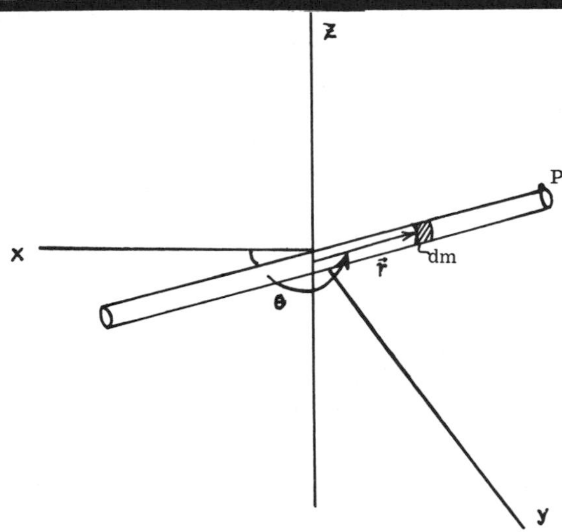

Solution: The angular momentum of an object about a fixed axis is

$$L = I\omega$$

where I is the moment of inertia of the object about that

axis, and ω is the angular velocity of the object.

To calculate L for a long thin rod, we must first find I. By definition,

$$I = \int r^2 dm \tag{1}$$

where dm is a mass element of the rod, and r is the distance of dm from the axis of rotation of the rod, z. The integral is evaluated over the total mass of the rod. If ϕ is the mass density of the rod, then by definition

$$\phi = \frac{dm}{dv}$$

and

$$dm = \phi dv$$

where dv is a volume element of the rod. If the rod is very thin, we may consider it to be one dimensional. Hence, using cylindrical coordinates (r, θ, z),

$$dv = dr \quad \text{and} \quad dm = \phi dr.$$

Using (1)

$$I = \int_{-\ell/2}^{\ell/2} \phi r^2 dr$$

where ℓ is the length of the rod.

$$I = \left.\frac{\phi r^3}{3}\right|_{-\ell/2}^{\ell/2} = \frac{\phi \ell^3}{12}.$$

But $\phi = M/\ell$

$$I = \frac{M\ell^2}{12}$$

Therefore $\quad L = \left(\frac{M\ell^2}{12}\right)\omega$

Using the given data

$$L = \frac{(2\text{ Kg})(36\text{ m}^2)(3\text{ rev/sec})}{12}$$

$$= \frac{18\text{ m}^2 \cdot \text{Kg} \cdot \text{rev}}{\text{sec}}$$

But $\quad \frac{1\text{ rev}}{\text{sec}} = 2\pi \frac{\text{rads}}{\text{sec}}$

$$L = (2\pi)(18)\frac{\text{m}^2 \cdot \text{Kg} \cdot \text{rad}}{\text{sec}}$$

$$L = 113.04\frac{\text{m}^2 \cdot \text{Kg} \cdot \text{rad}}{\text{sec}}$$

$$L = 1.13 \times 10^2 \left(\frac{\text{Kg} \cdot \text{m}}{\text{sec}^2}\right)\text{m} \cdot \text{sec} \cdot \text{rad}$$

$$L = 1.13 \times 10^2 \text{ Joules} \cdot \text{sec}$$

CHAPTER 7

GYROSCOPIC MOTION

• PROBLEM 344

A symmetrical top is described by the fact that its moments of inertia about 2 of its principal axes are equal (i.e., $I_1 = I_2 \neq I_3$). Assuming that no external torques act, derive and solve the equations of motion of this body.

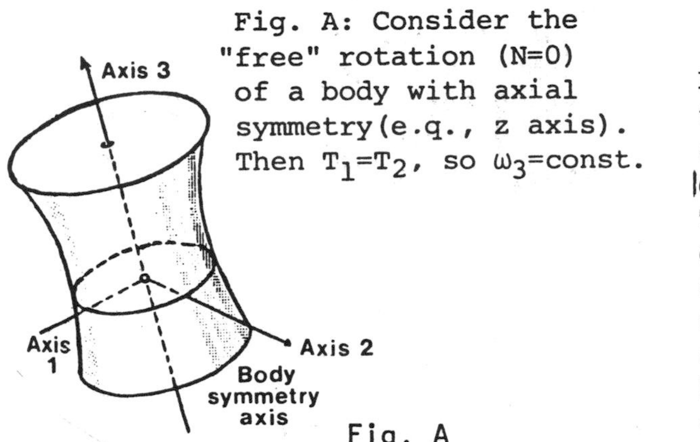

Fig. A: Consider the "free" rotation (N=0) of a body with axial symmetry(e.g., z axis). Then T_1=T_2, so ω_3=const.
Axis 3
Axis 1
Axis 2
Body symmetry axis
Fig. B: In these circumstances $|\omega|$ = const. The vector ω precesses at a constant rate around the body axis of symmetry.
Axis 3
Body axis
$\omega_\perp$
ω_3
ω
Body Cone

Fig. A

Fig. B

Solution: The general motion of a rigid body is very complex. For cases in which the object doesn't rotate about a fixed axis, we cannot relate the angular momentum (L) to the angular acceleration by

$$L = I\alpha$$

This relation only holds for rotations about a fixed axis. We must use

$$\vec{N} = \frac{d\vec{L}}{dt}$$

where $\vec{N}$ is the net external torque on the body for these rotations. Another alternative is to use the Euler Equations

$$I_1 \frac{d\omega_1}{dt} + \left(I_3 - I_2\right)\omega_3\omega_2 = N_1$$

$$I_2 \frac{d\omega_2}{dt} + \left(I_1 - I_3\right)\omega_1\omega_3 = N_2 \qquad (1)$$

$$I_3 \frac{d\omega_3}{dt} + \left(I_2 - I_1\right)\omega_2\omega_1 = N_3$$

where the subscript 1 refers to the first principal axis of the rigid body (see fig. (A)), and similarly for the subscripts 2 and 3. Furthermore, $\vec{\omega}$ is the angular velocity of rotation of the body with reference to an inertial frame.

In this example, $I_1 = I_2 \neq I_3$ and $\vec{N} = 0$, whence

$$I_1 \frac{d\omega_1}{dt} + \left(I_3 - I_2\right)\omega_3\omega_2 = 0$$

$$I_2 \frac{d\omega_2}{dt} + \left(I_1 - I_3\right)\omega_1\omega_3 = 0 \tag{2}$$

$$I_3 \frac{d\omega_3}{dt} = 0$$

Letting $I_1 = I_2 = I$, we obtain

$$\frac{d\omega_1}{dt} + \frac{\left(I_3 - I\right)}{I}\omega_3\omega_2 = 0$$

$$\frac{d\omega_2}{dt} + \frac{\left(I - I_3\right)}{I}\omega_1\omega_3 = 0$$

$$\frac{d\omega_3}{dt} = 0$$

Defining $\Omega \equiv \frac{I_3 - I}{I}\omega_3$, we may write

$$\frac{d\omega_1}{dt} + \Omega\omega_2 = 0$$

$$\frac{d\omega_2}{dt} - \Omega\omega_1 = 0 \tag{3}$$

$$\frac{d\omega_3}{dt} = 0$$

A solution of (3) is given by

$$\omega_1 = A \cos \Omega t; \quad \omega_2 = A \sin \Omega t ,$$

where A is a constant. We see that the component of the angular velocity perpendicular to the figure axis (axis 3) (see figure (A)) of the top rotates with a constant angular velocity Ω. The component ω_3 of the angular velocity along the figure axis is constant. Therefore the vector ω rotates uniformly with angular velocity Ω about the figure axis of the top. In other words, a top which spins about its figure axis with angular velocity ω_3 in force-free space will wobble with the frequency Ω.

For the earth I_3 is not exactly equal to I_1 because the earth is not exactly a sphere. The wobble is actually very well observed, giving rise to what is called the variation of latitude. The wobble is so interesting that the International Latitude Service maintains a number of observatories just for the purpose of measuring it.

• PROBLEM 345

For a uniform sphere with moments of inertia $I_1 = I_2 = I_3$, use the Euler equations to find the equation of motion of the sphere.

Solution: The Euler Equations are

$$I_1 \frac{d\omega_1}{dt} + \left(I_3 - I_2\right)\omega_3\omega_2 = N_1$$

$$I_2 \frac{d\omega_2}{dt} + \left(I_1 - I_3\right)\omega_1\omega_3 = N_2$$

$$I_3 \frac{d\omega_3}{dt} + \left(I_2 - I_1\right)\omega_2\omega_1 = N_3$$

where the subscript 1 refers to the first principal axis of the sphere. N and ω are the net external torque and angular velocity of the sphere. Noting that $I_1 = I_2 = I_3$, we obtain

$$I_1 \frac{d\omega_1}{dt} = N_1$$

$$I_2 \frac{d\omega_2}{dt} = N_2$$

$$I_3 \frac{d\omega_3}{dt} = N_3$$

Defining $I_1 = I_2 = I_3 = I$, we may write

$$\frac{d\omega_1}{dt} = \frac{N_1}{I}, \quad \frac{d\omega_2}{dt} = \frac{N_2}{I}, \quad \frac{d\omega_3}{dt} = \frac{N_3}{I} \qquad (1)$$

In free motion N = 0, and (1) tells us that ω = const. The result ω = const is a special feature of the free rotating sphere.

• PROBLEM 346

The flywheel in a delivery truck is mounted with its axis vertical, and thus acts as a stabilizing gyroscope for the truck. Calculate the torque that would have to be applied to it when it is rotating at full speed to make it precess in a vertical plane.

Figure (A)

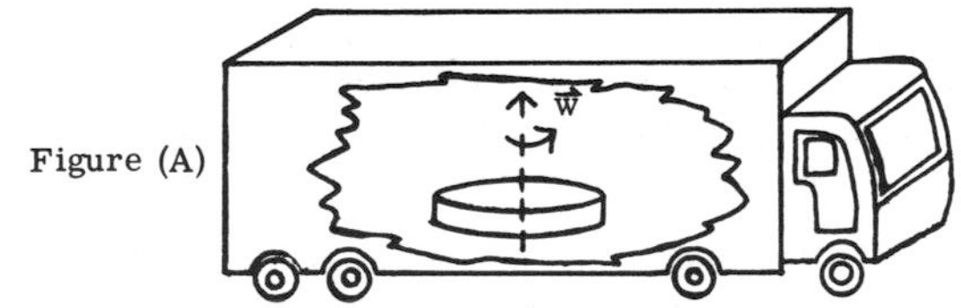

Figure (B): Blowup of Flywheel

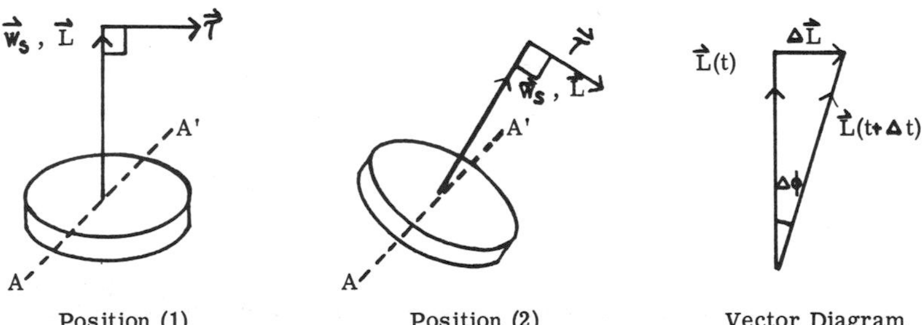

Position (1) Position (2) Vector Diagram

Solution: Figure (a) shows the situation. The flywheel is to precess about axis AA' as shown in figure (b). Originally, the angular momentum vector $\vec{L}$ is as shown in figure (b), position 1. After a time Δt, $\vec{L}$ has the new value $L(t + \Delta t)$, and the angular momentum vector has gone through an angle $\Delta\phi$, as shown in the vector diagram. Note that we have neglected the fact that there is a component of $\vec{L}$ along AA' due to the precession of the flywheel. This approximation is valid if the rate of precession, w_p, is small. By the relation

$$\frac{d\vec{L}}{dt} = \vec{\tau} \qquad (1)$$

where $\vec{\tau}$ is the net torque on the flywheel, we see that if we are to change $\vec{L}$, and thereby cause precession to occur, we must exert a torque $\vec{\tau}$. Now, the most efficient way for the torque to cause precession is if it acts in a direction perpendicular to $\vec{L}$, as shown in figure (b). As a result of (1), $d\vec{L}$ is also perpendicular to $\vec{L}$, and the length of $\vec{L}$ doesn't change. Hence

$$\frac{\Delta L}{\Delta t} \approx \tau$$

If $\Delta\vec{L}$ is small, and $\vec{\tau}$ is always perpendicular to $\vec{L}$,

$$\left|\frac{\Delta\vec{L}}{\vec{L}}\right| = \frac{\Delta L}{L} = \Delta\phi$$

or $$\tau \approx L\,\frac{\Delta\phi}{\Delta t} = L\,w_p$$

$$\tau \approx L\,w_p \qquad (2)$$

But $$L = I\,w_s \qquad (3)$$

where I is the moment of inertia of the flywheel about its symmetry axis and w_s is the spin angular velocity of the disc. Using (3) in (2)

$$\tau \approx I\,w_s\,w_p$$

Also $$I = \tfrac{1}{2} Mr^2$$

where M and r are the mass and radius of the disc. Finally

$$\tau \approx \tfrac{1}{2} Mr^2\,w_s\,w_p$$

CHAPTER 8

ELASTIC DEFORMATION

• PROBLEM 347

A steel bar, 20 ft long and of rectangular cross-section 2.0 by 1.0 in., supports a load of 2.0 tons. How much is the bar stretched?

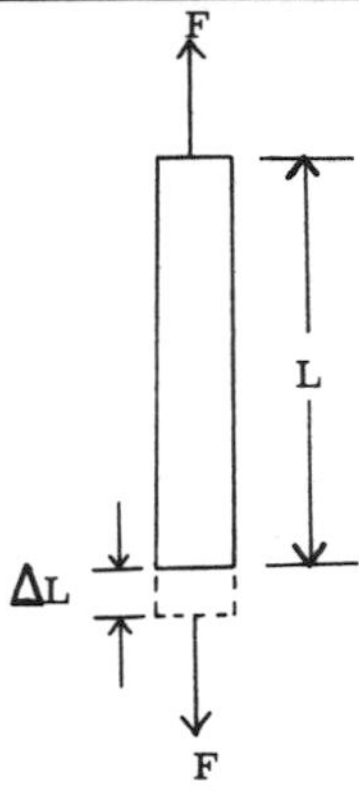

Solution: The Young's modulus of the metal bar is the ratio of longitudinal stress, F/A, to tensile strain ΔL/L (see the figure)

$$Y = \frac{F/A}{\Delta L/L} = \frac{FL}{A\Delta L}$$

Here, A is the bar's cross-sectional area. Therefore, the elongation ΔL of the bar is

$$\Delta L = \frac{\Delta FL}{YA}$$

$$\Delta F = 2.0 \text{ tons} = 2.0 \text{ ton} \times \frac{2000 \text{ lb}}{1 \text{ ton}} = 4000 \text{ lbs.}$$

$$A = (2.0 \text{ in.} \times 1.0 \text{ in.}) = 2.0 \text{ in.}^2$$

Young's modulus for steel is 29×10^6 lb/in.^{2}.

$$\Delta L = \frac{(4.0 \times 10^3 \text{ lb})(20 \text{ ft})}{(29 \times 10^6 \text{ lb/in.}^2)(2.0 \text{ in.}^2)} = 0.0014 \text{ ft}$$

$$= 0.017 \text{ in.}$$

• PROBLEM 348

If Young's Modulus for steel is 19×10^{11} dynes/cm^2, how much force will be required to stretch a sample of wire 1 sq mm in cross section by 10% of its original length?

Solution: The problem is recognized as one involving Young's Modulus, the defining equation for which is

$$Y = \frac{\text{Stress}}{\text{Strain}} = \frac{\frac{F}{A}}{\frac{\Delta x}{x}}$$

We are given that $\Delta x = .10x$ (or $\Delta x/x = 1/10$) and Y is given as 19×10^{11} dynes/cm². Moreover $A = 1\ mm^2 = 1\ mm^2 \times 1 cm^2/100\ mm^2 = .01\ cm^2$.

$$\frac{F}{A} = Y\frac{\Delta x}{x} \qquad \text{and} \qquad F = YA\frac{\Delta x}{x}$$

$$F = 19 \times 10^{11}\ dyne/cm^2 \times 10^{-2}\ cm^2 \times 10^{-1}$$

$$= 19 \times 10^{8}\ dynes.$$

• PROBLEM 349

A worker hangs a uniform bar of mass 12 kg horizontally from the roof of a laboratory by means of three steel wires each 1 mm in diameter. Two of the wires are 200 cm long and one, by an oversight, 200.05 cm long. The long wire is fastened to the middle of the bar, the others to the two ends. By how much is each wire stretched, and how much of the weight does each wire carry? Young's modulus for steel = 2.0×10^{12} dynes · cm^{-2}.

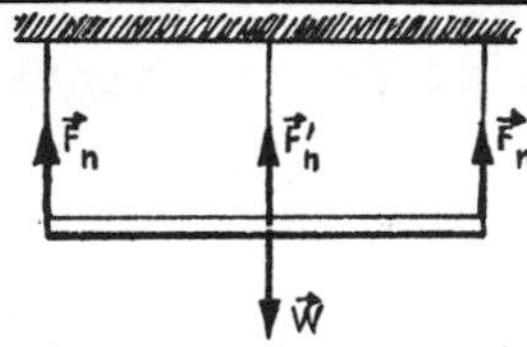

Solution: If the bar is hanging horizontally (see the figure), two of the wires will be extended Δl and one Δl - 0.05 cm. Now the formula for Young's modulus is

$$Y = \frac{stress}{strain} = \frac{F_n/A}{\Delta l/l_0},$$

where A is the cross sectional area of the steel wire, l_0 is the length of the wire with no stress acting on it, and F_n is the (stretching) force the bar exerts on the wire (equal in magnitude to the force the wire exerts on the bar). Thus

$$F_n = \frac{AY\Delta l}{l_0}.$$

Hence two wires exert upward forces on the bar of magnitude F_n, and one wire exerts a force of magnitude

$$F'_n = \frac{AY(\Delta l - 0.05\ cm)}{l_0 + 0.05\ cm}$$

Since the ratio $\frac{0.05}{l_0} = .00025$ is so small, we may ignore 0.05 in comparison with l_0 in the denominator of the expression for F'_n. Then, because the bar is in equilibrium, we obtain $W = 2F_n + F'_n = (AY/l_0)(2\Delta l + \Delta l - 0.05\ cm)$. Therefore

$$\Delta l = \frac{1}{3}\left(\frac{l_0 W}{AY} + 0.05\ cm\right)$$

However $A = \pi R^2 = \frac{\pi D^2}{4}$, where R and D are the radius and diameter, respectively, of the wire. We are given D = = 1 mm = 1 mm x $\frac{1 cm}{10 mm}$ = 0.1 cm. Hence

$$\Delta l = \frac{1}{3}\left(\frac{200 \text{ cm} \times 12 \text{ kg} \times 981 \times 10^3 \text{ dynes}}{(\pi/4) \times 10^{-2} \text{ cm}^2 \times 2 \times 10^{12} \text{ dynes} \cdot \text{cm}^{-2}} + 0.05 \text{ cm}\right)$$

$$= \frac{1}{3}(0.15 + 0.05)\text{cm} = 0.0667 \text{ cm} = 0.667 \text{ mm}.$$

Thus two of the wires are stretched by 0.667 mm and the other by (0.667 - 0.05)mm = 0.167mm. Also

$$\frac{F_n}{F'_n} = \frac{\Delta l}{\Delta l - 0.05 \text{ cm}} = \frac{0.667 \text{ mm}}{0.167 \text{ mm}} = 4;$$

$$12 \text{ kg} = W = 2F_n + F'_n = 9F'_n.$$

$$\therefore \quad F'_n = 1\tfrac{1}{3} \text{ kg} \quad \text{and} \quad F_n = 5\tfrac{1}{3} \text{ kg}.$$

• PROBLEM 350

To a good approximation, the force required to stretch a spring is proportional to the distance the spring is extended. That is,

$$F = kx$$

where k is the so-called spring constant or force constant and depends, of course, on the dimensions and material of the spring. Many elastic materials, if not stretched too far, obey this simple relationship - called Hooke's law after Robert Hooke (1635-1703), a contemporary of Newton.

Suppose that it requires 100 dynes to extend a certain spring 5 cm. What force is required to stretch the spring from its natural length to a length 20 cm greater? How much work is done in stretching the spring to 20 cm?

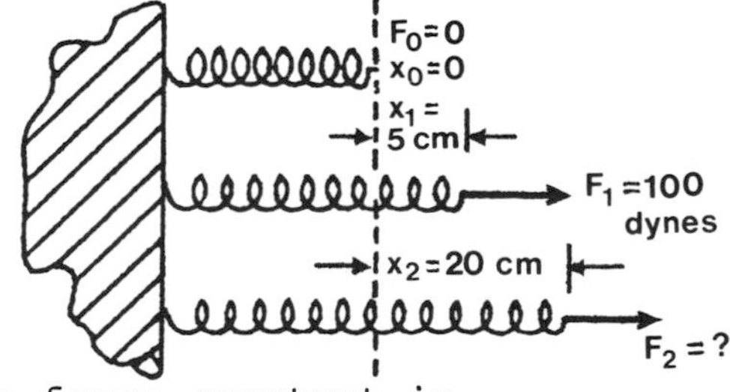

Solution: The force constant is

$$k = \frac{F_1}{x_1}$$

$$= \frac{100 \text{ dynes}}{5 \text{ cm}} = 20 \text{ dynes/cm}$$

Therefore, the force required to extend the spring to 20 cm is

$$F_2 = kx_2$$

$$= (20 \text{ dynes/cm}) \times (20 \text{ cm})$$

$$= 400 \text{ dynes}$$

The average force required to stretch the spring to 20 cm is

$$\bar{F} = \frac{F_2 + F_0}{2}$$

where: F_0 = initial force exerted on spring to keep its equilibrium length $= kx_0 = k \cdot 0 = 0$

F_2 = force required to stretch the spring to 20 cm $= kx_2$

Then $\bar{F} = \frac{F_2 + 0}{2} = \frac{kx_2}{2}$

and the work expended is the average force multiplied by the distance:

$$W = \bar{F}x_2 = \tfrac{1}{2} kx_2^2$$

$$= \tfrac{1}{2} \times (20 \text{ dynes/cm}) \times (20 \text{ cm})^2$$

$$= 4000 \text{ dynes - cm} = 4000 \text{ ergs}$$

since 1 erg = 1 dyne - cm.

• PROBLEM 351

A block of steel 2 ft. square and 1/4 in. thick is to be compressed .01 in. in length by application of a force F to faces A_1 and A_2. If Young's modulus for steel is 29×10^6 lb. in.^{2}, find F.

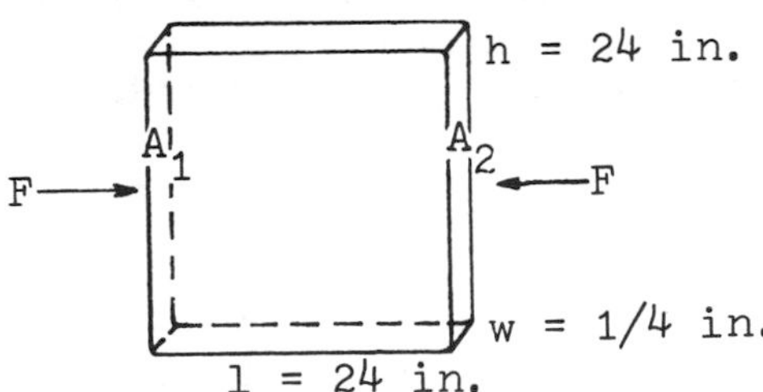

Solution: Young's modulus is defined as

$$Y = \frac{\text{STRESS}}{\text{STRAIN}} \qquad \text{(a)}$$

where

$$\text{STRESS} = \frac{\text{NORMAL FORCE}}{\text{AREA}} = \frac{F}{24 \times 1/4} = \frac{F}{6}$$

and

$$\text{STRAIN} = \frac{\text{CHANGE IN LENGTH}}{\text{ORIGINAL LENGTH}} = \frac{.01}{24} = \frac{1}{2400}$$

Substituting our values in (a),

$$29 \times 10^6 = \frac{F/6}{1/2400}$$

Thus

$$F = 72{,}500 \text{ lb.}$$

• PROBLEM 352

A steel shaft 12 ft long and 8 in. in diameter is part of a hydraulic press used to raise up cars in a garage. When it is supporting a car weighing 3200 lb, what is the decrease in length of the shaft? Young's modulus for steel is 29×10^6 lb·in^{-2}.

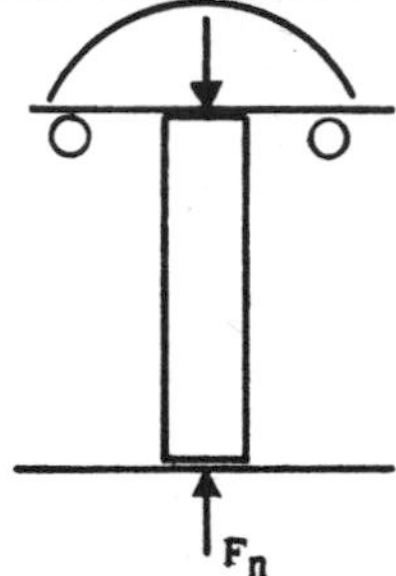

Solution: The formula for Young's modulus is

$$Y = \frac{\text{Stress}}{\text{Strain}} = \frac{F_n/A}{\Delta\ell/\ell_0}$$

where F_n is the normal force at the end of the shaft compressing it, A is the cross sectional area of the shaft, ℓ_0 is the length of the shaft when no stress is present and $\Delta\ell$ is the change in length due to the compression. A is given by $\pi R^2 = (\pi D^2)/4$, where R and D are the radius and diameter of the cross section of the shaft. Thus, the decrease in length is

$$\Delta\ell = \frac{F_n\ell_0}{YA} = \frac{3200 \text{ lb} \times 144 \text{ in.}}{29 \times 10^6 \text{ lb}\cdot\text{in}^2 \times 16\pi \text{ in}^2}$$

$$= 3.16 \times 10^{-4} \text{ in.}$$

• PROBLEM 353

A ship is being towed by a tug by means of a steel wire. If the drag on the ship is equivalent to 2×10^6 lb, and if the breaking strain of the wire is 0.025, what is the smallest permissible diameter of wire that may be used?

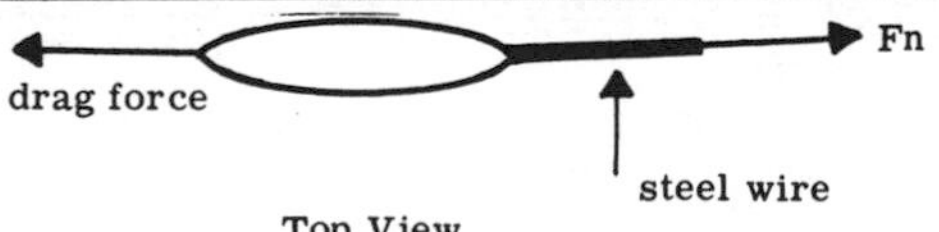

Top View

Solution: If the ship is being towed, it eventually settles down at a steady speed so that the force being exerted by the tow wire is equal and opposite to the drag on the ship. Now, the formula for Young's modulus is

$$Y = \frac{\text{Stress}}{\text{Strain}} = \frac{F_n/A}{\Delta l/l_0},$$

where the symbols have their usual significance. Thus $A = F_n l_0/Y\Delta l$, where F_n, the normal force on the wire, is equal to the force exerted by the wire on the ship, which balances the drag force. (See the fig.) Further, the strain $\Delta l/l_0$ must be less than 0.025, the strain at which the wire breaks. A table of Young's modului for different materials shows that for steel, $Y = 29 \times 10^6 \text{ lb}\cdot\text{in}^{-2}$. Hence

$$A \geq \frac{2 \times 10^6 \text{ lb}}{29 \times 10^6 \text{lb}\cdot\text{in}^{-2} \times 0.025}$$

The cross sectional area of the wire (A) is πR^2, where R is the radius of the wire. Since $R = \frac{D}{2}$ where D is the diameter of the wire, then $A = \pi\frac{D^2}{4}$ and $\frac{\pi D^2}{4} \geq \frac{80}{29}\text{in}^2$.

$$\therefore \; D \geq \sqrt{320/29\pi} \text{ in.} = 1.87 \text{ in.},$$

Hence, 1.87 in. is the smallest possible diameter for the tow wire.

• PROBLEM 354

A cubic foot of sea water at the surface weighs 64.0 lb. What volume of water weighs 100 lb at the sea bed, where the water pressure is 4000 $\text{lb}\cdot\text{ft}^{-2}$? The compressibility of sea water is $36 \times 10^{-7} \text{ in}^2\cdot\text{lb}^{-1}$.

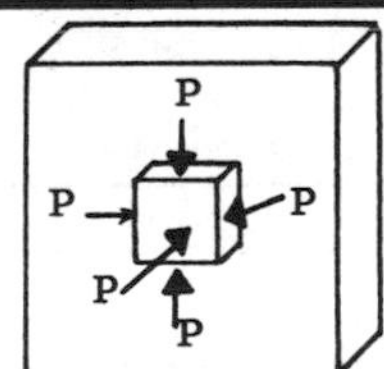

Solution: Using the definition of weight density D

$$D = \frac{\text{Weight}}{\text{Volume}}$$

then $$V = \frac{W}{D} = \frac{100 \text{ lb}}{64 \text{ lb/ft}^3} = 1.5625 \text{ ft}^3$$

where V is the volume 100 lb of water occupies at the surface. Where the water pressure P is 4000 $\text{lb}\cdot\text{ft}^{-2}$ $= 4000 \text{ lb}\cdot\text{ft}^{-2} \times 1 \text{ ft}^2/144 \text{ in}^2 = 4000/144 \text{ lb}\cdot\text{in}^{-2}$, the volume will have decreased by ΔV due to this additional pressure. The compressibility k of sea water is defined by

$$\frac{1}{k} = \frac{\text{Stress}}{\text{Strain}} = \frac{P}{\Delta V/V}$$

We are given that $k = 36 \times 10^{-7}\ \text{in}^2\cdot\text{lb}^{-1}$

$$\therefore \quad \frac{\Delta V}{V} = kp = \frac{4000}{144}\ \text{lb}\cdot\text{in}^{-2} \times 36 \times 10^{-7}\ \text{in}^2\cdot\text{lb}^{-1}$$

$$= 10^{-4}.$$

$$\therefore \quad 1 - \frac{\Delta V}{V} = \frac{V - \Delta V}{V} = 1 - 10^{-4} \qquad \text{or}$$

$$V - \Delta V = \frac{100}{64}(1 - 10^{-4})\,\text{ft}^3 = 1.5623\ \text{ft}^3$$

Thus the volume occupied at the lower level is $1.5623\ \text{ft}^3$.

• PROBLEM 355

> Find the weight density of water at a pressure of 4000 lb/in.^{2}, taking the weight density at normal atmospheric pressure as 62.4 lb/ft^3. (The bulk modulus of water is 2.97×10^5 lb/ft^2).

Solution: The change ΔV in the volume of water as a result of a change ΔP in the pressure acting on it is given by

$$-\frac{\Delta V}{V} = \frac{\Delta P}{B}$$

where B is the bulk modulus of water. It is defined as

$$\text{stress/strain} = \frac{\Delta P}{\Delta V/V} .$$

Initially, the pressure is that of air and it is increased to 4000 lb/in.^{2} Therefore,

$$\Delta P = 4000\ \text{lb/in}^2 - P_{air} = (4000\text{-}15)\ \text{lb/in.}^2$$

and

$$-\frac{\Delta V}{V} = \frac{(4000-15)\ \text{lb/in}^2}{(144\ \text{in}^2/\text{ft}^2)\times(2.97 \times 10^5\ \text{lb/ft}^2)} = 9.35 \times 10^{-5}$$

where we have converted the bulk modulus to lb/in^2. The weight density of water is mg/V, hence the fractional change in the density of water is

$$\Delta D = \frac{Mg}{V+\Delta V} - \frac{Mg}{V} = -\frac{Mg}{V}\left(1 - \frac{1}{1+\frac{\Delta V}{V}}\right)$$

where the weight Mg is unchanged. We find that

$$\Delta D = -D\left(\frac{\Delta V/V}{1 + \frac{\Delta V}{V}}\right)$$

and, since $\Delta V/V$ is much less than 1, we get

$$\frac{\Delta D}{D} \simeq -\frac{\Delta V}{V} = 9.35 \times 10^{-5}$$

The final density of water is

$$D_f = D + \Delta D = \left[62.4 + 9.35 \times 10^{-5} \times 62.4\right]\ \text{lb/ft}^3$$

$$= 62.406 \text{ lb/ft}^3 .$$

Since the compressibility of water is very small, there is not an appreciable increase in density.

• PROBLEM 356

The volume of oil contained in a certain hydraulic press is 5 ft^3. Find the decrease in volume of the oil when subjected to a pressure of 2000 lb/in^2. The compressibility of the oil is 20×10^{-6} per atm.

Solution: The volume decreases by 20 parts per million for a pressure increase of one atm. Since 2000 lb/in^2 = 136 atm., the volume decrease is 136 × 20 = 2720 parts per million. Since the original volume is 5 ft^3, the actual decrease is

$$\frac{2720}{1{,}000{,}000} \times 5 \text{ ft}^3 = 0.0136 \text{ ft}^3 = 23.5 \text{ in}^3.$$

Or, the change in volume of the oil is proportional to the original volume and the pressure exerted on the oil.

$$\Delta V = - k V_0 p$$

The constant of proportionality, k, equals the compressibility of the oil. Therefore, the change in volume can be found using the above equation.

$$\Delta V = - kV_0 p = - 20 \times 10^{-6} \text{ atm}^{-1} \times 5 \text{ ft}^3 \times 136 \text{ atm}$$

$$= - 0.0136 \text{ ft}^3.$$

• PROBLEM 357

A solid has a volume of 2.5 liters when the external pressure is 1 atm. The bulk modulus of the material is 2×10^{12} $dynes/cm^2$. What is the change in volume when the body is subjected to a pressure of 16 atm? What additional energy per unit volume is now stored in the material?

Solution. The bulk modulus is defined as the ratio of the net excess pressure Δp acting on a body and the volume strain $\frac{\Delta V}{V_0}$ resulting from this stress, where V_0 is the original volume. Hence,

$$B = - \frac{\Delta p}{\frac{\Delta V}{V_0}}$$

B is > 0 since, if $\Delta p > 0$, $\Delta V < 0$ and the solid is compressed $\Delta p = (16 - 1) = 15 \text{ atm} = 15 \times 1.013 \times 10^6 \text{ dynes cm}^{-2}$. Hence the decrease in the volume of the solid is

$$-\Delta V = \frac{\Delta p V_0}{B} = \frac{15 \times 1.013 \times 10^6 \text{ dynes/cm}^2 \times 2.5 \times 10^3 \text{ cm}^3}{2 \times 10^{12} \text{ dynes/cm}^2}$$

$= 18.99 \times 10^{-3}\ \text{cm}^3.$

For any small change of pressure dp, there will be a change of volume dV, and dp = -BdV/V. The work done on the system in that change and the energy stored in the material is dW = -p dV = (V/B)p dp.

In the change mentioned in the question the total work done is

$$W = -\int_{V_1}^{V_2} p\, dV = \int_{p_1}^{p_2} \frac{V}{B}\, p\, dp.$$

The minus sign results because the pressure on the gas opposes the volume change dV.

The volume V changes in the process, and account should be taken of this in the integration. In fact the change ΔV is negligible in comparison with V_0, and V may be treated as a constant throughout. Hence

$$W \simeq \frac{V_0}{B}\int_{p_1}^{p_2} p\, dp = \frac{1}{2}\,\frac{V_0}{B}\left(p_2^2 - p_1^2\right)$$

The extra energy stored per unit volume is thus

$$\frac{W}{V_0} = \frac{1}{2B}\left(p_2^2 - p_1^2\right) = \frac{1}{2} \times \frac{1}{2 \times 10^{12}\ \text{dynes/cm}^2}\left(16^2 - 1^2\right)\text{atm}^2$$

$$\times\ 1.013^2 \times 10^{12}\ \text{dynes}^2/\text{cm}^4 - \text{atm}^2$$

$$= 65.4\ \text{ergs/cm}^3.$$

CHAPTER 9

HARMONIC MOTION

• PROBLEM 358

An automobile moves with a constant speed of 50 mi/hr around a track of 1 mi diameter. What is the angular velocity and the period of the motion?

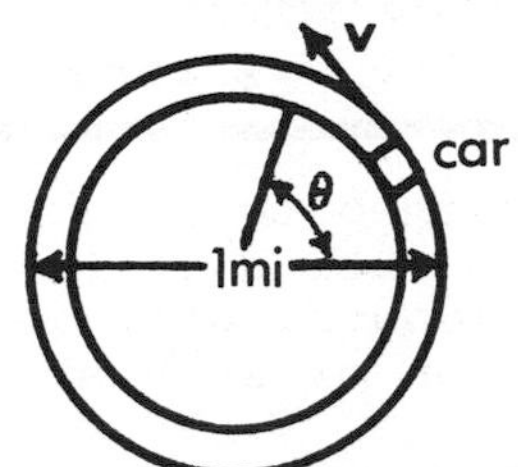

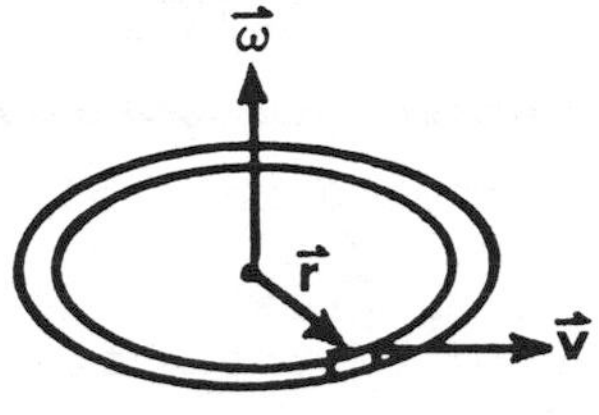

Solution: For circular motion, the angular velocity ω, the radius r, and the linear velocity v obey the relation: $\vec{v} = \vec{\omega} \times \vec{r}$ as shown in the figure. Since ω and r are perpendicular to each other, this reduces to v = ωr.

$$\omega = \frac{v}{r} = \frac{50 \text{ mi/hr}}{0.5 \text{ mi}} = 100 \text{ rad/hr}$$

The period τ is the time duration of one complete cycle of motion around the circular path. In linear motion, x = vt. This equation can be applied to circular motion with linear velocity v replaced by ω and linear distance x replaced by θ expressed in radians. In one cycle of motion, the automobile travels 2π **radians.** Therefore $\omega t = \theta \quad t = \theta/\omega \quad \tau = 2\pi/\omega$

$$\tau = \frac{2\pi}{\omega} = \frac{2\pi}{100 \text{ rad/hr}} = 0.063 \text{ hr} = 3.8 \text{ min.}$$

• PROBLEM 359

A uniform circular disk of radius 25 cm is pivoted at a point 20 cm from its center and allowed to oscillate in a vertical plane under the action of gravity. What is the period of its small oscillations? Take g as π^2 m·s^{-2}.

Solution: The moment of inertia of a uniform circular disk of radius R and mass M about an axis through its center perpendicular to its plane is $\frac{1}{2} MR^2$. By the parallel-axes theorem, the moment of inertia about a parallel axis a distance h from the first is

$$I = \frac{1}{2} MR^2 + Mh^2.$$

The disk is acting as a physical pendulum, and

hence its period for small oscillations is given by

$$T = 2\pi \sqrt{\frac{I}{Mgh}}$$

where I is the moment of inertia of the physical pendulum about its axis of suspension. Hence,

$$T = 2\pi \sqrt{\frac{\frac{1}{2}MR^2 + Mh^2}{Mgh}}$$

$$= 2\pi \sqrt{\frac{\frac{1}{2} \times 0.25^2 \text{ m}^2 + 0.2^2 \text{ m}^2}{\pi^2 \text{ m·s}^{-2} \times 0.2 \text{ m}}}$$

$$= 2 \sqrt{0.35625 \text{ s}} = 1.193 \text{ s}.$$

• PROBLEM 360

Suppose that a mass of 8 grams is attached to a spring that requires a force of 1000 dynes to extend it to a length 5 cm greater than its natural length. What is the period of the simple harmonic motion of such a system?

Solution: An interesting property of springs is that the length that they stretch is directly proportional to the applied force. The magnitude of this force is:

$$F = kx$$

where k is the force constant. The force constant is

$$k = \frac{F}{x} = \frac{1000 \text{ dynes}}{5 \text{ cm}}$$

$$= 200 \text{ dynes/cm}$$

Therefore, the period is by definition:

$$\tau = 2\pi \sqrt{\frac{m}{k}}$$

$$= 2\pi \sqrt{\frac{8 \text{ g}}{200 \text{ dynes/cm}}}$$

$$= 2\pi \sqrt{\frac{8 \text{ g}}{200 \text{ g-cm/cm-sec}^2}}$$

$$= 2\pi \times \sqrt{\frac{4}{100} \text{ sec}^2}$$

$$= 2\pi \times 0.2 \text{ sec}$$

$$= 1.26 \text{ sec}$$

and the frequency is by definition:

$$v = \frac{1}{\tau} = \frac{1}{1.26 \text{ sec}}$$

$$= 0.8 \text{ Hz}.$$

• PROBLEM 361

A 5.0-lb ball is fastened to the end of a flat spring. A force of 2.0 lb is sufficient to pull the ball 6.0 in. to one side. Find the force constant and the period of vibration.

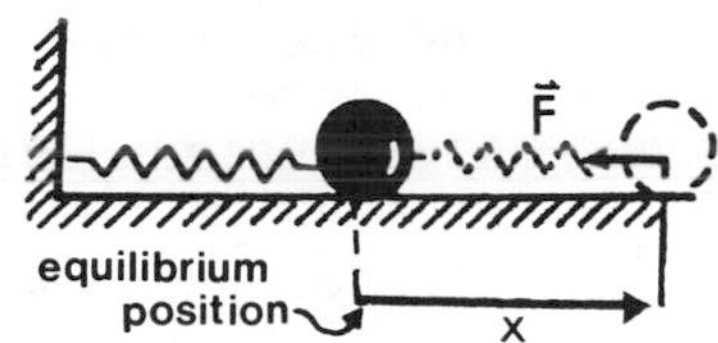

Solution: The restoring force on the ball as it is displaced from the equilibrium point 0 (see the figure) is, by Hooke's law,

$$\vec{F} = -k\vec{x}$$

where x is the displacement and k is the spring constant. Hence,

$$k = \frac{|\vec{F}|}{|\vec{x}|} = \frac{2.0 \text{ lb}}{0.50 \text{ ft}} = 4.0 \text{ lb/ft}$$

The mass of the ball is

$$m = \frac{W}{g} \text{ where W is the ball's weight. Hence,}$$

$$m = \frac{5.0 \text{ lb}}{32 \text{ ft/sec}^2} = 0.16 \text{ slug}$$

The period of oscillation is given by

$$T = 2\pi\sqrt{\frac{m}{k}} = 2\pi\sqrt{\frac{0.16 \text{ slug}}{4.0 \text{ lb/ft}}} = 1.2 \text{ sec.}$$

• PROBLEM 362

Let the mass of the body in the diagram be 25 gm, the force constant k be 400 dynes/ cm, and let the motion be started at t = 0 by displacing the body 10 cm to the right of its equilibrium position and imparting to it a velocity toward the right of 40 cm/sec. Compute (a) the period T, (b) the frequency f, (c) the angular frequency ω, (d) the total energy E, (e) the amplitude A, (f) the phase angle θ_0, (g) the maximum velocity v_{max}, (h) the maximum acceleration a_{max}, (j) the coordinate, velocity, and acceleration at a time $\pi/8$ sec after the start of the motion.

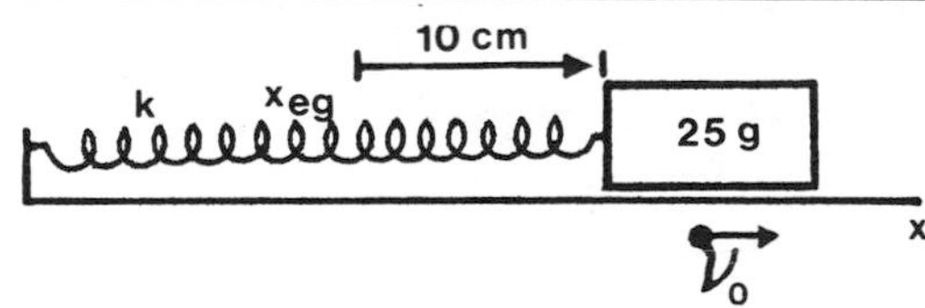

Solution: Note that the period is independent of amplitude or by implication, the initial velocity.

$$\text{(a)} \quad T = 2\pi\sqrt{\frac{m}{k}} = 2\pi\sqrt{\frac{25 \text{ gm}}{400 \text{ dynes/cm}}}$$
$$= \frac{\pi}{2} \text{ sec} = 1.57 \text{ sec.}$$

(b) $f = \frac{1}{T} = \frac{2}{\pi}\frac{\text{vib}}{\text{sec}} = 0.638 \frac{\text{vib}}{\text{sec}}$.

(c) $\omega = 2\pi f = 4$ rad/sec

(d) The total energy, (that is, the sum of potential and kinetic energies), stays constant as a spring oscillates . To find the spring's energy, we will compute its energy at time $t = 0$. The object has both kinetic and potential energy. Its kinetic energy is $\frac{1}{2} mv_0^2$, with m, the mass of the body, and v_0, its initial velocity. Its potential energy is $\frac{1}{2} kx_0^2$, where x_0 is the object's distance from equilibrium, and k is the spring constant. Then

$$E_{total} = \frac{1}{2} mv_0^2 + \frac{1}{2} kx_0^2$$

$$= \frac{1}{2} (25 \text{ gm})(40 \text{ cm/sec})^2 + \frac{1}{2}(400 \text{ dynes/cm})(10 \text{ cm})^2$$

$$= 20{,}000 \text{ ergs} + 20{,}000 \text{ ergs} = 40{,}000 \text{ ergs}$$

(e) The amplitude of oscillation is the distance between the equilibrium position x_{eq} and the point of maximum extension. To find the maximum extension we find the position at which the system's mechanical energy of 40,000 ergs is completely potential. This occurs when the kinetic energy is zero. Then

$$\frac{1}{2} kA^2 = 40{,}000 \text{ ergs}$$

$$\frac{1}{2} (400 \text{ dynes/cm})A^2 = 40{,}000 \text{ ergs}$$

$$A^2 = 200 \text{ cm}^2; \qquad A = 10\sqrt{2} \text{ cm}$$

(f) If x_0 is the displacement and A the amplitude, the initial angular displacement or phase angle θ_0 is defined by:

$$\sin \theta_0 = x_0/A = 1/\sqrt{2}, \qquad \theta_0 = \pi/4 \text{ rad.}$$

(g) To obtain v_{max} we find the point at which the energy is all kinetic. This occurs at the equilibrium point, $x = 0$. Then

$$E = KE + PE = KE + 0 = \frac{1}{2} mv_{max}^2$$

$$\frac{1}{2} mv_{max}^2 = 40{,}000 \text{ ergs}$$

$$\frac{1}{2} (25 \text{ gm})\left(v_{max}^2\right) = 40{,}000 \text{ ergs}$$

$$v_{max}^2 = 3{,}200 \text{ cm}^2/\text{sec}^2$$

$$v_{max} = 40\sqrt{2} \text{ cm/sec}$$

(h) The maximum acceleration occurs at the ends of the path where the force is a maximum. This force is given by Hooke's Law, $F = - kx$, where k is the spring constant and x is the displacement of the spring from equilibrium. At maximum extension, the displacement from equilibrium is just the amplitude. Hence,

$$F_{max} = -kx_{max} = -kA = -(400\ \text{dynes/cm})(10\sqrt{2}\ \text{cm})$$

$$= -4000\sqrt{2}\ \text{dynes}$$

Forces produce accelerations according to the law F = ma. Therefore

$$F_{max} = -4000\sqrt{2}\ \text{dynes} = ma_{max} = (25\ \text{gm})(a)$$

$$a_{max} = -160\sqrt{2}\ \text{cm/sec}^2$$

At maximum extension, the acceleration is greatest and in the direction of the equilibrium point of the spring and hence in a direction which we define as negative. The motion of an oscillating spring is highly symmetric and at the point of maximum compression, the acceleration will again reach this maximum but will this time be in the positive direction.

(j) The equation for the object's position is

$$x = A\sin(\omega t + \theta_0)$$

where A is the amplitude, ω is the angular velocity, t is the time variable, and θ_0 is the initial angular displacement. The velocity, v, and acceleration, a, are found from

$$v = \frac{dx}{dt}\ ; \qquad a = \frac{dv}{dt} = \frac{d^2x}{dt^2}$$

We then have

$$x = 10\sqrt{2}\sin\left(4t + \frac{\pi}{4}\right),$$

$$v = 40\sqrt{2}\cos\left(4t + \frac{\pi}{4}\right),$$

$$a = -160\sqrt{2}\sin\left(4t + \frac{\pi}{4}\right).$$

When t = (π/8) sec, the phase angle is

$$\left(4t + \frac{\pi}{4}\right) = \frac{3\pi}{4}\ \text{rad},$$

$$x = 10\sqrt{2}\sin(3\pi/4) = 10\ \text{cm},$$

$$v = 40\sqrt{2}\cos(3\pi/4) = -40\ \text{cm/sec},$$

$$a = -160\sqrt{2}\sin(3\pi/4) = -160\ \text{cm/sec}^2.$$

• PROBLEM 363

A simple pendulum consists of a mass m hung on the end of a string of length L. Find the natural frequency for small oscillations.

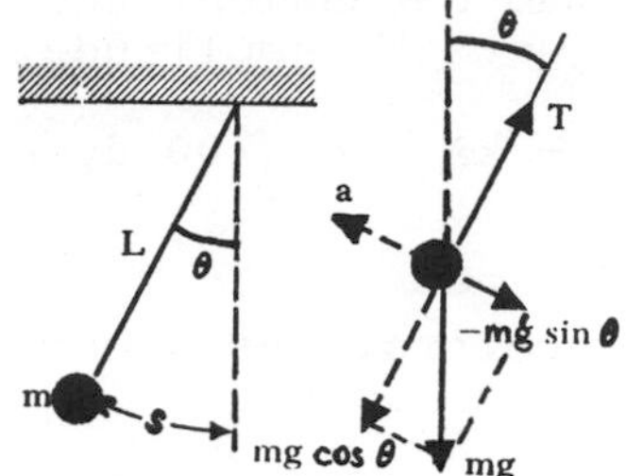

Solution: We start by drawing a diagram of the forces acting on the mass m. The restoring force in the direction of motion is $-mg \sin \theta$. Thus the equation of motion is

$$ma = -mg \sin \theta .$$

Now we can suppose that θ is small so that we can make the approximation $\sin \theta \cong \theta$. This is accurate to better than 1 per cent for $\theta = 15^\circ$ and is better than 5 per cent for $\theta = 30^\circ$.

The displacement of the mass is given by the arc s.

$$s = L\theta$$

Thus

$$v = \Delta s/\Delta t = L\Delta\theta/\Delta t = L\omega$$

where $\omega = \frac{\Delta\theta}{\Delta t}$ = angular velocity. And the acceleration a is given by

$$a = \Delta v/\Delta t = L\Delta\omega/\Delta t = L\alpha$$

where $\alpha = \frac{\Delta\omega}{\Delta t}$ = angular acceleration. Then finally the equation of motion reduces to

$$mL\alpha = -mg\theta$$

or

$$\alpha + (g/L)\theta = 0$$

The angular acceleration α is proportional to the negative of the angular displacement θ, so that the motion is simple harmonic with natural angular frequency ω_0 given by

$$\alpha + \omega_0^2\theta = 0$$

where $\omega_0^2 = g/L$

• PROBLEM 364

A simple pendulum has a period of 2.40 sec at a place where $g = 9.810\ m/sec^2$. What is the value of g at another place on the earth's surface where this pendulum has a period of 2.41 sec? (See figure).

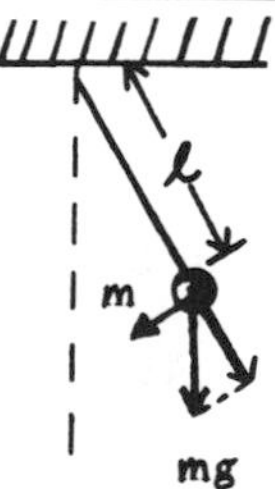

Solution: The period of oscillation is given by

$$T = 2\pi \sqrt{\frac{\ell}{g}} .$$

Therefore, two different periods, T_1 and T_2, will correspond to two different gravitational constants, g_1 and g_2, as follows.

$$\frac{T_1}{T_2} = \frac{2\pi\sqrt{\frac{\ell}{g_1}}}{2\pi\sqrt{\frac{\ell}{g_2}}} = \sqrt{\frac{g_2}{g_1}}$$

or

$$\frac{2.40}{2.41} = \sqrt{\frac{g_2}{9.810\text{m/sec}^2}}$$

$$g_2 = 9.729 \text{ m/sec}^2$$

• PROBLEM 365

Calculate the frequency of oscillation of the configuration shown in the figure. All surfaces are frictionless.

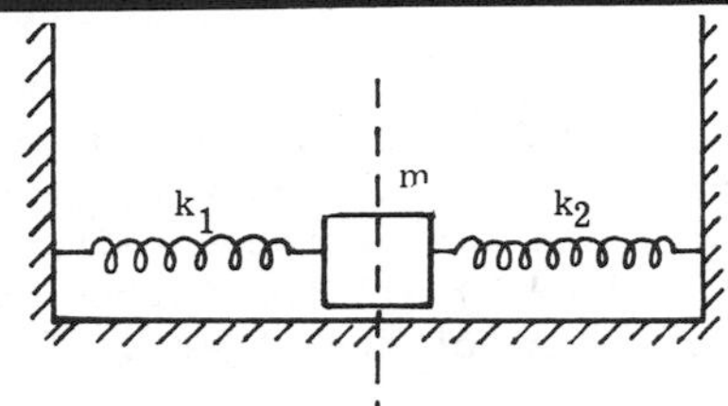

Solution: When the mass m moves, one spring is always stretched, and the other is always compressed by the same length. Thus:

$$\Delta x_1 = -\Delta x_2$$

where Δx_1 is the distance that the spring with force constant k_1 stretches, and Δx_2 that of the other spring. Note that a negative stretching distance represents a distance compressed. We denote the distance of the mass to the right of the origin 0 by Δx. Thus:

$$\Delta x_1 = \Delta x$$

$$\Delta x_2 = -\Delta x$$

taking positive displacement as pointing to the right. The force on the mass at any time is therefore:

$$F = -k_1\ \Delta x_1 - (-k_2\ \Delta x_2) = -k_1\ \Delta x + k_2(-\Delta x)$$

$$= -(k_1 + k_2)\ \Delta x$$

$$= -k'\ \Delta x$$

where we let $k' = k_1 + k_2$

Since the frequency of an oscillator having force constant k' is:

$$\nu = \frac{1}{2\pi}\sqrt{\frac{k'}{m}}$$

then: $$\nu = \frac{1}{2\pi}\sqrt{\frac{k_1 + k_2}{m}}$$

• PROBLEM 366

Let the force constant k of the spring in the figure be 24 newtons/meter, and let the mass of the body be 4 kgm. The body is initially at rest, and the spring is initially unstretched. Suppose that a constant force $\vec{P}$ of 10 newtons is exerted on the body, and that there is no friction. What will be the speed of the body when it has moved 0.50 meters?

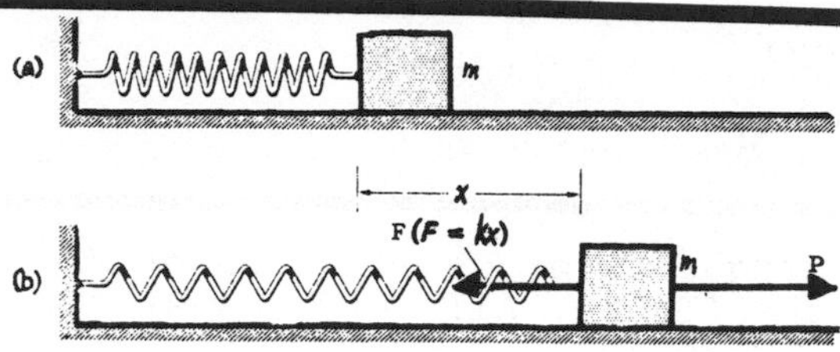

Solution: The equations of motion with constant acceleration cannot be used, since the resultant force on the body varies as the spring is stretched. However, the speed can be found using the work-energy theorem. This states that the work done by all the forces acting on a body is equal to the change in kinetic energy of the object. Then, if V_F is the final speed of the block,

$$\text{Work} = \int \vec{P} \cdot \vec{dx} + \int \vec{F} \cdot \vec{dx} = \tfrac{1}{2}\, m\left(V_F^2 - 0^2\right) = \Delta E_k$$

since the initial kinetic energy of the body is zero. P is constant, the angle between $\vec{P}$ and $\vec{dx}$ is 0° and the angle between $\vec{F}$ and $\vec{dx}$ is 180°. Also the magnitude of the restoring force is F = kx, by Hookes law. Then

$$P \int dx - \int kx\, dx = \tfrac{1}{2}\, mV_F^2$$

$$Px - \tfrac{1}{2}\, kx^2 = \tfrac{1}{2}\, mV_F^2$$

$$10n \times 0.5\text{ m} - \tfrac{1}{2} \times 24\,\frac{n}{m} \times 0.25\text{ m}^2 = \tfrac{1}{2} \times 4\text{kg} \times V_F^2$$

or

$$V_F = 1\,\frac{m}{sec}$$

• PROBLEM 367

Geologists on a plane are attempting to locate the exact position of the iron reserves in a region by measuring the variation of g in the area, since a large mass of iron will exert an appreciable additional gravitational attraction on a body in the vicinity. They hover above selected spots and observe the movement of a mass suspended from a light spring. If the system has a natural period of 2 s, and the smallest movement of the mass which can be detected is 10^{-6} m, what is the minimum change in g which they can observe?

Solution: At a point at which the acceleration due to gravity is g, the mass, when in equilibrium, has two forces acting on it: the weight mg down and the restoring force F = kx (i.e. Hooke's law) up, and these must be equal. Thus g = (k/m)x.

At another point, where local conditions vary, the stretching of the spring will be x + dx if the value of the acceleration due to gravity is g + dg (where dx and dg are very small changes in x and in g, respectively).

$$\therefore \quad g + dg = \frac{k}{m}(x + dx) \quad \text{or} \quad dg = \frac{k}{m}\,dx.$$

But, if the mass-spring system is allowed to oscillate, its period is given by

$$T = \frac{1}{f} = \frac{2\pi}{2\pi f} = \frac{2\pi}{\omega} = 2\pi\sqrt{\frac{m}{k}}$$

$$\therefore \quad \frac{k}{m} = \frac{4\pi^2}{T^2} \quad \text{and} \quad dg = \frac{4\pi^2}{T^2}dx.$$

If the smallest value of dx observable is 10^{-6} m, and we are given that T = 2 sec, the smallest value dg detectable is thus

$$dg = \frac{4\pi^2}{4\ s^2} \times 10^{-6}\ m = 9.87 \times 10^{-6}\ m\cdot s^{-2}.$$

• PROBLEM 368

A pendulum which has a period of 1 s in London, where $g = 32.200\ ft\cdot s^{-2}$, is taken to Paris, where it is found to lose 20 s per day. What is the value of g in Paris?

Solution: Since the period of the pendulum is 1 s in London, the number of oscillations it performs per day is

$$\frac{60\ sec}{1\ min} \times \frac{60\ min}{1\ hr} \times \frac{24\ hr}{1\ day} = 86{,}400\ \text{oscillations/day}$$

In Paris it looses 20 s per day, i.e., it makes only 86,380 complete oscillations per day.

In all pendulum formulas the period is $T = k/\sqrt{g}$, where k is a constant depending on the shape and possibly the mass of the pendulum. Thus, in London, $T = k/\sqrt{g}$, and in Paris, $T' = k/\sqrt{g'}$. Since $T = 1/f$, where f is the number of oscillations in a given time interval,

$$\frac{T}{T'} = \frac{1/f}{1/f'} = \frac{f'}{f} = \frac{86{,}380\ \text{oscillations/day}}{86{,}400\ \text{oscillations/day}} = \sqrt{\frac{g'}{g}}$$

$$\text{or} \qquad g' = \left(\frac{8638}{8640}\right)^2 g = \left(\frac{8640-2}{8640}\right)^2 g = \left(1 - \frac{2}{8640}\right)^2 g$$

$$\cong \left(1 - \frac{4}{8640}\right) g$$

since $(2/8640) << 1$.

Hence, $g' \approx (1 - 4/8640) \times 32.200\ ft\cdot s^{-2}$

$$= 32.185\ ft\cdot s^{-2}.$$

Neglecting rotational effects, Paris is slightly farther away from the center of the earth than London.

• PROBLEM 369

What is the acceleration of gravity at a place where the period of a simple pendulum 100 cm long is exactly 2 sec?

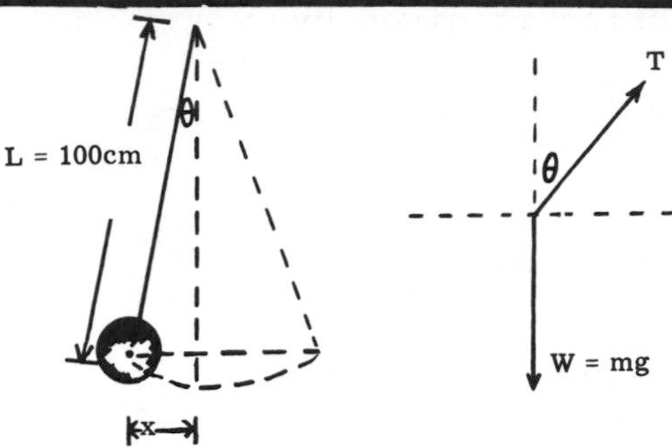

Solution: We assume that the pendulum bob are the tension of the string and the weight of the bob (it's mass is m). We assume that the dis- placement of the bob from the equilibrium position x = 0 (see figure) is small enough that the bob undergoes only a horizontal motion (i.e., the arc of motion of the bob is approximated by a straight line). The y direction of motion is then zero. Therefore there is no net force acting in the y direction. Hence

$$T\cos\theta = mg \quad \text{or} \quad T = \frac{mg}{\cos\theta} \qquad (1)$$

The net restoring force acting in the x direction is

$$F = T\sin\theta$$
$$= mg\frac{\sin\theta}{\cos\theta}$$
$$= mg\tan\theta$$

Here we made use of equation (1). Since the displacement of the bob is very small, then the following approximations can be made.

$$\sin\theta \approx \theta \quad \text{and} \quad \cos\theta \approx 1$$
$$F \cong mg\,\theta$$

The restoring force is then directly proportional to the angular dis- placement θ. Since the horizontal displacement x is approximately equal to the arc length of a circle of radius 1, then

$$x \cong 1\theta$$

where θ is in radians.
Therefore

$$F \cong \frac{mg}{\ell}x$$

The restoring force on the particle is then directly proportional to the displacement from the equilibrium position. This is the definition of harmonic motion. By Newton's second law,

$$F = ma = m\frac{d^2x}{dt^2} = \frac{mg}{\ell}x$$

$$\frac{d^2x}{dt^2} = \frac{g}{\ell}x$$

The solution of this differential equation, is

$$x = A\sin\sqrt{\frac{g}{\ell}}\,t + B\cos\sqrt{\frac{g}{\ell}} = C\sin\left(\sqrt{\frac{g}{1}}\,t + \phi\right) \qquad (1)$$

This can be verified by substitution into the differential equation. The constants A and B (or alternatively c and ϕ) can be found from the initial conditions of the problem (i.e., where the bob was located and its velocity, at $t = 0$). Equation (1) is of the form

$$x = c \sin(\omega t + \phi)$$

Therefore

$$\omega = 2\pi f = \sqrt{\frac{g}{\ell}}$$

where f is the frequency of motion. However $f = \frac{1}{T}$ where T is the time taken by the bob to undergo one oscillation. Then

$$\frac{2\pi}{T} = \sqrt{\frac{g}{\ell}}$$

$$T = 2\pi\sqrt{\frac{\ell}{g}}$$

$$2^2 = \frac{(2\pi)^2 (100)}{g}$$

therefore

$$g = \frac{4 \cdot \pi^2 \cdot 100 \text{ cm}}{4 \, s^2} = 1000 \text{ cm/sec}^2$$

• PROBLEM 370

One end of a fingernail file is clamped in a vise and the other end is given a to-and-fro vibration. The motion of the free end is approximately S.H.M. If the frequency is 10 vibrations per second and the amplitude is 4 millimeters, what is the velocity when the displacement of the free end is 2 millimeters?

Solution: The problem states that the motion is S.H.M. Therefore, we know that the displacement of the file is

$$x = A \sin(\omega t + \alpha) \qquad (1)$$

where A is the amplitude and α is a constant. ω is the angular frequency of the vibration. If f is the frequency of the motion

$$\omega = 2\pi f.$$

The velocity of the end of the file is, differentiating (1),

$$v = A\omega \cos(\omega t + \alpha) \qquad (2)$$

We need the velocity when x = 2 mm. At this position, using (1)

$$2 \text{ mm} = 4 \text{ mm} \sin(\omega t + \alpha)$$

$$\sin(\omega t + \alpha) = \tfrac{1}{2}$$

whence $(\omega t + \alpha) = 30°$

Hence, using (2),

$$v = A\omega \cos(30°)$$

or $v = A(2\pi f)\cos(30°)$

$$v = (4 \text{ mm})(6.28)(10 \text{ per sec})(\sqrt{3}/2)$$

$$v = \left(\frac{40\ \text{mm}}{\text{sec}}\right)(6.28)(.866) = 218\ \text{mm/sec.}$$

• PROBLEM 371

What must be the length of a simple pendulum that will have a period of 1 sec at the surface of the Earth?

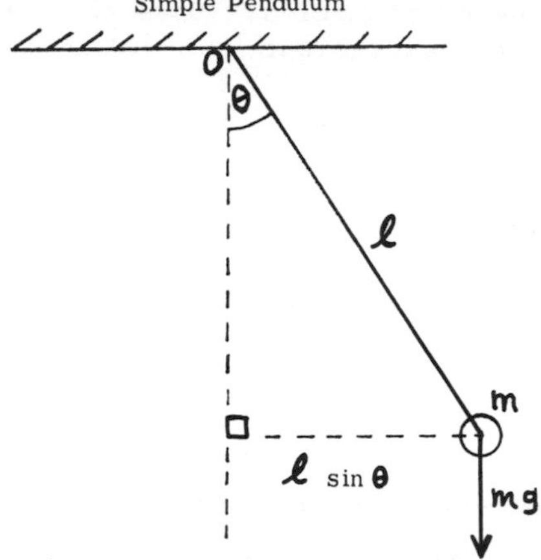

Solution: In the simple pendulum figure, the torque about point 0 is

$$\tau = -\ mg\ell \sin\theta,$$

where ℓ is the length of the string, and the negative sign is introduced to show that the torque acts to decrease θ.

For θ less than 30°, $\theta \cong \sin\theta$ is a good approximation, thus:

$$\tau = -\ mg\ell\ \theta$$

We note that this equation resembles the standard form for simple harmonic oscillators:

$$F = -\ kx$$

where $mg\ell$ is analogous to k, and θ to x.

We find the expression for the period T of a simple pendulum by analogy with the equation for that of the harmonic oscillator:

$$T = 2\pi\sqrt{\frac{m}{k}}$$

thus:

$$T = 2\pi\sqrt{\frac{I}{mg\ell}} = 2\pi\sqrt{\frac{m\ell^2}{mg\ell}} = 2\pi\sqrt{\frac{\ell}{g}}$$

where $I = m\ell^2$ is the moment of inertia of the mass m about point 0.

From the above equation:

$$\ell = \frac{T^2 g}{4\pi^2}$$

$$\ell = \frac{(1 \text{ sec})^2(9.8 \text{ m/sec}^2)}{4(3.14)^2} = 0.248 \text{ m}$$

• PROBLEM 372

What is the period of a small oscillation of an ideal pendulum of length ℓ, if it oscillates in a truck moving in a horizontal direction with acceleration a? (See figure a).

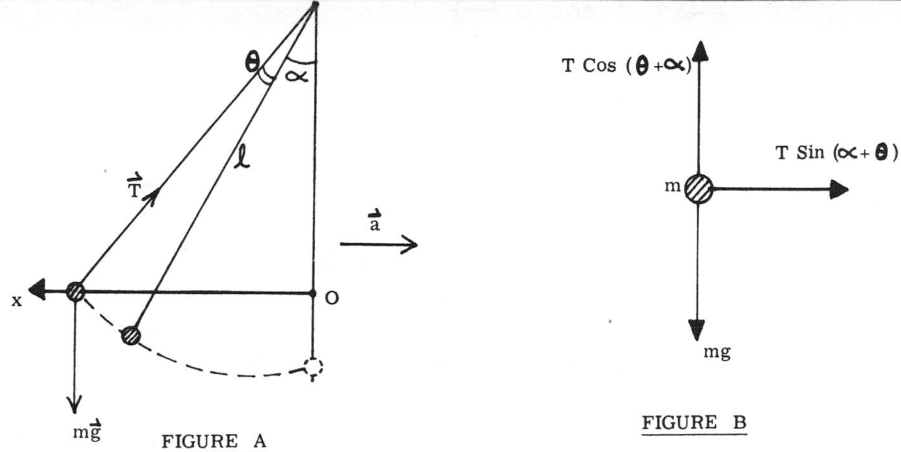

FIGURE A

FIGURE B

Solution. Let the equilibrium position be given by the angle α. In this position, the net force on m is along the horizontal axis and equals ma. The angle α is determined by the equations

$$T \sin \alpha = ma \tag{1}$$

$$T \cos \alpha = mg \tag{2}$$

where g is the gravitational acceleration. When the pendulum is displaced by a small amount θ, it will perform a simple harmonic motion around the equilibrium position. The force on m along the horizontal x-axis is $T \sin(\theta + \alpha)$, as shown in Fig. b. Newton's second law for the motion along this axis is

$$m\frac{d^2x}{dt^2} = -T \sin(\theta + \alpha) \tag{3}$$

where x is the distance from the vertical.

For small θ, we can expand $\sin(\theta + \alpha)$ as

$$\sin(\theta + \alpha) \simeq \sin \alpha + \theta \cos \alpha.$$

Substituting in (3)

$$m\frac{d^2x}{dt^2} \simeq -T \sin \alpha - \theta T \cos \alpha. \tag{4}$$

Combining (1), (2) and (4), we get

$$m\frac{d^2x}{dt^2} \simeq -ma - \theta mg$$

$$\frac{d^2x}{dt^2} \simeq -a - \theta g. \tag{5}$$

θ and ℓ are related geometrically as

$$x = \ell \sin(\theta + \alpha) = \ell \sin \alpha + \theta \ell \cos \alpha$$

therefore

$$\frac{d^2x}{dt^2} \simeq \ell \cos \alpha \frac{d^2\theta}{dt^2}$$

Substituting in (5),

$$\ell \cos \alpha \frac{d^2\theta}{dt^2} \simeq -\alpha - \theta g$$

$$\frac{d^2\theta}{dt^2} \simeq - \frac{g}{\ell \cos \alpha}\left[\theta + \frac{a}{g}\right] \tag{6}$$

If we make the following substitution in (6)

$$\phi = \theta + \frac{a}{g}$$

we get

$$\frac{d^2\phi}{dt^2} = - \frac{g}{\ell \cos \alpha}\phi .$$

This is the differential equation for a simple harmonic motion. Therefore its solution is

$$\phi = A \sin(\omega t + B)$$

where A and B are the constants of integration and

$$\omega = \sqrt{\frac{g}{\ell \cos \alpha}} .$$

The expression for θ is

$$\theta = A \sin(\omega t + B) - \frac{a}{g}.$$

The boundary conditions are $\theta = 0$ at $t = 0$ and $\theta = \theta_{max}$ at $t = \frac{\tau}{2}$ (where τ is the period).

Determine the constants A, B:

i) $t = 0$: $A \sin B = \frac{a}{g}$

ii) $t = \frac{\tau}{2}$: $A \sin\left(\frac{\omega\tau}{2} + B\right) - \frac{a}{g} = \theta_{max}$.

The period of the motion is

$$\tau = \frac{2\pi}{\omega} = 2\pi \sqrt{\frac{\ell \cos \alpha}{g}}.$$

A ball of mass 100 g is attached to the end of a string and is swung in a circle of radius 100 cm with a constant linear velocity of 200 cm/sec. While the ball is in motion, the string is shortened to 50 cm. What is the change in the velocity and in the period of the motion?

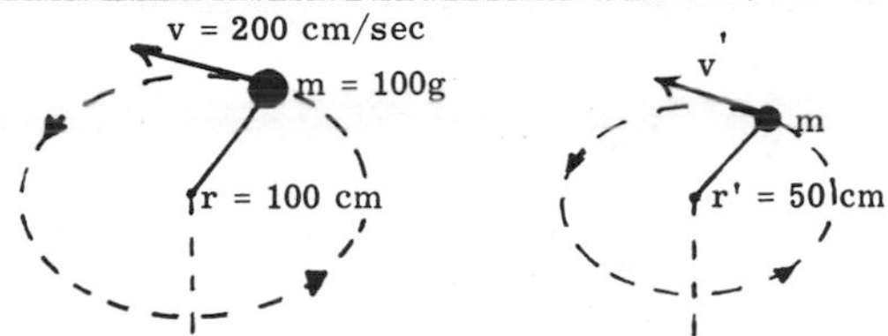

Solution: We define the initial state of the ball to be the circular path of 100 cm radius and the final state to be the path of 50 cm radius. The initial angular momentum of the object is

$$L = mvr$$

$$= (100\ g) \times (200\ cm/sec) \times (100\ cm)$$

$$= 2 \times 10^6\ g\text{-}cm^2/sec$$

The initial period is $T = \frac{1}{f}$ where f is the frequency of rotation of the ball in its initial motion. But

$$2\pi f = \omega$$

where ω is the initial angular velocity of the ball. Hence

$$T = \frac{1}{f} = \frac{2\pi}{\omega}$$

Also, $\omega = v/r$ where v is the velocity of the ball and r is its distance from the axis of rotation. Therefore

$$T = \frac{2\pi}{(v/r)} = \frac{2\pi r}{v}$$

$$= \frac{2\pi \times (100\ cm)}{200\ cm/sec}$$

$$= \pi\ sec$$

An alternate derivation is as follows. The velocity v of the object about the initial circular path is constant. Hence,

$$v = \frac{\text{distance}}{\text{time}}$$

In one period, however, the object moves a distance of one circumference length. Therefore

$$v = \frac{2\pi r}{T}$$

or

$$T = \frac{2\pi r}{v}$$

Shortening the string does not apply any torque to the ball because the applied force lies along the line connecting the ball with the center of rotation. Therefore, the torque is zero. However,

$$\tau = \frac{d\vec{L}}{dt}$$

Then

$$0 = \frac{d\vec{L}}{dt}$$

or $$\vec{L} = \text{constant} .$$

Hence the final angular momentum, L', is equal to the initial angular momentum L:

$$L' = mv'r' = L$$

Thus, the final velocity is

$$v' = \frac{L}{mr'}$$

$$= \frac{2 \times 10^6 \text{ g-cm}^2/\text{sec}}{(100 \text{ g}) \times (50 \text{ cm})}$$

$$= 400 \text{ cm/sec} .$$

The new period is

$$T' = \frac{2\pi r'}{v'}$$

$$= \frac{2\pi \times (50 \text{ cm})}{400 \text{ cm/sec}}$$

$$= \frac{\pi}{4} \text{ sec} .$$

Therefore, decreasing the radius by a factor of 2 has increased the linear velocity by the same factor but has decreased the period by a factor of 4.

• PROBLEM 374

The figure represents a small body of mass m revolving in a horizontal circle with velocity v of constant magnitude at the end of a cord of lenght L. As the body swings around its path, the cord sweeps over the surface of a cone. The cord makes an angle θ with the vertical, so the radius of the circle in which the body moves is $R = L \sin \theta$ and the magnitude of the velocity v, equals $v = 2\pi R/T = (2\pi L \sin \theta)/T$, where T is the period of revolution of the motion, the time for one complete revolution. Find T.

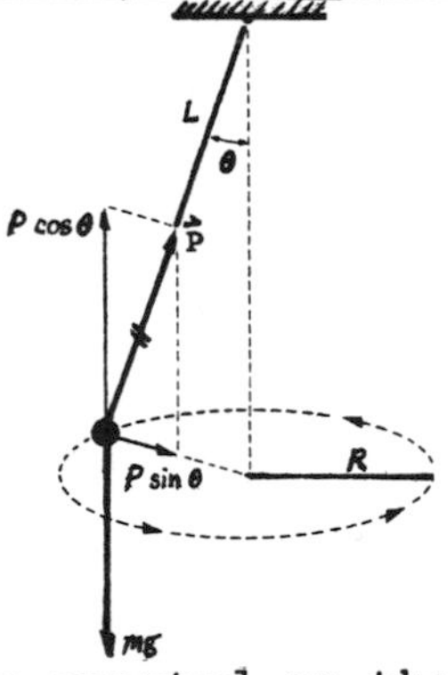

Solution: The forces exerted on the body when in the position shown are its weight mg and the tension P in the cord. Let P be resolved into a horizontal component P sin θ and a vertical component P cos θ. The body has no vertical acceleration, so the forces P cos θ and mg are equal, and the resultant inward, radial, or centripetal force is the component P sin θ. Then

$$P \sin \theta = m \frac{v^2}{R}, \quad P \cos \theta = mg.$$

When the first of these equations is divided by the second, we get

$$\tan \theta = \frac{v^2}{Rg}.$$

This equation indicates how the angle depends on the velocity v. As v increases, tan θ increases and θ increases. The angle never becomes 90°, however, since this requires that v = ∞.

Making use of the relations R = L sin θ and v = 2πL sin θ/T, we can also write

$$\tan \theta = \frac{\sin \theta}{\cos \theta} = \frac{v^2}{Rg} = \frac{4\pi^2 L^2 \sin^2 \theta}{T^2 \; L \sin \theta \; g}$$

$$\frac{\tan \theta}{\sin \theta} = \frac{1}{\cos} = \frac{4\pi^2 L}{gT^2}$$

$$\cos \theta = \frac{gT^2}{4\pi^2 L}$$

$$T = 2\pi\sqrt{L \cos \theta/g}.$$

This equation is similar in form to the expression for the time of swing of a simple pendulum for which $T = 2\pi\sqrt{L/g}$. Because of this similarity, the present device is called a conical pendulum.

• PROBLEM 375

Two springs are joined and connected to a mass m which rides on a frictionless surface (see figure (a)). What is the frequency ν of the oscillation that will result if the mass is displaced a small distance x?

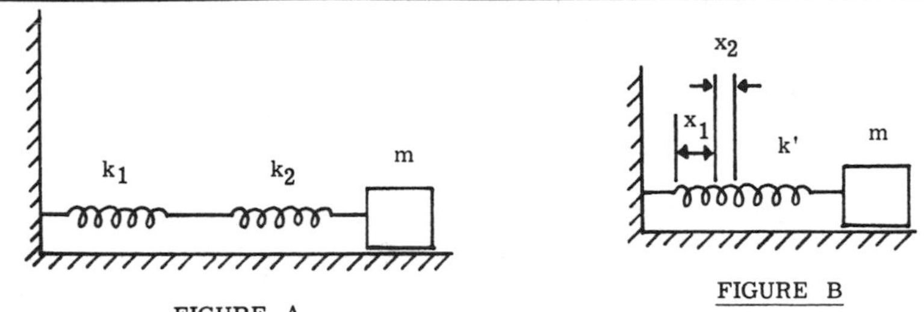

FIGURE A

FIGURE B

Solution: We must show that the configuration of figure (a), is equivalent to that of mass m, connected to a single spring having force constant k'. In figure (b), a mass m is shown connected to such a spring. A segment of the spring is divided into two sections of length x_1 and x_2. The tension in these two sections must be equal, as must be true of the tension in any other arbitrary sections into which the spring may be divided. If this were not the case, the spring would buckle. In general, when the spring is stretched or compressed by a force F, the changes in length Δx_1 and Δx_2 of sections x_1 and x_2 will not be equal since the magnitudes of such distortions will be proportional to the lengths of the segments involved. We can see this by symmetry. If a spring is stretched to twice its usual length, for example, each arbitrary section must stretch to twice its usual length. If we choose the sections to be of unequal length, the amount that each section stretches will be different. Thus:

$$F = -k_1 \Delta x_1 = -k_2 \Delta x_2$$

since we know that the force that the spring exerts on the mass equals the tension within each section. The force constants of sections x_1 and x_2 are represented by k_1 and k_2.

It is not unreasonable to assume that each arbitrary section of the spring can be considered to have a different force constant as long as:

$$F = -k_1 \Delta x_1 = -k_2 \Delta x_2 = -k_3 \Delta x_3 = \ldots -k_n \Delta x_n$$

$$= -k'x$$

where $x = \Delta x_1 + \Delta x_2 + \Delta x_3 + \ldots + \Delta x_n$

is the total displacement of the mass.

Thus we see that in the case of the two connected springs above, the tension in each must be equal:

$$F = -k_1 \Delta x_1 = -k_2 \Delta x_2 = -k'x$$

$$= -k'(\Delta x_1 + \Delta x_2)$$

$$\Delta x_1 = -\frac{F}{k_1}$$

$$\Delta x_2 = -\frac{F}{k_2}$$

Thus:

$$k' = -\frac{F}{\Delta x_1 + \Delta x_2} = \frac{-F}{-\frac{F}{k_1} - \frac{F}{k_2}} = \frac{1}{\frac{1}{k_1} + \frac{1}{k_2}}$$

$$= \frac{1}{\frac{k_1 + k_2}{k_1 k_2}} = \frac{k_1 k_2}{k_1 + k_2}$$

Since the frequency of an oscillator having force constant k' is:

$$\nu = \frac{1}{2\pi}\sqrt{\frac{k'}{m}}$$

then: $\nu = \frac{1}{2\pi}\sqrt{\frac{k_1 k_2}{(k_1 + k_2)m}}$

• PROBLEM 376

A metal disc is suspended from its center by a torsion bar, as shown in the figure. Find the period of oscillation for small angular displacements from equilibrium. Torsion bars have the property of exerting a torque which is proportional to the angular displacement and oppositely directed.

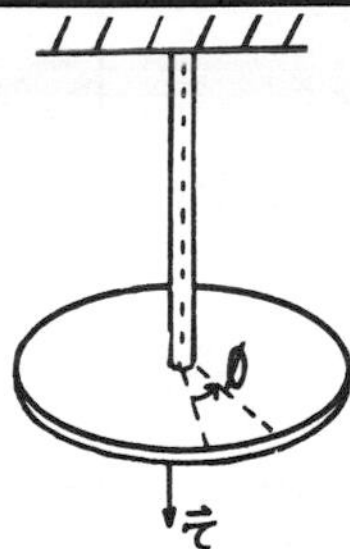

Solution: The angular displacement ϕ is opposed by a torque

$$\tau = -\kappa\phi$$

where κ is the torsion constant, and corresponds to the force constant of a tensile spring. The angular acceleration α and the moment inertia of the disc are related to τ by

$$\tau = I\alpha = I\frac{d^2\phi}{dt^2}$$

hence $I\dfrac{d^2\phi}{dt^2} = -\kappa\phi.$

The resulting differential equation for ϕ is

$$\frac{d^2\phi}{dt^2} + \Omega^2\phi = 0$$

where $\Omega = \sqrt{\dfrac{\kappa}{I}}$. This equation defines a simple harmonic motion, given by

$$\phi(t) = \phi_0 \sin \Omega t,$$

ϕ_0 is the maximum angular displacement and we assumed that $\phi = 0$ at $t = 0$. The period T is

$$T = \frac{2\pi}{\Omega} = 2\pi\sqrt{\frac{I}{\kappa}}\ .$$

• PROBLEM 377

A horizontal shelf moves vertically with simple harmonic motion, the period of which is 1 s and the amplitude of which is 30 cm. A light particle is laid on the shelf when it is at its lowest position. Determine the point at which the particle leaves the shelf and the height to which it rises from that position, g being taken as $\pi^2\ m\cdot s^{-2}$.

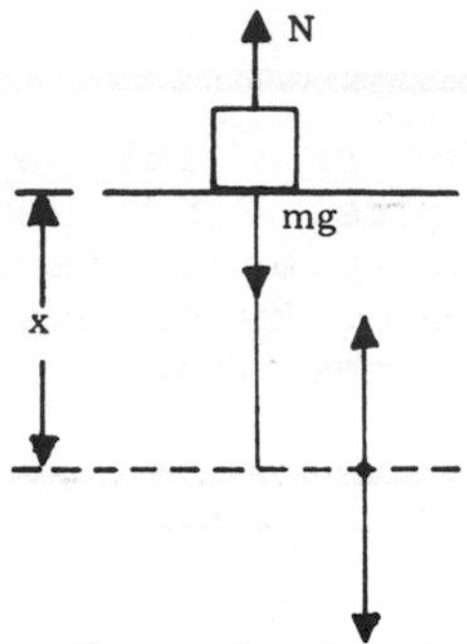

Solution: The period of a simple harmonic motion is given by the expression

$$T = \frac{1}{f} = \frac{2\pi}{2\pi f} = \frac{2\pi}{\omega}$$

Therefore, the angular frequency in this case is $\omega = 2\pi/T = 2\pi/1 \text{ s} = 2\pi \text{ rad}\cdot\text{s}^{-1}$.

The only forces acting on the particle are its weight $m\vec{g}$ downward and the normal force $\vec{N}$ exerted by the shelf upward. (See the figure.) At any time, according to Newton's second law, $N - mg = ma$, where a is the upward acceleration of shelf and particle. If $a = -g$, (i.e. the shelf accelerates downward with magnitude g) N becomes zero and, if a becomes more negative, the shelf is retarded at a greater rate than the particle; therefore the particle moves away from the shelf. Since the shelf undergoes simple harmonic motion, its displacement may be described by $x = A \cos(\omega t + \delta)$, where A is the amplitude of the oscillation, and δ is a phase factor dependent on the initial conditions (i.e. where the shelf is at $t = 0$). The acceleration $a = d^2x/dt^2 = -\omega^2 A \cos(\omega t + \delta)$ $= -\omega^2 x$. Hence, the displacement x at which the particle leaves the shelf is given by

$$-g = -\omega^2 x \qquad \text{or}$$

$$x = \frac{g}{\omega^2} = \frac{\pi^2 \text{ m}\cdot\text{s}^{-2}}{4\pi^2 \text{ rad}^2\cdot\text{s}^{-2}} = \frac{1}{4} \text{ m}.$$

$\left(\text{for } g = \pi^2 \text{ m}\cdot\text{s}^{-2} \text{ and } \omega = 2\pi \text{ rad}\cdot\text{sec}^{-1}\right)$.

The particle thus leaves the shelf when it is ¼ m above the mean position. At that point the common velocity of shelf and particle is given by the formula relating to velocity to displacement for simple harmonic motion:

$$v = \pm\, \omega\sqrt{A^2 - x^2}$$

Since the shelf is rising, v is positive and

$$v = 2\pi \text{ rad}\cdot\text{s}^{-1} \times \sqrt{(0.3 \text{ m})^2 - (0.25 \text{ m})^2}$$

$$= 2\pi \sqrt{0.0275} \text{ m}\cdot\text{s}^{-1}.$$

We now have a new problem concerning a particle thrown upward from a platform with an initial speed

v. If the platform level is taken as the reference level for measuring potential energy, then the law of conservation of energy requires that at each moment of time that the particle is in motion, the sum of its kinetic and potential energies must remain constant. At the time the particle leaves the platform, its potential energy is zero and

$$E_T = PE + KE = 0 + \tfrac{1}{2}\, mv^2$$

At its maximum height h, v = 0 and

$$E_T = PE + KE = mgh + 0$$

$$\therefore \quad \tfrac{1}{2}\, mv^2 = mgh \qquad \text{or}$$

$$h = \frac{v^2}{2g} = \frac{4\pi^2 \times 0.0275\ m^2 \cdot s^{-2}}{2 \times \pi^2\ m \cdot s^{-2}} = 0.055\ m = 5.5\ cm.$$

• PROBLEM 378

A vertical spring has an unstretched length L. When a mass m hangs at rest from its lower end, its length increases to L + ℓ. Find the period of small vertical oscillations of m (figure).

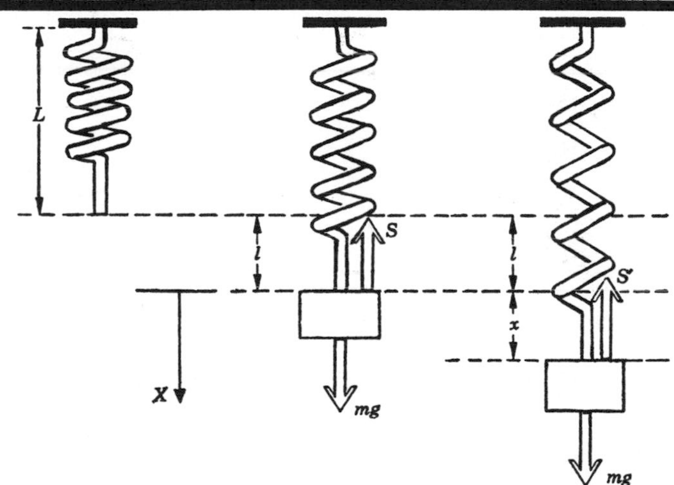

(a) No weight. (b) Weight at rest. (c) Weight oscillating.

Solution: When the mass is hanging at rest (figure b), the extension of the spring is ℓ and the force exerted by it on m is, according to Hooke's law,

$$S = -k\ell.$$

The positive direction is downward, but S is an upward force and therefore negative. Since the mass has no acceleration, this upward force exerted by the spring must be exactly counterbalanced by the weight, mg and by Newton's Second Law,

$$F_{net} = -k\ell + mg = 0.$$

Hence,

$$mg = k\ell. \tag{1}$$

Suppose that, during the oscillation, the mass is a distance x below its equilibrium position, so that the extension of the spring is $\ell + x$ (figure c). The force exerted on m by the spring is then

$$S' = -k(\ell + x)$$

$$= -k\ell - kx.$$

The total force F on m is the sum of S' and the weight mg.

$$F = S' + mg$$

$$F = -k\ell - kx + mg.$$

According to equation (1) $-k\ell$ cancels $+mg$, so

$$F = -kx \tag{2}$$

where x is the extension of the spring from its equilibrium position (figure c). In order to find the period of small vertical oscillations of m, we must solve the equation of motion (2) for x(t). Noting that

$$F = ma = m\,\frac{d^2x}{dt^2}$$

we may write, from (2)

$$m\,\frac{d^2x}{dt^2} = -kx$$

$$\frac{d^2x}{dt^2} + \left(\frac{k}{m}\right)x = 0 \tag{3}$$

We define

$$\omega_0^2 = \frac{k}{m}. \tag{4}$$

Using (3) and (4),

$$\frac{d^2x}{dt^2} + \omega_0^2 x = 0 \tag{5}$$

This is a linear, second order differential equation for x in terms of the variable t. A valid method of solution is to make an educated guess for x(t), substitute this guess into (5), and see if an identity results. If so, x(t) is the solution of (5). A good guess for x(t) is

$$x(t) = A\cos(at + \phi). \tag{6}$$

where a, A and ϕ are arbitrary constants. Noting that

$$\frac{dx(t)}{dt} = -aA\sin(at + \phi)$$

$$\frac{d^2x(t)}{dt^2} = -a^2A\cos(at + \phi)$$

and substituting these results into (5), we obtain

$$-a^2A\cos(at + \phi) + \omega_0^2 A\cos(at + \phi) = 0$$

which is an identity if $\omega_0^2 = a^2$. Hence, x(t) is a solution if $\omega_0 = a$ and

$$x(t) = A\cos(\omega_0 t + \phi).$$

To find the period of the motion, note that the cosine function goes through one complete cycle of variation when its argument $(\omega_0 t + \phi)$ has gone through 2π radians. Here, the change in the argument is

$$(\omega_0 t_f + \phi) - (\omega_0 t_0 + \phi)$$

or

$$\omega_0(t_f - t_0)$$

and this must equal 2π radians, or

$$\omega_0(t_f - t_0) = 2\pi$$

$$t_f - t_0 = \frac{2\pi}{\omega_0}. \tag{7}$$

But $t_f - t_0$ is the time required for cosine to go through one cycle, which is defined as the period of the function (T). Using (7) and (4),

$$T = \frac{2\pi}{\omega_0} = 2\pi\sqrt{\frac{m}{k}}. \tag{8}$$

From (1), $mg = k\ell$

or $k = \frac{mg}{\ell}$

Inserting this in (8), we obtain

$$T = 2\pi\sqrt{\frac{\ell}{g}}\ .$$

• PROBLEM 379

A mass $m = 2$ kg is hung on a spring of constant $k = 3.92 \times 10^3$ N/m. The natural angular frequency of the system is $\omega_0 = 44.3\ \text{sec}^{-1}$. Now we will force the system to vibrate at different frequencies by an alternating force

$$F = 2\cos\omega t \text{ newtons}$$

That is, the maximum force is two newtons. A static force of two newtons would cause a deflection of about ½ mm to the system. What will be the amplitude of vibration for $\omega = 15\ \text{sec}^{-1}$, and $60\ \text{sec}^{-1}$?

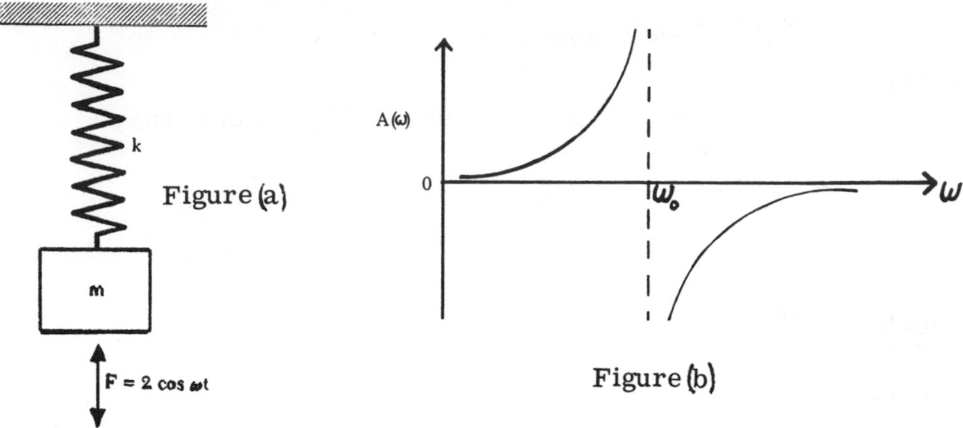

Solution: This problem is a case of harmonic motion with a periodic force applied to a vibrating mass. The forces acting on the mass m are the given applied force $F = 2 \cos \omega t$, and the restoring force $F_R = -ky$ due to the spring. y is the vertical displacement of the mass from its rest position. The negative sign indicates that the restoring force acts in such a direction as to oppose a change in vertical displacement. By Newton's second law,

$$-ky + 2 \cos \omega t = m \frac{d^2y}{dt^2}$$

or

$$\frac{d^2y}{dt^2} + \frac{k}{m} y = \frac{2}{m} \cos \omega t \qquad (1)$$

The following function is a solution to the above differential equation,

$$y(t) = A \cos \omega t \qquad (2)$$

where A is the amplitude of vibration. This can be verified by substitution into equation (1):

$$-\omega^2 A \cos \omega t + \frac{k}{m} A \cos \omega t = \frac{2}{m} \cos \omega t$$

Dividing out the common factor, and solving for A, we find

$$A = \frac{2/m}{k/m - \omega^2}$$

Let $k/m = \omega_0^2$ (where ω_0 is the natural frequency of vibration) then

$$A = \frac{2/m}{\omega_0^2 - \omega^2}$$

Since m = 2kg, we can calculate values of $|A|$ as shown in the table.

ω	$\lvert A \rvert$
15 sec^{-1}	5.8×10^{-4} m
44	3.8×10^{-2}
60	6.1×10^{-4}

When the frequency ω of the applied force is near the natural frequency ω_0 the amplitude becomes much larger (see figure (b)). We can also calculate the average total energy $\langle H \rangle$ of the system. The total energy H of the system at any moment is

$$H = \tfrac{1}{2} mv^2 + \tfrac{1}{2} ky^2 \qquad (3)$$

where the first term is the kinetic energy of the object and the second term is the elastic potential energy of the object. Upon differentiating equation (2), substituting it into equation (3), we obtain

$$H = \frac{1}{2} mA^2\omega^2 \sin^2\omega t + \frac{1}{2} kA^2 \cos^2\omega t .$$

But $k = \omega_0^2 m$ (by definition of ω_0^2). Therefore

$$H = \frac{1}{2} mA^2\omega^2 \sin^2\omega t + \frac{1}{2} mA^2\omega_0^2 \cos^2\omega t$$

The average value of $\cos^2\omega t$ over 1 period is, by definition

$$\langle\cos^2\omega t\rangle = \frac{1}{2\pi}\int_0^{2\pi} \cos^2\omega t \, d(\omega t) = \frac{1}{2}$$

Similarly, $\langle\sin^2 \omega t\rangle = 1/2$

Hence $\langle H\rangle = \frac{1}{4} mA^2\omega^2 + \frac{1}{4} mA^2\omega_0^2$

or

$$\langle H\rangle = \frac{1}{4} mA^2\left(\omega^2 + \omega_0^2\right)$$

which shows that the energy of the system becomes much larger as $\omega \to \omega_0$.

ω	$\langle H\rangle$
15 sec^{-1}	3.7×10^{-4}
44	2.8
60	1.0×10^{-3}

As the frequency of the applied force nears the resonance frequency it is possible to transfer considerably greater energy to the system.

• PROBLEM 380

Six students each of mass 80 kg decide to bounce an automobile of mass 1200 kg. They find that if they sit in the auto, the static deflection of the chassis is 1.5 cm. When they press down the bumpers in unison a maximum dynamic deflection of 10 cm is obtained. The auto also oscillates at a frequency of 0.8 sec^{-1}. Estimate the Q of the automobile suspension, and the damping factor ρ of the shock absorbers.

Solution: First we find the spring constant k. The total mass of the students is $6 \times 80 = 480$ kg; and their weight 480×9.8 N = Mg causes a deflection of 1.5×10^{-2} m. According to Hooke's law,

$$W = - kx$$

where x is the extension of the spring of the auto from its equilibrium position, and W is the force (the weight of an object in this case) on the spring. Then

$$k = \frac{W}{x} = \frac{Mg}{x} = \frac{480 \text{ kg} \times 9.8 \text{ m/sec}^2}{1.5 \times 10^{-2} \text{ m}} = 3.14 \times 10^5 \text{ N/m}$$

Next we estimate the work done by the students in pushing the car down. Suppose that in pushing down they take all their weight off their feet. Then in each push a force of (480×9.8) N travels through a distance of 0.10 m (10 cm). The work done in each oscillation is

$W = 480 \times 9.8 \times 0.10 = 470$ joules. The frequency is 0.8 sec^{-1}, so that the power expended per oscillation is found as follows:

$$p = \frac{\text{work/oscillation}}{\text{time for one oscillation}} = W \times f$$

$$= 470 \text{ j} \times 0.8 \text{ sec}^{-1} = 376 \text{ watt}$$

Here we made use of the relation $f = 1/T$.

The potential energy stored in the suspension is given by

$$H = \tfrac{1}{2} kA^2$$

where A is the maximum deflection. Thus

$$H = \tfrac{1}{2}\, 3.14 \times 10^5 \text{ N/m} \times (0.10 \text{ m})^2$$

$$= 1.57 \times 10^3 \text{ joules}$$

From this we can estimate Q of the system.

The Q of the system is a measure of the amount of energy dissipated in the system, per cycle of operation, relative to the energy present in the system. More precisely, we define Q as

$$Q = 2\pi \frac{H}{P}$$

where H is the energy stored in the system, and P is the energy dissipated, all in one cycle.

In our case we have

$$Q = 2\pi \frac{1.57 \times 10^3 \text{ j}}{470 \text{ j}}$$

$$\cong 21$$

1.57×10^3 j is the potential energy stored in the automobile springs.

Then we assume that f is the natural frequency (a moderately good assumption) we can calculate ρ using an alternate expression for Q.

Q can also be described in terms of the damping factor ρ. The damping factor is a measure of the time taken for the oscillations to die out. This in turn depends on the amount of energy dissipated by the system per oscillation. Q then, in terms of time, rather than in terms of energy, is given as follows:

$$Q = \frac{\omega_0}{\rho} = \frac{2\pi f}{\rho}$$

From this, we can find ρ. Then

$$\rho = 2\pi f/Q = 2\pi \times 0.8/21 = 0.24 \text{ sec}^{-1}$$

A particle which is performing simple harmonic motion passes through two points 20 cm apart with the same velocity, taking 1 s to get from one point to the other. It takes a further 2 s to pass through the second point in the opposite direction. What are the period and amplitude of the motion?

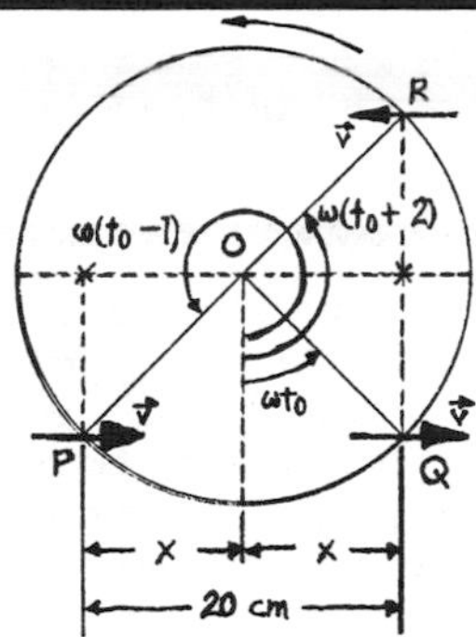

Solution: From the equations of simple harmonic motion, the velocity at any displacement x has a value $v = \omega\sqrt{A^2 - x^2}$, where ω is the angular frequency of the motion and A its amplitude. Thus v can be the same at two points only if the displacements of these points are $\pm$ x. If the origin of the time scale is taken at the mean position of the motion, as shown in the rotor diagram, and if the second point is reached t_0 thereafter, the displacement at the first point is

$$-x = A \sin \omega(t_0 - 1\text{ s}) \tag{1}$$

at the second point,

$$+x = A \sin \omega t_0, \tag{2}$$

and at the second point on the return journey,

$$+x = A \sin \omega(t_0 + 2\text{ s}) \tag{3}$$

Hence, using equations (1) and (2)

$$\sin \omega t_0 = x/A = -\sin \omega(t_0 - 1\text{ s})$$

Since

$$-\sin \omega(t_0 - 1\text{ s}) = \sin\left[-\omega\ (t_0 - 1\text{ s})\right] = \sin \omega t_0$$

$$t_0 = -(t_0 - 1\text{ s}) \quad \text{or} \quad t_0 = \tfrac{1}{2}\text{ s}.$$

Also, using equations (2) and (3),

$$\sin \omega(t_0 + 2\text{ s}) = x/A = \sin \omega t_0.$$

Since, in general, $\sin \theta_1 = \sin \theta_2$ implies $\theta_2 = \pi - \theta_1$ then, in this particular case

$$\omega(t_0 + 2\text{ s}) = \pi - \omega t_0 \text{ or } \pi/\omega = 2t_0 + 2\text{ s} = 3\text{ s}$$

$$\therefore \quad \omega = \frac{\pi}{3}\text{ rad}\cdot\text{s}^{-1}.$$

Also

$$\sin \omega(t_0 - 1\text{ s}) = \sin\left(\frac{\pi}{3}\text{ rad}\cdot\text{s}^{-1} \times -\tfrac{1}{2}\text{ s}\right)$$

$$= -\sin\frac{\pi}{6} = -\tfrac{1}{2}.$$

But $\sin \omega(t_0 - 1\text{ s}) = -x/A = -(0.1/A)\text{m}$.

$$\therefore \quad \tfrac{1}{2} = \frac{0.1}{A}\text{ m} \qquad \text{or} \qquad A = 0.2\text{ m}.$$

• PROBLEM 382

A 10 kg mass resting on a table is attached to a steel wire 5 m long which hangs from a hook in the ceiling. If the table is removed, the wire is momentarily stretched and the mass commences to oscillate up and down. Calculate the frequency of the oscillation if the cross-sectional area of the wire is 1 sq mm and the value of Young's Modulus is taken to be 19×10^{11} dynes/ cm^2.

Solution: Young's modulus is defined as

$$Y = \frac{\frac{F}{A}}{\frac{\Delta x}{x}}$$

where $\Delta x/x$ is the fractional change in length of the wire, A is its cross-section and F is the force normal to A.

$$\therefore F = Y\frac{\Delta x}{x}A$$

But F = ma (Newton's second law, where a = acceleration).

$$\therefore \quad a = \frac{F}{m} = \left(\frac{Y}{m}\frac{A}{x}\right)\Delta x \qquad (1)$$

Since a is proportional to the extension of the wire from its equilibrium length (Δx), the motion is simple harmonic. For this type of motion,

$$a = \omega_0^2 x \qquad (2)$$

where ω_0 is the angular frequency of the oscillation. Comparing (2) and (1)

$$\omega_0^2 = \frac{YA}{mx}$$

and $$\omega_0 = \sqrt{\frac{YA}{mx}}$$

If f is the frequency of the oscillation

$$\omega_0 = 2\pi f = \sqrt{\frac{YA}{mx}}$$

whence $$f = \frac{1}{2\pi}\sqrt{\frac{YA}{mx}}$$

Using the data supplied

$$f = \frac{1}{2\pi}\sqrt{\frac{(19 \times 10^{11}\ \text{dynes/cm}^2)(1\ \text{mm})^2}{(10\ \text{kg})(5\ \text{m})}}$$

Transforming all quantities to c.g.s. values

$$f = \frac{1}{2\pi}\sqrt{\frac{(19 \times 10^{11}\ \text{dynes/cm}^2)(10^{-2}\ \text{cm}^2)}{(10000\ \text{g})(500\ \text{cm})}}$$

$$f \approx 10\ \text{vib/s}$$

• PROBLEM 383

Derive the formulas for the period and the frequency of a simple harmonic oscillator.

Solution: A simple harmonic oscillator in one dimension is characterized by a mass which is acted upon by a force, F, proportional to and directed opposite to its displacement x:

$$F = -kx \tag{1}$$

From Newton's second law:

$$F = ma = m\frac{d^2x}{dt^2} = -kx,$$

$$\frac{d^2x}{dt^2} = -\frac{k}{m}x \tag{2}$$

From the theory of differential equations, a solution for x is:

$$x(t) = A\cos(\omega t + \delta) \tag{3}$$

where A, ω, and δ are constants. The constants A and δ are arbitrary. However, ω depends upon the physical characteristics of the oscillator, m and k. We can solve for ω by inserting the expression for x given in equation (3), into equation (2). We must first calculate the second derivative of x with respect to t:

$$\frac{dx}{dt} = -\omega A\sin(\omega t + \delta),\quad \frac{d^2x}{dt^2} = -\omega^2 A\cos(\omega t + \delta)$$

Then, making the substitution:

$$-\omega^2 A\cos(\omega t + \delta) = -\frac{k}{m}A\cos(\omega t + \delta)$$

Thus, $\omega^2 = \frac{k}{m}$, $\omega = \sqrt{\frac{k}{m}}$

Next, we can prove that the oscillator goes through one complete cycle in time $T = 2\pi/\omega$, by showing that at time $t + 2\pi/\omega$ the displacement x of the oscillator will be the same as at time t:

$$x\left(t + \frac{2\pi}{\omega}\right) = A \cos\left[\omega\left(t + \frac{2\pi}{\omega}\right) + \delta\right]$$

$$= A \cos (\omega t + 2\pi + \delta)$$

$$= A \cos \left[(\omega t + \delta) + 2\pi\right]$$

$$= A \cos (\omega t + \delta)$$

The last step is justified from the laws of trigonometry which state that:

$$\cos (y + 2\pi) = \cos y$$

where we let $y = \omega t + \delta$.

The time T it takes the oscillator to complete one cycle is called the period and is represented by T. Thus:

$$T = \frac{2\pi}{\omega} = 2\pi \sqrt{\frac{m}{k}}$$

The frequency of oscillation ν, is the number of cycles the oscillator goes through per unit time. This is the reciprocal of the period:

$$\text{cycles/sec} = \frac{1}{\text{sec/cycle}}$$

$$\nu = \frac{1}{T} = \frac{\omega}{2\pi} = \frac{1}{2\pi} \sqrt{\frac{k}{m}}$$

• PROBLEM 384

In an electric shaver, the blade moves back and forth over a distance of 2 mm, with a frequency of 60 cps. This constitutes a simple harmonic motion with amplitude R = 1 mm. (a) Find the maximum acceleration. (b) Find the maximum velocity. (c) Calculate the velocity and acceleration at point C, a distance x = 0.5 mm from 0, the center point (see diagram).

Solution: For simple harmonic motion, the force acting on the blade must be proportional to its displacement x, but opposite in direction. The limits of the oscillation are equidistant from the equilibrium position. We can then write

$$F = -kx = ma = m\frac{d^2x}{dt^2} \qquad (1)$$

where k is a constant, m is the mass of the blades, and the negative sign indicates that the force acts in the opposite direction to the displacement. Equation (1) can be written

$$\frac{d^2x}{dt^2} = -\frac{k}{m}x \tag{2}$$

which requires a solution where the second derivative of x(t) is proportional to - x(t). The sinusoidal functions have such a property. Assuming that at t = 0 sec, the displacement is at its maximum amplitude R, we can write

$$x = R \cos \omega t \tag{3}$$

where ω is a constant. Differentiating twice,

$$\frac{dx}{dt} = -\omega R \sin \omega t \tag{4}$$

$$\frac{d^2x}{dt^2} = -\omega^2 R \cos \omega t \tag{5}$$

Substituting equations (3) and (5) into (2), we find

$$-\omega^2 R \cos \omega t = -\frac{k}{m} R \cos \omega t$$

$$\omega^2 = \frac{k}{m}$$

Therefore, if the value for ω^2 is chosen to be k/m, then $x = R \cos \omega t$ is a solution of the equation obtained for the simple harmonic oscillation of the blade. From this solution, we see that ω must be the angular frequency of the motion since the function $\cos \omega t$ repeats itself after a time $2\pi/\omega$. The velocity and acceleration are dx/dt and d^2x/dt^2, respectively, as found in equations (4) and (5).

(a) Looking at the acceleration function

$$a = -\omega^2 R \cos \omega t \tag{6}$$

we note that the maximum value is attained when $\cos \omega t$ is one or $\omega t = n\pi$ where n is an integer. This occurs when the displacement is a maximum. The angular frequency for the blade is

$$\omega = 2\pi f = (2\pi)(60 \text{ sec}^{-1}) = 377 \text{ sec}^{-1}$$

Therefore, the maximum acceleration is

$$a_{max} = \omega^2 R = (377 \text{ sec}^{-1})^2 \times 1 \text{ mm}$$

$$= 1.42 \times 10^5 \text{ mm/sec}^2 = 1.42 \times 10^2 \text{ m/sec}^2$$

(b) To find the maximum velocity, see that

$$v = -\omega R \sin \omega t \tag{7}$$

has a maximum whenever $\sin \omega t = 1$. This happens whenever the blade is at its equilibrium position at which point $\omega t = n\pi/2$, where n is an integer. The maximum velocity is calculated to be

$$v_{max} = \omega R = 377 \text{ sec}^{-1} \times 10^{-3} \text{ m} = 0.377 \text{ m/sec}$$

(c) To express the velocity function in terms of the displacement x, we square equation (7). Then,

$$v^2 = \omega^2 R^2 \sin^2 \omega t = \omega^2 R^2 (1 - \cos^2 \omega t)$$

$$= \omega^2(R^2 - R^2 \cos^2 \omega t) = \omega^2(R^2 - x^2)$$

Expressing this in terms of $v_{max} = \omega R$, we write

$$v^2 = \omega^2 R^2 \left(1 - \frac{x^2}{R^2}\right) = v^2_{max} \left(1 - \frac{x^2}{R^2}\right)$$

At x = 0.5 mm

$$v = v_{max} \sqrt{1 - \frac{x^2}{R^2}} = 0.377 \text{ m/sec} \sqrt{1 - \left(\frac{0.5 \text{ mm}}{1.0 \text{ mm}}\right)^2}$$

$$v = 0.377 \sqrt{1 - (\tfrac{1}{2})^2} \text{ m/sec}$$

$$= 0.377 \times 0.865 \text{ m/sec} = 0.326 \text{ m/sec}$$

The acceleration function of equation (6) can be expressed as

$$a = -\omega^2 x$$

and at x = 0.5 mm = $(5)(10^{-4}$ m), the acceleration is

$$a = \omega^2 x = (377 \text{ sec}^{-1})^2 \times (5 \times 10^{-4} \text{ m})$$

$$= 71 \text{ m/sec}^2$$

• PROBLEM 385

The period of a compound pendulum is 2 s on the earth's surface. What is its period if it is aboard a rocket accelerating upward with an acceleration of 4.3 $m \cdot s^{-2}$?

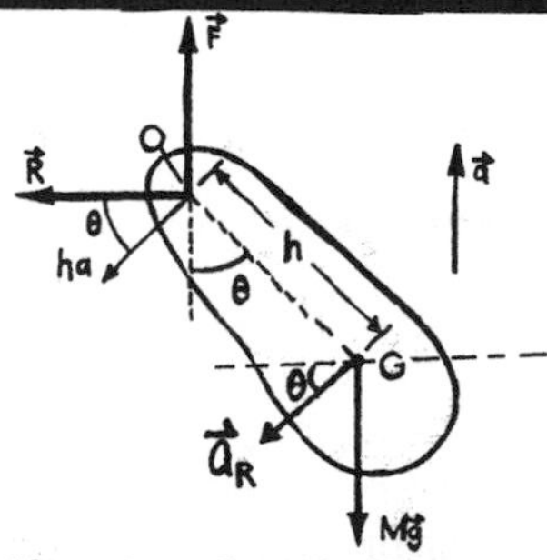

Solution: When on the surface the compound pendulum has a period $T = 2\pi \sqrt{I_0/Mgh}$, where M is the mass of the pendulum, I is its moment of inertia about the axis of rotation, h is the distance between the center of mass and the axis of rotation and g is the acceleration of gravity, as shown in the figure.

Under acceleration $\vec{a}$ upward, the forces acting on the body when it is displaced through an angle θ are those shown in the figure, the weight $M\vec{g}$ downward and the vertical force $\vec{F}$ and horizontal force $\vec{R}$ exerted by the pivot on the pendulum.

Consider the linear accelerations, horizontal and vertical, acting on the body at its center of mass and the rotational acceleration about the center of mass. Applying Newton's Law to the horizontal and vertical motions, we get

$$R = Ma_H \tag{1}$$

$$F - Mg = Ma_V \tag{2}$$

The equation of motion for the rotation is

$$\text{Net torque} = Rh \cos \theta - F\, h \sin \theta = I_G\, \alpha \tag{3}$$

where I_G is the moment of inertia with respect to the center of mass, and α is the angular acceleration.

The point O thus has an acceleration, a_H horizontally, an acceleration a_V vertically, and a further linear acceleration $a_R = h\alpha$ at right angles to OG, due to the rotation about G. But the point O does not move sideways, only upward with an acceleration a. Thus, there is no net horizontal acceleration

$$a_h + h\, \alpha \cos \theta = 0 \tag{4}$$

Substituting (4) in (1),

$$R = - Mh\, \alpha \cos \theta$$

The upward acceleration is

$$a = a_V - h\, \alpha \sin \theta$$

or $$a_V = a + h\, \alpha \sin \theta \tag{5}$$

Substituting (5) in (2)

$$F = Mg + M\,(a + h\, \alpha \sin \theta)$$

$$= M(g + a + h\, \alpha \sin \theta)$$

and finally equation (3) becomes

$$I_G\, \alpha = Rh \cos \theta - Fh \sin \theta$$

$$= - Mh^2 \alpha \cos^2 \theta - Mh^2 \alpha \sin^2 \theta - M(g + a)h \sin \theta$$

$$= - Mh^2 \alpha (\cos^2 \theta + \sin^2 \theta) - M(g + a)h \sin \theta$$

$$= - Mh^2 \alpha - M(g + a)h \sin \theta$$

or $\left(I_G + Mh^2\right) \alpha = I_0\alpha = - M(g + a) h \sin \theta$

where we used the equation $I_0 = I_G + Mh^2$.

But the angle θ is small, and $\sin \theta$ can be replaced by θ,

$$\alpha = \frac{d^2\theta}{dt^2} = - \frac{M(g + a)h}{I_0} \sin \theta \simeq - \frac{M(g + a)h}{I_0} \theta .$$

This is the differential equation of a simple harmonic motion, therefore it follows from the theory of simple harmonic motion that the period of oscillation is

$$T' = 2\pi \sqrt{\frac{I_0}{M(g + a)h}}$$

If T is the period of the motion when the pendulum is at rest on the earth

$$\frac{T'}{T} = \frac{2\pi\sqrt{\frac{I_0}{M(a + g)h}}}{2\pi\sqrt{\frac{I_0}{Mgh}}}$$

$$= \sqrt{\frac{g}{g + a}} = \sqrt{\frac{9.8\ m\cdot s^{-2}}{9.8\ m\cdot s^{-2} + 4.3\ m\cdot s^{-2}}}$$

$$= 0.83$$

Hence $T' = 0.83\ T = 0.83 \times 2\ s = 1.67\ s.$

Note that the result can be obtained more quickly if the idea of an accelerated frame of reference is applied. An observer in the rocket considers the point of support of the pendulum at rest relative to himself. To explain the observed equilibrium he finds it necessary to postulate a force $M\vec{a}$ acting downward on the body in addition to the weight $M\vec{g}$. Hence the pendulum acts as if the weight were $M(\vec{g} + \vec{a})$ instead of $M\vec{g}$, from which the formula follows immediately.

• PROBLEM 386

The simple harmonic motion of the pendulum in figure (a) is slowed as a result of air friction. If the frictional force is proportional to the velocity of the bob, (a) find the displacement of the pendulum as a function of time, (b) calculate the rate of energy dissipation by the damped harmonic motion of the pendulum. Assume that the oscillation frequency of the pendulum is much greater than the rate of damping (the weak damping limit).

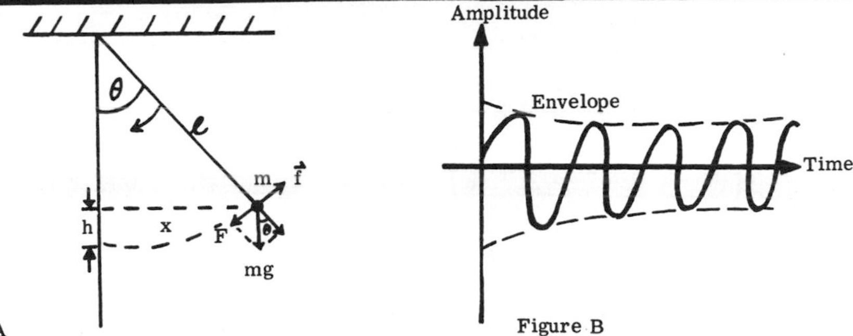

Figure A

Figure B

Solution: (a) The restoring force on the pendulum for a small angular displacement θ is

$$F = -mg \sin\theta \simeq -mg\theta$$

where m and g are the mass of the pendulum and the gravitational acceleration, respectively. The frictional force is

$$f = -bv$$

where b is a proportionality constant, and v is the velocity. The minus sign in the expressions for F and f means that they oppose an increase in θ and v, respectively. The displacement along the arc is

$$x = \ell\theta$$

The equation of motion for displacement x is

$$m\frac{d^2x}{dt^2} = F + f = -mg\theta - bv$$

$$= -mg\frac{x}{\ell} - b\frac{dx}{dt}$$

which gives the following differential equation for x:

$$\frac{d^2x}{dt^2} + \frac{b}{m}\frac{dx}{dt} + \frac{g}{\ell}x = 0 \qquad (1)$$

In the weak damping limit, b is small and the amplitude of the oscillation is damped as shown in Fig. b. Therefore, we try the solution

$$x(t) = Ae^{-t/\tau}\sin\omega t$$

in (1), where $e^{-t/\tau}$ is the equation of the amplitude envelope. We assumed that at t = 0, x =0.

We have

$$\frac{d^2x}{dt^2} = Ae^{-t/\tau}\left[\left(\frac{1}{\tau^2} - \omega^2\right)\sin\omega t - \frac{2\omega}{\tau}\cos\omega t\right]$$

$$\frac{b}{m}\frac{dx}{dt} = A\ e^{-t/\tau}\left[\ \frac{b\omega}{m}\cos\omega t - \frac{b}{m\tau}\sin\omega t\ \right]$$

$$\frac{g}{\ell}\,x = A\ e^{-t/\tau}\ \frac{g}{\ell}\sin\omega t.$$

Substituting in (1), we obtain

$$A\ e^{-t/\tau}\left\{\left(\frac{1}{\tau^2} - \omega^2 - \frac{b}{m\tau} + \frac{g}{\ell}\right)\sin\omega t + \left(\frac{b\omega}{m} - \frac{2\omega}{\tau}\right)\cos\omega t\right\} = 0$$

The coefficients of $\sin\omega t$ and $\cos\omega t$ must equal zero separately;

$$\frac{b\omega}{m} - \frac{2\omega}{\tau} = 0$$

$$\frac{1}{\tau^2} - \omega^2 - \frac{b}{m\tau} + \frac{g}{\ell} = 0$$

or $\quad \dfrac{1}{\tau} = \dfrac{b}{2m}$ (2)

$$\omega^2 = \frac{g}{\ell} + \frac{1}{\tau^2} - \frac{b}{m\tau} = \frac{g}{\ell} + \frac{b^2}{4m^2} - \frac{b^2}{2m^2}$$

$$= \frac{g}{\ell} - \frac{b^2}{4m^2}\ .$$

Hence the angular velocity of the motion is

$$\omega = \sqrt{\omega_0^2 - \frac{b^2}{4m^2}} = \omega_0\sqrt{1 - \left(\frac{b}{2m\omega_0}\right)^2}\ , \qquad (3)$$

where $\omega_0^2 = \dfrac{g}{\ell}$. For weak damping, $\dfrac{b}{2m\omega_0} = \dfrac{1}{\omega_0\tau} << 1$, and (3) becomes

$$\omega \simeq \omega_0\left(1 - \frac{b}{m\omega_0}\right) = \omega_0 - \frac{b}{m}\ . \qquad (4)$$

(b) The kinetic energy κ is

$$\kappa = \tfrac{1}{2}mv^2 = \tfrac{1}{2}m\left(\frac{dx}{dt}\right)^2$$

$$= \tfrac{1}{2}m\left\{A\ e^{-t/\tau}\left(\omega\cos\omega t - \frac{1}{\tau}\sin\omega t\right)\right\}$$

$$= \tfrac{1}{2}m\,A^2\,e^{-2t/\tau}\left(\omega^2\cos^2\omega t + \frac{1}{\tau^2}\sin^2\omega t - \frac{2\omega}{\tau}\sin\omega t\cos\omega t\right) \qquad (5)$$

Now, let us consider the time average of κ.

For this we substitute the following trigonometric identities in (5).

$$2 \sin \omega t \cos \omega t = \sin 2\omega t,$$

$$\cos^2 \omega t = \frac{1 + \cos 2\omega t}{2}$$

$$\sin^2 \omega t = \frac{1 - \cos 2\omega t}{2}$$

$$\kappa = \tfrac{1}{2} m A^2 e^{-2t/\tau}\left(\tfrac{1}{2}\omega^2 + \frac{1}{2\tau^2} + \tfrac{1}{2}\omega^2 \cos 2\omega t - \frac{1}{2\tau^2}\sin 2\omega t - \frac{\omega}{\tau}\sin 2\omega t\right)$$

The time average of a pure sine wave is zero, i.e.

$$< \cos 2\omega t > = < \sin 2\omega t > = 0$$

Therefore, only constant terms in the expression for κ survive when we take its time average

$$< \kappa > = \tfrac{1}{4} mA^2 e^{-2t/\tau}\left(\omega^2 + \frac{1}{\tau^2}\right) .$$

We see that the average kinetic energy decays exponentially. The potential energy U is

$$U = mgh = mg\ell\,(1 - \cos\theta) \simeq \tfrac{1}{2} mg\ell\,\theta^2$$

$$\simeq \tfrac{1}{2} mg\ell\left(\frac{x}{\ell}\right)^2 = \tfrac{1}{2}\frac{mg}{\ell}x^2$$

$$\simeq \tfrac{1}{2}\frac{mg}{\ell}A^2 e^{-2t/\tau}\sin^2\omega t$$

$$\simeq \tfrac{1}{4}\frac{mg}{\ell}A^2 e^{-2t/\tau}[1 - \cos 2\omega t]$$

The time average of U is

$$< U > \simeq \tfrac{1}{4}\frac{mg}{\ell}A^2 e^{-2t/\tau}$$

Therefore, the time average of total energy is

$$< E > = < U > + < \kappa > = \tfrac{1}{4} A^2 e^{-2t/\tau}\left(\frac{mg}{\ell} + m\omega^2 + \frac{m}{\tau^2}\right)$$

$$= \tfrac{1}{4} A^2 e^{-2t/\tau}\left(\frac{mg}{\ell} + \frac{mg}{\ell} - \frac{b^2}{4m} + \frac{b^2}{4m}\right)$$

$$= \tfrac{1}{2}\omega_0^2 A^2 e^{-2t/\tau}.$$

The rate of change of energy with time has a negative sign since the energy decreases. Therefore, the rate of dissipation, P, is positive since it is the rate of decrease (negative rate of increase) of the energy

$$< P > = - \frac{d}{dt} < E > = \frac{\omega_0^2 A^2}{\tau} e^{-2t/\tau}$$

$$= \frac{2 < E >}{\tau} .$$

• PROBLEM 387

At a carnival, the people who go on a certain ride sit in chairs around the rim of a horizontal circular platform which is oscillating rapidly with angular simple harmonic motion about a vertical axis through its center. The period of the motion is 2s and the amplitude .2 rad.

One of the chairs becomes unbolted and just starts to slip when the angular displacement is a maximum. Calculate the coefficient of static friction between chair and platform. (The rim is 12 ft. from the center).

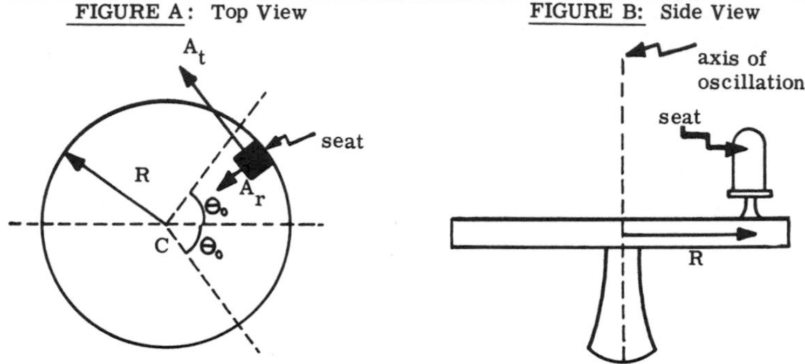

Solution: In order to find the coefficient of static friction, we must use Newton's Second Law to relate the acceleration of the seat to the net force acting on it. Now, the platform and seat are oscillating about an axis through C (see figure (A)) with a maximum angular displacement θ_0. Since the motion is simple harmonic, we may write

$$\theta = \theta_0 \cos(\omega_0 t + \rho) \qquad (1)$$

which gives us the angular displacement of a point on the disc (and, hence, the seat) as a function of time. Note that ρ is an arbitrary constant, which is determined by the way the angular motion begins, and ω_0 is the angular frequency of the motion. Differentiating (1) twice

$$\omega = \frac{d\theta}{dt} = - \theta_0 \omega_0 \sin(\omega_0 t + \rho) \qquad (2)$$

$$\alpha = \frac{d\omega}{dt} = - \theta_0 \omega_0^2 \cos(\omega_0 t + \rho) \qquad (3)$$

Here, ω and α are the angular velocity and acceleration of a point on the disc. Since the seat has an angular acceleration α, it also has a tangential acceleration

a_t, such that

$$a_t = \alpha R = -\theta_0\ \omega_0{}^2 R \cos\left(\omega_0 t + \rho\right) \qquad (4)$$

where R is the platform radius (and the distance of the seat from C, see figure (A)).

In addition, the seat also has a radial acceleration, a_r, pointing inward towards C. The value of a_r is

$$a_r = \omega^2\ R = \theta_0{}^2\ \omega_0{}^2\ R \sin^2\left(\omega_0 t + \rho\right) \qquad (5)$$

The net acceleration a is then

$$a^2 = a_t{}^2 + a_r{}^2$$

$$a^2 = \theta_0{}^2\ \omega_0{}^4\ R^2 \cos^2\left(\omega_0 t + \rho\right) + \theta_0{}^4\ \omega_0{}^4\ R^2 \sin^4\left(\omega_0 t + \rho\right)$$

$$a^2 = \theta_0{}^2\ \omega_0{}^4\ R^2 \left[\cos^2\left(\omega_0 t + \rho\right) + \theta_0{}^2 \sin^4\ \omega_0 t + \rho\ \right]$$

$$\text{or } a = \theta_0\ \omega_0{}^2 R\left(\cos^2\left(\omega_0 t + \rho\right) + \theta_0{}^2\ \sin^4\left(\omega_0 t + \rho\right)\right)^{\frac{1}{2}} \qquad (6)$$

If we assume the chair is unbolted, there are 2 sets of forces acting on the chair. In the vertical direction (perpendicular to the disc) 2 forces act - the normal force N of the disc on the chair, and its weight, mg (m is the chair's mass). Since the chair stays on the platform, there is no acceleration in the vertical direction, and N and mg balance:

$$N = mg \qquad (7)$$

In the plane of the disc, the only force acting is the force of static friction, f_s. By Newton's Second Law, this must equal the product of the chair's mass and acceleration. Using (6)

$$f_s = m\ \theta_0\ \omega_0{}^2\ R\left(\cos^2\left(\omega_0 t + \rho\right) + \theta_0{}^2\ \sin^4\left(\omega_0 t + \rho\right)\right)^{\frac{1}{2}}$$

But, $\qquad f_s \leq u_s\ N$

Hence, $\qquad f_s \leq u_s\ mg$

Combining the first, and last equation for f_s,

$$m\ \theta_0\ \omega_0{}^2 R\left(\cos^2\left(\omega_0 t + \rho\right) + \theta_0{}^2\ \sin^4\left(\omega_0 t + \rho\right)\right)^{\frac{1}{2}} \leq u_s\ mg$$

Solving for u_s

$$u_s \geq \frac{\theta_0\ \omega_0{}^2\ R\left(\cos^2\left(\omega_0 t + \rho\right) + \theta_0{}^2\ \sin^4\left(\omega_0 t + \rho\right)\right)^{\frac{1}{2}}}{g} \qquad (8)$$

This relation holds as long as the seat is stationary. Once the seat begins to slip, the maximum force of static friction is encountered, and (8) becomes a strict equality:

$$u_s = \frac{\theta_0 \omega_0^2 R}{g}\left(\cos^2(\omega_0 t + \varphi) + \theta_0^2 \sin^4(\omega_0 t + \varphi)\right)^{\frac{1}{2}} \quad (9)$$

Note that slippage occurs at the maximum value of θ, or θ_0. For this value of θ, (1) yields

$$\theta_0 = \theta_0 \cos(\omega_0 t + \alpha)$$

whence $\cos(\omega_0 t + \alpha) = 1$

As a result, $\sin(\omega_0 t + \alpha) = 0$

Using these facts in (9)

$$u_s = \frac{\theta_0 \omega_0^2 R \quad (1 + 0)^{\frac{1}{2}}}{g} = \frac{\theta_0 \omega_0^2 R}{g} \quad (10)$$

Note that we don't know ω_0, but we do know T, the period of the oscillation. By definition

$$\omega_0 = 2\pi f = \frac{2\pi}{T}$$

where f is the oscillation frequency. Using this in (10)

$$u_s = \frac{4\pi^2 \theta_0 R}{T^2 g}$$

Substituting the given data

$$u_s = \frac{(4)(9.89)(.2 \text{ rad})(12 \text{ ft})}{(2s)^2(32 \text{ ft/s}^2)}$$

$$u_s = .74$$

We could have done an easier (but less general) analysis by noting that, when $\theta = \theta_0$, the a_r term is zero, for the chair is instantaneously at rest.

• PROBLEM 388

Calculate the average over time of the kinetic and potential energy of a harmonic oscillator.

Solution: Assume that the harmonic oscillator we are dealing with is a mass on a spring. The position of the mass is then given by

$$x = A \sin(\omega_0 t + \varphi)$$

where A is the amplitude of the motion of the mass, and φ is a phase angle defining the initial position of the mass (at $t = 0$).

The kinetic energy is then

$$K = \tfrac{1}{2}M\dot{x}^2 = \tfrac{1}{2}M\left[\omega_0 A \cos(\omega_0 t + \varphi)\right]^2,$$

The time average of the kinetic energy over one period T of the motion is defined as

$$\langle K\rangle = \frac{\int_0^T K\,dt}{T}$$

But ω_0 is the angular frequency and

$$\omega_0 = 2\pi f$$

where f is the frequency of motion of the mass. Since $f = 1/T$

$$\omega_0 = 2\pi/T$$

and

$$T = 2\pi/\omega_0 .$$

Then

$$\langle K\rangle = \tfrac{1}{2} M\omega_0^2 A^2 \frac{\int_0^{2\pi/\omega_0} \cos^2(\omega_0 t + \varphi)dt}{2\pi/\omega_0}$$

Let

$$y = \omega_0 t + \varphi \tag{1}$$

and

$$dy = \omega_0\, dt$$

since φ is a constant. We then have

$$\langle K\rangle = \tfrac{1}{2} M\omega_0^2 A^2 \frac{\int_{\varphi}^{\varphi+2\pi} \cos^2 y\,(dy/\omega_0)}{2\pi/\omega_0} \tag{2}$$

where the limits are obtained by noting that, from (1), $y = \varphi$ at $t = 0$, and $y = 2\pi + \varphi$ at $t = 2\pi/\omega_0$. Rewriting (2)

$$\langle K\rangle = \tfrac{1}{2} \frac{M\omega_0^2 A^2}{2\pi} \left(\int_{\varphi}^{\varphi+2\pi} \cos^2 y\; dy\right)$$

But $\cos^2 y = \frac{1}{2}(1 + \cos 2y)$ and

$$\langle K\rangle = \frac{M\omega_0^2 A^2}{4\pi}\left(\int_{\varphi}^{\varphi+2\pi} \tfrac{1}{2}(1 + \cos 2y)dy\right)$$

$$\langle K\rangle = \frac{M\omega_0^2 A^2}{8\pi}\left[\int_{\varphi}^{\varphi+2\pi} dy + \int_{\varphi}^{\varphi+2\pi} \cos 2y\; dy\right]$$

$$\langle K\rangle = \frac{M\omega_0^2 A^2}{8\pi}\left[\int_{\varphi}^{\varphi+2\pi} dy + \tfrac{1}{2}\int_{\varphi}^{\varphi+2\pi} \cos 2y\,(2dy)\right]$$

$$\langle K\rangle = \frac{M\omega_0^2 A^2}{8\pi}\left[2\pi + \tfrac{1}{2}\left[\sin(2\varphi + 4\pi) - \sin(2\varphi)\right]\right]$$

Since $\sin(2\varphi + 4\pi) = \sin 2\varphi$

$$\langle K\rangle = \frac{M\omega_0^2 A^2}{4}$$

The potential energy is, with $x = A\sin(\omega_0 t + \varphi)$

$$U = \tfrac{1}{2}Cx^2 = \tfrac{1}{2}CA^2 \sin^2(\omega_0 t + \varphi)$$

where C is the spring constant. Now,

$$\langle U\rangle = \frac{\int_0^T U\,dt}{T} = \frac{\int_0^{2\pi/\omega_0} \frac{1}{2}CA^2 \sin^2(\omega_0 t + \varphi)\,dt}{2\pi/\omega_0}$$

Using (1)

$$\langle U\rangle = \frac{1}{2}CA^2 \frac{\int_{\varphi}^{\varphi+2\pi} \sin^2 y\,(dy/\omega_0)}{2\pi/\omega_0}$$

$$\langle U\rangle = \frac{CA^2}{4\pi} \int_{\varphi}^{\varphi+2\pi} \sin^2 y\,dy$$

Because $\sin^2 y = \frac{1}{2}(1 - \cos 2y)$

$$\langle U\rangle = \frac{CA^2}{4\pi}\left[\int_{\varphi}^{\varphi+2\pi} \frac{1}{2}(1 - \cos 2y)\,dy\right]$$

$$\langle U\rangle = \frac{CA^2}{8\pi}\left[\int_{\varphi}^{\varphi+2\pi} dy - \int_{\varphi}^{\varphi+2\pi} \cos 2y\,dy\right]$$

$$\langle U\rangle = \frac{CA^2}{8\pi}\left[\int_{\varphi}^{\varphi+2\pi} dy - \frac{1}{2}\int_{\varphi}^{\varphi+2\pi} \cos 2y\,(2dy)\right]$$

$$\langle U\rangle = \frac{CA^2}{8\pi}\cdot\left[2\pi - \frac{1}{2}[\sin(2\varphi + 4\pi) - \sin(2\varphi)]\right]$$

Since $\sin(2\varphi + 4\pi) = \sin(2\varphi)$

$$\langle U\rangle = \frac{CA^2}{4}$$

But, $\omega_0^2 = C/M$, by definition of the frequency of the simple harmonic oscillator. Therefore

$$\langle U\rangle = \frac{M\omega_0^2 A^2}{4}$$

Thus $\langle U\rangle = \langle K\rangle$ and the total energy of the harmonic oscillator is

$$E = \langle K\rangle + \langle U\rangle = \frac{1}{2} M\omega_0^2 A^2 .$$

Note that $E = \langle E\rangle$ because the total energy is a constant of the motion.

The equality of the average kinetic energy and potential energies is a special property of the harmonic oscillator. This property does not hold in general for anharmonic oscillators. It does hold for weakly damped oscillators.

• PROBLEM 389

If a tunnel were drilled through the earth along one of its diameters and if a stone were dropped into it from one end, how long would it be before the stone returned? Compare the answer with the period of an earth satellite in an orbit of minimum radius and comment on the two values. Assume the earth to be of uniform density, and make use of the information that a body inside the earth at a distance r from the center has a gravitational force acting on it due only to the portion of the earth of radius r.

Solution: Consider the regions I and II of the earth constructed out of the conical sections with pivot m (see the figure). Region I contains a smaller mass

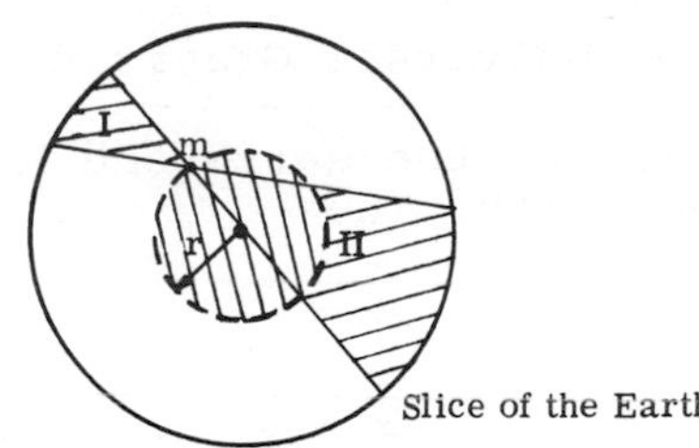

Slice of the Earth

than region II. It is, however, closer to m than region II. Since the gravitational force due to a mass is directly proportional to the mass, and inversely proportional to the square of distance, then it appears that regions I and II provide equal and opposite forces on m, due to the tradeoff between mass and distance. A detailed mathematical analysis verifies that regions I and II do neutralize each other and have no resultant effect on m. This is true for any such regions constructed by the above procedure, and the net effect of the portion of the earth outside the sphere of radius r is zero. At any distance r from the center the stone is acted on by a force of magnitude

$$F = -\frac{GM'm}{r^2} = -\frac{Gm}{r^2} \times \frac{4}{3}\pi\rho r^3 = -\frac{4}{3}\pi\rho Gmr,$$

where m is the mass of the stone, ρ the density of the earth, and M' the mass of that portion of the earth of radius r. We also used the fact that $M' = \rho V = \rho(4/3\ \pi r^3)$. The negative sign indicates that the force acts in a direction that opposes an increase in separation of the two bodies (it's attractive). Therefore, by Newton's second law,

$$F = ma = -\left(\frac{4}{3}\pi\rho Gm\right) r \quad \text{or} \quad F = -kr$$

where $k = 4/3\ \pi\rho Gm$.

The form of this equation indicates that the mass is undergoing simple harmonic motion about the center of the earth. The period of any simple harmonic oscillator of mass m is

$$T = 2\pi\sqrt{\frac{m}{k}}$$

where k is the effective spring constant.

Therefore, in this case,

$$T = \frac{2\pi}{\sqrt{\frac{4}{3}\pi\rho G}}$$

But at the surface of the earth the gravitational force of attraction on the mass m (i.e. its weight) is

$$W = mg = \frac{GMm}{R^2} = \frac{4}{3}\pi\rho GmR,$$

by Newton's Law of Universal Gravitation.

R is the radius of the earth and M is now the total mass of the earth. Thus

$$\frac{g}{R} = \frac{4}{3}\pi\rho G$$

Hence $\quad T = 2\pi\sqrt{\frac{R}{g}} = 2\pi\sqrt{\frac{6370 \times 10^3 \text{ m}}{9.8 \text{ m}\cdot\text{s}^{-2}}}$

$$= 5061.6 \text{ s} = 84.8 \text{ min.}$$

The time period of an earh satellite in a circular orbit is $T' = 2\pi d^{3/2}/R\sqrt{g}$, where d is the distance of the satellite from the center of the earth. If the height of the satellite above the earth's surface is negligible in comparison with the radius of the earth, then to a first approximation d = R, and $T' = 2\pi\sqrt{R/g}$, the same period as that of the stone undergoing simple harmonic motion along the tunnel. This is not surprising, since any simple harmonic motion may be considered the projection on a diameter of the motion of a point in a circle with constant speed. Thus we should expect the period of an earth satellite near the earth's surface to be the same as the period of a particle undergoing simple harmonic motion along a diameter of the circle.

• PROBLEM 390

Consider a pendulum which is oscillating with an amplitude so large that we may not neglect the θ^3 term in the expansion of sin θ, as we do for a harmonic oscillator. What is the effect on the motion of the pendulum of the term in θ^3? This is an elementary example of an anharmonic oscillator. Anharmonic or nonlinear problems are usually difficult to solve exactly (except by computers), but approximate solutions are often adequate to give us a good idea of what is happening.

Solution: The expansion of sin θ (for small θ) to terms of order θ^3, commonly expressed as "expansion to O (θ^3)," is

$$\sin\theta = \theta - \frac{1}{6}\theta^3 + \ldots,$$

so that the equation of motion of a simple oscillator becomes, to this order,

$$\frac{d^2\theta}{dt^2} + \omega_0{}^2\theta - \frac{\omega_0{}^2}{6}\theta^3 = 0, \qquad (1)$$

where $\omega_0{}^2$ denotes the quantity g/L. This is the equation of motion of an anharmonic oscillator.

We see if we can find an approximate solution

to (1) of the form

$$\theta = \theta_0 \sin \omega t + \varepsilon\theta_0 \sin 3\omega t, \tag{2}$$

It is now evident that (2) can only be an approximate solution at best. It remains for us to determine ε, and also ω; while ω must reduce to ω_0 at small amplitudes, it may differ at large amplitudes. For simplicity we suppose that $\theta = 0$ at $t = 0$.

An approximate solution of this type to a differential equation is called a perturbation solution, because one term in the differential equation perturbs the motion which would occur without that term. As you have seen, we arrived at the form of (2) by guided guesswork. It is easy enough to try several guesses and to reject the ones which do not work.

We have from (2)

$$\ddot{\theta} = -\omega^2\theta_0 \sin \omega t - 9\omega^2\varepsilon\theta_0 \sin 3\omega t;$$

$$\theta^3 = \theta_0{}^3(\sin^3 \omega t + 3\varepsilon \sin^2 \omega t \sin 3\omega t + \ldots),$$

where we have discarded the terms of order ε^2 and ε^3 because of our assumption that we can find a solution with $\varepsilon << 1$. Then the terms of (1) become

$$\omega_0^2\theta = \frac{\omega_0{}^2}{6}\theta^3 - \ddot{\theta}$$

$$\omega_0{}^2\,\theta_0 \sin \omega_0 t + \varepsilon\,\omega_0{}^2\theta_0 \sin 3\omega t \simeq \frac{\omega_0{}^2}{6}\theta_0{}^3 \times$$

$$(\sin^3 \omega t + 3\varepsilon \sin^2 \omega t \sin 3\omega t) +$$

$$\omega^2\theta_0 \sin \omega t + 9\,\omega^2\,\varepsilon\,\theta_0 \sin 3\omega t.$$

The coefficient of the term $\sin^2 \omega t \sin 3\omega t$ in the previous equation is small by $0(\varepsilon)$ or by $0(\theta_0{}^2)$, compared with the other terms in the equation. Since ε and θ_0 are small quantities, we neglect this term.

Using the trigonometric identity

$$\sin^3 \omega t = \frac{3 \sin \omega t - \sin 3\omega t}{4} \qquad \text{we get}$$

$$\omega_0{}^2\theta_0 \sin \omega t + \varepsilon\,\omega_0{}^2\theta_0 \sin 3\omega t \simeq \left(\frac{1}{8}\,\omega_0{}^2\theta_0 + \omega^2\theta_0\right) \times$$

$$\sin \omega t + \left(9\,\omega^2\varepsilon\theta_0 - \frac{1}{24}\,\omega_0{}^2\theta_0{}^3\right)\sin 3\omega t \tag{3}$$

In order for this equation to hold, the corresponding coefficients of $\sin \omega t$ and $\sin 3\omega t$ on each side of the equation must be equal:

$$\omega_0{}^2 = \frac{\omega_0{}^2\theta_0{}^2}{8} + \omega^2 \tag{4}$$

$$\varepsilon\omega_0{}^2 = -\frac{1}{24}\,\omega_0{}^2\theta_0{}^2 + 9\varepsilon\omega^2 \tag{5}$$

From (4), $\omega^2 \simeq \omega_0^2 \left(1 - \frac{1}{8}\theta_0^2\right)$

or $\omega \simeq \omega_0 \left(1 - \frac{1}{8}\theta_0^2\right)^{\frac{1}{2}} \simeq \omega_0 \left(1 - \frac{1}{16}\theta_0^2\right)$

using the binomial equation for the square root. We see that as $\theta_0 \to 0$, $\omega \to \omega_0$. The frequency shift $\Delta\omega$ is

$$\Delta\omega = \omega - \omega_0 = \frac{\omega_0}{16}\theta_0^2$$

In (5), we make the substitution $\omega^2 \simeq \omega_0^2$ and obtain an expression for ε.

$$\varepsilon\,\omega_0^2 \simeq -\frac{1}{24}\omega_0^2\theta_0^2 + 9\varepsilon\omega_0^2$$

$$\varepsilon \simeq \frac{\theta_0^2}{8 \times 24} = \frac{1}{16}\theta_0^2$$

We think of ε as giving the fractional admixture of the sin $3\omega t$ term in a solution for θ dominated by the sin ωt term.

Why did we not include in (2) a term in sin $2\omega t$? Try for yourself a solution of the form

$$\theta = \theta_0 \sin\omega t + \eta\theta_0 \sin 2\omega t,$$

and see what happens. You will find $\eta = 0$. The pendulum generates chiefly third harmonics, i.e., terms in sin $3\omega t$, and not second harmonics. The situation would be different for a device for which the equation of motion included a term in θ^2.

What is the frequency of the pendulum at large amplitudes? There is no single frequency in the motion. We have seen that the most important term (the largest component) is in sin ωt, and we say that ω is the fundamental frequency of the pendulum. To our approximation ω is given by (4). The term in sin $3\omega t$ is called the third harmonic of the fundamental frequency. Our argument following (2) suggests that an infinite number of harmonics are present in the exact motion, but that most of these are very small. The amplitude in (2) of the fundamental component of the motion is θ_0; the amplitude of the third harmonic component is $\varepsilon\theta_0$.

• PROBLEM 391

Suppose that the 2 atoms of a stable molecule oscillate along the line connecting their centers. Treating the system as an harmonic oscillator, calculate the vibration frequency. (Neglect any rotation of the system).

Solution: If we treat the given system as an harmonic oscillator, we may assume that the 2 atoms are coupled by a tiny spring connecting

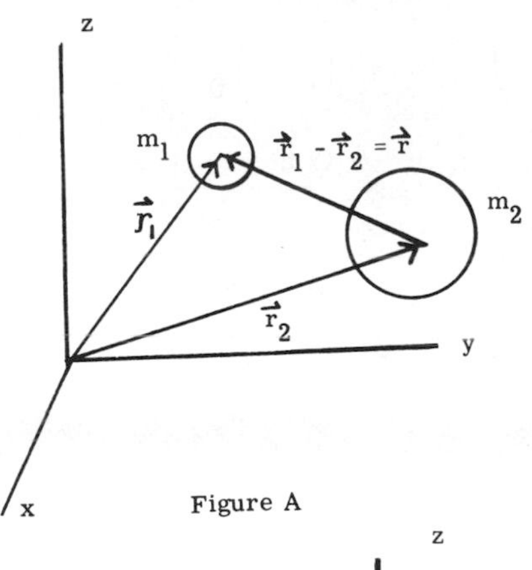

Figure A

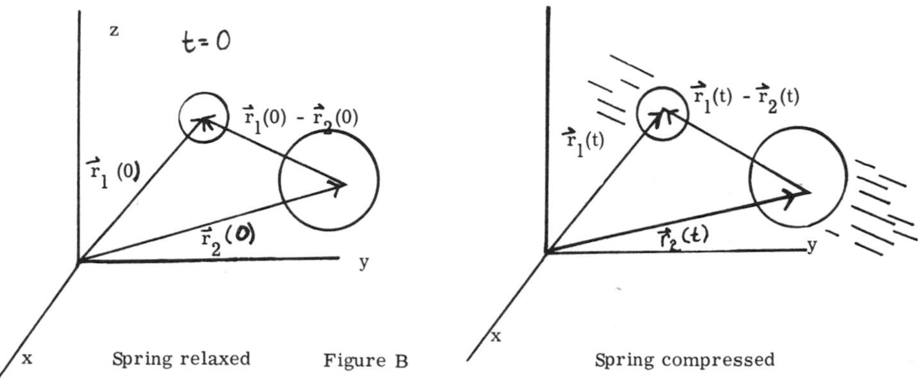

Spring relaxed Figure B Spring compressed

their centers. Then, using Newton's Second Law to relate the force on each atom to its acceleration, we obtain

$$\vec{F}_{12} = m_2 \ddot{\vec{r}}_2(t)$$
$$\vec{F}_{21} = m_1 \ddot{\vec{r}}_1(t) \tag{1}$$

where $\vec{F}_{12}$ is the force acting on atom 2 due to atom 1, and $\vec{F}_{21}$ is the force on atom 1 due to atom 2. Also, $\vec{r}_2(t)$ and $\vec{r}_1(t)$ are the initial positions of particles 2 and 1, respectively. (See figure (A)). Now, we may define the relative distance between the 2 atoms as

$$\vec{r} \equiv \vec{r}_1(t) - \vec{r}_2(t) \tag{2}$$

Looking at figure (B), we observe that, at $t = 0$,

$$\vec{r} = \vec{r}_0 = \vec{r}_1(0) - \vec{r}_2(0).$$

This is the initial relative separation of the 2 atoms. By Hooke's Law, we may write

$$\vec{F}_{12} = C\left(\vec{r} - \vec{r}_0\right)$$
$$\vec{F}_{21} = -C\left(\vec{r} - \vec{r}_0\right) \tag{3}$$

where $\vec{r} - \vec{r}_0$ is the extension of the "spring" and C is the spring constant. Note that particle 2 attracts particle 1 and vice versa. Inserting (3) in (1)

$$m_2 \ddot{\vec{r}}_2 = C\left(\vec{r} - \vec{r}_0\right) \tag{4}$$
$$m_1 \ddot{\vec{r}}_1 = -C\left(\vec{r} - \vec{r}_0\right) \tag{5}$$

Multiply (4) by m_1 and (5) by m_2 to obtain

$$m_1 m_2 \ddot{\vec{r}}_2 = m_1 C\left(\vec{r} - \vec{r}_0\right) \tag{6}$$

$$m_1 m_2 \ddot{\vec{r}}_1 = -m_2 C\left(\vec{r} - \vec{r}_0\right) \tag{7}$$

Subtracting (6) from (7)

$$m_1 m_2 \ddot{\vec{r}}_1 - m_1 m_2 \ddot{\vec{r}}_2 = -m_2 C\left(\vec{r} - \vec{r}_0\right) - m_1 C\left(\vec{r} - \vec{r}_0\right)$$

or

$$m_1 m_2\left(\ddot{\vec{r}}_1 - \ddot{\vec{r}}_2\right) = -C\left(\vec{r} - \vec{r}_0\right)(m_1 + m_2)$$

From (2)

$$\ddot{\vec{r}}_1 - \ddot{\vec{r}}_2 = \ddot{\vec{r}}$$

and

$$\frac{m_1 m_2}{m_1 + m_2} \ddot{\vec{r}} = -C\left(\vec{r} - \vec{r}_0\right)$$

Now, $m_1 m_2/m_1 + m_2$ is defined as the reduced mass u and

$$u \ddot{\vec{r}} = -C\left(\vec{r} - \vec{r}_0\right)$$

Finally

$$\ddot{\vec{r}} + \frac{C}{u}\left(\vec{r} - \vec{r}_0\right) = 0 \tag{8}$$

Redefining $\vec{r} - \vec{r}_0$ as $\vec{s}$, we note that

$$\ddot{\vec{s}} = \ddot{\vec{r}} - \ddot{\vec{r}}_0 = \ddot{\vec{r}}$$

since $\vec{r}_0$ = constant. Equation (8) now becomes

$$\ddot{\vec{s}} + \left(\frac{C}{u}\right) \vec{s} = 0$$

which is the equation of motion of a simple harmonic oscillator of angular frequency

$$\omega_0 = \sqrt{\frac{C}{u}} \tag{9}$$

It is known from spectroscopic measurements that the fundamental vibrational frequencies of the molecules HF and HCL are

$$\omega_0(\mathrm{HF}) = 7.55 \times 10^{14} \text{ rad/sec;}$$

$$\omega_0(\mathrm{HCl}) = 5.47 \times 10^{14} \text{ rad/sec.}$$

Let us use these data to compare the force constants C_{HF} and C_{HCl}. The reduced mass of HF is, in atomic mass units,

$$\frac{1}{u_{HF}} = \frac{1}{m_H} + \frac{1}{m_F} = \frac{1}{1 \text{ amu}} + \frac{1}{19 \text{ amu}} = \frac{20}{19} \text{ amu}$$

$$u_{HF} \approx .950 \text{ amu}$$

$$\frac{1}{u_{HCL}} = \frac{1}{m_H} + \frac{1}{m_{Cl}} = \frac{1}{1 \text{ amu}} + \frac{1}{35 \text{ amu}} = \frac{36}{35} \text{ amu}$$

(Here we have used the atomic mass of the most abundant isotope of chlorine, Cl^{35}.) Notice that the reduced masses are quite close to each other in value. This is because the hydrogen, being lightest, does most of the oscillating.

Now from (9) we have for the ratio of the force constants:

$$\frac{C_{HF}}{C_{HCl}} = \frac{\left(\mu\omega_0^2\right)_{HF}}{\left(\mu\omega_0^2\right)_{HCl}} \cong \frac{54.0 \times 10^{28} \text{ amu/s}^2}{29.0 \times 10^{28} \text{ amu/s}^2} \cong 1.86,$$

while for an individual force constant

$$C_{HF} = \left(54 \times 10^{28} \text{ amu/s}^2\right)\left(1.66 \times 10^{-24} \text{g/amu}\right) \approx 9 \times 10^5 \text{ dyne/cm}$$

Here we have inserted the factor which converts the mass from atomic mass units to grams.

Is this value of C reasonable? Suppose we stretch the molecule (which is about 1A or 1×10^{-8} cm in length) by 0.5 A. The work needed to do this would probably be nearly enough to break up the molecule into separate atoms of H and F. By using the formula for the potential energy of a compressed (or extended) spring, the work needed to stretch the molecule 0.5 A should be of the order of magnitude

$$\tfrac{1}{2}C\left(r - r_0\right)^2 \approx \tfrac{1}{2}\left(9 \times 10^5\right)\left(0.5 \times 10^{-8}\right)^2 \approx 1 \times 10^{-11} \text{ erg}$$

This is not unreasonable for an energy of decomposition into separate atoms. Therefore, the calculated value of C is reasonable.

CHAPTER 10

HYDROSTATICS/AEROSTATICS

DENSITY, SPECIFIC GRAVITY, PRESSURE

• PROBLEM 392

The density of a liquid can be measured by means of a "pyknometer" (see the figure). The pyknometer is a glass vessel with a ground glass stopper having a narrow hole along its axis. If you are given the mass, m_p, of the empty pyknometer, the mass $m_{p+\ell}$, of the pyknometer when filled with the liquid and the mass $m_{p+\omega}$ of the pyknometer filled with distilled water (all masses being determined at the same temperature), calculate the density of the liquid.

Solution: Let V be the volume of liquid contained by the pyknometer. Then

$$V = \frac{m_\omega}{\rho_\omega} = \frac{m_\ell}{\rho_\ell} \qquad (1)$$

where ρ_ω and ρ_ℓ are the water and the liquid densities respectively, and m_ω and m_ℓ are the masses of the water and the liquid in the pyknometer. Since

$$m_\omega = m_{p+\omega} - m_p$$

$$m_\ell = m_{p+\ell} - m_p$$

equation (1) becomes

$$V = \frac{m_{p+\omega} - m_p}{\rho_\omega} = \frac{m_{p+\ell} - m_p}{\rho_\ell} ,$$

giving ρ_ℓ in terms of ρ_ω:

$$\rho_\ell = \frac{m_{p+\ell} - m_p}{m_{p+\omega} - m_p} \ell_\omega \quad .$$

• PROBLEM 393

In order to determine their density, drops of blood

are placed in a mixture of xylene of density 0.867 $g \cdot cm^{-3}$, and bromobenzene of density 1.497 $g \cdot cm^{-3}$, the mixture being altered until the drops do not rise or sink. The mixture then contains 72% of xylene and 28% of bromobenzene by volume. What is the density of the blood?

Solution: Using the definition of density

$$\text{density} = \frac{\text{mass}}{\text{volume}}$$

every 72 cm^3 of xylene have a mass of 72 cm^3 × 0.867 $g \cdot cm^{-3}$ = 62.424 g, and every 28 cm^3 of bromobenzene have a mass of 28 cm^3 × 1.497 $gm \cdot cm^{-3}$ = 41.916 g. Thus, 100 cm^3 of the mixture have a mass of (62.424 + 41.916)g = 104.340 g. Thus the density of the mixture is 1.0434 $g \cdot cm^{-3}$.

But blood neither rises nor sinks in this mixture, showing that the blood has no net force acting on it. Thus the weight of any drop of blood is exactly equal to the upthrust acting on it. But, by Archimede's principle, the upthrust is the weight of an equal volume of mixture. Hence the blood and the mixture have the same densities; thus the density of blood is 1.0434 $g \cdot cm^{-3}$.

• PROBLEM 394

The mass of a rectangular bar of iron is 320 grams. It is 2 × 2 × 10 centimeters³. What is its specific gravity?

Solution: Specific gravity for solids is the ratio of the density of the solid to the density of water (approximately 1 gram per cubic centimeter). The specific gravity of iron is then

$$S = \frac{\rho_i}{\rho_\omega}$$

$$\text{But } \rho_i = \frac{320 \text{ gm}}{2 \times 2 \times 10 \text{ cm}^3} = 8 \text{ gm/cm}^3$$

$$\text{Since } \rho_\omega = 1 \text{ gm/cm}^3$$

$$S = \frac{8 \text{ gm/cm}^3}{1 \text{ gm/cm}^3} = 8$$

• PROBLEM 395

A water pipe in which water pressure is 80 lb/in.² springs a leak, the size of which is .01 sq in. in area. How much force is required of a patch to "stop" the leak?

Solution: This problem is quickly recognized as an application of the definition of fluid pressure.

Commencing with the definition of pressure as the ratio of the force f on an area a, and the area a, we find

$$p = \frac{f}{a}$$

It follows that: $f = pa$

Substituting values: $f = 80\ lb/in^2 \times .01\ in^2 = .8\ lb.$

• PROBLEM 396

> A piece of ice floats in a vessel filled with water. Will the water level change when the ice melts, if the final temperature of the water remains $0°C$?

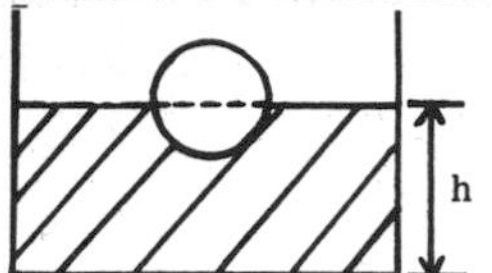

Figure A

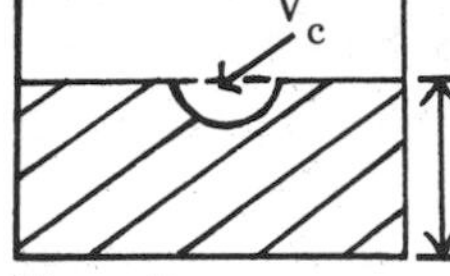

Figure B

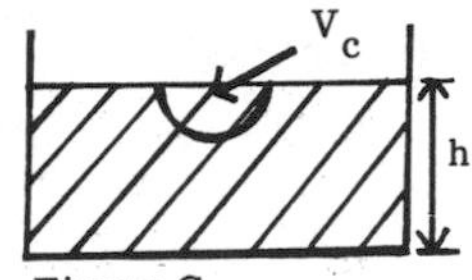

Figure C

Solution: The temperature of the system remains constant, therefore we do not expect any thermal expansion of the water. Now, suppose that somehow we were able to take the ice out of water while preserving the geometry of the water as shown in figures A and B. The volume V_c of the cavity that is going to result is the volume of the ice which was submerged in water. In order to keep the level of the water the same, the pressure we must exert on the walls of this cavity must be equal to that exerted by the weight of the ice. Therefore, we can fill the cavity with water whose weight is equal to that of ice in order to accomplish this. But, we already stated that this amount of water will have exactly the same volume as the submerged part of the ice, i.e., the volume of the cavity (Fig. C). As a result, we see that the level remains the same if the cavity is filled up by water.

When ice melts, the situation is equivalent to what has been described so far since ice becomes water upon melting and effectively fills up the volume vacated by the ice in water.

• PROBLEM 397

> A boy sits in a bus holding a balloon by a string. The bus accelerates forward. In which direction will the balloon move?

Solution: Our first guess is that the balloon moves backward. However, the balloon actually moves forward. This occurs due to the pressure gradient created by the motion of the bus. When the bus is at rest, the air molecules undergo random motions. On the average the molecules remain in one position. As the bus accelerates, the back of the bus "collects" the air molecules. The front of the bus leaves the air molecules behind. The net result is an increase in air density at the back of the bus, and a decrease in air density at the front. Just as a balloon rises due to the greater pressure at the lower end of the balloon than at the top of the balloon, similarly the greater pressure at the back of the balloon will cause it to move forward.

BUOYANCY EFFECTS

• PROBLEM 398

What is the apparent loss of weight of a cube of steel 2 in. on a side submerged in water if the weight density of H_2O is 62.4 lb/ft^3?

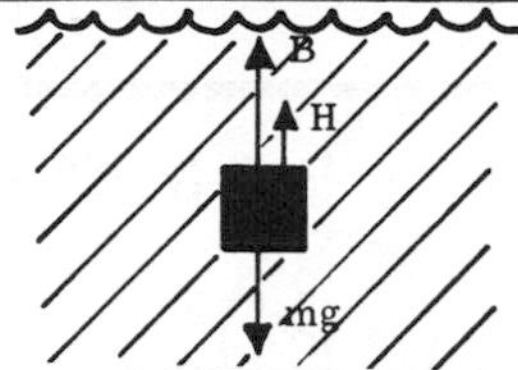

Solution: The situation is as depicted in the diagram. Assume that a diver's hand exerts an upward force H on the steel, which is just large enough to keep the block in equilibrium. In this case, from Newton's Second Law, the net force on the block is zero and

$$B + H - mg = 0 \tag{1}$$

where B is the buoyant force of the water on the steel. By Archimede's Principle, B is equal to the weight of water displaced by the block. Hence,

$$B = \rho_w gV \tag{2}$$

where V is the block's volume, and ρ_w is the density of water. Therefore, solving (1) for H, and using (2),

$$H = mg - B = mg - \rho_w gV$$

But m may be written as

$$m = \rho_s V \tag{3}$$

where ρ_s is steel's density. Finally, then,

$$H = \rho_s gV - \rho_w gV$$

But H is the apparent weight of the steel, since this is the force we exert on the block to keep it in equilibrium. The weight of the block outside the water is given by (3) as

$$mg = \rho_s gV$$

The difference between "apparent" and "actual" weights is then

$$\Delta = H - mg = \left(\rho_s gV - \rho_w gV\right) - \rho_s gV$$

$$|\Delta| = \rho_w gV$$

which is B. Hence,

$$|\Delta| = \left(62.4\ \text{lb/ft}^3\right)(2\ \text{in.})^3$$

$$= \left(62.4\ \text{lb/ft}^3\right)(1/6\ \text{ft})^3$$

$$|\Delta| = \frac{62.4}{216}\ \text{lb} = .29\ \text{lb.}$$

• PROBLEM 399

How far does a wooden (spherical) ball of specific gravity 0.4 and radius 2 feet sink in water?

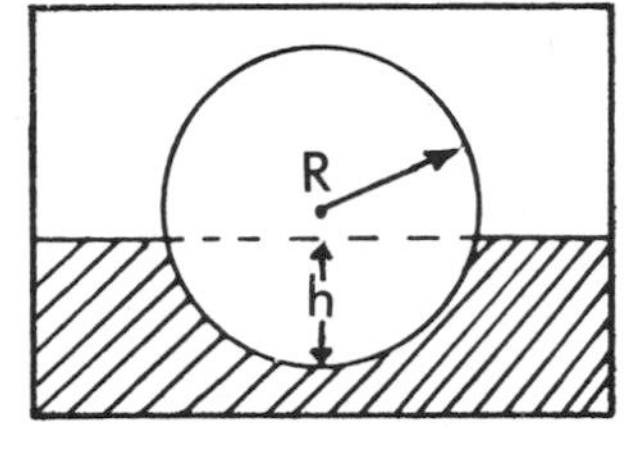

Fig. A

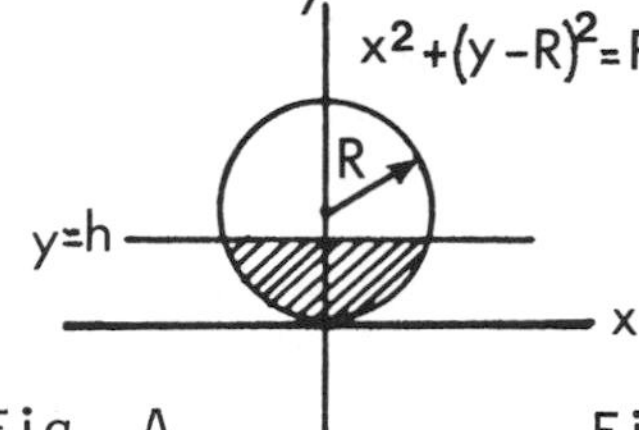

Fig. B

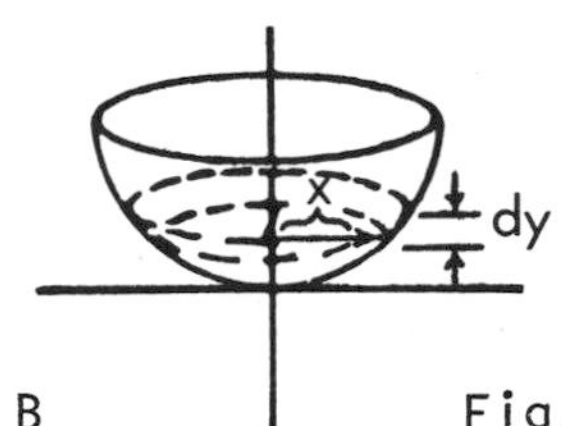

Fig. C

Solution: By "Archimedes' principle" we know that the ball will sink until it displaces a weight of water equal to the entire weight of the ball:

(weight of ball) = (weight of displaced water)

We know that:

(weight of ball) = (volume)(specific gravity)(density of water)

where the density of water w is measured in pounds per cubic foot.

We must first calculate the volume of the part of the sphere immersed in water when the sphere sinks to a depth of h, and then solve for h from the given information (figure A).

Finding this volume is equivalent to finding the volume generated by rotating the area between the curves $x^2 + (y - R)^2$ and $y = h$, about the y-axis, (see figure (B))

We note that the general formula for a circle is $(x - h)^2 + (y - k)^2 = r^2$, where (h,k) are the coordinates of its center and r is the length of its radius. In this case the coordinates of the center are $(0,R)$, and $r = R$.

Recall that (see figure (C)) :

$$dV = \pi x^2\,dy = \pi[R^2 - (y - R)^2]^2 dy = \pi(2Ry - y^2)dy$$

where dV is the differential cylindrical volume element, x being its radius and dy its height. Finally, we integrate dV between $y = 0$ and $y = h$.

$$V = \pi\int_0^h (2Ry - y^2)dy$$

$$= \pi\left[2R\frac{y^2}{2} - \frac{y^3}{3}\right]_0^h = \pi\left(Rh^2 - \frac{h^3}{3}\right) = \pi h^2\left(R - \frac{h}{3}\right)$$

Hence, from the equation for the weight of the ball:

(weight of ball) = (volume of submerged portion)(density of water)

$$\left(\frac{4}{3}\pi R^3\right)(0.4)w = \pi h^2\left(R - \frac{h}{3}\right)w$$

$$\frac{4}{3}(2)^3(0.4) = h^2\left(2 - \frac{h}{3}\right)$$

$$h^3 - 6h^2 + 12.8 = 0$$

We find by synthetic division that $h \approx 1.75$ feet.

• PROBLEM 400

Army engineers have thrown a pontoon bridge 10 ft in width over a river 50 yd wide. When twelve identical trucks cross the river simultaneously the bridge sinks 1 ft. What is the weight of one truck? The density of water is 1.94 $slugs \cdot ft^{-3}$.

Solution: When the trucks are on the bridge, the extra volume of the bridge immersed is 1 ft deep, 10 ft wide, and 50 yd = 150 ft long, i.e., 1500 ft^3. The upthrust on this extra volume immersed in water is the weight of an equal volume of water according to Archimedes' principle. Thus

$$U = v\rho_w g = 1500\ ft^3 \times 1.94\ slugs \cdot ft^{-3} \times 32\ ft \cdot s^{-2}$$

$$= 9.312 \times 10^4\ lb.$$

where ρ_w is the density of water, and g is the gravitational acceleration. But this upthrust just balances the weight of the twelve trucks. Hence one truck has a weight

$$W = \frac{U}{12} = \frac{9.312 \times 10^4\ lb}{12} = 7760\ lb.$$

• PROBLEM 401

How many cubic feet of life preserver of specific gravity .3, when worn by a boy of weight 125 lb and having a specific gravity .9, will just support him $\frac{8}{10}$ submerged in fresh water of which 1 cu ft weighs 62.4 lb?

Solution: In this problem the boy b is $\frac{8}{10}$ submerged while the life preserver p must be completely submerged to give the maximum buoyancy.

The weight of the boy W_b and the weight of the preserver W_p acting downward are just balanced by the buoyant force of the preserver B_p and the buoyant force of the boy B_b.

$$B_b + B_p = W_b + W_p \tag{1}$$

B_b and B_p are equal to the weight of fluid displaced by the boy and the preserver respectively. Hence

$$B_b = Mg$$

where M is the mass of the water displaced by the boy. Since density d = M/V and the volume of the displaced water V = 8/10 V_b where V_b is the volume of the boy, then

$$B_b = \left(\frac{8}{10} V_b\right) d_w g$$

where d_w is the density of water.

The weight of the boy is

$$W_b = \left(V_b d_b\right) g = 125 \text{ lb}$$

where $V_b d_b$ is the mass of the boy and d_b is the density of the boy.

Similarly,

$$B_p = V_p d_w g \qquad \text{and} \qquad W_p = V_p d_p g$$

where V_p is the volume of fluid displaced by the preserver, and d_p is the density of the preserver.

$$V_b = \frac{W_b}{g d_b}$$

Now, $$dw = \frac{\text{mass of 1 cu ft of water}}{\text{1 cu ft of water}}$$

$$= \frac{\dfrac{\text{weight of 1 cu ft of water}}{g}}{\text{1 cu ft of water}}$$

$$= \frac{62.4 \text{ lb}}{\text{1 cu ft of water}} \times \frac{1}{g}$$

Also, the specific gravity (or relative density) of the preserver with respect to water

$$S_p = \frac{d_p}{d_w} = \frac{3}{10}\ ; \quad \text{and} \quad S_{boy} = \frac{d_b}{d_w} = \frac{9}{10}$$

Therefore, equation (1) becomes

$$\therefore \quad \frac{8}{10} V_b d_w g + V_p d_w g = W_b + V_p d_p g$$

$$\frac{8}{10}\frac{125}{g d_b} d_w g + V_p d_w g = 125 + V_p \frac{3}{10} d_w g$$

$$V_p = \frac{\frac{8}{10}(125)\frac{d_w}{d_b} - 125}{\frac{3}{10} d_w g - d_w g} = \frac{\frac{8}{10}(125)\frac{1}{S_b} - 125}{-\frac{7}{10} d_w g}$$

$$= \frac{\frac{8}{10}\left(\frac{\frac{125}{9}}{\frac{}{10}}\right) - 125}{-\frac{7}{10}\frac{62.4}{\not g}\not g} = \frac{125 - \frac{8}{9}(125)}{\frac{7}{10}(62.4)}$$

$$= \frac{\frac{1}{9}(125)}{\frac{7}{10}(62.4)} = \frac{13.9}{43.7} = .32 \text{ cu ft (approx)}.$$

• PROBLEM 402

A barge of mass 15,000 kg, made from metal of density 7500 $kg \cdot m^{-3}$, is being loaded in a closed dock of surface area 6633 m^2 with ore of density 3 $g \cdot cm^{-3}$. When 80,000 kg of ore are aboard, the barge sinks. How does the water level in the dock alter? The area of the barge is assumed negligible in comparison with the area of the dock.

Solution: Before sinking the total mass of barge plus load was 95,000 kg. Since the barge floated, the upthrust of the water must have equaled the weight of 95,000 kg. The mass of displaced water was thus 95,000 kg and, since the density of water is 10^3 kg/m^3 the volume of the barge is

$$V = \frac{m}{\rho}$$

where m is the mass of the barge plus its load. Hence

$$V = \frac{95 \times 10^3 \text{ kg}}{10^3 \text{ kg/m}^3} = 95 \text{ m}^3$$

The volume of the material of the barge is, similarly, 15,000 kg/7500 $kg \cdot m^{-3}$ = 2 m^3, and the volume of the ore density 3 $g \cdot cm^{-3} = 3 \times 10^3$ $kg \cdot m^{-3}$ is $\frac{80}{3} = 26\frac{2}{3}$ m^3. The total volume occupied by the metal of the barge and the ore in the water after sinking is thus 28 2/3 m^3. This is the amount of displaced water after the barge sinks.

The displaced water has therefore decreased by 66 1/3 m^3. The water level in the dock thus falls by an amount h, equal to the decrease in volume divided by the surface area of the dock, the surface area of the barge being negligible. Therefore

$$h = \frac{66\ 1/3}{6633} = \frac{1}{100} \text{ m} = 1 \text{ cm}.$$

• PROBLEM 403

When a metal cylinder of height 14 cm. which is floating upright in mercurcy is set into vertical oscillation, the period of the motion is found to be .56 s. What is the density of the metal? The density of mercury is 13,600 $kg \cdot m^{-3}$ and g is π^2 $m \cdot s^{-2}$.

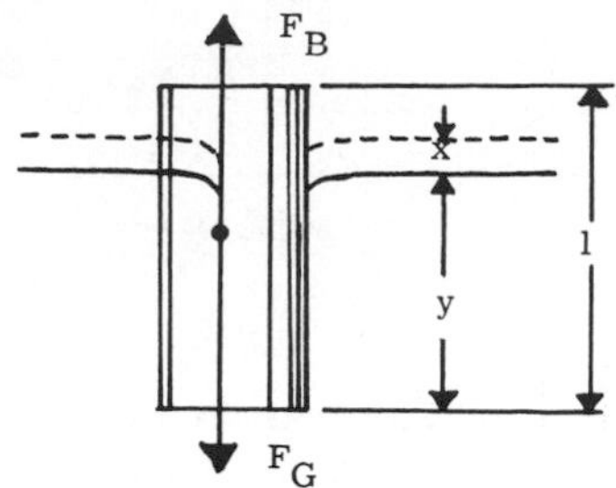

Solution: Let the cylinder have a cross-sectional area A, length l, and density ρ, and let it float in the mercury of density ρ' immersed to a height y. In this position, shown by the solid line in the diagram, the cylinder is in equilibrium. Hence, the net force on the cylinder, composed of its weight (F_G) and the buoyant force (F_B) is zero. Then, taking the positive direction downward,

$$F_G - F_B = 0$$

or $$F_G = F_B \tag{1}$$

But $F_G = m_c\, g$

where m_c is the cylinder mass. Since

$$\rho = \frac{m_c}{\text{Volume of cylinder (V)}}$$

$$m_c = \rho V = \rho A \ell$$

and $$F_G = \rho A \ell g \tag{2}$$

The buoyant force is equal to the weight of fluid displaced by the object. Hence

$$F_B = m_m\, g$$

where m_m is the mass of mercury displaced. But

$$m_m = \rho'\, V'$$

where V' is the fluid volume displaced. Hence,

$$m_m = \rho'\, A(\ell - y)$$

and $$F_B = \rho'\, A(\ell - y)g \tag{3}$$

Using (3) and (2) in (1)

$$\rho A \ell g = \rho'\, Ayg$$

If the cylinder is pushed in a further distance x, the upthrust is greater than the weight, and there is a restoring force attempting to return the cylinder to its original position. If a is the downward acceleration, we find, from Newton's Second Law

$$F_{net} = m_c a$$

Again, $F_{net} = F_G - F_B = m_c a$

or $\rho A\ell g - \rho' A(y + x)g = \rho A\ell a$

Since $\rho A\ell g = \rho' Ayg$

$$- \rho' Axg = \rho A\ell a$$

and $a = -\dfrac{\rho' g}{\rho\ell} x$

Comparing this with the equation of motion of a simple harmonic oscillator, we realize that

$$\omega^2 = \frac{\rho' g}{\rho \ell}$$

Since $T = 2\pi/\omega$, where T and ω are the period and angular frequency of the motion, we note that

$$\omega = 2\pi/T$$

and $\dfrac{4\pi^2}{T^2} = \dfrac{\rho' g}{\rho\ell}$

$$\rho = \frac{\rho' g T^2}{4\pi^2 \ell}$$

$$= \frac{(13,600 \text{ kg} \cdot \text{m}^{-3})(\pi^2 \text{ m} \cdot \text{s}^{-2})(.56)^2 \text{ s}^2}{(4\pi^2)\ (.14 \text{ m})}$$

$$\rho = 7616 \text{ kg} \cdot \text{m}^{-3}.$$

• PROBLEM 404

A rectangular post 4 in. thick is floating in a pond with three-quarters of its volume immersed. An oil tanker skids off the road and ends up overturned at the edge of the pond with oil of 1.26 slugs $\cdot$ ft^{-3} density leaking from it into the water. When the upper face of the post is just level with the surface of the liquid, what is the depth of the oil layer? What happens if more oil keeps pouring into the pond?

Solution: Before the oil is spilled, the post is floating in the water symmetrically. Let its cross-sectional area be A and its density ρ. Then, if three-quarters of the volume is immersed, only 1 in. is above the surface and 3 in. below the surface. The weight downward, F_G, and the buoyant force F_B balance, since the post is in equilibrium vertically. Hence if ρ_0

is the density of water, we may write

$$F_G - F_B = 0$$

$$\rho Ag \times 4" - \rho_0 Ag \times 3" = 0 \qquad (1)$$

or $\quad \dfrac{\rho}{\rho_0} = \dfrac{3}{4}$

Note that the buoyant force is equal to the weight of water displaced by the post. (We have taken the positive direction downward).

When the oil density ρ' pours on, it stays above the water. The water extends up to a height y and the oil fills the other (4 in. - y). Since equilibrium is still achieved, the weight downward must equal the sum of the two buoyant forces due to the water and the oil. Hence $\rho Ag \times 4" = \rho_0 Agy + \rho' Ag(4" - y)$. Using (1)

$$\rho \times 4" = \rho_0 \times 3" = \rho_0 y + \rho'(4" - y).$$

$$\therefore \quad y = \frac{\rho_0 \times 3" - \rho' \times 4"}{\rho_0 - \rho'}$$

$$= \frac{1.94 \text{ slugs} \cdot \text{ft}^{-3} \times 3" - 1.26 \text{ slugs} \cdot \text{ft}^{-3} \times 4"}{(1.94 - 1.26) \text{ slugs} \cdot \text{ft}^{-3}}$$

$$= \frac{0.78}{0.68}" = 1.15"$$

Thus the depth of the oil layer is 2.85".

If oil keeps pouring onto the pond, the post must stay as it is with respect to the water-oil interface. While the oil poured on initially, the post rose from the water to compensate for the extra upthrust from the oil by diminishing the upthrust from the water. Once the post is totally immersed, it is at the correct position with respect to the water-oil interface for the sum of the two upthrusts to equal the weight. Adding further oil cannot alter this.

• PROBLEM 405

Brass weights are used in weighing an aluminum cylinder whose approximate mass is 89 gm. What error is introduced if the buoyant effect of air ($\rho = 0.0013$ gm/cm^3) is neglected?

$\rho_{brass} = 8.9$ gm/cm^3

$\rho_{Al} = 2.7$ gm/cm^3

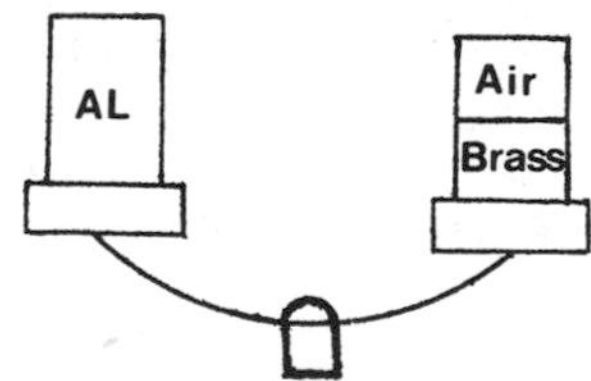

Solution: If the objects on the pans occupy different volumes, then the volume, and therefore the weight of the air is different on the two objects and must be accounted for. The additional weight on the object with less volume is just equal to the weight of the additional volume of air.

$$V = \frac{m}{\rho}$$

$$V_B = \frac{89 \text{ gm}}{8.9 \text{ gm/cm}^3} = 10 \text{ cm}^3$$

$$V_{Al} = \frac{89 \text{ gm}}{2.7 \text{ gm/cm}^3} = 33 \text{ cm}^3$$

The difference in volume V of air displaced on the two pans of the balance is

$$V = V_{Al} - V_B = 33 \text{ cm}^3 - 10 \text{ cm}^3 = 23 \text{ cm}^3$$

Hence, the mass error

$$m = V\rho = 23 \text{ cm}^3 \times 0.0013 \text{ gm/cm}^3 = 0.030 \text{ gm}$$

The error introduced is only a small fraction of the total mass, but in many experiments where accuracy is important an error of 0.030 gm in 89 gm is too great to allow.

• PROBLEM 406

A tank of water is placed on a scale, which registers its weight as W = Mg. What is the change in the scale reading if a block of steel, of weight w = mg, is lowered into the tank, as shown in figure (B)?

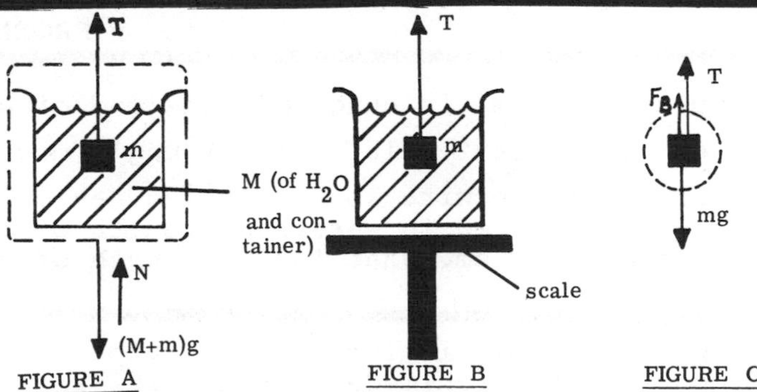

Solution: The figure shows the situation. The steel is held in the water by a string with tension T. We wish to find the force exerted by the system on the scale. By Newton's Third Law, this is equal in magnitude to the force exerted by the scale on the system, shown in figure (A). Since this system is in equilibrium, the net force acting on it is zero and

$$T + N - (M + m)g = 0$$

or $$N = (M + m)g - T \qquad (1)$$

However, in order to solve for N, we must know T. We can obtain T by applying Newton's Second Law to the system shown in figure (C). Since this system is in equilibrium, we may write

$$T + F_B - mg = 0$$

where F_B is the buoyant force on the block. By Archimede's Principle, F_B is equal to the weight of water displaced by the steel. Hence,

$$F_B = \rho_w gV$$

where V is the volume of the cube and ρ_w is the density of water. Then,

$$T = mg - F_B = mg - \rho_w gV \qquad (2)$$

Using (2) in (1),

$$N = (M + m)g + \rho_w gV - mg$$

or $N = Mg + \rho_w gV$

This is the "weight" registered by the scale. If the tank were weighed without the steel, we'd find

$$N' = Mg$$

The difference in these 2 readings is

$$N - N' = Mg + \rho_w gV - Mg = \rho_w gV$$

or the buoyant force.

• PROBLEM 407

A ball of volume 500 cm^3 is hung from the end of a wire of cross-sectional area 2×10^{-3} cm^2. Young's modulus for the material of the wire is 7×10^{11} $dynes \cdot cm^{-2}$. When the ball is immersed in water the length of the wire decreases by 0.05 cm. What is the length of the wire?

Solution: When the ball is immersed in water, it suffers (according to Archimede's Principle) an upthrust equal to the weight of a similar volume of water. Thus immersion causes a compressive force on the wire of magnitude

$$F = 500\ cm^3 \times \rho g$$

where ρ is the density of water. Hence

$$F = 500\ cm^3 \times 1\ g \cdot cm^{-3} \times 981\ cm \cdot s^{-2} = 49 \times 10^4\ dynes.$$

But Young's modulus for the wire is given by the formula $Y = (F/A)(\Delta\ell/\ell_0)$, where $\Delta\ell/\ell_0$ is the fractional change in length of the wire, A is the latter's cross-sectional area, and F is the force normal to the cross-section of the wire. Hence

$$\ell_0 = \frac{AY\Delta\ell}{F}$$

$$= \frac{2 \times 10^{-3}\ \text{cm}^2 \times 7 \times 10^{11}\ \text{dynes}\cdot\text{cm}^{-2} \times 5 \times 10^{-2}\ \text{cm}}{49 \times 10^4\ \text{dynes}}$$

$$= 142.9\ \text{cm}.$$

FLUID FORCES

• PROBLEM 408

Find the force acting on the bottom of an aquarium having a base 1 foot by 2 feet and containing water to a depth of one foot.

Solution: Pressure, p, is given by height times density (when density is weight per volume). The density of the water is $\frac{62.4\ \text{lb}}{\text{ft}^3}$. Therefore,

$$p = hw = 1\ \text{ft} \times \frac{62.4\ \text{lb}}{\text{ft}^3} = 62.4\ \frac{\text{lb}}{\text{ft}^2}$$

Force = pressure × Area of bottom, therefore,

$$F = pA = 62.4\ \frac{\text{lb}}{\text{ft}^2} \times (1\ \text{ft} \times 2\ \text{ft}) = 124.8\ \text{lb}.$$

Note that the shape of the vessel is not considered in this solution. It would be the same even if the sides were sloping outward or inward.

• PROBLEM 409

Find the pressure due to a column of mercury 74.0 cm high.

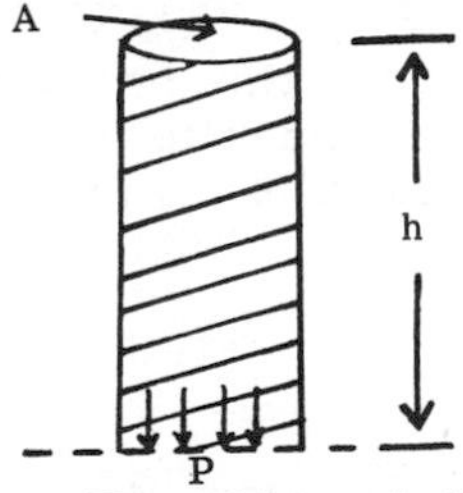

Solution: The total force F acting at the bottom of the column of mercury is due to the weight of the mercury. Or, by Newton's Second Law

$$F = W = mg.$$

Since $\quad \text{Density}(\rho) = \frac{\text{mass}(m)}{\text{volume}(V)}$

and $V = Ah$ where A is the cross sectional area of the column and h is its height. We then have

$$F = \rho Vg = \rho Ahg$$

The pressure P at the bottom of the column is defined as

$$P = \frac{F}{A} = \frac{pAhg}{A} = hPg =$$

$$= (0.740\text{m})\left(1.36 \times 10^4 \text{ kg/m}^3\right)\left(9.80\text{m/sec}^2\right)$$

$$= 9.86 \times 10^4 \text{ nt/m}^2 .$$

In the equation derived above, the pressure is that due to the liquid alone. If there is a pressure on the surface of the liquid, this pressure must be added to that due to the liquid to find the pressure at a given level. The pressure at any level in the liquid is then

$$P = P_s + hpg$$

where P_s is the pressure at the surface of the liquid.

• PROBLEM 410

A rectangular tank 6.0 by 8.0 ft is filled with gasoline to a depth of 8.0 ft. The pressure at the surface of the gasoline is 14.7 lb/in^2. (The density of gasoline is 1.325 sl/f^3). Find the pressure at the bottom of the tank and the force exerted on the bottom.

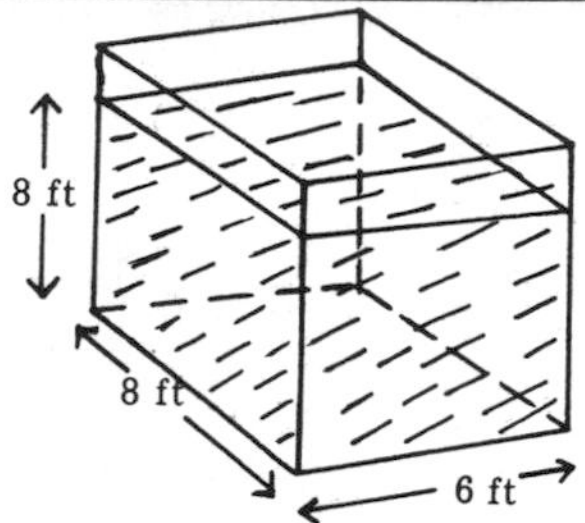

Solution: The total pressure at the tank's bottom is the sum of the air pressure at the surface of the fluid and the pressure due to the gasoline above the tank bottom:

$$P_{air} = 14.7 \quad \text{lb/in}^2$$

Since 1 lb/in^2 = 144 lb/f^2

$$P_{air} = 14.7 \text{ lb/in}^2 = (14.7)(144 \text{ lb/f}^2) = 2120 \text{ lb/f}^2 \quad (1)$$

To find the pressure on the bottom of the tank due to the gasoline, we note that the pressure is equal to the force on the bottom of the tank divided by the area of the bottom

$$P_{gas} = \frac{F}{A}$$

But $F_{gas} = \rho gV$ where ρ is the density of gasoline, g is 9.8 m/s^2, and V is the volume of the gasoline in the tank. Hence

$$P_{gas} = \frac{\rho gV}{A}$$

But V = hA, where h is the height of the gasoline in the tank. Therefore

$$P_{gas} = \rho gh = (1.313\ sl/f^3)(32\ f/s^2)(8\ f)$$

$$P_{gas} = 336\ lb/f^2 \qquad (2)$$

Hence, using (1) and (2)

$$P_{total} = (336 + 2120)lb/f^2$$

$$P_{total} = 2456\ lb/f^2$$

Noting that

$$P_{total} = \frac{F_{total}}{A}$$

and $$F_{total} = P_{total}\ A$$

$$= (2456\ lb/f^2)(48\ f^2)$$

$$= 117888\ lb$$

• PROBLEM 411

How much pressure is needed to raise water to the top of the Empire State Building, which is 1250 feet high?

Solution: Pressure is given by height times density (when density is weight per volume). This is seen from the diagram. Since pressure is force per unit area, the force the column of water exerts is equal to its height times the density of the material.

$$p = hw = 1250\ ft \times \frac{62.4\ lb}{ft^3} \qquad \text{or}$$

$$= \frac{78,000\ lb}{ft^2} \times \frac{1\ ft^2}{144\ in.^2} = 542\ lb/in.^2$$

• PROBLEM 412

A capillary tube of length 50 cm is closed at both ends. It contains dry air at each end separated by a mercury column 10 cm long. With the tube horizontal, the air columns are both 20 cm long, but with the tube vertical the columns are 15 cm and 25 cm long. What is the pressure in the capillary tube when it is horizontal?

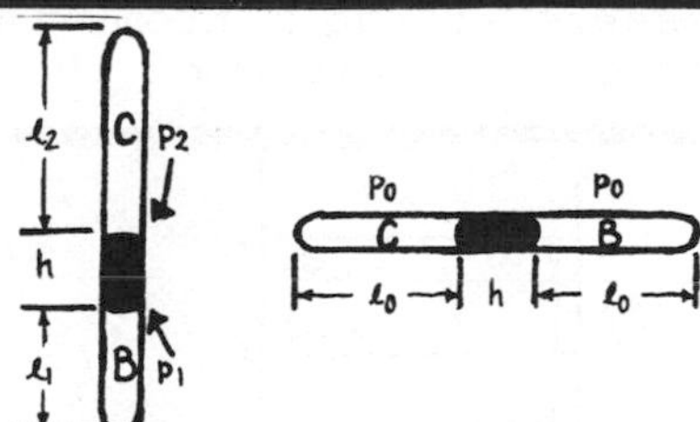

Solution: When the mercury column is vertical, the pressure on the gas in the two parts is as shown in the diagram, where p_1 is the pressure at the foot of the mercury column and p_2 the pressure at the top. But the difference in pressure at two levels in a vertical column of liquid is known from the laws of hydrostatic pressure. Thus measuring distance from the top of the mercury colum,

$$p_2 = p_2$$

and $p_1 = \rho g(h) + p_2$

whence $p_2 - p_1 = -\rho gh$

Here, ρ is the density of mercury.

Applying Boyle's law to section C of the gas when the capillary is in its 2 positions, we obtain

$$p_1 A\ell_1 = p_0 A\ell_0$$

Similarly, for section B

$$p_2 A\ell_2 = p_0 A\ell_0$$

where p_0 and ℓ_0 refer to conditions when the tube is horizontal. Thus

$$p_1 = p_0 \frac{\ell_0}{\ell_1} \quad \text{and} \quad p_2 = p_0 \frac{\ell_0}{\ell_2} .$$

$$\therefore \quad p_1 - p_2 = \rho gh = p_0 \ell_0 \left(\frac{1}{\ell_1} - \frac{1}{\ell_2}\right) = p_0 \ell_0 \left(\frac{\ell_2 - \ell_1}{\ell_1 \ell_2}\right)$$

$$\therefore \quad p_0 = \frac{\rho gh \ \ell_1 \ell_2}{\ell_0 (\ell_2 - \ell_1)}$$

$$\therefore \quad \frac{p_0}{\rho g} = \frac{\ell_1 \ell_2}{\ell_0 (\ell_2 - \ell_1)} h = \frac{15 \text{ cm} \times 25 \text{ cm}}{20 \text{ cm } (25 - 15)\text{cm}} \times 10 \text{ cm}$$

$$= 18.75 \text{ cm of mercury.}$$

• PROBLEM 413

A rectangular cistern 6 ft × 8 ft is filled to a depth of 2 ft with water. On top of the water is a layer of oil 3 ft deep. The specific gravity of the oil is .6. What is the absolute pressure at the bottom, and what is the total thrust exerted on the bottom of the cistern?

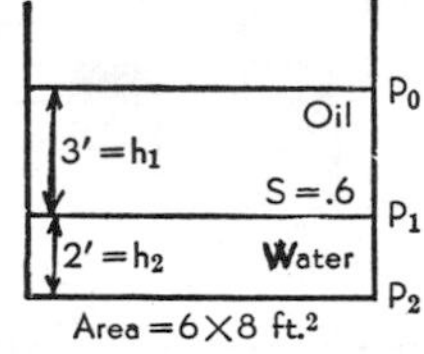

Solution: The total force F acting at the bottom of the cistern is the sum of the weights of the water Wg, the oil W_0, and the air in the atmosphere above the cistern $\left(F_{atm}\right)$. Since

$$\text{Density (d)} = \frac{\text{Mass}}{\text{Volume}} \quad \text{and} \quad \text{Pressure} = \frac{\text{Force}}{\text{Area}}$$

Then

$$F = M_w g + M_0 g + F_{atm} \quad = d_w V_w g + d_0 V_0 g + P_{atm} A$$

where V_w and V_0 are the volumes of water and oil respectively, and A is the cross sectional area of the cistern.

$$V_w = h_2 A$$

$$V_0 = h_1 A$$

Therefore $F = \left(d_w h_2 g + d_0 h_1 g + P_{atm}\right) A$

$$d_w = \frac{62.4 \text{ slug}}{32 \text{ ft}^3}$$

By definition of specific gravity (or relative density) of oil

$$S_0 = \frac{d_0}{d_w}$$

Since we are given that $S_0 = .6$ we have

$$d_0 = .6\, d_w = (.6)\left(\frac{62.4 \text{ slug}}{32 \text{ ft}^3}\right)$$

Also $P_{atm} = 14.7 \text{ lb/in}^2 = 14.7 \text{ lb/in}^2 \times 144 \text{ in}^2/1 \text{ ft}^2$

$h_1 = 3$ ft and $h_2 = 2$ ft

Therefore

$$F = \left[\left(\frac{62.4 \text{ slug}}{32 \text{ ft}^3}\right)(2 \text{ ft})\left(32 \text{ ft/sec}^2\right) + .6\left(\frac{62.4 \text{ slug}}{32 \text{ ft}^3}\right)\left(32 \text{ ft/sec}^2\right) + (14.7)\ (144)\text{lb/ft}^2\right] A$$

or $F = \left(2357 \text{ lb/ft}^2\right) A$

$$P_{bottom} = \frac{F}{A} = 2357 \text{ lb/ft}^2$$

Since $A = 6 \text{ ft} \times 8 \text{ ft}$

$$F = \left(2357 \text{ lb/ft}^2\right)\left(6 \times 8 \text{ ft}^2\right) = 113{,}000 \text{ lb.}$$

• PROBLEM 414

What is the force due to the liquid only acting on a circular plate 2 in. in diameter which covers a hole in the bottom of a tank of oil 4 ft high, if the specific gravity of oil is .5?

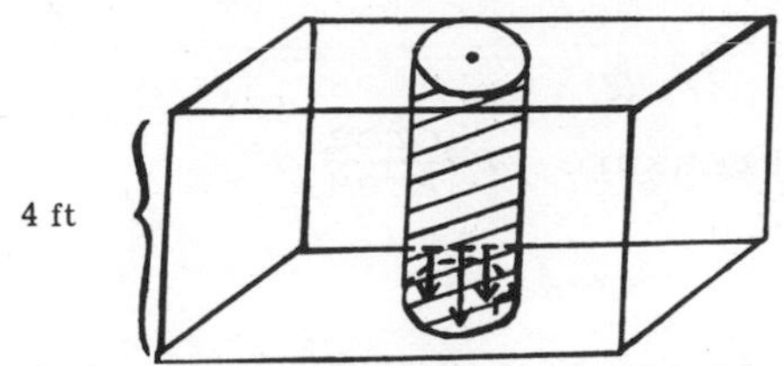

The force on the circular plate is due to the shaded cylinder of fluid.

Solution: Since the liquid in the tank is in equilibrium, it can exert only a vertical force on the bottom of the tank, as shown in the figure. Furthermore, the net force on the bottom surface of the tank is due only to the weight of the water above this surface. Hence,

$$F_{net} = Mg \tag{1}$$

where M is the mass of fluid in the tank. Since the density of the fluid is

$$\rho = \frac{M}{V}$$

where V is the tank volume, we obtain

$$M = \rho V$$

and

$$F_{net} = \rho g V \tag{2}$$

The force on the circular plate of radius r is, using (2)

$$F_{plate} = F_{net}\frac{\pi r^2}{A} = \rho g V\left(\frac{\pi r^2}{A}\right) \tag{3}$$

where A is the area of the tank bottom. We may write the volume of the tank as

$$V = hA \tag{4}$$

Here, **h** is the depth of fluid in the tank. Combining (4) and (3)

$$F_{plate} = \rho g h A \frac{\left(\pi r^2\right)}{A} = \pi \rho g h r^2$$

$$F_{plate} = \pi \rho g h r^2$$

Now, the specific gravity of a substance, δ, is defined as

$$\delta = \frac{\rho}{\rho_w}$$

where ρ' is the density of the substance and ρ_w is water's density. Hence

$$F_{plate} = \pi\ \rho_w\ \delta\ g h r^2$$

$$F_{plate} = (3.14)\left(1.94\ sl/ft^3\right)(.5)\left(32\ ft/s^2\right)(4\ ft)\left(1\ in^2\right)$$

In order to keep our units consistent,

$$1\ in = 1/12\ ft$$

$$1\ in^2 = 1/144\ ft^2$$

whence

$$F_{plate} = (3.14)\left(1.94\ sl/ft^3\right)(.5)\left(32\ ft/s^2\right)(4\ ft)\left(1/144\ ft^2\right)$$
$$= 2.71\ lb.$$

• PROBLEM 415

A triangular plate is immersed in water (of density ρ) with one vertex at the surface and the others at depths of 6 in. and 12 in. What is the thrust on the plate due to the pressure of the water only? Its areas is 63 in^2. (See figure (a)).

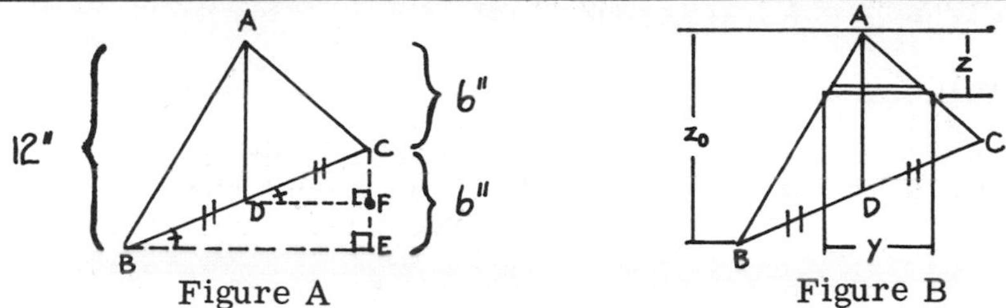

Figure A Figure B

Solution: At depth z from the water's surface, the pressure is $g\rho z$, the symbols having their usual significance. The total thrust on the small element, parallel to the surface, shown in figure (a) is

$$dF = g\rho zy\,dz.$$

The total thrust on the plate is found by summing this differential element of force over the entire triangle.

$$F = \int_0^{z_0} g\rho yz\,dz$$

$$= g\rho \left[\frac{\int_0^{z_0} \rho' yz\,dz}{\int_0^{z_0} \rho' y\,dz} \right] \times \int_0^{z_0} y\,dz \qquad \text{where}$$

ρ' is the density of the plate material.

Here, $\int_0^{z_0} \rho' y\,z\,dz \Big/ \int_0^{z_0} \rho' y\,dz$ is the location of the plate's center of mass relative to the water's surface. $\int_0^{z_0} y\,dz$ is the area of the plate.

The total thrust on the plate is thus seen to be the pressure at the center of mass of the plate multiplied by the area of the plate. This is a general result for all plates, as can be seen from the general nature of the derivation.

In the particular case of the triangular plate, the area of 63 in^2 = 63/144 ft^2 is given. The center of mass of a triangular plate is two-thirds of the way from a vertex to the middle of the opposite side. From figure (b), we see that triangles BEC and DFC are similar. Hence

$$\frac{CF}{CE} = \frac{CD}{CB}$$

$$CF = \left(\frac{CD}{CB}\right) CE$$

Since D is the mid-point of BC

$$CF = (\tfrac{1}{2})CE = \tfrac{1}{2}(6") = 3"$$

Hence, D is 9" below the water's surface. But the center of mass is two-thirds of AD from A and must be 6 in. = ½ ft from the surface. In this case, therefore,

$$F = g\rho \,\{\text{location of C.M.}\} \times \{\text{area of plate}\}$$

$$= 32 \text{ ft/s}^2 \times 1.94 \text{ sl/ft}^3 \times \tfrac{1}{2} \text{ ft} \times 63/144 \text{ ft}^2$$

$$= 15.58 \text{ lb}$$

where we used the fact that $\rho = 1.94$ sl/ft^3 for water.

• PROBLEM 416

Compute the atmospheric pressure on a day when the height of the barometer is 76.0 cm.

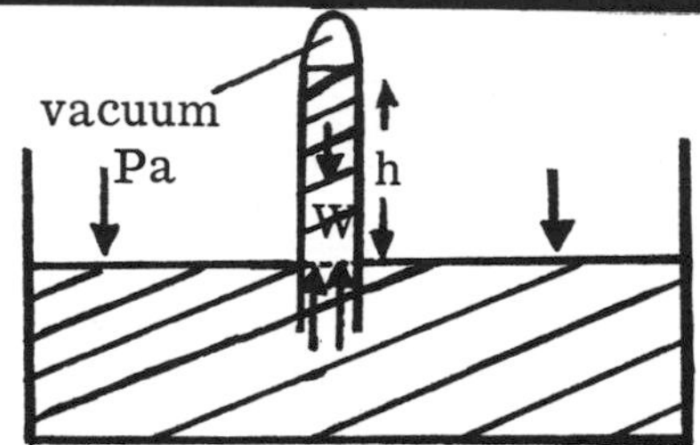

Solution: The height of the mercury column of the barometer depends on density ρ and g as well as on the atmospheric pressure. Hence both the density of mercury and the local acceleration of gravity must be known. The density varies with the temperature, and g with the latitude and elevation above sea level. All accurate barometers are provided with a thermometer and with a table or chart from which corrections for temperature and elevation can be found. Let us assume $g = 980$ cm/sec^2 and $p = 13.6$ gm/cm^3. The pressure due to the atmosphere supports the weight of mercury in the column of the barometer (see the figure). If the cross sectional area of the column is A, then the weight of mercury in the column is

$$W = mg$$

where m is the mass of the mercury. Since

$$\text{Density } (\rho) = \frac{\text{mass}}{\text{volume}}$$

then

$$W = \rho(Ah)g$$

where V = Ah, h being the height of mercury in the column. Therefore

$$\frac{W}{A} = \rho gh$$

is the pressure due to the weight of the mercury acting downward. It must equal p_a for equilibrium to be maintained in the fluid. (see figure). Hence

$$p_a = pgh = 13.6 \frac{\text{gm}}{\text{cm}^3} \times 980 \frac{\text{cm}}{\text{sec}^2} \times 76 \text{ cm}$$

$$= 1{,}013{,}000 \frac{\text{dynes}}{\text{cm}^2}$$

(about a million dynes per square centimeter). In British engineering units,

$$76 \text{ cm} = 30 \text{ in.} = 2.5 \text{ ft},$$

$$\rho g = 850 \frac{\text{lb}}{\text{ft}^3}$$

$$p_a = 2120 \frac{\text{lb}}{\text{ft}^2} = 14.7 \frac{\text{lb}}{\text{in}^2} \ .$$

• PROBLEM 417

A horizontal capillary tube closed at one end contains a column of air imprisoned by means of a small volume of water. At 7°C and a barometric pressure of 76.0 cm of mercury, the length of the air column is 15.0 cm. What is the length at 17°C if the saturation pressures of water vapor at 7°C and 17°C are 0.75 cm and 1.42 cm of mercury, respectively?

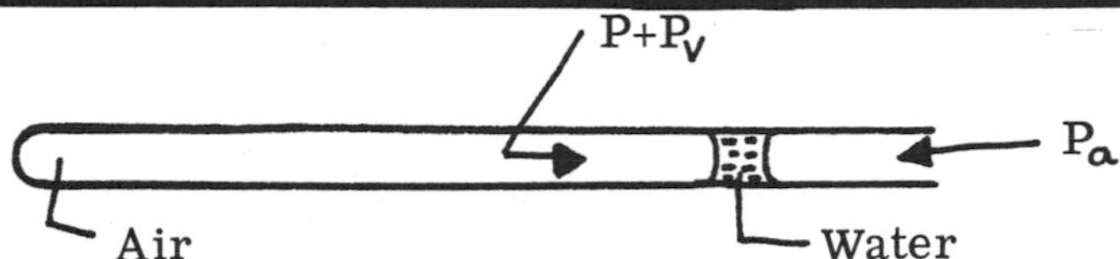

Solution. Since the tube is horizontal and the pressure at the open end of the water column is always atmospheric, the pressure at the closed end of the water column is also always atmospheric. The pressure in the moist air is made up of the partial pressures of air and of water vapor. When the equilibrium between the liquid and gas phases of a liquid is reached in a closed volume, the pressure of the vapor acting on the liquid equals the saturated vapor pressure. The evaporation process effectively stops once this pressure is attained by the vapor. The air and water vapor act on the liquid surface independently, therefore the pressure on the inner surface of the water is the sum of the pressures p and p_V, due to the air and vapor in the tube, respectively (as shown in the figure).

$$p_a = p + p_V .$$

Hence, for the two cases, the air pressure inside is

$$p = (76.00 - 0.75) \text{ cm Hg at } 7°\text{C},$$

and $$p' = (76.00 - 1.42) \text{cm Hg at } 17°\text{C}.$$

Applying the gas law to the air alone, since the air and water vapor exert effects independent of one another,

$$\frac{pV}{T} = \frac{p'V'}{T}$$

where p, V, T are the pressure, volume and temperature (in °K) of the air.

or $$\frac{75.25 \text{ cm} \times 15 \text{ cm} \times A}{280°\text{K}} = \frac{74.58 \text{ cm} \times yA}{290°\text{K}},$$

where A is the cross-sectional area of the tube and y is the length of the column at the temperature of 17°C. Hence

$$y = \frac{290 \times 75.25 \times 15}{280 \times 74.58} \text{cm} = 15.68 \text{ cm.}$$

• PROBLEM 418

The pressure in a static water pipe in the basement of an apartment house is 42 lb · in^{-2}, but four floors up it is only 20 lb · in^{-2}. What is the height between the basement and the fourth floor?

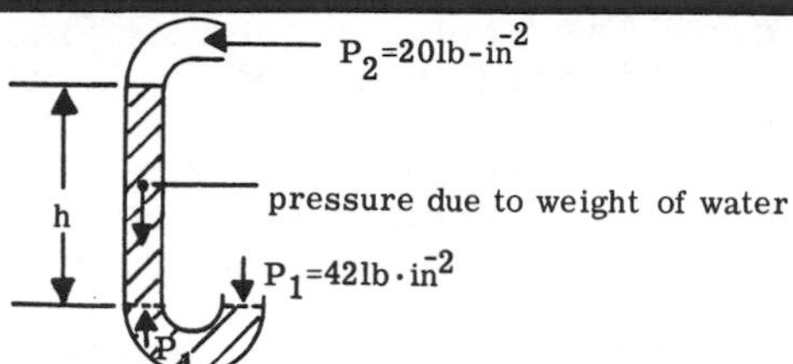

Solution: If A is the cross sectional area of the pipe, then the pressure $\left(P_1 = \frac{F1}{A} \text{ where } F_1 \text{ is the force exerted}\right)$ in the pipe at the basement must balance both the pressure $P_2 \left(= \frac{F_2}{A}\right)$ in the pipe at the fourth floor and the weight of the water in the column of height h (see the figure). If ρ is the density of water, then by definition

$$\rho = \frac{m}{v}$$

where m is the mass of the water in the column of volume $v = Ah$. Then $m = \rho Ah$ and the weight of the water is $W = mg = \rho ghA$. Thus the pressure due to the weight of the water is $\frac{W}{A} = \rho gh$. Hence

$$P_1 = P_2 + \rho gh$$

$$\left(P_1 - P_2\right) = (42 - 20) \text{ lb} \cdot \text{in}^{-2} = 22\frac{\text{lb}}{\text{in}^2} \times \frac{144 \text{ in}^2}{1 \text{ ft}^2}$$

$$= \rho gh = 1.94 \text{ slug} \cdot \text{ft}^{-3} \times 32 \text{ ft} \cdot \text{s}^{-2} \times h$$

$$\therefore \quad h = \frac{(22 \times 144) \text{ lb} \cdot \text{ft}^{-2}}{1.94 \text{ slug} \cdot \text{ft}^{-3} \times 32 \text{ lb} \cdot \text{ft}^{-3}} = \frac{99}{1.94} \text{ ft}$$

$$= 51.03 \text{ ft.}$$

• PROBLEM 419

A circular cylinder of cross-sectional area 100 ft^2 and height 8 ft is closed at the top and open at the bottom and is used as a diving bell. (a) To what depth must it be lowered into water so that the air inside is compressed to 5/6 of its original volume, if the atmospheric pressure at that time is 30 in. of mercury? (b) Air is pumped from the surface to keep the bell full of air. How many moles of air have passed through the pump when it is at the depth calculated above, if the atmospheric temperature is 10°C?

Solution: Applying Boyle's law to the first part of the problem, we obtain

$$p_0 V_0 = p \times V_f = p \times \frac{5}{6} V_0$$

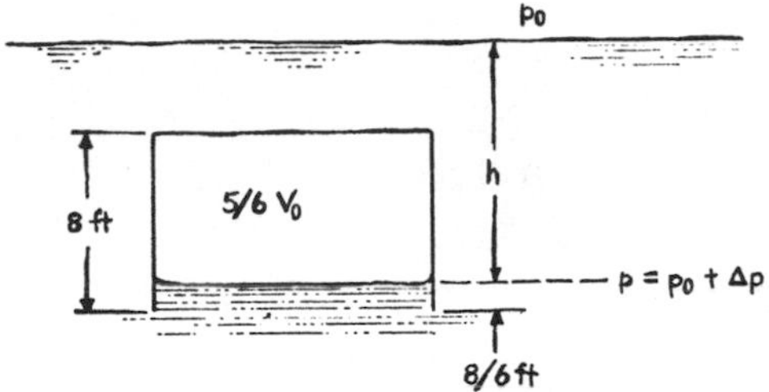

where p_0 and V_0 are the initial pressure and volume of the air inside the diving bell. p and V_f are the final pressure and volume of the air in the bell.

$$p = \frac{6}{5} p_0$$

Now, the pressure change that the air experiences can only be due to a change in pressure of the water with depth. The relation between pressure (p) and depth (h) in a fluid is given by

$$p = p_0 + \rho gh \qquad (1)$$

where p_0 is the ambient pressure at the surface of the fluid (see figure) and ρ is the fluid density. Now, the change in pressure caused by submerging the bell a distance h in the water is

$$p - p_0 = \rho gh \qquad (2)$$

But, the change in pressure experienced by the air in the bell is

$$\Delta p = \frac{6}{5} p_0 - p_0 = \frac{1}{5} p_0 \qquad (3)$$

and this must be caused by the submerging of the bell a distance h in the fluid. Therefore, using (3) and (2)

$$\frac{1}{5} p_0 = \rho gh$$

or $$h = \frac{p_0}{5\rho g} \qquad (4)$$

The ambient pressure is given as 30 in. of mercury. This is to be interpreted as meaning that the ambient pressure is equal to the pressure exerted by a column of mercury 30 in. long. Thus

$$p_0 = (30 \text{ in.})\ \rho'\ g \qquad (5)$$

where ρ' is mercury's density. Thus, inserting (5) in (4)

$$h = \frac{(30 \text{ in})\rho'\ g}{5\ \rho g} = \frac{(30 \text{ in})\rho'}{5\ \rho}$$

Since the relative density of mercury is defined as

$$R = \frac{\rho'}{\rho}$$

we obtain

$$h = \frac{(30\ \text{in})R}{5} = (6\ \text{in.})\ R$$

But $R = 13.6$, and

$$h = (6\ \text{in})(13.6) = (\tfrac{1}{2}\ \text{ft})(13.6)$$

$$h = 6.8\ \text{ft}.$$

The water level in the bell is thus at a depth of 6.80 ft below the surface of the fluid. But 1/6 of the bell's volume, V_0, is water. Noting that

$$V_0 = A \times 8\ \text{ft}$$

where A is the bell's cross-sectional area, we find that

$$\frac{1}{6} V_0 = \frac{8\ \text{ft}}{6} \times A$$

is water. Hence, the height of water in the bell is $\frac{8}{6}$ ft. (See figure). The depth of the foot of the bell is thus 6.80 ft + 8/6 ft = 8.13 ft. The bell has thus been lowered 8.13 ft into the water.

(b) If air filled the whole jar at this depth, the pressure on it would be that due to atmospheric pressure plus 8.13 ft of water. Using (1)

$$p = p_0 + \rho g\ h$$

$$p = 1\ \text{atm} + \left(1.95\ \text{sl/ft}^3\right)\left(32\ \text{ft/s}^2\right)(8.13\ \text{ft})$$

$$p = 1\ \text{atm} + \left(62.4\ \text{lb/ft}^3\right)(8.13\ \text{ft})$$

$$p = 1\ \text{atm} + 507.312\ \text{lb/ft}^2$$

Since atmospheres can't be added to lb/ft^2, we note that

$$1\ \text{lb/ft}^2 = 4.725 \times 10^{-4}\ \text{atm}$$

Then

$$p = 1\ \text{atm} + \left(507.312\ \text{lb/ft}^2\right)\left(4.725 \times 10^{-4}\ \text{atm/lb/ft}^2\right)$$

$$p = 1.239\ \text{atm}.$$

The pressure acting on the air in the bell is thus 1.239 atm. The bell's volume, V_0, is constant at

$$V_0 = 8\ \text{ft} \times A = 8\ \text{ft} \times 100\ \text{ft}^2$$

$$V_0 = 800\ \text{ft}^3$$

The number of moles in this volume is obtained from the gas equation

$$p\ V_0 = n\ R\ T$$

where R is the gas constant, T is the gas temperature in Kelvin degrees, and n is the number of moles of gas. Hence, at its submerged position

$$n = \frac{pV_0}{RT} = \frac{(1.239 \text{ atm})(800 \text{ ft}^3)}{\left(.0821 \frac{\text{liter}\cdot\text{atm}}{\text{mole}\cdot{}^\circ\text{K}}\right)(283^\circ\text{K})}$$

where we used the fact that

$$10^\circ \text{ C} = (273 + 10)^\circ\text{K} = 283^\circ\text{K}$$

In order to be consistent, we transform 800 ft^3 to liters by noting that 1 ft^3 = 28.32 liters. Then

$$n = \frac{pV_0}{RT}$$

$$= \frac{1.239 \text{ atm} \times 800 \times 28.32 \text{ liters}}{0.0821 \text{ liter}\cdot\text{atm}\cdot\text{mole}^{-1}\cdot\text{K deg}^{-1} \times 283^\circ\text{K}}$$

$$= 1208 \text{ moles.}$$

On the surface of the water the number of moles in the diving bell was

$$n_0 = \frac{p_0V_0}{RT}$$

$$= \frac{1 \text{ atm} \times 800 \times 28.32 \text{ liters}}{0.0821 \text{ liter}\cdot\text{atm}\cdot\text{mole}^{-1}\cdot\text{K deg}^{-1} \times 283^\circ\text{K}} = 975 \text{ moles.}$$

The number of moles that have passed through the pump is thus 1208 - 975 = 233.

• PROBLEM 420

In a hydraulic press the small cylinder has a diameter of 1.0 in., while the large piston has a diameter of 8.0 in. If a force of 120 lb is applied to the small piston, what is the force on the large piston, neglecting friction?

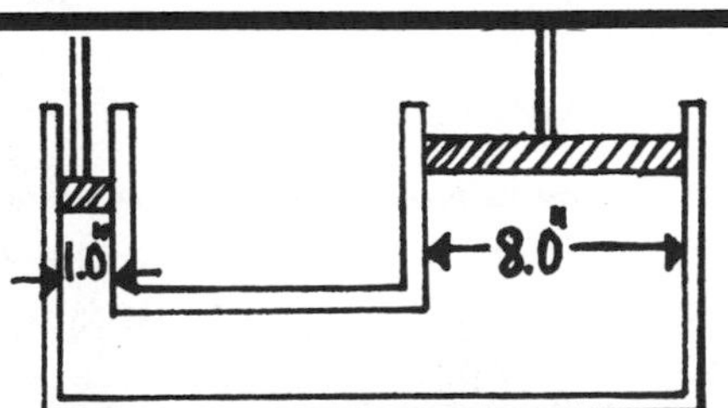

Hydraulic Press

Solution: Pascal's law states that pressure applied to an enclosed fluid is transmitted throughout the fluid in all directions without loss. In the hydraulic press shown, this means that the pressure applied to the smaller piston is transmitted unchanged to the larger piston. Since it has a larger area, it experiences a greater force since F = PA. Hence, we have

$$P_2 = P_1 \qquad \frac{F_2}{A_2} = \frac{F_1}{A_1}$$

$$F_2 = \frac{A_2}{A_1} F_1 = \frac{\pi(4.0 \text{ in.})^2}{\pi(0.50 \text{ in.})^2} 120 \text{ lb} = 7.7 \times 10^3 \text{ lb}$$

• PROBLEM 421

What is the diameter of the small piston of a hydraulic press when a force of 20 pounds on it produces a force of 4 tons on the large piston whose diameter is 20 inches, assuming that friction can be neglected? What is the mechanical advantage?

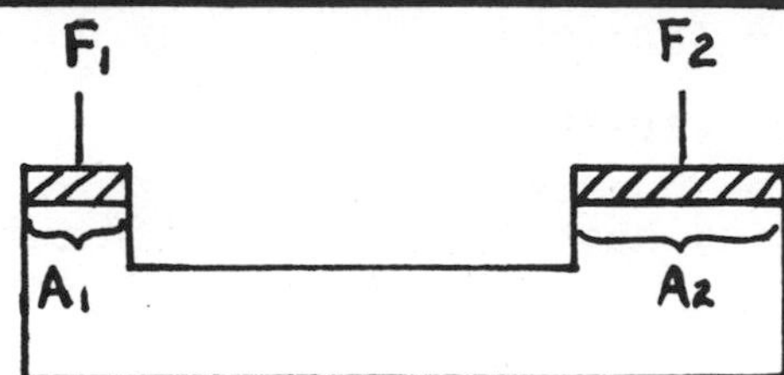

Solution: The force exerted on each piston is proportional to its area. This means:

$$\frac{F_1}{F_2} = \frac{A_1}{A_2}$$

where F_1 is the force on the small cylinder, F_2 the force on the large cylinder, and A_1 and A_2 their respective areas. Therefore,

$$\frac{20 \text{ lbs}}{4 \text{ tons} \times 2000 \frac{\text{lbs}}{\text{ton}}} = \frac{\pi \quad r^2}{\pi(10 \text{ in})^2}$$

$$r_1 = \frac{1}{2} \text{ in}^2$$

If friction is neglected, then AMA = IMA. The IMA of a hydraulic press is the ratio of the areas of its pistons.

$$\text{IMA} = \text{AMA} = \frac{A_2}{A_1} = \frac{\pi \ (10 \text{ in})^2}{\pi(\frac{1}{2} \text{ in})^2} = \frac{F_2}{F_1} = 400.$$

CAPILLARY ACTION

• PROBLEM 422

A capillary tube of internal radius 0.25 mm is dipped into water of surface tension 72 dynes • cm^{-1}. How high does the water rise in the tube? The capillary tube is gradually lowered into the water until only 1 cm is left above the surface. Explain what happens to the water in the tube.

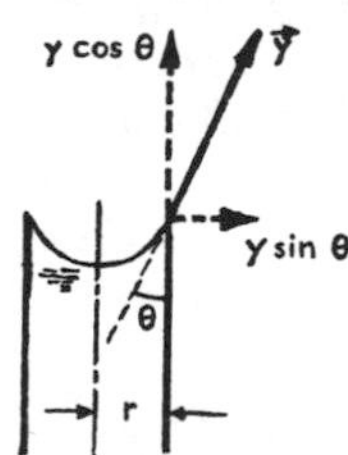

Solution: Consider a capillary tube of radius r. The liquid in it makes contact with the tube along a line of length $2\pi r$. Let the liquid in the tube be a height y above the surface of the liquid in which it is dipped. The upward force, T, is defined as the product of the surface tension, γ, and the length perpendicular to the force, along which it acts. Then

$$T = (\gamma)(2\pi r)(\cos\theta)$$

where θ is the contact angle. The downward force on the liquid in the tube is equal to its weight w. Then w equals the liquid's weight density, ρg, multiplied by its volume $\pi r^2 y$.

$$w = \rho g \pi r^2 y$$

For the liquid in the tube to be in equilibrium, these forces must be equal.

$$w = T$$

$$\rho g \pi r^2 y = \gamma 2\pi r \cos\theta$$

Then $$y = 2\gamma \cos\theta / \rho g r.$$

Since the liquid in this case is water, the angle of contact is 0°, and the density is $1\ g\cdot cm^{-3}$. Hence

$$y = \frac{2 \times 72 \text{ dynes} \cdot cm^{-1}}{1\ g \cdot cm^{-3} \times 980\ cm \cdot s^{-2} \times 0.025\ cm} = 5.88\ cm.$$

As long as more than 5.88 cm of tube shows above the liquid surface, there is no problem. The liquid rises to that height. But, as the tube is lowered, a stage will be reached when less than 5.88 cm are above the surface.

What can not happen is that liquid pour out over the top. If it did, the liquid pouring over the edge could be used to drive a water wheel to provide energy; and the process would continue as liquid would always rise up the tube to take the place of that pouring from the end. In other words, a perpetual motion machine would be established, which is in direct contradiction with the principle of conservation of energy.

What does happen is that the angle of contact at the top of the tube increases. Only the vertical component of the surface tension is used to balance the weight of the water column held up. As the height of the projecting tube gets smaller and smaller, the angle of contact gets larger and larger until, with $y = 0$, $\theta = 90°$, and the surface at the top of the tube is flat.

In particular, when y = 1 cm,

$$1\ cm = \frac{2\gamma \cos\theta}{\rho g r} = 5.88 \cos\theta\ cm.$$

$$\therefore \quad \cos\theta = \frac{1}{5.88} = 0.17 \qquad \therefore \quad \theta = 80.2°.$$

• PROBLEM 423

Find the coefficient σ of surface tension of a liquid if it rises to a height h = 32.6 mm. in a capillary of diameter D = 1 mm. The density of the liquid is δ = 1 gr/cm^3. The contact angle of the surface film is zero.

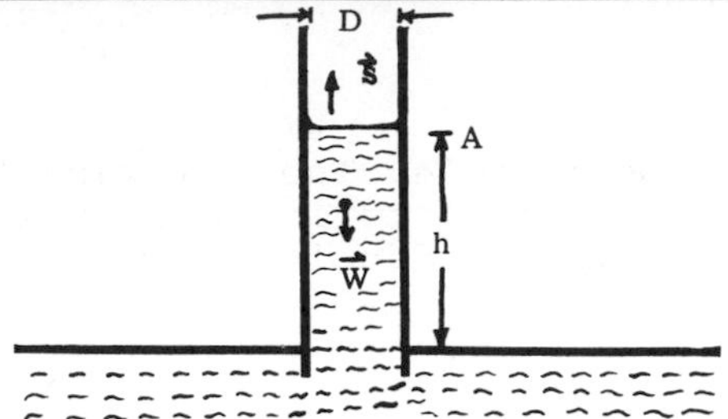

Solution: The surface force acting along the circumference of the water surface in the tube (as shown in the figure) supports the weight of the water column. Surface force is given by

$$S = \sigma\pi D.$$

Hydrostatic equilibrium requires that

$$S = W,$$

$$\sigma\pi D = g \times \text{mass} = g\delta \times \text{volume}$$

$$= g\delta h\pi \frac{D^2}{4}.$$

where g is the acceleration due to gravity. The coefficient of surface tension is

$$\sigma = \frac{1}{4} g\ \delta\ h\ D$$

$$= \frac{1}{4} \times \left(980 \text{ cm/s}^2\right) \times \left(1 \text{ gr/cm}^3\right) \times (3.26 \text{ cm}) \times \left(10^{-1}\text{cm}\right)$$

$$= 80.4 \text{ dyne/cm}$$

• PROBLEM 424

A thin square metal sheet of side 6 cm is suspended vertically from a balance so that the lower edge of the sheet dips into water in such a way that it is parallel to the surface. If the sheet is clean, the angle of contact between water and metal is 0°, and the sheet appears to weigh 4700 dynes. If the sheet is greasy, the contact angle is 180° and the weight appears to be 3000 dynes. What is the surface tension of water?

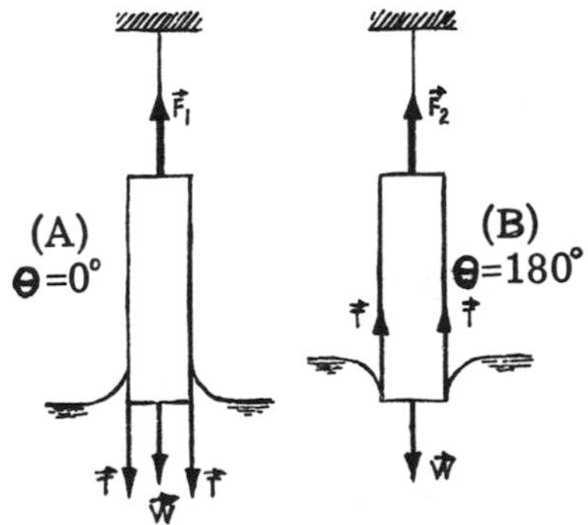

Solution: The contact angle θ is a measure of the curvature of the liquid surface adjacent to the metal sheet (see figure). In either case there are three forces acting on the sheet: the tension in the suspension which gives the apparent weight, the actual weight of the sheet, and the total surface-tension force. In the first case the angle of contact is zero and the surface tension force acts downward since it tries to restore the liquid to its original level. Thus since the sheet is in equilibrium $F_1 = W + 2T$, the factor 2 being necessary since thereare two sides to the sheet. In the second case the angle of contact is 180° and thus the surface-tension force is acting upward. Hence $F_2 = W - 2T$.

The surface tension γ is defined as the ratio of the surface force T, to the length, ℓ, along which the force acts. Each force T acts along one side of the sheet, the thickness of the sheet assumed negligible with respect to the length of the sheet. This length is perpendicular to T and is given to be 6 cm. We have

$$T = \gamma\ell$$

Subtracting F_2 from F_1, we get

$$F_1 - F_2 = (W + 2T) - (W - 2T) = 4T$$

$$F_1 - F_2 = 4\gamma\ell$$

Therefore

$$\gamma = \frac{F_1 - F_2}{4\ell} = \frac{(4700 - 3000)\,\text{dynes}}{4 \times 6\ \text{cm}} = 70.8\ \text{dynes} \cdot \text{cm}^{-1}.$$

• PROBLEM 425

A soap bubble consists of two spherical surface films very close together, with liquid between. A soap bubble formed from 5 mg of soap solution will just float in air of density 1.290 g • liter when filled with hydrogen of density 0.090 g • liter. The surface tension of soap solution is 25 dynes • cm^{-1}. What is the excess pressure in the bubble?

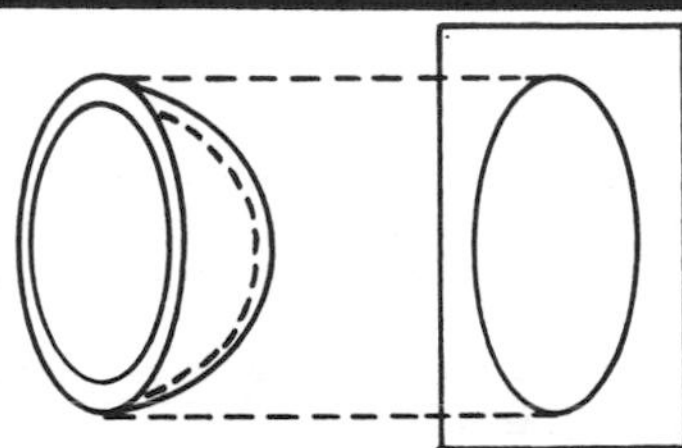

Solution: When the bubble is floating in air, the weight of soap solution plus the weight of the hydrogen must just be balanced by the upthrust due to the displaced air. The buoyant force of the air is equal to the volume of air displaced by the bubble multiplied by the weight density of air. Hence, if the bubble has a volume of y,

$$g(5 \times 10^{-3}\ g) + (0.09 \times 10^{-3}\ g \cdot cm^{-3})gy$$
$$= (1.29 \times 10^{-3} g \cdot cm^{-3})gy.$$
$$\therefore y = \frac{5\ cm^3}{1.2} = \frac{25}{6}\ cm^3.$$

But the bubble is spherical and of radius r. Thus

$$y = \frac{4}{3}\pi r^3 = \frac{25}{6}\ cm^3.$$

$$\therefore r^3 = \frac{25 \times 3\ cm^3}{24\pi} \qquad \text{or } r = 1\ cm.$$

Consider half of the bubble, as shown in the figure. The other half exerts a force to the left equaling twice the surface tension, γ, multiplied by the perimeter or

$$F_{left} = (2\gamma)(2\pi r)$$

We use twice the surface tension since the soap bubble has both an inner and an outer surface producing tension. The thickness of the bubble is assumed small in comparison with its radius letting us use the average value of r for both inner and outer surfaces. The force on the bubble to the right equals the pressure difference, P, between the outer and inner surfaces of the bubble times the area of the bubble in the direction being considered. This area is obtained by projecting the half-bubble on a plane perpendicular to this direction, as shown in the figure. The projected area of a sphere on a plane is a circular area and is equal to πr^2. Then,

$$F_{right} = (P)(\pi r^2)$$

Since the half-bubble is in equilibrium, we have from the first condition of equilibrium that

$$F_{left} = F_{right}$$

and $\quad 4\pi r\gamma = P\pi r^2$

yielding $P = \frac{4\gamma}{r}$

for a soap bubble. The excess pressure in the bubble is then

$$P = \frac{4\gamma}{r} = \frac{4 \times 25\ dynes \cdot cm^{-1}}{1\ cm} = 100\ dynes \cdot cm^{-2}.$$

• PROBLEM 426

What is the difference in the levels of a liquid in two connecting capillaries of diameters D_1 and D_2? The surface tension of the liquid is σ. The edge angles of the surface films are zero.

Solution: The surface forces, S_1 add S_2, acting on the water surfaces in capillaries 1 and 2 (as shown in the figure), respectively are

$$S_1 = \pi D_1 \sigma, \qquad S_2 = \pi D_2 \sigma.$$

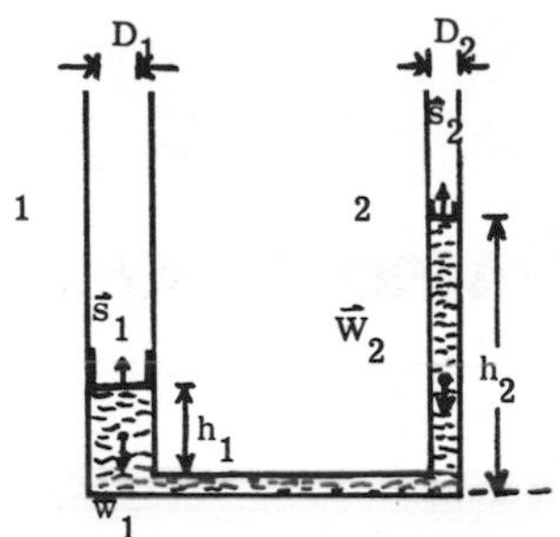

If $\vec{W}_1$ and $\vec{W}_2$ are the weights of the water columns in tubes 1 and 2, the net force (neglecting the air pressure), at the bottom of each capillary is

$$\vec{F}_1 = \vec{W}_1 + \vec{S}_1,$$

$$\vec{F}_2 = \vec{W}_2 + \vec{S}_2$$

Corresponding pressures are

$$P_1 = \frac{F_1}{A_1} = \frac{W_1}{A_1} - \frac{S_1}{A_1} = gh_1\delta - \frac{S_1}{A_1}$$

$$P_2 = \frac{F_2}{A_2} = \frac{W_2}{A_2} - \frac{A_2}{A_2} = gh_2\delta - \frac{S_2}{A_2}$$

where g is the gravitational acceleration, δ is the density of the liquid, and A_1 and A_2 are the cross-sectional areas of the tubes. The hydrostatic pressures at the bottoms of the tubes should be equal, hence we have

$$P_1 = P_2$$

giving

$$gh_1\delta - \frac{S_1}{A_1} = gh_2\delta - \frac{S_2}{A_2} \quad ,$$

or

$$\delta g(h_2 - h_1) = \frac{S_2}{A_2} - \frac{S_1}{A_1} \quad ,$$

$$\delta g(h_2 - h_1) = \frac{\pi D_2\sigma}{\frac{1}{4}\pi D_2^2} - \frac{\pi D_1\sigma}{\frac{1}{4}\pi D_1^2} \, ,$$

$$= 4\sigma\left(\frac{1}{D_2} - \frac{1}{D_1}\right).$$

The difference in the levels of the water columns is therefore,

$$h_2 - h_1 = \frac{4\sigma\left(D_1 - D_2\right)}{\delta g\ D_1\ D_2} \quad .$$

CHAPTER 11

HYDRODYNAMICS/AERODYNAMICS

• **PROBLEM** 427

Water flows into a water tank of large cross-sectional area at a rate of 10^{-4} m^3/s, but flows out from a hole of area 1 cm^2, which has been punched through the base. How high does the water rise in the tank?

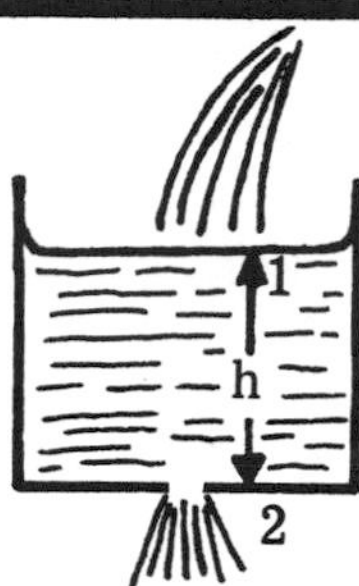

Solution: When the water reaches its maximum height in the tank the pressure head is great enough to produce an outflow exactly equal to the inflow. Equilibrium is then reached and the water level in the tank stays constant.

Since the cross-sectional area of the tank is large in comparison with the area of the hole, the water in the tank may be considered to have zero velocity. Further, the air above the tank and outside the holes are each at atmospheric pressure. Apply Bernoulli's theorem,

$$p_1 + \rho g y_1 + \tfrac{1}{2}\rho v_1^2 = p_2 + \tfrac{1}{2}\rho g y_2 + \tfrac{1}{2}\rho v_2^2$$

with point 1 at the surface of the water at a height h above the hole and point 2 the hole itself. Then

$$p_a + \rho g h + 0 = p_a + 0 + \tfrac{1}{2}\rho v^2,$$

where v is the velocity of efflux from the hole. Hence, $v = \sqrt{2gh}$.

But at equilibrium v is the rate of influx divided by the area of the hole. That is,

$$v = \frac{10^{-4}\ m^3/s}{10^{-4}\ m^2} = 1\ m/s.$$

Therefore the maximum height of water in the tank is

$$h = \frac{v^2}{2g} = \frac{1^2\ m^2/s^2}{2 \times 9.8\ m/s^2} = 5.1\ cm.$$

• PROBLEM 428

An observation balloon has a volume of 300 m^3 and is filled with hydrogen of density 0.1 g/liter. The basket and passengers have a total mass of 350 kg. Find the initial acceleration when the balloon is released, assuming that the air resistance is zero when the velocity is zero. The density of air is 1.3 g/liter and the upward force on the balloon is equal to the weight of air displaced by the balloon.

Solution: The weight of air that the balloon displaces equals the upward force U on it, as a consequence of Archimides' principle. This law states that a body, wholly or partly immersed in a fluid(either a liquid or a gas), is buoyed up with a force equal to the weight of the fluid displaced by the body. This force is then

$$U = W_{air} = \rho_{air}\ g\ V$$

where ρ_{air} is the density of the air, g is the acceleration due to gravity, and V is the volume of the balloon. We have

$$\rho_{air} = (1.3\ g/liter)\left(10^3\ liter/m^3\right)\left(10^{-3}\ kg/g\right)$$

$$= 1.3\ kg/m^3$$

Then $U = \left(1.3\ kg/m^3\right)\left(9.8\ m/sec^2\right)\left(300\ m^3\right) = 3822\ N$

The mass that must be moved consists of the basket and passengers (350 kg) and that of the balloon. The mass m_b of the balloon is

$$m_b = \rho_h\ V$$

where ρ_h is the density of the hydrogen gas

$$\rho_h = (0.1\ g/liter)\left(10^3\ liter/m^3\right)\left(10^{-3}\ kg/g\right) = 0.1\ kg/m^3$$

Therefore $m_b = \left(0.1\ kg/m^3\right)\left(300\ m^3\right) = 30\ kg$

and the total mass m is

$$m = 350\ kg + m_b = 350\ kg + 30\ kg = 380\ kg.$$

Due to the gravitational force acting on this mass, there is a force W acting downward and equal to the weight of the total mass.

$$W = mg = (380\ kg)(9.8\ m/sec) = 3724\ N$$

From Newton's second law, the sum of the forces acting on a body equals the product of its mass m and its acceleration.

$$\sum F = ma.$$

The total initial force is equal to the sum of the weight of the balloon and the upward buoyant force. Taking the upward direction as positive,

$$U - W = ma$$

$$3822\text{ N} - 3724\text{ N} = (380\text{ kg})\, a$$

The initial acceleration is

$$a = \frac{98\text{ N}}{380\text{ kg}} = 0.258\text{ m/sec}^2.$$

• PROBLEM 429

> Spherical particles of pollen are shaken up in water and allowed to stand. The depth of water is 2 cm. What is the diameter of the largest particles remaining in suspension 1 hr later? Density of pollen = 1.8 g/cm^3.

Solution: The terminal velocity of the particles after they are allowed to settle will very quickly be reached. After 1 hr the only particles left in suspension are those which take longer than 1 hr to fall 2 cm. The larger, heavier particles have already settled. The particles which have just not settled are those which take exactly 1 hr to fall 2 cm. That is,

$$v_T = \frac{2\text{ cm}}{(1\text{ hr})(3600\text{ s/hr})} = \frac{1}{1800}\text{ cm/sec}$$

We need another expression for the terminal velocity. Stoke's law states that when a sphere moves through a viscous fluid at rest, the resisting force f exerted by the fluid on the sphere is given by

$$f = 6\pi\eta rv$$

where η is the viscosity of the fluid, r is the radius of the sphere, and v is its velocity with respect to the fluid. The other forces which act on the sphere are its weight mg and the upward buoyant force B of the fluid. Let ρ be the density of the sphere and ρ' the density of the fluid. Then

$$mg = \frac{4}{3}\pi r^3 \rho g$$

$$B = \frac{4}{3}\pi r^3 \rho' g \qquad \text{(Archimedes' principle)}$$

The net force on the sphere equals the product of its mass and acceleration. Taking the downward direction as positive,

$$mg - B - R = ma$$

$$a = g - \frac{B + R}{m}$$

Assuming the initial velocity is zero, this net acceleration imparts a downward velocity to the sphere. As this velocity increases, so does the retarding force. At some terminal v_T, the retarding force has increased an amount such that the downward acceleration equals zero. At this point, the velocity of the sphere stays constant and is found by setting the acceleration equal to zero. Then

$$mg = B + R$$

$$\frac{4}{3}\pi r^3 \rho g = \frac{4}{3}\pi r^3 \rho' g + 6\pi\eta r v_T$$

$$v_T = \frac{2}{9}\frac{r^2 g}{\eta}(\rho - \rho')$$

The radius of the largest particles still just in suspension is thus given by

$$r^2 = \frac{9}{2}\frac{\eta\, v_T}{g(\rho - \rho')}$$

$$= \frac{9}{2}\frac{1 \times 10^{-2}\text{ poise} \times \frac{1}{1800}\text{ cm/s}}{980\text{ cm/s}^2(1.8 - 1)\text{g/cm}^3} = \frac{10^{-4}}{64 \times 49}\text{ cm}^2$$

$$d = 2r = \frac{2 \times 10^{-2}}{8 \times 7}\text{ cm} = 3.57 \times 10^{-4}\text{ cm.}$$

• PROBLEM 430

A water tank standing on the floor has two small holes vertically above one another punched in one side. The holes are 3.6 cm and 10 cm above the floor. How high does water stand in the tank when the jets from the holes hit the floor at the same point?

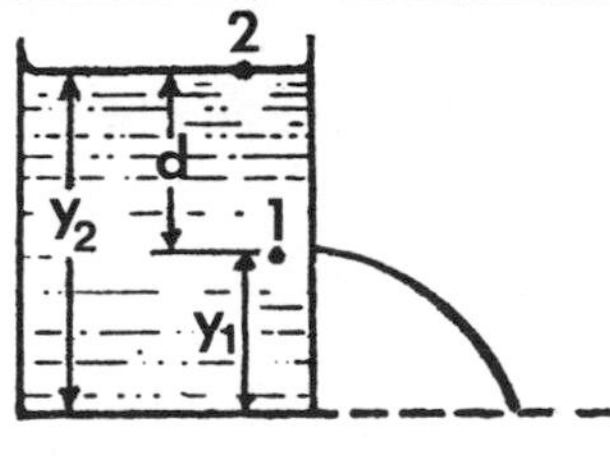

FIGURE 1

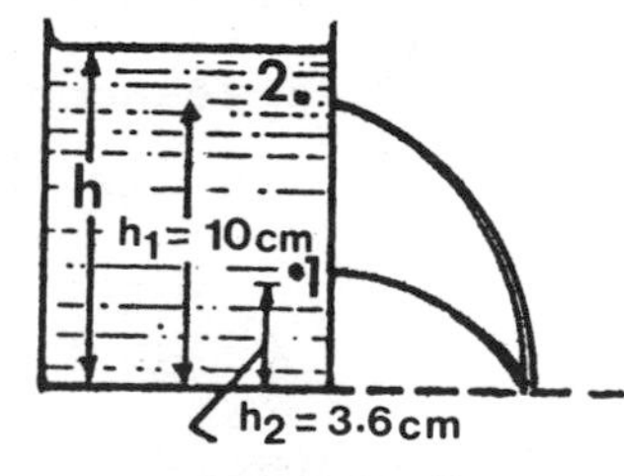

FIGURE 2

Solution: For any hole in a tank, the velocity of discharge of the liquid is given by Torricelli's theorem. To derive it, consider a hole a distance d below the surface of the liquid in the tank (see figure 1). Using Bernoulli's equation,

$$p_1 + \tfrac{1}{2}\rho v_1^2 + \rho g y_1 = p_2 + \tfrac{1}{2}\rho v_2^2 + \rho g y_2$$

take point 1 to be at the hole and point 2 at the surface of the liquid. The pressure at each point is the atmospheric pressure p_a since both are open to the atmosphere. If the hole is small, the level of the liquid in the tank falls slowly and its velocity v_2 can be assumed to be zero. Using the bottom of the tank as the reference level,

$$p_a + \tfrac{1}{2}\rho v_1^2 + \rho g y_1 = p_a + 0 + \rho g y_2$$

or $\quad v_1^2 = 2g\left(y_2 - y_1\right) = 2g\,d$

Therefore, the velocity of discharge from a hole in a tank is given by

$$v = \sqrt{2gd}$$

In this problem, the velocities of efflux are horizontal from both holes. Using Torricelli's theorem, one gets for the upper hole (see figure 2),

$$v_1 = \sqrt{2g(h - h_1)},$$

and for the lower one,

$$v_2 = \sqrt{2g(h - h_2)}.$$

Water from the upper hole has a horizontal velocity v_1 and no initial vertical velocity u. In time t_1, applying the formula $\left(y-y_0\right) = ut_1 + 1/2\ gt_1^2$ to the vertical motion , one obtains $h_1 = 0 + 1/2\ gt_1^2$ or $t_1 = \sqrt{2h_1/g}$.

In that time the horizontal distance gone is $v_1 t_1$, which is the distance from the tank at which the jet strikes the floor.

Similarly, the distance at which the jet from the lower holes strikes the floor is $v_2 t_2$, where $t_2 = \sqrt{2h_2/g}$.

But these distances are equal, and thus $v_1 t_1 = v_2 t_2$ or $(v_1 t_1)^2 = (v_2 t_2)^2$. Then

$$2g(h - h_1) \times \frac{2h_1}{g} = 2g(h - h_2) \times \frac{2h_2}{g}$$

$$(h - h_1) \times h_1 = (h - h_2) \times h_2$$

$$hh_1 - h_1^2 = hh_2 - h_2^2$$

$$hh_1 - hh_2 = h_1^2 - h_2^2$$

$$h = \frac{h_1^2 - h_2^2}{h_1 - h_2} = h_1 + h_2 \ . \qquad \therefore \ h = 13.6 \text{ cm.}$$

• **PROBLEM 431**

A stream of gas is escaping through a small opening at one end of a large cylinder under the action of an excess pressure (relative to air pressure) $\Delta P = 10^4$ dynes/cm². If the density of gas in the cylinder is $\rho = 8 \times 10^{-4}$ gm/cm³, find the escape velocity v.

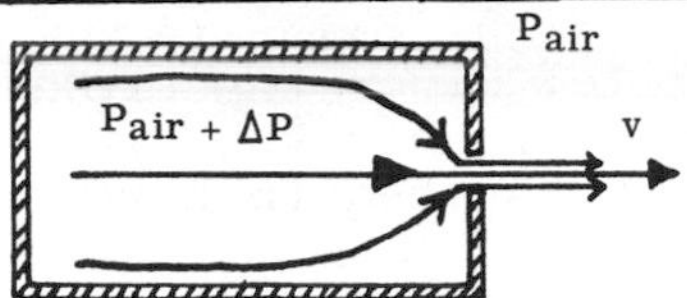

Solution: The excess pressure is about 10^4 dynes/cm² $\simeq$ 10.2 cm of water, whereas the normal air pressure P_{air} is about 98.3 cm of water. Since the excess pressure is much smaller than the outside pressure, we can assume that there is no appreciable compression of the gas. Then, we can treat the gas escaping through the hole as incompressible and apply Bernoulli's equation. The pressures inside and outside the cylinder are related by

$$P_{inside} = P_{outside} + \tfrac{1}{2}\rho v^2$$

or

$$v^2 = \frac{2}{\rho}\left[P_a + \Delta P - P_a\right]$$

$$v = \sqrt{\frac{2\Delta P}{\rho}}$$

$$= \sqrt{\frac{2 \times 10^4 \text{ dyne/cm}^2}{8 \times 10^{-4} \text{ gm/cm}^3}}$$

$$= 5 \times 10^3 \text{ cm/sec.}$$

• **PROBLEM 432**

The seal over a circular hole of diameter 1 cm in the side of an aquarium tank ruptures. The water level is 1 m above the hole and the tank is standing on a smooth plastic surface. What force must an attendant apply to the tank to prevent it from being set into motion?

Solution: For streamline flow of an incompressible, nonviscous fluid, Bernoulli's equation can be applied. It states

$$p_1 + \tfrac{1}{2}\rho v_1^2 + \rho g y_1 = p_2 + \tfrac{1}{2}\rho v_2^2 + \rho g y_2$$

where the subscripts 1 and 2 refer to quantities pertaining to any two points along the flow. The absolute pressure is p, ρ the density, v the velocity, g the gravitational acceleration, and y the elevation above some arbitrary reference level.

Take point 1 to be at the surface of the water in the tank, a height h above the hole which is taken to be point 2. The pressures above the tank and outside the hole are both atmospheric pressure. Applying Bernoulli's theorem to this case, we thus have

$$p_a + 0 + \rho gh = p_a + \tfrac{1}{2}\rho v^2 + 0.$$

Here v is the velocity of efflux from the hole, the reference level for height being taken as the horizontal level through the hole. Since the cross section of the tank is very much larger than the area of the hole, the liquid in the tank is assumed to have zero velocity. Thus $v = \sqrt{2gh}$.

Let A be the area of the hole. The mass of fluid ejected in time dt is $dm = \rho dv = \rho A d\ell = \rho A\, d\ell/dt\ dt = \rho\ Av\ dt$, and thus the momentum P acquired in time dt is $\rho Av^2\ dt$. The escaping fluid therefore has a rate of change of momentum of $dP/dt = \rho Av^2$ and thus by Newton's second law $F = dP/dt$ the force causing this is ρAv^2. By Newton's third law, an equal and opposite force acts on the tank. Hence, to prevent the tank from moving backward, the attendant must apply to the tank a force of magnitude

$$F = \rho Av^2 = \rho \frac{\pi d^2}{4} \times 2gh$$

$$= 10^3\ \text{kg/m}^3 \times \frac{\pi}{4} \times 10^{-4}\ \text{m}^2 \times 2 \times 9.8\ \text{m/s}^2 \times 1\ \text{m}$$

$$= 1.54\ \text{N}.$$

• PROBLEM 433

At two points on a horizontal tube of varying circular cross-section carrying water, the radii are 1 cm and 0.4 cm and the pressure difference between these points is 4.9 cm of water. How much liquid flows through the tube per second?

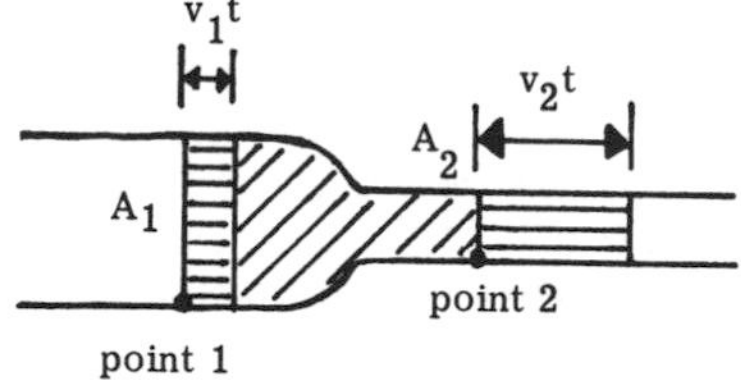

Discharge rate of a tube

Solution: Since the tube is horizontal there is no pressure difference along the tube due to hydrostatic effects because the static pressure due to the weight of the fluid plays no part in the problem. Thus Bernoulli's equation is

$$p_1 + \tfrac{1}{2}\rho v_1^2 = p_2 + \tfrac{1}{2}\rho v_2^2 \qquad (1)$$

where ρ is the density of the liquid, v its velocity, p its pressure, and the subscripts 1 and 2 refer to any two points along the tube. In time t, those particles of the fluid which were originally at point 1 (see figure), move a distance v_1t. The total volume of fluid which moves past point 1 in time t is therefore A_1v_1t. Its rate of flow per unit time is then A_1v_1. Similarly, the rate of flow past point 2 is A_2v_2. Assuming the fluid is incompressible, these two rates of flow must be equal. We have

$$A_1v_1 = A_2v_2 \tag{2}$$

This is the equation of continuity which states that the quantity of an incompressible liquid which flows through a tube per second is constant at all points.

The pressure difference is given as 4.9 cm of water. This equals the pressure produced by the weight of 4.9 cm of water or

$$p_1 - p_2 = \rho g \times 4.9 \text{ cm} \tag{3}$$

From equations (1) and (3),

$$v_2^2 - v_1^2 = \frac{2(p_1 - p_2)}{\rho} = \frac{2(\rho g)(4.9 \text{ cm})}{\rho} = (2g)(4.9 \text{ cm})$$

$$= (2)(980 \text{ cm/sec}^2)(4.9 \text{ cm})$$

and $$v_2^2 - v_1^2 = 98^2 \text{ cm}^2/\text{sec}^2 \tag{4}$$

Using equation (2),

$$\frac{v_1}{v_2} = \frac{A_2}{A_1} = \frac{\pi \times 0.4^2 \text{ cm}^2}{\pi \times 1^2 \text{ cm}^2} = 0.16.$$

Substituting $v_1^2 = 0.16^2\ v_2^2$ in equation (4) yields

$$v_2^2(1 - 0.16^2) = 98^2 \text{ cm}^2\cdot\text{s}^{-2}$$

or $$v_2 = \sqrt{\frac{98^2 \text{ cm}^2\cdot\text{s}^{-2}}{0.9744}}$$

The quantity of water flowing through the tube per second is thus

$$A_1v_1 = A_2v_2 = \pi \times (0.4 \text{ cm})^2 \times \sqrt{\frac{98^2 \text{ cm}^2\cdot\text{s}^{-2}}{0.9744}}$$

$$= 50 \text{ cm}^3\cdot\text{s}^{-1}.$$

• PROBLEM 434

An aircraft wing requires a lift of 25.4 lb/ft^2. If the speed of flow of the air along the bottom surface of the wing is to be 500 ft/s, what must be the speed of flow over the top surface to give the required lift? The density of air is 2.54×10^{-3} slug/ft^3.

Lines of flow about an aircraft wing

Solution: Below an aircraft wing, there is little disturbance of the air flow. Because of the shape of the wing, the streamlines crowd together above it, effectively decreasing the cross-sectional area A for the air flow. The equation of continuity states that for an incompressible fluid (such as air), Av = constant. Therefore, the velocity v of the air above the wing must increase. Consider two points in the air flow at the same height, the first at a point to the left of the wing (see figure), where the flow has yet been disturbed and the second at a point above the wing. Bernoulli's equation states that

$$p_1 + \tfrac{1}{2}\rho v_1^2 = p_2 + \tfrac{1}{2}\rho v_2^2$$

where the "y" terms in the equation cancel since the two points are at the same elevation. From this equation, we see that since v_2 is greater than v_1, p_2 must be less than p_1. Since p_1 is also the pressure of the air under the wing, we see that the pressure is less above the wing than below it. This pressure differential gives rise to the lift on the wing. In Bernoulli's equation, let the subscript 1 refer to the lower surface and the subscript 2 to the upper surface of the wing. Thus the dynamic lift per unit area is

$$p_1 - p_2 = 25.4 \text{ lb/ft}^2$$

Solving for the speed of flow v_2 over the top of the wing in the first equation, we get

$$v_2^2 = \frac{2(p_1 - p_2)}{\rho} + v_1^2$$

$$= \frac{(2)\ (25.4 \text{ lb/ft}^2)}{(2.54)\ (10^{-3}) \text{ slug-ft}^3} + (25)\ (10^4) \text{ ft}^2/\text{sec}^2$$

$$= \left[(2)\ (10^4) + (25)\ (10^4)\right] \text{ ft}^2/\text{sec}^2$$

$$= (27)\ (10^4) \text{ ft}^2/\text{sec}^2$$

$$v_2 = 519.6 \text{ ft/sec.}$$

• PROBLEM 435

Water flows at the rate of 300 ft^3/min through an inclined pipe as shown in the figure. At A, where the diameter is 12 in., the pressure is 15 lb/in.^2 What is the pressure at B, where the diameter is 6.0 in. and the center of the pipe is 2.0 ft lower than at A?

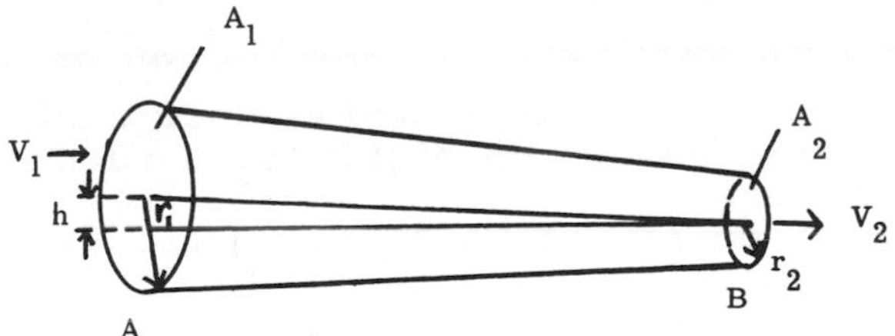

Inclined Tube

Solution: The mass of liquid entering the tube at point A, in a time Δt, should be equal to the mass leaving it at point B in Δt. Let the velocities and the densities at A and B be v_1, v_2 and ρ_1, ρ_2, respectively. In a time Δt, the liquid entering at A moves a distance $v_1 \Delta t$, hence the volume of liquid entering is $Av_1\Delta t$. Therefore, the mass of this fluid is $\rho_1 v_1 A_1 \Delta t$. Similarly, the mass of liquid leaving at B is $\rho_2 v_2 A_2 \Delta t$. Dividing both terms by Δt, we get the continuity equation for the flow

$$\rho_1 v_1 A_1 = \rho_2 v_2 A_2 \ .$$

For all practical purposes, we can assume liquids to be incompressible, therefore the density of liquid during flow remains constant

$$\rho_1 = \rho_2$$

and we have

$$v_1 A_1 = v_2 A_2 \ .$$

For this problem

$$A_1 v_1 = \frac{300\ \text{ft}^3/\text{min}}{60\ \text{sec/min}} = 5.0\ \text{ft}^3/\text{sec}$$

Hence

$$v_1 = \frac{A_1 v_1}{A_1} = \frac{A_1 v_1}{\pi r_1^2} = \frac{5.0\ \text{ft}^3/\text{sec}}{3.14 \times (\frac{1}{2}\text{ft})^2} = 6.4\ \text{ft/sec}$$

$$v_2 = \frac{A_1}{A_2} v_1 = \frac{\pi(\frac{1}{2}\ \text{ft})^2}{\pi(\frac{1}{4}\ \text{ft})^2} v_1 = 4v_1$$

$$v_2 = 26\ \text{ft/sec.}$$

The pressure P_1 at point A is

$$P_1 = \left(15\ \text{lb/in.}^2\right)\left(144\ \text{in.}^2/\text{ft}^2\right) = 2200\ \text{lb/ft}^2$$

The weight density of water

$D = 62.4\ \text{lb/ft}^3$, and therefore $\rho = 1.94\ \text{slugs/ft}^3$.

The Bernoulli equation for the pressures at A and B is

$$P_1 - P_2 = \tfrac{1}{2}\rho g h + \tfrac{1}{2}\rho\left(v_2^2 - v_1^2\right)$$

where h is the difference between the heights of the centers of the cross-sections at the two ends of the pipe. The pressure at point B is

$$\begin{aligned} P_2 &= P_1 + \rho g\left(h_1 - h_2\right) + \frac{\rho}{2}\left(v_1^2 - v_2^2\right) \\ &= 2200\ \text{lb/ft}^2 + \left(62.4\ \text{lb/ft}^3\right)(2.0\ \text{ft}) + \frac{1.94\ \text{slug/ft}^3}{2} \left[(6.4 - 26)^2\text{ft}^2/\text{sec}^2\right] \\ &= 2200\ \text{lb/ft}^2 + 120\ \text{lb/ft}^2 - 620\ \text{lb/ft}^2 \\ &= 1700\ \text{lb/ft}^2 = 12\ \text{lb/in.}^2 \end{aligned}$$

An old-fashioned water clock consists of a circular cylinder 10 cm in diameter and 25 cm high with a vertical capillary tube 40 cm in length and 0.5 mm in diameter attached to the bottom. The viscosity of water is 0.01 poise. What is the distance between hour divisions at the top of the vessel and at the bottom of the vessel?

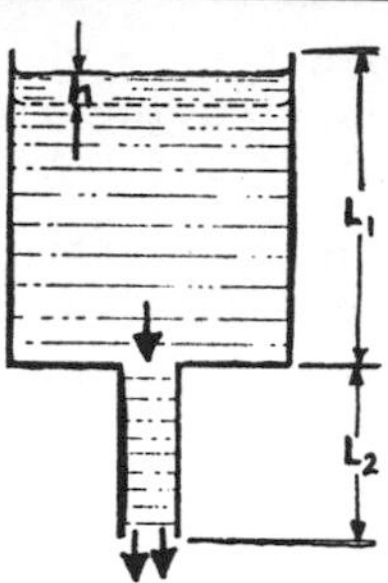

Solution: The total volume of liquid Q which flows across the entire cross-section of a cylindrical tube in time t, is given by Poiseuille's law,

$$Q = \frac{\pi}{8}\frac{R^4}{\eta L}\ \Delta p\ t$$

where R is the radius, η is the viscosity of the liquid, and Δp is the pressure difference between the two cross-sectional surfaces separated by a distance L. The water in the capillary flows as a result of the pressures due to the water in the cylinder and its own weight, as shown in the figure. Under its own weight, it would have a rate of flow given by,

$$\frac{Q_1}{t} = \frac{\pi}{8}\frac{R^4}{\eta L_2}\left(\rho g L_2\right)$$

where ρ is the density of water and g is the gravitational acceleration. The weight of the water exerts a pressure ρ gL_1 on the upper cross-section of the capillary and gives rise to another pressure difference between the two ends of the capillary. The rate of flow due to this pressure difference is,

$$\frac{Q_2}{t} = \frac{\pi}{8}\frac{R^4}{\eta L_2}\left(\rho g L_1\right)$$

The total rate of flow is therefore,

$$\frac{Q}{t} = \frac{Q_1}{t} + \frac{Q_2}{t} = \frac{\pi}{8}\frac{R^4}{\eta L_2}\rho g\left(L_1 + L_2\right)$$

The quantity of water, Q, flowing from the capillary in

time t causes a drop in the level of the cylinder, h. The area of the cylinder is A, and thus Q/t = Ah/t.

$$\therefore \frac{h}{t} = \frac{\pi}{8A} \frac{R^4}{\eta} \frac{\rho g\left(L_1 + L_2\right)}{L_2}$$

When the cylinder is full, $L_1 = 25$ cm, and

$$\frac{h}{t} = \frac{\pi \times \left(0.25 \times 10^{-3}\text{m}\right)^4 \times 10^3\text{kg/m}^3 \times 9.8\text{m/s}^2 \times 0.65\text{m}}{8 \times \pi/4 \times 10^{-2}\text{m}^2 \times 10^{-3}\text{Ns/m}^2 \times 0.40\text{m}}$$

$$= 3.11 \times 10^{-6}\text{m/s} = 1.12\text{cm/hr}$$

When the cylinder is empty, $L_1 = 0$ cm, and,

$$\frac{h'}{t} = \frac{\pi R^4}{8A\eta L_2} \rho g L_2 = \frac{\pi R^4}{8A\eta L_2}\left(L_1 + L_2\right) \cdot \frac{L_2}{L_1 + L_2}$$

$$= \frac{h}{t}\frac{L_2}{L_1 + L_2} = \frac{h}{t}\frac{0.40}{0.65}$$

$$= 1.12\text{ cm/hr} \cdot \frac{0.40}{0.65} = 0.69\text{ cm/hr}$$

Thus hour divisions are separated by 1.12 cm at the top and 0.69 cm at the bottom. Note that L_1 varies slightly during the hour and, to be quite exact, an integration ought to be performed. The error involved is, however, slight, since the variation in L_1 is very small in comparison with $L_1 + L_2$.

• PROBLEM 437

A Venturi meter is a device by means of which the velocity of flow of a fluid can be measured. The diagram illustrates the operation of one type of such a meter. If the value of A is 10 times that of a, and colored water is used in the U-tube, what is the velocity v_1 of flow of water when the difference in levels h is 6 in.? See Fig.

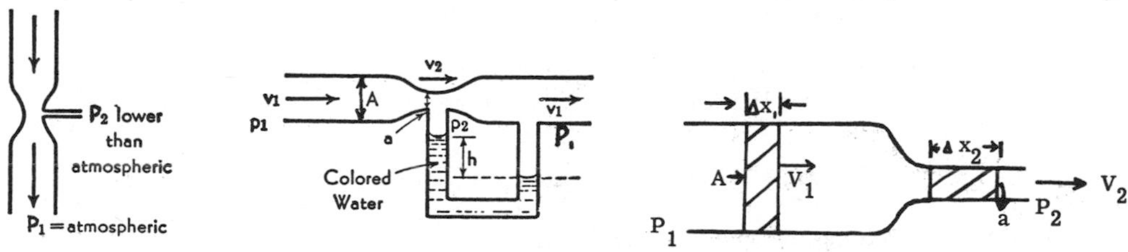

Figure A Figure B Figure C

Solution: The operation of the meter, according to diagrams A and B is based upon Bernoulli's Principle. The indicator tube shows that the pressure at the constriction (p_2) is less than p_1. The pressure p_1 due to the flowing fluid in the wide tube must balance both p_2 as well as the pressure due to the weight of water in the column, hence it must be greater than p_2. By the law of continuity

$$Av_1 = av_2$$

This result follows from the assumed incompressability of the fluid. In the same time interval Δt, the same volume of fluid which enters the constriction must leave it. Or (see figure C).

$$\frac{A\Delta x_1}{\Delta t} = \frac{a\Delta x_2}{\Delta t}$$

where A and a are the cross-sections indicated in figure B. By definition of velocity

$$v_1 = \frac{\Delta x_1}{\Delta t} \text{ and } \tfrac{1}{2} = \frac{\Delta x_2}{\Delta t} .$$

Then

$$Av_1 = av_2$$

We are given that $A = 10a$, then

$$10\ av_1 = av_2$$

$$10v_1 = v_2 \qquad (1)$$

By Bernoulli's Principle

$$\tfrac{1}{2}\ dv_1^2 + p_1 = \tfrac{1}{2}\ dv_2^2 + p_2$$

where d is the density of the fluid. This principle follows from the work-energy theorem.
Consider a volume of fluid (fig. C) which flows into the constriction. The total work done on this element of fluid, is equal to the work done on it by the fluid behind it in pushing it through the constriction minus the work it does on the fluid in front of it when it pushes this fluid forward. This total work is equal to the change in kinetic energy of this element of fluid. Or

$$\int \vec{F}_1 \cdot \vec{dx}_1 - \int \vec{F}_2 \cdot \vec{dx}_2 = F_1\Delta x_1 - F_2\Delta x_2 = \tfrac{1}{2}\ mv_2^2 - \tfrac{1}{2}\ mv_1^2 \qquad (2)$$

Here F_1 is the constant force exerted on the element of fluid, by the fluid to the left of it, F_2 is the force it exerts on the fluid to the right of it, and v_1 and v_2 are the velocity of the fluid element before it enters the constriction, and after it enters the constriction, respectively. M is the mass of the fluid element. Equation (2) may be written as

$$F_1\Delta x_1 + \tfrac{1}{2}\ mv_1^2 = F_2\Delta x_2 + \tfrac{1}{2}\ mv_2^2 \qquad (3)$$

Using the fact that the volume of fluid element pushed to the right equals the volume of fluid element pushed to the left (i.e., $A\Delta x_1 = a\Delta x_2$) then

$$F_1\Delta x_1 + \tfrac{1}{2}\ mv_1^2 = F_2\ \frac{A}{a}\ \Delta x_1 + \tfrac{1}{2}\ mv_2^2$$

Dividing both sides by the volume $A\Delta x_1$

$$\frac{F_1}{A} + \tfrac{1}{2}\ \frac{m}{A\Delta x_1}\ v_1^2 = \frac{F_2}{a} + \tfrac{1}{2}\ \frac{m}{A\Delta x_1}\ v_2^2$$

or

$$p_1 + \tfrac{1}{2}\, dv_1^2 = p_2 + \tfrac{1}{2}\, dv_2^2$$

since density $= \dfrac{\text{Mass}}{\text{Volume}}$ and Pressure $= \dfrac{\text{Force}}{\text{Area}}$.

d is the density of water. Then

$$p_1 - p_2 = \tfrac{1}{2}\, d\left(v_2^2 - v_1^2\right) = \tfrac{1}{2}d\left(100v_1^2 - v_1^2\right)$$

$$= \tfrac{1}{2}d\left(100v_1^2\right) \text{ (approx)}$$

where we used equation (1) But

$$p_1 - p_2 = \frac{F_1 - F_2}{A_x}$$

where A_x is the cross sectional area of the indicator tube, and the difference of these forces (due to the fluid in motion) must equal the weight of water in the column of height h. Then

$$F_1 - F_2 = mg = d(Ah)g$$

where m is the mass of water in the column, d is the density of water, and Ah is the volume of the water. Upon division of both sides by A_x,

$$p_1 - p_2 = \frac{F_1 - F_2}{A_x} = dhg$$

Therefore

$$hdg = \tfrac{1}{2}d(100)v_1^2$$

$$v_1^2 = \frac{2g}{100}\, h = \frac{2(32)}{100}\, h = .64h$$

$$v_1 = .8\sqrt{h}$$

Substituting h = 6 in. = .5 ft:

$$v_1 = .8(.7 \text{ ft})_s = .56 \text{ ft/sec}$$

• PROBLEM 438

A space vehicle ejects fuel at a velocity u relative to the vehicle. Its mass at some instant of time is m. Fuel is expelled at the constant rate $\dfrac{\Delta m}{\Delta t}$. Set up and solve the equation of motion of the space vehicle, neglecting gravity.

Solution: At any given time t, the momentum is mv. At time t + Δt the mass of the rocket is m + Δm where Δm is negative since the total mass of the vehicle is decreasing, while the velocity is v + Δv and the momentum is (m + Δm)(v + Δv). However, after time Δt, since Δm in mass leaves the rocket, it introduces its own momentum. In the inertial frame of reference, the velocity of the fuel is v - u which is the velocity of the rocket minus the velocity of the fuel with respect to the rocket. The mass of the fuel ejected during time Δt is Δm, and so its momentum is $\Delta m(v - u)$. The law of conservation of momentum tells us that, in an isolated system the momentum at time t equals the momentum at $t + \Delta t$. Therefore,

$$mv = (m + \Delta m)(v + \Delta v) - \Delta m\ (v - u)$$

Simplifying, we have

$$m\Delta v = - \Delta m\ (u + \Delta v)$$

If we let $\Delta v \to 0$ to get instantaneous velocity and $\Delta m \to 0$ we have

$$mdv = - dm(u)$$

$$dv = - dm \frac{u}{m}$$

Integrating from v_0 to v (initial and instantaneous velocities) and from M to m (where M is the initial mass and m is the instantaneous mass) we have:

$$\int_{v_0}^{v} dv = - \int_{M}^{m} u \frac{dm}{m}$$

Integrating, we have

$$v = u \ln \left(1 + \frac{m}{M}\right) + v_0$$

CHAPTER 12

TEMPERATURE, THERMOMETRY, THERMAL EXPANSION

• PROBLEM 439

A Celsius thermometer indicates a temperature of 36.6°C. What would a Fahrenheit thermometer read at that temperature?

Solution: The relationship between the Celsius and Fahrenheit scales can be derived from a knowledge of their corresponding values at the freezing and boiling points of water. These are 0°C and 32°F for freezing and 100°C and 212°F for boiling. The temperature change between the two points is equivalent for the two scales and a temperature difference of 100 Celsius degrees equals 180 Frhrenheit degrees. Therefore one Celsius degree is $\frac{9}{5}$ as large as one Fahrenheit degree. We can then say

$$°F = \frac{9}{5}°C + B$$

where B is a constant. To find it, substitute the values known for the freezing point of water:

$$32° = \frac{9}{5} \times 0° + B = B.$$

We therefore have

$$°F = \frac{9}{5}°C + 32°.$$

For a Celsius temperature of 36.6°, the Fahrenheit temperature is

$$F = \frac{9}{5} \times 36.6° + 32° = 65.9° + 32° = 97.9°.$$

• PROBLEM 440

What Fahrenheit temperature corresponds to -40° Centigrade?

Solution: -40°C is 40 Centigrade degrees below the freezing point of water. Now 40°C = 9/5(40) = 72°F since 1 Centigrade degree is 9/5 of 1 Fahrenheit degree. But 72°F below the freezing point, which is 32°F, is 40°F below 0°F (72 - 32 = 40). Thus -40°C = -40°F. This could have been obtained directly as follows.

The formula for converting temperature in degrees Centigrade to degrees Fahrenheit is

$$°F = \frac{9}{5}°C + 32$$

If °C = -40° then

$$°C = \frac{9}{5}(-40) + 32$$

$$= -40°$$

• PROBLEM 441

What temperature on the Centigrade scale corresponds to the common room temperature of 68°F?

Solution: Because 68 - 32 = 36, note that +68°F is 36 Fahrenheit degrees above the freezing point of water. 36°F above the freezing point corresponds to 5/9(36) = 20°C above the freezing point since 1°F = 5/9(1°C). But since the freezing point is 0°C, this temperature is +20°C. Thus +68°F = 20°C.

This result could have been obtained directly as follows.
The formula for converting temperature in degrees Fahrenheit to degrees Centigrade is

$$°C = \frac{5}{9}(°F - 32)$$

If $°F = 68°$ then

$$°C = \frac{5}{9}(68 - 32)$$

$$= 20°$$

• PROBLEM 442

The extremes of temperature in New York, over a period of 50 years, differ by 116 Fahrenheit degrees. Express this range in Celsius degrees.

Solution: Fahrenheit and Celsius temperature scales are related by

$$C° = \frac{5}{9}(F° - 32).$$

Since in this example, only a change in temperature is being converted from one linear scale to the other, we have

$$\Delta C° = \frac{5}{9}\Delta F°$$

Substituting, we get

$$C° = \frac{5}{9} \times 116\ °F = 64.5\ C°$$

• PROBLEM 443

Express 20°C and - 5°C on the Kelvin scale.

Solution: The relationship between the Celsius and Kelvin scale is

$$K° = 273° + C°$$

Therefore 20°C is

$$T = 273° + 20° = 293°K$$

and - 5°C is

$$T = 273° + (-5°) = 268°K$$

• PROBLEM 444

A certain platinum-resistance thermometer has a resistance of 9.20 ohms when immersed in a triple-point cell. When the thermometer is placed in surroundings where its resistance becomes 12.40 ohms, what temperature will it show?

Solution: The triple-point of water occurs when water can co-exist in its three forms: liquid, gas, and solid. This can happen at a temperature of 273.16° K and a water vapor pressure of 4.58 mm-Hg. Since the resistance of a thermometer is directly proportional to the temperature, we can write

$$\frac{T_1}{R_1} = \frac{T_2}{R_2}$$

or

$$T_2 = T_1 \ (R_2/R_1)$$

$$T_2 = 273.16° \text{ K} \left(\frac{12.40}{9.20}\right) = 368.1° \text{ K}$$

• PROBLEM 445

A copper bar is 8.0 ft long at 68°F and has a linear expansivity of 9.4×10^{-6}/F°, What is the increase in length of the bar when it is heated to 110°F?

Solution: Change in this object's dimensions is proportional to the change in temperature and the original length. Therefore the change in length of the bar is

$$\Delta L = L_0 \alpha \ \Delta t = (8.0 \text{ ft})(9.4 \times 10^{-6}/\text{F°})(110°\text{F} - 68°\text{F})$$

$$= 0.0032 \text{ ft.}$$

• PROBLEM 446

An iron steam pipe is 200 ft long at 0°C. What will its increase in length when heated to 100°C? ($\alpha = 10 \times 10^{-6}$ per celsius degree).

Solution: The change in length, ΔL, of a substance due to a temperature change is proportional to the change, ΔT, and to the original length, L_0, of the object:

$$\Delta L = \alpha \ L_0 \ \Delta T$$

where α is the proportionality constant and is called the coefficient of linear expension.

$L_0 = 200$ ft, $\alpha = 10 \times 10^{-6}$ per C°,

$T = 100°$C, $T_0 = 0°$C.

$$\text{Increase in length} = \Delta L = \alpha \ L_0 \Delta T$$

$$= (10 \times 10^{-6})(200)(100)$$

$$= 0.20 \text{ ft.}$$

• PROBLEM 447

A certain weight of alcohol has a volume of 100 cm^3 at 0°C. What is its volume at 50°C?

Solution: The coefficient of volume expansion of alcohol is 0.00112/°C. Thus, the increase of 100 cubic centimeter for a 50°C rise is

$$\frac{0.00112}{°C} \times 100\ cm^3 \times 50°C = 5.60\ cm^3$$

The new volume is therefore 105.60 cubic centimeters.

• PROBLEM 448

A brass plug has a diameter of 10.000 cm at 150°C. At what temperature will the diameter be 9.950 cm?

Solution: It is observed experimentally that when a sample is exposed to a temperature change ΔT, the sample experiences a change in length ΔL, proportional to ΔT and L, the original length of the sample. This (approximate) result may be written as:

$$\Delta L = \alpha L\ \Delta T \qquad (1)$$

where α is the coefficient of linear thermal expansion. Solving (1) for ΔT, we find that

$$\Delta T = \frac{\Delta L}{\alpha L} \qquad (2)$$

is the change in temperature required to implement a change in length ΔL. Substituting the given data into (2), we obtain:

$$\Delta T = \frac{(9.950 - 10.00)\ cm.}{(19 \times 10^{-6}/°C)\ (10.000\ cm)}$$

$$T = -\ 260°\ C$$

But we want the final value of T, not ΔT. Since

$$\Delta T = T_f - T_o$$

$$T_f = \Delta T + T_o$$

$$T_f = 150°\ C - 260°\ C = -\ 110°\ C.$$

This is the value to which the temperature must be lowered in order to shrink the diameter of the plug to 9.950 cm.

• PROBLEM 449

Two rods of the same diameter, one made of brass and of length 25 cm, the other of steel and of length

50 cm, are placed end to end and pinned to two rigid supports. The temperature of the rods rises to 40°C. What is the stress in each rod? Young's moduli for steel and brass are 20×10^{11} dynes $\cdot$ cm^{-2} and 10×10^{11} dynes $\cdot$ cm^{-2}, respectively, and their respective coefficients of expansion are 1.2×10^{-5} C deg^{-1} and 1.8×10^{-5} C deg^{-1}.

Solution: The temperature rises and the rods, if permitted to, would expand. Since they are rigidly held, they cannot do so and therefore suffer a compressive stress. The forces in the two rods must be the same. If they were not, then at the interface between them, the forces would not balance, equilibrium would not exist, and the interface would move until the forces were equal.

Young's Modulus $Y = \dfrac{\text{Stress}}{\text{Strain}}$, where the stress is the normal force per unit (cross sectional) area acting at the end of the bar, and the strain is the fractional change of length $\Delta\ell/\ell$ of a bar due to the stress. If Y_B and Y_S are, respectively, Young's modulii for brass and for steel, then, since the stresses are equal $Y_B \dfrac{\Delta\ell_B}{\ell_B} = Y_S \dfrac{\Delta\ell_S}{\ell_S}$. ℓ_B and ℓ_S are the lengths of the brass and the steel, respectively, when no stress is applied.

But the total decrease in length $(\Delta\ell_B + \Delta\ell_S)$ is the amount the rods have not been allowed to expand when the temperature rose. To compute this sum, we use the formula relating the fractional change in length, $\Delta\ell$, of a bar to a change in temperature t, $\Delta\ell = \ell\alpha t$. ℓ is the original length of the bar, and α is the coefficient of expansion of the bar. Hence

$$\Delta\ell_B + \Delta\ell_S = \ell_B\alpha_B \times 40°C + \ell_S\alpha_S \times 40°C.$$

But $\Delta\ell_S = \dfrac{Y_B}{Y_S}\dfrac{\ell_S}{\ell_B}\Delta\ell_B$. Then

$$\Delta\ell_B\left[1 + \frac{Y_B}{Y_S}\frac{\ell_S}{\ell_B}\right] = \left(\ell_B\alpha_B + \ell_S\alpha_S\right) \times 40°C.$$

$$\therefore \Delta\ell_B = \frac{40°C\times\left(25\ \text{cm}\times1.8\times10^{-5}\text{deg}^{-1}+50\ \text{cm}\times1.2\times10^{-5}\text{deg}^{-1}\right)}{1 + (10\times10^{11}/20\times10^{11})\times(50/25)}$$

$$= 2.1 \times 10^{-2}\ \text{cm}$$

and $\Delta\ell_S = \dfrac{Y_B}{Y_S}\dfrac{\ell_S}{\ell_B}\Delta\ell_B = \frac{1}{2} \times \dfrac{50}{25} \times\Delta\ell_B = 2.1 \times 10^{-2}$ cm.

The stress in each rod is

$$Y_B \frac{\Delta\ell_B}{\ell_B} = Y_S \frac{\Delta\ell_S}{\ell_S}$$

$$= 10 \times 10^{11} \text{ dynes} \cdot \text{cm}^{-2} \times \frac{2.1 \times 10^{-2} \text{ cm}}{25 \text{ cm}}$$

$$= 0.84 \text{ dyne} \cdot \text{cm}^{-2}.$$

• PROBLEM 450

In the design of a modern steel bridge, provisions must obviously be made for expansion. How much does this amount to in the case of a bridge two miles long which is subjected to temperatures ranging from $-40°F$ to $+110°F$, assuming an average expansion coefficient of $.000012/°C$?

Solution: By definition of the coefficient of linear expansion

$$\alpha = \frac{\Delta\ell}{\ell_0 \ \Delta T}$$

where $\Delta\ell/\ell_0$ is the fractional change in length of an object due to a temperature change ΔT.

In our case

$$\Delta\ell = \alpha \ \ell_0 \ \Delta T$$

$$\Delta\ell = \left(.000012 \ °C^{-1}\right)\left(2 \text{ miles}\right)\left(110°F - (-40°F)\right)$$

$$\Delta\ell = (.000012 \ °C^{-1})(2 \text{ miles})(150°F)$$

Since $150°F = \frac{5}{9} \cdot 150°C = \frac{750°C}{9}$

$$\Delta\ell = (1.2 \times 10^{-5})(2 \text{ miles})(750/9)$$

$$\Delta\ell = .002 \text{ miles}$$

• PROBLEM 451

The volume of the bulb of a mercury thermometer at $0°C$ is V_0, and the cross section of the capillary is A_0. The coefficient of linear expansion of the glass is α_G per $C°$, and the coefficient of cubical expansion of mercury is β_M per $C°$. If the mercury just fills the bulb at $0°C$, what is the length of the mercury column in the capillary at a temperature of $t°C$?

Solution: An exaggerated view of the expansion is shown in figure (b). Figure (a) represents the initial situation. When exposed to a temperature change ΔT, the cross section of the capillary, the volume of the bulb, and the volume occupied by the mercury all change (see figures).

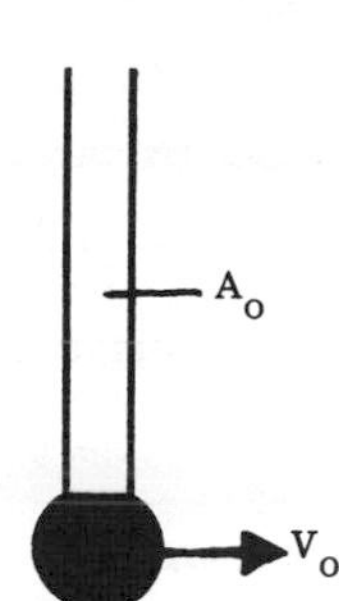

FIGURE A

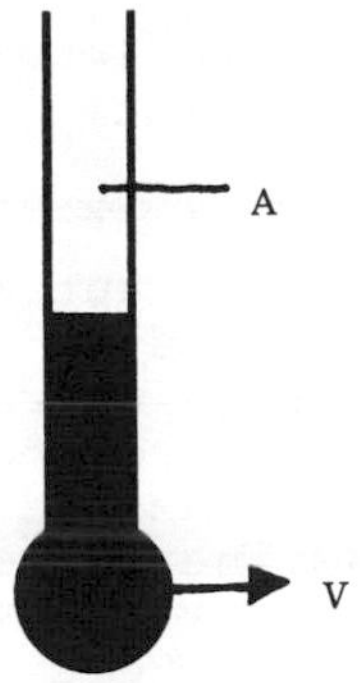

FIGURE B

The final volume occupied by the mercury is

$$V_{Hg} = V_0 \left(1 + \beta_M \, \Delta T\right) \tag{1}$$

where β_M is the coefficient of volume expansion of mercury. The new cross section of the capillary will be

$$A = A_0 \left(1 + 2\alpha_G \, \Delta T\right) \tag{2}$$

where α_G is the coefficient of linear expansion of glass. Similarly, the new volume of the bulb is

$$V_g = V_0 \left(1 + 3\alpha_G \, \Delta T\right) \tag{3}$$

(Note that, initially, the volume of Hg = the volume of the bulb).

Now, the volume of mercury outside the bulb in figure (b) will be

$$V_{Hg} - V_g = V_0 \left(1 + \beta_M \, \Delta T - 1 - 3\alpha_G \, \Delta T\right)$$

$$V_{Hg} - V_g = V_0 \left(\beta_M - 3\alpha_G\right)\Delta T \tag{4}$$

If the length of the mercury column in figure (b) is h, then

$$V_{Hg} - V_g = hA = hA_0 \left(1 + 2\alpha_G \, \Delta T\right) \tag{5}$$

where we have used (2). Equating (5) and (4)

$$hA_0\left(1 + 2\alpha_G \, \Delta T\right) = V_0 \left(\beta_M - 3\alpha_G\right) \Delta T$$

or $$h = \frac{V_0}{A_0} \left(\frac{\beta_M - 3\alpha_G}{1 + 2\alpha_G \Delta T}\right) \Delta T$$

Since $\Delta T = t^\circ C - 0^\circ C$

$$h = \frac{V_0}{A_0} \left(\frac{\beta_M - 3\alpha_G}{1 + 2\alpha_G t}\right) t$$

This is the length of the mercury column in the capillary at temperature t.

• PROBLEM 452

A 20 gallon automobile gasoline tank is filled exactly to the top at 0°F just before the automobile is parked in a garage where the temperature is maintained at 70°F. How much gasoline is lost due to expansion as the car warms up? Assume the coefficient of volume expansion of gasoline to be .0012/°C.

Solution: Here, we assume that the tank doesn't expand or contract. By definition of the coefficient of volume expansion

$$\beta = \frac{\Delta V}{V_0 \ \Delta T}$$

where V_0 is the original volume occupied by the liquid, and ΔV is the change in volume of the liquid due to a temperature change ΔT.

The gasoline lost is then

$$\Delta V = \beta \ V_0 \ \Delta T$$

$$\Delta V = (.0012\ {}^\circ C^{-1})(20 \text{ gal})(70^\circ F)$$

But $70^\circ F = \left(\frac{5}{9}\right) \cdot (70^\circ C) = \frac{350}{9}\ {}^\circ C$ and

$$\Delta V = (.0012)(20 \text{ gal})(350/9)$$

$$\Delta V = .94 \text{ gal.}$$

• PROBLEM 453

The brass scale attached to a barometer reads correctly at 20°C. The barometer height is read as 75.34 cm of mercury when the temperature is 25°C. What is the true height at 0°C? The coefficients of volume expansion of mercury and of linear expansion of brass are $\beta_M = 18 \times 10^{-5}/°C$ and $\alpha_B = 1.8 \times 10^{-5}/°C$, respectively.

Solution. The brass scale reads correctly at 20°C, but at 25°C, the scale expands and therefore indicates a smaller length than the true length of the measured object. Hence, the true length is given by the measured length plus the expansion of the brass scale due to the temperature rise from 20°C to 25°C. Note that, the brass scale readings always give the true length of the scale at 20°C. The true length, ℓ, of the mercury then becomes

$$\ell = 75.34 \text{ cm} + (75.34 \text{ cm})\alpha_B(25°C - 20°C)$$

$$= 75.34\left(1 + 9 \times 10^{-5}\right)\text{cm.}$$

The height ℓ_0 of the mercury column at 0°C will be

smaller than ℓ since the density increases with decreasing temperature and the same mass of mercury occupies a smaller volume. The volume at 0°C is

$$V_0 = V - V\beta_M(25° - 0°C)$$

$$= V\left(1 - \beta_M \cdot 25°C\right)$$

where V is the volume at 25°C. The cross-section A, of the glass tube containing the mercury remains practically constant as the temperature changes. Hence, the change of the volume of the mercury is reflected as the change in its length;

$$\frac{V_0}{A} = \frac{V}{A}\left(1 - \beta_M \times 25°C\right) \qquad \text{or}$$

$$\ell_0 = \ell\left(1 - \beta_M \times 25°C\right) = \ell\left(1 - 4.5 \times 10^{-3}\right)$$

$$= 75.34\left(1 + 9 \times 10^{-5}\right)\left(1 - 4.5 \times 10^{-3}\right)\text{cm}$$

$$= 75.01 \text{ cm.}$$

• PROBLEM 454

Find the change in volume of an aluminum sphere of 5.0-cm radius when it is heated from 0 to 300° C.

Solution: In the case of one dimensional thermal expansion, we may relate the change in length of a sample to the temperature change which it experiences by

$$\Delta L = \alpha L \ \Delta T \tag{1}$$

where α is the coefficient of linear thermal expansion. Dividing both sides of (1) by ΔT, and taking the limit as $\Delta T \to 0$, we obtain the exact relation:

$$\frac{dL}{dT} = \alpha L \tag{2}$$

We are specifically concerned with the change in the volume of a sphere due to a change in temperature, or

$$\frac{dV}{dT} \tag{3}$$

where V is the volume of the sphere. Using the chain rule,

$$\frac{dV}{dT} = \left(\frac{dV}{dR}\right)\left(\frac{dR}{dT}\right)$$

assuming that V changes only as a result of a change in radius of the sphere (R).

$$\frac{dV}{dR} = \frac{d}{dR}\left(\frac{4}{3}\pi R^3\right) = 4\pi R^2$$

$$\frac{dV}{dT} = 4\pi R^2 \frac{dR}{dT}$$

Also, from (2),

$$\frac{dR}{dT} = \alpha R \quad \text{hence,}$$

$$\frac{dV}{dT} = \frac{\left(4\pi R^3\right)}{3}(3\alpha) = 3\alpha V \tag{4}$$

where V is the original volume of the sphere.

If ΔT is small, we may write

$$\Delta V = 3\alpha V\, \Delta T \tag{5}$$

Substituting the information provided into (5), we obtain:

$$\Delta V = 3\left(2.2 \times 10^{-5}/C°\right)\left(\frac{4}{3}\right)(\pi)\left(5 \times 10^{-2}\ m\right)^3(300°C)$$

$$\Delta V = 10\ cm^3$$

• PROBLEM 455

A steel tube, whose coefficient of linear expansion is 18×10^{-6} per °C, contains mercury, whose coefficient of absolute expansion is 180×10^{-6} per °C. The volume of mercury contained in the tube is 10^{-5} m^3 at 0°C, and it is desired that the length of the mercury column should remain constant at all normal temperatures. This is achieved by inserting into the mercury column a rod of silica, whose thermal expansion is negligible. Calculate the volume of the silica rod. (See figure.)

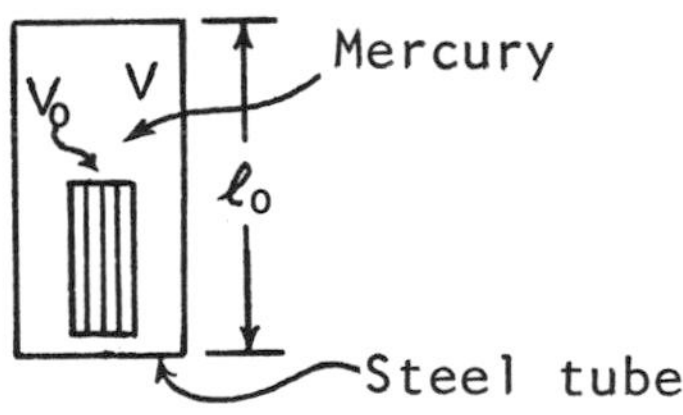

Solution: At 0°C, let the volume of the silica rod be V_0, the volume of mercury be V, and the cross-sectional area and length of the column be A_0 and ℓ_0, respectively. Then at t = 0°C

$$\ell_0 A_0 = V + V_0 \tag{1}$$

At any temperature t, V and A_0 will change to their new values as a result of thermal expansion. These new values, are, respectively V' and A, where

$$V' = V(1 + \beta t)$$

and

$$A = A_0\ (1 + 2\alpha t)$$

Here, α and β are the coefficient of linear expansion of steel and the coefficient of absolute expansion of mercury. Note that we have imposed the constraint that the column length, ℓ_0, be constant. Hence, at temperature t, we may write

$$\ell_0 A = V' + V_0$$

or $$\ell_0 A_0(1 + 2\alpha t) = V(1 + \beta t) + V_0 \tag{2}$$

Using (1) in (2)

$$(V + V_0)(1 + 2\alpha t) = V(1 + \beta t) + V_0.$$

$$V_0(1 + 2\alpha t - 1) = V(1 + \beta t - 1 - 2\alpha t)$$

or $$V_0 = \frac{V(\beta - 2\alpha)t}{2\alpha t} = \frac{V(\beta - 2\alpha)}{2\alpha}.$$

$$V_0 = \frac{10^{-5}\ m^3(180 \times 10^{-6} - 36 \times 10^{-6})deg^{-1}}{36 \times 10^{-6}\ deg^{-1}}$$

$$= \frac{10^{-5} \times 144}{36}\ m^3 = 4 \times 10^{-5}\ m^3.$$

• PROBLEM 456

A glass bulb with volumetric expansion coefficient β_B is weighed in water at temperatures T and T_1. The weights of the displaced water are W and W_1, respectively. Find the volumetric expansion coefficient β_W of the water in the temperature interval from T to T_1.

Solution: The volumetric expansion coefficient β relates the change ΔV in the volume of a substance to a small change ΔT in the temperature of that substance:

$$\frac{\Delta V}{V} = \beta\, \Delta T$$

where V is the initial volume.

The volume of the displaced water equals the volume of the bulb since the bulb is completely immersed in the water while being weighed. The change in the volume of the bulb is due to the change in the volume of the glass since the gas inside the bulb cannot appreciably enlarge the glass. If the specific weights of water at T and T_1 are ρ_ω and ρ_{ω_1}, respectively, then

$$V_B = \frac{W}{\rho_\omega}, \tag{1}$$

$$V_{B_1} = V_B + \Delta V_B = \frac{W_1}{\rho_{\omega_1}} \tag{2}$$

are respectively the volumes of the bulb at T and T_1. The specific weight of water will decrease as a result of the thermal expansion of its volume since its weight remains constant. If the weight of water is

W_w and its volume at T is V_w, we can write

$$W_w = V_w \rho_\omega = \left(V_w + \Delta V_w\right)\rho_{\omega_1}$$

where ΔV_w is the volumetric expansion of water. Hence

$$\rho_{\omega_1} = \frac{V_w}{V_w + \Delta V_w}\rho_\omega = \frac{1}{1 + \frac{\Delta V_w}{V_w}}\rho_\omega \tag{3}$$

The volumetric expansions ΔV_B and ΔV_w are given as

$$\Delta V_B = \beta_B V_B \Delta T = \beta_B \frac{W}{\rho_\omega}\left(T_1 - T\right) \tag{4}$$

$$\Delta V_w = \beta_w V_w \Delta T = \beta_w V_w \left(T_1 - T\right) \tag{5}$$

From (1) and (2), we get

$$\Delta V_B = \frac{W_1}{\rho_{\omega_1}} - \frac{W}{\rho_\omega}$$

or, using (3),

$$\Delta V_B = \frac{W_1}{\rho_\omega}\left(1 + \frac{\Delta W_w}{V_w}\right) - \frac{W}{\rho_\omega}$$

$$= \frac{1}{\rho_\omega}\left(W_1 - W\right) + \frac{W_1}{\rho_\omega}\frac{\Delta V_w}{V_w}$$

Substituting the expressions (4) and (5) for ΔV_B and ΔV_W in the above equation,we get

$$\beta_B \frac{W}{\rho_\omega}\left(T_1 - T\right) = \frac{W_1}{\rho_\omega}\beta_w\left(T_1 - T\right) + \frac{W_1 - W}{\rho_\omega}$$

or

$$\beta_B = \frac{W_1}{W}\beta_w + \frac{W_1 - W}{W\left(T_1 - T\right)}$$

The volumetric expansion coefficient for water is

$$\beta_w = \frac{W}{W_1}\beta_B + \frac{W - W_1}{W_1\left(T_1 - T\right)} = \beta_B + \frac{W - W_1}{W_1}\left(\beta_B + \frac{1}{\Delta T}\right)$$

The above relation will hold for small $\Delta T = \left(T_1 - T\right)$. This corresponds to a small volumetric change for the bulb in the sense that

$$\frac{\Delta V_B}{V_B} \ll 1 .$$

• PROBLEM 457

A clock is controlled by a pendulum which correctly beats seconds at 20° C. The pendulum is a light iron rod, of coefficient of linear expansion 16×10^{-6} C deg^{-1}, with a concentrated mass at one end. How many seconds does it lose in a week if the temperature is kept at 30° C?

Solution: If the length of the pendulum is ℓ at 20°C,

at 30°C its length will be $\ell(1 + \alpha \times 10 \text{ deg})$, where α is the coefficient of linear expansion of iron.

The period of the pendulum is given by $T = 2\pi\sqrt{\ell/g}$. Since it is easier to differentiate the log of T with respect to ℓ than to differentiate T directly with respect to ℓ, we obtain

$$\log T = \log 2\pi \left(\frac{\ell}{g}\right)^{\frac{1}{2}} = \log \left(\frac{4\pi\ell}{g}\right)^{\frac{1}{2}}$$

$$\log T = \tfrac{1}{2} \log \frac{4\pi\ell}{g}$$

$$\frac{d}{d\ell}[\log T] = \frac{d}{d\ell}[\tfrac{1}{2} \log \frac{4\pi\ell}{g}]$$

$$\frac{1}{T}\frac{dT}{d\ell} = \tfrac{1}{2}\frac{g}{4\pi\ell} \cdot \frac{4\pi}{g}$$

$$\frac{dT}{T} = \frac{d\ell}{2\ell}$$

This is an exact relation between dT and $d\ell$. If ΔT and Δl represent small changes in T and in ℓ respectively, then,

$$\frac{\Delta T}{T} \approx \tfrac{1}{2}\frac{\Delta\ell}{\ell} = \tfrac{1}{2}\alpha \times 10 \text{ deg.}$$

$$\Delta T = 2 \text{ s} \times \tfrac{1}{2} \times 16 \times 10^{-6} \text{ deg}^{-1} \times 10 \text{ deg}$$

$$= 1.6 \times 10^{-4} \text{ s.}$$

Note that T = 2s, since each "tick" of the pendulum encompasses 1/2 of its periodic motion. The number of seconds lost in a week is thus

$$(\Delta T)(\#\text{ secs. in 1 wk.}) = (1.6 \times 10^{-4}) \times (302400 \text{ s})$$

$$= 48.4 \text{ s.}$$

• PROBLEM 458

Compute the average kinetic energy in electronvolts of a gas molecule at room temperature.

Solution: Absolute kinetic energy does not depend on the mass of the molecule; therefore, the molecules of all gases have the same absolute kinetic energy at a given temperature.

$$\overline{KE} = \frac{3}{2}kT$$

where k is the Boltzmann constant and the temperature T is expressed in the Kelvin scale. Room temperature is 20°C or 293°K. Substituting values:

$$\overline{KE} = \frac{3}{2} \times (8.62 \times 10^{-5} \text{ eV/°K}) \times (293\text{°K})$$

$$= 0.038 \text{ eV}$$

CHAPTER 13

HEAT/CALORIMETRY

THERMAL ENERGY

• PROBLEM 459

How many Btu are required to raise the temperature of 2 pounds of water from 32°F to 212°F?

Solution: The temperature rise is 180 degrees Fahrenheit. The number of Btu necessary is

$$2 \times 180° = 360 \text{ Btu},$$

since one Btu is required to raise the temperature of one pound of water one degree Fahrenheit.

• PROBLEM 460

A gallon of gasoline will deliver about 110,000 Btu when burned. To how many foot-pounds is this equivalent?

Solution:

$$1 \text{ Btu} = 778 \text{ foot-pounds}$$

$$110{,}000 \text{ Btu} = 778 \frac{\text{ft-lb}}{\text{Btu}} \times 110{,}000 \text{ Btu}$$

$$= 85{,}580{,}000 \text{ foot-pounds}.$$

• PROBLEM 461

How many calories of heat are required to raise 1,000 grams of water from 10°C to 100°C?

Solution: The temperature rise is 90 degrees centigrade. The number of calories needed is

$$1000 \times 90° = 90{,}000 \text{ calories},$$

since one calorie is required to raise the temperature of one gram of water one degree centigrade.

• PROBLEM 462

The density, ρ, of air at STP is 0.00129 g/cm^3, the specific heat capacity at constant pressure is 0.238 cal/g -°K, and the ratio of the principal specific heats is 1.40. What is the mechanical equivalent of heat?

Solution: The equation of state of an ideal gas for one mole is PV = RT, where R is the gas constant, P is the pressure of the gas, T is its temperature in °K and V is the molar volume. This equation may be written as,

$$p\frac{M}{\rho} = RT$$

where M is the molecular weight, and ρ is the density of air. Thus,

$$\frac{R}{M} = \frac{p}{\rho T} = \frac{1.013 \times 10^6 \text{ dynes cm}^{-2}}{0.00129 \text{ g}\cdot\text{cm}^{-3} \times 237°K} = \frac{1.013 \times 10^9}{1.29 \times 273}$$

ergs/g -°K

Also $C_p - C_v = R$, where C_p and C_v are the molar heat capacities at constant pressure and constant volume respectively. Thus $C_p - C_v = R/M$, where C_p and C_v are the corresponding specific heat capacities per unit mass. Further, $C_p/C_v = \gamma$. Therefore,

$$\frac{R}{M} = \left(C_p - C_v\right) = C_p\left(1 - \frac{1}{\gamma}\right) = 0.238 \text{ cal/g - °K} \times \left(1 - \frac{1}{1.40}\right)$$

$$= \frac{0.238 \quad 0.40}{1.40} \text{ cal/g - °K.}$$

The value of R/M is thus given in two systems of units, one mechanical and the other thermal. The mechanical equivalent of heat is thus obtained by dividing one by the other. Hence

$$J = \frac{1.013 \times 10^9}{1.29 \times 273} \text{ergs/g - °K} \times \frac{1.40}{0.238 \times 0.40 \text{ cal/g - °K}}$$

$$= 4.23 \times 10^7 \text{ ergs/cal.}$$

• PROBLEM 463

How many calories are developed in 1.0 min in an electric heater which draws 5.0 amp when connected to a 110-volt line?

Solution: A resistance (the electric heater) which draws 5.0 amp when connected to a 110 volt line develops power (or energy per unit time) given by

$$P = \frac{\text{energy}}{\text{time}} = I^2R$$

But, by Ohm's Law, V = IR, hence

$$P = I(IR) = IV$$

The energy developed in 1.0 min is then

$$E = IVt = 5 \text{ amp} \times 110 \text{ volts} \times 1 \text{ min} \times \frac{60 \text{ sec}}{\text{min}}$$

$$= 33{,}000 \text{ Joules}$$

(The unit of time was converted to seconds to make it compatible with the MKS system being used.)

Since 1 calorie = 4.19 Joules

$$E = 33{,}000 \text{ Joules} \times \frac{1 \text{ cal}}{4.19 \text{ Joules}} = 7.9 \times 10^3 \text{ cal.}$$

• PROBLEM 464

A 1000-gram metal block fell through a distance of 10 meters. If all the energy of the block went into heat energy, how many units of heat energy appeared?

Solution:

Work is given by the force acting on the block times the distance travelled by the block, when force and distance are in the same direction. Hence,

$$\text{Work} = (980 \times 1000)\text{dynes} \times 1000 \text{ cm}$$

$$= 98 \times 10^7 \text{ erg.}$$

Since 1 joule = 10^7 ergs, 98×10^7 ergs equals 98 joules. There are 4.19 joules/cal. Therefore,

$$\text{Heat} = \frac{98 \text{ joules}}{4.19 \text{ joules/cal}}$$

$$= 23.5 \text{ cal approximately.}$$

• PROBLEM 465

Protons of mass 1.67×10^{-27} kg and moving with a velocity of 2×10^7 m $\cdot$ s^{-1} strike a target of mass 1 g and specific heat capacity 0.334 cal $\cdot$ g^{-1} $\cdot$ C deg^{-1}. The proton stream corresponds to a current of 4.8 μA. At what rate does the temperature of the target initially rise if one-third of the energy of the protons is converted into heat?

Solution: Each proton carries a charge of 1.60×10^{-19} C. If the current I flowing is 4.8 μA, the number of protons striking the target in 1 s must be n, where

$$I = nQ = \frac{n \times 1.60 \times 10^{-19} \text{ C}}{1 \text{ s}} = 4.8 \times 10^{-6} \text{ A.}$$

$$n = 3.00 \times 10^{13} \text{ protons.}$$

In one second the total kinetic energy lost by the protons is $KE = n \times \frac{1}{2} m_p v^2$ where $\frac{1}{2} m_p v^2$ is the kinetic energy of each proton. We are given that one-third of this energy is converted into heat in the target. If in one second the temperature rise of the target is t, the heat gained by the target is Q = mct, where c is the specific heat of the target (of mass m) and Q = 1/3 KE. Therefore, $mct = 1/3 \times \frac{1}{2} nm_p v^2$ or

$$t = \frac{nm_p v^2}{6 \text{ mc}}$$

$$= \frac{3.00\times10^{13}\times1.67\times10^{-27}\text{kg}\times4\times10^{14}\text{m}^2\cdot\text{s}^{-2}}{6\times 1\text{g}\times 4.18 \text{ J}\cdot\text{cal}^{-1}\times0.334 \text{ cal}\cdot\text{g}^{-1}\cdot\text{C deg}^{-1}}$$

$$= 2.39°\text{C.}$$

Water flows at a rate of $2.5\ m^3 \cdot s^{-1}$ over a waterfall of height 15 m. What is the maximum difference in temperature between the water at the top and at the bottom of the waterfall and what usable power is going to waste? The density of water is $10^3\ kg \cdot m^{-3}$ and its specific heat capacity is $10^3\ cal \cdot kg^{-1} \cdot C\ deg^{-1}$.

Solution: The water loses potential energy and gains kinetic energy in falling over the waterfall. The maximum possible temperature difference between the water at the top and at the bottom of the falls occurs if all this kinetic energy is converted to heat. The potential energy lost, mgh, is completely converted to heat in this case. The power available is the potential energy lost in a time τ, or

$$P = \frac{mgh}{\tau} = \frac{\rho Vgh}{\tau} \tag{1}$$

where m is the mass contained in a volume of water V, and ρ is the mass density of water. Note that V/τ is the volume of water passing over the waterfall per unit time. Hence,

$$P = 10^3\ kg \cdot m^{-3} \times 2.5\ m^3 \cdot s^{-1} \times 9.8\ m \cdot s^{-2} \times 15\ m$$

$$= 3.675 \times 10^5\ W = 367.5\ kW.$$

Under the conditions we have assumed, all this power goes into heat.

The rise in temperature, Δt, of a mass of material m, caused by an amount of heat Q is given by the relation

$$Q = mc\ \Delta t$$

where c is the specific heat capacity of the material. Hence

$$\Delta t = \frac{Q}{mc} = \frac{Q/\tau}{cm/\tau}$$

In our case, $P = Q/\tau$ and

$$\Delta t = \frac{P}{cm/\tau} = \frac{P\tau}{mc}$$

Furthermore, m is the mass of water in a volume V, or

$$m = \rho V$$

whence $\Delta t = \dfrac{\rho Vgh}{\rho Vc} = \dfrac{gh}{c}$

$$\Delta t = \frac{9.8\ m \cdot s^{-2} \times 15\ m}{4.186 \times 10^3\ J \cdot kg^{-1} \cdot C\ deg^{-1}} = 0.035^\circ\ C.$$

This is the temperature change experienced by a mass m of water in falling through a distance h.

(a) How much heat energy is produced by a 5-kg rock that falls a vertical distance of 10 m before it strikes the surface of the earth? Assume that the rock was initially at rest.
(b) How much would the temperature of 1 kg of water be raised by the rock striking the earth's surface? (4.19×10^3J of heat energy is required to raise the temperature of 1 kg of water 1°K.)

Solution: (a) For this motion the kinetic energy is initially zero since the rock was released from rest. Just before colliding with the earth, the kinetic energy is a maximum. The conservation of energy requires that the increase in kinetic energy of the rock must equal the change in its potential energy,

$$U - U_0 = mgh - mgh_0 = mg(h - h_0)$$

Since $h - h_0 = 0m - 10m$, $m = 5$ kg, and $g = 9.8$ m/s^2, the change in the potential energy is

$$U - U_0 = (5 \text{ kg})(9.8\text{m/s}^2)(-10 \text{ m}) = -4.9 \times 10^2 \text{J}$$

The minus sign means that the potential energy has decreased. The increased kinetic energy is then

$$4.9 \times 10^2 \text{ J} .$$

This kinetic energy is all converted into heat upon collision with the earth. Consequently, the heat energy Q of the rock and earth is

$$Q = 4.9 \times 10^2 \text{J}$$

(b) Since 4.19×10^3J of heat energy will raise the temperature of 1 kg of water 1°K, 4.9×10^2 J of heat energy will cause a temperature rise of

$$T = \frac{4.9 \times 10^2 \text{J}}{4.19 \times 10^2 \text{J}/^\circ\text{K}} = 1.2 \times 10^{-1}\ ^\circ\text{K}$$

in 1 kg of water.

• PROBLEM 468

A 10-g lead bullet is traveling with a velocity of 10^4 cm/sec and strikes a heavy wood block. If, in coming to rest in the block, half of the initial kinetic energy of the bullet is transformed into thermal energy in the block and half into thermal energy in the bullet, calculate the rise of temperature of the bullet. (The block remains stationary during the collision.)

Figure A

Figure B

Solution: This problem involves the transfer of energy of one form (kinetic energy) into energy of another form (heat). The total energy of the bullet-block system before the bullet strikes the block is just the kinetic energy of the bullet. Or

$$E_T = \frac{1}{2} mv^2 = \frac{1}{2} \times (10 \text{ g}) \times (10^4 \text{ cm/sec})^2$$
$$= 5 \times 10^8 \text{ ergs}$$

After the bullet strikes the block, it loses its kinetic energy. The law of conservation of energy demands that this energy appear as thermal energy in the block and bullet. Or

$$E_T = KE = Q_{block} + Q_{bullet} = 2Q_{bullet}$$

for we are given that $Q_{block} = Q_{bullet}$. Hence,

$$Q_{bullet} = E_T/2 .$$

But $Q_{bullet} = cm\Delta T$ where c is the specific heat of the lead bullet (the amount of heat required to raise the temperature of one gram of the substance one degree centigrade), m is the mass of the bullet, and ΔT is the rise in temperature of the bullet due to the thermal energy. The specific heat for lead is 0.0310 cal/g.c°. We then have

$$\Delta T = \frac{Q_{bullet}}{mc} = \frac{\frac{1}{2}ET}{mc} =$$

$$= \frac{\frac{1}{2} \times 5 \times 10^8 \text{ ergs}}{(4.186 \times 10^7 \text{ ergs/cal})(0.0310 \text{ cal/g-}^\circ\text{C}) \times 10 \text{ g}}$$

$$= 19.3^\circ\text{C}$$

• PROBLEM 469

Near the absolute zero of temperature, the specific heats of solids obey the Debye equation, $c = kT^3$, where T is measured in °K. For a particular solid k has the value 2.85×10^{-2} cal/g·K deg^4. Calculate the heat that must be supplied to raise 50 g of the solid from 10°K to 20°K and the mean specific heat capacity of the solid in this interval.

Solution: The specific heat capacity varies markedly with temperature. The mean value of the specific heat is defined by

$$\bar{c} = \frac{1}{T_2 - T_1} \int_{T_1}^{T_2} c \, dT$$

Over the range 10°K to 20°K its mean value will be

$$\bar{c} = \frac{1}{(20 - 10)^\circ K} \int_{10^\circ K}^{20^\circ K} cdT = \frac{1}{10^\circ K} \int_{10^\circ K}^{20^\circ K} kT^3 \, dT$$

$$= \frac{1}{10^\circ K} \left[\tfrac{1}{4} kT^4 \right]_{10^\circ K}^{20^\circ K} = \frac{1}{40^\circ K} \times 2.85$$

$$\times 10^{-2} \text{ cal/g·K deg}^4 [20^4 - 10^4] \text{K deg}^4$$

$$= 106.9 \text{ cal/g·K deg.}$$

This compares with a magnitude for c of 28.5 cal/g·K deg

at 10°C and 228 cal/g·K deg at 20°C.

The heat that must be applied to raise the temperature of 50 g through the range of temperature is

$$Q = m\bar{c}(T_2 - T_1)$$

$$= 50\ \text{g} \times 106.9\ \text{cal/g·K deg} \times 10\ \text{K deg}$$

$$= 53{,}450\ \text{cal.}$$

HEAT OF FUSION

• PROBLEM 470

A skier descends a slope of 30° at a constant speed of 15 m/s. His total mass is 80 kg. How much snow melts beneath his skis in 1 min, if the latent heat of fusion of snow is 340 J/g and it is assumed that all the friction goes into melting snow?

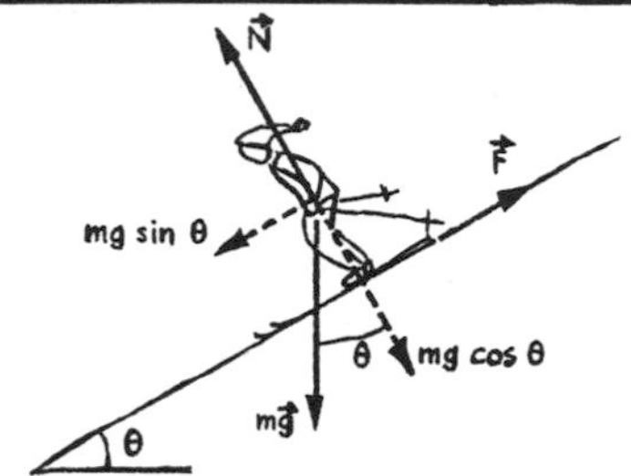

Solution: When the skier is descending the slope, the forces acting on him are his weight $\vec{mg}$ vertically downward and the two forces exerted on him by the slope, the normal force $\vec{N}$ at right angles to the slope and the frictional force $\vec{F}$ opposing the motion (see figure). Since the skier does not rise from the snow and is traveling with constant speed, all forces perpendicular to the slope, and all forces parallel to the slope, must cancel out, as a result of Newton's Second Law. Hence $N = mg \cos\theta$ and $F = mg \sin\theta$.

By Newton's third law, an equal and opposite force $\vec{F}$ is exerted by the skier on the snow. This equal and opposite force moves its point of application a distance $\vec{v}$ in 1 s, where $\vec{v}$ is the constant velocity of the skier. Hence the rate of working of the frictional force acting on the snow is

$$P = \vec{F} \cdot \vec{v} = Fv = mg \sin\theta v$$

$$= 80\ \text{kg} \times 9.8\ \text{m/s}^2 \times \tfrac{1}{2} \times 15\ \text{m/s} = 5880\ \text{W}.$$

If all this power is used in melting snow, the energy available per min is $Q = 5880$ J/s × 60 s/min = 352,800 J/min. But if a mass m of snow is melted per min, the heat required is mL, where L is the latent heat of fusion of snow. Hence

$$m \times 340 \text{ J/g} = 352{,}800 \text{ J/min} \qquad \text{or}$$

$$m = \frac{5880 \times 60 \text{ g/min}}{340} = 1038 \text{ g/min} = 1.038 \text{ kg/min.}$$

• PROBLEM 471

How much heat is required to change 25 kg of ice at -10°C to steam at 100°C?

Solution. We have 4 separate situations which we must consider in this problem. First, the ice is heated to its melting point, which involves a change in temperature. Next, the ice changes state to form water during which there is no change of temperature. Then, as heat is added the water reaches its boiling point and any further addition of heat serves only to finally change the state of the water to steam and will not raise the temperature of the boiling water. Note that the specific heat of ice is different from that of water.

Heat to raise temperature of ice to its melting point = $m_i c_i \Delta t_i$ = 25 kg(0.51 Cal/kg C°)[0 - (-10°C)] = 128 Cal.

Heat to melt ice = $m_l L_v$ = 25 kg(80 Cal/kg) = 2000 Cal.

Heat to warm water to its boiling point = $m_w c_w \Delta t_w$ = 25 kg(1.0 Cal/kg C°)(100°C - 0°C) = 2500 Cal

Heat to vaporize water = $m_w L_v$ = 25 kg(540 Cal/kg) = 13,500

Total heat required	128 Cal
	2,000
	2,500
	14,000
	19,000 Cal

Note that in this summation 128 is negligible and may be disregarded, since there is a doubtful figure in the thousands place in 14,000.

• PROBLEM 472

What must be the speed v of a lead bullet if it melts when striking a steel slab? The initial temperature of the bullet is $T_0 = 300°$ K, its melting point is $T_1 = 700°$ K, its heat of melting q = 5 cal gr^{-1}, and its specific heat c = 0.03 cal gr^{-1} $K^{\circ\,-1}$.

Solution: Assume that all the kinetic energy of the bullet is transformed to heat energy upon impact. The heat released first raises the temperature of the bullet to its melting point T_1, and then supplies the heat of melting the lead. The amount of heat Q_1 required to raise the temperature of the bullet to the melting point is

$$\begin{aligned} Q_1 &= mc(T_1 - T_0) \\ &= (m \text{ gr}) \times (0.03 \text{ cal gr}^{-1} \text{ K}^{\circ\,-1})(700 - 300)\text{K}^\circ \\ &= 12 \text{ m cal.} \end{aligned}$$

where m is the bullet's mass.

Melting requires another amount of heat Q_2, where

$$Q_2 = mq$$
$$= (m\ gr) \times (5\ cal\ gr^{-1})$$
$$= 5\ m\ cal.$$

Therefore, the total amount of heat used up after the collision, is

$$Q = Q_1 + Q_2 = (12m + 5m)\ cal$$
$$= 17\ m\ cal.$$

The conservation of energy principle in this problem can be stated as

$$E_{kinetic} = Q$$

or $\frac{1}{2}\ mv^2$ ergs $= 17$ m cal $\times 4.19 \times 10^7$ ergs/cal

$$v^2 = 2 \times 17 \times 4.19 \times 10^7$$
$$= 14.2 \times 10^8\ cm^2/sec^2$$
$$v = 3.8 \times 10^4\ cm/sec = 380\ m/sec$$

• PROBLEM 473

500 g of lead shot at a temperature of 100° C are poured into a hole in a large block of ice. If the specific heat of lead is .03, how much ice is melted?

Solution: As the lead is poured into the hole in the ice, the latter will melt (gain heat energy) and the former will cool off (lose heat energy). By the principle of conservation of energy, we may write

heat lost by lead = heat gained by ice (1)

Now assuming that the lead doesn't undergo a phase change during the process, we have

heat lost by lead $= m_\ell\ c_\ell |\Delta T|$ (2)

where m_ℓ is the mass of the lead, c_ℓ is the specific heat, and $|\Delta T|$ is the magnitude of the temperature change experienced by the lead. Unlike the lead, the ice changes phase during the process. Assuming that not all of the ice is melted, the portion that is melted will be in equilibrium with the remaining ice. Hence,

heat gained by ice $= m_i\ L$ (3)

where m_i is the mass of ice melted, and L is the heat of fusion of ice. Then using (3) and (2) in (1)

$$m_\ell\ c_\ell\ \Delta T_\ell = m_i\ L$$

or $$m_i = \frac{m_\ell c_\ell |\Delta T_\ell|}{L}$$

$$m_i = \frac{(500\ g)(.03\ cal/g°C)\,|(0°C - 100°C)|}{80\ cal/g}$$

$$m_i = 18.75\ g$$

Note that the final temperature of the lead is 0°C. Since not all the ice is melted, the lead comes into equilibrium with the ice and water at 0°C.

• PROBLEM 474

A 200 g ice cube is placed in 500 g of water at 20°C. Neglecting the effects of the container, what is the resultant situation?

Solution: Note that a cube of ice at 0°C will lower the temperature of the water, and that for every 80 calories of heat energy absorbed by the ice, one gram will be melted without any change in temperature. If the heat given off by the 500 g of water cooling to 0°C exceeds the amount necessary to melt the 200 g of ice, then the water will not cool to 0°C. If, however, it is less than sufficient to melt all 200 g of ice, only a fraction of the ice will be melted, and the resultant temperature will be 0°C.

The amount of heat that must be withdrawn from the water to lower its temperature to 0°C is

$$Q = mc\ \Delta T$$

where m is the mass of water, c is its specific heat, and ΔT is the change in temperature that the water experiences.

$$Q = (500\ g)(1\ cal/g°C)(20°C)$$

$$Q = 10000\ cal$$

The amount of ice that 10000 calories will melt at 0°C is

$$\frac{10000}{80} = 125\ g$$

This is less than 200 g, the original amount of ice. Therefore a 75 g block of ice finds itself floating in water at 0°C.

• PROBLEM 475

A piece of iron of mass, M = 20g is placed in liquid air until thermal equilibrium is achieved. When it is quickly taken out and placed in water at 0°C, a coating of ice of mass, M = 5.22g forms on it. The mean specific heat, c_i of iron over the range of temperature of the experiment is 0.095 cal/g -°C and the heat of fusion L, of water is 80 cal/g. What is the temperature of the liquid air?

Solution: The iron is initially at the same temperature T as the liquid air. When placed in water, it takes heat from the water until its temperature reaches 0°C. The amount of heat Q lost by the water can be found from the amount of ice formed as a result of this transfer of heat.

$$
\begin{aligned}
Q &= ML \\
&= (5.22\text{gr})(80\text{cal/gr}) \\
&= 417.6 \text{ cal.}
\end{aligned}
$$

The heat acquired by the iron as its temperature is raised by 0°C - T°C = - T°C, must be equal to the heat Q lost by the water in turning to ice. Then, if M is the mass of the iron,

$$Q = -C_i MT$$

$$417.6 \text{ cal} = -(0.095 \text{ cal/gr-°C})(20\text{gr})\ T$$

giving

$$T = -\frac{417.6}{20 \times 0.095}\ °\text{C}$$

$$= -220°\text{C}$$

CALORIMETRY

• PROBLEM 476

A 100-gram piece of ice at 0°C is added to 400 grams of water at 30°C. Assuming we have a perfectly insulated calorimeter for this mixture, what will be its final temperature when the ice has all been melted?

Solution: The heat gained by the ice must equal the heat lost by the water. In addition energy is lost because the ice changes from the solid state to the liquid state, which requires the addition of the heat of fusion (which is 80 cal/gm for ice).

The heat gained by the ice is H_g.

$$
\begin{aligned}
H_g &= (\text{mass} \times \text{heat of fusion}) \\
&\quad + (\text{mass} \times \text{specific heat of ice} \times \text{change in temperature}) \\
&= mL + mc\Delta t
\end{aligned}
$$

$$
\begin{aligned}
H_g = {} & 100 \text{ gm} \times 80 \text{ cal/gm} + 100 \text{ gm} \\
& \times (1 \text{ cal/gm} \times °\text{C}) \times (t - 0°)\text{C}
\end{aligned}
$$

where t is the final temperature.

The heat lost by the warm water is H_1

$$H_1 = mc\Delta t$$

$H_1 = 400 \text{ gm} \times (1 \text{ cal/gm} \times {}^\circ C) \times (30^\circ - t^\circ)C$

Since heat gained must equal heat lost,

$100 \times 8,000 \text{ cal} + 100t^\circ \text{ cal} = 12,000 - 400t^\circ \text{ cal}$

whence

$(100 + 400)t^\circ \text{ cal} = 12,000 \text{ cal} - 8000 \text{ cal}$

and

$t = 8$ degrees centigrade,

• PROBLEM 477

Five kg of aluminum ($c_v = 0.91$ J/gm°K.) at 250°K. are placed in contact with 15 kg of copper ($c_v = 0.39$ J/gm°K.) at 375°K. If any transfer of energy to the surroundings is prevented, what will be the final temperature of the metals?

Solution: If the final temperature is T the change in the internal energy of the aluminum will be

$$\Delta U_{Al} = mc_v \Delta T$$

where m is the mass of Al, c_v is the specific heat of Al, and ΔT is the temperature change the sample experiences. Hence

$$\Delta U_{Al} = 5 \times 0.91 \; (T - 250)$$

Similarly, for Cu

$$\Delta U_{Cu} = 15 \times 0.39 \; (T - 375)$$

According to conservation of energy

$$\Delta U_{Total} = \Delta U_{Al} + \Delta U_{Cu} = 0$$

Thus $\quad 5 \times 0.91(T - 250) + 15 \times 0.39(T - 375) = 0$

from which we can calculate $T = 321^\circ$ K.

• PROBLEM 478

The entire power from a 100-hp automobile engine is used to agitate 50 kg of water thermally insulated from its surroundings. How long will it take for the temperature of the water to rise 10 Celsius degrees?

Solution: Since 1 hp = 746 watts (W), the power available is 7.46×10^4 W. All this power is turned to heat in the agitation of the water. A watt equals a joule/sec. Therefore the rate at which heat is supplied to the water is

$$\frac{(7.46 \times 10^4 \text{ joule/sec})}{(4.186 \text{ joule/cal})} = 1.782 \times 10^4 \text{ cal/sec.}$$

In time τ the heat supplied is thus 1.782×10^4 cal/s $\times \tau$.

The temperature rise takes place according to the following equation, the specific heat capacity of water being assumed constant and of value 1 cal/g•C deg over the range of temperature considered: $Q = mc(t_2 - t_1)$, the symbols having their usual significance. Thus

$$1.782\tau \times 10^4 \text{ cal/s} = 5 \times 10^4 \text{ g} \times 1 \text{ cal/g·C deg} \times 10 \text{ C deg}$$

or $\tau = \dfrac{50}{1.782}$ s $= 28$ s.

• PROBLEM 479

500 g of alcohol at 75° C are poured into 500 g of water at 30° C in a 300 g glass container (c_{glass} = .14). The mixture displays a temperature of 46° C. What is the specific heat of alcohol?

Solution: When the alcohol is poured into the glass-water system, the former loses heat energy, and its temperature drops. The latter gains heat energy and its temperature rises. Hence, by the principle of conservation of energy

$$\text{heat loss by alcohol} = \text{heat gained by } H_2O + \text{heat gained by glass} \qquad (1)$$

In general, if a sample of mass m, composed of a substance of specific heat c, is exposed to a temperature change ΔT, it will lose or gain heat energy

$$Q = m\,c\,\Delta T.$$

Using this fact, we may write

$$\text{heat gained by } H_2O = m_{H_2O}\, c_{H_2O}\, \Delta T_{H_2O}$$

$$= (500 \text{ g})(1 \text{ cal/g°C})(46°\text{C} - 30°\text{C})$$

$$= 8000 \text{ cal}$$

$$\text{heat gained by glass} = m_g\, c_g\, \Delta T_g$$

$$= (300 \text{ g})(.14 \text{ cal/g°C})(46°\text{C} - 30°\text{C})$$

$$= 672 \text{ cal}$$

$$\text{heat lost by alcohol} = m_a\, c_a\, \Delta T_a$$

$$= (500 \text{ g})(c_a)(75°\text{C} - 46°\text{C})$$

$$= (14500 \text{ cal})\, c_a$$

(Note that the heat gained by the alcohol is negative. Hence, the heat lost by the alcohol is positive. This is the reason why $\Delta T_a > 0$). Using these facts in (1)

$$(14500 \text{ g } ^\circ\text{C})c_a = 8000 \text{ cal} + 672 \text{ cal} = 8672 \text{ cal}$$

or $$c_a = \frac{8672}{14500} \frac{\text{cal}}{\text{g}^\circ\text{C}} = .598 \frac{\text{cal}}{\text{g}^\circ\text{C}}$$

• PROBLEM 480

The temperatures of three different liquids are maintained at 15°C, 20°C, and 25°C, respectively. When equal masses of the first two liquids are mixed, the final temperature is 18°C, and when equal masses of the last two liquids are mixed, the final temperature is 24°C. What temperature will be achieved by mixing equal masses of the first and the last liquid?

Solution: Let the mass used in all cases be m, and label the specific heat capacities of the liquids c_1, c_2, and c_3, respectively. The heat Q which must be supplied to a body of mass m and specific heat c to raise its temperature through an increment Δt is given by

$$Q = m\,c\,\Delta T$$

In the first mixing, the heat lost by the second liquid must equal the heat gained by the first. Thus

$$mc_2 \times (20 - 18)^\circ\text{C} = mc_1 \times (18 - 15)^\circ\text{C}$$

or

$$2c_2 = 3c_1.$$

Similarly, for the second mixing,

$$mc_3 \times (25 - 24)^\circ\text{C} = mc_2 \times (24 - 20)^\circ\text{C}$$

or $c_3 = 4c_2$.

It follows that $c_3 = 6c_1$.

If the third mixing produces a final temperature t, then one applies the same argument as before, to obtain $mc_3 \times (25^\circ\text{C} - t) = mc_1 \times (t - 15^\circ\text{C})$.

$$\therefore \quad 6c_1(25^\circ\text{C} - t) = c_1(t - 15^\circ\text{C})$$

$$150^\circ\text{C} - 6t = t - 15^\circ\text{C}.$$

$$\therefore \quad t = \frac{165}{7}\,^\circ\text{C} = 23\tfrac{4}{7}\,^\circ\text{C}.$$

• PROBLEM 481

A 1.4447-gm sample of coal is burned in an oxygen-bomb calorimeter. The rise in temperature of the bomb (mass m_c) and the water surrounding it $\left(\text{mass } m_w\right)$ is 7.795 F° = 4.331 C°. The water equivalent of the calorimeter $\left[= m_w + m_c\left(c_c/c_w\right)\right]$ is 2511 gm. What is the heating value of the coal sample?

Solution: The heat flowing in or out of a body of mass m with specific heat c is given by

$$Q = mc\Delta T$$

where ΔT is the change in temperature of the body. Therefore,

$$\text{Heat liberated} = (2511\ \text{gm})(1\ \text{cal/gm C}^\circ)(4.331\ \text{C}^\circ) = 10{,}875\ \text{cal}$$

$$\text{Heating value} = \frac{\text{heat liberated}}{\text{mass of heating agent}} = \frac{10{,}875\ \text{cal}}{1.4447\text{gm}}$$

$$= 7525\ \frac{\text{cal}}{\text{gm}} = 13{,}520\ \frac{\text{Btu}}{\text{lb}}$$

• PROBLEM 482

An aluminum calorimeter of mass 50 g contains 95 g of a mixture of water and ice at 0°C. When 100 g of aluminum which has been heated in a steam jacket is dropped into the mixture, the temperature rises to 5°C. Find the mass of ice originally present if the specific heat capacity of aluminum is 0.22 cal/g·C deg.

Solution: The heat lost by the cooling aluminum must equal the heat gained by the calorimeter and contents. If a mass y of ice were originally present, the total heat gained would have to include the heat acquired by the ice in melting, the heat gained by the 95 g of water in rising in temperature, and the heat gained by the calorimeter in doing likewise. The heat Q absorbed by a mass m of specific heat c as its temperature rises an amount Δt is:

$$Q = m\ c\ \Delta T$$

Also one gram of ice absorbs 80 calories of heat in changing into water. Thus,

heat gained by the aluminum calorimeter $= (50\ \text{g})(0.22\ \text{cal/g·C deg})(5 - 0)°\text{C}$

heat gained by ice as it melts $= (y)(80\ \text{cal/g})$

heat gained by water $= (95\ \text{g})(1\ \text{cal/g·C deg})(5 - 0)°\text{C}$

heat lost by chunk of aluminum $= (100\ \text{g})(0.22\ \text{cal/g·C deg})(100 - 5)°\text{C}$

since steam has a temperature of 100°C. Thus

$$100\ \text{g} \times 0.22\ \text{cal/g·C deg} \times (100 - 5)°\text{C}$$

$$= y \times 80\ \text{cal/g} + 95\ \text{g} \times 1\ \text{cal/g·C deg} \times (5 - 0)°\text{C} + 50\ \text{g} \times 0.22\ \text{cal/g·C deg} \times (5 - 0)°\text{C}$$

$\therefore \quad 80\ y\ \text{cal/g} = \left[0.22(9500 - 250) - 95 \times 5\right]\ \text{cal.}$

$\therefore \quad y = \frac{1560}{80} = 19.50\ \text{g.}$

• PROBLEM 483

An immersion heater in an insulated vessel of negligible heat capacity brings m_w = 100 g of water to the boiling point from 16°C in 7 min. The water is replaced by m_a = 200 g of alcohol, which is heated from the same initial temperature to the boiling point of 78°C in 6 min 12 s. Then 30 g are vaporized in 5 min 6 s. Determine the specific heat and the heat of vaporization of alcohol, and the power of the heater.

Solution: In 7 min 100 g of water are raised in temperature by (100 -16) °C = 84°C. The amount of heat provided by the heater to the water is,

$$Q_w = C_w m_w \Delta T$$

where C_w is water's specific heat, and M_w is the mass of water.

$$Q_w = (1\ \text{cal/gr.°C})(100\ \text{gr})(100°\text{C} - 16°\text{C})$$

$$= 8.4 \times 10^3\ \text{cal}$$

$$= \left(8.4 \times 10^3\ \text{cal}\right) \times (4.186\ \text{J/cal})$$

$$= 3.52 \times 10^4\ \text{J}$$

The rate of delivery of the heat energy is,

$$P = \frac{Q_w}{t} = \frac{Q_w}{(7\ \text{min})(60\ \text{sec/min})} = \frac{8.4 \times 10^3}{420}\ \text{cal/s}$$

$$= 20\ \text{cal/s}$$

$$= \frac{3.52 \times 10^4}{420}\ \text{J/s} = 83.7\ \text{W}$$

Therefore the power of the heater is 83.7 W. With 200 gr. of alcohol in the vessel, the temperature rises from 16°C to 78°C in 6 min 12 s. If C_a is the specific heat of alcohol and M_a is the alcohol's mass, it absorbs,

$$Q_a = C_a M_a\ (78°\text{C} - 16°\text{C})$$
$$= C_a\ (200\ \text{gr})(62°\text{C})$$

amount of heat during the temperature rise. The power of the heater remains the same while heating the water or the alcohol, hence, in calories per second, we have,

$$P = \frac{Q_a}{(6 \text{ min})(60\text{s/min}) + 12 \text{ s}} = \frac{Q_a}{372 \text{ s}}$$

$$20 \text{ cal/s} = \frac{C_a \times (200 \text{ gr}) \times (62°C)}{372 \text{ s}}$$

giving

$$C_a = \frac{(20 \text{ cal/s})(372 \text{ s})}{(200 \text{ gr}(*62°C)}$$

$$= 0.6 \text{ cal/ C°.gr}$$

30 gr of alcohol are vaporized in 5 min 6 s = 306 s, hence the amount of heat, Q', required to vaporize it at 78°C is,

$$Q' = p \times (306 \text{ s})$$

$$= (20 \text{ cal/s})(306 \text{ s}) = 6.12 \times 10^3 \text{ cal.}$$

If L is the heat of vaporization of alcohol, Q' is given by,

$$Q' = L\ (30 \text{ gr})$$

Then,

$$L = \frac{Q'}{30 \text{ gr}} = \frac{6.12 \times 10^3 \text{ cal}}{30 \text{ gr}}$$

$$= 204 \text{ cal/gr}$$

• PROBLEM 484

In a typical experiment performed to measure the mechanical (electrical) equivalent of heat the following data were obtained: resistance of the coil, 55 ohms; applied voltage, 110 volts; mass of water, 153 gm; mass of calorimeter, 60 gm; specific heat of calorimeter, 0.10cal/(gm C°); time of run, 1.25 min; initial temperature of water, 10.0°C; final temperature, 35.0°C. Find the value of J.

Solution: The current through the coil resistance is, by Ohm's Law

$$I = \frac{V}{R} = \frac{110 \text{ volts}}{55.0 \text{ ohms}} = 2.00 \text{ amp}$$

The power (or energy per unit time) developed by the coil is

$$p = \frac{\text{energy dissipated}}{\text{time}} = I^2 R$$

In 1.25 min. the energy dissipated by the coil, to the surrounding water and calorimeter container, is

$$E = I^2 R t = (2.00 \text{ amp})^2 (55.0 \text{ ohm}) \left(1.25 \text{ min} \times \frac{60 \text{ sec}}{1 \text{ min}}\right)$$

$$= 16.5 \times 10^3 \text{ Joules}$$

By the principle of conservation of energy, this electrical energy generated by the coil is converted entirely to heat energy. This heat energy is absorbed by the surrounding water and calorimeter container. As a consequence, the temperature of the water-calorimeter system increases from the initial temperature, 10.0°C to the final temperature, 35.0°C. Consequently, the heat energy absorbed by the two bodies in this system is given by

$$Q = \left(M_\omega C_\omega + M_c C_c\right)\left(T_F - T_i\right) \qquad (1)$$

where C_ω and C_c are the specific heats (that is, the amount of heat required to raise the temperature of one gram of the substance one degree centigrade) of water and of the container, respectively. Substituting the given values in (1), and noting that C_ω is defined as 1 cal/gm°C,

$$Q = [(153 \text{ gm})(1 \text{ cal/gm°C}) + (60 \text{ gm})(.10 \text{ cal/gm°C})]$$

$$[35.0°C - 10.0°C]$$

$$= 3975 \text{ cal.}$$

But from the principle of conservation of energy, electrical energy = heat energy or

$$16.5 \times 10^3 \text{ Joules} = 3975 \text{ cal.}$$

Therefore, in order to find how many Joules are equivalent to 1 calorie, we develop the proportion

$$J = \frac{x \text{ Joules}}{1 \text{ cal}} = \frac{16.5 \times 10^3 \text{ Joules}}{3975 \text{ cal}}$$

or $J = 4.15$ Joules/cal.

Alternatively, 4.15 Joules = 1 cal.

• PROBLEM 485

A 100 g block of copper ($s_{cu} = .095$) is heated to 95°C and is then plunged quickly into 1000 g of water at 20° C in a copper container whose mass is 700 g. It is stirred with a copper paddle of mass 50 g until the temperature of the water rises to a steady final value. What is the final temperature?

Solution: The heat lost by the hot copper block as it cools to temperature t_f

$$m_{block} s_{cu} \left(t_{95} - t_f\right) = (100 \text{ g})(.095 \text{ cal/g}) \left(95° \text{ C} - t_f\right)$$

where s_{cu} is the specific heat of copper.

The heat gained by the water, the container, and the paddle is

$$\left(m_{water}s_{H_2O} + m_{container}s_{cu} + m_{paddle}s_{cu}\right)\left(t_f - t_{20}\right)$$

Here s_{H_2O} is the specific heat of water. Then

$$\left((1000\ g)(1\ cal/g) + (700\ g)(.095\ cal/g) + (50\ g)(.095\ cal/g)\right)\left(t_f - 20°\ C\right)$$

Equating the heat lost to the heat gained:

$$(100\ g)(.095\ cal/g)\left(95°\ C - t_f\right) = \left((1000\ g)(1\ cal/g) + (700\ g)(0.95\ cal/g) + (50\ g)(.095\ cal/g)\right)\left(t_f - 20°\ C\right)$$

Regrouping and solving for t_f:

$$(9.5)\left(95°\ C - t_f\right) = (1000 + 66.5 + 4.75)\left(t_f - 20°\ C\right)$$

$$902.5°\ C - 9.5\ t_f = 1071.3\left(t_f - 20\right) = 1071.3t_f - 21430°C$$

$$22330°\ C = 1081t_f$$

$$t_f = \frac{22330}{1081}\ °C = 20.6\ °C.$$

• PROBLEM 486

When 2.00 lb of brass at 212°F is dropped into 5.00 lb of water at 35.0°F the resulting temperature is 41.2°F. Find the specific heat of the brass. (Neglect the effect of the container.)

Solution: The quantity of heat Q_w added to the water is

$$Q_w = m_w c_w \Delta T_w$$

where m_w and c_w are respectively the mass and specific heat of the water, and ΔT_w is the increase in temperature of the water. Similarly, the heat Q_B lost by the brass to the water is

$$Q_B = m_B c_B \Delta T_B\ ,$$

ΔT_B being the decrease in the temperature of the brass. The heat will flow from the brass to the water until they are at the same temperature. Since the total energy of the system is conserved, the heat leaving the brass equals the heat entering the water,

$$m_B c_B \Delta T_B = m_w c_w \Delta T_w$$

$$(2.00\ lb)(c_B)(212°F - 41.2°F) = (5.00\ lb)(1.00\ Btu/lbF°)(41.2°F - 35.0°F)$$

$$c_B = 0.091\ Btu/lbF°$$

• PROBLEM 487

Given the necessary precautions, water can be cooled to a

temperature T = -10°C. What mass of ice m is formed from M = 1 kg. of such water when a particle of ice is thrown into it and freezing thereby produced? Regard the specific heat of the supercooled water as independent of the temperature and equal to the specific heat of ordinary water.

Solution: The ice particle causes some of the water to freeze. The physics behind this process is somewhat involved. However, we can solve the problem if we consider what happens in the final state.

The partial freezing caused by the ice particle releases heat into the system consisting of ice and water. This heat is the latent heat of freezing released by all freezing water and must be absorbed by the rest of the system. Therefore, the freezing can continue only as long as the water is capable of absorbing the heat released in the process. Equilibrium is attained when the water reaches 0°C at which point water must first freeze if it is to attain a higher temperature. Since water gives off heat when it freezes and there is nothing to absorb this heat, freezing stops at this point.

The latent heat of water is 80 cal/gr. Therefore the heat released in forming m grams of ice is

$$\Delta Q = (m \text{ gr}) \times (80 \text{ cal/gr}).$$

The same heat is used to raise the temperature of the 1 kg. of supercoded water by 10°C;

$$\Delta Q = cM \, \Delta T$$

$$= (1 \text{ cal/gr C°}) \times \left(10^3 \text{ gr}\right) \times (10°\text{C})$$

where c is the specific heat of water. Therefore we get

$$(m \text{ gr}) \times (80 \text{ cal/gr}) = 10^4 \text{ cal}$$

and the amount of ice produced is

$$m = \frac{10^4}{80} \text{gr} = 125 \text{ gr} = 0.125 \text{ gr}.$$

CHAPTER 14

GASES

ATOMIC/MOLECULAR CHARACTERISTICS OF GASES

• PROBLEM 488

About how many molecules are there in 1 cm^3 of air and what is their average distance apart?

Solution: The number of molecules in 1 cm^3 can be calculated from the ideal gas equation:

$$N = \frac{pV}{kT}$$

The pressure of the air is approximately $p = 10^6$ dyne cm^{-2}. The temperature of the air is approximately $300°$ K. If $V = 1\ cm^3$,

$$N = \frac{10^6\ dyne/cm^2 \times 1\ cm^3}{(1.38 \times 10^{-16}\ erg/°K \times 300°\ K)}$$

$$N = \frac{10^6\ dyne/cm^2 \times 1\ cm^3}{1.38 \times 10^{-16}\ dyne\text{-}cm/°K \times 300°\ K}$$

$$= 2.5 \times 10^{19}$$

In 1 cm^3 of air there are approximately 2.5×10^{19} molecules. Imagine the 1 cm^3 to be divided up into little cubes of side a, each of which contains a molecule. Then the volume of each cube is a^3. Hence, in 1 cm^3, there are 1 cm^3/a^3 cubes. Since there is 1 molecule in each cube, the number of cubes must equal the number of molecules in 1 cm^3.

$$\frac{1\ cm^3}{a^3} = 2.5 \times 10^{19}$$

$$a^3 = \frac{1\ cm^3}{2.5 \times 10^{19}} = 4 \times 10^{-20}\ cm^3$$

$$a = 3.4 \times 10^{-7}\ cm$$

This is the average distance apart of the molecules and is about 20 times the size of an oxygen or nitrogen molecule.

• PROBLEM 489

The best vacuum that can be produced corresponds to a pressure of about 10^{-10} dyne cm^{-2} at $300°$ K. How many molecules remain in 1 cm^3?

Solution: We can use the ideal gas equation to calculate N, the number of molecules in the given volume:

$$N = \frac{pV}{kT}$$

$$= \frac{10^{-10}\ \text{dyne/cm}^2 \times 1\ \text{cm}^3}{1.38 \times 10^{-16}\ \text{dyne-cm/°K} \times 300°\ \text{K}}$$

$$\simeq 2{,}500$$

There is still a large number of molecules left.

• **PROBLEM 490**

What is the average velocity of the molecules of the air at 27° C?

Solution: From a simple atomic model in which we consider the atom as a hard spherical body subject to completely elastic collisions we can develop an equation for the average kinetic energy of a molecule which is:

$$\tfrac{1}{2}\, mv_a^2 = \frac{3kT}{2}$$

where m is the mass of one molecule, v_a is its average velocity, k is Boltzmann's constant, and T is the absolute temperature of the environment of the molecule. Multiply both sides by Avogadro's number N_A and 2

$$N_A m v_a^2 = 3N_A kT$$

But $N_A m = M_m$ and $N_A k = R$ since M_m is the mass of one mole of molecules, and R is the gas constant which is Boltzmann's constant times Avogadro's number. Substituting and rearranging we have:

$$v_a^2 = \frac{3RT}{M_m} \quad .$$

Air consists mainly of nitrogen, which is diatomic, and its effective molecular mass is approximately twice the atomic mass of nitrogen. So

$$M_m \simeq 2 \times 14 = 28\ \text{gm/mole}$$

$$v_a^2 = \frac{(3)(8.32\ \text{Joule/mole °K})(273 + 27)°\text{K}}{28\ \text{gm/mole}}$$

where we have used the fact that 27° C = (273 + 27)°K. Hence

$$v_a^2 = 267.43\ \frac{\text{Joule}}{\text{gm}}$$

But 1 Joule = 1 nt • m = 1 kg • m^2/s^2 = 10^7 gm • cm^2/s^2 and

$$v_a^2 = 267.43 \times 10^7 \frac{gm \cdot cm^2}{gm \cdot s^2} = 267.43 \times 10^7 \ cm^2/s^2$$

Therefore $v_a = 5.17 \times 10^4$ cm/s.

This is equivalent to 1,160 miles per hour!

• PROBLEM 491

Compute the r.m.s. speed of O_2 at room temperature.

Solution: The r.m.s. speed of a gas molecule is

$$V_{r.m.s.} = \sqrt{\frac{3RT}{M}}$$

where M is the molar mass of the gas, T is its temperature in degrees Kelvin, and R is the gas constant. Hence,

$$V_{r.m.s.} = \sqrt{\frac{(3)(8.31 \text{ joule/mole}^\circ K)(273^\circ K)}{(32 \times 10^{-3} \text{ kg/mole})}}$$

Here, we have used the fact that $0°C = (0 + 273)°K$.

$$V_{r.m.s.} = \sqrt{2.13 \times 10^5 \ m^2/s^2}$$

$$V_{r.m.s.} = 4.61 \times 10^2 \ m/s.$$

• PROBLEM 492

Show that the average distance, ℓ, a molecule travels between collisions in a gas is related to the number density n and the molecular diameter d by

$$\ell = \frac{1}{n\pi d^2}.$$

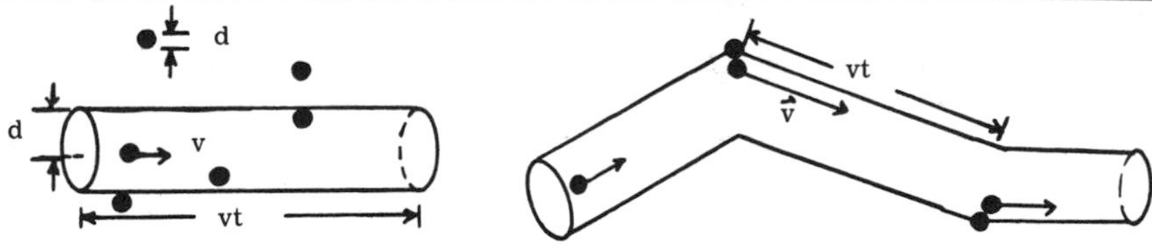

Figure A Figure B

Solution: Consider a molecule moving through a region of stationary molecules. It can collide with those molecules whose centers are at a distance less than or equal to d from its center. If the speed of the molecule is v, it moves a distance vt in time t and collides with every molecule in the cylindrical volume $vt \pi d^2$ (Fig.A).

The molecules in this cylinder cannot avoid the incident molecule because the diameter of the cylinder is 2d, twice that of a molecule. If there are n molecules per unit volume, the number of molecules in the cylinder is

$$N = nvt\pi d^2.$$

Actually, after each collision, the molecule changes its direction and the cylinder mentioned before makes zigzags as shown in Fig. B. The number of collisions is just the number of molecules in the cylinder, hence the average distance per collision is

$$\ell \simeq \frac{vt}{nvt\pi d^2} = \frac{1}{n\pi d^2} .$$

ℓ is called the mean free path.

• PROBLEM 493

A container with a pressure of 3 atmospheres and a temperature of 200° C. contains 36 gm of nitrogen. What is the average speed of the nitrogen molecules? What is the mean distance between molecules (assuming that the container has a cubic shape), and approximately what distance will a molecule travel before it collides with another?

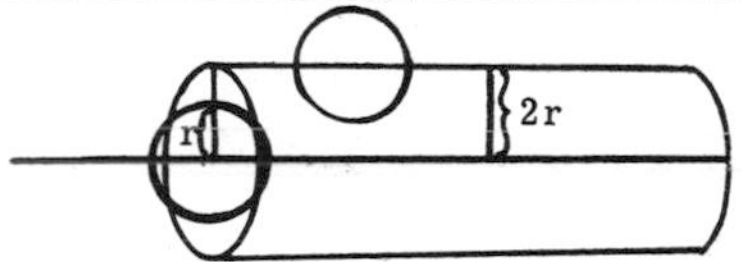

Solution: The number of moles of gas present is the mass of gas present divided by the molecular mass of nitrogen, or

$$n = \frac{36}{28} = 1.29$$

The pressure is

$$p = 3 \text{ atm}$$

$$= 3 \times 1.013 \times 10^5 \text{ N/m}^2 = 3.04 \times 10^5 \text{ N/m}^2$$

Thus the volume of the container is by the ideal gas law

$$V = \frac{nRT}{p}$$

$$= \frac{1.29 \text{ moles} \times 8.313 \text{ joules/°k} \times 473° \text{ k}}{3.04 \times 10^5 \text{ N/m}^2}$$

$$= \frac{1.29 \text{ moles} \times 8.313 \text{ N-m/°k} \times 473° \text{ k}}{3.04 \times 10^5 \text{ N/m}^2}$$

$$= 16.7 \times 10^{-3} \text{ m}^3$$

That is, the volume is a cube with sides 25.6 cm. The total number of molecules is the number of moles of gas times Avogadro's number, or

$$(1.29 \text{ moles})\left(6.02 \times 10^{23} \frac{\text{molecules}}{\text{moles}}\right)$$

$$= 1.29 \times 6.02 \times 10^{23} \text{ molecules}$$

so that the volume per molecule is

$$\frac{16.7 \times 10^{-3} \text{ m}^3}{1.29 \times 6.02 \times 10^{23}} = 2.15 \times 10^{-26} \text{ m}^3$$

$$= 2.15 \times 10^{-20} \text{ cm}^3$$

This corresponds to a cube with sides 2.8×10^{-7} cm, which is the mean distance between molecules.

The mean square speed is calculated from

$$\frac{1}{2} m\overline{v^2} = \frac{3}{2} kT$$

where m is the mass of one molecule of nitrogen, $\overline{v^2}$ is the mean square speed of the molecule, k is Boltzmann's constant, and T is the absolute temperature. Furthermore, since $k = R/N_o$ where R is the gas constant and No is Avogadro's number, and $mN_o = M$ where M is the mass of one mole of gas, we have:

$$\overline{v^2} = \frac{3kT}{m} = \frac{3RT}{N_o m} = \frac{3RT}{M}$$

$$\overline{v^2} = \frac{3 \times 8.313 \text{ joule}/°\text{k mole} \times 473° \text{ k}}{28 \times 10^{-3} \frac{\text{kg}}{\text{mole}}}$$

$$= \frac{3 \times 8.313 \text{ kg-m}^2/\text{s}^2 \ °\text{k mole} \times 473° \text{ k}}{28 \times 10^{-3} \text{ kg/mole}}$$

$$= 4.21 \times 10^5 \text{ m}^2/\text{sec}^2$$

Thus the average speed c of a molecule is

$$c = \sqrt{\overline{v^2}} = 6.5 \times 10^2 \text{ m/sec.}$$

When two molecules of radius r collide, their centers are a distance 2r apart. Therefore, a molecule travelling along a straight line will collide with other molecules within a distance 2r of its center (we assume a simplified model in which one molecule moves and the others remain stationary and in which all collisions are elastic). During a time Δt, the molecule which we are following travels a distance $c\Delta t$. Thus, the molecules with which our molecule will collide are all found within a cylinder of base radius 2r and height $c\Delta t$. This cylinder is called the collision cylinder. If N is the number of molecules in volume V, then the density of molecules is N/V. If we multiply the volume of the cylinder by the density of molecules we will have the number of molecules in the cylinder $(4\pi r^2 \ c\Delta t \ N/V)$. Dividing this quantity by Δt we have the number of collisions per unit time $(4\pi r^2 c \ N/V)$. The average time between collisions is the reciprocal of this, called the mean free time ($V/4\pi r^2 cN$). If we multiply this by the average velocity, we have the average distance a molecule travels before colliding with another (the mean free path):

$$L = \frac{cV}{4\pi r^2 cN}$$

$$= \frac{V}{4\pi r^2 N}$$

Substituting our values, we have (in the present case let $r = 1.3 \times 10^{-10}$ m):

$$L = \frac{16.7 \times 10^{-3}\ m^3}{4\pi(1.3 \times 10^{-10}\ m)^2 (1.29\ moles)(6.023 \times 10^{23}\ moles^{-1})}$$

$$= 1.01 \times 10^{-7}\ m$$

• PROBLEM 494

How many kilograms of O_2 are contained in a tank whose volume is 2 ft^3 when the gauge pressure is 2000 lb/in^2 and the temperature is 27°C?

Solution: Assume the ideal gas laws to hold. The molecular weight of O_2 is 32 gm/mole. The volume V is

$$V = 2\ ft^3 = 2\ ft^3 \times 28.3\ \frac{liters}{ft^3} = 56.6\ liters.$$

Gauge pressure is the pressure above air pressure. Air pressure is 14.7 lb/in^2. Therefore

$$P_{abs} = 2000\ lb/in^2 + 14.7\ lb/in^2 = 2015\ lb/in^2$$

$$= \frac{2015\ lb/in^2}{14.7\ atm/(lb/in^2)} = 137\ atm$$

The temperature must be expressed in Kelvin degrees in order for us to be able to use the ideal gas laws.

$$T = t + 273 = 300°K.$$

Hence the number of moles of gas in the tank is then

$$n = \frac{P_{abs}V}{RT} = \frac{137\ atm \times 56.6\ liters}{0.082\ liter\cdot atm/mole\cdot°K \times 300°K} = 315\ moles.$$

The mass of this amount of gas is

$$m = (315\ moles)(32\ gm/mole) = 10{,}100 gm = 10.1\ kgm$$

Note that we had to convert P and V to the appropriate units in order for them to be consistent with the units of the ideal gas law.

Compute the r.m.s. speed of the molecules of oxygen at 76.0 cm. Hg. pressure and 0°C, at which temperature and pressure the density of oxygen is 0.00143 gm/cm3.

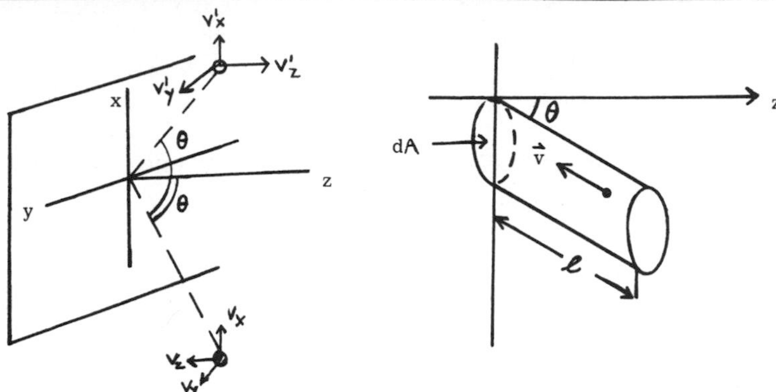

Figure A: Elastic Collision with wall.

Figure B

Solution: The pressure exerted on a wall by an ideal gas can be calculated as follows. In Fig. (a), the elastic collision of a molecule with the wall is shown. If the force exerted on the molecule during the collision is perpendicular to the wall, then the x and y components of the molecule's velocity are not affected. The collision is assumed to be elastic, therefore the z component of the velocity is reversed in direction but remains unchanged in magnitude

$$v'_x = v_x$$

$$v'_y = v_y$$

$$v'_z = -v_z$$

The z-component of momentum of the molecule changes by an amount

$$\Delta p_z = p'_z - p_z = m\left(v'_z - v_z\right)$$

$$= -2mv_z \; .$$

Now, we need to know the number of molecules that strike the wall with velocities $\vec{v}$, per unit time per unit area. Let us consider an infinitesimal area dA on the wall and the molecules incident on it with velocities parallel to $\vec{v}$. These molecules will be included in the tube shown in Fig. (b). Molecules in the tube that strike the wall with a velocity $\vec{v}$ in time dt must be at most a distance $\ell = v dt$ from the wall. Therefore, if we restrict the length of the tube to vdt, all the molecules inside it with velocity $\vec{v}$ will strike the wall within the time dt. The molecules lying outside this tube with the same velocity $\vec{v}$ will not strike dA during the same period. Since the molecules move in random directions, we expect that the number of molecules per unit volume, moving with velocity $\vec{v}$, does not depend on the direction of $\vec{v}$ but rather on its magnitude v. If the density of the molecules with speed v is n(v), the total number of the molecules in the tube with speed v is

$$= n(v) \times \text{volume}$$
$$= n(v) \times v dt \, dA \cos\theta$$
$$= n(v) \, v_z \, dt \, dA \; .$$

Because of the randomness of the motion, the average number of molecules moving toward the wall with velocity $\vec{v}$ is equal to the average number moving away from the wall with velocity $-\vec{v}$. Therefore, the number of the molecules in the tube striking the wall is half the number we found for those with speed v;

$$dN(\vec{v}) = \frac{1}{2} n(v)\, v_z\, dt\, dA .$$

Therefore, the total number of particles incident on an area dA per unit time is

$$\frac{dN(\vec{v})}{dt} = \frac{1}{2} n(v)\, v_z\, dA .$$

The total rate of change of momentum is the number of collisions per unit time multiplied by the momentum change in each collision. Using Newton's Second Law,

$$dF_z = \frac{dp_z}{dt} = \frac{1}{2} n(v)\, v_z \left(-2mv_z\right) dA$$

$$= -mv_z^2\, n(v)\, dA$$

where dF_z is the element of force which the area dA exerts on the molecules which strike it. The reaction force exerted on the wall by the molecules, using Newton's third law, is

$$dF = -dF_z$$

thus the pressure on the wall becomes

$$p = -\frac{dF_z}{dA} = mv_z^2\, n(v) .$$

Now, we have to find the total average pressure, since not all molecules have the same $\vec{v}$. For this, we re-express the average of the quantity $v_z^2\, n(v)$ as

$$\langle v_z^2\, n(v) \rangle_{av} = \overline{v_z^2}\, \bar{n}$$

where $\bar{n}$ is the average number of particles per unit volume;

$$\bar{n} = \frac{\text{total number}}{\text{total volume}} = \frac{N}{V} .$$

The average of v^2, for a gas, is the sum of the averages of its components

$$\overline{v^2} = \overline{v_x^2} + \overline{v_y^2} + \overline{v_z^2} .$$

The motion is completely random, therefore all the directions of motion are equally probable. Therefore we may take

$$\overline{v_x^2} = \overline{v_y^2} = \overline{v_z^2} = \frac{1}{3}\overline{v^2}$$

which gives

$$p = \frac{1}{3} m\, \overline{v^2}\, \frac{N}{V} .$$

In this problem, the pressure of oxygen is the weight of a 0.76 m. mercury column with unit area:

$$p = \text{volume} \times \text{density} \times g = h\rho_{Hg}\, g$$

$$= 0.76\ \text{m} \times 13.6 \times 10^3\ \text{kg/m}^3 \times 9.8\ \text{m/sec}^2$$

$$= 1.01 \times 10^5\ \text{nt/m}^2 .$$

Pressure can be expressed as

$$p = \frac{1}{3}\, \overline{v^2}\left(\frac{mN}{V}\right) = \frac{1}{3}\, \overline{v^2}\left(\frac{M_{\text{total}}}{V}\right) = \frac{1}{3}\, \overline{v^2}\, \rho_{ox}$$

giving

$$\overline{v^2} = \frac{3p}{\rho_{ox}}$$

Hence, the r.m.s speed is

$$\overline{v^2} = \frac{3 \times 1.01 \times 10^5 \text{ nt/m}^2}{1.43 \text{ kg/m}^3} = 2.12 \times 10^5 \text{ m}^2/\text{sec}^2$$

$$v_{rms} = \sqrt{\overline{v^2}}$$

$$= 461 \text{ m/sec.}$$

• PROBLEM 496

Calculate (a) the root-mean-square speed of the molecules of nitrogen under standard conditions, and (b) the kinetic energy of translation of one of these molecules when it is moving with the most probable speed in a maxwellian distribution.

Solution: (a) Each molecule of an ideal gas may have a velocity with rectangular components v_x, v_y, v_z. Hence, the square of the velocity of one molecule is

$$v^2 = \left(v_x^2 + v_y^2 + v_z^2\right)$$

If we calculate this for every gas molecule, add the results, and divide by the number of molecules in the box, N, we find

$$\frac{\sum_{i=1}^{N} v_i^2}{N} = \overline{v^2} = \overline{v_x^2} + \overline{v_y^2} + \overline{v_z^2}$$

where the bar over a quantity indicates an average value. (The summation symbol $\sum$ indicates that we calculate v^2 for each gas molecule and add the results.) Since no direction of motion is preferred for the gas molecule,

$$\overline{v_x^2} = \overline{v_y^2} = \overline{v_z^2}$$

and

$$\overline{v^2} = 3\overline{v_x^2}$$

we call $\sqrt{\overline{v^2}}$ the root mean square speed, v_{rms}.

Now, the average kinetic energy of one molecule is related to the temperature T of the gas by

$$\frac{1}{2}m\overline{v^2} = \frac{3}{2}kT \qquad (1)$$

where m is the mass of one gas molecule, and k is Boltzmann's constant. Then the kinetic energy of 1 mole of molecules is found by multiplying (1) by N_0, Avogadro's number, or

$$\frac{1}{2}N_0 m v_{rms}^2 = \frac{3}{2}N_0 kT$$

The gas constant, R, is, however

$$R = kN_0$$

and $mN_0 = M$ the mass of 1 mole of gas. Hence

$$\frac{1}{2}M\overline{v^2} = \frac{3}{2}RT \qquad \text{and} \qquad \overline{v^2} = \frac{3RT}{M}$$

If we consider a kg mole of the gas, we have

$$\overline{v^2} = 3 \times 8.31 \times 10^3 \frac{\text{joule}}{°\text{K}\cdot\text{mole}} \times 273°\text{K} \times \frac{1 \text{ mole}}{28 \text{ kgm}} = 2.43 \times 10^5 \frac{\text{m}^2}{\text{sec}^2} ;$$

$$v_{rms} = \sqrt{\overline{v^2}} = \sqrt{2.43 \times 10^5 \text{m}^2/\text{sec}^2} = 492 \text{ m/sec.}$$

(b) $E_k = \frac{1}{2}mv_m^2$, where v_m is the most probable speed.

The mass of a nitrogen molecule can be calculated from its molecular weight and Avogadro's number:

$$m = M/N_0$$

$$= 28 \frac{\text{kg}}{\text{kmole}} \times \frac{1 \text{ kmole}}{6.02 \times 10^{26} \text{ molecules}}$$

$$= 4.64 \times 10^{-26} \text{ kg/molecule.}$$

$$v_m = \sqrt{8/3\pi}\, v_{rms} = .921\, v_{rms}$$

$$\text{Hence } E_k = \frac{1}{2}mv_m^2 = \frac{1}{2}m\left(.921\, v_{rms}\right)^2$$

$$= \left(\frac{1}{2}\right)\left(4.64 \times 10^{-26}\text{kg}\right)(.921)^2\left(2.43 \times 10^5 \frac{\text{m}^2}{\text{s}^2}\right)$$

$$= 3.76 \times 10^{-21} \text{ Joule}$$

• PROBLEM 497

Show that $(\bar{v})^2$ does not equal $\overline{v^2}$.

Solution: Consider four particles with the following velocities: 1,2,3, and 4 cm/sec. The square of the average of v is

$$(\bar{v})^2 = \left(\frac{1+2+3+4}{4}\right)^2 \text{cm}^2/\text{s}^2 = \left(\frac{10}{4}\right)^2 \text{cm}^2/\text{s}^2 = 6.25(\text{cm/sec})^2$$

whereas the average of v^2 is

$$\overline{v^2} = \left(\frac{(1)^2 + (2)^2 + (3)^2 + (4)^2}{4}\right)\text{cm}^2/\text{s}^2$$

$$= \left(\frac{1+4+9+16}{4}\right)\text{cm}^2/\text{s}^2 = 7.5(\text{cm/sec})^2$$

so that there is a substantial difference between the two methods of averaging.

If the individual velocities are +1, -2, -3 and +4 cm/sec, there will, of course, be no change in the value of $\overline{v^2}$, but the average velocity $\bar{v}$ will be zero.

• PROBLEM 498

The constant b in van der Waals' equation for helium is 23.4 $\text{cm}^3 \cdot \text{mole}^{-1}$. Obtain an estimate of the diameter of a helium molecule.

Solution. At low densities, real gases obey the ideal gas law $PV = \mu RT$. When the density of a real gas increases, we can no longer neglect the fact that the molecules occupy a fraction of the volume available to the gas and that the range of molecular forces is greater than the diameters of the molecules. Van der Waals developed an equation to take these factors into account. Assume the molecules have a diameter d. Then they can't approach within a distance d/2 of the walls and a distance d from the center of another molecule. Therefore, the volume available to the molecules is less than the volume V of the container that is used in the ideal gas law. The free volume per mole is less than the "geometric" volume per mole, V/μ, by a volume b. Modifying the ideal gas law,

$$p(v-b) = RT$$

where v is the "geometric" volume per mole, V/μ. To account for the intermolecular forces, we note that they vary as the square of the number of particles per unit volume. Inversely, they then vary as the square of the volume per mole, as $(1/v)^2$. The gas acts as though it experienced a pressure in excess of that applied externally. This pressure is equal to a constant a times $(1/v)^2$. The excess pressure $(a/v)^2$ causes the gas to occupy less volume than if it was ideal. Further modifying the ideal gas law gives van der Waals equation of state of a gas,

$$\left(p + \frac{a}{v^2}\right)(v-b) = RT.$$

The equation linking the constant b in van der Waals' equation to the molecular diameter is $b = \frac{2}{3}N_0\pi d^3$.

$$\therefore \quad d^3 = \frac{3b}{2\pi N_0} = \frac{3 \times 23.4\ \text{cm}^3 \cdot \text{mole}^{-1}}{2\pi \times 6.02 \times 10^{23}\ \text{mole}^{-1}} \text{ or}$$

$$d = \sqrt[3]{\frac{3 \times 23.4}{2\pi \times 6.02 \times 10^{23}}}\ \text{cm} = 2.65\ \text{Å}.$$

• PROBLEM 499

Find the minimum radius for a planet of mean density $5500\ \text{kg} \cdot \text{m}^{-3}$ and temperature 400°C which has retained oxygen in its atmosphere.

Solution. The escape velocity from a planet is given by the relation

$$V = \sqrt{\frac{2GM}{r}} = \sqrt{2}\sqrt{\frac{G \times \frac{4}{3}\pi r^3 \rho}{r}} = \sqrt{\frac{8}{3}G\pi\rho r^2}, \tag{1}$$

where r is the planet radius, M is its mass, and ρ is its density

If most oxygen molecules have velocities greater than this, then, when they are traveling upward near the top of the atmosphere, they will escape into space and never return. A slow loss of oxygen from the atmosphere will therefore take place. In this case, however, we are told that the planet has retained its oxygen and we can assume that escape velocity from the planet is greater than the rms velocity of the oxygen molecules. When the two are equated, the minimum radius for the planet results. We need the rms velocity of oxygen molecules. This speed V is so defined that the internal energy U would be the same if all the atoms had this speed. For a gas consisting of N atoms, V is defined by

$$U = N\frac{1}{2}mv^2 \tag{2}$$

where m is the mass of one atom.

If the gas is ideal and monatomic, then we also know that

$$U = N\frac{3}{2}kT \tag{3}$$

where k is Boltzmann's constant and T is the temperature of the gas in °K. Oxygen is neither ideal or monatomic but equation (3) is still a good approximation since the gas is not very dense and therefore interatomic forces can be ignored.

Equating equations (2) and (3), we get

$$mv^2 = 3kT.$$

Multiplying both sides by Avogadro's number N_A (the number of molecules in one mole of the gas),

$$N_A mv^2 = 3N_A kT \tag{4}$$

But $N_A m$ equals the mass, M', of one mole of the gas. Also, by definition $N_A k = R$ where R is the universal gas constant. Substituting these two expressions in equation (4) yields

$$M'v^2 = 3RT.$$

Solving for the velocity, we have

$$v = \sqrt{\frac{3RT}{M'}}. \tag{5}$$

Set equations (1) and (5) equal to each other so as to find the minimum radius. Then

$$\sqrt{\frac{8}{3}G\pi\rho r_{min}^2} = \sqrt{3RT/M'}.$$

where T is the absolute temperature in the atmosphere, and M' is the mass per mole of O_2.

The temperature of the oxygen is 400°C + 273° = 673°K. Oxygen gas is diatomic, and its effective molecular mass is therefore twice the atomic mass of monatomic oxygen

$$M' = (2 \times 16)g \cdot mole^{-1} = 32 \times 10^{-3}\ kg \cdot mole^{-1}$$

$$r_{min} = \sqrt{\frac{9RT}{8G\pi\rho M'}}$$

$$= \sqrt{\frac{9 \times 8.315\ J \cdot mole^{-1} \cdot K\ deg^{-1} \times 673\ K\ deg}{8 \times 6.67 \times 10^{-11} N \cdot m^2 \cdot kg^{-2} \times \pi \times 5500\ kg \cdot m^{-3} \times 32 \times 10^{-3} kg \cdot mole^{-1}}}$$

$$\therefore\ r_{min} = \sqrt{1.708 \times 10^{11} m^2} = 4.131 \times 10^5 m = 413.1\ km.$$

• PROBLEM 500

What is the average kinetic energy of air molecules at a temperature of 300° K? What would be a typical speed for nitrogen molecules, which are the major constituent of air? The mass of a nitrogen molecule is approximately 4.68 x x 10^{-26} kg.

Solution: The kinetic energy of a particle can have more than one term which is quadratic in velocities. If the molecules of an ideal gas display only three dimensional translational motion, then the kinetic energy of a molecule is

$$k = \frac{1}{2} mv_x^2 + \frac{1}{2} mv_y^2 + \frac{1}{2} mv_z^2$$

where v_x, v_y, v_z are the velocity components respectively along the x, y, and z directions. There are three independent quadratic terms and we say that the system has three degrees of freedom. The equipartition theorem states that the average kinetic energy $\overline{E}_k$ of a particle when the system is in thermal equilibrium is

$$\overline{E}_k = \frac{1}{2} nkT$$

where n is the number of degrees of freedom of the system.

For T = 300° K, we have

$$\overline{E}_k = \frac{3}{2} kT = \left(\frac{3}{2}\right)(1.38 \times 10^{-23}\ J/°K)(300°\ K)$$

$$= 6.21 \times 10^{-21}\ J$$

The average speed of a nitrogen gas molecule may be found using the kinetic-energy relation, $E_k = \frac{1}{2} mv^2$. For the nitrogen molecule, then, the average speed v is

$$v^2 = \frac{\overline{E}_k}{2m}$$

$$\overline{E}_k = \frac{(2)(2.61 \times 10^{-21}\ J)}{4.68 \times 10^{-26}\ kg} = 0.265 \times 10^6\ m^2/s^2$$

$$= 26.5 \times 10^4\ m^2/s^2$$

or $v = 5.15 \times 10^2$ m/s

Considering air to be an ideal gas to a first approximation, calculate the ratio of the specific heats of air, given that at sea level and STP the velocity of sound in air is 334 $m \cdot s^{-1}$, and that the molecular weight of air is 28.8 $g \cdot mole^{-1}$.

Solution: The speed of sound in air is

$$c = \sqrt{\frac{\beta}{\rho}} \qquad (1)$$

where ρ is the density of air, and β is its bulk modulus. The latter is given by

$$\beta = -\Delta p/(\Delta V/V)$$

where $\Delta V/V$ is the fractional change in volume of a volume element of air when it is exposed to a change in pressure Δp. For infinitesimal increments, we may write

$$\beta = -\frac{dp}{(dV/V)} \quad \text{or} \quad -\frac{V\,dp}{dV} \qquad (2)$$

Now, the compressions and rarefactions of the sound waves travelling through air are adiabatic. Hence, the pressure experienced by a volume of air, V, must satisfy

$$pV^{\gamma} = \text{constant} = \alpha \qquad (3)$$

where $r = Cp/Cv$, the ratio of the molar specific heat at constant pressure and the molar specific heat at constant volume. Then, using (3)

$$\frac{dp}{dV} = \frac{d}{dV}\left(\frac{\alpha}{V^{\gamma}}\right) = \frac{d}{dV}\,(\alpha V^{-\gamma})$$

$$\frac{dp}{dV} = -\gamma\ \alpha V^{-\gamma-1}$$

Since $\alpha = pV^{\gamma}$, this becomes

$$\frac{dp}{dV} = -\gamma\, p\, V^{\gamma}\, V^{-\gamma-1} = -\gamma\, p\, V^{-1}$$

Using this relation in (2)

$$\beta = -V(-\gamma\ p\ V^{-1}) = \gamma p$$

Inserting this in (1)

$$c = \sqrt{\frac{\gamma p}{\rho}} \qquad (4)$$

But, if air is assumed to be an ideal gas, it must follow the ideal gas law, or

$$pV = \mu RT$$

where T is the temperature of air in degrees Kelvin, and μ is the number of moles of air in a given volume of the gas, V. Then

$$p = \frac{\mu RT}{V}$$

Now $\mu = \frac{M}{M_0}$

where M is the mass of air in a volume V, and M_0 is the mass of one mole of air. Hence

$$p = \frac{MRT}{M_0 V} = \frac{\rho RT}{M_0}$$

by definition of ρ. Using this in (4)

$$c = \sqrt{\frac{\gamma RT}{M_0}}$$

whence $\gamma = \frac{M_0 c^2}{RT}$

$$= \frac{28.8\ \text{g}\cdot\text{mole}^{-1} \times 33.400^2\ \text{cm}^2\cdot\text{s}^{-2}}{8.31 \times 10^7\ \text{ergs}\cdot\text{mole}^{-1}\cdot\text{K deg}^{-1} \times 273\ \text{K deg}}$$

$$= 1.415.$$

GAS LAWS

• PROBLEM 502

A volume of 50 liters is filled with helium at 15° C to a pressure of 100 standard atmospheres. Assuming that the ideal gas equation is still approximately true at this high pressure, calculate approximately the mass of helium required.

Solution: From the ideal gas equation, PV = nRT (where P, V, T are the pressure, temperature and volume of the gas, R is a constant, and n is the number of moles of gas in V.) We can find the number of moles required, and from the atomic mass we can calculate the total mass required. Thus, converting all data to cgs units, we have

$$P = 100\ \text{atmospheres} \times 1.0 \times 10^6\ \frac{\text{dyne}}{\text{cm}^2\ \text{atmospheres}}$$

$$= 1.0 \times 10^8\ \frac{\text{dyne}}{\text{cm}^2}$$

$$V = 50 \text{ liters} \times 10^3 \frac{cm^3}{liter} = 5.0 \times 10^4 \text{ cm}^3$$

$$T = 15° + 273° = 288° \text{ K}$$

Substituting into the ideal gas equation,

$$1.0 \times 10^8 \frac{dyne}{cm^2} 5.0 \times 10^4 \text{ cm}^3$$

$$= n \frac{8.3 \times 10^7 \text{ erg}}{°K \text{ mole}} 288° \text{ K}$$

$$n = \frac{5 \times 10^{12} \text{ dyne} \cdot \text{cm}}{\left(8.3 \times 10^7 \frac{erg}{°K \cdot mole}\right)(288° \text{ K})} = 2.09 \times 10^2 \text{ moles}$$

The atomic mass of helium is approximately 4 gm/mole, and since helium is a monoatomic gas, one mole of helium contains 4 gm of matter. Therefore, 210 moles of gas contains

$$210 \text{ moles} \times 4 \text{ gm/mole} = 840 \text{ gm.}$$

The helium has a mass of 840 gm.

• PROBLEM 503

Does an ideal gas get hotter or colder when it expands according to the law pV^2 = Const?

Solution: The ideal-gas equation states that

$$pV = nRT$$

where V is the molar volume, R is the gas constant, T is the temperature and n is the number of moles. Therefore, for pV^2 = Const., we have

$$(pV)V = \text{Const.}$$

$$nRTV = \text{Const.}$$

or $$V = \frac{\text{Const.}}{nRT}$$

We see that as the volume increases, temperature must decrease since V is inversely proportional to T.

• PROBLEM 504

A certain quantity of a gas has a volume of 1200 cm^3 at 27°C. What is its volume at 127°C if its pressure remains constant?

Solution: Charles' law states that for constant pressure the volume of a gas is directly proportional to its absolute temperature (in degrees Kelvin). Converting the temperatures into Kelvin's temperatures by adding 273 we have,

$$T_1 = 27° + 273° = 300° \text{ K}$$

$$T_2 = 127° + 273° = 400° \text{ K}$$

Using Charles' law, we obtain

$$v_1 = kT_1 \quad \text{and} \quad v_2 = kT_2$$

where k is a constant.

Taking the ratio of these 2 equations, we find

$$\frac{v_2}{v_1} = \frac{T_2}{T_1}, \quad \frac{v_2}{1200 \text{ cm}^3} = \frac{400° \text{ K}}{300° \text{ K}}$$

then

$$v_2 = 1200 \text{ cm}^3 \times 400° \text{ K} = 1600 \text{ cm}^3$$

• PROBLEM 505

An ideal gas is contained within a volume of 2ft^3, when the pressure is 137 atmosphere and the temperature is $27°$C. What volume would be occupied by this gas if it were allowed to expand to atmospheric pressure at a temperature of $50°$C?

Solution: We may use the ideal gas law to analyze the behavior of the ideal gas.

$$PV = nRT$$

where P is the pressure of a container (of volume V) of gas at an absolute temperature T. n is the number of moles of the gas and R is the universal gas constant. Since we are dealing with a fixed mass of gas, we may write

$$\frac{PV}{T} = nR = \text{constant.}$$

Alternatively,

$$\frac{P_1V_1}{T_1} = \frac{P_2V_2}{T_2}$$

where (V_1, P_1, T_1) and (V_2, P_2, T_2) are the conditions which describe the behavior of the gas before and after it expands, respectively. Since $T_1 = 273° + 27° = 300°$K and $T_2 = 273° + 50° = 323°$K then

$$V_2 = V_1 \frac{P_1}{P_2} \frac{T_2}{T_1} = \left(2 \times \frac{137}{1} \times \frac{323}{300}\right)\text{ft}^3 = 295\text{ft}^3 .$$

• PROBLEM 506

A 5000-cm^3 container holds 4.90 gm of a gas when the pressure is 75.0 cm Hg and the temperature is 50° C. What will be the pressure if 6.00 gm of this gas is confined in a 2000-cm^3 container at 0° C?

Solution: From the ideal gas law,

$$\frac{P_1V_1}{m_1T_1} = \frac{P_2V_2}{m_2T_2}$$

Note we can use masses instead of number of moles since they are proportional.

$$\frac{P_1 \times 2000 \text{ cm}^3}{6.00 \text{ gm} \times 273° \text{ K}} = \frac{75.0 \text{ cm Hg} \times 5000 \text{ cm}^3}{4.90 \text{ gm} \times 323° \text{ K}}$$

$$P_1 = 194 \text{ cm Hg}$$

• PROBLEM 507

An automobile tire of volume 5.6×10^3 cc is filled with nitrogen to a gauge pressure of 29 psi at room temperature 300° K. How much gas does the tire contain? If, during a trip, the temperature of the tire rises to 320° K., what will be the pressure?

Solution. First we convert the data to MKS units. Gauge pressure is the pressure above atmospheric pressure (14.7 psi). Thus the total pressure is

$$p = 29 + 14.7 = 43.7 \text{ psi}$$

Using the conversion factor 1 psi = 6.9×10^3 N/m^2,

$$p = 43.7 \times 6.9 \times 10^3 \text{ N/m}^2$$

$$= 3.02 \times 10^5 \text{ N/m}^2.$$

The volume is $V = 5.6 \times 10^3 \text{ cm}^3$

$$= 5.6 \times 10^{-3} \text{ m}^3.$$

The amount of gas in moles is

$$n = \frac{pV}{RT}$$

$$= \frac{3.02 \times 10^5 \times 5.6 \times 10^{-3}}{8.31 \times 300}$$

$$= 0.68.$$

The molecular weight of nitrogen (N_2) is 28 gm. Since there are 0.68 moles of nitrogen in the tire, the mass in grams is

$$m_{N_2} = 0.68 \text{ moles } N_2 \times 28 \text{ gm/mole } N_2 = 19.0 \text{ gm}.$$

As the temperature rises, n and V are constant (for this example); therefore the ideal gas law

$$\frac{p_1V_1}{n_1T_1} = \frac{p_2V_2}{n_2T_2}$$

reduces to

$$\frac{p_2}{p_1} = \frac{T_2}{T_1}.$$

Substituting values,

$$\frac{p_2}{43.7 \text{ psi}} = \frac{320}{300}$$

$$p_2 = 46.6 \text{ psi}.$$

The gauge pressure will be 46.6 - 14.7 = 31.9 psi, and this will be the pressure read by the service station attendant.

• PROBLEM 508

To what volume must a liter of oxygen be expanded if the mean free path of the molecules is to become 2m? The molecules of oxygen have a diameter of 3 Å. Assume that the gas starts at STP.

Solution. The mean free path L is the average distance between successive collisions of a gas molecule and is given by

$$L = \frac{1}{\pi\sqrt{2}nd^2} = \frac{0.707}{\pi nd^2}$$

where n is the number of molecules per unit volume and d is the molecule's diameter. If L is 200 cm, then

$$n = \frac{0.707}{L\pi d^2} = \frac{0.707}{200 \text{ cm} \times \pi\left(3 \times 10^{-8}\right)^2 \text{ cm}^2}.$$

The gas equation is $pV = n_0RT$, where n_0 is the number of moles present in the volume V. But n_0/V is the number of moles of gas per unit volume. Multiplying it by Avogadro's number, N_0, (the number of molecules in one mole of a substance) yields the number of molecules of oxygen in a unit volume. Therefore,

$$\frac{n_o}{V} N_o = n \quad \text{and} \quad \frac{n_0}{V} = \frac{n}{N_0}.$$

Substitution into the gas equation gives

$$p = \frac{n}{N_0}RT =$$

$$\frac{0.707 \times 8.3 \times 10^7 \text{ dynes} \cdot \text{cm} \cdot \text{mole}^{-1} \cdot \text{K deg}^{-1} \times 273 \text{ K deg}}{200 \text{ cm} \times \pi\left(3 \times 10^{-8}\right)^2 \text{ cm}^2 \times 6.02 \times 10^{23} \text{ mole}^{-1}}$$

$$= 0.047 \text{ dyne} \cdot \text{cm}^{-2}.$$

But since the temperature remains unchanged, the expansion takes place according to Boyle's law.

$$p_1V_1 = p_2V_2.$$

The gas starts at STP (standard temperature and pressure). This corresponds to a temperature of 0°C and a pressure of 1 atm.

Thus 1 liter changes to a volume V_2, while the pressure changes from 1 atm to 0.047 dyne $\cdot$ cm^{-2}.

To keep the units consistent, use is made of the fact that 1 atm = 1.013×10^6 dynes $\cdot$ cm^{-2} and 1 liter = 10^3 cm^3. Then

$$1.013 \times 10^6 \text{ dynes} \cdot \text{cm}^{-2} \times 10^3 \text{ cm}^3 = 0.047 \text{ dyne} \cdot \text{cm}^{-2} \times V_2$$

$$\therefore \quad V_2 = \frac{1.013 \times 10^9}{0.047} \text{cm}^3 = 2.155 \times 10^{10} \text{ cm}^3$$

• PROBLEM 509

Find the number, n, of cycles that the piston of the air pump in Fig. B must go through in order to pump a vessel of volume V from a pressure P_1 to a pressure P_2, if the change in the volume corresponding to one cycle of the piston is v. Assume that the air in the vessel is in good thermal contact with the surroundings.

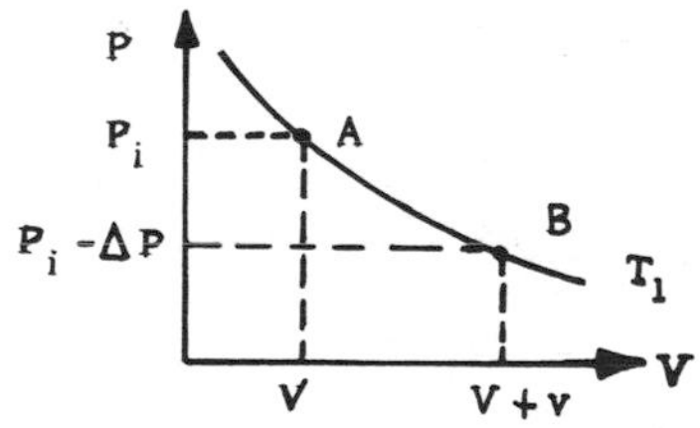

Figure A

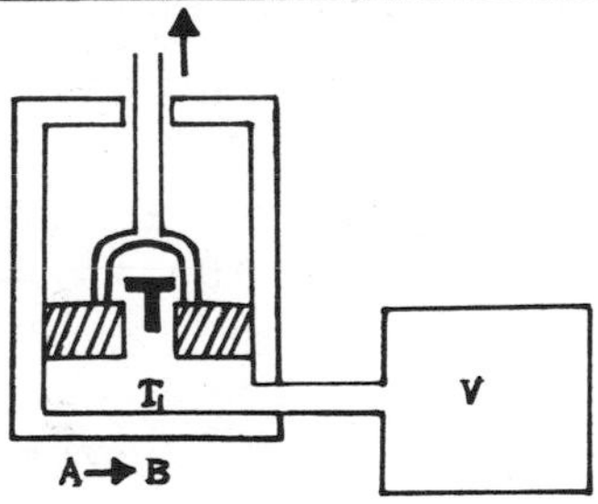

Figure B

Solution: The expansion of air during pumping is an isothermal (constant temperature) process since, as a result of thermal contact with the surroundings, the air in the vessel will have the same temperature as that of the air outside. The process is shown in Fig. A, where expansion proceeds from the initial state A to the final state B. It is governed by the ideal gas law

$$PV = nRT_1 = \text{Constant}.$$

If the volume is increased by an infinitesimal amount dV; then the pressure change can be obtained from

$$d(PV) = 0$$

$$PdV + VdP = 0,$$

or $\frac{dP}{P} = - \frac{dV}{V}$. (1)

The volume changes by an amount v during one cycle. This corresponds to a decrease ΔP in the pressure of the vessel. Integrating (1) from initial to final parameters of the system during one cycle, we get

$$\int_{P_i}^{P_i-\Delta P} \frac{dP}{P} = - \int_{V}^{V+v} \frac{dV}{V}$$

or

$$\ln P \Big]_{P_i}^{P_i-\Delta P} = - \ln V \Big]_{V}^{V+v}$$

$$\ln \frac{P_i - \Delta P}{P_i} = - \ln \frac{V+v}{V} \qquad (2)$$

When the next cycle starts, the pressure of the vessel goes down to $P_i - \Delta P$, but the volume of the vessel is again V. Therefore at the end of the second cycle the pressure becomes $P_i - 2\Delta P$ and (2) for this case is

$$\ln \frac{P_i - 2\Delta P}{P_i - \Delta P} = - \ln \frac{V+v}{V} \qquad (3)$$

Rearranging (3), we have

$$\ln \left(\frac{P_i - 2\Delta P}{P_i} \cdot \frac{P_i}{P_i - \Delta P} \right) = - \ln \frac{V + v}{V}$$

$$\ln \frac{P_i - 2\Delta P}{P_i} - \ln \frac{P_i - \Delta P}{P_i} = - \ln \frac{V + v}{V}$$

$$\ln \frac{P_i - 2\Delta P}{P_i} = - \ln \frac{V + v}{V} + \ln \frac{P_i - \Delta P}{P_i} . \qquad (4)$$

Now, we substitute (2) in (4),

$$\ln \frac{P_i - 2\Delta P}{P_i} = - \ln \frac{V + v}{V} - \ln \frac{V + v}{V} = - 2 \ln \frac{V + v}{V}$$

If we repeat the cycle n times;

$$\ln \frac{P_i - n\Delta P}{P_i} = - n \ln \frac{V + v}{V} .$$

If P_i is the original pressure P_1 of the vessel, then $(P_1 - n\Delta P)$ is the final pressure P_2,

$$\ln \frac{P_2}{P_1} = - n \ln \frac{V + v}{V} .$$

Thus, the number of pumping cycles required to achieve the pressure P_2 is

$$n = \frac{\ln p_1/p_2}{\ln(V + v)/V}$$

• PROBLEM 510

Find the decrease of air pressure with elevation under the assumption that the atmosphere is a homogenous ideal gas at a uniform temperature. (Neglect the variation of the gravitational acceleration g, with elevation).

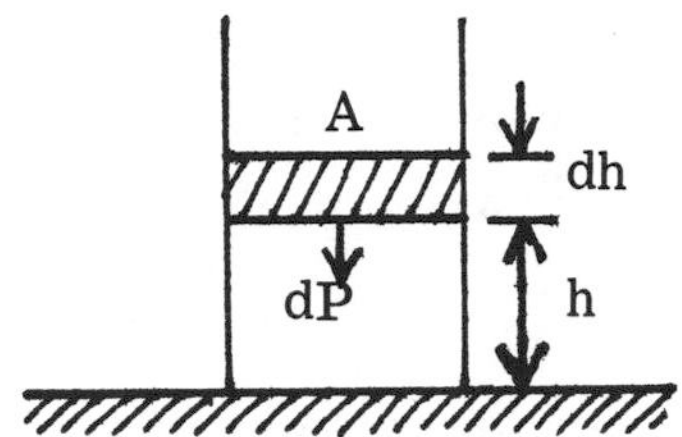

Solution: For this purpose, consider an air column of cross section A and height h, as shown in the figure. In the equilibrium state, the pressure at any elevation is produced solely by the weight of the gas above it. The differential volume element of height dh in the figure increases the force on the lower cross-section by

$$dW = (Adh)\ \rho g$$

where ρ is the density of the air, and $(Adh)\rho$ is the mass of gas in the volume Adh. The resulting decrease in pressure is

$$dP = - \frac{dW}{A} = \rho\ g\ dh \tag{1}$$

(pressure decreases as height increases). Then the ideal gas law, written for one mole of the gas, is

$$PV_M = R\ T.$$

If M is the molar mass of the air, then ρ is

$$\rho = \frac{M}{V_M} = \frac{MP}{RT} \tag{2}$$

Substituting (2) in (1)

$$dP = - \frac{MP}{RT}\ g\ dh$$

$$\frac{dP}{P} = - \frac{Mg}{RT}\ dh.$$

Integration of this equation gives

$$P(h) = P_0 e^{-Mg/RT\ h}$$

where P_0 is the pressure at the earth's surface.

• PROBLEM 511

Gas expanding in a gas engine moves a piston in a cylinder and does 2000 ft-lb of work at a constant pressure of 3000 lb/sq ft. How much does the volume change?

Solution: The work done by a gas in expanding a piston a distance ds is

$$dW = \vec{F} \cdot d\vec{s}$$

where $\vec{F}$ is the force exerted by the gas on the piston of area A. Since $\vec{F}$ and $d\vec{s}$ are in the same direction,

$$dW = F\ ds$$

By definition of the gas pressure, p, we have

$$p = \frac{F}{A}$$

or $\quad F = pA$

Using this in the expression for dW,

$$dW = p\ A\ ds = p\ dV$$

where dV is the change in volume of the gas during the expansion. The net work done by the gas, in expanding at constant pressure from volume V_1 to volume V_2, is

$$W = \int_{V_1}^{V_2} p\ dV = p \int_{V_1}^{V_2} dV = p(V_2 - V_1)$$

Solving for $V_2 - V_1$, we obtain

$$V_2 - V_1 = \frac{W}{p} = \frac{2000\ \text{ft lb}}{3000\ \text{lb/ft}^2} = \frac{2}{3}\ \text{ft}^3$$

for the volume change of the gas.

• PROBLEM 512

Bubbles of air escaping from a cylinder of compressed air at the bottom of a pond 34 ft deep are observed to expand as they rise to the surface. Approximately how much do they increase in volume if it can be assumed that there is no change in temperature?

Solution: Recognizing this as a situation involving Boyle's Law, it follows that

$$\frac{V_t}{V_b} = \frac{p_b}{p_t}$$

where the subscripts b and t refer to bottom and top respectively. Furthermore, p and V represent the pressure and volume, respectively. But p_t is atmospheric pressure $\left(1 \text{ atmosphere} = 14.7 \text{ lb/in.}^2\right)$.

The pressure at the bottom of the pond is

$$p_b = p_t + (\rho g)h$$

where ρ is the density of water, $g = 32 \text{ ft/s}^2$, and h is the depth of point b relative to the surface of the pond (point t). Therefore,

$$p_b = 1 \text{ atm} + \left(62.4 \text{ lb/ft}^3\right)(34 \text{ ft})$$

$$p_b = 1 \text{ atm} + 2121.6 \text{ lb/ft}^2$$

Since $1 \text{ lb/ft}^2 = 1/144 \text{ lb/in}^2$

$$2121.6 \text{ lb/ft}^2 = \frac{2121.6}{144} \text{ lb/in}^2 = 14.73 \text{ lb/in}^2$$

Because $14.7 \text{ lb/in}^2 = 1 \text{ atm}$

$$2121.6 \text{ lb/ft}^2 \approx 1 \text{ atm}$$

Hence $p_b = 2 \text{ atmospheres } \left(29.4 \text{ lb/in.}^2\right)$

It follows that $\dfrac{V_t}{V_b} = \dfrac{2}{1}$

• PROBLEM 513

A cylindrical glass tube of length L is half submerged in mercury, as shown in Figure a. The tube is closed by a finger and withdrawn. Part of the mercury flows out. What length of mercury column remains in the tube? (Figs. b and c). Take the atmospheric pressure P_a to be H cm Hg.

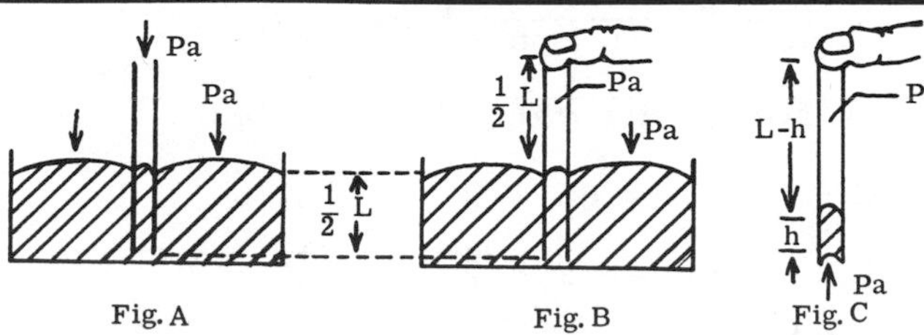

Fig. A Fig. B Fig. C

Solution: When the tube is submerged in mercury with both

ends open, mercury rises in the tube until the levels of mercury in the tube and in the container are the same (Fig. a). We expect no change in the level of the mercury inside the tube if we close the top of the tube since the air trapped inside was previously in equilibrium with the atmospheric pressure P_a. Closing the top does not change the state of the air inside so that the air pressure on the mercury inside the tube is still P_a (Fig. b). When the tube is in air with its top still closed, the mercury flows out until the pressure at the bottom of the tube equals air pressure (Fig. c). If P is the pressure of the air in the tube and h is the length of the remaining mercury, we can write

$$P_a = P + \frac{\text{weight of the mercury}}{\text{cross-sectional area}} = P + \frac{W_{Hg}}{A}$$

$$= P + \frac{\rho_{Hg}\ A \cdot h}{A} = P + h\rho_{Hg} \tag{1}$$

where ρ_{Hg} is the specific weight of mercury.

We can find P by using Boyle's law for the air trapped in the tube. Since the temperature remains constant, we have,

$$(P_a) \times (\text{Volume in Fig. b}) = (P) \times (\text{Volume in Fig. c})$$

or $$P_a \frac{1}{2}LA = P(L - h)A$$

giving $$P = \frac{LP_a}{2(L - h)}. \tag{2}$$

Substituting (2) in (1), we get

$$P_a = P_a \frac{L}{2(L - h)} + h\rho_{Hg}. \tag{3}$$

We are told that P_a is equal to the weight of H cm long mercury column with unit cross-sectional area,

$$P_a = H\rho_{Hg}.$$

Hence, (3) becomes

$$H\rho_{Hg} = H\rho_{Hg} \frac{L}{2(L - h)} + h\rho_{Hg}$$

or $$H = H \frac{L}{2(L - h)} + h. \tag{4}$$

If we solve (4) for h, we get

$$2H(L - h) = HL + 2h(L - h)$$

$$2HL - 2Hh = HL - 2hL + 2h^2 = 0$$

$$2h^2 - 2h(H + L) + LH = 0.$$

The roots of this equation are, by the quadratic formula,

$$h = \frac{H + L \pm \sqrt{(H + L)^2 - 2LH}}{2} = \frac{H + L \pm \sqrt{H^2 + L^2}}{2}$$

Since $P < P_a$, we see that $h\rho_{Hg} < H\rho_{Hg}$, or $h < H$.

The root

$$\frac{H + L + \sqrt{H^2 + L^2}}{2}$$

is greater than H, therefore it can not be the physical choice. Hence

$$h = \frac{H + L - \sqrt{H^2 + L^2}}{2} .$$

• PROBLEM 514

Air at pressure 1.47 lb/in.^{2} is pumped into a tank whose volume is 42.5 ft^3. What volume of air must be pumped in to make the gage read 55.3 lb/in.^{2} if the temperature is raised from 70 to 80°F in the process?

Solution: $P_1 = 14.7$ lb/in.^{2}

Gage pressure is the pressure present minus the air pressure. Therefore, when the gage reads 55.3 lb/in.^{2}, the actual pressure P_2 is

$$P_2 = 14.7 \text{ lb/in.}^2 + 55.3 \text{ lb/in.}^2 = 70.0 \text{ lb/in.}^2$$

$$T_1 = 70°F = 294°K$$

$$T_2 = 80°F = 320°K$$

$$V_2 = 42.5 \text{ ft}^3$$

The volume of air V_1 pumped in can be found from

the ideal gas law. $\dfrac{P_1V_1}{n_1T_1} = \dfrac{P_2V_2}{n_2T_2}$

Since the number of moles of air is constant, this reduces to

$$\frac{P_1V_1}{T_1} = \frac{P_2V_2}{T_2}$$

$$\frac{(14.7 \text{ lb/in.}^2)V_1}{294°K} = \frac{(70.0 \text{ lb/in.}^2)(42.5 \text{ ft}^3)}{320°K}$$

$$V_1 = \frac{(70.0)(42.5)(294)}{(14.7)(320)} \text{ ft}^3 = 186 \text{ ft}^3$$

• PROBLEM 515

An automobile tire whose volume is 1500 in.^{3} is found to have a pressure of 20.0 lb/in.^{2} when read on the tire gage. How much air (at standard pressure) must be forced in to bring the pressure to 35.0 lb/in.^{2}?

Solution: The 1500 in.^{3} of the air at 20 lb/in.^{2} is compressed into a smaller volume at 35.0 lb/in.^{2}

$$P_1V_1 = P_2V_2$$

We must remember to add, 14.7 lb/in.^{2}, the atmospheric pressure to the value read on the tire gauge.

$$P_1 = 20.0 \text{ lb/in.}^2 + 14.7 \text{ lb/in.}^2 = 34.7 \text{ lb/in.}^2$$

$$P_2 = 35.0 \text{ lb/in.}^2 + 14.7 \text{ lb/in.}^2 = 49.7 \text{ lb/in.}^2$$

$$(34.7 \text{ lb/in.}^2)(1500 \text{ in.}^3) = (49.7 \text{ lb/in.}^2)V_2$$

$$V_2 = 1050 \text{ in.}^3$$

The volume of air added to the tire is

$$1500 \text{ in.}^3 - 1050 \text{ in.}^3 = 450 \text{ in.}^3$$

when its gage pressure is 35.0 lb/in^2.

The volume at atmospheric pressure will be found from Boyle's law,

$$14.7 \text{ lb/in.}^2 \times V = 49.7 \text{ lb/in.}^2 \times 450 \text{ in.}^3$$

$$V = \frac{49.7}{14.7} 450 \text{ in.}^3 = 1500 \text{ in.}^3$$

• PROBLEM 516

A cyclinder containing gas at 27°C is divided into two parts of equal volume, each of 100 cm^3, and at equal pressure, by a piston of cross-sectional area 15 cm^2. The gas in one part is raised in temperature to 100°C; the other volume is maintained at the original temperature. The piston and walls are perfect insulators. How far will the piston move during the change in temperature?

Solution. The heating of one side of the cylinder increases the pressure of the gas in that portion. If the piston were fixed, the volumes on the two sides would stay equal and there would be a pressure difference across the piston. Since the piston is movable, it alters its position until there is no pressure difference between its two sides: the hotter gas expands and thus drops in pressure, and the cooler gas is compressed and thus increases in pressure. When equilibrium has been reached, the two pressures are equal at p_0; the cooler gas now occupies a volume smaller by an amount dV and the hotter gas a volume greater by a corresponding amount dV. The ideal gas equations for both compartments are

$$p_0(V - dV) = nRT$$
$$p_0(V + dV) = nRT' \qquad (1)$$

where n is the number of moles in each compartment, T and T' are the temperatures. Dividing (1) by (2), we get

$$\frac{V - dV}{V + dV} = \frac{T}{T'}$$

$$VT' - dVT' = VT + dVT$$

$$V\left(T' - T\right) = dV\left(T + T'\right)$$

or

$$\frac{dV}{V} = \frac{T' - T}{T' + T}$$

Therefore, the change in the volume of each compartment is

$$dV = \frac{(373 - 300)°C}{(373 + 300)°C} \times 100 \text{ cm}^3 = 10.85 \text{ cm}^3.$$

The piston has an area of 15 cm^2. Hence it moves a distance of 10.85 cm^3/15 cm^2 = 0.723 cm.

• PROBLEM 517

Two bulbs of equal volume joined by a narrow tube of negligible volume contain hydrogen at 0°C and 1 atm pressure.
1) What is the pressure of the gas when one of the bulbs is immersed in steam at 100°C and the other in liquid oxygen at -190°C?
2) The volume of each bulb is 10^{-3} m^3 and the density of hydrogen is 0.09 kg·m^{-3} at 0°C and 1 atm. What mass of hydrogen passes along the connecting tube?

Solution. 1) When the two bulbs are at different temperatures, one bulb contains n_1 moles at temperature T_1 occupying volume V, and the other n_2 moles at temperature T_2 also occupying volume V. Once equilibrium has been attained, both must be at the same pressure p. Originally, the gas in the bulbs was at T_0 = 0°C = 273°K with the pressure p_0 = 1 atm. It had $\left(n_1 + n_2\right)$ moles in a volume of 2V. The gas equation in this case is pV = nRT where R is the gas constant. Then $p_0(2V) = \left(n_1 + n_2\right)RT_0$ or

$$p_0V = \frac{n_1 + n_2}{2}RT_0 \qquad (1)$$

When the bulbs are immersed in steam and liquid oxygen, the gas equation for each bulb is

$$pV = n_1RT_1, \quad T_1 = 100°C = 373°K \qquad (2)$$

$$pV = n_2RT_2, \quad T_2 = -190°C = 83°K \qquad (3)$$

Dividing (2) by (1), we get,

$$\frac{p}{p_0} = \frac{n_1RT_1}{\frac{1}{2}\left(n_1+n_2\right)RT_0}$$

$$= \frac{2n_1T_1}{\left(n_1+n_2\right)T_0} = \frac{2T_1}{\left(1 + \frac{n_2}{n_1}\right)T_0} \tag{4}$$

From (2) and (3), we see that

$$pV = n_1RT_1 = n_2RT_2$$

or

$$\frac{n_2}{n_1} = \frac{T_1}{T_2}. \tag{5}$$

Substituting in (4),

$$\frac{p}{p_0} = \frac{2T_1}{\left(1 + \frac{T_1}{T_2}\right)T_0} = \frac{2 \times 373°K}{\left(1 + \frac{373°K}{83°K}\right)273°K} = 0.497.$$

Hence

$$p = 0.497\ p_0 = 0.497\ \text{atm}.$$

At the initial temperature T_0, one bulb contained $\frac{1}{2}\left(n_1 + n_2\right)$ moles and at temperature T_1 it had n_1 moles. Since $T_1 = 100°C > T_0 = 0°C$, gas in this bulb expands and some of it flows into the other bulb. The number of moles that pass along the connecting tube is

$$\frac{1}{2}\left(n_1 + n_2\right) - n_1 = \frac{1}{2}\left(n_2 - n_1\right).$$

The equation $\frac{n_2}{n_1} = \frac{T_1}{T_2}$ from (5) is identical to

$$\frac{n_2 - n_1}{n_1 + n_2} = \frac{T_1 - T_2}{T_2 + T_1} \qquad \text{or}$$

$$\frac{\frac{1}{2}\left(n_2 - n_1\right)}{\frac{1}{2}\left(n_1 + n_2\right)} = \frac{T_1 - T_2}{T_2 + T_1} = \frac{373°K - 83°K}{373°K + 83°K} = \frac{290}{456}.$$

Thus $\frac{290}{456}$ of the mass in the bulb at 0°C passed along the tube as the temperature varied from 0°C to 100°C. But each bulb held $10^{-3}\ m^3$ at 0°C, corresponding to a mass of

$$10^{-3}\ m^3 \times 0.09\ kg \cdot m^{-3} = 9 \times 10^{-5}\ kg.$$

The mass passing along the tube is thus

$$\frac{290}{456} \times 9 \times 10^{-5}\ \text{kg} = 5.72 \times 10^{-5}\ \text{kg} = 0.0572\ \text{g}.$$

• PROBLEM 518

A factory chimney of height h = 50 m carries off smoke at a temperature $T_1 = 60°$ C. Find the static pressure ΔP producing the draught in the chimney. The air temperature is $T_0 = 0°$ C. The density of air is $d_0 = 1.29 \times 10^{-3}$ g cm^{-3} at 0° C.

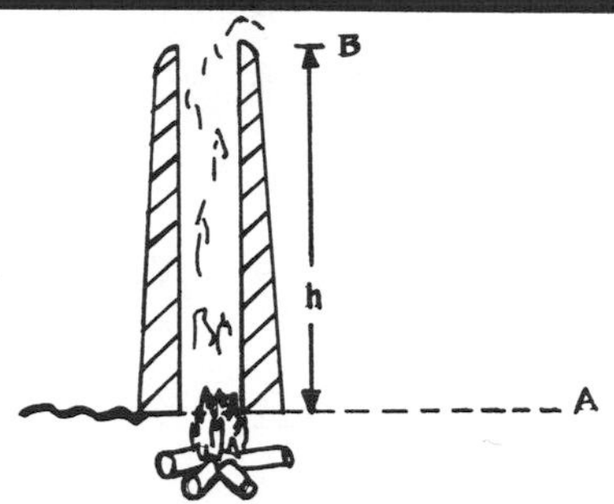

Solution: Let us assume that initially the chimney has no smoke. The pressure A (see the figure) is the sum of the air pressure P_B at B plus the pressure at A due to the air column in the chimney

$$P_A = P_B + gd_0h$$

where g is the gravitational acceleration, and d_0 is the density of air at $T_0 = 0°C$.

When hot smoke fills the chimney, the temperature inside becomes T_1. We can take the density of the smoke-air mixture as approximately equal to that of the air d_1 at T_1. The pressure at A in this case, is

$$P'_A = P_B + gd_1h.$$

Right before A, where hot air is being produced, pressure is equal to the air pressure P_A. Since $P'_A < P_A$, hot air is pushed upward by the difference

$$\Delta P = P_A - P'_A = gh(d_0 - d_1).$$

We can arrive at this result in a simpler manner if we realize that the warm air in the chimney is less dense than the surrounding cold air and is in touch with the cold air at the two ends of the chimney. Hence, as a result of Archimedes' principle for fluids, hot air will be buoyed up with a force equal to the weight of the cold air displaced by the warm air. The net force ΔF acting on the warm air column therefore equals the difference between this buoyant force and the weight of the warm air

$$\Delta F = gd_0V - gd_1V = gAh(d_0 - d_1).$$

The resulting draught pressure ΔP is

$$\Delta P = \frac{\Delta F}{A} = gh\left(d_0 - d_1\right).$$

Let us assume that air can be thought of as an ideal gas. We do not expect the pressure inside the chimney to differ appreciably from the outside pressure since it is mainly the higher temperature that determines the volume of the warm air:

$$V \approx \text{Constant x temperature.}$$

Under the assumption that pressure is approximately constant, the volume of a gas at two different temperatures T_1 and T_0 obeys the relation

$$\frac{V_0}{V_1} = \frac{T_0}{T_1} .$$

The mass of air in both cases is the same

$$\text{Mass} = V_0 d_0 = V_1 d_1 ,$$

giving

$$\frac{V_0}{V_1} = \frac{d_1}{d_0} .$$

The density of warm air at T_1° C is related to the density of air at 0°C by

$$d_1 = d_0 \frac{T_0}{T_1} .$$

The final expression for ΔP is therefore

$$\Delta P = ghd_0\left(1 - \frac{d_1}{d_0}\right) = ghd_0\left(1 - \frac{T_0}{T}\right).$$

or

$$= \left(980 \text{ cm/sec}^2\right) \times \left(50 \text{ m} \times 10^2 \text{ cm/m}\right) \times$$
$$\times \left(1.29 \times 10^{-3} \text{ gm/cm}^3\right) \times \left(1 - \frac{273°\text{K}}{(273° + 60°)\text{K}}\right)$$
$$= 1.14 \times 10^3 \text{ dynes/cm}^2$$

• PROBLEM 519

A barometer tube extends 89.4 cm above a free mercury surface and has air in the region above the mercury column. The height of the column is 74.5 cm at 25°C when the reading on a true barometer is 76 cm. On a day when the temperature is 11°C it reads 75.2 cm. What is the true atmospheric pressure?

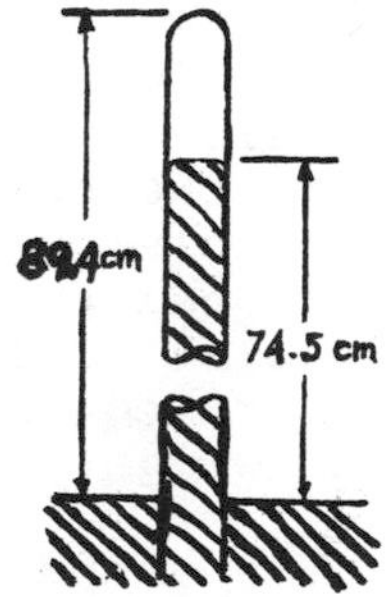

<u>Solution:</u> Since there is a fixed mass of air at all times

in the top of the barometer tube, the gas law (pV/T) = const may be applied to it directly.

In the first case when the temperature is 25°C=25 +273= 298°K, the barometric height is 76 cm of mercury. This is the pressure exerted at the free surface of mercury and thus, by the laws of hydrostatic pressure, at the same horizontal level inside the barometer tube. At points in the tube higher than this, the pressure drops off with height.

If there were true vacuum instead of air above the mercury column in the tube, the mercury would rise to a height of 76 cm, which is the atmospheric pressure. However, the rise of the mercury is resisted by the pressure of the air trapped in the tube (see the figure), therefore the pressure of the trapped air must be equal to that exerted by (76 - 74.5) = 1.5 cm of mercury. The volume of the trapped air is $(89.4 - 74.5)A\ cm^3 = 14.9A\ cm^3$, where $A\ cm^2$ is the cross-sectional area of the tube.

In the second case, when the temperature is 11°C = 284°K, the pressure of the trapped air is (p_0 - 75.2 cm of mercury), where p_0 is the atmospheric pressure on that day. The volume of trapped air is

$(89.4 - 75.2)A\ cm^3 = 14.2A\ cm^3$. Hence

$$\frac{1.5\ cm \times 14.9A\ cm^3}{298°C} = \frac{(p_0 - 75.2\ cm)14.2A\ cm^3}{284°C}..$$

$$\therefore\quad p_0 - 75.2\ cm = 1.5\ cm \quad or \quad p_0 = 76.7\ cm\ of\ mercury.$$

• PROBLEM 520

The dew point (the temperature at which the water vapor in a given sample of air becomes saturated and condensation becomes possible) of a mass of air at 15°C is 10°C. Calculate the relative humidity and the mass of 1 liter of the moist air if the barometric height is 76 cm of mercury. The gram-molecular weight of air is 28.9 g and the saturated aqueous vapor pressures at 10°C and 15°C are 9.2 mm of mercury and 12.8 mm of mercury, respectively.

Solution. The relative humidity is defined as

$$100 \times \frac{\text{saturated vapor pressure at the dew point}}{\text{saturated vapor pressure at the given temperature}}.$$

Therefore the relative humidity is

$$RH = \frac{9.2}{12.8} \times 100\% = 71.9\%$$

Using the gas law, one can calculate the number of moles present independently for (a) the dry air and (b) the water vapor. Measuring the pressure p in atmospheres and the volume V in liters gives

$$(a)\ n = \frac{pV}{RT} = \frac{1\ atm \times 1\ liter}{0.082\ liter\text{-}atm/mole - °K \times 288°K} = 0.0424\ mole$$

and

$$\text{(b)}\ n' = \frac{p'V}{RT} = \frac{\frac{9.2 \text{ mm Hg}}{760 \text{ mm Hg/atm}} \times 1 \text{ liter}}{0.082 \text{ liter-atm/mole - °K} \times 288°K}$$

$$= 0.00051 \text{ mole.}$$

The mass of moist air consists of dry air and water vapor. In one liter of moist air, there are 0.0424 moles of dry air and 0.00051 mole of water vapor, hence its mass is

$$M = 0.0424 \text{ mole} \times 28.9 \text{ g/mole} + 0.00051 \text{ mole} \times 18.0 \text{ g/mole}$$

$$= (1.2254 + 0.0092)\text{g} = 1.2346 \text{ g.}$$

• PROBLEM 521

The pressure of the nitrogen in a constant-volume gas thermometer is 78.0 cm at 0°C. What is the temperature of a liquid in which the bulb of the thermometer is immersed when the pressure is seen to be 87.7 cm?

Solution: In a thermometer there is one physical property (thermometric property) whose change is used to indicate a change of temperature. The thermometric property of the thermometer, in this case the pressure, is taken as being directly proportional to the Kelvin temperature. Therefore

$$T = cp$$

where c is a constant of proportionality. We can then state that for two temperatures on this scale, the following relationship holds:

$$\frac{T_1}{T_2} = \frac{p_1}{p_2}$$

Let T_1 be 0°C or 273°K. Substituting the known values, we get

$$T_2 = \frac{T_1 p_2}{p_1} = \frac{(273°K)(87.7 \text{ cm})}{(78.0 \text{ cm})} = 307°K$$

Reconverting to the Celsius scale,

$$T_2 = 307°K - 273°K = 34°C$$

• PROBLEM 522

In a Wilson cloud chamber at a temperature of 20°C, particle tracks are made visible by causing condensation on ions by an approximately reversible adiabatic expansion of the volume in the ratio

$$\frac{\text{final volume}}{\text{initial volume}} = 1.375 \text{ to } 1.$$

The ratio of the specific heats of the gas is 1.41. Estimate the gas temperature after the expansion.

Solution. The adiabatic expansion of an ideal gas obeys the law

$$pV^{\gamma} = \text{constant}$$

where γ is the ratio of the specific heats at constant volume and at constant pressure,

$$\gamma = \frac{C_P}{C_V}.$$

Also, by the ideal gas law $P = \frac{nRT}{V}$, we also have $\frac{pV}{T} =$ constant (for the number of moles of gas within the chamber is constant).

Then $TV^{\gamma-1} =$ constant. If T_1 and V_1 are the initial temperature and volume respectively, and T_2, V_2 are the final ones,

$$T_1V_1^{\gamma-1} = T_2V_2^{\gamma-1}$$

or

$$\frac{T_2}{T_1} = \left(\frac{V_1}{V_2}\right)^{\gamma-1}$$

Taking the logarithm of both sides,

$$\log\left(\frac{T_2}{T_1}\right) = (\gamma - 1)\log\left(\frac{V_1}{V_2}\right) = 0.41 \log\left(\frac{1}{1.375}\right) = -0.0567$$

$$= \bar{1}.9433.$$

From the logarithmic table, we get

$$\frac{T_2}{T_1} = 0.878.$$

$$T_2 = 0.878T_1 = 0.878 \times 293°K = 257.2°K = -15.8°C.$$

CHAPTER 15

THERMODYNAMICS

ENTROPY

• PROBLEM 523

What is the change in entropy of a gas if the temperature increases from 100°K to 101°K when heat is added and the volume is kept constant?

Solution: Consider a system containing a large number of particles. When heat is added to this system, the average kinetic energy of the particles will increase. This is reflected as an increase in the temperature of the system. The system will have a higher internal disorder as a result of increased thermal motion of its constitutents.

The entropy of a system is a measure of the tendency of a system to increase its internal disorder. Therefore, as heat is added, entropy increases. In our problem, let the increase in entropy be Δs when the system reaches a new equilibrium after its temperature increases by $\Delta T = 1°K$ Since $\Delta T \ll T = 100°K$, the amount of the heat added must be very small, and the entropy change is

$$\Delta s = \frac{Q}{T}$$

where Q is the quantity of heat added.

The heat added to a gas is equal to the gas' increase in internal energy plus the work done on the gas while expanding. The volume is kept constant, therefore the mechanical work done is zero . Using N for Avogadro's number and k for Boltzmann's constant, we have (for an ideal monatomic gas) $Q = \Delta E = \frac{3}{2} Nk\, \Delta T$

where ΔE is the increase in the internal energy of the gas. Hence,

$$\Delta s = \frac{3}{2} Nk \frac{\Delta T}{T} = \frac{3}{2} \frac{\left(6.02 \times 10^{23} \text{mole}^{-1}\right) \times \left(1.38 \times 10^{-23} J/°k\right) 1°k}{100°K}$$

$$= 0.125 \text{ joule/mole}°K$$

• PROBLEM 524

Find the entropy rise ΔS of an ideal gas of N molecules occupying a volume V_1 when it expands to a volume V_2 under constant pressure.

Solution: If dQ is the heat added to the system, dW is the work done by the system and dU is the change in the internal energy of the system, the first law of thermodynamics states that

$$dQ = dU + dW,$$

or

$$TdS = dU + PdV, \quad (1)$$

where S is the entropy, and P, V, T are, respectively, the pressure, the volume and the temperature of the gas. The internal energy of an ideal gas (whose molecules have only translational motion) is

$$U = \frac{3}{2} NkT$$

where k is Boltzmann's constant.

Since for an ideal gas

$$PV = NkT, \qquad (2)$$

its internal energy can be expressed as

$$U = \frac{3}{2} PV.$$

If P is constant, we get

$$dU = \frac{3}{2} PdV. \qquad (3)$$

Substituting (3) in (1),

$$TdS = \frac{3}{2} PdV + PdV = \frac{5}{2} PdV$$

or

$$dS = \frac{5}{2} \frac{P}{T} dV.$$

From (2), we see that $\frac{P}{T} = \frac{Nk}{V}$. Therefore

$$dS = \frac{5}{2} Nk \frac{dV}{V}. \qquad (4)$$

Integrating (4) between initial and final states as the gas expands, we get the entropy rise

$$\Delta S = \frac{5}{2} Nk \int_{V_1}^{V_2} \frac{dV}{V} = \frac{5}{2} Nk \ln \frac{V_2}{V_1} .$$

• PROBLEM 525

When 100 g of water at 0°C are mixed with 50 g of water at 50°C, what is the change of entropy on mixing?

<u>Solution.</u> The 100 g of water at 0°C are arbitrarily said to have zero entropy. The 50 g of water at 50°C have a greater entropy than the same quantity of water at 0°C, since it contains more heat energy. Entropy S is defined as

$$ds = \frac{dQ}{T} \qquad (1)$$

where ds is the infinitesimal change in the entropy due to an infinitesimal quantity of heat dQ in the system. T is the instantaneous temperature in Kelvin degrees. Integrating both sides of equation (1) gives

$$S_2 - S_1 = \int_{Q_1}^{Q_2} \frac{dQ}{T}. \qquad (2)$$

In raising its temperature from a temperature t_1 to t_2, a substance absorbs heat dQ given by

$$dQ = mcdT \tag{3}$$

where m is the mass of the substance, c is its specific heat, and dT is its change in temperature in Kelvin degrees (same as change in Celsius degrees). Substitution of equation (3) into equation (2) yields

$$S_2 - S_1 = \int_{t_1}^{t_2} mc \frac{dT}{T} \tag{4}$$

In degree Kelvin, 0°C = (0 + 273)°K = 273°K and 50°C = (50 + 273)°K = 323°K. Let m_2 = 50 gm and m_1 = 100 g. The specific heat of water is given by $c = 1 \text{ cal} \cdot g^{-1} \cdot K\ deg^{-1}$. Then

$$S_2 - S_1 = \int_{273°K}^{323°K} m_2 c \frac{dT}{T} = m_2 c \ln\left(\frac{323}{273}\right) = 50 \text{ g} \times 1 \text{ cal} \cdot g^{-1} \cdot K\ deg^{-1} \times 2.303 \times 0.0730$$

$$= 8.4 \text{ cal} \cdot K\ deg^{-1}.$$

Since $S_1 = 0$, it follows that $S_2 = 8.4 \text{ cal} \cdot K\ deg^{-1}$.

When the water is mixed, the heat gained by the cold water is equal to the heat lost by the hot water. Therefore, $m_1 c\left(t_3 - t_1\right) = m_2 c\left(t_2 - t_3\right)$, where t_1 is the original temperature (0°C) of the 100 g of water, t_2 is the original temperature (50°C) of the 50 g of water and t_3 is the final, intermediate temperature of the system.

$$100 \text{ g} \times \left(t_3 - 0°C\right) = 50 \text{ g} \times \left(50°C - t_3\right). \therefore t_3 = \frac{2500°C}{150}$$

$$= 16.67°C.$$

Converting to Kelvin degrees in order to be able to use equation (4), we have t_3 = 16.67°C = (16.67 + 273)°K = 289.67°K.

The entropy of the final mixture is

$$S_3 = \int_{t_1}^{t_3} \frac{dQ}{T} = \int_{273°K}^{289.67°K} \left(m_1 + m_2\right) c \frac{dT}{T} = \left(m_1 + m_2\right) c \ln\left(\frac{289.67}{273}\right)$$

$$= 150 \text{ g} \times 1 \text{ cal} \cdot g^{-1} \cdot K\ deg^{-1} \times 2.303 \times 0.0257$$

$$= 8.9 \text{ cal} \cdot K\ deg^{-1}.$$

The increase in entropy is thus $0.5 \text{ cal} \cdot K\ deg^{-1}$.

A 5-gm block of aluminum at 250°K is placed in contact with a 15-gm copper block at 375°K. The equilibrium temperature of the system is 321°K. The specific heat of aluminum is $c_v = 0.91$ joules/gm-°K, and that of copper $c_v = 0.39$ joules/gm- K. What is the change in entropy of the system when the two blocks of metal are placed in contact?

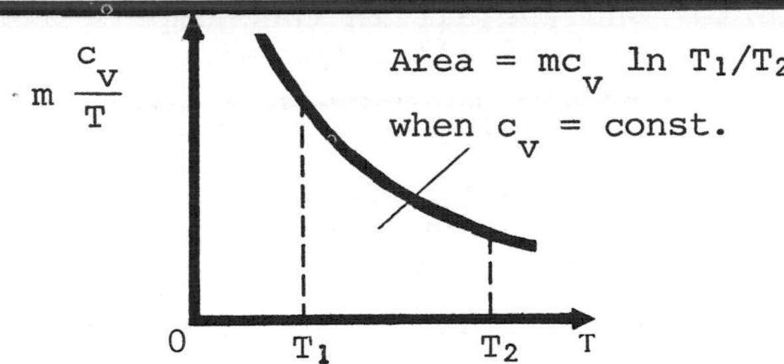

Solution: The entropy is defined as being the area under the mc_v/T vs T curve. We can always find this area by drawing the curve and counting the squares. However, if c_v is a constant, we can obtain the answer from a formula. The area is just

$$\Delta S = \int_{T_1}^{T_2} m \frac{c_v}{T} dt = mc_v \ln T_2/T_2$$

where T_2 is the final temperature, T_1 the initial and m is the mass of material. The above expression is correct when v = const., which is approximately true for a solid.

Now, the aluminum warmed up from 250°K.; thus,

$$\Delta S_{Al} = 5 \text{ gm} \times 0.91 \frac{\text{joules}}{\text{gm-°K}} \times \ln \frac{321°K}{250°K} = 1.14 \text{ joules/°K}$$

The copper was cooled from 375°K to 321°K.

$$\Delta S_{Cu} = 15 \text{ gm} \times 0.39 \frac{\text{joules}}{\text{gm-°K}} \times \ln \frac{321°K}{375°K}$$

$$= - 15 \times 0.39 \ln \frac{375}{321} \text{ joules/°K}$$

$$= - 0.91 \text{ joules/°K}$$

We can then determine that

$$\Delta S = \Delta S_{Al} + \Delta S_{Cu} = (1.14 - 0.91) \text{ joules/°K}$$

$$= 0.23 \text{ joules/°K.}$$

There was net increase in entropy of the system by 0.23 joules/°K. even though the internal energy remained constant.

• PROBLEM 527

A small boy pumps up his bicycle tires on a day when the temperature is 300°K. Find the temperature of the air in the bicycle pump if the tire pressures are to be 24.5 lb/in^2 and the air in the pump is assumed to be compressed adiabatically. For air, $\gamma = 1.40$.

Solution: During an adiabatic process, the quantity $p^{(1-\gamma)/\gamma}T$ remains constant, when p and T are the pressure and the temperature of the gas. In the final stages of the pumping, air at $T_1 = 300°K$ and atmospheric pressure $p_1 = 14.7$ lb/in^2 is drawn into the bicycle pump and compressed adiabatically to a pressure of $p_2 = 24.5$ lb/in^2 and a temperature T_2. Therefore

$$p_1^{(1-\gamma)/\gamma}T_1 = p_2^{(1-\gamma)/\gamma}T_2$$

or
$$\frac{T_2}{T_1} = \left(\frac{p_1}{p_2}\right)^{(1-\gamma)/\gamma}$$

Taking the logarithm of both sides

$$\log\left(\frac{T_2}{T_1}\right) = \frac{1-\gamma}{\gamma}\log\left(\frac{p_1}{p_2}\right)$$

$$= -\frac{0.40}{1.40}\log\left(\frac{14.7}{24.5}\right) = 0.0634.$$

Using the logarithmic table, we get

$$\frac{T_2}{T_1} = 1.157$$

and
$$T_2 = 1.157\ T_1 = 1.157 \times 300°K$$

$$= 347°K = 74.1°C.$$

• PROBLEM 528

One liter of an ideal gas under a pressure of 1 atm is expanded isothermally until its volume is doubled. It is then compressed to its original volume at constant pressure and further compressed isothermally to its original pressure. Plot the process on a p-V diagram and calculate the total work done on the gas. If 50 J of heat were removed during the constant-pressure process, what would be the total change in internal energy?

Solution. During an isothermal change, T is constant. The

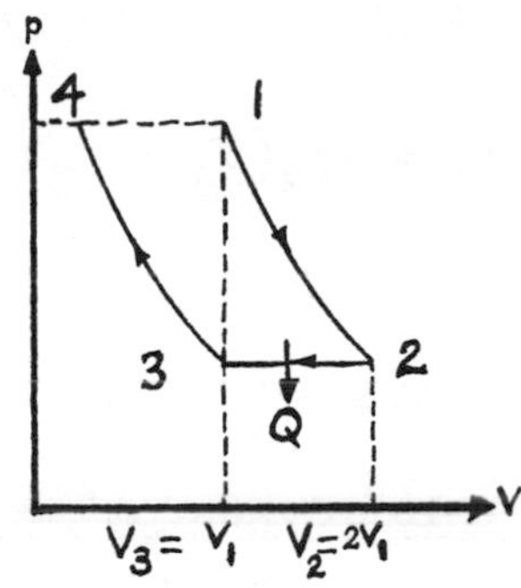

work done on the gas in such a change is

$$W = -\int_{V_i}^{V_f} pdV.$$

This is negative because the pressure on V_i the gas is in opposition to the volume change. From the ideal gas law, $pV = nRT$, we get

$$W = -\int_{V_i}^{V_f} \frac{nRT}{V}dV = -nRT \int_{V_i}^{V_f} \frac{dV}{V} = -nRT \ln \frac{V_f}{V_i} = -p_iV_i \ln \frac{Vf}{Vi}$$

$$= -p_iV_i \ln \frac{p_i}{p_f}.$$

where the subscripts i and f refer to initial and final states respectively.

Thus the work done on the gas in the first change is (from (1) to (2), as shown in the figure)

$$W_1 = -p_1V_1 \ln \frac{V_2}{V_1}$$

$$= -\left(1 \text{ atm} \times 1.013 \times 10^6 \text{ dynes/cm}^2\cdot\text{atm}\right)$$

$$\times \left(1 \text{ liter} \times 10^3 \text{ cm}^3/\text{lit}\right) \times \ln 2$$

$$= -1.013 \times 10^6 \text{ dynes/cm}^2 \times 10^3 \text{ cm}^3 \times \ln 2$$

$$= -7.022 \times 10^8 \text{ ergs} = -70.22 \text{ J}.$$

Further, since the volume is doubled, by the application of Boyle's law $p_1V_1 = p_2V_2$, we see that the pressure is halved at (2)

$$p_2 = p_1 \frac{V_1}{V_2} = \frac{1}{2}p_1.$$

The work done on the gas in the second change is (from (2) to (3))

$$W_2 = -p_2\int_{V_2}^{V_3} dV = -p_2\left(V_3 - V_2\right) = -\tfrac{1}{2}p_1\left(V_1 - 2V_1\right)$$

$$= \tfrac{1}{2}p_1V_1$$

$$= \frac{1.013 \times 10^6 \text{ dynes/cm}^2 \times 10^3 \text{ cm}^3}{2 \times 10^7 \text{ ergs/J}} = 50.65 \text{ J.}$$

The work done on the gas in the final change from (3) to (4) is

$$W_3 = -p_3V_3 \ln \frac{p_3}{p_4} = -\tfrac{1}{2}p_1V_1 \ln \frac{p_2}{p_1}$$

$$= \tfrac{1}{2}p_1V_1 \ln \tfrac{1}{2} = \tfrac{1}{2}\, p_1V_1 \ln 2$$

$$= \frac{1.013 \times 10^6 \text{ dynes/cm}^2 \times 10^3 \text{ cm}^3 \times \ln(2)}{2 \times 10^7 \text{ ergs/J}} = 35.11\text{J}$$

The total work done on the gas is thus $W_1 + W_2 + W_3 =$ $(50.65 + 35.11 - 70.22)$J = 15.54 J. In the first and third processes the temperature does not change. In an ideal gas the internal energy depends only on the temperature, so that no change of internal energy takes place in the first and third processes. Any work done on the gas in these changes is equal to the heat transfer taking place.

The second process is isobaric. The change in internal energy during the process is given by the first law of thermodynamics as $\Delta U = Q - W$, where Q is the heat energy added to the system and W the work done by the system. Hence $\Delta U = -50 \text{ J} - (-50.65 \text{ J}) = +0.65$ J. The internal energy thus increases by 0.65 J during the three processes.

• PROBLEM 529

What is the maximum efficiency of a steam engine if the temperature of the input steam is 175° C and the temperature of the exhaust is 75° C?

Solution: Carnot's Theorem states that the efficiency of all reversible engines operating between the same 2 temperatures is the same. Furthermore, no irreversible engine (including our steam engine) can have an efficiency greater than this. The efficiency of a reversible engine is

$$e = 1 - \frac{T_2}{T_1}$$

where T_2 and T_1 are the Kelvin temperatures of the low and high temperature sinks, respectively, of the engine. Hence, for our steam engine

$$e_{max} = 1 - \frac{T_2}{T_1} = 1 - \frac{(75 + 273)^\circ K}{(175 + 273)^\circ K}$$

We have used the fact that

$$T\ (^\circ K) = T\ (^\circ C) + 273^\circ$$

Then $$e_{max} = 1 - \frac{348}{448} = \frac{100}{448} = .223$$

In terms of percentage

$$e_{max} = 22.3\ \%.$$

• PROBLEM 530

A house near a lake is kept warm by a heat engine. In winter, water from beneath the ice covering the lake is pumped through the heat engine. Heat is extracted until the water is on the point of freezing when it is ejected. The outside air is used as a sink. Assume that the air temperature is -15°C and the temperature of the water from the lake is 2°C. Calculate the rate at which water must be pumped to the engine. The efficiency of the engine is one-fifth that of a Carnot engine and the house requires 10 kW.

Solution: The thermal efficiency of a heat engine is defined as the ratio of the heat converted to mechanical work by the engine to the heat Q_2 supplied to it. If Q_1 is the heat rejected to the reservoir, efficiency is,

$$\eta = \frac{Q_1 - Q_2}{Q_2}$$

The efficiency of a Carnot engine operating between two reservoirs at temperatures $T_2 > T_1$, is given by the ratio,

$$\eta_c = \frac{T_2 - T_1}{T_2}$$

Hence, for the practical heat engine of the problem we have,

$$\eta = \frac{Q_1 - Q_2}{Q_2} = \frac{1}{5}\eta_c = \frac{T_2 - T_1}{T_2}$$

Heat is taken from the lake water as it cools from 2°C to 0°C before ejection. The mean temperature of the hot-temperature source is thus 274°K. If m is the mass of water flowing through in time t, the heat taken in at the hot reservoir in unit time is $Q_2/t = (m/t)c \times 2^\circ C$, where c is the specific heat capacity of water. Heat is rejected to the air as sink at a temperature of $-15^\circ C = 258^\circ K$, the amount of air available being assumed infinite so that the temperature remains constant. Further, the work done $(Q_2 - Q_1)$ is given as $10\ kW = 10^4 J \cdot s^{-1}$. Thus, from the first equation, we have,

$$\frac{10^4 \text{J/s}}{(m/t)\times 4.18 \text{ J/g}-°\text{C}\times 2\text{C deg}} = \frac{1}{5}\,\frac{(275 - 258)°\text{K}}{274°\text{K}}$$

$$\therefore \frac{m}{t} = \frac{5 \times 274 \times 10^4}{2 \times 4.18 \times 16}\text{g/s} = 102.4 \times 10^3\text{g/s}.$$

The rate of water flow necessary is thus 102.4 liters/s.

• PROBLEM 531

One gram of water (1 cm^3) becomes 1671 cm^3 of steam when boiled at a pressure of 1 atm. The heat of vaporization at this pressure is 539 cal/gm. Compute the external work and the increase in internal energy.

Solution: The work done by the water in expanding from volume V_1 to volume V_2 is

$$W = \int_{V_1}^{V_2} p\, dV$$

where p is the pressure exerted by the water on its container. In our problem, p is constant, whence

$$W = p(V_2 - V_1) = p\left(V_V - V_L\right)$$

where V_V is the volume occupied by the steam, and V_L is the volume occupied by the water. Hence,

$$W = p\left(V_V - V_L\right)$$

$$= 1.013 \times 10^6 \text{ dynes/cm}^2 \ (1671 - 1)\text{cm}^3$$

Here we used the fact that

$$1 \text{ atm} = 1.013 \times 10^6 \text{ dynes/cm}^2$$

$$= 1.695 \times 10^9 \text{ ergs}$$

Since $1 \text{ erg} = 2.389 \times 10^{-8}$ cal

$$W = \left(1.695 \times 10^9 \text{ ergs}\right)\left(2.389 \times 10^{-8} \text{ cal/erg}\right)$$

$$W = 41 \text{ cal}$$

The Second Law of Thermodynamics is

$$\Delta U = \Delta Q - \Delta W$$

where ΔU is the change in internal energy of the water-steam system during the stated process. Also, ΔQ and ΔW are the heat added to and the work done by the system during the process, respectively. Denoting the gaseous state by the subscript V, and the liquid state by the subscript L, we obtain

$$U_V - U_L = \Delta Q - \Delta W$$

The heat, ΔQ, added to the system is the amount needed to vaporize the water, or

$$\Delta Q = mL = (1\ g)(539\ cal/g) = 539\ cal$$

Then $U_V - U_L = 539\ cal - 41\ cal = 498\ cal.$

Hence the external work, or the external part of the heat of vaporization, equals 41 cal, and the increase in internal energy, or the internal part of the heat of vaporization, is 498 cal.

• PROBLEM 532

A cylinder contains an ideal gas at a pressure of 2 atm, the volume being 5 liters at a temperature of 250°K. The gas is heated at constant volume to a pressure of 4 atm, and then at constant pressure to a temperature of 650°K. Calculate the total heat input during these processes. For the gas, C_v is 21.0 $J \cdot mole^{-1} \cdot K\ deg^{-1}$.

The gas is then cooled at constant volume to its original pressure and then at constant pressure to its original volume. Find the total heat output during these processes and the total work done by the gas in the whole cyclic process.

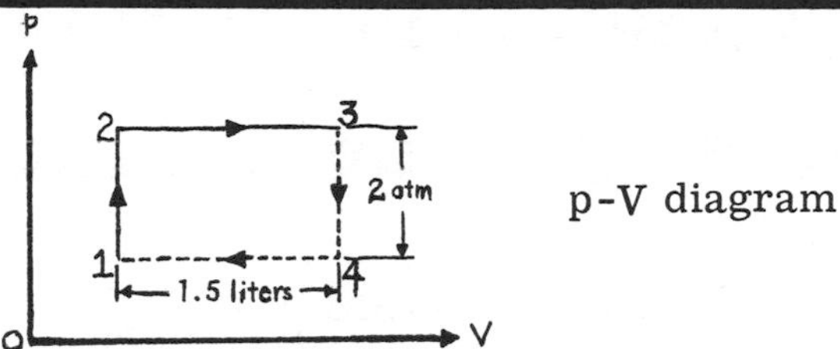

p-V diagram

Solution: The number of moles, n, originally present at point (1) in the P-V diagram can be calculated from the gas equation

$$n = \frac{pV}{RT}$$

$$= \frac{2\ atm \times 5\ liters}{0.0821\ liter \cdot atm \cdot mole^{-1} \cdot K\ deg^{-1} \times 250°K} = 0.487\ mole.$$

The specific heat C_p at constant pressure is

$$C_p = C_v + R\ (21.0 + 8.317) J \cdot mole^{-1} \cdot K\ deg^{-1}$$

$$= 29.317\ J \cdot mole^{-1} \cdot K\ deg^{-1}.$$

In going from (1) to (2), V is constant. Therefore in the first change, P/T remains constant: (from the universal gas law)

$$\frac{P_1}{T_1} = \frac{P_2}{T_2}$$

or $T_2 = T_1 \dfrac{P_2}{P_1}$

Since $\frac{P_2}{P_1} = \frac{4 \text{ atm}}{2 \text{ atm}} = 2,$

we have

$$T_2 = 2T_1 = 2 \times 250°K$$
$$= 500°K$$

The heat input along the change of state from (1) to (2) is

$$H_{12} = nC_v(T_2 - T_1)$$
$$= 0.487 \text{ mole} \times 21.0 \text{ J}\cdot\text{mole}^{-1}\cdot\text{K deg}^{-1} \times (500 - 250)°K$$
$$= 2558 \text{ J}$$

In the second change, from (2) to (3), P and therefore V/T are constant

$$\frac{V_2}{T_2} = \frac{V_3}{T_3}$$

or $V_3 = \frac{T_3}{T_2} V_2 = \frac{T_3}{T_2} V_1$

$$= \frac{650°K}{500°K} \text{ 5 lit} = 6.5 \text{ lit.}$$

Heat input during this change is

$$H_{23} = nC_p(T_3 - T_2)$$
$$= 0.487 \text{ mole} \times 29.317 \text{ J}\cdot\text{mole}^{-1}\cdot\text{K deg}^{-1} \times (650 - 500)°K$$
$$= 2143 \text{ J.}$$

The total heat input during these two processes is thus $H = H_{12} + H_{23} = 4701$ J.

During the change from (3) to (4), the gas cooled at constant volume. Hence

$$\frac{P_3}{T_3} = \frac{P_4}{T_4}$$

or $T_4 = \frac{P_4}{P_3} T_3$

Since $P_4/P_3 = \frac{1}{2}$ we get

$$T_4 = \tfrac{1}{2} T_3 = \tfrac{1}{2} \times 650°K = 325°K.$$

The heat rejected by the gas during this process is

$$H_{34} = nC_v(T_3 - T_4)$$
$$= 0.487 \text{ mole} \times 21.0 \text{ J}\cdot\text{mole}^{-1}\cdot\text{K deg}^{-1} \times (650 - 325)°K$$
$$= 3325 \text{ J}$$

In the second cooling process, from (4) to (1), P is

kept constant;

$$\frac{V_4}{T_4} = \frac{V_1}{T_1}$$

or $$T_1 = \frac{V_1}{V_4} T_4$$

Since $\frac{V_1}{V_4} = \frac{V_1}{V_3} = \frac{5 \text{ lit}}{6.5 \text{ lit}}$, we get

$$T_1 = \frac{5}{6.5} \times 325°K = 250°K$$

as expected. The heat output during this change is

$$H_{41} = nC_p(T_4 - T_1)$$
$$= 0.487 \text{ mole} \times 29.317 \text{ J·mole}^{-1} \text{ K deg}^{-1} \times (325 - 250)°K$$
$$= 1072 \text{ J}.$$

The total heat output during the cooling processes is thus

$$H' = H_{34} + H_{41} = 4397 \text{ J}.$$

The difference between heat input and heat output is 304 J. This must appear as work done by the gas, since the internal energy of the gas must be the same at the beginning and at the end of a cyclic process.

The mechanical work done during the cycle is given by

$$W = \int_1^2 P\,dV + \int_2^3 P\,dV + \int_3^4 P\,dV + \int_4^1 P\,dV,$$

which is the area enclosed by the rectangular figure in the P-V diagram.

This is a rectangle of height 2 atm and length 1.5 liters. The area under the curve is thus

$$W = 2 \times 1.013 \times 10^6 \text{ dynes·cm}^{-2} \times 1.5 \times 10^3 \text{ cm}^3$$

$$= 3.04 \times 10^9 \text{ ergs} = 304 \text{ J},$$

which agrees with the net heat input.

• PROBLEM 533

In a certain engine, fuel is burned and the resulting heat is used to produce steam which is then directed against the vanes of a turbine, causing it to rotate. What is the efficiency of the heat engine if the temperature of the steam striking the vanes is 400° K and the temperature of the steam as it leaves the engine is 373° K?

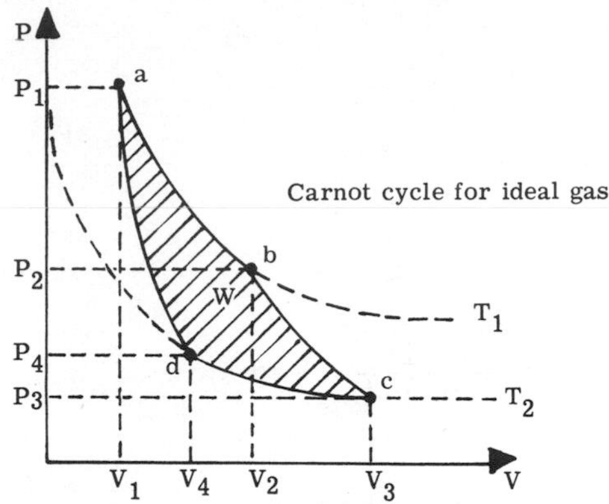

Solution: The efficiency E of a heat engine is the ratio of the net work W done by the engine in one cycle to the heat Q, absorbed from the high temperature source in one cycle.

$$E = \frac{W}{Q_1}$$

For the Carnot cycle, which describes the operation of a reversible heat engine, we know the efficiency to be,

$$E = \frac{W}{Q_1} = \frac{Q_1 - Q_2}{Q_1} = \frac{T_1 - T_2}{T_1}$$

where T_2 is the low temperature reservoir. Carnot stated that the efficiency of all Carnot engines operating between the same two temperatures is the same and that no irreversible engine working between these two temperatures can have a greater efficiency. This means that the maximum efficiency of this heat engine is given by,

$$\varepsilon = \frac{T_1 - T_2}{T_1} = \frac{400°K - 373°K}{400°K} = 0.068 = 6.8\%$$

• PROBLEM 534

Three moles of a diatomic perfect gas are allowed to expand at constant pressure. The initial volume is 1.3 m^3 and the initial temperature is 350°K. If 10,000 Joules are transferred to the gas as heat, what are the final volume and temperature?

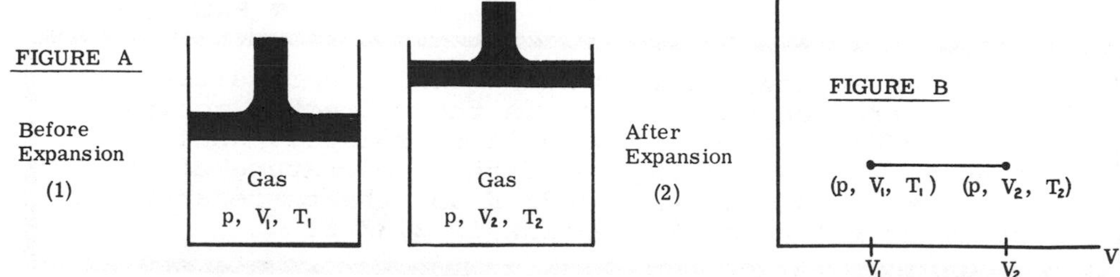

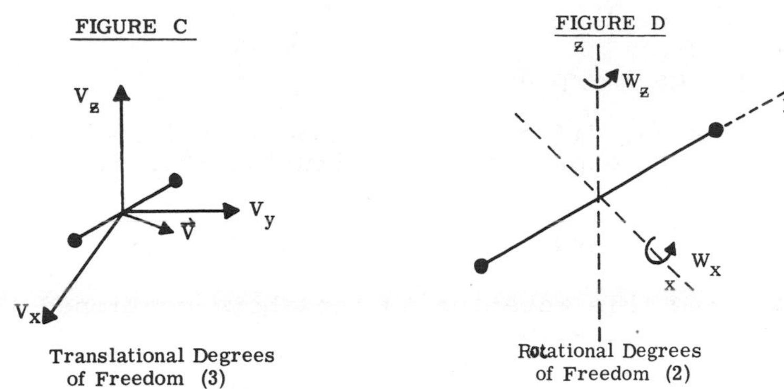

Solution: Since the process of heat (Q) addition occurs at constant pressure, we may write

$$Q = \mu\, C_p(T_2 - T_1)$$

where μ is the number of moles of gas in the system, C_p is the molar specific heat at constant pressure, and $T_2 - T_1$ is the temperature difference between the 2 equilibrium states (see figures (a) and (b)). Now, Q is given (10,000 Joules), as is μ and T. Hence, we may solve for T_2 as a function of C_p. If we can calculate the value of C_p from kinetic theory, we will have obtained T_2. We now perform the appropriate calculation.

Consider a gas moving from one equilibrium state to another, via some thermodynamic process. We assume that the process occurs at constant volume. Using the First Law of Thermodynamics, we obtain

$$\Delta U = Q - W \tag{1}$$

Here, ΔU is the change in internal energy of the gas during the process, and Q and W are the heat added to and the work done by the gas, respectively, during the process. Writing (1) in differential form

$$dU = dQ - dW \tag{2}$$

In general, the element of work done by the gas in an expansion is, by definition

$$dW = \vec{F} \cdot d\vec{s}$$

where $\vec{F}$ is the force the gas exerts on the piston (see figure (a)) and $d\vec{s}$ is the element of distance the piston moves during the expansion. Since $\vec{F}$ acts perpendicular to the face of the piston (that is, $\vec{F}$ and $d\vec{s}$ are parallel), we obtain

$$dW = F\, ds \tag{3}$$

But F may be written in terms of the pressure p, that the gas exerts on the piston face of area A

$$F = pA$$

Using this in (3)

$$dW = p\, ds\, A = p\, dV$$

where dV is the differential change in volume of the gas during the expansion. Substituting this in (2), we find

$$dU = dQ - p\, dV \tag{4}$$

Applying this equation to the above-mentioned isovolumic process, we obtain

$$dU = dQ$$

since dV = 0. By defintion, however

$$dQ = \mu\, C_v\, dT$$

where C_v is the molar specific heat of the gas at constant volume, and dT is the differential temperature change the gas experiences due to the addition of heat dQ. Then

$$d\mu = \mu\, C_v\, dT \tag{5}$$

We now assume that the change in internal energy of a gas is only a function of the temperature difference experienced by the gas. Then, no matter what thermodynamic process the gas experiences, (5) holds.

Consider next an isobaric thermodynamic process. Again, we apply (4)

$$dU = dQ - p\, dV \tag{4}$$

Since the process occurs at constant pressure,

$$dQ = \mu\, C_p\, dT \tag{6}$$

where C_p is the molar heat capacity at constant pressure. Furthermore, from the ideal gas law

$$pV = \mu RT$$

If p is constant,

$$p\, \frac{dV}{dT} = \mu R$$

or $$p\, dV = \mu\, R\, dT \tag{7}$$

Using (6), (7), and (5) in (4)

$$\mu\, C_v\, dT = \mu\, C_p\, dT - \mu\, R\, dT$$

or $$C_p = C_v + R \tag{8}$$

Equation (8) relates the molar specific heat at constant pressure to the molar specific heat at constant volume.

All the derivations up to now have been necessary in order to obtain certain relations involving molar specific heats, namely equations (5) and (8). We now turn to an examination of the internal energy of a diatomic gas. Each method of energy storage of a diatmoc molecule is called a degree of freedom. If we view a diatomic molecule as being dumbell-shaped, then it has 5 degrees of freedom (see figures (c) and (d)). The molecule may move translationally in 3 directions (x, y, z) with 3 kinetic energies $\left(\frac{1}{2}mv_x^2, \frac{1}{2}mv_y^2, \frac{1}{2}mv_z^2\right)$. Furthermore, it may rotate about 3 axes (x, y, z), again, with 3 kinetic energies $\left(\frac{1}{2}I_x\omega_x^2, \frac{1}{2}I_y\omega_y^2, \frac{1}{2}I_z\omega_z^2\right)$. However, the rotational kinetic energy about the y axis is negligible (see figure (d)) because $I_y << I_x, I_z$. Hence a diatomic molecule has 5 independent methods of energy absorption, or 5 degrees of freedom. Notice one important fact: each of these kinetic energy terms has the same form, mathematically. That is, they are all of the form of a positive constant times the square of a variable which has a domain extending from $-\infty$ to $+\infty$. The theorem of equipartition of energy tells us that, when Newtonian mechanics holds, and the number of gas particles is large, each term of this form has the same average value per molecule, namely, $\frac{1}{2}kT$. In other words, each degree of freedom of a gas molecule contributes an amount $\frac{1}{2}kT$ to the internal energy of the gas. For a diatomic gas, then, the internal energy per molecule is

$$U_i = 5\left(\frac{1}{2}kT\right) = \frac{5}{2}kT$$

The internal energy for μ moles of molecules is

$$U = \mu N_0 U_i = \frac{5}{2}\mu k N_0 T = \frac{5}{2}\mu RT$$

Using this in (5), we may solve for C_v

$$\frac{1}{\mu}\frac{d\left(\frac{5}{2}\mu RT\right)}{dT} = C_v$$

$$C_v = \frac{5}{2}R$$

Using this fact in (8)

$$C_p = C_v + R = \frac{5R}{2} + R = \frac{7}{2}R$$

Getting back to the original problem, use this value of C_p in the first equation

$$Q = \mu C_p(T_2 - T_1) = \frac{7}{2}\mu R(T_2 - T_1)$$

or $$T_2 = T_1 + \frac{Q}{\frac{7}{2}\mu R} = 350°K + \frac{10{,}000 \text{ Joules}}{\left(\frac{7}{2}\right)(3 \text{ moles})\left(8.31 \frac{\text{Joules}}{\text{mole °K}}\right)}$$

$$T_2 = 350°K + 114°K = 464°K$$

Using the ideal gas law for the 2 equilibrium states

$$pV_1 = \mu RT_1$$

$$pV_2 = \mu RT_2$$

or $$\frac{V_2}{V_1} = \frac{T_2}{T_1}$$

whence $$V_2 = \frac{T_2}{T_1} V_1 = \left(\frac{464}{350}\right) 1.3\ m^3 = 1.72\ m^3$$

• PROBLEM 535

A refrigerator which has a coefficient of performance one-third that of a Carnot refrigerator is operated between two reservoirs at temperatures of 200°K and 350°K. It absorbs 500 J from the low-temperature reservoir. How much heat is rejected at the high-temperature reservoir?

Solution: The coefficient of performance of a Carnot refrigerator is defined as the ratio of the heat extracted from the cold source and the work needed to run the cycle. Hence,

$$E_c = \frac{Q_1}{Q_2 - Q_1} \quad \text{or equivalently} \quad \frac{T_1}{T_2 - T_1}$$

where Q_1 is the heat absorbed at temperature T_1 and Q_2 is the heat rejected at the higher temperature T_2. Here all temperatures T are to be expressed in Kelvin degrees. The actual refrigerator has thus a coefficient of performance

$$\frac{Q_1}{Q_2 - Q_1} = \frac{1}{3} \frac{T_1}{T_2 - T_1}$$

or $$\frac{Q_2 - 500\ J}{500\ J} = \frac{3(350 - 250)°K}{250°K}$$

$$\therefore \quad Q_2 = 1100\ J.$$

• PROBLEM 536

In an airconditioning process a room is kept at 290°K., while the temperature outside is 305°K. The refrigerating machine has compression cylinders operating at 320°K. (located outside) and expansion coils inside the house operating at 280°K. If the machine operates reversibly, how much work must be done for each transfer of 5000 joules of heat from the house? What entropy changes occur inside and outside the house for this amount of refrigeration?

Solution: An engine works by accepting heat at a high temperature, converting part of it into work, and re-

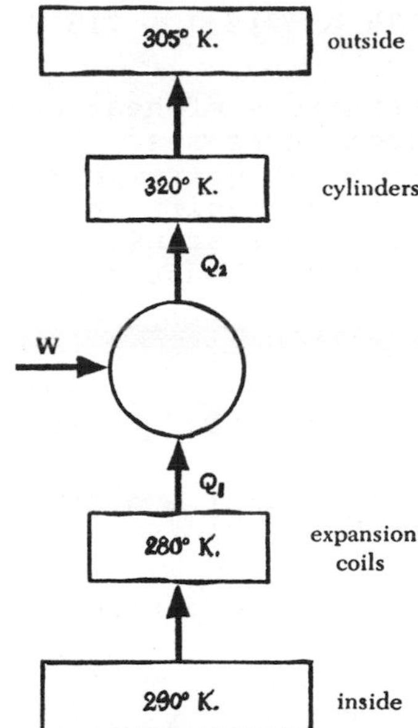

jecting the remainder at a lower temperature. A refrigerating machine works the opposite way. By supplying to it an amount of work W, it will accept heat Q_1 at a low temperature and reject heat $Q_2 = Q_1 + W$ at a higher temperature.

The efficiency η of a reversible heat engine is given by

$$\eta = \frac{W}{Q_1} = \frac{Q_1 - Q_2}{Q_1} = \frac{T_1 - T_2}{T_1}$$

where W is the net work done by the machine in one cycle and Q_1 is the heat absorbed in one cycle. Since a refrigerator and a heat engine operate in opposite ways, and $Q_2 > Q_1$, its efficiency can be defined as

$$\eta = \frac{W}{Q_2} = \frac{Q_2 - Q_1}{Q_2} = \frac{T_2 - T_1}{T_2} - 1 - \frac{T_1}{T_2}$$

where W is the work done on the machine.

The sequence of events is shown in the diagram. The machine operates between reservoirs at 280°K. and 320°K. If Q_1 = 5000 joules, we have

$$\eta = 1 - \frac{280}{320} = 0.125 = \frac{Q_2 - Q_1}{Q_2} = \frac{Q_2 - 5000\text{ J}}{Q_2}$$

$$Q_2 = 5715\text{ J}$$

The work done can be found from

$$\eta = \frac{W}{Q_2}$$

or $\quad W = \eta Q_2 = 0.125 \times 5715\ \text{J} \approx 715\ \text{J}$

Irreversible transfers of heat occur when the entropy of the system increases. This occurs for a transfer of heat from a high temperature reservoir to a low temperature reservoir. In this problem, there are two irreversible transfers of heat, one between the inside of the house and the low temperature reservoir, for which

$$\text{entropy, } \Delta S = Q_1 \left(\frac{1}{T_{\text{exp coil}}} - \frac{1}{T_{\text{inside}}} \right)$$

$$= Q_1 \left(\frac{1}{280} - \frac{1}{290} \right) = 0.62\ \text{J/°K}.$$

and one between the high temperature reservoir and the outside:

$$\Delta S = Q_2 \left(\frac{1}{T_{\text{out}}} - \frac{1}{T_{\text{cylinder}}} \right)$$

$$= Q_2 \left(\frac{1}{305} - \frac{1}{320} \right) = 0.88\ \text{J/°K}.$$

CHAPTER 16

HEAT TRANSFER

THERMAL CONDUCTIVITY

• PROBLEM 537

On either side of a pane of window glass, temperatures are 70°F and 0°F. How fast is heat conducted through such a pane of area 2500 cm^2 if the thickness is 2 mm?

Solution: The equation of heat conduction is

$$\frac{dQ}{dt} = - KA \frac{dT}{dx} \qquad (1)$$

where dQ/dt is the rate at which heat is transferred across a cross-section A of a material with coefficient of thermal conductivity K. dT/dx is the temperature gradient in the material.

In the steady state, the temperature at each point of the material remains constant in time. Hence, the rate of heat transfer across a cross-section is the same at all cross-sections. As a result of (1), dT/dx must be the same at all cross-sections. If T_1 is the temperature at a cross-section at x_1, and T_2 is the temperature at x_2, we obtain

$$\frac{dT}{dx} = \frac{\Delta T}{\Delta x} = \frac{T_2 - T_1}{x_2 - x_1} \qquad (2)$$

(Note that this is a direct consequence of the fact that dT/dx is constant). Using (2) in (1)

$$\frac{dQ}{dt} = - K\ A \left(\frac{T_2 - T_1}{x_2 - x_1}\right) = K\ A \left(\frac{T_1 - T_2}{x_2 - x_1}\right)$$

But $x_2 - x_1$ is equal to L, the length of the material across which the heat conduction is taking place.

$$\frac{dQ}{dt} = \frac{K\ A\ (T_1 - T_2)}{L}$$

For the pane of glass,

$$T_1 = 70°F \qquad @ \qquad x_1 = 0 \text{ mm}$$

$$T_2 = 0°F \qquad @ \qquad x_2 = 2 \text{ mm}$$

Furthermore, K = .0015 cal/cm·s·°C for glass, whence

$$\frac{dQ}{dt} = \frac{(.0015 \text{ cal/cm·s·°C})(2500 \text{ cm}^2)(70°F - 0°F)}{(2\text{mm} - 0 \text{ mm})}$$

Since 70°F = 5/9 · 70°C = 350°C/9, we obtain,

$$\frac{dQ}{dt} = \frac{(.0015 \text{ cal/cm·s·°C})(2500 \text{ cm}^2)(350\text{°C}/9)}{(.2 \text{ cm})}$$

$$\frac{dQ}{dt} = 729 \text{ cal/s}$$

Note that, by convention, temperature decreases as x increases. Hence, $T_2 < T_1$ and $x_2 > x_1$. As a result, $dQ/dt > 0$ in the direction in which $dT/dx < 0$.

• PROBLEM 538

How long will it take to form a thickness of 4 cm of ice on the surface of a lake when the air temperature is -6°C? The thermal conductivity K of ice is 4×10^{-3} cal/s - cm - °C and its density is $\rho = 0.92$ g/cm^3.

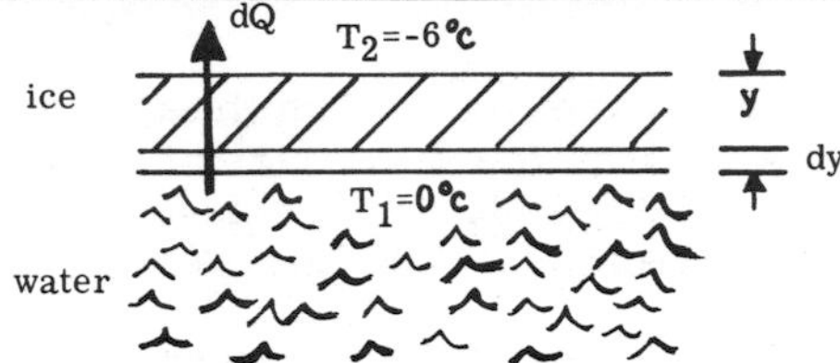

Solution. Let the thickness of the ice layer at any instant be represented by y. The next layer of thickness dy forms through the transfer of heat dQ from water to air through the ice as shown in the figure. Let this transfer take place in dt seconds. The heat lost by the freezing water, is

$$dQ = \rho A \, dy \, L$$

where A is the area of ice formed, ρ is its density, and L is the latent heat of water. This is equal to the heat transmitted through the layer of ice already formed,

$$dQ = \frac{-kA\left(T_2 - T_1\right)dt}{y}$$

where T_1 and T_2 are the temperatures of the water (near the ice) and air, respectively and k is a constant. Hence

$$\rho A \, dy \, L = \frac{-kA\left(T_2 - T_1\right)}{y}dt$$

or $$dt = \frac{\rho L}{k\left(T_2 - T_1\right)} y dy$$

Integrating the above equation from y = 0 to y = 4 cm, we get

$$\int_0^t dt = \frac{-\rho L}{k\left(T_2 - T_1\right)} \int_0^{4 \text{ cm}} y dy = \frac{\rho L}{k\left(T_2 - T_1\right)} \left[\frac{1}{2}y^2\right]_0^{4 \text{ cm}}$$

where t is the time it takes for the ice to grow 4 cm thick.

$$t = \frac{-\rho L \times 8\ cm^2}{k\left(T_2 - T_1\right)} = \frac{8\ cm^2 \times 0.92\ gr/cm^3 \times 80\ cal/gr}{4 \times 10^{-3}\ cal/s\ °C\ deg \cdot cm \times 6°C\ deg.}$$

$$= 24.53 \times 10^3\ s$$

$$= 409\ min$$

$$= 6\ hr\ 49\ min.$$

• PROBLEM 539

A cubical tank of water of volume 1 m^3 is kept at a steady temperature of 65°C by a 1-kW heater. The heater is switched off. How long does the tank take to cool 50°C if the room temperature is 15°C?

Solution: While the heater is operating, the heat supplied by it, 1 kW = 240 $cal \cdot s^{-1}$, is just sufficient to make up for the heat loss that would take place according to Newton's law of cooling.

$$\frac{dt}{d\tau} = -k\left(t - t_s\right) \qquad (1)$$

where t is the temperature of the cooling body at $\tau = 0$, t_s is the ambient temperature, and k is a constant. Furthermore, $dt/d\tau$ is the rate of change of temperature with time. Before using this law, we must evaluate k for the case at hand. In order to do this, note that the definition of the specific heat of a substance is

$$c = \frac{dQ}{mdt}$$

where m is the mass of the substance, dQ is an increment of heat energy, and dt is an increment of temperature. Then

$$dt = \frac{dQ}{mc} \qquad (2)$$

and $$\frac{dt}{d\tau} = \frac{dQ}{mcd\tau} \qquad (3)$$

But $dt/d\tau < 0$ in (1) if $\left(t - t_s\right) > 0$, and $dt/d\tau > 0$ in (3) if $dQ > 0$. But, if $dQ > 0$, the temperature change $dt > 0$, as in (2). Hence, there is an inconsistency in the sign of $dt/d\tau$ between (1) and (3).

For consistency, replace $dt/d\tau$ in (2) by $-dt/d\tau$. Now $dt/d\tau$ has the same meaning in (1) and (2). Taking account of this, and inserting (2) in (1)

$$-\frac{dQ}{mcd\tau} = -k\left(t - t_s\right)$$

or $$mck = \frac{1}{\left(t - t_s\right)} \frac{dQ}{d\tau}$$

But $dQ/d\tau$ is the heat power supplied to the tank. Thus

$$mck = \frac{240\ cal \cdot s^{-1}}{(65 - 15)^\circ C} = 4.8\ cal \cdot s^{-1} \cdot C\ deg^{-1}.$$

But the mass of 1 m^3 of water is 10^6 g and the specific heat capacity of water is 1 $cal \cdot g^{-1} \cdot C\ deg^{-1}$. Hence, $k = 4.8 \times 10^{-6}\ s^{-1}$. When the heater is switched off, the tank cools according to the equation $dt/d\tau = -k(t - t_s)$.

$$\therefore \quad \int_{65^\circ C}^{50^\circ C} \frac{dt}{t - t_s} = -k \int_0^\tau d\tau.$$

where $t = 65^\circ C$ at $\tau = 0$ and $t = 50^\circ C$ at $\tau = \tau$. Then

$$\int_{65^\circ C}^{50^\circ C} \frac{dt}{t - t_s} = -k\tau$$

$$\ln |t - t_s| \Big|_{65^\circ C}^{50^\circ C} = -k\tau$$

$$\ln |50^\circ C - 15^\circ C| - \ln |65^\circ C - 15^\circ C| = -k\tau$$

$$\ln |65^\circ C - 15^\circ C| - \ln |50^\circ C - 15^\circ C| = k\tau$$

$$\ln \left(\left| \frac{50^\circ C}{35^\circ C} \right| \right) = k\ \tau$$

$$\tau = \frac{1}{k} \ln |10/7|$$

$$\therefore \quad \tau = \frac{10^6}{4.8} \ln \frac{10}{7}\ s = \frac{10^6 \times 0.3567}{4.8}\ s$$

$$= 74313.5\ s = 20.64\ hr.$$

• PROBLEM 540

A copper kettle, the circular bottom of which is 6.0 in. in diameter and 0.062 in. thick, is placed over a gas flame. On assuming that the average temperature of the outer surface of the copper is 214°F and that the water in the kettle is at its normal boiling point, how much heat is conducted through the bottom in 5.0 sec? The thermal conductivity may be taken as 2480 Btu/(ft^2 hr F°/in).

Solution: The heat Q conducted through the bottom of the kettle in time t is given by

$$Q = K\ At \frac{\Delta T}{\Delta x}$$

where $\Delta T/\Delta x$ is the temperature gradient in F°/in, K is the thermal conductivity and A is the area of the bottom in ft^2. We have

$$A = \pi r^2 = \pi \left(\frac{3.0}{12}\ ft \right)^2 = 0.20\ ft^2$$

$$t = 5.0 \text{ sec} = \frac{5.0}{3600} \text{ hr} = 0.0014 \text{ hr}$$

The temperature on the inside of the bottom of the kettle is the same as that of boiling water (212°F). Since the temperature on the outside of the bottom is 214°F and the thickness of the bottom of the kettle is 0.062 in, the temperature gradient across the bottom is

$$\frac{\Delta T}{\Delta x} = \frac{214°F - 212°F}{0.062 \text{ in}} = 32°F/\text{in}$$

The heat conducted through the bottom is then

$$Q = \left(2480 \frac{\text{Btu}}{\text{ft}^2 \text{ hr } °F/\text{in}}\right)(0.20 \text{ ft}^2)(0.0014 \text{ hr})(32°F/\text{in})$$

$$= 22 \text{ Btu}$$

• PROBLEM 541

Sheets of brass and steel, each of thickness 1 cm, are placed in contact. The outer surface of the brass is kept at 100°C and the outer surface of the steel is kept at 0°C. What is the temperature of the common interface? The thermal conductivities of brass and steel are in the ratio of 2 : 1.

Solution: Once equilibrium conditions have been attained, the same quantity of heat must pass through all sections of the system in unit time. In other words, the heat current flowing through the system is constant; otherwise alterations in the temperature at various points would take place. This would be contrary to the condition that equilibrium had been established. The heat H flowing in unit time across the brass is

$$H = K_1 A \frac{100°C - t}{L} \qquad (1)$$

where K_1 is the thermal conductivity of brass,

A is the cross-sectional area of the brass slab, and t is the temperature of the common interface. Heat flows from the inner surface of the steel to its outer surface with the same rate,

$$H = K_2 A \frac{t - 0°C}{L} \qquad (2)$$

where K_2 is the thermal conductivity of steel. From (1) and (2), we get

$$K_1 A \frac{100°C - t}{L} = K_2 A \frac{t - 0°C}{L}$$

or $$\frac{K_1}{K_2} = \frac{t}{100°C - t}$$

But we are given that $K_1/K_2 = 2$, hence

$$\frac{t}{100°C - t} = 2$$

$$200°C - 2t = t$$

or $t = \frac{200°C}{3} = 66.7°C.$

• PROBLEM 542

A steel rod of length L = 20 cm and cross-sectional area $A = 3\ cm^2$ is heated at one end to $T_1 = 300°k$ while the other end rests in ice. Assuming that heat transmission occurs exclusively through the rod (without losses from the walls), calculate the mass m of the ice melting in time $\Delta t = 10$ min. The thermal conductivity of steel is $k = 0.16\ cal\ deg^{-1}\ sec^{-1}\ cm^{-1}$.

Solution: Thermal conductivity k as given above, indicates the amount of heat transferred per second per square centimeter per degree centigrade through 1 cm length of steel.

The rate of heat transfer through the steel rod is given by

$$\frac{heat}{sec} = \frac{\Delta Q}{\Delta t} = k \times \frac{A \times (T_1 - T_2)}{L}$$

where T_2 is the temperature of the colder end of the rod. Hence,

$$\frac{\Delta Q}{\Delta t} = \frac{(0.16\ cal\ K°^{-1}\ sec^{-1}\ cm^{-1}) \times (3\ cm^2) \times (300 - 273)K°}{20\ cm}$$

$$= 0.648\ cal/sec.$$

In time Δt = 10 min., the amount of heat transferred by the rod to the ice is

$$\Delta Q = (0.648\ cal/sec) \times \Delta t$$

$$= (0.648\ cal/sec) \times (10 min \times 60 sec/min)$$

$$= 388.8\ cal.$$

The heat of fusion of ice is 80 cal/gr, which means in order to melt 1 gr. of ice, 80 cal. must be added to the ice. Therefore, 388.8 calories will melt

$$m = \frac{\Delta Q\ cal}{80\ cal/gr} = \frac{388.8}{80} gr = 4.86\ gr.$$

of ice.

• PROBLEM 543

Determine the power required to maintain a temperature difference of 20° C between the faces of a glass window of area $2\ m^2$ and thickness 3 mm. Why does a much lower power suffice to keep a room with such a window at a temperature 20° C above the outside? The thermal conductivity of glass is 25×10^{-4} cal·s^{-1}·cm^{-1}·C deg^{-1}.

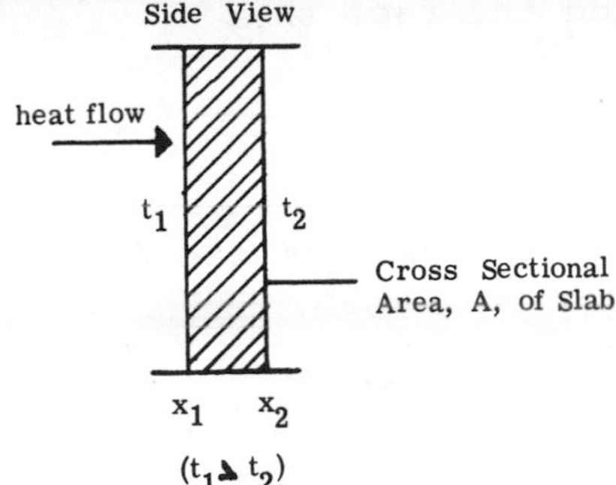

Solution: The equation appropriate to thermal conductivity is

$$\frac{dQ}{d\tau} = - k A \frac{dt}{dx} \tag{1}$$

where $dQ/d\tau$ is the rate of heat transfer across a cross section of area A of a slab of material of thermal conductivity k. dt/dx is the temperature gradient in the material.

Now, if we assume that the heat transfer is occurring as a steady state process, the temperature of each point of the slab will be time independent. If this is the case, $dQ/d\tau$ is the same at all cross-sections of the slab. However, by (1), this means that dt/dx is constant at all cross-sections. Hence dt/dx decreases linearly along the slab. Using the figure,

$$\frac{dt}{dx} = \frac{t_2 - t_1}{x_2 - x_1}$$

But $x_2 - x_1 = L$, the slab thickness, whence

$$\frac{dt}{dx} = \frac{t_2 - t_1}{L}$$

and $\dfrac{dQ}{d\tau} = - k A \dfrac{(t_2 - t_1)}{L}$

Since $t_2 < t_1$, we may rewrite this as

$$\frac{dQ}{d\tau} = k A \frac{(t_1 - t_2)}{L}$$

In this equation, t_1 and t_2 are the temperatures of the slab at positions x_1 and x_2. (See figure.) In this particular case, $t_1 = t_2 + 20°C$ and

$$\frac{dQ}{d\tau} = 25 \times 10^{-4} \text{ cal·s}^{-1}\text{·cm}^{-1}\text{·C deg}^{-1} \times 2 \times 10^{4} \text{ cm}^2$$

$$\times \frac{20 \text{ C deg}}{0.3 \text{ cm}}$$

$= 3.33 \times 10^3 \text{ cal}\cdot\text{s}^{-1}$.

Here we have used the fact that

$$2 \text{ m}^2 = 2 \times 10^4 \text{ cm}^2$$

and 3 mm = .3 cm

These conversions follow from the definitions of a cm. and mm.

Since 1 cal = 4.19 Joules

$$\frac{dQ}{d\tau} = 3.3 \times 10^3 \text{ cal}\cdot\text{s}^{-1} = \left(3.3 \times 10^3 \text{ cal}\cdot\text{s}^{-1}\right)\left(4.19 \text{ J}\cdot\text{cal}^{-1}\right)$$

$$\frac{dQ}{d\tau} = 13.95 \times 10^3 \text{ J}\cdot\text{s}^{-1}.$$

Thus 3.33×10^3 cal = 13.95×10^3 J are required per second to replace the lost heat. The power required is thus 13.95 kilowatts (kW).

A much smaller power than this is required in practice because the inner surface of the window and the air in contact with it drops in temperature because of the heat loss through the glass. Heat is conducted from the rest of the room through air, the thermal conductivity of which is very low. The inner surface of the window is thus not maintained at a temperature 20°C above the outside. A similar effect will occur on the outside of the window. The temperature difference across the window may well drop to only a few degrees, in which case only a fraction of the above power needs to be supplied, giving a much more reasonable figure for the heat that needs to be supplied per second.

• PROBLEM 544

Two vessels, filled with liquids at temperatures T_{1i} and T_{2i} are joined by a metal rod of length L, cross-section A and thermal conductivity k. The masses and specific heats of the liquids are m_1, m_2 and c_1, c_2 respectively. The vessels and rod are thermally insulated from the surrounding medium. What is the time t required for the temperature difference to be halved?

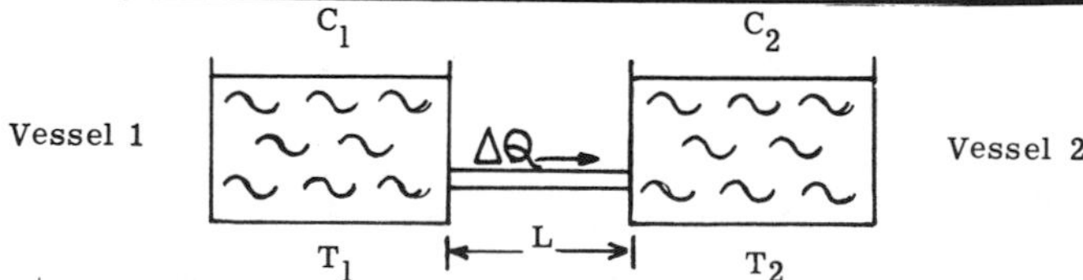

Solution: Let the vessels have instantaneous temperatures T_1 and T_2 (as shown in the figure) with $T_1 > T_2$. After they are joined by the metal rod, heat flows from vessel 1 to vessel 2 at a rate

$$\frac{\text{heat}}{\text{sec}} = \frac{dQ}{dt} = kA\left(\frac{T_1 - T_2}{L}\right). \qquad (1)$$

As heat is transferred, the temperatures of the vessels tend to equalize. Therefore the rate of heat transfer decreases in time. The temperature variations dT_1 and dT_2 caused by the transfer of heat can be obtained by noting that the same heat dQ which leaves vessel 1 must enter vessel 2. Therefore

$$dQ = c_1m_1\left(-dT_1\right) = c_2m_2dT_2$$

where $(-dT_1)$ indicates a decrease in T_1. Substituting for dQ in (1), we get

$$\frac{-c_1m_1dT_1}{dt} = \frac{kA\left(T_1 - T_2\right)}{L} \quad \text{and} \tag{2}$$

$$\frac{c_2m_2dT_2}{dt} = \frac{k\ A\left(T_1 - T_2\right)}{L}. \tag{3}$$

Let us rearrange equations (2) and (3) as follows

$$\frac{dT_1}{dt} = -\frac{k\ A\left(T_1 - T_2\right)}{c_1m_1L}, \tag{4}$$

$$\frac{dT_2}{dt} = \frac{k\ A\left(T_1 - T_2\right)}{c_2m_2L}. \tag{5}$$

Then, if we subtract (5) from (4), we obtain the rate of change of the temperature difference $T_1 - T_2$ with time:

$$\frac{dT_1}{dt} - \frac{dT_2}{dt} = \frac{d\left(T_1 - T_2\right)}{dt} = -\frac{k\ A}{L}\left(\frac{1}{c_1m_1} + \frac{1}{c_2m_2}\right)\left(T_1 - T_2\right).$$

The solution of the above differential equation gives the time dependence of $\left(T_1 - T_2\right)$:

$$\left(T_1 - T_2\right) = \left(T_1 - T_2\right)_{\text{initial}}\ e^{-\frac{kA}{L}\left(\frac{1}{c_1m_1} + \frac{1}{c_2m_2}\right)t}$$

where $\left(T_1 - T_2\right)_{\text{initial}}$ is the temperature difference at $t = 0$.

The time t required for $\left(T_1 - T_2\right)$ to equal one half of its initial value $\left(T_1 - T_2\right)_{\text{initial}}$ is

$$e^{-\frac{kA}{L}\left(\frac{1}{c_1m_1} + \frac{1}{c_2m_2}\right)t} = \frac{\left(T_1 - T_2\right)(t)}{\left(T_1 - T_2\right)_{\text{initial}}} = \frac{1}{2}.$$

Taking the natural logarithm of both sides of the above equation, we get

$$-\frac{kA}{L}\left(\frac{1}{c_1m_1} + \frac{1}{c_2m_2}\right)t = \ln\frac{1}{2} = -\ln 2.$$

or $$t = \frac{L}{kA\left(\frac{1}{c_1m_1} + \frac{1}{c_2m_2}\right)} \ln 2$$

$$= \frac{L\, c_1c_2m_1m_2}{kA\left(m_1c_1 + m_2c_2\right)} \ln 2.$$

• PROBLEM 545

The passenger compartment of a jet transport is essentially a cylindrical tube of diameter 3 m and length 20 m. It is lined with 3 cm of insulating material of thermal conductivity 10^{-4} cal·cm^{-1}·C deg^{-1}·s^{-1}, and must be maintained at 20°C for passenger comfort, although the average outside temperature is - 30°C at its operating height. What rate of heating is required in the compartment neglecting the end effects?

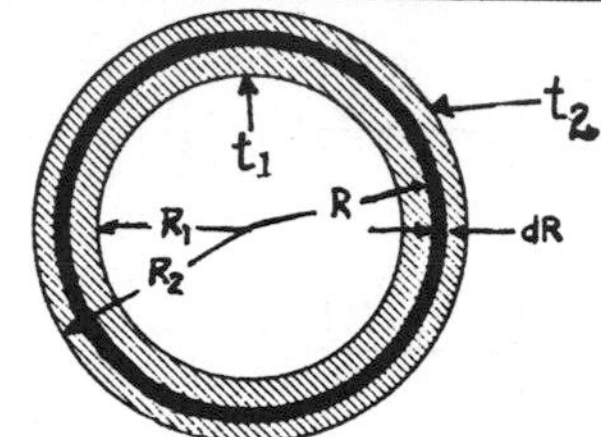

Solution: The hull of the aircraft is a good conductor of heat and may be considered to be at the outside temperature. The circular cylinder of insulating material has thus a temperature of 20°C inside and - 30°C outside (see figure).

Consider a cylinder of the material at distance R from the center of the craft and of thickness dR. By the normal equation of conductivity, the flow of heat across this infinitesimal cylinder per second is

$$H = KA\,\frac{dt}{dR}$$

where dt/dR is the variation of temperature with R (the temperature gradient) and A is the area of the surface across which the heat flow occurs. Hence

$$A = 2\pi\ R\ L$$

and $H = 2\pi\ R\ L\ K\ dt/dR$

Therefore $$dR = \frac{2\pi\ R\ L\ K\ dt}{H}$$

where L is the length of the cylinder. Thus

$$\frac{dR}{R} = \frac{2\pi KL}{H}\ dt.$$

The quantity H is a constant since the system is in

equilibrium. If the same quantity of heat did not pass over every cross section of the insulating material, heat would build up somewhere and the temperature would rise. This is contrary to the condition that equilibrium shall have been attained.

For the whole cylinder of insulating material, then

$$\int_{R_1}^{R_2} \frac{dR}{R} = \frac{2\pi KL}{H} \int_{t_1}^{t_2} dt$$

where the temperature at R_1 is t_1, and the temperature at $R_2 = t_2$ (see figure). Then

$$\ln \frac{R_2}{R_1} = \frac{2\pi KL}{H} \left(t_2 - t_1\right)$$

Hence

$$H = \frac{2\pi KL\left(t_2 - t_1\right)}{\ln\left(R_2/R_1\right)}$$

$$= \frac{2\pi \times 10^{-4} \text{cal}\cdot\text{cm}^{-1}\cdot\text{Cdeg}^{-1}\cdot\text{s}^{-1} \times 20 \times 10^2 \text{cm}\left[20-(-\ 30)\right]\ ^\circ\text{C}}{\ln\ (300/294)}$$

$$= 3100\ \text{cal}\cdot\text{s}^{-1} = 12{,}980\ \text{J}\cdot\text{s}^{-1} \approx 13.0\ \text{kW}.$$

Here we have used the fact that

$$1\ \text{cal/s} = 4.186\ \text{J/s}$$

This is the heat which flows through the walls. In order to keep the temperature of the cabin constant, an equal amount of heat power must be supplied to the cabin by external means.

HEAT RADIATION

• PROBLEM 546

The heat energy E radiated from the surface of a solar storage tank at a temperature T each second is

$$E = \text{constant}\left(T^4 - T_a^4\right)A$$

where T_a is the ambient temperature of the room and A is the total surface area of the storage tank. How much larger is the energy loss when water at 340°K is used to store the solar energy as compared to Glauber salts at 310°K? Assume the ambient termperature is 293°K.

Solution: If we assume that identical storage tanks are used for storing the solar energy, then the surface area of each tank is the same. We obtain

$$\frac{\text{energy lost by radiation from water}}{\text{energy lost by radiation from salt}} = \frac{\text{constant}\left(340^4 - 293^4\right)A}{\text{constant}\left(310^4 - 293^4\right)A}$$

$$= 3.2.$$

The heat loss from the water would be 3.2 times greater than for salt.

• PROBLEM 547

The solar constant, or the quantity of radiation received by the earth from the sun is 0.14 $W \cdot cm^{-2}$. Assuming that the sun may be regarded as an ideal radiator, calculate the surface temperature of the sun. The ratio of the radius of the earth's orbit to the radius of the sun is 216.

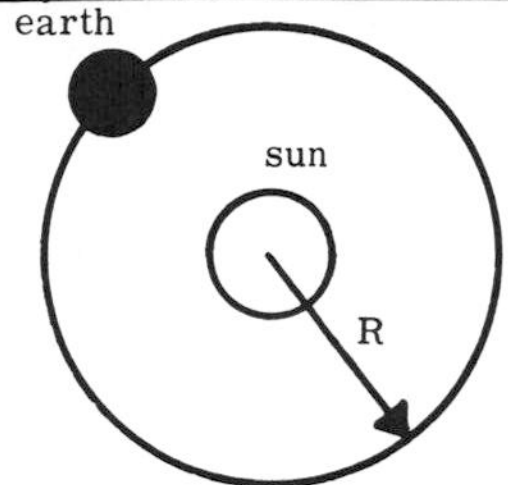

Solution: To calculate the temperature of the sun, T, we use Stefan's Law

$$R = e\,\sigma\,T^4$$

Here, e is the emissivity of the radiator, σ is a constant, T is the temperature of the radiator in Kelvin degrees, and R is the rate of emission of radiant energy per unit area of the radiator. Hence,

$$T^4 = \frac{R}{e\sigma} \qquad (1)$$

Regarding the sun as an ideal radiator, e = 1. Furthermore,

$$R = \frac{P}{A}$$

where A is the surface area of the sun, and P is the power provided by the sun as a result of radiation. Using these facts in (1)

$$T^4 = \frac{P}{\sigma A} \qquad (2)$$

Now, the power per unit area intercepted by the earth is

$$\frac{P}{A'} = .14\ W/cm^2$$

where A' is the surface area of a sphere having a radius equal to that of the earth's orbit. Hence,

$$P = (.14\ W/cm^2)\ A' \qquad (3)$$

Using (3) in (2)

$$T^4 = \frac{(.14\ W/cm^2)}{\sigma}\frac{A'}{A}$$

Now $\frac{A'}{A} = \frac{4\pi\ r^2}{4\pi\ R^2}$, where r and R are the radius of the earth's orbit and the radius of the sun, respectively. Then,

$$T^4 = \frac{(.14\ W/cm^2)}{\sigma}\left(\frac{r}{R}\right)^2 \qquad \text{or}$$

$$T^4 = \frac{0.14\ W\cdot cm^{-2}}{5.6 \times 10^{-12}\ W\cdot cm^{-2}\cdot K\ deg^{-4}} \times (216)^2$$

$$\therefore \quad T = 5.84 \times 10^{3}\,^{\circ}K.$$

• PROBLEM 548

In some underdeveloped nations dung is used as fuel for cooking. This is wasteful because it deprives the soil of valuable nutrients. It should be possible to use solar cookers in some of these countries. Generally, the "stove" consists of a curved aluminum mirror which focuses the heat energy on a collector plate (see figure). Calculate how long it takes to raise the temperature of 1 liter of water from 293°K to the boiling point, 373°K. Assume that the diameter of the mirror is 1 m and that 70 percent of the incident solar energy is actually available for heating the water. To raise the temperature of 1 liter of water 1°K, 4.186×10^3 J of thermal energy is required. The power radiated by the sun at the surface of the earth is $5.5 \times 10^2\ W/m^2$.

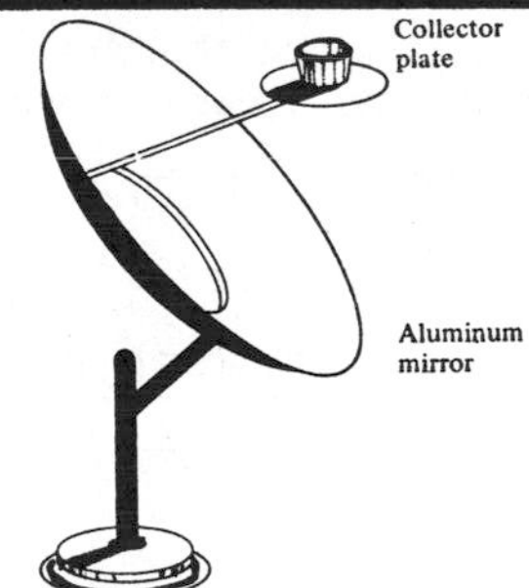

Solution: The collection area A of the mirror is,

$$A = \pi r^2 = \pi(5 \times 10^{-1}\ m)^2 = 7.9 \times 10^{-1}\ m^2$$

The total power P incident on the reflector is,

$$P = (7 \times 10^2 W/\not{m}^2)(7.9 \times 10^{-1}\ \not{m}^2)$$

$$= 5.5 \times 10^2\ W$$

Since the conversion efficiency is only 70 percent, the power converted to thermal power H is,

$$H = P(7.0 \times 10^{-1}) = (5.5 \times 10^2 W)(7 \times 10^{-1}) = 3.9 \times 10^2\ J/s$$

The temperature must be increased by 80° K (from 293 to 373° K). The total thermal energy Q required is then,

$$Q = (4.19 \times 10^3 \text{ J/°}\cancel{K})(8 \times 10^{1}\text{°}\cancel{K}) = 3.35 \times 10^5 \text{J}$$

The time would be the amount of thermal energy needed devided by the rate at which thermal energy is produced. Hence,

$$t = \frac{Q}{H} = \frac{3.35 \times 10^5 \cancel{J}}{3.9 \times 10^2 \cancel{J}/s} = 8.59 \times 10^2 \text{ s}$$

$$= \frac{8.59 \times 10^2 \cancel{s}}{60 \cancel{s}/\text{min}} = 1.4 \times 10^1 \text{ min}$$

• PROBLEM 549

A wire 0.5 mm in diameter is stretched along the axis of a cylinder 5 cm in diameter and 25 cm in length. The wire is maintained at a temperature of 750°K by passing a current through it, the cylinder is kept at 250°K, and the gas in it has a thermal conductivity of 6×10^{-5} cal·cm^{-1}·C deg^{-1}·sec^{-1}. Find the rates at which the heat is dissipated both by conduction through the gas and by radiation, if the wire is perfectly black.

Solution: The heat flow due to conductivity through a hollow cylinder is given by

$$H = \frac{2\pi KL(t_2 - t_1)}{\ln (R_2/R_1)}$$

where R_1 and R_2 are the inner and outer radii of the cylinder, L is its length, and K is the coefficient of thermal conductivity of the material of which the cylinder is composed. Also, t_1 is the cylinder temperature at its inner radius, and similarly for t_2. In this case, therefore

$$H = \frac{2\pi \times 6 \times 10^{-5} \text{cal}\cdot\text{cm}^{-1}\cdot\text{C deg}^{-1}\cdot\text{s}^{-1} \times 25 \text{ cm} \times (750-250)\text{C deg}}{\ln (2.5 \text{ cm}/0.025 \text{ cm})}$$

$$= 1.02 \text{ cal}\cdot\text{s}^{-1}.$$

The rate of emission of energy per unit area by radiation is the net outflow according to Stefan's Law. Thus, in the usual notation,

$$R = e\,\sigma\,(T^4 - T_0^4)$$

where T is the absolute temperature of the outer cylinder surface, and similarly for T_0, e is the emissivity of the cylinder's surface, and σ is a constant. However,

$$H' = RA = e\,\sigma\,A(T^4 - T_0^4)$$

where A is the area of the surface which emits the

radiation. Since the wire is emitting the energy, and it is to be considered a black body,

$$e = 1$$

and $A = 2\pi R_1 L$

$$H' = \frac{5.67\times10^{-12}\,W\cdot cm^{-2}\cdot Kdeg^{-4}\times2\pi\times0.025\ cm\times25\ cm(750^4-250^4)(K\ deg)^4}{4.186\ J\cdot cal^{-1}}$$

$$= 1.67\ cal\cdot s^{-1}.$$

CHAPTER 17

ELECTROSTATICS- FUNDAMENTALS

• **PROBLEM** 550

What is the electric field intensity at a point 30 centimeters from a charge of 0.10 coulombs?

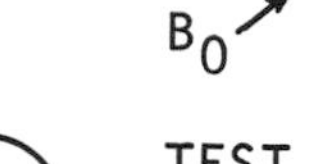

Solution: The electrostatic force on the test charge q, due to the charge Q is, by Coulomb's law, (see figure)

$$F = \frac{kQq}{r^2}$$

The electric field intensity at point B is defined as:

$$\varepsilon = \frac{F}{q} \quad \left(= \frac{kQq/r^2}{q}\right)$$

$$= \frac{kQ}{r^2}$$

In the problem we are presented with, we have

$$Q = 0.10 \text{ coulomb},$$

$$r = 30 \text{ cm} = 3.0 \times 10^{-1} \text{ m}$$

Then

$$\varepsilon = 9 \times 10^9 \frac{\text{nt - m}^2}{\text{coulombs}^2} \times \frac{0.10 \text{ coulombs}}{\left(3.0 \times 10^{-1}\right)^2 \text{ m}^2}$$

$$= 10^{10} \text{ nt/coulombs}$$

• **PROBLEM** 551

Show how two metallic balls that are mounted on insulating glass stands may be electrostatically charged with equal amounts but opposite sign charges.

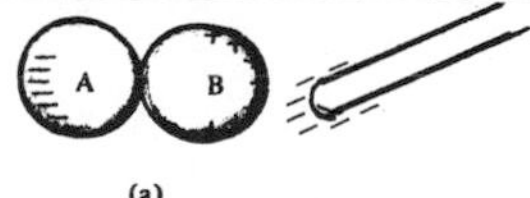

(a)

(b)

Solution: The two metal balls are assumed to be initially uncharged and touching each other. (Any charge on them may first be removed by touching them to the earth. This will provide a path for the charge on the spheres to move to the ground). A charged piece of amber is brought near one of the balls (B) as shown in the Figure. The negative charge of the amber will repel the electrons in the metal and cause them to move to the far side of A, leaving B charged positively. If the balls are now separated, A retains a negative charge and B has an equal amount of positive charge. This method of charging is called charging by induction, because it was not necessary to touch the objects being electrified with a charged object (the amber). The charge distribution is induced by the electrical forces associated with the excess electrons present on the surface of the amber.

• PROBLEM 552

What is the intensity of the electric field 10 cm from a negative point charge of 500 stat-coulombs in air?

Solution: The electrostatic force on a positive test charge q' at a distance r from a charge Q is, by Coulomb's law, (in the CGS system of units)

$$\vec{F} = k \frac{Qq'}{r^2}$$

The electric field intensity E is defined as the force per unit charge, or

$$\vec{E} = \frac{\vec{F}}{q'} = \frac{kQ}{r^2}$$

$\vec{E}$ points in the direction the force on the test charge acts. In a vacuum, k = 1 (to a good approximation, k = 1 for air as well), therefore the electric field 10 cm from a point charge of 500 stat-coulomb is

$$\vec{E} = (1) \frac{500 \text{ stat-coul}}{(10 \text{ cm})^2} = 5 \text{ dyne/stat-coul} \quad \text{pointing}$$

directly toward the negative charge.

• PROBLEM 553

If 5 joules of work are done in moving 0.025 coulomb of positive charge from point A to point A', what is the difference in potential of the points A and A'?

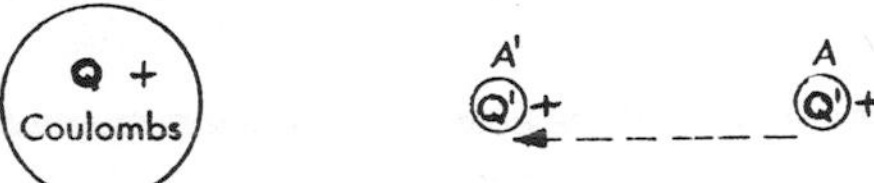

Solution: To solve this problem we use our formula for the definition of the volt, $E = \frac{W}{Q}$.

The work is 5 joules and the charge Q is 0.025 coulomb. Then the potential difference

$$E = \frac{5 \text{ joules}}{0.025 \text{ coulomb}} = 200 \text{ volts}$$

• PROBLEM 554

Suppose that a small, electrically charged metal ball is lowered into a metal can as illustrated in the Figure. Show how the charge is distributed when (a) the ball is inside the can but not touching and (b) after the ball touches the inside of the can.

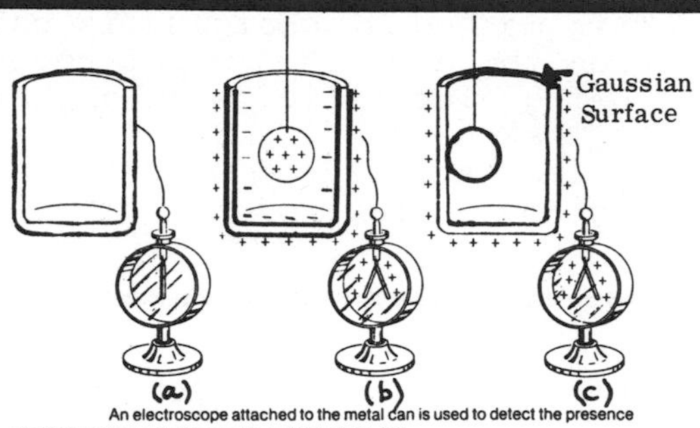

An electroscope attached to the metal can is used to detect the presence of electric charge on the outside surface of the can.

Solution: When the charged sphere is lowered to the position as in Figure (b), free electrons from atoms in the metal migrate to the inner surface because the positive charge of the ball exerts an attractive force. Since the net charge of the isolated can was originally zero, there is now a charge imbalance within the conductor. An excess of positive charge results. In a fraction of a second, due to transient currents within the conductor, the positive charges can be thought to mutually repel, spreading to the outside surface of the can. The outside surface then has a positive charge equal to the negative charge on the inside surface. As the ball and can touch, they form a single conductor and the electrons on the inner surface of the can move onto the metal ball and neutralize the positive charge carried by the ball. The final result is that the excess charge of the metallic sphere, placed in contact with an insulated metal can, resides entirely on its outside surface (see Figure c). This experiment provides a verification of Gauss's law. If a Gaussian surface is constructed inside the outer surface of the metal can, then there is no net charge within the surface. Then, according to Gauss's law,

$$\Phi = \frac{Q}{\varepsilon_0}$$

where Φ is the electric flux through the Gaussian surface due to the net charge Q within the surface. This then becomes $\Phi = 0$. Any excess charge must therefore reside on the outer surface of the conductor, outside the Gaussian surface.

• PROBLEM 555

A charge is placed on a string of infinite length so that the linear charge density on the string is n coulombs/m. Find the electric field due to this charge distribution.

Solution: This problem can be solved using Gauss's Law.

We construct as our Gaussian surface a cylinder, whose axis of symmetry coincides with the string, of

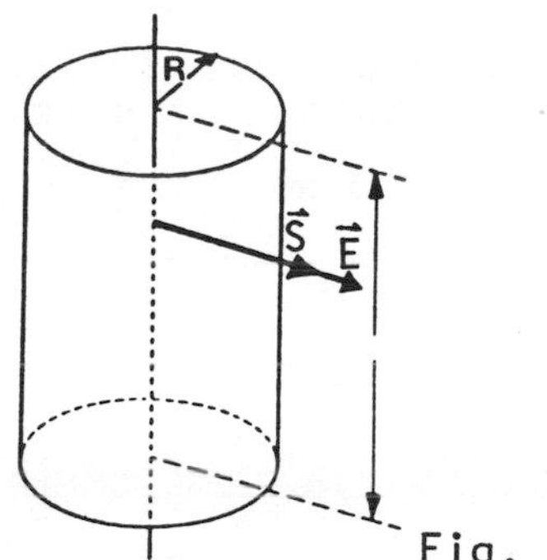

Fig. 1

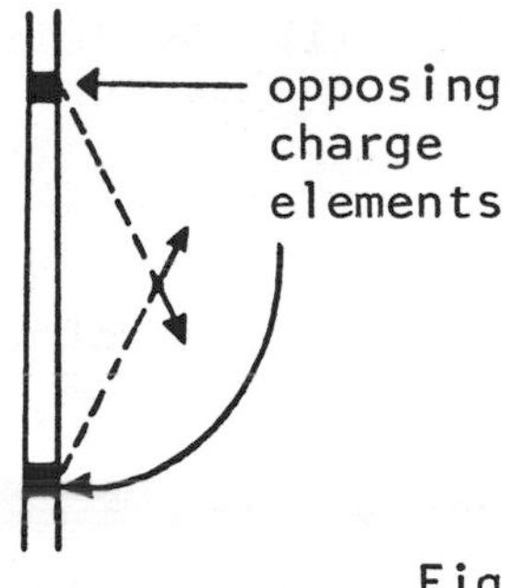

Fig. 2

length L, and of radius R. It can be seen from symmetry that there can be no component of the electric field parallel to the string, since all contributions to the field in that direction will cancel (see Fig. 2.). Since the field vector can be expressed in terms of components that are either perpendicular or parallel to the string, the resulting field will be radial. It can also be seen from symmetry that the magnitude of the field will be uniform over the surface of the cylinder, excluding the circular top and bottom. The flux through these portions is zero, however, since the field lines do not pass through their area.

The flux through the cylinder is therefore:

$$\Phi_E = \int \vec{E} \cdot d\vec{S} = E \int \cos 0° \, dS = E \int dS = ES =$$
$$= E \cdot 2\pi RL$$

Since the field is constant in magnitude it can be factored outside of the integral sign. The field lines coincide with the surface vector elements of the cylinder, which is the same as saying that they make an angle of zero degrees with each other. The corresponding term cos 0° in the integral reduces to 1, leaving only dS in the integrand which reduces to S, the total surface area of the cylinder (excluding the top and bottom).

The charge on length L of string is nL, thus by Gauss's Law:

$$\Phi_E = 4\pi k_E q = 4\pi \frac{1}{4\pi\varepsilon_o} q = \frac{q}{\varepsilon_o}$$

$$E \cdot 2\pi RL = \frac{nL}{\varepsilon_o}$$

$$E = \frac{n}{2\pi\varepsilon_o R} = 2 k_E \frac{n}{R}$$

where $k_E = \dfrac{1}{4\pi\varepsilon_o}$.

• PROBLEM 556

(1) What is the electric intensity in a copper conductor of resistivity $\phi = 1.72 \times 10^{-8}$ ohm meter having a current density $J = 2.54 \times 10^6$ amp/m^2? (2) What is the potential difference between two points of a copper wire 100 m apart?

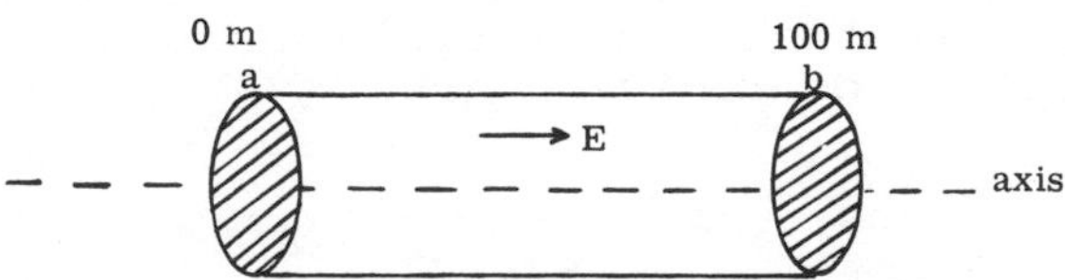

Solution: (1) By definition, $\vec{E}$, the electric field, is related to the current density, $\vec{J}$, through the relationship

$$\vec{E} = \frac{\vec{J}}{\sigma}$$

But $\sigma = \frac{1}{\phi}$, and therefore,

$$|\vec{E}| = \phi|\vec{J}|$$

$$= (1.72 \times 10^{-8} \text{ ohm}\cdot\text{m})(2.54 \times 10^{6} \text{ amp/m}^2)$$

$$= 4.37 \times 10^{-2} \text{ volt/m.}$$

(2) E is related to V by

$$V_v - V_a = -\int_a^b \vec{E} \cdot d\vec{\ell}. \tag{1}$$

From the figure, $\vec{E}$ is parallel to the axis of the cylindrical wire. If we evaluate (1) along a line in the direction of E and parallel to the cylinder axis, we obtain

$$V_b - V_a = E(a - b)$$

$$V_b - V_a = \left(4.37 \times 10^{-2} \frac{\text{volt}}{\text{m}}\right)(0 - 100 \text{ m})$$

$$V_b - V_a = -4.37 \text{ volts.}$$

Therefore, V_b is at a lower potential than V_a.

A second method of solution is to calculate the resistance (R) of a length ℓ of the wire from

$$R = \frac{\phi\ell}{A}$$

where A is the cross sectional area of the wire. Using Ohm's Law,

$$V_a - V_b = \left[\frac{\phi\ell}{A}\right] I$$

If A and the current I are given, $V_a - V_b$ may be found.

• PROBLEM 557

The spherical shell of a Van de Graaff generator is to be charged to a potential of 10^6 V. Calculate the minimum radius the shell can have if the dielectric strength of air is 3×10^6 V·m^{-1}.

Solution: The potential and electric intensity at the surface of a sphere of radius R are

$$V = \frac{Q}{4\pi\varepsilon_0 R} \qquad \text{and} \qquad E = \frac{Q}{4\pi\varepsilon_0 R^2} = \frac{V}{R}$$

Note that these relations are the same as the formulae for the potential and electric field of a point charge at a distant R from the charge. Thus, the field due to a sphere of charge Q is the same as that due to a point charge of charge Q. Therefore, R = V/E. But the maximum acceptable value of E is 3×10^6 V•m^{-1} for, at any higher value of E, the air will break down, and arc discharges through the air will result. Hence, the maximum radius for the spherical shell is

$$R = \frac{10^6 \text{ V}}{3 \times 10^6 \text{ V}\cdot\text{m}^{-1}} = \frac{1}{3} \text{ m}.$$

• **PROBLEM 558**

A mechanical device moves a charge of 1.5 coulombs for a distance of 20 cm through a uniform electric field of 2×10^3 newtons/coulomb. What is the emf of the device?

Solution: The electromotive force or emf ε is the work done by transporting a unit charge through an opposing electric field E. This input of work becomes available as an electric potential (as in a battery). In order to move the charge q, a force of magnitude F = Eq must act opposite to the electric force on the charge. An amount of work

$$W = \vec{F} \cdot \vec{d} = Eqd$$

will be supplied over a distance d. The emf is this work per unit charge, therefore

$$\varepsilon = \frac{W}{q} = Ed$$

$$= (2 \times 10^3 \text{ N/coul})(0.2\text{m}) = 400 \text{ volts}.$$

• **PROBLEM 559**

A metal sphere of radius 5 cm has an initial charge of 10^{-6} coul. Another metal sphere of radius 15 cm has an initial charge of 10^{-5} coul. If the two spheres touch each other what charge will remain on each?

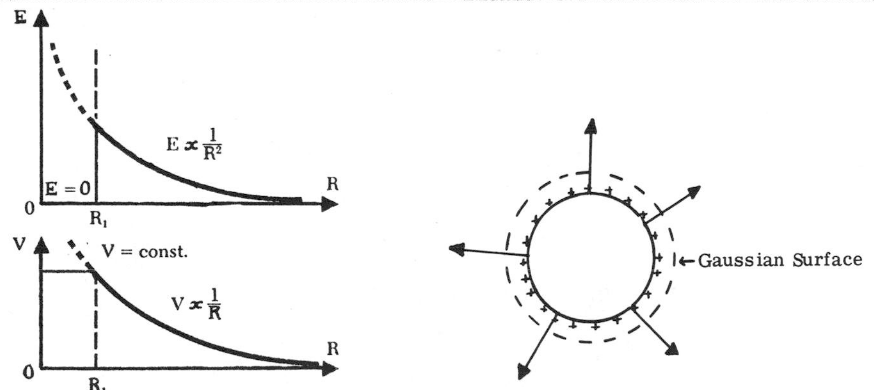

Solution: First we find the field of the charged sphere by using Gauss's law,

$$\int \vec{E} \cdot d\vec{S} = \frac{q}{\varepsilon_0}$$

Here, q is the total charge enclosed by the Gaussian surface and the integral is a surface integral. Consider a spherical Gaussian surface of radius R centered at the center of the sphere.

The magnitude of $\vec{E}$ is the same at all points on the Gaussian surface by symmetry considerations. $\vec{E}$ and $d\vec{A}$ are in the same directions, as well (i.e., both point radially outward). Gauss' law then reduced to

$$E\int dA = E\,4\pi R^2 = \frac{q}{\epsilon_0}$$

For $4\pi R^2$ is the surface area of the sphere. Thus,

$$E = \frac{1}{4\pi\epsilon_0}\frac{q}{R^2}$$

The field external to the sphere is as if all the charge were concentrated at the center; the field internal to the sphere must be zero. Since the sphere is a conductor. Similarly the potential external to the sphere will be as if all the charge were concentrated at the center. The potential inside the sphere must be constant since E, the potential gradient, (i.e.,

$$E = -\frac{dV}{dr}\Big),$$

is zero (see figure). The potential, then, at any point on the sphere or external to the sphere, is, by definition

$$V(R) - V(\infty) = -\int_{\infty}^{R} E\,dR = -\frac{q}{4\pi\epsilon_0}\int_{\infty}^{R}\frac{dR}{R^2} = \frac{1}{4\pi\epsilon_0}\left.\frac{q}{R}\right|_{\infty}^{R}$$

But $V(\infty) = 0$, $V(R) = \frac{1}{4\pi\epsilon_0}\frac{q}{R}$. If we set $K_E = \frac{1}{4\pi\epsilon_0}$, $V(R) = \frac{K_E q}{R}$.

When the two spheres are touched, their potentials must become equal. This is accomplished by a movement of charge from one sphere to the other, until the potentials equalize. After touching,

$$V_1 = V_2 \quad \text{or} \quad K_E\frac{q_1}{R_1} = K_E\frac{q_2}{R_2}$$

where q_1 and q_2 are the charged on spheres 1 and 2 respectively.

Thus

$$\frac{q_1}{q_2} = \frac{R_1}{R_2} = \frac{15}{5} = 3$$

$$q_1 = 3q_2$$

But the total charge is

$$\begin{aligned} q_1 + q_2 &= 10^{-5}\text{ coul} + 10^{06}\text{ coul} \\ &= 10^{-5}(1 + 0.1)\text{ coul} \qquad (1) \\ &= 1.1 \times 10^{-5}\text{ coul} \end{aligned}$$

Also, $3q_2 = q_1$, and using (1)

$$\begin{aligned} 4q_2 &= 1.1 \times 10^{-5}\text{ coul} \\ q_2 &= 2.75 \times 10^{-6}\text{ coul} \\ q_1 &= 8.25 \times 10^{-6}\text{ coul} \end{aligned}$$

Initially we had $q_1 = 10^{-5}$ coul and $q_2 = 10^{-6}$ coul.

• PROBLEM 560

An electron is released from rest at one point in a uniform electric field and moves a distance of 10 cm in 10^{-7} sec. What is the electric field strength and what is the voltage between the two points?

Solution: To find the electric field strength we divide the force exerted on the test charge, the electron, by the magnitude of the electron.

$$E = \frac{F}{q}$$

We are given the distance the electron travels and the time it takes. We must try to find a relationship to use in solving for the unknown F, in order to determine E.

Then: For a uniform electric field, the force on the electron is constant; hence, the acceleration, $a = F_E/m_e$, is also constant. The distance traveled is

$d = \frac{1}{2} at^2$, so

$$d = \frac{1}{2} at^2 = \frac{1}{2} \left(\frac{F_E}{m_e}\right) t^2$$

and $$F_E = \frac{2m_e d}{t^2}$$

The field strength is the force divided by the charge:

$$E = \frac{F_E}{e} = \frac{2m_e d}{et^2}$$

$$= \frac{2 \times (9.1 \times 10^{-28} \text{ g}) \times 10 \text{ cm}}{(4.8 \times 10^{-10} \text{ statC}) \times (10^{-7} \text{ sec})^2}$$

$$= 3.8 \times 10^{-3} \text{ statV/cm}$$

The voltage is

$$V = E \times d$$

$$= (3.8 \times 10^{-3} \text{ statV/cm}) \times 10 \text{ cm}$$

$$= 0.038 \text{ statV}$$

$$= 0.038 \times 300 = 11.4 \text{ V}$$

• PROBLEM 561

A charge of 1 C flows from a 100-V outlet through a 100-W light bulb each second. How much work is done each second by this electrical source?

Solution: The voltage, V = 100 V, and the charge, q = 1 C, are given. By definition of potential

$$V = \frac{W}{q}$$

where W is the work done in moving the charge q through a potential difference V. Then

$$W = qV = (1\ C)(100\ V) = 1 \times 10^2\ J$$

Alternatively, since the power rating of the light bulb is given as 100 watt, it dissipates 100 joules of energy per second. Therefore, for each second, the source must supply 100 joules of energy (or do 100 joules of work per second) to provide the energy dissipated by the light bulb resistance.

• PROBLEM 562

An isolated sphere 10 cm in radius is charged in air to 500 volts. How much charge is required? If this charge is then shared with another isolated sphere of 5 cm radius by connecting them together quickly with a fine wire, what is the final charge on each and what is the final potential of each?

FIGURE A FIGURE B

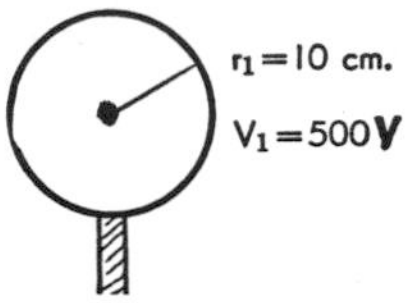

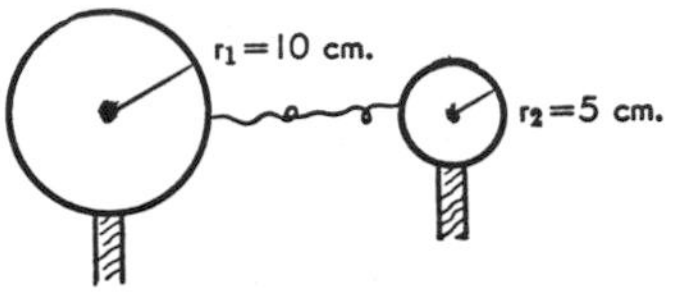

Solution: Figure A shows the first situation. (We assume both spheres are made of a conducting material.) The potential of a sphere is

$$V = \frac{1}{4\pi\varepsilon_0}\frac{q}{R}$$

where ε_0 is the permittivity of free space, and q is the charge on the sphere of radius R. Solving for q, and using the given data

$$q = 4\pi\varepsilon_0 RV$$

$$q = \frac{(5 \times 10^{-2}\ m)(500\ V)}{(9 \times 10^9\ N{\cdot}m^2/c^2)} \approx 2.8 \times 10^{-9}\ C \qquad (1)$$

This is the charge needed to raise the sphere of 10 cm radius to 500 V.

In figure B, we show the 2 spheres connected by a fine wire. In this situation, they have equal potentials and

$$V_1 = V_2$$

or $$\frac{1}{4\pi\varepsilon_0}\frac{q_1}{R_1} = \frac{1}{4\pi\varepsilon_0}\frac{q_2}{R_2}$$

whence $$q_1 = \frac{R_1}{R_2}q_2 \qquad (2)$$

Here, the subscript 1, refers to variables involved

with the larger sphere, and similarly for the subscript 2 and the smaller sphere. Furthermore, since both spheres share the charge initially on the larger sphere,

$$q_1 + q_2 = q \qquad (3)$$

where q is given by (1). Using (2) in (3), we solve for q_2,

$$\left(\frac{R_1}{R_2} + 1\right) q_2 = q$$

$$q_2 = \frac{q}{\frac{R_1}{R_2} + 1} = \frac{q}{2 + 1} = \frac{q}{3}$$

whence $\quad q_2 = \frac{2.8}{3} \times 10^{-9}\ C \approx .93 \times 10^{-9}\ C$

Furthermore, $\quad q_1 = q - q_2 \approx (2.8 - .93) \times 10^{-9}\ C$

$$q_1 \approx 1.87 \times 10^{-9}\ C$$

The final potential of the larger sphere is the same as the final potential of the smaller sphere. Both spheres then have a final potential of

$$V = V_1 = V_2 = \frac{q_1}{4\pi\varepsilon_0 R_1}$$

$$V \approx \frac{(1.87 \times 10^{-9}\ C)(9 \times 10^9\ N\cdot m^2/c^2)}{(10 \times 10^{-2}\ m)}$$

$$V \approx 168.3 \text{ Volts}$$

• PROBLEM 563

Prove the following theorem: The electric field outside of an infinite cylindrically symmetrical charge distribution is equivalent to the field due to an infinite line charge of equal linear charge density.

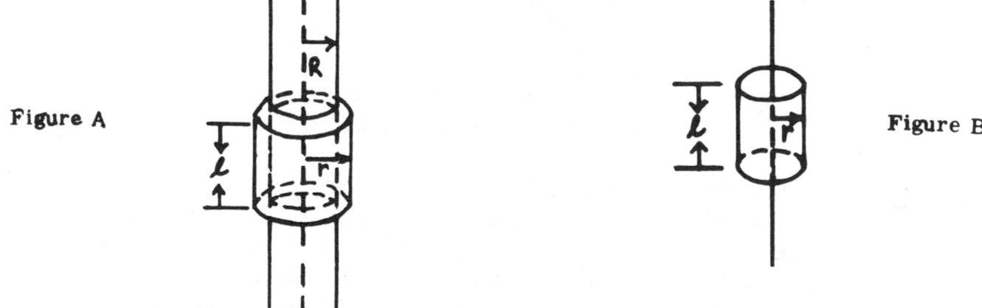

Solution: First, we compute the field due to a cylindrical shell of charge. We note that the field must be radial since no other direction is preferred. We erect as a Gaussian surface, a cylinder, of radius r (r > R) and height ℓ, concentric to the shell. (See figure (a)). By Gauss' law (since E is constant along any cylinder concentric to the axis):

$$\int \vec{E} \cdot d\vec{A} = 4\pi q \ , \quad 2\pi r\ell E = 4\pi(2\pi R\ell\sigma)$$

where $\sigma = \frac{q}{\text{area}}$ is the surface charge density of the shell. We note that since the field is radial, the flux through the top and bottom of the Gaussian cylinder is zero. Thus:

$$E = \frac{4\pi R\sigma}{r} = 2\,\frac{2\pi R\;\frac{q}{2\pi R\ell}}{r} = \frac{2\,\frac{q}{\ell}}{r} = \frac{2\lambda}{r}$$

where $\lambda = q/\ell$ is the linear charge density. This formula holds for a cylindrically symmetrical charge distribution since we can consider such a configuration as the superposition of many cylindrical shells of charge density λ_i, $i = 1,2,3,\ldots$

$$E = \frac{2\lambda_1}{r} + \frac{2\lambda_2}{r} + \frac{2\lambda_3}{r} + \ldots = \frac{2}{r}(\lambda_1 + \lambda_2 + \lambda_3 + \ldots)$$
$$= \frac{2\lambda'}{r}$$

where $\lambda' = \lambda_1 + \lambda_2 + \lambda_3 + \ldots = \frac{q_1}{\ell} + \frac{q_2}{\ell} + \frac{q_3}{\ell} + \ldots = \frac{q\text{ total}}{\ell}$

Now, we compute the field due to an infinite line charge. Figure (b) depicts an infinite line of charge of linear charge density λ, with a cylindrical Gaussian surface of radius r and height ℓ, surrounding it. Again, we see as with the cylindrical shell, that the field must be radial since no other direction is preferred. Thus, the flux through the top and bottom of the Gaussian surface is zero. Applying Gauss's law:

$$\int \vec{E}\cdot d\vec{A} = 2\pi r\ell\, E = 4\pi\ell\lambda = 4\pi q$$

$$E = \frac{2\lambda}{r}\,.$$

The same result is thus obtained.

• PROBLEM 564

A very large conducting plate has a surface charge density of 10^{-2} coul/m^2. What is the energy density of the field produced by this charge distribution?

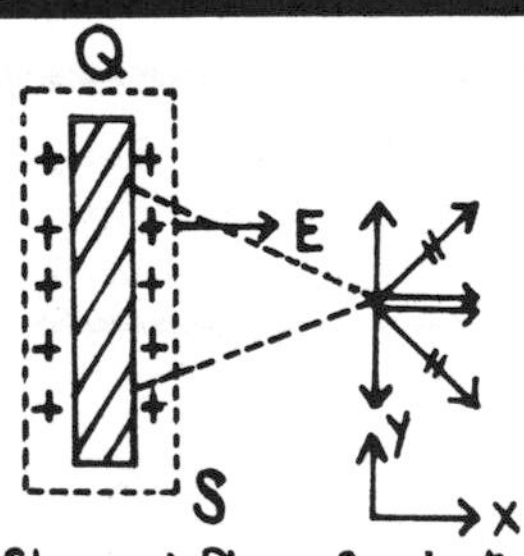

Charged Plane Conductor

Solution: The electric field due to the evenly charged sheet can be obtained by applying Gauss' Law at the surface of the sheet (see figure). By the definition of a conductor, the electric field at the surface of the conductor must be at right angles to it. (The y components of $\vec{E}$ due to 2 symmetrically placed elements of the conductor's surface cancel, whereas the x components reinforce.)

If we allow the Gaussian surface S to be very close to the surface of the conductor and neglect the fringing at the edges, we may use Gauss' Law,

$$\varepsilon_0 \int_S \vec{E} \cdot d\vec{S} = Q, \quad \text{or} \quad \varepsilon_0 AE = \delta A,$$

where A is the total surface area of the conductor. Therefore,

$$E = \frac{\delta}{\varepsilon_0}$$

where δ is the surface charge density. The energy density of the field E is, by definition,

$$u = \frac{\varepsilon_0 E^2}{2} \qquad \text{or}$$

$$u = \frac{\varepsilon_0}{2}\left(\frac{\delta}{\varepsilon_0}\right)^2 = \frac{\delta^2}{2\varepsilon_0}$$

But $\varepsilon_0 = \dfrac{1}{4\pi K_E}$, where $K_E = 9 \times 10^9 \dfrac{N \cdot m^2}{c^2}$.

Hence $u = \dfrac{\delta^2}{2} 4\pi K_E = 2\pi K_E \delta^2$

In this problem

$$u = 2\pi \times \left(9 \times 10^9 \frac{N \cdot m^2}{c^2}\right) \times 10^{-4} \frac{c^2}{m^4}$$

$$u = 56.52 \times 10^5 \frac{N}{m^2}$$

Because 1 Joule = 1 N • m

$$u = 56.52 \times 10^5 \frac{\text{Joules}}{m^3}$$

• PROBLEM 565

In the figure, a fine wire, having a positive charge per unit length λ, lies on the y-axis. Find the electric intensity set up by the wire at point P.

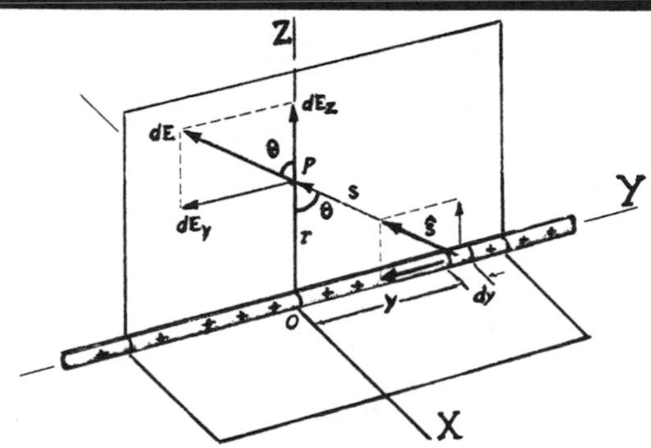

Charged Wire

Solution: Let the wire be subdivided, in imagination, into short elements of length dy. The charge dq on an element is then λ dy. Let r represent the perpendicular distance from P to the wire and $\vec{s}$ the vector from dq to P. If we view dq as a point charge, then it sets up a field $d\vec{E}$ at P given by

$$d\vec{E} = k \frac{\hat{s}\, dq}{s^2} = k \frac{\hat{s} \lambda dy}{s^2},$$

where $\hat{s}$ is a unit vector in the direction of $\vec{s}$, and $k = 9 \times 10^9\ N \cdot m^2/c^2$, and the resultant intensity $\vec{E}$ is the sum of all these infinitesimal fields $d\vec{E}$ along the y-axis, or

$$\vec{E} = k \int \frac{\hat{s}\lambda dy}{s^2} .$$

The unit vector $\hat{s}$ lies in the yz-plane, so its x-component is zero. The magnitude of its y-component is $\sin\theta$ and that of its z-component is $\cos\theta$. The vector equation above is then equivalent to the three scalar equations

$$E_x = 0$$

$$E_y = k\lambda \int_{-\infty}^{+\infty} \frac{\sin\theta\ dy}{s^2}$$

$$E_z = k \int_{-\infty}^{+\infty} \frac{\cos\theta\ dy}{s^2} .$$

The wire is considered to be sufficiently long so that the limits of integration are from $-\infty$ to $+\infty$.

Let us change the integration variable from y to θ, so $y = r\tan\theta$, $s = r\sec\theta$ and θ varies from $-\frac{\pi}{2}$ to $\frac{\pi}{2}$ as y varies between $-\infty$ and $+\infty$. Since

$$y = r\tan\theta,$$

$$dy = r\sec^2\theta\ d\theta.$$

Hence,

$$E_y = k\lambda \int_{-\frac{\pi}{2}}^{\frac{\pi}{2}} \frac{(\sin\theta)(r\sec^2\theta)d\theta}{s^2}$$

Since $\sec\theta = \frac{s}{r}$,

$$E_y = k\lambda \int_{-\frac{\pi}{2}}^{\frac{\pi}{2}} \frac{(\sin\theta)(s^2/r)d\theta}{s^2} = \frac{k\lambda}{r} \int_{-\frac{\pi}{2}}^{\frac{\pi}{2}} \sin\theta\ d\theta = 0.$$

This result is not unexpected since in the figure we see that for each dq at $y = Y$, there is another dq at $y = -Y$. The y-components of the electric fields of these two charges cancel, whereas the z-components add up.

$$E_z = k\lambda \int_{-\frac{\pi}{2}}^{\frac{\pi}{2}} \frac{dy\cos\theta}{s^2}$$

$$= k\lambda r \int_{-\frac{\pi}{2}}^{\frac{\pi}{2}} \frac{(\cos\theta)(\sec^2\theta)d\theta}{s^2}$$

$$= k\lambda r \int_{-\frac{\pi}{2}}^{\frac{\pi}{2}} \frac{(\cos\theta)(\not{s}^2/r^2)}{\not{s}^2}$$

$$= \frac{k\lambda}{r} \int_{-\frac{\pi}{2}}^{\frac{\pi}{2}} \cos\theta \, d\theta = \frac{2k\lambda}{r}$$

• PROBLEM 566

In the figure, positive charge is distributed uniformly over the entire xy-plane, with a charge per unit area, or surface density of charge, σ. Find the electric intensity at the point P.

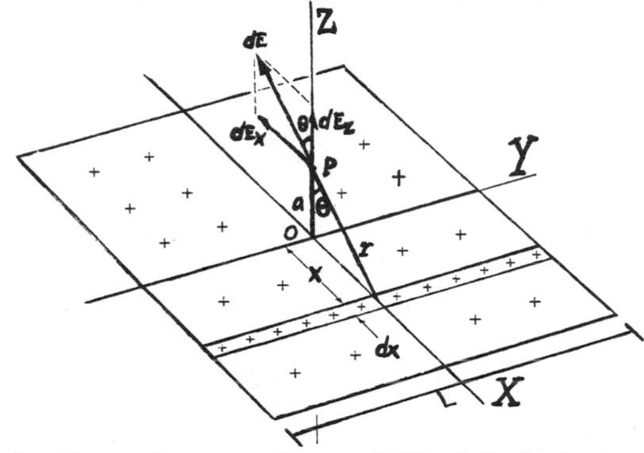

Solution: Let the charge be subdivided into narrow strips parallel to the y-axis and of width dx. Each strip can be considered a line charge.

The area of a portion of a strip of length L is L dx, and the charge dq on the strip is

$$dq = \sigma L \, dx.$$

The charge per unit length, dλ, is therefore

$$d\lambda = \frac{dq}{L} = \sigma \, dx.$$

Considered as a line of charge the strip sets up at point P a field $d\vec{E}$, lying in the xz-plane and of magnitude

$$dE = 2k\sigma \frac{dx}{r},$$

which is the field due to a line of charge.

The field can be resolved into components dE_x and dE_z. The components dE_x will sum to zero when the entire sheet of charge is considered. To see this consider the lines of charge at points x and - x. The x-components of each pair cancel each other. The resultant field at P is therefore in the z-direction, perpendicular to the sheet of charge. It will be seen from the diagram that

$$dE_z = dE \cos \theta$$

and hence

$$E = \int dE_z = 2k \int_{-\infty}^{+\infty} \frac{\cos \theta \, dx}{r} .$$

If we use θ as the integral variable (which varies between $-\frac{\pi}{2}$ and $\frac{\pi}{2}$), and note that

$$r = \frac{a}{\cos \theta}, \quad x = a \tan \theta, \; dx = a \sec^2 \theta \, d\theta$$

we obtain

$$E = 2k\sigma \int_{-\infty}^{\infty} \frac{\cos \theta}{r} dx$$

$$= 2k\sigma \int_{-\frac{\pi}{2}}^{\frac{\pi}{2}} \frac{(\cos^2 \theta)(a \sec^2 \theta)}{a} d\theta = 2k \, \sigma\pi$$

Note that the distance a from the plane to the point P does not appear in the final result. This means that the intensity of the field set up by an infinite plane sheet of charge is independent of the distance from the charge. In other words, the field is uniform and normal to the plane of charge.

The same result would have been obtained if point P, had been taken below the xy-plane. That is, a field of the same magnitude but in the opposite sense is set up on the opposite side of the plane.

• **PROBLEM 567**

The nucleus of an atom has a charge +2e, where e is the electronic charge. Find the electric flux through a sphere of radius 1 Å (10^{-10} m).

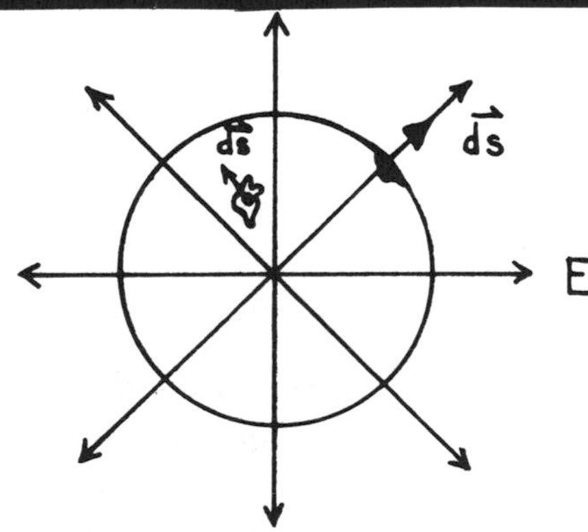

Solution: This problem is solved most directly by using Gauss's Law:

$$\Phi_E = 4\pi k_E q$$

where q is the total charge enclosed by the sphere. The orientation of the charge within the sphere does not matter. Gauss's Law yields:

$$\Phi_E = 4\pi k_E (2e) = 8\pi k_E e$$

We can also find the flux from its definition:

$$\Phi_E = \int \vec{E} \cdot d\vec{S}$$

where $d\vec{S}$ is the differential surface area vector which is always perpendicular to the surface. Taking the nucleus to be at the center of the sphere, we see that the field, being radial, is perpendicular to the sphere surface. Since the nucleus is equidistant from all points on the sphere, the magnitude of the field is constant over the entire surface, and is, by definition:

$$E = k_E \frac{2e}{R^2}$$

where R is the radius of the sphere.

Thus, we may take $\vec{E}$ outside of the integral sign:

$$\Phi_E = 2k_E \frac{e}{R^2} \int \cos 0° \, dS = 2k_E \frac{e}{R^2} \int dS =$$

$$= 2k_E \frac{e}{R^2} S = 2k_E \frac{e}{R^2} \cdot 4\pi R^2 = 8\pi k_E e$$

The $\vec{E}$ vector makes an angle of 0° with the $d\vec{S}$ vector, since both are perpendicular to the surface of the sphere (see diagram).

The cosine is introduced since the integrand is the inner product of the two vectors $\vec{E}$ and $d\vec{S}$, and by definition, if $\vec{A}$ and $\vec{B}$ are vectors then:

$$\vec{A} \cdot \vec{B} = |\vec{A}||\vec{B}| \cos (A,B)$$

where (A,B) is the angle between $\vec{A}$ and $\vec{B}$.

$S = 4\pi R^2$ is the surface area of the sphere.

Substituting

$$k_E = 9 \times 10^9 \frac{\text{N-m}^2}{\text{coul.}^2} \quad \text{and } e = 1.6 \times 10^{-19} \text{ coulombs}$$

we obtain the magnitude of the flux.

$$\Phi_E = (8)(3.14)\left(9\text{x}10^9 \frac{\text{N-m}^2}{\text{coul.}^2}\right)\left(1.6 \times 10^{-19} \text{ coul.}\right)$$

$$= 3.61 \times 10^{-8} \frac{\text{N-m}^2}{\text{coul.}}$$

We note that this result is independent of the radius of the sphere. We could have seen this immediately from Gauss's Law, since the flux through the sphere is entirely determined by the amount of charge enclosed within it.

• PROBLEM 568

Consider a sphere of radius a which has a charge q evenly distributed on its surface. What is the electric field outside the sphere?

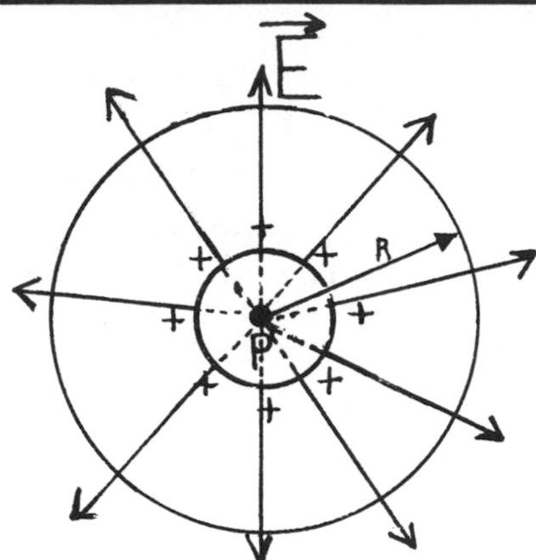

Solution: Due to the fact that the charge is uniformly distributed over the surface of the sphere (and therefore symmetric), we realize that the electric field must have the same strength at any point a distance r away from the center of the charged sphere. Furthermore, we expect the lines of $\vec{E}$ to begin on the positive surface charges and emanate radially from the surface of the sphere. Consider a spherical surface of radius R and with the same center as the charged sphere. If the field at this surface is E, then the total electric flux through the surface is

$$\Phi_E = \int \vec{E} \cdot d\vec{S} = \int E\, dS$$

because $\vec{E}$ and $d\vec{S}$ are parallel. Hence,

$$\Phi_E = 4\pi R^2 E$$

where $4\pi R^2$ is the surface area of the spherical surface. Since the charge enclosed by the surface is q, then by Gauss's Law,

$$\Phi_E = \frac{q}{\varepsilon_0}\ .$$ Therefore,

$$4\pi R^2 E = \frac{q}{\varepsilon_0}$$ from which

$$E = \frac{1}{4\pi\varepsilon_0} \frac{q}{R^2}$$

$$= K_E \frac{q}{R^2}$$

Thus the field outside the sphere is just as if all the charge q were located at the center of the sphere.

• PROBLEM 569

A positively charged ring of radius R lies in the Y-Z plane. Compute the electric intensity at point P on the axis of the ring.

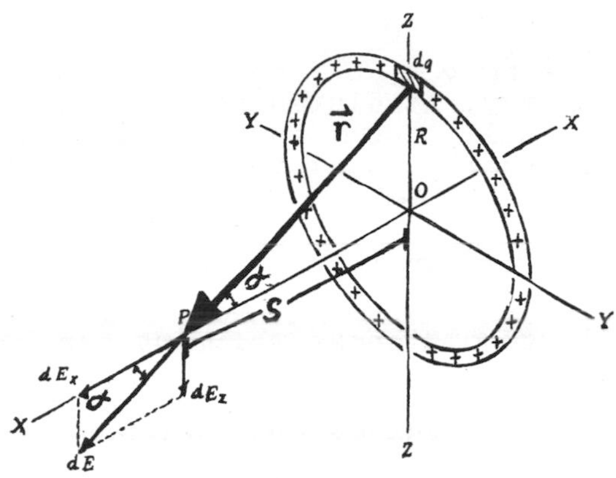

<u>Solution:</u> To calculate the electric field intensity at a point P from a continuous distribution, we calculate the electric field intensity due to one arbitrary element of charge, dq, at the point P, and then integrate this over the entire region under consideration. The electric field intensity, due to a differential charge element dq is given by

$$d\vec{E} = \frac{dq\ \vec{r}}{4\pi\varepsilon_0\ r^3} \tag{1}$$

where $d\vec{E}$ is the field intensity due to dq, dq is an element of charge, $\vec{r}$ is a vector from dq to P, and r is the magnitude of this vector. In this problem, however, we can simplify the integral in (1). Note from the figure that the Z components of the field intensities due to charge elements dq on opposite sides of the ring will cancel because they are of equal magnitude, but opposite in direction. Hence, the net electric field intensity will point along the x-axis and will be due to the x component of $d\vec{E}$, which is of magnitude (dE) cos α. Now we may neglect the vector nature of the integrand in (1), because the problem has been reduced to a calculation in one dimension. Therefore,

$$E_{net} = \int dE \cos\alpha .$$

From (1), we obtain

$$E_{net} = \int \frac{dq \cos\alpha}{4\pi\varepsilon_0\ r^2} .$$

Because cos α, $4\pi\varepsilon_0$, and r are constants, we may write

$$E_{net} = \frac{1}{4\pi\varepsilon_0} \frac{\cos\alpha}{r^2} \int dq . \tag{2}$$

Integrating (2), we find

$$E_{net} = \frac{q \cos\alpha}{4\pi\varepsilon_0\ r^2} \tag{3}$$

where q is the total charge on the ring. Note that this field intensity is directed along the x-axis, and varies inversely with r^2.

At the center of the ring, $\alpha = 90°$, $\cos\alpha = 0$, and $E = 0$, as is evident by symmetry. At distances large compared to R, the angle α is small, $\cos\alpha$ is approximately 1, and s^2 (see figure) is nearly equal to r^2. Hence at large distances

$$E = \frac{1}{4\pi\varepsilon_0}\frac{q}{s^2}$$

In other words, at large distances the ring can be considered a point charge.

• PROBLEM 570

A circular hoop of radius 0.3 m receives a charge of 0.2 pC (picoCoulomb). Determine the potential and the field strength at the center of the hoop and at a point on the axis of the hoop 0.4 m from the center. Where on the axis is the field strength a maximum?

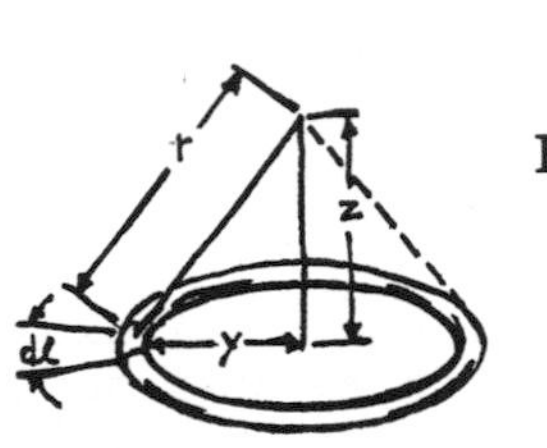

FIGURE A

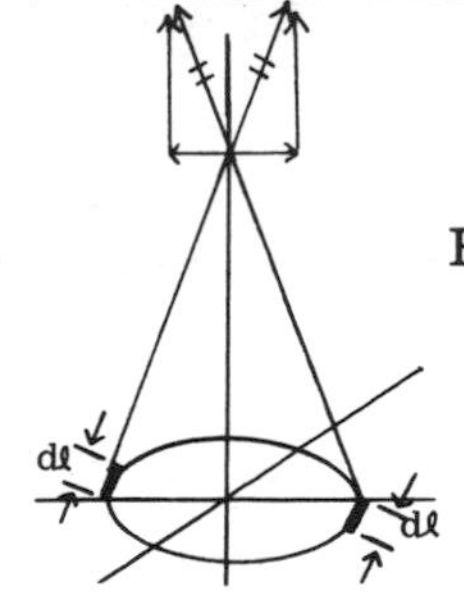

Figure B

Solution: Consider a small element $d\ell$ of the hoop carrying a charge dq (see fig. A). The potential at a point a distance z along the axis of the hoop due to dq is

$$dV = \frac{dq}{4\pi\varepsilon_0 r} = \frac{dq}{4\pi\varepsilon_0\sqrt{y^2+z^2}}.$$

The total potential at the point due to the charge on the whole hoop is thus

$$V = \int dV = \int \frac{dq}{4\pi\varepsilon_0 r} = \frac{1}{4\pi\varepsilon_0 r}\int dq$$

$$= \frac{q}{4\pi\varepsilon_0\sqrt{y^2+z^2}}$$

r is constant, for every line element $d\ell$ is equidistant from the point of interest. q is the total charge of the hoop. Thus the potential at the center of the hoop occurs for z = 0 m, and

$$V_0 = \frac{q}{4\pi\varepsilon_0 y}$$

$$= \frac{0.2\times10^{-12}\ \text{C}\times9\times10^9\ \text{N}\cdot\text{m}^2\cdot\text{C}^{-2}}{0.3\ \text{m}}$$

$$= 6\times10^{-3}\ \text{V}.$$

Also, when z = 0.4 m,

$$V_{0.4} = \frac{0.2 \times 10^{-12}\ C \times 9 \times 10^9\ N \cdot m^2 \cdot C^{-2}}{\sqrt{0.3^2 + 0.4^2}\ m}$$

$$= \frac{1.8 \times 10^{-3}}{0.5}\ V = 3.6 \times 10^{-3}\ V.$$

The electric intensity at the general point on the axis is

$$E = -\frac{dV}{dz} = +\frac{qz}{4\pi\varepsilon_0 (y^2 + z^2)^{3/2}} ,$$

From symmetry considerations, the direction of $\vec{E}$ must be along the z-axis. Let the electric field due to the charge dq of each segment $d\ell$ be resolved into a vertical and a horizontal component (see fig. B). From the symmetry of the hoop about its center, the horizontal components of the electric field due to the charges on any two segments $d\ell$ on opposite ends of the center will cancel one another. The vertical components are in the same direction and add algebraically. The direction, then, of the total $\vec{E}$ due to all pairs of segments $d\ell$ at opposite ends of the center, will be vertically upward, or along the positive z-axis. Thus at the center of the hoop where there is no vertical component of the electric field due to the charge dq on a segment $d\ell$, E is zero and at the position where z = 0.4 m, using (1)

$$E_{0.4} = \frac{9 \times 10^9\ N \cdot m^2 \cdot C^{-2} \times 0.2 \times 10^{-12} C \times 0.4\ m}{(\sqrt{(0.3\ m)^2 + (0.4\ m)^2})^3}$$

$$= \frac{0.2 \times 10^{-12}\ C \times 0.4\ m \times 9 \times 10^9\ N \cdot m^2 \cdot C^{-2}}{(0.5)^3\ m^3}$$

$$= 5.76 \times 10^{-3}\ V \cdot m^{-1}.$$

Note that when z is positive, E is positive, and when z is negative, E is negative. The direction of $\vec{E}$ is thus always along the axis away from the hoop.

The electric intensity E is zero when z = 0 and also when z = ∞; E must therefore pass through a maximum value somewhere between these two points. For a maximum dE/dz = 0, or using the product rule for differentiation,

$$\frac{q}{4\pi\varepsilon_0 (y^2 + z^2)^{3/2}} - \frac{3qz^2}{4\pi\varepsilon_0 (y^2 + z^2)^{3/2}} = 0.$$

$$\therefore\ y^2 + z^2 - 3z^2 = 0 \qquad \text{or} \qquad z = \pm \frac{y}{\sqrt{2}} .$$

Thus, at a distance along the axis of $(0.3/\sqrt{2})$ m = 0.21 m, E has its maximum value of

$$E_{max} = \frac{0.2 \times 10^{-12}\ C \times 0.21\ m \times 9 \times 10^9\ N \cdot m^2 \cdot C^{-2}}{(0.3^2 + 0.21^2)^{3/2}\ m^3}$$

$$= 7.70 \times 10^{-3}\ V \cdot m^{-1}.$$

By direct calculation, determine the value of the electric intensity at any distance from an infinite plane sheet of uniformly distributed charge. Show that the result follows at once from an application of Gauss's law.

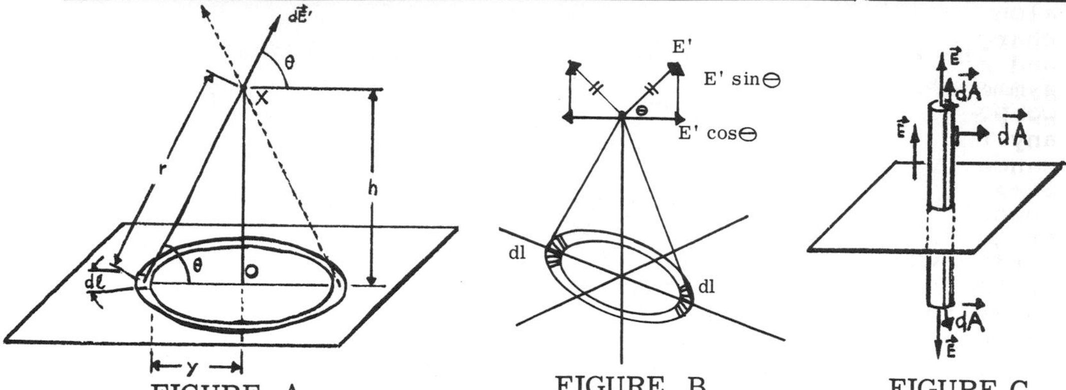

FIGURE A FIGURE B FIGURE C

Solution: Consider any point X at a perpendicular distance h from the plane sheet of charge density ρ. See figure A. Drop the perpendicular from the point to the sheet, cutting the latter at 0, and draw two circles, centered at 0, at radii of y and y + dy. Take a small portion of the annulus so formed, of length dℓ, and consider the electric intensity dE' at the point X due to the small (almost point-like) element of charge. Then the electric field due to a point charge is

$$dE' = \frac{dq}{4\pi\varepsilon_0 r^2}$$

Since the charge density $\rho = \frac{dq}{dA} = \frac{dq}{d\ell dy}$ then,

$$dE' = \frac{\rho\, d\ell\, dy}{4\pi\varepsilon_0\, r^2}\, .$$

The direction of dE' is the same as that of r, and dE' may therefore be resolved into components along OX and at right angles to it. The component along OX has the same value; no matter what position on the annulus dℓ occupies. But the element of the annulus diametrically opposite dℓ produces a component perpendicular to OX equal but opposite to that produced by dℓ. (See figure B). These two components thus cancel out, as do all components from diametrically opposite elements. The electric intensity from the whole annulus is thus perpendicular to the sheet and has magnitude

$$dE = \oint dE' \sin\theta = \frac{\rho\, dy}{4\pi\varepsilon_0 r^2} \sin\theta \oint d\ell$$

$$= \frac{\rho\ dy}{4\pi\varepsilon_0 r^2} \cdot \frac{h}{r} \quad 2\pi y = \frac{h\rho y\ dy.}{2\varepsilon_0 \left(h^2 + y^2\right)^{3/2}}.$$

We used the fact that $\sin\theta = h/r$ (geometric considerations in figure A) and that the sum of all the infinitesimal elements of length dℓ about the whole ring is equal to the circumference of the ring. Also used was the fact that $r = (h^2 + y^2)^{\frac{1}{2}}$.

For the whole sheet of charge the electric intensity is the sum of contributions due to all the annulii of radius $y = 0$ to $y = \infty$ (for the infinite plane sheet). Or

$$E = \int dE = \int_0^\infty \frac{h\rho y\, dy}{2\varepsilon_0 (h^2 + y^2)^{3/2}} = \frac{h\rho}{2\varepsilon_0} \int_0^\infty \frac{y\, dy}{(h^2 + y^2)^{3/2}}$$

$$= -\frac{h\rho}{2\varepsilon_0} \left[(h^2 + y^2)^{-\frac{1}{2}} \right]_0^\infty$$

$$= -\frac{h\rho}{2\varepsilon_0} \left[0 - \frac{1}{h} \right] = \frac{\rho}{2\varepsilon_0} .$$

To apply Gauss's law to the same problem, construct a cylinder of small and uniform cross-sectional area dA at right angles to the sheet and bisected by the sheet (see figure C). Since the sheet is infinite and the charge uniformly distributed, the electric intensity must be the same at all points equidistant from the sheet, and thus by symmetry must be everywhere perpendicular to the sheet. Hence E is everywhere parallel to the sides of the cylinder and thus the flux of E from the cylinder through its sides is zero. The magnitude of E at each end of the cylinder will be the same if the cylinder is bisected by the sheet, and E will be perpendicular to each end. Hence, applying Gauss's law, we obtain

$$\int \vec{E} \cdot d\vec{A} = \int \left[(\vec{E} \cdot d\vec{A})_{top} + (\vec{E} \cdot d\vec{A})_{side} + (\vec{E} \cdot d\vec{A})_{bottom} \right]$$

Since $d\vec{A}$ is small, $\int \vec{E} \cdot d\vec{A} \approx \vec{E} \cdot d\vec{A}$ and

$$\int \vec{E} \cdot d\vec{A} = \left(EdA + 0 + EdA = 2EdA \right) = \frac{dq}{\varepsilon_0} ;$$

but $\rho = \dfrac{dq}{dA}$ and

$$2EdA = (\rho dA/\varepsilon_0).$$

Therefore $E = \rho/2\varepsilon_0$. Thus E is everywhere perpendicular to the sheet and has the same value $\rho/2\varepsilon_0$ at all points.

• PROBLEM 572

(a) What is the magnitude of the electric field at a distance of 1Å(= 10^{-8} cm) from a proton?
(b) What is the electrostatic potential at this distance?
(c) What is the potential difference in volts between positions 1Å and 0.2Å from a proton?
(d) A proton is released from rest at a distance of 1Å from another proton. What is the kinetic energy

when the protons have moved infinitely apart? If one proton is kept at rest while the other moves, what is the terminal velocity of the moving proton?

(e) A proton is accelerated from rest by a uniform electric field. The proton moves through a potential drop of 100 volts. What is its final kinetic energy? (Note that 100 volts ≅ 0.33 statvolts.)

Solution:

(a) From Coulomb's law

$$E = \frac{e}{r^2} \cong \frac{5 \times 10^{-10} \text{ esu}}{(1 \times 10^{-8} \text{ cm})^2} = 5 \times 10^6 \text{ statvolt/cm}$$

Statvolt/cm is the dimension of electric field. The field is directed radially outward from the proton.

(b) Electrostatic potential is given by $\int_r^\infty \vec{E} \cdot d\vec{s}$. By convention, we shall assume that the potential is 0 at infinity, and we shall set our limits of integration accordingly.

$$\phi(r) = \int_r^\infty \frac{e}{r^2} dr = -\frac{e}{r}\Big|_r^\infty = \frac{e}{r}$$

$$\cong \frac{5 \times 10^{-10} \text{ esu}}{1 \times 10^{-8} \text{ cm}} \cong 5 \times 10^{-2} \text{ statvolts.}$$

(c) The potential difference between two points is $\int_{p_1}^{p_2} \vec{E} \cdot d\vec{s}$ where p_1 and p_2 are the two points. Therefore,

$$\int_{p_1}^{p_2} \vec{E} \cdot d\vec{s} = \int_{p_1}^{p_2} \frac{e}{r^2} dr = \int_{0.2\times10^{-8} \text{ cm}}^{1\times10^{-8} \text{ cm}} \frac{e}{r^2} dr$$

$$= -\frac{e}{r}\Bigg|_{0.2\times10^{-8} \text{ cm}}^{1\times10^{-8} \text{ cm}}$$

$$\cong -\frac{5 \times 10^{-10} \text{ esu}}{1 \times 10^{-8} \text{ cm}} + \frac{5 \times 10^{-8} \text{ esu}}{0.2 \times 10^{-8} \text{ cm}}$$

$$\cong 0.2 \text{ statvolts}$$

(d) By conservation of energy we know that the kinetic energy must equal the original potential energy. Potential energy is given by $\int \vec{F} \cdot d\vec{s}$, where potential energy is zero at infinity. The force is given by qE. Therefore,

$$\int_{1\times10^{-8} \text{ cm}}^{\infty} qE \cdot ds = \int_{1\times10^{-8} \text{ cm}}^{\infty} \frac{e^2}{r^2} \cdot dr$$

$$= -\frac{e^2}{r}\Bigg|_{1\times 10^{-8}\ \text{cm}}^{\infty}$$

$$= \frac{(4.8 \times 10^{-10}\ \text{esu})^2}{1 \times 10^{-8}\ \text{cm}} \cong 23 \times 10^{-12}\ \text{erg}$$

If one proton is kept at rest while the other moves, the terminal velocity of the moving proton is given by (using conservation of energy)

$$\tfrac{1}{2} Mv^2 \cong 23 \times 10^{-12}\ \text{erg}$$

$$v^2 \cong \frac{2 \times 23 \times 10^{-12}\ \text{erg}}{1.67 \times 10^{-24}\ \text{gm}}$$

$$\cong \frac{2 \times 23 \times 10^{-12}\ \frac{\text{gm - cm}^2}{\text{sec}^2}}{1.67 \times 10^{-24}\ \text{gm}}$$

$$\cong 27 \times 10^{12}\ \frac{\text{cm}^2}{\text{sec}^2}$$

$$v \cong 5 \times 10^6\ \frac{\text{cm}}{\text{sec}}$$

(e) The kinetic energy will be equal to the change in potential energy. This is equal to

$\int_{p_1}^{p_2} F \cdot ds$. Here $F = qE$ and energy is $\int_{p_1}^{p_2} qE \cdot ds$

$$= q \int_{p_1}^{p_2} E \cdot ds = q\phi_{12}\quad, \text{ or}$$

$$(4.8 \times 10^{-10}\ \text{statcoul})(0.33\ \text{statvolt})$$

$$\cong 1.6 \times 10^{-10}\ \text{erg}$$

• PROBLEM 573

> **A ring of charge with radius 0.5 m has a 0.02 m gap (see figure (a)). Compute the field at the center if the ring carries a charge of +1 coulomb.**

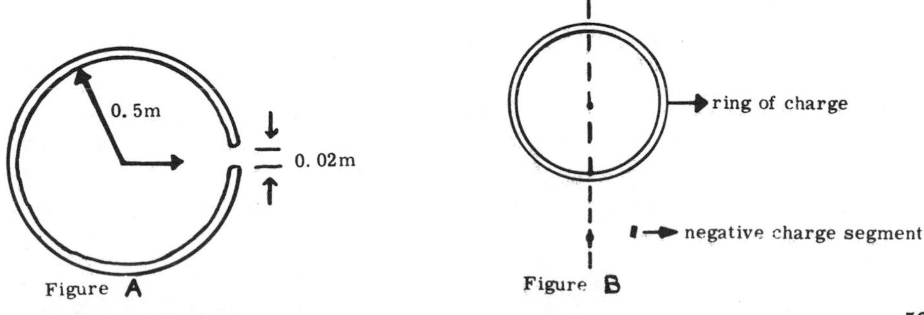

Solution: The field can be found by superposition of the fields of an imaginary ring of charge, and a hegative charge segment located where the gap would be (see figure (b)).

We must first calculate the linear charge density of the incomplete ring.

$$\sigma = \frac{q}{\text{length of ring}} = \frac{q}{2\pi R - 0.02} = \frac{1 \text{ coulomb}}{[2\pi(0.5) - 0.02]\text{m}}$$

$$= 0.321 \text{ coulombs/m}$$

where σ is the linear charge density and $R = 0.5$ is the radius. We can approximate the arc length of the gap with the linear distance between the ends since this chordal length is small compared with the radius.

The field at the center due to the complete ring is zero. Since all charge elements are diametrically opposite to the center, all field elements must cancel. Thus the field is entirely due to the negative charge segment. Both the ring and the segment must have charge densities whose absolute values (since the segment is negative) equal the charge density of the incomplete ring. Thus, the charge on the segment is:

$$q' = (0.02\text{m})(-0.321 \text{ coulombs/m}) = -6.42 \times 10^{-3} \text{coulombs}$$

The field at the center is:

$$E = k\frac{q'}{r^2} = 9 \times 10^9 \frac{N - m^2}{C^2} \frac{6.42 \times 10^{-3} C}{(0.5 \text{ m})^2} = 2.31 \times 10^8 \text{ N/C}$$

where we have treated the segment as if it were a point source.

• PROBLEM 574

A small metallic ball is charged positively and negatively in a sinusoidal manner at a frequency of 60 cps. The maximum charge on the ball is 10^{-6} coul. What is the displacement current due to this alternating charge? What would the displacement current be if the charging frequency were 10^6 cps?

Solution: The charge on the ball can be written as

$$q = q_0 \sin \omega t$$

where q_0 is the maximum charge on the ball (10^{-6} coul), $\omega = 2\pi f$ ($f = 60$ cps) and the sine function expresses the sinusoidal variation of the charge. According to Gauss's law, the total electric flux through a Gaussian surface about the sphere is given by

$$\Phi_E = \int \vec{E} \cdot d\vec{s} = \frac{q}{\epsilon_0} = \frac{q_0 \sin \omega t}{\epsilon_0}$$

The displacement current i_0 is defined as

$$i_0 \equiv \epsilon_0 \frac{d\Phi E}{dt} = \omega q_0 \sin \omega t = \frac{dq}{dt} \tag{1}$$

It is called a displacement current because even though there is no actual movement of charge from one position to another, the mathematical form of i_0 has the form of an actual charge flow. (See equation (1)).

The maximum value of the displacement current occurs when $|\cos \omega t| = 1$. Then

$$i_{D_{max}} = \omega q_0 = 2\pi f q_0$$

At 60 cps

$$i_{D_{max}} = 2\pi \times 60 \text{ sec}^{-1} \times 10^{-6} \text{ coul}$$
$$= 3.77 \times 10^{-4} \text{ amp}$$

If the frequency were 10^6 cps, then

$$i_{D_{max}} = 2\pi \times 10^6 \text{ sec}^{-1} \times 10^{-6} \text{ coul}$$
$$= 6.28 \text{ amp}$$

• PROBLEM 575

Charge is uniformly distributed over a spherical volume. Show that the electric intensity at any point inside the volume is the same as if all the charge closer to the center were concentrated there, and the rest of the charge removed.

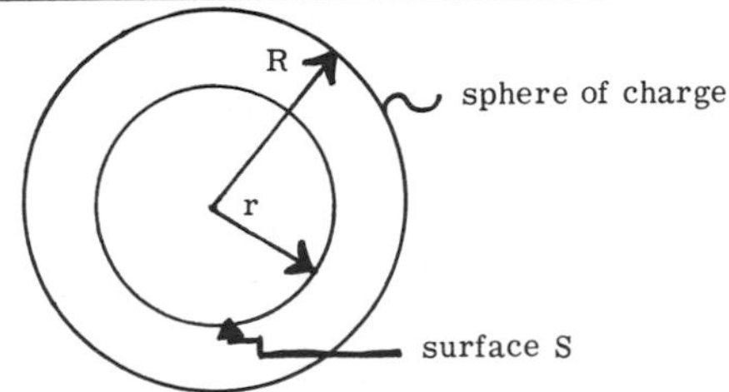

Solution: Consider any sphere concentric with the charged volume and of lesser radius r than the charged volume (see figure). By symmetry, the electric intensity must be the same at all points on the surface of a sphere of radius r since the charge is uniformly distributed within the sphere. Thus, the electric field intensity must be purely radial in direction. Hence the flux of intensity from such a sphere is, by definition,

$$\Phi_e = \int_S \vec{E} \cdot d\vec{S}$$

In this surface integral, $\vec{E}$ is the electric field intensity, and $d\vec{S}$ is a vector element of area for the surface S. In this case, S will be the above-mentioned sphere of radius r. Since $\vec{E}$ is a function of r only, and radial in direction, we may write

$$\vec{E} = E(r)\hat{r}$$

where $\hat{r}$ is a unit vector in the radial direction, originating at the center of the sphere shown in the figure. But $d\vec{S}$ is also in the radial direction, since it is an element of surface area of the sphere of radius r. Then

$$d\vec{S} = dS\ \hat{r}$$

Using the last 2 equations, we evaluate Φ_e:

$$\Phi_e = \int_S E(r)\hat{r} \cdot \hat{r}\ dS = \int_S E(r)\ dS$$

Since E(r) is constant over any sphere of radius r,

$$\Phi_e = E(r) \int_S dS = E(r) \times 4\pi r^2 \qquad (1)$$

where $4\pi r^2$ is the surface area of S. But by Gauss' Law,

$$\Phi_e = \frac{Q}{\varepsilon_0} \qquad (2)$$

where Q is the net charge enclosed by the surface over which Φ_e is evaluated (S).

Combining (1) and (2)

$$E(r) = \frac{Q}{4\pi\varepsilon_0 r^2}$$

where Q is the total charge inside the sphere of radius r.

But the same equation would have been obtained if all the charge inside a radius r were concentrated at the center and the rest removed, which proves the premise stated in the problem.

CHAPTER 18

ELECTROSTATIC INTERACTIONS AMONG PARTICLES & BODIES

ELECTROSTATIC INSTRUMENTS

• **PROBLEM** 576

Calculate the electrostatic force on q_1 due to $q_2(F_{12})$ and the force on q_2 due to $q_1(F_{21})$ for the case illustrated in the figure.

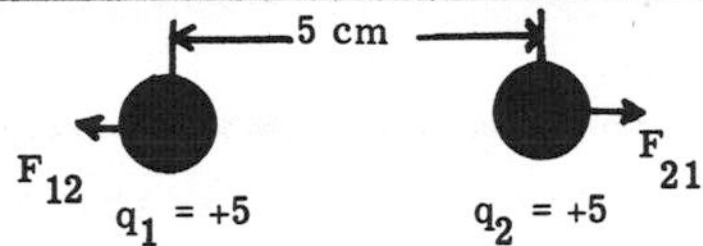

Solution: Using Coulomb's law and doing the calculation in the CGS system, of units we have

$$F_{12} = \frac{(+3 \text{ stat C})(+5 \text{ stat C})}{(5\text{cm})^2} = +\ 0.6 \text{ dyne (to the left)}$$

$$F_{21} = \frac{(+5 \text{ stat C})(+3 \text{ stat C})}{(5 \text{ cm})^2} = +\ 0.6 \text{ dyne (to the right)}$$

Both forces have the same magnitude (Newton's third law for electrostatis forces) and are repulsive.

• **PROBLEM** 577

Calculate the resultant force, on the charge q_3 in the figure.

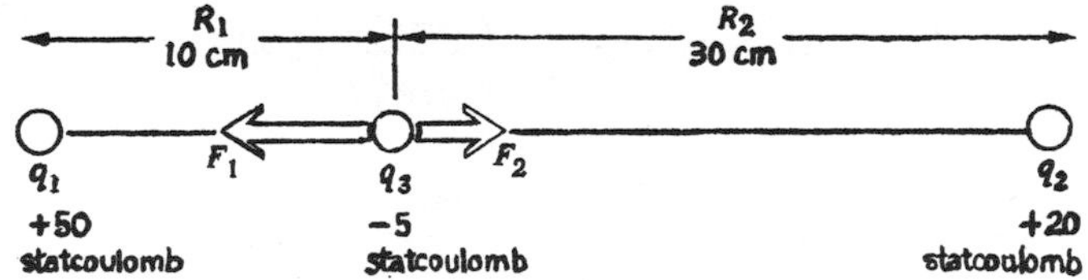

Solution: The force exerted by q_1 on q_3 is

$$F_1 = \frac{q_1 q_3}{R_1^2}$$

$$= \frac{(50)(-5)}{(10)^2} = -\ 2.5 \text{ dyne}$$

The negative sign denotes an attractive force. The force exerted on q_3 by q_2 is

$$F_2 = \frac{q_2 q_3}{R_2^2}$$

$$= \frac{(20)(-5)}{(30)^2} = \frac{-100}{900}$$

$$= -0.111 \text{ dyne}$$

Since q_2 is positive and q_3 is negative this force is attractive and is directed to the right toward q_2.

The resultant force on q_3 is

$$F_R = F_1 - F_2 = -2.5 - (-0.111)$$
$$= -2.389 \text{ dyne}$$

and is directed to the left.

• PROBLEM 578

Suppose we have two charges, $q_1 = +4$ statC and $q_2 = -6$ statC, with an initial separation of $r_1 = 3$ cm. What is the change in potential energy if we increase the separation to 8 cm?

Solution : The potential energy of two point charges, q_1 and q_2, separated by a distance r_1, is given by

$$V_{12} = \frac{q_1 q_2}{r_1} .$$

Therefore, as the separation is increased from r_1 to r_2, the change in potential energy is

$$\Delta V_{12} = q_1 q_2 \left(\frac{1}{r_2} - \frac{1}{r_1} \right)$$

$$= (4 \text{ statC})(-6 \text{ statC}) \times \left(\frac{1}{8\text{cm}} - \frac{1}{3\text{cm}} \right)$$

$$= (-24 \text{ statC}^2) \left(\frac{-5\text{cm}}{24\text{cm}^2} \right)$$

$$= +5 \frac{\text{statC}^2}{\text{cm}}$$

$$= +5 \text{ ergs}$$

In this case, there is a net increase in the electrostatic potential energy (that is, $\Delta V_{12} > 0$) because work was done by an outside agent against the attractive electrostatic force.

• PROBLEM 579

What is the force between two positive charges of 100μ coulombs and 200μ coulombs, respectively, when they are separated a distance of 3 centimeters?

Solution: Using Coulomb's Law,

$$F = k \frac{Q_1 Q_2}{r^2}$$

we have

$$Q_1 = 100\mu \text{ coulombs} = 10^{-4} \text{ coulombs}$$

$$Q_2 = 2 \times 10^{-4} \text{ coulombs}$$

$$k = \text{electrostatic constant} = 9 \times 10^9 \frac{(\text{nt-m}^2)}{\text{coulombs}^2}$$

and $r = 3 \text{ cm} = 3 \times 10^{-2}$ m

$$\text{Then } F = 9 \times 10^9 \frac{(\text{nt- m}^2)}{\text{coulombs}^2}$$

$$\times \frac{10^{-4} \text{ coulombs} \times 2 \times 10^{-4} \text{ coulombs}}{(3 \times 10^{-2})^2 \text{ m}^2}$$

$$= 2 \times 10^5 \text{ nt}$$

• PROBLEM 580

Alpha particles are subatomic objects that have a mass of about 6.7×10^{-27} kg and a charge of 3.2×10^{-19} C. Calculate the force on an alpha particle when it is in an electric field ξ whose strength is 1×10^3 N/C.

Solution: The charge, $q = 3.2 \times 10^{-19}$ C, and the electric field, $\xi = 1 \times 10^3$ N/C, are given. By definition of the electric field,

$$\xi = \frac{F}{q}$$

where F is the force on the charge. Therefore,

$$F = q\xi = (3.2 \times 10^{-19} \not{C})(1 \times 10^3 \text{ N}/\not{C}) = 3.2 \times 10^{-16} \text{ N}.$$

The weight of the alpha particle is

$$W = mg$$

$$= (6.7 \times 10^{-27} \text{ kg})\left(9.8 \frac{\text{m}}{\text{sec}^2}\right) \simeq 7 \times 10^{-26} \text{ N}.$$

We see that the force due to the electric field is very much larger than the gravitational force on the particle (10^{10} orders of magnitude greater!).

• PROBLEM 581

Two equal conducting spheres of negligible size are charged with 16.0×10^{-14}C and -6.4×10^{-14} C, respectively, and are placed 20 cm apart. They are then moved to a distance of 50 cm apart. Compare the forces between them in the two positions. The spheres are connected by a thin wire. What force does each now exert on the other?

Solution: The equation giving the force between the spheres, which may be considered as point charges, is by Coulomb's law,

$$F = \frac{1}{4\pi\varepsilon_0}\frac{q_1 q_2}{r^2}$$

where q_1, q_2 are the charges on the spheres, and r is their separation. Thus

$$F_1 = \frac{1}{4\pi\varepsilon_0}\frac{q_1 q_2}{(0.2)^2\ m^2} \quad \text{and} \quad F_2 = \frac{1}{4\pi\varepsilon_0}\frac{q_1 q_2}{(0.5)^2\ m^2}$$

$$\therefore \quad \frac{F_1}{F_2} = \frac{(0.5)^2}{(0.2)^2} = 6\tfrac{1}{4}$$

If the spheres are joined by a wire, the charges, which are attracted to one another, can flow in the wire under the influence of the forces acting on them. The charges will neutralize as far as possible and $\left[16.0 \times 10^{-14} + (-6.4 \times 10^{-14})\right] = 9.6 \times 10^{-14}$ C will be left distributed over the system. Neglecting the effect of the wire, by symmetry 4.8×10^{-14} C will reside on each sphere. The force between the two spheres is now

$$F = \frac{1}{4\pi\varepsilon_0}\frac{q^2}{r^2}$$

$$= 9 \times 10^9\ N\cdot m^2\cdot C^{-2} \times \frac{(4.8 \times 10^{-14})^2 C^2}{(0.5)^2\ m^2}$$

$$= 8.29 \times 10^{-17}\ N.$$

• PROBLEM 582

(a) What is the magnitude of the electric field at a distance of 1 Å $\left(= 10^{-8}\ \text{cm}\right)$ from a proton? (b) What is the potential at this point? (c) What is the potential difference, in volts, between positions 1 and 0.2 Å from a proton?

Solution: (a) From Coulomb's law

$$E = \frac{e}{r^2} \approx \frac{5 \times 10^{-10}\ \text{statcoulomb}}{\left(1 \times 10^{-8}\ \text{cm}\right)^2} \approx 5 \times 10^6\ \text{statvolts/cm}$$

$$\approx (300)\left(5 \times 10^6\right)\text{V/cm} \approx 1.5 \times 10^9\ \text{V/cm}$$

Here, e is the unit of electronic charge, and r is the distance between the proton and the point at which we calculate the field. We have also used the fact that

$$\frac{1\ \text{statvolt}}{\text{cm}} = 300\ \frac{\text{V}}{\text{cm}}$$

The field is directed radially outward from the proton.

(b) The electrostatic potential at a distance r from the proton is

$$\Phi(r) = \frac{e}{r} \approx \frac{5 \times 10^{-10} \text{ statcoulomb}}{1 \times 10^{-8} \text{ cm}}$$

$$\approx 5 \times 10^{-2} \text{ statvolts} \approx 15 \text{ V}$$

from the conversion factor given above.

(c) The potential at 1×10^{-8} cm is 15 V; at 0.2×10^{-8} cm it is 75 V. The difference 75 - 15 = 60 V.

• PROBLEM 583

In the Bohr model of the hydrogen atom, the electron is considered to move around the nuclear proton in a circular orbit that has a radius of 0.53×10^{-8} cm. In what electric field and in what potential does the electron move?

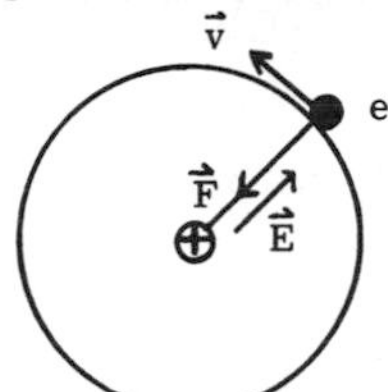

Hydrogen Atom

Solution: The electric field, $\vec{E}$, experienced by the electron is radial and has a magnitude of

$$E = \frac{e}{r^2}$$

where e is the electronic charge of a proton, and r is the distance between electron and proton.

$$E = \frac{4.8 \times 10^{-10} \text{ statC}}{(0.53 \times 10^{-8} \text{ cm})^2}$$

$$= 1.7 \times 10^{7} \text{ statV/cm}$$

which is a very large field indeed. Sparking usually occurs in air when a field strength of 100 statV/cm is reached. The electric potential of the electron is

$$\Phi_E = \frac{e}{r} .$$

$$= \frac{4.8 \times 10^{-10} \text{ statC}}{0.53 \times 10^{-8} \text{ cm}}$$

$$= 0.09 \text{ statV}$$

which is rather small. The potential difference between the terminals of a flashlight is 1.5 V or 0.005 statV.

The electric field E depends on $1/r^2$, whereas the potential Φ_E depends on $1/r$; since r is extremely small $(0.5 \times 10^{-8} \text{cm})$ in the case of the hydrogen atom, the field strength is large while the potential is small.

• PROBLEM 584

Consider the array of three charges shown in the diagram. Find the force on charge 1 caused by the other two charges. Calculate the field at the position of 1 due to the other two charges.

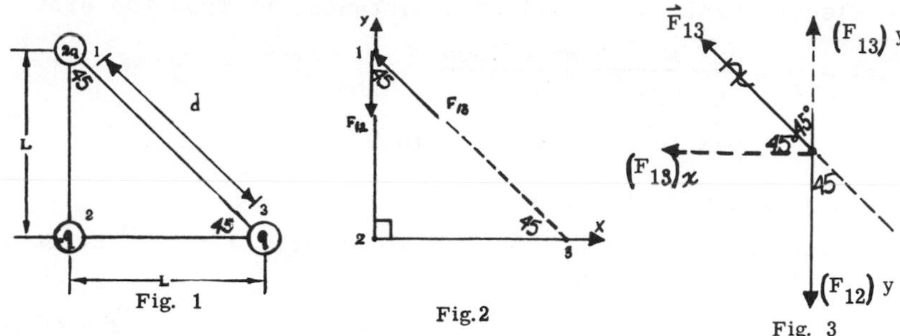

Fig. 1

Fig. 2

Fig. 3

Solution: The force at 1 will be the vector sum of forces caused by charges 2 and 3. The magnitudes of these forces are

$$F_{12} = K_E \frac{(2q)q}{L^2} = K_E \frac{2q^2}{L^2}$$

$$F_{13} = K_E \frac{(2q)q}{d^2}$$

But $d^2 = 2L^2$ (figure 1). Therefore

$$F_{13} = \frac{K_E q^2}{2L^2}$$

F_{12} is an attractive force, and F_{13} repulsive. Their x- and y-components are (figure 3).

$$\left(F_{12}\right)_x = 0$$

$$\left(F_{12}\right)_y = -K_E \frac{2q^2}{L^2}$$

$$\left(F_{13}\right)_x = -K_E \frac{q^2}{2L^2} \cos 45^\circ$$

$$\left(F_{13}\right)_y = K_E \frac{q^2}{2L^2} \sin 45^\circ$$

Thus the resultant force F at 1 is

$$F_x = \left(F_{12}\right)_x + \left(F_{13}\right)_x = -K_E \frac{q^2}{2L^2} \frac{1}{\sqrt{2}} \quad \text{for} \quad \cos 45^\circ = \frac{1}{\sqrt{2}}$$

$$F_y = \left(F_{12}\right)_y + \left(F_{13}\right)_y = -K_E \frac{2q^2}{L^2} + K_E \frac{q^2}{2L^2} \frac{1}{\sqrt{2}} \quad \text{for} \sin 45^\circ = \frac{1}{\sqrt{2}}$$

The magnitude of F is

$$F = \sqrt{F_x^2 + F_y^2} = 1.59\, K_E \frac{q^2}{L^2}$$

If $q = e$ and $L = 1\ \mathring{A} = 10^{-10}$ m, then

$$F = 1.59 \times \left(9\times10^9 \frac{\text{nt-m}^2}{\text{coul}^2}\right) \times \frac{\left(1.6\times10^{-19} \text{ coul}\right)^2}{\left(10^{-10} \text{ m}\right)^2}$$

$$= 2.24 \times 10^{-8} \text{ N}$$

The electric field E at position 1 is given by the force at 1 divided by the net charge at 1, 2q:

$$E = \frac{F}{2q} = 1.59\ K_E \frac{q}{2L^2}$$

$$= \frac{2.24 \times 10^{-8}\ N}{2\left(1.6 \times 10^{-19}\ \text{coul}\right)} = 2.1 \times 10^{11}\ \frac{N}{\text{coul}}$$

• PROBLEM 585

In the simple case of the field due to a single point charge q, check the method for obtaining E from ϕ. See the figure.

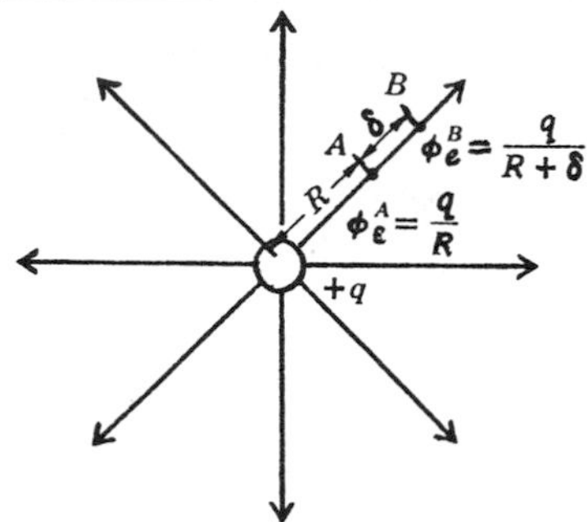

Solution: Choose the points A and B to be on the same radius, in which case the component of E in the direction $\overrightarrow{AB}$ is the total field. Let A be at a distance R from q and B at a distance $(R + \delta)$, where δ is very small. In general,

$$\text{work} = \int \vec{F} \cdot d\vec{r}$$

where the integral is evaluated over the path of travel of the object which we are working on. For this problem, $\vec{F}$ and $d\vec{r}$ are parallel because we are moving q along a radius. Hence,

$$\text{work} = \int_R^{\delta+R} F\ dr$$

Now, because δ is very small, F will be essentially constant along the path of travel, and we may replace it by its average value, $\overline{F}$. Therefore

$$\text{work} \simeq \overline{F}\ \delta \tag{1}$$

(This relation becomes more exact as δ gets smaller.) Also note that, by definition of the potential difference, between R and R + δ, we obtain

$$\text{work} = q\Delta V$$

Substituting this in (1), we find

$$q\Delta V = \overline{F}\ \delta$$

But $\quad \overline{F} = q\overline{E}$

Hence $\quad \Delta V = \overline{E}\ \delta$

or $$\bar{E} = \frac{\Delta V}{\delta} \qquad (2)$$

As $\delta \to 0$, we will obtain E, the exact value of the electric field intensity.

The potential at A is by definition

$$\phi_e^A = \frac{q}{R}$$

The potential at B is

$$\phi_e^B = \frac{q}{R + \delta}$$

Using equation (2), $\bar{E} = \dfrac{\frac{q}{R} - \frac{q}{R + \delta}}{\delta}$

$$= \frac{1}{\delta}\left(\frac{q(R + \delta)}{R(R + \delta)} - \frac{qR}{(R + \delta)R}\right)$$

$$= \frac{1}{\delta}\,\frac{(qR + q\delta - qR)}{R(R + \delta)}$$

$$= \frac{q}{R(R + \delta)}$$

$$= \frac{q}{R^2\left(1 + \frac{\delta}{R}\right)}$$

Taking the limit as $\delta \to 0$, we find

$$E = \frac{q}{R^2}$$

for the value of E at a distance R from q.

• PROBLEM 586

Compute the electric field and the electric potential at point P midway between two charges, $Q_1 = Q_2 = +5$ statC, separated by 1 m.

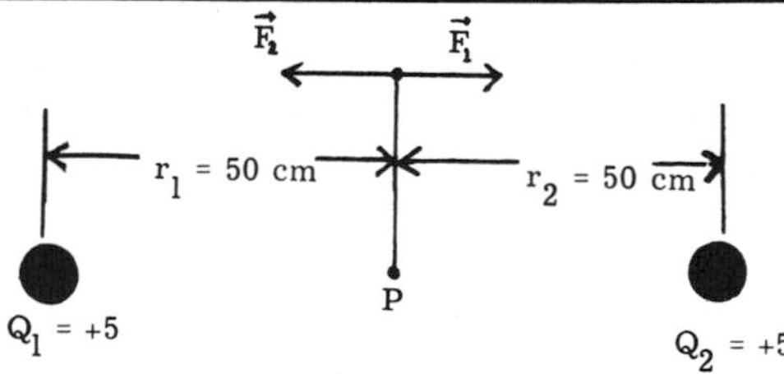

Solution: The magnitude of a test charge is +1 unit of charge. The forces on a test charge placed midway between two identical charges Q_1 and Q_2 are

$$\vec{F}_1 = \frac{Q_1}{r_1^2}\,\hat{r}_{12}$$

$$\vec{F}_2 = \frac{Q_2}{r_2^2}\,\hat{r}_{21} = \frac{-Q_2}{r_2^2}\,\hat{r}_{12}$$

where the unit vector $\hat{r}_{12}$ points from Q_1 to Q_2 ,r_1,r_2 are the distances between the test charge and Q_1 and Q_2, and $\vec{F}_1$ and $\vec{F}_2$ are equal in magnitude but opposite in direction. The net force is therefore zero at P;

$$F = F_1 + F_2 = 0 .$$

The force on a unit charge gives the electric field strength at that point, then the electric field $\vec{E}$ at P is also zero.
Although the electric field at P is zero, this does not imply that the electric potential is also zero. The total potential $\Phi_{E\ total}$ is the sum (the algebraic sum since potential is a scalar) of the potentials due to Q_1 and Q_2 :

$$\Phi_{E,1} = \frac{Q_1}{r_1} = \frac{5}{50} = 0.1 \text{ statV}$$

$$\Phi_{E,2} = \frac{Q_2}{r_2} = \frac{5}{50} = 0.1 \text{ statV}$$

Therefore,

$$\Phi_{E,total} = \Phi_{E,1} + \Phi_{E,2} = 0.2 \text{ statV}$$

Notice that if either Q_1 or Q_2 is changed from +5 statC to -5 statC, the electric potential will vanish but the electric field will not. Therefore, the fact that either the field or the potential is zero in any particular case does not necessarily mean that the other quantity will also be zero; each quantity must be calculated separately.

• PROBLEM 587

Two small conducting balls, each of mass 0.25 g, are hanging from the roof on insulating threads of length 50 cm so that they just touch. A charge, which they share equally, is given to them and each takes up a position such that the thread by which it hangs makes an angle of 45° with the vertical. What is the charge on each?

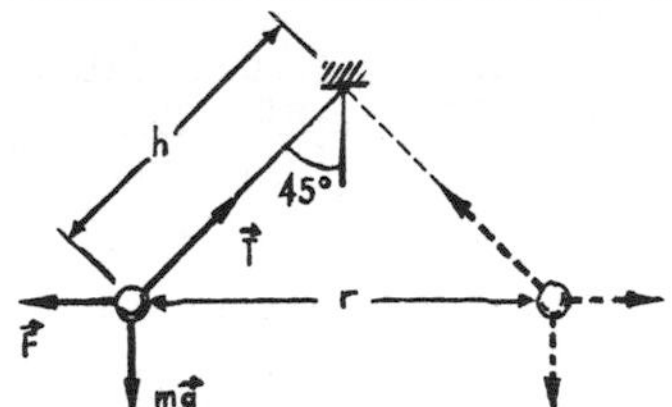

Solution: There are three forces acting on each ball, the weight $m\vec{g}$ acting downward, the Coulombian repulsive force $\vec{F}$ acting horizontally, and the tension $\vec{T}$ in the supporting thread. Since the ball is in equilibrium, horizontal and vertical components must separately balance (see figure). Thus

$$mg = T \cos 45° \qquad \text{and} \qquad F = T \sin 45°$$

or, dividing these 2 equations:

$$F = mg \tan 45° = mg.$$

But, by Coulomb's Law

$$F = \frac{q^2}{4\pi\varepsilon_0 r^2} = \frac{q^2}{4\pi\varepsilon_0 (2h \sin 45°)^2},$$

where q is the charge on each ball, and r is the separation of the 2 balls.

$$\therefore \quad q^2 = 4\pi\varepsilon_0 (2h \sin 45°)^2 mg$$

$$= \frac{[2 \times 0.5 \text{ m} \times (1/\sqrt{2})]^2 \times 2.5 \times 10^{-4} \text{ kg} \times 9.8 \text{ m·s}^{-2}}{9 \times 10^9 \text{ N·m}^2\text{·C}^{-2}}$$

$$= 13.6 \times 10^{-14} \text{ C}^2.$$

$$\therefore q = 3.7 \times 10^{-7} \text{ C}.$$

• PROBLEM 588

(a) Determine the field intensity midway between two identical positive charges of 200 stat-coulombs each, in oil of dielectric constant 5, if the charges are 6 cm apart.

(b) What is the answer if one charge is positive and the other is negative?

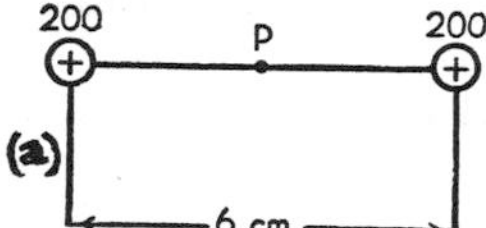

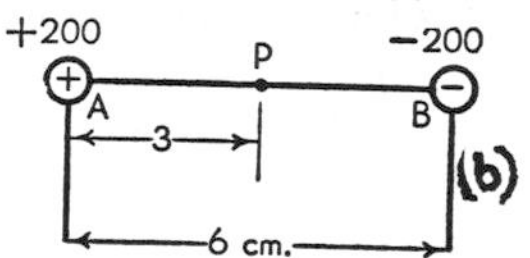

Solution: (a) Before attempting to calculate the numerical value of the field intensity E at point P due to each charge, note that if unit positive charge is placed at P, the forces acting on it due to each charge will point in opposite directions and will balance each other to give a resultant field intensity of zero. (See figure (a).)

E at P is zero.

(b) A unit positive charge placed at P will experience a force due to A: (see figure (b))

$$E_1 = \frac{q}{Kr^2} = \frac{200 \text{ stataC}}{\left(5\frac{\text{stataC}^2}{\text{dyne-cm}^2}\right)(9\text{cm}^2)} = 4.4 \text{ dynes/stat-}$$

coulomb to the right. K is the dielectric constant of the media. It accounts for the influence the media has on the electric field of a charge.

Also due to B:

$$E_2 = \frac{2}{Kr^2} = 4.4 \text{ dynes/stat-coulomb also to the right}$$

therefore

$$E = E_1 + E_2 = 8.8 \text{ dynes/stat-coulomb from + charge}$$

to - charge.

• PROBLEM 589

Two point charges + 2q and - q are separated by a distance L. At what point on the line between their centers is the electric field zero?

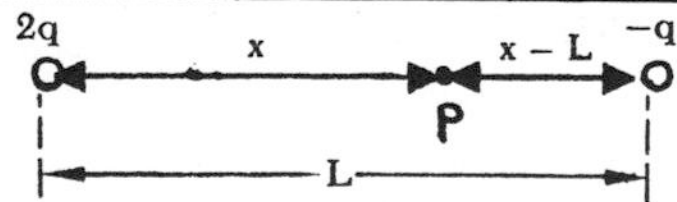

Solution: Suppose that this point is a distance x from the + 2q charge, as shown in the figure.

By definition, the electric field at a point P is

$$E = \frac{K_E q}{r^2},$$

where q is the charge producing the field, r is the distance from q to P, and K_E is a constant ($K = 9 \times 10^9 N \cdot m^2/c^2$).

The field at x due to 2q is

$$E_+ = K_E \frac{2q}{x^2}$$

The electric field E_- due to the negative charge is

$$E_- = - K_E \frac{q}{(x - L)^2}$$

The resultant electric field at the point P is then, by the principle of superposition, equal to the sum of the fields due to the individual charges 2q and - q. Because we want E_{net} at P to be zero, we have

$$E = 0 = E_+ + E_-$$

$$= K_E \frac{2q}{x^2} - \frac{K_E q}{(x - L)^2}$$

or $$x^2 = 2(x - L)^2$$

$$x^2 = 2x^2 - 4xL + 2L^2$$

$$x^2 - 4xL + 2xL^2 = 0$$

$$x = \frac{4L \pm \sqrt{16L^2 - 8L^2}}{2} = \frac{4L \pm \sqrt{(2 \cdot 4)L^2}}{2}$$

$$= 2 L \pm \sqrt{2} L$$

$$= 3.41 \text{ L or } 0.588 \text{ L}$$

All we have done so far is to find two points along the axis where the fields due to +2q and - q are equal in magnitude. We have yet to take account of the vector nature of the fields. At the interior point x = 0.588 L the vectors are in the same direction, so that the fields are added. However at x = 3.41 L the field vectors are in opposite directions, so that the resultant field is zero.

• PROBLEM 590

An electric field is set up by two point charges q_1 and q_2, of the same magnitude (12×10^{-9} coul; see diagram) but opposite sign, as shown in the figure. What is the electric intensity at points a, b, and c?

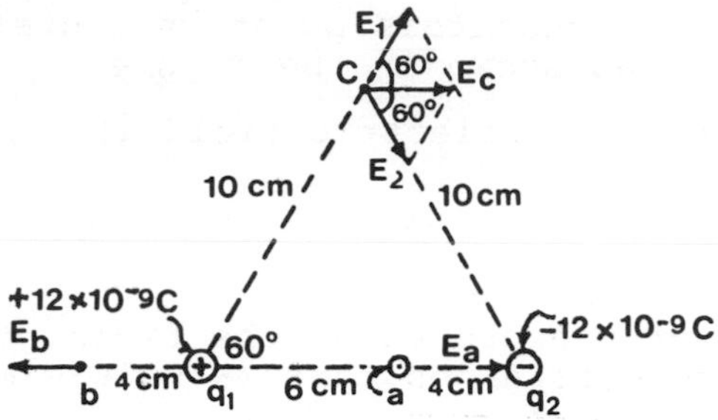

Solution: By definition, the magnitude of the electric field intensity, $\vec{E}$, is

$$E = \frac{kq}{r^2}$$

where q is the charge causing the field, and r is the distance from q to the point at which we wish to calculate $\vec{E}$. ($k = 9 \times 10^9 \ N \cdot m^2/\ c^2$). If the field is due to more than one charge, then the total field at a point is the vector sum of the fields due to each charge at that point.

At every point, the intensity due to the positive charge is directed radially away from that charge, and the intensity due to the negative charge is radially inward toward the charge.

At point a, the intensity due to each charge is directed toward the right. The resultant intensity E_a is also toward the right and its magnitude is the arithmetic sum of the individual intensities. Hence,

$$E_a = \frac{kq_1}{r_1{}^2} - \frac{kq_2}{r_2{}^2}$$

$$E_a = \left(9 \times 10^9 \ \frac{N \cdot m^2}{C^2}\right)\left(\frac{(12 \times 10^{-9}\ C)}{36 \times 10^{-4}\ m^2} - \frac{(-12 \times 10^{-9}\ C}{16 \times 10^{-4}\ m^2}\right)$$

$$E_a = 9.75 \times 10^4 \ N/C \quad \text{toward the right.}$$

At point b, the intensity set up by q_1 is directed toward the left and that set up by q_2 is toward the right. The magnitude of the first is greater than that of the second because q_1 is closer to b than q_2. The resultant intensity $\vec{E}_b$ is toward the left and its magnitude is the difference between the individual intensities. Therefore,

$$E_b = -\frac{kq_1}{(4\ cm)^2} - \frac{kq_2}{(14\ cm)^2}$$

$$E_b = \left(-9 \times 10^{-9}\ \frac{N{\cdot}m^2}{C^2}\right)\left(\frac{12 \times 10^{-9}\ C}{16 \times 10^{-4}\ m^2} - \frac{12 \times 10^{-9}\ C}{196 \times 10^{-4}\ m^2}\right)$$

$$E_b = -6.2 \times 10^4 \ N/C, \text{ which is toward the left.}$$

At point c, the individual intensities have the directions shown and the resultant intensity $\vec{E}_c$ is their vector sum. Note, from the figure, that the vertical components of $\vec{E}_1$ and $\vec{E}_2$ will cancel, and their horizontal components will reinforce. Hence,

$$E_c = \left|\vec{E}_1\right| \cos 60° + \left|\vec{E}_2\right| \cos 60°$$

$$= \frac{|\vec{E}_1|}{2} + \frac{|\vec{E}_2|}{2}$$

$$= \frac{1}{2}\left(\left|\frac{kq_1}{(10\text{ cm})^2}\right|\right) + \frac{1}{2}\left(\left|\frac{kq_2}{(10\text{ cm})^2}\right|\right)$$

$$= \frac{1}{2}\left(\left|\frac{\left[9 \times 10^{-9}\ \frac{\text{N}\cdot\text{m}^2}{\text{C}^2}\right](12 \times 10^{-9}\text{ C})}{100 \times 10^{-4}\text{ m}^2}\right|\right)$$

$$+ \frac{1}{2}\left(\left|\frac{\left[9 \times 10^{-9}\ \frac{\text{N}\cdot\text{m}^2}{\text{C}^2}\right](-\ 12 \times 10^{-9}\text{ C})}{100 \times 10^{-4}\text{ m}^2}\right|\right)$$

$$= 1.08 \times 10^4 \text{ N/C} \quad \text{toward the right.}$$

• PROBLEM 591

The square ABCD has a side of 10 cm length. Equal positive charges of+50 statcoulombs are placed at A and B and equal negative charges of - 100 statcoulombs are placed at C and D. Calculate the electric field at P, the center of the square.

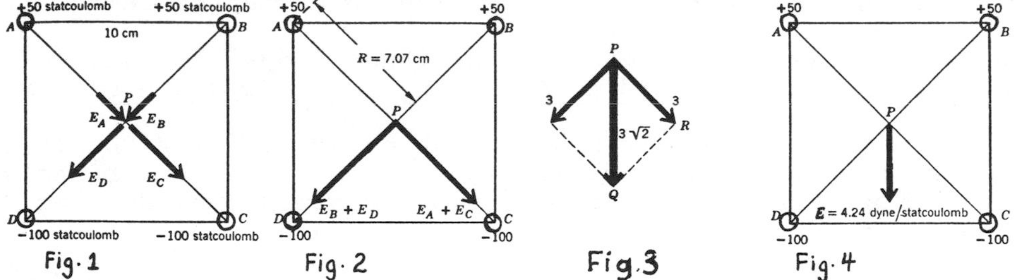

Solution: P is the point where the two diagonals AC and BD cross. Let AP = BP = CP = DP = R. Then, applying Pythagoras' theorem to the right angle triangle APB,

$$AP^2 + BP^2 = AB^2$$

$$2R^2 = 10^2 \text{ cm}^2$$

$$R^2 = 50 \text{ cm}^2$$

$$R = 7.07 \text{ cm}$$

The charge q_A at A produces a contribution E_A to the field at P given by definition as

$$E_A = \frac{q_A}{R^2}$$

$$= \frac{50 \text{ statcoul.}}{50 \text{ cm}^2}$$

Since $1 \frac{\text{statcoul}}{\text{cm}^2} = 1 \frac{\text{dyne}}{\text{statcoul}}$

$$E_A = 1 \text{ dyne per statcoulomb}$$

Since the charge at A is positive, E_A points directly away from A, (see figure). Similarly, the charge at B produces a contribution

$$E_B = 1 \text{ dyne per statcoulomb}$$

which points directly away from B. The negative charge q_C at C produces a contribution

$$E_C = \frac{q_C}{R^2}$$

$$= \frac{100 \text{ statcoul}}{50 \text{ cm}^2}$$

$$= 2 \text{ dyne per statcoulomb}$$

Since q_C is negative this contribution points directly toward C. Similarly, the charge at D produces a contribution

$$E_D = 2 \text{ dyne per statcoulomb}$$

which points directly toward D.

Adding together E_A and E_C, which point in the same direction, we get a vector of magnitude 3 dyne per statcoulomb pointing toward C. Adding E_B to E_D we get a vector of magnitude 3 dyne per statcoulomb pointing toward D. This is shown in the figure. This figure also gives the triangle of vectors PQR used to add the two vectors shown. Here we are using the parallogram law of vector addition.

The resultant field $E = \overrightarrow{PQ}$ is obviously vertically downward and its magnitude is obtained from Pythagoras' theorem.

$$PQ^2 = PR^2 + RQ^2$$

$$E^2 = (3^2 + 3^2) \text{dyne}^2/\text{statcoul}^2$$

$$= 18 \text{ dyne}^2/\text{statcoul}^2$$

$$E = 4.24 \text{ dyne per statcoulomb.}$$

The resultant field at P is therefore 4.24 dyne per statcoulomb pointing in the direction $\overrightarrow{AD}$.

• **PROBLEM 592**

How many electrons must be added to a spherical conductor (radius 10 cm) to produce a field of 2×10^{-3} N/coul just above the surface?

Solution: The electric field $\vec{E}$ at a point in space, due to a spherical conductor having a total charge Q is given by

$$E = \frac{KQ}{R^2},$$

where K is a constant having a value of $9 \times 10^9 \frac{N \cdot m^2}{c^2}$,

and R is the distance from the center of the sphere to the point at which we wish to calculate $\vec{E}$. The charge needed to produce a field of 2×10^{-3} N/coul. at the surface of the sphere (R = 10 cm = .1 m) is then

$$Q = \frac{R^2 E}{K}$$

$$Q = \frac{(.1\ m)^2 (2\times10^{-3} N/c)}{(9\times10^9\ N\cdot m^2/c^2)} = 2.22 \times 10^{-15}\ C$$

(The radius was converted to meters in order to make it compatible with the MKS system being used.) Since one electron has a charge of 1.6×10^{-19} coul., n electrons will produce a charge of 2.22×10^{-15} coul. Setting up the following proportion,

$$\frac{1 \text{ electron}}{1.6\times10^{-19} \text{ coul}} = \frac{n \text{ electrons}}{2.22\times10^{-15} \text{ coul}}$$

We may solve for n

$$n = \frac{2.22 \times10^{-15} \text{ coul}}{1.6 \times10^{-19} \text{ coul}} = 1.39 \times 10^4.$$

• **PROBLEM 593**

Compare the electrostatic and gravitational forces that exist between an electron and a proton.

Solution: The electrostatic force law and the gravitational force law both depend on $1/r^2$:

$$F_G = G \frac{m_1 m_2}{r^2}$$

where $G = 6.67 \times 10^{-8} \frac{\text{dyne-cm}^2}{g^2}$, and r is the distance between masses m_1 and m_2. Furthermore, $F_E = \frac{q_1 q_2}{r^2}$, in the c.g.s. system, where r is the distance between q_1 and q_2. Therefore, the ratio F_E/F_G is independent of the distance of separation:

$$\frac{F_E}{F_G} = \frac{q_1 q_2}{Gm_1 m_2}$$

For the case of an electron and a proton this becomes

$$\frac{F_E}{F_G} = \frac{(e)(e)}{Gm_e m_p} = \frac{e^2}{Gm_e m_p}$$

Substituting the values of the quantities, we find

$$\frac{F_E}{F_G} = \frac{\left(4.80 \times 10^{-10} \text{ statC}\right)^2}{\left(6.67 \times 10^{-8} \text{dyne-cm}^2/\text{g}^2\right) \times \left(9.11 \times 10^{-28} \text{ g}\right) \times \left(1.67 \times 10^{-24} \text{ g}\right)}$$

$$= 2.3 \times 10^{39}$$

Thus, the electrostatic force between elementary particles is enormously greater than the gravitational force. Therefore, only the electrostatic force is of importance in atomic systems. In nuclei, the strong nuclear force overpowers even the electrostatic force but not to the extent that electrostatic forces are completely negligible. Many important nuclear effects are the result of electrostatic forces.

• **PROBLEM** 594

Show that, for a given dipole, V and E cannot have the same magnitude in MKS units at distances less than 2 m from the dipole. Suppose that the distance is $\sqrt{5}$ m; determine the directions along which V and E are equal in magnitude.

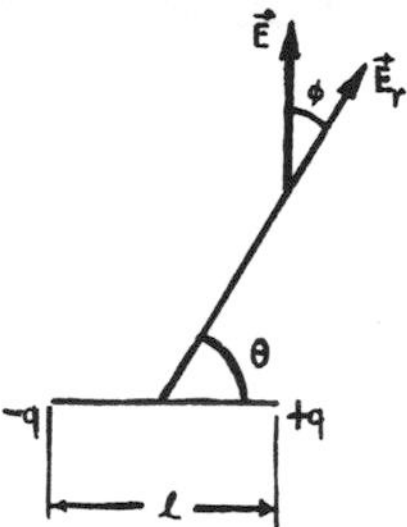

Solution: The expression for the magnitude of the potential due to a dipole is

$$V = \frac{p \cos \theta}{4\pi\varepsilon_0 r^2}$$

where p is the dipole moment ($p = q\ell$) of the dipole, r is the distance from the dipole to the point at which we calculate V, and θ is as shown in the figure. $\frac{1}{4\pi\varepsilon_0}$ is a constant equal to $9 \times 10^9 \text{N}\cdot\text{m}^2/\text{c}^2$. The magnitude of the electric field intensity is

$$E = \frac{p}{4\pi\varepsilon_0 r^3} \sqrt{4 \cos^2 \theta + \sin^2 \theta}$$

If these are to be equal in magnitude,

$$\cos\theta = \frac{\sqrt{4\cos^2\theta + \sin^2\theta}}{r}$$

$$\text{or} \quad r^2 = \frac{4\cos^2\theta + \sin^2\theta}{\cos^2\theta} = 4 + \tan^2\theta$$

The minimum value of r^2 occurs when $\tan\theta = 0$. Hence the minimum value of r for V and E to be equal in magnitude occurs for $r^2 = 4$; that is, r = 2 m, in MKS units.

If $r = \sqrt{5}$ m, then V and E are equal in magnitude when

$$(\sqrt{5})^2 = \frac{4\cos^2\theta + \sin^2\theta}{\cos^2\theta}$$

$$5\cos^2\theta = 4\cos^2\theta + \sin^2\theta$$

$$\cos^2\theta = \sin^2\theta$$

Thus $\theta = 45°, 135°, 225°$, or $315°$.

• PROBLEM 595

Calculate the potential energy of the charge distribution shown in the diagram.

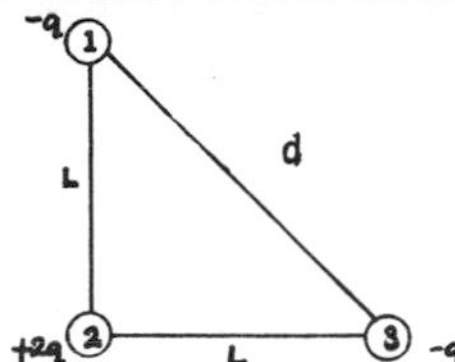

Solution: The potential energy of any two charges q_i and q_j is

$$U_{ij} = K_E \frac{q_i q_j}{R_{ij}}$$

where R_{ij} is the distance between the two charges, and

$$K_E = 9 \times 10^9 \frac{N \cdot m^2}{c^2}.$$

The potential energy of the charge distribution is the sum of the potential energies of every possible pair of charges within the distribution. Hence,

$$U = U_{12} + U_{13} + U_{23} = K_E\left[\frac{(q)(2q)}{L} + \frac{(-q)(-q)}{d} + \frac{(+2q)(-q)}{L}\right]$$

Since $d^2 = L^2 + L^2$ we have $d = \sqrt{2L}$ and

$$U = K_E\left[\frac{-2q^2}{L} + \frac{q^2}{\sqrt{2L}} - \frac{2q^2}{L}\right]$$

$$= -3.29\ K_E \frac{q^2}{L} \text{ joules} \quad .$$

If $q = e$ and $L = 1\ \mathring{A} = 10^{-8}$ m, then

$$U = -3.29 \times 9 \times 10^{9} \frac{\text{nt-m}^2}{\text{coul}^2} \times \frac{\left(1.6\times10^{-19}\ \text{coul}\right)^2}{10^{-8}\ \text{m}}$$

$$= -7.58 \times 10^{-20}\ \text{J}$$

The negative sign indicates that work would be required to disassemble the charge distribution (i.e., work must be done against attractive electrical forces).

• PROBLEM 596

Compute the electrostatic force of repulsion between two α-particles at a separation of 10^{-11} cm, and compare with the force of gravitational attraction between them.

Solution. For this problem, we use Coulomb's Law which states that the electrostatic force between two charges is directly proportional to the product of the two charges and inversely proportional to the square of the distance by which the charges are separated. The constant of proportionality is written as $1/4\pi\varepsilon_0$ where ε_0 has the value of

8.85×10^{-12} coul^2/nt - m^2.

Each α-particle has a charge of +2e, or $2 \times 1.60 \times 10^{-19} = 3.20 \times 10^{-19}$ coul. The force of repulsion at a separation of 10^{-11} cm or 10^{-13} m is

$$F = \frac{1}{4\pi\varepsilon_0} \frac{qq'}{r^2}$$

$$= 9 \times 10^{9} \frac{\left(3.20 \times 10^{-19}\right)^2}{\left(10^{-13}\right)^2}$$

$$= 9.18 \times 10^{-2}\ \text{newton}$$

and since 1 newton $= 10^5$ dynes,

$$F = 9180\ \text{dynes}.$$

This is a sizable force, equal to the weight of nearly 10 grams! To find the force of gravitational attraction we use Newton's Law of Universal Gravitation. This has the same form as Coulomb's Law(an inverse square law) but instead of charges we have masses and the constant of proportionality is called G. The mass of an α-particle (2 protons + 2 neutrons) is

$4 \times 1.67 \times 10^{-24} = 6.68 \times 10^{-24}$ gm $= 6.68 \times 10^{-27}$ kgm.

The gravitational constant G is

$$G = 6.67 \times 10^{-11} \frac{\text{newton-m}^2}{\text{kgm}^2}.$$

The force of gravitational attraction is

$$F = G\frac{mm'}{r^2}$$

$$= 6.67 \times 10^{-11} \frac{\left(6.68 \times 10^{-27}\right)^2}{\left(10^{-13}\right)^2}$$

$$= 2.97 \times 10^{-37} \text{ newton.}$$

The gravitational force is evidently negligible in comparison with the electrostatic force.

• **PROBLEM 597**

Calculate the magnitude of the electrostatic force exerted by the proton on the electron in a hydrogen atom and compare it with the weight of the electron.

Solution: In a hydrogen atom the nucleus is a single proton and a single electron moves around it at an average distance away of 0.53×10^{-8} cm. The charge on each particle is e and the electrostatic force is, by Coulomb's Law,

$$F_e = \frac{e^2}{R^2} = \frac{\left(4.8 \times 10^{-10} \text{esu}\right)^2}{\left(0.53 \times 10^{-8} \text{ cm}\right)^2}$$

Since 1 dyne $\cdot$ cm^2 = 1 esu^2

$$F_e = 8.2 \times 10^{-3} \text{ dyne}$$

The mass of an electron is

$$m_e = 9.11 \times 10^{-28} \text{ gram}$$

By Newton's Second Law, the gravitational force on m_e is

$$F_g = m_e g$$

where g is the acceleration of m_e due to gravity. F_g is then the weight of m_e. Hence

$$F_g = \left(9.11 \times 10^{-28} \text{gm}\right)\left(980 \text{ cm/s}^2\right)$$

$$= 8.9 \times 10^{-25} \text{ dyne}$$

The ratio of the electrostatic force to the weight is

$$\frac{F_e}{m_e g} = \frac{8.2 \times 10^{-3}}{8.9 \times 10^{-25}}$$

The electrostatic force is therefore overwhelmingly larger than the weight. We never have to worry about gravitational forces when we are considering the theory of the hydrogen atom.

• **PROBLEM 598**

If the electrode spacing is 1×10^{-3} m and the voltage is 1×10^4 V, how large is the Coulomb force that is responsible for the separation of dust particles from the air? Assume that the particle's charge is + 200 quanta.

Solution: The electric field ε existing between two plates is

$$\varepsilon = \frac{V}{d} = \frac{1 \times 10^{4}\ V}{1 \times 10^{-3}\ m} = 1 \times 10^{7}\ V/m$$

Quanta represent the number of unit charges present on the dust particle. A unit charge is the charge present on a proton or 1.6×10^{-19} coul. Therefore, the electrostatic force experienced by the particle is

$$F = q\varepsilon = (2 \times 10^{2})(1.6 \times 10^{-19}\ C)(1 \times 10^{7}\ V/m)$$

$$= 3.2 \times 10^{-10}\ N$$

This is approximately 10 to 100 times larger than the gravitational force on the particle.

• PROBLEM 599

What electric field intensity is just sufficient to balance the earth's gravitational attraction on an electron? If this electric field were to be produced by a second electron how far away must it be put?

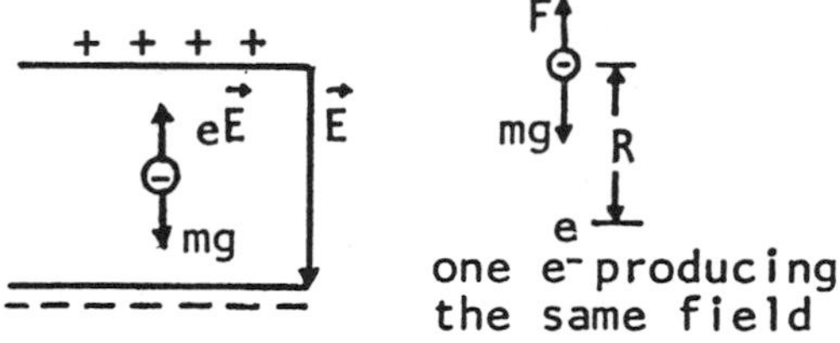

Solution: The gravitational force on the electron is mg and the force due to the field E is eE. Thus if they are to balance (see the figure)

$$eE = mg$$

$$E = \frac{mg}{e}$$

$$= \frac{(9.1 \times 10^{-31}\ kg)(9.8\ m/s^{2})}{(-\ 1.6 \times 10^{-19}\ c)}$$

$$= -5.57 \times 10^{-11}\ N/coul$$

If this field is supplied by another electron a distance R away (see figure) then by definition, the electric field due to this electron at R is

$$E = \frac{ke}{R^{2}}$$

where $k = 9 \times 10^{9}\ \frac{N \cdot m^{2}}{c^{2}}$, and e is the signed charge of an electron. Hence, solving for R,

$$R^{2} = \frac{ke}{E}\ .$$

Using the previous calculation of E,

$$R^2 = \frac{\left(9 \times 10^9 \frac{N\cdot m^2}{c^2}\right)(-1.6 \times 10^{-19}\ c)}{(-5.57 \times 10^{-11}\ N/c)}$$

$$R^2 = 25.8\ m^2$$

$$R = 5.1\ m$$

• PROBLEM 600

An electron is separated from a proton by a distance of 10^{-10} m. What is the gravitational and electrostatic potential energy due to the proton at the position of the electron? How much work is required against each field to move the electron to a position of separation 5×10^{-10} m?

Solution. The mass of the proton is $m_p = 1.67 \times 10^{-27}$ kg, and the mass of the electron is $m_e = 9.11 \times 10^{-31}$ kg. The magnitude of the charge on each is $e = 1.60 \times 10^{-19}$ coul. The gravitational potential energy is given by

$$U_G = -G\frac{m_p m_e}{R}$$

$$= \frac{\left(-6.67 \times 10^{-11}\right) \times \left(1.67 \times 10^{-27}\right) \times \left(9.11 \times 10^{-31}\right)}{R}$$

$$= \frac{-1.01 \times 10^{-67}}{R}\ \text{joules}$$

$$U_E = -k_E \frac{e^2}{R}$$

$$= \frac{-\left(8.99 \times 10^9\right) \times \left(1.60 \times 10^{-19}\right)^2}{R}$$

$$= \frac{-2.30 \times 10^{-28}}{R}\ \text{joules}$$

Thus at $R = 10^{-10}$ m, $U_G = -1.01 \times 10^{-57}$ J and $U_E = -2.30 \times 10^{-18}$ J. At $R = 5 \times 10^{-10}$ m, $U_G = -2.03 \times 10^{-58}$ J and $U_E = -4.60 \times 10^{-19}$ J. The work required to move from one point to the other is

$$W_G = \Delta U_G = 8.1 \times 10^{-58}\ J$$

$$W_E = \Delta U_E = 1.84 \times 10^{-18}\ J.$$

In both cases work had to be done on the electron, thus W is positive. Notice that W_E is greater than W_G by the enormous factor of about 10^{40}, which indicates the weakness of the gravitational interaction.

• PROBLEM 601

> Suppose that all of the electrons in a gram of copper could be moved to a position 30 cm away from the copper nuclei. What would be the force of attraction between these two groups of particles?

Solution: The atomic mass of copper is 63.5. Therefore, 1 g of copper contains a number of atoms given by Avogadro's number divided by the mass of 1 mole (that is, 63.5 g):

$$\text{No. atoms} = \frac{6.02 \times 10^{23} \text{ atoms/mole}}{63.5 \text{ g/mole}} = 0.92 \times 10^{22} \text{ atoms/g}$$

The atomic number of copper is 29; in other words, each neutral copper atom contains 29 electrons. Therefore, the number of electrons in 1 g of copper is

$$\text{No. electrons in 1 g} = 29 \times 0.92 \times 10^{22} = 2.7 \times 10^{23} \text{ electrons}$$

Thus, the total charge on the group of electrons is

$$\begin{aligned} q_e &= 2.7 \times 10^{23} \times (-e) \\ &= 2.7 \times 10^{23} \times \left(-4.8 \times 10^{-10} \text{ statC}\right) \\ &= -1.3 \times 10^{14} \text{ statC} \end{aligned}$$

A similar positive charge resides on the group of copper nuclei. Hence, the attractive electrostatic force (in the CGS system)

$$F_E = \frac{q_1 q_2}{r^2}$$

where r is the distance between charges q_1 and q_2. Therefore, since the 2 groups of charges with which we are concerned both have magnitude q_e

$$\begin{aligned} F_E &= \frac{q_e^2}{r^2} = \frac{\left(1.3 \times 10^{14} \text{ statC}\right)^2}{(30 \text{ cm})^2} \\ &= 1.9 \times 10^{25} \text{ dyne} \end{aligned}$$

Because the nuclei and electrons have opposite charges, this force is attractive. It is as great as the gravitational force between the Earth and the moon!

• PROBLEM 602

> A shower of protons from outer space deposits equal charges $+q$ on the earth and the moon, and the electrostatic repulsion then exactly counterbalances the gravitational attraction. How large is q?

Solution: If R is the distance between the earth and the moon, the electrostatic force in the CGS system is

$$F_e = \frac{q^2}{R^2}$$

If M_e and M_i are the masses of the earth and the moon respectively, the gravitational force is

$$F_G = \frac{GM_e M_i}{R^2}$$

Since the two forces are equal,

$$\frac{q^2}{R^2} = \frac{GM_e M_i}{R^2}$$

$$q = \sqrt{GM_e M_i}$$

• PROBLEM 603

How much energy in electron volts must be expended to separate the atoms in the potassium iodide molecule, $^{39}K\ ^{127}I$, if the ions are originally separated by a distance $R = 3.04 \times 10^{-10}$ m? The potential energy for Coulomb's law of force is,

$$E_p = \frac{-ke^2}{d}$$

where e is the electric charge of each ion and d is the distance between the charges.

$$K = 9 \times 10^9\ N \cdot m^2/c^2$$

Solution: When the ions are bonded together their separation distance is R, so the potential energy is,

$$E_p(R) = \frac{-ke^2}{R} = -\frac{\left[9 \times 10^9 N\left(m^{\not 2}/C^2\right)\right]\left(1.6 \times 10^{-19} C\right)^2}{3.04 \times 10^{-10}\ \not m}$$

$$= -7.6 \times 10^{-19} J$$

When the ions are very far apart, the separation distance d becomes very large and may be assumed to be infinite. The potential energy for infinite separation distance is zero:

$$E_p(\infty) = \frac{-ke^2}{\infty} = 0$$

The binding energy of the molecule is the difference between these two potential energies (the amount of energy needed to breakup the molecule).

$$\text{Binding energy} = E_p(\infty) - E_p(R) = 7.5 \times 10^{-19} J$$

Since I eV = 1.6×10^{-19} J, the energy to separate the atoms may be written,

$$\frac{7.6 \times 10^{-19}\ \not J}{1.6 \times 10^{-19}\ \not J/eV} = 4.8\ eV$$

The photoneutron effect is the absorption of a photon by a heavy nucleus with subsequent emission of a neutron. The threshold energy of the photon is found to be about 10 MeV. Assume that the neutron is removed from the nucleus by applying to it a constant force which has to move it through a distance of 10^{-13} cm outward. Calculate the order of magnitude of this "average nuclear force" and compare it with the electrostatic force between two protons separated by 1.9×10^{-13} cm.

Solution: The minimum energy needed to remove the neutron from the nucleus (the threshold energy) is 10 MeV. This is the work which must be done by the constant force to "pluck out" the neutron.

$$\text{Work done by force} = 10 \text{ MeV}$$

$$= 10 \times 10^6 \text{eV} \times \frac{1.60\ 2 \times 10^{-12} \text{erg}}{1 \text{eV}}$$

$$= 1.602 \times 10^{-5} \text{ erg.}$$

But, $\quad \text{Work} = \text{Force} \times \text{distance}$

because, in this case, the force is constant and parallel to the displacement. Hence,

$$\text{Force} \times (10^{-13} \text{ cm}) = 1.602 \times 10^{-5} \text{ erg}$$

$$\text{Force} = 1.602 \times 10^{8} \text{ dyne.}$$

Notice, first, that this force, which is present inside a single nucleus, is equivalent to the weight of about 160 kilograms. It could support the weight of two men.

The electrostatic force between the two protons (in c.g.s. units) is

$$\text{Electrostatic force} = \frac{e^2}{R^2}$$

$$= \left(\frac{4.8 \times 10^{-10} \text{ esu}}{1.9 \times 10^{-13} \text{ cm}}\right)^2$$

$$= 6.4 \times 10^{6} \text{ dyne.}$$

The "average nuclear force" is about 25 times larger than the electrostatic force. Since, in reality, the nuclear force falls off very rapidly as the neutron is pulled outward, the force in the initial position is considerably larger than the average.

• **PROBLEM 605**

If a 1,000-V battery is connected to two parallel plates separated by 1 mm $\left(10^{-3}\text{ m}\right)$, what is the electric field?

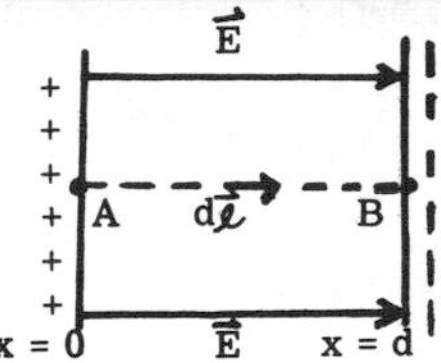

Solution: The potential of the battery, V = 1,000 V, and the distance between the plates, $d = 10^{-3}$ m, are given. By definition, the difference in potential experienced by moving a charge from point A to point B is

$$V_B - V_A = -\int_A^B E \cdot d\ell \tag{1}$$

where E is the electric field and d is an element of the path traversed in moving the charge. Now, looking at the figure, we see that, for the plates of a battery, E is perpendicular to the plates. If we evaluate (1) over a straight line path parallel to E, we find

$$V_B - V_A = -\int_A^B E\, d\ell = -\int_0^d E\, d\ell = -E\, d$$

where d is the plate separation. Then

$$|E| = \frac{|V_b - V_a|}{d} = \frac{10^3\text{ V}}{10^{-3}\text{ m}} = 10^6\text{ V/m}.$$

• **PROBLEM 606**

The plates of a parallel plate capacitor are 5 mm apart and 2 m^2 in area. The plates are in vacuum. A potential difference of 10,000 volts is applied across the capacitor. Compute (a) the capacitance, (b) the charge on each plate, and (c) the electric intensity.

Solution:

(a)

$$C_o = \varepsilon_o \frac{A}{d}$$

$$= 8.85 \times 10^{-12} \times \frac{2}{5 \times 10^{-3}}$$

$$= 3.54 \times 10^{-9}\text{ farad}$$

$$= 3.54 \times 10^{-3}\ \mu f$$

$$= 3540\ \mu\mu f.$$

(b) The charge on the capacitor is

$$q = CV_{ab}$$

$$= 3.54 \times 10^{-9} \times 10^{4}$$

$$= 3.54 \times 10^{-5} \text{ coulomb.}$$

(c) The electric intensity is

$$E = \frac{1}{\varepsilon_o}\sigma = \frac{1}{\varepsilon_o}\frac{q}{A}$$

$$= \left(36\pi \times 10^{9}\right) \times \left(1.77 \times 10^{-5}\right)$$

$$= 20 \times 10^{5} \text{ volts/meter.}$$

The electric intensity may also be computed from the potential gradient.

$$E = \frac{V_{ab}}{d}$$

$$= \frac{10^{4}}{5 \times 10^{-3}} = 20 \times 10^{5} \text{ volts/meter.}$$

• **PROBLEM 607**

An electron in an oscilloscope tube is situated midway between two parallel metal plates 0.50 cm apart. One of the plates is maintained at a potential of 60 volts above the other. What is the potential gradient between the plates? What is the force on the electron?

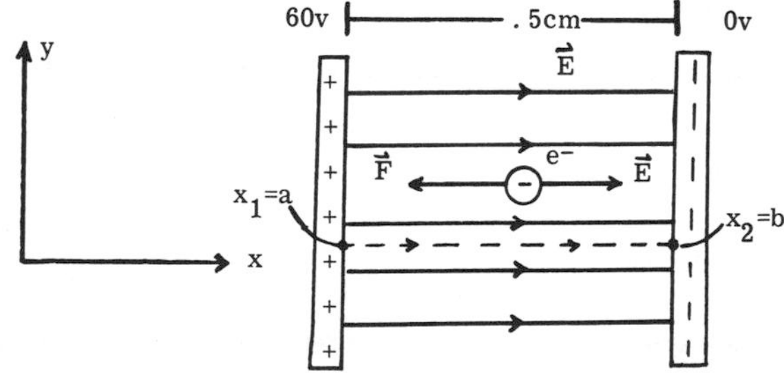

Solution: The difference of potential between points a and b, is, by definition

$$V_b - V_a = -\int_a^b \vec{E} \cdot d\vec{\ell} \qquad (1)$$

where the integral is evaluated over an arbitrary path between a and b and $\vec{E}$ is the electric field intensity.

In this example, $\vec{E}$ is constant between the plates (see figure), and

$$V_b - V_a = -\vec{E} \cdot \int_a^b d\vec{\ell} \qquad (2)$$

Also, we evaluate (2) over the path shown in the figure, since $\vec{E}$ and $d\vec{\ell}$ are in the same direction for this path. Then

$$V_{x_2} - V_{x_1} = -\vec{E} \cdot \int_{x_1}^{x_2} d\vec{\ell} = -E(x_2 - x_1)$$

and
$$E = -\frac{\left(V_{x_2} - V_{x_1}\right)}{(x_2 - x_1)} = -\frac{\Delta V}{\Delta x} \qquad (3)$$

By definition, $\Delta V/\Delta x$ is the potential gradient. Hence, for this case, by (3)

$$-E = \frac{\Delta V}{\Delta x} = -\frac{60 \text{ Volts}}{.5 \times 10^{-2} \text{ m}}$$

$$-E = \frac{\Delta V}{\Delta x} = -\frac{60 \text{ Volts}}{5 \times 10^{-3} \text{ m}} = -12 \times 10^3 \frac{V}{m}$$

Therefore, $\dfrac{\Delta V}{\Delta x} = -12 \times 10^3 \dfrac{V}{m}$

$$E = 12 \times 10^3 \frac{V}{m}$$

By definition, the force on the electron is the product of E and the electron charge, or

$$F = Eq = (1.2 \times 10^4 \text{ nt/coul}) \times (-1.60 \times 10^{-19} \text{ coul})$$

$$= -1.92 \times 10^{-15} \text{ nt}$$

This force is toward the plate of higher potential.

• PROBLEM 608

Consider two large parallel plates of area $1m^2$ separated by 1mm. (a) What is the capacitance of the system? (b) Suppose that the **capacitor** is charged so that there is a charge $+q$ on the upper surface and $-q$ on the lower where $q = 10^{-3}$coul. How much work must be done to charge the capacitor? (c) What is the force between the plates?

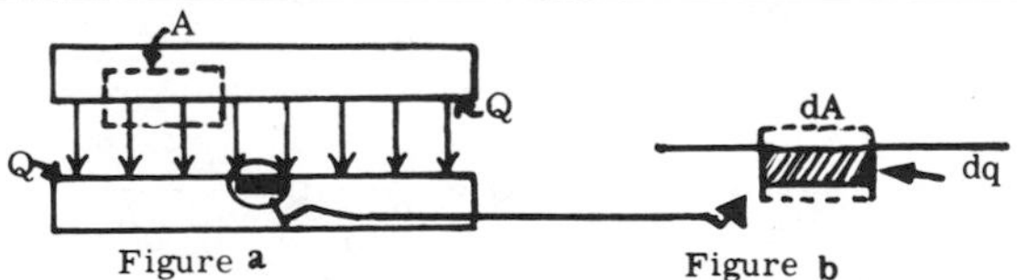

Figure a Figure b

Solution: (a) The capacitance of a parallel plate capacitor is given by:

$$C = \frac{\epsilon_0 A}{d} = \frac{A}{4\pi k_E d}$$

where A is the area of each of the plates, d is the separation of the plates, and $k_E = \dfrac{1}{4\pi\epsilon_0}$

$$C = \frac{1m^2}{4(3.14)(9 \times 10^9 nt - m^2/coul^2)(10^{-3}m)} = 8.05 \times 10^{-9} \frac{coul^2\text{-}sec^2}{kg\text{-}m^2}$$

$$= 8.05 \times 10^{-9} \text{ farads}$$

(b) The work done in charging the **capacitor** equals the energy stored in it:

$$W = E = \frac{1}{2}\frac{q^2}{C} = \frac{1}{2}\frac{(10^{-3}coul)^2}{8.05 \times 10^{-9}\frac{coul^2\text{-}sec^2}{kg\text{-}m^2}} = 62.1 \frac{kg\text{-}m^2}{sec^2} = 62.1 \text{ joules}$$

(c) To find the force between the plates, we must first calculate the field between the plates. We construct as a Gaussian surface, a rectangular box with one face within the top plate and another between the plates, as in the diagram (a). Since the plates are separated by a distance which is small compared to their length, the field between them is uniform. Therefore:

$$\int \vec{E} \cdot d\vec{S} = \frac{q}{\epsilon_0} = \frac{\sigma A}{\epsilon_0}, \quad E = \frac{\sigma A}{A\epsilon_0} = \frac{\sigma}{\epsilon_0}$$

where A is the area of the face of the Gaussian surface between the plates. We see that since the vertical sides are parallel to the field, they make no contribution to the flux. The face within the top plate also makes no contribution to the flux since the field within a conductor is zero.

Next, we must calculate the force on an infinitesimal charge element dq on the bottom plate. Part of the field between the plates is due to charge elements such as this one. Therefore, in order to obtain the net external field acting on dq (which we use to calculate the force on dq) we must subtract the field due to dq, from the field between the plates. We construct as a Gaussian surface a rectangular box (see figure (b)) with horizontal faces very close to the surface of dq. Close to dq, the field is vertical and uniform. This occurs because, at this distance, dq appears to be a long sheet of charge. Since dq has an almost infinitesimal width, the flux through the vertical faces is negligible.

By Gauss's law:

$$\int \vec{E} \cdot d\vec{S} = 2dAE_i = \frac{dq}{\epsilon_0} = \frac{\sigma dA}{\epsilon_0}, \quad E_i = \frac{\sigma}{2\epsilon_0}$$

Thus, the net external field acting on dq is:

$$E' = E - E_i = \frac{\sigma}{\epsilon_0} - \frac{\sigma}{2\epsilon_0} = \frac{\sigma}{2\epsilon_0}$$

The force on dq then is:

$$dF = E'dq = \frac{\sigma}{2\epsilon_0}dq$$

Therefore the total force on a plate is

$$F = \int dF = \int \frac{\sigma}{2\epsilon_0}dq = \frac{\sigma}{2\epsilon_0}Q = \frac{Q/A}{2\epsilon_0}Q = \frac{Q^2}{2\epsilon_0 A}$$

$$F = \frac{(10^{-3}coul)^2}{2(8.85 \times 10^{-12}farads/m)(1m^2)} = 5.65 \times 10^4 \frac{coul^2}{farad\text{-}m}$$

$$= 5.65 \times 10^4 \frac{coul^2}{\frac{coul^2\text{-}sec^2}{kg\text{-}m^2}\text{-}m} = 5.65 \times 10^4 \frac{kg\text{-}m}{sec^2} = 5.65 \times 10^4 N$$

• **PROBLEM 609**

The electric field in the space between the plates of a discharge tube is 3.25×10^4 newtons/coul. What is the force of the electric field on a proton in this field? Compare this force with the weight of the proton, if the mass of the proton is 1.67×10^{-27} kg and its charge is 1.60×10^{-19} coul.

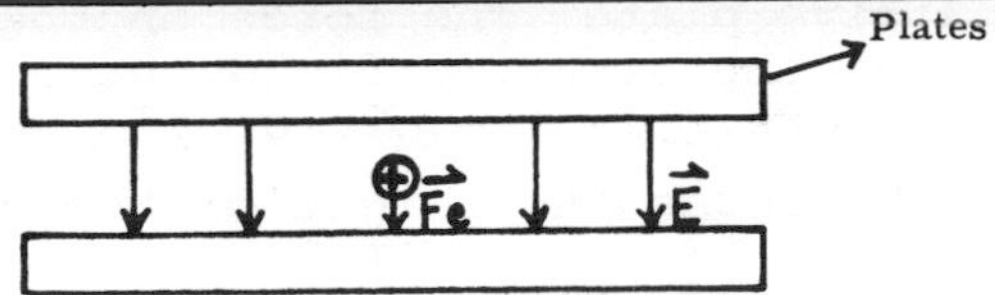

Solution: $\vec{E}$, the electric field strength, is defined as the force per unit charge q, or

$$\vec{E} = \vec{F}/q$$

The magnitude of $\vec{F}$ is

$$F = Eq = 3.25 \times 10^4 \text{ nt/coul} \times 1.60 \times 10^{-19} \text{ coul}$$

$$= 5.20 \times 10^{-15} \text{ nt}$$

The weight of the proton is given by the force of gravitational attraction on m. By Newton's Second Law,

$$F_g = ma$$

where a is the acceleration of m and F_g is the force of gravitational attraction on m (the weight of m). Because the acceleration of m is due to the earth's gravity, we may write

$$F_g = mg = (1.67 \times 10^{-27} \text{ kg})(9.80 \text{ m/s}^2)$$

$$= 1.64 \times 10^{-26} \text{ nt}$$

To compare the force on the proton in the electric field to the weight on a proton (also a force), we take their ratio. Hence

$$\frac{F}{W} = \frac{5.20 \times 10^{-15} \text{ nt}}{1.64 \times 10^{-26} \text{ nt}} = 3.17 \times 10^{11}$$

This emphasizes the fact that the force caused by an electric field may be much greater than that due to a gravitational field.

• **PROBLEM 610**

A charged oil drop of mass 2.5×10^{-4} g is in the space between the two plates, each of area 175 cm^2, of a parallel-plate capacitor. When the upper plate has a charge of 4.5×10^{-7} C and the lower plate an equal negative charge, the drop remains stationary. What charge does it carry?

Solution: The electric intensity between equal and oppositely charged parallel plates is given by the equation $E = \sigma/\varepsilon_0$, where σ is the surface charge density on one of the plates. By definition,

$$\sigma = \frac{Q}{A}$$

and $E = Q/A\varepsilon_0$, where Q and A are the charge on, and area of, the positive plate. The force on the oil drop is, by definition of the electric field intensity, $F = qE = qQ/A\varepsilon_0$, where q is the oil drop's charge. Since this force balances the weight of the drop, $mg = qQ/A\varepsilon_0$, or

$$q = \frac{mg\ A\varepsilon_0}{Q}$$

$$= \frac{2.5\times10^{-7}\ \text{kg}\times9.8\ \text{m}\cdot\text{s}^{-2}\times175\times10^{-4}\ \text{m}^2\times8.85\times10^{-12}\text{C}^2\cdot\text{m}^{-2}\cdot\text{N}^{-1}}{4.5\times10^{-7}\ \text{C}}$$

$$= 8.43\times10^{-13}\ \text{C}.$$

• PROBLEM 611

Suppose that in Millikan's experiment an oil drop weighing 1.6×10^{-13}N remains stationary when the electric field between the plates is adjusted to a value of 5×10^5N/C. What is the charge on the oil drop in this case, and how many units of the charge quantum does this represent if the particle is moving with a constant velocity between the plates?

Solution: In the experiment, the charged particle is attracted upward by the electrostatic force. If the electric field in which the particle is moving is E, the electrostatic force is

$$F_e = qE$$

where q is the charge. The gravitational force pulling the particle downward is its weight

$$W = 1.6 \times 10^{-13}\text{N}.$$

The particle is moving with a constant velocity (i.e., zero acceleration) therefore the net force acting on it must be zero. This means that

$$F_e = qE = W \quad \text{or}$$

$$q = \frac{W}{E} = \frac{1.6 \times 10^{-13}\not{N}}{5 \times 10^5\not{N}/C} = 3.2 \times 10^{-19}\text{C}.$$

Electric charge in nature exists in integral multiples of 1.6×10^{-19}C, hence the particle of the problem has

$$\frac{3.2 \times 10^{-19}\not{C}}{1.6 \times 10^{-19}\not{C}/\text{quantum}} = 2 \text{ quanta of charge.}$$

A plane parallel plate capacitor consisting of two metal circular plates 5 cm in radius separated 1 mm in air, is charged to 300 stat-volts, whereupon it is connected in parallel to another similarly charged capacitor (positive terminals connected together and negative terminals connected) (see Figure A). How much energy would be released if the combinations were discharged by a short circuit?

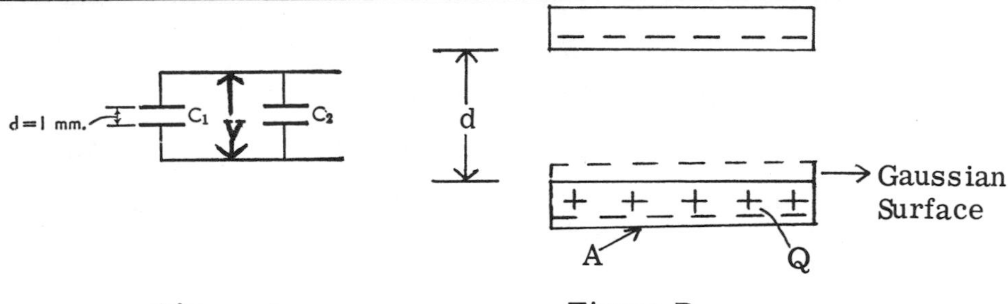

Figure A Figure B

Solution: For a plane parallel plate capacitor:

$$C = \frac{KA}{4\pi d}$$

This result can be obtained as follows. According to the definition of capacitance C,

$$C = \frac{Q}{V}$$

where Q is the total charge on one plate, and V is the potential difference between the plates. According to Gauss's law, if the Gaussian Surface is constructed as shown in Figure B, then

$$\frac{K}{4\pi}\,\Phi_E = \frac{K}{4\pi}\,EA = Q \qquad (1)$$

in the CGS system.

This relation holds because the electric field E is a constant in the parallel plate capacitor. Q is the charge enclosed by the Gaussian Surface. It is also the total charge on either plate, due to the construction of the surface. Also, for a parallel plate capacitor

$$V = Ed \qquad (2)$$

Therefore combining (1) and (2), we get the result for the capacitance of the parallel plate capacitor.

$$\therefore\ C_1 = \frac{\not{\pi} r^2}{4\not{\pi} d} = \frac{5^2}{4 \times 1\text{ mm} \times 1\text{ cm}/10\text{ mm}}$$

$$= \frac{25}{.4} = 62.5\text{ stat-farads.}$$

Recalling that the energy stored in a capacitor is

$$W = \frac{1}{2}QV = \frac{1}{2}CV = \frac{1}{2}\frac{Q^2}{C}$$

and choosing the second form because C and V are known

$$W_1 = \frac{1}{2} C_1V_1{}^2 = \frac{1}{2}(62.5)(300)^2 = 31.25(90,000)$$

$$= 2,820,000 \text{ ergs}$$

But the total energy stored in the two capacitors is

$$W_1 + W_2 = 2W_1$$

$$\therefore \quad W = 2(2,820,000) = 5,640,000 \text{ ergs}$$

$$= .564 \text{ joules} \qquad \text{Ans.}$$

This is the energy available and able to be released if the combination were discharged by a short circuit.

Solution in Mks Units: Data:

plate radius $= 5 \times 10^{-2}$ m $d = 10^{-3}$ m $V = 9 \times 10^4$ volts

$$C = \frac{1}{4\pi k}\frac{A}{d} = \frac{\not\pi\ 25 \times 10^{-4}}{4\not\pi\ 9 \times 10^9 \times 10^{-3}} = 6.94 \times 10^{11} \text{ farads}$$

But 1 farad $= 9 \times 10^{11}$ stat-farads

$$\therefore C = 6.94 \times 10^{-11} \times 9 \times 10^{11} = 62.5 \text{ stat-farads}$$

Check.

$$W = \frac{1}{2} C_1V_1^2 = \frac{1}{2}6.94 \times 10^{-11} \times 81 \times 10^8$$

$$= 28.1 \times 10^{-2} \text{ joules}$$

But 1 joule $= 10^7$ ergs.

$$\therefore W = 28.1 \times 10^{-2} \times 10^7 = 2.81 \times 10^6 \text{ ergs}$$

Total $W = 2 \times 28.1 \times 10^{-2} = .562$ joules

$= 5.62 \times 10^6$ ergs Check.

• PROBLEM 613

The space between the plates of a parallel-plate capacitor is filled with dielectric of coefficient 2.5 and strength $5 \times 10^5 \text{V}\cdot\text{m}^{-1}$. The plates are 2mm apart. What is the maximum voltage which can be applied between the plates? What area of plates will give a capacitance of $10^{-3}\mu\text{F}$, and at maximum voltage what are the free and bound charges per unit area of the plate and dielectric surface?

Solution: The dielectric strength of the dielectric is the largest electric field which it can withstand before becoming a conductor. We must relate the voltage between the capacitor plates to E_{max} (dielectric strength). This can be done by realizing that voltage differences are defined by

$$V_b - V_a = -\int_a^b \vec{E} \cdot d\vec{\ell} \qquad (1)$$

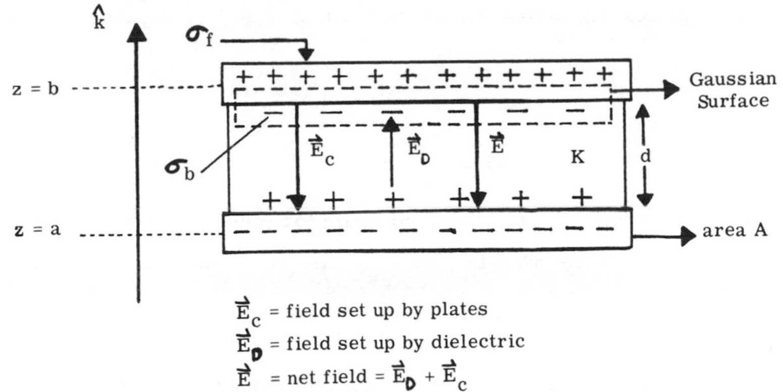

$\vec{E}_c$ = field set up by plates
$\vec{E}_D$ = field set up by dielectric
$\vec{E}$ = net field = $\vec{E}_D + \vec{E}_c$

where V_b, V_a refer to the potentials at $z = b$ and $z = a$, respectively (see figure), and $\vec{E}$ is the electric field. The integral in (1) is a line integral, and it is to be evaluated over an arbitrary path connecting a and b, $d\vec{\ell}$ being a small element of path length. Looking at the figure, we see that $\vec{E}$ is composed of contributions from two sources- the conducting plates $(\vec{E}_c)$ and the dielectric material $(\vec{E}_D)$. Note that the latter is in opposition to $\vec{E}_c$. Since $\vec{E}$ is uniform in direction and magnitude for a parallel-plate capacitor, (1) becomes

$$V_b - V_a = -\vec{E} \cdot \int_a^b d\vec{\ell} \tag{2}$$

The easiest path to evaluate this line integral along is a straight line path from z = a to z = b. In this case.

$$d\vec{\ell} = d\ell\ \hat{k}$$

Since

$$\vec{E} = -E\ \hat{k}$$

(2) becomes

$$V_b - V_a = -(-E\hat{k}) \cdot \int_a^b (d\ell\ \hat{k})$$

$$V_b - V_a = E(b - a)$$

But $b - a = d$ (see figure) and we define

$$V_b - V_a = \Delta V$$

as the potential difference between the plates. Therefore,

$$\Delta V = Ed \tag{3}$$

The maximum voltage which can be applied between the plates is

$$\Delta V_{max} = E_{max} d = \left(5 \times 10^6 \frac{V}{m}\right)\left(2 \times 10^{-3} m\right)$$

$$\Delta V_{max} = 10^4 V$$

To answer the second part of the problem, we must relate the capacitance of the capacitor to its geometry. We do this by beginning with the definition of capacitance (C)

$$C = \frac{Q}{\Delta V} \tag{4}$$

where Q is the charge on 1 capacitor plate. If the free charge density on the plate of cross-sectional area A is σ_f, (see figure) then

$$Q = \sigma_f A \tag{5}$$

Using (5) and (3) in (4)

$$C = \frac{\sigma_f A}{Ed} \tag{6}$$

Since we don't know E in this portion of the problem, we must eliminate it from (6). This may be done by using Gauss' Law for a dielectric

$$\oint_s \vec{E} \cdot \vec{ds} = \frac{Q}{\epsilon} \text{net} \tag{7}$$

where ϵ is a constant, and Q_{net} is the total free charge enclosed by the surface s over which the integral is evaluated. Evaluating (7) over the Gaussian surface indicated in the figure,

$$\oint_s \vec{E} \cdot \vec{ds} = \int_{s_T} \vec{E}(s_T) \cdot \vec{ds} + \int_{s_B} \vec{E}(s_B) \cdot \vec{ds} = \frac{Q_{net}}{\epsilon} \tag{8}$$

where s_T and s_B are the top and bottom of the rectangular surface. Now, $\vec{ds}$ is a vector element of surface area. For s_T, $\vec{ds} = ds\,\hat{k}$ and for s_B, $\vec{ds} = -ds\,\hat{k}$. Then, using the fact that $\vec{E} = -E\hat{k}$ everywhere, (8) becomes

$$\oint_s \vec{E} \cdot \vec{ds} = \int_{s_T} \left(-E(s_T)\hat{k}\right) \cdot (ds\,\hat{k}) + \int_{s_B} \left(-E(s_B)\hat{k}\right) \cdot (-ds\,\hat{k}) = \frac{Q_{net}}{\epsilon}$$

$$\oint_s \vec{E} \cdot \vec{ds} = -\int_{s_T} E(s_T) ds + \int_{s_B} E(s_B) ds = \frac{Q_{net}}{\epsilon}$$

Now, $E(s_T)$ is the value of E at s_T, which lies in the top conducting plate. By definition of a conductor, then, $E(s_T) = 0$. Therefore

$$\oint_s \vec{E} \cdot \vec{ds} = \int_{s_B} E(s_B) ds = \frac{Q_{net}}{\epsilon} \tag{9}$$

But $E(s_B) = E$, the electric field between the capacitor plates. This is constant, and (9) becomes

$$E \int_{s_B} ds = EA = \frac{Q_{net}}{\epsilon}$$

since the area of s_B is A. Hence

$$E = \frac{Q_{net}}{\epsilon A}.$$

Now, Q_{net} includes the free charge found within the Gaussian surface. Therefore (see figure)

$$Q_{net} = \sigma_f A$$

and

$$E = \frac{\sigma_f}{\epsilon} \tag{10}$$

Using (10) in (6)

$$C = \frac{\sigma_f A}{\frac{\sigma_f}{\epsilon} d} = \frac{\epsilon A}{d}$$

But K, the dielectric constant, is defined by

$$K = \frac{\epsilon}{\epsilon_0}$$

Hence, $\epsilon = \epsilon_0 K$ and

$$C = \frac{K\epsilon_0 A}{d} \tag{11}$$

Solving for A

$$A = \frac{Cd}{K\epsilon_0} \tag{12}$$

Substituting the given data in (12)

$$A = \frac{(10^{-3}\mu F)(2 \times 10^{-3} m)}{(2.5)(8.85 \times 10^{-12} C^2/N.m^2)}$$

$$A = .09m^2$$

The free charge density can be found using (10)

$$\sigma_f = \epsilon E = \epsilon_0 KE$$

or

$$\sigma_f = (5 \times 10^6 V/m)(2.5)(8.85 \times 10^{-12} C^2/N\cdot m^2)$$

$$\sigma_f = 110.6 \times 10^{-6} C/m^2$$

From the figure, note that the net field $\vec{E}$ is the superposition of the field due to the bound charges of the dielectric $(\vec{E}_D)$ and the field due to the free charge on the capacitor plates $(\vec{E}_c)$. Then

$$\vec{E} = \vec{E}_c + \vec{E}_D \tag{13}$$

But, by (10) and the figure, $\vec{E} = -\frac{\sigma_f}{\epsilon}\hat{k}$. Since the bound charge accumulates only on the surface of the dielectric, we may consider the dielectric slab to be equivalent to a parallel plate capacitor with surface density σ_b and an air dielectric.

$$\vec{E}_D = \frac{\sigma_b}{\epsilon_0}\hat{k}$$

Similarly,

$$\vec{E}_c = -\frac{\sigma_f}{\epsilon_0}\hat{k}$$

Hence, from (13)

$$-\frac{\sigma_f}{\epsilon}\hat{k} = -\frac{\sigma_f}{\epsilon_0}\hat{k} + \frac{\sigma_b}{\epsilon_0}\hat{k}$$

or

$$-\sigma_f = -\sigma_f \frac{\epsilon}{\epsilon_0} + \sigma_b \frac{\epsilon}{\epsilon_0}$$

$$\sigma_f\left(\frac{\epsilon}{\epsilon_0} - 1\right) = \sigma_b \frac{\epsilon}{\epsilon_0}$$

Since

$$K = \varepsilon/\varepsilon_0$$

$$\sigma_b = \sigma_f \frac{(K-1)}{K} = \frac{1.5}{2.5}\sigma_f = \frac{3}{5}\sigma_f$$

Noting that

$$\sigma_f = 110.6 \times 10^{-6} C/m^2$$

$$\sigma_b = \frac{331.8}{5} \times 10^{-6} C/m^2$$

$$\sigma_b = 66.4 \times 10^{-5} C/m^2$$

• PROBLEM 614

Two hollow spherical shells are mounted concentrically, but are insulated from one another. The inner shell has a charge Q and the outer shell is grounded. What is the electric intensity and potential in the space between them?

When the outer shell is not grounded, why does a charge outside the system experience a force when the inner shell is charged?

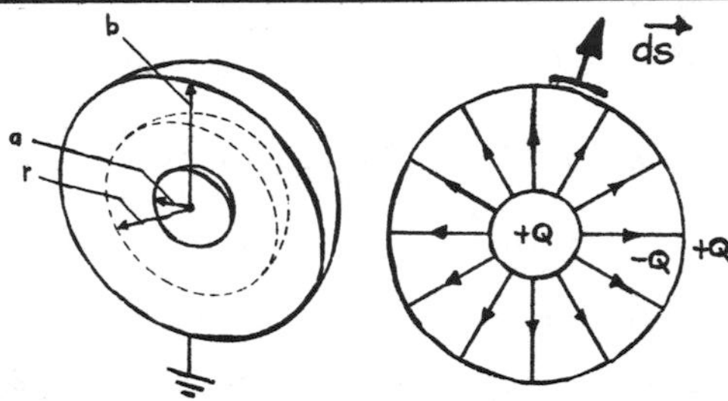

Solution: In the region between the shells, because of the symmetry of the arrangement, the electric intensity $\vec{E}$ must have the same magnitude at all points a distance r from the common center, and must thus be everywhere radial in direction. Hence, applying Gauss's law to a region bounded by a spherical surface of radius r (see the figure), we have

$$\int \vec{E} \cdot d\vec{S} = \frac{Q}{\varepsilon_0} \tag{1}$$

where Q is the total charge enclosed by the Gaussian surface, and dS is an element of surface area of the Gaussian surface. $\vec{E}$ is parallel to $d\vec{S}$, thus (1) becomes

$$E \int dS = 4\pi r^2 E = \frac{Q}{\varepsilon_0} \qquad \text{or} \qquad E = \frac{Q}{4\pi\varepsilon_0 r^2} \quad .$$

But $E = -dV/dr$ by definition of E as a potential gradient.

$$\therefore \quad dV = -\frac{Q}{4\pi\varepsilon_0 r^2}\,dr \qquad \text{or} \qquad V = \frac{Q}{4\pi\varepsilon_0 r} + C,$$

where C is a constant of integration. But at the outer spherical shell of radius $r = b$, $V = 0$.

$$\therefore \quad 0 = \frac{Q}{4\pi\varepsilon_0 b} + C \qquad \text{or} \qquad C = -\frac{Q}{4\pi\varepsilon_0 b} .$$

$$\therefore \quad V = \frac{Q}{4\pi\varepsilon_0}\left(\frac{1}{r} - \frac{1}{b}\right) .$$

Lines of force come from the inner shell and all end on the outer shell. The same number of lines of force end on the outer shell as start on the inner shell; hence the charge induced on the inside of the outer shell is equal and opposite to that on the inner shell. Thus a charge - Q is induced on the inside of the outer shell. But this shell was initially uncharged. Hence a charge + Q must be left on the outside of the outer shell.

If the outer shell is grounded, electrons flow from the earth to neutralize this positive charge. In the absence of grounding, the positive charge remains on the outside of the shell and produces a field of force around the system which affects any other charge in the vicinity.

• PROBLEM 615

Two parallel plates of area $A = 1\ m^2$ are given equal and opposite charges of Q = 30 microcoulombs each. A sheet of dielectric of permittivity $\varepsilon = 15 \times 10^{-12}$ $coul^2/newton\text{-}m^2$ occupies the space between the plates (see Fig. A). Compute (a) the resultant electric intensity in the dielectric, (b) the induced charge per unit area on the faces of the dielectric.

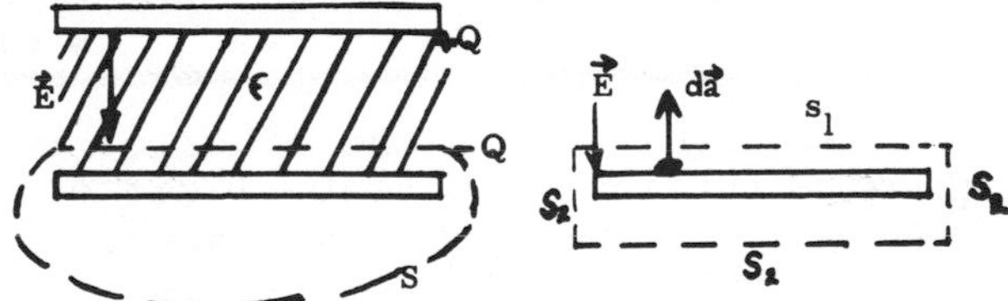

Figure A Figure B

Solution: (a) The charge per unit area on the plates is

$$\sigma = \frac{q}{A} = 30 \times 10^{-6}\ coul/m^2.$$

The resulting electric field between the plates can be obtained by applyi·g Gauss' Law to surface S in Fig. b.

$$\int_S \vec{E} \cdot d\vec{a} = \frac{Q}{\varepsilon}$$

In Fig. B, we see that on surface S_1 $\vec{E} \cdot d\vec{a} =$ $- E\ da$ and on the rest of the surface $\vec{E} \cdot d\vec{a} = 0$ since the field through the sides S_2 of the surface is zero. The electric field is constant between the plates. Therefore

$$\int_S \vec{E} \cdot d\vec{a} = - E \int_{S_1} da = - EA,$$

giving $E = \frac{-Q}{\varepsilon A} = -\frac{\sigma}{\varepsilon}$

$$|E| = \frac{30 \times 10^{-6} \text{ coul/m}^2}{15 \times 10^{-12} \text{ coul}^2/\text{n-m}^2}$$

$$= 2 \times 10^6 \text{ volts/m.}$$

(b) The dielectric coefficient is

$$K = \frac{\varepsilon}{\varepsilon_0} = \frac{15 \times 10^{-12}}{8.85 \times 10^{-12}}$$

$$= 1.7.$$

The induced charge on the dielectric of a capacitor is given by

$$Q_{ind} = Q\left(1 - \frac{1}{K}\right).$$

Then the induced charge density in the dielectric is

$$\sigma_{ind} = \frac{Q_{ind}}{A} = \frac{Q}{A}\left(1 - \frac{1}{K}\right)$$

$$= \sigma\left(1 - \frac{1}{K}\right)$$

or $\sigma_{ind} = 30 \times 10^{-6} \ (1 - 1/1.7) \text{coul/m}^2$

$$= 12.3 \times 10^{-6} \text{ coul/m}^2.$$

• PROBLEM 616

An electron travels from one to the other of two plates, between which is maintained a potential difference of 1000 V. With what speed and with what energy does the electron arrive at the positive plate?

A positively charged particle with equal and opposite charge but 3680 times the mass is then released at the positive plate. With what velocity and what energy does it reach the negative plate?

Solution: The electron travels through a potential difference of 1000 V. The energy acquired is thus E = eV, where e is the charge of the electron $(= 1.60 \times 10^{-19}$ C) and V is the potential difference between the plates. Thus E $(1.60 \times 10^{-19}$ C) (1000 V) $= 1.60 \times 10^{-16}$ J. However, the energy required to move an electron through a potential difference of 1 volt is an electron volt (eV). Hence, the energy required to move the electron through a potential difference of 1000 volt is 1000 eV, whence 1000 eV $= 1.60 \times 10^{-16}$ J. As required by the conservation of energy, all this potential energy is converted to kinetic energy on arrival of the electron at the positive plate. Hence

$\frac{1}{2} mv^2 = 1.60 \times 10^{-16}$ J or

$$v^2 = \frac{3.20 \times 10^{-16} \text{ J.}}{9.1 \times 10^{-31} \text{ kg}}$$

$$\therefore \quad v = 1.88 \times 10^7 \text{ m} \cdot \text{s}^{-1}.$$

For the positively charged particle, the charge it possesses is the same in magnitude as that of the electron and it moves through the same potential difference in the opposite direction. Hence, it acquires the same energy of 1.60×10^{-16} J. The velocity, however, is smaller because of the much larger mass. Thus

$\frac{1}{2} m_1 v_1^2 = 1.60 \times 10^{-16}$ J or

$$v_1^2 = \frac{3.20 \times 10^{-16} \text{ J}}{9.1 \times 10^{-31} \times 3680 \text{ kg}}$$

$$\therefore \quad v_1 = 3.10 \times 10^5 \text{ m} \cdot \text{s}^{-1}.$$

• PROBLEM 617

A parallel plate capacitor of 2 meter^2 in area and with charge $q = 3.54 \times 10^{-5}$ coulomb is insulated while a sheet of dielectric 5 mm thick, of dielectric coefficient 5, is inserted between the plates. Compute (a) the electric intensity in the dielectric, (b) the potential difference across the capacitor, (c) its capacitance.

Solution:

(a) The insertion of a dielectric between the capacitor plates alters the electric intensity because of the reversed field set up by the induced charges on the dielectric.

The electric intensity is

$$E = \frac{\sigma}{K \varepsilon_o} = \frac{1}{K \varepsilon_o} \frac{q}{A}$$

$$= \frac{1}{5 \times 8.85 \times 10^{-12}} \frac{3.54 \times 10^{-5}}{2}$$

$$= 4 \times 10^5 \text{ volts/meter.}$$

(b) The potential difference across the capacitor is reduced to

$$V_{ab} = Ed$$

$$= 4 \times 10^5 \times 5 \times 10^{-3}$$

$$= 2000 \text{ volts.}$$

(c) The capacitance is increased to

$$C = \frac{q}{V_{ab}}$$

$$= \frac{3.54 \times 10^{-5}}{2000}$$

$$= 1.77 \times 10^{-8} \text{ farad}$$

$$= 17{,}700 \ \mu\mu f.$$

The capacitance may also be computed from

$$C = \varepsilon \frac{A}{d} = K \varepsilon_o \frac{A}{d}$$

$$= 5 \times 8.85 \times 10^{-12} \frac{2}{5 \times 10^{-3}}$$

$$= 17{,}700 \ \mu\mu f.$$

• PROBLEM 618

Suppose the plates in the figures have an area of 2000 cm^2 or 0.20 m^2, and are 1 cm or 10^{-2} m apart. The potential difference between them in vacuum, $\vec{V}_0$, is 3000 volts, and it decreases to 1000 volts when a sheet of dielectric 1 cm thick is inserted between the plates. Compute the following: (a) the relative permittivity K of the dielectric, (b) its permittivity ε, (c) its susceptibility χ, (d) the electric intensity between the plates in vacuum, (e) the resultant electric intensity in the dielectric, (f) the electric intensity set up by the bound charges, and (g) the ratio of the surface density of bound charge, σ_b, to that of free charge, σ_f.

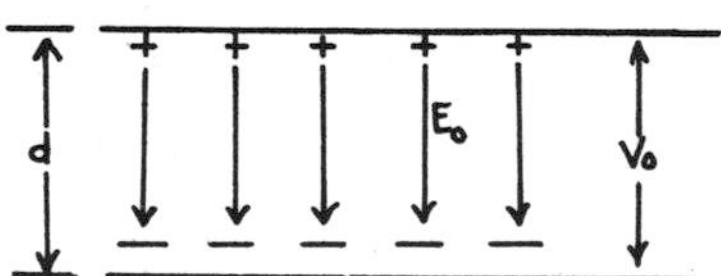

Fig. 1 Parallel Plate Capacitor

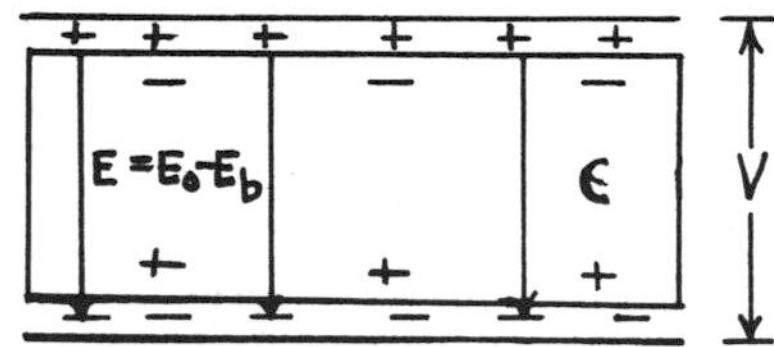

Fig. 2 The Effect of the Dielectric

Solution: The dielectric is polarized when inserted between the plates and the polarization charges (or bound charges) effectively neutralize some of the surface charges on the plates, as shown in figure 2. This then reduces the field strength in the dielectric, thus lowering the voltage difference across the plates, since the latter is proportional to the electric field (V = Ed). What remains unchanged in this case is the true charge density on the plates, i.e. the total charge on the plates. The ratio of the field in the dielectric to that in the vacuum gives the relative permittivity of the dielectric

(a) $K = \frac{E}{E_0} = \frac{V}{V_0} = \frac{3000}{1000} = 3$

(b) $\varepsilon = K_{\varepsilon 0} = 3_{\varepsilon 0}$

(c) $\chi = \varepsilon - \varepsilon_0 = 2_{\varepsilon 0}$

(d) $E_0 = \frac{V_0}{l} = \frac{3 \times 10^3 \text{ volts}}{10^{-2} \text{ m}} = 3 \times 10^5 \frac{\text{volts}}{\text{m}}$

(e) $E = \frac{V}{l} = \frac{1 \times 10^3 \text{ volts}}{10^{-2} \text{ m}} = 10^5 \frac{\text{volts}}{\text{m}}$

The bound charges of the dielectric set up a new electric field E_b in the slab which opposes the electric field E_0 due to the plate charges. The new field E is the resultant of these two

(f) $$E_b = E_0 - E = 2 \times 10^5 \text{ volts/m.}$$

The surface charge density σ is given by

(g) $$\sigma = \varepsilon_0 E_0 = 3 \times 10^5 \varepsilon_0 \frac{\text{coul}}{\text{m}^2}$$

The bound charges on the surface of the slab have a density

$$\sigma_b = \varepsilon_0 E_b = \varepsilon_0 (E_0 - E) = \varepsilon_0 E(K - 1)$$

$$= \chi E = 2 \times 10^5 \varepsilon_0 \text{ coul/m}^2,$$

and we get

$$\frac{\sigma_b}{\sigma_f} = \frac{2}{3} .$$

CHAPTER 19

ELECTRODYNAMICS

• PROBLEM 619

A convenient unit of energy in atomic physics and in nuclear physics is the electron volt (ev). One electron volt is defined as the potential energy difference of a charge e between two points having a potential difference of one volt. What is the equivalent of electron volts in ergs? What is the kinetic energy of an alpha particle (He^4 nucleus or doubly ionized helium atom) accelerated from rest through a potential difference of 1000 volts?

Solution: Potential energy is equal to $e\Delta\phi$. This is so since the change in energy is

$$\int F \cdot ds \quad \text{and } F = qE$$

so that energy is $q \int E \cdot ds$ or $q\Delta\phi$, and here $q = e$.

Therefore,

$$1 \text{ electron volt} = e\Delta\phi \cong (4.80 \times 10^{-10} \text{ esu}) \left(\frac{1}{300} \text{ statvolt}\right)$$

$$[300 \text{ volts} = 1 \text{ statvolt}]$$

$$\cong 1.60 \times 10^{-12} \text{ erg}$$

The potential energy of the alpha particle is:

$$2e(1000 \text{ volts}) = 2000 \text{ electron volts}$$

where

$$2000 \text{ ev} = (2 \times 10^3 \text{ ev})\left(\frac{1}{300}\right)(4.80 \times 10^{-10} \text{ esu})$$

$$= 3.2 \times 10^{-9} \text{ erg}$$

• PROBLEM 620

A proton, starting from rest, falls through a potential difference of 10^6 V. What is its final kinetic energy and final velocity?

Solution: At its rest position, the proton has only potential energy and no kinetic energy. As it falls, it loses potential energy but gains kinetic energy. In its final position, the proton has only kinetic energy and no potential energy. However, the law of conservation of energy demands that at all times, the sum of the kinetic and potential energies remain constant. Consequently, the sum of the two energies at the rest position must equal the sum of the two energies at the final position. Or

$$PE + 0 = 0 + KE$$

By definition of potential V,

$$V = \frac{\text{Energy}}{\text{Charge}} = \frac{E}{q}$$

Then

$$PE = eV$$

where e is the charge of the proton and V is the potential difference through which it falls. Therefore

$$10^6 \text{ elec.volts} = \tfrac{1}{2} m_p v^2 ,$$

where an electron volt is the energy required to move a charge e through a potential of 1 volt. The final kinetic energy is then

$$10^6 eV = 10^6 \text{ eV} \times \frac{1.602 \times 10^{-12} \text{ erg}}{1 \text{ eV}} = 1.602 \times 10^{-6} \text{ erg} = \tfrac{1}{2} m_p v^2 .$$

To compute the final velocity, we use this relation, then

$$v = \sqrt{\frac{2 \times (1.60 \times 10^{-6} \text{ erg})}{1.67 \times 10^{-24} \text{ g}}} .$$

where $m_p = 1.67 \times 10^{-24}$ g. Consequently,

$$v = 1.38 \times 10^9 \text{ cm/sec} .$$

• PROBLEM 621

An electron initially at rest is accelerated through 1 cm by an electric field of 3×10^4 V/m. What is the terminal speed?

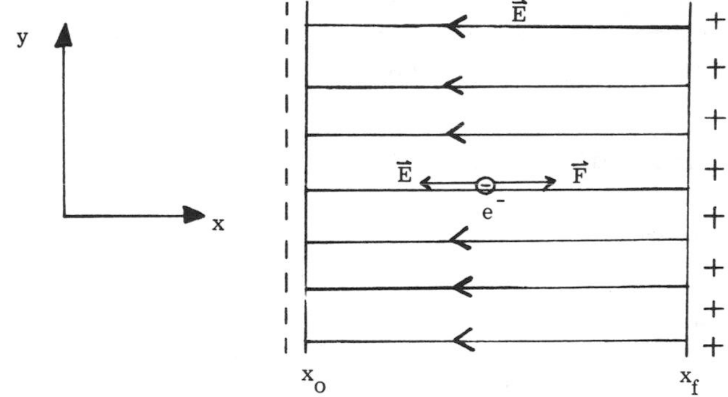

Solution: In order to solve for kinematical variables such as position, velocity, and acceleration, we must use Newton's Second Law to relate the net force on our system to its acceleration. We then integrate this equation to obtain v(t) and x(t).

In this problem, the only force acting on the electron is that due to the electric field $\vec{E}$. By definition

$$\vec{E} = \frac{\vec{F}}{q}$$

where $\vec{F}$ is the force acting on q. Hence,

$$\vec{F} = q\vec{E}$$

Since the electron charge is - e, where e = 1.6×10^{-19} coul. we may write

$$\vec{F} = -e\vec{E}$$

But, by the second law,

$$\vec{F} = m\vec{a}$$

where m and $\vec{a}$ are the electron mass and acceleration, respectively. Therefore,

$$m\vec{a} = -e\vec{E}$$

or $$\vec{a} = \frac{-e}{m}\vec{E}$$

For our problem, $\vec{E}$ is constant. Since e and m are also constants, the same must be true of $\vec{a}$. Looking at the figure, we see that $\vec{E}$ is in the negative x direction. If $\hat{\imath}$ is a unit vector in the positive x direction

$$\vec{E} = -E\hat{\imath}$$

and $$\vec{a} = \left(\frac{-e}{m}\right)(-E\hat{\imath}) = \frac{eE}{m}\hat{\imath} \qquad (1)$$

Noting that $\vec{a}$ is only in the x direction we may drop the vector notation in (1) and resort to scalar notation.

$$a = \frac{eE}{m} \qquad (2)$$

where a is positive when in the positive x direction But we want to know v in terms of x. Using the fact that

$$a = \frac{dv}{dt} = \left(\frac{dv}{dx}\right)\left(\frac{dx}{dt}\right) = \left(\frac{dv}{dx}\right)(v)$$

we obtain $$a = v\frac{dv}{dx}$$

or $$adx = vdv$$

Using (2),

$$\left(\frac{eE}{m}\right)dx = vdv$$

$$\frac{eE}{m}\int_{x_0}^{x_f} dx = \int_{v_0}^{v_f} vdv \qquad (3)$$

where the subscripts "f" and "0" indicate final and initial values, respectively. Integrating (3)

$$\frac{eE}{m}(x_f - x_0) = \frac{1}{2}v^2\Big|_{v_0}^{v_f} = \frac{1}{2}(v_f^2 - v_0^2)$$

Solving for v_f

$$\frac{eE}{m}(x_f - x_0) = \frac{1}{2}(v_f^2 - v_0^2)$$

$$\frac{2eE}{m}(x_f - x_0) + v_0^2 = v_f^2$$

$$v_f = \sqrt{\frac{2eE}{m}(x_f - x_0) + v_0^2}$$

But $v_0 = 0$ since the electron is initially at rest, and $x_f - x_0 = 1$ cm. Therefore,

$$v_f = \sqrt{\frac{2(1.6 \times 10^{-19}\ \text{coul})(3 \times 10^2\ \text{V/cm})(1\ \text{cm})}{(9.11 \times 10^{-31}\ \text{kg})}}$$

$$v_f = \sqrt{1.054 \times 10^{14}\ \text{m/s}^2}$$

$$v_f = 1.03 \times 10^7\ \text{m/s}$$

• PROBLEM 622

An electron is released from rest in a uniform electric field E = 1 N/coul. What velocity will it acquire in traveling 1 cm? What will then be its kinetic energy? How long a time is required? (Neglect the gravitational force.)

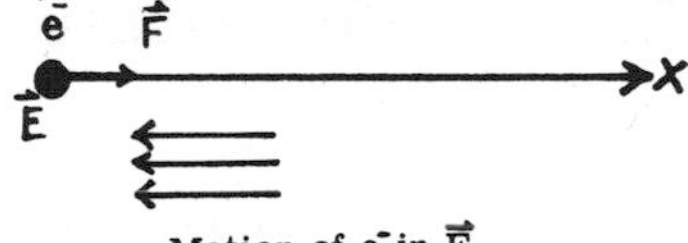

Motion of e⁻ in $\vec{E}$

Solution: The force on the electron is constant, therefore the electron moves with a constant acceleration (see the figure). By Newton's Second Law

$$a = \frac{F}{m} = \frac{eE}{m} = \frac{1.60 \times 10^{-15}\ \text{n}}{9.1 \times 10^{-31}\ \text{kg}} = 1.8 \times 10^{15}\ \frac{\text{m}}{\text{sec}^2}\ .$$

Its velocity after traveling 1 cm, or 10^{-2} m, is

$$v^2 = v_0{}^2 + 2a(x - x_0)$$

where v_0 and x_0 are the initial velocity and position of the electron. Both of these are zero in this problem. Hence,

$$v = \sqrt{2ax} = \sqrt{(2)(1.8 \times 10^{15}\ \text{m/s}^2)(10^{-2}\ \text{m})}$$

$$= 6.0 \times 10^6\ \frac{\text{m}}{\text{sec}}\ .$$

Its kinetic energy is

$$\tfrac{1}{2}mv^2 = (\tfrac{1}{2})\left(9.11 \times 10^{-31}\ \text{kg}\right)\left(36 \times 10^{12}\ \text{m}^2/\ \text{s}^2\right)$$

$$= 1.6 \times 10^{-17}\ \text{joules.}$$

and it represents the work done by the electric force $\vec{F}$ on the electron.

The time is found from $v = v_0 + at$. But $v_0 = 0$ hence

$$t = \frac{v}{a} = 3.3 \times 10^{-9} \text{ sec.}$$

• PROBLEM 623

A proton is at rest a long way away from the earth. It falls toward the earth under the influence of the earth's gravitational attraction. When it reaches the earth, all its kinetic energy is converted into the energy of a single quantum of light. What is the frequency of this quantum?

Solution: When the proton is at an infinite distance from the earth, the mutual gravitational potential energy of the earth-proton system is zero. When the proton reaches the surface of the earth, the mutual potential energy of the system is

$$\Phi_G = -\frac{GM_e m}{R_e}$$

where m is the mass of the proton, M_e is the mass of the earth, and R_e is the radius of the earth. The kinetic energy gained by the proton is equal to the potential energy lost, and so, if v is the velocity with which the proton strikes the earth,

$$\frac{1}{2}mv^2 = \frac{GM_e m}{R_e}.$$

All of this energy is converted into the energy of the quantum of light. The energy of a quantum of light is given by $h\nu$, where ν is the frequency of the light. Therefore

$$h\nu = \frac{GM_e m}{R_e}$$

$$\nu = \frac{GM_e m}{hR_e}$$

$$= \frac{\left(6.67 \times 10^{-11} \frac{\text{N m}^2}{\text{kg}^2}\right)(6 \times 10^{24} \text{ kg})(1.67 \times 10^{-27} \text{ kg})}{(6.63 \times 10^{-34} \text{ J·s})(6.37 \times 10^6 \text{ m})}.$$

$$= 1.6 \times 10^{14} \text{ sec}^{-1}.$$

This frequency is in the infrared.

• PROBLEM 624

A proton is accelerated from rest for 1 nanosecond $(= 10^{-9} \text{ s})$ by an electric field $E = 3 \times 10^4$ volts/meter. What is the final velocity (see figure)?

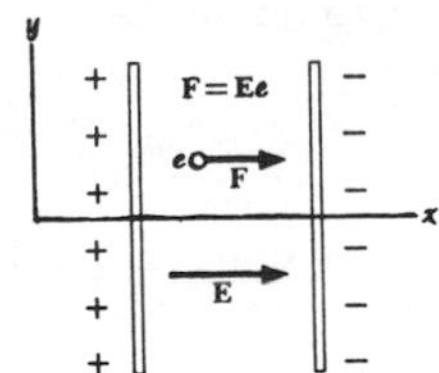

Solution. The general equation of motion involving time, constant acceleration, and velocity is $v_f = v_0 + at$. The acceleration is given by the electric force, eE, divided by the mass of the proton. v_0, the initial velocity, is zero. Therefore, the expression for v_f is:

$$v_f = at = \frac{eE}{M_p}t$$

$$e = 1.6 \times 10^{-19} \text{ coulombs}$$

$$E = 3 \times 10^{4} \text{ volts/meter}$$

$$M_p = 1.67 \times 10^{-27} \text{ kg}$$

$$t = 1 \times 10^{-9} \text{ sec}$$

$$v_f = \frac{\left(1.6 \times 10^{-19}\right)\left(3 \times 10^{4}\right)\left(1 \times 10^{-9}\right)}{1.67 \times 10^{-27}} \simeq 2.9 \times 10^{3} \text{ meters/sec}$$

• PROBLEM 625

What potential difference V in an electron gun is required to accelerate an electron that was initially at rest to a final speed of 1×10^7 m/s?

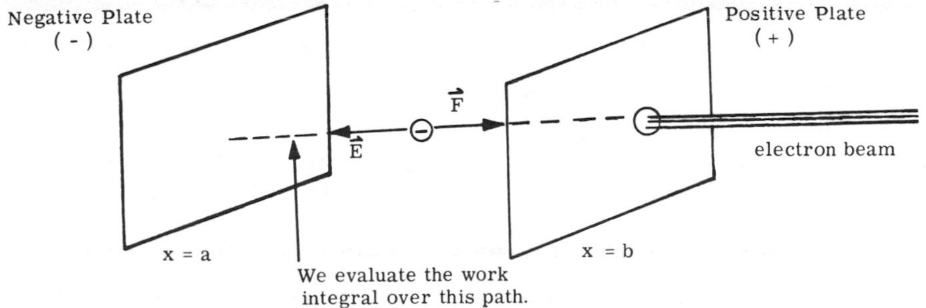

Solution: The electron starts from rest at the negative plate and accelerates straight across to the positive plate and then escapes through a small hole to form the electron beam. (See figure). By the work-energy theorem the change in kinetic energy of the electron is equal to the work done on the electron by the net force acting on it. Looking at the diagram, the net force on the electron is that due to the electric field $\vec{E}$. By definition,

$$\vec{E} = \vec{F}/q$$

where $\vec{F}$ is the force on charge q. Since $q = -e$, the electronic charge,

$$\vec{F} = q\vec{E} = -e\vec{E}$$

Hence, the work done on the electron is

$$W = \int_a^b \vec{F} \cdot d\vec{r} = \int_a^b -e\vec{E} \cdot d\vec{r}$$

where the integral is evaluated over a path between points a and b. Using the work-energy theorem,

$$\tfrac{1}{2} mv_b^2 - \tfrac{1}{2} mv_a^2 = -e \int_a^b \vec{E} \cdot d\vec{r} .$$

Here, v_b and v_a are the electron speeds at points a and b, and m is its mass. Since the electron starts from rest, $v_a = 0$ and

$$\tfrac{1}{2} mv_b^2 = -e \int_a^b \vec{E} \cdot d\vec{r} . \qquad (1)$$

By definition,

$$-\int_a^b \vec{E} \cdot d\vec{r} = V_b - V_a \qquad (2)$$

where V_b, V_a are the potentials at points b and a. Then, using (2) in (1)

$$\tfrac{1}{2} mv_b^2 = e\left(V_b - V_a\right)$$

Hence

$$V_b - V_a = \frac{mv_b^2}{2e}$$

Using the given speed and the known values of electron mass and charge,

$$V_b - V_a = \frac{\left(9.11 \times 10^{-31} kg\right)\left(10^{14} m^2/s^2\right)}{2\left(1.6 \times 10^{-19} \text{ coul}\right)}$$

$$V_b - V_a = \frac{9.11 \times 10^{-17} \text{ Joules}}{3.2 \times 10^{-19} \text{ Coul}}$$

But $1 \frac{\text{Joule}}{\text{Coul}} = 1$ volt

$$V_b - V_a = 2.8 \times 10^2 \text{ volts}$$

• PROBLEM 626

The SLAC accelerator is capable of accelerating electrons to an energy of 4×10^{10} eV. If the number of electrons in the beam corresponds to a current of 6×10^{-5} A, (a) how many electrons arrive at the target each second and (b) how much energy, in joules, is deposited in the target each second?

Solution: (a) Since a current of 1 A is defined as the flow of 1 C of charge each second, the beam current 6×10^{-5} A implies that 6×10^{-5} C of charge strikes the target each second. The charge of each electron is 1.6×10^{-18} C; therefore, the number of electrons N arriving each second is

$$N = \frac{6 \times 10^{-5} \text{ C/s}}{1.6 \times 10^{-19} \text{ C/electron}} = 3.75 \times 10^{14} \text{ electrons/s}$$

(b) The energy of the electrons can be expressed in joules:

$$E = (4 \times 10^{10}\ eV)(1.6 \times 10^{-19}\ J/eV) = 6.4 \times 10^{-9}\ J$$

Therefore, the energy deposited in the target by N electrons per second is

$$E = (6.4 \times 10^{-9}\ J)(3.75 \times 10^{14}\ electrons/s)$$

$$= 2.4 \times 10^{6}\ J/s.$$

This energy consumption is about the same as the amount of electrical energy used by a town of 1,000 people.

• PROBLEM 627

If an electron is projected into an upward electric field with a horizontal velocity v_0, find the equation of its trajectory.

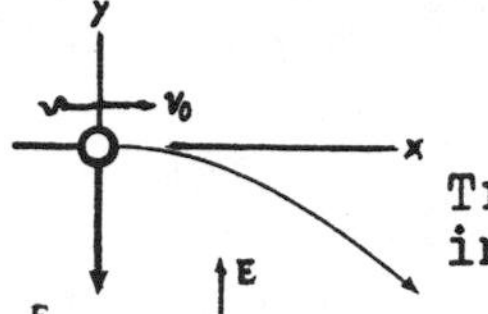

Trajectory of an electron in an electric field.

Solution: The direction of the field is upward (see the figure) and the force on e is $e\vec{E}$, where e is the electronic charge, and $\vec{E}$ is the electric field intensity. Since $e < 0$ the force on the electron points downward. The initial velocity is along the positive x-axis. The only force is in the - y-direction, therefore the acceleration along the x-axis is zero. The y-acceleration is

$$\vec{a}_y = \frac{\vec{F}_y}{m} = \frac{e\vec{E}}{m} \qquad (1)$$

where $e < 0$.

After a time t, the position of the electron will be

$$x = x_0 + v_{0x}t + \tfrac{1}{2} a_x t^2$$

$$y = y_0 + v_{0y}t + \tfrac{1}{2} a_y t^2$$

(x_0, y_0) and (v_{0x}, v_{0y}) are the components of the initial position and velocity of the particle. If we take $x_0 = 0$, $y_0 = 0$ as the starting point of the particle, and note that $a_x = 0$, $v_{0y} = 0$, we may write

$$x = v_{0x}t$$
$$y = \tfrac{1}{2} a_y t^2 \qquad (2)$$

Substituting (1) in (2)

$$x = v_{0x}t$$

$$y = \frac{e\vec{E}}{2m} t^2 \qquad (3)$$

Writing $\vec{E}$ in terms of a unit vector ($\hat{j}$) in the direction of the y - axis

$$\vec{E} = E\,\hat{j}$$

Substituting this in the equation for y appearing in (3), we obtain

$$y = \left(\frac{eEt^2}{2m}\right)\hat{j} \qquad (4)$$

Solving the x equation of (3) for t, and substituting this in (4),

$$t = \frac{x}{v_{0x}}$$

$$y = \left(\frac{eEx^2}{2mv_{0x}^{\ 2}}\right)\hat{j} \qquad (5)$$

Note that $e < 0$, and since all the other quantities in (5) are positive, $y < 0$ which is the equation of a parabola. The motion is the same as that of a body projected horizontally in the earth's gravitational field. The deflection of electrons by an electric field is used to control the direction of an electron stream in many electronic devices, such as the cathode-ray oscilloscope.

• PROBLEM 628

A proton is released from rest at a distance of 1 Å from another proton. What is the kinetic energy when the protons have moved infinitely far apart? What is the terminal velocity of one of the protons if the other is kept at rest? If both are free to move, what is their velocity?

Solution: When protons are moved infinitely far apart, the mutual potential energy of the protons is zero. Thus they have only kinetic energy.

By conservation of energy we know that the kinetic energy must equal the original potential energy, which is

$$E_p = \frac{e^2}{r} \approx \frac{\left(4.8 \times 10^{-10}\,\text{statcoulomb}\right)^2}{1 \times 10^{-8}\ \text{cm}} \approx 23 \times 10^{-12}\ \text{erg}$$

Here, r is the original separation of the protons, and e is the unit of electronic charge. The terminal velocity of the moving proton is given by (using conservation of energy)

$$E_k = \frac{1}{2} Mv^2 \approx 23 \times 10^{-12}\ \text{erg}$$

$$v^2 \approx \frac{2 \times 23 \times 10^{-12}\ \text{erg}}{1.67 \times 10^{-24}\ \text{g}} \approx 27 \times 10^{12} (\text{cm/s})^2$$

or

$$v \approx 5 \times 10^6\ \text{cm/s}$$

Using MKS units,

$$E_p = \left(9 \times 10^9 \frac{N\text{-}m^2}{kg^2}\right)\frac{(1.6 \times 10^{-19} coul)^2}{10^{-10} m} \approx 23 \times 10^{-19} J$$

$$v^2 \approx \frac{2 \times 23 \times 10^{-19}}{1.67 \times 10^{-27}} \approx 27 \times 10^8 \; m^2/s^2$$

$$v \approx 5 \times 10^4 \; m/s$$

If both protons are free to move, each proton will have equal and opposite momenta as a result of conservation of the initial momentum, which is zero in this case. The particles are identical, therefore their speeds and their kinetic energies will be the same. The total energy of the system in the final state is

$$\frac{1}{2} Mv_1^2 + \frac{1}{2} Mv_2^2 = Mv^2 \approx 23 \times 10^{-12} \text{ erg}$$

Hence the final speed of each particle is

$$v \approx \frac{5 \times 10^6 \text{ cm/s}}{\sqrt{2}} \approx 3.5 \times 10^6 \text{ cm/s}$$

• PROBLEM 629

An electron of charge -1.60×10^{-19} coul is in a circular orbit of radius $R = 5.5 \times 10^{-11}$ m around a proton of equal and opposite charge. The mass of the electron m_e is 9.11×10^{-31} kg and the mass of the proton m_p is 1.67×10^{-27} kg. Compare the electrostatic and gravitational forces between the two particles. Neglecting relativistic corrections, calculate the speed of the electron and the period of its orbit.

Solution: The electrostatic force is:

$$F_E = k_E \frac{q^2}{R^2}$$

and the gravitational force is:

$$F_G = G \frac{m_e m_p}{R^2}$$

The ratio is:

$$\frac{F_E}{F_G} = \frac{k_E \dfrac{q^2}{R^2}}{G \dfrac{m_e m_p}{R^2}} = \frac{k_E q^2}{G m_e m_p}$$

$$= \frac{(9 \times 10^9 \text{ N-m}^2/\text{coul.}^2)(1.60 \times 10^{-19} \text{ coul.})^2}{(6.67 \times 10^{-11} \text{ N-m}^2/\text{kg}^2)(9.11 \times 10^{-31} \text{ kg})(1.67 \times 10^{-27} \text{ kg})}$$

$$= 2.26 \times 10^{39}$$

The electrostatic force is gigantic compared to the gravitational force.

If the speed of the electron in orbit is V, then:

$$F_E = k_E \frac{q^2}{R^2} = m_e a = \frac{m_e V^2}{R}$$

$$V = q \left(\frac{k_E}{m_e R}\right)^{1/2}$$

$$= (1.60 \times 10^{-19} \text{ coul.}) \left[\frac{9 \times 10^9 \text{ N - m}^2/\text{coul.}^2}{(9.11\times10^{-31} \text{ kg})(5.5\times10^{-11} \text{ m})}\right]^{1/2}$$

$$= 2.1 \times 10^6 \text{ m/sec.}$$

The period T is the time it takes for the electron to complete a single orbit:

$$T = \frac{2\pi R}{V} = \frac{2(3.14)(5.5 \times 10^{-11} \text{ m})}{2.1 \times 10^6 \text{ m/sec}}$$

$$= 1.64 \times 10^{-16} \text{ sec.}$$

• PROBLEM 630

An electron with velocity $v = 10^9$ cm/s enters a region of length $L = 1$ cm in which there exists a transverse deflecting field $E = .1$ statvolt/cm (see figure). What angle with the x axis does the electron make on leaving the deflecting region?

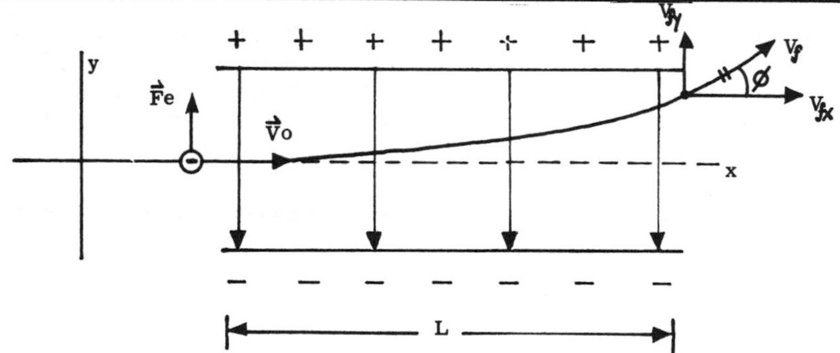

Solution: From the figure, we see that the angle made by v_f (the exit velocity) with the x axis is

$$\tan \phi = \frac{v_{f_y}}{v_{f_x}} \tag{1}$$

where v_{f_y}, v_{f_x} are the y and x components of the electron's final velocity.

We note that since there is no acceleration in the x-direction, the x component of the electron's velocity must remain constant. Hence

$$v_{f_x} = v_{0_x} = v = 10^9 \text{ cm/s} \tag{2}$$

We must now calculate v_{f_y}.

In order to find v_{f_y}, we must apply Newton's Second

Law (F = ma) to the vertical (y) component of motion of the electron. By definition of electric field intensity

$$\vec{E} = \frac{\vec{F}}{q}$$

where $\vec{F}$ is the force acting on charge q. For the electron, q = - e where e is the electron charge. Therefore

$$\vec{F} = - e\,\vec{E}$$

Furthermore, from the figure

$$\vec{E} = - E\,\hat{j}$$

where $\hat{j}$ is a unit vector in the positive y direction. Then

$$\vec{F} = (- e)(- E\hat{j}) = eE\hat{j}$$

But $$\vec{F} = m\vec{a}$$

where m, $\vec{a}$ are the mass and acceleration of the electron. Hence

$$m\vec{a} = eE\hat{j}$$

and $$\vec{a} = \frac{eE\hat{j}}{m}$$

We note that $\vec{E}$ is constant, and, therefore, $\vec{a}$ is constant. We may then use the kinematics equations for constant acceleration to find v_{f_y}. Also, $\vec{a}$ is one dimensional and we may use a scalar relation for v_{f_y}

$$v_{f_y} = v_{0_y} + at = v_{0_y} + \left(\frac{eE}{m}\right) t$$

where t is the time it takes for the electron to travel the distance L, and $v_{0_y} = 0$, as shown in the figure. Then

$$v_{f_y} = \left(\frac{eE}{m}\right) t$$

But by definition of v_x, (and since v_x is constant)

$$t = \frac{L}{v_{0_x}}$$

Therefore, $$v_{f_y} = \left(\frac{eE}{m}\right)\left(\frac{L}{v_{0_x}}\right) = \frac{eEL}{mv_{0_x}}$$

Substituting in (1), and using (2)

$$\tan\phi = \frac{v_{f_y}}{v_{f_x}} = \left(\frac{eEL}{mv_{0_x}}\right)\left(\frac{1}{v_{0_x}}\right)$$

$$\tan\phi = \frac{eEL}{mv_{0_x}^2}$$

$$\tan\phi = \frac{(4.8 \times 10^{-10} \text{ esu})(10^{-1} \text{ statvolt/cm})(1 \text{ cm})}{(9.11 \times 10^{-28} \text{ gm})(10^{18} \text{ cm}^2/\text{ s}^2)}$$

But 1 statvolt = 1 esu, and

$$\tan\phi = \frac{(4.8 \times 10^{-11})\text{esu}^2}{(9.11 \times 10^{-10})\text{gm} \cdot \text{cm}^2/\text{ s}^2}$$

Also, $1 \frac{\text{esu}^2}{\text{cm}} = 1 \text{ dyne}$

Hence $1 \text{ dyne} \cdot \text{cm} = 1 \text{ esu}^2$

and $1 \text{ gm} \cdot \text{cm}^2/\text{s}^2 = 1 \text{ dyne} \cdot \text{cm}$

Therefore $\tan\phi = .0527$

$$\phi \simeq 3°$$

• PROBLEM 631

We consider a particle with charge q which moves along the x axis with a high momentum p_0 and enters a region of length L in which there is a transverse electric field $\varepsilon\hat{y}$. Find the angle through which the particle is deflected by the electric field.

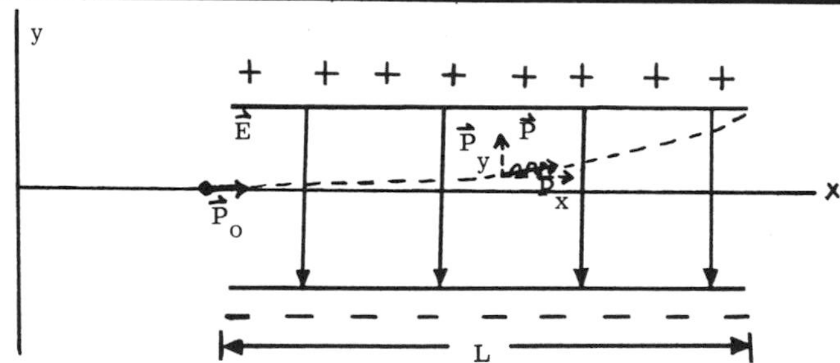

Solution: Since we are given the momentum and not the mass of the particle, we use a momentum-energy approach. We first note that we are given the electric field ε. We can translate this into the force exerted on the particle by multiplying the field by the charge on the particle ($q\varepsilon$). But, force is the derivative of momentum. Since the field is only present in the y direction, the resulting force is exerted solely in the y direction. Thus,

$$\frac{dp_x}{dt} = 0; \qquad \frac{dp_y}{dt} = q\varepsilon,$$

Integrating, we have $p_x = p_{0_x}$, $p_y = q\varepsilon t + p_{0_y}$

where p_{0_x} is the initial x momentum, and p_{0_y} is the initial y momentum. Since the particle initially has no y velocity

$$p_{0_y} = 0$$

and $\quad p_x = p_{0_x} \qquad p_y = q\varepsilon t \qquad (1)$

We want to find the velocity v. If we can find the energy E, then we can find the velocity from the momentum by using the relation $v = pc^2/E$.

The energy is given by

$$E^2 = M^2c^4 + p^2c^2 = M^2c^4 + \left(p_{0_x}^2 + q^2\varepsilon^2t^2\right)c^2$$

from (1). But $E_0^2 = M^2c^4 + p_0^2\ c^2$ and, then,

$$E^2 = \left(M^2c^4 + p_{0_x}^2 c^2\right) + (q\varepsilon tc)^2$$

Since $p_0 = p_{0_x}$

$$E^2 = E_0^2 + (q\varepsilon tc)^2 \qquad (2)$$

where E_0 is the initial energy. Therefore from (1), (2) and the velocity-momentum relation we have

$$v_x = \frac{p_x c^2}{[E_0^2 + (q\varepsilon tc)^2]^{\frac{1}{2}}} = \frac{p_{0x}\ c^2}{[E_0^2 + (q\varepsilon tc)^2]^{\frac{1}{2}}}$$

$$v_y = \frac{p_y c^2}{[E_0^2 + (q\varepsilon tc)^2]^{\frac{1}{2}}} = \frac{q\varepsilon tc^2}{[E_0^2 + (q\varepsilon tc)^2]^{\frac{1}{2}}}$$

Note that v_x decreases as t increases. At a time t, the angle θ the trajectory makes with the x axis is given by

$$\tan\theta(t) = \frac{v_y}{v_x} = \frac{q\varepsilon tc^2}{p_0c^2} = \frac{q\varepsilon t}{p_0}\ .$$

• PROBLEM 632

Let us assume that the conduction electrons in a metal are completely free except for a retarding force which is proportional to the speed. a) Find the variation of the electron velocity with time when a constant electric field is set up in a metal. b) How long does it take for the electrons to reach maximum velocity?

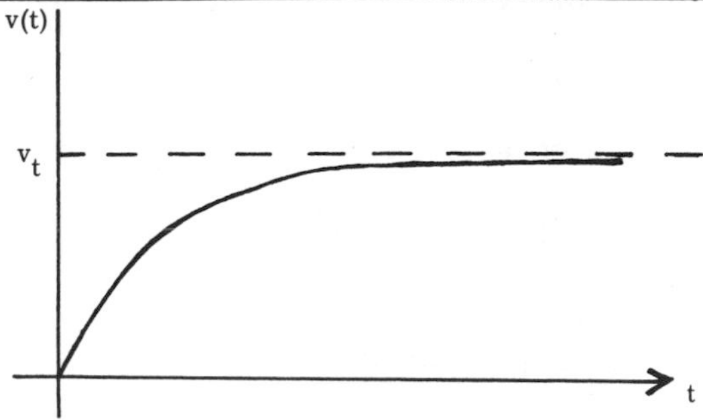

Solution: a) The acceleration of an electron due to an electric field is given by

$$m_e \left(\frac{dv}{dt}\right)_1 = Ee$$

where v is the velocity of the electron, and e is the electronic charge. The retarding force gives rise to a deceleration given by

$$m_e \left(\frac{dv}{dt}\right)_2 = -bv$$

where b is some constant. The equation of motion is then

$$m_e \frac{dv}{dt} = Ee - bv.$$

The solution of this equation is (see the figure)

$$v(t) = \frac{eE}{b}\left(1 - e^{-t/T}\right)$$

where $T = \frac{m_e}{b}$ is called the relaxation time. We see that as t becomes large, a terminal velocity $v_t = \frac{eE}{b}$ is established.

b) If we write v_t as

$$v_t = \frac{eE}{m_e}\frac{m_e}{b} = \frac{eE}{m_e} T$$

it turns out to be just that velocity which an electron would attain in a time T with acceleration $\frac{eE}{m_e}$,

$$v_t = aT = \frac{eE}{m_e} T.$$

• PROBLEM 633

A parallel plate capacitance is charged (linearly) to 10^{-3} coul in a time of 10^{-3} sec. Calculate the displacement current between the plates.

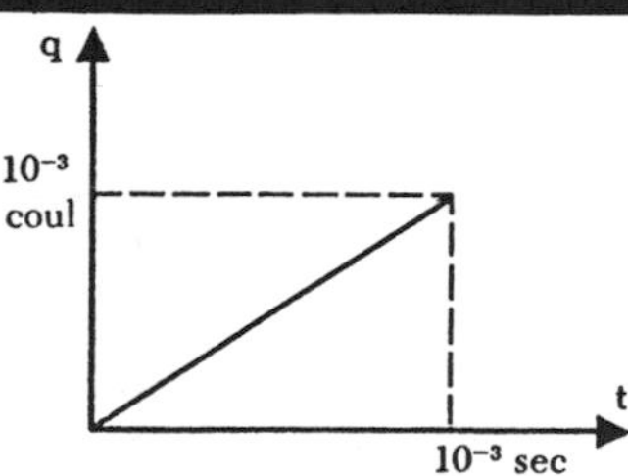

Solution: A plot of charge on one plate versus time is shown in the figure. The charge density on a surface of the parallel plate capacitance, as a function of time, is given by,

$$\sigma(t) = \frac{q(t)}{A}$$

where q is the charge on a plate of A. The field as a function of time is

$$E(t) = \frac{\sigma(t)}{\epsilon_0} = \frac{q(t)}{\epsilon_0 A}$$

The electric flux is then

$$\Phi_E = EA = \frac{q(t)}{\epsilon_0}$$

A change in charge on the plate Δq will then produce a change of electric flux given by

$$\Delta\Phi_E = \frac{\Delta q}{\epsilon_0}$$

Dividing both sides by Δt, we have

$$\frac{\Delta\Phi_E}{\Delta t} = \frac{1}{\epsilon_0}\frac{\Delta q}{\Delta t}$$

This expression relates a change in flux with time to a change in charge with time,

$$\frac{\Delta q}{\Delta t} \cdot \frac{\Delta q}{\Delta t}$$

can be viewed as a current through the capacitance. It is called a displacement current, I_D, to distinguish it from an actual movement of charge. From the graph we see that

$$\Delta q = 10^{-3} \text{ coul} - 0 \text{ coul}$$

for

$$\Delta t = 10^{-3} \text{ sec} - 0 \text{ sec}$$

Therefore

$$I_D = \frac{\Delta q}{\Delta t} = \frac{10^{-3}}{10^{-3}} = 1 \text{ coul/sec}$$

• PROBLEM 634

How much silver is deposited on a spoon which is plated for 20 minutes at 0.50 ampere?

Solution: In order to check this problem, we must understand what happens during the electroplating process. As each silver ion migrates to the spoon, it is reduced to a metallic silver atom. All the silver ions are in a plus 1 ionized state. This means that for every electron passing through the circuit, one silver ion will be turned into metallic silver and deposited. The problem then reduces to one of charge transport - as many atoms (or moles of atoms) of silver will be deposited as electrons (or moles of electrons) that pass through the circuit. We merely have to equate the two. The number of moles of deposited silver is given by the mass of the liberated silver (an unknown quantity) divided by the atomic mass of silver (107.9):

$$\frac{\text{Mass liberated in grams}}{107.9 \text{ gm/mole}}$$

To discover the amount of charge transported, and hence the number of moles transported, we use the relationship

$$I = \frac{q}{t} \quad \text{or} \quad q = It$$

where I is current, q is charge, and t is time. Since we know that there are 96,500 coulombs of charge per mole of electrons, we can calculate the number of moles of electrons by using

$$\frac{q}{96{,}500 \text{ coulombs/mole}} \quad \text{or} \quad \frac{It}{96{,}500 \text{ coulombs/mole}}$$

Equating the number of moles of silver plated, and the number of electrons which have passed through the circuit during the given time period, we have

$$\frac{\text{Mass liberated in grams}}{107.9 \text{ gm/mole}} = \frac{It}{96{,}500 \text{ coulombs/mole}}$$

Since I = 0.50 amp and t = 20 min = 1200 sec. we have

$$\frac{\text{Mass}}{107.9 \text{ gm/mole}} = \frac{0.50 \text{ amp} \times 1200 \text{ sec}}{69{,}500 \text{ coulombs/mole}}$$

Solving, we obtain

Mass = 0.671 gm, approximately.

• PROBLEM 635

How many coulombs are required to deposit 0.10 gram of zinc, the atomic mass of zinc being 65.38 and its valence 2?

Solution: In order to do this problem, we must realize that for every 2 electrons transported through the circuit, one zinc atom will de deposited. We therefore know that exactly half as many zinc molecules (or moles of zinc molecules) will be deposited as transported electrons (or moles of transported electrons). We may calculate the number of moles of zinc we need to deposit by dividing the mass of material we want by the atomic mass of zinc. Equating this with one half the number of moles of electrons transported (obtainable by dividing the amount of transported charge by 96,500 coulombs/mole) we have

$$\frac{0.10 \text{ gm}}{65.38 \text{ gm/mole}} = \left(\frac{1}{2}\right) \frac{Q \text{ in coulombs}}{96{,}500 \text{ coulombs/mole}}$$

Solving for Q we have:

$$Q = \frac{0.10 \text{ gm} \times 96{,}500 \text{ coulombs/mole}}{32.69 \text{ gm/mole}}$$

$$= 295 \text{ coulombs, approximately.}$$

• PROBLEM 636

The type of wall socket commonly found in the house is capable of delivering a current of 5 amperes. If this current flows through a copper wire with a diameter of 0.1 cm, what is the drift velocity v_d of the electrons?

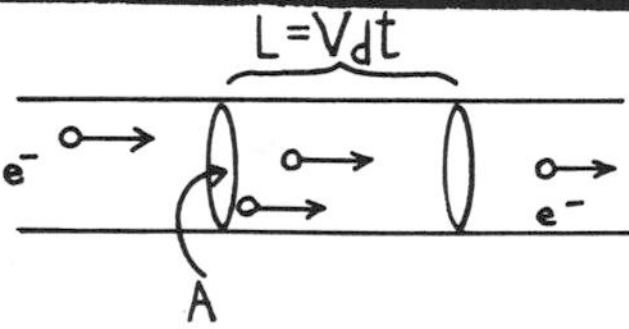

Solution: The drift velocity (v_d) is the velocity of the electrons in the wire due to the accelerating field $\vec{E}$. But, v_d is constant because the electrons are constantly colliding with the copper atoms of the wire. Hence, the net effect of the collisions and accelerating field is to propel the electrons at constant velocity v_d. Our aim is to relate the number of electrons per unit volume of the wire to the current carried by the wire. We will then find a relation for v_d.

We shall need to know n_0, the number of free electrons per cm^3. The copper atom is known to have one loosely bound electron, so we shall assume that one free electron is provided by each copper atom. n_0 is therefore equal to the number of copper atoms in $1 cm^3$. The atomic mass of copper is 64 which is the gram mass of Avogadro's number of copper atoms. Since the density of copper is 9.0 gm/cm^3, 1 cm^3 of copper has a mass of 9.0 gms. Therefore,

$$\frac{6 \times 10^{23} \text{ atoms}}{64 \text{ gm}} = \frac{n \text{ atoms in } 1 \text{ cm}^3}{9 \text{ gm}}$$

$$n = \frac{(9 \text{ gm})(6 \times 10^{23} \text{ atoms})}{(64 \text{ gm})}$$

$$n = 8.4 \times 10^{22}$$

Hence, there are 8.4×10^{22} atoms in 1 cm^3 of copper, and

$$n_0 = 8.4 \times 10^{22} \frac{\text{atoms}}{\text{cm}^3} .$$

The current is

$$5 \text{ amps} = 5 \text{ amp} \times \frac{3 \times 10^9 \text{ stata amp}}{1 \text{ amp}}$$

or

$$i = 1.5 \times 10^{10} \text{ statamps}$$

The cross-sectional area of the wire in the Figure is

$$A = \pi r^2$$
$$= \pi \times \left(\frac{.1}{2} \text{ cm}\right)^2$$

The charge on the electron is 4.80×10^{-10} statcoulomb. Then the net charge passing a point of the wire in a time t is the amount of charge in a cylinder (see figure) of length $v_d t$, where v_d is the drift velocity of the charges, and base area A. This is equal to the number of electrons in the cylinder times the charge of an electron.

$$Q = n_0 A v_d t e \quad \text{and} \quad L = \frac{Q}{t} = n_0 A v_d e$$

Hence

$$v_d = \frac{i}{n_0 A e}$$

$$= \frac{1.5 \times 10^{10} \text{ stata amp}}{(4.80 \times 10^{-10} \text{ stata coul})\left(8.4 \times 10^{22} \frac{1}{\text{cm}^3}\right)(7.854 \times 10^{-3} \text{cm}^2)}$$

Drift velocity, $v_d = 4.74 \times 10^{-2}$ cm/sec

If the wire is 1 meter long, the time taken for an electron to drift from one end to the other is $100/(4.74 \times 10^{-2})$sec $= 2.11 \times 10^3$ sec = 35 minutes!

Notice that we chose to work in CGS units throughout. In this particular example we could have obtained the correct answer if we had left i in amps and expressed e in coulombs. To be consistent, we would then have had to express n_0 in atoms per m^3, A in m^2 and v_d in m/sec. We would, however, have obtained the correct answer if we had left n_0, A and v_d in CGS units, but this cannot be relied upon without careful consideration of the problem. The student is advised never to mix systems of units and then he can be certain of not running into trouble.

After each collision in a solid, the valence electrons rebound in a random direction. However, when an electric field is present, there is a general drift of the electrons superimposed on this random motion, as shown in the figure. Show that the average drift velocity v_d may be written,

$$v_d = \frac{at}{2}$$

Where a is the acceleration produced by the electric field and t is the average time interval between collisions. If the acceleration is 7×10^{10} m/s^2, what is the numerical value of the drift velocity for free electrons in copper metal? How long does it take these electrons to drift 1 m in the presence of the electric field? The mean free time between collisions with the crystal lattice for an electron in a crystal is $3/3 \times 10^{-14}$ sec.

The presence of an electric field $\mathcal{E}$ in a metal crystal produces a general drift of electrons which is superimposed upon their random motion.

Solution: We assume that each time an electron suffers a collision within the crystal, it rebounds in a random fashion and on the average has no component of motion parallel to the field. So the initial velocity v_o in the field direction must be zero. The electric force accelerates the electron until its next collision with an ion. The final velocity acquired during the time interval t between collisions is v. The distance traveled in the direction of the force can be found from the kinematics equations for constant acceleration, or

$$x = x_o + v_o t + 1/2\ at^2$$

But $v_o = 0$, and $x - x_o = d$, the distance travelled by the electron in the direction of E. Hence,

$$d = x - x_o = 1/2\ at^2$$

Since the average drift speed during this time interval is given by the distance travelled by the electron divided by the time t, we have,

$$v_d = \frac{d}{t}$$

Because $d = 1/2\ at^2$, $v_d = \dfrac{1/2\ at^2}{E} = 1/2\ at$

The average drift velocity of free electrons in copper is, therefore,

$$v_d = \frac{\left(7 \times 10^{10}\ m/s^2\right)\left(3.3 \times 10^{-14} s\right)}{2} = 1.2 \times 10^{-3} m/s$$

This number is very small compared to the average speed 1.21×10^6 m/s associated with the random electron motion. The time t required for electrons to drift a distance of 1 m is,

$$t = \frac{1 \not{m}}{1.2 \times 10^{-3} \not{m}/s} = 8.3 \times 10^2 \text{ s}$$

• PROBLEM 638

What is the flux density $\vec{B}$ in the region between the plates of a circular capacitor that is being charged?

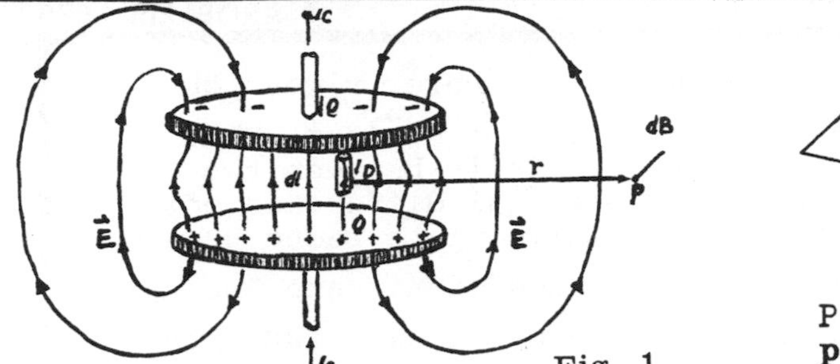

Fig. 1

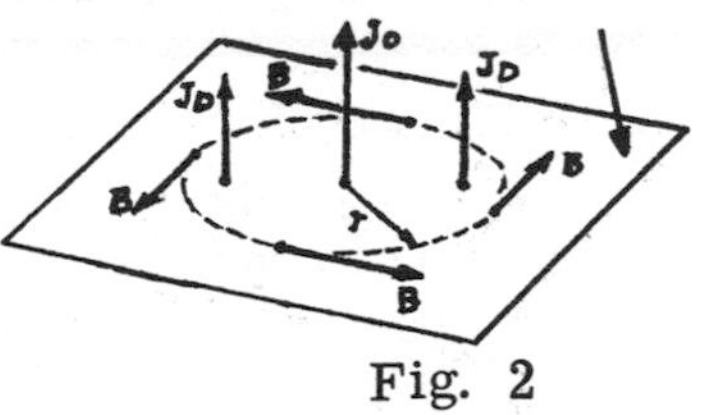

Fig. 2

Plane midway between plates of Fig. 1.

Solution: Figure 2 represents a plane midway between the plates of the capacitor in Fig. 1. During the process of charging, an effective current will pass across the plates as a result of charge transfer between the plates over a finite period of time. The electric field inside the capacitance will incrase in time from zero to a maximum value, and give rise to the displacement current density $\vec{J}_D$, which is given by Maxwell's equations as

$$\mu_0 \varepsilon_0 \frac{\partial \vec{E}}{\partial t} = \vec{J}_D .$$

The magnetic field due to $\vec{J}_D$ can be obtained from Stoke's theorem

$$\int_C \vec{B} \cdot d\vec{r} = \mu_0 \int_S \vec{J}_D \cdot d\vec{A} \tag{1}$$

where $\vec{B}$ is the magnetic induction.

For the first integral, let the circle of Fig. 2 be the contour C about which we evaluate the left side of (1). The integral involving $\vec{J}_D$ is then evaluated about the area S enclosed by C. Because of the circular symmetry of the charge distribution on the plates, i.e., the uniformity of the $\vec{J}_D$ lines, the induced magnetic field $\vec{B}$ will be circular. Then, we find using (1), that at every radius r

$$2\pi r\ B_r = \mu_0 I_{D,r} \quad , \quad B_r = \frac{\mu_0}{2\pi} \frac{I_{D,r}}{r}$$

where $I_{D,r}$ is the displacement current passing through the indicated surface. If r is less than the radius of the plates, then $I_{D,r}$ is smaller than the conduction current I_C, because not all the electric field lines go through S.

In the idealized case in which fringing fields are neglected, and $\vec{r}$ equals the radius of the plates, the displacement current equals the conduction current and

$$B_r = \frac{\mu_0}{2\pi} \frac{I_C}{r}$$

which is the same as the field at a distance $\vec{r}$ from an infinitely long straight conductor.

• PROBLEM 639

An oil drop carries a net charge of three times the electronic charge and has a radius of 10^{-4} cm. What is its terminal velocity when it falls between two horizontal plates kept at a potential difference of 1000 V and 2 cm apart, the positive plate being uppermost? The densities of the oil and of air are 800 $kg \cdot m^{-3}$ and 1.29 $kg \cdot m^{-3}$ and the visocity of air is 1.80×10^{-5} $N \cdot s \cdot m^{-2}$.

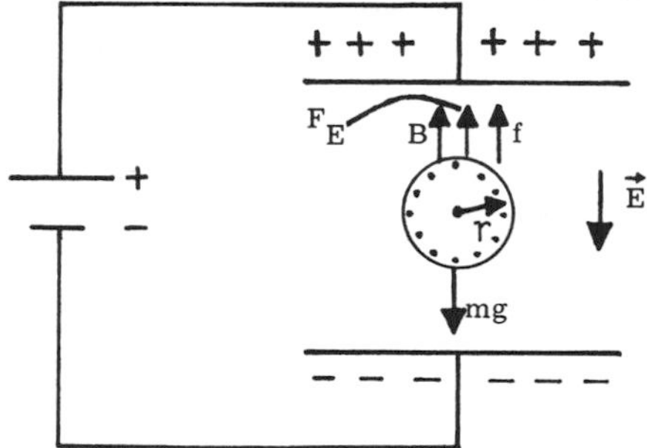

Solution: Between two parallel plates, separated by a distance d and maintained at a difference of potential V, the electric intensity E is E = V/d. The electrostatic force acting on the drop is upward, and of magnitude $F_E = qE = qV/d$. This follows from the defintion of E ($q = 3e^-$). Three other forces are acting on the drop; its weight downward and two upward forces, the viscous retarding force f, due to the surrounding air, and the buoyant upthrust B (see figure). When the terminal velocity is achieved, the forces balance, by definition of terminal velocity. The magnitude of the viscous retarding force is given by Stoke's law: $f = 6\pi\eta rv$. r is the radius of the drop, ρ its density, η the viscosity of air and v its terminal velocity. The buoyant force is equal to the weight of air displaced by the drop (Archimede's principle).

The volume of the (spherical) drop is $4/3\ \pi r^3$ and the density of air is σ. The weight of the displaced air (equal to B) is then $(4/3\pi r^3)\sigma g = B$. The weight of the drop is $W = mg = (4/3\pi r^3)\rho g$, where ρ is oil's density. Therefore

$$W = B + f + F_E$$

$$\frac{4}{3}\pi r^3 \rho g = \frac{4}{3}\pi r^3 \sigma g + 6\pi\eta r v + \frac{qV}{d}, \qquad (1)$$

Hence,

$$v = \frac{\frac{4}{3}\pi r^3 g(\rho - \sigma) - (qV/d)}{6\pi\eta r}$$

$$= \frac{\frac{4}{3}\pi \times 10^{-18} m^3 \times 9.8\ m\cdot s^{-2}(800-1.29)kg\cdot m^{-3} - \frac{3\times 1.6\times 10^{-19}C\times 10^3 V}{0.02\ m}}{6\pi \times 1.80 \times 10^{-5}\ N\cdot s\cdot m^{-2} \times 10^{-6}\ m}$$

$$= \frac{(3.27 - 2.40) \times 10^{-14}}{3.40 \times 10^{-10}}\ m\cdot s^{-1} = 2.56 \times 10^{-5}\ m\cdot s^{-1}.$$

In the classical Millikan oil drop experiment, the same set up is used to determine the electronic charge. A microscope is used to find the terminal velocity v of the drop. Equation (1) is then used to solve for q.

• PROBLEM 640

An instrument that has been used to measure atomic masses with great accuracy is the 180° mass spectrometer shown in the figure. Ionized atoms from a source pass through a potential difference and enter a region in which there is a uniform magnetic field B. The magnetic force acts at right angles to the direction of the velocity vector and causes the ions to move along a circular path. After completing one-half revolution (180°), the ions strike a detector, usually a photographic film. (a) Show that the charge/mass ratio, q/m, of these ions is given by

$$\frac{q}{m} = \frac{v}{BR}$$

where v is the speed of the ions, B the magnetic field strength, and R the orbit radius. (b) In an experiment the orbit radius is observed to be 0.2 m for singly ionized atoms of speed 2.1×10^5 m/s in a magnetic field of 0.13 T. What is the charge/mass ratio of these ions? (c) What is the mass of these atoms?

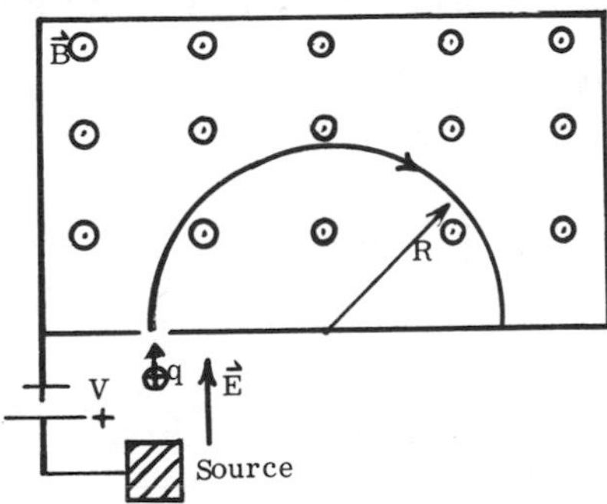

Solution: (a) For circular motion the centripetal acceleration is

$$a = \frac{v^2}{R}.$$

Newton's second law of motion requires that the force exerted on the ion be

$$F = ma = m\frac{v^2}{R}.$$

The magnitudes of the electric potential and magnetic fields determine the value of q/m for protons. The charge of the proton, $q = 1.6 \times 10^{-19}C$, is known; therefore, the mass may be computed as follows: An ion of charge q is accelerated through a potential difference V. It attains a velocity given by

$$\frac{1}{2}mv^2 = Vq$$

since the potential energy of the ion at the source is Vq with respect to the inlet of the magnetic deflection area. The deflecting force on the charge due to the magnetic field is

$$F = qvB$$

$$= m\frac{v^2}{R} \quad \text{(by Newton's second law) giving}$$

$$v = \frac{qBR}{m}.$$

Therefore the ratio $\frac{q}{m}$ for the spectrometer is,

$$\frac{q}{m} = \frac{v}{BR}.$$

The value of q/m for protons from this type of experiment is approximately $9.57 \times 10^7 C/kg$. We find that for the proton

$$\frac{q}{m} = 9.57 \times 10^7 C/kg \quad \text{but } q = 1.6 \times 10^{-19}C$$

$$m = \frac{1.6 \times 10^{-19}\not{C}}{9.57 \times 10^7 \not{C}/kg} = 1.67 \times 10^{-27}kg.$$

(b) The given quantities are $v = 2.1 \times 10^5$ m/s, $B = 0.13$ T, and $R = 0.2$ m.

The charge/mass ratio for these ions is found to be

$$\frac{q}{m} = \frac{2.1 \times 10^5 \not{m}/s}{(1.3 \times 10^{-1}T)(2 \times 10^{-1}\not{m})} = 8.1 \times 10^6 C/kg.$$

(c) The charge q of the ions is $1.6 \times 10^{-19}C$; therefore, the mass is given by

$$m = \frac{q}{q/m} = \frac{1.6 \times 10^{-19}\not{C}}{8.1 \times 10^6 \not{C}/kg} = 2.0 \times 10^{-26}kg.$$

CHAPTER 20

ELECTRIC CIRCUITS

D. C. CIRCUIT ELEMENTS & INSTRUMENTS

• PROBLEM 641

What is the resistance of a piece of nichrome wire 225 centimeters long with a cross-sectional area of 0.015 square centimeter?

Solution: To solve this problem we use the relation

$$R = \rho \frac{L}{A}$$

Where R = resistance, ρ = resistivity, L = wire length, A = cross sectional area

This basic relationship tells us that resistance is directly proportional to resistivity and length and inversely proportional to cross sectional area. In the case of a wire this means that the resistance depends on the nature of the substance (which appears in the equation as the resistivity), that the resistance increases as the wire gets longer and decreases as the wire gets thicker.

The resistivity (ρ) for nichrome is 100×10^{-6} ohm-centimeter. The length is 225 centimeters, and the area is 0.015 square centimeter.

Then $$R = \frac{10^{-4} \text{ ohm-cm} \times 225 \text{ cm}}{0.015 \text{ cm}^2} = 1.5 \text{ ohms.}$$

• PROBLEM 642

In order to find how much insulated wire he has left on a bobbin, a scientist measures the total resistance of the wire, finding it to be 5.18 Ω. He then cuts off a 200-cm length and finds the resistance of this to be 0.35 Ω. What was initially the length of wire on the bobbin?

Solution: The resistance of the wire on the bobbin is related to its length by the formula $R_0 = \rho\ell_0/A$. That is, the resistance is directly proportional to the length (ℓ_0) of the resistor and inversely proportional to the cross-sectional area A of the resistor. ρ is a constant of proportionality (the resistivity). The cut-off length has the same resistivity and cross-sectional area. Hence its resistance is $R = \rho\ell/A$.

$$\therefore \quad \frac{\ell_0}{\ell} = \frac{R_0}{R} \quad \text{or} \quad \ell_0 = 200 \text{ cm} \times \frac{5.18\ \Omega}{0.35\ \Omega} = 2960 \text{ cm.}$$

• **PROBLEM 643**

Find the current through the filament of a light bulb with a resistance of 240 ohms when a voltage of 120 volts is applied to the lamp.

Solution: Since we wish to find the current, we use Ohm's Law in the form

$$I = \frac{E}{R} .$$

$$E = 120 \text{ volts}, \qquad R = 240 \text{ ohms}$$

Therefore

$$I = \frac{120 \text{ volts}}{240 \text{ ohms}} = 0.5 \text{ ampere.}$$

• **PROBLEM 644**

What is the resistance of an electric toaster if it takes a current of 5 amperes when connected to a 120-volt circuit?

Solution: This is an application of Ohm's law. Since we wish to find the resistance, we use

$$R = \frac{E}{I} .$$

$$E = 120 \text{ volts}, \quad I = 5 \text{ amperes}$$

Therefore

$$R = \frac{120 \text{ volts}}{5 \text{ amperes}} = 24 \text{ ohms}$$

• **PROBLEM 645**

What voltage will send a current of 2 amperes through a bell circuit if the resistance of the circuit is 3 ohms?

Solution: Since we wish to find the voltage, we use Ohm's Law in the form $E = IR$.

$$I = 2 \text{ amperes}, \qquad R = 3 \text{ ohms}$$

Therefore

$$E = 2 \text{ amperes} \times 3 \text{ ohm} = 6 \text{ volts.}$$

• **PROBLEM 646**

The difference of potential V_1 between the terminals of a resistor is 120 volts when there is a current I_1 of 8.00 amp in the resistor. What current will be maintained in the resistor if the difference of potential is increased to 180 volts?

Solution: Ohm's law indicates that the resistance R will remain the same when the potential difference is increased; hence we can write

$$R = \frac{V_1}{I_1} = \frac{120 \text{ volts}}{8.00 \text{ amp}} = 15.0 \text{ ohms}$$

$$I_2 = \frac{V_2}{R} = \frac{180 \text{ volts}}{15.0 \text{ ohms}} = 12.0 \text{ amp.}$$

• PROBLEM 647

How much heat is produced in 5 minutes by an electric iron which draws 5 amperes from a 120-volt line?

Solution: Work is given in joules by

$$W = EIt$$

To convert this to units of heat (calories) we use the conversion factor of 0.239 $\frac{\text{calorie}}{\text{joule}}$. This gives us

$$H = \left(0.239 \frac{\text{calorie}}{\text{joule}}\right) EIt$$

$$E = 120 \text{ volts,} \qquad I = 5 \text{ amperes}$$

$$t = 5 \text{ minutes} = 300 \text{ seconds}$$

$$H = \left(0.239 \frac{\text{calorie}}{\text{joule}}\right) \times 120 \text{ volts}$$

$$\times 5 \text{ amperes} \times 300 \text{ seconds}$$

$$= 43{,}000 \text{ calories approximately.}$$

• PROBLEM 648

A battery of 50 cells is being charged from a dc supply of 230 V and negligible internal resistance. The emf of each cell on charge is 2.3 V, its internal resistance is 0.1 Ω and the necessary charging current is 6 A. What extra resistance must be inserted in the circuit?

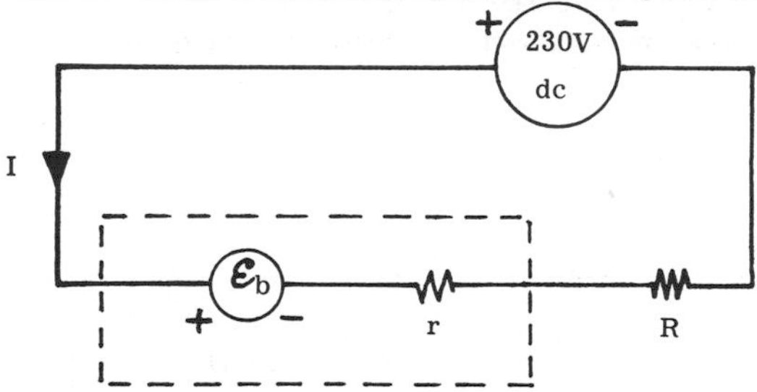

Solution: Let R be the extra resistance needed in the circuit. The 50 cells have a total emf of 50 cells × 2.3 V/cell = 115 V and a total internal resistance of 50 cells × 0.1Ω/cell = 5 Ω. Let us then represent the battery by an emf source $\mathcal{E}_b$ in series with a resistance r. Since the battery is being charged, its polarity will be in the direction opposite to that of the dc supply source. The net emf $\mathcal{E}$ of the circuit is then the difference between the 230 volt dc supply voltage and $\mathcal{E}_b$ = 115 V. The charging current I = 6 A. We apply Ohm's law $\mathcal{E} = I(R + r)$ to obtain

$$(230 - 115)\text{V} = 6\ \text{A}(R + 5\Omega).$$

$$\therefore \quad R = \frac{115\ \text{V}}{6\ \text{A}} - 5\ \Omega = 14.2\ \Omega.$$

• PROBLEM 649

The voltage across the terminals of a resistor is 6.0 volts and an ammeter connected as in the diagram reads 1.5 amp. (a) What is the resistance of the resistor? (b) What would the current be if the potential difference were raised to 8.0 volts?

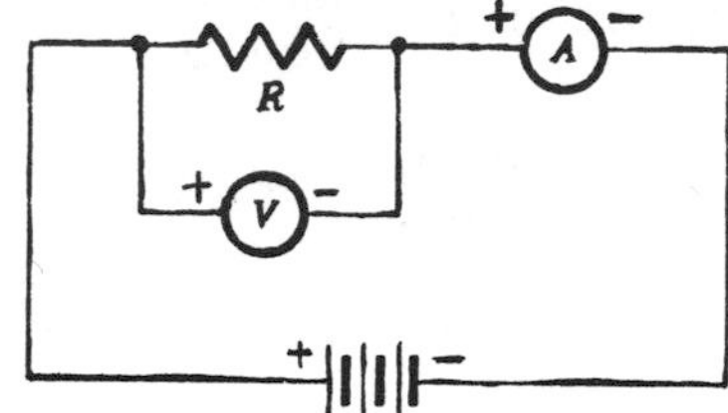

Solution:

$$\text{(a)} \quad R = \frac{V}{I} = \frac{6.0\ \text{volts}}{1.5\ \text{amp}} = 4.0\ \text{ohms}$$

$$\text{(b)} \quad I = \frac{V}{R} = \frac{8.0\ \text{volts}}{4.0\ \text{ohms}} = 2.0\ \text{amp.}$$

In part a of this solution we have used merely the definition of resistance. But in part b we have used Ohm's law, that is, the fact that R is constant.

• PROBLEM 650

If the cost of electricity is 5 cents per kilowatt-hour, what does it cost to run a motor 2 hours if the motor draws 5 amperes from a 120-volt line?

Solution:

$$E = 120\ \text{volts}, \quad I = 5\ \text{amp}, \quad t = 2\ \text{hours}$$

$$\text{Work} = \text{Power} \times \text{Time} = EI \times t$$

$$W = EIt = 120\ \text{volts} \times 5\ \text{amp} \times 2\ \text{hr}$$

$$= 1200\ \text{watt-hours} = 1.2\ \text{kw-hr}$$

This is the work done by the motor in the given time period. Multiplying this by the cost per hour we have:

$$\text{Cost} = 1.2\ \text{kw-hr} \times 5¢/\text{kw-hr} = 6¢.$$

• PROBLEM 651

Two conductors of the same length and material but of different cross-sectional area are connected (a) in series, and (b) in parallel. When a potential difference is applied across the combinations, in which conductor will the heating be greater in each case?

Solution: The resistance of each conductor has the form $R = \rho \ell / A$. That is, R is directly proportional to the length of the conductor and inversely proportional to the cross-sectional area of the conductor. ρ is the constant of proportionality (the resistivity). Since the resistivity and length are the same in each case then $R_1 = \rho\ \ell/A_1$ and $R_2 = \rho\ \ell/A_2$ or $R_1/R_2 = A_2/A_1$.

(a) When the conductors are in series, the same current passes through each, by definition of a series connection. Hence, the ratio of the heating produced (or the power developed) in the wires is

$$\frac{H_1}{H_2} = \frac{i^2 R_1}{i^2 R_2} = \frac{R_1}{R_2} = \frac{A_2}{A_1} .$$

The heating is thus greater in the conductor with the smaller cross-sectional area.

(b) When the conductors are in parallel, different currents pass through them but the potential difference across each is the same, by definition of a parallel connection. Hence,

$$\frac{H_1'}{H_2'} = \frac{V^2/R_1}{V^2/R_2} = \frac{R_2}{R_1} = \frac{A_1}{A_2} .$$

We made use of the alternate form of power development, $P = IV = I^2R = V^2/R$.

In this case, the heating is greater in the conductor with the larger cross-sectional area.

• PROBLEM 652

A car battery supplies a current I of 50 amp to the starter motor. How much charge passes through the starter in ½ min?

Solution: Current (I) is defined as the net amount of charge, Q, passing a point per unit time. Therefore,

$$Q = It = (50 \text{ amp})(30 \text{ sec}) = 1500 \text{ coul.}$$

• PROBLEM 653

An automobile battery produces a potential difference (or "voltage") of 12 volts between its terminals. (It really consists of six 2 volt batteries following one after the other.) A headlight bulb is to be connected directly across the terminals of the battery and dissipate 40 watts of joule heat. What current will it draw and what must its resistance be?

Solution. To find the current, we use the formula P = IV where P is the power dissipated (40 watts), I is the current, and V is the voltage.

Therefore,

$$I = \frac{P}{V} = \frac{40 \text{ watts}}{12 \text{ volts}} = \frac{40 \text{ joules/sec}}{12 \text{ joules/coulomb}} = 3.33 \text{ coulombs/sec}$$

$$= 3.33 \text{ amps.}$$

The bulb draws 3.33 amps from the battery.

From Ohm's law

$$i = \frac{V}{R}$$

$$R = \frac{V}{i}$$

$$R \text{ ohms} = \frac{12 \text{ volts}}{3.33 \text{ amps}}$$

$$R = 3.6 \text{ ohms.}$$

The resistance of the bulb must be 3.6 ohms.

We may also compute the resistance using the formula

$$P = \frac{V^2}{R}. \quad \text{Therefore } R = \frac{V^2}{P} = \frac{(12)^2}{40} = 3.6 \text{ ohms.}$$

This second formula for power may be obtained from the first as follows:

$$P = iV$$

but from Ohm's Law $i = \frac{V}{R}$. Therefore $P = \frac{(V)(V)}{R} = \frac{V^2}{R}$.

• PROBLEM 654

An electric kettle contains 2 liters of water which it heats from 20°C to boiling point in 5 min. The supply voltage is 200 V and a kWh (kilowatt-hour) unit costs 2 cents. Calculate (a) the power consumed (assume that heat losses are negligible), (b) the cost of using the kettle under these conditions six times, (c) the resistance of the heating element, and (d) the current in the element.

Solution: The heat gained by the water in being raised to the boiling point is given by the expression $H = mc(t_2 - t_1)$ where c is the specific heat of water (the amount of heat required to raise the temperature of the substance 1°C), m is the mass of the water being heated and $(t_2 - t_1)$ is the temperature difference before and after heating.

(a) $$H = 2 \times 10^3 \text{ cm}^3 \times 1 \text{ g}\cdot\text{cm}^{-3} \times 4.18 \text{ J}\cdot\text{g}^{-1}\cdot\text{C deg}^{-1}$$

$$\times (100 - 20)\text{C deg} = 6.69 \times 10^5 \text{ J.}$$

Since heat losses are neglected, the conservation of energy requires that the heat energy generated be equal to the electrical energy consumed by the kettle.

Thus the electric energy $E = 6.69 \times 10^5$ J.

The power is the energy consumed per second, which is thus

$$P = \frac{H}{\tau} = \frac{6.69 \times 10^5 \text{ J}}{5 \times 60 \text{ s}} = 2.23 \times 10^3 \text{ J}\cdot\text{s}^{-1}$$

$$= 2.23 \text{ kW.} \qquad \left(\text{for IW} = 1 \text{ J}\cdot\text{s}^{-1}.\right)$$

(b) The kettle uses 2.23 kW for 5 min each time the water is boiled. When it is used six times, 2.23 kW is used for 30 min = ½ hr. The cost is thus

$$2.23 \text{ kW} \times \tfrac{1}{2} \text{ hr} \times 2 \text{ cents} \cdot \text{kWh}^{-1} = 2.23 \text{ cents.}$$

(c) The power P consumed is 2.23 kW and the supply voltage V is 200 V. But $P = V^2/R$, where R is the resistance of the kettle's heating element.

$$R = \frac{V^2}{P} = \frac{200^2 V^2}{2.23 \times 10^3 \text{ W}} = 17.9 \ \Omega.$$

(d) But one may also write the power as $P = IV$, where I is the current through the heating element.

$$I = \frac{P}{V} = \frac{2.23 \times 10^3 \text{ W}}{200 \text{ V}} = 11.2 \text{ A.}$$

• PROBLEM 655

A variable resistor in series with a 2-V cell and an ammeter is adjusted to give a full-scale deflection on the meter, which occurs for a curent of 1 mA. What resistance placed in series in the circuit will reduce the meter readings by 1/f?

The meter is calibrated to measure resistance on this basis, but the emf of the cell drops by 5% and the variable resistor is readjusted so that the full-scale deflection again corresponds to the zero of the resistance scale. What percentage error is now given on a resistor which has a true resistance of 3800 Ω?

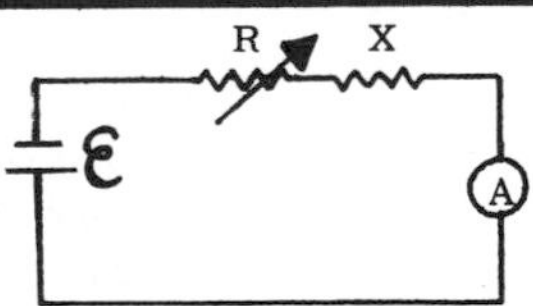

Solution: The total resistance in the circuit when the meter is giving full-scale deflection is

$$R = \frac{\mathcal{E}}{I} = \frac{2 \text{ V}}{10^{-3} \text{ A}} = 2000 \ \Omega,$$

for we are given that full scale deflection on the ammeter occurs for a current of $1 \text{ mA} = 1 \times 10^{-3}$ A.

If an unknown resistance X is added to the circuit and produces a meter reading of (1/f) mA, then

$$R + X = \frac{2\ V}{(1/f) \times 10^{-3}\ A} = 2000\ f\ \Omega.$$

$$\therefore\quad X = (2000f - 2000)\Omega = 2000(f - 1)\Omega. \qquad (1)$$

The emf of the cell now drops to 95/100 (= 95%) of 2 V = 1.9 V. Alternatively since we are given that the emf of the cell drops by 5%, then the emf loss is 5/100 of 2 V = .1 V. The new emf is now 2V - .1 V = 1.9 V. For full-scale deflection the resistance in the circuit is now

$$R' = \frac{1.9\ V}{10^{-3}\ A} = 1900\ \Omega,$$

and if a further resistance of 3800 Ω is inserted in the circuit, the current is 1.9 V/(1900 + 3800)Ω = 1/3 mA.

But from the meter calibration, when the current drops to one-third of its value (i.e. the meter reading is reduced by 1/f = 1/3, or f = 3) the inserted resistance should have a value given by (1)

$$X = [2000(3 - 1)]\Omega = 4000\ \Omega.$$

The error in the reading is thus (4000 - 3800)Ω = 200 Ω, and the percentage error is

$$\frac{200}{3800} \times 100\% = 5.3\%.$$

• PROBLEM 656

A 12-V automobile battery supplies 20C of charge in 5 s to a stereo tape player. What is the electrical current flowing into the device and how much work is done by the battery.

Solution: The charge supplied by the battery, q = 20 C, and the time interval, t = 5 s, are given. The current is, by definition,

$$I = \frac{q}{t} = \frac{20\ C}{5\ s} = 4\ A$$

The potential of the battery, V = 12 V, is also given. However, the potential difference between two points is the work required to move a unit charge from the point at lower potential to that of higher potential. Or

$$V = \frac{W}{q}$$

Then $\quad W = Vq = (12\ V)(20\ C) = 2.4 \times 10^2\ J$

The work done by the automobile battery is 240 J.

• **PROBLEM 657**

A dynamo driven by a steam engine which uses 10^3 kg of coal per day produces a current I = 200 A at an emf V of 240 V. What is the efficiency of the system if the calorific value of coal is $6.6 \times 10^3\ \text{cal}\cdot\text{g}^{-1}$?

Solution: The energy supplied by the coal per second is equal to the product of the calorific value of coal and the mass of coal used, divided by the time it takes to burn the coal. Hence,

$$E_0 = \frac{6.6 \times 10^3\ \text{cal}\cdot\text{g}^{-1} \times 10^6\ \text{g}}{24 \times 60 \times 60\ \text{s}} = \frac{4.2 \times 6.6 \times 10^9}{24 \times 60 \times 60}\ \text{J}\cdot\text{s}^{-1}$$

$$= 3.2 \times 10^5\ \text{W}.$$

The electric power supplied by the dynamo is

$$P = IV = 200\ \text{A} \times 240\ \text{V} = 4.8 \times 10^4\ \text{W}$$

The efficiency of the system is thus

$$\frac{P}{E_0} \times 100\% = \frac{4.8 \times 10^4}{3.2 \times 10^5}\ \% = 15\%.$$

• **PROBLEM 658**

The variable capacitor in the figure is connected to a battery of e.m.f. V and internal resistance r. The current in the circuit is kept constant by changing the capacitance. (Assume that we are able to increase the capacitance indefinitely in order to accomplish this).

a) Calculate the power supplied by the battery.

b) Compare the rate at which energy is supplied by the battery with the rate of change of the energy stored in the capacitor.

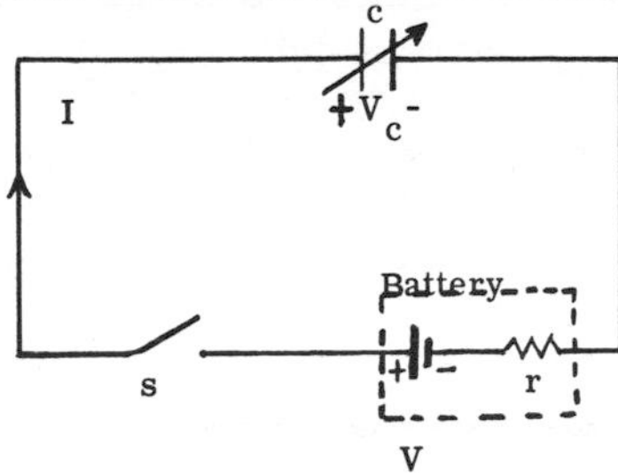

Solution: a) The current in the circuit is related to the voltage across the capacitor as

$$C\,\frac{dV_c}{dt} = I$$

As the capacitor charges up, V_c rises toward its limiting value and its rate of change goes to zero. Therefore, in order to keep I constant, capacitance, C, should compensate for this drop in $\frac{dV_c}{dt}$ (observe that, as time $t \to \infty$, $\frac{dV_c}{dt} \to 0$ and we should have $C_\infty \to \infty$). Ignoring the practical difficulties of maintaining a constant I, asymptotically we have a continuous charge flow in the circuit

$$\frac{dq}{dt} = I,$$

and
$$V_c = V.$$

The battery supplies a constant power since its e.m.f. is constant,

$$P_B = VI.$$

b) The capacitor is being continuously charged. Once the voltage across the capacitor stabilizes at $t \to \infty$, we have

$$V = Ir + V_{c,\infty}$$

or
$$V_{c,\infty} = V - Ir.$$

The energy stored in the capacitor becomes

$$W = \frac{1}{2} q_\infty V_{c,\infty}$$

$$= \frac{1}{2} q_\infty (V - Ir).$$

The rate of change of W with time is

$$P_c = \frac{dE}{dt} = \frac{1}{2} \frac{dq_\infty}{dt} V_{c,\infty} = \frac{1}{2} I (V - Ir)$$

The rate of dissipation of energy in the resistor r is

$$P_r = Ir,$$

Therefore the power supplied directly to the capacitor is

$$P = P_B - P_r = IV - I^2r = I(V - Ir),$$

which is twice as large as that used in charging the capacitor:

$$P = 2P_c.$$

The battery supplies twice as much energy to the capacitor as is stored in the capacitor. The difference is the work done by the capacitor against the external agent that is changing the capacitance.

• PROBLEM 659

Explain how a diode may be used to convert alternating current (AC) into direct current (DC).

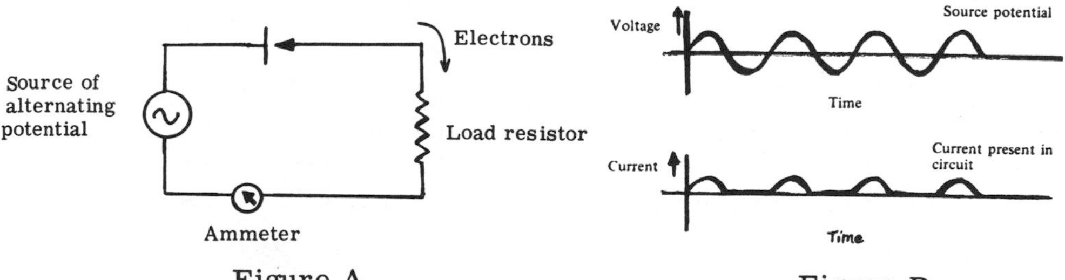

Figure A

Figure B

Solution: Figure (a) shows the arrangement of an AC generator, the diode, and the resistive load represented by a resistor R through which a direct current flows. The polarity of the generator terminals reverses twice during each cycle. (See figure (b), voltage diagram). When the generator lead connected to the negative terminal of the diode is negatively charged, the diode is forward biased and electrons readily flow through the diode, the resistor, and back to the positive terminal of the generator. One half-cycle later, the polarity of the generator lead connected to the negative terminal is positive, the diode is reverse biased, and the current through the diode is essentially zero. The current through the resistor will vary like the voltage does during the half-cycle that conduction occurs in the diode, so the current will change as indicated in figure (b).

• PROBLEM 660

The coil of a galvanometer has 150 turns of mean area 1 cm^2 and the restoring couple of the suspension is 10^{-6} N•m per radian. The magnitude of the radial magnetic induction in which the coil swings is 0.2 Wb•m^{-2}. What deflection will be produced when a current of 10 μA passes through the coil?

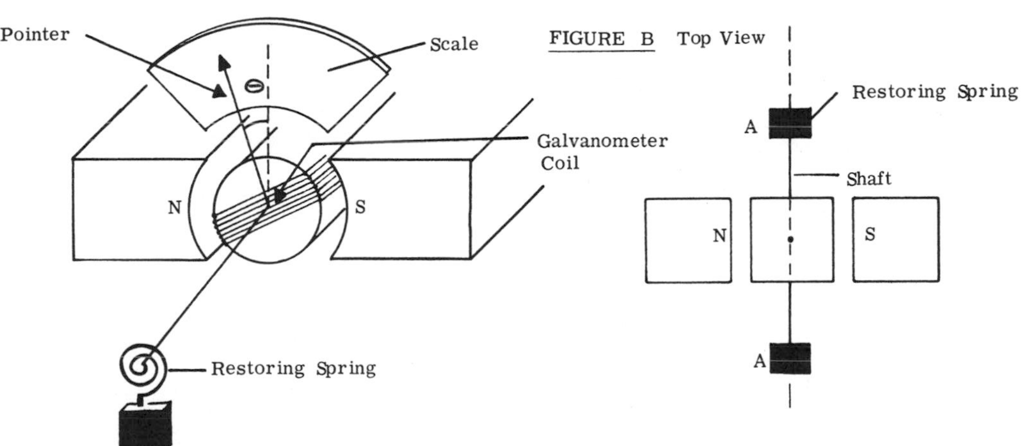

Solution: Our first task is to relate the deflection of the galvanometer coil (measured by the angle θ in figure (a)) to the coil characteristics. Before we do this, we briefly review the method of operation of a galvanometer.

The coil of the galvanometer is wrapped around a cylindrical form. The shaft of this form (figure (a)) is mechanically connected to two restoring coil springs, present at supports A (figure (b)). The entire coil apparatus is placed between the poles of a permanent magnet. When no current passes through the coil, it is in equilibrium between the poles, as shown by the dotted line in figure (a). Now, any current carrying coil possesses a magnetic moment $\vec{\mu}$. If the current passes through the coil from left to right in figure (a), $\vec{\mu}$ will be in the direction of the pointer. However, a magnetic moment in a field of magnetic induction $\vec{B}$ will experience a torque $\vec{T}$ given by

$$\vec{T} = \vec{\mu} \times \vec{B} \tag{1}$$

Since the field lines of $\vec{B}$ are radial, the coil will rotate about the form axis. Since the shaft of the form is attached to restoring springs, the motion of the coil will not be unimpeded, and it will tend to return to its equilibrium position. We now show that θ is related to the current I flowing in the coil.

From (1), the magnitude of the torque experienced by the coil due to $\vec{B}$ is

$$T = \mu B \sin \phi \tag{2}$$

where ϕ is the angle between $\vec{\mu}$ and $\vec{B}$. When the coil has attained its maximum deflection, it **will** rotate no more.

Hence, the torque in (2) will then equal the restoring torque due to the springs. This latter torque is given by

$$T' = -k\theta \tag{3}$$

where k is the torsional constant of the spring. At θ_{max}, the net torque is zero, and

$$T + T' = 0$$

or $$k\,\theta_{max} = \mu B \sin 90° = \mu B$$

Now, for a planar coil $\mu = nIA$

where n is the number of turns the coil has, and A is its cross-sectional area. Hence

$$k\,\theta_{max} = nIAB \qquad \text{or} \qquad \theta_{max} = \frac{nIAB}{k}$$

We see that the maximum coil deflection is related to the current it carries. We may therefore use the galvanometer as the basis of a current-measuring device. In our case,

$$\theta_{max} = \frac{150 \times 10^{-4}\ m^2 \times 10^{-5}\ A \times 0.2\ Wb\cdot m^{-2}}{10^{-6}\ N\cdot m}$$

$$= 0.03 \text{ rad.}$$

RESISTANCE - TEMPERATURE CHARACTERISTICS

• PROBLEM 661

The cross-sectional area of the copper wire used in a household wiring system is approximately 3 mm^2 = $3 \times 10^{-6}\ m^2$. Find the resistance of a copper wire 10 m long, at 20°C, if the resistivity of copper is 1.72×10^{-8} ohm. m.

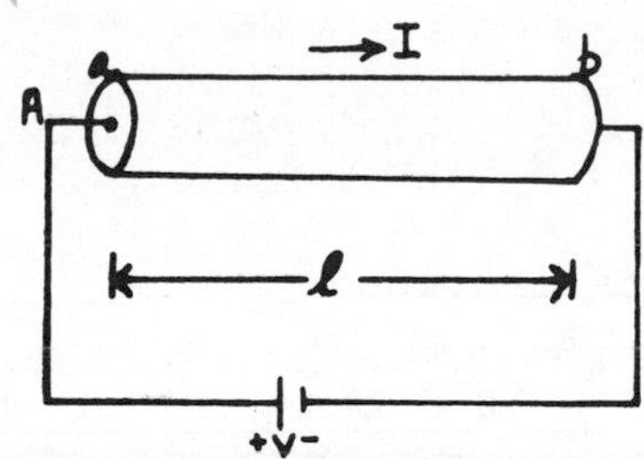

<u>Solution:</u> The resistivity ρ of an isotropic material is defined as the ratio of the electric field E it is placed in and the current density J flowing through it as a result of this electric field:

$$\rho = \frac{E\ \frac{\text{volts}}{\text{m}}}{J\ \frac{\text{amp.}}{\text{m}^2}} = \frac{E}{J}\ \frac{\text{ohms}}{\text{m}} \qquad (1)$$

As in the figure, we take the wire to be a cylindrical conductor and apply a voltage across the ends. A finite current I and a non-zero electric field will be set up in the wire since we have an imperfect conductor ($\rho \neq 0$). The cross-sections at each end are small enough to be assumed to be equipotential surfaces. By definition,

$$V_b - V_a = -\int_a^b \vec{E} \cdot d\vec{\ell} \qquad (2)$$

and

$$I = \int \vec{J} \cdot d\vec{S} \qquad (3)$$

where $\vec{E}$ and $\vec{J}$ are the electric field intensity and curent density, respectively. In this case, $\vec{E}$ is parallel to the axis of the wire, and if we evaluate (1) along a path parallel to the axis of the wire, we obtain

$$V_b - V_a = E\ell \qquad (4)$$

Similarly, $\vec{J}$ is parallel to the axis of the wire, and (3) may be evaluated. Hence,

$$I = JA \qquad (5)$$

Using (4) and (5) in (1), we obtain

$$\rho = \frac{E}{J} = \frac{(V_b - V_a)/\ell}{I/A}$$

$$\rho = \frac{(V_b - V_a)A}{I\ell}$$

But $\frac{V_b - V_a}{I} = R$, by Ohm's Law, where R is the resistance of the wire. Hence

$$\rho = \frac{RA}{\ell}$$

Solving for R, $R = \frac{\rho \ell}{A}$.

Using the data provided

$$R = \frac{(1.72 \times 10^{-8} \text{ ohm} \cdot \text{m})(10 \text{ m})}{(3 \times 10^{-6} \text{ m}^2)}$$

$$R = .057 \text{ ohm.}$$

• PROBLEM 662

The resistance of a copper wire 2500 cm long and 0.090 cm in diameter is 0.67 ohm at 20°C. What is the resistivity of copper at this temperature?

Solution: The resistivity of a conductor is directly proportional to the cross-sectional area A and its resistance, and inversely proportional to its length ℓ. Therefore, knowing the resistance, we have

$$\rho = R\,\frac{A}{\ell} = \frac{0.67 \text{ ohm}}{2500 \text{ cm}}\;\frac{\pi(0.090 \text{ cm})^2}{4}$$

$$= 1.7 \times 10^{-6} \text{ ohm-cm}$$

Resistivity is a characteristic of a material as a whole, rather than of a particular piece of it. For a given temperature, it is constant for the particular medium, as opposed to resistance which depends on the dimensions of the piece.

• PROBLEM 663

A copper coil has a resistance of 100 ohms at 20°C. What is its resistance at 50°C if the temperature coefficient of resistivity for copper is 0.0038 ohm per ohm per degree centigrade?

Solution: We are given the resistance of a wire at one temperature, and are asked to calculate its resistance at another temperature given the temperature coefficient of resistivity. The new resistance is given by the old resistance plus a factor proportional to the old resistance, the temperature change, and the constant coefficient for the substance.

R_{20} = 100 ohms, t = 50°C, α = 0.0038 ohm/ohm/°C.

Using $R_t = R_{20} + R_{20}\,\alpha(t - 20°C)$, we have

$$R_t = 100 \text{ ohms} + 100 \text{ ohms} \times 0.0038 \text{ ohm/ohm/°C } (50°C - 20°C)$$

$$= 100 \text{ ohms} + 11.4 \text{ ohms}$$

$$= 111 \text{ ohms, approximately.}$$

• PROBLEM 664

The total resistance of a wire wound rheostat when "cold" is 300 ohms. In use it experiences a rise in temperature. How does the current which it draws on a 100 volt line after its temperature has risen 50° C, compare with that drawn at the start when it is "cold"?

Solution: This problem involves a combination of Ohm's Law and the dependence of resistance upon temperature.

$$I = \frac{V}{R} \quad \text{(Ohm's Law)}$$

But $R = R_0(1 + \alpha t)$ where α for metals is $.0038/°C$ (approx). That is the resistance of the metal increases at a rate directly proportional to the increase in temperature.

When "cold" $R_1 = 300$ ohms.

$$\therefore I_1 = \frac{V}{R_1} = \frac{100}{300} = .333 \text{ ampere}$$

But when "hot" $R_2 = 300[1 + .0038(50)]$

or $R_2 - 300 = 300(.0038)(50)$

$$= 3 \times 3.8 \times 5 \times 10^0 = 57$$

$$\therefore R_2 = 357$$

And $I_2 = \frac{V}{R_2} = \frac{100}{357} = .280$ ampere

Thus $I_2 = \frac{.280}{.333} I_1 = .84\, I_1$ (approx).

• PROBLEM 665

A silver wire has a resistance of 1.25 ohms at 0°C and a temperature coefficient of resistance of 0.00375/C°. To what temperature must the wire be raised to double the resistance?

Solution: The change in resistance $R_t - R_0$ is directly proportional to the change in temperature and the original resistance R_0. It is known from experiment that

$$\Delta R = \alpha R_0 \Delta t.$$

Substituting values, we have

$$\Delta t = \frac{\Delta R}{\alpha R_0} = \frac{R_t - R_0}{\alpha R_0}$$

$$t - 0°\,C = \frac{(2.50 - 1.25)\text{ ohms}}{0.00375/C° \times 1.25 \text{ ohms}}$$

since $R_t = 2R_0 = 2(1.25) = 2.50$

$$t = 266°C.$$

A wire of diameter 1 mm carrying a heavy current has a temperature of 1200°K when equilibrium has been achieved. We assume that the heat lost from the wire is purely by radiation. The temperature of the surroundings is 300°K, the resistivity of the wire at this temperature is 5×10^{-8} Ω·m, and the temperature coefficient of resistance of the wire is 4×10^{-3} per C deg. What is the magnitude of the current in the wire?

Solution: Since the heat is being lost by radiation only, the energy lost per second by a 1-m length of the wire (i.e. the intensity of radiation emitted by the wire)is given by Stefan's law $W = A\sigma\,(T^4 - T_0^4)$, where A is the surface area of the length of wire and σ is Stefan's constant. The wire is assumed to radiate as a blackbody (i.e. it emits all of the radiation produced by the excited atoms of the wire). T_0 is the wire temperature and T is the ambient temperature.

But this energy is supplied by the current flowing. Thus, if R is resistance of 1 m of the wire, then the energy supplied per second is Power = $I^2R = W = A\sigma\left(T^4 - T_0^4\right)$. But

$$R = \frac{\rho \ell}{A'}$$

where A' is the cross-sectional area, ℓ is the length and ρ is the resistivity of the wire at temperature T. It is related to T by the following relation: $\rho = \rho_0[1 + \alpha(T - T_0)]$, where ρ_0 is the resistivity at 300°K, and α is the temperature coefficient of resistance. Hence

$$R = \frac{\rho_0[1 + \alpha(T - T_0)]\ell}{A'}$$

But, for 1 meter of wire, P = W and

$$I^2 = \frac{A\sigma\left(T^4 - T_0^4\right)}{\dfrac{\rho_0[1 + \alpha(T - T_0)]\ell}{A'}} = \frac{AA'\sigma\left(T^4 - T_0^4\right)}{\rho_0[1 + \alpha(T - T_0)]\ell}$$

$$= \frac{1\text{m}\times 2\pi\times \tfrac{1}{2}\times 10^{-3}\text{m}\times\pi\left(\tfrac{1}{2}\times 10^{-3}\right)^2\text{m}^2\times 5.67\times 10^{-8}\text{W}\cdot\text{m}^{-2}(\text{K deg})^{-4}}{5\times 10^{-8}\Omega\cdot\text{m}[1+4\times 10^{-3}(\text{K deg})^{-1}(1200-300)\text{K deg}]\times 1\text{m}}$$

$$\times\ \left(1200^4 - 300^4\right)(\text{K deg})^4$$

$$= 1258\ \text{A}^2.$$

$$\therefore \qquad I = 35.5\ \text{A}.$$

• PROBLEM 667

Find the total resistance in the circuit in the figure.

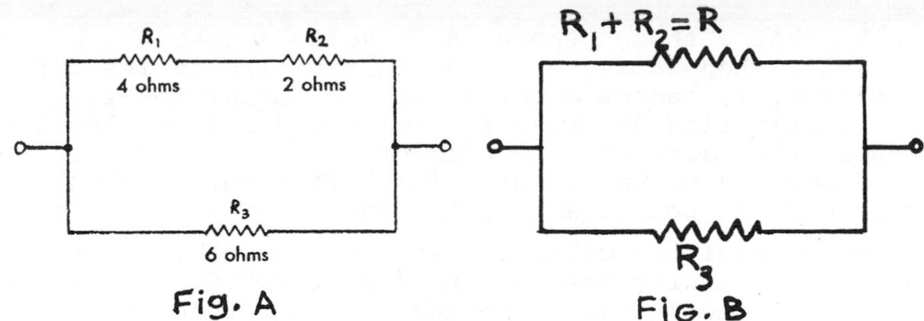

Solution: This problem is simplified by observing that the circuit can be resolved into its component parts. Since resistors R_1 and R_2 are in series, we may take their sum and consider it as a single resistor (see diagram) with resistance R.

Combining the first two resistances,

$$R = R_1 + R_2 = 4 \text{ ohms} + 2 \text{ ohms} = 6 \text{ ohms}$$

Now we have a simple parallel circuit and can easily solve for the total resistance of the circuit. Letting R' be the total resistance of the circuit we obtain:

$$\frac{1}{R'} = \frac{1}{R} + \frac{1}{R_3} = \frac{1}{6 \text{ ohms}} + \frac{1}{6 \text{ ohms}} = \frac{1}{3 \text{ ohms}}$$

whence

$$R' = 3 \text{ ohms.}$$

• PROBLEM 668

Consider the simple circuit in the figure grounded at point b. Compute the potentials of points a and c.

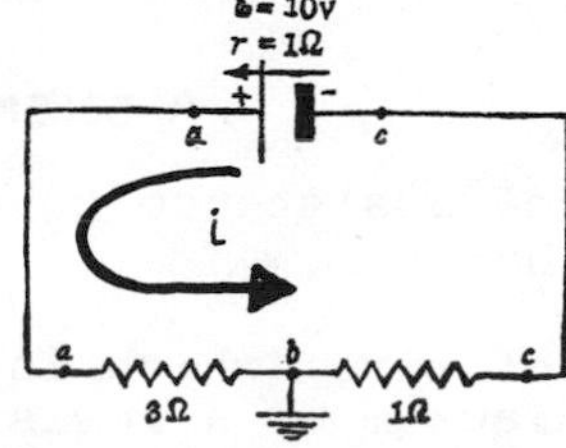

Solution. In this circuit point B is grounded. When dealing with circuits, the grounded point is considered as zero potential and we express potentials relative to this reference level. The direction of current flow is counterclockwise so we will traverse the circuit in this direction. Kirchoff's loop theorem states that the sum of the changes in potential around any closed loop must be equal to zero. Note that this is just a statement of conservation of energy. Applying this theorem gives the following equation:

$$\varepsilon - ir - i(3 \text{ ohms}) - i(1 \text{ ohms}) = 0$$

Observe that although there is 10 volts across the battery by itself, when it is connected to the circuit its internal resistance, r, causes a potential drop equal to -ir.

Substituting 1Ω for r and solving for i, yields 2 amperes as the value for the current.

Since the potential at point b is zero, we start there and proceed to points a or c to find V_a or V_c respectively. We may go in either direction so long as we take into account the proper sign for the current (negative if counterclockwise, positive if clockwise). Proceeding counterclockwise from b to c yields:

$$V_c = -i(1\Omega) = -2 \text{ volts}$$

Proceeding clockwise from b to a and remembering that in this direction the current is -2 amp, we see that $V_a = -(-2)(3) = +6$ volts.

That is, point a is 6 volts above ground and point c is 2 volts below ground. The potential difference V_{ac} can now be found by subtraction

$$V_{ac} = V_a - V_c = 6 -(-2) = +8 \text{ volts}$$

• PROBLEM 669

A bell circuit consists of 150 feet of No. 18 wire which has a resistance of 1 ohm, a bell which has a resistance of 5 ohms, and a battery of two dry cells, each having an emf of 1.5 volts. What is the current through the circuit,assuming that the resistance of the battery is negligible?

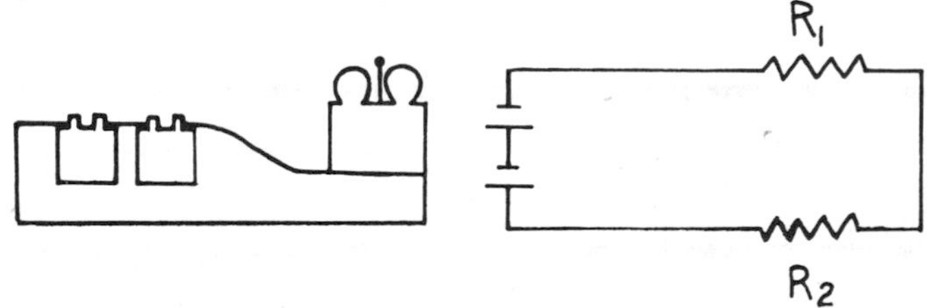

(a) ACTUAL CIRCUIT (b) SCHEMATIC DIAGRAM

Solution: It may be of assistance to draw a diagram (see diagram). Note that

R_1 = resistance of wire (which is represented in the schematic diagram as a resistor in the circuit).

R_2 = resistance of bell in the schematic diagram.

Since the bell and the wire are in series, the total resistance is the sum of 5 ohms and 1 ohm; that is, 6 ohms.

From Ohm's law:

$$I = \frac{E}{R} = \frac{3 \text{ volts}}{6 \text{ ohms}} = 0.5 \text{ amp.}$$

• PROBLEM 670

A galvanometer of resistance 20 Ω gives a full-scale deflection when a current of 1 mA passes through it. What modification must be made to the instrument so that it will give full-scale deflection for (a) a current of 0.5 A, and (b) a potential difference of 500 V?

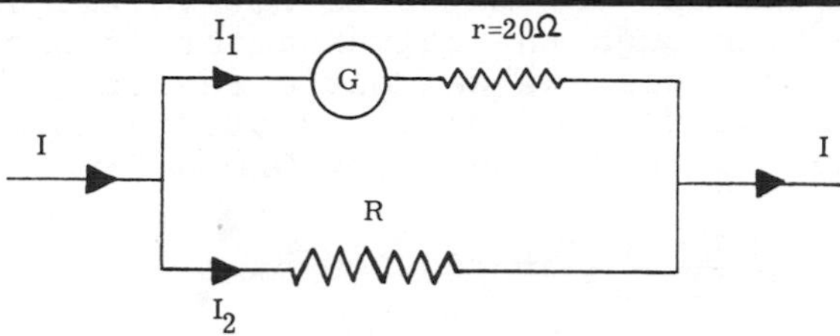

Solution: If a galvanometer has a resistance R of 20 Ω and gives full-scale deflection for a current I of 1 mA, then the voltage drop across it under these circumstances is given by Ohm's Law as

$$V = IR = 10^{-3} \text{ A} \times 20 \ \Omega = 0.02 \text{ V}.$$

(a) If we want a full-scale deflection of the galvanometer for a current of .5 A, we must arrange things so that only 1 mA of this current passes through the galvanometer. Referring to figure (a), a shunt resistor R must be added to the galvanometer. This resistor must take 499 mA, allowing only 1 mA through the galvanometer. But since r and R are in parallel, the potential difference across each is the same. Thus, if R is the resistance of the shunt, then, by Ohm's Law,

$$1 \text{ mA} \times 20 \ \Omega = 499 \text{ mA} \times R$$

$$R = \frac{20 \ \Omega}{499} = 0.0401 \ \Omega.$$

(b) The galvanometer's full-scale deflection occurs when a voltage of .02 V is across the galvanometer resistance. Hence, to convert to a voltmeter reading up to 500 V, one must add a series resistor to the galvanometer. Only 0.02 V is dropped across the galvanometer for the maximum current of 1 mA. Thus 499.98 V must be dropped across the resistor of resistance R. The same current flows through both resistor and galvanometer. Hence, by Ohm's Law

$$R = \frac{499.98 \text{ V}}{10^{-3} \text{ A}} = 499{,}980 \ \Omega.$$

A galvanometer has a resistance of 5 ohms with 100 divisions on its face. Maximum deflection of the meter occurs when the current through it is 2 ma. What series resistance should be used with the galvanometer in order to employ it as a voltmeter of range 0 to 200 volts?

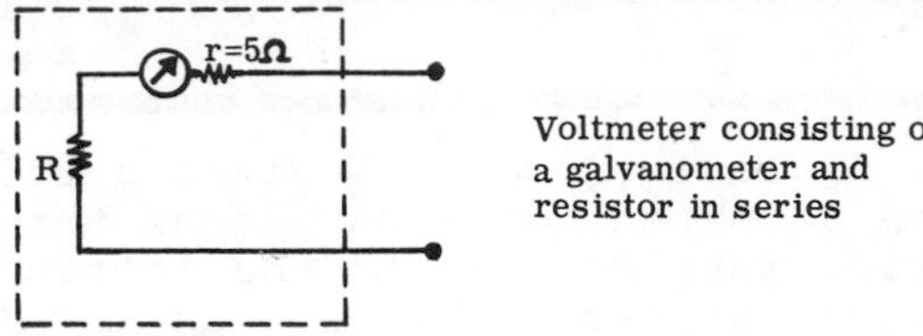

Voltmeter consisting of a galvanometer and resistor in series

Solution: The maximum voltage we need to read is 200 volts. We therefore want maximum deflection to occur when the voltage across the voltmeter is 200 volts. This occurs when the current through the galvanometer is 2ma or 0.002 amp. To accomplish this, we can put a resistor R in series with the galvanometer. The total resistance in the circuit, R + r (see figure), must then be, by Ohm's Law,

$$R + r = \frac{V}{I} = \frac{200 \text{ volts}}{0.002 \text{ amp}} = 100{,}000 \text{ ohms}$$

and $$R = 100{,}000 - 5 = 99{,}995 \text{ ohms}$$

Since the voltage across the terminals is proportional to the current flowing through the galvanometer, each division of the meter corresponds to

$$\frac{200 \text{ volts}}{100 \text{ divisions}} = 2 \text{ volts/division.}$$

• PROBLEM 672

Compute the resistance across the terminals in figure A.

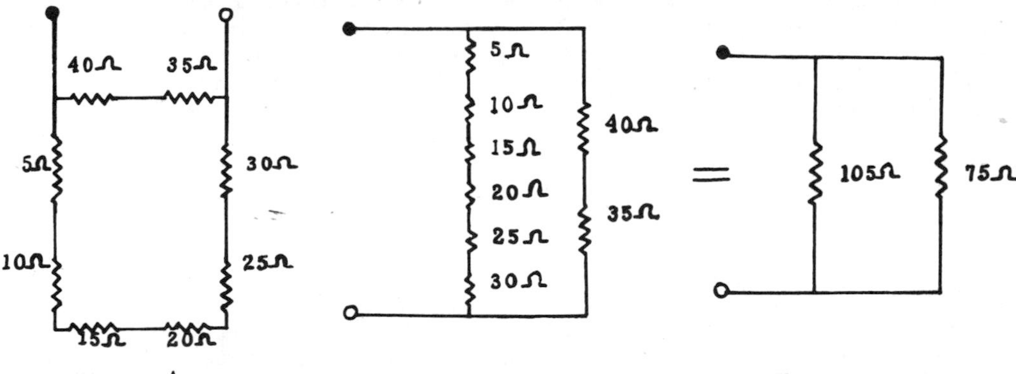

Figure A Figure B Figure C

Solution: First we regroup the resistors to simplify our calculations. We are allowed to do this as long as we do not change the orientation of the resistors with respect to each other and to the terminals. An equivalent arrangement is shown in figure B.

In figure C we sum the resistors in series. We are left with two resistances in parallel which we find from the formula:

$$\frac{1}{R_T} = \frac{1}{R_1} + \frac{1}{R_2} = \frac{1}{105} + \frac{1}{75} = \frac{12}{525} = \frac{4}{173}$$

where R_T is the total resistance across the terminals. Thus:

$$R_T = \frac{173}{4} = 43.25$$

• PROBLEM 673

In the figure $\mathcal{E}_1 = 12$ volts, $r_1 = 0.2$ ohm; $\mathcal{E}_2 = 6$ volts, $r_2 = 0.1$ ohm; $R_3 = 1.4$ ohms; $R_4 = 2.3$ ohms; compute (a) the current in the circuit, in magnitude and direction, and (b) the potential difference V_{ac}.

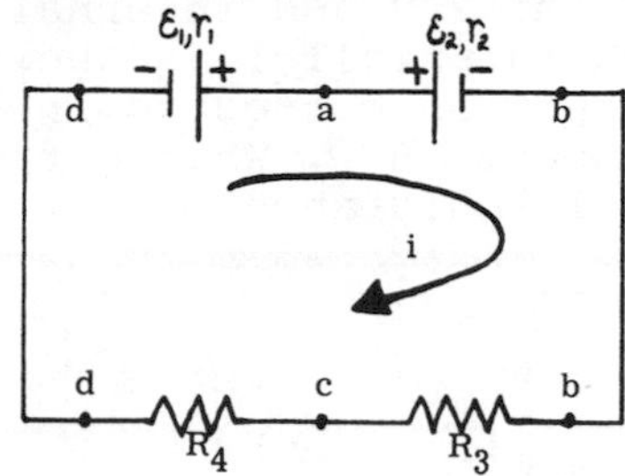

Solution: (a) From conservation of energy we know that the sum of the changes in potential (voltage changes) around any closed loop must equal zero. Therefore the current (which is conventionally taken as the flow of positive charge) is in a clockwise direction because $\varepsilon_1 > \varepsilon_2$; but let us choose it as going counterclockwise to show that it doesn't make any difference. Note that each battery has an internal resistance. Starting at point A and traversing counterclockwise yields the following equation:

$$-\varepsilon_1 - ir_1 - iR_4 - iR_3 - ir_2 + \varepsilon_2 = 0$$

$$i(r_1 + r_2 + R_3 + R_4) = \varepsilon_2 - \varepsilon_1$$

$$i = \frac{\varepsilon_2 - \varepsilon_1}{(r_1+r_2+R_3+R_4)} = \frac{-6}{4}$$

$$= -1.5 \text{ amp.}$$

The negative value for the current merely means that we chose the wrong direction (i.e., the current flows clockwise)

(b) We may use either a clockwise or counterclockwise path from point A to point C to find V_{AC}. Since we are only concerned with differences in potential, let us assume a zero potential of A and then traverse the loop clockwise from A to C. Taking into account the clockwise flow of current this yields,

$$-\varepsilon_2 - ir_2 - iR_3 = -6 - (1.5)(.1) - (1.5)(1.4)$$

$$= -8.25 \text{ volts}$$

This means that the potential is 8.25 volts lower at point C than at point A. If we go from point A to point C in a counterclockwise direction we must remember to use the negative value for the current. This path yields:

$$-\varepsilon_1 - ir_1 - iR_4 = -12 - (-1.5)(.2) - (-1.5)(2.3)$$

$$= -12 + .3 + 3.45 = -8.25 \text{ volts.}$$

Again, we see that the potential at point C is 8.25 volts lower than that at point A.

• PROBLEM 674

Two cells, one of emf 1.2 V and internal resistance 0.5 Ω, the other of emf 2 V and internal resistance 0.1 Ω, are connected in parallel as shown in the figure and the combination connected in series with an external resistance of 5 Ω. What current passes through this external resistance?

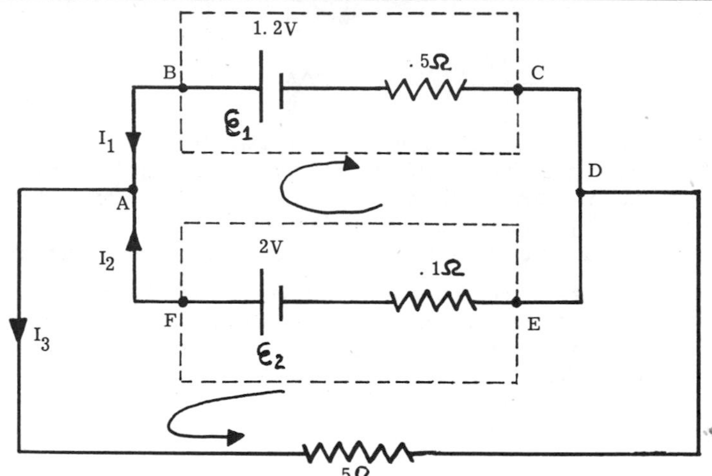

Solution: The diagram is labeled and current values have been inserted in each part of the circuit. Applying Kirchhoff's current law to point A, we have

$$I_1 + I_2 = I_3 \qquad (1)$$

Note that in the figure, boxes have been drawn representing the 2 batteries in the circuit. The given voltages, ε_1 and ε_2, are the voltages of the batteries assuming zero internal resistance. (The terminal voltages are V_{BC} and V_{FE}, not ε_1 and ε_2.)

Applying Kirchhoff's voltage law to the closed circuit containing both cells, and then to the closed circuit through the lower cell and the external resistance (see figure for the directions in which the loops are traversed) we have

$$+\varepsilon_2 - \varepsilon_1 + (.5\ \Omega)I_1 - (.1\ \Omega)(I_2) = 0$$

and $$+\varepsilon_2 - (5\ \Omega)(I_3) - (.1\ \Omega)(I_2) = 0$$

Hence, $\varepsilon_2 - \varepsilon_1 = (2 - 1.2)V$

$$= (.1\ \Omega)(I_2) - (.5\ \Omega)(I_1)$$

$$\varepsilon_2 = 2V = (5\ \Omega)(I_3) + (.1\ \Omega)(I_2)$$

or, upon multiplication of both sides of each equation by 10,

$$8\ V = (1\ \Omega)(I_2) - (5\ \Omega)(I_1) \quad (2)$$

$$20\ V = (1\ \Omega)(I_2) + (50\ \Omega)(I_3) \quad (3)$$

Substituting equation (1) in (3)

$$20\ V = (1\ \Omega)(I_2) + (50\ \Omega)(I_1 + I_2)$$

$$20\ V = (51\ \Omega)(I_2) + (50\ \Omega)I_1 \quad (4)$$

Multiplying (2) by 10,

$$80\ V = (10\ \Omega)(I_2) - (50\ \Omega)(I_1) \quad (5)$$

Adding (4) and (5), we may solve for I_2

$$100\ V = (61\ \Omega)I_2$$

and $$I_2 = \frac{100\ V}{61\ \Omega} = 1.64\ A \quad (6)$$

since 1 ampere = 1 volt/ohm.

Substituting (6) in (3), we obtain I_3,

$$20\ V = (1\ \Omega)(1.64\ A) + (50\ \Omega)(I_3)$$

$$\frac{18.46\ V}{50\ \Omega} = I_3$$

or $I_3 \approx .37$ A.

• PROBLEM 675

Two devices, whose resistances are 2.8 and 3.5Ω, respectively, are connected in series to a 12-V battery. Compute the current in either device and the potential applied to each.

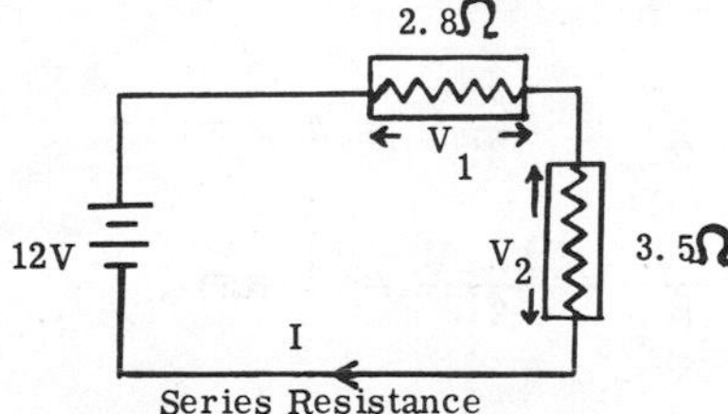

Series Resistance

Solution: Resistances in series add. The equivalent resistance of the two devices is given by

$$R = 2.8\Omega + 3.5\Omega = 6.3\Omega.$$

The current supplied by the battery can be computed using

Ohm's law,

$$I = \frac{V}{R} = \frac{12\ V}{6.3\Omega} = 1.9\ A.$$

This current I flows through both devices since they are in series. Ohm's law may be applied to calculate the potential applied to each device: (see figure)

$$V_1 = IR_1 = (1.9\ A)(2.8\Omega) = 5.3V$$

$$V_2 = IR_2 = (1.9\ A)(3.5\Omega) = 6.7V.$$

Note that the sum of these potentials is equal to the battery potential, 12V.

• PROBLEM 676

Suppose that three devices are connected in parallel to a 12-V battery. Let the resistances of the devices be $R_1 = 2\Omega$, $R_2 = 3\Omega$, and $R_3 = 4\Omega$. What current is supplied by the battery and what is the current in each device?

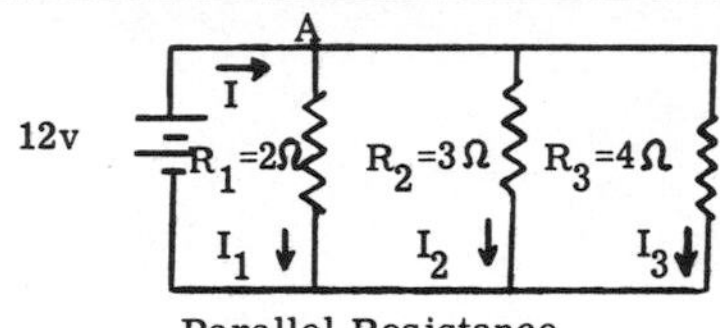

Parallel Resistance

Solution: Since the resistors are in parallel, we have for the equivalent resistance R,

$$\frac{1}{R} = \frac{1}{R_1} + \frac{1}{R_2} + \frac{1}{R_3} = \frac{1}{2\Omega} + \frac{1}{3\Omega} + \frac{1}{4\Omega} = \frac{13}{12}\Omega^{-1}.$$

The equivalent resistance, therefore, is

$$R = \frac{12}{13}\Omega = 0.92\Omega.$$

The voltage across each device is 12 volts since they are in parallel to the battery. Therefore, using Ohm's law and the figure,

$$I_1 = \frac{V}{R_1} = \frac{12\ V}{2\Omega} = 6\ \text{amp}$$

$$I_2 = \frac{V}{R_2} = \frac{12\ V}{3\Omega} = 4\ \text{amp}$$

$$I_3 = \frac{V}{R_3} = \frac{12\ V}{4\Omega} = 3\ \text{amp}.$$

The current supplied by the battery is found by applying Kirchoff's node equation at point A. Hence

$$I = I_1 + I_2 + I_3 = (6 + 4 + 3)\text{amp}$$

$$I = 13\ \text{amp}.$$

Compare the cost of operating 3 lamps in series and in parallel on a 115 volt circuit, if each lamp has a resistance of 100 ohms.

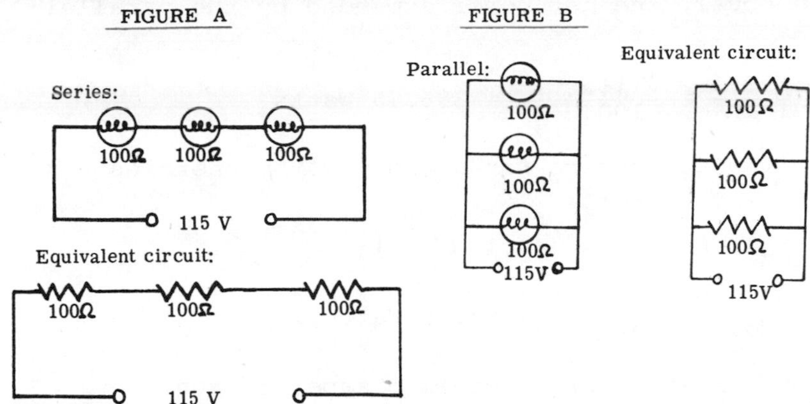

Solution: We calculate the cost of operation for each configuration (see figures) by calculating the net power expended by each circuit. Assuming both circuits run for the same time, the energy used by each can then be found. The circuit using less energy is the more economical.

For the series circuit, the same current I flows through each lamp. Each one then uses power

$$P = I^2 R$$

where R is the lamp resistance. Since the resistance of each lamp is the same, the net power expended in the series circuit is

$$P_{net} = 3I^2R \tag{1}$$

Looking at the equivalent circuit in figure (a), we realize that the net resistance of the series configuration is

$$R_{net} = 3R$$

By Ohm's Law, the current in this circuit is

$$I = \frac{V}{R_{net}} = \frac{V}{3R} \tag{2}$$

Using (2) in (1)

$$P_{net} = \frac{3\ V^2}{9\ R^2}\ R = \frac{V^2}{3R}$$

Using the given data, the series configuration uses power

$$P_{net} = \frac{(115\ V)^2}{300\ \Omega} = 44.1\ \text{Watts}$$

For the parallel connection, each lamp has the

same voltage V applied across it. Each one uses power

$$P' = \frac{V^2}{R}$$

where R is the lamp resistance. Since all the resistances are equal, the net power expended by the parallel circuit is

$$P'_{net} = \frac{3V^2}{R} = \frac{3(115\ V)^2}{100\ \Omega} = 396.75\ \text{Watts}$$

If both circuits operate for a time τ, the energies used are

$$E_{series} = P_{net}\ \tau = (44.1\ \text{Watts})\tau$$

$$E_{parallel} = P'_{net}\ \tau = (396.75\ \text{Watts})\tau$$

Hence, the series combination is cheaper to run.

• PROBLEM 678

Determine the current in each of the resistors in figure A.

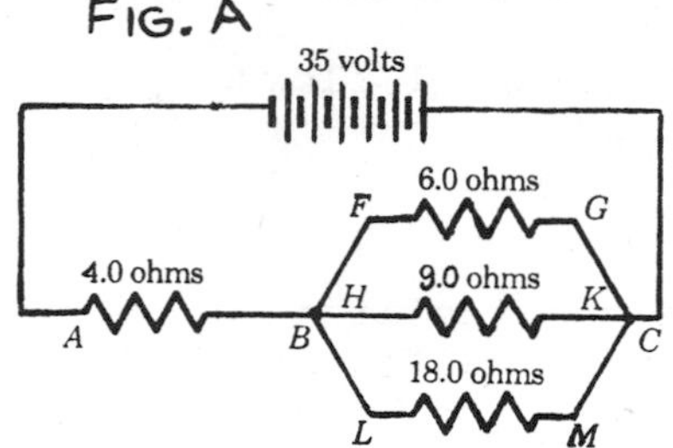

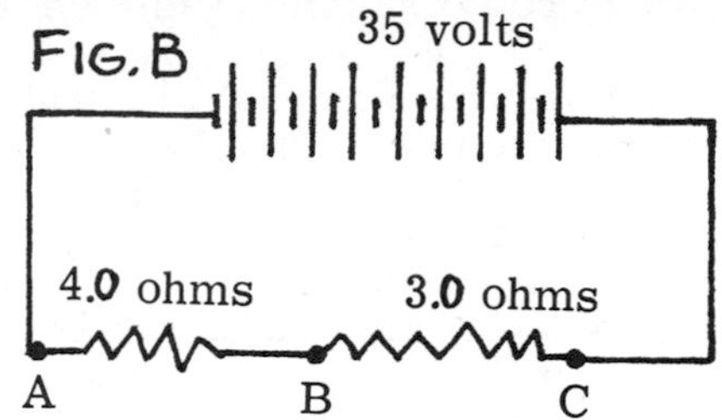

Solution: We find the resistance between points B and C (R_{BC}) by using the relation for resistors $R_1, R_2, \ldots$ in parallel (see figure (A)).

$$\frac{1}{R_{Total}} = \frac{1}{R_1} + \frac{1}{R_2} + \ldots$$

$$\frac{1}{R_{BC}} = \frac{1}{6.0\ \text{ohms}} + \frac{1}{9.0\ \text{ohms}} + \frac{1}{18.0\ \text{ohms}}$$

$$= \frac{6.0}{18.0\ \text{ohms}}$$

$$R_{BC} = \frac{18.0}{6.0}\ \text{ohms} = 3.0\ \text{ohms}$$

Using the formula for resistors in series,

$$R_{Total} = R_1 + R_2 + \ldots ,$$

we find the resistance between points A and C in the circuit. (see figure (B))

$$R_{AC} = R_{AB} + R_{BC} = 4.0\ \text{ohms} + 3.0\ \text{ohms}$$

$$= 7.0\ \text{ohms}$$

The current I_t in the circuit is obtained from Ohm's Law

$$I_t = \frac{V_{AC}}{R_{AC}} = \frac{35 \text{ volts}}{7.0 \text{ ohms}} = 5.0 \text{ amp.}$$

The current through each individual resistor is, by Ohm's Law, equal to the voltage across the resistor divided by its resistance. Hence

$$I_{FG} = \frac{V_{FG}}{R_{FG}} = \frac{15 \text{ volts}}{6.0 \text{ ohms}} = 2.5 \text{ amp}$$

$$I_{HK} = \frac{V_{HK}}{R_{HK}} = \frac{15 \text{ volts}}{9.0 \text{ ohms}} = 1.7 \text{ amp}$$

$$I_{LM} = \frac{V_{LM}}{R_{LM}} = \frac{15 \text{ volts}}{18.0 \text{ ohms}} = 0.83 \text{ amp.}$$

Note that $I_t = I_{FG} + I_{HK} + I_{LM}$ by Kirchoff's Current Law.

$$I_t = (2.5 + 1.7 + 0.8) \text{ amp} = 5.0 \text{ amp.}$$

• PROBLEM 679

A bank of cells having a total emf of 12 V and negligible internal resistance is connected in series with two resistors. A voltmeter of resistance 5000 Ω is connected across the resistors in turn, and measures 4 V and 6 V, respectively. What are the resistances of the two resistors?

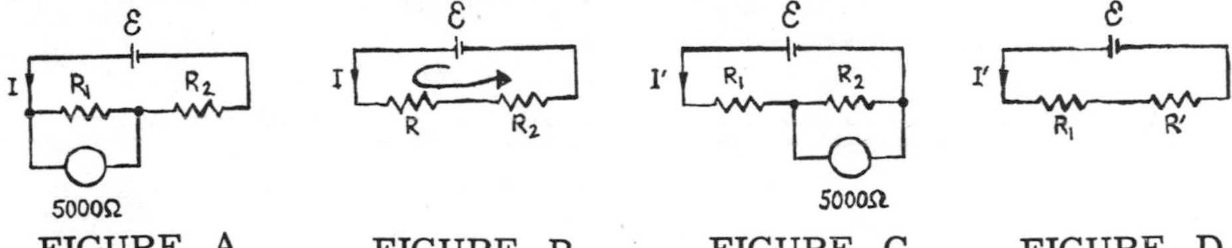

FIGURE A FIGURE B FIGURE C FIGURE D

Solution: The voltmeter is connected across R_1 as in diagram (a) and since the resistance of the voltmeter is in parallel with R_1 the circuit is equivalent to that shown in diagram (b), where

$$\frac{1}{R} = \frac{1}{R_1} + \frac{1}{5000 \ \Omega} = \frac{5000 \ \Omega + R_1}{5000 \ \Omega \ R_1}$$

$$R = \frac{5000 \ R_1 \ \Omega}{5000 \ \Omega + R_1} \qquad (1)$$

Now, the voltmeter measures a 4 V drop across R_1. By Kirchoff's Voltage Law, the net voltage around the circuit shown in figure (b) is zero. Hence, traversing the circuit as shown

$$\varepsilon - IR - IR_2 = 0 \qquad (2)$$

But we know that the voltage drop across R_1 equals the voltage drop across R, since R_1 and the voltmeter are in parallel. Then

$$IR = 4 \text{ V}$$

and, from (2) $IR_2 = \varepsilon - IR = 12\text{ V} - 4\text{ V} = 8\text{ V}$

Therefore, $\frac{IR_2}{IR} = \frac{8}{4} = 2$

or $R = \frac{1}{2} R_2$

Using (1) $R = \frac{5000\ R_1\ \Omega}{5000\ \Omega + R_1} = \frac{R_2}{2}$

Similarly, from diagrams (c) and (d), showing the second connection of the voltmeter and the equivalent circuit, we have

$$R' = \frac{5000\ R_2\ \Omega}{5000\ \Omega + R_2} \qquad \text{and } 6\text{ V} = I'R_1 = I'R'.$$

$$R' = \frac{5000\ R_2\ \Omega}{5000\ \Omega + R_2} = R_1.$$

Hence, from the two equations obtained, we have (by cross multiplication)

$$10{,}000\ R_1\ \Omega = 5000\ R_2\ \Omega + R_1R_2 \qquad (3)$$

and $$5000\ R_2\ \Omega = 5000\ R_1\ \Omega + R_1R_2. \qquad (4)$$

Subtracting these equations,

$$10{,}000\ R_1\ \Omega - 5000\ R_2\ \Omega = 5000\ R_2\ \Omega - 5000\ R_1\ \Omega$$

or

$$15{,}000\ R_1 = 10{,}000\ R_2 \qquad \text{or} \qquad R_1 = \frac{2}{3} R_2.$$

Substituting back into equation (3), we get

$$10{,}000 \left(\frac{2}{3} R_2\right) \Omega = 5000\ R_2\ \Omega + \left(\frac{2}{3} R_2\right)(R_2)$$

$$10{,}000\ \Omega = 7500\ \Omega + R_2$$

$$R_2 = 2500\ \Omega$$

and $$R_1 = \frac{2}{3} R_2 = \frac{2}{3} (2500\ \Omega)$$

$$R_1 = 1667\ \Omega$$

• PROBLEM 680

An enquiring physics student connects a cell to a circuit and measures the current drawn from the cell to be I_1. When he joins a second, identical cell in series with the first, the current becomes I_2. When he connects the cells in parallel, the current through the circuit is I_3. Show that the relation he finds between the currents is $3I_2I_3 = 2I_1(I_2 + I_3)$. (See figures (a), (b) and (c)).

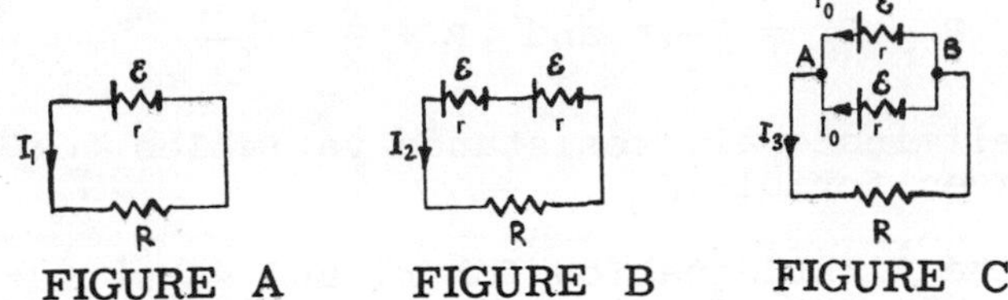

FIGURE A FIGURE B FIGURE C

Solution: Let the emf of any of the cells be ε and its internal resistance be r. Let the external circuit have a resistance R. When a single cell is used (see figure (a)) R and r will be in series. Hence, the equivalent circuit resistance R_{eq} is

$$R_{eq} = R + r$$

Ohm's Law yields

$$I_1 = \frac{\varepsilon_{net}}{R_{net}} = \frac{\varepsilon}{R_{eq}} = \frac{\varepsilon}{R + r}$$

If two identical cells are connected in series, their emf's act in the same sense. Hence, again using Ohm's Law (see figure (b))

$$I_2 = \frac{\varepsilon_{net}}{R_{net}} = \frac{2\varepsilon}{R + r}$$

When the cells are connected in parallel, since they are identical, by the symmetry of the arrangement identical currents I_0 must flow through each cell. Further, since no charge accumulates at point A in this circuit, (by conservation of charge)

$$I_3 = I_0 + I_0 = 2I_0$$

Considering the passage of current through either cell, we have

$$V_{AB} = \varepsilon - I_0 r = \varepsilon - \frac{I_3}{2} r.$$

This follows because, each charge passing through ε is raised in potential an amount ε. However, by Ohm's Law, each charge also loses potential $I_0 r$ by crossing the battery's internal resistance. When we consider the passage of current through the external circuit, then $V_{AB} = I_3 R$, by Ohm's Law. Hence

$$I_3 R = \varepsilon - \frac{I_3 r}{2}$$

or $$\varepsilon = I_3 \left(R + \frac{r}{2}\right)$$

Rewriting the three equations obtained, we find that

$$R + r = \frac{\varepsilon}{I_1}\ , \quad R + 2r = \frac{2\varepsilon}{I_2}, \quad \text{and} \quad R + \frac{r}{2} = \frac{\varepsilon}{I_3}$$

We must eliminate all resistance variables to obtain the given formula.

Solving the first equation for r, and substituting this value in the second equation, we obtain

$$r = \frac{\varepsilon}{I_1} - R$$

$$R + 2\left(\frac{\varepsilon}{I_1} - R\right) = \frac{2\varepsilon}{I_2}$$

$$\text{or} \ - R = \frac{2\varepsilon}{I_2} - \frac{2\varepsilon}{I_1}$$

$$R = 2\varepsilon\left(\frac{1}{I_1} - \frac{1}{I_2}\right) \qquad (1)$$

Inserting the calculated value of r in the third equation

$$R + \tfrac{1}{2}\left(\frac{\varepsilon}{I_1} - R\right) = \frac{\varepsilon}{I_3} \qquad \text{or} \qquad \tfrac{1}{2}R = \frac{\varepsilon}{I_3} - \tfrac{1}{2}\frac{\varepsilon}{I_1}$$

$$R = \varepsilon\left(\frac{2}{I_3} - \frac{1}{I_1}\right) \qquad (2)$$

Dividing equations (1) and (2) gives

$$1 = \frac{2[(1/I_1) - (1/I_2)]}{(2/I_3) - (1/I_1)}$$

$$\frac{2}{I_3} - \frac{1}{I_1} = \frac{2}{I_1} - \frac{2}{I_2}$$

$$\text{or} \ \frac{2}{I_3} = \frac{3}{I_1} - \frac{2}{I_2}$$

Multiplying both sides by $I_1 I_2 I_3$

$$2I_1I_2 = 3I_2I_3 - 2I_1I_3$$

$$\text{or} \ 3I_2I_3 = 2I_1(I_3 + I_2)$$

$$\therefore\ 2I_1I_2 - I_2I_3 = 2I_2I_3 - 2I_1I_3.\ \therefore\ 3I_2I_3 = 2I_1(I_2 + I_3)$$

• PROBLEM 681

Five resistors, each of resistance 10 Ω, are connected to form a letter H, a 2-V cell of internal resistance 1.86 Ω being connected across the upper ends and an ammeter of resistance 5 Ω across the lower ends. What current passes through the ammeter?

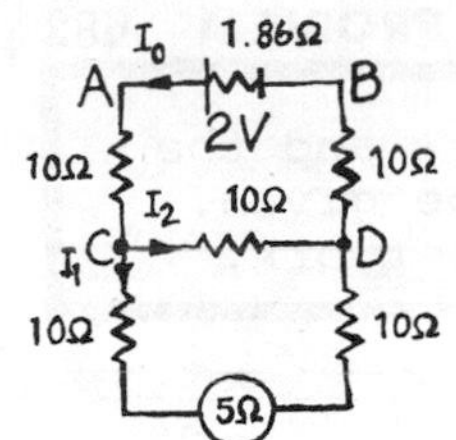

FIGURE A

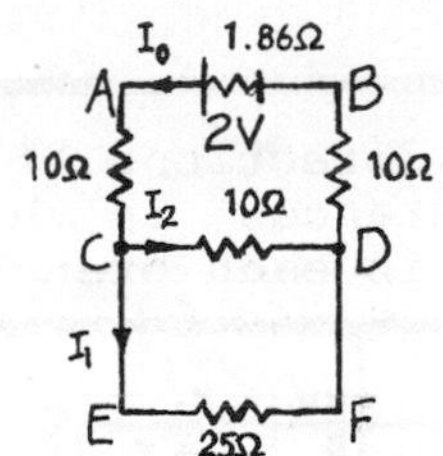

FIGURE B

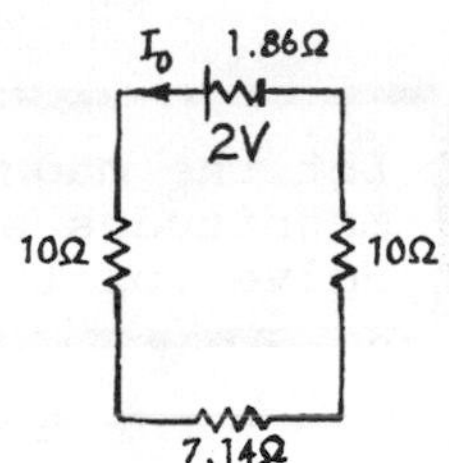

FIGURE C

Solution: Because the 5 Ω resistance of the ammeter and the 10 Ω resistance of the lower branch of the circuit in figure (A) are in series, figure (A) is equivalent to figure (B). This follows because the equivalent resistance of n resistors in series is equal to the sum of their individual resistances. The resistances of 10 Ω and 25 Ω are in parallel. Hence the equivalent resistance is R, where

$$\frac{1}{R} = \frac{1}{10\ \Omega} + \frac{1}{25\ \Omega} = \frac{35\ \Omega}{250\ \Omega^2}$$

$$\therefore\ R = \frac{50}{7}\ \Omega = 7\frac{1}{7}\ \Omega = 7.14\ \Omega.$$

The circuit is therefore equivalent to the one shown in diagram (C). It is now possible to find the current I_0 in the battery circuit, for, by Ohm's Law

$$I_0 = \frac{\varepsilon}{R} = \frac{2\ V}{(10 + 10 + 7.14 + 1.86)\Omega} = \frac{2}{29}\ A. \qquad (1)$$

This current splits up into currents I_1 and I_2 through the lower parts of the circuit, as shown in diagrams (A) and (B). Using figure (B), note that branches CD and EF are in parallel. Therefore, the voltage drops across CD and EF are equal. Using Ohm's Law

$$V_{CD} = V_{EF}$$

or $$(10\ \Omega)I_2 = (25\ \Omega)I_1$$

$$\frac{I_1}{I_2} = \frac{R_2}{R_1} = \frac{10\ \Omega}{25\ \Omega} = \frac{2}{5}$$

Since no charge can accumulate in the circuit, then $I_1 + I_2 = I_0$. Therefore,

$$I_1 + \frac{25}{10} I_1 = I_0$$

$$I_1 = \frac{10}{35} I_0 = \frac{10}{35} \times \frac{2}{29}\ A = 0.0197\ A,$$

where we have used (1). This is the current flowing through the ammeter.

Let the magnitudes and directions of the emf's, and the magnitudes of the resistances in the figure be given. Solve for the currents in each branch of the network.

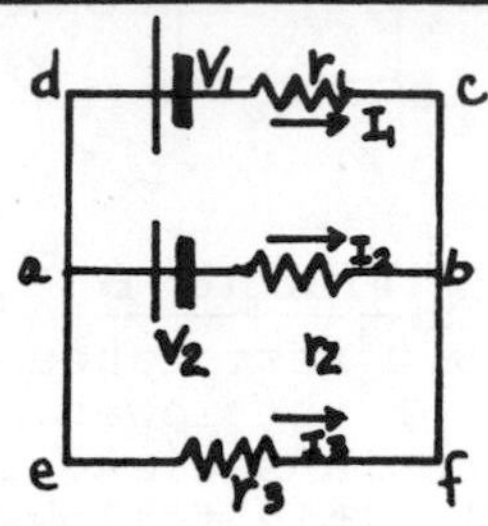

Resistive Network

Solution: We assign a direction and a letter to each unknown current. The assumed directions are entirely arbitrary. Note that the currents in source 1 and resistor 1 are the same, and require only a single letter I_1. The same is true for source 2 and resistor 2; the current in both is represented by I_2.

At any branch point we may apply Kirchoff's current law, which states that the current entering a branch point must equal the current leaving a branch point.

There are only two branch points, a and b. At point b,

$$\Sigma I = I_1 + I_2 + I_3 = 0 \qquad (1)$$

Since there are but two branch points, there is only one independent "point" equation. If the point rule is applied at the other branch point, point a, we get

$$\Sigma I = - I_1 - I_2 - I_3 = 0 \qquad (2)$$

which is the same equation with signs reversed.

We now apply Kirchoff's voltage law to the two loops of the figure. This law states that the sum of the voltage drops around any closed loop of a circuit must be zero. Hence, for loop defc,

$$v_1 - I_3 r_3 + I_1 r_1 = 0 \qquad (3)$$

and for loop aefb

$$v_2 - I_3 r_3 + I_2 r_2 = 0 \qquad (4)$$

We first solve for I_3. Solving (1) for I_1,

$$I_1 = - I_2 - I_3 \qquad (5)$$

Substituting this in (3)

$$v_1 - I_3 r_3 + (- I_2 - I_3) r_1 = 0$$

or $$v_1 - I_3 r_3 - I_2 r_1 - I_3 r_1 = 0$$

$$v_1 - I_3 (r_1 + r_3) - I_2 r_1 = 0 \qquad (6)$$

Solving this for I_2

$$I_2 r_1 = v_1 - I_3 (r_1 + r_3)$$

$$I_2 = \frac{v_1 - I_3 (r_1 + r_3)}{r_1} \qquad (7)$$

Substituting (7) in (4)

$$v_2 - I_3 r_3 + \left[\frac{v_1 - I_3 (r_1 + r_3)}{r_1}\right] r_2 = 0$$

Solving for I_3

$$v_2 - I_3 r_3 + \frac{v_1 r_2}{r_1} - I_3 \frac{(r_1 + r_3)}{r_1} r_2 = 0$$

or $$I_3 \left[r_3 + \frac{(r_1 + r_3)}{r_1} r_2\right] = v_2 + \frac{v_1 r_2}{r_1}$$

Hence

$$I_3 = \frac{\left[v_2 + \frac{v_1 r_2}{r_1}\right]}{\left[r_3 + \frac{(r_1 + r_3)}{r_1} r_2\right]} \qquad (8)$$

Now, we solve for I_2 by substituting (8) in (4)

$$v_2 - \frac{\left[v_2 + \frac{v_1 r_2}{r_1}\right] r_3}{\left[r_3 + \frac{(r_1 + r_3) r_2}{r_1}\right]} + I_2 r_2 = 0$$

$$I_2 r_2 = \frac{\left[v_2 + \frac{v_1 r_2}{r_1} \quad r_3\right]}{\left[r_3 + \frac{(r_1 + r_3)\ r_2}{r_1}\right]} - v_2$$

$$I_2 = \frac{\left(v_2 + \frac{v_1 r_2}{r_1}\right)\frac{r_3}{r_2}}{\left(r_3 + \frac{(r_1 + r_3)r_2}{r_1}\right)} - \frac{v_2}{r_2} \qquad (9)$$

Substituting (9) and (8) in (5), we may solve for I_1

$$I_1 = \frac{v_2}{r_2} - \frac{\left(v_2 + \frac{v_1 r_2}{r_1}\right)\frac{r_3}{r_2}}{\left(r_3 + \frac{(r_1 + r_3)r_2}{r_1}\right)} - \frac{\left(v_2 + \frac{v_1 r_2}{r_1}\right)}{\left(r_3 + \frac{(r_1 + r_3)r_2}{r_1}\right)}$$

Hence

$$I_1 = \frac{v_2}{r_2} - \frac{\left(v_2 + \frac{v_1 r_2}{r_1}\right)}{\left(r_3 + \frac{(r_1 + r_3)r_2}{r_1}\right)}\left(\frac{r_3}{r_2} + 1\right)$$

• PROBLEM 683

Discuss the operation of (1) a voltmeter across a 12v. battery with an internal resistance $r = 2\Omega$, (2) an ammeter in series with a 4Ω resistor connected to the terminals of the same battery.

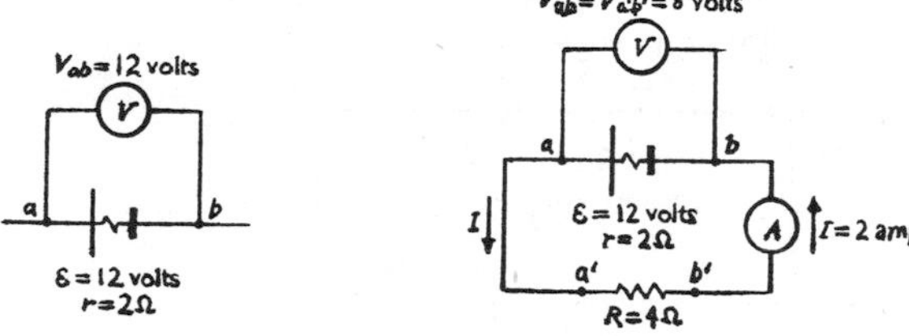

Fig. 1. A source on open circuit. Fig. 2. A source on closed circuit.

Solution: (1) Consider a source whose emf ϵ is constant and equal to 12 volts, and whose internal resistance r is 2 ohms. (The internal resistance of a commercial 12-volt lead storage battery is only a few thousandths of an ohm.) Figure 1 represents the source with a voltmeter V connected between its terminals a and b . A voltmeter reads the potential difference between its terminals. If it is of the conventional type, the voltmeter provides a conducting path between the terminals and so there is a current in the source (and through the voltmeter). We shall assume, however, that the resistance of the voltmeter is so large (essentially infinite) that it draws no appreciable current. The source is then an open circuit, corresponding to a source with open terminals and the voltmeter reading V_{ab} equals the emf ϵ of the source, or 12 volts.

(2) In Fig. 2, an ammeter A and a resistor of resistance $R = 4\Omega$ have been connected to the terminals of the source to form a closed circuit. The total resistance of the circuit is the sum of the resistance R, the internal resistance r, and the resistance of the

ammeter. The ammeter resistance, however, can be made very small, and we shall assume it so small (essentially zero) that it can be neglected. The ammeter (whatever its resistance) reads the current I through it. The circuit corresponds to a source with a 4Ω resistance across its terminals.

The wires connecting the resistor to the source and the ammeter, shown by straight lines, ideally have zero resistance and hence there is no potential difference between their ends. Thus points a and a' are at the same potential and are electrically equivalent, as are points b and b'. The potential differences V_{ab} and $V_{a'b'}$ are therefore equal.

The current I in the resistor (and hence at all points of the circuit) could be found from the relation $I = V_{ab}/R$, if the potential difference V_{ab} were known. However, V_{ab} is the terminal voltage of the source, equal to $\varepsilon - Ir$, and since this depends on I it is unknown at the start. We can, however, calculate the current from the circuit equation:

$$I = \frac{\varepsilon}{R + r} = \frac{12 \text{ volts}}{4\Omega + 2\Omega} = 2 \text{ amp.}$$

The potential difference V_{ab} can now be found by considering a and b either as the terminals of the resistor or as those of the source. If we consider them as the terminals of the resistor,

$$V_{a'b'} = IR = 2 \text{ amp} \times 4\Omega = 8 \text{ volts.}$$

If we consider them as the terminals of the source,

$$V_{ab} = \varepsilon - Ir = 12 \text{ volts} - 2 \text{ amp} \times 2\Omega = 8 \text{ volts.}$$

The voltmeter therefore reads 8 volts and the ammeter reads 2 amp. •

• PROBLEM 684

Compute the equivalent resistance of the network in Figure1, and find the current in each resistor.

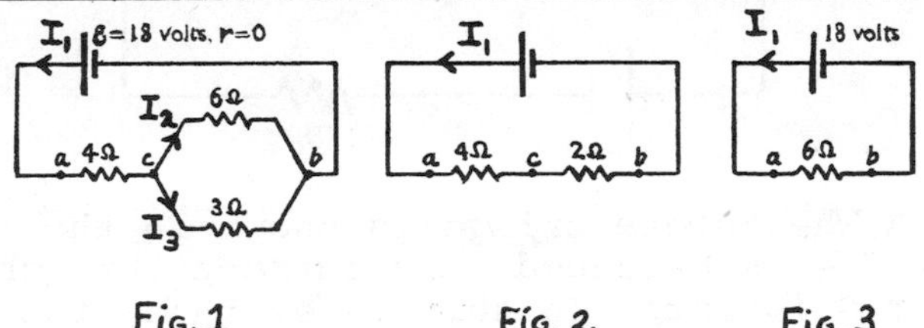

Fig. 1 Fig. 2 Fig. 3

Solution: Successive stages in the reduction to a single equivalent resistance are shown in Figs. 1 and 2. The 6Ω and 3Ω resistors in Fig. 1 are in parallel, hence they are equivalent to the

$$\frac{6\Omega \times 3\Omega}{6\Omega + 3\Omega} = 2\Omega$$

resistor in Fig. 2. The series combination of this 2Ω resistor with the 4Ω resistor gives the 6Ω resistor in Fig. 3.

The total current I_1 in the circuit is

$$I_1 = \frac{18\text{v}}{6\Omega} = 3 \text{ amp.}$$

The current I_2 through the 6Ω resistor in Fig. 1 is

$$I_2 = \frac{V_{cb}}{6\Omega}$$

where V_{cb} is the potential across the 6Ω and 3Ω resistors. Similarly, the current I_3 through the 3Ω resistor is

$$I_3 = \frac{V_{cb}}{3\Omega} .$$

V_{cb} is obtained by considering the loop equation for Fig. 2;

$$V_{cb} = I_1 \times 2\Omega = 3 \text{ amp} \times 2\Omega = 6\text{v}.$$

Therefore

$$I_2 = \frac{6\text{v}}{6\Omega} = 1 \text{ amp} ,$$

$$I_3 = \frac{6\text{v}}{3\Omega} = 2 \text{ amp}.$$

• PROBLEM 685

A coil of wire is connected across one gap of a Wheatstone bridge and a temperature-controlled standard 1-Ω resistor across the other. If the temperature of the coil is 0°C, the other arms of the bridge have resistances in the ratio 0.923. If the temperature of the coil is 100°C the ratio is 1.338. What is the temperature coefficient of resistance of the wire?

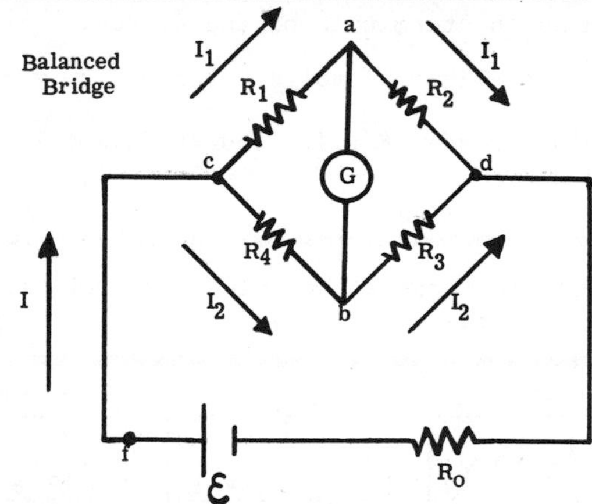

Solution: A Wheatstone bridge is shown in the figure. When the bridge is balanced, the current through galvanometer G is zero. In this case, then, the potential between points a and b is the same, whether we calculate it by path cab or path dab. Using Kirchoff's Voltage Law around these 2 loops, we find

$$- I_1R_1 + I_2R_4 = 0$$

and $\quad I_1R_2 - I_2R_3 = 0$

Solving each equation separately for the ratio I_1/I_2

$$\frac{I_1}{I_2} = \frac{R_4}{R_1}$$

$$\frac{I_1}{I_2} = \frac{R_3}{R_2}$$

and, therefore, $\frac{R_4}{R_1} = \frac{R_3}{R_2}$

or $\frac{R_1}{R_2} = \frac{R_4}{R_3}$

Let R_1 be the coil, and R_2 the temperature-controlled standard. In the first case,

$$\frac{R_1(0°C)}{1\ \Omega} = .923$$

or $R_1(0°C) = .923\ \Omega$

In the second case

$R_1(100°C) = 1.338\ \Omega$

But $R_1(100°C) = R_1(0°C)(1 + \alpha\ t)$, where α is the temperature coefficient of resistance of the wire and t is the difference in temperature experienced by the resistor (100°C). Thus

$$\alpha = \frac{R_1(100°C) - R_1(0°C)}{t\ R_1(0°C)} = \frac{1.338\ \Omega - .923\ \Omega}{(100°C)(.923\ \Omega)}$$

$\alpha = .0045$ per °C

• PROBLEM 686

A piece of uniform wire is made up into two squares with a common side of length 4 in. A current enters the rectangular system at one of the corners and leaves at the diagonally opposite corner. Show that the current in the common side is one-fifth of the entering current. What length of wire connected between input and output terminals would have an equivalent resistive effect?

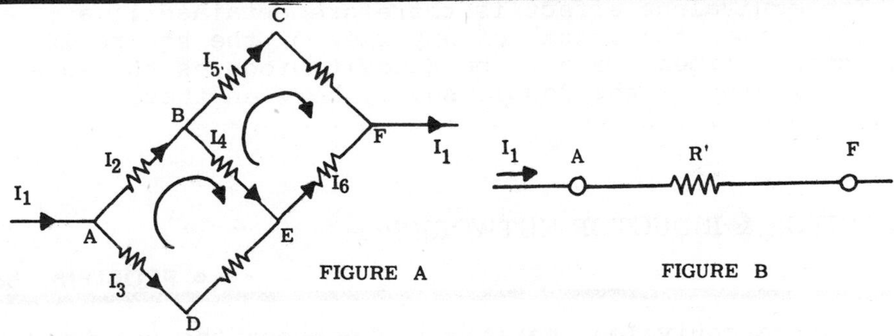

FIGURE A

FIGURE B

Solution: Let each side of the double square have resistance R, and let the lettering of the diagram and the currents flowing be as shown in Figure A. Applying the Kirchoff current rule, $\Sigma I = 0$, to the junctions A, B and E in turn (with the convention that current entering a junction is positive, and current leaving a junction is negative), gives

$$I_1 - I_2 - I_3 = 0, \qquad (1)$$

$$I_2 - I_4 - I_5 = 0, \qquad (2)$$

$$I_3 + I_4 - I_6 = 0. \qquad (3)$$

Applying the Kirchoff voltage rule to the loops ABED and BCFE gives

$$I_2R + I_4R - I_3 \times 2R = 0, \qquad (4)$$

$$I_5 \times 2R - I_6R - I_4R = 0. \qquad (5)$$

Eliminating I_5 and I_6 from Eqs. (2), (3) and (5), we obtain

$$I_1 - I_2 - I_3 = 0 \qquad (6)$$

$$I_2 - 2I_3 + I_4 = 0 \qquad (7)$$

$$2I_2 - I_3 - 4I_4 = 0 \qquad (8)$$

Eliminating I_2 from these three equations gives

$$I_1 - 3I_3 + I_4 = 0, \qquad (9)$$

and $$2I_1 - 3I_3 - 4I_4 = 0, \qquad (10)$$

or $$I_4 = \frac{1}{5} I_1. \qquad (11)$$

Further, the potential drop from A to F by route ADEF is

$$V_{AF} = I_3 \times 2R + I_6 \times R = R(2I_3 + I_3 + I_4)$$

using equation (3). By (9) this becomes

$$V_{AF} = R(I_1 + 2I_4)$$

and using (11), $$V_{AF} = I_1R\left(1 + \frac{2}{5}\right) = \frac{7}{5} RI_1$$

The equivalent effect is therefore obtained if a wire 7/5 times the length of any side of the square is connected between A and F, because it produces the same potential drop as the double square between these points (see fig. B).

CAPACITOR & INDUCTOR NETWORKS

• PROBLEM 687

What is the equivalent capacitance between the points A and B in diagram (A)? The charge on the 6-μF capacitor is 90 μC. What potential difference exists between the points A and R?

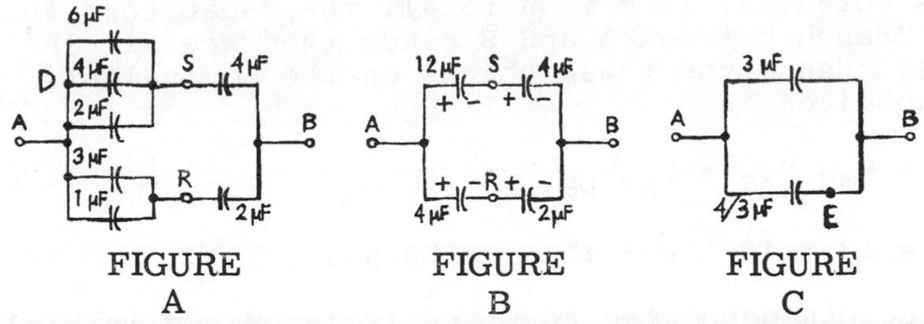

FIGURE A FIGURE B FIGURE C

Solution: In the arrangement shown in diagram (A) there are two sets of capacitors in parallel. Since the net capacitance of n capacitors in parallel is

$$C_{net} = C_1 + C_2 + \ldots + C_n$$

the arrangement is equivalent to that shown in diagram (B).

In each branch there are now two capacitors in series. If we have n capacitors in series, their net capacitance is

$$\frac{1}{C_{net}} = \frac{1}{C_1} + \frac{1}{C_2} + \ldots + \frac{1}{C_n}$$

For each branch, then,

$$\frac{1}{C_{net}} = \frac{1}{C_1} + \frac{1}{C_2} .$$

For the top branch

$$\frac{1}{C_{net}} = \frac{1}{12\ \mu F} + \frac{1}{4\ \mu F} = \frac{4\ \mu F + 12\ \mu F}{48\ \mu F^2}$$

$$C_{net} = 3\ \mu F$$

For the lower branch

$$\frac{1}{C_{net}} = \frac{1}{4\ \mu F} + \frac{1}{2\ \mu F} = \frac{2\ \mu F + 4\ \mu F}{8\ \mu F^2}$$

$$C_{net} = \frac{4}{3}\ \mu F.$$

Thus, the arrangement is equivalent to that shown in diagram (C). Here we have two capacitors in parallel. Their capacitances add. Hence, the equivalent capacitance between A and B is

$$C = \left(3 + \frac{4}{3}\right)\mu F = 4\ \frac{1}{3}\ \mu F.$$

The charge on the 6-μF capacitor is 90 μC. Hence, the potential across it is, by definition of capacitance

$$V_{DS} = \frac{Q_{DS}}{C_{DS}} = \frac{90 \times 10^{-6}\ C}{6 \times 10^{-6}\ F} = 15\ V.$$

This potential is common to all the capacitors in the top branch between A and S since they are all in parallel. Hence, the total charge on the equivalent 12-μF capacitor is

$$Q_{AS} = C_{AS}\ V_{AS} = C_{AS}V_{DS}$$

$$= 12 \times 10^{-6}\ F \times 15\ V = 180\ \mu C.$$

The conductors connected to S are isolated and initially must have been uncharged. If a charge of - 180 μC appears on the negative plate of the equivalent 12-μF capacitor connected to S, a corresponding charge of + 180 μC must be induced on the positive plate of the 4-μF capacitor connected to S, leaving the net charge at S zero. A corresponding - 180-μC charge is induced on the negative terminal of the 4- μF capacitor, and the voltage between its plates is thus

$$V_{SB} = \frac{Q_{SB}}{C_{SB}} = \frac{180 \times 10^{-6}\ C}{4 \times 10^{-6}\ F} = 45\ V.$$

The total potential difference between A and B is thus

$$V = V_{AS} + V_{SB} = (15 + 45)V = 60\ V.$$

This is the potential difference between A and B by either branch. Referring to diagram (C), the charge on the equivalent 4/3-μF capacitor is thus

$$Q_{AE} = C_{AE}\ V_{AE} = C_{AE}\ V = \frac{4}{3} \times 10^{-6}\ F \times 60\ V = 80\ \mu C.$$

This is the charge on the plate attached to A in either the equivalent circuit or the original circuit, since the two produce identical effects. Hence, the equivalent 4-μF capacitor between A and R has charges of ± 80 μC on each of its plates. Hence the potential difference across it is

$$V_{AR} = \frac{Q_{AR}}{C_{AR}} = \frac{80 \times 10^{-6}\ C}{4 \times 10^{-6}\ F} = 20\ V.$$

• PROBLEM 688

In the figure below, $C_1 = 6\ \mu f$, $C_2 = 3\ \mu f$ and $V_{ab} = 18\ v$. Find the charge on each capacitor. What is the value of the equivalent capacitance (see figure)?

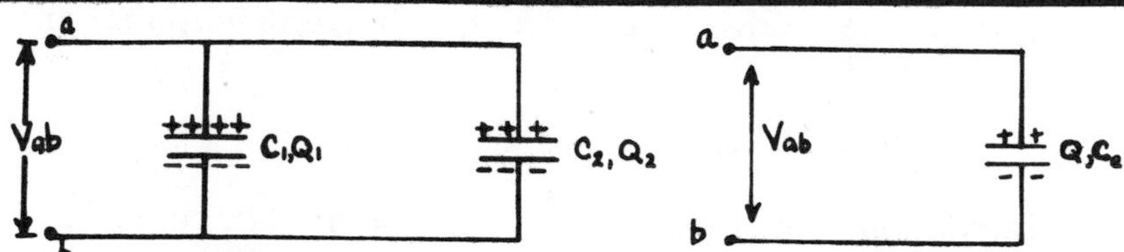

Fig. 1-Two Capacitors in parallel. Fig. 2-Their Equivalent

Solution: The charge Q on a capacitor having capacitance C is Q = VC, where V is the potential difference across the capacitor. Then,

$$Q_1 = V_{ab}C_1 = (18v) \times (6 \times 10^{-6} f) = 108 \times 10^{-6} C$$

$$Q_2 = V_{ab}C_2 = (18v) \times (3 \times 10^{-6} f) = 54 \times 10^{-6} C$$

The equivalent capacitance must carry the same total charge as the original system, since charge is conserved (none leaks out of the system). Hence

$$Q_{net} = Q_1 + Q_2 = 162 \times 10^{-6} C$$

Then, the equivalent capacitance is

$$C_e = \frac{Q_{net}}{V_{ab}} = \frac{162 \times 10^{-6} C}{18 v} = 9 \times 10^{-6} f$$

• PROBLEM 689

How should 5 capacitors, each of capacitance 1 μF, be connected so as to produce a total capacitance of 3/7 μF?

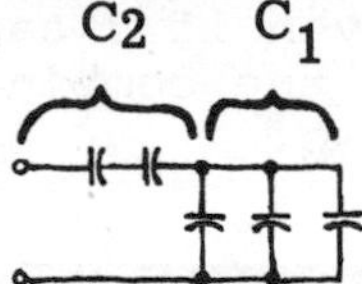

Series connection of C_1 and C_2

Solution: If all capacitors are joined in parallel, the resultant capacitance is 5 μF. (For the resultant capacitance of a set of capacitors connected in parallel equals the sum of the individual capacitances). If the capacitors are connected in series, the resultant capacitance is 1/5 μF (for the resultant capacitance of a set of capacitors connected in series equals the reciprocal of the sum of the reciprocals of the individual capacitances). The connection is thus more complicated.

Suppose that n capacitors are connected in parallel and 5 - n in series. The resultant capacitances are thus such that

$$C_1 = (\underbrace{1 + 1 + \ldots}_{n \text{ times}})\mu F = n\ \mu F$$

$$\text{and } \frac{1}{C_2} = \underbrace{\left(\frac{1}{1} + \frac{1}{1} + \ldots\right)}_{(5-n) \text{ times}} = (5 - n)\mu F^{-1}$$

$$\text{or} \qquad C_2 = \frac{1}{5 - n}\ \mu F.$$

If C_1 and C_2 are connected in parallel, then

$$C_r = C_1 + C_2 = \left(n + \frac{1}{5 - n}\right)\ \mu F = \frac{3}{7}\ \mu F.$$

$$5n - n^2 + 1 = \frac{15 - 3n}{7}$$

$$35n - 7n^2 + 1 = 15 - 3n$$

or $$7n^2 - 38n + 8 = 0$$

By the quadratic formula, $n = \dfrac{-(-38) \pm \sqrt{(-38)^2 - 4(7)(8)}}{2(7)}$

There is thus no integral solution for n.

But if C_1 and C_2 are connected in series (see figure), then

$$\frac{1}{C_r} = \frac{1}{C_1} + \frac{1}{C_2} = \left(\frac{1}{n} + 5 - n\right) \mu F^{-1} = \frac{7}{3} \mu F^{-1}.$$

$$\therefore \quad 3 + 15n - 3n^2 = 7n \quad \text{or} \quad 3n^2 - 8n - 3 = 0.$$

$$\therefore \quad (3n + 1)(n - 3) = 0.$$

This has an integral solution for n, n = 3. Thus the required capacitance is given if 3 capacitors are connected in parallel, and the combination is connected in series with the other two.

• PROBLEM 690

A particular type of x-ray equipment discharges a capacitor to obtain its electrical energy. The capacitor of capacitance 0.25 μF is charged to 100 kV and discharged to 40 kV during a 0.1-s exposure. Calculate the quantity of charge supplied to the x-ray tube, the average current through it, and the energy dissipated.

Solution: The charge possessed by the capacitor initially is

$$Q_1 = CV_1 = 0.25 \times 10^{-6} \text{ F} \times 10^5 \text{ V} = 0.025 \text{ C}.$$

At the end of the exposure the capacitor is left with charge

$$Q_2 = CV_2 = 0.25 \times 10^{-6} \text{ F} \times 4 \times 10^4 \text{ V} = 0.01 \text{ C}.$$

The charge supplied to the x-ray set is thus $Q_1 - Q_2 = 0.015$ C. This charge is supplied in $\tau = 0.1$ s. The average current flowing is thus

$$i = \frac{Q_1 - Q_2}{\tau} = \frac{0.015 \text{ C}}{0.1 \text{ s}} = 150 \text{ mA}.$$

The energy dissipated in this time is the difference in the energy stored in the capacitor before and after discharge:

$$W = \tfrac{1}{2}CV_1^2 - \tfrac{1}{2} CV_2^2 = \tfrac{1}{2} \times 0.25 \times 10^{-6} \text{ F}\left(10^{10} - 16 \times 10^8\right)\text{V}^2$$

$$= 1050 \text{ J}.$$

A 1-μF capacitor charged to 200 V and a 2-μF capacitor charged to 400 V are connected; the positive plate of each is connected to the negative plate of the other. Find the difference of potential and charge on each capacitor and the loss of energy that has taken place.

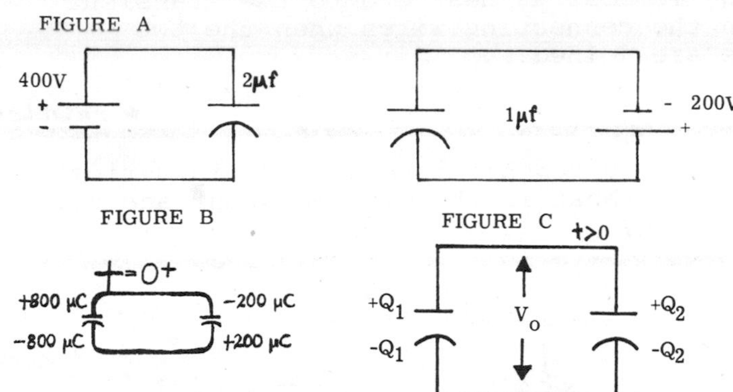

FIGURE A

FIGURE B

FIGURE C

Solution: The charge Q on a charged capacitor of capacitance C is Q = CV where V is the potential difference between the plates of the capacitor. Thus the charge on the 1-μF capacitor before connection is 1 μf × 200 V = 200 μC and on the 2-μF capacitor is 2 μf × 400 V = 800 μC. Fig. A depicts the situation before connection of the two capacitors.

If the two capacitors are now connected positive to negative, a charge of + 800 μC and one of - 200 μC are joined, as are charges of - 800 μC and + 200 μC. The situation just after the connection is depicted in Figure B. The composite capacitor thus has charges of ± 600 μC on its plates, since charge cannot be created or destroyed, but only neutralized. These charges will be shared between the individual capacitors, with $\pm Q_1$ on the first capacitor, and $\pm Q_2$ on the second, since the charge flows from one to the other until a common potential V_0 is achieved. Fig. C depicts this situation. Thus

$$Q_1 = C_1V_0 \quad \text{and} \quad Q_2 = C_2V_0, \quad \text{where } Q_1 + Q_2 = 600 \ \mu C.$$

Thus combining the above three equations

$$(Q_1 + Q_2) = (C_1 + C_2)V_0 \qquad \text{or}$$

$$600 \times 10^{-6} \ C = (1 \times 10^{-6} \ F + 2 \times 10^{-6} \ F)V_0 \qquad \text{or}$$

$$V_0 = \frac{600 \times 10^{-6} \ C}{3 \times 10^{-6} \ F} = 200 \ V.$$

$$\therefore \quad Q_1 = 200 \ \mu C, \qquad Q_2 = 400 \ \mu C.$$

The initial energy of the charged capacitors minus the final energy is

$$W = \tfrac{1}{2}C_1V_1^2 + \tfrac{1}{2}C_2V_2^2 - \tfrac{1}{2}C_1V_0^2 - \tfrac{1}{2}C_2V_0^2$$

$$= \tfrac{1}{2} \times 10^{-6}\ F \times (200)^2\ V^2 + \tfrac{1}{2} \times 2 \times 10^{-6}\ F \times (400)^2\ V^2 - \tfrac{1}{2} \times 10^{-6}\ F \times (200)^2\ V^2 - \tfrac{1}{2} \times 2 \times 10^{-6}\ F \times (200)^2\ V^2$$

$$= 12 \times 10^4 \times 10^{-6}\ J = 0.12\ J.$$

This energy is lost as heat due to the transient current in the connecting wires when the two capacitors are joined.

• PROBLEM 692

A resistor R = 10 megohms is connected in series with a capacitor 1 μf. What is the time constant and half-life of this circuit?

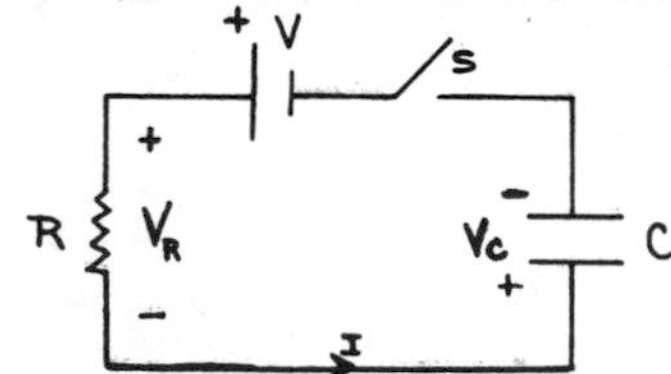

RC Circuit

Solution: Suppose that we introduce an e.m.f. in the circuit above, for example by connecting a battery to the circuit. (See the figure). In this case a current I will flow in the loop until C is charged up to the battery voltage V. Therefore, by Kirchoff's Voltage Law, V_R and I approach zero as V_C increases. The same current goes through R and C in the loop as we close the switch S;

$$I = \frac{V_R}{R} = \frac{dQ}{dt} = \frac{d}{dt}\left(C\ V_C\right) = C\ \frac{dV_C}{dt}$$

where Q is the charge on the capacitor.

As a result of Kirchoff's second rule, $V_C + V_R = V$ and we obtain

$$RC\ \frac{dV_C}{dt} + \left(V_C - V\right) = 0$$

or $$\frac{dV_C}{dt} + \frac{1}{RC}\left(V_C - V\right) = 0$$

The general solution of this differential equation is

$$V_C(t) = -\ A\ e^{-t/\tau} + V \tag{1}$$

where $\tau = RC$ is the time constant of the circuit and A is the integration constant. At t = 0, $V_C = 0$ because the voltage is initially only across R. Thus, substitut- in (1), A = V, and we get

$$V_C(t) = V\left(1 - e^{-t/\tau}\right).$$

Note that as t becomes very large

$V_C(t = \infty) = V.$

The current I is

$$I(t) = C\frac{dV_C}{dt} = C\frac{d}{dt}\left[V\left(1 - e^{-t/\tau}\right)\right]$$

$$I(t) = \frac{CV}{\tau}e^{-t/\tau} = \frac{V}{R}e^{-t/\tau}$$

For the circuit under consideration

$$\tau = RC = 10 \times 10^6 \text{ ohms} \times 10^{-6} \text{ f} = 10 \text{ sec.}$$

The half-life is the time required for the decay factor $(e^{-t/\tau})$ to be $\frac{1}{2}$; or

$$e^{-\frac{t_h}{\tau}} = \frac{1}{2}$$

$$t_h = \tau \ln 2$$

$$t_h = 10 \text{ sec} \times \ln 2 = 6.9 \text{ sec.}$$

On the other hand, if R = 10 ohms the time constant is only 10×10^{-6} sec, or 10 μsec.

• PROBLEM 693

A capacitor of capacitance 0.1 μF is charged until the difference in potential between its plates is 25 V. Then the charge is shared with a second capacitor which has air as the dielectric between its plates; the potential difference falls to 15 V. The experiment is repeated with a dielectric between the plates of the second capacitor, and the final potential difference is 8 V. What is the dielectric coefficient of the dielectric used? (See figures (a), (b) and (c)).

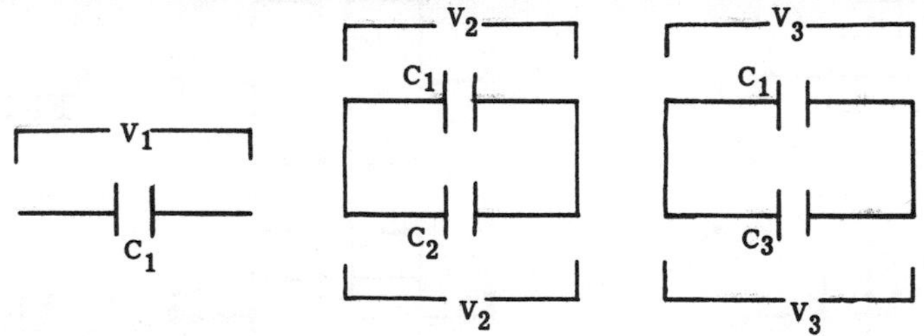

FIGURE A FIGURE B FIGURE C

Solution: The situation is illustrated in figures (a) through (c). The charge possessed by the first capacitor initially, is, by the definition of capacitance (see figure (a))

$$Q = C_1V_1 = 10^{-7} \text{ F} \times 25 \text{ V} = 2.5 \text{ μC}.$$

This charge is shared with a second capacitor of capacitance C_2, no charge being lost. Hence $Q = Q_1 + Q_2$ where Q_1 is the charge on C_1 and Q_2 is the charge on C_2 (see figure (B)). Therefore

$$Q = (C_1 + C_2)V_2 \qquad \text{or}$$

$$C_2 = \frac{Q}{V_2} - C_1 = \frac{2.5 \times 10^{-6}\ C}{15\ V} - 10^{-7}\ F$$

$$= \frac{2}{3} \times 10^{-7}\ F.$$

If a dielectric of coefficient κ is placed between the plates of capacitor C_2 and the experiment is repeated, the capacitance of C_2 is increased to $C_3 = \kappa C_2$, where κ is the dielectric coefficient. In this case, Q is shared by C_3 and C_1. Hence $Q = (C_1 + \kappa C_2)V_3$.

$$\therefore \quad \kappa = \frac{1}{C_2}\left(\frac{Q}{V_3} - C_1\right) = \frac{3}{2} \times 10^7\ F^{-1}\left(\frac{2.5 \times 10^{-6}\ C}{8\ V} - 10^{-7} F\right)$$

$$= \frac{3}{2} \times 10^7 \times \frac{17}{8} \times 10^{-7} = 3.2.$$

In this analysis, we have used the fact that κ for air is equal to κ for vacuum, or $\kappa_{air} = \kappa_{vac} = 1$.

• PROBLEM 694

A radio capacitor consists of a stack of five equally spaced plates each of area 0.01 m^2, the separation between neighbors being 2.0 mm. Calculate the capacitance (a) if the top and bottom plates are connected to form one conductor and the center three are connected to form the other, and (b) if the top, center, and bottom plates are connected to form one conductor and the other two plates are connected to form the other conductor. (See figs. (a) and (b)).

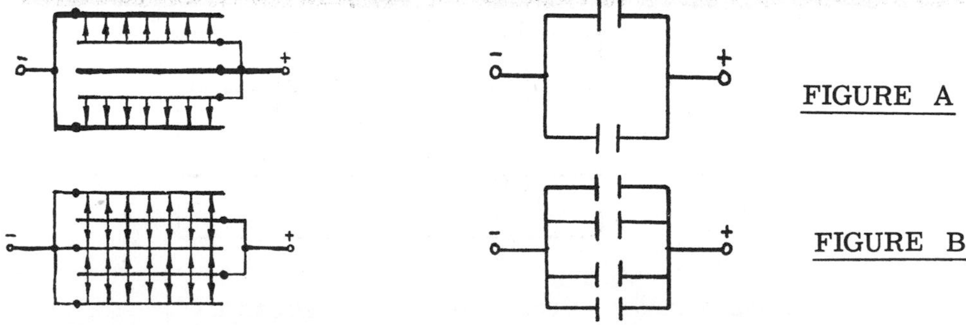

Solution: (a) Since the middle three plates are at the same potential, no field exists between them. The capacitor essentially consists of two capacitors of equal capacitance in parallel, one formed from the top two plates, the other from the bottom two plates (see figure (a)). The capacitance of a parallel plate capacitor is

$$C = \frac{\varepsilon_0 A}{d}$$

where ε_0 is the permittivity of free space, d is the plate separation, and A is the area of 1 capacitor plate. Since the equivalent capacitance of 2 capacitors in parallel is equal to the sum of their individual capacitances, we obtain

$$C_1 = 2\varepsilon_0 \frac{A}{d}$$

$$= \frac{2 \times 8.85 \times 10^{-12}\ C^2 \cdot N^{-1} \cdot m^{-2} \times 0.01\ m^2}{0.002\ m}$$

$$= 8.85 \times 10^{-11}\ F.$$

(b) Here a field exists between any pair of plates. Each of the two connected plates acts as the positive plate for each of two capacitors formed between itself and the outer and middle plates. There are effectively four equal capacitors all connected in parallel. Hence

$$C_2 = 4\varepsilon_0 \frac{A}{d} = 17.7 \times 10^{-11}\ F,$$

which is twice the capacitance of the previous arrangement.

• PROBLEM 695

A conductor of capacitance 10^{-2} μF to the ground is insulated from the ground by a silica plate 2.5 mm thick and 5 cm^2 in cross-sectional area. What is the minimum resistivity of the silica if the rate of decrease of potential is to be no greater than 0.1% per min of its instantaneous value?

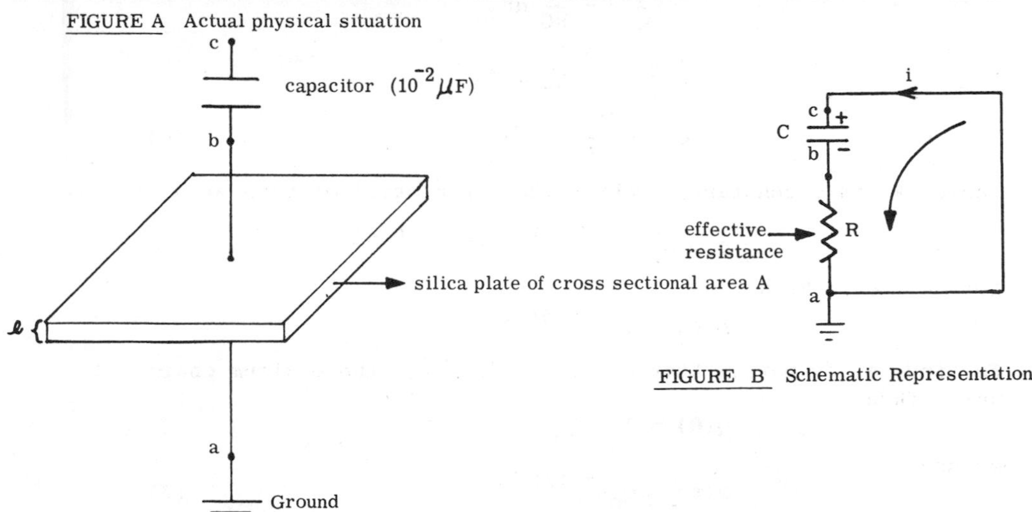

Solution: In this problem, the capacitor is initially charged to its maximum value, and then discharges to ground through the silica plate (see figure (a)). The latter may be considered to be an effective resistance (see figure (b)). Before solving the problem, we must know the voltage across the capacitor as a function of time.

Kirchoff's Voltage Law states that the net voltage around a closed circuit loop is zero. Hence,

$$V_{cb} + V_{ba} = 0 \tag{1}$$

Starting at c, and traversing the loop in the given direction (see figure (b)), we note that c is at a higher potential than b. Hence, $V_c > V_b$ or $V_b - V_c = V_{cb} < 0$. But, by definition of capacitance

$$C = \frac{|Q|}{V_{bc}}$$

or

$$V_{bc} = \frac{|Q|}{C}$$

where $|Q|$ is the absolute value of the charge on 1 plate of the capacitor. Therefore,

$$V_{cb} = -V_{bc} = \frac{-Q}{C} \tag{2}$$

where $Q > 0$. (2a)

Furthermore, $V_b > V_a$ or $V_a - V_b = V_{ba} < 0$. By Ohm's Law,

$$V_{ba} = -iR \tag{3}$$

Using (3) and (2) in (1),

$$\frac{-Q}{C} - iR = 0 \tag{4}$$

But $i = \frac{dQ}{dt}$, where Q is the net charge passing a point of the circuit per unit time. Equation (4) then becomes

$$\frac{1}{C} Q + R \frac{dQ}{dt} = 0$$

or

$$Q + RC \frac{dQ}{dt} = 0 \tag{5}$$

Solving (5)

$$\frac{dQ}{Q} = -\frac{1}{RC} dt$$

$$\int \frac{dQ}{Q} = -\frac{1}{RC} \int dt$$

$$\ell n\, Q = -\frac{1}{RC} t + F \tag{6}$$

where F is a constant. Taking the exponential of both sides of (6)

$$Q = e^{-t/RC + F} = e^{F} e^{-t/RC}$$

Let $A = e^F$. Then

$$Q(t) = Ae^{-t/RC}.$$

We find A by noting that at $t = 0$, $Q = Q_0$, the maximum charge C has. Then

$$Q(0) = A = Q_0$$

whence

$$Q(t) = Q_0 e^{-t/RC} \tag{7}$$

The voltage across C is then, by definition of C

$$V = \frac{|Q|}{C} = \frac{Q_0}{C} e^{-t/RC}$$

Note that $Q_0 > 0$ because $Q(t) > 0$. (See eq. (2a)). Defining the initial voltage across C as

$$V_0 = \frac{Q_0}{C}$$

we find

$$V(t) = V_0 e^{-t/RC} \tag{8}$$

The time rate of change of (8) is

$$\frac{dV(t)}{dt} = -\frac{1}{RC} V_0 e^{-t/RC} = -\frac{1}{RC} V(t)$$

But, the question states that

$$\frac{dV(t)}{dt} \le \left(.001 \text{ min}^{-1}\right) V(t)$$

or

$$-\frac{1}{RC} \le .001 \text{ min}^{-1}$$

Hence, solving for R

$$-1 \le \left(.001 \text{ min}^{-1}\right) RC$$

or

$$R \ge \frac{-1}{\left(.001 \text{ min}^{-1}\right)(C)} \tag{9}$$

Now, R is the resistance of the silica, which may be written as

$$R = \frac{\rho \ell}{A} \tag{10}$$

where ρ is silica's resistivity, and ℓ and A are the thickness and cross-sectional area of the plate. Using (9) in (8), and solving for ρ

$$\rho \ge -\frac{A}{\left(.001 \text{ min}^{-1}\right)(\ell)(C)}$$

Using the given values

$$\rho \ge \frac{\left(5 \times 10^{-4} \text{ m}^2\right)}{\left(\frac{.001}{605}\right)\left(2.5 \times 10^{-3}\right)\left(10^{-2} \mu F\right)}$$

Since $1\mu F = 10^{-6} F$

$$\rho \ge \frac{\left(5 \times 10^{-4} \text{m}^2\right)(60S)}{\left(10^{-3}\right)\left(2.5 \times 10^{-3} \text{m}\right)\left(10^{-8} F\right)}$$

$$\rho \ge 1.2 \times 10^{12} \ \Omega \cdot m$$

We have used the fact that $1F = 1 \text{ C/V}$.

Then

$$\rho_{min} = 1.2 \times 10^{12} \text{ m} \cdot \Omega$$

• PROBLEM 696

An inductor of inductance 3 henrys and resistance 6 ohms is connected to the terminals of a battery of emf 12 volts and of negligible internal resistance. (a) Find the initial rate of increase of current in the circuit. (b) Find the rate of increase of current at the instant when the current is 1 ampere. (c) What is the instantaneous current 0.2 sec after the circuit is closed?

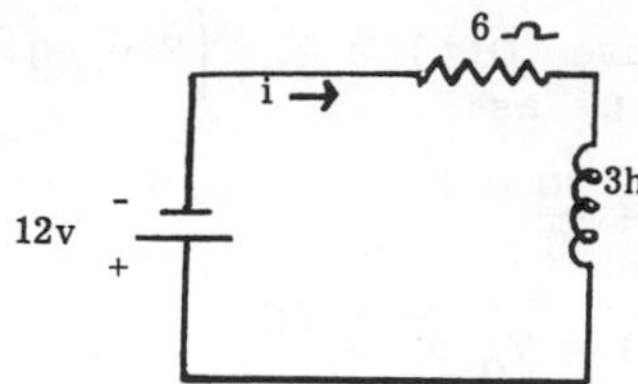

Solution: (a) Using Kirchoffs voltage law around the circuit yields

$$V = Ri(t) + L\frac{di(t)}{dt}$$

or $\frac{di(t)}{dt} = \frac{V}{L} - \frac{R}{L}i(t).$ (1)

Here, $L\frac{di}{dt}$ is the EMF induced in the inductance due to the changing current. Equation (1) relates the rate of change in current at a time t, to the current at time t. At t = 0, the initial current is zero. Hence the initial rate of increase of current is

$$\frac{di}{dt} = \frac{V}{L} = \frac{12\ V}{3h} = 4\ \text{amp/sec.}$$

(b) When i = 1 amp,

$$\frac{di}{dt} = \frac{12\ V}{3h} - \frac{6\Omega}{3h} \times 1 = 2\ \text{amp/sec.}$$

(c) The current at any time can be found by solving equation (1) for i. The function

$$i = \frac{V}{R}\left(1 - \varepsilon^{-\frac{R}{L}t}\right)$$

can be shown by substitution into the differential equation to satisfy both equation (1) and the initial condition i = 0 at t = 0. At t = 0.2 sec, we then have

$$i = \frac{V}{R}\left(1 - \varepsilon^{-\frac{Rt}{L}}\right) = \frac{12\ V}{6}\left(1 - \varepsilon^{-6\times.2/3}\right) = 2\left(1 - \varepsilon^{-.4}\right)\text{amps}$$

$$= 2(1 - .672)\text{amps} = 0.65\ \text{amps.}$$

• PROBLEM 697

A solenoid switch is activated when the magnetic induction on the axis is $5 \times 10^{-4}\ \text{Wb}\cdot\text{m}^{-2}$. The solenoid has 50 turns per cm and an inductance of 180 mH, and is operated by a 12V battery. Find the time lag when it is employed in a circuit of resistance 90 Ω.

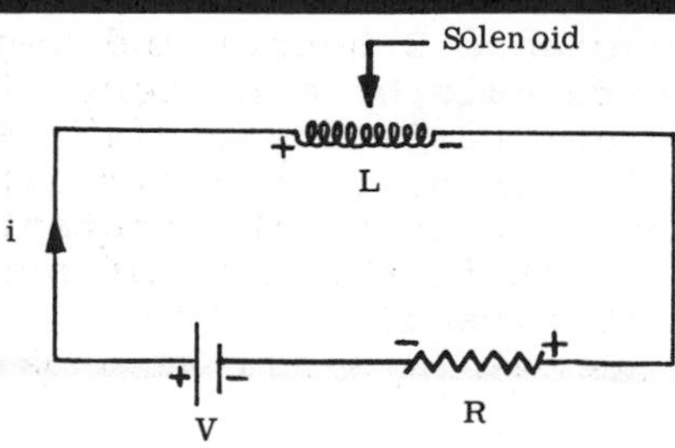

Solution: The situation is shown in the figure. When the magnetic induction in the solenoid has the value B, the current i passing through the coil is given by the equation

$$B = \mu_0 ni ,$$

where n is the number of turns per unit length of the solenoid. Further, the current at any time t after the solenoid circuit is switched on is given by the relation

$$i' = \frac{V}{R}\left[1 - e^{-Rt/L}\right]$$

where L is the solenoid inductance. (See figure). Hence,

$$B = \mu_0 ni' = \frac{\mu_0 nV}{R}\left[1 - e^{-Rt/L}\right]$$

Solving for t as a function of B,

$$\frac{BR}{\mu_0 nV} = 1 - e^{-Rt/L}$$

$$e^{-Rt/L} = 1 - \frac{BR}{\mu_0 nV}$$

Taking the logarithm of both sides of the equation

$$-\frac{Rt}{L} = \ln\left[1 - \frac{BR}{\mu_0 nV}\right]$$

Then

$$t = -\frac{L}{R}\ln\left[1 - \frac{BR}{\mu_0 nV}\right]$$

Hence, when $B = 5 \times 10^{-4}\ W{\cdot}m^{-2}$, t is

$$t = -\frac{180 \times 10^{-3}H}{90\ \Omega}\ln\left(1 - \frac{90\Omega \times 5 \times 10^{-4} Wb{\cdot}m^{-2}}{4\pi \times 10^{-7} N{\cdot}A^{-2} \times 5 \times 10^{3} m^{-1} \times 12V}\right)$$

$$= -2 \times 10^{-3} \times 2.303 \log(1 - 0.597)s = + 4.606 \times 10^{-3}\log\left(\frac{1}{0.403}\right)s$$

$$= 1.818 \times 10^{-3}\ s.$$

The time lag is thus 1.82×10^{-3}s .

• PROBLEM 698

A series-wound D.C. motor has an internal resistance of 2.0 ohms. When running at full load on a 120 volt line, a current of 4.0 amp is drawn. (a) What is the emf in the armature? (b) What is the power delivered to the motor? (c) What is the rate of dissipation of energy in the motor? (d) What is the mechanical power developed?

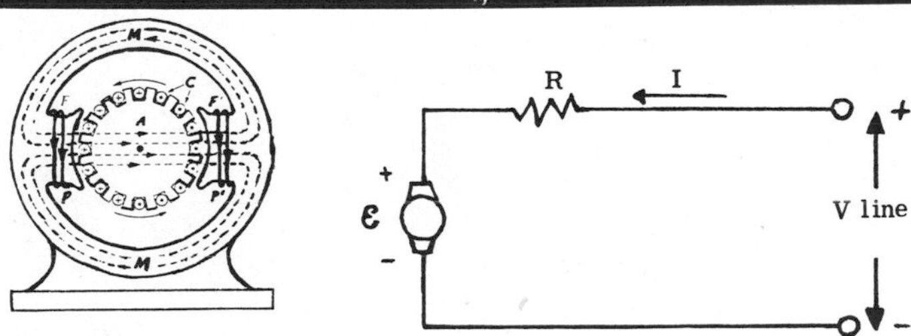

Fig. 1. Schematic diagram of a DC motor.

Fig. 2. The Electrical Circuit.

Solution:

(a) As the armature rotates between the poles F and F' of the magnet (see figure 1), an emf is induced in the loops C. According to Lenz's Law, this emf will always be in opposition to the emf applied to run the motor. This induced emf is called the "back emf" since its polarity is opposite to that of the line voltage (the voltage which runs the motor. See Figure 2).

Kirchoff's Voltage Law states that the sum of the voltage drops around a circuit loop must be zero. Using this law along with Ohm's Law,

$$\varepsilon + IR - V_{line} = 0$$

Hence $$\varepsilon = V_{line} - IR = 120\text{ V} - (2\Omega)(4\text{A}) = 112\text{ V}$$

and opposes V_{line}, as shown in the diagram.

(b) By definition, the power delivered to the motor is equal to the product of the line voltage and the current or

$$P_s = IV_\ell = (4\text{ amp})(120\text{ volt}) = 480\text{ watts.}$$

(c) The power dissipated in the motor is

$$P_d = I^2R = (16\text{ amp}^2)(2\text{ ohms}) = 32\text{ watts.}$$

(d) The mechanical power developed is the power supplied to the motor (P_s) less the power dissipated (P_d)

$$P_m = P_s - P_d = 448\text{ watts.}$$

The mechanical power developed may also be found from

$$\text{Mechanical Power} = \text{back emf} \times \text{current}$$

$$= (112\text{ v}) \times (4\text{ amp})$$

$$= 448\text{ watts.}$$

CHAPTER 21

MAGNETICS

MAGNETIC FIELDS, FLUX, INTENSITY, PERMEABILITY

• PROBLEM 699

What is the magnetic field intensity at a point in air 30 cm away from and on the extension of the line of a bar magnet 10 cm long whose magnetic moments is 400 poles cm, if the point in question is nearer the north pole of the magnet?

10 cm. 30 cm. P
S N

Solution: Draw a diagram. Recall that field intensity H is a vector quantity, which with respect to a pole strength m is given by the expression

$$H = \frac{m}{\mu r^2} \text{ which follows directly from Coulomb's Law } F = \frac{mm'}{\mu r^2}$$

where, by definition $H = \dfrac{F}{m'}$

where m' is a test pole with a north polarity. Hence $H = \dfrac{m}{\mu r^2}$.

In this problem, the pole strength can be evaluated because the nagnetic moment is given by the defining equation $M = mL$, where M is 400 poles cm, and L is 10 cm.

$$m = \frac{M}{L} = \frac{400}{10} = 40 \text{ poles.}$$

It follows that due to the north pole of the magnet, the field intensity H_1 at P is

$$H_1 = \frac{m}{\mu r^2} = \frac{40 \text{ poles}}{(1)(30\text{cm})^2} = \frac{40}{900}\ \frac{\text{poles}}{\text{cm}^2} = .044 \text{ oersteds to the}$$

right. Also, the field intensity H_2 due to the south pole is

$$H_2 = \frac{40 \text{ poles}}{1(40\text{cm})^2} = \frac{1}{40}\ \frac{\text{poles}}{\text{cm}^2}$$

Therefore H is the vector sum of H_1 and H_2

or

$$H = \overrightarrow{.044} - \overleftarrow{.025} = .019 \text{ oersteds to the right.}$$

This problem is completely analogous to the problem of finding the electric field intensity at point p, due to two charges, one positive and one negative, at a distance 30 cm and 40 cm from the point P. Coulomb's law for the electrostatic force between charges would be the electrostatic analogue for Coulomb's law for the magnetic force between poles.

• PROBLEM 700

A bar with a cross-sectional area of 6 square centimeters and a permeability of 1000 units is placed in a magnetic field of intensity 5 oersteds. What is the total number of lines of magnetic flux in the iron?

Solution: Let

B = flux density

μ = magnetic permeability

H = magnetic field intensity

$B = \mu H$ and total flux $\phi = B \times$ area

Since

$$H = 5 \text{ oersteds},$$

$$B = 1000 \times 5 \text{ oersteds} = 5000 \text{ gauss}$$

Then

$$\text{the flux } \phi = 5000 \text{ gauss} \times 6\text{cm}^2$$

$$= 30{,}000 \text{ lines of flux.}$$

• PROBLEM 701

What is the magnetic field 10 cm from a long straight wire carrying a current of 10 amp?

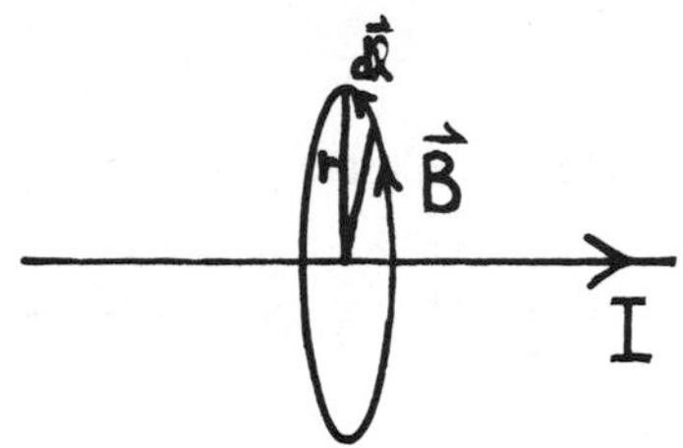

Solution: The magnitude of the current in the CGS system of units is

$$10 \text{ amp} = (10 \text{ A}) \times 3 \times 10^9 \text{ statA/A} = 3 \times 10^{10} \text{ statA}$$

The magnetic field, $\vec{B}$, due to the current I in the wire can be found by applying Ampere's law to the circular path shown in the figure,

$$\oint \vec{B} \cdot d\vec{l} = \frac{4\pi}{c} I .$$

From the symmetry of the configuration, the lines of $\vec{B}$ form concentric circles around the wire, then $\vec{B} \cdot d\vec{l} = B \; dl$. B at a distance r from the wire is

$$B \int dl = \frac{4\pi}{c} I$$

or

$$B = \frac{4\pi I}{c \; 2\pi r}$$

$$B = \frac{2I}{cr}$$

$$= \frac{2 \times \left(3 \times 10^{10} \text{ statA}\right)}{\left(3 \times 10^{10} \text{ cm/sec}\right) \times 10 \text{ cm}}$$

$$= 0.2 \text{ gauss}$$

For comparison, this is approximately equal to the magnitude of the Earth's magnetic field at the surface of the Earth and at middle latitudes.

In the figure, a long straight conductor perpendicular to the plane of the paper carries a current i going into the paper. A bar magnet having point poles of strength m at its ends lies in the plane of the paper. What is the magnitude and direction of the magnetic intensity H at point P?

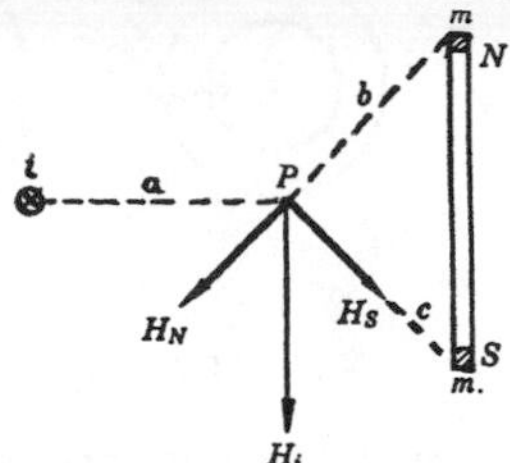

Solution: The assumption that the ends of the magnet can be taken to be point sources of magnetic flux is not a realistic one although it greatly simplifies the calculation.

The vectors H_i, H_N, and H_S, as shown in the figure, represent the components of H due respectively to the current, and to the N and S poles of the magnet. Consider first H_i. The flux density B at point P, due to the current i in a long straight conductor at a distance "a" from the conductor is known to be

$$B = \frac{\mu_0}{2\pi} \frac{i}{a} .$$

In free space, the magnetic field strength H is related to B by

$$H = \frac{B}{\mu_0}$$

hence $$H_i = \frac{1}{2\pi} \frac{i}{a} .$$

Analogous to the electric field, the magnetic field due to a magnetic pole of strength m at a distance r from the magnetic pole is

$$H = \frac{1}{4\pi\mu_0} \frac{m}{r^2} ,$$

therefore, the components H_N and H_S are respectively

$$H_N = \frac{1}{4\pi\mu_0} \frac{m}{b^2}$$

$$H_S = \frac{1}{4\pi\mu_0} \frac{m}{c^2} .$$

The resultant of these three vectors is the magnetic intensity H at the point P.

• PROBLEM 703

The current from a dc supply is carried to an instrument by two long parallel wires, 10 cm apart. What is the magnetic flux density midway between the wires when the current carried is 100 A?

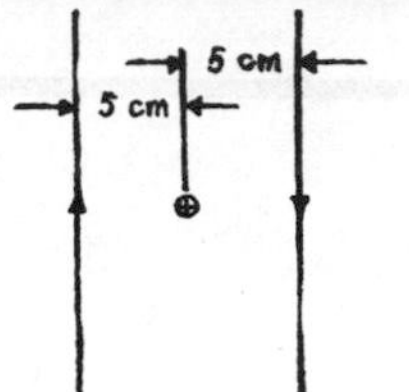

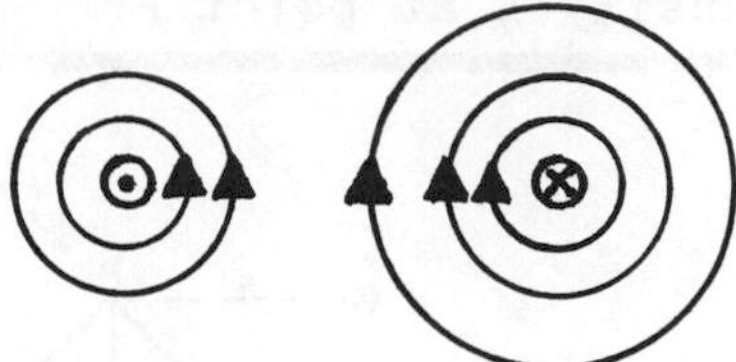

FIGURE A: Side View FIGURE B: Top View

Solution: The magnetic field due to each wire in the diagram at the point midway between them will be into the paper. This may be seen by use of the right hand rule. If the thumb of the right hand points in the direction of current through the wire, then the fingers will curl in the direction of the magnetic field (or magnetic flux density) created by the current. Application of this rule to both current carrying wires indicates that the field of each is into the page (see figures A and B). The effects due to the wires are therefore additive at that point and the total effect is twice the effect of either alone. Hence, midway between the wires the magnetic field due to one wire is

$$B = \frac{\mu_0}{2\pi} \frac{I}{r}$$

where the permeability $\mu_0 = 4\pi \times 10^{-7}$ N - A^{-2}, I is the current through the wire, and r is the distance from the point being considered to the wire. Thus

$$B = 2 \times 10^{-7} \text{ N - A}^{-2} \times \frac{100 \text{ A}}{0.05 \text{ m}} = 4 \times 10^{-4} \text{ Wb - m}^{-2}$$

The magnetic field due to both wires is then

$$B_T = 2B = 8 \times 10^{-4} \text{ Wb - m}^{-2}.$$

• PROBLEM 704

Calculate B at the center of a circular loop of wire (point P in the diagram).

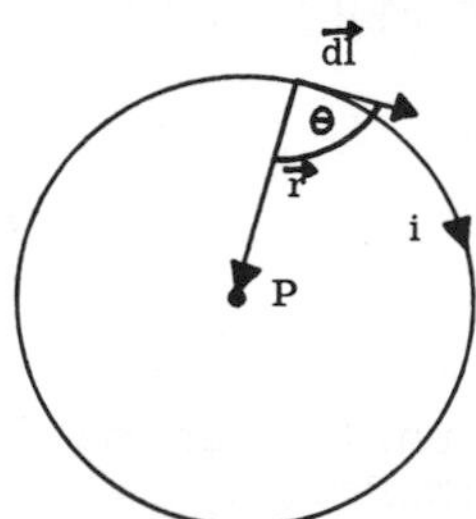

Solution. For this problem we apply the Biot-Savart Law which gives us the magnitude and direction of the magnetic field at a certain point due to a current carrying wire,

$$d\vec{B} = \frac{\mu_0 i}{4\pi} \frac{d\vec{\ell} \times \vec{r}}{r^3}$$

where $\vec{r}$ is a displacement vector from a current element to P, and $d\vec{\ell}$ is the length of this current element in the direction of current flow.

Since the contribution from any current element will be in the same direction (into the page), we may add (integrate) these contributions directly neglecting the vector nature.

The magnitude, dB, is given by

$$dB = \frac{\mu_0 i}{4\pi} \frac{d\ell \sin\theta}{r^2}$$

where θ is the angle between $d\vec{\ell}$ and $\vec{r}$.

Since we are dealing with a circular current loop, θ is 90° and $\sin\theta = 1$.

The magnetic field strength at point P is found by integrating dB over the entire loop

$$B = \int dB = \int \frac{\mu_0 i}{4\pi} \frac{d\ell}{r^2}$$

But $\frac{\mu_0 i}{4\pi}$ and r are constants. Therefore, $B = \frac{\mu_0 i}{4\pi r^2} \int d\ell$.

The integral of $d\ell$ is just $2\pi r$, the circumference.

Therefore $B = \frac{\mu_0 i}{2r}$ (directed into the page).

• PROBLEM 705

A toroidal coil has 3000 turns. The inner and outer diameters are 22 cm and 26 cm, respectively. Calculate the flux density inside the coil when there is a current of 5.0 amp.

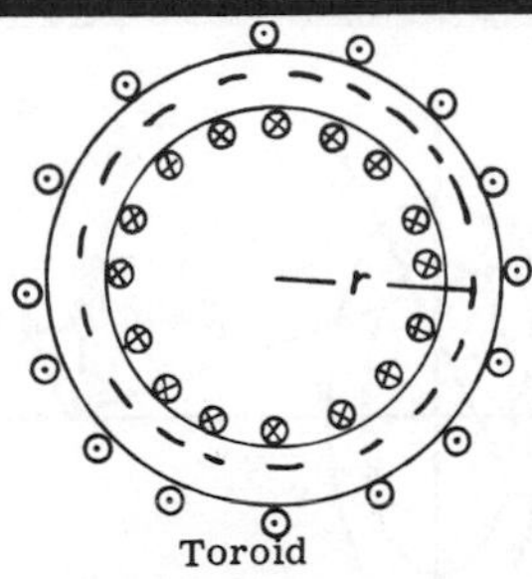

Toroid

Solution: A toroid is a wire wound in a helix and bent into the shape of a doughnut with a current i running through it. The magnetic field $\vec{B}$ forms concentric circles inside the toroid. Let r be the mean radius of the toroid. Apply Ampere's law around the circular path of radius r,

$$\oint \vec{B} \cdot d\vec{\ell} = \mu_0 I$$

where the symbol $\oint$ indicates that the integral is taken over a closed path and I is the total current enclosed by the path of integration. We get

$$(B)(2\pi r) = \mu_0 \; N \; i$$

Therefore, $B = \dfrac{\mu_0 N i}{2\pi r}$

For the toroid given,

$$\text{mean diameter} = \frac{22 \text{ cm} + 26 \text{ cm}}{2} = 24 \text{ cm} = 0.24 \text{ m}$$

$$\text{mean radius} = r = \frac{0.24 \text{ m}}{2} = 0.12 \text{ m}$$

The magnetic field is

$$B = \frac{\left(4\pi \times 10^{-7} \text{ weber/amp-m}\right)(3000)(5.0 \text{ amp})}{(2\pi)(0.12 \text{ m})}$$

$$= 0.025 \text{ weber/m}^2$$

Note that the magnetic field is not constant over the cross section of the toroid, but is inversely proportional to the radius. The magnetic field outside the toroid is zero since around any closed path encircling the toroid the net current enclosed is zero, due to equal amounts of current travelling in opposite directions.

• PROBLEM 706

Two 250-turn circular Helmholtz coils are placed parallel to one another and separated by a distance equal to their common radius. Find the value of the magnetic induction at a point on the axis between them when current flows through both coils in the same sense, and show that the field is almost uniform about the midpoint.

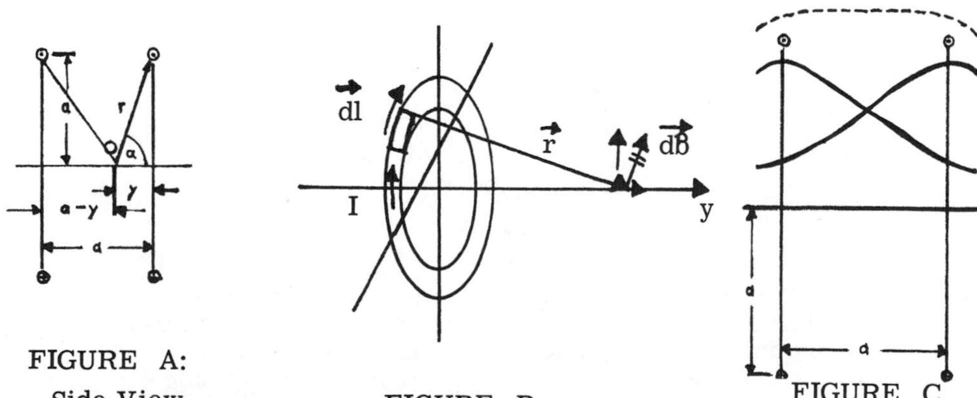

FIGURE A: Side View

FIGURE B

FIGURE C

Solution: The magnetic induction due to a single coil at a point along the axis a distance y from the plane of the coil can be found, using the Biot-Savart law

$$\vec{dB} = \frac{\mu_0}{4\pi} \frac{I\, \vec{d\ell} \times \vec{r}}{r^3}$$

(see figures A and B).

Due to the symmetry of the loop, the vertical components of the $\vec{dB}$ contributions by all the elements of current carrying wire $\vec{d\ell}$, cancel. The horizontal components add, however (see figure B). The magnitude of dB is

$$dB = \frac{\mu_0}{4\pi} \frac{I\, d\ell\, r \sin\alpha}{r^3}$$

where α is the angle between $\vec{d\ell}$ and $\vec{r}$.

$$B_1 = \frac{\mu_0}{2} \frac{Ia \sin\alpha}{r^2} = \frac{\mu_0}{2} \frac{Ia^2}{r^3} = \frac{\mu_0}{2} \frac{Ia^2}{(a^2 + y^2)^{3/2}}$$

Similarly, at the same point the magnetic induction due to a single turn of the second coil is (see figure A)

$$B_2 = \frac{\mu_0}{2} \frac{Ia^2}{\left[a^2 + (a - y)^2\right]^{3/2}}$$

These act in the same direction, (for the direction is determined by the direction of the vector $\vec{d\ell} \times \vec{dr}$, which is the same for both coils) and thus the total effect at 0 due to the n (= 250) turns of both coils is

$$B = n(B_1 + B_2)$$

$$= \frac{250\ \mu_0 I a^2}{2} \left(\frac{1}{(a^2 + y^2)^{3/2}} + \frac{1}{[a^2 + (a - y)^2]^{3/2}} \right)$$

If $y = a/2$, then $B = (8 \times 250\ \mu_0 I)/5^{3/2}\, a$. Further,

$$\frac{dB}{dy} = \frac{250\ \mu_0 I a^2}{2} \left(\frac{-3y}{(a^2 + y^2)^{5/2}} + \frac{3(a - y)}{[a^2 + (a - y)^2]^{5/2}} \right) = 0$$

if $y = a/2$.

Also

$$\frac{d^2B}{dy^2} = \frac{250\ \mu_0 I a^2}{2} \left(\frac{-3}{(a^2 + y^2)^{5/2}} - \frac{3}{[a^2 + (a - y)^2]^{5/2}} \right.$$

$$\left. + \frac{15y^2}{(a^2 + y^2)^{7/2}} + \frac{15(a - y)^2}{[a^2 + (a - y)^2]^{7/2}} \right)$$

$$= \frac{250\mu_0 I a^2}{2} \left(\frac{15y^2 - 3(a^2 + y^2)}{(a^2 + y^2)^{7/2}} + \right.$$

$$\left.\frac{15(a-y)^2 - 3\left[a^2 + (a-y)^2\right]}{\left[a^2 + (a-y)^2\right]^{7/2}}\right) = 0$$

if $y = a/2$.

Thus dB/dy and d^2B/dy^2 are each equal to zero at the point $y = a/2$, midway between the coils. Hence B hardly varies around that point, giving a large region of uniform field midway between the coils.

With this particular spacing of the coils, the dropping off in the value of B due to one coil as we move away from it is compensated for by the increase in B due to the other coil for much of the region between them. The situation is illustrated in figure C. The solid lines give the magnitude of B due to each coil separately at various distances along the axis. The dashed line shows the combined effect of the two coils, and the region of uniform field around the midpoint of the system is clearly seen.

• PROBLEM 707

An electron, charged -1.6×10^{-19} coul, moves at some instant of time in the +x-direction with velocity $v = 0.8$ c. A magnetic field $B = 10$ W/m^2 is present in the +y-direction. What is the direction and magnitude of the magnetic force?

B= 10W/m²

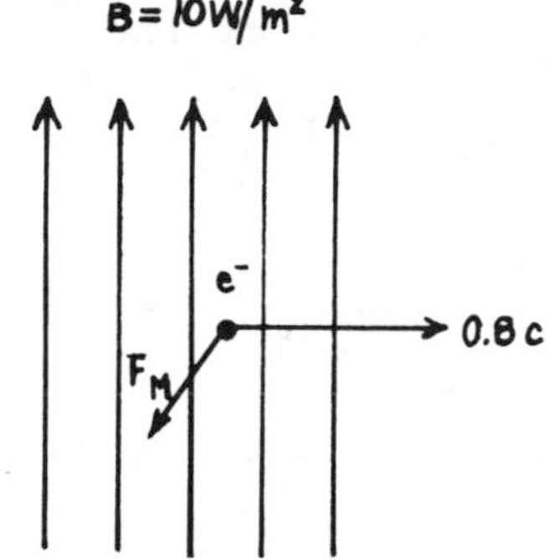

Solution: To find the magnetic force acting on a charged particle moving through a magnetic field, one uses the formula

$$\vec{F}_m = q\vec{v} \times \vec{B}$$

where $\vec{F}_m$ is the resulting magnetic force, $\vec{v}$ is the velocity of the particle and $\vec{B}$ is the magnetic field vector.

In this problem $\vec{v}$ is $0.8\text{ c} = 0.8 \times 3 \times 10^8$ m/sec in the +x-direction, $\vec{B}$ is 10 W/m^2 in the +y-direction, and q is $e^- = -1.6 \times 10^{-19}$ coul.

So:

$$\vec{F}_m = \left(-1.6 \times 10^{-19}\text{ coul.}\right)(0.8)\left(3 \times 10^8\text{ m/sec}\right)\hat{i}$$

$$\times (10 \text{ W/m}^2)\hat{j}$$

$$= -3.84 \times 10^{-10} \frac{\text{coul.} - \text{m} - \text{W}}{\text{m}^2 - \text{sec}} (\hat{i} \times \hat{j})$$

$$= -3.84 \times 10^{-10} \text{ N } \hat{k}$$

where we used the fact that $\hat{i} \times \hat{j} = \hat{k}$, $\hat{i}$, $\hat{j}$, and $\hat{k}$ being the unit vectors in the +x, +y, and +z-directions, respectively.

• PROBLEM 708

A particle is projected horizontally with a velocity of 10^4 m · s^{-1} in such a direction that it moves at right angles to a horizontal magnetic field of induction, of magnitude 4.9×10^{-5} Wb · m^{-2}. The particle, which carries a single electronic charge, stays in the same horizontal plane. What is its mass?

Solution: The upward acting magnetic force is $\vec{F} = q(\vec{v} \times \vec{B})$, where q is the charge of the particle, $\vec{v}$ its velocity, and $\vec{B}$ the magnetic induction. Since the motion is at right angles to the direction of the magnetic induction, it follows that the magnitude of $\vec{F}$, $|\vec{F}| = q\,v\,B \sin 90° = q\,v\,B$. Since the particle stays in the same horizontal plane during the motion, the magnetic force on it must, by Newton's Second Law, just balance its weight (= mg). Thus, mg = qvB or m = qvB/g.

$$\therefore m = \frac{1.6\times10^{-19}\text{C}\times10^4 \text{ m}\cdot\text{s}^{-1}\times4.9\times10^{-5} \text{ Wb}\cdot\text{m}^{-2}}{9.8 \text{ m} \cdot \text{s}^{-2}}$$

$$= 8.0 \times 10^{-21} \text{ kg}.$$

• PROBLEM 709

What is the radius of the orbit of a 1-MeV proton in a 10^4-gauss field?

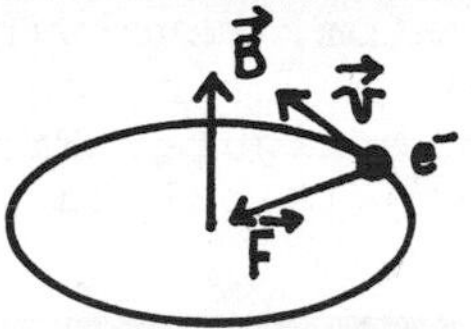

Solution: An electron which is moving in a magnetic field $\vec{B}$ with velocity $\vec{v}$, experiences a force

$$\vec{F} = -\frac{1}{c} e\vec{v} \times \vec{B}.$$

As a result of this force, the electron moves on a circular path in the plane of $\vec{v}$. The radius of the orbit is obtained from the expression for the centripetal force

$$F_{center} = F = \frac{mv^2}{R}$$

or

$$\frac{1}{c} evB = \frac{mv^2}{R}$$

$$R = \frac{mvc}{eB}.$$

The velocity of a 1-MeV proton is obtained as follows

$$KE = \text{total energy-rest energy} = \frac{m_0c^2}{\sqrt{1-\beta^2}} - m_0c^2$$

$$= \left[\frac{1}{\sqrt{1-\beta^2}} - 1\right]m_0c^2 = 1 \text{ MeV}$$

$$= 1.6 \times 10^{-6} \text{ ergs}$$

The rest energy of a proton is

$$m_0c^2 = 1.67 \times 10^{-24}\text{gr} \times \; 3 \times 10^{10}\text{cm/sec}^{2}$$

$$= 1.5 \times 10^{-3} \text{ ergs}$$

Since $KE \ll m_0c^2$, we have a non-relativistic motion. In this case, $\beta = \frac{v}{c} \ll 1$, hence we can use the approximation

$$\frac{1}{\sqrt{1-\beta^2}} \simeq 1 + \tfrac{1}{2}\beta^2$$

and

$$\tfrac{1}{2}\beta^2 \simeq \frac{KE}{m_0c^2} = \frac{1.6 \times 10^{-6}\text{ergs}}{1.5 \times 10^{-3}\text{ergs}} = 1.07 \times 10^{-3}$$

$$\beta = \sqrt{2.14 \times 10^{-3}} = 0.046$$

$$v = \beta c = 0.046 \times 3 \times 10^{10}\text{cm/sec} = 1.38 \;\; 10^{9}\text{cm/sec}$$

In the expression for R we can use the nonrelativistic (rest mass) m_0 for m. Therefore

$$R \simeq \frac{m_0vc}{eB}$$

Since $m_o = 1.67 \times 10^{-24}\text{g}$, $e = 4.8 \times 10^{-8}\text{stat C}$

or

$$R = \frac{\left(1.67 \times 10^{-24}\text{g}\right) \times \left(1.38 \times 10^{9}\text{cm/sec}\right) \times \left(3 \times 10^{10}\text{cm/sec}\right)}{\left(4.8 \times 10^{-10}\text{statC}\right) \times 10^{4}\text{gauss}}$$

$$= 14.4 \text{ cm}$$

• PROBLEM 710

The electron of a hydrogen atom, revolving in the first Bohr orbit can be thought of as being equivalent to a current loop, as shown in the figure. Find the magnetic moment μ_B of this loop (which is called one Bohr magneton).

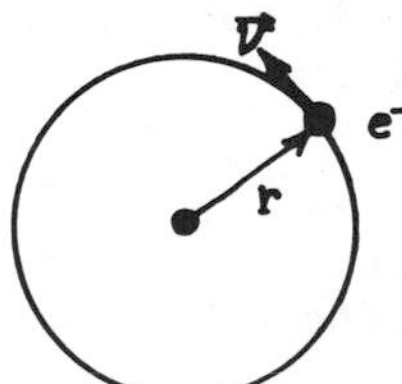

The First Bohr Orbit

Solution: The average charge, per unit time, passing a point of the orbit, or the average current I is $\frac{e}{T}$, where T is the period of rotation. The angular momentum of the first Bohr radius is given by

$$L = mvr = \frac{h}{2\pi} ,$$

or $$v = \frac{h}{2\pi mr} .$$

Then, the period and average current are

$$T = \frac{2\pi r}{v} = \frac{4\pi^2 r^2 m}{h} .$$

$$I = \frac{eh}{4\pi^2 r^2 m} .$$

The magnetic moment of the loop is $\mu_B = IA$, where A is its area, πr^2. Therefore,

$$\mu_B = \frac{h}{4\pi} \cdot \left(\frac{e}{m}\right)$$

$$= \frac{6.62 \times 10^{-34} \text{ joule-sec} \times 1.76 \times 10^{11} \text{ coul/kg}}{12.57}$$

$$= 9.27 \times 10^{-24} \text{ amp} \cdot \text{m}^2 .$$

• PROBLEM 711

The energy of the doubly charged α-particles of mass 6.64×10^{-27} kg emitted from ThC is 6.048 MeV. What is their velocity and what magnetic field applied perpendicular to a collimated beam of such particles would bend the beam into a circle of radius 40 cm?

Solution: The energy of the α-particles is 6.048 MeV $= 6.048 \text{ MeV} \times 1.602 \times 10^{-13} \text{ J/ 1 MeV} = 9.689 \times 10^{-13}$ J. The energy of the particle refers to its kinetic energy or $KE = \frac{1}{2} mv^2 = 9.689 \times 10^{-13}$ J, or

$$v = \sqrt{\frac{19.378 \times 10^{-13} \text{ J}}{6.64 \times 10^{-27} \text{ kg}}} = 1.709 \times 10^7 \text{ m} \cdot \text{s}^{-1} .$$

In the magnetic field the magnetic force supplies the centripetal force necessary to keep the particles moving in a circle. This centripetal force, F, due to the magnetic field has magnitude $F = qvB \sin\theta$ where θ is the angle between $\vec{v}$ and $\vec{B}$. Since we are given that this angle is 90°, then $\sin\theta = 1$. The centripetal acceleration of a particle with velocity v about a circle of radius R is $a = v^2/R$. By Newton's second law, $F = mv^2/R = qvB$ or $v = qBR/m$. Therefore $B = mv/qR$.

The α-particles carry twice the electronic charge (for they contain two positively charged protons and two neutral neutrons).

$$\therefore B = \frac{6.64 \times 10^{-27} \text{ kg} \times 1.709 \times 10^7 \text{ m} \cdot \text{s}^{-1}}{2 \times 1.602 \times 10^{-19} \text{ C} \times 0.40 \text{ m}}$$

$$= 0.885 \text{ Wb} \cdot \text{m}^{-2} .$$

• **PROBLEM 712**

A hydrogen atom consists of a proton and an electron separated by about 5×10^{-11} m. If the electron moves around the proton in a circular orbit with a frequency of 10^{13} sec^{-1}, what is the magnetic field at the position of the proton due to the moving electron?

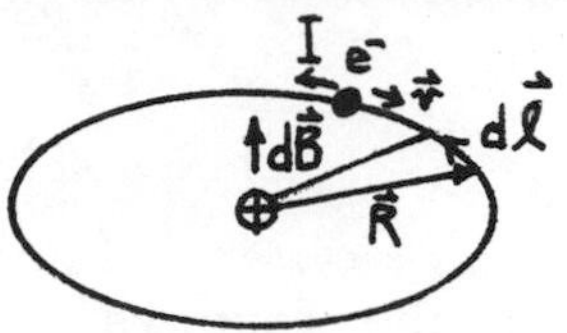

Hydrogen Atom

Solution: The motion of the electron is equivalent to an electric current. That is, the charge e moves by a point on the orbit in time T, where T is the period of revolution. Thus the equivalent current is

$$i = \frac{\text{charge pass a point}}{\text{time}}$$

$$= \frac{e}{T} = ef \ .$$

The magnetic field at the center of the circular loop of radius R is obtained from the Biot-Savart Law;

$$d\vec{B} = \frac{\mu_0 i}{4\pi} \frac{d\vec{\ell} \times \vec{R}}{R^3} \qquad (1)$$

where the permeability constant $\mu_0 = 4\pi \times 10^{-7} \frac{\omega}{a\text{-}m}$.

As shown in the diagram, all the infinitesimal contributions to $\vec{B}$ from the infinitesimal circuit elements are in the direction perpendicular to the plane of the orbit. In this case we may neglect the vector nature of (1) and obtain

$$dB = \frac{\mu_0 i}{4\pi} \frac{d\ell R \sin 90^\circ}{R^3} = \frac{\mu_0 i}{4\pi} \frac{d\ell}{R^2}$$

since $\vec{R}$ and $d\vec{\ell}$ are perpendicular to each other. Therefore, the total magnetic field is the sum of the infinitesimal contributions dB or

$$B = \int dB = \frac{\mu_0 i}{4\pi} \frac{1}{R^2} \int d\ell = \frac{\mu_0 i}{4\pi} \frac{2\pi R}{R^2} = \frac{\mu_0}{2} \frac{i}{R}$$

$$= 2\pi \times 10^{-7} \frac{\omega}{a\text{-}m} \times \frac{1.6 \times 10^{-19} \text{coul} \times 10^3 \text{sec}^{-1}}{5 \times 10^{-11} \text{ m}}$$

$$= 2.0 \times 10^{-2} \frac{\omega}{m^2} \ .$$

• **PROBLEM 713**

Deuterons with a mass of 3.3×10^{-27} kg may have a velocity of 5×10^7 m/s and an orbit radius of 0.8 m in a cyclotron. (a) Find the frequency at which the accelerating field must change. (b) What is the energy of the deuterons in MeV.

Solution: As shown in the figure, the particles move in circular orbits in the dees under the influence of the mag-

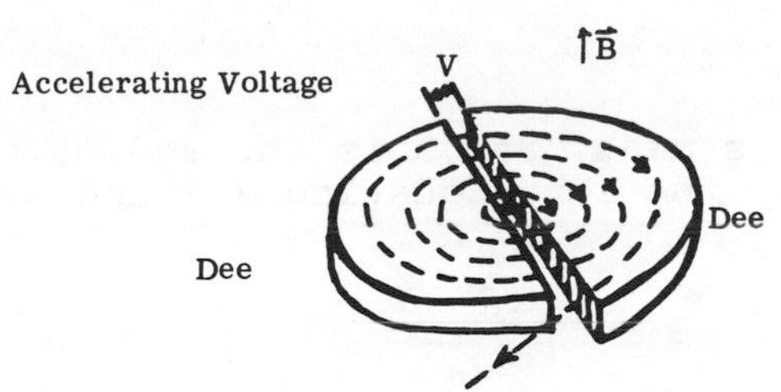

netic field and are accelerated across the gap by the electric field. Therefore, the polarity of the electric field varies with time in such a way that each time the particle enters the gap, it is accelerated rather than decelerated.

Deuterons travel during each cycle a distance

$$d = 2\pi r = 2 \times \pi \times \left(8 \times 10^{-1}\ m\right) = 5.0\ m$$

in the cyclotron. The frequency of the electric field should be equal to the frequency of the deuteron's revolutions in the dee.

$$f = \frac{1}{\text{period}} = \frac{\text{particle speed}}{\text{distance traveled during one revolution}}$$

$$= \frac{5 \times 10^7\ m/s}{5m} = 1 \times 10^7\ Hz$$

$$= 10\ MHz.$$

b) Since the deuteron speed is much less than the speed of light we can use the non-relativistic expression for kinetic energy:

$$K = \frac{1}{2}mv^2 = \left(\frac{1}{2}\right)\left(3.3 \times 10^{-27}\ kg\right)\left(5 \times 10^7 m/s\right)^2$$

$$= 4.13 \times 10^{-12}\ J$$

Since 1 eV equals 1.6×10^{-19}J, the kinetic energy may be written

$$K = \frac{4.13 \times 10^{-12}\ \not{J}}{1.6 \times 10^{-19}\ \not{J}/eV} = 2.58 \times 10^7\ eV = 25.8\ MeV$$

• PROBLEM 714

In one type of mass spectrometer the charged particles pass through a velocity selector before entering the magnetic field. In another the particles pass through a strong electric field before entering the magnetic field. Compare the ratio of the radii of singly charged lithium ions of masses 6 amu and 7 amu in the two cases.

Solution: In the magnetic field, an ion moves in a circle, the centripetal force necessary being provided by the magnetic force on it. If the velocity $\vec{v}$ of the ion is perpendicular to the field of magnetic induction $\vec{B}$, then the magnetic force on the ion of charge q, is

$$F = q\ v\ B \qquad (1)$$

Since this is the required centripetal force,

$$F = \frac{mv^2}{R} \qquad (2)$$

where m is the ion's mass, and R is the radius of the circle traversed by the ion. Equating (1) and (2),

$$q\ v\ B = \frac{mv^2}{R}$$

or $$v = \frac{q\ B\ R}{m} \qquad (3)$$

When the ions have passed through a velocity selector, both lithium ions have the same velocity in the field. Further, they have the same charge and are in the same magnetic flux density. Thus, using (3), $R_6/m_6 = R_7/m_7$.

$$\frac{R_6}{R_7} = \frac{m_6}{m_7} = \frac{6}{7} = 0.857.$$

If the ions have passed through a strong electric field, they have both acquired the same kinetic energy. But, from equation (3) we have

$$\tfrac{1}{2}\ mv^2 = \frac{q^2\ B^2\ R^2}{2m}$$

Therefore, since q and B are the same for both isotopes,

$$\frac{r_6^2}{m_6} = \frac{r_7^2}{m_7} \qquad \text{or} \qquad \frac{r_6}{r_7} = \sqrt{\frac{m_6}{m_7}} = 0.926.$$

• PROBLEM 715

Gyroradius:–What is the radius of the cyclotron orbit in a 10-kilogauss field for an electron of velocity 10^8 cm/sec normal to $\vec{B}$?

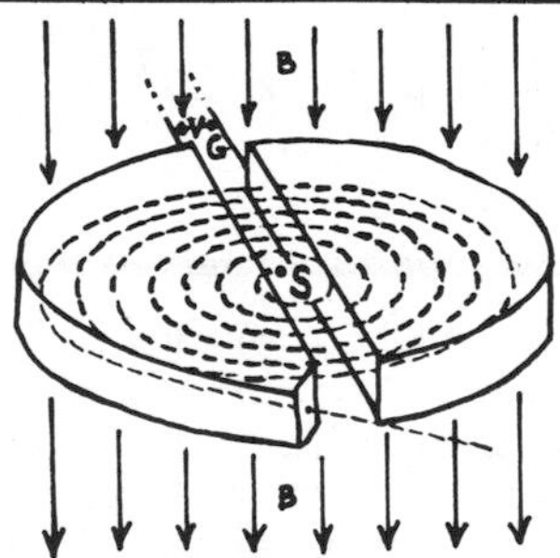

Solution: In the cyclotron, a particle is launched from point S. A voltage v is applied across the "gap" (G). A magnetic field B exerts a centripetal force towards the center. The particle is accelerated by the voltage v each time it crosses the gap, which increases the radius of the orbit. Thus the particle describes a spiral. The centripetal force which keeps the particle in orbit is given by

$$\vec{F} = \frac{q}{c}\ \vec{v} \times \vec{B}$$

The magnetic field is perpendicular to the linear

velocity of the particle so that the force exerted on the particle is towards the center of the cyclotron. The magnitude of the force is

$$\frac{q}{c} \text{ v B sin } \theta \text{, and since sin } 90° = 1 \text{, we have}$$

$$F = \frac{q}{c} vB.$$

Since within each orbit we can think of the particle as describing a circle, its acceleration is simply $\omega^2 R$ or

$\frac{v^2}{R}$ where v is the linear velocity. Since F = ma

$$\frac{q}{c} vB = m \frac{v^2}{R}$$

$$R = \frac{mvc}{qB}$$

Substituting our values we have:

$$R = \frac{0.911 \times 10^{-27} \text{ gm } 10^8 \text{ cm/sec } 3 \times 10^{10} \text{ cm/sec}}{4.8 \times 10^{-10} \text{ esu } 10^4 \text{ gauss}}$$

$$\simeq 5.7 \times 10^{-4} \text{ cm}$$

• PROBLEM 716

What is the radius of the cyclotron orbit in a field of magnetic induction of 1 weber/m^2 for an electron traveling with velocity 10^6 m/s in a direction normal to $\vec{B}$? (This radius is termed the gyroradius).

Solution: Before starting this problem, we must recognize what type of motion the electron is executing. Since the electron is a charged particle traveling perpendicular to a uniform magnetic field (a field having the same value over all space), the particle will travel in a circle.

To find the exact radius of this circular motion, we relate the magnetic force acting on the electron to the electron's acceleration via Newton's Second Law, $\vec{F} = m\vec{a}$. The magnetic force for a particle of charge q traveling perpendicular to a magnetic field with velocity $\vec{v}$ is

$$F = qvB \tag{1}$$

Using Newton's Second Law,

$$qvB = ma \tag{2}$$

Then because the motion is circular, we know that the acceleration the electron experiences is centripetal (that is, it always points to the center of the circle) and has the value $\frac{v^2}{R}$, where v is the speed of the electron, and R is the radius of its orbit. Substituting this into equation (2), we find

$$qvB = \frac{mv^2}{R} \tag{3}$$

Solving for R, we obtain

$$R = \frac{mv}{qB} \tag{4}$$

Now, the charge of an electron is $q = 1.6 \times 10^{-19}$ Coulombs, and its mass is $m = 9.11 \times 10^{-31}$ kilograms. Substituting this information and the values of v and B given in the statement of the problem into (4)

$$R = \frac{(9.11 \times 10^{-31}\ \text{kg})(10^6\ \text{m/s})}{(1.6 \times 10^{-19}\ \text{C})(1\ \text{w/m}^2)}$$

$$R = 5.7 \times 10^{-6}\ \text{m}$$

• PROBLEM 717

A cyclotron has an oscillator frequency of $11.4\ \text{Mc}\cdot\text{s}^{-1}$ and a radius of 60 cm. What magnetic induction is required to accelerate protons of mass 1.67×10^{-27} kg and charge 1.6×10^{-19} C, and what is the final energy that they acquire?

What error is made by assuming that the mass of the protons remains constant?

Solution: The force on a particle of charge q, travelling with velocity $\vec{v}$, in a field of magnetic induction $\vec{B}$, is

$$\vec{F} = q\vec{v} \times \vec{B}$$

Assuming that $\vec{B}$ and $\vec{v}$ are perpendicular,

$$F = qvB \tag{1}$$

Since a particle in this situation will execute a circular orbit, F is a centripetal force and the particle's acceleration is $a = v^2/R$. Using Newton's Second Law,

$$F = ma = mv^2/R \tag{2}$$

where m is the mass of the particle, and R is the radius of its orbit. Inserting (2) in (1)

$$\frac{mv^2}{R} = qvB$$

or, solving for v

$$v = \frac{qBr}{m} \tag{1}$$

Now, we must eliminate v, since it is unknown. But, since the path is circular, and v is constant, we may write

$$v = \frac{2\pi R}{T}$$

where T is the time it takes the particle to traverse its orbit once, or the period of the motion. Since

$$T = \frac{1}{f}$$

where f is the frequency of the motion

$$v = 2\pi Rf \qquad (2)$$

Substituting (2) in (1) gives us B in terms of known quantities.

$$2\pi Rf = \frac{qBR}{m}$$

Solving for B

$$B = \frac{2\pi fm}{q}$$

$$= \frac{2\pi \times 11.4 \times 10^{6}\ s^{-1} \times 1.67 \times 10^{-27}\ kg}{1.6 \times 10^{-19}\ C} = 0.748\ Wb \cdot m^{-2}.$$

where we have used the fact that in the cyclotron, the orbital frequency of the particle equals the oscillator frequency.

The final energy of the protons is, using (1)

$$\frac{1}{2}mv^2 = \frac{q^2 B^2 R^2}{2m}$$

$$= \frac{\left(1.6 \times 10^{-19}\right)^2 C^2 \times (0.748)^2\ Wb^2 \cdot m^{-4} \times 0.6^2\ m^2}{2 \times 1.67 \times 10^{-27}\ kg}$$

$$= 0.154 \times 10^{-11}\ J$$

Since $E = mc^2$, this energy is equivalent to an increase of mass

$$\Delta m = \frac{0.154 \times 10^{-11}\ J}{9 \times 10^{16}\ m^2 \cdot s^{-2}} = 0.017 \times 10^{-27}\ kg.$$

The error is thus

$$\frac{\Delta m}{m} \times 100 = \frac{0.017}{1.67} \times 100 = 1.02\%.$$

• PROBLEM 718

What is the gyrofrequency of an electron in a magnetic field of 10 kilograms, or 1×10^4 gauss? (A field of 10 to 15 kilogauss is typical of ordinary laboratory iron core electromagnets.)

Solution: The centripetal force keeping the electron in its orbit is provided by the magnetic field. This is given by

$$\vec{F} = \frac{q}{c}\, \vec{v} \times \vec{B}$$

Since the velocity is perpendicular to the magnetic field, this reduces to

$$F = \frac{q}{c}\, vB$$

In circular motion, $v = R\omega$. Therefore

$$F = \frac{q}{c}\, R\omega B$$

Newton's third law tells us that $F = ma$, and since in circular motion $a = \omega^2 R$, we have $F = m\omega^2 R$. Equating this with the above expression for force we have:

$$\frac{q}{c}\, R\omega B = m\omega^2 R$$

$$\omega = \frac{qB}{mc}$$

Substituting for our values:

$$\omega = \frac{4.8 \times 10^{-10}\ \text{esu}\,(1 \times 10^4\ \text{gauss})}{.911 \times 10^{-27}\ \text{gm}\ (3 \times 10^{10}\ \text{cm/sec})}$$

$$= \frac{4.8 \times 10^{-6}\ \text{esu}\ \dfrac{\text{gm - cm}}{\text{sec}^2\ \text{esu}}}{2.7 \times 10^{-17}\ \text{gm}\ \dfrac{\text{cm}}{\text{sec}}} = 1.8 \times 10^{11}\ \ \text{sec}^{-1}$$

Dividing the angular velocity by 2π we arrive at the frequency ν

$$\nu = \frac{1.8 \times 10^{11}\ \text{sec}^{-1}}{2\pi} = 2.8 \times 10^{10}\ \text{cps}$$

Electromagnetic wavelength is given by $\lambda = \frac{c}{\nu}$.

Therefore, this gyrofrequency is equivalent to an electromagnetic wavelength of

$$\lambda = \frac{3 \times 10^{10}\ \frac{\text{cm}}{\text{s}}}{2.8 \times 10^{10}\ \text{s}^{-1}} \cong 1\ \text{cm}.$$

• PROBLEM 719

The combination of electric and magnetic fields used in J.J. Thomson's experiment can be used to measure the speed of the electrons. This measurement is possible if the electric and magnetic fields are arranged so that they produce forces acting in opposite directions. The strength of the electric and magnetic fields are then adjusted so that the resultant force is zero and the beam is undeflected. (a) Show in this case that the electron speed v is given by,

$$v = \frac{E}{B}$$

Where E and B are the electic and magnetic field

strengths, respectively. (b) Compute the velocity of an electron beam that is undeflected in passing through electric and magnetic fields of 3.7 × 104 N/C and 0.23 Weber $/m^2$ respectively.

Solution: Thomson measured the ratio of the charge q of the electron to its mass m. Electrons were emitted from a hot filament and accelerated by an applied potential difference in a direction perpendicular to an electric field E and a magnetic field B. E and B are also at right angles so that they accelerate the electron along the same direction. The resultant force F on the electron is,

$$F = qE + qv \times B$$

For the electron not to be deflected, this force must be equal to zero. The above equation reduces to,

$$qE = qvB$$

Since v and B are perpendicular.

Solving this equation for v,

$$v = \frac{E}{B}$$

(b) Since the values of the electric and magnetic fields are 3.7×10^4 N/C and 2.3×10^1 Weber/m^2 respectively.

$$v = \frac{E}{B} = \frac{3.7 \times 10^4 \text{ N/C}}{2.3 \times 10^{-1} \text{ Weber }/m^2}$$

Since,

$$1 \frac{\text{Weber}}{m^2} = 1 \frac{N}{A \cdot m}$$

$$v = 1.6 \times 10^5 \text{ m/s}$$

The speed of the electrons is 1.6×10^5 m/s. Electic and magnetic fields arranged in this manner are used as a velocity selector for charged particles (ions) in several types of apparatus.

• PROBLEM 720

In a cloud chamber, a proton crosses at right angles a uniform magnetic field of 1.0 weber/m^2. From the photograph of the proton's path the radius of curvature is measured as 0.22 m. Calculate the speed of the proton.

Solution. The centripetal force acting on the proton causes it to curve. This force is due to the magnetic deflecting force Bqv where q, the charge on the proton, is 1.6×10^{-19} coulombs. The force can also be represented in terms of the radius of curvature and the velocity of the proton as $\frac{mv^2}{r}$, with the mass of the proton, m, equaling 1.67×10^{-27} kg. Setting the two expressions equal and solving for the velocity,

$$Bqv = \frac{mv^2}{r}$$

$$v = \frac{Bqr}{m} = \frac{(1.0 \text{ weber/m}^2)(1.60 \times 10^{-19} \text{ coul})(0.22 \text{ m})}{1.67 \times 10^{-27} \text{ kg}}$$

$$= 2.1 \times 10^7 \text{ m/sec}.$$

(Since this speed is less than a tenth the speed of light, we are justified in neglecting any relativistic change in the mass of the proton.)

MAGNETIC FORCES

• PROBLEM 721

A magnetic south pole of 15 units strength, when placed 10 cm away from another pole in air, experiences a repulsion of 300 dynes. What is the nature and strength of the second pole?

Solution: Since the force is one of repulsion, the second pole is a like pole, i.e., a south pole. Until the advent of quantum theory, the nature of the magnetic force of a magnet was not well understood. The concept of magnetic pole strength due to a magnetic pole was then developed in a manner analogous to the concept of electric field strength and charge. The analogue to Coulomb's law for the electrostatic force between two charges is Coulomb's law for the magnetic force between two poles of field strength m and m' separated by a distance r. It is

$$F = \frac{1}{\mu}\frac{mm'}{r^2}$$

where $\mu = 1$ for the CGS system being used. We are given that $F = 300$ dynes, m is 15 poles, $\mu = 1$ for air, and $r = 10$ cm. Therefore,

$$m' = \frac{\mu r^2 F}{m} = \frac{(1)(10 \text{ cm})^2(300 \text{ dynes})}{(15 \text{ poles})} = 2000 \text{ poles}$$

Although this model of magnetic poles correctly predicts experimentally observed magnetic forces between poles, magnetic monopoles have never been observed.

• PROBLEM 722

An electron is projected into a magnetic field of flux density $B = 10$ w/m^2 with a velocity of 3×10^7 m/sec in a direction at right angles to the field. Compute the magnetic force on the electron and compare with the weight of the electron.

Solution. The force on the electron in a magnetic field is given by $\vec{F} = q\vec{v} \times \vec{B}$ where $\vec{v}$ is the velocity of the electron and $\vec{B}$ is the flux density of the magnetic field. In this case the velocity is perpendicular to the magnetic field so the force may be computed by a straightforward multiplication instead of taking the cross product.

The magnetic force is

$$F = qvB = 1.6 \times 10^{-19} \times 3 \times 10^{7} \times 10 = 4.8 \times 10^{-11} \text{ newton}$$

The gravitational force, or the weight of the electron, is

$$F = mg = 9 \times 10^{-31} \times 9.8 = 8.8 \times 10^{-30} \text{ newton.}$$

The gravitational force is therefore negligible in comparison with the magnetic force.

• PROBLEM 723

Two very long straight parallel wires carry currents i_1 and i_2 and are a distance r apart. Calculate the force on a length I_2 of the wire with current i_2. Verify that the force is attractive when the currents are in the same direction, but repulsive when they are in opposite directions.

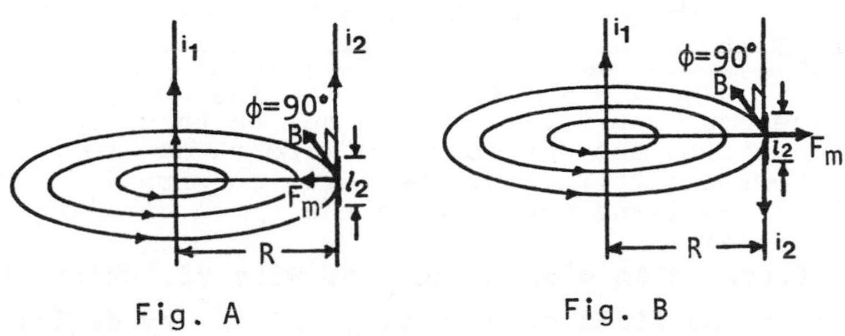

Solution: Figure a is the case of the two currents flowing in the same direction. The magnetic lines of forces due to i_1 are circles that go around clockwise for an observer looking in the direction of i_1. The magnetic field produced by i_1 at a point on the other wire is (in the CGS system)

$$B = \frac{2i_1}{cr} \tag{1}$$

This field is perpendicular to i_1 and to the radius r drawn perpendicular to i_1 and to the radius drawn perpendicularly to both wires. Since B is also perpendicular to i_2, $\phi = 90°$, $\sin \phi = 1$. The force exerted by the field on a length I_2 of the wire with current i_2 is given by

$$F_m = \frac{1}{c} i_2 \vec{I}_2 \times \vec{B} .$$

$\vec{I}$ and $\vec{B}$ are perpendicular to each other (see the diagram). Therefore,

$$F_m = \frac{i_2 I_2 B}{c} \tag{2}$$

Combining equations (1) and (2), the required force is

$$F_m = \frac{2i_1 i_2 I_2}{c^2 r}$$

In figure a the magnetic field is into the plane of the paper. Applying the right hand rule the thumb would point to the left, toward i_1. Figure b is the case of currents flowing in opposite directions, i_1 is still upward and B is still into the plane of the paper. Using the right hand rule. The thumb would point to the right, so the force is repulsive.

• PROBLEM 724

Two straight parallel wires each 90 cm long are 1.0 mm apart. There are currents of 5.0 amp in opposite directions in the wires. What are the magnitude and sense of the force between these currents?

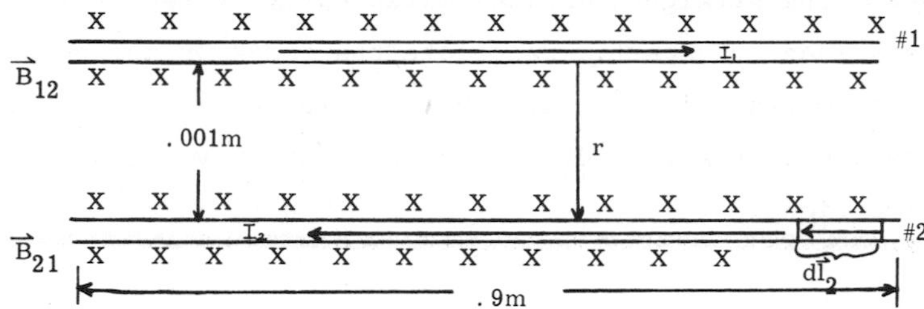

Solution: There are 2 steps in the solution of problems like these. First we find the magnetic field due to current #1 at any point on wire #2. (See figure). This field ($\vec{B}_{21}$) exerts a force on each moving charge that constitutes current #2. It is the sum of these forces which constitute the net force on wire #2 due to wire #1. (By Newton's Third Law, the force on wire #1 due to wire #2 is equal and opposite to the force on wire #2 due to wire #1).

The force on an element $d\vec{\ell}_2$ of wire #2, which is immersed in the field of wire #1 ($\vec{B}_{21}$) is, by definition,

$$d\vec{F}_{21} = I_2 \, d\vec{\ell}_2 \times \vec{B}_{21}$$

and $$\vec{F}_{21} = I_2 \int d\vec{\ell}_2 \times \vec{B}_{21} \qquad (1)$$

where the integral in (1) is evaluated over the length of wire #2 and $d\ell_2$ has the direction of I_2. In order to calculate $\vec{F}_{21}$, we must find $\vec{B}_{21}$.

The lines of magnetic induction of a long wire are circles centered on the axis of the wire. Hence, to calculate $\vec{B}_{21}$, we may use Ampere's Law, which is

$$\oint \vec{B} \cdot d\vec{\ell} = \mu_0 I_{enc} \qquad (2)$$

In (2), the integral is evaluated over a closed path (this is the meaning of the circle on the integral sign) and I_{enc} is the net current enclosed by the closed path. In evaluating $\vec{B}_{21}$, we take the integral about a circular line of magnetic induction, of radius r, centered on wire

#1. Therefore,

$$2\pi r\ B_{21} = \mu_0 I_1$$

since I_1 is enclosed by the path. Then

$$B_{21} = \frac{\mu_0 I_1}{2\pi r} \qquad (3)$$

The direction of this field is shown in the figure by the "X" symbol, which indicates that the field is perpendicular to the plane of the figure and directed into the figure.

Now, we may write the magnitude of $\vec{F}_{21}$ as

$$F_{21} = I_2 \int d\ell_2\ B_{21}\ \sin\ \phi$$

where ϕ is the angle between $d\vec{\ell}_2$ and $\vec{B}_{21}$. Looking at the figure, ϕ is 90° and

$$F_{21} = I_1 \int d\ell_2\ B_{21}$$

Using (3) $$F_{21} = I_2 \int \frac{\mu_0 I_1}{2\pi r}\ d\ell_2$$

$$F_{21} = \frac{\mu_0 I_1 I_2 \ell_2}{2\pi r}$$

$$F_{21} = \frac{\left(4\pi\times\ 10^{-7}\ \frac{\text{Weber}}{\text{amp.m}}\right)\left(25\ \text{amp}^2\right)\left(90\ \times\ 10^{-2}\ \text{m}\right)}{(2\pi)\left(10^{-3}\ \text{m}\right)}$$

$$F_{21} = 4.5\ \times\ 10^{-3}\ \text{nt}$$

By Newton's Third Law,

$$\left|\vec{F}_{21}\right| = \left|\vec{F}_{12}\right|$$

• PROBLEM 725

Two long, straight wires, each carrying a current of 9 A in the same direction are placed parallel to each other. Find the force that each wire exerts on the other when the separation distance is 1×10^{-1} m.

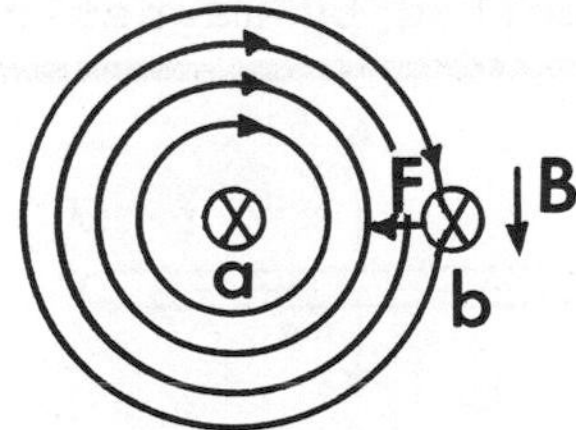

Solution: The currents carried by the wires i_a = 9 A, i_b = 9 A, and the distance between them, $d = 1 \times 10^{-1}$ m, are given. The first current carrying wire (a) produces a field of induction B at all nearby points around it. The magnitude of B is

$$B = \frac{\mu_0}{2\pi} \frac{i_a}{d} \qquad (1)$$

where i_a is the current through wire a, d is the distance separating the two wires and the permeability constant $\mu_0 = 4\pi \times 10^{-7}$ W/(A · m). The other wire will find itself immersed in the field due to the first wire. The magnetic field it creates, that is its own self field, has no influence on its behavior. The magnetic force on this second current carrying wire (of length ℓ) is

$$\vec{F} = i_b \vec{\ell} \times \vec{B}$$

where i_b is the current through the second wire. Since the wire length is perpendicular to the magnetic field vector B, we then have

$$F = i_b \ell B \qquad (2)$$

F is directed inward toward the first wire. It is perpendicular to both B and to the length vector. Therefore, combining equations (1) and (2) we have

$$F = \frac{\mu_0}{2\pi} \frac{i_a i_b}{d} \ell$$

The force per unit length on a wire is then

$$\frac{F}{\ell} = \frac{\mu_0}{2\pi} \frac{i_a i_b}{d} = 2 \times 10^{-7} \text{ N/A}^2 \frac{i_a i_b}{d}$$

$$= 2 \times 10^{-7} \text{ N/A}^2 \frac{(9 \text{ A})(9 \text{ A})}{1 \times 10^{-1} \text{ m}} = 1.62 \times 10^{-4} \frac{\text{N}}{\text{m}}$$

• PROBLEM 726

A long, horizontal, rigidly supported wire carries a current of 50 A. Directly above it and parallel to it is a fine wire, the weight of which is 0.075 N per meter, which carries a current of 25 A. How far above the first wire should the second wire be strung in order for it to be supported by magnetic repulsion?

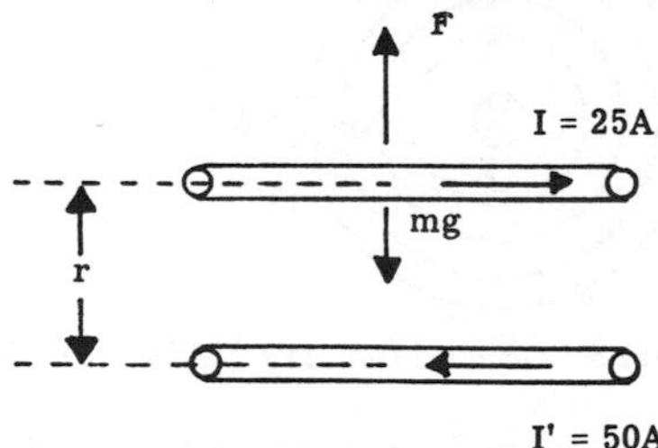

Solution: If the upper wire is to be supported by magnetic repulsion, the magnetic force per unit length (F/ℓ) must just equal the weight of a unit length of the wire (mg/ℓ). Further, the currents in the two wires must be in opposite directions in order for the force between the wires to be one of repulsion. Hence

$$\frac{mg}{\ell} = \frac{F}{\ell}$$

but $$\frac{F}{\ell} = \frac{\mu_0}{2\pi}\,\frac{I\,I'}{r} \quad \text{(see the figure)}$$

$$\therefore \quad \frac{mg}{\ell} = \frac{\mu_0}{2\pi}\,\frac{I\,I'}{r}$$

$$r = \frac{\mu_0 \ell I I'}{2\pi mg} = \frac{2 \times 10^{-7}\ \text{N} \cdot \text{A}^{-2} \times 50\text{A} \times 25\ \text{A}}{0.075\ \text{N} \cdot \text{m}^{-1}}$$

$$= 0.33 \times 10^{-2}\ \text{m} = 0.33\ \text{cm}.$$

The wires must therefore be very thin in order to allow their centers to be so close together.

• PROBLEM 727

A scientifically minded Romeo has found a method of sending secret messages to a beautiful Juliet who is immured in the top floor of a castle 50 ft from the ground. Romeo places two light metal rods (too light to use for climbing up)against her windowsill, and between the rods he mounts a wire 10 cm long, to which is attached the message and a magnet so placed that the wire is permanently in a magnetic field of strength $0.049\ \text{Wb} \cdot \text{m}^{-2}$, at right angles to the plane of the rods. When he passes a current of 10 A up one rod, through the connecting wire and back down the other rod, the message,wire, and magnet travel at uniform speed up the rods. The moving assembly weighs 0.25 kg. Neglecting friction, calculate what the length of the rods must be.

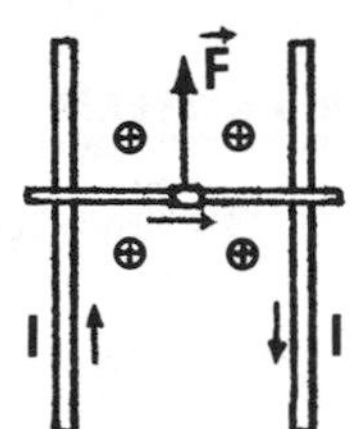

FIGURE A: Front View

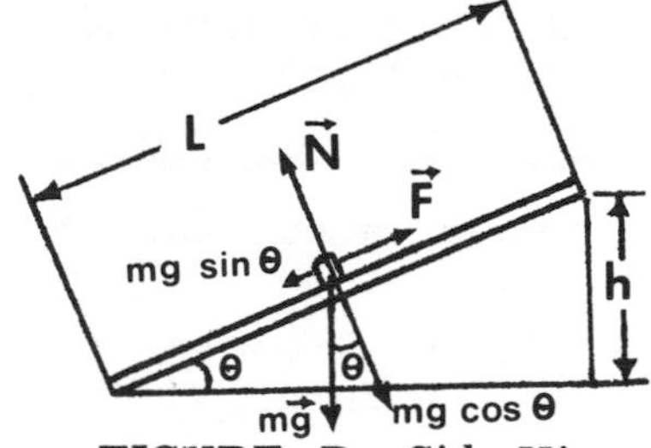

FIGURE B: Side View

Solution: From figure A, we see that the magnetic field must be at right angles to the plane of the rods and acting downward. The magnetic field vector is perpendicular to both the direction of current and to the force. The right hand rule determines that the direction is downward. The magnitude of the force experienced by the wire and attachments is

$|\vec{F}| = \ell IB \sin \phi$ where ϕ is the angle between the direction of I and $\vec{B}$. $\phi = 90°$, and

$$F = \ell IB = 0.1\ \text{m} \times 10\ \text{A} \times 0.049\ \text{Wb} \cdot \text{m}^{-2} = 0.049\ \text{N}.$$

Considering fig. B, we see that the forces acting on the wire and attachments are three in number: the weight acting vertically downward, the force F acting up the plane of the rods, and N, the normal reaction of the rods on the wire acting at right angles to the plane of the rods. Since the assembly moves up the rods at uniform speed, $F = mg \sin\theta$.

$$\therefore \quad \sin\theta = \frac{0.049 \text{ N}}{0.25 \text{ kg} \times 9.8 \text{ m} \cdot \text{s}^{-2}} = 0.02.$$

From the diagram, $h/L = \sin\theta = 0.02$.

$$\therefore \quad L = \frac{h}{0.02} = \frac{50 \text{ ft}}{0.02} = 2500 \text{ ft}.$$

• PROBLEM 728

Find the force on an electrically charged oil drop when it moves at a speed of 1×10^2 m/s across a magnetic field whose strength is 2 T. Assume that the charge on the oil-drop is 2×10^{-17} C.

Solution: The speed of the particle, $v = 1 \times 10^2$ m/s, the field strength, $B = 2$ T, and the charge, $q = 2 \times 10^{-17}$ C, are given.

The force on the drop due to its motion through the magnetic field is given by

$$\vec{F} = \vec{q}\,\vec{v} \times \vec{B} \qquad (1)$$

Since the drop moves across the magnetic field, the angle between $\vec{v}$ and $\vec{B}$ is 90°. Equation (1) then reduces to

$$|\vec{F}| = qvB = \left(2 \times 10^{-17}\text{C}\right)\left(1 \times 10^2 \text{ m/s}\right)(2 \text{ T}) = 4 \times 10^{-15} \text{ N}$$

The force acts in a direction perpendicular to both $\vec{B}$ and to $\vec{v}$. This force is very small compared with the weight of even a very small oil drop.

• PROBLEM 729

The figure shows a current of 25 amp in a wire 30 cm long and at an angle of 60° to a magnetic field of flux density 8.0×10^{-4} weber/m^2. What are the magnitude and direction of the force on this wire?

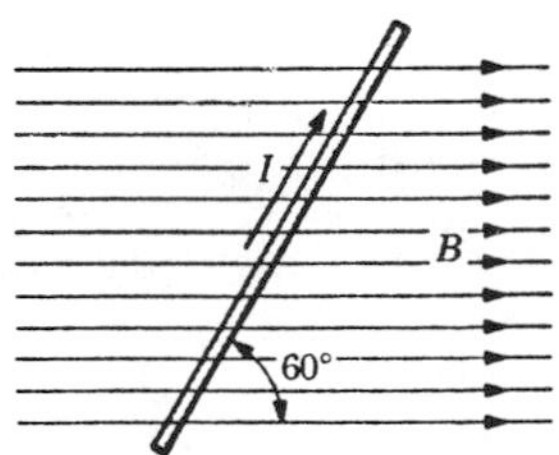

Solution: We must find the magnetic force on a wire placed in a magnetic field. The force on a differential element of the current carrying wire,

$d\vec{\ell}$, is $\quad d\vec{F} = I\, d\vec{\ell} \times \vec{B}$ (1)

where I is the current in the wire, $d\vec{\ell}$ is a vector tangent to the wire in the direction of I, and $\vec{B}$ is the magnetic induction. The net force on the wire is found by integrating $d\vec{F}$ over the length of the wire (this amounts to adding the contributions of each current element $d\vec{\ell}$ to the net force). Hence,

$$\vec{F} = \int_0^{\ell} I\, d\vec{\ell} \times \vec{B} \qquad (2)$$

where ℓ is the length of the wire. Because I is constant and $\vec{B}$ is uniform (independent of position) we may rewrite (2) as

$$\vec{F} = I \left[\int_0^{\ell} d\vec{\ell}\right] \times \vec{B} \quad \text{or } \vec{F} = I\, \vec{\ell} \times \vec{B} \qquad (3)$$

where $\vec{\ell}$ is a vector whose magnitude is the length of the wire, and whose direction is the direction of current flow in the wire. Now, in general, the magnitude of a cross product (such as $|\vec{\ell} \times \vec{B}|$) is defined as:

$$|\vec{\ell} \times \vec{B}| = \ell B \sin\theta$$

where ℓ is the magnitude of $\vec{\ell}$, B is the magnitude of $\vec{B}$, and θ is the angle between the directions of $\vec{\ell}$ and $\vec{B}$. Because we are asked to find the magnitude of the force, we have:

$$F = I\ell B \sin\theta \qquad (4)$$

Substituting the given values into (4), we obtain:

$$F = (25\text{ amp})(.3\text{ m})\left(8 \times 10^{-4}\ \frac{\text{weber}}{\text{m}^2}\right)(\sin 60°)$$

or $\quad F = 5.2 \times 10^{-3}$ Newtons

The wire is pushed away from the reader, from the stronger toward the weaker field.

• PROBLEM 730

A current-carrying wire in the form of a semicircle lies in a plane at right angles to the direction of a uniform magnetic induction. Show that the force on the wire is the same as that experienced by a straight wire lying along the diameter between the ends of the semicircle.

Solution: Let the semicircle carrying a current i have radius r, and let the magnetic induction have magnitude B. Consider Fig. A, in which a vector element $\vec{dl}$ of the current-carrying wire is shown in a direction from the center 0 of the semicircle making an angle θ with the radius of symmetry. The force on that element due to the magnetic field is $\vec{dF} = i(\vec{dl} \times \vec{B})$. Here $\vec{dl}$ and $\vec{B}$ are at

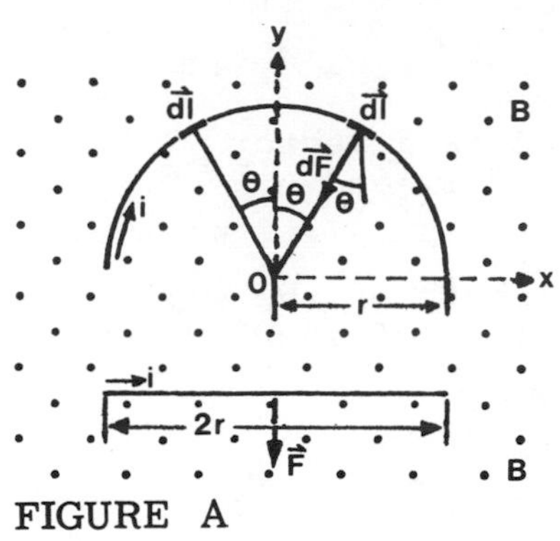

FIGURE A

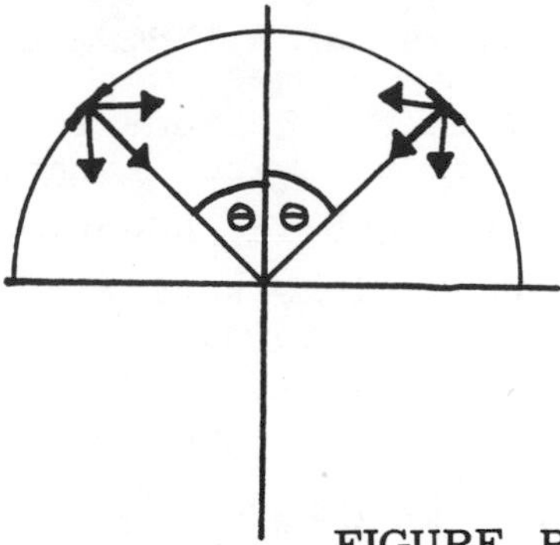

FIGURE B

right angles, and thus $\vec{dF}$ lies perpendicular to both $\vec{dl}$ and $\vec{B}$, or along the radius from $\vec{dl}$ to 0. Also $\vec{dF}$ has components, in the x- and y-directions shown, of $- i\,dlB \sin\theta$ and $- i\,dlB \cos\theta$, respectively (see figure B). But there is a corresponding element $\vec{dl}$ in a direction from 0 making an angle $-\theta$ with the radius of symmetry. This element is subjected to a force which has x- and y-components of $+ i\,dlB \sin\theta$ and $- i\,dlB \cos\theta$, respectively. The x-components of the forces of these two elements thus cancel out, and this is true of all pairs of elements chosen at all possible angles θ on the semicircle. It follows that the total force $\vec{F}$ on the semicircle has a y-component only. Now $dl/r = d\theta$ radians or $dl = rd\theta$. Also, when $l = 0$, $\theta = -\pi/2$ and when l = unity, $0 = +\pi/2$. Therefore,

$$F = \int_0^1 dF_y = F = \int_0^1 - i\,dlB \cos\theta$$

$$= \int_{-\pi/2}^{\pi/2} - ir\,d\theta B \cos\theta = - iBr \Big[\sin\theta\Big]_{-\pi/2}^{\pi/2}$$

$$= - 2iBr.$$

Consider the straight wire; the force $\vec{F}'$ on it is $\vec{F}' = i(2\vec{r} \times \vec{B})$. Thus $\vec{F}'$ has magnitude $2iBr$ and points in the negative y-direction. This is the same force as that which acts on the semicircle.

One may arrive at this result and a more general result by noting that a closed current-carrying loop lying in a plane at right angles to the magnetic field experiences no net force. If the semicircular loop is closed by allowing the current to return along a wire occupying the vacant diameter (or by any loop whatsoever lying in the plane and joining the two ends of the semicircle), the complete circuit so formed experiences no net force. It follows that the forces on the semicircle and on the return wire are equal and opposite. Since reversing the direction of the current reverses the magnetic force on it, it immediately follows that the force on the semicircle is equal to the force on any current-carrying conductor lying in the plane and having the same endpoints.

A rectangular coil 30 cm long and 10 cm wide is mounted in a uniform field of flux density 8.0×10^{-4} nt/amp -m. There is a current of 20 amp in the coil, which has 15 turns. When the plane of the coil makes an angle of 40° with the direction of the field, what is the torque tending to rotate the coil?

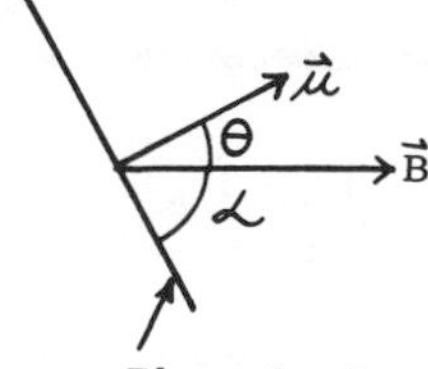

Plane of coil

Solution: The torque on a circuit in a field of magnetic induction, $\vec{B}$, is

$$\vec{T} = \vec{\mu} \times \vec{B} \qquad (1)$$

where $\vec{\mu}$ is the magnetic moment of the circuit. (This is the property of the circuit which causes the torque to be exerted.) The magnitude of the magnetic moment is

$$\mu = NIA \qquad (2)$$

where N is the number of turns in the circuit, I is the current in the circuit, and A is the area it encloses. The direction of $\vec{\mu}$ is given by the right hand rule: wrap the fingers of your right hand around the circuit in the direction of the current, and the direction in which your thumb points will then be the sense of $\vec{\mu}$. Since we only want the magnitude of $\vec{T}$, we write

$$T = \mu B \sin\theta \qquad (3)$$

where T, μ, B are the magnitudes of $\vec{T}$, $\vec{\mu}$, $\vec{B}$, and θ is the angle between the directions of $\vec{\mu}$ and $\vec{B}$ (see figure). Substituting (2) into (3), we obtain

$$T = NiAB \sin\theta \qquad (4)$$

However, the data is given in terms of flux density, not in terms of B. But flux density is actually equal to B because

$$\text{Flux density} = \frac{\Phi}{A} = \frac{BA}{A} = B$$

where A is the area enclosed by the circuit, and Φ is the flux cutting through the circuit. We still cannot proceed yet, because we do not have θ. The question gives us the angle between the plane of the coil and the direction of $\vec{B}$. (In the figure this is α.) The angle we need, θ, is $90° - \alpha = 50°$. Inserting the given data in

(4), we find

$$T = \left[8 \times 10^{-4} \frac{nt}{A \cdot m}\right](15)(20A)(.3m)(.1m)(.77)$$

$$T = .0055 \text{ nt} \cdot \text{m}$$

MAGNETIC CIRCUITS

• PROBLEM 732

The mean length of a Rowland ring is 50 cm and its cross section is 4 cm^2. Use the permeability curve given below to compute the magnetomotive force needed to establish a flux of 4×10^{-4} weber in the ring. (a) What current is required if the ring is wound with 200 turns of wire? (b) If an air gap one millimeter in length is cut in the ring, what current is required to maintain the same flux?

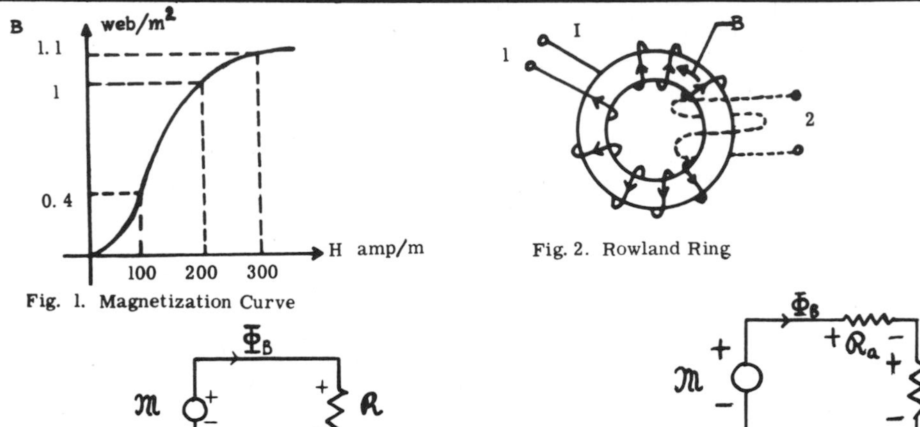

Fig. 1. Magnetization Curve

Fig. 2. Rowland Ring

Fig. 3. Magnetic Circuit

Fig. 4. Circuit with Air Gap

Solution: (a) As can be seen from Fig. 2, a Rowland ring is a torus of a given ferromagnetic material with two coils around. The first long coil is used to set up the circular magnetic field B inside the ring. As the current I in the first coil changes, an induced e.m.f. will be set up in the second coil. Thus, by measuring the voltage at the terminals of the second coil, we can measure B.
If the ferromagnetic material is not present, the magnetic field B_0 in the toroidal coil is given by (similar to a solenoid)

$$B_0 = \mu_0 nI$$

where n is the number of turns of the first coil per unit length. We can find B_0 by measuring I. As we insert the ferromagnetic core inside the coil, B_0 will induce a magnetic field (called the magnetization M) in the direction of B_0, in the core. The resultant magnetic field B will be the sum of these fields. (for magnetic materials, M is often much larger than B_0). Defining the magnetic intensity H as

$$B_0 = \mu_0 H ,$$

the expression for B is given by

$$B = \mu_0(H + M) = \mu H$$

where M is the magnetization and μ the permeability of the core.

From the magnetization curve, the H required to set up a magnetic field is 2×10^2 amp/m . At this point the permeability is

$$\mu = \frac{B}{H} = 5 \times 10^{-3} \text{ w/amp.m}$$

$$B = \frac{\Phi}{A} = \frac{4 \times 10^{-4} \text{w}}{4 \times 10^{-4} \text{m}^2} = 1 \text{ w/m}^2 .$$

In analogy with electric circuits, one can represent a magnetic material subject to a magnetic flux as a magnetic circuit. The circuit for this problem is given in Fig. 3, where the loop variable is magnetic flux and the magnetomotive force that gives rise to Φ_B in a coil is taken to be $n I \ell$. With these definitions, the reluctance of our ring with Φ_B through it, is given by

$$R = \frac{\mathfrak{M}}{\Phi_B} = \frac{n I \ell}{BA}$$

The magnetic field B inside the ring is

$$B = \mu H = \mu \frac{B_0}{\mu_0} = \mu n I ,$$

thus

$$R = \frac{1}{\mu A} = \frac{0.5 \text{ m}}{5 \times 10^{-3} (\text{w/amp.m}) \times 4 \times 10^{-4} \text{m}^2} = 2.5 \times 10^5 \text{ amp/w},$$

and since $\mathfrak{M} = \Phi R$, the required magnetomotive force is

$$\mathfrak{M} = 4 \times 10^{-4} \text{w} \times 2.5 \times 10^5 (\text{amp/w}) = 100 \text{ amp-turns.}$$

Using the expression for the magnetomotive force

$$\mathfrak{M} = NI$$

where N is the total number of turns in the coil, the required current is obtained as

$$I = \frac{\mathfrak{M}}{N} = \frac{100 \text{ amp turns}}{200 \text{ turns}} = 0.5 \text{ amp.}$$

(b) The air gap will introduce a new reluctance R_a into the magnetic circuit, in series with the reluctance of the ring (see Fig. 4). Since the same flux Φ_B goes through both of the reluctances, the loop equation for this magnetic circuit is

$$\mathfrak{M} = (R + R_a) \Phi_B$$

where

$$R_a = \frac{\ell_a}{\mu_0 A} = \frac{10^{-3} \text{m}}{12.57 \times 10^{-7} \text{w/amp.m} \times 4 \times 10^{-4} \text{m}^2}$$

$$= 20 \times 10^5 \text{ amp/w} .$$

Hence, assuming that the change in length of the ring is negligible and Φ_B in the ring is kept constant, the new magnetomotive force for this arrangement is

$$\mathfrak{M} = (2.5 \times 10^5 + 20 \times 10^5) \times 4 \times 10^{-4}$$

$$= 900 \text{ amp-turns.}$$

Therefore the current in the first coil should be increased to

$$I = \frac{\mathfrak{M}}{N} = \frac{900 \text{ amp-turns}}{200 \text{ turns}} = 7.5 \text{ amp.}$$

A Rowland ring, made of iron, of mean circumferential length 30 cm and cross section 1 cm^2, is wound uniformly with 300 turns of wire. Ballistic galvanometer measurements made with a search coil around the ring show that when the current in the windings is 0.032 amp, the flux in the ring is 2×10^{-6} weber(see figure). Compute (a) the flux density in the ring, (b) the magnetic intensity, (c) the permeability, (d) the relative permeability.

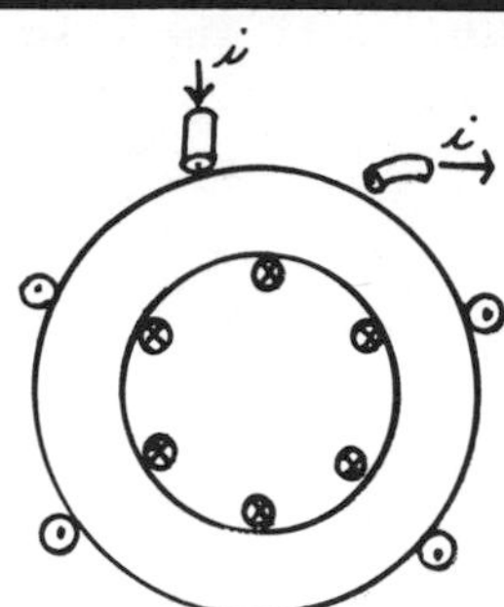

Solution: a) The flux, Φ, through the ring is defined as

$$\Phi = \int \vec{B} \cdot d\vec{A}$$

where B is the flux density and $d\vec{A}$ is an infinitesimal cross sectional element through which the flux passes. B is constant in the iron, and the angle between $\vec{B}$ and the area vector is zero. Therefore

$$\Phi = B \int dA = BA$$

where A is the cross section of the iron. Hence

$$B = \frac{\Phi}{A}$$

$$= \frac{2 \times 10^{-6} \text{ w}}{1 \text{ cm}^2 \times 1 \text{ m}^2/10^4 \text{ cm}^2}$$

$$= 2 \times 10^{-2} \text{ w/m}^2.$$

b) Magnetic intensity $H = \frac{Ni}{\ell}$

$$= \frac{300 \times .032}{.30}$$

$$= 32 \text{ amp-turns/m}.$$

c) Permeability $\mu = \frac{B}{H}$ (by definition)

$$= \frac{2 \times 10^{-2} \text{ w/m}^2}{32 \text{ amp/m}}$$

$$= 6250 \times 10^{-7} \text{ w/amp-m}.$$

d) Relative permeability $K_m = \frac{\mu}{\mu_0}$

$$= \frac{6250 \times 10^{-7}}{12.57 \times 10^{-7}}$$

$$= 498 \text{ (no units)}.$$

A Rowland ring made of iron has a mean circumferential length of 50 cm and a cross-sectional area of 4 cm^2. It is wound with 450 turns of wire which carry a current of 1.2 A. The relative permeability of iron under these conditions is 550. What is the magnetic flux through the ring? What would be the flux through the ring if a gap of 2 cm were to be cut in its length, assuming that the flux did not spread from the gap?

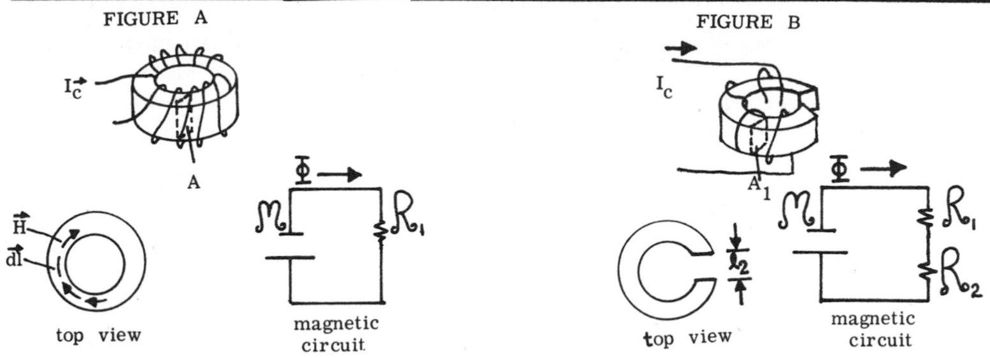

Solution: Assume that the iron in the Rowland ring is operated in the linear region. Then the magnetic induction through a Rowland ring (see fig. A) is given by the formula

$$B = \mu H$$

Applying Ampere's circuital law about the circumference (of length ℓ) of the Rowland ring,

$$\int \vec{H} \cdot \vec{d\ell} = NI_c$$

$\vec{H}$ is constant along the circumference and is parallel to $\vec{d\ell}$, an infinitesimal element of length. N is the number of windings of current-carrying wire around the ring. Then

$$H \int d\ell = H\ell = NI_c \qquad \text{and}$$

$$H = \frac{NI_c}{\ell}$$

Hence $B = \mu \dfrac{NI_c}{\ell} = K_m \mu_0 \dfrac{NI_c}{\ell}$

where the relative permeability of iron $K_m = \mu/\mu_0$. The flux through the ring is

$$\phi = \int \vec{B} \cdot \vec{dA} = BA = K_m \mu_0 A \frac{NI_c}{\ell} \qquad (1)$$

where A is the cross-sectional area of the ring. Since we are given $A = 4\ cm^2$, $N = 450$, $\ell = 50\ cm = 0.5\ m$, $I_c = 1.2$ A and $K_m = 550$, then

$$\phi = 550 \times 4\pi \times 10^{-7}\ N \cdot A^{-2} \times (4 \times 10^{-4}\ m^2) \times \frac{450 \times 1.2\ A}{0.5\ m}$$

$$= 2.99 \times 10^{-4}\ Wb.$$

Equation (1) may be written as

$$\phi = \frac{NI_c}{\ell/\mu A} = \frac{M}{R_1}$$

where M is the magnetomotive force, and R the reluctance of the ring. This is the magnetic analogue of Ohm's law, with Φ the analogue of current, M the analogue of emf and R the analogue of resistance (see figure A).

When a gap is cut in the ring (see fig. B), the flux may be obtained by use of the magnetic circuit relation

$$\phi = \frac{M}{R_1 + R_2},$$

where R_1 and R_2 are the reluctance of ring and gap, respectively (see fig. B). Thus

$$\phi = \frac{NI_c}{(\ell_1/\mu_1 A_1) + (\ell_2/\mu_2 A_2)}$$

ℓ_1 is the length of the ring minus the gap (= 0.5 cm - .02m = 0.48 m), μ_1 the permeability of iron (= 550 μ_0), A_1 the cross sectional area of the ring, ℓ_2 the length of the gap (= 0.02 m), $\mu_2 = \mu_0$ and $A_2 = A_1$. Thus

$$\phi = \frac{450 \times 1.2\ A}{[0.48\ m/(550 \times 4\pi \times 10^{-7} N \cdot A^{-2} \times 4 \times 10^{-4} m^2)] + [0.02\ m/(4\pi \times 10^{-7} N \cdot A^{-2} \times 4 \times 10^{-4} m^2)]}$$

$$= \frac{450 \times 1.2 \times 4\pi \times 10^{-7} \times 4 \times 10^{-4}}{[(0.48/550) + 0.02]}\ Wb$$

$$= 1.30 \times 10^{-5}\ Wb.$$

• PROBLEM 735

An experiment is done using Thomson's apparatus for positive-ray analysis. A set of positive-ray parabolas are examined and it is found that for the same horizontal displacement y, the corresponding vertical displacements for the three parabolas observed are 3.24 mm, 3.00 mm, and 2.81 mm. The parabola with the largest displacement is known to correspond to C^{12} and all ions are singly charged. What are the other ions present?

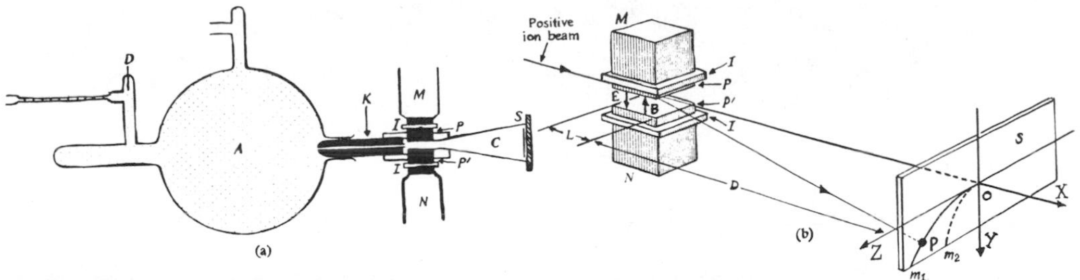

Solution: In Thompson's apparatus (figures (a) and (b)) a gas of the element to be examined fills discharge tube A. An electrical discharge ionizes the gas, and the positive ions are accelerated by an electric field between the anode D and cathode K. In travelling towards K, many of the positive ions bombard the latter, and heat it, but a few of the ions pass through the canal in the cathode, and are thereby collimated. The positive ion beam next passes through the pole faces of a magnet, where a uniform field of magnetic induction, $\vec{B}$, and a uniform electric field intensity, $\vec{E}$, exist. (The $\vec{E}$ field is produced by a parallel plate capacitor (PP') attached to the pole faces by dielectric slabs (I)). After passing through the field region, the ions travel in free space until they strike fluorescent screen S. If the fields are off during this process, the beam ions will not be accelerated in the pole face region, and will strike the screen at point 0. If the fields are on, the ions are deflected and accelerated, and strike the screen at point P having coordinates Y and Z relative to 0. It is our task to find an expression relating Y and Z, which can be measured off the screen, to q/m, the charge to mass ratio of the ions.

Suppose an ion, with charge to mass ratio q/m, enters the field region at time t = 0. The force acting on the ion is then

$$\vec{F} = q\vec{E} + q\vec{v} \times \vec{B} \tag{1}$$

where $\vec{v}$ is the ion velocity. During the period it is within the pole faces, the ion is accelerated in the y direction by $\vec{E}$, and in the z direction by $\vec{B}$. Since $\vec{v}$ can be written as

$$\vec{v} = v_x\,\hat{\imath} + v_y\,\hat{\jmath} + v_z\,\hat{k} \tag{2}$$

where v_x is the x-component of $\vec{v}$, etc., and $\vec{E} = E\,\hat{\jmath}$, $\vec{B} = -B\,\hat{\jmath}$, (1) becomes

$$\vec{F} = q\,E\,\hat{\jmath} + q(-v_x\,B\,\hat{k} + v_z\,B\,\hat{\imath})$$

However, by Newton's Second Law, the acceleration $\vec{a}$ of an object of mass m acted on by a net force $\vec{F}$ is $\vec{a} = \vec{F}/m$, whence

$$\vec{a} = \frac{q}{m}(v_z\,B\,\hat{\imath} + E\,\hat{\jmath} - v_x\,B\,\hat{k}) \tag{3}$$

Using the example of (2), we may write

$$\vec{a} = a_x \hat{\imath} + a_y \hat{\jmath} + a_z \hat{k} \qquad (4)$$

Comparing (3) and (4), we find

$$a_x = \frac{q\, v_z\, B}{m}$$

$$a_y = \frac{q\, E}{m} \qquad (5)$$

$$a_z = -\frac{q\, v_x\, B}{m}$$

Note that $a_r^2 = a_x^2 + a_z^2 = \frac{q^2 B^2}{m^2} (v_x^2 + v_z^2)$

$$a_r = \frac{q\, B\, v'}{m}$$

is the centripetal acceleration caused by $\vec{B}$. Since the magnetic force is always perpendicular to $\vec{v}$, it does not change the magnitude of $\vec{v}$, only its direction. Furthermore, in general, the magnitude of only the y-component of $\vec{v}$ is changed, and this by the $\vec{E}$ field. Hence,

$$v' = \sqrt{v_x^2 + v_z^2}$$

is constant in magnitude. Therefore, the initial value of v' is equal to its value at any other time. Since the initial value of v' is v_{xo} (assuming the ion to be travelling parallel to the x-axis before entering the field region), we obtain

$$v_{xo} = \sqrt{v_x^2 + v_z^2} \qquad (6)$$

Now, in practice, $v_z << v_x$, and we can write

$$v_{xo} \approx v_x$$

This means that in this experiment, the effect of $\vec{B}$ is to deflect the ion beam, and not to change v_x appreciably. Then (5) becomes

$$a_x \approx 0$$

$$a_y = \frac{q\, E}{m}$$

$$a_z \approx -\frac{q\, v_{xo}\, B}{m}$$

Since a_x, a_y and a_z are constant, we may relate the velocity and position of the ion just after leaving the pole faces $\left[(x, y, z) \text{ and } (v_x, v_y, v_z)\right]$ to its velocity and position just before entering the latter $\left[(x_o, y_o, z_o) \text{ and } (v_{xo}, v_{yo}, v_{zo})\right]$ by

$$v_x = v_{ox} \qquad\qquad x = x_o + v_{ox}\, t$$

$$v_y = v_{oy} + \frac{qEt}{m} \qquad\qquad y = y_o + v_{oy}\, t + \frac{qEt^2}{2m}$$

$$v_z = v_{oz} - \frac{q\, v_{xo}\, Bt}{m} \qquad\qquad z = z_o + v_{oz}\, t - \frac{qv_{xo}\, Bt^2}{2m}$$

Here, t is the time needed to cross the pole faces. Since v_{xo} is constant, and the beam traverses a distance approximately equal to L, (see figure (b)) we find

$$t = \frac{L}{v_{xo}}$$

Furthermore, calling the initial position $(x_o, y_o, z_o) = (0, 0, 0)$ the origin, and noting that the initial velocities v_{oy} and v_{oz} are zero, we obtain

$$v_x = v_{xo} \qquad\qquad x = L$$

$$v_y = \frac{qEl}{mv_{xo}} \qquad\qquad y = \frac{qEL^2}{2mv_{xo}^{\;2}} \qquad (7)$$

$$v_z = -\frac{qBL}{m} \qquad\qquad z = -\frac{qBL^2}{mv_{xo}}$$

We must now use (7) to help us locate the final coordinates of the ion on the screen.

After leaving the pole faces, the ion moves with constant velocity until it traverses a distance D in the x direction. Since v_x is constant, the time needed to do this is

$$t' = \frac{D}{v_x} = \frac{D}{v_{xo}}$$

Hence, in the force free region, the ion travels a further distance (relative to its position given in equation (7)) in each direction of

$$x' = v_{ox}\, t' = D$$

$$y' = v_y\, t' = \frac{q\, E\, L\, D}{mv_{ox}^{\;2}}$$

$$z' = v_z \; t' = -\frac{q\,B\,L\,D}{mv_{ox}}$$

The final position of the ion (on the screen) relative to its point of entry into the pole face region is then

$$X = x + x' = L + D$$

$$Y = y + y' = \frac{q\,E\,L^2}{2mv_{ox}^{\;2}} + \frac{q\,E\,L\,D}{mv_{ox}^{\;2}} = \frac{q\,E\,L}{mv_{ox}^{\;2}}\left(\frac{L}{2} + D\right)$$

$$Z = z + z' = -\frac{q\,B\,L^2}{mv_{ox}} - \frac{q\,B\,L\,D}{mv_{ox}} = -\frac{q\,B\,L}{mv_{ox}}\,(L + D)$$

Because $L < < D$, $L + D \approx D$ and we obtain

$$X \approx D$$

$$Y \approx \frac{q\,E\,L\,D}{mv_{ox}^{\;2}} \qquad (8)$$

$$Z \approx -\frac{q\,B\,L\,D}{mv_{ox}}$$

as the position of the ion relative to the position it had before entering the field region. However, point 0 has the same x and y coordinates as this entry point. Hence, the values of Y and Z given in (8) are the screen coordinates of the ion relative to 0.

The formulas in (8) locate one ion of the beam on the screen. But each ion has a different value of v_{ox}, and possibly, a different value of q/m. Hence, we do not see a single point on the screen, but a locus of points. Since

$$Z^2 = \frac{q^2B^2L^2D^2}{m^2v_{ox}^{\;2}} = \frac{q\,B^2\,L\,D}{m}\left(\frac{q\,L\,D}{mv_{ox}^{\;2}}\right)$$

$$Z^2 = \frac{q\,B^2\,L\,D}{mE}\;Y$$

we see that the locus generated by (8) is a parabola in general. Knowing Y, Z, B, L, D and E, one can find q/m.

In our case, we know that q, B, L, D and E are the same for all ions.

Thus, for fixed y, $z^2 = k/m$, where k is constant for all ions.

Since, when z = 3.24 mm, m is 12.000 amu, then $k = (3.24)^2\ mm^2 \times 12.000\ amu = 126\ mm^2 \cdot amu$. Thus when z = 3.00 mm,

$$m = \frac{k}{z^2} = \frac{126\ mm^2 \cdot amu}{9\ mm^2} = 14.00\ amu.$$

The ion is thus N^{14}.

When z = 2.81 mm,

$$m = \frac{k}{z^2} = \frac{126\ mm^2 \cdot amu}{(2.81)^2\ mm^2} = 15.96\ amu.$$

This ion is thus O^{16}.

CHAPTER 22

MAGNETIC INDUCTION

• **PROBLEM** 736

A closed loop of wire is placed in a magnetic field in such a way that flux points into the coil as shown in the figure where the ×'s indicate the tail ends of flux lines. If the flux density suddenly increases, will current be induced in the loop, and if so will it point clockwise or counterclockwise?

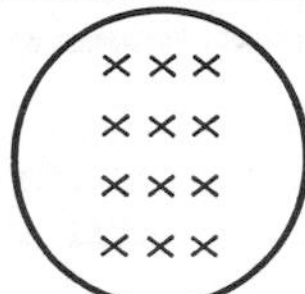

Solution: This problem is an application of Lenz's Law, by virtue of which a current will be induced in the loop.

The direction of the current is found by noting that a change in flux induces a current which by its own electromagnetic action opposes the change responsible for it. This suggests that the current, whatever its direction, develops a magnetic field out of the paper inside the loop, i.e., opposed to the original field. The right hand rule is used to find the current direction in the coil. If the thumb of the right hand points in the direction of the magnetic field developed by the loop, then the fingers will curl in the direction of the current in the loop. In this case the current must point in a counterclockwise direction.

• **PROBLEM** 737

What is the inductive reactance of a coil of 20 millihenries inductance when it is connected to a 60cycle line?

Solution: Here inductance L = 20 millihenries = 0.020 henry and f = 60 cps. Then the inductive reactance of the coil =

$$X_L = 2\pi fL = 2\pi \times 60 \text{ cps} \times 0.020 \text{ h}$$

$$= 7.5 \text{ ohms}$$

• **PROBLEM** 738

If a wire carrying 2 amperes lies perpendicularly across a uniform magnetic field of flux density 5×10^{-2} weber/meter^2 in such a manner that 15 cm of the wire are subjected to the field (i.e., if the pole pieces of the magnet are 15 cm across), how much side thrust is experienced by the wire, and which way does it act?

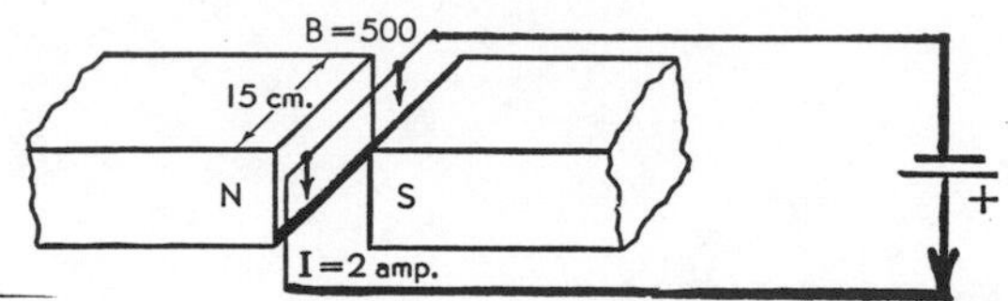

Solution: By the right-hand rule, it is seen that the thrust is downward. The magnitude of the thrust is given by

$$\vec{F} = I\vec{L} \times \vec{B}$$

where $\vec{B}$ is the magnetic induction, and I is the current in a wire of length L. Since the angle between $\vec{L}$ and $\vec{B}$ is 90°, then

$$F = BLI$$

therefore

$$F = 5 \times 10^{-2} \frac{w}{m^2} \times 15\text{cm} \times \frac{1\text{m}}{100\text{cm}} \times 2 \text{ amp}$$

$$= 15 \times 10^{-3} \text{ n} = .015 \text{ nt}$$

where we have used the fact that $1 \text{ cm} = \frac{1}{100} \text{ n}$.

• PROBLEM 739

A coil has a self-inductance of 1.26 millihenrys. If the current in the coil increases uniformly from zero to 1 amp in 0.1 sec, find the magnitude and direction of the self-induced emf.

(a) (b)

Direction of a self-induced emf. (a) i increasing, $\mathcal{E}$ opposite to i, point a at a higher potential than b. (b) i decreasing, $\mathcal{E}$ and i in same direction, b at higher potential than a. (R = 0.)

Solution: The self-induced emf on the inductance is given by

$$\varepsilon = -L \frac{di}{dt}$$

$$\varepsilon = \left(-1.26 \times 10^{-3} \text{ henry}\right)\left(\frac{1\text{amp}}{.1 \text{ sec}}\right).$$

Since $1 \text{ henry} = \frac{1 \text{ volt} \cdot \text{sec}}{\text{amp}}$

$$\mathcal{E} = \left(-1.26 \times 10^{-3} \frac{\text{volt} \cdot \text{sec}}{\text{amp}}\right)\left(\frac{10 \text{ amp}}{\text{sec}}\right)$$

$$= -12.6 \text{ millivolts.}$$

Since the current is increasing, the direction of this emf is opposite to that of the current.

• PROBLEM 740

What is the magnetic induction B at the center of a circular cable consisting of 100 turns of wire having a common radius of 20 cm carrying 15 amperes?

Solution: Consider the circular contour about the circular loop shown in the figure. By the Biot-Savart law the contribution to the magnetic induction at the center of the circular loop, due to an infinitesimal element, $d\vec{\ell}$, of the loop, is given by

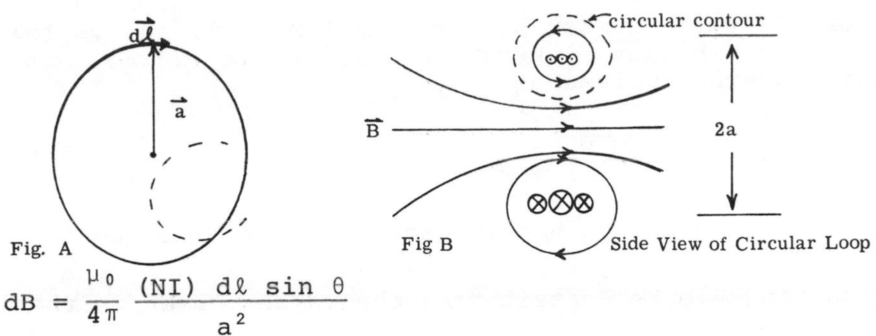

$$dB = \frac{\mu_0}{4\pi} \frac{(NI)\, d\ell \sin\theta}{a^2}$$

where $\mu_0 = 4\pi \times 10^{-7}$ Weber/A·m is the constant of permeability, θ is the angle between $d\vec{\ell}$ and the radius vector $\vec{a}$ ($\theta = 90°$), and NI is the total current through the loop. At the center of the loop, B is directed perpendicular to the plane of the loop.

$$B = \int dB = \frac{\mu_0}{4\pi} \frac{NI}{a^2} \int d\ell \qquad \text{for } \sin 90° = 1$$

$$B = \frac{\mu_0}{4\pi} \frac{NI}{a^2} 2\pi a$$

$$= \frac{\mu_0}{2} \frac{NI}{a}$$

We are given that N = 100 turns, I = 15 amp and a = 20 cm × 1 m/100 cm then

$$B = \frac{2\pi \times 10^{-7} \frac{W}{A\text{-}m} \times 100 \times 15A}{0.2\ m} = 1.5 \times 10^{-4}\,\pi \text{ weber}$$

• PROBLEM 741

A coil of 600 turns is threaded by a flux of 8.0×10^{-5} weber. If the flux is reduced to 3.0×10^{-5} weber in 0.015 sec, what is the average induced EMF?

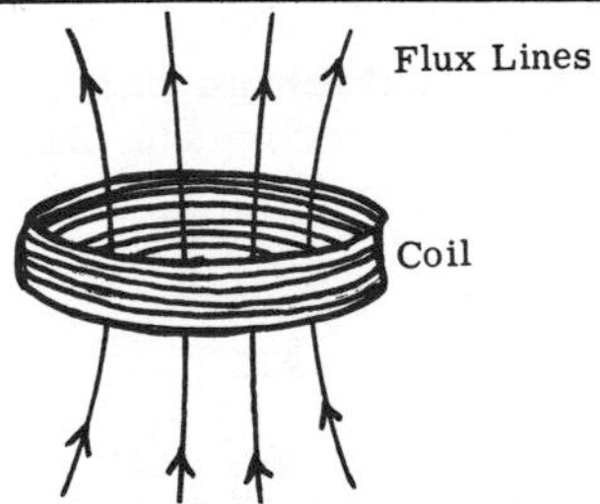

Solution: We note that there is a change in magnetic flux. This immediately implies the use of Faraday's Law, which relates a change in magnetic flux to an induced E.M.F. (electromotive force). The flux linking the coil will induce an E.M.F. in the coil. Faraday's Law states:

$$\text{E.M.F.} = \frac{-N d\Phi_B}{dt} \qquad (1)$$

where N is the number of turns in the coil, and Φ_B is the magnetic flux linking the coil. We may write this using average values as

$$\overline{E.M.F.} = -N \frac{\Delta\Phi_B}{\Delta t} \quad (2)$$

where $\Delta\Phi_B$ is the change in magnetic flux over the interval Δt, and $\overline{E.M.F.}$ is the average value of the resulting E.M.F. Substituting the values given in the statement of the problem into equation (2), we obtain

$$\overline{E.M.F.} = -\frac{(600)\left(8 \times 10^{-5} \text{ weber} - 3 \times 10^{-5} \text{ weber}\right)}{(.015 \text{ s})}$$

$$= -2 \frac{\text{weber}}{\text{sec}}$$

But $\quad 1 \text{ weber} = 1 \dfrac{\text{Joule - sec}}{\text{coul}}$

Therefore,

$$\overline{E.M.F.} = -2 \frac{\text{Joule - sec}}{\text{coul - sec}} = -2 \text{ Volts}$$

• PROBLEM 742

A current of 30 amp is maintained in a thin, tightly wound coil of 15 turns, with a radius of 20 cm. What is the magnetic induction at the center of the coil?

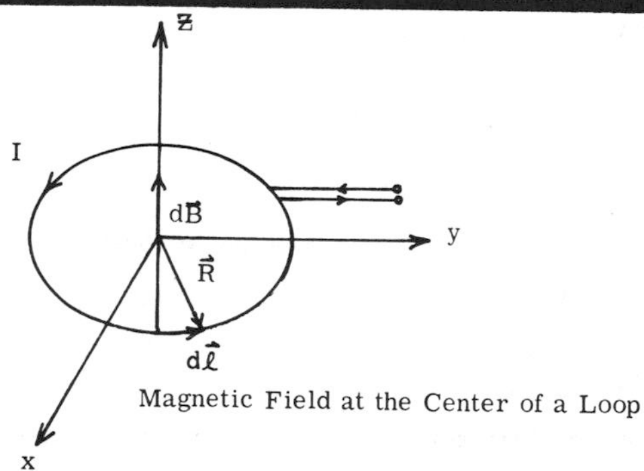

Magnetic Field at the Center of a Loop

Solution: The magnetic induction at the center of a coil of radius R with one turn can be found by using the Biot-Savart Law.

$$d\vec{B} = \frac{\mu_0 i}{4\pi} \frac{d\vec{\ell} \times \vec{R}}{R^3}$$

where the permeability constant $\mu_0 = 4\pi \times 10^{-7} \frac{\omega}{\text{a-m}}$, and $d\vec{\ell}$ is an element of the coil in the direction of the current i. From the figure we have

$$dB = \frac{\mu_0 i}{4\pi} \frac{d\ell R \sin 90^\circ}{R^3} = \frac{\mu_0 i}{4\pi} \frac{d\ell}{R^2}$$

where $\vec{R}$ and $d\vec{\ell}$ are 90° apart. We have used the magnitude of $d\vec{B}$ because all the infinitesimal contributions to the magnetic induction from the infinitesimal lengths $d\vec{\ell}$ are in a direction perpendicular to the plane of the coil. Therefore the total magnetic field at the center is the sum of the infinitesimal contributions dB or

$$B = \int dB = \frac{\mu_0 i}{4\pi} \frac{1}{R^2} \int d\ell = \frac{\mu_0 i}{4\pi} \frac{2\pi R}{R^2} = \frac{\mu_0}{2} \frac{i}{R}$$

The magnetic induction at the center of a coil containing N coils will be equal to the sum of the contributions due to each of the coils, or

$$B_T = NB = \frac{\mu_0 Ni}{2R}$$

$$= \left(4\pi \times 10^{-7} \text{weber/amp-m}\right) \frac{15 \times 30 \text{ amp}}{2 \times 0.20 \text{ m}}$$

$$= 1.4 \times 10^{-3} \text{weber/m}^2$$

The direction of B_T is perpendicular to the plane of the orbit.

• PROBLEM 743

Calculate the magnetic induction B along the axis of a very long 2.5×10^{-1} meters solenoid of 1000 turns of wire if the radius of the coil is 2×10^{-2} meters and the current in the wire is 15 amperes.

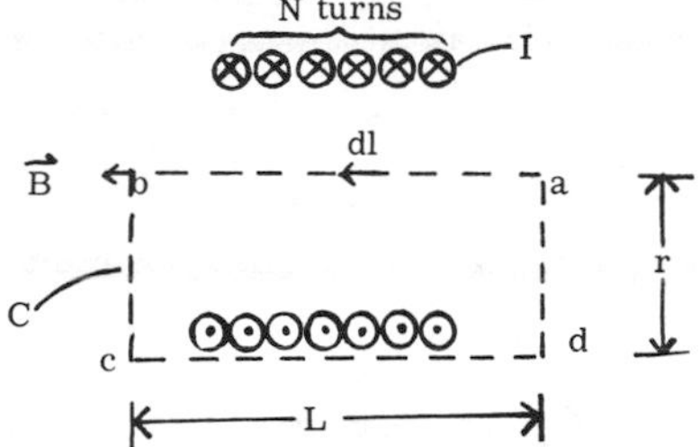

Solution: Consider the rectangular contour (C) about the solenoid as shown in the figure. It encloses a total current NI where I is the current through the wire and N is the number of turns. By Ampere's Law

$$\oint_C \vec{B} \cdot d\vec{\ell} = \mu_0 (NI)$$

where the constant of permeability $\mu_0 = 4\pi \times 10^{-7}$ Weber/amp-m and $d\vec{\ell}$ is the vector infinitesimal element of contour length. Assume there is no magnetic field outside the solenoid, and neglect fringing effects. Then,

$$\oint \vec{B} \cdot d\vec{\ell} = \int_a^b \vec{B} \cdot d\vec{\ell} + \int_b^c \vec{B} \cdot d\vec{\ell} + \int_c^d \vec{B} \cdot d\vec{\ell} + \int_d^a \vec{B} \cdot d\vec{\ell}$$

$$= BL \cos 0° + Br \cos 90° + (0)L + Br \cos 90°$$

$$= BL$$

Hence, Ampere's law for the solenoid becomes

$$BL = \mu_0 NI$$

$$B = \frac{\mu_0 NI}{L}$$

If N = 1000 turns, I = 15 amp, and L = 2.5×10^{-1} m then

$$B = \frac{4\pi \times 10^{-7} \frac{W}{a\text{-}m} \times 1000 \times 15a}{2.5 \times 10^{-1}\ m}$$

$$= 7.54 \times 10^{-2} \frac{\text{Weber}}{m^2}$$

$$= .0754 \frac{W}{m^2}$$

The radius of the solenoid does not appear in any of the calculations and is extraneous information.

• PROBLEM 744

An air-core toroid of cross-sectional area A and of mean circumferential length ℓ is closely wound with N turns of wire. If N = 100, A = 10 cm^2, ℓ = 0.50 m, find its self inductance, L.

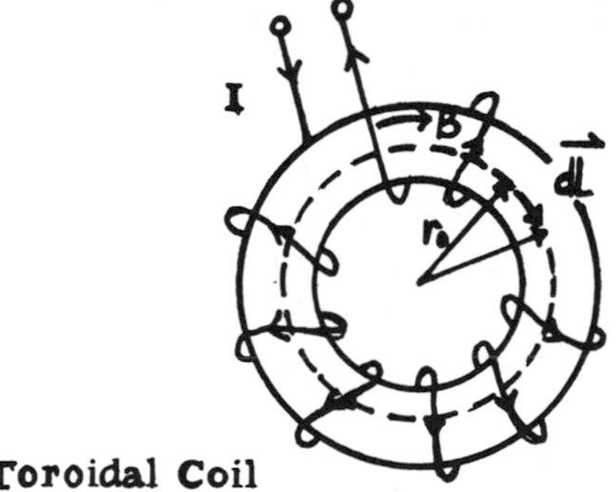

Toroidal Coil

Solution: The magnetic flux density B throughtout the coil will not deviate appreciably from its value at the mean radius r_0 of the torus, if its width is much smaller than $\ell = 2\pi r_0$. Applying Ampere's Law around the circle with radius r_0, we get

$$\oint B \cdot d\ell = \mu_0 NI$$

or

$$B\ell = \mu_0 NI$$

$$B = \frac{\mu_0 NI}{\ell}$$

and the flux is

$$\Phi_B = BA = \frac{\mu_0 NAI}{\ell}.$$

If a current I sets up a magnetic flux, Φ_B in a coil, then Φ_B and I are related through the self inductance of the coil as follows,

$$L = \frac{N\Phi_B}{I}$$

where N is the number of turns. Hence

$$L = \frac{\mu_0 N^2 A}{\ell}$$

or

$$L = \frac{\left(4\pi \times 10^{-7} \frac{w}{a\text{-}m}\right) \times (100)^2 \times \left(\frac{1\,m^2}{10^4\,cm^2} \times 10\,cm^2\right)}{0.50\,m}$$

$$\approx 25 \times 10^{-6} \text{ henry.}$$

• PROBLEM 745

A long straight wire in a house carries an alternating current which has a maximum value of 20 amp. Calculate the maximum magnetic induction a distance 1m away from the wire.

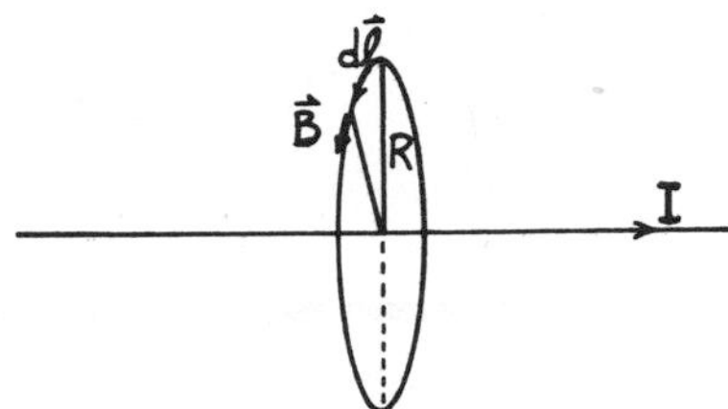

Solution: The magnetic induction at a distance R from a wire containing a current i can be found by using Ampere's Law. Given a closed path c, and a current i through the closed curve, the following relation holds:

$$\oint_c \vec{B} \cdot d\vec{\ell} = \mu_0 i$$

where the circle on the integral sign indicates that c is closed, and the permeability constant $\mu_0 = 4\pi \times 10^{-7}$ weber/amp-meter . Let the closed curve c of the above integral be in the shape of a circle of radius R, concentric with the current carrying wire as shown in the figure. Ampere's Law then becomes:

$$\int_c B \cos\theta \, d\ell = \int_c B \, d\ell$$

since $\vec{B}$ and $d\vec{\ell}$ are collinear and $\theta = 0^\circ$. $\vec{B}$ is constant along the path c, therefore

$$B \int d\ell = \mu_0 i$$

$$B \cdot 2\pi R = \mu_0 i$$

or

$$B = \frac{\mu_0 i}{2\pi R}$$

from which we have

$$B_{max} = \frac{\mu_0}{2\pi} \frac{i_{max}}{R} = 2 \times 10^{-7} \frac{\omega}{a\text{-}m} \times \frac{20a}{1m}$$

$$= 4 \times 10^{-6} \frac{W}{m^2}$$

This can be compared with the earth's magnetic field, which has an intensity of the order of 5×10^{-5} W/m^2.

• PROBLEM 746

Calculate the self-inductance of a coil if a rate of change of current of 5 amperes per second produces a back emf of 2 volts.

Solution: A change in current through the coil produces a change in magnetic flux through the coil. By Faraday's law, this changing flux induces an EMF in the coil, in such a direction as to oppose the flux change which produced it. This EMF is termed the back EMF of the coil. The magnitude of this back EMF, E, is

$$E = L \frac{\Delta I}{\Delta t}$$

where L is a constant of proportionality which depends on the geometry of the coil. It is termed the self-inductance of the coil. We are given that E = 2 volts and $\frac{\Delta I}{\Delta t}$ = 5 amp/sec. Therefore

$$L = \frac{E}{\Delta I/\Delta t} = \frac{2}{5} = 0.4 \text{ henry.}$$

• PROBLEM 747

A coil of 60 ohms inductive reactance in series with a resistance of 25 ohms is connected to an a-c line of 130 volts. What will be the current through the circuit?

Solution:

X_L = 60 ohms, R = 25 ohms, and E = 130 volts

The impedance of an a-c circuit is given by

$$Z = \sqrt{R^2 + (X_L - X_C)^2},$$

where the minus sign results because X_C and X_L are 180° out of phase.

Then

$$Z = \sqrt{(25 \text{ ohms})^2 + (60 \text{ ohms})^2} = 65 \text{ ohms}$$

From Ohm's law for an a-c circuit I = E/Z, we have

$$I = 130 \text{ volts}/65 \text{ ohms} = 2.0 \text{ amp.}$$

• PROBLEM 748

With a certain current in circuit 1 of the figure, a flux of 5×10^{-4} weber links with circuit 2. When circuit 1 is opened the flux falls to zero in 0.001 sec. What average e.m.f. is induced in circuit 2?

Solution: The induced e.m.f. ε in circuit 2 opposes the reduction of the magnetic flux Φ linking it by setting up its own flux in the direction of Φ. (see figure).

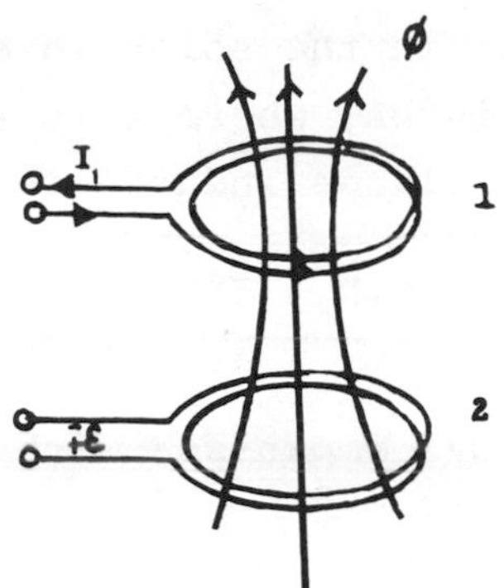

The average rate of decrease of flux in circuit 2 is

$$\frac{\Delta\Phi}{\Delta t} = \frac{5 \times 10^{-4}\ \text{w}}{.001\ \text{sec}} = 0.5\ \text{weber/sec.}$$

The average induced e.m.f. is therefore, by Faraday's Law,

$$\bar{\varepsilon} = -\frac{\Delta\Phi}{\Delta t} = -\ 0.5\ \text{volt}$$

since 1 volt = 1 weber/sec.

• PROBLEM 749

A long solenoid of length l and cross-sectional area A is closely wound with N_1 turns of wire. A small coil of N_2 turns surrounds it at its center, as in the figure. Find the mutual inductance of the coils.

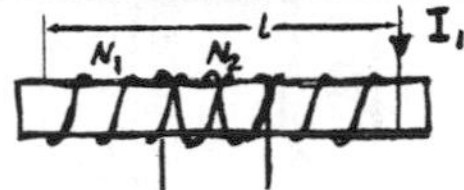

Solution: If a current I in a coil is changing at a rate $\frac{dI}{dt}$, then a voltage across the coil will be induced in the direction to oppose the change,

$$V_{coil} = -\ L\frac{dI}{dt}$$

where L is the self inductance of the coil. Similarly, if the time varying magnetic flux of one coil links another coil, then it will induce a voltage in the second coil equal to

$$V'_{coil} = -\ M\frac{dI}{dt} \qquad (1)$$

where I is the current in the first coil. The constant M is the mutual inductance of two coils. Its value is determined only by the geometry and positioning of the coils. In our problem, the magnetic field in the solenoid (away from the edges) is given by

$$B = \frac{\mu_0 N_1 I_1}{l}$$

where I_1 is the current in the solenoid coil. The flux Φ through the N_2 coil is BA, where A is the area of the second coil. Then the voltage induced in the second coil by I_1 is, by Faraday's Law,

$$V_{12} = -N_2 \frac{d\Phi}{dt} = -\frac{\mu_0 N_1 N_2 A}{l} \frac{dI_1}{dt} .$$

Therefore we see by comparison with (1) that the mutual inductance of this system is

$$M = \frac{\mu_0 A N_1 N_2}{l} .$$

If $l = 0.50$ m, $A = 10\ cm^2 = 10^{-3}\ m^2$, $N_1 = 1000$ turns, $N_2 = 10$ turns,

$$M = \frac{(4\pi \times 10^{-7}\ \text{henry/m})(10^{-3}\ m^2)(1000\ \text{turns})(10\ \text{turns})}{(.5\ m)}$$

$$\simeq 25 \times 10^{-6}\ \text{henry} \simeq 25\ \mu h.$$

• PROBLEM 750

A current of 10 A is flowing in a long straight wire situated near a rectangular loop, as indicated in the diagram. The current is switched off and falls to zero in 0.02 s. Find the emf induced in the loop and indicate the direction in which the induced current flows.

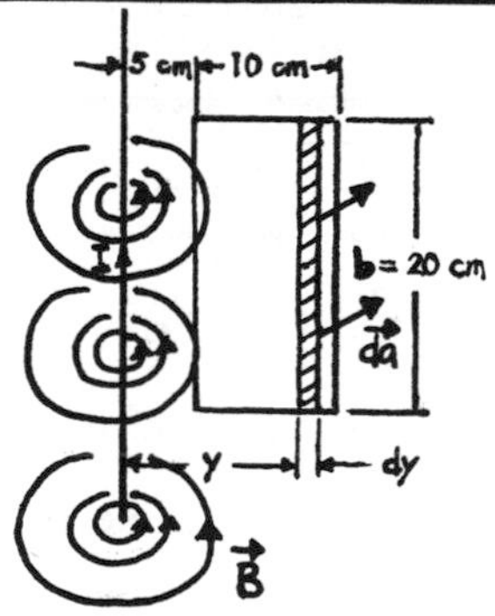

Solution: Consider the diagram, and in particular the shaded portion of width dy situated distance y from the straight current-carrying wire. The magnetic induction at all points of the shaded portion due to the current-carrying wire has the value

$$dB = \frac{\mu_0}{2\pi} \frac{I}{y} ,$$

where the permeability $\mu_0 = 4\pi \times 10^{-7}\ N \cdot A^{-2}$.

Therefore the flux through the shaded area is

$$d\Phi = (\vec{dB}) \cdot \vec{dA}.$$

Since $\vec{dB}$ is constant throughout the shaded portion and $\vec{dB}$ is parallel to $\vec{dA}$ where $\vec{dA}$ is an element of area within the shaded portion, then

$$d\Phi = (dB)\int dA = (dB)(bdy) = \frac{\mu_0}{2\pi}\frac{I}{y}\,b\,dy.$$

The flux through the whole loop is thus

$$\phi = \int d\phi = \frac{\mu_0}{2\pi}\,Ib\int_{0.05\text{ m}}^{0.15\text{ m}}\frac{dy}{y} = \frac{\mu_0}{2\pi}\,Ib\ln 3. \qquad (1)$$

The limits of integration are taken from y = 5cm = 0.05 m to y = 15 cm = 0.15 m to include the flux within the whole loop.

The emf induced in the loop is by Faraday's law,

$$\varepsilon = -\Delta\Phi/\Delta t.$$

Thus, the magnitude of the induced emf is (since the flux goes from the value in (1) to 0 in .02 s)

$$\varepsilon = \frac{\mu_0 Ib}{2\pi}\ln 3 \times \frac{1}{\Delta t}$$

$$= \frac{4\pi \times 10^{-7}\text{ N}\cdot\text{A}^{-2} \times 10\text{ A} \times 0.2\text{ m} \times \ln 3}{2\pi \times 0.02\text{ s}}$$

$$= 22.0 \times 10^{-6}\text{ V}.$$

The flux through the loop is decreasing. The induced current must produce effects tending to oppose the change causing it. The current must therefore be in such a direction as to produce a flux through the loop in the same direction as that produced by the current in the straight wire, i.e., into the plane of the paper. Thus the induced current traverses the loop in a clockwise direction. The negative sign in Faraday's law signifies this opposition of the induced emf to the charge causing it (Lenz's law).

• PROBLEM 751

A copper bar laid perpendicularly across a pair of parallel metal tracks running north-south, one meter apart, is slid in a northerly direction. At one end, the tracks are connected through a galvanometer. At the given location the vertical component of the earth's magnetic field is .55 oersted. Is there any reason to suppose that the galvanometer will read a deflection as the bar is moved at the rate of 150 cm/sec? If so, what is it, which way does the current point, how much electromotive force is developed in the bar between the rails, and which end of the bar is at the higher potential?

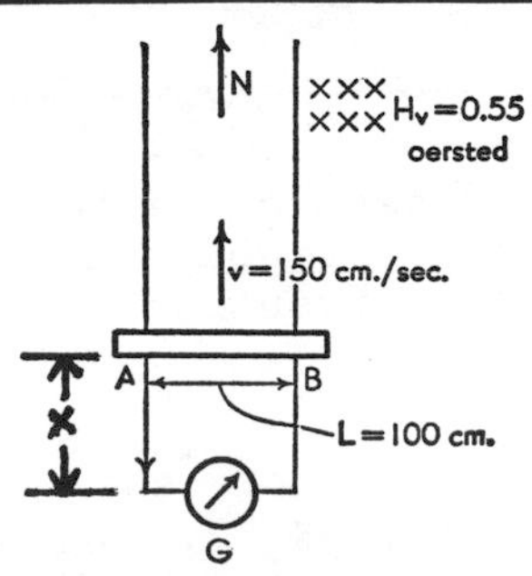

Solution: Note that as the bar moves along the track, as indicated in the diagram, it cuts the vertical component of the earth's field, which points downward, or into the paper. Hence, an electromotive force must be generated between the points A and B, and a current must be established in the circuit, to be detected by the galvanometer. This results from Faraday's Law because the magnetic flux is changing. The direction of this current follows from Lenz' Law, which states that the induced current will flow in a direction such as to set up an induced flux opposite in direction to the change in flux. The current points from B to A in the bar. This means that the point A is at a higher potential than point B. To determine the magnitude of the electromotive force induced, use Faraday's law

$$E = -\frac{d\Phi}{dt}$$

where the negative sign indicates that the EMF is induced in such a direction as to oppose the change in flux that created it. The flux Φ through the loop formed by the bar and the galvanometer is

$$\Phi = \int \vec{B} \cdot d\vec{A} = BLx$$

for B is constant in the loop and it is parallel to the area vector (i.e., $\theta = 0^\circ$). Then

$$E = -BL\frac{dx}{dt}$$

Since $v = \frac{dx}{dt}$

$$E = -BLv$$

where B here is 5.5×10^{-5} weber/meter^2, L = 1.0 m, and $v = 1.5 \frac{m}{sec}$

$$E = -\left(5.5 \times 10^{-5} \frac{W}{m^2}\right)(1.0\ m)\left(1.5 \frac{m}{sec}\right)$$

$$= -8.25 \times 10^{-5} \text{ volt.}$$

• PROBLEM 752

A wire of length 1 m is moving at a speed of 2 m·s^{-1} perpendicular to a magnetic field of induction of 0.5 Wb·m^{-2}. What is the potential difference induced between the ends of the wire? The ends are joined by a circuit of total resistance R = 6 Ω. At what rate is work being done to keep the wire moving at constant velocity?

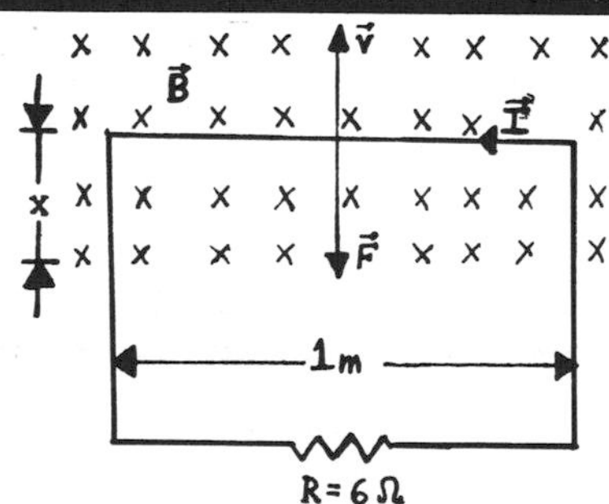

Solution: Since the direction of motion and the magnetic induction are at right angles, the induced emf will have magnitude given by Faraday's law

$$\mathcal{E} = \frac{d\Phi}{dt} \tag{1}$$

where the flux, $\Phi = \int \vec{B} \cdot d\vec{A}$, is evaluated over the area enclosed by the circuit, $\vec{B}$ is the constant magnetic induction passing through the loop of area A. The angle between the direction of the vectors $\vec{B}$ and $\vec{dA}$ is 0°.

Thus $\Phi = BA$ (for $A = \int dA$). However, $A = \ell x$, where ℓ is the length of the wire, and x is the position of the wire within the magnetic field (see the figure). Hence, (1) becomes

$$\mathcal{E} = B\ell \frac{dx}{dt} = B\ell\, v$$

where v is the velocity of the wire. Hence,

$$\mathcal{E} = vB\ell = 2\ \text{m}\cdot\text{s}^{-1} \times 0.5\ \text{Wb}\cdot\text{m}^{-2} \times 1\ \text{m} = 1\ \text{V}.$$

The power dissipated in the external circuit is

$$P = \frac{\mathcal{E}^2}{R} = \frac{1^2 V^2}{6\ \Omega} = \frac{1}{6}\ \text{W},$$

and this must equal the rate at which work is being done to keep the wire moving at constant velocity. If the closed system is the loop, magnetic field, and the agent moving the loop, then the energy given up by the agent is used to heat the resistance. Only an energy exchange occurred, and not a change in energy, as required by the principle of conservation of energy.

This can be checked by considering that a current

$$I = \frac{\mathcal{E}}{R} = \frac{1}{6}\ \text{A}$$

will flow in the wire in the direction shown in the diagram for only in this direction will the current create a flux which will oppose the flux of the magnetic field in accordance with Faraday's Law. Using the right hand rule, if the fingers of the right hand curl in the direction of the current about the loop, then the thumb will point in the direction of the magnetic field created by this current. In this case, the created B points out of the page, opposite to the direction of the given field. When a current flows in a wire in a magnetic field, the wire experiences a force of magnitude

$$F = I\ell B,$$

which will be in this case in the direction shown. The work done per second to keep the wire traveling at uniform speed v is

$$F\frac{x}{t} = Fv = I\ell vB$$

$$= \frac{1}{6}\text{A} \times 1\ \text{m} \times 2\ \text{m}\cdot\text{s}^{-1} \times 0.5\ \text{Wb}\cdot\text{m}^{-2} = \frac{1}{6}\ \text{W},$$

in agreement with the result obtained above.

A metal bar of length 1 m falls from rest under gravity while remaining horizontal with its ends pointing toward the magnetic east and west. What is the potential difference between its ends when it has fallen 10 m? The horizontal component of the earth's magnetic induction is 1.7×10^{-5} Wb•m^{-2}.

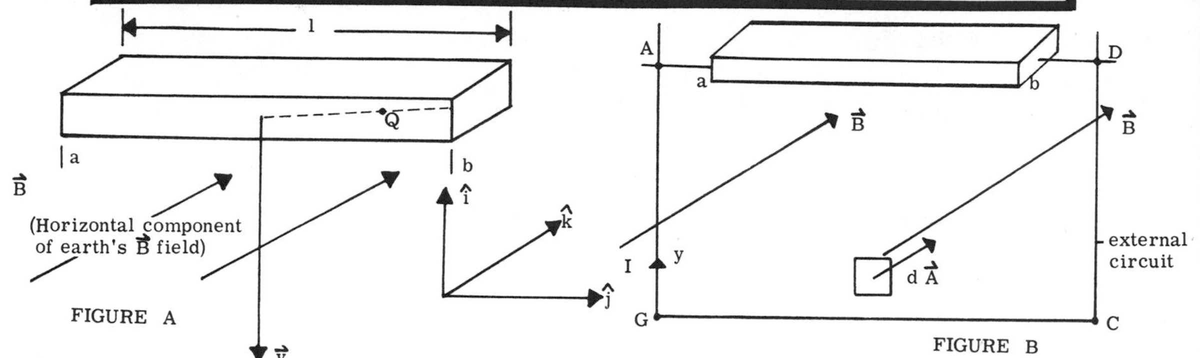

Solution: Figure (A) shows the bar, of length ℓ, moving with a velocity $\vec{v}$ in a field of magnetic induction $\vec{B}$. Each charge Q of the bar will experience a force

$$\vec{F} = Q\vec{v}' \times \vec{B}$$

where $\vec{v}'$ is the velicity of Q. Note that, at t = 0, when we let go of the bar, $\vec{v}' = \vec{v}$, the velocity of the bar due to its free-fall motion. The force at t = 0, then, accelerates the charges Q along the bar. Hence, at any time t after t = 0, the charge Q has 2 components of velocity - one is parallel to the bar, and the other component is equal to $\vec{v}$. The first component of $\vec{v}'$ will tend to curve the paths of the charges in the bar (see figure (A)). However, since Q and $\vec{B}$ are very small, the curvature of the actual path of the charges will be extremely large, and we may approximate the trajectory of Q by a straight line parallel to the bar. Furthermore, $\vec{F}$ will be small, so that $\vec{v}'$ will be very close to $\vec{v}$. We may then write

$$\vec{v}' \approx \vec{v}$$

and $\vec{F} = Q\vec{v} \times \vec{B}$

where $\vec{v}$ is the bar's velocity. This means that the net effect of $\vec{F}$ is not to change the velocity of Q by an appreciable amount, but, rather, to separate the oppositely charged particles in the bar. These charges will accumulate at points a and b, and will then set up an e.m.f. in the bar. We now evaluate this e.m.f.

By definition, the work done by $\vec{F}$ on a charge Q in moving it along an arbitrary path from point a to point b is

$$W = \int_a^b \vec{F} \cdot d\vec{s} = \int_a^b (Q\vec{v} \times \vec{B}) \cdot d\vec{s}$$

where $d\vec{s}$ is a differential element of the path. Hence,

$$\frac{W}{Q} = \int_a^b (\vec{v} \times \vec{B}) \cdot d\vec{s} \qquad (1)$$

Now, an agent that performs work on charge carriers (thereby instituting a current) can be viewed as an e.m.f., ε, where

$$\varepsilon = \frac{W}{Q} \qquad (2)$$

and W/Q is the work done by the agent on charge Q. In our problem, the agent is the magnetic field $\vec{B}$, doing work through the force $\vec{F}$. Using (1) in (2), we obtain

$$\varepsilon = \int_a^b (\vec{v} \times \vec{B}) \cdot d\vec{s} \qquad (3)$$

Now, $\vec{v}$ and $\vec{B}$ are uniform throughout the bar, and we may rewrite (3) as

$$\varepsilon = (\vec{v} \times \vec{B}) \cdot \int_a^b d\vec{s}$$

Using the coordinate system shown in figure (a)

$$\vec{v} = -v\hat{i}$$

$$\vec{B} = B\,\hat{k}$$

$$d\vec{s} = ds\,\hat{j}$$

and $\varepsilon = (-v\hat{i} \times B\,\hat{k}) \cdot \int_a^b ds\,\hat{j}$

$$\varepsilon = v\,B\,\hat{j} \cdot \int_a^b ds\,\hat{j} = vB\,(b - a)$$

But $b - a = \ell$, and we find

$$\varepsilon = v\,B\,\ell$$

Since the motion of the bar is free fall, the velocity of the bar is $v^2 = v_0^2 - 2\,gs$, where v_0 is the initial velocity of zero. When s is 10 m,

$$v^2 = \left(-\,2 \times 9.8\ \text{m}\cdot\text{s}^{-2}\right) \times (-\,10\ \text{m})$$

or $\quad v = 14\ \text{m}\cdot\text{s}^{-1}$.

The magnitude of the induced e.m.f. is then

$$\varepsilon = vB\ell = 14\ m\cdot s^{-1} \times 1.7 \times 10^{-5}\ Wb\cdot m^{-2} \times 1\ m$$

$$= 2.38 \times 10^{-4} V.$$

(b) We may also do this problem as indicated in figure (b). We consider the bar to be connected to an imaginary external circuit (AGCD). As the bar moves down, the flux through this imaginary circuit changes. Using Faraday's Law, the induced e.m.f. is

$$\varepsilon = -\frac{d\Phi}{dt} \qquad (4)$$

where Φ is the magnetic flux through the circuit, or

$\Phi = \int \vec{B} \cdot d\vec{A}$. This integral is evaluated over the area enclosed by the circuit. $d\vec{A}$ is a vector element of area (see figure (B)).

$$\Phi = \vec{B} \cdot \int d\vec{A}$$

Again, using the coordinate system shown in figure (A)

$$\vec{B} = B\,\hat{k} \qquad d\vec{A} = dA\,\hat{k}$$

and $\Phi = B \int dA = BA$

But the area A is a function of time. Measuring the height of the bar from the surface of the earth by y, we obtain

$$A = y\,\ell$$

and $\Phi = B\,y\,\ell \qquad (5)$

Using (5) in (4)

$$\varepsilon = -\frac{d}{dt}(\cdot By\ell) = -B\ell\frac{dy}{dt} = -B\ell v$$

where v is the velocity of the bar.

The magnitude of ε is then

$$\varepsilon = 2.38 \times 10^{-4}\ V.$$

• PROBLEM 754

A rectangular coil of 300 turns has a length of 25.0 cm and a width of 15.0 cm. The coil rotates with a constant angular speed of 1800 rev/min in a uniform field of induction 0.365 weber/m^2. (a) What EMF is induced in a quarter revolution after the plane of the coil is perpendicular to the field? (b) What is the EMF for a rotation of 180° from the zero position? (c) What is the EMF for a full rotation?

Solution: The flux through a coil of N turns, is, because $\vec{B}$ is constant,

$$\Phi = \vec{B} \cdot \vec{A} = BA \cos\theta$$

where θ is the angle between $\vec{B}$ and $\vec{A}$. The angular velocity ω,

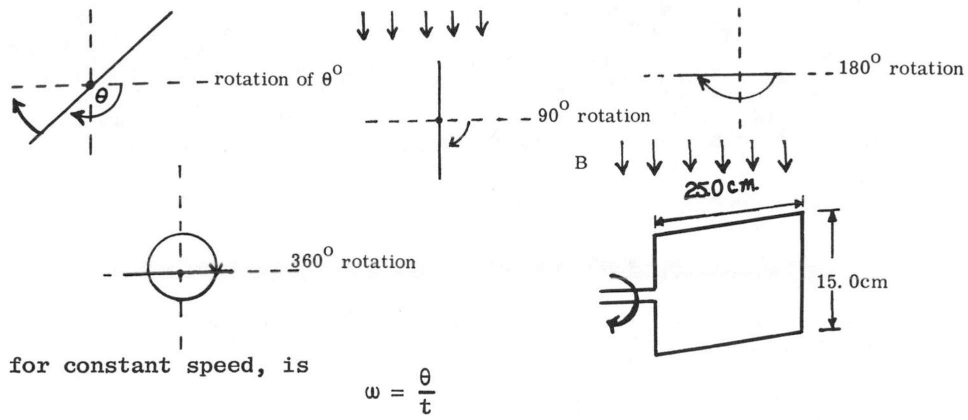

for constant speed, is

$$\omega = \frac{\theta}{t}$$

where ω is the angular velocity of the coil. By definition, $\omega = 2\pi n$, where n is the frequency of rotation of the coil. According to Faraday's law of induction, the EMF induced in a coil due to a changing flux is given by

$$\epsilon = \frac{-Nd\Phi}{dt}$$

The negative sign indicates that the EMF is induced in such a direction as to oppose the change in flux which induced it. Then

$$\epsilon = -N\frac{d}{dt}(BA \cos \omega t) = \omega NBA \sin \omega t = \omega NBA \sin \theta = 2\pi n \text{ NBA} \sin \theta$$

Therefore,

$$\epsilon = 2\pi\left(1800 \text{ sec}^{-1}\right)(300)\left(0.365 \frac{\omega}{m^2}\right)\left(25\text{cm} \times 15 \text{ cm} \times \frac{1\text{cm}^2}{10^{-4}m^2}\right) \times \sin \theta$$

or

$$\epsilon = 4.6 \times 10^{12} \times \sin \theta \text{ volts.}$$

a) When $\theta = 90^\circ$ $\sin \theta = 1$ therefore $\epsilon = 4.6 \times 10^{12}$ v.

b) When $\theta = 180^\circ$ $\sin \theta = 0$ therefore $\epsilon = 0$

c) When $\theta = 360^\circ$ $\sin \theta = 1$ therefore $\epsilon = 4.6 \times 10^{12}$ v.

• PROBLEM 755

A single circular loop of wire is rotated in a uniform field of magnetic induction $\vec{B}$. We can suppose that the magnetic field is in the +z-direction, and the axis of rotation of the loop is in the x-direction along a diameter. If the speed of rotation ω is constant, find the induced EMF in the coil.

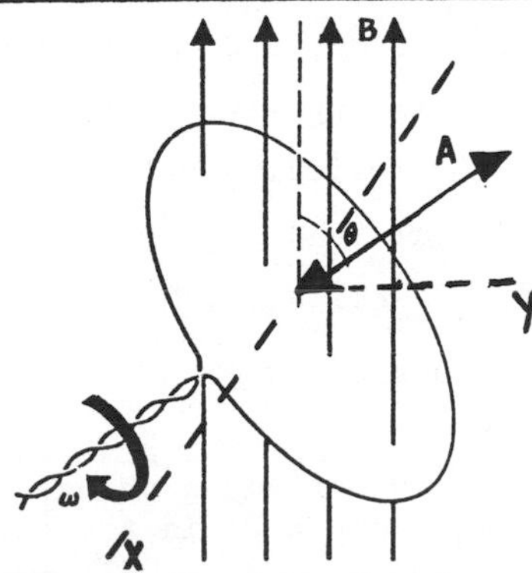

Solution: The flux through the circular loop is, since $\vec{B}$ is constant,

$$\Phi_M = B \cdot A$$
$$= BA \cos \theta$$

where θ is the angle between B and A (as shown in the Figure.) The angular velocity ω, for constant speed of rotation, is

$$\omega = \frac{\theta}{t} \qquad \theta = \omega t$$

Therefore,

$$\Phi_M = BA \cos \omega t$$

According to Faraday's law of induction, the EMF induced in a coil, due to a changing flux, is given by

$$\epsilon = -\frac{d\Phi_M}{dt}$$

where the negative sign indicates that the EMF is induced in such a direction as to oppose the change in flux which created it. Substituting for Φ_M and differentiating, we then have

$$\epsilon = \omega BA \sin \omega t = \omega BA \sin \theta$$

In this case the induced EMF varies with time in a sinusoidal way.

• PROBLEM 756

To measure magnetic fields, rotating coils are often used. A circular coil of radius 1 cm and with 100 turns is rotated at 60 cps in a magnetic field. The emf induced in the coil has a maximum value of 12.3 volts. Calculate the intensity of the field.

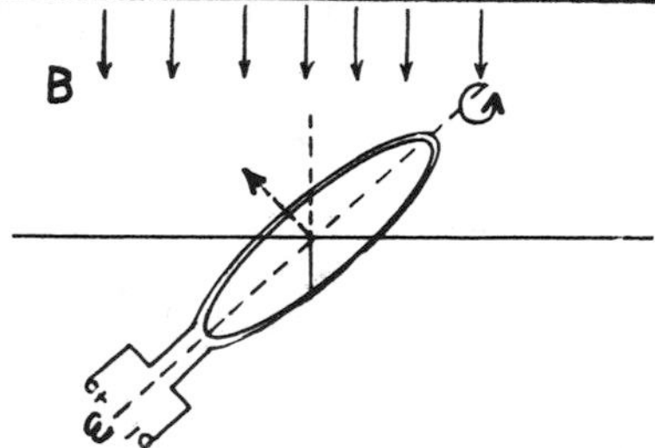

Solution: The magnetic flux (Φ) through one coil is defined as follows:

$$\Phi_m = \int_A \vec{B} \cdot d\vec{A} = \int_A B \cos \theta \, dA = B \cos \theta \int_\theta dA = BA \cos \theta$$

B is a constant in this problem, and θ is a function of time, so they were taken out of the integral. θ is the angle between the plane of the coil and the direction of $\vec{B}$, and A is the area of the loop, $\left(= \pi R^2\right)$. Since the coil is rotating with a constant angular velocity ω, θ is related to time by the following relation;

$$\theta = \omega t$$

Therefore, the flux through N coils is, N times the flux through one coil,

$$\Phi_m = NBA \cos \omega t$$

According to Faraday's law of induction, a change in flux through a coil with N turns will induce an EMF in the coil. The induced EMF is

$$\epsilon = -\frac{d\Phi_m}{dt}$$

The negative sign signifies the fact that the EMF is induced in such a direction as to oppose the change in flux that created it.

The EMF induced in the coil is then

$$\epsilon = \omega NBA \sin \omega t$$

The sine function has values ranging from +1 to -1. ϵ will then attain its maximum value when

$$\sin \omega t = \pm 1$$

Then

$$|\epsilon_{max}| = |\omega NBA|$$

or, since $\omega = 2\pi n$ where n is the number of revolutions per second,

$$|\epsilon_{max}| = 2\pi n \; NBA = 2\pi n \; NB(\pi R^2)$$

or

$$B = \frac{\epsilon_{max}}{2\pi n N/(\pi R^2)} = \frac{12.3 \text{ volts}}{2\pi \times 60 \text{ sec}^{-1} \times 100 \times \pi \times (.01\text{m})^2}$$

$$= 1.04 \frac{\text{volt-sec}}{\text{m}^2} = 1.04 \frac{\text{Weber}}{\text{m}^2}$$

The unit of length of the radius, R, was changed to meters to be consistent with the MKS system being used.

• PROBLEM 757

A square coil of 50 cm² area consisting of 20 loops is rotated about a transverse axis at the rate of 2 turns per second in a uniform magnetic field of flux density 500 gauss. The coil has a resistance of 20 ohms. (a) What is the average electromotive force induced in the coil during one quarter cycle of a revolution? (b) What is the average current in a complete cycle? (c) How much charge is passed through the coil in this interval?

Solution: (a) Note that in one quarter of a revolution, the flux threading the coil is completely changed once. Therefore $\Phi = NAB$ represents the number of lines cut in 1/8 second, since 1/8 second is one quarter of the period of rotation, and since N is the number of loops intercepting the changing flux at all times. Therefore, by Faraday's law,

$$E = \frac{\Delta\Phi}{\Delta t} = \frac{NAB}{\frac{1}{8}} = \frac{20\ (50\ \text{cm}^2)(500\ \text{gauss})}{\frac{1}{8}\ \text{sec}}$$

$$= 2 \times 5 \times 5 \times 8 \times 10^4 \text{ ab-volts}$$

$$= 400 \times 10^4 \text{ ab-volts}$$

$$= 400 \times 10^4 \text{ ab-volt} \times \frac{1 \text{ volt}}{10^8 \text{ ab-volt}} = 0.04 \text{ volt}$$

(b) By Ohm's Law $I = \frac{E}{R}$

$$= \frac{.04}{20} \text{ amperes} = .002 \text{ amperes}$$

(c) But by definition of current

$$I = \frac{Q}{t}$$

where Q is the quantity of charge passing through a point in the conductor in a time t. Then

$$Q = It = .002\left(\frac{1}{8}\right) \text{ coulomb} = .00025 \text{ coulomb}$$

• **PROBLEM 758**

An anemometer (a gauge for measuring the pressure or velocity of the wind) is made by attaching cups to each end of a metal rod 50 cm long fixed rigidly to a central vertical column which can rotate freely. A square vertical coil of side 10 cm is attached to the column and the wind speed is measured by finding the emf induced in the coil due to rotation in the earth's magnetic field. (a) Given that the maximum wind velocity to be measured is 120 mph and the maximum induced emf cannot exceed 15 mV, how many turns must the coil have?

(b) Calculate the emf induced in the metal rod during rotation at maximum speed. Assume that the horizontal and vertical components of the earth's magnetic induction are 1.5×10^{-5} Wb•m^{-2} and 5.5×10^{-5} Wb•m^{-2}, respectively.

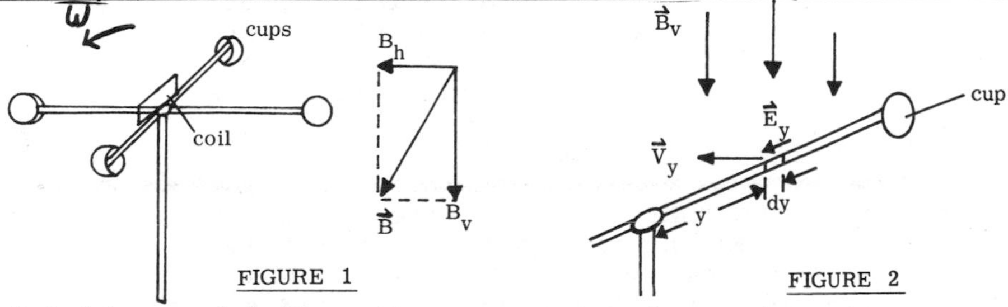

FIGURE 1

FIGURE 2

Solution: (a) When the anemometer is moving at maximum speed, the cups are moving at 120 mph = 53.64 m•s^{-1}. The angular velocity of rotation of the cups is thus

$$\omega = \frac{v}{r} = \frac{53.64 \text{ m}\cdot\text{s}^{-1}}{0.25 \text{ m}} = 214.6 \text{ rad}\cdot\text{s}^{-1}.$$

The plane of the coil is vertical, and thus the vertical component of the earth's magnetic induction produces no effect during rotation, as shown in Fig. 1. Only the horizontal component is involved. The maximum emf induced during rotation of a coil in a magnetic field of induction B is $\varepsilon_{max} = n\omega AB$, where n is the number of turns of the coil and A is its area. In this case ε_{max} must not exceed 15 mV. Hence the number of turns on the coil is

$$n = \frac{\varepsilon_{max}}{\omega AB}$$

$$= \frac{15 \times 10^{-3}\ V}{214.6\ s^{-1} \times 10^{-2} m^2 \times 1.5 \times 10^{-5}\ Wb \cdot m^{-2}}$$

$= 470$ turns.

(b) The rod which holds the cups is rotating at right angles to the vertical component of the earth's magnetic induction, and is therefore acting as a crude form of Faraday disk dynamo. (The horizontal component is in the plane of rotation and thus has no effect.)

Let us consider an element, dy of the rod at a distance y from the center of the rod as shown in Fig. 2. This element is moving with velocity $\vec{v}_y$ perpendicular to the vertical component of the earth's magnetic field. The electric field $\vec{E}y$ set up in this element is, $\vec{E}y = \vec{v}_y \times \vec{B}_v$ acting in a radial direction. Since $v_y = \omega y$, its magnitude is given by

$$Ey = v_y B_v = y \omega B_v .$$

The e.m.f. established between the center and either end of the rod has the magnitude

$$\mathcal{E} = \int_0^a dy\ Ey = \omega B_v \int_0^a dy\ y$$

$$= \frac{1}{2} \omega B_v a^2$$

$$= \frac{1}{2} \times 214.6\ s^{-1} \times 5.5 \times 10^{-5}\ wb.m^{-2} \times (0.25)^2 m^2$$

$$= 3.69 \times 10^{-4} v.$$

• PROBLEM 759

The long solenoid in Fig. 1 is wound with n = 1000 turns per meter, and the current in its windings is increased at the rate of 100 amp/sec. The cross-sectional area A of the solenoid is $4\ cm^2 = 4 \times 10^{-4}\ m^2$.

(a) Find the rate of change of magnetic flux inside the solenoid.

(b) What is the induced electric field E at a distance d = 10 cm from the axis of the solenoid?

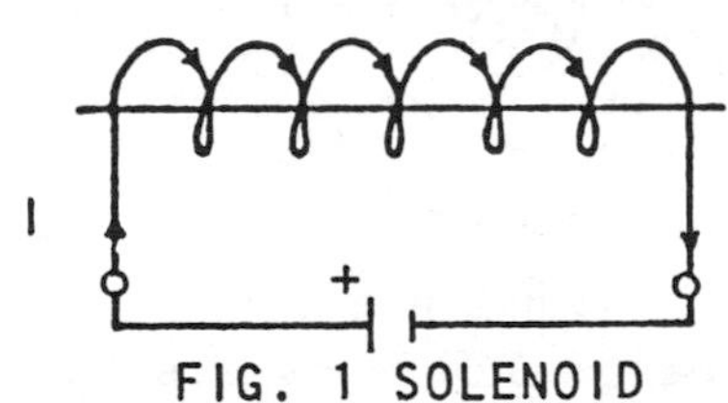

FIG. 1 SOLENOID

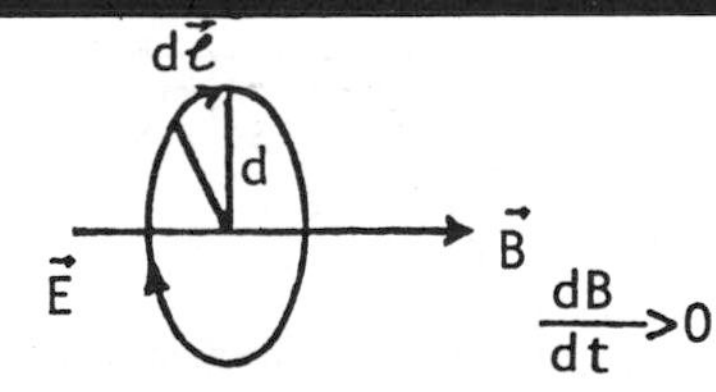

FIG. 2 B AND E FIELDS

Solution: (a) The magnetic field B inside the solenoid, due to current I flowing in it, is given by

$$B = \mu_0 n I .$$

Then, the magnetic flux Φ_B inside the coil becomes

$$\Phi_B = BA = \mu_0 n A I$$

and the rate of change of this flux is

$$\frac{d\Phi_B}{dt} = A\,\frac{dB}{dt} = \mu_0 nA\,\frac{dI}{dt}$$

$$= \left(4\pi \times 10^{-7}\,\frac{w}{a\text{-}m}\right)\left(1000\,\frac{\text{turns}}{m}\right)\left(4 \times 10^{-2} m^2\right)\left(100\,\frac{amp}{sec}\right)$$

$$= 16\pi \times 10^{-7}\ w/_{sec}$$

(b) A long solenoid can be thought of as a long cylindrical current with the magnetic field outside becoming negligible in comparison to the field inside (at least far away from the edges). Therefore, the problem reduces to that of finding the electric field induced by a time varying uniform magnetic field B while it is increasing (see Fig. 2). For this, we shall employ Faraday's law around the circle with radius d:

$$\oint \vec{E}.d\vec{\ell} = -\frac{d\Phi_B}{dt}$$

The direction and shape of the electric field can be obtained by remembering that, it will tend to set up a new flux to oppose the increase in magnetic flux through the coil. The electric field is circular and it is constant around the path we defined for the above integral. Therefore it can be taken outside the integral sign.

$$\vec{E}.\oint d\vec{\ell} = E\ell = E\,2\pi d = -\frac{d\Phi_B}{dt}$$

or

$$E = -\frac{1}{2\pi d}\,\frac{d\Phi_B}{dt}$$

$$= 8 \times 10^{-5}\,\frac{w}{m\cdot sec} = 8 \times 10^{-5}\,\frac{v}{m}\,.$$

• PROBLEM 760

Electrons with energies of 1 MeV are injected into the vacuum tube of a betatron of radius 1 m, through the center of which is a magnetic flux which changes at the rate of 100 Wb · s^{-1}. The electrons make 250,000 revolutions before being ejected from the betatron. What is their final energy?

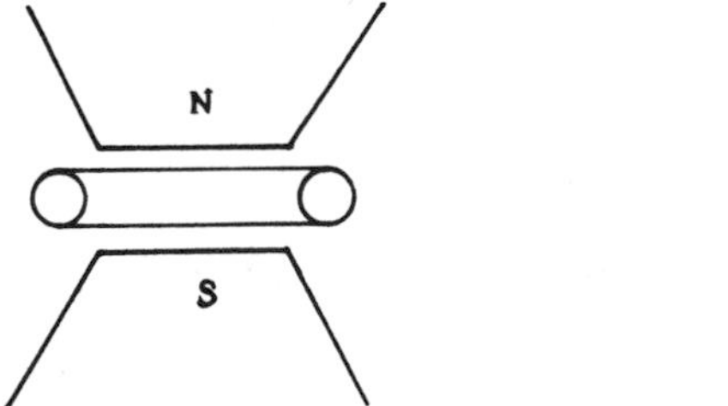

FIGURE A: Side view of betatron

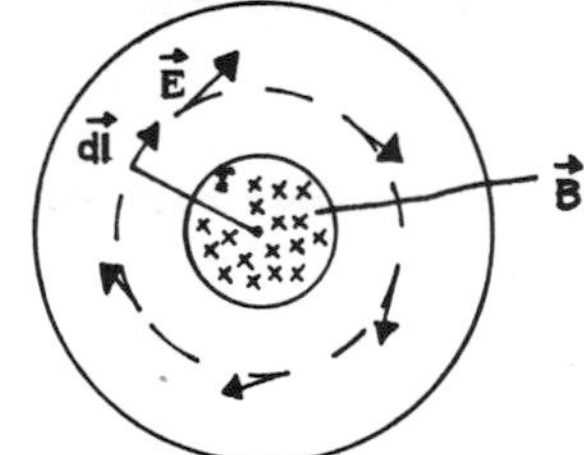

FIGURE B

Solution: A betatron (see Fig. A) basically consists of an evacuated tube in the shape of a circular ring with a magnetic field passing through the center of the ring. The magnetic field is slowly increased. This induces an increasing tangential electric field around the circumference of the ring by Faraday's Law. An electron placed in the ring will be accelerated around the ring by this electric field. The tube is evacuated to prevent collisions between the accelerating electrons and air particles. The force due to the changing magnetic flux acting on the electron is found using Faraday's law and the definition of emf ε.

$$\varepsilon \equiv \oint_C \vec{E} \cdot \vec{d\ell} = -\frac{d\phi}{dt} \equiv -\dot{\phi} \qquad (1)$$

The line integral is taken about the contour C defined by the circumference of the circular ring. $\vec{E}$ is the electric field vector induced by the changing magnetic field and $\vec{d\ell}$ is an element of arc length (see figure B). $\dot{\phi}$ is the rate of change of magnetic flux through the contour. The magnitude of $\vec{E}$ is constant at all points on the contour. $\vec{E}$ is also parallel to $\vec{d\ell}$ at any point on the contour. Thus (1) becomes

$$E \int_C d\ell = E(2\pi r) = \dot{\phi} \qquad (2)$$

where r is the radius of the circular contour within the evacuated tube. But by definition of electric field, E is equal to the force per unit charge, or

$$E = \frac{F}{q}$$

The work, then, done on the electron (of charge e) by the induced electric field in moving the electron once around the ring is the product of the force acting on it times the distance it moves. Or

$$W = Fs = eE(2\pi r) = e\dot{\phi}$$

Here, we used equation (2). This is equal to the energy gained by the electron in one revolution. Making use of the electronvolt-joule conversion factor,

$$W = e\dot{\phi} \text{ Joules} \times \frac{1 \text{ eV}}{1.6 \times 10^{-19} \text{ J}}$$

$$= \left(1.6 \times 10^{-19}\, \dot{\phi}\right)\text{J} \times \frac{1 \text{ eV}}{1.6 \times 10^{-19} \text{ J}}$$

$$= \dot{\phi} \text{ eV}$$

The total energy the electrons acquire while in the betatron is thus the energy gained per revolution times the number of revolutions performed (= 250,000).

$$\therefore \quad W = 100 \times 250{,}000 \text{ eV} = 25 \text{ MeV}.$$

The final energy is thus E = 1 MeV + W = 26 MeV.

• PROBLEM 761

The current i in a long straight wire is increasing at a steady rate $i = 3.36(1 + 2t) \times 10^{-2}$ amps. A small circular loop of wire of radius a = 0.1 cm is in a plane through the wire and its center is a distance r = 100 cm from the wire (figure). If the resistance of the loop is $R = 8.99 \times 10^{-4}$ ohms what is the induced current i_l flowing round it and in which direction does it flow?

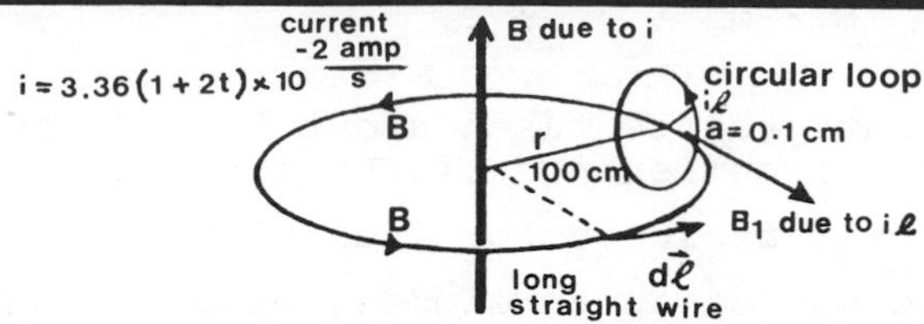

Solution: The current i in the straight wire produces circular magnetic lines of force. In the vicinity of the loop these lines are perpendicular to the plane of the loop. Because the current in the long wire is time dependent, the magnetic field which it sets up at the site of the circular coil will change with time. Furthermore, being that magnetic flux is defined as

$$\Phi = \int \overline{B} \cdot d\overline{s}, \tag{1}$$

(where $\vec{B}$ is the magnetic induction and the integral is a surface integral), Φ will also be time dependent. Then, by Faraday's Law

$$\text{E.M.F.} = -\frac{d\Phi}{dt}, \tag{2}$$

an E.M.F. (electromotive force) will be induced in the coil of wire. If the resistance of this loop is R, then by Ohm's Law, the current in the loop is

$$i_\ell = \frac{\text{E.M.F.}}{R} = -\frac{1}{R}\frac{d\Phi}{dt} \tag{3}$$

To evaluate this current, we must find Φ, and, hence, $\vec{B}$. To calculate the latter, we use Ampere's Law, or

$$\oint \vec{B} \cdot d\vec{\ell} = \mu_0 i_{enc} \tag{4}$$

This integral must be evaluated over a closed path. i_{enc} is the net current passing through this path and $\mu_0 = 4\pi \times 10^{-7}$ Weber/amp. m. The lines of magnetic induction, $\vec{B}$, for a long wire are circles centered on the wire. Hence, to evaluate (4), we use a circular path of radius r centered on the wire. In this way, $\vec{B}$ and $d\vec{\ell}$ will be parallel, and, from (4)

$$B2\pi r = u_0 i_{enc}$$

and

$$B = \frac{\mu_0 i_{enc}}{2\pi r}.$$

We may next find Φ. Because the area elements $d\vec{s}$ of the circular loop are all parallel to the lines of $\vec{B}$ set up by the long wire, Φ reduces to

$$\Phi = \int \vec{B} \cdot d\vec{s} = \int B ds.$$

Since the radius a of the loop is very small compared with its distance r from the wire, it is reasonable to assume that the magnetic field has this value at all points inside the loop. The flux through the loop is therefore

$$\Phi = BA$$

$$= \frac{\mu_0 i_{enc}}{2\pi r}(\pi a^2).$$

But $i_{enc} = 3.36(1 + 2t) \times 10^{-2}$ amp/s and

$$\Phi = \frac{(\mu_0 (3.36)(1 + 2t)10^{-2}\ \text{amp/s})a^2}{2r}$$

Using (3)

$$i_\ell = -\frac{1}{R}\frac{d}{dt}\frac{\mu_0(3.36)(1 + 2t)10^{-2}\ \text{amp/s})a^2}{2r}$$

$$= -\frac{1}{R}\frac{\mu_0(3.36)(2)\left(10^{-2}\ \frac{\text{amp}}{\text{s}}\right)a^2}{2r}$$

$$= -\frac{\left(4\pi \times 10^{-7}\ \frac{\text{Weber}}{\text{amp.m}}\right)(6.72)\left(10^{-2}\ \frac{\text{amp}}{\text{s}}\right)(10^{-6}\text{m}^2)}{(2)(1\text{m})(8.99\quad 10^{-4}\ \text{ohms})}$$

$$= \frac{4.22 \times 10^{-14}\ \text{Weber}}{8.99 \times 10^{-4}\ \text{ohms} \cdot \text{s}}$$

$$= 4.70 \times 10^{-11}\ \frac{\text{Weber}}{\text{ohms}\cdot\text{s}}\ .$$

But 1 Weber= 1 $\frac{\text{Newton} \cdot \text{m}}{\text{amp}}$ and 1 ohm = $\frac{1\ \text{volt}}{\text{amp}} = \frac{1\ \text{joule}}{\text{amp coul}}$.

$$i_\ell = 4.70 \times 10^{-11}\ \frac{\text{Newton} \cdot \text{m}}{\text{amp}\quad \text{s}} \cdot \frac{\text{amp. coul}}{\text{joule}}$$

$$= 4.70 \times 10^{-11}\ \frac{\text{Newton} \cdot \text{m} \cdot \text{coul}}{\text{Newton} \cdot \text{m} \cdot \text{s}} = 4.69 \times 10^{-11}\ \text{amp}$$

The magnetic field produced by the straight wire goes through the loop into the page in the figure and it is increasing with time. The current i_l in the loop tries to counteract this by producing a magnetic field coming out of the page. The induced current must therefore flow counterclockwise round the loop.

CHAPTER 23

ALTERNATING CURRENTS/CIRCUITS

• PROBLEM 762

What is the maximum value of a 6.0-amp alternating current?

Solution. The 6.0-amp characterizing the alternating current is the rms or the root mean square value equal to 0.707 of the maximum current. The rms value is used as the effective current for power calculations $\left(P = I^2R\right)$.

$$I = 0.707I_m = 6.0 \text{ amp}$$

Hence, $i_m = \frac{6.0}{0.707}\text{amp} = 8.5 \text{ amp.}$

• PROBLEM 763

A capacitor is found to offer 25 ohms of capacitive reactance when connected in a 400-cps circuit. What is its capacitance?

Solution: Capacitive resistance, X_C, is given by

$$X_C = \frac{1}{2\pi fC}$$

Here X_C = 25 ohms and f = 400 cps. Then

$$X_C = 25 \text{ ohms} = \frac{1}{2\pi \times 400 \text{ cps} \times C}$$

or $$C = \frac{1}{2\pi \times 400 \text{ cps} \times 25 \text{ ohms}}$$

Since $1 \text{ farad} = 1 \frac{\text{coul}}{\text{volt}} = \frac{1 \text{ coul}}{\text{amp} \cdot \text{ohm}} = 1 \frac{\text{sec}}{\text{ohm}}$

$$C = \frac{1}{2\pi \times 400 \times 25} \text{ farad}$$

$$= 1.6 \times 10^{-5} \text{ farad} = 16 \text{ } \mu\text{f}$$

• PROBLEM 764

What is the impedance of a 1-μf capacitor at angular frequencies of 100, 1000 and 10,000 rad/sec?

Solution: The circuit element is a capacitor, therefore the impedance

is purely reactive.
At an angular frequency of 1000 rad/sec, the reactance of a 1-μf capacitor is

$$X_c = \frac{1}{wC} = \frac{1}{\left(10^3 \text{ rad/sec}\right) \times 10^{-6} f} = 1000 \text{ ohms}.$$

At a frequency of 10,000 rad/sec the reactance of the same capacitor is only 100 ohms, and at a frequency of 100 rad/sec it is 10,000 ohms.

• PROBLEM 765

What is the impedance of a 1-henry inductor at angular frequencies of 100, 1000 and 10,000 rad/sec?

Solution: The circuit element is an inductor, therefore the impedance is purely reactive.
At an angular frequency of 1000 rad/sec, the reactance of a 1-henry inductor is

$$X_L = wL = 10^3 \frac{\text{rad}}{\text{sec}} \times 1 \text{ h} = 1000 \text{ ohms}.$$

At a frequency of 10,000 rad/sec the reactance of the same inductor is 10,000 ohms, while at a frequency of 100 rad/sec it is only 100 ohms.

• PROBLEM 766

The voltage in an ac circuit of resistance 30 ohms varies sinusoidally with time with a maximum of 170 volts. What is the instantaneous voltage when it has reached 45° in its cycle? What is the current then?

Solution. The instantaneous voltage can be represented by sine wave multiplied by the maximum voltage or $e = e_m \sin \theta$. At $\theta = 45°$

$$e = e_m \sin \theta = 170 \sin 45° = 170 \text{ volts} \times 0.71 = 120 \text{ volts}.$$

In a circuit of pure resistance, the current i is in phase with the voltage. Therefore,

$$i = \frac{e}{R} = \frac{e_m \sin \theta}{R} = \frac{170 \text{ volts}}{30 \text{ ohms}} \times 0.71 = 4.0 \text{ amp}.$$

• PROBLEM 767

A coil having resistance and inductance is connected in series with an ac ammeter across a 100 volt dc line. The meter reads 1.1 amperes. The combination is then connected across a 110 volt ac 60 cycle line and the meter reads .55 ampere. What are the resistance, the impedance, the reactance, and the inductance of the coil?

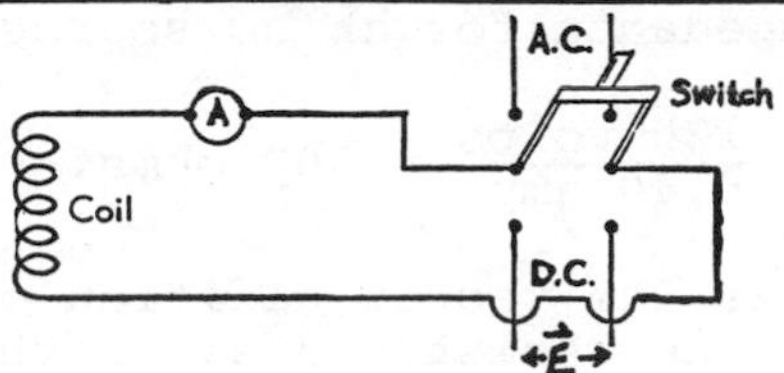

Solution: Note that with dc by Ohm's law,

$$I = \frac{E}{R} \qquad\qquad R = \frac{E}{I}$$

$$R = \frac{110 \text{ v}}{1.1 \text{ A}} = 100 \text{ ohms}$$

(Resistance)

On ac, however the reactance of the inductance must also be taken into account (it is zero for dc current). Ohm's law still applies with the impedance taking the place of resistance. Therefore

$$\frac{E}{I} = Z = \frac{110}{.55} = 200 \text{ ohms (Impedance)}$$

But

$$Z = \sqrt{R^2 + X^2}$$

where X is the impedance of the inductance.

$$= 100^2 + X^2 = (200\ \Omega)^2$$

therefore

$$X^2 = (40000 - 10000)\Omega^2 = 30000\ \Omega^2$$

$$X = \sqrt{30000\ \Omega^2} = 173\ \Omega \text{ (Reactance)}$$

And

$$X = 2\pi nL$$

where n is the number of times per second the current alternates. For dc current, n = 0, and the inductance has no effect on the circuit. (The effect of the inductance on the behavior of the circuit increases appreciably as the frequency of the ac current increases).

Therefore

$$L = \frac{X}{2\pi n} = \frac{173\ \Omega}{2\pi(60)S^{-1}} = .459 \text{ henry (inductance)}$$

• PROBLEM 768

It is found that the current in the circuit of Fig. A is 0.50 amp with the dc source, 0.40 amp with the ac source. The voltage ε for dc is 120 volts and for ac ε is 120 volts, with frequency f = 60 cycles/sec. What are the resistance R, impedance Z, reactance X_L, and inductance L?

Figure A

Figure B

Solution. The reactance of the inductor L is zero for dc operation since $X_L = 2\pi fL$ and f is zero. Therefore, for a dc source, the impedance is equal to R. The resistance R is the same for both dc and ac operation.

$$R = \frac{\varepsilon}{I} = \frac{120 \text{ volts}}{0.50 \text{ amp}} = 240 \text{ ohms}$$

The effective impedance for an ac source is

$$Z = \frac{\varepsilon}{I} = \frac{120 \text{ volts}}{0.40 \text{ amp}} = 300 \text{ ohms.}$$

The impedance Z is the vector addition of the reactance of the inductor and the resistance since the reactance of the inductor causes current to lead voltage by a phase shift of 90°.

From Fig. B

$$Z^2 = R^2 + X_L^2$$

$$300^2 = 240^2 + X_L^2$$

$$X_L^2 = 32,400$$

$$X_L = 180 \text{ ohms.}$$

From $X_L = 2\pi fL$

$$180 \text{ ohms} = 2\pi(60 \text{ cycles/sec})L$$

$$L = 0.48 \text{ henry.}$$

• PROBLEM 769

In the circuit of fig. A, the values are as follows: C = 30 μf, V = 120 volts, and R = 25 ohms. The voltage is alternating with frequency f = 60 cycles/sec. What is the current? What is the phase angle?

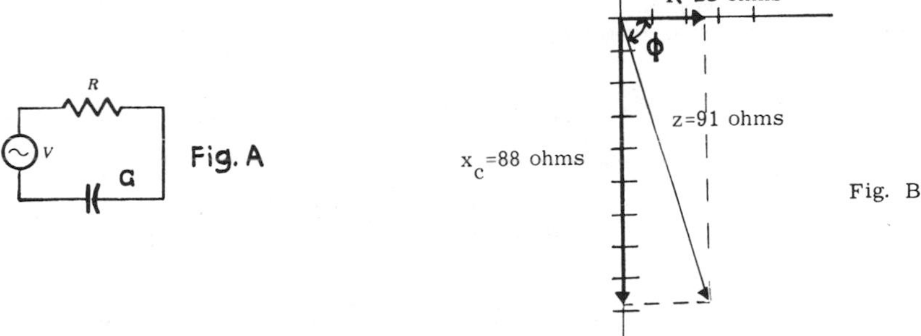

Solution. The reactance of the capacitor depends on frequency.

$$X_c = \frac{-1}{2\pi fC} = \frac{-1}{2\pi \times 60 \times 30 \times 10^{-6}} = -88 \text{ ohms.}$$

The impedance Z is the vector addition of the reactance and pure resistance, since the reactance of the capacitor causes the current to lag the voltage by a phase of 90°.

$$Z = \sqrt{R^2 + X_c^2} = \sqrt{25^2 + 88^2} = 91 \text{ ohms}$$

$$I = \frac{V}{Z} = \frac{120 \text{ volts}}{91 \text{ ohms}} = 1.3 \text{ amp.}$$

The phase angle ϕ is the angle between the impedance and the pure resistance of the circuit (see figure B).

$$\cos \phi = \frac{R}{Z}$$

$$\phi = \cos^{-1} \frac{R}{Z} = \cos^{-1} \frac{25 \text{ ohms}}{-91 \text{ ohms}} = -74.2°.$$

A 600-ohm resistor is in series with a 0.5 henry inductor and a 0.2 μf capacitor. Compute the impedance of the circuit and draw the vector impedance diagram (a) at a frequency of 400 cycles/sec, (b) at 600 cycles/sec.

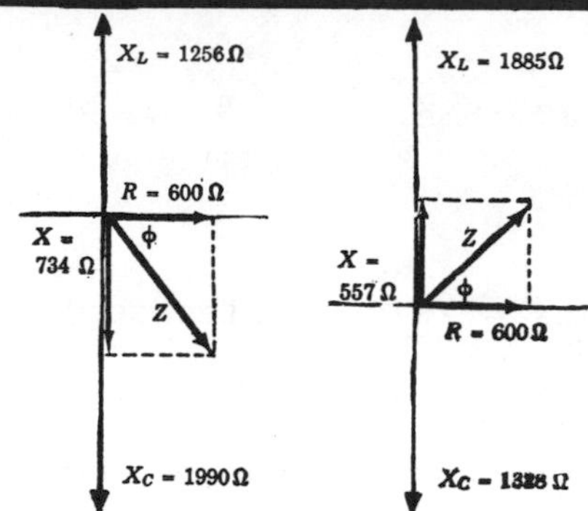

Solution: The formula for the total impedance is

$$Z = \sqrt{R^2 + (X_L - X_C)^2}$$

(a) At 400 cycles/sec,

$$X_L = 2\pi \times 400 \times 0.5 = 1256 \text{ ohms,}$$

$$X_C = \frac{1}{2\pi \times 400 \times 0.2 \times 10^{-6}} = 1990 \text{ ohms,}$$

$$X = X_L - X_C = 1256 - 1990 = -734 \text{ ohms,}$$

$$Z = \sqrt{(600)^2 + (-734)^2} = 949 \text{ ohms.}$$

(see figure, part (a).)

(b) At 600 cycles/sec,

$$X_L = 2\pi \times 600 \times 0.5 = 1885 \text{ ohms,}$$

$$X_C = \frac{1}{2\pi \times 600 \times 0.2 \times 10^{-6}} = 1328 \text{ ohms,}$$

$$X = X_L - X_C = 1885 - 1328 = 557 \text{ ohms,}$$

$$Z = \sqrt{(600)^2 + (557)^2} = 818 \text{ ohms.}$$

(see figure, part (b).)

• PROBLEM 771

When a 2-V cell is connected in series with two electrical elements, the current in the circuit is 200 mA. If a 50-

cycle · s^{-1}, 2-V ac source replaces the cell, the current becomes 100 mA. What are the values of the circuit elements? Suppose that the frequency is increased to 1000 cycles · s^{-1}. What is the new value of the current?

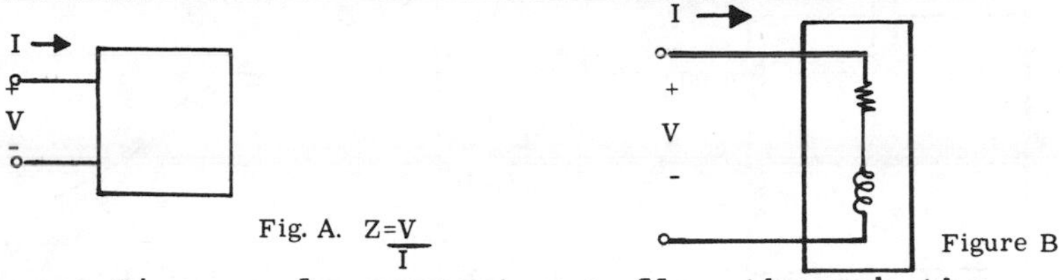

Fig. A. $Z = \frac{V}{I}$ Figure B

Solution: Since a dc current can flow through the elements, neither of them can be a capacitor, which offers an infinite resistance to direct current. The resistance of the elements is

$$R = \frac{V}{I} = \frac{2\ V}{200 \times 10^{-3}\ A} = 10\ \Omega.$$

Since the current changes when alternating current is supplied, the circuit must also contain an inductor of inductance L. The reactance (the ac analogue of resistance) of an inductor is $X = \omega L$ where $\omega = 2\pi n$. n is the frequency of variation of voltage. The impedance Z (i.e. the ratio of V to I at a set of terminals of a circuit as shown in Figure A) of the series combination of the resistor and inductor (Fig. B) is

$$Z^2 = R^2 + X^2$$

$$Z = \sqrt{R^2 + \omega^2 L^2} = \frac{V'}{I'} = \frac{2\ V}{100 \times 10^{-3}\ A} = 20\ \Omega.$$

$$\therefore\quad 100\ \Omega^2 + \omega^2 L^2 = 400\ \Omega^2 \quad \text{or } L^2 = \frac{300\ \Omega^2}{\omega^2}.$$

$$\therefore\quad L = \frac{17.32\ \Omega}{2\pi \times 50\ s^{-1}} = 0.055\ H.$$

When the frequency is increased to 10^3 cycles · s^{-1},

$$I' = \frac{V'}{Z'} = \frac{2\ V}{\sqrt{100\ \Omega^2 + (2\pi \times 10^3 \times 0.055)^2 \Omega^2}} = \frac{2}{346}\ A$$

$$= 5.77\ mA.$$

We see that when the frequency n = 0, I = 200 mA. When n = 50 sec^{-1}, I = 100mA, and when n = 1000 sec^{-1}, I = 5.77 mA. The inductor does then act as a resistor. Its opposition to current (the reactance) is directly proportional to frequency as is seen by the relation $X = (L)\omega = (2\pi L)n = Kn$ where K is a constant.

• PROBLEM 772

(a) Find the current in a circuit consisting of a coil and capacitor in series, if the applied voltage is v = 110 volts, frequency f = 60 cycles/sec; the inductance of the coil is L = 0.80 henry; the resistance of the coil is R = 50.0 ohms; and the capacitance of the capacitor is C = 8.0 μf. (b) Find the power used in the circuit.

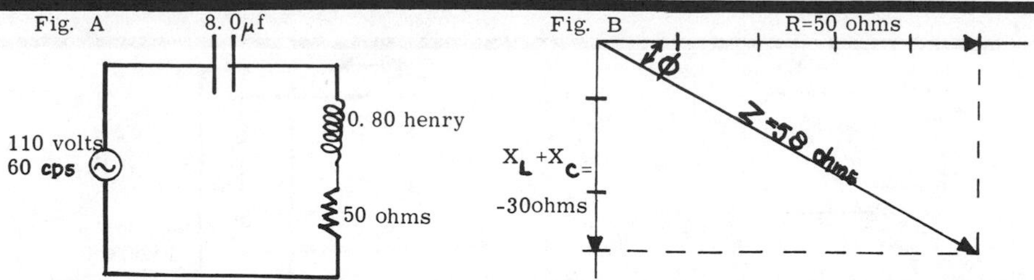

Solution. (a) The coil can be represented by an inductance and resistance in series (see figure A).

The effective impedance of the inductor and capacitor depend on frequency. Since the inductor and capacitor cause the current to either lead or lag the voltage by a phase shift of 90°, the impedance Z is the vector addition of their combined reactance and the pure resistance (see figure B).

$$X_L = 2\pi fL = 2\pi(60)(0.80)\text{ohms} = 300 \text{ ohms}$$

$$X_C = \frac{-1}{2\pi fC} = \frac{-1}{2\pi \times 60 \times 8.0 \times 10^{-6}} \text{ ohms}$$

$$= -330 \text{ ohms}$$

$$X_L + X_C = 300 - 330 = -30 \text{ ohms}$$

$$Z = \sqrt{R^2 + (X_L + X_C)^2}$$

$$= \sqrt{(50)^2 + (300 - 330)^2} \text{ ohms}$$

$$= \sqrt{50^2 + (-30)^2} \text{ ohms} = 58 \text{ ohms}$$

$$I = \frac{V}{Z} = \frac{110 \text{ volts}}{58 \text{ ohms}} = 1.9 \text{ amp}$$

(b) The power is equal to $P = I^2R$ or $P = VI \cos$ where is the angle between the impedance and the pure resistance in the circuit.(see figure b)

$$\cos \quad = \frac{R}{Z} = \frac{50 \text{ ohms}}{58 \text{ ohms}} = 0.86$$

$$P = VI \cos \theta = 110 \text{ volts} \times 1.9 \text{ amp} \times 0.86$$

$$= 180 \text{ watts.}$$

Using $P = I^2R$ as a check,

$$P = I^2R = (1.9 \text{ amp})^2 \times 50 \text{ ohms} = 180 \text{ watts.}$$

• PROBLEM 773

A transmission line delivers power at a potential of 240,000V to a transformer designed to step the potential down to 2,400 V. If the primary coil has 10,000 turns, how many turns should the secondary coil contain? Suppose that the transformer delivers 500 A of current at the secondary. What would be the current in the primary coil?

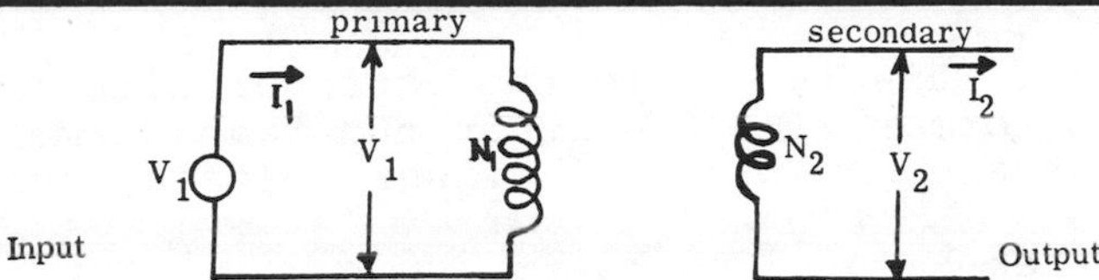

Step-Down Transformer

Solution: The voltage output of a transformer depends on the input voltage and on the turns ratio according to the relationship (See figure),

$$\frac{V_1}{V_2} = \frac{N_1}{N_2}$$

Substituting, we find the turns N_2 in the secondary coil to be,

$$N_2 = \frac{N_1 \; V_2}{V_1} = \frac{(1 \times 10^4 \text{ turns})\;(2.4 \times 10^3 \text{ V})}{(2.4 \times 10^5 \text{ V})} = 1 \times 10^2 \text{turns}$$

If we assume that power is transferred from primary to the secondary of this transformer at 100 per cent efficiency, the power in equals power out because of the principle of conservation of energy. Therefore,

$$V_1 \; I_1 = V_2 \; I_2$$

or

$$I_1 = \frac{V_2 \; I_2}{V_1} \; \frac{(2.4 \times 10^3 \text{ V})\;(5 \times 10^2 \text{ A})}{(2.4 \times 10^5 \text{ V})} = 5 \text{ A}$$

• PROBLEM 774

A step-down transformer at the end of a transmission line reduces the voltage from 2400 volts to 120 volts. The power output is 9.0 kw, and the overall efficiency of the transformer is 92 percent. The primary ("high-tension") winding has 4000 turns. How many turns has the secondary, or "low-tension," coil? What is the power input? What is the current in each of the two coils?

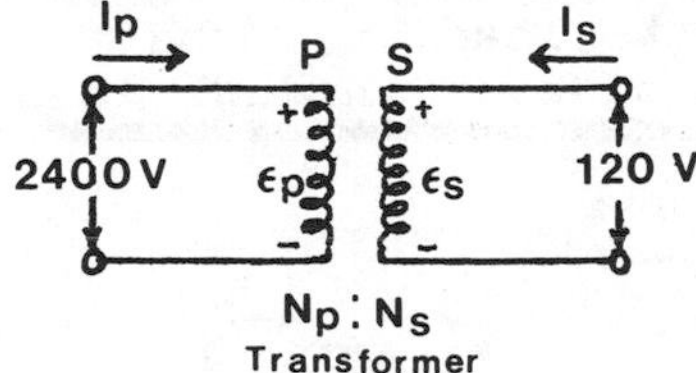

Transformer

Solution: ε_p and ε_s are the voltages induced by the currents I_p and I_s, respectively (as shown in the figure above). ε_p and ε_s are related by the following formula:

$$\frac{\varepsilon_p}{\varepsilon_s} = \frac{N_p}{N_s}$$

where N_p and N_s are the number of turns in coils P and S, respectively. This is due to the configuration of the coils in the transformer. The fact that the transformer is step-down indicates ε_p must be the higher voltage, and ε_s the lower. We then have,

$$\frac{2400 \text{ v.}}{120 \text{ v.}} = \frac{4000 \text{ turns}}{N_s}$$

Hence $N_s = 200$ turns.

The power output P_s is the power available at the secondary terminals (S), or $P_s = 9.0$ kw = 9000 watts. But

$$\text{Efficiency} = \frac{P_s}{P_p}$$

or $$0.92 = \frac{9000 \text{ watts}}{P_p}$$

Then $$P_p = 9800 \text{ watts.}$$

To find the currents, note that

$$P_p = I_p \varepsilon_p$$

or $$I_p = \frac{P_p}{\varepsilon_p} = \frac{9800 \text{ watts}}{2400 \text{ volts}} = 4.1 \text{ amp}$$

Similarly,

$$P_s = I_s \varepsilon_s$$

or $$I_s = \frac{P_s}{\varepsilon_s} = \frac{9000 \text{ watts}}{120 \text{ volts}} = 75 \text{ amp.}$$

• PROBLEM 775

An ac source of internal resistance 9000 Ω is to supply current to a load of resistance 10 Ω. How should the source be matched to the load, and what is then the ratio of the currents passing through load and source?

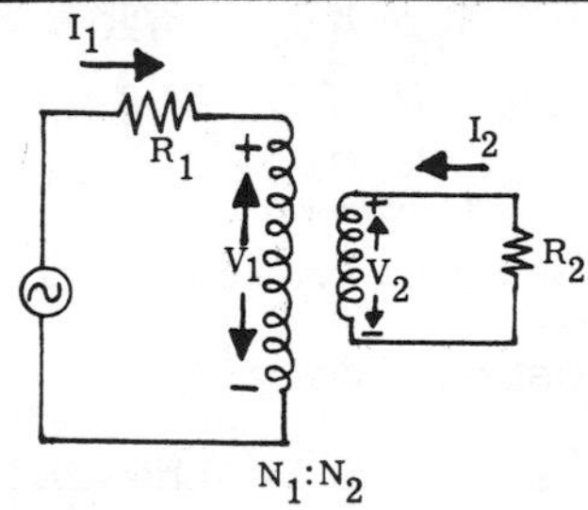

Solution: The matching may be done by means of a transformer (see the figure). If the numbers of turns on primary and secondary windings are N_1 and N_2, then the internal resistance of the source, R_1, and load resistance, R_2, are related by the equation $R_1 = (N_1/N_2)^2 R_2$.

$$\therefore \quad \left(\frac{N_1}{N_2}\right)^2 = \frac{R_1}{R_2} = \frac{9000}{10} = 900 \quad \text{or} \quad \frac{N_1}{N_2} = 30.$$

Therefore, a transformer with a turns ratio of 30 : 1 must be employed. The transformer lowers the voltage in the ratio 30 : 1, but correspondingly increases the current in the same ratio, for

$$\frac{V_1}{V_2} = \frac{N_1}{N_2} \qquad \text{and} \qquad \frac{I_1}{I_2} = \frac{1}{\left(\frac{N_1}{N_2}\right)}$$

• PROBLEM 776

The primary of a transformer, consisting of 20 turns, is connected to a varying voltage source which a voltmeter indicates to have a value of 110 volts. If the secondary circuit has 1000 turns and a resistance of 20,000 ohms, what voltage would a meter read if connected across it? What is the current in the primary if 100% efficiency is assumed?

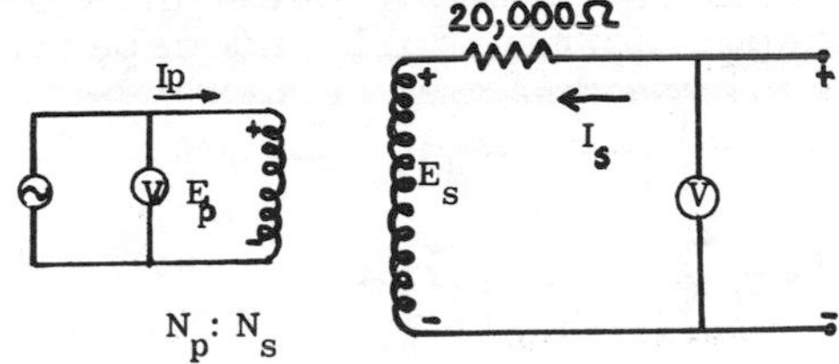

Solution: The voltmeter reads the root mean square (rms) value of the actual voltage. That is, if the actual instantaneous voltage is given by

$$e = E_{max} \sin \omega t$$

where ω is the angular frequency of the voltage variation, then

$$E_{rms} = E = \sqrt{\frac{1}{2\pi} \int_0^{2\pi} E_{max}^2 \sin^2 \omega t \quad d(\omega t)}$$

If E_p and E_s are the rms values of the voltages on the primary (i.e. the side where the voltage source is located) and on the secondary sides, respectively, of the transformer, then according to the principle of the transformer

$$\frac{E_s}{E_p} = \frac{N_s}{N_p}$$

$$\therefore\ E_s = \frac{N_s}{N_p} E_p = \frac{1000}{20}(110) = 5500 \text{ volts}$$

The efficiency of a transformer is defined as

$$E_{ff} = \frac{\text{Power out}}{\text{Power in}} \times 100$$

If 100% efficiency is assumed, the power output is equal to the power input, where P = EI.

By Ohm's Law, $I_s = \frac{E_s}{R_s} = \frac{5500}{20000} = .275$ ampere

$$\therefore \quad P = E_s I_s = E_p I_p$$

$$\therefore \quad I_p = \frac{E_s I_s}{E_p} = \frac{5500}{110}(.275)$$

$$= 50(.275) = 13.75 \text{ amperes.}$$

• PROBLEM 777

A coil of resistance 10 ohm and inductance 0.1 H is in series with a capacitor and a 100-V 60-cycle $\cdot\ s^{-1}$ source. The capacitor is adjusted to give resonance in the circuit. Calculate the capacitance of the capacitor and the voltages across coil and capacitor.

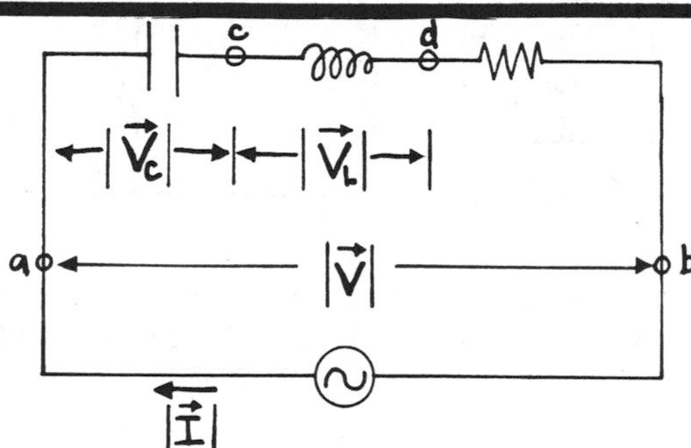

Solution: The (complex) impedance Z (seen looking into the terminals a-b) of the series R-L-C circuit (see figure) is

$$\vec{Z} = \frac{\vec{V}}{\vec{I}} = R + j\left(X_L - X_c\right)$$

where the reactances $X_L = 2\pi fL = \omega L$ and $X_c = 1/2\pi fC = 1/\omega C$. f is the frequency of variation of voltage. The negative sign is introduced above because the inductive and capacitive reactances tend to cancel one another's effect. In the series combination, the voltages tend to cancel because they are in phase opposition. The (complex) voltage $\vec{V} = |\vec{V}|\ e^{j\theta_1}$ where $|\vec{V}|$ is the magnitude of the voltage and θ_1 is the phase angle of the voltage relative to the current $\vec{I}\ \left(= |\vec{I}|\ e^{jo} = |\vec{I}|\right)$.

The magnitude and phase of the impedance are respectively

$$|\vec{Z}| = \sqrt{R^2 + \left(X_L - X_C\right)^2} \qquad \theta = \arctan \frac{\left(X_L - X_C\right)}{R}$$

Then $\vec{Z} = |\vec{Z}|\, e^{j\theta}$

At resonance, $X_L = X_C$.

$$\frac{1}{\omega C} = \omega L$$

$$\therefore \quad C = \frac{1}{\omega^2 L} = \frac{1}{4\pi^2 \times 60^2\ s^{-2} \times 0.1\ H} = 70.4\ \mu F.$$

Further, the circuit becomes purely resistive for $|\vec{Z}| = \sqrt{R^2 + 0^2}$ or $|\vec{Z}| = R$, and $\theta = \arctan 0 = 0°$. Thus

$$|\vec{I}| = \frac{|\vec{V}|}{R} = \frac{100\ V}{10\ \Omega} = 10\ A.$$

The voltage difference across the inductor is $\vec{V}_L = \vec{I}\vec{Z}_L$ where Z_L is the impedance looking into the terminals a - c (see the figure). However, the only impedance present is the inductive reactance X_L. Then $|\vec{Z}_L| = X_L = 2\pi fL$

$$|\vec{V}_L| = |\vec{I}|\, X_L = 10A \times 2\pi \times 60\ s^{-1} \times 0.1\ \text{Henry} = 377\ V.$$

The voltage difference across the capacitor is, similarly, $\vec{V}_C = \vec{I}\,\vec{Z}_C$ where Z_L is the impedance looking into the terminals c - d (see the figure). But $|\vec{Z}_C| = X_C = 1/2\pi fC$, hence

$$|\vec{V}_C| = |\vec{I}|\, X_C = 10\ A \times \frac{1}{2\pi \times 60 s^{-1} \times 70.4 \times 10^{-6}\ F}$$

$$= 377\ V.$$

Thus, $|\vec{V}_C| = |\vec{V}_L|$. However $\vec{V}_C$ and $\vec{V}_L$ are in phase opposition or $|\theta_C - \theta_L| = \pi$, hence, their effects cancel. Therefore, at any time, $V_{ad} = V_{ac} + V_{cd} = 0$ and the voltage of the source appears across the resistor only. Notice that $|\vec{V}_C|$ and $|\vec{V}_L|$, individually, may have values greater than the source voltage.

• PROBLEM 778

A radio receiving set is tuned to a certain station by the use of a .25 millihenry (2.5×10^{-4} henry) inductance, and a 32.2 microfarad (32.2×10^{-12}farad) condenser. What is the frequency of the station? What is its wave length?

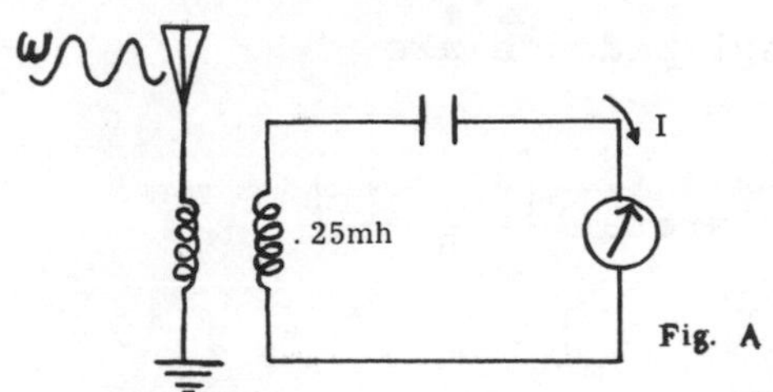

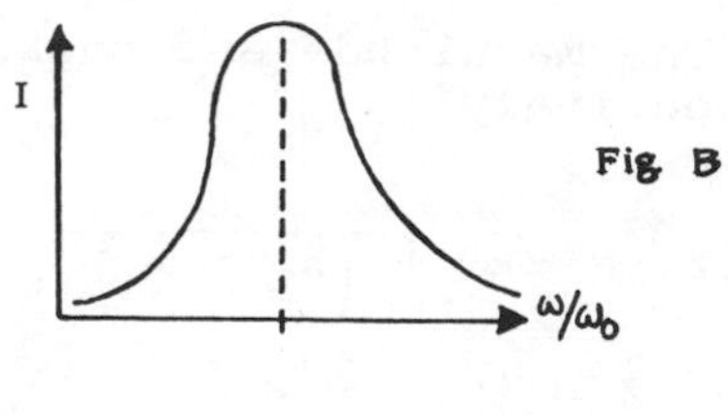

Solution: The heart of the receiving set of the radio station is the tank or tuning circuit as shown in figure (A). The circuit is more responsive to certain frequencies than to others. At a frequency ω_0, denoted the resonance frequency, the current through the circuit is much greater than the current response of the circuit at any other frequency. This resonance peak is shown in figure (B). This resonant frequency is determined by the condition that the impedance of the capacitance equal the impedance of the inductance. Or

$$\frac{1}{\omega_0 C} = \omega_0 L$$

$$\omega_0 = 2\pi f = \sqrt{\frac{1}{LC}}$$

$$f = \frac{1}{2\pi}\sqrt{\frac{1}{LC}}$$

$$f = \frac{1}{2\pi}\sqrt{\frac{1}{2.5 \times 10^{-4}\ \text{h} \times 32.2 \times 10^{-12}\ \text{f}}}$$

$$= \frac{1}{2\pi}\sqrt{\frac{10^{16}}{81}}$$

$$f = \frac{10^8}{2\pi 9} = \frac{10^8}{56.5} = 1.77 \times 10^6 \text{ cycles per sec}$$

The velocity of radio waves is the same as that of the speed of any electromagnetic wave. It is therefore,

3×10^{10} cm/sec,

and $v = f\lambda$ for all waves

$$\therefore \lambda = \frac{v}{f} = \frac{3 \times 10^{10}}{1.77 \quad 10^6} = 1.7 \times 10^4 = 17{,}000 \text{ cm}$$

$$= 170 \text{ m}$$

• PROBLEM 779

When a cathode-ray tube has its deflector plates connected across a 100-V battery, the spot on the fluorescent screen is deflected 12 cm. If the plates are now connected across a resistance of 20 Ω in parallel with an ac voltmeter and in series with a 50-cycle$\cdot$s^{-1} ac generator, the length of trace on the screen is 17 cm and the voltmeter reads 50 V. How can these apparently contradictory figures be explained?

Suppose that the resistance is replaced by a coil of resistance 5 Ω and reactance 0.1 H, and that the current drawn from the generator is adjusted to the same value as before. What length of trace will be obtained and what is the rate of heat production in the coil?

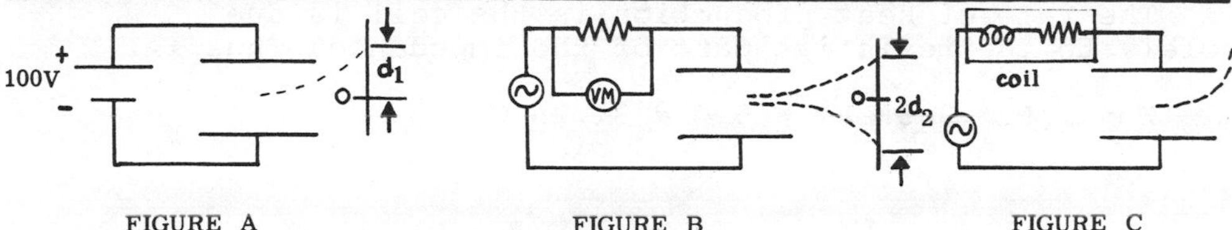

FIGURE A FIGURE B FIGURE C

Solution: When the 100-V battery is applied to the deflector plates, a deflection of 12 cm (= d_1 in Fig. A) is obtained. The displacement per volt is thus 1.2 mm. (See Fig. A).

When the ac voltage across the resistor is applied to the cathode ray tube, a trace of length 17 cm is obtained and the voltmeter reads only 50 V. At first sight this might appear to give a different displacement per volt, but this is not so. The reading on the voltmeter is the root-mean-square (rms) value of the alternating voltage. The peak value is given by the rms value multiplied by $\sqrt{2}$ or $50\sqrt{2} = 70.7$ V. The trace on the screen is responsive to the instantaneous voltage applied to the plates. It therefore marks a movement of the spot from the position where it is subjected to the peak value to the position where it is subjected to minus the peak voltage. (See Figure B). In other words, the length of the trace corresponds to a deflection due to a change of 70.7 - (- 70.7) = 141.4 V. The displacement per volt is 17 cm/141.4 = 1.2 mm, in agreement with the dc measurement.

The rms current through the resistor is

$$I = \frac{V}{R} = \frac{50\ \text{V}}{20\ \Omega} = 2.5\ \text{A}.$$

This is the current an ammeter would read.

When the resistor is replaced by a coil, we are given that the (rms) current remains the same (see Fig. C). The rms voltage across the coil is $V = IZ$, where Z is the magnitude of the impedance of the series combination of the resistance and the inductance. If $X_L = 2\pi fL$ is the reactance of the inductance (where f is the frequency of voltage variation) then

$$Z = \sqrt{R^2 + X_L^2} = \sqrt{R^2 + (2\pi fL)^2}$$

and $$V = IZ = 2.5\ \text{A} \times \sqrt{5^2\ \Omega^2 + (2\pi \times 50 \times 0.1)^2\Omega^2}$$

$$= 2.5 \times 31.8\ \text{V} = 79.5\ \text{V}.$$

The peak value of voltage is the rms voltage times $\sqrt{2}$ or $V' = \sqrt{2} \times 79.5\ \text{V} = 112.4$ V. The peak to peak value is twice this or 224.8 V. From the discussion above, the displacement per volt is 1.2 mm =

$0.12\ cm \cdot V^{-1}$ and the trace on the screen is $224.8\ V \times 0.12\ cm \cdot V^{-1} = 27\ cm$ in length.

The rate of heat production in the coil is due solely to the resistive part of the impedance. Thus

$$W = I^2R = 2.5^2\ A^2 \times 5\ \Omega = 31.25\ W.$$

CHAPTER 24

ELECTRIC POWER

• PROBLEM 780

An electric heater takes 4 amperes from a 120-volt line. What is its power rating?

Solution:

$$E = 120 \text{ volts}, \qquad I = 4 \text{ amp}$$

$$P = E \times I = 120 \text{ volts} \times 4 \text{ amp} = 480 \text{ watts}.$$

• PROBLEM 781

A 2.4 kilowatt generator delivers 10 amperes. At what potential difference does the generator operate?

Solution: In most situations we are given the voltage and amperege of a device, and are asked to calculate its power. Here we must work in reverse, calculating the potential difference (voltage) from the power and the current. Nevertheless, we resort to the same formula, namely P = EI.

$$P = 2.4 \text{ kilowatts} = 2400 \text{ watts}, \quad I = 10 \text{ amp}$$

$$P = E \times I$$

Then

$$E = \frac{P}{I} = \frac{2400 \text{ watts}}{10 \text{ amp}} = 240 \text{ volts}.$$

• PROBLEM 782

A 60-ohm electric lamp is left connected to a 240-volt line for 3.00 min. How much energy is taken from the line?

Solution: The current through the resistance of the electric lamp is, by Ohm's Law,

$$I = \frac{V}{R} = \frac{240 \text{ volts}}{60 \text{ ohms}} = 4.0 \text{ amp}$$

The power (or energy per unit time) dissipated by the resistance is

$$P = \frac{\text{energy}}{\text{time}} = I^2 R \qquad \text{or}$$

$$E = I^2 Rt = (4.0 \text{ amp})^2 \times 60 \text{ ohm} \times \left(3 \text{ min} \times \frac{60 \text{ sec}}{\text{min}}\right)$$

$$= 1.72 \times 10^4 \text{ Joules}$$

(The unit of time was converted to seconds to make it compatible with the MKS system being used.)

• PROBLEM 783

How many amperes will a 720-watt electric iron take from a 120-volt line?

Solution:

$$P = 720 \text{ watts}, \qquad E = 120 \text{ volts}$$

$$P = E \times I$$

Then

$$I = \frac{P}{E} = \frac{720 \text{ watts}}{120 \text{ volts}} = 6 \text{ amp}$$

• PROBLEM 784

The figure shows a battery and a resistor in series. What is the power P supplied by the battery and the power dissipated as heat?

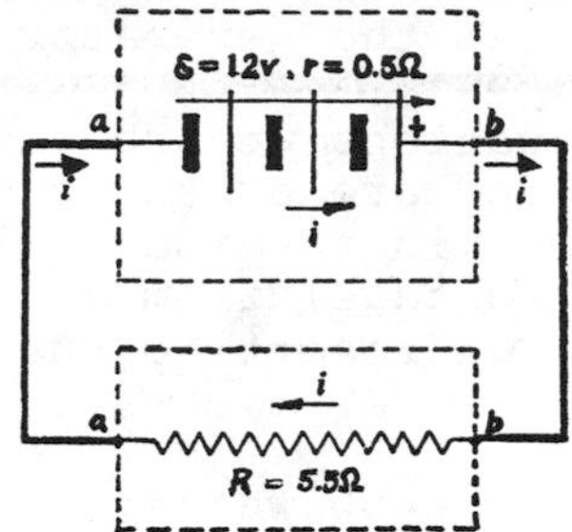

Solution: The total resistance of the circuit is

$$R_t = r + R = (5.5 + 0.5)\ \Omega = 6\ \Omega$$

Therefore the current in the circuit is, by Ohm's Law,

$$i = \frac{\varepsilon}{R_t} = \frac{12 \text{ v}}{6 \text{ amp}} = 2 \text{ amp.}$$

Point b is at a higher potential than point a, and

$$V_{ba} = iR = 2 \text{ amp } (5.5\Omega) = 11 \text{ volts}$$

or, by Kirchoff's Law

$$V_{ba} = \varepsilon - ir = 12 - (2 \times 0.5) = 11 \text{ volts}$$

and $V_{ab} = - V_{ba} = - 11$ volts.

In the lower rectangle, the direction of the current is from b to a, hence the power dissipated in R is

$$P_R = V_{ba} \times i = (2 \text{ amp}) \times (11 \text{ v}) = + 22 \text{ watts.}$$

The energy supplied to R is converted to heat at a

rate

$$\text{energy/time} = i^2R = (2\text{ amp})^2 \times 5.5\ \Omega$$
$$= 22 \text{ watts}$$

which equals the power input to R.

The energy loss in the battery is due to the internal resistance r;

$$P_r = i^2r = (2\text{ amp})^2 \times 0.5\ \Omega$$
$$= 2 \text{ watts.}$$

The rate of conversion of nonelectrical to electrical energy in the seat of emf is given by

$$P_\varepsilon = i\varepsilon = (2\text{ amp}) \times (12\text{ v}) = 24 \text{ watts.}$$

The total rate of energy dissipation in the resistors should add up to the rate at which energy is supplied by the emf,

$$\text{or}\quad P_\varepsilon = P_R + P_r$$
$$= (22 + 2)\text{ watts} = 24 \text{ watts.}$$

• PROBLEM 785

An electric motor, rated at 1 hp, operates from a 100-V line for 1 hr. How much current does the motor require and how much electrical energy was expended?

Solution: The power expended in an electric circuit is given by the product of the voltage across its terminals and the current passing through the terminals. Hence, the current in the motor is

$$I = \frac{P_E}{V} = \frac{1\text{ hp}}{100\text{ V}} = \frac{746\text{ W}}{100\text{ V}}$$
$$= 7.46\text{ A}$$

The power of the motor indicates the amount of electrical energy it draws from the electrical source.per unit time and converts to mechanical energy. Then, the electrical energy expended in one hour is

$$E_E = P_E \times t = 1\text{ hp} \times 1\text{ hr}$$
$$= 746\text{ W-hr}$$
$$= 0.746\text{ kW-hr}$$

or, in CGS units,

$$E_E = (746\text{ W-hr}) \times \left(\frac{10^7\text{ ergs/sec}}{1\text{ W}}\right) \times \left(\frac{3600\text{ sec}}{1\text{ hr}}\right)$$
$$= 2.68 \times 10^{13}\text{ ergs}$$

• PROBLEM 786

What is the cost of operating for 24 hr a lamp requiring 1.0 amp on a 100-volt line if the cost of electric energy is \$0.50/kw-hr?

Solution: The power P developed by the lamp resistance is

$$P = \frac{\text{energy dissipated}}{\text{time}} = VI$$

The energy dissipated by the lamp in 24 hours is then

$$E = VIt = (100 \text{ volts})(1.0 \text{ amp})(24 \text{ hr})$$

$$= 2400 \text{ watt-hr}$$

$$= 2.4 \text{ kw-hr}$$

But each kilowatt-hour of electrical energy costs \$0.050. Therefore the cost of 2.4 kw-hr is

$$\text{Cost} = 2.4 \text{ (kw-hr)} \times \frac{\$0.050}{\text{(kw-hr)}}$$

$$= \$0.12.$$

• PROBLEM 787

A dc series motor operates at 120 volts and has a resistance of 0.300 ohm. When the motor is running at rated speed, the armature current is 12.0 amp. What is the counter EMF in the armature?

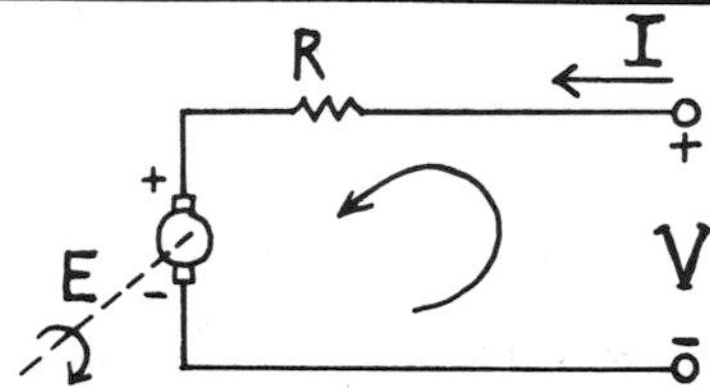

Solution: An electric circuit containing a series motor (that is a motor whose coil resistance is in series with the motor) is drawn schematically above. The motor draws current, and uses it to produce the mechanical motion of a shaft.

By Kirchoff's voltage law, the sum of the voltage drops around the circuit must be zero. Using this fact along with Ohm's Law (V = IR) we obtain

$$V = \varepsilon + IR$$

or $$\varepsilon = V - IR = 120 \text{ volts} - 12.0 \text{ amp} \times 0.300 \text{ ohm}$$

$$= 116 \text{ volts.}$$

• PROBLEM 788

In a transistor amplifier circuit it is found that a microphone converts sound energy into an electrical current of 0.01 A at a potential of 0.5 V. Compare the power from the microphone with the power delivered to the loudspeaker if the collector current for the particular transistor used is 50 times as great as the base current and the voltage of the amplified signal at the loudspeaker is 2V.

Solution: The power delivered by the microphone is equal to the product of the current the microphone produces and the voltage at which it produces this current. Hence,

$$P = VI = \left(5 \times 10^{-1} V\right)\left(1 \times 10^{-2} A\right) = 5 \times 10^{-3} W$$

The loudspeaker is connected to the collector. Therefore, the collector current delivered to the loudspeaker by the transistor is,

$$(50)\left(1 \times 10^{-2} A\right) = 5 \times 10^{-1} A$$

so the loudspeaker power is,

$$P = VI = (2V) \times \left(5 \times 10^{-1} A\right) = 1 W$$

The additional energy required to "drive" the speaker is supplied by the batteries.

• PROBLEM 789

The starter motor in an automobile draws a current of 200A from a 12-V car battery. What is the electrical power consumed by the motor? If the motor has an efficiency of 80 per cent, how much mechanical power is done by the starter motor?

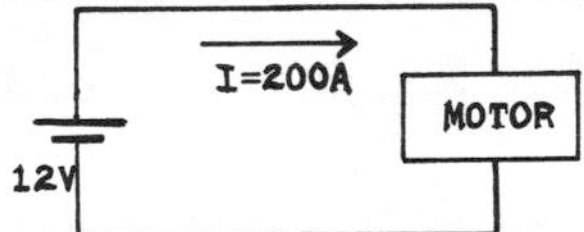

Solution: Electrical power is the rate at which electrical energy is produced or consumed. It is equal to the product of the current in a device and the fall of potential across its terminals or, for the motor,

$$P = VI = \left(1.2 \times 10^{1} V\right)\left(2 \times 10^{2} A\right) = 2.4 \times 10^{3} W.$$

Since the motor only has an efficiency of 80%, 20% of the available power goes into losses such as heat. The other 80% is available to the motor to do mechanical work. The mechanical power delivered by the motor, is

$$\left(2.4 \times 10^{3} W\right)\left(8 \times 10^{-1}\right) = 1.92 \times 10^{3} W.$$

• PROBLEM 790

A 1,000-horsepower steam engine produces about 750,000 W of mechanical power. If this engine operates a generator with an efficiency of 95 per cent, what is the electrical power produced?

Solution: Efficiency ε is defined by

$$\varepsilon = \frac{P_{output}}{P_{input}} \times 100\%$$

The steam engine delivers 750,000 W to the generator. The generator operates at an efficiency of 95% where P_{output} is its power output. For the generator,

$$\frac{P_{output}}{\left(7.5 \times 10^{5} W\right)} = 95\% = \frac{95}{100} = 9.5 \times 10^{-1}$$

The electric power delivered in this energy-transformation process is,

$$P = \left(7.5 \times 10^5 \text{ W}\right)\left(9.5 \times 10^{-1}\right) = 7.125 \times 10^5 \text{ W}$$

The 5 per cent difference (37,500 W) appears as heat that must be dissipated by either passing air through cooling fins or circulating water.

• PROBLEM 791

How much power is required to service a city of 100,000 homes, each of which draws an average current of 20 A at a potential of 120 V? If the transmission lines that carry power were capable of carrying a current of 1,000 A, what potential would be required to transmit the power from the source?

Solution: The total power which must be supplied is equal to the total power dissipated in all the homes. Since power equals the product of the current used (or supplied) by a device and the voltage across the device, we calculate,

$$P = IV$$

for each home. Here I is current and V is voltage. Each home uses power,

$$P = (20A)(120V) - 2400 \text{ watts}$$

But there are 10^5 homes and

$$P_{net} = \left(2.4 \times 10^3 \text{ watts}\right)\left(10^5\right)$$

$$P_{net} = 2.4 \times 10^8 \text{ watts}$$

If the current is 1,000 A, the required voltage is

$$V = \frac{Pnet}{I} = \frac{2.4 \times 10^8 \text{Watts}}{1.3 \times 10^3 \text{ A}} = 2.4 \times 10^5 \text{V}$$

• PROBLEM 792

An electric iron with a resistance of 24 ohms is connected to a 120-volt line. What power is being used?

Solution: The formula for power is $P = \frac{E^2}{R}$. This formula has two equivalent forms. From

$$P = \frac{E^2}{R} \quad \text{with } E = IR \text{ (Ohm's law) we get}$$

$$P = \frac{(IR)^2}{R}$$

$$= I^2R \qquad (1)$$

$$= I(IR)$$

$$= EI \qquad (2) \text{ (again by Ohm's law)}$$

Using the original form $\left(P = \frac{E^2}{R}\right)$ we arrive at solution 1:

Solution 1:

$$E = 120 \text{ volts}, \qquad R = 24 \text{ ohms}$$

$$P = \frac{E^2}{R} = \frac{120^2 \text{ (volts)}^2}{24 \text{ ohms}} = 600 \text{ watts}$$

For both the other solutions we need to know the current I.

$$I = \frac{E}{R} = \frac{120 \text{ volts}}{24 \text{ ohms}} = 5 \text{ amp}$$

Solution 2: Here we use form (1) of the equation.

$$P = I^2R = 5^2 \text{ (amp)}^2 \times 24 \text{ ohms} = 600 \text{ watts}$$

Solution 3: Here we use form (2) of the equation.

$$P = EI = 120 \text{ volts} \times 5 \text{ amp} = 600 \text{ watts.}$$

• PROBLEM 793

For underground electrical transmission cables using insulating materials, the power loss in the insulator is proportional to V^2, where V is the potential applied to the cable. Compare the power loss per meter for two standard transmission voltages, 69,000 V and 345,000 V.

Solution: The available power is given by the relationship,

$$P = VI \tag{1}$$

where I is the current through the cable. I can be replaced by $I = \frac{V}{R}$, by Ohm's Law, where R is the cable resistance. Then, from (1),

$$P = \frac{V^2}{R}$$

If R is constant,

$$P \propto V^2 \tag{2}$$

For the transmission cable, power loss is proportional to the available power and, by (2), is therefore also proportional to V^2. If the same cable is used for both potentials, the following ratio provides a comparison:

$$\frac{\text{power loss of 345,000-V line}}{\text{power loss of 69,000-V line}} = \frac{(3.45 \times 10^5 V)^2}{(6.9 \times 10^4 V)^2} = 25$$

In the 1930s F.T. Bacon designed hydrogen fuel cells with extremely good performance. Using his concepts Pratt and Whitney has constructed hydrogen fuel cells that produce a potential of 0.9 V and generate a current of about 2.3×10^3 A for each square meter of anode area. If a Bacon battery is to deliver 100 W of power, how large must the anode be?

Solution: Recall that the power dissipated (or produced) by a device is,

$$P = IV$$

Where I is the current going through a device, and V is the voltage across its terminals. In this example $P = 1 \times 10^2$W and $V = 0.9$V. Therefore, the current required to deliver 100W of energy is,

$$I = \frac{P}{V} = \frac{1 \times 10^2 \text{ W}}{9 \times 10^{-1} \text{ V}} = 1.1 \times 10^2 \text{ A}$$

The surface area A required is,

$$A = \frac{1.1 \times 10^2 \not{A}}{2.3 \times 10^3 \not{A}/m^2} = 4.8 \times 10^{-2} \text{ m}^2$$

If the anode is designed to have a square shape, then the area A is equal to d^2, where d is the length of one edge. We find that,

$$d^2 = 4.8 \times 10^{-2} \text{ m}^2$$

$$d = 2.2 \times 10^{-1} \text{ m}$$

A very compact energy supply may be constructed using a hydrogen fuel cell.

• PROBLEM 795

A shunt generator has a terminal potential difference of 120 volts when it delivers 1.80 kw to the line. Resistance of the field coils is 240 ohms, and that of the armature is 0.400 ohm. Find the EMF of the generator and the efficiency.

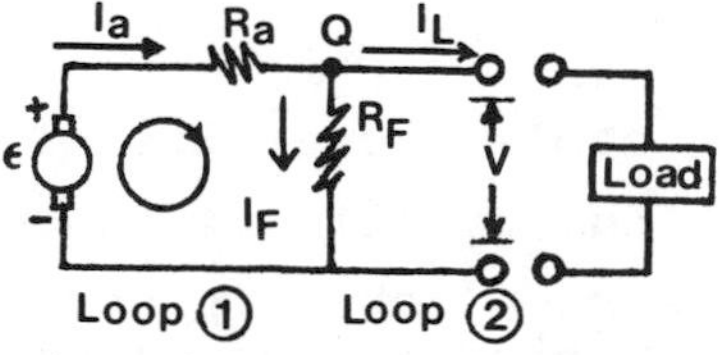

Solution: An electric circuit containing a shunt generator (that is, a generator whose field resistance R_F is in parallel with the generator) can be described schematically as shown above. The potential difference at the terminals where a load (or resistance) is connected is the terminal voltage, V. The load, when connected will draw a line current I_L, from the circuit. Therefore, the power delivered to the load is $P = I_L V$. Solving for

$$I_L = \frac{1800 \text{ watts}}{120 \text{ volts}} = 15.0 \text{ amp.},$$

Using Ohm's Law, $V = I_f R_f$, (1)

or $$I_F = \frac{V}{R_F} = \frac{120 \text{ volts}}{240 \text{ ohms}} = 0.500 \text{ amp}$$

By Kirchoff's current law, the sum of the currents entering a junction equals the sum of the current leaving the junction. Therefore, at point Q

$$I_A = I_F + I_L = 0.50 \text{ amp} + 15.0 \text{ amp} = 15.5 \text{ amp.}$$

By Kirchoff's voltage law, the sum of the voltage drops about a loop is zero. Applying this law to loop (1), we obtain

$$\varepsilon = I_f R_f + I_A R_A$$

Using (1)

$$\varepsilon = V + I_A R_A$$

$$\varepsilon = 120 \text{ volts} + (15.5 \text{ amp})(.4 \text{ ohms})$$

$$\varepsilon = 126 \text{ volts}$$

The input power

$$P_i = I_A \varepsilon = 15.5 \text{ amp} \times 126 \text{ volts} = 1950 \text{ watts}$$

and it is delivered by the generator. The output power is the power delivered to the line, and it is given as 1800 watts. Hence,

$$\text{Efficiency} = \frac{P_o}{P_i} = \frac{1800 \text{ watts}}{1950 \text{ watts}} = 0.923 = 92.3\%.$$

• PROBLEM 796

What is the power factor of a circuit if the following meter readings prevail? Ammeter reads .15 amperes, voltmeter reads 115 volts, and wattmeter reads 15.9 watts.

Solution: The ammeter and voltmeter read root mean square (RMS) values of the actual current and voltage. If

$$V = V_0 \cos \omega t$$

and $$I = I_0 \cos (\omega t + \rho)$$

are the actual current and voltages through the circuit, then the instantaneous power (i.e. the instantaneous rate at which energy flows in the circuit) is

$$P = VI = V_0 I_0 \cos \omega t \cos(\omega t + \rho)$$

$$= V_0 I_0 (\cos^2 \omega t \cos \rho - \cos \omega t \sin \omega t \sin \rho)$$

Now $\cos \omega t \sin \omega t = \frac{1}{2} \sin 2\omega t$, and the time average of $\sin 2\omega t$ is zero (since its graph is symmetric about the horizontal axis). The average of $\cos^2 \omega t$ is $\frac{1}{2}$, for its graph is symmetric about the value of 1/2. This is to say that its value is greater than $\frac{1}{2}$ as often as it is less than $\frac{1}{2}$, and by the same amount. Therefore the average power is:

$$\overline{P} = V_0 I_0 \left(\overline{\cos^2 \omega t \longleftrightarrow \cos \rho} - \overline{\cos \omega t \sin \omega t \sin \rho} \right)$$

$$= V_0 I_0 (\tfrac{1}{2} \cos \rho - 0)$$

$\cos \rho$ is called the power factor of the circuit. It is a measure of the phase relation between the current and voltage in the circuit.

According to the definition of the RMS value of a function,

$$I_{RMS} = \sqrt{\frac{1}{2\pi} \int_0^{2\pi} I^2 dt} = \sqrt{\frac{1}{2\pi} \int_0^{2\pi} I_0^2 \cos^2(\omega t + \rho) dt}$$

$$= \frac{1}{\sqrt{2}} I_0$$

Similarly,

$$V_{RMS} = \sqrt{\frac{1}{2\pi} \int_0^{2\pi} V^2 dt} = \sqrt{\frac{1}{2\pi} \int_0^{2\pi} V_0^2 \cos^2 \omega \, t dt}$$

$$= \frac{1}{\sqrt{2}} V_0$$

Hence $\quad \overline{P} = \frac{1}{2} \left(\sqrt{2}\, I_{RMS} \right) \left(\sqrt{2}\, V_{RMS} \right) \cos \rho = I_{RMS} V_{RMS} \cos \rho$

The wattmeter reads the average power of a circuit. Then given $I_{RMS} = .15$ amp, $V_{RMS} = 115$ v $\overline{P} = 1.59$ watt,

the power factor is

$$\cos \rho = \frac{\overline{P}}{I_{RMS} V_{RMS}} = \frac{15.9 \text{ w}}{(.15 \text{ a})(115 \text{ v})} = 0.92$$

• PROBLEM 797

A 10,000-ohm, 1-watt resistor has been connected up with two capacitors of capacitance 0.2 and 0.5 microfarads (μF). We propose to plug this into the 120-volt, 60-cycle outlet (see Figures). Will the 1-watt resistor get too hot?

Solution: (i) The angular frequency $\omega = 2\pi f = 2\pi \times 60 \text{ sec}^{-1} = 377 \text{ sec}^{-1}$. At times we will work with the reciprocal of impedance, or admittance. Admittance of

(i) $\quad C_2 = i\omega C_2 = (377)(2 \times 10^{-7})i$

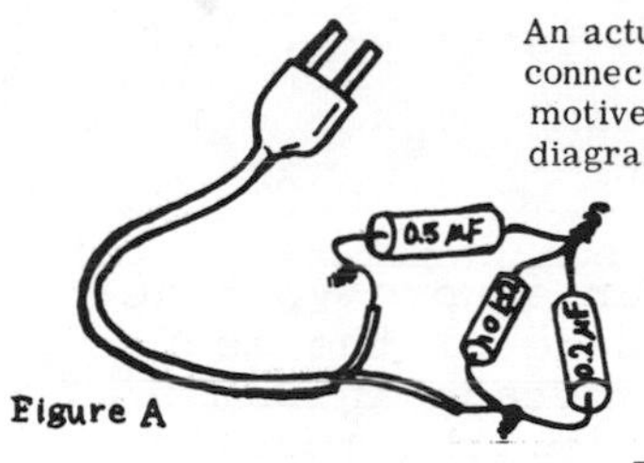

Figure A

An actual network (a) ready to be connected to a source of electromotive force, and (b) the circuit diagram.

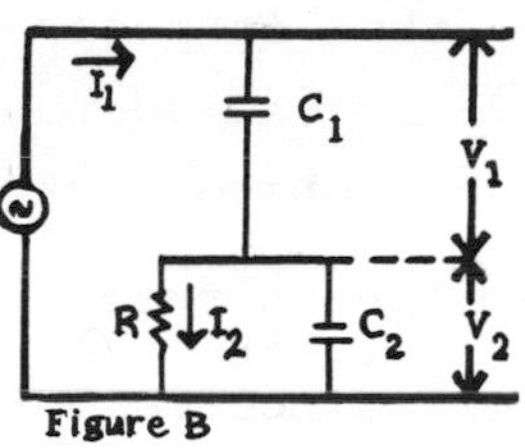

Figure B

$$= 0.754 \times 10^{-4} i \text{ ohm}^{-1}$$

(ii) Admittance of the resistor $= \frac{1}{R} = 10^{-4}$ ohm^{-1}

(iii) Admittance of [resistor ∥ capacitor] $= (i) + (ii) =$

$$= 10^{-4}(1 + 0.754i) \text{ ohm}^{-1}$$

(iv) Impedance of [resistor ∥ capacitor] $= \dfrac{1}{10^{-4}(1 + 0.754i)}$

$$= \frac{10^4}{(1+0.754i)} \frac{(1-0.754i)}{(1-0.754i)}$$

$$= \frac{10^4(1 - 0.754i)}{1^2 + 0.754^2}$$

$$= (6360 - 4800i) \text{ ohms}$$

(v) Impedance of $C_1 = \dfrac{1}{i\omega C} = -\dfrac{i}{\omega C} = -\dfrac{i}{(377)(5 \times 10^{-7})}$

$$= -5300 \, i \text{ ohms}$$

Here we used the fact that $1/i = -i$.

(vi) Impedance of the entire circuit = (iv) + (v)

$$= (6360 - 10{,}100i) \text{ ohms}$$

(vii) By Ohm's law $I_1 = \dfrac{V}{Z} = \dfrac{120 \text{ v}}{(6360 - 10100i)\Omega}$

$$= \frac{120 \text{ v}}{(6360 - 10100)\Omega} \frac{(6360 + 10100i)}{(6360 + 10100i)}$$

$$= \frac{120(6360 + 10{,}100i)}{(6360)^2 + (10{,}100)^2}$$

$$= (5.37 + 8.53i) \times 10^{-3} \text{ amp}$$

In polar form

$$I_1 = [(5.37)^2 + (8.53)^2]^{\frac{1}{2}} \times 10^{-3} \; \underline{/\tan^{-1} 8.53/5.37}$$

$$= 10.0 \times 10^{-2} \; \underline{/1.01 \text{ rad}}.$$

for if a number A is expressed in rectangular form, A =

x + jy, then in polar form $A = \sqrt{x^2 + y^2}\ \tan^{-1} y/x$. $\sqrt{x^2 + y^2}$ is called the modulus of $A \cdot \tan^{-1} y/x = \phi$ is called the phase factor.

The 120-volt source is the root mean square voltage (rms) (i.e., the square root of the square of the mean voltage). Since we have used this rms voltage in Ohm's law above, we obtain rms current. That is, the modulus of the complex number I_1, which is 10.0mA, is the rms current in amperes. An ac milliammeter inserted in series with the line would read 10mA. This current has a phase angle ϕ =1.01 radians with respect to the line voltage. The average power delivered to the entire circuit is then:

$$\text{(viii)} \quad \overline{P} = VI \cos \phi = (120 \text{ volts})(0.010 \text{ amp}) \cos 1.01$$

$$= 0.64 \text{ watt}$$

In this circuit the resistor is the only dissipative element, so this must be the average power dissipated in it. Just as a check, we can find the voltage V_2 across the resistor:

$$\text{(ix)} \quad V_1 = I_1 \frac{1}{i\omega C_1} = I_1 \frac{-i}{\omega C_1} = (5.37 + 8.53i)(-5300i)10^{-3}$$

$$= (45.2 - 28.4i) \text{ volts}$$

$$\text{(x)} \quad V_2 = 120 - V_1 = (74.8 + 28.4i)\text{volts}$$

The current I_2 in R will be in phase with V_2, of course, so the average power in R will be

$$\overline{P} = \frac{V_2{}^2}{R} = \frac{(74.8)^2 + (28.4)^2}{10^4} = 0.64 \text{ watt}$$

which checks.

Thus the rating of the resistor isn't exceeded, for what that assurance is worth. Actually, whether the resistor will get too hot depends not only on the average power dissipated in it but also on how easily it can get rid of the heat. The power rating of a resistor is only a rough guide.

• PROBLEM 798

A flat coil consisting of 500 turns, each of area 50 cm^2, rotates about a diameter in a uniform field of intensity 0.14 $Wb \cdot m^{-2}$, the axis of rotation being perpendicular to the field and the angular velocity of rotation being 150 $rad \cdot s^{-1}$. The coil has a resistance of 5 Ω, and the induced emf is connected via slip rings and brushes to an external resistance of 10 Ω.

Calculate the peak current flowing and the average power supplied to the 10-Ω resistor.

Solution: The emf generated by the motion is given by

the equation

$$\varepsilon = NAB\omega \sin \omega t.$$

where ω is the loop's angular velocity, A is the coil's cross sectional area, and N is the number of turns in the coil. Also, B is the field of magnetic induction at the site of the coil.

The current flowing is thus, by Ohm's Law,

$$I = \frac{\varepsilon}{R} = \frac{NAB\omega}{R} \sin \omega t. \tag{1}$$

where R is the coil resistance.

The peak value of the current is found when $\sin \omega t$ is a maximum ($t = \pi/2\omega$). Hence,

$$I_{max} = \frac{NAB\omega}{R}$$

$$= \frac{500 \times 50 \times 10^{-4}\ m^2 \times 0.14\ Wb\cdot m^{-2} \times 150 s^{-1}}{15\ \Omega}$$

$$= 3.5\ A.$$

The average power supplied to the external resistor is

$$P = I^2_{rms} R$$

where I_{rms} is the root mean square value of the current given in (1). Now

$$I_{rms} \equiv \sqrt{\langle I^2(t) \rangle} \tag{2}$$

where $\langle\ \rangle$ indicates the time average of I^2 over one cycle of I^2. By definition,

$$\langle I^2 \rangle = \frac{1}{T} \int_0^T I^2(t) dt \tag{3}$$

where T is the period of I^2. The period of $I^2(t)$ is the smallest non-zero value of T for which

$$I^2(t + T) = I^2(t)$$

Using (1), we find

$$\frac{N^2A^2B^2\omega^2}{R^2} \sin^2 (\omega(t + T) = \frac{N^2A^2B^2\omega^2}{R^2} \sin^2 \omega t$$

or $\quad \sin^2 (\omega t + \omega T) = \sin^2 \omega t \qquad (4)$

Thus, the values of T for which (4) holds are $\omega T = \pm 0, \pm \pi, \pm 2\pi....$ Hence,

$$T = \pm 0, \pm \pi/\omega, \pm 2\pi/\omega$$

The smallest non-zero value of T is then

$$T = \frac{\pi}{\omega} \tag{5}$$

Inserting (5) into (3) and utilizing (1)

$$\langle I^2 \rangle = \frac{\omega}{\pi} \int_0^{\frac{\pi}{\omega}} \frac{N^2A^2B^2\omega^2}{R^2} \sin^2 \omega t \, dt$$

$$= \frac{\omega}{\pi} \int_0^{\frac{\pi}{\omega}} \frac{N^2A^2B^2\omega^2}{R^2} \sin^2 \omega t \, d(\omega t)$$

Since $\sin^2 \omega t = \dfrac{1 - \cos 2\omega t}{2}$

$$\langle I^2 \rangle = \frac{\omega^2N^2A^2B^2}{\pi \ R^2} \left\{ \frac{1}{2} \int_0^{\frac{\pi}{\omega}} d(\omega t) - \frac{1}{2} \int_0^{\frac{\pi}{\omega}} \cos 2\omega t \, d(\omega t) \right\}$$

$$= \frac{\omega^2N^2A^2B^2}{\pi \ R^2} \left\{ \frac{1}{2} \int_0^{\frac{\pi}{\omega}} d(\omega t) - \frac{1}{4} \int_0^{\frac{\pi}{\omega}} \cos 2\omega t \, d(2\omega t) \right\}$$

$$= \frac{\omega^2N^2A^2B^2}{\pi \ R^2} \left\{ \frac{1}{2}(\pi - 0) - \frac{1}{4}(\sin 2\omega \times \pi/\omega - \sin 0) \right\}$$

$$\langle I^2 \rangle = \frac{\omega^2N^2A^2B^2}{2R^2}$$

Finally, from (2)

$$I_{rms}^2 = \langle I^2 \rangle = \frac{\omega^2N^2A^2B^2}{2R^2}$$

But $I_{max}^2 = \dfrac{\omega^2N^2A^2B^2}{R^2}$

whence $I_{rms}^2 = \dfrac{I_{max}^2}{2}$

Hence, $P = I_{rms}^2 \ R = \frac{1}{2} \ I_{max}^2 \ R = \frac{1}{2}(3.5 \text{ A})^2 \ 10 \ \Omega$

$P = 61.25$ W.

CHAPTER 25

WAVE MOTION

TRAVELING & STANDING WAVES

• PROBLEM 799

A wave is represented by the equation $y = 0.20 \sin 0.40\pi(x - 60t)$, where all distances are measured in centimeters and time in seconds. Find: (a) the amplitude, (b) the wavelength, (c) the speed, and (d) the frequency of the wave. (e) What is the displacement at $x = 5.5$ cm and $t = 0.020$ sec?

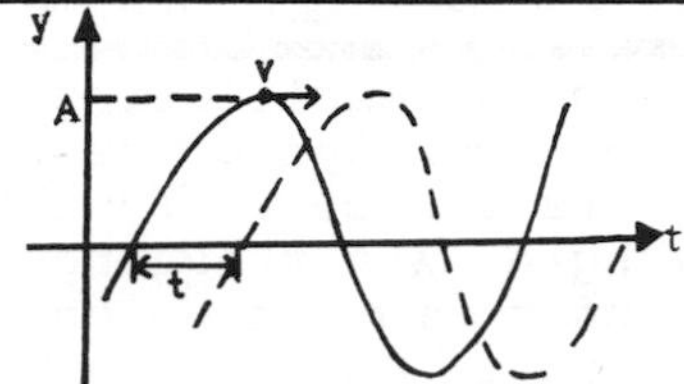

Solution: The displacement y of the medium due to wave motion at a position x and at a time t is (see the figure)

$$y = A \sin \frac{2\pi}{\lambda}(x - vt)$$

where A is the amplitude, λ is the wavelength, and v is the velocity with which the wave is traveling along the x-axis. If we compare this equation with the expression given in the question, we see that

(a) $A = 0.20$ cm

(b) $\frac{2\pi}{\lambda} = 0.40\pi$

$$\lambda = \frac{2}{0.40} \text{ cm} = 5.0 \text{ cm}$$

(c) $v = 60$ cm/sec

(d) $f = \frac{v}{\lambda} = \frac{60 \text{ cm/sec}}{5.0 \text{ cm}} = 12/\text{sec}$

(e)
$$\begin{aligned} y &= (0.20 \text{ cm})\sin 0.40\pi(5.5 - 60 \times 0.020) \\ &= (0.20 \text{ cm})\sin 0.40\pi(5.5 - 1.2) \\ &= (0.20 \text{ cm})\sin(0.40 \times 3.3\pi) \\ &= (0.20 \text{ cm})\sin 1.32\pi \\ &= (0.20 \text{ cm})(-0.86) = -0.17 \text{ cm} \end{aligned}$$

• PROBLEM 800

A compressional wave of frequency 250/sec is set up in an iron rod and passes from the rod into air. The speed of the wave is 1.6×10^4 ft/sec in iron and 1.1×10^3 ft/sec in air. Find the wavelength in each material.

Solution: The frequency f of a wave remains constant as it passes from one medium to another. The velocity v and wavelength λ of the wave vary in accordance with the relationship

$$v = \lambda f$$

In iron

$$\lambda = \frac{v}{f} = \frac{1.6 \times 10^4 \text{ ft/sec}}{250/\text{sec}} = 64 \text{ ft}$$

In air

$$\lambda = \frac{v}{f} = \frac{1.1 \times 10^3 \text{ ft/sec}}{250/\text{sec}} = 4.4 \text{ ft}$$

• PROBLEM 801

If the frequency of an oscillating source on the surface of a pool of water is 3 Hz, what is the speed of the wave if the wavelength is observed to be 0.5 m?

Solution: An example of an oscillating wave is a sinusoidal wave. Three important properties of an oscillating wave are its velocity of propagation, frequency, and wavelength. Its frequency f is the number of cycles per unit time at which any point oscillates or, expressed in another way, the number of waves that pass a given point per unit time. The wavelength λ is the distance between two adjacent crests of the wave. For a relation between these quantities, note that the time t required for the wave to make one oscillation is 1/f. During this time, the wave moves a distance $d = \lambda$. From

$$d = vt$$

we have $\lambda = v \cdot \frac{1}{f} = \frac{v}{f}$

or $v = f\lambda$

Substituting the known values,

$$v = (3 \text{ Hz})(5 \times 10^{-1} \text{ m}) = 1.5 \text{ m/sec}$$

(Note: 1 Hz = sec^{-1}.)

• PROBLEM 802

Find the speed of a compressional wave in an iron rod whose specific gravity is 7.7 and whose Young's modulus is 27.5×10^6 lb/in.^{2}

Solution: A wave in an iron rod will move with a speed

$$v = \sqrt{\frac{E}{\rho}}$$

where E is Young's modulus, and ρ is the specific weight of iron.

$$E = 27.5 \times 10^6 \text{ lb/in}^2 = 27.5 \times 10^6 \times \frac{\text{lb}}{\text{in}^2} \times \frac{144 \text{ in}^2}{\text{ft}^2}$$

where we've used the fact that

$$1 \text{ lb/in}^2 = 144 \text{ lb/ft}^2$$

$$\rho = \frac{D}{g} = \frac{7.7 \times 62.4 \text{ lb/ft}^3}{32 \text{ ft/sec}^2} = 15.0 \text{ slugs/ft}^3$$

Hence,

$$v = \sqrt{\frac{27.5 \times 10^6 \times 144 \text{ lb/ft}^2}{15.0 \text{ slugs/ft}^3}}$$

$$= 1.6 \times 10^4 \text{ ft/sec} .$$

• PROBLEM 803

The speed of a certain compressional wave in air at standard temperature and pressure is 330 m/sec. A point source of frequency 600/sec radiates energy uniformly in all directions at the rate of 5.00 watts. What is the intensity of the wave at a distance of 20.0 m from the source? What is the amplitude of the wave there?

Solution: At any concentric spherical surface the energy from a point source is spread over an area $4\pi r^2$. At a distance of $r = 20.0$ m, the intensity I is

$$I = \frac{E}{tA} = \frac{P}{A} = \frac{5.00 \text{ watts}}{4\pi \times (20.0 \text{ m})^2}$$

$$= 0.99 \times 10^{-3} \text{ watt/m}^2$$

The rate of transfer of energy depends on the square of the wave amplitude and the square of the wave frequency for all types of waves, with I the average intensity and the density of air $\rho = 1.29$ gm/liter $= 1.29$ kg/m^3, we have,

$$A^2 = \frac{I}{2\pi^2 v\rho f^2}$$

$$= \frac{0.99 \times 10^{-3} \text{ watt/m}^2}{2\pi^2 (330 \text{ m/sec})(1.29 \text{ kg/m}^3)(300/\text{sec})^2}$$

$$= 1.32 \times 10^{-12} \text{ m}^2$$

$$A = 1.15 \times 10^{-6} \text{ m} = 1.15 \times 10^{-4} \text{ cm}$$

• PROBLEM 804

Standing waves are produced by the superposition of two waves of the form

$$y_1 = 15 \sin (3\pi t - 5x) \quad (1)$$

$$y_2 = 15 \sin (3\pi t + 5x) \quad (2)$$

Find the amplitude of motion at x = 21.

Solution: We note that the two waves are of the form

$$y = A \sin(wt \pm kx)$$

where y is the displacement of the wave at position x and time t.

A is the amplitude of the wave (i.e., the maximum displacement), w is the angular frequency (= $2\pi f$) and k is the angular wavelength $\left(= \frac{2\pi}{\lambda}\right)$ of the wave. Both waves have the have the same characteristics (i.e., the same amplitude, frequency and wavelength). They differ only in that they travel in opposite directions. The negative sign in wave (1) indicates that it is travelling to the right. Wave (2) is travelling to the left. The resultant wave produced by the superposition of these two waves can be found as follows.

We use the relationships

$$\sin(\alpha + \beta) = \sin\alpha \cos\beta + \cos\alpha \sin\beta$$

$$\sin(\alpha - \beta) = \sin\alpha \cos\beta - \cos\alpha \sin\beta$$

Therefore

$$\sin(\alpha + \beta) + \sin(\alpha - \beta) = 2 \sin\alpha \cos\beta \qquad (3)$$

Thus, comparing (3) with (2) and (1),

$$y = y_1 + y_2 = 2(15) \sin (3\pi)t \cos(5) x$$

$$= 30 \sin 3\pi t \cos 5x$$

This wave pattern is called a standing wave (as opposed to a travelling wave). The wave remains in one location; or alternatively, the energy associated with the wave is not transferred from one location to another. With

$$x = 21,\ 5x = 105 \text{ radians}$$

$$= 38.4\pi \text{ radians.}$$

Now $\cos 38.4 = \cos(.4\pi + 38\pi) = \cos .4\pi = \cos 72° = 0.309$.

Thus, x = 21,

$$y = 30 \sin 3\pi t \cos 5x$$
$$y = (30)(.309) \sin 3\pi t$$

$$y = 9.27 \sin 3\pi t.$$

The amplitude of this wave is the maximum value of y. This maximum value is 9.27.

• PROBLEM 805

A string 4.0 m long has a mass of 3.0 gm. One end of the string is fastened to a stop, and the other end hangs over a pulley with a 2.0-kg mass attached. What is the speed of a transverse wave in this string?

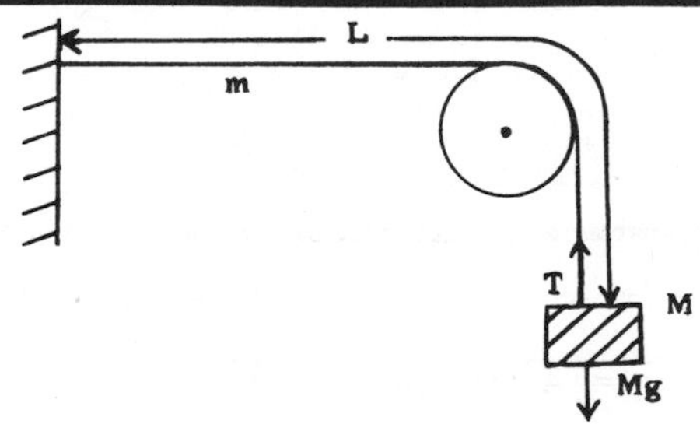

Solution: The string is stretched by a force (the tension), which is in equilibrium with the weight of the mass:

$$T = Mg = 2.0 \text{ kg} \times 9.8 \text{ m/sec}^2 = 19.6 \text{ nt.}$$

The linear density μ (mass per unit length) of the string is

$$\mu = \frac{m}{1} = 0.0030 \text{ kg/4.0m} = 7.5 \times 10^{-4} \text{ kg/m}$$

A transverse wave can be set up in the string by moving the weight at one end up and down. The speed v of this wave is given by

$$v = \sqrt{\frac{T}{\mu}} = \sqrt{\frac{19.6 \text{ kg-m/sec}^2}{7.5 \times 10^{-4} \text{ kg/m}}}$$

$$= \sqrt{2.6 \times 10^4 \text{ m}^2/\text{sec}^2} = 160 \text{ m/sec}$$

• PROBLEM 806

An electrical transmission line is strung across a valley between two utility towers. The distance between the towers is 200 m, and the mass of the line is 40 kg. A lineman on one tower strikes the line and a wave travels to the other tower, is reflected, and is detected by the lineman when it returns. If the elapsed time measured by the lineman is 10 s, what is the tension force in the wire?

Solution: The distance d traveled by the wave pulse is $d = 2 \times 200 \text{ m} = 400 \text{ m}$. The speed of the wave is computed using

$$v = \frac{d}{t} = \frac{400 \text{ m}}{10 \text{ s}} = 40 \text{ m/s}$$

For the stretched line, the tension F is given by

$$F = \mu v^2$$

where μ is the inertia characteristic of the wire and is equal to the mass per unit length m/L. Therefore,

$$F = \frac{m}{L} v^2 = \frac{mv^2}{L} = \frac{(40 \text{ kg})(40 \text{ m/s})^2}{200 \text{ m}} = 3.2 \times 10^2 \text{ N}$$

• PROBLEM 807

Two sources separated by 10 m vibrate according to the equations $y_1 = 0.03 \sin \pi t$ and $y_2 = 0.01 \sin \pi t$. They send out simple waves of velocity 1.5 m/sec. What is the equation of motion of a particle 6 m from the first source and 4 m from the second?

FIGURE A: Motion of the particle due to source ①

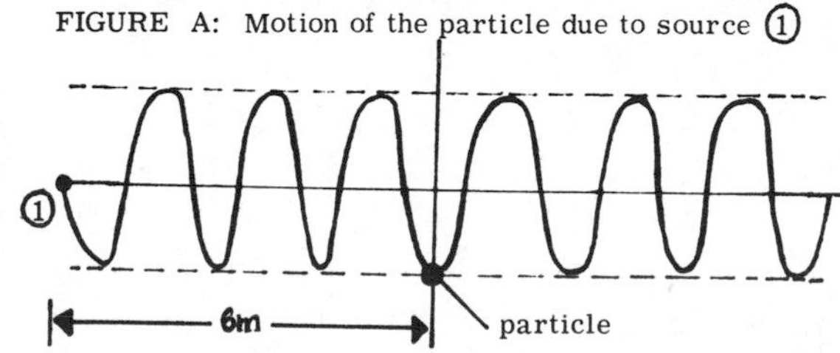

FIGURE B: Motion of particle due to source ②

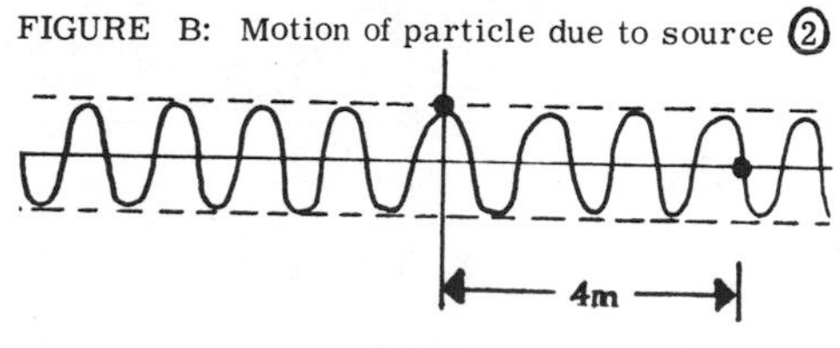

FIGURE C: Resultant motion

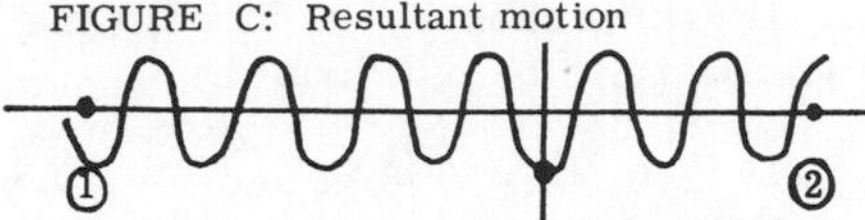

<u>Solution:</u> The equation of a wave travelling along the x - axis is

$$y = A \sin (\omega t \pm Kx)$$

where ω is the angular frequency of the wave A is its amplitude and K is its wave number. The factor $\pm Kx$ accounts for the direction of travel of the wave; $-Kx$ indicates that the wave travels towards increasing values of x, and vice-versa. Note that this equation assumes that, at $x = 0$, $t = 0$, the y displacement is zero. Since $\omega = 2\pi f$, where f is the frequency of the wave, and $k = 2\pi/\lambda$, where λ is its wavelength, we obtain,

$$y = A \sin (\omega t \pm Kx)$$

$$y = A \sin \left(2\pi ft \pm \frac{2\pi x}{\lambda}\right)$$

But $\lambda = \frac{v}{f}$, where v is the wavespeed. Therefore,

$$y = A \sin 2\pi \left(ft \pm \frac{fx}{v}\right)$$

$$y = A \sin 2\pi f\left(t \pm \frac{x}{v}\right)$$

We suppose that source 1 sends out waves in the +x direct tion, with amplitude a_1, and frequency f_1.

$$y_1 = a_1 \sin 2\pi f_1 \left(t - \frac{x_1}{v}\right) \qquad (1)$$

and that source 2 sends out waves in the -x direction, with amplitude a_2 and frequency f_2.

$$y_2 = a_2 \sin 2\pi f_2 \left(t + \frac{x_2}{v}\right) \qquad (2)$$

In these equations x_1 and x_2 measure position from sources 1 and 2 as origin, respectively. Comparing equations (1) and (2) with the equations given in the question, we find that,

$$2\pi f_1 = \pi \text{ and } 2\pi f_2 = \pi$$

or

$$f_1 = f_2 = 1/2$$

Furthermore,

$$v = 1.5 \text{ m/sec}$$

$$a_1 = 0.03 \text{ m} \qquad\qquad a_2 = 0.01 \text{ m}$$

$x_1 = 6$ m $\qquad\qquad\qquad\qquad x_2 = -4$ m

Thus,

$$y_1 = (.03 \text{ m}) \sin \pi(t - 4)$$

$$y_1 = (.03 \text{ m}) [\sin \pi t \cos 4\pi - \cos \pi t \sin 4\pi]$$

$$Y_1 = (.03 \text{ m}) \sin \pi t$$

$$Y_2 = (.01 \text{ m}) \sin \pi (t - 8/3)$$

$$y_2 = (.01 \text{ m}) [\sin \pi t \cos 8\pi/3 - \cos\pi t \sin 8\pi/3]$$

$$y_2 = (.01 \text{ m}) [\sin \pi t (-1/2) - \cos \pi t(\sqrt{3}/2)]$$

$$y_2 = -.005 \text{ m} \sin \pi t - .00866 \cos \pi t$$

The resultant wave motion of the particle is,

$$y = y_1 + y_2$$

$$= (.03 \text{ m}) \sin \pi t - (.005 \text{ m}) \sin \pi t - (.00866 \text{ m}) \cos \pi t$$

$$= (.025\text{m}) \sin \pi t - .00866 \cos \pi t \qquad (3)$$

We will write this in the form,

$$y = A \sin (\pi t + \phi)$$

$$= A \sin \pi t \cos \phi + A \cos \pi t \sin \phi \qquad (4)$$

Comparing (4) with (3),

$$A \cos \phi = .025 \text{ m}$$

$$A \sin \phi = -.00866 \text{ m}$$

$$A^2 (\sin^2 \phi + \cos^2 \phi) = A^2 = (.025 \text{ m})^2 + (.00866 \text{ m})^2$$

$$A = .0264 \text{ m}$$

and,

$$\tan \phi = \frac{-.00866}{.025} = -.346$$

$$-\tan \phi = .346$$

But,

$$-\tan \phi = \tan (-\phi) \text{ and}$$

$$\tan (-\phi) = .346$$

$$-\phi = \tan^{-1} (.346)$$

$$-\phi = 19.1°$$

ELECTROMAGNETIC WAVES, POLARIZATION

• PROBLEM 808

What is the speed of an electromagnetic wave in empty space?

Solution. The speed of an electromagnetic wave in a substance can be determined by using:

$$V = \frac{1}{\sqrt{\mu\varepsilon}}$$

where μ is the permeability and ε the permittivity of the substance.

$$\mu_0 = 4\pi \times 10^{-7}\ \text{nt/amp}^2$$

$$\varepsilon_0 = 8.55 \times 10^{-12}\ \text{coul}^2/\text{nt-m}^2$$

$$V = \frac{1}{\sqrt{\mu_0\varepsilon_0}}$$

$$= \frac{1}{\sqrt{4\pi \times 10^{-7} \times 8.85 \times 10^{-12}\ \text{coul}^2/\text{amp}^2\text{-m}^2}}$$

$$= 3.00 \times 10^8\ \text{m/sec.}$$

• PROBLEM 809

H. Hertz produced radio waves whose wavelength was about 3 m. What was the frequency of the oscillating electric charges responsible for this electromagnetic radiation?

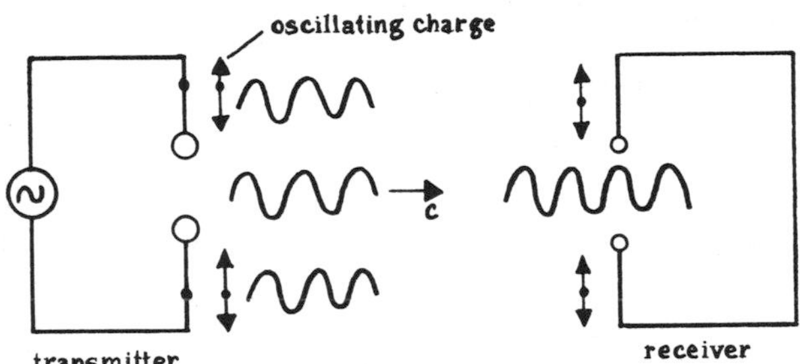

Solution: Hertz produced radio waves by use of an induction coil. This alternating current generator was connected in series with a metal loop containing a gap in it (see the figure). A second loop (the receiver) with a similar gap was placed a few feet away from the first loop (the transmitter). The induction coil created an arc discharge across the gap of the transmitting circuit. A similar discharge appeared across the gap of the receiving circuit. Apparently, the disturbance at the first circuit was transmitted to the second circuit. This disturbance was shown to propagate with the speed of light c.

The effect of the AC generator is to cause the electric charge within the wire in the transmitting circuit to oscillate about an equilibrium position. An oscillating charge undergoes acceleration and emits electromagnetic radiation with a frequency equal to the oscillating frequency of the charge. The electromagnetic wave disturbance is transmitted through space.

When it reaches the receiving circuit, it causes the charge in the wire to oscillate. An AC current is then created. An arc discharge is then developed across the gap due to this current.

If the wavelength of the wave is given, the frequency of the wave can be found by use of the following relation.

$$c = f\lambda$$

Since the value of the wavelength, $\lambda = 3m$, and the speed of light, $c = 3 \times 10^8$ m/s, are known, the frequency is then

$$f = \frac{c}{\lambda} = \frac{3 \times 10^8 \text{ m/s}}{3 \text{ m}} = 1 \times 10^8 \text{ Hz}$$

This frequency falls within the present-day FM radio band. The frequency of the source (i.e. the oscillating charge) is the same as that of the wave, so the current (i.e. the movement of charge) is oscillating at a frequency of 1×10^8 Hz also.

• PROBLEM 810

The solar constant, the power due to radiation from the sun falling on the earth's atmosphere, is $1.35 \text{ kW}\cdot\text{m}^{-2}$. What are the magnitudes of $\vec{E}$ and $\vec{B}$ for the electromagnetic waves emitted from the sun at the position of the earth?

Solution: Starting with the electromagnetic waves at the earth, it is possible to determine $\vec{E}$ and $\vec{B}$ by two methods. (a) The Poynting vector

$$\vec{S} = \frac{1}{\mu_0} \vec{E} \times \vec{B}$$

gives the energy flow across any section of the field per unit area per unit time.

Here, $\vec{E}$ and $\vec{B}$ are the instantaneous electric field and magnetic induction, respectively, at a point of space, and μ_0 is the permeability of free space. If we approximate the sun as a point source of light, then we realize that it radiates electromagnetic waves in all directions uniformly. However, the distance between earth and sun is very large, and we may approximate the electromagnetic waves arriving at the surface of the earth as plane waves. For this type of wave, $\vec{E}$ and $\vec{B}$ are perpendicular. Thus

$$|\vec{S}| = \left|\frac{1}{\mu_0} \vec{E} \times \vec{B}\right| = EH = 1.35 \times 10^3 \text{ W}\cdot\text{m}^{-2}$$

where we have used the fact that $|\vec{B}| = \left|\frac{\vec{H}}{\mu_0}\right|$ in vacuum. ($\vec{H}$ is the magnetic field intensity.)

But in the electromagnetic field in vacuum,

$\varepsilon_0 E^2 = \mu_0 H^2$, or $E\sqrt{\varepsilon_0/\mu_0} = H$. Then

$$E \times \sqrt{\varepsilon_0/\mu_0}\, E = EH = 1.35 \times 10^3 \text{ W}\cdot\text{m}^{-2}$$

or $$E^2 = \sqrt{\mu_0/\varepsilon_0} \times 1.35 \times 10^3 \text{ W}\cdot\text{m}^{-2}$$

$$= 377\ \Omega \times 1.35 \times 10^3 \text{ W}\cdot\text{m}^{-2}.$$

$$E = \sqrt{5.09 \times 10^5}\ \text{V}\cdot\text{m}^{-1} = 0.71 \times 10^3 \text{ V}\cdot\text{m}^{-1}.$$

Similarly,

$$B = \mu_0 H = \frac{\mu_0(1.35 \times 10^3 \text{ W}\cdot\text{m}^{-2})}{E}$$

$$B = \frac{(4\pi \times 10^{-7} \text{ Weber}\cdot\text{A}^{-1}\cdot\text{m}^{-1})(1.35 \times 10^3 \text{ W}\cdot\text{m}^{-2})}{.71 \times 10^3 \text{ V}\cdot\text{m}^{-1}}$$

$$B = 2.39 \times 10^{-6}\ \frac{\text{Weber}\cdot\text{W}\cdot\text{A}^{-1}\cdot\text{m}^{-2}}{\text{V}}$$

But $1 \text{ W} = 1 \text{ J}\cdot\text{s}^{-1}$ and $1 \text{ V} = 1 \text{ J}\cdot\text{C}^{-1}$ whence

$$B = 2.39 \times 10^{-6}\ \frac{\text{Weber}\cdot\text{J}\cdot\text{s}^{-1}\cdot\text{A}^{-1}\cdot\text{m}^{-2}}{\text{J}\cdot\text{C}^{-1}}$$

$$B = 2.39 \times 10^{-6} \text{ Weber}\cdot\text{m}^{-2}.$$

(b) The electromagnetic energy density (or, energy per unit volume) in an electromagnetic field in vacuum is $\mu_0 H^2 = \varepsilon_0 E^2$. The energy falling on 1 m^2 of the earth's atmosphere in 1 s is the energy initially contained in a cylinder 1 m^2 in cross section and 3×10^8 m in length; for all this energy travels to the end of the cylinder in the space of 1 s. Hence the energy density near the earth is

$$\mu_0 H^2 = \varepsilon_0 E^2 = \frac{1.35 \times 10^3 \text{ W}\cdot\text{m}^{-2}}{3 \times 10^8 \text{ m}\cdot\text{s}^{-1}}$$

Here, ε_0 is the permittivity of free space.

$$E^2 = \frac{1.35 \times 10^3 \text{ W}\cdot\text{m}^{-2}}{8.85 \times 10^{-12} \text{ C}^2\cdot\text{N}^{-1}\cdot\text{m}^{-2} \times 3 \times 10^8 \text{ m}\cdot\text{s}^{-1}}$$

$$E^2 = \frac{1.35 \times 10^7}{26.55}\ \frac{\text{W}}{\text{C}^2\cdot\text{N}^{-1}\cdot\text{m}\cdot\text{s}^{-1}}$$

But $1 \text{ W} = 1 \text{ J}\cdot\text{s}^{-1} = 1 \text{ N}\cdot\text{m}\cdot\text{s}^{-1}$

$$E^2 = 5.085 \times 10^5 \text{ N/C N}^{-1} = 5.085 \times 10^5 \text{ N}^2/\text{C}^2$$

or $$E = .71 \times 10^3 \text{ N}\cdot\text{C}^{-1} = .71 \times 10^3 \text{ V}\cdot\text{m}^{-1}$$

Also $$\mu_0 H^2 = \frac{B^2}{\mu_0} = \frac{1.35 \times 10^3 \text{ W}\cdot\text{m}^{-2}}{3 \times 10^8 \text{ m}\cdot\text{s}^{-1}}$$

$$B^2 = \frac{4\pi \times 10^{-7}\ N\cdot A^{-2} \times 1.35 \times 10^3\ W\cdot m^{-2}}{3 \times 10^8\ m\cdot s^{-1}}$$

or

$$B = 2.36 \times 10^{-6}\ Wb\cdot m^{-2}.$$

• PROBLEM 811

Show that a particle subjected to two simple harmonic vibrations of the same frequency, at right angles and out of phase, traces an elliptical path which degenerates to two coincident straight lines if the phase difference is π. Indicate the relevance of this to a half-wave plate.

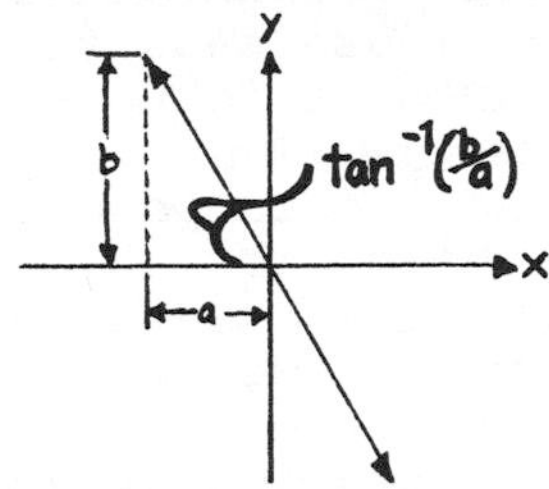

Solution: Let the vibrations be taking place along the x- and y-axes with a phase difference of ϕ between them. Then if $x = a \sin \omega t$, $y = b \sin (\omega t + \phi)$. Since $\sin (\alpha + \beta) = \sin \alpha \cos \beta + \cos \alpha \sin \beta$

$$\frac{y}{b} = \sin \omega t \cos \phi + \cos \omega t \sin \phi$$

$$= \frac{x}{a} \cos \phi + \sqrt{1 - \frac{x^2}{a^2}} \cdot \sin \phi$$

Here we have used the fact that

$$\cos \omega t = \sqrt{1 - \sin^2 \omega t}$$

$$\frac{y^2}{b^2} + \frac{x^2}{a^2} \cos^2 \phi - \frac{2xy}{ab} \cos \phi = \left(1 - \frac{x^2}{a^2}\right) \sin^2 \phi$$

$$\frac{x^2}{a^2} (\cos^2 \phi + \sin^2 \phi) + \frac{y^2}{b^2} - \frac{2xy}{ab} \cos \phi = \sin^2 \phi$$

or $$\frac{x^2}{a^2} + \frac{y^2}{b^2} - \frac{2xy}{ab} \cos \phi = \sin^2 \phi$$

This is the general equation of an ellipse where the major and minor axes do not coincide with the x- and y-axes. Thus the particle always has x- and y-coordinates such that the point they define lies on an ellipse. The particle thus follows an elliptical path.

If $\phi = \pi/2, 3\pi/2, 5\pi/2, \ldots$, the equation of the path reduces to $(x^2/a^2) + (y^2/b^2) = 1$, which is an ellipse with the major and minor axes coincident with the coordinate axes.

When $\phi = \pi$, the equation of the path becomes

$$\frac{x^2}{a^2} + \frac{y^2}{b^2} + \frac{2xy}{ab} = 0,$$

that is $\left(\frac{x}{a} + \frac{y}{b}\right)^2 = 0.$

This is the equation of two coincident straight lines $x/a = -y/b$, inclined to the negative x-axis at an angle $\tan^{-1}(b/a)$. (See figure.)

In the case of a half-wave plate, plane-polarized light striking the plate is split up in two components, O and E, plane-polarized at right angles to one another and initially in phase. These pass through the plate at different speeds and the thickness is such that on emergence the two beams are out of phase by π. Any particle affected by the two components will thus be affected by two simple harmonic vibrations at right angles, out of phase by π. As can be seen from the above analysis, the particle would trace a straight-line path. This means that the two components are equivalent to a single vibration at an angle $\tan^{-1}(b/a)$ to the slower component, b/a being the ratio of the amplitudes of the components of the incident light on entering the plate. If the plane-polarized light is striking the plate at an angle of 45° to the two transmission directions, then it is resolved into two equal components so that $b = a$. The emerging light is thus plane-polarized in a direction making an angle of $-45°$ with each of the principal directions in the plate.

• PROBLEM 812

The captain of a submarine fitted with a directional transmitter finds that he receives bad echoes from the sea bed when he is submerged if the transmission direction makes an angle greater than 45° with the vertical (see Figure (A)). He wishes to transmit a message to shore using radiation which is completely horizontally polarized. How far from the coast should he surface if the receiving point is a house on top of a coastal cliff 500 ft high and he intends to polarize his radiation by reflection on the sea surface? Take the location of the transmitter as 12 ft above the water when the submarine has surfaced.

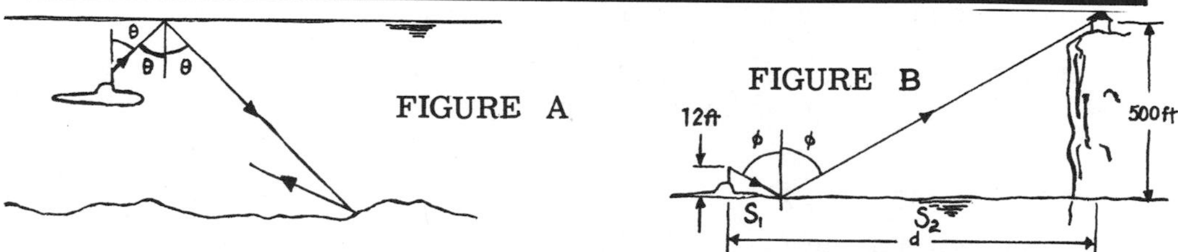

FIGURE A

FIGURE B

Solution: If the transmission direction makes a small angle with the vertical, most of the radiation passes through the water surface into the air and only a small fraction is reflected back to the ocean bed to produce echoes. The amount reflected increases with the angle until, when the critical angle is reached, reflection is total, and the echo becomes troublesome. The refractive index of water for the radiation used is found from Snell's Law,

$$n \sin \theta_i = n_{air} \sin \theta_r$$

where θ_i and θ_r are the angles of incidence and refraction for the transmitted signal. We are told that the critical angle is $\theta_i = 45°$. At the critical angle, $\theta_r = 90°$. Hence,

$$n = \frac{1}{\sin 45°} = \sqrt{2} = 1.414.$$

When the submarine has surfaced, it can produce a completely plane-polarized beam by reflection of the radiation at the Brewster angle from the surface of the sea. The angle required is $\tan \phi = n = 1.414$. That is, $\phi = 54.75°$. (See figure (B)).

Thus, the distance of the submarine from the cliff is

$$d = s_1 + s_2$$

From figure (B), however,

$$\frac{12 \text{ ft}}{s_1} = \tan (90 - \phi) = \tan 35.25°$$

and $$\frac{500 \text{ ft}}{s_2} = \tan (90 - \phi) = \tan 35.25°$$

or $$d = \frac{500 \text{ ft}}{\tan 35.25°} + \frac{12 \text{ ft}}{\tan 35.25°} = \frac{512}{0.707} \text{ ft} = 724 \text{ ft}.$$

VIBRATING RODS & STRINGS

• PROBLEM 813

A string 100 centimeters long has a frequency of 200 vibrations per second. What is the frequency of a similar string under the same tension but 50 centimeters long?

Solution: Since the frequency is inversely proportional to length, the frequency of the 50-centimeter string is 2×200, or 400 vps.

• PROBLEM 814

A string 100 centimeters long has a mass of 4 grams and emits a frequency of 250 vibrations per second. Another string 100 centimeters long has a mass of 1 gram. What is the frequency of the second string if it is put under the same tension as the first?

Solution: The second string has one-fourth the mass of

the first. The square root of ¼ is ½. Since the frequency varies inversely as the square root of the mass per unit length, the frequency of the second string is 2 × 250, or 500 vps.

• PROBLEM 815

A brass rod of density 8.5 $g\cdot cm^{-3}$ and length 100 cm is clamped at the center. When set into longitudinal vibration it emits a note two octaves above the fundamental note emitted by a wire also of 100-cm length weighing 0.295 g and under a tension of 20 kg weight which is vibrating transversely. What is Young's modulus for brass?

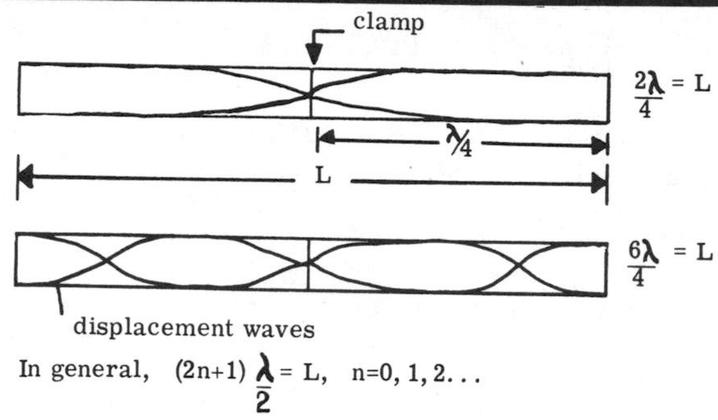

Solution: The rod vibrates with its center clamped (see figure). Its fundamental frequency of vibration is thus such that the center of the rod is a node and each of the ends an antinode. The length of the rod, L, is half a wavelength (λ). Thus λ = 2L. Further, the speed of sound in the rod is $c = \sqrt{Y/\rho}$, where Y is Young's modulus for brass and ρ its density. Hence the frequency of vibration is

$$f = \frac{c}{\lambda} = \frac{1}{2L}\sqrt{\frac{Y}{\rho}}$$

For the vibrating wire the length is the same and, if μ is the mass per unit length of the wire ($\mu = m/L$) the frequency of the fundamental vibration is

$$f_1 = \frac{1}{2L}\sqrt{\frac{S}{\mu}} = \frac{1}{2L}\sqrt{\frac{SL}{m}}\ ,$$

where m is the mass of the wire. But $f = 4f_1$, since one frequency is two octaves above the other. Hence

$$\frac{1}{2L}\sqrt{\frac{Y}{\rho}} = \frac{4}{2L}\sqrt{\frac{SL}{m}}$$

$$\text{or } Y = \frac{16\rho SL}{m}$$

$$= \frac{16 \times 8.5\ g\cdot cm^{-3} \times 2 \times 10^4\ kg \times 981\ cm\cdot s^{-2} \times 100\ cm}{0.295\ g}$$

$$= 9.04 \times 10^{11}\ dynes\cdot cm^{-2}.$$

• **PROBLEM 816**

A string under a tension of 256 newtons has a frequency of 100 vibrations per second. What is its frequency when the tension is changed to 144 newtons?

Solution: The tension is only $\frac{144}{256}$ as much as it was at first. The square root of $\frac{144}{256}$ is $\frac{12}{16}$, or $\frac{3}{4}$. Since the frequency is directly proportional to the square root of the tension, the new frequency is

$$\frac{3}{4} \times 100, \text{ or } 75 \text{ vps.}$$

• **PROBLEM 817**

One end of a horizontal wire is fixed and the other passes over a smooth pulley and has a heavy body attached to it. The frequency of the fundamental note emitted when the wire is plucked is 392 cycles$\cdot s^{-1}$. When the body is totally immersed in water, the frequency drops to 343 cycles$\cdot s^{-1}$. Calculate the density of the body.

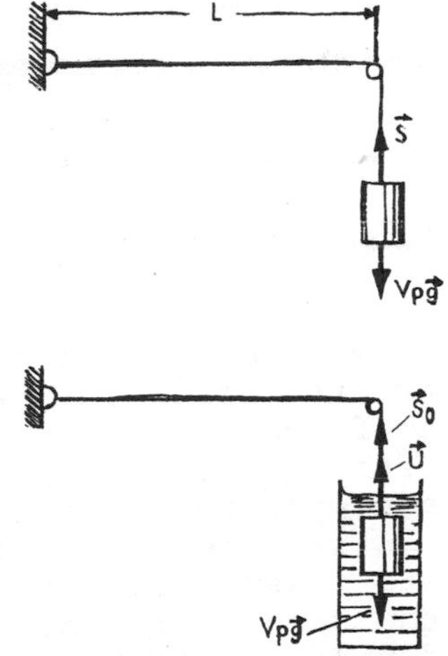

Solution: Let the density of the body be ρ and its volume be V. The density of water is 1 $g\cdot cm^{-3} = \rho_0$. In the first case, the weight of the body is balanced by the tension $\vec{S}$ in the wire. In the second case, a third force, the buoyancy, enters into the calculation. (See the figure.) The weight of the body is balanced partly by the new tension in the wire, $\vec{S}_0$, and partly by the buoyancy, $\vec{U}$, acting on it according to Archimedes' principle. That is, U is equal to the weight of water displaced by the body. Since the volume of the displaced water is equal to the volume of the body, then $U = (V\rho_0)g$ where $V\rho_0$ is the mass of the displaced water. Thus

$$S = V \rho g$$

where $V\rho$ is the mass of the body and

$$S_0 + U = S_0 + V \rho_0 g = V \rho g,$$

the buoyancy due to the air in the first case being ignored.

The frequencies of the fundamental notes emitted in the two cases are

$$f_1 = \frac{1}{2L}\sqrt{\frac{S}{\mu}} \qquad \text{and} \qquad f_0 = \frac{1}{2L}\sqrt{\frac{S_0}{\mu}}$$

where μ is the mass of the wire per unit length (the mass density). Thus

$$\frac{f_0^2}{f_1^2} = \frac{S_0}{S} = \frac{V\rho g - V\rho_0 g}{V\rho g} = \frac{\rho - \rho_0}{\rho}$$

$$\therefore \quad \rho = \frac{f_1^2 \rho_0}{f_1^2 - f_0^2} = \frac{392^2\ s^{-2} \times 1\ g\cdot cm^{-3}}{(392^2 - 343^2)\ s^{-2}}$$

$$= 4.27\ g\cdot cm^{-3}.$$

• PROBLEM 818

A flexible wire 80 cm long has a mass of 0.40 gm. It is stretched across stops that are 50 cm apart by a force of 500 nt. Find the frequencies with which the wire may vibrate.

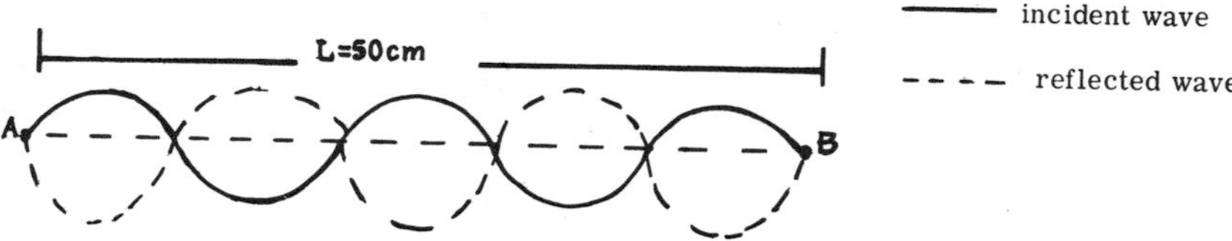

Solution: The speed of a wave through a medium is determined by its elasticity and inertia. The elasticity is what causes a restoring force to act on any part of the medium displaced from its equilibrium position. The reaction of the displaced portion of the medium to the restoring force depends on its inertia. For a stretched wire, the tension T is a measure of its elasticity; the greater the tension, the greater is the elastic restoring force on the displaced portion of wire. The inertia is measured by m, the mass per unit length of the wire. The speed of the wave has been found both analytically and experimentally to be,

$$v = \sqrt{\frac{T}{\mu}} = \sqrt{\frac{500\ nt}{0.40 \times 10^{-3}\ kg/0.80\ m}}$$

$$= \sqrt{10^6\ m^2/sec^2} = 1000\ m/sec$$

The wire can only vibrate in a standing wave pattern, since it is stopped at two points (see figure). The incident wave is reflected at points A and B and reinforces the later incident waves, producing the pattern shown. Hence, λ is related to L by,

$$L = \frac{n\lambda}{2} \qquad (1)$$

Hence,

$$\lambda = \frac{2L}{n}$$

Since the velocity of a sound wave is related to its frequency f and wavelength   by

$$v = f$$

we obtain,

$$\frac{v}{f} = \frac{2L}{n}$$

or,

$$f = \frac{nv}{2L} = \frac{n\left(10^3 \text{ m/s}\right)}{(2)\left(50 \times 10^{-2} \text{ m}\right)}$$

$$f = n \times 10^3 \text{ s}^{-1}$$

Putting in values of n, we find,

$$f_1 = 10^3 \text{ s}^{-1}$$

$$f_2 = 2 \times 10^3 \text{ s}^{-1}$$

$$f_3 = 3 \times 10^3 \text{ s}^{-1}$$

$$\cdot \qquad \cdot$$

$$\cdot \qquad \cdot$$

$$f_n = n \times 10^3 \text{ s}^{-1}$$

The other possible frequencies are the integral multiples of 1000 vibrations/sec, that is, 2000, 3000, 4000,....., vibrations/sec.

• PROBLEM 819

To what tension must a brass wire of cross-sectional area 10^{-2} cm^2 be subjected so that the speed of longitudinal and transverse waves along it may be the same? Young's modulus for brass is 9.1×10^{11} dynes·cm^{-2}. Is this situation physically realizable?

Solution: The speed of transverse waves in the wire is $\sqrt{S/\mu}$, and of longitudinal waves $\sqrt{Y/\rho}$, where Y is the Young's modulus of brass, S is the tension in the wire, ρ is the density of brass, and μ is the mass per unit length of the wire.

In this problem we require that $\sqrt{S/\mu} = \sqrt{Y/\rho}$.

$$\therefore \quad S = \frac{\mu}{\rho} Y = \frac{\text{mass per unit length}}{\text{mass per unit volume}} Y = AY$$

where A is the cross-sectional area of the wire. Therefore

$$S = 10^{-2}\ cm^2 \times 9.1 \times 10^{11}\ dynes \cdot cm^{-2}$$

$$= 9.1 \times 10^9\ dynes$$

Since the formula for Young's modulus is $Y = (S/A)(\Delta\ell/\ell)$, then $S = AY$ implies $\Delta\ell/\ell = 1$. In other words, the wire must stretch by an amount equal to its length ℓ. The elastic limit would have been passed long before this point. The situation is therefore physically unrealizable and longitudinal waves will always travel faster than transverse ones in the wire.

• PROBLEM 820

Two identical wires are stretched by the same tension of 100 N, and each emits a note of frequency 200 cycles$\cdot s^{-1}$. The tension in one wire is increased by 1 N. Calculate the number of beats heard per second when the wires are plucked.

Solution: The frequency of the fundamental note emitted by each wire before the tension change occurs is

$$\nu = \frac{1}{2L}\sqrt{\frac{T}{\mu}} \qquad (1)$$

If T changes, ν will also change. We can find the relation between these 2 changes by taking the derivative of (1) with respect to T

$$\frac{d\nu}{dT} = \frac{1}{2L}\left(\frac{1}{2}\left(\frac{T}{\mu}\right)^{-\frac{1}{2}}\frac{1}{\mu}\right)$$

$$\frac{d\nu}{dT} = \frac{1}{4L}\sqrt{\frac{\mu}{T}}\ \frac{1}{\mu}$$

$$\frac{d\nu}{dT} = \frac{1}{4LT}\sqrt{\frac{T^2\mu}{T\mu^2}} = \frac{1}{4LT}\sqrt{\frac{T}{\mu}}$$

From (1)

$$\frac{d\nu}{dT} = \frac{\nu}{2T}$$

Hence, $\Delta\nu \approx \frac{\nu}{2}\frac{\Delta T}{T}$

where $\Delta\nu$ is the frequency difference induced in the string as a result of a change in tension ΔT. In other words, $\Delta\nu$ is the number of beats observed if the string's tension is changed by an amount ΔT. Using the given data

$$\Delta\nu = \left(\frac{200}{2}\ cycles \cdot s^{-1}\right)\left(\frac{1N}{100N}\right)$$

$$\Delta\nu = 1\ cycle \cdot s^{-1}$$

Calculate the velocity of a transverse pulse in a string under a tension of 20 lb if the string weighs 0.003 lb/ft.

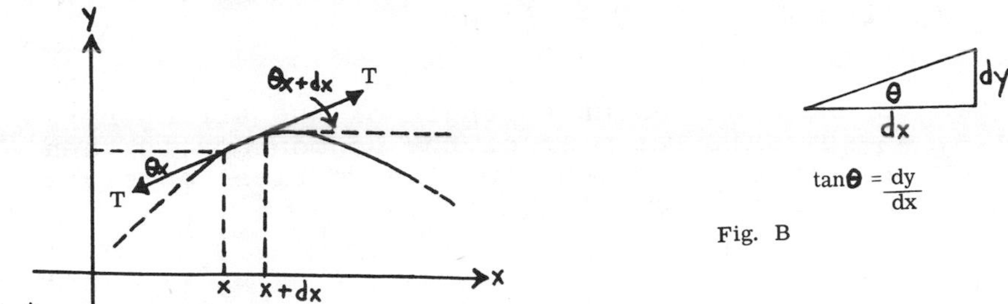

Fig. A

Fig. B

Solution: Consider the section of string shown in figure A, which is under the tension T. This segment can be interpreted as being part of the pulse being transmitted along the string. The net force acting in the y direction is

$$F_y = T \sin \theta_{x + dx} - T \sin \theta_x$$

Since θ_x and $\theta_{x + dx}$ are small, we have approximately,

$$\sin \theta_x \approx \theta_x \approx \tan \theta_x$$

$$\sin \theta_{x + dx} \approx \theta_{x + dx} \approx \tan \theta_{x + dx}$$

Therefore, $F_y = T(\tan \theta_{x + dx} - \tan \theta_x)$

but $\tan \theta_{x + dx} = \left(\frac{\partial y}{\partial x}\right)_{x + dx}$

$\tan \theta_x = \left(\frac{\partial y}{\partial x}\right)_x$ (See fig. B)

∂y and ∂x have the same meaning as dy and dx, they are small increments of y and of x, respectively. The ∂ symbol indicates that more than one variable is under consideration.

$$\text{Hence, } F_y = T\left[\left(\frac{\partial y}{\partial x}\right)_{x + dx} - \left(\frac{\partial y}{\partial x}\right)_x\right] \qquad (1)$$

Now, by Taylor's theorem, given a continuous and differentiable function G(x),

$$G(x + dx) = G(x) + \frac{\partial G}{\partial x} dx + \ldots$$

$$G(x + dx) - G(x) \approx \frac{\partial G}{\partial x} dx \qquad (2)$$

Higher order terms have been neglected because dx is so small that terms involving $(dx)^2$ or higher must necessarily be negligible. If $G(x) = \partial y/\partial x$, then we have from (2)

$$\left(\frac{\partial y}{\partial x}\right)_{x + dx} - \left(\frac{\partial y}{\partial x}\right)_{x} = \frac{\partial}{\partial x}\left(\frac{\partial y}{\partial x}\right) dx = \frac{\partial^2 y}{\partial x^2} dx$$

Hence, (1) becomes $F_y = T \dfrac{\partial^2 y}{\partial x^2} dx$

Denote the mass per unit length of the string by μ (i.e. $\mu = dm/dx$). The mass of the segment dx is then $m = \mu dx$. By Newton's second law, the vertical acceleration of the string segment, a_y, is

$$F_y = ma_y$$

$$T \frac{\partial^2 y}{\partial x^2} dx = (\mu dx) \frac{\partial^2 y}{\partial t^2}$$

$$\frac{\partial^2 y}{\partial x^2} = \frac{\mu}{T} \frac{\partial^2 y}{\partial t^2} \qquad (3)$$

Equation (3) is of the form of the wave equation

$$\frac{\partial^2 y}{\partial x^2} = \frac{1}{v^2} \frac{\partial^2 y}{\partial t^2}$$

where $y(x, t)$ is the displacement of the wave at position x and at time t, and v is the velocity of the wave. For the transverse wave, then

$$v = \sqrt{\frac{T}{\mu}}$$

Returning to our original problem,

$T = 20$ lb,

$$\mu = \frac{0.003}{32} \frac{\text{lb/ft}}{\text{ft/sec}^2},$$

$$v = \sqrt{\frac{20 \text{ lb} \times 32 \text{ ft/sec}^2}{0.003 \text{ lb/ft}}} = 461 \frac{\text{ft}}{\text{sec}}.$$

CHAPTER 26

ACOUSTICS

• PROBLEM 822

What is the frequency of a 2-cm sound wave in sea water? The velocity of sound in sea water is $\upsilon = 1.53 \times 10^5$ cm/sec.

Solution: The 2-cm is the wavelength λ of the sound wave. The frequency is given by

$$\nu = \frac{\upsilon}{\lambda}$$

$$= \frac{1.53 \times 10^5 \text{ cm/sec}}{2 \text{ cm}}$$

$$= 7.6 \times 10^4 \text{ Hz} = 76 \text{ kHz}$$

which is an ultrasonic wave (that is, above the human audible range). A 2-cm sound wave in air would be audible.

• PROBLEM 823

The frequency of middle C is 256 sec^{-1}. What is its wavelength in air?

Solution: The velocity of sound in air varies with temperature. At 18° C, which is a common room temperature it is 3.4×10^4 cm/sec. Hence, since

Wave velocity = Frequency × Wavelength

we see that

$$\text{Wavelength} = \frac{\text{Wave velocity}}{\text{Frequency}}$$

$$= \frac{3.4 \times 10^4 \text{ cm/sec.}}{256 \text{ sec}^{-1}}$$

$$= 133 \text{ cm.}$$

This is approximately 4 feet. When the pianist plays middle C, the high pressure regions traveling toward a listener through the air are about 4 feet apart, but they are moving with the very high speed of 3.4×10^4 cm/sec (760 mph) and so 256 of them arrive at the listener's ear every second.

• PROBLEM 824

A sound with a frequency of 1,000 cycles per second is produced when the air temperature is 15° centigrade. What is the wavelength of this sound?

Solution: Velocity (v), frequency (n) and wavelength (λ) are related by the relation $v = n\lambda$. The speed of sound at sea level at $0°C$ is 1090 ft/sec. This speed increases by 2 ft/sec for every degree centigrade above $0°C$. Hence,

$$\text{Velocity in ft/sec} = 1090 + (2 \times 15)$$
$$= 1090 + 30$$
$$= 1120$$

Since $v = n\lambda$,

$$\lambda = v/n$$
$$= \frac{1120 \text{ ft/sec}}{1000 \text{ cycles/sec}}$$
$$= 1.12 \text{ ft/cycle.}$$

• PROBLEM 825

Find the theoretical speed of sound in hydrogen at $0°C$. For a diatomic gas $\gamma = 1.40$, and for hydrogen $M = 2.016$ gm/mole.

Solution: Sound waves are longitudinal mechanical waves. That is, they are propagated in matter and the particles transmitting the wave oscillate in the direction of propagation of the wave. The speed of the wave is determined by the elastic and inertial properties of the medium. For a gaseous medium, the elastic property depends on the undisturbed gas pressure p_0 and the inertial property on ℓ_0, the density/mole of the gas. With γ a constant called the ratio of specific heats for the gas, the velocity is

$$v = \sqrt{\gamma p_0/\rho_0}$$

Since for one mole of gas,

$$p_0 = \frac{RT}{V} = \frac{RT\rho_0}{M} \qquad \text{we have}$$

$$v = \sqrt{\frac{\gamma RT}{M}}$$

$$= \sqrt{\frac{1.40\ [8.317 \text{ joules/(mole K°)}](273°K)}{2.016 \times 10^{-3} \text{ kg/mole}}}$$

$$= \sqrt{\frac{1.40 \times 8.317 \times 273 \text{ joules}}{2.016 \times 10^{-3} \text{ kg}}}$$

$$= 1.25 \times 10^3 \text{ m/sec}$$

• PROBLEM 826

A sound is returned as an echo from a distant cliff in 4 sec. How far away is the cliff, assuming the velocity of sound in air to be 1100 ft/sec?

Solution: The sound travels the distance (s) between cliff and observer twice. Hence

$$2s = v \times t$$

where v is the velocity of sound, and t is the time required for the entire trip. Therefore,

$$s = \frac{v \times t}{2} = \frac{(1100\ \text{ft/sec}) \times (4\ \text{sec})}{2} = 2200\ \text{ft.}$$

• PROBLEM 827

Using the speed of sound at sea level as approximately 750 miles per hour, what is the velocity of a jet plane traveling at Mach Number 2.2?

Solution:

$$\text{Mach Number} = \frac{\text{velocity of body}}{\text{velocity of sound}}, \quad \text{and}$$

$$\text{velocity of body} = \text{Mach Number} \times \text{velocity of sound},$$

whence

$$\text{Velocity of sound} = 750\ \text{mph} \times 2.2$$

$$= 1650\ \text{mph} = 2200\ \text{ft/sec approximately.}$$

• PROBLEM 828

Compute the speed of sound in the steel rails of a railroad track. The weight density of steel is 490 lb/ft^3, and Young's modulus for steel is $29 \times 10^6 lb/in^2$.

Solution: For an elastic medium, the speed of longitudinal waves is given by

$$v = \sqrt{\frac{Y}{\rho}} = \sqrt{\frac{Yg}{D}}$$

Where Y is Young's modulus, ρ is the density of the medium and $\rho = \frac{D}{g}$ where D is the weight density of the medium.

$$v = \sqrt{\frac{(29 \times 10^6\ \text{lb/in}^2)\ (32\ \text{ft/ s}^2)}{490\ \text{lb/ft}^3}}$$

In order to keep all length dimensions consistent, we must change $29 \times 10^6\ lb/in^2$ to lb/ft^2, Hence,

$$29 \times 10^6\ \text{lb/in}^2 = \frac{29 \times 10^6\ \text{lb}}{\frac{1}{144}\ \text{ft}^2}$$

$$29 \times 10^6\ \text{lb/in}^2 = 29 \times 144 \times 10^6\ \text{lb/ft}^2$$

Therefore,

$$v = \sqrt{\frac{\left(29 \times 10^6 \times 144 \text{ lb/ft}^2\right)\left(32 \text{ ft/sec}^2\right)}{490 \text{ lb/ft}^3}}$$

$$= 1.6 \times 10^4 \text{ ft/sec}$$

• PROBLEM 829

A small sports arena is designed by an architect in the form of a dome with radius of curvature R = 115 ft mounted on a cylindrical base 75 ft in radius and 30 ft in height.

The dome acts as a spherical mirror with a focal length f = 1/2R = 57.5 ft. The top of the dome is the vertex of the mirror. It is of interest to calculate the location of the focal point with respect to the ground surface of the arena.

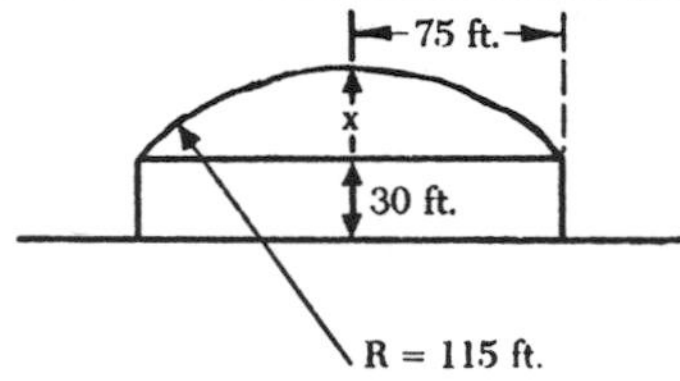

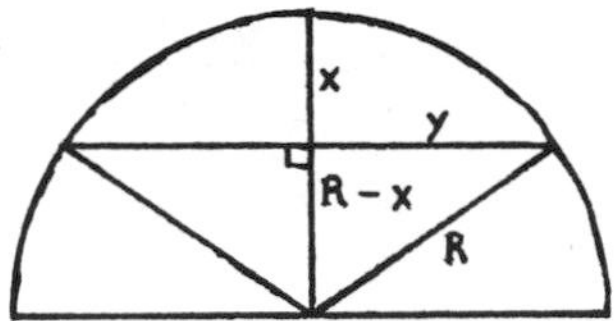

Solution: From the diagram

$$y^2 + (R - x)^2 = R^2$$

$$(R - x)^2 = R^2 - y^2$$

$$= \left(115^2 - 75^2\right)\text{ft}^2$$

$$= 87^2 \text{ft}^2$$

$$R - x = 87 \text{ ft}$$

$$x = (115 - 87)\text{ft}$$

$$x = 28 \text{ ft}$$

The distance from the vertex of the dome to the ground surface is x + 30 = 58 ft, the same as the focal length. Thus the focal point of the mirror lies on the ground surface at the center of the arena.

As a result of this there will be a tendency for spectator noise to be focused at the center of the ground surface, and the noise there is liable to be deafening. There exists a hockey arena that has been designed this way (accidentally), and in the center ice region the noise is of such intensity that the players can not hear the whistles of the officials.

• PROBLEM 830

What is the wavelength of the sound wave emitted by a standard 440 cycles per second tuning fork?

Solution: Noting that the velocity (v), frequency (n), and wavelength (λ) of sound are related by $v = n\lambda$, and assuming the velocity of sound to be 34,000 cm/sec, or approx. 1100 ft/sec, we find

$$\lambda = v/n = \frac{1100 \text{ ft}}{440} = 2.5 \text{ ft (approx.)}$$

• PROBLEM 831

> When two tuning forks are sounded simultaneously, a beat note of 5 cycles per second is heard. If one of the forks has a known frequency of 256 cycles per second, and if a small piece of adhesive tape fastened to this fork reduces the beat note to 3 cycles per second, what is the frequency of the other fork?

Solution: This problem involves the phenomenon of beats. When two similar waves are superimposed, the beat frequency represents the numerical difference in their frequencies. Hence, for the case in question,

$$n = (256 \pm 5) \text{cycles/sec}$$

where n represents the unknown frequency.

It appears that n has two possible values, either 251 or 261. Now, when the standard fork is loaded with the tape, its frequency will decrease. Since the beat frequency is then reduced to 3 cycles per second, the unknown frequency must be less rather than more than 256. Hence,

$$n = 251.$$

• PROBLEM 832

> Two trains moving along parallel tracks in opposite directions converge on a stationary observer, each sounding its whistle of frequency 350 cycles$\cdot$ s^{-1}. One train is traveling at 50 mph. What must be the speed of the other if the observer hears 5 beats per second. The speed of sound in air is 750 mph.

Solution: When a source is moving toward a stationary observer, the latter hears a frequency for the emitted note which is related to the frequency of the source by the expression $f = uf_s/(u - v_s)$ where u is the speed of sound in air, v_s is the speed of the source and f_s is the frequency of the sound emitted by the source. If one of the trains is moving toward the observer with v_1 and the other with speed v_2, then since both have the same frequency whistle,

$$f_1 = \frac{uf_s}{u - v_1} \qquad \text{and}$$

$$f_2 = \frac{uf_s}{u - v_2} = \frac{750 \text{ mph} \times 350 \text{ s}^{-1}}{(750 - 50) \text{ mph}} = 375 \text{ cycles}\cdot\text{s}^{-1}.$$

But the observer hears 5 beats per second. This corresponds to a frequency difference $f_1 - f_2 = \pm 5$ cycles $\cdot$ sec^{-1}. Hence, $f_1 = 370$ cycles $\cdot$ s^{-1} or

380 cycles · s^{-1}.

$$\therefore \quad f_1 = \frac{uf_s}{u - v_1} = 370\ s^{-1} \quad \text{or} \quad 380\ s^{-1}.$$

$$\therefore u - v_1 = \frac{750 \text{ mph} \times 350\ s^{-1}}{370\ s^{-1}} \quad \text{or}$$

$$\frac{750 \text{ mph} \times 350\ s^{-1}}{380\ s^{-1}} = 709.5 \text{ mph} \quad \text{or} \quad 690.8 \text{ mph}.$$

$$\therefore \quad v_1 = 40.5 \text{ mph} \quad \text{or } 59.2 \text{ mph}.$$

• PROBLEM 833

Estimate the upper limit to the frequency of "sound" waves in ordinary matter.

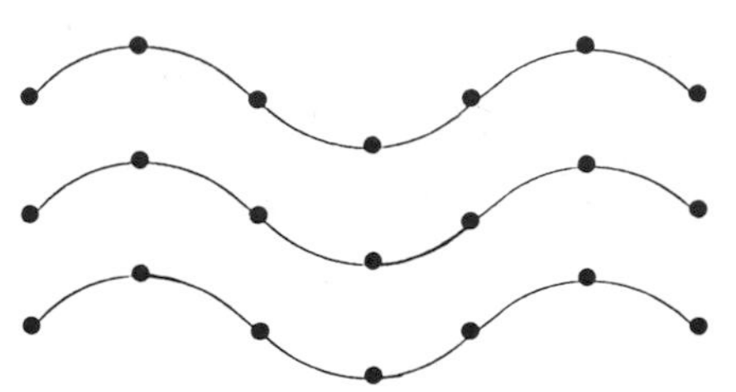

(a) The behavior of the atoms for a transverse wave with a wavelength longer than the distance between atoms

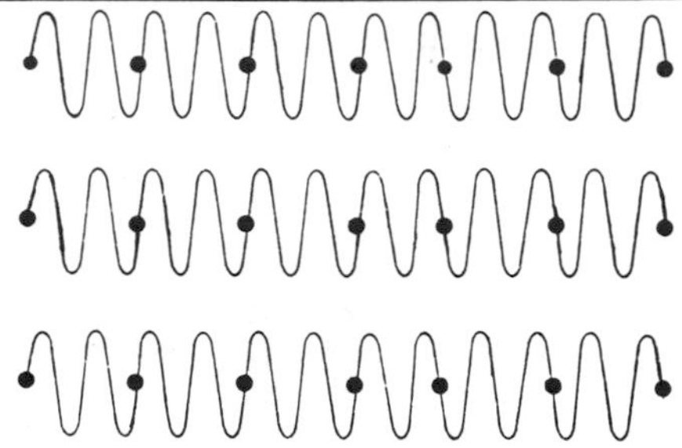

(b) There is no meaning in a wavelength shorter than the distance between atoms because there is nothing in between the atoms to oscillate.

Solution: The relation $\nu = \frac{v}{\lambda}$, (1)

where ν, v, and λ are the frequency, velocity and wavelength of the sound wave, respectively, makes it clear that the higher the frequency the shorter is the wavelength. We are therefore asking what is the shortest wavelength sound can have. The answer is that, when the wavelength becomes shorter than the distance apart of the atoms, the concept of a wave breaks down because there is nothing in between the atoms to oscillate (see figure). The atoms are closest together in solids and highly compressed gases.

However, when two atoms are about 10^{-8} cm apart they repel one another very strongly and it is difficult to force them any nearer. Consequently, in no material are the atoms or molecules found to be closer together than about 10^{-8} cm. This is therefore the order of magnitude of the shortest wavelength of sound.

The highest value found for the velocity of sound is about 10^6 cm/sec. Using equation (1).

$$\text{Highest frequency} = \frac{\text{Largest wave velocity}}{\text{Shortest wavelength}}$$

$$= \frac{10^6}{10^{-8}} \text{ approximately}$$

$$= 10^{14} \text{ sec}^{-1} \text{ approximately.}$$

This is much larger than the highest frequency yet produced experimentally, which is $2.5 \times 10^{10}\ sec^{-1}$.

The reader should note the character of these arguments, which are not precise calculations, but rather intelligent guesses. We have made it very plausible that the highest frequency is not very much bigger than $10^{14}\ sec^{-1}$. It is conceivable that, by applying a very high pressure to the right gas or solid, we could force its atoms a little closer than 10^{-8} cm and achieve a velocity of sound a little larger than 10^6 cm/sec. In this way we might perhaps realize a frequency of, say, $2 \times 10^{14}\ sec^{-1}$. We should be very surprised, though, if we ever pushed the frequency up to $10^{15}\ sec^{-1}$. In fact we know that there is a limit to the procedure, because there is reason to believe that, when the pressure on a substance becomes extremely large, its atoms break up into separate electrons and nuclei.

• PROBLEM 834

What is the lowest frequency of the standing sound wave that can be set up between walls that are separated by 25 ft?

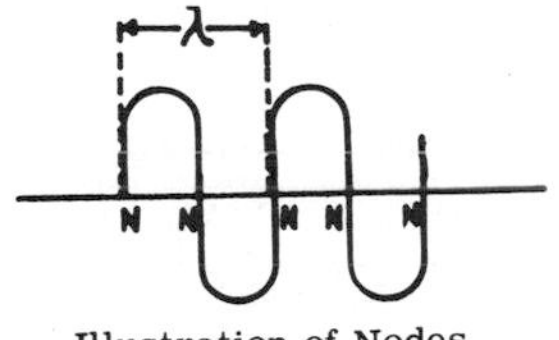

Illustration of Nodes

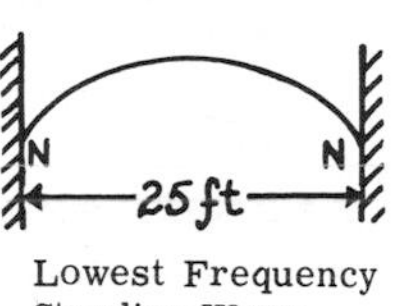

Lowest Frequency Standing Wave

Solution: A sinusoidal wave that maintains its overall shape between two termination points is called a standing wave. Its amplitude does change with time. For such a wave, the end points have zero amplitude at all times. Zero amplitude points are called nodes and occur every half wavelength.

The wave of lowest frequency has the longest wavelength. For a given distance L, the standing wave of longest wavelength has $\lambda = 2L$ with the only nodes occurring at the termination points. Therefore,

$$\lambda = 2L = 2 \times 25\ ft = 50\ ft$$

The frequency of the wave is

$$\nu = \frac{\upsilon}{\lambda} = \frac{1100\ ft/sec}{50\ ft}$$

$$= 22\ Hz$$

which is close to the lowest frequency that can be heard by a human ear. Therefore, a room somewhat larger than 25 ft is necessary in order to set up standing waves of the lowest audible frequency (for example, organ notes of 16 Hz).

• PROBLEM 835

A sonar device emits waves of frequency 40,000 cycles·s^{-1}. The velocities of the wave in air and water are 1100 ft·s^{-1} and 4200 ft·s^{-1}, respectively. What are the frequency of the wave in air and the wavelengths in air and water?

Suppose that the device is fixed to the bottom of a ship. It emits a signal and the echo from the ocean bed returns 0.8 s later. What is the depth of the ocean at that point?

Solution: The frequency of the waves emitted is the same in air or water. The surrounding medium has no influence on the vibration mechanism. Since $\lambda = c/f$ where c is the wavespeed, and f and λ are the frequency and wavelength of the sound, respectively, we have (a) in air

$$\lambda = \frac{1100 \text{ ft}\cdot\text{s}^{-1}}{4 \times 10^4 \text{ s}^{-1}} = 2.75 \times 10^{-2} \text{ ft}$$

and (b) in water

$$\lambda' = \frac{4200 \text{ ft}\cdot\text{s}^{-1}}{4 \times 10^4 \text{ s}^{-1}} = 10.50 \times 10^{-2} \text{ ft.}$$

Since the velocity of sound in water is 4200 ft·s^{-1} and the echo returns in 0.8 s after traversing 2d, where d is the ocean depth at that point, we have s = ct or 2d = 4200 ft·s^{-1} × 0.8 s.

$$\therefore \quad d = 1680 \text{ ft.}$$

• PROBLEM 836

Two small loudspeakers A and B vibrate in phase at 800 cps, and are set apart by 10 ft. The speakers emit spherical waves which obey the inverse square law with respect to intensity. The intensity variation (for distances away from the speakers greater than a few inches) is

$$I_A = \frac{60}{R_A^2} \qquad I_B = \frac{30}{R_B^2}$$

The units are arbitrary; R_A is the distance from speaker A, R_B is the distance from speaker B. Find the point of minimum intensity along the line joining the speakers. Find the first three points of zero intensity that are nearest to the speakers.

Solution: Assume that points of minimum and zero intensity occur only at points of destructive interference. Destructive interference of two waves occurs when the waves are 180° out of phase. The resultant amplitude at the point of interference will be the difference of the amplitude of the two waves at the

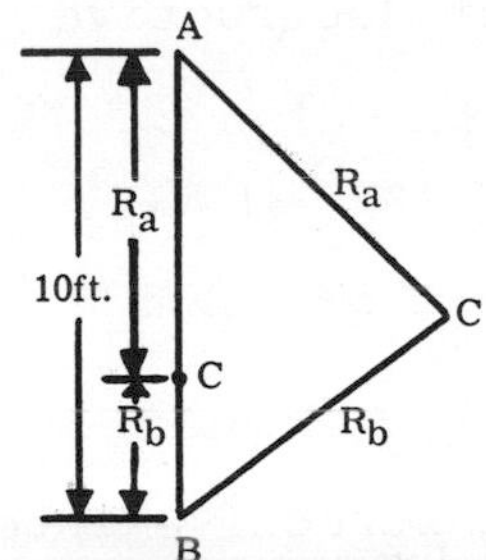

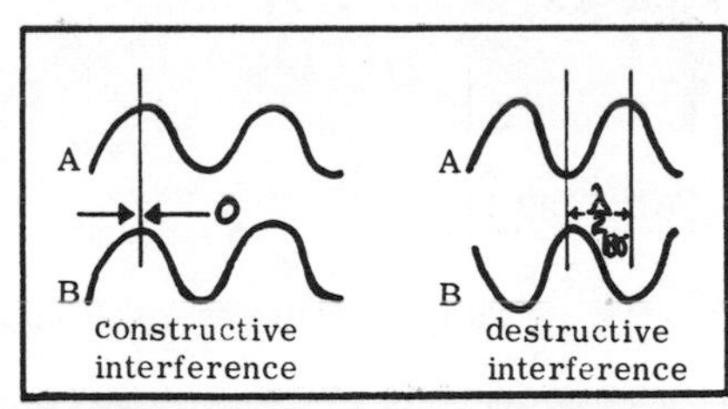

point. The speed of sound is 1200 ft/sec. Consider point C (in the **figure**) such that

$$R_A = \overline{CA} \qquad\qquad R_B = \overline{CB}$$

Wave cancellation occurs when the two waves are 180° out of phase. Since the two waves originate with a 0° phase difference, one wave must undergo a 180° phase shift (relative to the second wave) for destructive interference to occur. In our case, the phase change is effected by letting the two waves move through different path lengths before they meet and interfere. Destructive interference will then occur when this path difference is an odd number of half wavelengths. This will insure a phase shift of 180°. Therefore,

$$|R_A - R_B| = (2n - 1)\frac{\lambda}{2} \qquad n = 1, 2, 3, \ldots$$

Now, if λ and f are the wavelength and frequency of the sound wave, and c is its velocity,

$$\lambda f = c$$

$$\lambda = \frac{c}{f} = \frac{1200 \text{ ft/sec}}{800 \text{ sec}^{-1}} = 1.5 \text{ ft}$$

We are also given that $\overline{AB} = 10 \text{ ft} = R_A + R_B$, when C is on the line joining $\overline{AB}$; thus

$$|R_A - R_B| = \left|R_A - (10 - R_A)\right| = |2R_A - 10|$$

and cancellation will occur for

$$2R_A - 10 = (2n - 1)\,\frac{\lambda}{2} \qquad n = 1, 2, 3, 4, \ldots$$

$$= (1)\,\frac{1.5}{2} = 0.75 \qquad \text{if } n = 1$$

$$= (3)\,\frac{1.5}{2} = 2.25 \qquad \text{if } n = 2$$

$$= (5)\,\frac{1.5}{2} = 3.75 \qquad \text{if } n = 3$$

$$= (7)\,\frac{1.5}{2} = 5.25 \qquad \text{if } n = 4 \text{ and so forth.}$$

The resultant intensity at the point of destructive interference is

$$I_C = |I_A - I_B|$$

$$= \left|\frac{60}{R_A^2} - \frac{30}{R_B^2}\right|$$

This follows from the very nature of destructive interference; **the intensities** of **the interfering waves** tend to **try to cancel** one another.

• PROBLEM 837

A vibrating tuning fork of frequency 384 cycles·s^{-1} is held over the end of a vertical glass tube, the other end of which dips into water. Resonance occurs when the top of the tube is 21.9 cm and also 66.4 cm above the water surface. Calculate the speed of sound in air and the end correction of the tube.

Assuming that the temperature is 13°C, what is the velocity of sound at 0°C (v_0)?

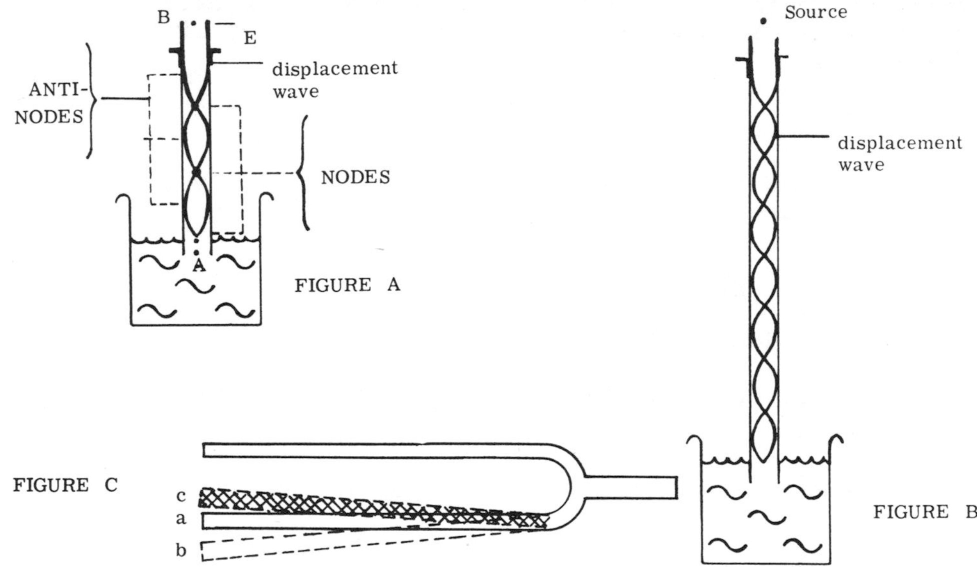

Solution: Figure (C) shows the tuning fork in vibration. In order to send a compression wave down the tube, one tine of the fork is pulled back to position c, and then is let go. During one oscillation, the tine moves from c to b and then back to c. Now, the pipes with which we are dealing have water at one end. This end must then be a displacement node, for the air at this end of the column is always at rest. Alternatively, it is a pressure antinode. Similarly, the open end of the tube is a displacement maximum, or a pressure node. Now, suppose the fork starts at point c and sends a compression wave down the tube. When this wave reaches the bottom of the tube, it must be reflected as a compression if that end is to remain a pressure antinode. The reflected compression travels back up the tube. If resonance is to occur, the compression must reach the tine of the tuning fork when the latter is ready to move from b to c. (In this situation, the tine is preparing to send a rarefaction down the tube). If this does not occur, the top of the tube will not remain a pressure node, for the reflected pressure wave and the new pressure wave will not cancel. Hence, in ½ oscillation of the tuning fork, the wave travels a distance 2L (twice the tube length). In general, resonance will occur if the wave travels a distance 2L in an odd number of half oscillations of the fork. If the wave velocity is $\mathbf{v}$ and the frequency of the fork is ν_{source}, the resonance condition is

$$2L = v(n + \tfrac{1}{2})/\nu_{source} \qquad (n = 0, 1, 2 \ldots) \quad (1)$$

Since the wave frequency equals the source frequency, we may write

$$\nu_{wave} = \nu_{source} = \nu$$

But $\quad \nu_{wave}\, \lambda = v$

where λ is the wavelength of the wave. Hence, (1) becomes

$$2L = \frac{v(n + \frac{1}{2})}{\nu}$$

Solving this for v

$$v = \frac{2L\nu}{(n + \frac{1}{2})} \qquad (n = 0, 1, 2 \ldots) \qquad (2)$$

Therefore, we may measure v if we know the tube length, the source frequency, and the value of n. In practice, the tube is put in the water, and slowly drawn out as the fork vibrates. When the first resonance occurs, n = 0, and the length of tube extending out of the water is measured. Again, the tube is drawn out of the water. When the second resonance occurs, n = 1, and the tube length is again measured, etc. Each resonance will give us the same value for v, as equation (2) indicates.

Using the relation

$$v = \nu\lambda$$

where λ is the wavelength of the wave, we may also write (2) as

$$v = \frac{2L}{(n + \frac{1}{2})} \frac{v}{\lambda}$$

$$\text{or} \quad L = (n + \tfrac{1}{2}) \frac{\lambda}{2} \qquad (n = 0, 1, 2 \ldots) \quad (3)$$

In practice, an antinode never occurs quite at the end of an open pipe. Its position is just beyond the end of the pipe, the maximum displacement slightly overshooting the end (see figs. (a) and (b)). Thus for the first resonance (n = 0 in (3)) the length of the tube will be almost a quarter of a wavelength, and $\lambda/4 = L + E$, where L is the length of the air column and E is the end correction. Similarly, for the second resonance, $3\lambda/4 = L' + E$, where L' is the length of the air column when the second resonance occurs. Thus, using our data,

$$\frac{\lambda}{2} = L' - L = (66.4 - 21.9)\ \text{cm}$$

$$= 44.5\ \text{cm} \qquad \text{or } \lambda = 89\ \text{cm}.$$

Therefore the velocity of sound is

$$v = f\lambda = 384\ s^{-1} \times 89\ \text{cm} = 34176\ \text{cm}\cdot s^{-1}$$

$$= 341.8\ m\cdot s^{-1}.$$

Further, $E = \lambda/4 - L = (22.25 - 21.9)\ \text{cm} = 0.35\ \text{cm}$.

The velocity of sound in a gas is proportional to the square root of the absolute temperature. Hence $v_0/v = \sqrt{T_0/T} = \sqrt{273°K/286°K} = 0.977$.

$$\therefore \quad v_0 = 0.977 \times 341.8\ m\cdot s^{-1} = 333.9\ m\cdot s^{-1}.$$

• PROBLEM 838

When a Kundt's tube contains air, the distance between several nodes is 25 cm. When the air is pumped out and replaced by a gas, the distance between the same number of nodes is 35 cm. The velocity of sound in air is 340 $m\cdot s^{-1}$. What is the velocity of sound in the gas?

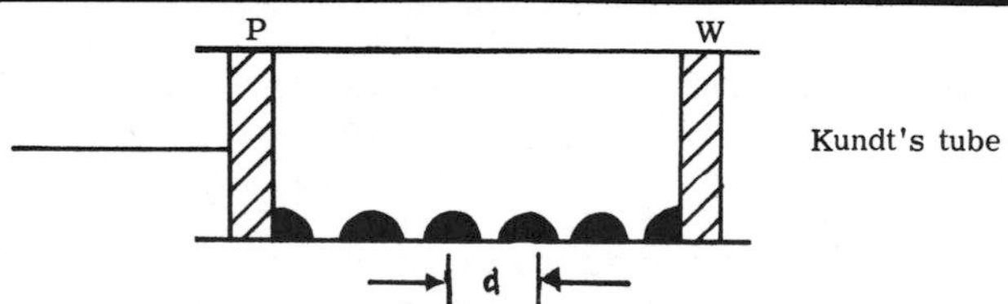

Kundt's tube

Solution: A Kundt's tube (see the figure) is a glass tube with sawdust spread over its interior. A piston P is set into longitudinal vibration and the wall W moved until a standing wave pattern of nodes and antinodes is set up within the tube. The sawdust will accumulate at all the nodal points, for these are the points of the wave for which there is no vibration of the gas. By measuring the distance d between the nodes, we may find the velocity of sound of the gas in the tube. Let the number of nodes involved be 2n + 1. There are 2n intervals between these 2n + 1 nodes, and the total distance thus corresponds to 2n half-wavelengths, or to n full wavelengths.

The frequency of the emitted sound is the same in both cases, for it depends only on the frequency of the vibrating membrane which is causing the standing wave within the Kundt's tube. Thus $c_A = f\lambda_A$ and $c_G = f\lambda_G$.

Since there are, in the case of the air filled tube, n wavelengths in 25 cm of space, then the number of centimeters of space one wavelength will contain is found by the following proportion.

$$\frac{25 \text{ cm}}{n \text{ wavelength}} = \frac{x \text{ cm}}{1 \text{ wavelength}} = \lambda_A$$

Similarly for the case of the gas filled tube,

$$\frac{35 \text{ cm}}{n \text{ wavelength}} = \frac{x \text{ cm}}{1 \text{ wavelength}} = \lambda_G$$

Thus

$$\frac{c_G}{c_A} = \frac{\lambda_G}{\lambda_A} = \frac{(35/n)\text{cm}}{(25/n)\text{cm}} = \frac{7}{5}. \quad \therefore \quad c_G = \frac{7}{5} \times 340 \text{ m}\cdot\text{s}^{-1} = 476 \text{ m}\cdot\text{s}^{-1}.$$

If the number of nodes involved is 2n, then there are 2n - 1 intervals between these 2 nodes. The total distance thus corresponds to 2n - 1 half-wavelengths, or to $n - \frac{1}{2}$ full wavelengths. The same analysis as before holds, and

$$\frac{c_G}{c_A} = \frac{\lambda_G}{\lambda_A} = \frac{\left(35/n - \frac{1}{2}\right)\text{cm}}{\left(25/n - \frac{1}{2}\right)\text{cm}} = \frac{7}{5}$$

The same result is obtained, as it must, if an odd number of nodes are counted as if an even number of nodes are counted.

• PROBLEM 839

(a) What will be the frequencies of the first and the second overtones of a pipe closed at one end of length 2 ft? (b) What will be the frequencies of the first and second overtones of an open pipe 2.5 ft long? (c) Will there be any common beat frequency between these overtones?

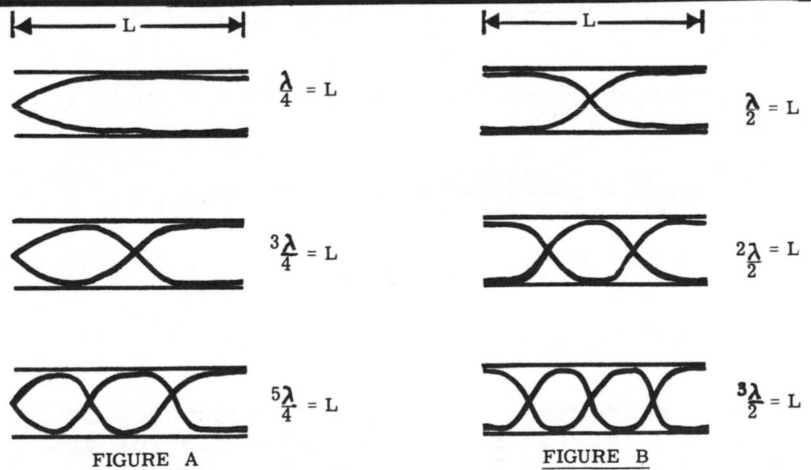

FIGURE A

FIGURE B

Solution: (a) Not all wave shapes can be fitted into a closed (or semi-closed) pipe. Only those waves which satisfy certain boundary conditions can exist in the enclosure. Only those waves which have a node (a point of zero amplitude) at a closed end of the pipe and which have an antinode (a point of maximum amplitude) at an open end, can exist in the pipe. The wave with the lowest frequency which can exist in a pipe closed at one end is one which has only one node (at the closed end) and one antinode (at the open end). (See figure A). Its wavelength is $\lambda = 4\ell$ and its frequency n_f (the fundamental frequency) is, using the relation $\lambda n_f = v$, where v is the velocity of sound,

$$n_f = \frac{v}{\lambda} = \frac{v}{4\ell} = \frac{1100 \text{ ft/sec}}{4 \times 2 \text{ ft}} = 137.5 \text{ sec}^{-1}$$

The first overtone contains two nodes and two antinodes. The second overtone contains three nodes and three antinodes. In general, the nth overtone will contain n + 1 nodes and n + 1 antinodes. The first and second overtones of the pipe will then be the third and the fifth harmonic respectively, i.e., frequencies 3 times and 5 times that of the fundamental (see figure A).

$$\therefore n_{1st} = 3(137.5) = 412.5 \text{ sec}^{-1}$$

$$n_{2nd} = 5(137.5) = 687.5 \text{ sec}^{-1}$$

The only waves which can exist in an open pipe are those which have antinodes at both ends, of the pipe. The enclosed wave with the lowest possible frequency, n_f(the fundamental) space will contain two antinodes and one node (see figure B). The first overtone contains three antinodes and two nodes. The second overtone contains four antinodes and three nodes. In general, the nth overtone contains n + 2 antinodes and n + 1 nodes. The first and second overtones will then be the second and third harmonics, i.e., frequencies 2 times and 3 times that of the fundamental.

The wavelength of the fundamental is $\lambda = 2\ell$ and its frequency n_f' is

$$n_f' = \frac{v}{\lambda} = \frac{v}{2\ell} = \frac{1100 \text{ ft/sec}}{2 \times 2.5 \text{ ft}} = 220 \text{ sec}^{-1}.$$

Hence $$n'_{1st} = 2(220) = 440 \text{ sec}^{-1}$$

$$n'_{2nd} = 3(220) = 660 \text{ sec}^{-1}$$

The frequency difference for the first overtones is 440 - 412.5 = 27.5. The frequency difference for the second overtones is 687.5 - 660 = 27.5.

Thus a common beat frequency is 27.5 cycles per sec.

• PROBLEM 840

A source emits sound waves at 1000 cycles/second (frequency f_0) and the speed of the wave with respect to the source is 1000 ft/second (v_w)

(a) Calculate the wavelength a listener observes if he is at rest with respect to the source (λ_0)?

(b) If the source moves with a velocity of 100 ft/second (v_s) towards the listener, what frequency (f_{s1}) and wavelength (λ_{s1}) does he observe?

(c) If the source moves at a velocity v_s away from the listener, what frequency (f_{s2}) and wavelength (λ_{s2}) does he observe?

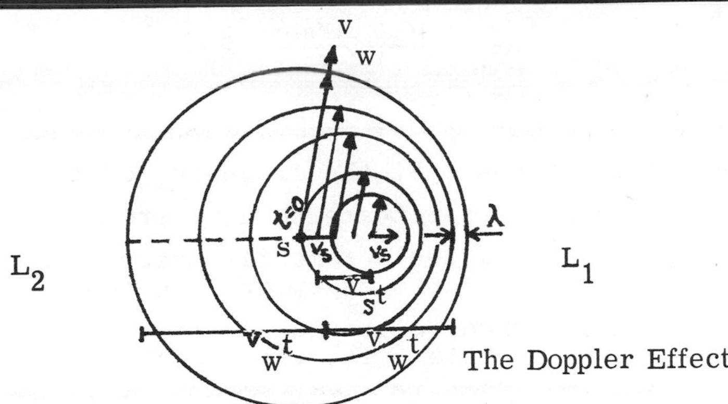

The Doppler Effect

Solution: Everyone has heard the drop in pitch of a passing train's whistle. The Doppler effect is the apparent change of wave frequency observed by a listener when he and the wave source are in relative motion. In this problem, we deal with sound waves and derive the change in observed frequency and wavelength for two kinds of relative motion: motion of the observer and motion of the source. For any observer, $v = \lambda f$, which means that the velocity at which he observes the wave to move is equal to the product of its observed frequency and wavelength. This is no more than an application of the conventional velocity definition $v = \Delta s/\Delta t$ if we remember $f = 1/T$ where T is the wave's period. Then $v = \lambda f = \lambda/T$ where λ is the observed displacement in time T.

(a) Using $v = \lambda f$, $v_w = \lambda_0 f_0$, $\lambda_0 = v_w/f_0 = \dfrac{1000 \text{ ft/second}}{1000/\text{second}} = 1 \text{ ft.}$

(b) It is known that the velocity of waves in a medium depend only on the mechanical properties of that medium. When the source moves towards the listener (see L_1 in figure) a "bunching up" of waves is noted by the listener, as shown in the figure. We seek a mathematical relation to determine by what amount their wavelength is effectively reduced, and how the frequency is affected.

In a time, t, the source emits $t/T = f_0 t$ waves. Along the line between listener and source these waves are spread over a distance $v_w t - v_s t$. Thus, if the wavelength is smaller by a constant amount, it must now be

$$\lambda_{s1} = \frac{v_w t - v_s t}{f_0 t} = \frac{v_w - v_s}{f_0} = \frac{1000 \text{ ft/sec} - 100 \text{ ft/sec}}{1000/\text{sec}}$$

$$= \frac{900 \text{ ft/sec}}{1000/\text{sec}} - 0.9 \text{ ft.}$$

As the speed of the wave is unchanged, the listener will observe an increase in the wave's frequency, according to

$$v_w = \lambda_{s1} f_{s1};\ f_{s1} = v_w/\lambda_{s1} = \frac{1000 \text{ ft/sec}}{.9 \text{ ft}} = 1111 \text{ sec}^{-1}$$

(c) As the source recedes a listener observes the waves to occupy more space than those of a stationary source, as can be seen by looking at L_2 in the figure. In a time, t, $f_0 t$ waves are emitted, spread over a distance $v_w t + v_s t$. As before, we find the wavelength

$$\lambda_{s2} = \frac{v_w t + v_s t}{f_0 t} = \frac{v_w + v_s}{f_0} = \frac{1000 \text{ ft/sec} + 100 \text{ ft/sec}}{1000/\text{sec}}$$

$$= 1.1 \text{ ft.}$$

And, as in (b), we have for the observed frequency,

$$f_{s2} = \frac{v_w}{\lambda_{s2}} = \frac{1000 \text{ ft/sec}}{1.1 \text{ ft}} = \frac{909}{\text{sec}} .$$

• PROBLEM 841

> A researcher notices that the frequency of a note emitted by an automobile horn appears to drop from 284 cycles$\cdot s^{-1}$ to 266 cycles$\cdot s^{-1}$ as the automobile passes him. From this observation he is able to calculate the speed of the car, knowing that the speed of sound in air is 1100 ft$\cdot s^{-1}$. What value does he obtain for the speed?

Solution: This is an example illustrating the Doppler effect. When there is no movement of the surrounding medium the relation between the frequency as heard by a moving observer and that emitted by a moving source is

$$\frac{f_L}{u \pm v_L} = \frac{f_s}{u \mp v_s}$$

where f_L is the frequency heard by the listener, f_s the frequency emitted by the moving source, v_L the velocity of the listener, v_s the velocity of the source, and u the velocity of sound $\left(= 1100 \text{ ft}\cdot s^{-1}\right)$. The upper signs (+ left side of equation, - right side) correspond to the source and observer moving along the line joining the two and approaching each other and the lower signs (- left, + right) correspond to source and observer receding from one another.

In this case the frequencies heard by the stationary listener $\left(v_L = 0\right)$ will be $f_L = uf_s/\left(u \mp v_s\right)$. As the automobile approaches the observer he records a frequency of 284 cycles$\cdot s^{-1}$, and as the automobile moves away from him, he records 266 cycles$\cdot s^{-1}$. Thus

$$284 \text{ s}^{-1} = \frac{uf_s}{u - v_s} \tag{1}$$

and

$$266 \text{ s}^{-1} = \frac{uf_s}{u + v_s} \tag{2}$$

Dividing (1) by (2)

$$\frac{u + v_s}{u - v_s} = \frac{284}{266}$$

$$266\left(u + v_s\right) = 284\left(u - v_s\right)$$

$$(266 + 284)v_s = (284 - 266)u$$

or $$\frac{v_s}{u} = \frac{18}{550}.$$

$$\therefore\ v_s = \frac{18}{550} \times 1100\ \text{ft}\cdot\text{s}^{-1} = 36\ \text{ft}\cdot\text{s}^{-1} = 36\ \text{ft}\cdot\text{s}^{-1}$$

$$= 36\ \text{ft}\cdot\text{s}^{-1} \times \frac{1\ \text{mile}}{5280\ \text{ft}} \times \frac{60\ \text{s}}{1\ \text{min}} \times \frac{60\ \text{min}}{1\ \text{hr}} = 24.5\ \text{mph}$$

• PROBLEM 842

An airplane is flying at Mach 0.5 and carries a sound source that emits a 1000-Hz signal. What frequency sound does a listener hear if he is in the path of the airplane after the airplane has passed?

Solution: The frequency of a wave disturbance depends on the relative motion of the source and observer. This phenomenon is called the Doppler effect and can be determined. The wavelength λ of a wave can be defined as

$$\lambda = \frac{\text{distance}}{\text{no. of waves}}$$

The no. of waves that a source of frequency ν_s emits in time t is just $\nu_s t$. If the medium permits the waves to travel at velocity **v** then the distance they cover in time t due to their own motion is **vt**. Since the source is also moving toward the listener at velocity $\mathbf{v}_s$ and covers a distance $\mathbf{v}_s t$, this means that the waves have a distance $\mathbf{v}t - \mathbf{v}_s t$ to be spread out in. Therefore

$$\lambda = \frac{\mathbf{v}t - \mathbf{v}_s t}{\nu_s t} = \frac{\mathbf{v} - \mathbf{v}_s}{\nu_s}$$

The frequency ν_L of the wave as observed by the listener as the source moves toward him is

$$\nu_L = \frac{\mathbf{v}}{\lambda_L} = \mathbf{v} \times \frac{\nu_s}{\mathbf{v} - \mathbf{v}_s} = \nu_s \left(\frac{\mathbf{v}}{\mathbf{v} - \mathbf{v}_s}\right) = \frac{\nu_s}{1 - \mathbf{v}_s/\mathbf{v}}$$

If the source moves away from the listener, the $\mathbf{v}_s$ is considered negative in the above expression.

A speed of Mach 0.5 means that the airplane moves at half the speed of sound in air. Therefore $\mathbf{v}_s/\mathbf{v} = 0.5$. As the airplane moves toward the listener

$$\nu_L = \frac{\nu_s}{1 - 0.5} = 2\nu_s$$

so that the listener hears a 2000-Hz sound.

After the airplane has passed the listener, the frequency he hears is

$$\nu_L = \frac{\nu_s}{1 + \mathbf{v}_s/\mathbf{v}}$$

$$= \frac{\nu_s}{1 + 0.5} = \frac{2}{3}\,\nu_s$$

so that the listener hears a 667-Hz sound.

CHAPTER 27

GEOMETRICAL OPTICS

REFLECTION

• PROBLEM 843

Prove that the virtual image observed in a plane mirror is the same distance behind the mirror as the object is in front of the mirror.

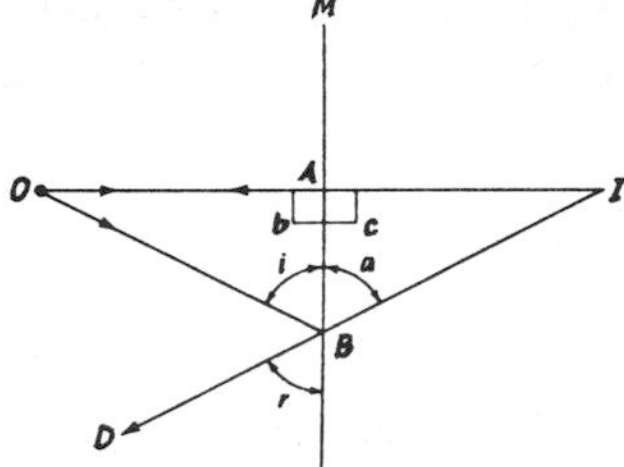

Solution: As shown in the figure, let OA be the ray of light that strikes normal to the reflecting surface, while OB represents the ray that strikes the mirror at point B. The law of reflection states that the angle of incidence i equals the angle of reflection r,

$$i = r.$$

Rays DB and OA are extended back through the mirror to form triangle AIB, where point I is the apparent position of the image. Angle r must equal a; therefore, we obtain

$$a = r = i.$$

Angles b and c are equal since they are both right angles. Therefore, we have shown that the two triangles OAB and IAB are congruent, that is, coincide perfectly when superimposed because they share a common side, AB. We conclude that OA = IA and that the virtual image appears as far behind the mirror as the object is in front of the mirror.

• PROBLEM 844

What is the minimum length L of a wall mirror so that a person of height h can view herself from head to shoes?

Solution: This is not easily solved by a diagram. We suppose that the person stands a distance x from the wall and that her eyes (E) are a distance y from the top of her head (H). To look at her toes (F) she looks at point A which is the point of reflection of a light ray from her foot. A must be at a height halfway between her eyes and feet (so that the angle of incidence equals the angle of reflection). Similarly to look at the top of her head she looks at point B. If OP = h and BP =

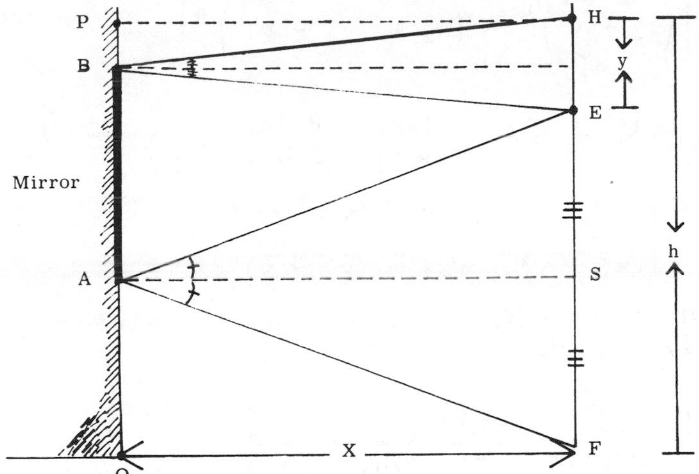

y/2 ,then the length of the mirror is AB = PO- BP -OA = h - y/2 - 1/2(h-y) = h/2. Thus the minimum length of the mirror is h/2, and this does not depend on the distance x that the person is standing away from the mirror.

• PROBLEM 845

Prove that when light goes from one point to another via a plane mirror, the path chosen is the one which takes the least time.

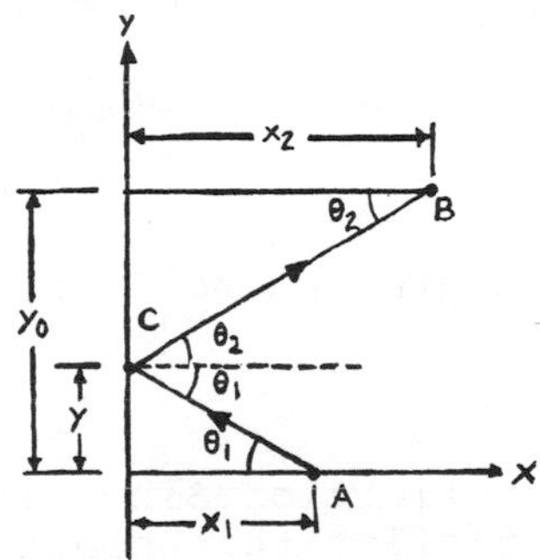

Solution: Let the points be A and B, and let C be any general point on the mirror. Orient the diagram so that the x- and y-axes are as shown. Draw the normals to the mirror surface passing through A, B and C. Now in specular reflection, the reflected ray lies in the plane determined by the incident ray and the normal to the mirror at the point of reflection. Hence A, B and C must be in the same plane.

The coordinates of the three points are $A(x_1, 0)$; $B(x_2, y_0)$; $C(0, y)$.

The length of the path ACB is, by the Pythagorean theorem,

$$p = \sqrt{x_1^2 + y^2} + \sqrt{x_2^2 + (y_0 - y)^2}$$

But the time of travel of light by this path, the velocity of light being, c, is $t = p/c$. For the path to be traveled in minimum time, we must have $dt/dy = 0$, where y is the variable which changes with path. Thus

$$t = \frac{1}{c}\left[\left(x_1^2 + y^2\right)^{\frac{1}{2}} + \left(x_2^2 + (y_0 - y)^2\right)^{\frac{1}{2}}\right]$$

$$\frac{dt}{dy} = \frac{1}{c}\left[\frac{1}{2}\left(x_1^2 + y^2\right)^{-\frac{1}{2}}(2y) + \frac{1}{2}\left(x_2^2 + (y_0 - y)^2\right)^{-\frac{1}{2}} \times 2(y_0 - y)(-1)\right]$$

$$\frac{dt}{dy} = \frac{1}{c}\left(\frac{y}{\sqrt{x_1^2 + y^2}} - \frac{(y_0 - y)}{\sqrt{x_2^2 + (y_0 - y)^2}}\right)$$

To find the values of y which make t a minimum, we set $dt/dy = 0$. Hence,

$$0 = \frac{1}{c}\left(\frac{y}{\sqrt{x_1^2 + y^2}} - \frac{y_0 - y}{\sqrt{x_2^2 + (y_0 - y)^2}}\right).$$

But since $c \neq \infty$, the quantity in the braces must be zero. Therefore,

$$\frac{y}{\sqrt{x_1^2 + y^2}} = \frac{y_0 - y}{\sqrt{x_2^2 + (y_0 - y)^2}} \qquad (1)$$

$$\sin\theta_1 = \frac{y}{\sqrt{x_1^2 + y^2}} \qquad \sin\theta_2 = \frac{y_0 - y}{\sqrt{x_2^2 + (y_0 - y)^2}}$$

Hence, (1) becomes

$$\sin\theta_1 = \sin\theta_2$$

and consulting the diagram we see that,

$$\theta_1 = \theta_2$$

which is the law of reflection.Since light reflected specularly always satisfies this condition, the light ray follows the path which takes the least time.

• PROBLEM 846

An object is 12 feet from a concave mirror whose focal length is 4 feet. Where will the image be found?

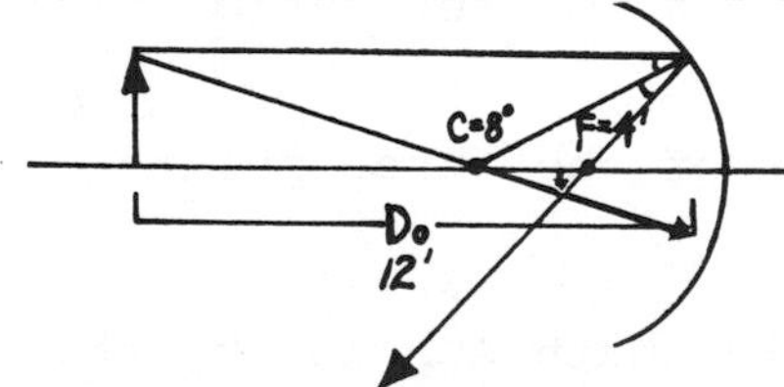

Solution: We first construct a ray diagram.

The image is a real image (inverted) between the center of curvature and the focal point. It is smaller than the object.

We now solve mathematically:

D_0 is 12 feet and f is 4 feet. Substituting in

$$\frac{1}{D_0} + \frac{1}{D_I} = \frac{1}{f}$$

$$\frac{1}{12 \text{ ft}} + \frac{1}{D_I} = \frac{1}{4 \text{ ft}}$$

whence

$$D_I = 6 \text{ ft.}$$

• PROBLEM 847

An object is 4 inches from a concave mirror whose focal length is 12 inches. Where will the image be formed?

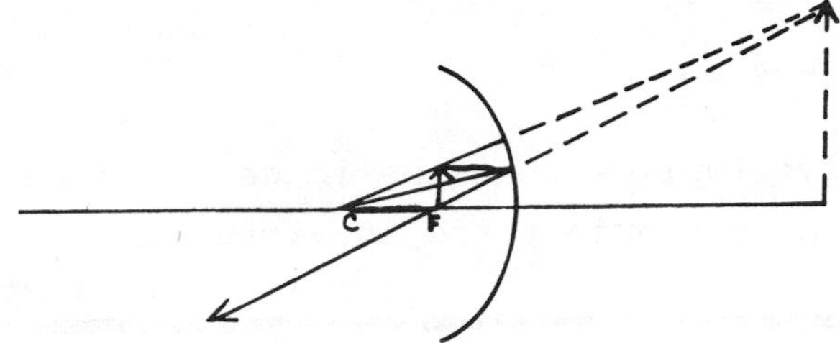

Solution: First make a ray-diagram.

Solving mathematically,

D_0 is 4 inches and f is 12 inches. Substitution in

$$\frac{1}{D_0} + \frac{1}{D_I} = \frac{1}{f}$$

$$\frac{1}{4 \text{ in.}} + \frac{1}{D_I} = \frac{1}{12 \text{ in.}}$$

whence $D_I = - 6$ in.

which means that since D_I is negative the image is 6 inches from the lens on the same side on the lens as the object and is virtual.

• PROBLEM 848

An object is placed 12 centimeters from a convex mirror whose focal length is 6 centimeters. Where will the image be formed?

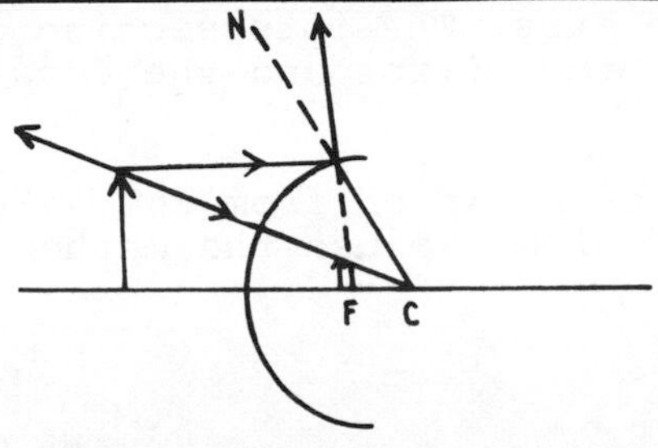

Solution: First, we construct a ray-diagram.

Here we trace the path of two rays - one parallel to the axis, and one through the center of curvature. The image is virtual and smaller than the object (for the convex mirror this is true for all positions of the object).

We may now solve mathematically.

D_0 is 12 centimeters, f is - 6 centimeters. Substituting in

$$\frac{1}{D_0} + \frac{1}{D_I} = \frac{1}{f}$$

$$\frac{1}{12\text{ cm}} + \frac{1}{D_I} = \frac{1}{-6\text{ cm}}$$

whence $D_I = -4$ cm

D_I is negative implies that the image is on the same side of the lens as the object and is virtual.

• PROBLEM 849

Where would an object have to be located in front of a concave mirror in order to have a virtual image formed? Precisely where would it be located if the radius of the mirror were 20 cm and the image were 20 cm behind (i.e., to the right of) the mirror?

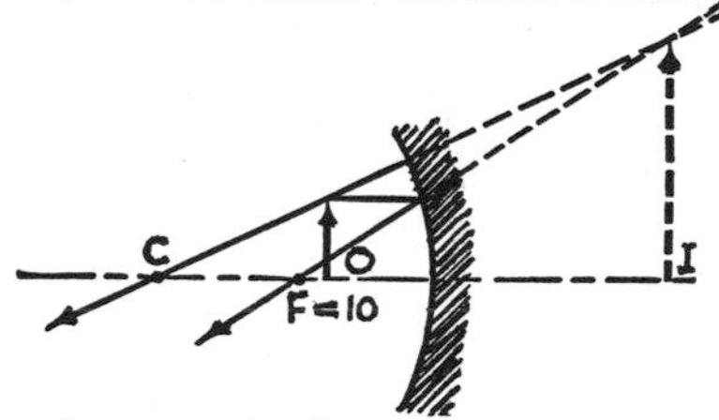

Solution: Formula Method

A virtual image is one which is uninverted and cannot be focused on a screen, and in the case of a concave mirror, occurs to the right of the mirror. Referring to the figure, we reason back to the intersection of two light rays "emitted" from the tip of the image. The ray reflected back through the center of curvature must have originated there, since the angle of incidence is equal to the angle of reflection, and the angle of incidence is zero. The ray reflected through the focal point must have originated as a ray parallel to the axis. The intersection of these two rays is between the mirror and the focal point (see figure).

To find the exact position from the values specified in the problem, we use the mathematical relationship:

$$\frac{1}{0} + \frac{1}{i} = \frac{2}{R}$$

Substituting, we have

$$\frac{1}{0} - \frac{1}{20 \text{ cm}} = \frac{2}{20 \text{ cm}}$$

$$\frac{1}{0} = \frac{3}{20 \text{ cm}}$$

$$0 = 6\frac{2}{3} \text{ cm}$$

Note that i is negative because the image is located behind the mirror.

Ray-Diagram Method

To form a virtual image with a concave mirror, the object must lie between the focal point and the mirror.

For an image to be 20 cm to the right of the mirror, the ray approaching the head end of the image from the focal point must have been reflected through the focal point, whereupon it must have been parallel to the axis before reflection.

The ray approaching the head end of the image from the center of curvature must have experienced no change in direction.

Consequently, by tracing these two rays back to their origin, the head end of the object is located as in the diagram, at approximately 6 2/3 cm in front of the concave mirror. The diagram checks the calculations.

• PROBLEM 850

A candle is held 3.0 in. in front of a convex mirror whose radius is 24 in. Where is the image of the candle?

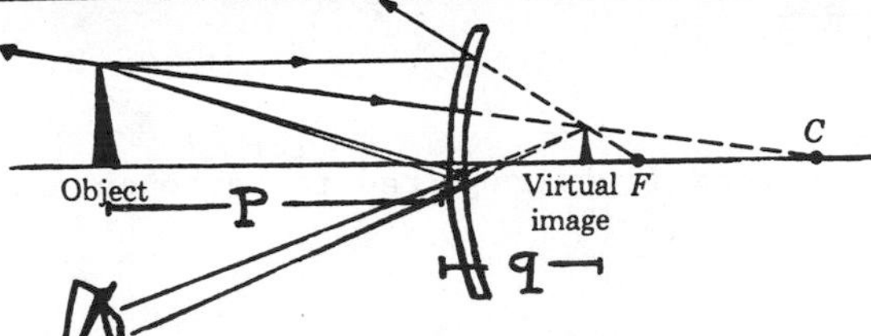

The image produced by a convex mirror is always diminished, erect, and vertical.

Solution. The figure illustrates the conditions of the problem. The relative location of the candle can be found from the general mirror equation

$$\frac{1}{p} + \frac{1}{q} = \frac{1}{f}$$

where p is the distance between the candle and the mirror, q is the distance between the image and the mirror, and f is the focal length of the mirror. For a spherical mirror of small arc, as this is assumed to be, the focal length is approximately equal to one-half the radius of the mirror.

Therefore $f = -\frac{r}{2} = -\frac{24 \text{ in.}}{2} = -12$ in.

We have

$$\frac{1}{3.0 \text{ in.}} + \frac{1}{q} = \frac{-1}{12 \text{ in.}}$$

$$\frac{1}{q} = \frac{-1 - 4}{12 \text{ in.}} = -\frac{5}{12 \text{ in.}}$$

$$q = -\frac{12}{5} \text{ in.}$$

The negative sign for q indicates that the image lies behind the mirror and is a virtual image.

• PROBLEM 851

What type of mirror is required to form an image, on a wall 3 m from the mirror, of the filament of a headlight lamp 10 cm in front of the mirror? What is the height of the image if the height of the object is 5 mm?

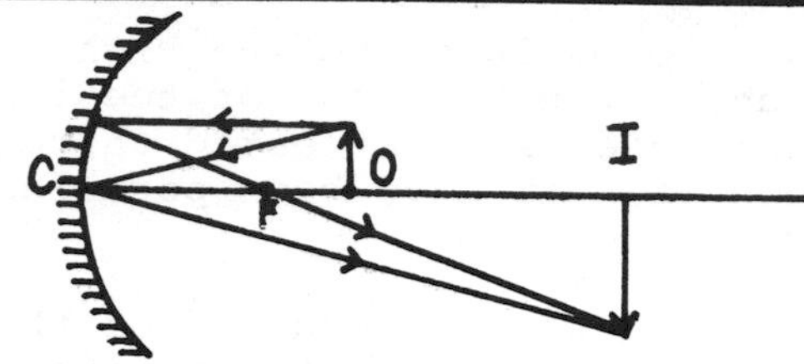

Solution: The image I has to be real since it appears on the wall. Therefore, we must use a concave mirror and the object 0 must be placed beyond the focal point F for a real image (see the figure). We rule out a convex mirror since one cannot obtain images that can be shown on a screen with a convex mirror.

If p and q are the object and image distances from the mirror respectively, the first mirror equation is

$$\frac{1}{p} + \frac{1}{q} = \frac{1}{f}$$

where $f = \frac{R}{2}$ is the focal distance of the mirror. Therefore, we have

$$p = 10 \text{ cm}, \qquad q = 300 \text{ cm}.$$

$$\frac{1}{10 \text{ cm}} + \frac{1}{300\text{cm}} = \frac{2}{R},$$

and

$$R = 19.4 \text{ cm}.$$

The radius R has a positive sign, as it is required for a concave mirror. The optical magnification m is

$$m = -\frac{q}{p}$$

where the negative sign is required because we want m to come out negative to signify an inverted image. The image height is obtained as follows.

$$h_1 = h_0 m = -h_0 \frac{q}{p} = -0.5\text{mm} \times \frac{300 \text{ cm}}{10 \text{ cm}} = -15 \text{ cm}.$$

The image is therefore 30 times bigger than the object and is inverted.

• PROBLEM 852

A small object lies 4 in. to the left of the vertex of a concave mirror of radius of curvature 12 in. Find the position and magnification of the image.

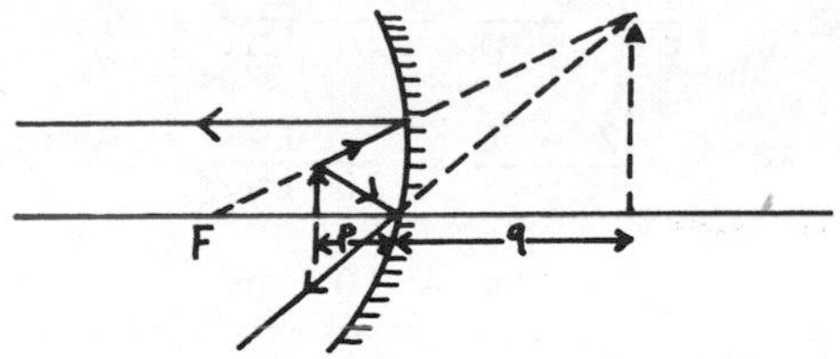

Concave Mirror

Solution: The mirror equation for a concave mirror is

$$\frac{1}{p} + \frac{1}{q} = \frac{2}{R}$$

with a positive R. The object distance is p = +4 in. and R is +12 in. Then,

$$\frac{1}{4 \text{ in.}} + \frac{1}{q} = \frac{2}{12 \text{ in.}}$$

$$q = -12 \text{ in.},$$

Magnification m is given by

$$m = -\frac{q}{p}$$

$$= -\frac{-12 \text{ in.}}{4 \text{ in.}} = 3$$

The image is therefore 12 in. to the right of the vertex (q is negative), is virtual (q is negative), erect(m is positive), and 3 times the height of the object. See the figure.

• PROBLEM 853

A man has a concave shaving mirror whose focal length is 20 in. How far should the mirror be held from his face in order to give an image of two-fold magnification?

Solution: An erect, virtual, magnified image is desired. With q as the distance between the mirror and image, and p the distance between the mirror and the man's face, the equation

$$M = \frac{q}{p}$$

can be used. M represents the ratio of the size of the image to the size of the actual object. This relation between p and q is without regard to sign. Since the image is virtual, it lies behind the mirror. Distances in front of the mirror are positive and distances behind the mirror are negative. Therefore q is negative. To compensate for this, a negative sign is placed in front of q so as to make the overall expression positive. For a two-fold magnification,

$$M = \frac{-q}{p} = 2$$

$$q = -2p.$$

Substitution in the general mirror equation

$$\frac{1}{p} + \frac{1}{q} = \frac{1}{f}$$

gives
$$\frac{1}{p} + \frac{1}{-2p} = \frac{1}{20\text{ in.}}$$

$$\frac{2 - 1}{2p} = \frac{1}{20\text{ in.}}$$

$$p = 10\text{ in.}$$

• PROBLEM 854

Derive the mirror formula for rays incident on a mirror of radius of curvature R, if the rays make a small angle with the mirror's axis.

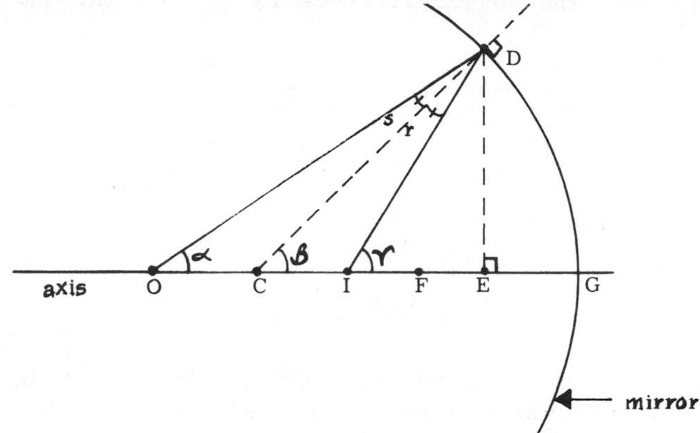

Solution: Our proof will be totally geometrical. (See figure.) Ray OD is incident on mirror DG, at an angle s with the normal to the mirror CD. (C is the center of curvature of the arc forming the mirror.) It is reflected at an angle r, and intersects the mirror axis at point I. By the law of reflection, angle i is equal to angle r. Hence

$$s = r \tag{1}$$

Furthermore, $$\beta = \frac{DG}{CG} \tag{2}$$

But CG is the mirror radius R, whence

$$\beta = \frac{DG}{R}$$

Also $$\tan\alpha = \frac{DE}{OE}$$

(3)

and $$\tan r = \frac{DE}{IE}$$

However, if α, β and r are small angles (that is, ray OD is close to the mirror axis) we may write

$$\tan\alpha \approx \alpha$$

(4)

$$\tan\gamma \approx \gamma$$

Furthermore, $$DE \approx DG \tag{5}$$

Using (5) and (4) in (3)

$$\alpha \approx \frac{DG}{OE}$$

(6)

$$\gamma \approx \frac{DG}{IE}$$

We also note that, since γ is an exterior angle of triangle ICD

$$\gamma = \beta + r \qquad (7)$$

Similarly, $\beta = \alpha + s$ (8)

Using (1) in (7) and (8)

$$\gamma = \beta + s \qquad (9)$$

$$\beta = \alpha + s \qquad (10)$$

Eliminating s in (9) and (10),

$$\gamma - \beta = \beta - \alpha$$

or $2\beta - \gamma - \alpha = 0$ (11)

Substituting (6) and (2) in (11)

$$\frac{2DG}{R} - \frac{DG}{IE} - \frac{DG}{OE} = 0$$

or $\frac{1}{IE} + \frac{1}{OE} = \frac{2}{R}$ (12)

However, if α, β and γ are small,

$$IE \approx IG = i$$

(13)

$$OE \approx OG = O$$

where i and O are the distances of the image from the mirror (image distance) and the object from the mirror (object distance). Hence, using (13) in (12) we have the mirror formula

$$\frac{1}{i} + \frac{1}{O} = \frac{2}{R}$$

REFRACTION

• PROBLEM 855

How fast does light travel in glass of refractive index 1.5?

Solution: By definition, refractive index n is the ratio of the velocity of light in vacuum (3.00×10^{10} cm/sec) to the velocity of light in the medium in question.

Therefore $n = \frac{3 \times 10^{10} \text{ cm/s}}{v} = 1.5$

Therefore $v = \frac{3 \times 10^{10} \text{ cm/s}}{1.5}$

$= 2.00 \times 10^{10}$ cm/sec.

An incident wavefront of light makes an angle of 60° with the surface of a pool of water. The speed of light in water is 2.3×10^8 m/s. What angle does the refracted wavefront make with the surface of water?

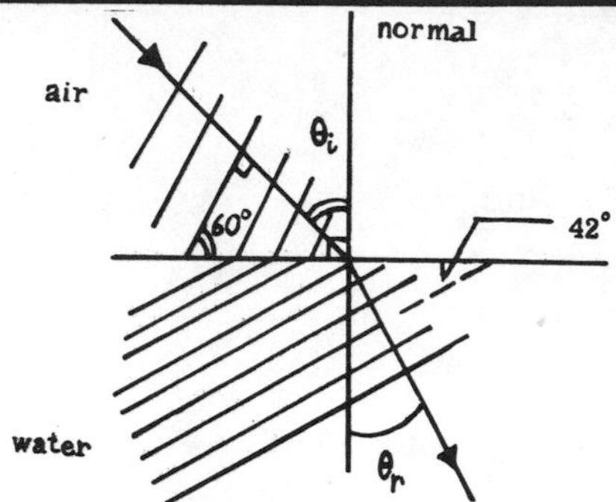

Solution: The angle θ_i between the incident ray and the normal to the surface (as shown in the figure), equals the angle between the incident wavefront and the water surface, and

$$\theta_i = 60°.$$

Snell's Law, relating the angle of incidence, θ_i, to the angle of refraction, θ_r of the light, is

$$n_1 \sin \theta_i = n_2 \sin \theta_r$$

where n_1 and n_2 are the refractive indices of air and water, respectively. Hence

$$\sin \theta_r = \frac{n_1}{n_2} \sin \theta_i$$

But

$$n_1 = \frac{\text{speed of light (vacuum)}}{\text{speed of light (air)}} \qquad n_2 = \frac{\text{speed of light (vacuum)}}{\text{speed of light (water)}}$$

Hence $\quad \sin \theta_r = \left(\dfrac{2.3 \times 10^8 \text{ m/s}}{3 \times 10^8 \text{ m/s}}\right) \sin 60° = .664$

or $\quad \theta_r = 42°.$

θ_r also equals the angle the refracted wavefront makes with the water surface.

• PROBLEM 857

A flat bottom swimming pool is 8 ft. deep. How deep does it appear to be when filled with water whose refractive index is 4/3?

Solution: In order to see why we would expect to observe a different depth for the pool when it is filled with water, examine the figure.

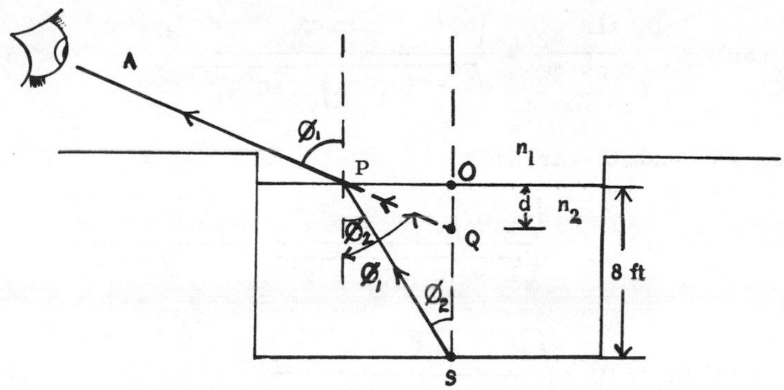

If no water is in the pool, light coming from a point S on the bottom of the pool will travel directly to the observer's eye. If the pool is filled with water, light emanating from point S will be refracted at P, as shown. Upon reaching the observer's eye, the light appears to be coming from Q and he perceives the depth of the pool to be the distance OQ, rather than the actual depth OS. Our problem is to find the distance d.

Note that, from the figure,

$$\tan \varphi_1 = \frac{OP}{d}$$

$$\tan \varphi_2 = \frac{OP}{8 \text{ ft.}}$$

Hence

$$\frac{\tan \varphi_1}{\tan \varphi_2} = \frac{OP}{d} \cdot \frac{8 \text{ ft.}}{OP} = \frac{8 \text{ ft.}}{d}$$

and

$$d = \frac{(8 \text{ ft})\tan \varphi_2}{\tan \varphi_1} \tag{1}$$

From Snell's Law,

$$n_1 \sin \varphi_1 = n_2 \sin \varphi_2$$

where n_1 and n_2 are the indices of refraction of air and water, respectively. Therefore

$$\left(\frac{n_1}{n_2}\right) \text{in } \varphi_1 = \sin \varphi_2 \tag{2}$$

To calculate the tangents in (1), we must also know $\cos \varphi_1$ and $\cos \varphi_2$. These we may find by observing that

$$\cos \varphi = \sqrt{1 - \sin^2 \varphi} \tag{3}$$

Using (2) in (3)

$$\cos \varphi_2 = \sqrt{1 - \sin^2 \varphi_2}$$

$$\cos \varphi_2 = \sqrt{1 - \left(\frac{n_1}{n_2}\right)^2 \sin^2 \varphi_1} \tag{4}$$

$$\cos \varphi_1 = \sqrt{1 - \sin^2 \varphi_1}$$

Hence

$$\tan \varphi_1 = \frac{\sin \varphi_1}{\cos \varphi_1} = \frac{\sin \varphi_1}{\sqrt{1 - \sin^2 \varphi_1}} \tag{5}$$

and using (2) with (4)

$$\tan \varphi_2 = \frac{\sin \varphi_2}{\cos \varphi_2} = \frac{(n_1/n_2) \sin \varphi_1}{\sqrt{1 - (n_1/n_2)^2 \sin^2 \varphi_1}} \tag{6}$$

Substituting (5) and (6) in (1)

$$d = (8 \text{ ft}) \frac{(n_1/n_2) \sin \varphi_1}{\sqrt{1 - (n_1/n_2)^2 \sin^2 \varphi_1}} \cdot \frac{\sqrt{1 - \sin^2 \varphi_1}}{\sin \varphi_1}$$

$$d = (8 \text{ ft})(n_1/n_2) \sqrt{\frac{1 - \sin^2 \varphi_1}{1 - (n_1/n_2)^2 \sin^2 \varphi_1}} \tag{7}$$

Now, since we don't know the angle φ_1, we make an approximation. Suppose φ_1 is very small. (This means that the observer is looking almost directly down into the pool.) Then $\sin \varphi_1 \approx 0$ and the square root in (7) becomes 1. Therefore

$$d = (8 \text{ ft})\left(\frac{n_1}{n_2}\right) = (8 \text{ ft})\left(\frac{1}{4/3}\right) = 6 \text{ ft.}$$

The pool appears to be 6 ft. deep.

• PROBLEM 858

Show that the optical length of a light path, defined as the geometrical length times the refractive index of the medium in which the light is moving, is the equivalent distance which the light would have traveled in a vacuum.

Solution: Suppose that light travels a distance ℓ in a medium of refractive index n. The optical length is then

$$\text{optical length} = n\ell$$

and, since $n = c/v$

$$\text{optical length} = c\ell/v$$

Here c and v are the speeds of light in vacuum and the medium, respectively.

But light travels with constant velocity in the medium, and hence $\ell/v = t$, where t is the time taken to traverse the light path.

$$n\ell = \frac{c\ell}{v} = ct = \ell_0$$

where ℓ_0 is the distance the light would have traveled at velocity c, that is, in a vacuum. Thus the optical length is the equivalent distance which the light would have traveled in the same time in a vacuum.

• PROBLEM 859

Describe the phenomena of the critical angle in optics. What is the critical angle for a glass-air interface, if the index of refraction of glass with respect to air is 1.33?

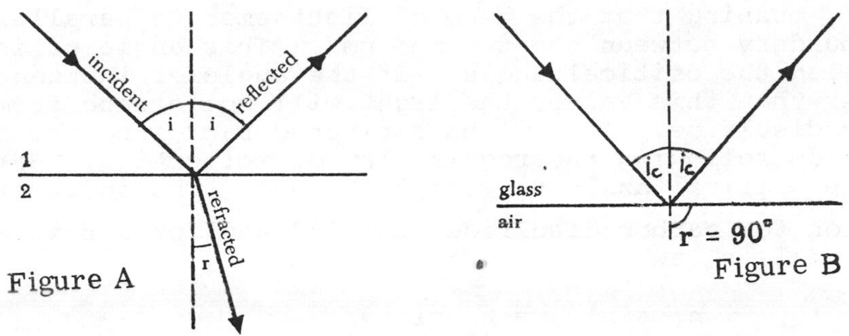

Solution: Consider two media, 1 and 2, such that the index of refraction of 1 with respect to 2 is less than unity, as shown in Fig. A. That is, medium 1 is "denser", and the angle of refraction will be greater than the angle incidence.

In general part of the incident ray is reflected and part refracted. As the angle of incidence is increased, the angle of refraction will increase until $r = 90°$. At this critical angle, i_c, (see Fig. B), we have

$$\frac{\sin i_c}{\sin 90°} = \sin i_c = n_{21}$$

At the critical angle, and for values of i greater than i_c, refraction cannot occur and all the energy of the incident beam appears in the reflected beam. This phenomenon is called total internal reflection.

The index of refraction of air with respect to glass is

$$\frac{1}{1.33} = 0.75.$$

The critical angle for a glass-air interference is therefore

$$\sin i_c = 0.75$$

or

$$i_c = 48.6°$$

Thus, for angles of incidence $\geq 48{,}6°$, total internal reflection will occur for a glass-air combination similar to the one shown in the figure.

• PROBLEM 860

What is the critical angle between carbon disulfide and air?

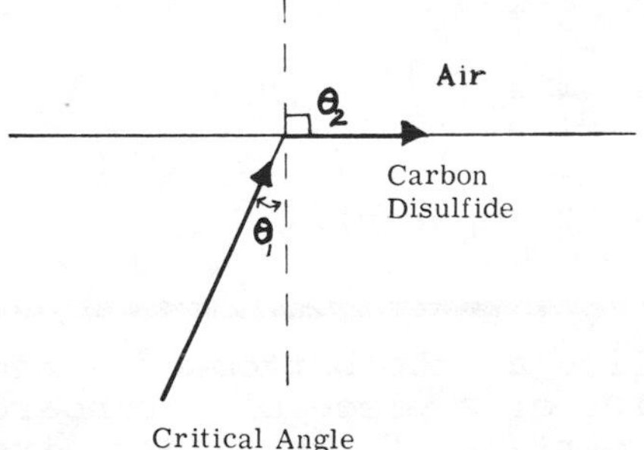

Critical Angle

Solution. Carbon disulfide is a more optically dense material than air. Therefore, as a beam of light passes from carbon disulfide to air, the angle of refraction is larger than the angle of incidence. There is an angle of incidence smaller than 90° for which the angle of refraction is equal to 90°, meaning that the beam of light emerges parallel to the boundary between the two mediums. This angle of incidence is called the critical angle. If the angle of incidence is greater than this value, the light will not escape from the carbon disulfide. It will be reflected back into the carbon disulfide following the regular law of reflection. Solving for the critical angle θ_1, let θ_2 be 90°. The index of refraction for carbon disulfide is 1.643 and for air it is 1.00 Using Snell's law

$$n_1 \sin \theta_1 = n_2 \sin \theta_2$$

$$1.643 \sin \theta_1 = 1.00 \sin 90°$$

$$\sin \theta_1 = \frac{1.00}{1.643} = 0.608$$

$$\theta_1 = 37.4°.$$

• PROBLEM 861

What is the critical angle of incidence for a ray of light passing from glass into water. Assume n_{glass} = 1. 50 and n_{water} = 1.33

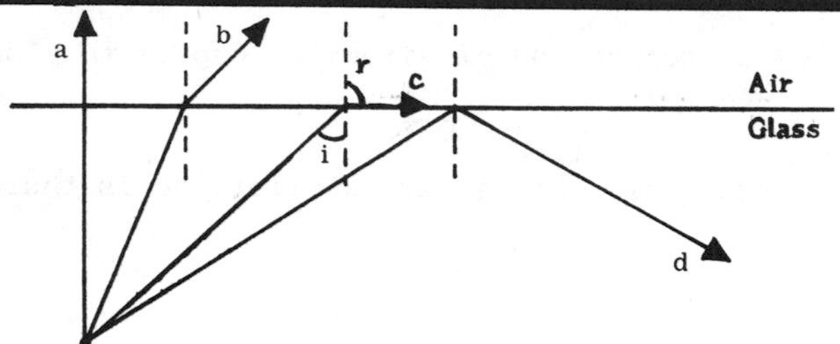

Solution: When light passes from a more optically dense to a less optically dense medium, there is an angle of incidence i, called the critical angle, at which the light ray (ray c of the diagram) will be refracted parallel to the interface of the media. The angle of refraction r will be 90° in this case. Therefore, by Snell's Law, $n_1 \sin i = n_2 \sin r$. Also critical angle of incidence means $\sin r = 1$.

$$\therefore \quad \sin i = \frac{n_2}{n_1} = \frac{1.33}{1.50} = .887$$

$$\therefore i_c = 62° \text{ (approx)}.$$

• PROBLEM 862

A small pebble lies at the bottom of a tank of water. Determine the size of a piece of cardboard which, when floating on the surface of the water, directly above the pebble, totally obscures the latter from view.

Solution: We can consider the pebble as a point source of light. If the cardboard is big enough for its purpose, then all rays of light from the pebble which would be

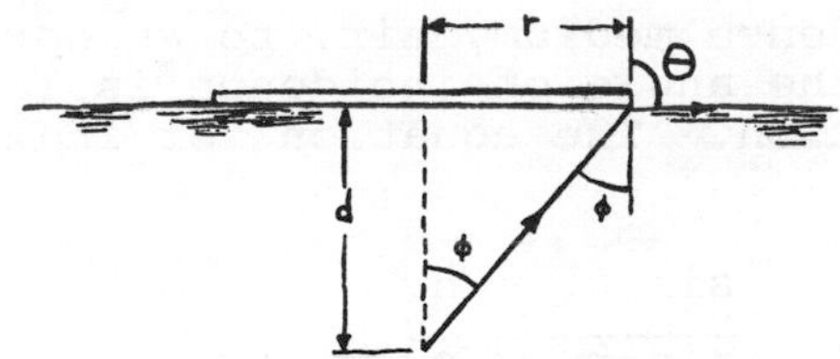

refracted into the air at the surface must be blocked off by the cardboard, and all rays striking the surface of the water outside the cardboard must be totally internally reflected (see figure).

The cardboard must obviously be circular, and, if its center is directly above the pebble, a ray of light striking the edge of the cardboard must do so at an angle $\phi \geq$ the critical angle.

By Snell's Law,

$$n_w \sin \phi = n_a \sin \theta$$

where ϕ is the angle of incidence, θ is the angle of refraction, n_a is the index of refraction of air $(n_a = 1)$ and n_w is that of water. Then,

$$n_w \sin \phi = 1$$

because $\theta = 90°$ to satisfy the requirement that ϕ be a critical angle. Therefore, using the figure

$$n_w \frac{r}{\sqrt{r^2 + d^2}} = 1$$

$$r^2 + d^2 = n_w^2 r^2 \qquad \text{or} \qquad r^2 = \frac{d^2}{n_w^2 - 1}$$

$$r = \frac{24 \text{ ft}}{\sqrt{\frac{16}{9} - 1}} = \frac{72 \text{ ft}}{\sqrt{7}} = 27.2 \text{ ft.}$$

• PROBLEM 863

A beam of light in air falls on a glass surface at an angle of incidence of 20.0°. Its angle of refraction in the glass is 12.4°. What is the index of refraction of the glass?

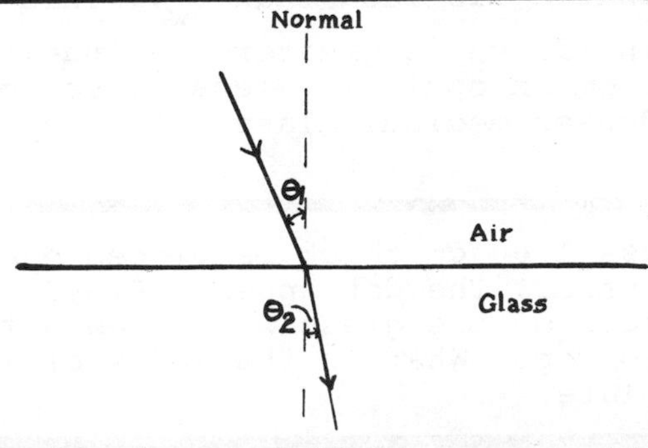

Solution. Since the beam of light passes obliquely from an

optically less dense medium, air, to an optically denser medium, glass, the angle of incidence is larger than the angle of refraction. The equation for indices of refraction is

$$\frac{\sin \theta_1}{\sin \theta_2} = \frac{n_2}{n_1}.$$

Since the index of refraction for air is approximately one, this reduces to

$$n_2 = \frac{\sin \theta_1}{\sin \theta_2} = \frac{\sin 20.0°}{\sin 12.4°} = \frac{0.342}{0.215} = 1.58.$$

• **PROBLEM 864**

A ray of light in water is incident on a plate of crown glass at an angle of 45°. What is the angle of refraction for the ray in the glass?

Solution. The indices of refraction are inversely proportional to the sine of their respective angles, or, by Snell's law,

$$n_g \sin \theta_g = n_w \sin \theta_w.$$

From a table,

$$n_g = 1.517$$

$$n_w = 1.333.$$

Substituting these values in the equation above,

$$1.517 \sin \theta_g = 1.137 \sin 45°.$$

Solving for θ_g, the angle of refraction in the glass,

$$\sin \theta_g = \frac{1.333 \times 0.707}{1.517} = 0.624$$

$$\theta_g = 38.6°.$$

Notice that θ_g is less than θ_w. This occurs because the angle of incidence is greater than the angle of refraction when passing from an optically less dense medium, water, to an optically denser medium, glass.

• **PROBLEM 865**

A plate of glass 1.00 cm thick is placed over a dot on a sheet of paper. The dot appears 0.640 cm below the upper surface of the glass when viewed from above through a microscope. What is the index of refraction of the glass plate?

Solution: The eye records the direction from which a

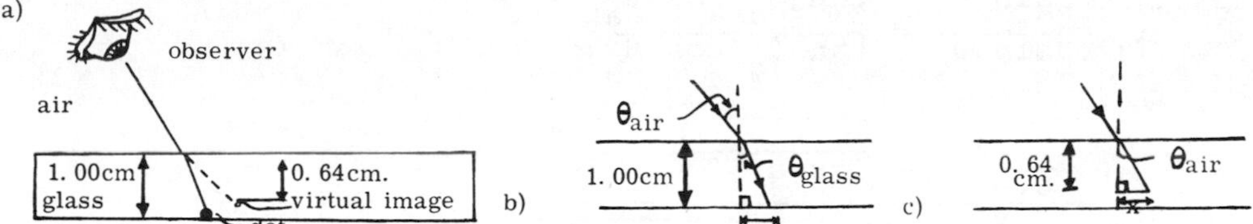

light ray enters it as though it has traveled in a straight line from the source. It cannot compensate for refraction of the light. Therefore, the observer sees the dot 0.640 cm below the upper surface of the glass when in actuality it is 1.00 cm below the surface.

Assuming the index of refraction of air to be one (n_{air} = 1.00029), we have from Snell's law,

$$n_{glass} \sin \theta_{glass} = n_{air} \sin \theta_{air} \tag{1}$$

$$n_g = \frac{n_g}{n_a} = \frac{\sin \theta_a}{\sin \theta_g} \quad \text{since } n_a \approx 1 \tag{2}$$

The sine function can be expressed as

$$\sin \theta = \tan \theta \cos \theta \tag{3}$$

We know from the figure that

$$\tan \theta_a = \frac{x}{0.64 \text{ cm}}$$

$$\tan \theta_g = \frac{x}{1.00 \text{ cm}}$$

From the trigonometric relation

$$\cos \theta = \sqrt{1 - \sin^2 \theta}$$

we have $\cos \theta_a = \sqrt{1 - \sin^2 \theta_a}$

$$\cos \theta_g = \sqrt{1 - \sin^2 \theta_g} \tag{4}$$

From equation (1),

$$\sin \theta_g = \frac{n_a}{n_g} \sin \theta_a \tag{5}$$

Substituting equation (5) into equation (4),

$$\cos \theta_g = \sqrt{1 - \left(\frac{n_a}{n_g}\right)^2 \sin^2 \theta_a}$$

Using the values found for the cosines and tangents of the angles and equation (3), substitute into equation (2)

$$n_g = \frac{\sin\theta_a}{\sin\theta_g} = \frac{\tan\theta_a \cos\theta_a}{\tan\theta_g \cos\theta_g}$$

$$= \frac{\dfrac{x}{0.64\ \text{cm}}\sqrt{1-\sin^2\theta_a}}{\dfrac{x}{1.00\ \text{cm}}\sqrt{1-\left(\dfrac{n_a}{n_g}\right)^2 \sin^2\theta_a}} \qquad (6)$$

The observer looks at the dot through a microscope. This means that he looks at the dot from directly above and θ_a must be very small. We can then make the approximation

$$\sin\theta_a \approx \sin 0° = 0$$

Substituting this value in equation (6), we find

$$n_g = \frac{\dfrac{x}{0.64\ \text{cm}}\sqrt{1-0}}{\dfrac{x}{1.00\ \text{cm}}\sqrt{1-\left(\dfrac{n_a}{n_g}\right)^2 (0)}}$$

$$= \frac{1.00}{0.64} = 1.57$$

• PROBLEM 866

One end of a cylindrical glass rod is ground to a hemispherical surface of radius R = 2 cm. An object of height h_0 = 1 mm. is placed on the axis of the rod, p = 8 cm to the left of the vertex. Find the image distance q and the image height h_I (a) when the rod is in air, (b) the rod is in water. The indices of refraction of glass and water are 1.50 and 1.33 respectively.

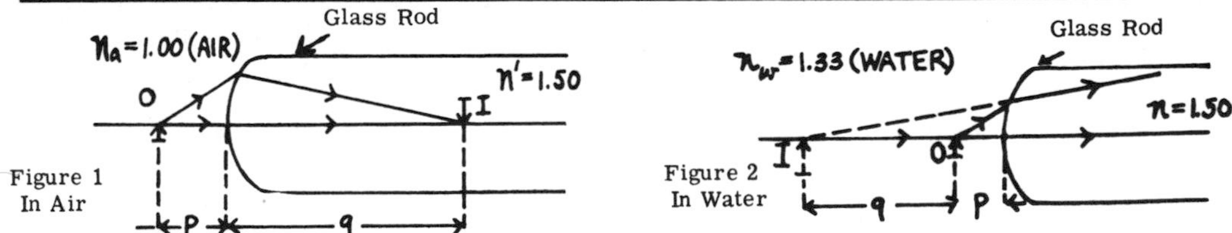

Solution: (a) The optical equation for the spherical end of the rod (which is a spherical refracting surface), is given by

$$\frac{n}{p} + \frac{n'}{q} = \frac{n' - n}{R}$$

where the object is in the region of refraction index n, the rays are going from the region of refractive index n to the region of refractive index n', and R is the curvature of the refractive surface. The radius R for the glass hemisphere has a positive sign because the center of curvature of the glass surface lies inside the glass, which is the real image region (see Fig. 1). R is negative when the curvature center lies in the virtual image region.

As shown in Fig. 1 above, p = +8 cm, R = +2 cm. Therefore, the image distance q is obtained as

$$\frac{1.5}{q} + \frac{1}{8\text{ cm}} = \frac{1.5 - 1}{2\text{cm}}$$

or

$$q = + 12 \text{ cm}$$

q is positive, i.e., the image is formed at the right of the vertex of the glass surface and is real.

The magnification m for this problem is given by

$$m = - \frac{n}{n'} \frac{q}{p}$$

$$= - \frac{1}{1.5} \times \frac{12 \text{ cm}}{8 \text{ cm}} = -1$$

that is, the image has the same height as the object, but is inverted,

$$h_I = -h_0 = - 0.1 \text{ cm}.$$

(b) When the rod is in water, the optical equation yields for q (Fig.2)

$$\frac{1.5}{q} + \frac{1.33}{8\text{ cm}} = \frac{1.50 - 1.33}{2\text{ cm}}$$

or

$$q = - 18 \text{ cm}.$$

Since q is negative, the image is formed in the water and is imaginary. For magnification, we have

$$m = - \frac{1.33}{1.5} \times \frac{-18 \text{ cm}}{8 \text{ cm}} = 1.99 ,$$

and the image is erect and has a height

$$h_I = 1.99\, h_0 = 0.99 \text{ cm}.$$

• PROBLEM 867

A man standing symmetrically in front of a plane mirror with beveled edges can see three images of his eyes when he is 3 ft from the mirror (see figure (a)). The mirror is silvered on the back, is 2 ft 6 in. wide, and is made of glass of refractive index 1.54. What is the angle of bevel of the edges?

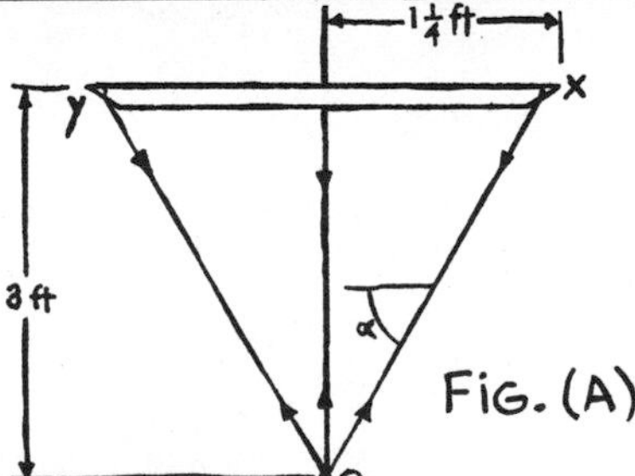

FIG. (A)

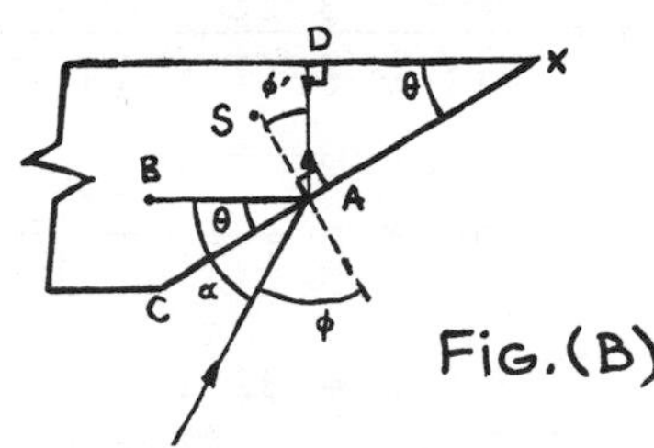

FIG. (B)

Solution: The man can only see an image of his eyes if light leaves them, strikes the mirror, and is reflected back along the same path. The central image is thus formed by light traversing the perpendicular from his eyes to the mirror. The outer images are formed by light striking the beveled edges at the point A (see figure (b)) at an angle of incidence ϕ such that the angle of refraction ϕ' makes the refracted ray strike the silvered surface normally. This must be the case if the ray of light is to leave the beveled edge by the same path with which it arrived. The angle ϕ' lies between the normal to the beveled edge and the normal to the back surface. Since $\sphericalangle SAX = 90°$ (see figure (b))

$$\phi' + \sphericalangle DAX = 90°$$

But $\sphericalangle DAX = 90° - \theta$

Hence $\phi' = 90° - 90° + \theta = \theta$

Draw BA, a construction line at A parallel to the back of the mirror. Angle BAC is also equal to θ.

But by Snell's Law $n_1 \sin \phi = n \sin \phi'$, where n_1 is the refractive index of air ($n_1 = 1$) and n is that of glass. Then $\sin \phi = n \sin \phi' = n \sin \theta$. Also $\alpha = \theta + (90 - \phi)$. (See figure (b)).

$$\sin[90 - (\alpha - \theta)] = n \sin \theta.$$

But $\sin (90 - \psi) = \cos \psi$ and

$$\cos (\alpha - \theta) = n \sin \theta.$$

By the trigonometric relation for double angles

$$\cos \alpha \cos \theta + \sin \alpha \sin \theta = n \sin \theta.$$

$$\cos \alpha + \sin \alpha \tan \theta = n \tan \theta$$

$$\cos \alpha = \tan \theta \,[n - \sin \alpha]$$

$$\tan \theta = \frac{\cos \alpha}{n - \sin \alpha}$$

Looking at figure (a)

$$\cos \alpha = \frac{1\tfrac{1}{4} \text{ ft}}{\sqrt{(1\tfrac{1}{4} \text{ ft})^2 + (3 \text{ ft})^2}} = \frac{5}{13}$$

$$\sin \alpha = \frac{3 \text{ ft}}{\sqrt{(1\tfrac{1}{4} \text{ ft})^2 + (3 \text{ ft})^2}} = \frac{12}{13}$$

whence $$\tan \theta = \frac{5/13}{1.54 - (12/13)} = 0.625.$$

$$\theta = 32°.$$

• PROBLEM 868

In hunting a submarine, two ships A and B, separated by 3000 ft, find a sonar echo on the line between them but 30° from vertical for A and 60° for B. However, 200 ft below the surface, the water temperature changes suddenly so that the velocity of sound in the depths is 0.9 that in the shallows. (a) For what depth will the depth charges be set, if the ship captains do not know of this? (b) What is the actual depth of the submarine? (c) What will the ship captains think the submarine's horizontal distance from ship A is? (d)

What is the submarine's actual horizontal distance from ship A?

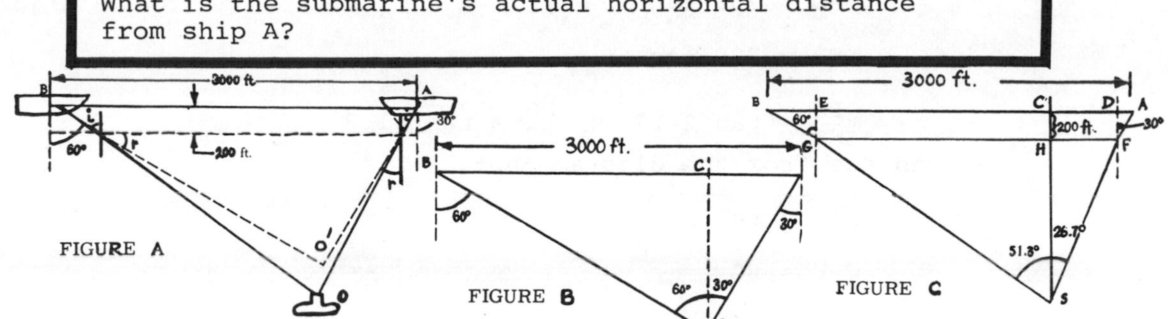

Solution: Figure (a) shows the actual paths of the sonar waves represented by solid lines, and their apparent paths as broken lines. The submarine will appear to the ship captains to be at point 0' when in reality it is at point 0, as shown.

(a) First we calculate the apparent depth. From triangle ABS, in figure (b):

$$AC + CB = 3000$$

$$\frac{AC}{CS} = \tan 30$$

$$\frac{CB}{CS} = \tan 60$$

$$AC + CB = CS\ (\tan 30 + \tan 60)$$

$$CS = \frac{AC + CB}{\tan 30 + \tan 60}$$

$$= \frac{3000 \text{ ft}}{0.577 + 1.732}$$

$$= 1310 \text{ ft}$$

since $\tan 30 = 0.577$

$\tan 60 = 1.732$

(b) In actual fact the sound waves are refracted at a depth of 200 ft. By definition, the refraction is such that:

$$\frac{\sin i}{\sin r} = \frac{v_s}{v_d} = \frac{v_s}{0.9\ v_s} = \frac{1}{0.9}$$

where i is the angle that the path the sonar wave takes in the shallow water makes with an imaginary line normal to the interface between shallow and deep water. The letter r stands for a similar angle for the path in deep water, and v_s and v_d represent the velocities of sound in the shallow and deep water, respectively.

If $i = 30°$, then $r = 26.7°$ and if $i = 60°$, $r = 51.3°$. We see from figure (c) that:

$$AD + DC' + C'E + EB = 3000 \text{ ft}$$

$$AD = 200 \tan 30$$

$$EB = 200 \tan 60$$

$$\frac{FH}{HS} = \tan 26.7 \qquad \frac{HG}{HS} = \tan 51.3$$

We can see from the diagram that:

$$DC' = FH$$

$$C'E = HG$$

Thus, from the first equation in the above group:

$$AD + FH + HG + EB = 3000 \text{ ft.}$$

$$200 \tan 30 + HS(\tan 26.7 + \tan 51.3) + 200 \tan 60 = 3000$$

$$HS = \frac{3000 - 115 - 346}{0.503 + 1.248}$$

$$= 1450 \text{ ft}$$

The actual depth of the submarine is 200 + 1450 = 1650 ft.

The horizontal distance of the submarine from ship A will appear to be AC in figure (b):

$$AC = 1310 \tan 30 = 755 \text{ ft}$$

The submarine's actual horizontal distance is AC' in figure (c):

$$AC' = 200 \tan 30 + 1450 \tan 26.7$$

$$= 115 + 730 = 845 \text{ ft}$$

Thus without knowledge of the water temperature the depth charges will be shallow by 340 ft and off in a horizontal direction by 90 ft. That is, the explosion will be 350 ft away from the submarine, a near miss rather than a direct hit.

PRISMS

• PROBLEM 869

A ray of light enters the face BA of a right-angled prism of refracting material at grazing incidence. It emerges from the adjacent face AC at an angle θ to the normal. If ϕ_c is the critical angle for the material, show that $\sin \theta = \cot \phi_c$. (See figure.)

Will a ray always emerge from AC? If not, explain what happens, and deduce for what values of the refractive index of the material the ray actually emerges.

Solution: Since the ray strikes the prism at grazing

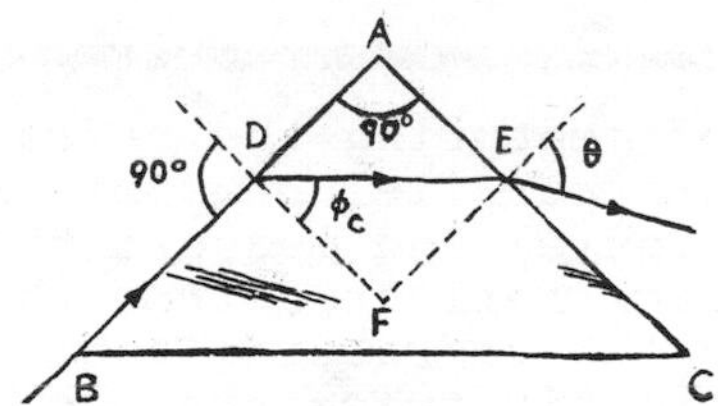

incidence, the refracted ray DE must enter at the critical angle ϕ_c. Now angles DAE, ADF, and AEF are all right angles. This follows because the prism is right-angled, and also since DF and FE are normals to the surfaces BA and AC. Thus DFE must be a right angle also, since the four angles of a quadrilateral (ADFE) add up to 360°.

The angles of a triangle must add up to 180°, and therefore $\angle DEF = 90° - \phi_c$. (1)

Applying Snell's law to the refraction at face AC, we have $n_1 \sin \angle DEF = n_2 \sin \theta$, where n_1 and n_2 are the refractive indices of the prism and air, respectively. Since the medium to the right of face AC is air, $n_2 = 1$, whence

$$n_1 \sin \angle DEF = \sin \theta. \quad (2)$$

At surface BA, we obtain

$$n_2 \sin 90° = n_1 \sin \phi_c$$

or $(1)(1) = n_1 \sin \phi_c$

Then $$\sin \phi_c = 1/n. \quad (3)$$

Using (3) and (1) in (2)

$$\left(\frac{1}{\sin \phi_c}\right)(\sin (90 - \phi_c)) = \sin \theta$$

But $\sin(90 - \phi_c) = \cos \phi_c$, whence

$$\frac{\cos \phi_c}{\sin \phi_c} = \cot \phi_c = \sin \theta$$

The ray will emerge from AC only if $\angle DEF$ is less than the critical angle. If it is greater, total internal reflection occurs and the ray is directed along AC.

Thus, for the ray to emerge, $\angle DEF < \phi_c$. That is, $90° - \phi_c < \phi_c$ or $\phi_c > 45°$. Using (3)

$$\therefore \quad \sin \phi_c = \frac{1}{n_1} > \sin 45° = \frac{1}{\sqrt{2}}. \therefore n_1 < \sqrt{2}.$$

• PROBLEM 870

The easiest method of measuring the refracting angle of a prism is to direct a parallel beam of light on to the angle (vertex A in figure) and measure the angular separation of the beams reflected from the two sides of the prism containing the refracting angle. Show that this angular separation is twice the angle of the prism.

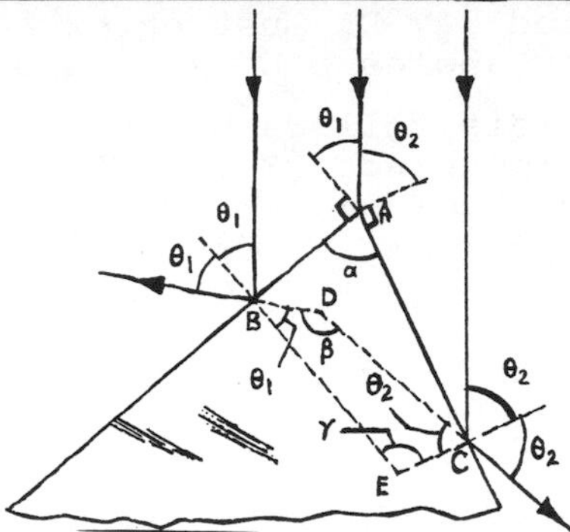

Solution: Consider three incoming rays, all parallel and striking the prism at points A, B and C. Erect normals to AB at A and B and to AC at A and C. Designate the angles as in the diagram.

The rays striking at B and C are reflected according to the laws of optics, as shown and the angle between the reflected rays is β. E is the point at which the normals at B and C meet.

The sum of the angles of quadrilateral ABEC is 360°. Since ∡ ABE and ∡ ACE are each 90°,

$$\alpha + \gamma = 180°. \qquad (1)$$

In the quadrilateral BDCE,

$$\beta + \gamma + \theta_1 + \theta_2 = 360°. \qquad (2)$$

Since two of the angles surrounding A are right angles,

$$\alpha + \theta_1 + \theta_2 = 180°. \qquad (3)$$

Add Eqs. (1) and (3)

$$2\alpha + \gamma + \theta_1 + \theta_2 = 360° \qquad (4)$$

Subtract (2) from (4)

$$2\alpha - \beta = 0$$

or $2\alpha = \beta$

Thus, the angle between the reflected beams, β, is twice the refracting angle of the prism, α.

• PROBLEM 871

A parallel beam of light falls normally on the first face of a prism of small angle α. At the second face it is partly transmitted and partly reflected, the reflected beam striking the first face again and emerging from it in a direction making an angle of $6^\circ 30'$ with the reversed direction of the incident beam. The refracted beam is found to have undergone a deviation of $1^\circ 15'$ from the original direction. Calculate the refractive index of the glass and the angle of the prism.

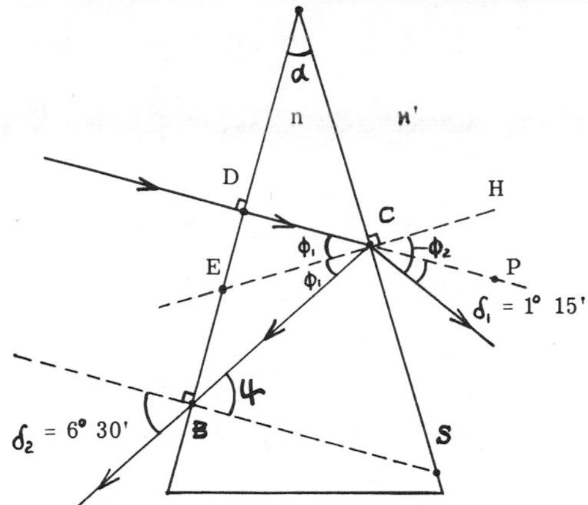

Solution: We must first solve for the refractive index, n, of the prism glass. Applying Snell's Law to the refraction at point c (see figure), we obtain

$$n \sin \phi_1 = n' \sin \phi_2$$

But n' is the refractive index of air, which is 1. Hence,

$$n \sin \phi_1 = \sin \phi_2 \tag{1}$$

Similarly, applying Snell's Law to the refraction at point B

$$n \sin \psi = \sin \delta_2 \tag{2}$$

Now, we must relate ϕ_1, ϕ_2 and ψ to known quantities.

Note that $\measuredangle$ HCP = $\measuredangle$ DCE, since they are vertical angles. Therefore,

$$\measuredangle HCP = \measuredangle DCE$$

$$\phi_2 - \delta_1 = \phi_1$$

or

$$\delta_1 = \phi_2 - \phi_1 \tag{3}$$

Noting that DC and BS are parallel,

$$\psi = 2\phi_1 \tag{4}$$

We need one more equation relating any of O_1, O_2 and ψ to α. $\measuredangle ACD = 90^\circ - \alpha$. But

$$\measuredangle ACD + \phi_1 = 90^\circ$$

Hence

$$90^\circ - \alpha + \phi_1 = 90^\circ$$

and

$$\phi_1 = \alpha \tag{5}$$

If all the angles $(\phi_1, \phi_2, \psi, \delta_1, \delta_2)$ are small, we may approximate the sine of an angle by the angle itself. Using (1) and (2)

$$n \phi_1 \approx \phi_2$$

$$n \psi \approx \delta_2 \tag{6}$$

Taking the ratio of each equation in (6)

$$\frac{\varphi_1}{\psi} \approx \frac{\varphi_2}{\delta_2}$$

Hence,

$$\varphi_1 \approx \frac{\psi\phi_2}{\delta_2}$$

Using (4)

$$\varphi_1 \approx \frac{2\varphi_1\varphi_2}{\delta_2}$$

or

$$\delta_2 = 2\varphi_2 \qquad (7)$$

Hence, solving (3) for φ_1

$$\varphi_1 = \varphi_2 - \delta_1$$

Since

$$\varphi_2 = \frac{\delta_2}{2}$$

$$\varphi_1 = \frac{\delta_2}{2} - \delta_1 \qquad (8)$$

Solving the first equation of (6) for n

$$n \approx \frac{\varphi_2}{\varphi_1}$$

with (7) and (8)

$$n = \frac{\delta_2/2}{\frac{\delta_2}{2} - \delta_1} = \frac{1}{1 - \frac{2\delta_1}{\delta_2}}$$

Using the given data

$$n = \frac{1}{1 - \frac{2(1^\circ 15')}{(6^\circ 30')}}$$

$$n = \frac{1}{1 - \frac{2(1\ 1/4^\circ)}{(6\ 1/2^\circ)}}$$

$$n = \frac{1}{1 - \frac{5/2}{13/2}} = \frac{1}{1 - 5/13}$$

$$n = \frac{13}{13 - 5} = \frac{13}{8} = 1.625$$

Furthermore, from (5)

$$\alpha = \varphi_1$$

But, equation (8) tells us that

$$\alpha = \varphi_1 = \frac{\delta 2}{2} - \delta_1 = \frac{6^\circ 30'}{2} - 1^\circ 15'$$

Hence $\quad \alpha = 3^\circ 15' - 1^\circ 15' = 2^\circ$

CHAPTER 28

LENSES & OPTICAL INSTRUMENTS

• **PROBLEM** 872

An object is 24 inches from a convex lens whose focal length is 8 inches. Where will the image be?

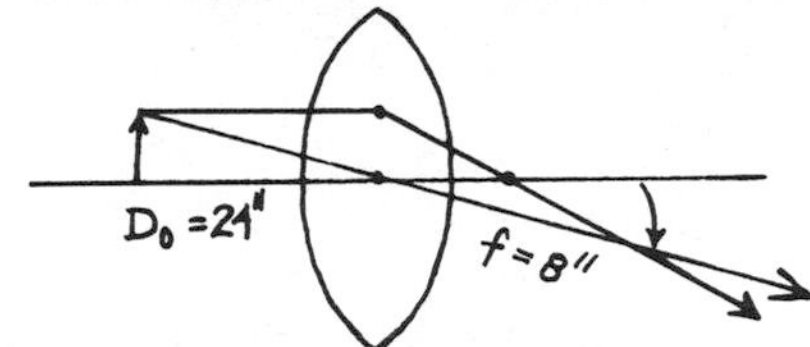

Solution: The use of a ray diagram is helpful here.

We can see that the image is real (on the far side of the lens and inverted).

We then solve mathematically:

D_0 is 24 inches and f is 8 inches. Substituting in

$$\frac{1}{D_0} + \frac{1}{D_I} = \frac{1}{f}$$

$$\frac{1}{24 \text{ in.}} + \frac{1}{D_I} = \frac{1}{8 \text{ in.}}$$

Solving

$$D_I = 12 \text{ in.}$$

Hence

$$D_I = 12 \text{ in.}$$

which means that the image is 12 inches from the lens on the side away from the object.

• **PROBLEM** 873

If an object is in a position 8 cm in front of a lens of focal length 16 cm, where and how large is the image? (See figure.)

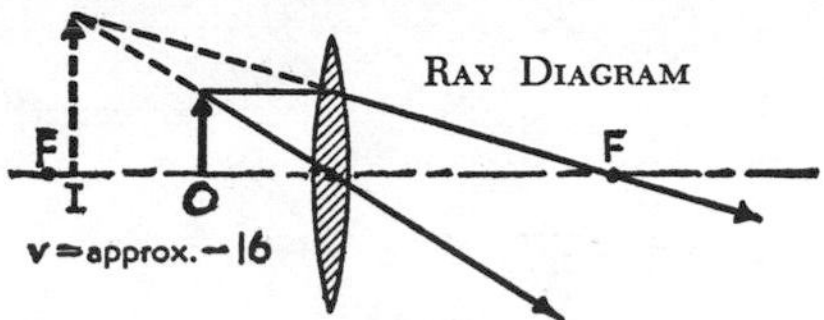

Solution: We refer here to the relationship

$$\frac{1}{0} + \frac{1}{i} = \frac{1}{f}$$

Here, the image distance, i, is the unknown. The object distance, 0, is 8 cm, while the focal length, f, is 16 cm. Thus,

$$\frac{1}{0} + \frac{1}{i} = \frac{1}{f}$$

$$\frac{1}{8\text{ cm}} + \frac{1}{i} = \frac{1}{16\text{ cm}}$$

$$\frac{1}{i} = \frac{1}{16\text{ cm}} - \frac{1}{8\text{ cm}}$$

$$\frac{1}{i} = -\frac{1}{16\text{ cm}}$$

$$i = -16\text{ cm}$$

This means that the image is 16 cm in front of the lens.

To calculate the image size, we first calculate the magnification. Thus,

$$m = \frac{-i}{0} = \frac{+16}{8} = 2$$

This means that the image is erect, therefore virtual, and twice as large as the object, or 16 cm high.

• PROBLEM 874

An object is 4 inches from a concave lens whose focal length is - 12 inches. Where will the image be?

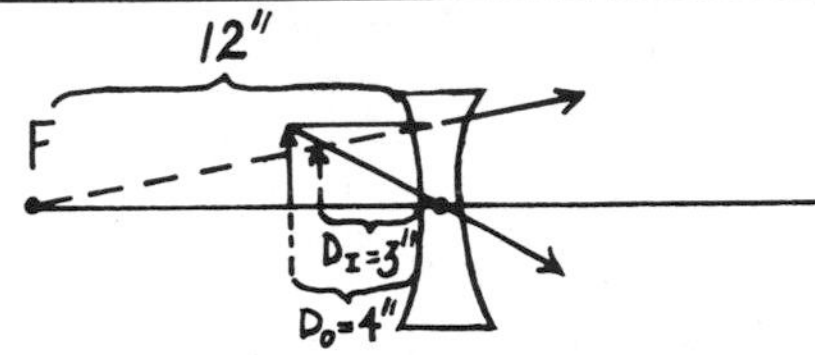

Solution: It may be useful to construct a ray-diagram first (see diagram). We draw two rays - one parallel to the axis and one through the center of the lens.

From the diagram it can be seen that the image is virtual and that it is smaller than the object.

We now attempt a mathematical solution:

D_0 is 4 inches and f is - 12 inches. Substituting in

$$\frac{1}{D_0} + \frac{1}{D_I} = \frac{1}{f}$$

$$\frac{1}{4\text{ in.}} + \frac{1}{D_I} = \frac{1}{-12\text{ in.}}$$

Solving $D_I = -3$ in. Hence $D_I = -3$ in.

which means that since D_I is negative, the image is 3 inches from the lens on the same side on the lens as the object and is virtual.

• PROBLEM 875

A converging lens with a focal length of 3 m forms an image of an object placed 9 m from it. Find the position of the image and the magnification.

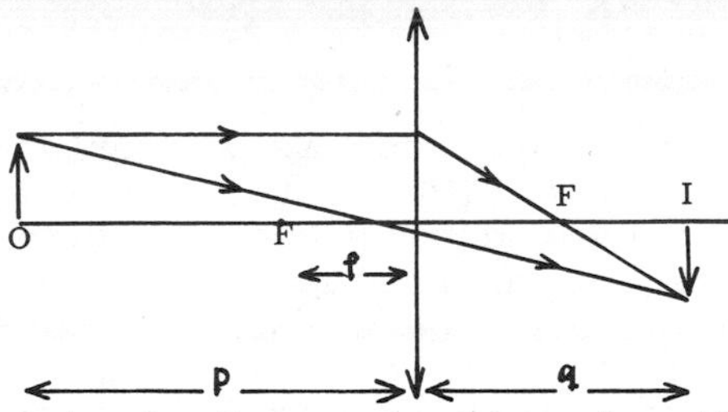

Solution: The simple lens equation for the converging lens of this problem is

$$\frac{1}{f} = \frac{1}{p} + \frac{1}{q}$$

where f, p and q are respectively the focal length of the lens and the distances of the object and the image from the lens. The image is real and inverted (see the figure). Substituting the given values in the above equation, we get

$$\frac{1}{q} = \frac{1}{f} - \frac{1}{p} = \frac{1}{3m} - \frac{1}{9m} = \frac{2}{9}m^{-1} \qquad \text{and}$$

$$q = \frac{9}{2}m = 4.5m.$$

Since the value of q is positive, the image occurs on the right side of the lens. The magnification M is

$$M = \frac{q}{p} = \frac{4.5\ m}{9\ m} = 0.5$$

so the image is one-half as high as the object.

• PROBLEM 876

A converging lens of 5.0 cm focal length is used as a simple magnifier, producing a virtual image 25 cm from the eye. How far from the lens should the object be placed? What is the magnification?

Solution. The image produced is virtual, on the same side of the lens as the object. Therefore, the distance q of the image from the lens is negative. Using the general lens equation

$$\frac{1}{p} + \frac{1}{q} = \frac{1}{f}; \quad \frac{1}{p} = \frac{1}{f} - \frac{1}{q}.$$

Solve for p and substitute values.

$$p = \frac{fq}{q - f} = \frac{5.0\ cm(-25\ cm)}{-25\ cm - 5.0\ cm} = 4.2\ cm.$$

Using absolute values to find the magnification,

$$M = \left|\frac{q}{p}\right| = \left|\frac{-25\ \text{cm}}{4.2\ \text{cm}}\right| = 5.9.$$

Since the image is on the same side of the lens as the object, the light has been focused in a way that produces an erect image. In a real image, which is seen on the opposite side of the lens in relation to the object, the object is inverted.

• PROBLEM 877

The length of a microscope tube is 10 centimeters. The focal length of the objective is 0.5 centimeters and the focal length of the eyepiece is 2 centimeters. What is the magnifying power of the microscope?

Solution: The magnification of this compound microscope is equal to the product of the magnifications of its component lenses or

$$M = M_1 \times M_2$$

which in this case is

$$\frac{25\ \text{cm}}{f_0} \times \frac{10\ \text{cm}}{f_E}.$$

We use 25 cm since in most cases we want the image to be formed at that distance from the ocular. Therefore, the solution is:

$$\frac{25L}{f_0 f_E} = \frac{25 \times 10}{0.5 \times 2} = 250$$

• PROBLEM 878

The lens system of a certain portrait camera may be taken as equivalent to a thin converging lens of focal length 10.0 in. How far behind the lens should the film be located to receive the image of a person seated 50.0 in. from the lens? How large will the image be in comparison with the object?

Solution. The general equation for thin lenses states

$$\frac{1}{p} + \frac{1}{q} = \frac{1}{f}$$

where p is the distance of the object, in this case the person, in front of the lens, and q is the distance between the image formed and the lens. The focal length is represented by f. All distances are measured with respect to the optical center of the lens. This center is defined as the point through which light can pass without being bent. Since the lens is a converging one, it is convex. This means that it is thicker at the center than at the edges. Substitute values in the above equation noting that q is positive when it is on the opposite side of the lens in relation to the object.

$$\frac{1}{q} = \frac{1}{10} - \frac{1}{50} = \frac{50 - 10}{(10)(50)} = \frac{4}{50}$$

$$q = \frac{50}{4} = 12.5 \text{ in.}$$

To find the magnification M, the equation $M = \frac{q}{p}$ can be used. Substituting,

$$M = \frac{12.5 \text{ in.}}{50.0 \text{ in.}} = 0.250.$$

The image will be one-fourth as large as the object.

• PROBLEM 879

In one of Edgar Allan Poe's stories, the author describes his terrifying experience of focusing a telescope on a distant hill and observing a "dragon" crawling up it. The punch line comes when he realizes that the dragon is an ant crawling up the windowpane through which he is observing the hill. Explain why this is impossible.

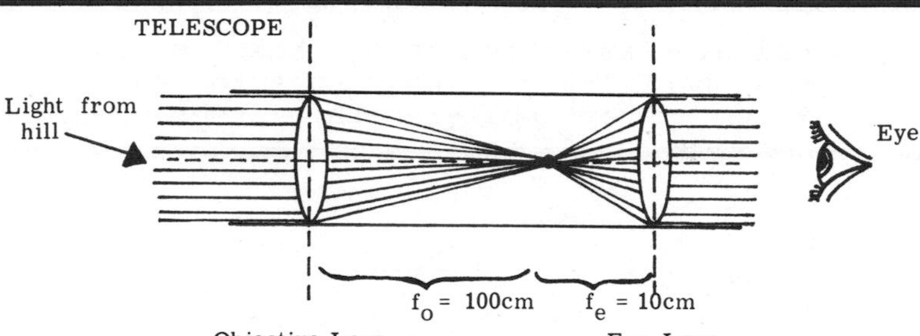

Solution: The distant hill is, for all practical purposes, at infinity. The objective lens of the telescope forms an image of it at its second focal point, which is also the first focal point of the eye lens (see figure). The final image is being viewed at infinity. Unless the ant is at infinity or at the second focal point of the objective lens, i.e., unless it occupies the same position as the object or the intermediate image, its final image cannot be at infinity also, and thus it will not be viewed at the same position as the image of the hill.

In fact, assuming that the telescope has focal lengths of 100 cm and 10 cm for its objective and eye lenses, respectively, and that the ant is 200 cm from the objective, we can work out where the final image of the ant lies.

Treating the objective, we find that

$$\frac{1}{s_1} + \frac{1}{s_1'} = \frac{1}{f_1}$$

where s_1 and s_1' are the object and image distances, respectively.

$$\frac{1}{200 \text{ cm}} + \frac{1}{s_1'} = \frac{1}{100 \text{ cm}}.$$

$$\frac{1}{s_1'} = \frac{2}{200 \text{ cm}} - \frac{1}{200 \text{ cm}} = \frac{1}{200 \text{ cm}}$$

$s_1' = 200$ cm.

The objective lens and eye lens are 110 cm apart (see figure) and the image formed by the objective will act as a virtual object for the eye lens. The object distance is $s_2 = (110 - 200)$ cm = - 90 cm.

$$-\frac{1}{90\text{ cm}} + \frac{1}{s_2'} = \frac{1}{10\text{ cm}}$$

$$\frac{1}{s_2'} = \frac{9}{90\text{ cm}} + \frac{1}{90\text{ cm}} = \frac{10}{90\text{ cm}}$$

or $\quad s_2' = 9$ cm

The final image is a real one on the observer's side of the eye lens and therefore Poe, when he looked through the telescope, could not see an image of the ant.

• PROBLEM 880

A certain farsighted person has a minimum distance of distinct vision of 150 cm. He wishes to read type at a distance of 25 cm. What focal-length glasses should he use?

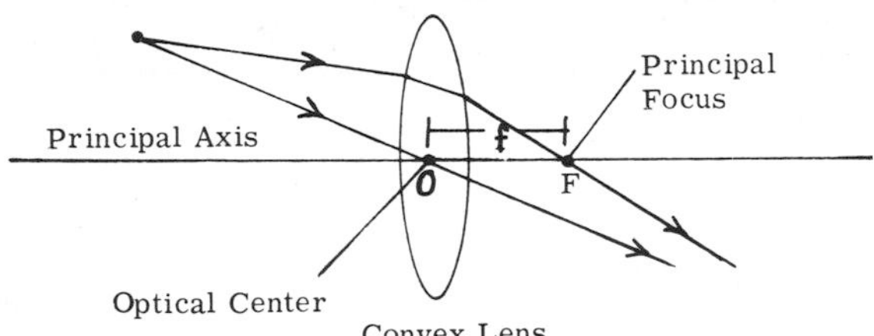

Solution. The principal axis is the line passing through the centers of curvature of the faces of the lens. The optical center is the point in the lens through which light can pass without being bent. All rays of light parallel to the principal axis pass through F, the point of principal focus. The distance f between F and the optical center is called the focal length of the lens. It is positive for converging, convex lenses, negative for concave, diverging lenses.

Since the person cannot see clearly objects closer than 150 cm, the lens must form a virtual image at that distance. Since the image is formed on the same side of the lens as the object, its distance q from the lens is negative.

$$p = 25\text{ cm}$$

$$q = -150\text{ cm}.$$

Substituting in the general equation for lenses,

$$\frac{1}{p} + \frac{1}{q} = \frac{1}{f}$$

$$\frac{1}{25\text{ cm}} + \frac{1}{-150\text{ cm}} = \frac{1}{f}$$

$$f = 30\text{ cm}.$$

Since f is positive, this lens is converging and is convex.

A microscope has an objective lens of 10.0 mm focal length and an eyepiece of 25.0 mm focal length. What is the distance between the lenses, and what is the magnification if the object is in sharp focus when it is 10.5 mm from the objective?

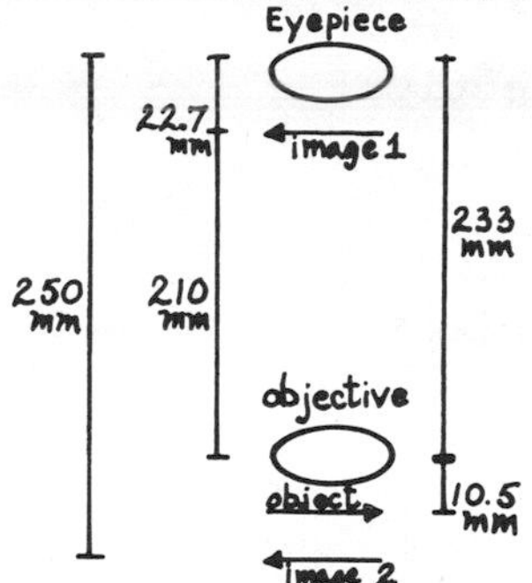

Solution: This is a compound microscope which uses converging lenses to produce large magnification. A short-focus lens, the objective, is placed near the object. It produces a real, inverted and magnified image. The eyepiece further magnifies this inverted image and produces a virtual image 250 mm from the eyepiece. This is the distance of most distinct vision.

Considering the image produced by the objective, we use the optics equation

$$\frac{1}{p} + \frac{1}{q} = \frac{1}{f}$$

p represents the distance of the object from the objective lens, q the distance of image 1 from the lens, and f is the focal length. Substituting,

$$\frac{1}{10.5 \text{ mm}} + \frac{1}{q} = \frac{1}{10.0 \text{ mm}}$$

$$q = 210 \text{ mm}$$

Therefore image 1 is 210 mm from the objective lens, and is real.

The eyepiece magnifies image 1 and produces a second virtual image 250 mm from the lens so as to provide most distinct vision. Since image 2 is virtual, on the same side of the lens as image 1, the distance q' of image 2 from the eyepiece is negative. Using the optics equation again,

$$\frac{1}{p'} + \frac{1}{q'} = \frac{1}{f'}$$

$$\frac{1}{p'} + \frac{1}{-250 \text{ mm}} = \frac{1}{25.0 \text{ mm}}$$

$$p' = 22.7 \text{ mm}$$

Therefore the eyepiece is 22.7 mm from image 1. The

distance between lenses is

$$q + p' = 210 \text{ mm} + 22.7 \text{ mm} = 233 \text{ mm} = 23.3 \text{ cm}$$

To find the magnification, first find the magnification produced by each lens using the equation

$$M = \frac{q}{p}$$

Magnification by objective:

$$M_0 = \frac{210 \text{ mm}}{10.5 \text{ mm}} = 20.0$$

Magnification by eyepiece:

$$M_e = \frac{-\ 250 \text{ mm}}{22.7 \text{ mm}} = -\ 11.0$$

Total magnification:

$$M = M_e M_0 = -\ 11.0 \times 20.0 = -\ 220$$

• PROBLEM 882

A projector with a lens of 40 cm focal length illuminates an object slide 4.0 cm long and throws an image upon a screen 20 m from the lens. What is the size of the projected image?

Solution: We use the lens formula $\frac{1}{p} = \frac{1}{f} - \frac{1}{q}$ where p is the object distance, f is the focal length of the lens, and q is the image distance. Upon substitution of the given values in the formula, we have

$$\frac{1}{p} = \frac{1}{40 \text{ cm}} - \frac{1}{20 \text{ m}}$$

In order to do the subtraction, we must change 20 m to centimeters. Since 1 m = 10^2 cm, 20 m = 2000 cm and

$$\frac{1}{p} = \frac{1}{40 \text{ cm}} - \frac{1}{2000 \text{ cm}}$$

$$\frac{1}{p} = \frac{2000 \text{ cm} - 40 \text{ cm}}{8000 \text{ cm}^2} = \frac{1960}{80000 \text{ cm}}$$

$$p = \frac{80000 \text{ cm}}{1960} = 40.8 \text{ cm}$$

This is the object distance.

The magnification M of the lens is defined as

$$M = \frac{q}{p} = \frac{2000 \text{ cm}}{40.8 \text{ cm}} = 49.$$

Given, then, an object 4 cm long, the size of its projected image is

$$\text{Image length} = M \times \text{object length}$$

$$= 49 \times 4 \text{ cm} \simeq 200 \text{ cm}$$

• PROBLEM 883

The frames in a home movie must be magnified 143 times before the picture formed on a screen 12 ft from the projection lens is large enough to please the family watching. What distance must the film be from the lens and what is the focal length of the lens?

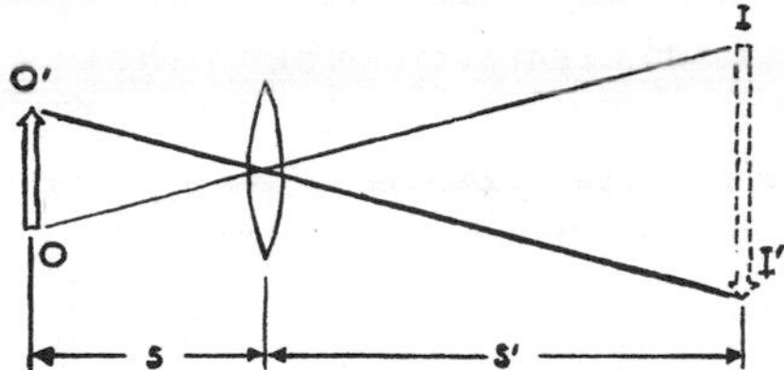

Solution: The magnification produced by the lens is given by

$$m = -\frac{s'}{s} = -\frac{12 \text{ ft}}{s} = -143.$$

where s' and s are the image and object distance, respectively. (The image must be inverted that is, the magnification is negative, since s must be positive (see figure)). Thus the film-to-lens distance is

$$s = \frac{12}{143} \text{ ft} = \frac{144}{143} \text{ in.} = 1.007 \text{ in.}$$

Applying the lens formula, we can obtain the focal length, since

$$\frac{1}{f} = \frac{1}{s} + \frac{1}{s'} = \frac{143}{12 \text{ ft}} + \frac{1}{12 \text{ ft}} = \frac{144}{12 \text{ ft}}$$

$$f = \frac{12}{144} \text{ ft} = 1 \text{ in.}$$

• PROBLEM 884

When an object is placed 20 in. from a certain lens, its virtual image is formed 10 in. from the lens. Determine the focal length and character of the lens.

Solution. Since the image is virtual, on the same side of the lens as the object, its distance from the lens, q, is negative. Substitution in the general equation for lenses yields

$$\frac{1}{p} + \frac{1}{q} = \frac{1}{f}$$

$$\frac{1}{20 \text{ in}} + \frac{1}{-10 \text{ in}} = \frac{1}{f}$$

$$\frac{1}{f} = \frac{-10 \text{ in} + 20 \text{ in}}{(20 \text{ in}) \times (-10 \text{ in})} = -\frac{10}{200 \text{ in}}$$

$$f = -20 \text{ in.}$$

The negative sign for the focal length indicates that the lens is diverging. Diverging lenses are concave.

A luminous object and a screen are placed at a fixed distance D apart. Show that if a converging lens of focal length f, where f < D/4, is inserted between them it will produce a real image of the object on the screen for two positions separated by a distance $d = \sqrt{D(D - 4f)}$, and that the ratio of the two image sizes for these two positions of the lens is $(D - d)^2/(D + d)^2$.

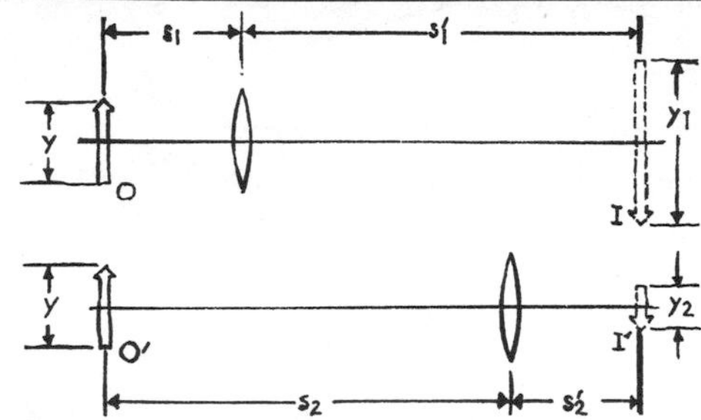

Solution: In both cases,

$$\frac{1}{s} + \frac{1}{s'} = \frac{1}{f}$$

where s is the object distance, and s' is the image distance.

$$\frac{ss'}{s + s'} = f \qquad \text{or} \qquad \frac{ss'}{D} = f.$$

since s + s' = D (see figure)

$$ss' = fD \tag{1}$$

and

$$s + s' = D \tag{2}$$

Let d = s - s'.

$$d^2 = (s - s')^2 = (s + s')^2 - 4ss' = D^2 - 4fD.$$

Therefore $d = \sqrt{D(D - 4f)}$. Also, from Eqs. (1) and (2),

$$s + \frac{fD}{s} = D \qquad \text{or} \qquad s^2 - Ds + fD = 0.$$

$$s = \frac{D \pm \sqrt{D^2 - 4fD}}{2} = \frac{D \pm d}{2}$$

This is a general formula for s. It has 2 roots, one of which must be s_1, and the other of which must be s_2. (See figure).

$$s_1 = \tfrac{1}{2}(D - d) \qquad \text{and} \qquad s_2 = \tfrac{1}{2}(D + d)$$

From (2),

$$s_1' = D - s_1 = \tfrac{1}{2}(D - d) \quad \text{and} \quad s_2' = D - s_2 = \tfrac{1}{2}(D - d).$$

Therefore $s_2 - s_1 = d$, and the two positions of the lens are separated by the distance $d = \sqrt{D(D - 4f)}$. Also, the magnifications for the 2 positions are

$$m_1 = -\frac{s_1'}{s_1} = \frac{y_1}{y} \quad \text{and} \quad m_2 = -\frac{s_2'}{s_2} = \frac{y_2}{y}.$$

$$\therefore \frac{y_2}{y_1} = \frac{m_2}{m_1} = \frac{s_1 s_2'}{s_1' s_2} = \frac{\frac{1}{4}(D - d)^2}{\frac{1}{4}(D + d)^2} = \frac{(D - d)^2}{(D + d)^2}.$$

Note that this method only works if $f < D/4$; for otherwise d^2 is negative and d is thus imaginary.

PHOTOMETRY

• PROBLEM 886

What is the illumination 5 feet from a 75 candlepower lamp?

Solution: Illumination is defined as flux divided by area $\left(E = \frac{F}{A}\right)$. Making the simplifying assumption that our lamp is a point source, the total flux that it emits is $4\pi I$ where I is the intensity of the source. If we construct a sphere enveloping the point source with the point source at its center, and having a radius of 5 ft., we can find the illumination at this distance.

Hence,

$$E = \frac{F}{A} = \frac{4\pi I}{4\pi r^2} = \frac{I}{r^2}$$

$$\text{And Illumination} = \frac{75 \text{ candlepower}}{(5 \times 5)\text{ft}^2}$$

$$= 3 \text{ foot-candles.}$$

• PROBLEM 887

A spotlight equipped with a 32-candle bulb concentrates the beam on a vertical area of 125 ft^2 at a distance of 100 ft. What is the luminous intensity of the spot of light in the beam direction?

Solution: In a lamp, electrical power is supplied and radiation is emitted. The radiant energy emitted per unit of time is called the radiant flux. Only a fraction of this lies within the wavelength interval (400mμ to 700 mμ) which can produce a visual sensation in the human eye. The part of the radiant flux which affects the eye is called the luminous flux F and is measured in lumens. The luminous intensity I of a source is defined as the flux it emits per unit solid angle ($I = F/\omega$). The solid angle ω is a measure of the size of the cone of radiation and is defined in steradians as

$$\omega = \frac{A}{R^2}$$

where R is any distance and A is the area of a spherical surface surrounding the source which is irradiated by the light source at this radius R.

Assuming that the spotlight radiates in all directions, the total area illuminated at a distance R is equal to the area of a sphere of radius R or $4\pi R^2$. Therefore the total solid angle

$$\omega_{total} = \frac{4\pi R^2}{R^2} = 4\pi \quad \text{sterad.}$$

and the total flux emitted by the bulb is given by

$$F_{total} = I\,\omega_{total} = (32 \text{ candles})(4\pi \text{ steradians}) = 400 \text{ lu}$$

This total flux is concentrated into a beam with a small solid angle through the use of a reflector and lens. This solid angle is

$$\omega = \frac{A}{R^2} = \frac{125 \text{ ft}^2}{(100 \text{ ft})^2} = 0.0125 \text{ sterad.}$$

The intensity of this beam is then

$$I = \frac{F_{total}}{\omega} = \frac{400 \text{ lu}}{0.0125 \text{ sterad}} = 32{,}000 \text{ candles}$$

• PROBLEM 888

A "point-source" unshaded electric lamp of luminous intensity 100 candles is 4.0 ft above the top of a table. Find the illuminance of the table (a) at a point directly below the lamp and (b) at a point 3.0 ft from the point directly below the lamp.

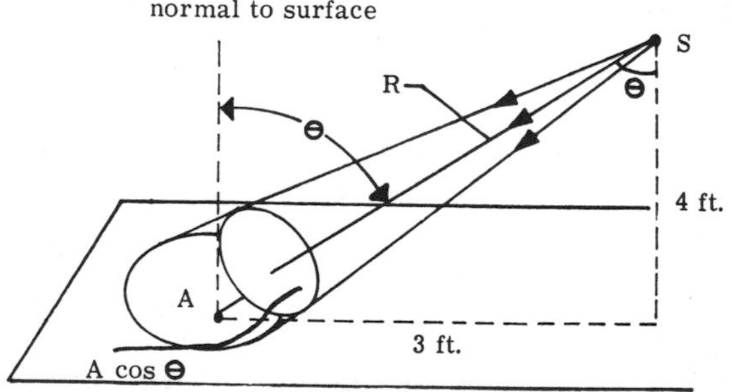

Illuminance of a surface by a point source

Solution: a) Illuminance E is the luminous flux F incident per unit area A. Then

$$E = \frac{F}{A}$$

Also $$F = I\omega$$

and $$\omega = \frac{A}{R^2}$$

If the area A is perpendicular to the path of radiation from the point source, the illuminance can also be expressed as

$$E = \frac{F}{A} = \frac{I\omega}{A} = \frac{I(A/R^2)}{A} = \frac{I}{R^2}$$

which is the equation needed since the given quantities are the luminous intensity I and the distance R from the point source. Furthermore, we know that the area is perpendicular to the radiation being emitted by the lamp. Therefore,

$$E = \frac{I}{R^2} = \frac{100 \text{ candles}}{(4.0 \text{ ft})^2} = 6.25 \text{ lu/ft}^2$$

b) For this second point, the area illuminated is a distance

$$R = \sqrt{(4.0 \text{ ft})^2 + (3.0 \text{ ft})^2} = 5.0 \text{ ft}$$

from the lamp, which was found by using the trigonometric relation for a right triangle. The illuminance is

$$E = \frac{F}{A}$$

where $$F = I\omega.$$

The solid angle ω is defined as the ratio of the area upon which the source radiates at a radius R to this distance R. The area upon which the source radiates for this case can be seen from the figure to be A cos θ. Therefore,

$$\omega = \frac{A \cos \theta}{R^2}$$

and $$E = \frac{F}{A} = \frac{I\omega}{A} = \frac{I\left(A \cos \theta/R^2\right)}{A} = \frac{I \cos \theta}{R^2}$$

Using trigonometry, cos θ is found to be

$$\cos \theta = \frac{4.0 \text{ ft}}{5.0 \text{ ft}} = 0.80$$

Then the illuminance on the area A is

$$E = \frac{I \cos \theta}{R^2} = \frac{(100 \text{ candles})(0.80)}{(5.0 \text{ ft})^2} = 3.2 \text{ lu/ft}^2$$

• PROBLEM 889

A standard 48-candle lamp is placed 36 in. from the screen of a photometer and produces there the same illuminance as a lamp of unknown intensity placed 45 in. away. What is the luminous intensity of the unknown lamp?

Solution: Illuminance E is equal to the ratio of the luminous intensity I to the square of the distance R from the source. Since the illuminance of the two lamps is equal,

$$E_1 = E_2$$

where the subscripts 1 and 2 refer to the lamps at distances of 45 in. and 36 in. respectively. Then

$$\frac{I_1}{R_1} = \frac{I_2}{R_2}$$

and substituting values,

$$\frac{I_1}{(45 \text{ in})^2} = \frac{48 \text{ candles}}{(36 \text{ in})^2}$$

$$I_1 = \frac{(45 \text{ in})^2 (48 \text{ candles})}{(36 \text{ in})^2} = 75 \text{ candles}$$

Note that the distances can be expressed in any unit as long as they are consistent.

CHAPTER 29

OPTICS-INTERFERENCE

• PROBLEM 890

> Derive a relation describing the interference effects observed when light is reflected from a thin film. (See figure).

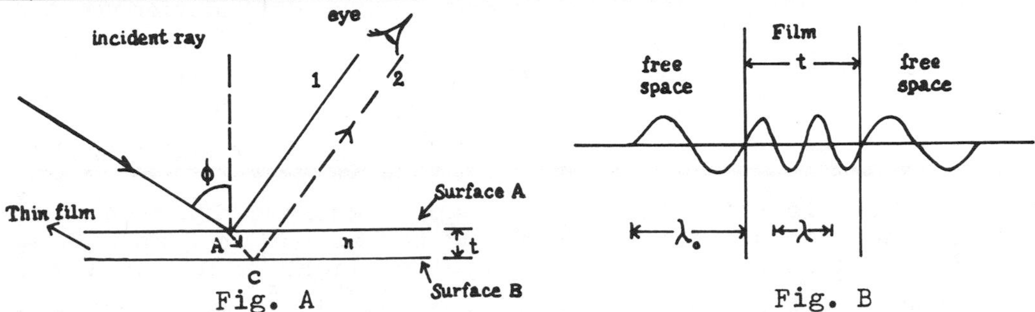

Fig. A

Fig. B

Solution: In order to understand the interference effects produced by a thin film, we trace the path of an incident ray of light, as shown in figure (a). The incident ray first encounters surface A, where it is partially reflected and partially absorbed. Since the refractive index of the film is greater than the refractive index of air, the reflected ray undergoes a 180° phase change. The transmitted part of the incident ray now encounters interface B, where it is partially reflected and partially absorbed. However, this time the reflected ray undergoes no phase change since it is traveling from a region of high refractive index to a region of low refractive index. Hence, rays 1 and 2 differ in phase by 180°, or $\lambda_0/2$ where λ_0 is the wavelength of the incident light in free space.

In addition to the 180° phase change due to reflection, ray 2 travels a distance 2t greater than ray 1. (This holds only if the rays shown are incident at an angle ϕ which is very small.) Then, if we want to observe destructive interference, the distance 2t must contain an integral number of wavelengths, $N\lambda$, where $N = 0,1,2,\dots$. But, λ is not the wavelength of the light in free space, but rather, the wavelength of light in the film (see figure(b)). However, the wavelengths λ_0 and λ are related. By definition of the refractive index of the film

$$n = c/v$$

where c is the speed of light in free space, and v is its speed in the film. If λ_0 and f_0 are the free space wavelength and frequency of light, we may write

$$c = \lambda_0 f_0$$

Similarly,

$$v = \lambda f$$

where λ and f are the wavelength and frequency of light in the film. But the frequency of light is the same in all media. Then

$$v = \lambda f_0$$

Hence

$$n = \frac{\lambda_0 f_0}{\lambda f_0} = \frac{\lambda_0}{\lambda}$$

and

$$\lambda_0 = n\lambda$$

Combining this fact with the previous discussion, we obtain

$$2t = N\lambda = \frac{N\lambda_0}{n} \qquad N = 0,1,2,\ldots \qquad \text{destructive interference}$$

$$2t = (N+\tfrac{1}{2})\lambda = \frac{(N+\tfrac{1}{2})\lambda_0}{n} \qquad N = 0,1,2,\ldots \qquad \text{constructive interference}$$

or

$$t = \frac{N\lambda_0}{2n} \qquad N = 0,1,2,\ldots \qquad \text{destructive interference}$$

$$t = \frac{(N+\tfrac{1}{2})\lambda_0}{2n} \qquad N = 0,1,2,\ldots \qquad \text{constructive interference}$$

• PROBLEM 891

In a double slit interference experiment the distance between the slits is 0.05 cm and the screen is 2 meters from the slits. The light is yellow light from a sodium lamp and it has a wavelength of 5.89×10^{-5} cm. What is the distance between the fringes?

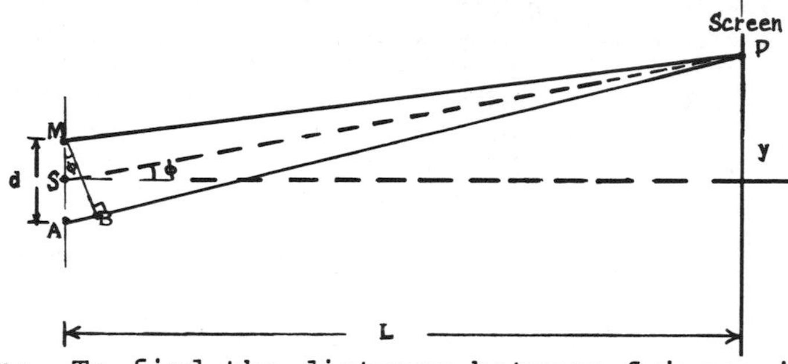

Solution: To find the distance between fringes in the double slit experiment, we must first derive the formulas for the location of the maxima and minima of the fringe pattern. Let us examine this experiment in more detail.

Light is incident on the 2 slits from the left. (See figure) MP and AP represent 2 rays of light, one from each slit, arriving at P. Typically, L >> d, and we may consider MP to be equal to BP. Assuming that the light rays emerging from the slits are in phase, the two light rays arriving at P will be out of phase because light from A must travel the extra distance AB when compared with light from M. If this path difference ($AB = d \sin\phi$) is equal to an even number of half wavelengths, P will be a maximum point. If AB equals an odd number of half wavelengths, P will be a minimum point. Hence,

$$\text{For a maximum } \sin\phi = (2n)\frac{\lambda}{2d} \qquad (n = 0,1,2,\ldots)$$

$$\text{For a minimum } \sin\phi = (2n+1)\frac{\lambda}{2d} \qquad (n = 0,1,2,\ldots)$$

Therefore, the angular location of adjacent maxima on the screen (say the nth and (n+1)th maxima,) is

$$\sin\left(\phi_{n+1}\right) = \frac{(2(n+1))\lambda}{2d} = \frac{(n+1)\lambda}{d} \tag{1}$$

$$\sin\left(\phi_n\right) = \frac{(2n)\lambda}{2d} = \frac{n\lambda}{d}$$

But, if ϕ is small,

$$\sin\left(\phi_{n+1}\right) \approx \tan\left(\phi_{n+1}\right)$$

$$\sin\left(\phi_n\right) \approx \tan\left(\phi_n\right).$$

Hence, using (1) and the figure,

$$\frac{Y_{n+1}}{L} = \frac{(n+1)\lambda}{d}$$

$$\frac{Y_n}{L} = \frac{n\lambda}{d} \qquad \text{hence,}$$

$$Y_{n+1} - Y_n = \frac{(n+1)\lambda L}{d} - \frac{n\lambda L}{d}$$

$$Y_{n+1} - Y_n = \frac{\lambda L}{d}.$$

This is the screen separation of 2 adjacent maxima.

If $\lambda = 5.89 \times 10^{-5}$ cm

$L = 200$ cm

$d = 0.05$ cm.

$$Y_{n+1} - Y_n = \frac{\left(5.89 \times 10^{-5} \times 200\right)\text{cm}^2}{0.05\ \text{cm}}$$

$$= .233\text{cm}.$$

• PROBLEM 892

With two slits spaced 0.2 mm apart, and a screen at a distance of ℓ = 1m, the third bright fringe is found to be displaced h = 7.5 mm from the central fringe. Find the wavelength λ of the light used. See the figure.

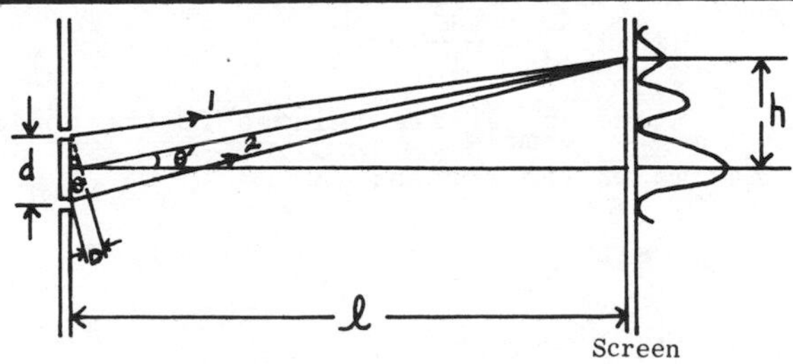

Double Slit

Solution: When the difference D between the path lengths of the rays 1 and 2 is an integral multiple of the wavelength λ, one obtains a maximum (bright fringe) of the interference pattern on the screen. From the figure we see that

$$D = d \sin \theta .$$

If ℓ is much larger than the distance between the two slits, we see that $\theta' \simeq \theta$, where θ' relates the position of the maximum on the screen to the distance between slits and the screen,

$$\tan \theta' = \frac{h}{\ell} .$$

The approximation $\ell \gg d$ also means that θ is small; for which case we have

$$\tan \theta' \simeq \sin \theta' .$$

Therefore, for the third maximum to occur at h, D must be 3λ;

$$D = d \sin \theta = 3\lambda$$

or

$$\sin \theta \simeq \sin \theta' = \frac{3\lambda}{d}$$

$$\frac{h}{\ell} = \frac{3\lambda}{d}$$

which gives λ as

$$\lambda = \frac{dh}{3\ell}$$

$$= \frac{0.75 \text{ cm} \times 0.02 \text{ cm}}{3 \times 100 \text{ cm}} = 5 \times 10^{-5} \text{ cm}$$

$$= 500 \times 10^{-9} \text{m} = 500 \text{ nm}.$$

• PROBLEM 893

In a double-slit experiment, D = 0.1 mm and L = 1 m. If yellow light is used, what will be the spacing between adjacent bright lines?

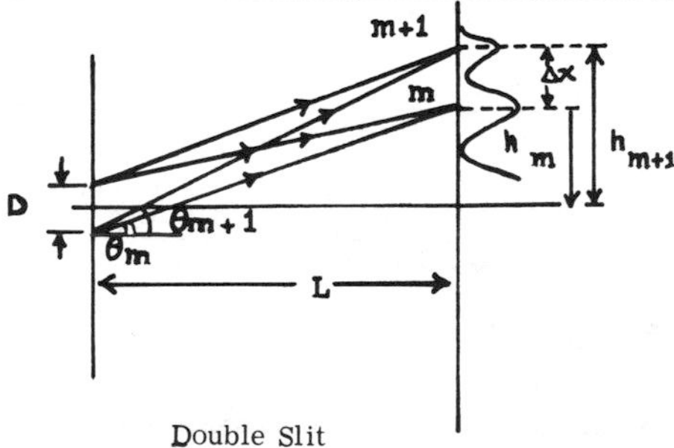

Double Slit

Solution: The wavelength of yellow light is approximately 6×10^{-5} cm. Let the separation between the (n+1)th and m'th maxima be Δx, as shown in the figure. Then,

$$\sin \theta_m = \frac{m}{D} \lambda$$

$$\sin \theta_{m+1} = \frac{m+1}{D} \lambda .$$

The angles θ_m and θ_{m+1} are related to the positions h_m, and h_{m+1} of these maxima on the screen;

$$\sin \theta_m \simeq \frac{h_{m+1}}{L}$$

$$\sin \theta_{m+1} \simeq \frac{h_m}{L} ,$$

hence,

$$\sin \theta_{m+1} - \sin \theta_m = \frac{\lambda}{D}$$

$$\frac{h_{m+1} - h_m}{L} \simeq \frac{\lambda}{D}$$

or

$$\frac{\Delta x}{L} \approx \frac{\lambda}{D}$$

$$\Delta x \cong \frac{L}{D}$$

$$= \frac{(6 \times 10^{-5}\text{cm}) \times (100 \text{ cm})}{10^{-2} \text{ cm}}$$

$$= 0.6\text{cm}$$

Thus, the spacing between lines is about 6 mm or 1/4 of an inch.

• PROBLEM 894

The double-slit experiment can be simulated using two small blocks of wood oscillating up and down together in a pool of water as shown in the figure. Suppose that the blocks are 3 cm apart and the wavelength of the water waves is 1 cm. Locate the points 10 cm from one of the blocks where constructive interference occurs.

The points on the circle are the positions where constructive interference occurs.

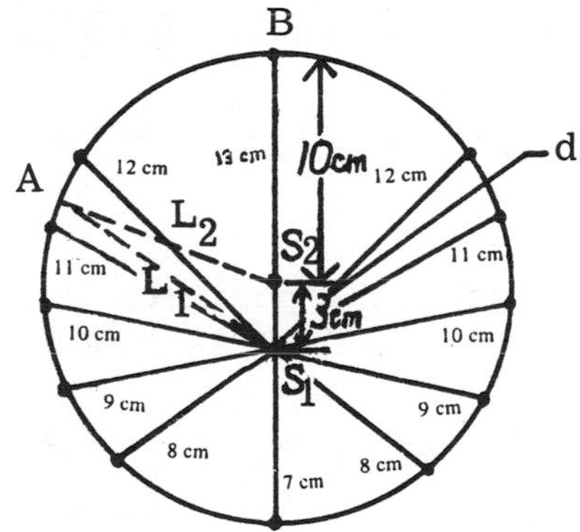

Solution: The motion of the blocks produce circular waves which are emanating from two sources S_1 and S_2 separated by $d = 3$ cm. In order to observe the interference pattern that forms at 10 cm from one of the blocks, draw a circle of radius 10 cm around source S_2 as shown in the figure. Constructive interference occurs at points where the difference in the distances to the two blocks is either zero or some whole number of wavelengths.

Let A be a point on the circle at a distance L_1 from S_1. All the points on the circle are $L_2 = 10$ cm from S_2. Constructive interference occurs at points for which the length $|L_1 - L_2|$ is an integer multiple of the wavelength $\lambda = 1$ cm. Therefore, we have constructive interference at points on the circle that are

$$L_1 = 10 \text{ cm} - 3 \text{ cm} = 7 \text{ cm}$$

$$= 10 \text{ cm} - 2 \text{ cm} = 8 \text{ cm}$$

$$= 10 \text{ cm} - 1 \text{ cm} = 9 \text{ cm}$$

$$= 10 \text{ cm}$$

$$= 10 \text{ cm} + 1 \text{ cm} = 11 \text{ cm}$$

$$= 10 \text{ cm} + 2 \text{ cm} = 12 \text{ cm}$$

$$= 10 \text{ cm} + 3 \text{ cm} = 13 \text{ cm}$$

from S_1.

• PROBLEM 895

A student sets up a Young's experiment using a sodium vapor lamp as a light source and placing his slits 1 m from a screen. He is unsure of the slit separation and, standing beside the slits, he varies the separation and finds the interference pattern vanishes if the slits are too far apart. If the angular resolution of his eye is 1 minute of arc, how far apart are the slits when he just cannot see the interference fringes?

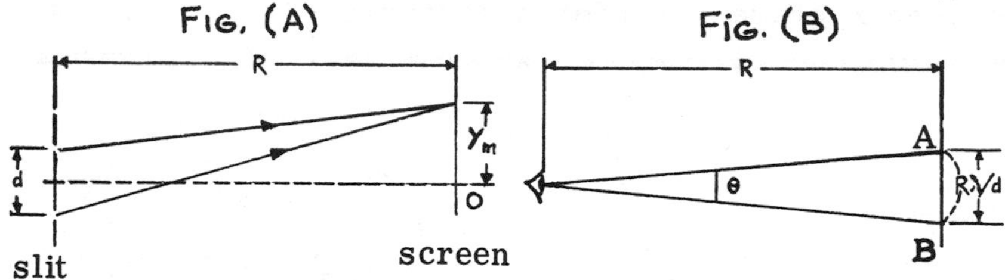

Solution: The position of the mth bright fringe of the fringe system from the center O is given by

$$y_m = \frac{mR\lambda}{d} ,$$

where λ is the wavelength used (see figure (A)). Similarly, for the (m + 1)th fringe,

$$y_{m+1} = \frac{(m + 1)R\lambda}{d}$$

Thus, the fringe separation is

$$y_{m+1} - y_m = \frac{R\lambda}{d} ,$$

a quantity independent of m and thus constant throughout the fringe system.

The angle subtended by this fringe separation at the student's eye is (see figure (B))

$$\theta = \frac{R\lambda/d}{R} = \frac{\lambda}{d} \text{ rad.}$$

Here, we have approximated the arc shown in figure (B) (dotted line) by the straight line distance $\overline{AB}$.

But the student cannot see the fringes as distinct unless the angle neighboring fringes subtend at his eye $\geq$ 1 minute of arc. But 1 minute of arc is $1/60° = \pi/60 \times 180$ rad. Hence,

$$\theta_{min} = \frac{\lambda}{d_{max}} = \frac{\pi}{180 \times 60} \text{ rad}$$

$$\therefore \quad d_{max} = \frac{180 \times 60 \times 5.89 \times 10^{-5}}{\pi \text{ rad}} \text{ cm} = 2.025 \text{ mm.}$$

• PROBLEM 896

When a flat plate of glass and a lens are placed in contact, a distinctive interference pattern, known as Newton's Rings, is observed. (See figure A). Derive a formula giving the location of the fringes of the interference pattern relative to the center of the lens. (See figure B).

Figure A: Interference Pattern (Top View)

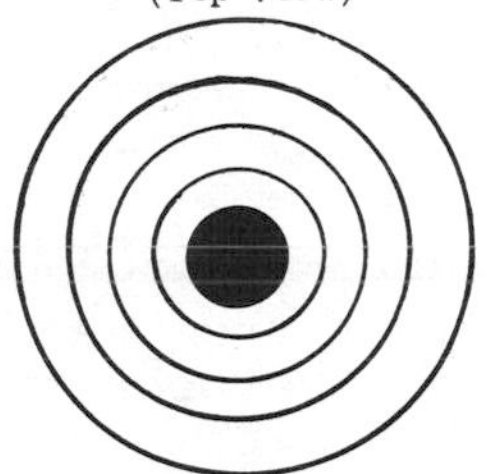

Figure B

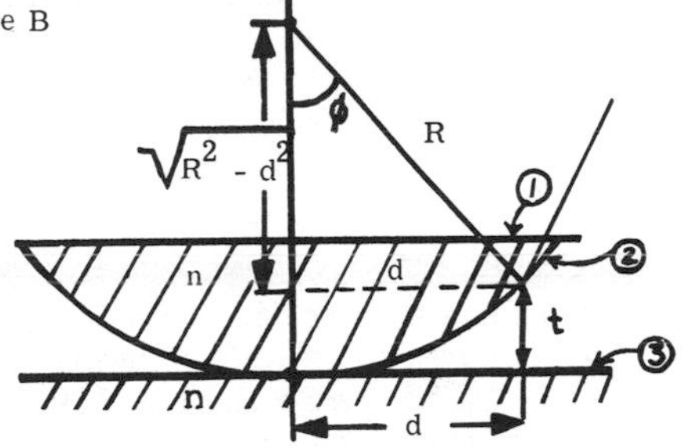

Solution: Destructive interference will result when the waves reflected from the apparatus shown in figure (B) are 180° out of phase. Let us trace the path of an incident ray. The ray will be partially reflected and partially transmitted at surface (1). When a ray of light is tramsmitted from a region of low refractive index to a medium of higher refractive index, it undergoes a phase change of 180°. Hence, the ray reflected at surface (1) is 180° out of phase with the incident ray. The transmitted ray next encounters surface (2). At this surface there is no phase change, since the light leaves an area of high refractive index and enters a region of low refractive index. In addition, part of this light is reflected at surface (2). The light transmitted at surface (2) next encounters surface (3) and is reflected with a 180° or $\lambda/2$ phase change. (λ is the wavelength the light). Hence, the ray reflected at (2), and the ray reflected at (3) are 180° out of phase.

Now, the ray reflected at (3) travels a distance $2t$ greater than the ray reflected at (2). We will see destructive interference whenever $2t$ is an integral number of wavelengths, since the additional $\lambda/2$ required for destruction is provided by the phase change due to reflection. Hence

$$2t = n\lambda \qquad n = 0,1,2,\ldots \qquad \text{destructive interference} \quad (1)$$

$$2t = (n+\tfrac{1}{2})\lambda \qquad n = 0,1,2,\ldots \qquad \text{constructive interference}$$

We must now find the location of the interference fringes in terms of the geometry of figure (B).

From figure (B),

$$t = R - \sqrt{R^2 - d^2} \qquad (2)$$

$$t = R - R\sqrt{1 - d^2/R^2}$$

$$t = R\left\{1 - \sqrt{1 - d^2/R^2}\right\} \qquad (3)$$

But $d \ll R$ and $d/R \ll 1$. (This means that the radius of curvature of the lens is large). We may therefore approximate the square root in (3) by the binomial theorem. Therefore,

$$\sqrt{1 - d^2/R^2} \approx 1 - d^2/2R^2 \qquad (4)$$

Substituting (4) in (3)

$$t = R(1 - 1 + d^2/2R^2$$

$$t = d^2/2R$$

$$d = \sqrt{2tR}$$

Using (1)

$$d = \sqrt{n\lambda R} \qquad n = 0,1,2,\ldots \qquad \text{destructive interference}$$

$$d = \sqrt{(n+\tfrac{1}{2})\lambda R} \qquad n = 0,1,2,\ldots \qquad \text{constructive interference}$$

The first equation locates the dark rings relative to the center of the lens, and the second equation locates the bright rings.

• PROBLEM 897

An interferometer illuminated with red light from cadmium (λ= 6438 A) is used to measure the distance between two points. Calculate this distance, D, if 120 minima pass the reference mark as the mirror is moved from one of the points to the other.

Solution: The fringes observed represent the interference of light rays. Consider 2 rays of light, initially in phase. (That is, they interfere to produce areas of high light intensity, or maxima). If the phase of one ray is varied until a minima is observed, we will find that the phase difference of the 2 rays is now $\frac{\lambda}{2}$, where λ is the wavelength of the light. Hence, 2 minima are separated by λ. Therefore,

$$D = N\lambda = 120\left(6.438 \times 10^{-5}\ \text{cm}\right) = 0.00773\ \text{cm}.$$

• PROBLEM 898

To produce a minimum reflection of wavelengths near the middle of the visible spectrum (550 mμ), how thick a coating of MgF_2 (n = 1.38) should be vacuum-coated on a glass surface?

Solution: Consider light to be incident at near-normal incidence. We wish to cause destructive interference between rays r_1 and r_2 so that maximum energy passes into

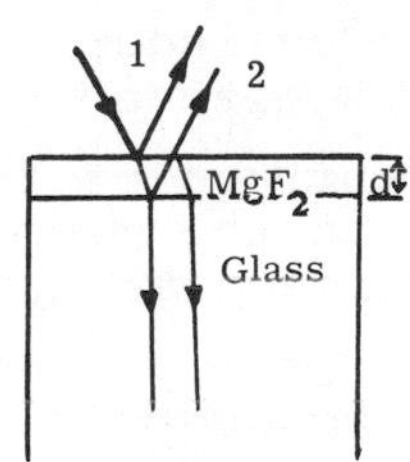

Ray striking coated glass

the glass. A phase change of 1/2λ occurs in each ray, for at both the upper and lower surfaces of the MgF_2 film, the light is reflected by a medium of greater index of refraction. When striking a medium of lower index refraction, the light is reflected with no phase change. Since in this problem both ray 1 and 2 experience the same phase shift, no net change of phase is produced by these two reflections. Hence the only way a phase change can occur is if the 2 rays travel through different optical path lengths. (the optical path length is defined as the product of the geometric distance a ray travels through and the refractive index of the medium in which the ray is travelling). For destructive interference, the 2 rays must be out of phase by an odd number of half wavelengths. Therefore, the optical path difference needed for destructive interference is,

$$2nd = (2N + 1)\ \lambda/2 \qquad N = 0,1,2\ldots \quad \text{for minima}$$

Note that 2nd is the total optical path length that the rays traverse. When N = 0,

$$d = \frac{1/2\lambda}{2n} = \frac{\lambda}{4n} = \frac{550\ \text{m}\mu}{4 \times 1.38} = 100\ \text{m}\mu$$

$$= 1.0 \times 10^{-5}\ \text{cm}$$

• PROBLEM 899

A thin lens of long focal length is supported horizontally a short distance above the flat polished end of a steel cylinder. The cylinder is 5 cm high and its lower end is rigidly held. Newton's rings are produced between the lens and the upper end of the cylinder, using normally incident light of wavelength 6000 Å, and viewed from above by means of a microscope. When the temperature of the cylinder is raised 25 C deg, 50 rings move past the cross-wires of the microscope. What is the coefficient of linear expansion of steel.

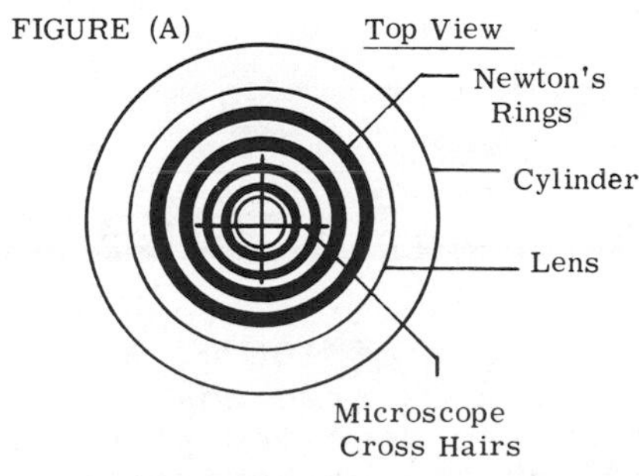

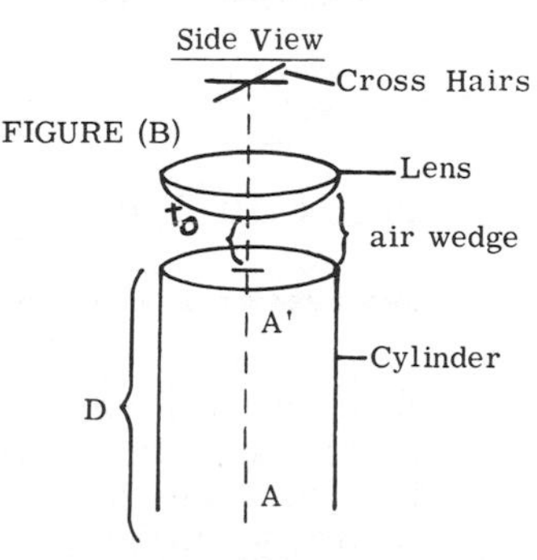

Solution: Initially, the cylinder has a length d, and a gap of length t_0 exists between the top of the cyliner and the bottom surface of the lens in the portion of the air wedge viewed in the microscope at the same position as the cross-wires. (Technically, t_0 is the distance of the lens from the cylinder as measured along axis AA' in figure (B). However, since the lens is thin, t_0 is the distance of any point on the bottom surface of the lens from the top of the cylinder). Let us now see how interference fringes are produced.

Light is incident upon the lens from above. Light is transmitted through both lens surfaces with no phase change. However, the light reflected from the bottom lens surface and the top of the cylinder are 180° (or $\lambda/2$) out of phase. This phase change is due to the reflection from the cylinder. In addition, the wave reflected from the cylinder travels a distance $2t_0$ greater than the ray reflected from the lens in traversing the air gap. If this distance is equal to an odd number of half-wavelengths (odd because the waves are already $\lambda/2$ out of phase due to reflection) constructive interference will occur. Hence

Constructive Interference $$2t_0 = (2n + 1)\frac{\lambda}{2} \quad (n = 0, 1, 2, \ldots)$$

or $$2t_0 = (n + \tfrac{1}{2})\lambda \quad (n = 0, 1, 2 \ldots)$$

Hence, for a bright fringe to appear at the cross-wires, $2t_0 = (n + \frac{1}{2})\lambda$, where n is an unknown integer.

After one heats the cylinder through a temperature difference T, the length of the cylinder is $d(1 + \alpha T)$, where α is the coefficient of linear expansion of steel, and the gap will have been reduced to t, where $t_0 - t = d\alpha T$.

If a bright fringe is again seen at the position of the cross-wires, then, similarly, $2t = (m + \frac{1}{2})\lambda$, where m is an integer. $(m \neq n)$

$$\therefore \quad 2(t_0 - t) = 2d\alpha T = (n - m)\lambda.$$

During the heating process, (n - m) bright fringes must have passed over the cross-wires. Thus

$$\alpha = \frac{(n - m)\lambda}{2dT} = \frac{50 \times 6 \times 10^{-5}\ \text{cm}}{2 \times 5\ \text{cm} \times 25\ \text{C deg}}$$

$$= 1.2 \times 10^{-5} \text{ per } {}^\circ\text{C}.$$

• PROBLEM 900

A radio telescope sited on the edge of a cliff overlooking the sea operates on a wavelength of 100 m. A radio star rises above the horizon and is tracked by the telescope. The first minimum of the received signal occurs when the star is 30° above the horizontal.

Explain why the minimum occurs and determine the height of the cliff, assuming that radio waves suffer a phase change of π on reflection at a water surface. (See figure.)

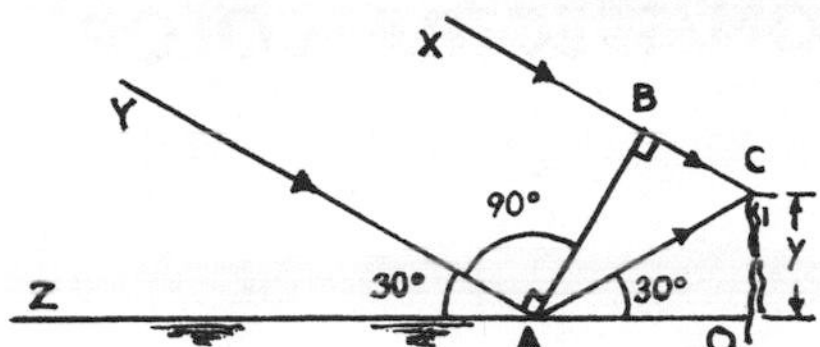

Solution: The radio telescope is receiving signals direct from the star (ray XBC) and also by reflection from the water surface, (YAC) which is acting like a plane mirror. In this case the source of radiation is far enough away to be considered at infinity and the rays are descending on the earth in a parallel beam. When the path difference between rays YAC and XBC (see figure) is such that they reach the telescope exactly out of phase, destructive interference occurs and the signal at C will be a minimum.

Consider the diagram. If AB is drawn perpendicular to XC, it will also be perpendicular to YA, and AB is a plane wave front of the incoming beam. Thus the disturbances at A and B have the same phase at all times. A phase change of π occurs at A and this is equivalent to an increase in path of $\lambda/2$. Thus the path difference between the two rays is $\delta = AC + (\lambda/2) - BC$. But by the laws of reflection $\angle YAZ = \angle CAO = 30°$, and therefore $\angle BAC = 180° - 90° - 30° - 30° = 30°$.

$$\delta = AC + \frac{\lambda}{2} - AC \sin 30° = \frac{\lambda}{2} + AC(1 - \sin 30°)$$

Since $\sin 30° = Y/AC$, $AC = Y/\sin 30°$ and

$$\delta = \frac{\lambda}{2} + \frac{y}{\sin 30°}(1 - \sin 30°) = \frac{\lambda}{2} + y.$$

In order for minima to occur, the path difference δ must equal an odd number of half wavelengths,

$$\text{or} \quad \delta = (2n + 1)\frac{\lambda}{2} \qquad n = 0, 1, 2, \ldots$$

$$\text{Then} \quad (2n + 1)\frac{\lambda}{2} = \frac{\lambda}{2} + y.$$

If $n = 0$, $\delta = \lambda/2$, $y = 0$, and this corresponds to the center of the interference pattern being a minimum. Since this is the first minimum the telescope receives, C must be at the first minimum above O for the situation shown in the diagram. (Were it a minimum other than the first, a previous minimum must have occurred for an angle lower than 30°. But we are told that this doesn't happen.) Therefore, $n = 1$ and δ must be $3\lambda/2$.

$$\text{Hence,} \quad \frac{3\lambda}{2} = \frac{\lambda}{2} + y \qquad \text{and} \quad y = \lambda = 100 \text{ m}.$$

CHAPTER 30

OPTICS: DIFFRACTION/SPECTRA/COLOR

• PROBLEM 901

When light is incident on a thin slit, a diffraction pattern, shown in figure (a), is produced. Find an expression which gives the location of the minima of the diffraction pattern in terms of the angle φ. (See figure (b)).

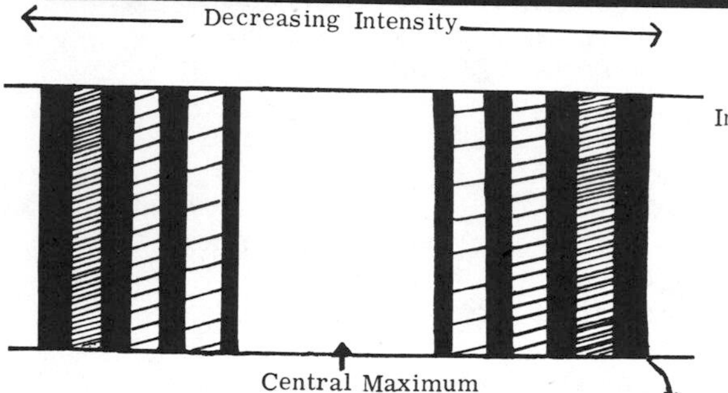

Figure A Single Slit Diffraction Pattern

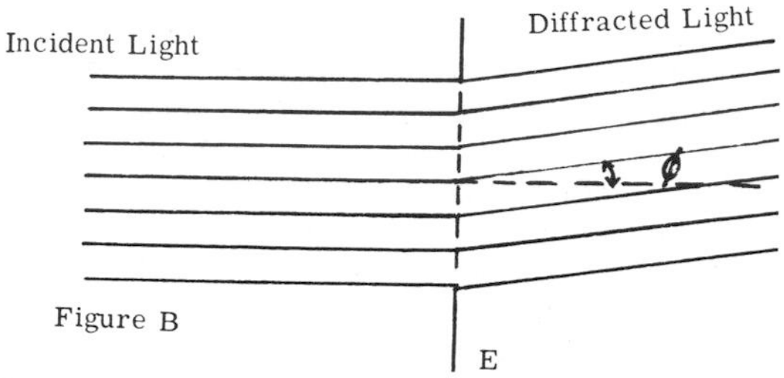

Figure B

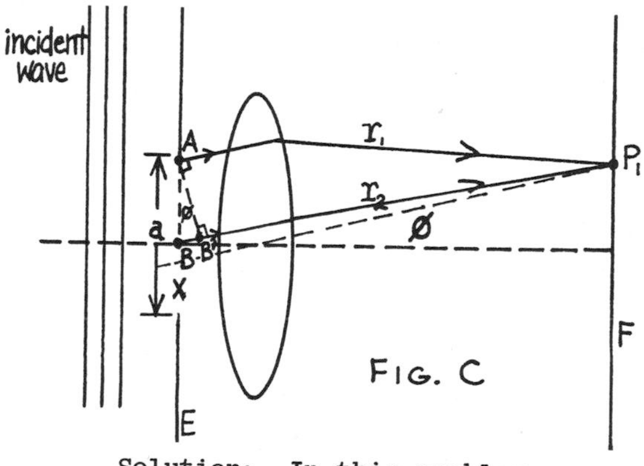

FIG. C

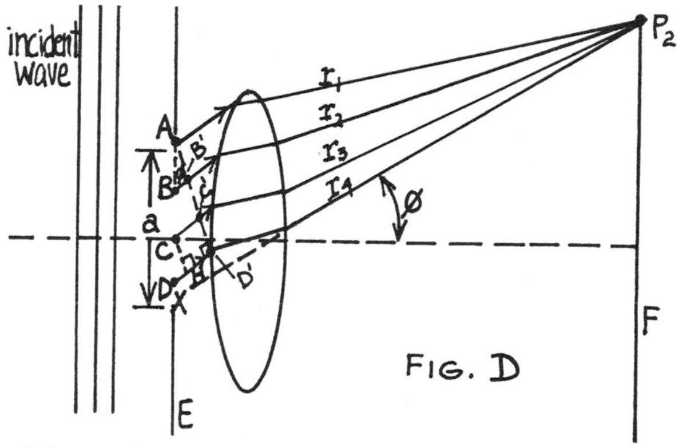

FIG. D

Solution: In this problem, we consider only Fraunhofer diffraction. (See figure (b).) This type of diffraction is characterized by parallel, incident light rays encountering a slit, and being diffracted, again parallel to one another. In practice, this restriction may be effected in 2 ways. The light source is placed very far away from the slit, and the screen is far from the slit. Another method employs a converging lens to the left of the slit, and a converging lens to the right. Light rays incident upon the first converging lens leave parallel to one another, encounter the slit, and are defracted parallel to one another (see figure (c)). They then are focused by the second converging lens on screen F, and the diffraction pattern results.

Using figure (c), we can derive an equation locating the minima of the diffraction pattern. Let us focus on rays coming from points A and B. Since the incident light is in phase, the only phase difference between r_1 and r_2 must occur because r_2 travels a larger distance than r_1. (Here, we assume that the rays are effectively parallel). If this distance, BB', is equal to $\frac{1}{2}\lambda$, where λ is the wavelength of light, the rays r_1 and r_2 will interfere destructively and p_1 will be a minimum. Since

$$BB' = a/2 \sin \varphi ,$$

minima will be observed when

$$a/2 \sin \varphi = \lambda/2$$

Hence,

$$a \sin \varphi = \lambda \qquad \text{minima} .$$

This formula gives the 1st order minima of the diffraction pattern.

Now, examine figure (d), where the slit has been divided into 4 equal portions of length $a/4$. Looking at rays r_1 and r_2, we note that the only phase difference between them occurs because they travel unequal distances. Ray r_2 travels a distance BB' greater than r_1. If $BB' = \lambda/2$, r_1 and r_2 will destructively interfere. Furthermore, r_3 and r_4 will also destructively interfere since $DH = \lambda/2$. Hence, each pair of similar rays will destructively interfere, and P_2 will be a minimum of the diffraction pattern. Therefore, since

$$BB' = a/4 \sin \varphi$$

the second order minimum is described by

$$a/4 \sin \varphi = \lambda/2 \qquad \text{minimum}$$

Then

$$a \sin \varphi = 2\lambda \qquad \text{minimum} .$$

In general, if we divide the slit into n equal segments, where n is an even integer, we will find

$$a/n \sin \varphi = \lambda/2 \qquad \text{minima}$$

and

$$a \sin \varphi = n\lambda/2 \qquad \text{minima} \quad n \text{ even}$$

Since $n = 2m$ where $m = 1,2,\ldots$ we obtain

$$a \sin \varphi = m\lambda \qquad \text{minima} \quad m = 1,2,\ldots$$

Note that n must be even because each pair of rays emanating from the slit interfere.

• PROBLEM 902

A slit of width **a** is placed in front of a lens of focal length 50 cm and is illuminated normally with light of wavelength 5.89×10^{-5} cm. The first minima on either side of the central maximum of the diffraction pattern **observed** in the focal plane of the lens are separated by 0.20 cm. What is the value of **a**?

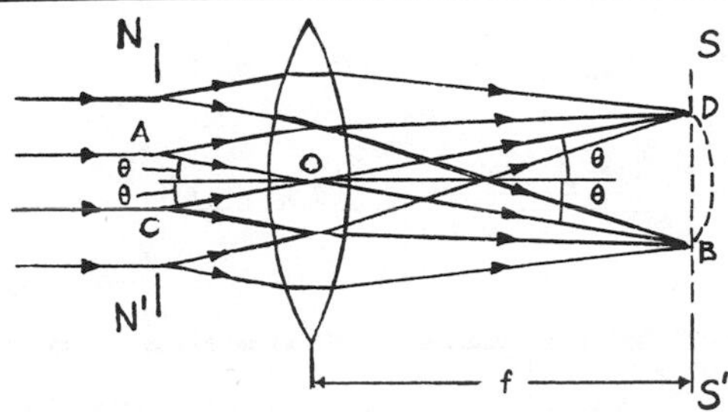

Solution: This is an example of Fraunhofer diffraction (see figure). Parallel rays of light are incident on slit NN' from the left. The rays are diffracted and encounter the lens of focal length f. The rays are then focused on a screen (SS') lying in the lens' focal plane, and a diffraction pattern is observed. The minima of this diffraction pattern are described by the formula

$$\sin\theta = \frac{m\lambda}{a}$$

where θ locates the minima fringes, a is the slit width, m is the minima number, and λ is the wavelength of the light used. In this problem, the first minima on either side of the central maximum is found at angle θ, such that

$$\theta = \sin^{-1}\frac{\lambda}{a}\,.$$

The angular separation of the 2 minima is then (see figure)

$$\delta = 2\theta = 2\sin^{-1}\frac{\lambda}{a} \qquad (1)$$

But, we may write

$$2\theta \approx \frac{\overline{DB}}{f} \qquad (2)$$

where DB is the linear separation of the 2 minima. Here, we have approximated the arc DB (shown dotted in the figure) by the linear distance $\overline{DB}$. Using (2) in (1)

$$\frac{\overline{DB}}{f} \approx 2\sin^{-1}\frac{\lambda}{a}$$

or $$\sin\left(\frac{\overline{DB}}{2f}\right) \approx \frac{\lambda}{a}$$

and $$a \approx \frac{\lambda}{\sin\left(\frac{\overline{DB}}{2f}\right)}$$

Hence $$a \approx \frac{5.89 \times 10^{-5}\ \text{cm}}{\sin\left(\frac{.20\ \text{cm}}{100\ \text{cm}}\right)} = \frac{5.89 \times 10^{-5}\ \text{cm}}{\sin(.0020)}$$

Since .0020 rad is a very small angle, we may write

$$\sin(.0020) \approx .0020 = 2 \times 10^{-3}$$

whence $$a \approx \frac{5.89 \times 10^{-5}\ \text{cm}}{2 \times 10^{-3}} = 2.945 \times 10^{-2}\ \text{cm}$$

• PROBLEM 903

A plane wave of monochromatic light of wavelength 5893 Å passes through a slit 0.500 mm wide and forms a diffraction pattern on a screen 1.00 m away from the slit and parallel to it. Compute the separation of the first dark bands on either side of the central bright band, that is, the width of the central bright band.

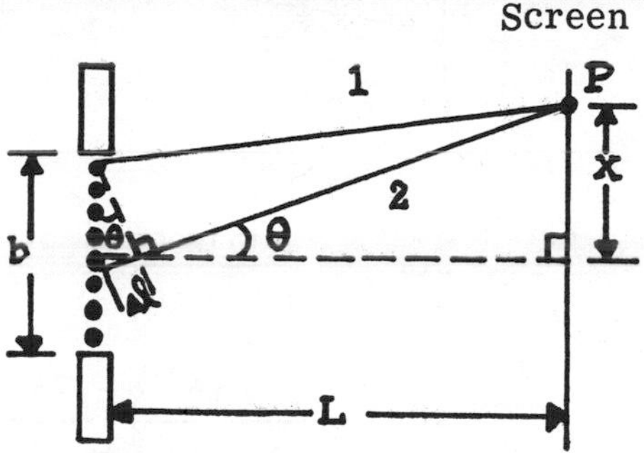

Single Slit Interference

Solution: According to Huygens' principle, each point in the slit may be considered to behave as a single point source of light. Consider a pair of corresponding points in each half of the slit as shown in the figure. For a dark band to occur (corresponding to destructive interference) at P, the two rays must be out of phase by 180° or $\lambda/2$. This phase difference results because ray 2 travels a distance $\Delta\ell$, greater than ray 1 (see figure). Therefore, since P is a point of destructive interference

$$\Delta\ell = \lambda/2 = \frac{b}{2}\sin\theta$$

$$\lambda = b\sin\theta.$$

If L is much greater than b, we can make the following approximations: The hypotenuse of the large right triangle is equal to L, and in considering any two corresponding points in the two halves of the slit, the angle θ remains unchanged. Then, we can write

$$\sin\theta = x/L.$$

But $\sin\theta = \frac{\lambda}{b}$ and $\frac{x}{L} = \frac{\lambda}{b}$ or

$$x = \frac{\lambda L}{b} = \frac{(0.00005893\text{ cm})(10)}{0.0500\text{ cm}} = 0.118\text{ cm}$$

where x is the distance of the first dark band from the middle of the central bright band. The separation of the two first-order dark bands is

$$2x = 2(0.118\text{ cm}) = 0.236\text{ cm} = 2.36\text{ mm}.$$

• PROBLEM 904

Find the angular width of the central maximum of a Fraunhofer diffraction pattern if the light used has wavelength $\lambda = 6000$ Å and the slit width is $.1 \times 10^{-3}$ m.

Solution: The angular location of the minima of a Fraunhofer diffraction pattern is given by

$$\sin\varphi = m\lambda/a \qquad (m = 1, 2, \ldots)$$

where a is the slit width. The central maximum is flanked on either side by the first order minima (m = 1). The angular position of this

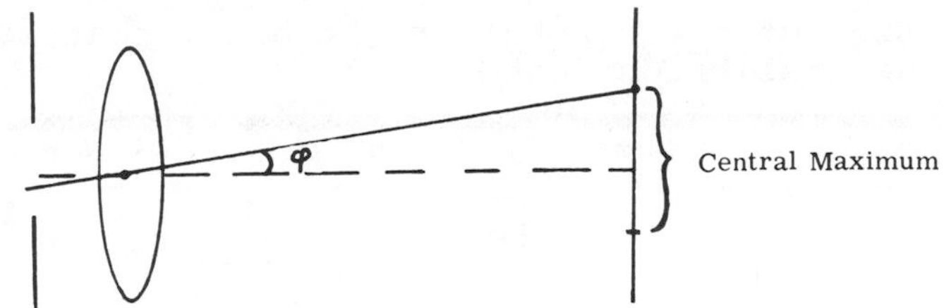

minimum is

$$\sin \varphi = \frac{(1)(6000\ \text{Å})}{(.1 \times 10^{-3}\ \text{m})}$$

Since $1\text{Å} = 10^{-10}$ m

$$\sin \varphi = \frac{6 \times 10^{3} \times 10^{-10}\ \text{m}}{1 \times 10^{-4}\ \text{m}}$$

$$\sin \varphi = 6 \times 10^{-3} = .006$$

$$\varphi = 1/3^{\circ}$$

Hence, the angular breadth of the central maximum is (see figure)

$$2\varphi = 2/3^{\circ}.$$

• PROBLEM 905

Sodium yellow light, which consists of the two wavelengths 5890 Å and 5896 Å, falls normally on a plane diffraction grating with 1500 rulings per centimeter. What is the angular separation of the two lines observed in the first-order spectrum, and under what conditions will they be seen as separated?

Solution: The grating formula is $a \sin \theta = m\lambda$ where m is the order number, λ is the wavelength of the light incident on the grating, and a is the grating spacing. The angle θ locates the diffraction maxima. But the number of rulings per unit distance p is equal to 1/a. Therefore $\sin \theta = m\lambda/a = mp\lambda$. In this problem, a small change in wavelength to $\lambda + d\lambda$ produces a change in the angle of diffraction to $\theta + d\theta$. Then

$$\frac{d}{d\lambda}(\sin \theta) = \frac{d}{d\lambda}(mp\lambda)$$

or $$\cos \theta \frac{d\theta}{d\lambda} = mp$$

whence $$d\theta = \frac{mp\ d\lambda}{\cos \theta} = \frac{mp\ d\lambda}{\sqrt{1 - m^2p^2\lambda^2}}$$

Note that we've used the fact that

$$\cos \theta = \sqrt{1 - \sin^2 \theta} = \sqrt{1 - m^2p^2\lambda^2}$$

The separation of the sodium lines in the first order is thus

$$d\theta = \frac{1 \times 1500\ \text{cm}^{-1} \times 6 \times 10^{-8}\ \text{cm}}{\sqrt{1 - 1^2 \times 1500^2\text{cm}^{-2} \times 5893^2 \times 10^{-16}\ \text{cm}^2}}$$

$$= \frac{9 \times 10^{-5}}{0.9961} = 9.04 \times 10^{-5} \text{ rad.}$$

We have used the average value of the 2 wavelengths of sodium light in this formula (5890 Å + 5896 Å/2 = 5893 Å).

The resolving power of a grating $R = \lambda/d\lambda = mn$, where n is the total number of lines on the grating. If we are to resolve the given wavelength difference $d\lambda$ in the first order, we must have

$$n = \frac{\lambda}{md\lambda}$$

$$n = \frac{5893 \times 10^{-8} \text{ cm}}{1 \times 6 \times 10^{-8} \text{ cm}} = 982 \text{ rulings.}$$

As long as the grating is wide enough to contain 982 rulings, the sodium yellow lines will be resolved in the first order.

• PROBLEM 906

The deviation of the second-order diffracted image formed by an optical grating having 5000 lines/cm is 32°. Calculate the wavelength of the light used.

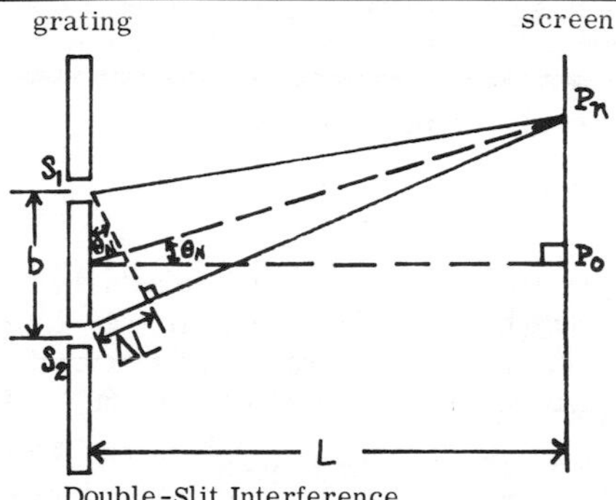

Double-Slit Interference

Solution: An optical grating is a transparent piece of glass or plastic on which there are closely spaced parallel scratches. These scratches behave like opaque barriers and the spaces between slits like narrow slits. Each adjacent pair of slits produces a double-slit diffraction pattern so that this problem can be analyzed using double-slit interference.

Point P_n in the diagram receives light from both slits. The path lengths from slits S_1 and S_2 to P_n differ by an amount very close to ΔL. If the two waves are in phase as they leave slits S_1 and S_2, then they will also be in phase at P_n if ΔL is an integral multiple of the wavelength of the light. That is, if $\Delta L = n\lambda$ then reinforcement occurs at P_n and a bright band occurs there.

If b is small compared to L, then the angle θ in the small right triangle is nearly equal to θ in the larger right triangle. Therefore, we can say

$$\sin \theta_N = \frac{N\lambda}{b}$$

or $$b \sin \theta_N = N\lambda$$

where θ_N is the deviation of the Nth order diffracted image and b is the distance between slits.

$$b = 1/5000 \text{ cm} = 0.00020 \text{ cm}$$

$$\lambda = \frac{b \sin \theta_N}{N} = \frac{0.00020 \text{ cm} \times 0.53}{2}$$

$$= 0.000053 \text{ cm} = 5\bar{3}00 \text{ A}$$

• PROBLEM 907

The spectrum of a particular light source consists of lines and bands stretching from a wavelength of 5.0 $\times 10^{-5}$ cm to 7.5 $\times 10^{-5}$ cm. When a diffraction grating is illuminated normally with this light it is found that two adjacent spectra formed just overlap, the junction of the two spectra occurring at an angle of 45°. How many lines per centimeter are ruled on the grating?

Solution: The grating formula is

$$d \sin \theta = n\lambda$$

where λ is the wavelength of light incident upon the grating, d is the grating spacing, n is the order number, and θ locates the maxima of the diffraction pattern. At the angle of 45°, we have d sin 45° = m × 7.5 × 10^{-5} cm, and also d sin 45° = (m + 1) × 5.0 × 10^{-5} cm. (We can see why the smaller wavelength has the larger order number by examining the grating formula, d sin θ = nλ. Since θ and d are the same for both λ's, we obtain nλ = const. Hence, at a particular θ, the larger the wavelength, the smaller must be n, and vice-versa).

$$\therefore \quad \frac{m+1}{m} = \frac{7.5}{5.0} = \frac{3}{2} . \qquad \therefore \quad m = 2.$$

The second-order spectrum thus just overlaps with the third. Also, using the first formula above,

$$d = \frac{2 \times 7.5 \times 10^{-5} \text{ cm}}{\sin 45°} = 2.12 \times 10^{-4} \text{ cm}.$$

This is the separation of the rulings. Hence the number of rulings per centimeter, n, is

$$n = \frac{1}{d} = \frac{10^4}{2.12 \text{ cm}} = 4715 \text{ per cm}.$$

The limits of the visible spectrum are approximately 400 nm to 700 nm. (a) Find the angular breadth of the first-order visible spectrum produced by a plane grating having 15,000 lines per inch, when light is incident normally on the grating. (b) Show that the violet of the third-order spectrum overlaps the red of the second-order spectrum:

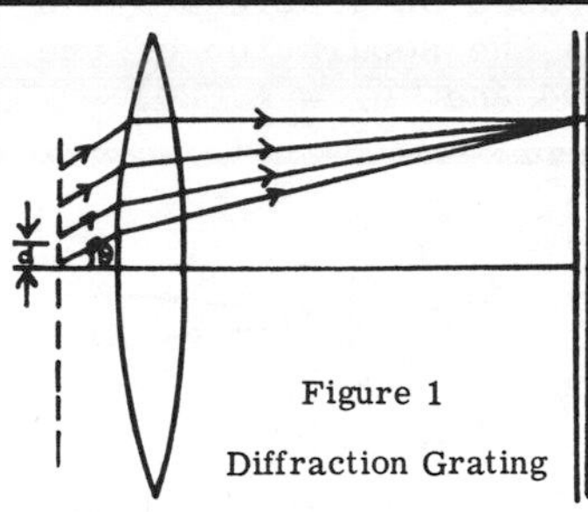

Figure 1

Diffraction Grating

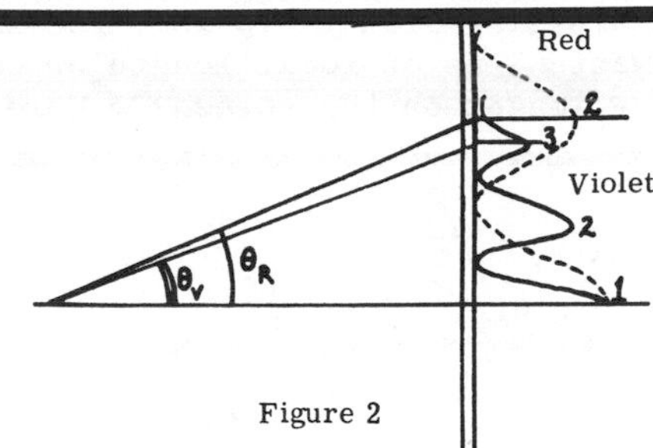

Figure 2

Solution: (a) The diffraction grating, shown in Fig. 1 has a grating spacing d given by

$$d = \frac{2.54 \text{ cm/in.}}{15,000 \text{ lines/in.}} = 1.69 \times 10^{-4} \text{ cm.}$$

The nth order angular deviation for wavelength λ is

$$\sin\theta = \frac{n\lambda}{d}$$

therefore the angular deviation of the violet is

$$\sin\theta_v = \frac{\lambda_v}{d} n = \frac{4 \times 10^{-5} \text{ cm}}{1.69 \times 10^{-4} \text{cm}} = 0.237,$$

$$\theta_v = 13^\circ 40'.$$

The angular deviation of the red is

$$\sin\theta_R = \frac{\lambda_R}{d} n = \frac{7 \times 10^{-5} \text{ cm}}{1.69 \times 10^{-4} \text{ cm}} = 0.415,$$

$$\theta_R = 24^\circ 30'.$$

The first order deviations (n = 1) for the highest and lowest frequencies (violet and red respectively) of the visible spectrum will have an angular difference $\theta_R - \theta_v$. Hence, the first order visible spectrum includes an angle of

$$\theta_R - \theta_v = 24^\circ 30' - 13^\circ 40' = 10^\circ 50'.$$

(b) For n = 3, violet light has the angular deviation

$$\sin\theta_v = \frac{3\lambda_v}{d} = \frac{3 \times \left(4 \times 10^{-5} \text{ cm}\right)}{d}$$

The second-order deviation for the red light is

$$\sin\theta_R = \frac{2\lambda_R}{d} = \frac{2 \times \left(7 \times 10^{-5} \text{ cm}\right)}{d}$$

The first angle θ_v is smaller than the second angle θ_R, therefore whatever the grating spacing, the third order will always overlap the second, as can be seen in Fig. 2.

The spectrum from a hydrogen discharge tube contains the red C line and the violet F line. A parallel beam from the discharge tube is passed through a refracting prism of 60° angle with the red C light suffering minimum deviation. What are the deviations suffered by the red C light and the violet F light?

On emerging from the prism, the light is focused on a screen by an achromatic lens of focal length 30 cm. What is the separation of the C and F images on the screen? $\left(\text{Here } n_C = 1.604 \text{ and } n_F = 1.620\right)$

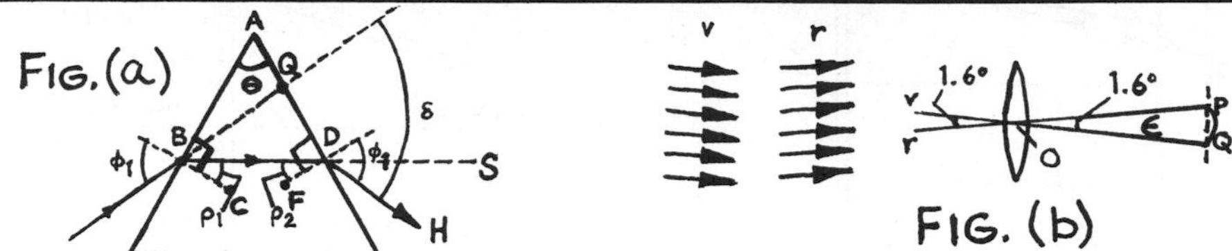

Solution: The geometry is shown in figure (a). For minimum deviation, $\varphi_1 = \varphi_2$. The physics of this problem lies in the fact that the refractive index, n, of the glass of which the prism is constructed is different for different colors of light passing through the prism. That is,

$$n = n(\lambda)$$

where λ is the wavelength of the incident light. Hence, if the different colored incident light rays are all parallel, they will leave the prism in a non-parallel manner. We now derive a formula for the deviation, δ, of a light ray incident on the prism face at an angle φ_1.

Note, first, that

$$\delta = \sphericalangle QBD + \sphericalangle SDH$$

But, $\sphericalangle SDH = \varphi_1 - \rho_2$ and $\sphericalangle QBD = \varphi_1 - \rho_1$. Then,

$$\delta = 2\varphi_1 - \left(\rho_1 + \rho_2\right)$$

Apply Snell's Law at both interfaces, and noting that the refractive index of air is 1, we obtain

$$\sin\varphi_1 = n(\lambda)\sin\rho_1 \qquad n(\lambda)\sin\rho_2 = \sin\varphi_1 \tag{1}$$

Equating these 2 equations

$$n(\lambda)\sin\rho_1 = n(\lambda)\sin\rho_2$$

whence

$$\rho_1 = \rho_2 = \rho$$

Therefore,

$$\delta = 2\varphi_1 - 2\rho = 2\left(\varphi_1 - \rho\right) \tag{2}$$

But, since the prism is in the shape of an equilateral triangle,

$$\sphericalangle ABD = 90 - \rho_1 = 90 - \rho = 60^\circ$$

Hence,

$$\rho = 30^\circ \tag{3}$$

Using this fact in (2)

$$\delta = 2\left(\varphi_1 - 30^\circ\right) \tag{4}$$

Substituting (3) in equation (1), we can find φ_1

$$\sin\varphi_1 = n(\lambda)\sin 30^\circ = \frac{n(\lambda)}{2}$$

whence

$$\varphi_1 = \sin^{-1}\left(\frac{n(\lambda)}{2}\right) \qquad (5)$$

Using (5) in (4)

$$\delta = 2\left(\sin^{-1}\left[\frac{n(\lambda)}{2}\right] - 30^\circ\right)$$

We may use this formula for all the colors incident on the prism, since they all enter the latter at the same angle φ_1. Hence, for the red C line,

$$\delta_C = 2\left(\sin^{-1}\left[\frac{n_C}{2}\right] - 30^\circ\right)$$

$$\delta_C = 2\left(\sin^{-1}\left[\frac{1.604}{2}\right] - 30^\circ\right) = 2\left(\sin^{-1}(.802) - 30^\circ\right)$$

$$\delta_C = 2\left(53.3^\circ - 30^\circ\right) = 46.6^\circ$$

and, for the violet F line,

$$\delta_F = 2\left(\sin^{-1}\left[\frac{n_F}{2}\right] - 30^\circ\right)$$

$$\delta_F = 2\left(\sin^{-1}\left[\frac{1.620}{2}\right] - 30^\circ\right)$$

$$\delta_F = 2\left(\sin^{-1}(.810) - 30^\circ\right)$$

$$\delta_F = 2\left(54.1^\circ - 30^\circ\right) = 48.2^\circ$$

A parallel beam of red light is emerging from the prism at an angle of $48.2^\circ - 46.6^\circ = 1.6^\circ$ to a similarly parallel beam of violet light. Parallel beams are brought to a focus in the focal planes of lenses, and thus both the red and violet beams give sharp images in the focal plane of the inserted lens.

The real image of a point object is the place at which all rays converge. Hence if we can find the point at which any violet ray, and the point at which any red ray, strike the focal plane of the lens, we have located the images, and their separation gives us the answer required. The easiest rays to choose are the red and violet rays which pass through the center of the lens, since these are undeviated.

It can be seen from figure (b) that the separation of the images is PQ. Now, if ϵ is small, we can find its value (in radian measure), by

$$\epsilon = \frac{\widehat{PQ}}{R} \qquad (6)$$

where $\widehat{PQ}$ is the arc PQ, and R is the radius which sweeps out PQ. If ϵ is small,

$$\widehat{PQ} \approx \overline{PQ}$$

and

$$R \approx f$$

where f is the focal length of the lens and $\overline{PQ}$ is the straight line PQ. This follows since both P and Q lie in the lens' focal plane. Then, using (6)

$$\overline{PQ} \approx \epsilon f$$

where ϵ is in radians. Noting that

$$1^\circ = 2\pi/180 \text{ rad}$$

$$1.6^\circ = 3.2\pi/180 \text{ rad} = .028 \text{ rad}$$

and

$$\overline{PQ} \approx (.028 \text{ rad})(30 \text{ cm}) = .84 \text{ cm}.$$

CHAPTER 31

ATOMIC/MOLECULAR STRUCTURE

• PROBLEM 910

In the Bohr model of the hydrogen atom, the electron is considered to move in a circular orbit around the nuclear proton. The radius of the orbit is 0.53×10^{-8} cm. What is the velocity of the electron in this orbit?

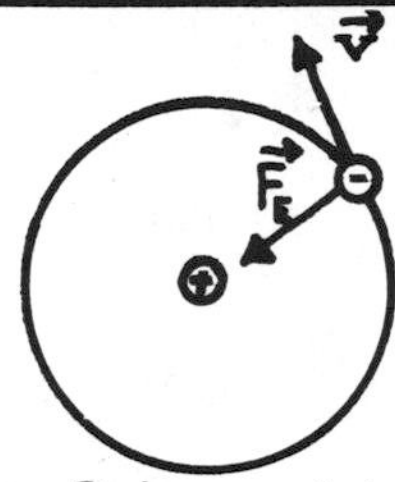

Bohr Model

Solution: If we assume that the only force acting is the electrostatic force,

$$F_E = -\frac{q_1 q_2}{r^2} = \frac{e^2}{r^2}$$

$$= \frac{(4.80 \times 10^{-10} \text{ statC})^2}{(0.53 \times 10^{-8} \text{ cm})^2}$$

$$= 8.2 \times 10^{-3} \text{ dyne}$$

In order to maintain a circular orbit, the electron must be subject to a centripetal acceleration:

$$a_c = \frac{v^2}{r} .$$

The mass of the electron times this acceleration must equal the force on the electron:

$$m_e a_c = \frac{m_e v^2}{r} = F_E$$

or, solving for v,

$$v = \sqrt{\frac{rF_E}{m_e}}$$

$$= \sqrt{\frac{(0.53 \times 10^{-8}\text{cm} \times 8.2 \times 10^{-3}\text{dyne})}{(9.11 \times 10^{-28}\text{g})}}$$

$$= 2.18 \times 10^8 \text{ cm/sec}$$

Hence, the electron velocity is about 1 percent of the velocity of light.

• PROBLEM 911

How many nuclei are there in 1 kg of aluminum?

Solution: The mass m of a single aluminum atom $^{27}_{31}Al$, is 26.98153 amu. 1 a.m.u. corresponds to the mass of a proton or 1.66×10^{-27} kg, therefore

$$m = (26.98 \text{ amu})\left(1.66 \times 10^{-27} \frac{\text{kg}}{\text{amu}}\right) = 4.48 \times 10^{-26}\text{kg}$$

This mass value is also approximately equal to the mass of an aluminum nucleus since the electron mass is so much smaller than the mass of the atom. Therefore, the number of aluminum nuclei is

$$N = \frac{1.0 \text{ kg}}{4.48 \times 10^{-26} \text{ kg/nuclei}} = 2.23 \times 10^{25} \text{ nuclei.}$$

• PROBLEM 912

Natural boron is made up of 20 per cent ^{10}B and 80 per cent ^{11}B. What is the approximate atomic weight of natural boron on the scale of 16 units for ^{16}O (chemical scale)?

Solution. The scale of 16 units for ^{16}O means that the superscript represents the atomic weight of the atom. Therefore:

atomic weight of $^{10}B = 10$

atomic weight of $^{11}B = 11$

average atomic weight of boron (natural)

$$= \frac{20 \times 10 + 80 \times 11}{100} = 10.8.$$

• PROBLEM 913

A cube of copper metal has a mass of 1.46×10^{-1} kg. If the length of each edge of the cube is 2.5×10^{-2} m and a copper atom has a mass of 1.06×10^{-25} kg, determine the number of atoms present in the sample and then estimate the size of a copper atom. Although the actual crystal structure is more complex, assume a simple cubic lattice.

Solution: The number of atoms, N, is found in the following manner:

Mass of N atoms = (Mass of 1 atom)(number of atoms, N)

$$1.46 \times 10^{-1} \text{ kg} = \left(1.06 \times 10^{-25} \frac{\text{kg}}{\text{atom}}\right)(\text{N atoms})$$

$$N = \frac{1.46 \times 10^{-1} \text{ kg}}{1.06 \times 10^{-25} \frac{\text{kg}}{\text{atom}}} = 1.38 \times 10^{24} \text{ atoms.}$$

Let us assume that each copper atom may be represented by

a sphere whose diameter is d. If the atoms are touching one another, there will be the same number, say n, along each edge of the cube. The total number of atoms N is related to n by the volume relationship

$$n^3 = N = 138 \times 10^{24}.$$

The number of atoms along one edge is then approximately

$$n = 1.1 \times 10^8 \text{ atoms}$$

This number is approximate due to the inaccuracy of the initial assumption that each atom has the shape of a sphere. Also,

Length of an edge of the cube = (diameter, d, of one copper atom)(number, n, of atoms along an edge)

Then $nd = 2.5 \times 10^{-2}$ m. Therefore, the diameter of a copper atom is approximately

$$d = \frac{2.5 \times 10^{-2} \text{ m}}{1.1 \times 10^8} = 2.27 \times 10^{-10} \text{ m}$$

This value agrees reasonably well with the value of 2.56×10^{-10} m obtained using other methods.

• PROBLEM 914

What is the energy of a photon of green light (frequency = 6×10^{14} vps)?

Solution: Planck's hypothesis states that $E = h\upsilon$, where υ is the frequency of the radiation, and h is Planck's constant. Therefore,

$$E = (6.63 \times 10^{-34} \text{ joule-sec})(6 \times 10^{14} \text{ vps})$$

$$E = 3.98 \times 10^{-19} \text{ joules.}$$

• PROBLEM 915

What is the energy content of 1 gm of water?

Solution. If the mass of the gram of water was completely converted to energy, the amount of energy released would be

$$E = mc^2$$

$$= 1 \times 10^{-3} \times (3 \times 10^8)^2$$

$$= 9 \times 10^{13} \text{ joules}$$

• PROBLEM 916

If the average distance the free electrons travel between collisions in copper is 4×10^{-8} m, how many collisions per second do the electrons make? What is the time between collisions? The average electron speed in copper is 1.21×10^6 m/s.

Solution: The number of collisions per second, N, is,

$$N = \frac{v}{\bar{\ell}} = \frac{1.21 \times 10^6 \text{ m/s}}{4 \times 10^{-8} \text{ m/collision}} = 3.0 \times 10^{13} \text{ collisions/s}$$

The average time t between collisions is

$$t = \frac{1}{N} = \frac{1}{3.0 \times 10^{13}} \text{ s} = 3.3 \times 10^{-14} \text{ s} .$$

• **PROBLEM 917**

Find the energy equivalent to 1 amu.

Solution: The atomic mass unit is 1/12 of the mass of a C^{12}_{6} atom and is equal to 1.660×10^{-24} gm. The amount of energy released by the conversion of this mass to energy is,

$$E = \Delta mc^2 = 1.660 \times 10^{-24} \text{ gm} \times (2.998 \times 10^{10} \text{ cm/sec})^2$$

$$= 14.94 \times 10^{-4} \text{ erg} = 14.94 \times 10^{-11} \text{ joule}$$

Converting to units of electron volts, since the energies on the molecular level are small,

$$1 \text{ Mev} = 10^6 \text{ volts} \times 1.602 \times 10^{-19} \text{ coul}$$

$$= 1.602 \times 10^{-13} \text{ joule}$$

$$1 \text{ amu} = \frac{14.94 \times 10^{-11}}{1.602 \times 10^{-13}} \text{ Mev}$$

$$= 931 \text{ Mev}$$

• **PROBLEM 918**

Estimate the radius of the nucleus of mercury. The radius R varies with atomic weight A according to

$$R = 1.2 \times 10^{-13} A^{1/3} \text{ cm.}$$

Solution. For mercury, A = 200, thus

$$R = 1.2 \times 10^{-13} \sqrt[3]{200}$$

$$= 7 \times 10^{-13} \text{ cm.}$$

The variation of R with A quoted above holds for any nucleus. From it we can see that the density of nuclear matter is the same for every nucleus. That is,

$$\text{density} = \frac{\text{mass}}{\text{volume}} = \frac{m}{V}.$$

The mass of a nucleus of atomic weight A is

$$m = 1.66 \times 10^{-27} \text{ A.}$$

If the nucleus is assumed to be spherical with radius R, its volume will be

$$V = \frac{4\pi R^3}{3} = \frac{4\pi}{3} \times (1.2 \times 10^{-13})^3 \text{ A.}$$

Thus the density does not depend on A, and is approximately

$$\text{density} = \frac{3}{4\pi} \times \frac{1.66 \times 10^{-27}}{(1.2 \times 10^{-13})^3}$$

$$= 2.3 \times 10^{11} \text{ gm/cm}^3.$$

This is a truly fantastic density; one cubic centimeter of nuclear matter has a mass of about 200,000 tons!

• PROBLEM 919

At a counting rate of 5 atoms per second, how long would it take to count the atoms in a spherical droplet of water 0.1 cm in diameter?

Solution: We can calculate the number of atoms in the water droplet from the density of water and the gram molecular weight of a water molecule.

The density of water is defined as its mass per unit volume, or

$$\rho = \frac{m}{v}$$

Hence, $m = \rho v.$ (1)

Now, the volume of water in the spherical droplet is the volume of a sphere of radius .05 cm. The volume of a sphere of radius $r = 4/3\ \pi r^3$.

$$\text{Volume of droplet} = 4/3\ \pi(0.05)^3$$

$$= 5.24 \times 10^{-4} \text{ cm}^3$$

The density of water is 1 gm per cubic centimeter, and from (1), the mass of water in the droplet is

$$m = (1 \text{ gm/cm}^3)(5.24 \times 10^{-4} \text{ cm}^3)$$

$$m = 5.24 \times 10^{-4} \text{ gm}$$

We may now find the number of molecules in this mass by dividing it by the mass of one molecule.

A molecule of water contains two atoms of ${}_1H^1$ and one atom of ${}_8O^{16}$ and its molecular mass is therefore

$$(2 \times 1.0078 \text{ amu}) + 15.995 \text{ amu} = 18 \text{ amu}$$

But 1 amu $= 1.66 \times 10^{-24}$ gms.

Therefore, a water molecule has a mass, in grams, of

$(18)(1.66 \times 10^{-24}$ gms$) = 29.88 \times 10^{-24}$ gms

The total number of molecules in 5.24×10^{-24}gms is then

$$n = \frac{5.24 \times 10^{-4} \text{ gm}}{2.99 \times 10^{-23} \text{ gm/molec.}} = 1.75 \times 10^{19} \text{ molecules}$$

to sufficient accuracy.

Since each molecule contains 3 atoms, the number of atoms in the water droplet is

$3n = (1.75 \times 10^{19}$ molecules$)(3$ atoms/molecule$)$

$3n = 5.25 \times 10^{19}$ atoms

At a rate of 5 per second the time taken to count these atoms would be

$$\frac{5.25 \times 10^{19} \text{ atoms}}{5 \text{ atoms/sec}} = 1.05 \times 10^{19} \text{ sec}$$

There are approximately 3.16×10^{7} sec in a year, so the time taken would be

$$\frac{1.05 \times 10^{19} \text{ sec}}{3.16 \times 10^{7} \text{ sec/yr}} = 3.3 \times 10^{11} \text{ years.}$$

• PROBLEM 920

Calculate the mass of the electron by combining the results of Millikan's determination of the electron charge q and J.J. Thomson's measurement of q/m.

Solution: The charge of the electron, $q = 1.6 \times 10^{-19}$ C, and the ratio of charge to mass, $q/m = 1.76 \times 10^{11}$ C/kg, are known.

$$\frac{q}{m} = 1.76 \times 10^{11} \frac{\text{C}}{\text{kg}} \quad \text{but} \quad q = 1.6 \times 10^{-19} \text{ C}$$

Therefore,

$$m = \frac{1.6 \times 10^{-19} \not{\text{C}}}{1.76 \times 10^{11} \not{\text{C}}/\text{kg}} = 9.1 \times 10^{-31} \text{ kg}$$

The mass of the electron is about 9.1×10^{-31} kg.

• PROBLEM 921

Find the deBroglie wavelength corresponding to an electron with energy 1, 10^{4}, or 10^{5} eV. Neglect any corrections connected with the theory of relativity.

Solution: DeBroglie knew that light has a dual, wave-particle nature given by the relationship

$$\lambda = \frac{h}{p}$$

which relates the wavelength λ of a light wave with the momentum p of its photons through Planck's constant h. DeBroglie reasoned that matter also has a wave-particle nature, and that the wavelength of the matter wave was given by the same equation used for light with p the momentum of the particle of matter. We then have

$$\lambda = \frac{h}{mv}$$

The energy given for the electron is its kinetic energy K. This is equal to

$$K = \tfrac{1}{2} mv^2$$

or $$v = \sqrt{\frac{2K}{m}}$$

We can therefore say

$$\lambda = \frac{h}{m\sqrt{\frac{2K}{m}}} = \sqrt{\frac{h^2}{2Km}}$$

where m is the mass of the electron.

Substituting values, we find

$$\lambda = \sqrt{\frac{(6.6 \times 10^{-34}\ \text{joule/sec})^2}{(2)\times(\text{KeV})\times(1.6\ \times 10^{-19}\text{joule/eV})\times(9.1\times 10^{-31}\text{kg})}}$$

$$= \sqrt{\frac{150}{K}}\ 10^{-10}\ \text{m} = \sqrt{\frac{150}{K}}\ \text{A}$$

where K is in electron volts and λ in Angstroms.

For $K_1 = 1$ eV

$$\lambda_1 = \sqrt{\frac{150}{1}}\ \text{A} = 12.2\ \text{A}$$

For $K_2 = 10^4$ eV

$$\lambda_2 = \sqrt{\frac{150}{10^4}}\ \text{A} = 0.122\ \text{A}$$

For $K_3 = 10^5$ eV

$$\lambda_3 = \sqrt{\frac{150}{10^5}}\ \text{A} = 0.039\ \text{A}$$

• PROBLEM 922

Calculate the wavelength of the first line in the visible (Balmer) series of the hydrogen spectrum, for which the electron transition is from orbit 3 to orbit 2.

Solution: The total energy of the nth orbit of the hydrogen atom is given by

$$E_n = -\tfrac{1}{2} K \frac{e^2}{r_n}$$

where $r_n = n^2 r_1$, r_1 being the first Bohr radius. If an electron jumps from a higher orbit to a lower orbit, it will emit photons (electromagnetic waves) because it has to decrease its energy to match the binding energy of the new orbit. Therefore, the energy carried away by radiation is equal to the difference between the two energy levels

$$E^{ph} = E_{n_1} - E_{n_2} = -\frac{1}{2} k \frac{e^2}{r_1}\left[\frac{1}{n_1^2} - \frac{1}{n_2^2}\right]$$

where n_1 and n_2 denote the initial and final energy levels. If the emitted electromagnetic wave has a wave length, λ, its energy is $\frac{hc}{\lambda}$. We have, then, for the wave length:

$$\frac{1}{\lambda} = \frac{1}{2}\frac{ke^2}{hcr_1}\left[\frac{1}{n_2^2} - \frac{1}{n_1^2}\right].$$

Substituting for the constants, we get

$$\frac{1}{\lambda} = R\left(\frac{1}{n_2^2} - \frac{1}{n_1^2}\right)$$

where

$$R = \frac{ke^2}{2hcr_1} = \frac{\left(9 \times 10^9 \text{ m/farads}\right) \times \left(1.6 \times 10^{-19} \text{ coul}\right)^2}{(2) \times \left(5.29\times10^{-11}\text{m}\right) \times \left(6.63\times10^{-34}\text{J-sec}\right) \times \left(3\times10^8\text{m/sec}\right)}$$

$$= 1.097 \times 10^7 \text{ m}^{-1}$$

$$= 1.097 \times 10^7 \text{ m}^{-1} \times 10^{-10}\text{m/A}$$

$$= 1.097 \times 10^{-3} \text{ A}^{-1}$$

For $n_1 = 3$ and $n_2 = 2$, the wavelength is

$$\frac{1}{\lambda} = 1.097 \times 10^{-3} \text{ A}^{-1}\left(\frac{1}{2^2} - \frac{1}{3^2}\right)$$

$$= 1.52 \times 10^{-4} \text{ A}^{-1}$$

$$\lambda = 6560 \text{ A}$$

• PROBLEM 923

As the explosive TNT burns, it releases about 4.2×10^6 joules/kg. The molecular weight of TNT is 227. Find the energy released by one molecule of TNT in the process. What is the fractional change in mass that occurs as one kg of TNT explodes?

Solution. The molecular weight is expressed in terms of atomic mass units. One amu equals 1.66×10^{-27} kg. Therefore, the mass of one molecule is $1.66 \times 10^{-27} \times 227$ kg. The amount of energy released by one molecule is,

$$\text{energy release} = 4.2 \times 10^6 \times 1.66 \times 10^{-27} \times 227 \text{ joule}$$

$$= 1.58 \times 10^{-18} \text{ joule}$$

$$= 9.8 \text{ eV}.$$

This energy should be compared with the quantity 7.6×10^{10} joules involved in the fission of a uranium atom into zirconium and neodymium. We can easily calculate the fraction of mass converted into energy in an explosion of TNT. The energy released by 1 kg is 4.2×10^6 J; thus the mass change is

$$\Delta m = \frac{E}{c^2} = \frac{4.2 \times 10^6}{(3 \times 10^8)^2}$$

$$= 4.7 \times 10^{-11} \text{ kg}.$$

The fractional change in mass is

$$\frac{\Delta m}{m} = \frac{4.7 \times 10^{-11} \text{ kg}}{1 \text{ kg}} = 4.7 \times 10^{-11}.$$

• PROBLEM 924

Show that for large values of the principal quantum number, the frequencies of revolution of an electron in adjacent energy levels of a hydrogen atom and the radiated frequency for a transition between these levels all approach the same value.

Solution: We use the Bohr model of the hydrogen atom in the analysis of this problem. Assuming that the electron is orbiting about the proton in a circular orbit, we observe that its period is given by

$$T = \frac{2\pi r}{v} \qquad (1)$$

where r is the orbit radius, and v is the velocity of the electron. Bohr's condition on the angular momentum of the electron is

$$L = nh/2\pi \qquad n = 0,1,2,\ldots$$

In a circular orbit,

$$L = mvr$$

whence

$$mvr = nh/2\pi$$

and

$$v = \frac{nh}{2\pi mr} \qquad (2)$$

Inserting (2) in (1)

$$T = 2\pi r \cdot \frac{2\pi mr}{nh}$$

$$T = \frac{4\pi^2 mr^2}{nh} \qquad (3)$$

To eliminate r in (3), we note that the Coulomb force acting on the electron is centripetal, and

$$\frac{1}{4\pi\epsilon_0} \frac{e^2}{r^2} = \frac{mv^2}{r}$$

where e is the electronic charge. Hence

$$e^2 r = mv^2 r^2 4\pi\epsilon_0$$

$$r = \frac{e^2}{4\pi\epsilon_0 v^2 m} \qquad (4)$$

Substituting (2) in (4)

$$r = \frac{e^2}{4\pi\epsilon_0 m} \left(\frac{4\pi^2 m^2 r^2}{n^2 h^2} \right)$$

$$1 = \frac{e^2 \pi m r}{n^2 h^2 \epsilon_0}$$

and

$$r = \frac{n^2 h^2 \epsilon_0}{e^2 \pi m} \qquad (5)$$

Substituting (5) in (3)

$$T = \frac{4\pi^2 m}{nh} \cdot \frac{n^4 h^4 \epsilon_0^2}{e 4\pi^2 m^2}$$

$$T = \frac{4n^3 h^3 \epsilon_0^2}{e^4 m}$$

Hence, the orbital frequency of the electron is

$$\nu = \frac{me^4}{4\epsilon_0^2 n^3 h^3} \qquad (6)$$

We must now find how the energy of a hydrogen atom is quantized.
The energy of the atom is potential and kinetic

$$E = \tfrac{1}{2} mv^2 - \frac{e^2}{4\pi\epsilon_0 r} \qquad (7)$$

To transform E into a function of n, we eliminate v and r in (7) by using (2) and (5)

$$v = \frac{nh}{2\pi m r} = \frac{nh}{2\pi m}\left(\frac{e^2 \pi m}{n^2 h^2 \epsilon_0}\right)$$

$$v = \frac{e^2}{2\epsilon_0 nh}$$

$$r = \frac{n^2 h^2 \epsilon_0}{e^2 \pi m}$$

and

$$E = \frac{m}{2}\left(\frac{e^4}{4\epsilon_0^2 n^2 h^2}\right) - \frac{e^2}{4\pi\epsilon_0}\left(\frac{e^2 \pi m}{n^2 h^2 \epsilon_0}\right)$$

$$E = \frac{me^4}{8\epsilon_0^2 n^2 h^2} - \frac{me^4}{4\epsilon_0^2 n^2 h^2}$$

$$E = \frac{-me^4}{8\epsilon_0^2 n^2 h^2}$$

But, the energy is quantized and

$$h\nu_n = \frac{-me^4}{8\epsilon_0^2 n^2 h^2}$$

$$\nu_n = \frac{-me^4}{8\epsilon_0^2 n^2 h^3}$$

The radiated frequency for a transition between 2 adjacent energy levels is

$$\nu_n - \nu_{n-1} = \frac{-me^4}{8\epsilon_0^2 h^3}\left(\frac{1}{n^2} - \frac{1}{(n-1)^2}\right)$$

$$\nu_n - \nu_{n-1} = \frac{-me^4}{8\epsilon_0^2 h^3}\left(\frac{n^2-2n+1-n^2}{n^2(n-1)^2}\right)$$

$$\nu_n - \nu_{n-1} = \frac{me^4}{8\epsilon_0^2 h^3}\left(\frac{2n-1}{n^2(n-1)^2}\right) \qquad (7)$$

We must show that (6) and (7) approach the same value for large n. If $n \gg 1$, $2n-1 \approx 2n$ and $n-1 \approx n$. Hence,

$$\nu_n - \nu_{n-1} \approx \frac{me^4}{8\epsilon_0^2 h^3}\left(\frac{2n}{n^2 n^2}\right)$$

$$\nu_n - \nu_{n-1} \approx \frac{me^4}{4n^3 \epsilon_0^2 h^3}$$

which is (6).
At large quantum numbers, classical and quantum mechanical results agree for the energy levels lose their discrete characteristics. This is an example of Bohr's correspondence principle.

• PROBLEM 925

When a small drop of stearic acid is placed on the surface of water, the liquid spreads out on the water to form a single layer of molecules which are all standing on end, as shown in the figure. In a stearic acid molecule, one end is polar. This occurs in the O-H bond, since the electron the two atoms share does not orbit an equal time around the individual atoms. The electron spends more time in orbit around the oxygen atom, causing it to be slightly negative and the hydrogen atom to be slightly positive. The charge of the two atoms as a whole remains neutral. Since water molecules (H_2O) contain O-H bonds, they are also polarized. The stearic acid and water molecules therefore attract each other causing the acid molecules to stand on end. Estimate the length of the stearic acid molecule if the volume of the drop was 1.56×10^{-10} m^3 and the area of the stearic acid film is 6.25×10^{-2} m^2. Also compute the approximate size of an atom, assuming that the carbon, oxygen, and hydrogen atoms are the same size. The chain is 20 atoms long.

Solution: The volume V is related to the area, A, of the liquid and L, the length of the stearic acid molecule, as follows:

$$V = LA$$

The length of the molecule is, therefore,

$$L = \frac{V}{A} = \frac{1.56 \times 10^{-10}\ \text{m}^3}{6.25 \times 10^{-2}\ \text{m}^2} = 2.5 \times 10^{-9}\ \text{m}$$

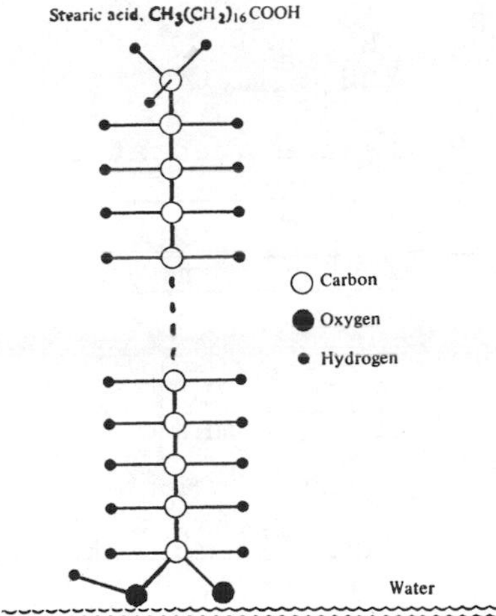

Since the chain is 20 atoms long, (see figure), each atom has a diameter d that is approximately

$$d = \frac{L}{20} = \frac{2.5 \times 10^{-9}\ \text{m}}{2.0 \times 10^{1}} = 1.3 \times 10^{-10}\ \text{m}$$

This method is a very simple way to estimate the length of linear molecules. The technique was suggested independently in 1890 by both W.C. Röntgen and Lord Rayleigh.

• PROBLEM 926

An electron with angular momentum $L = 6 \times 10^{-35}$ N-sec and total energy $H_0 = - 4 \times 10^{-18}$ J is in orbit around a proton. What are the distances of nearest approach and farthest separation?

Solution: The electrostatic potential is given by

$$V_E = -k_E \frac{e^2}{R}$$

where the negative sign indicates its attractive nature. The kinetic energy of the electron is

$$\text{k.E.} = \tfrac{1}{2}mv^2 = \frac{m^2 v^2 R^2}{2mR^2} = \frac{L^2}{2mR^2}$$

since, by definition of angular momentum, $L = mvR$.

The total energy of the electron in its orbit is

$$H_0 = \text{k.E.} + V_E = \frac{L^2}{2mR^2} - k_E \frac{e^2}{R}$$

or
$$H_0 = \frac{L^2}{2mR^2} - \frac{k_E e^2}{R},$$

$$R^2 H_0 = \frac{L^2}{2m} - k_E e^2 R$$

$$R^2 = \frac{L^2}{2mH_0} - \frac{k_E e^2 R}{H_0}$$

$$R^2 + \frac{k_E e^2 R}{H_0} - \frac{L^2}{2mH_0} = 0$$

Solving for R via the quadratic equation

$$R = -\frac{\frac{k_E e^2}{H_0} \pm \sqrt{\frac{k_E^2 e^4}{H_0{}^2} + \frac{2L^2}{mH_0}}}{2}$$

or $$2R = -\frac{k_E e^2}{H_0} \pm \left(\frac{k_E^2 e^4}{H_0^2} + \frac{2L^2}{mH_0}\right)^{\frac{1}{2}}$$ Now,

$$\frac{k_E e^2}{H_0} = \frac{\left(9 \times 10^9 \frac{N \cdot m^2}{c}\right)(2.56 \times 10^{-38}\ c^2)}{-\ 4 \times 10^{-18}\ J}$$

$$\frac{k_E e^2}{H_0} = -\ 5.76 \times 10^{-11}\ m$$

$$\frac{2L^2}{mH_0} = \frac{2(36 \times 10^{-70}\ N^2 \cdot s^2)}{(9.1 \times 10^{-31}\ kg)(.4 \times 10^{-18}\ J)}$$

$$\frac{2L^2}{mH_0} = -\ 1.98 \times 10^{-21}\ m^2$$

Thus

$$2R = 5.76 \times 10^{-11}\ m$$

$$\pm\ (3.32 \times 10^{-21}\ m^2 - 1.98 \times 10^{-21}\ m^2)^{\frac{1}{2}}$$

$$= 5.76 \times 10^{-11}\ m \pm 3.66 \times 10^{-11}$$

Thus

$$R = 1.05 \times 10^{-11}\ m \text{ or } 4.71 \times 10^{-11}\ m$$

which gives the nearest approach and farthest separation.

• PROBLEM 927

An α-particle (mass 6.64×10^{-27} kg, charge 3.20×10^{-19} coul) is scattered through 120° by a gold nucleus (mass 3.28×10^{-25} kg, charge 1.26×10^{-17} coul). The initial kinetic energy of the α-particle was 1.5×10^{-12} J. Calculate the impact parameter, and the distance of nearest approach of the α-particle to the nucleus.

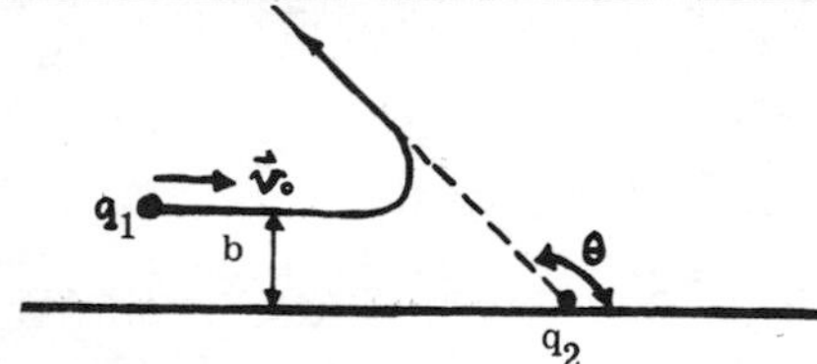

Solution: When a charged particle q_1 is scattered by another stationary charge q_2, the scattering angle θ is determined by the Coulomb force between the two charges, the speed of the incident particle, V_o, and the distance b between the initial trajectory of the incoming particle and the line parallel to this trajectory passing through q_2. The distance b is called the impact parameter, as shown in the figure.

Rutherford's formula for the scattering angle is

$$\tan\frac{\theta}{2} = \frac{k_E q_1 q_2}{mv_0^2 b}$$

Therefore, the impact parameter b is

$$b = \frac{k_E q_1 q_2}{mv_0^2 \tan\frac{\theta}{2}}$$

$$= \frac{9 \times 10^9 \times 3.20 \times 10^{-19} \times 1.26 \times 10^{-17}}{2 \times 1.5 \times 10^{-12} \times 1.732}$$

$$= 7.0 \times 10^{-15} \text{ m}$$

CHAPTER 32

RELATIVISTIC EFFECTS

• PROBLEM 928

Find the length of a meter stick (L_0 = 1 m) that is moving lengthwise at a speed of 2.7×10^8 m/s.

Solution: The length of the stick seems to be smaller when it is moving with respect to the observer. The relativistic formula giving the contracted length L, is

$$L = L_0\sqrt{1 - v^2/c^2}$$

where v is the speed of the stick with respect to the observer. Hence,

$$L = (1m) \times \sqrt{1 - \left(\frac{2.7 \times 10^8 \text{ m/s}}{3 \times 10^8 \text{ m/s}}\right)^2}$$

$$L = (1m) \times 0.44 = 0.44 \text{ m}.$$

• PROBLEM 929

Express the rest mass energy of an electron in ergs and in electron volts.

Solution: The rest mass energy of any object is given by the product of the mass of that object as observed by an observer travelling with the object (m_0), and c^2 (c = the speed of light).

In ergs,

$$E_{rest} = m_0c^2 = (9.11 \times 10^{-28} \text{ g})(9 \times 10^{20} \text{ cm}^2/\text{s}^2)$$

$$m_0c^2 = 8.2 \times 10^{-7} \text{ erg}$$

Since 1 erg = 6.24×10^{11} eV

$$E_{rest} = m_0c^2 = (8.2 \times 10^{-7} \text{ erg})\left(6.24 \times 10^{11} \frac{\text{eV}}{\text{erg}}\right)$$

$$m_0c^2 = 0.512 \times 10^6 \text{ eV}.$$

The rest mass energy of an electron is 0.512 MeV.

• PROBLEM 930

At what velocity is the mass of a particle twice its rest mass?

Solution: When the mass of an object that is travelling at a velocity approaching the speed of light, c, is measured, it is found to be larger than the mass measured when the object is at rest. The mass associated with an object travelling at any velocity $\vec{v}$ is called the particle's relativistic mass, and is given by the formula

$$m(v) = \frac{m_o}{\sqrt{1 - v^2/c^2}} \qquad (1)$$

where m_o is the rest mass of the particle.

We are asked to find the velocity at which the mass of a particle (meaning its relativistic mass) is equal to twice the particle's rest mass. Writing this as an equation,

$$m(v) = 2m_o$$

Using (1), this may be written as

$$\frac{m_o}{\sqrt{1 - \frac{v^2}{c^2}}} = 2m_o$$

$$\frac{1}{\sqrt{1 - \frac{v^2}{c^2}}} = 2$$

Multiplying both sides by $\frac{1}{2}\sqrt{1 - \frac{v^2}{c^2}}$, we obtain

$$\sqrt{1 - \frac{v^2}{c^2}} = \frac{1}{2}$$

$$1 - \frac{v^2}{c^2} = \frac{1}{4}$$

$$\frac{v^2}{c^2} = \frac{3}{4}$$

$$\frac{v}{c} = \frac{\sqrt{3}}{2}$$

$$\frac{v}{c} = 0.866$$

$$v = 0.866 \times 3 \times 10^{10} \text{ cm/sec}$$

$$v = 2.664 \times 10^{10} \text{ cm/sec}$$

• **PROBLEM 931**

An observer moves past a meter stick at a velocity that is one-half the velocity of light. What length does he measure for the meter stick?

Solution: Einstein stated two postulates which form the basis for the theory of special relativity. They are

1. All physical laws are the same in all inertial reference frames.

2. The velocity of light in a vacuum is constant for an observer regardless of the relative motion between the light source and the observer.

From these postulates, it is found that the length of an object viewed by an observer travelling with velocity v with respect to the object is less in the direction of motion than the length seen by a person stationary with respect to the object. The apparent shortened length ℓ' of the meter stick as it moves with respect to the observer (Lorentz contraction) is given by

$$\ell' = \ell\sqrt{1 - (v/c)^2} = \ell\sqrt{1 - \beta^2}$$

where ℓ is the length seen by a person stationary with respect to the object and β is v/c.

For this problem, $\beta = v/c = 0.5c/c = 0.5$ and the length ℓ' measured by the observer is

$$\ell' = \ell\sqrt{1 - \beta^2}$$

$$= (100 \text{ cm}) \times \sqrt{1 - (0.5)^2}$$

$$= (100 \text{ cm}) \times \sqrt{0.75}$$

$$= 86.6 \text{ cm}$$

• **PROBLEM 932**

If a 1-kg object could be converted entirely into energy, how long could a 100-W light bulb be illuminated? A 100-W bulb uses 100 J of energy each second.

Solution: Einstein's mass-energy relation can be used to calculate the energy derived from this mass:

$$E = mc^2 = (1 \text{ kg})(3 \times 10^8 \text{ m/s})^2 = 9 \times 10^{16} \text{ J}.$$

A 100 Watt bulb uses 100 Joules of energy in 1 second, by definition of the watt. Hence, for every 100 Joules of energy supplied, the bulb remains lit for 1 second. The time t the bulb is lighted by 9×10^{16} Joules is

$$t = \frac{9 \times 10^{16} \not{J}}{1 \times 10^2 \not{J}/s} = 9 \times 10^{14} \text{ s}$$

One year is approximately 3.1×10^7 s, so the time may be written

$$t = \frac{9 \times 10^{14} \not{s}}{3.1 \times 10^7 \not{s}/\text{year}} = 2.9 \times 10^7 \text{ years}$$

Mass is indeed a very compact form of energy!

• PROBLEM 933

Show how two clocks, one at the origin and the other a distance d from the origin, may be synchronized.

Solution: The velocity of light is the same for all observers regardless of the relative motion between the light source and the observer. If the distance d between the clocks is measured, then the time t required for light to travel from one clock to the other is

$$t = \frac{d}{c}$$

Suppose that a flash of light is produced at the origin when the clock at the origin is recording exactly 12:00 noon. This flash of light will arrive at the other clock when the origin clock reads 12:00 plus d/c. Hence the other clock should be pre-set so that it reads 12:00 o'clock plus d/c. When the flash of light arrives from the origin, the second clock should then be allowed to begin recording time. This process is said to synchronize the two clocks.

• PROBLEM 934

10 calories of heat are supplied to 1 g of water. How much does the mass of the water increase?

Solution: The increase in total energy of the water is

$$\Delta\varepsilon = 10 \text{ cal} = 10 \times (4.19 \times 10^7 \text{ ergs})$$

$$= 4.19 \times 18^8 \text{ ergs}$$

Then using the mass-energy conversion formula:

$$\Delta m = \frac{\Delta\varepsilon}{c^2}$$

$$= \frac{4.19 \times 10^8 \text{ ergs}}{(3 \times 10^{10} \text{ cm/sec})^2}$$

$$= 4.7 \times 10^{-13} \text{ g}$$

So that the mass of the water increases from 1 g to 1.00000000000047 g, a negligible increase indeed! But the mass has increased. Where does this additional mass come from? It is just the mass associated with the increase of kinetic energy that has been given to the water molecules by the addition of thermal energy.

• PROBLEM 935

A spaceship moving away from the Earth at a velocity $v_1 = 0.75\ c$ with respect to the Earth, launches a rocket (in the direction away from the Earth) that attains a velocity $v_2 = 0.75\ c$ with respect to the spaceship. What is the velocity of the rocket with respect to the Earth?

Solution: Newtonian relativity states that the laws of mechanics are the same in all inertial reference frames but that the laws of electrodynamics are not. Since such a theory was not acceptable, the theory of relativity was developed and resolved this problem. One of the statements of this new theory was that the velocity of light is independent of any relative motion between the light source and the observer. Experiments have shown this to be true. In support of this statement Einstein showed that ordinary mechanical velocities do not add algebraically. Instead, for the addition of two velocities v_1 and v_2, the sum is

$$V = \frac{v_1 + v_2}{1 + \frac{v_1 v_2}{c^2}}$$

For small velocities ($v << c$), this reduces to

$$V = v_1 + v_2,$$

as in Newtonian mechanics, since the term $v_1 v_2/c^2$ is very small compared to one and can be ignored.

Since the velocities in this problem are large, the velocity of the rocket with respect to the Earth is

$$V = \frac{v_1 + v_2}{1 + \frac{v_1 v_2}{c^2}} = \frac{0.75c + 0.75c}{1 + \frac{(0.75c)(0.75c)}{c^2}}$$

$$= \frac{1.5c}{1 + 0.5625} = 0.96c$$

Therefore, in spite of the fact that the simple sum of the two velocities exceeds c, the actual velocity relative to the Earth is slightly less than c.

• PROBLEM 936

It is known that the sun radiates approximately 3.8×10^{26} J of energy into space each second. Determine how much mass must be converted into energy each second, and how many years these thermonuclear reactions may continue at this rate if the sun's total mass is 2×10^{30} kg.

Solution: The mass, m, converted to energy, E, in each second may be obtained from the relationship,

$$E = mc^2$$

$$m = \frac{E}{c^2} = \frac{3.8 \times 10^{26}\ J}{(3 \times 10^8\ m/s)^2} = 4.2 \times 10^9\ kg$$

Since 1 year equals 3.1×10^7 s, the mass lost in 1 year is,

$$m = (4.2 \times 10^9\ kg/s)\ (3.1 \times 10^7\ s/year)$$

$$= \quad 1.3 \times 10^{17}\ kg/year$$

The time t required to consume the sun's mass is,

$$t = \frac{\text{sun's mass}}{\text{mass loss per year}} = \frac{2 \times 10^{30}\ \cancel{k}g}{1.3 \times 10^{17}\ \cancel{k}g/year}$$

$$= 1.5\ \ 10^{13}\ years$$

• PROBLEM 937

What is the Lorentz contraction of an automobile traveling at 60 mph? (60 mph is equivalent to 2682 cm/sec.)

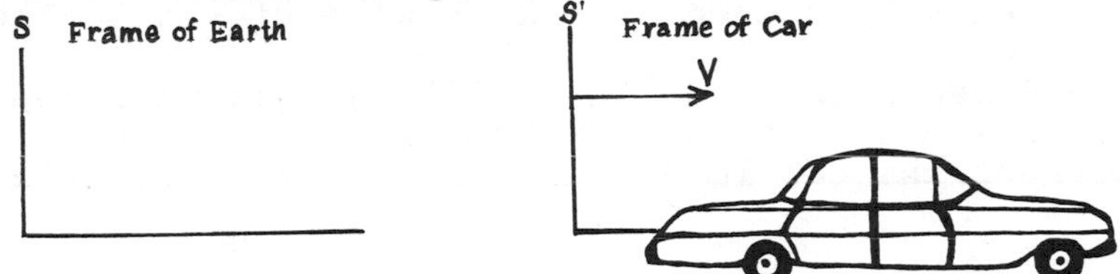

Solution: Suppose we are given two frames of reference moving relative to one another with a velocity v (see figure). If we are dealing with classical physics and want to relate the coordinates of an event occurring in the S-frame (x, y, z, t) to the coordinates of an event occurring in the S'-frame (x', y', z', t'), we use the Galilean transformation, or

$$x' = x - vt$$

$$y' = y \quad \text{(If v is in the x-direction only).}$$

$$z' = z$$

$$t' = t.$$

In relativistic physics, this transformation is invalid, and must be replaced by the Lorentz transformation, or

$$x' = \frac{x - vt}{\sqrt{1 - v^2/c^2}}$$

$$y' = y$$

$$z' = z$$

$$t' = \frac{t - vx/c^2}{\sqrt{1 - v^2/c^2}}.$$

Now, we may relate distances measured in S' to distances as measured in S. Let us imagine the measurement of a distance parallel to the x'-axis in the S' frame. In order to measure the length of a rod in S, we must locate both ends of the rod (x_1, x_2) at the same time $(t_1 = t_2)$ in S. Hence, the length in S' is

$$x'_2 - x'_1 = \frac{(x_2 - x_1) - v(t_2 - t_1)}{\sqrt{1 - v^2/c^2}}.$$

But $t_1 = t_2$, therefore

$$x'_2 - x'_1 = \frac{x_2 - x_1}{\sqrt{1 - v^2/c^2}}.$$

$$\text{Hence } (x_2 - x_1) = (x'_2 - x'_1)\sqrt{1 - v^2/c^2}. \qquad (1)$$

Since $\sqrt{1 - \frac{v^2}{c^2}} < 1$ we then have $x_2 - x_1 < x'_2 - x'_1$. The observer in S measures a smaller rod length (contracted) than the observer in the rod's rest frame, S'. Now, we calculate the length of the car in S, $(x_2 - x_1)$. If V_r is 2682 cm/sec.

$$\frac{V_r}{c} = \frac{2682}{3 \times 10^{10}}$$

$$= 8.94 \times 10^{-8}$$

$$\left(\frac{V_r}{c}\right)^2 = 8.0 \times 10^{-15}.$$

When x is very much less than 1,

$$\sqrt{1 - x} = 1 - \tfrac{1}{2}x \text{ approximately.}$$

Therefore,

$$\sqrt{1 - \left(\frac{V_r}{c}\right)^2} \simeq \left[1 - \left(4.0 \times 10^{-15}\right)\right].$$

Substituting in (1)

$$x_2 - x_1 \simeq \left(x'_2 - x'_1\right)\left(1 - 4.0 \times 10^{-15}\right).$$

This means that the change in length of a meter rule is only 4.0×10^{-15} meters, or 4.0×10^{-13} cm. Since the diameter of an atom is about 10^{-8} cm, the diameter of a nucleus is about 10^{-12} cm and the size of the electron is about 10^{-13} cm, this contraction is clearly negligible. Again we see that the difference between relativistic and classical physics is not important for the velocities we are normally concerned with.

• PROBLEM 938

A particle of rest mass M moving with speed v_0 collides with and sticks to a stationary particle of rest mass m. What is the speed of the composite system after collision?

Solution: In fact, we are asked to find the speed of the center of mass of the system, since it coincides with the composite particle after the collision. The velocity, momentum and total energy of a relativistic particle are related to each other as

$$\frac{\vec{v}}{c} = \frac{\vec{P}\,c}{E}$$

Therefore, we can define the center of mass of a composite system as

$$\frac{\vec{v}_{Cm}}{c} = \frac{\sum_i \vec{P}_i\, c}{\sum_i E_i}$$

Since there are no forces acting on the system, the velocity of the center of mass does not change during the collision. Before the collision, we have

$$\vec{P}_m = 0, \qquad E_m = mc^2$$

$$\vec{P}_M = M\,\gamma_0 \vec{v}_0, \qquad E_M = Mc^2\gamma_0,$$

where $\gamma_0 = \dfrac{1}{\sqrt{1 - \dfrac{v_0^2}{C^2}}}$.

Hence
$$\frac{\vec{v}_{Cm}}{c} = \frac{\vec{P}_M\, c}{mc^2 + Mc^2\gamma_0}$$

$$\frac{v_{Cm}}{c} = \frac{M\gamma_0 v_0}{(m + M\gamma_0)c},$$

$$v_{Cm} = \frac{M\gamma_0}{m + M\gamma_0}\, v_0 .$$

• PROBLEM 939

What is the fractional increase of mass for a 600-mi/hr jetliner?

Solution: Fractional increase of mass is defined as change in mass divided by the original mass or $\Delta m/m_0$. The equation for the variation of mass with velocity is

$$m = \frac{m_0}{\sqrt{1 - \beta^2}}, \qquad \beta^2 = \frac{v^2}{c^2}$$

Therefore the change in mass is

$$\Delta m = m - m_0 = m_0 \left(\frac{1}{\sqrt{1 - \beta^2}} - 1 \right)$$

and

$$\frac{\Delta m}{m_0} = \frac{1}{\sqrt{1 - \beta^2}} - 1$$

For velocities much less than light, $\beta = v/c$ is very small and $1/\sqrt{1 - \beta^2}$ cam be approximated by $1 + \beta^2/2$. Since 600 mi/hr is small compared to c, we can say that for this problem the fractional mass is

$$\frac{\Delta m}{m_0} \cong (1 + \beta^2/2) - 1 = \beta^2/2$$

$$v = 600 \text{ mi/hr} \cong 2.7 \times 10^4 \text{ cm/sec}$$

$$\beta = \frac{v}{c} = \frac{2.7 \times 10^4 \text{ cm/sec}}{3 \times 10^{10} \text{ cm/sec}} \cong 10^{-6}$$

Therefore,

$$\frac{\Delta m}{m_0} \cong \tfrac{1}{2}\beta^2 \cong .5 \times 10^{-12}$$

so that the mass is increased by only a trivial amount.

• PROBLEM 940

Suppose Stan is on the earth and Mavis is flying past the earth in a spaceship with a speed $v = \frac{3}{4}c$, as shown in the figure. Another spaceship is approaching the earth in the opposite direction and Stan measures its velocity of approach $v_s = -\frac{3}{4}c$. The negative sign denotes the fact that the spaceship is moving to the left along the x-axis. What is the speed of the other spaceship as measured by Mavis?

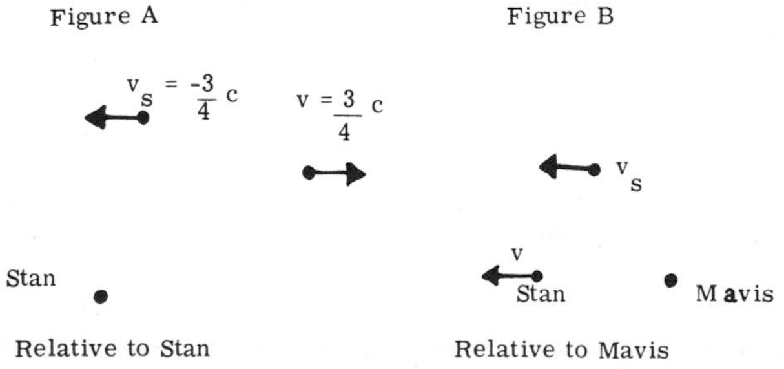

Figure A

$v_s = -\frac{3}{4}c$ $\quad v = \frac{3}{4}c$

Stan

Relative to Stan

Figure B

v_s

v

Stan Mavis

Relative to Mavis

Solution: The given quantities are $v = \frac{3}{4}c$ and $v_s = -\frac{3}{4}c$. In the nonrelativistic case (i.e., where the speeds of the objects are much less than the speed of light, c) the speed of the other spaceship relative to Mavis is, by the law of addition of velocities, equal to the sum of the velocity of the spaceship relative to Stan and the velocity of Stan relative to Mavis. Or

$$v_m = v_s + (-v).$$

The negative sign here indicates the velocity of Stan relative to Mavis. It is equal but opposite to the velocity of Mavis relative to Stan (v).

In the relativistic case, (where, as in this case, the velocities of the objects are comparable to the speed of light), the result above must be modified according to the special theory of relativity, as follows

$$v_m = \frac{v_s + (-v)}{1 + \frac{v_s(-v)}{c^2}}$$

$$= \frac{v_s - v}{1 - vv_s/c^2} = \frac{\left(-\frac{3}{4}c\right) - \frac{3}{4}c}{1 - \left[\left(\frac{3}{4}c\right)\left(-\frac{3}{4}c\right)\right]/c^2}$$

$$= \frac{-\frac{3}{2}c}{1 + \frac{9}{16}} = -\frac{24}{25}c.$$

Thus Mavis measures a speed less than the speed of light.

• PROBLEM 941

Two electrons A and B have speeds of 0.90c and 0.80c, respectively. Find their relative speeds (a) if they are moving in the same direction and (b) if they are moving in opposite directions.

Solution: For speeds close to that of light, when adding velocities, the relativistic law must be used. For the relative velocity V_r between two objects A and B, measured relative to A

$$V_r = \frac{V_A - V_B}{1 - \frac{V_A V_B}{c^2}}$$

When V_A and V_B are small, the term $V_A V_B/c^2$ is small compared to unity and the above equation reduces to the classical expression for relative velocity,

$$V_r = V_A - V_B$$

The relativistic equation for relative velocity

must be used for speeds close to that of light, since, according to the theory of relativity, the maximum speed V_r between two objects is c, regardless of the reference frame used.

(a) For the relative speed between the two electrons A and B, if they move in the same direction

$$V_{ab} = \frac{0.90c - 0.80c}{1 - \frac{(0.90c)(0.80c)}{c^2}}$$

$$= \frac{0.90c - 0.80c}{1 - 0.72c^2/c^2} = \frac{0.10c}{0.28} = 0.36c$$

(b) When the electrons are moving in opposite directions,

$$V_{ab} = \frac{0.90c - (-\ 0.80c)}{1 - \frac{(0.90c)(-\ 0.80c)}{c^2}}$$

$$= \frac{0.90c + 0.80c}{1 + \frac{0.72c^2}{c^2}} = \frac{1.70c}{1.72} = 0.99c$$

If classical physics had been used to compute the relative velocity in the two cases, the relative speeds would have been found to be 0.10c and 1.70c, respectively.

• PROBLEM 942

If two 1 gram masses with equal and opposite velocities of 10^5 cm/sec collide and stick together, what is the additional rest mass of the joined pair?

Solution: In figure 1, both particles are moving towards each other with the same velocity in our frame of reference. In figure 2 they have collided and stuck together. The velocity of the joined body would seem to be zero, but we must prove that this is so. By the law of conservation of momentum, the total momentum before and after collision must be conserved. We are told that the velocities of the two particles are equal but opposite and we assume that they are collinear so that the problem is one dimensional making the velocities v and - v respectively. Therefore, the momentum before the collision is mv + m(- v). Since this is equal to 0, the momentum after the collision must also equal 0, or $m_{final}v_{final} = 0$. Since no energy is produced in the collision, no mass can be lost (it can only be gained) so that m_{final} is not 0, meaning that v_{final} is 0.

Further, we note that the two particles had total kinetic energy $2 \cdot \frac{1}{2} mv^2$ before the collision, and 0 kinetic energy after the collision. Therefore, all this energy must have been converted to heat. Since $E = mc^2$ in the rest frame, this heat energy has an equivalent mass given by $\Delta E = \Delta Mc^2$. Hence,

$$\Delta m = \frac{mv^2 - 0}{c^2}$$

$$\Delta m = \frac{1 \text{ gm } (10^5 \text{ cm/sec})^2}{(3 \times 10^{10} \text{ cm/sec})^2} = 1.1 \times 10^{-11} \text{ gm}$$

• PROBLEM 943

The Berkeley synchrocyclotron was designed to accelerate protons to a kinetic energy of 5.4×10^{-11} J, which corresponds to a particle speed of about 2×10^8 m/s. At this speed the relativistic mass increase is important and must be taken into account in the design of the accelerator. Calculate the percentage increase in the proton mass encountered in this instrument.

Solution: The relation between relative mass, m, and rest mass, m_0, is given by

$$m = \frac{m_0}{\sqrt{1 - v^2/c^2}}, = \frac{m_0}{\sqrt{1 - (2 \times 10^8/3 \times 10^8)^2}}$$

$$= \frac{m_0}{\sqrt{1 - \frac{4}{9}}} = \frac{m_0}{\sqrt{\frac{5}{9}}} = \frac{3m_0}{\sqrt{5}} = 1.34\ m_0.$$

The percentage increase in mass is the fractional increase in mass times 100, or

$$\frac{m - m_0}{m_0} \times 100 = \frac{1.34m_0 - m_0}{m_0} \times 100 = 34 \text{ per cent.}$$

The proton mass at a speed of 2×10^8 m/s is 34 per cent greater than its rest mass.

• PROBLEM 944

An observer on earth finds that the lifetime of a neutron is 6.42×10^2 s. What will the lifetime of a neutron be as measured by an observer in a spacecraft moving past the laboratory at a speed of 2×10^8 m/s?

Solution: If we measure the time required for the neutron to decay, first from the laboratory, and then relative to the neutron, we do not record the same time. The decay of the neutron takes longer for the observer in the lab. It is known that the faster the observer moves with respect to an event the slower the event seems to take place. This phenomenon is called time dilation and is a result of the laws of relativistic kinematics. The lifetime of an unstable (i.e. decaying) particle will therefore be longer when viewed from the rocket. The formula relating the lifetime t_R observed from the rocket to one t_L observed in the laboratory is

$$t_R = \frac{1}{\sqrt{1 - \frac{v^2}{c^2}}} t_L$$

where **v** is the speed of the rocket with respect to the laboratory. Hence, for t_R we get

$$t_R = \frac{1}{\sqrt{1 - \left(\frac{2 \times 10^8 \text{ m/s}}{3 \times 10^8 \text{ m/s}}\right)^2}} \times 6.42 \times 10^2 \text{ s}$$

$$= 1.34 \times 6.42 \times 10^2 \text{ s} = 8.6 \times 10^2 \text{ s}.$$

• PROBLEM 945

The mean proper lifetime (T) of π^+ mesons is 2.5×10^{-8} s. In a beam of π^+ mesons of speed 0.99c, what is the average distance a meson travels before it decays? What would this value be if the relativtistic time dilation did not exist?

Solution: The proper lifetime, T, of a particle is the lifetime of the particle as measured by an observer traveling with the particle. In a coordinate system S' moving with the mesons the average lifetime of the mesons is 2.5×10^{-8} s. A laboratory observer makes his measurements in a system S fixed in the laboratory, with respect to which S' is moving at a speed of 0.99 c. According to the theory of special relativity, an event occurring in space-time will have coordinates (x, y, z, t) relative to S, and coordinates (x', y', z', t') relative to S'. If the relative velocity between the 2 frames is v, these 2 sets of coordinates are related by the Lorentz Transformation

$$x = \frac{x' + vt'}{\sqrt{1 - (v/c)^2}} \quad (1a)$$

$$y = y' \quad (1b)$$

$$z = z' \quad (1c)$$

$$t = \frac{t' + (vx'/c^2)}{\sqrt{1 - (v/c)^2}} \quad (1d)$$

where c is the speed of light.

Now, note that the equations in (1) relate the coordinates of one event as recorded in 2 different reference frames. We need 2 events to describe the lifetime of the meson: its "birth" and its "death". If we travel with the meson, we record the following coordinates for these 2 events:

Birth: $(x_1', y_1', z_1', t_1') = (0, 0, 0, 0)$

Death: $(x_2', y_2', z_2', t_2') = (0, 0, 0, T)$

Here, $x_2' = 0$ because, if we travel with the meson, we do not see it move. It appears stationary. The coordinates of these 2 events in S are found from equations (1), using the above data:

$$x_1 = \frac{(0) + v(0)}{\sqrt{1 - (v/c)^2}} = 0$$

$$y_1 = 0$$

$$z_1 = 0$$

$$t_1 = \frac{(0) + \left(v(0)/c^2\right)}{\sqrt{1 - (v/c)^2}} = 0$$

and $$x_2 = \frac{vT}{\sqrt{1 - (v/c)^2}}$$

$$y_2 = 0$$

$$z_2 = 0$$

$$t_2 = \frac{T}{\sqrt{1 - (v/c)^2}}$$

Relative to S, the meson travels a distance

$$x_2 - x_1 = \frac{vT}{\sqrt{1 - (v/c)^2}}$$

in a time

$$t_2 - t_1 = \frac{T}{\sqrt{1 - (v/c)^2}}$$

Hence, $t_2 - t_1$ is the lifetime of the particle relative to S. (Notice that $t_2 - t_1 > T$)

Using the given data

$$x_2 - x_1 = \frac{(.99c)(2.5 \times 10^{-8}\ s)}{\sqrt{1 - (.99)^2}}$$

$$x_2 - x_1 = \frac{(2.5 \times 10^{-8}\ s)(.99)(3 \times 10^8\ m/s)}{.141}$$

$$x_2 - x_1 = 52.7\ m.$$

If time dilation did not exist, the distance traveled would be d_0, where

$$d_0 = 2.5 \times 10^{-8}\ s \times 0.99 \times 3.0 \times 10^8\ m{\cdot}s^{-1}$$

$$= 7.43\ m.$$

• PROBLEM 946

An electron is observed moving at 50 per cent of the speed of light, $v = 1.5 \times 10^8$ m/s. (a) What is the relativistic mass of the electron? (b) What is the kinetic energy of the electron?

Solution: (a) The known observables are $v = 1.5 \times 10^8$ m/s, and $m_0 = 9.1 \times 10^{-31}$ kg. The relativistic expression for mass as a function of velocity is

$$m = \frac{m_0}{\sqrt{1 - v^2/c^2}} = \frac{9.1 \times 10^{-31}\ kg}{\sqrt{1 - \left(\frac{1.5 \times 10^8\ \cancel{m}/\cancel{s}}{3 \times 10^8\ \cancel{m}/\cancel{s}}\right)^2}} = \frac{9.1 \times 10^{-31}\ kg}{\sqrt{1 - (0.5)^2}}$$

$$\frac{9.1 \times 10^{-31}\ kg}{\sqrt{0.75}} = \frac{9.1 \times 10^{-31}\ kg}{8.7 \times 10^{-1}} = 1.05 \times 10^{-30}\ kg$$

(b) The relativistic energy, E, of the particle is the sum of its kinetic energy, T, and its rest mass energy

$$E = m_0c^2 + T$$

$$T = E - m_0c^2$$

$$T = \left(m - m_0\right)c^2$$

$$T = \left(10.5 \times 10^{-31}\ kg - 9.1 \times 10^{-31}\ kg\right)\left(3 \times 10^8\ m/s\right)^2$$

$$= \left(1.4 \times 10^{-31}\ kg\right)\left(9 \times 10^{16}\ m^2/s^2\right) = 1.26 \times 10^{-14}\ J.$$

• PROBLEM 947

With what speed is an electron moving if its kinetic energy is 1% larger than the value that would be calculated if relativistic effects were not present? What is the value of the kinetic energy of the electron?

Solution: The relativistic expression for the kinetic energy of a particle of rest mass m_0 and mass m traveling with speed v is

$$T = E - m_0c^2 = \frac{M_0c^2}{\sqrt{1 - v^2/c^2}} - m_0c^2$$

$$= m_0c^2\left(\frac{1}{\sqrt{1 - (v^2/c^2)}} - 1\right) = m_0c^2\left(\left(1 - \frac{v^2}{c^2}\right)^{-\frac{1}{2}} - 1\right)$$

If the error involved in using the classical formula for T is only 1%, the particle is traveling at a speed such that

$$\frac{v^2}{c^2} \ll 1$$

Hence, using a Taylor expansion for

$$\left(1 - v^2/c^2\right)^{-\frac{1}{2}} = \left(1 + v^2/2c^2 + 3v^4/8c^4 + \ldots\right)$$

$$T = m_0c^2\left(\frac{1}{2}\frac{v^2}{c^2} + \frac{3}{8}\frac{v^4}{c^4} + \ldots\right) = \frac{1}{2} m_0v^2\left(1 + \frac{3}{4}\frac{v^2}{c^2}\right),$$

when we ignore terms of higher order than those in v^2/c^2. But $\frac{1}{2}m_0v^2$ is the nonrelativistic expression for the kinetic energy of the particle, and thus, for the electron in the problem,

$$\frac{1}{2}m_0v^2\left(1 + \frac{3}{4}\frac{v^2}{c^2}\right) = \frac{1}{2}m_0v^2 + (1\%)\left(\frac{1}{2}m_0v^2\right) = 1.01\left(\frac{1}{2}m_0v^2\right)$$

or

$$1 + \frac{3v^2}{4c^2} = 1.01$$

$$\frac{3v^2}{4c^2} = .01$$

$$v^2 = \frac{.04c^2}{3} = \frac{4c^2}{300}$$

$$v = 0.1155c.$$

$$T = \frac{101}{100} \times \frac{1}{2}m_0v^2 = \frac{101}{100} \times \frac{1}{2} \times 9.108 \times 10^{-31}\text{kg} \times \frac{4}{300} \times 2.998^2 \times 10^{16}\ m^2 \cdot s^2$$

$$= 5.512 \times 10^{-16}\ J.$$

Since $1\ eV = 1.602 \times 10^{-19}\ J$

$$T = 5.512 \times 10^{-16}\ J/1.602 \times 10^{-19}\ J/eV = 3442\ eV.$$

• PROBLEM 948

Suppose that two particles are traveling opposite to each other with velocity $v'_x = \pm\ 0.9\ c$ as observed in the S' system. What is the velocity of one particle with respect to the other, that is as measured by the other?

Solution: In the reference frame S', the two particles move with velocities $-v'_{1x} = v'_{2x} = 0.9\ c$ (see Fig. 1).

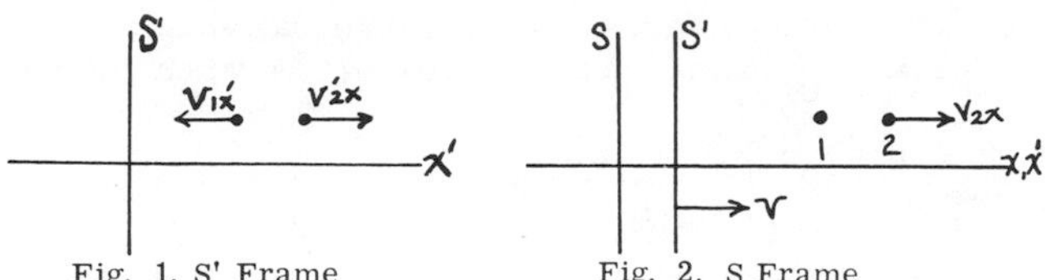

Fig. 1. S' Frame Fig. 2. S Frame

If we observe from the reference frame S in which the first particle is at rest, then S' will appear to move with velocity + 0.9 c with respect to this particle, i.e. S' has velocity v = + 0.9 c relative to S (see Fig. 2).

The velocity of the second particle in S, as observed by the first particle, will be given by the formula for the relativistic addition of v_{2x}' and v:

$$v_{2x} = \frac{v_{2x}' + v}{1 + \frac{v_{2x}'v}{c^2}} = \frac{1.8\ c}{1 + (0.9)^2} = 0.994\ c,$$

(i.e. we transformed the velocity of the second particle from S' to S). Notice that the relative velocity of the two particles is less than c.

If a photon is travelling at velocity + c in S', and S' is traveling relative to S at velocity + c, the photon as viewed from S is traveling only at velocity + c, and not at + 2c. If v_s' is the velocity of the photon in S' and v the relative velocity of S' with respect to S, then in S we have

$$v_s = \frac{v_s' + v}{1 + \frac{v_s'v}{c^2}} = \frac{c + c}{1 + \frac{c^2}{c^2}} = c,$$

for the photon. The fact of an ultimate speed is a consequence of the structure of the velocity-addition equations which we have derived from the Lorentz transformation. Note further that there is no frame in which a photon (light quantum) is at rest.

• PROBLEM 949

A physicist, Mavis, walks at a speed of 1 m/s past a stationary physicist, Stan. They each have measuring sticks and clocks and they observe a bird hop from a tree branch to the lawn. Each measures the position and the time when this event occurred. Show in the special case of small velocities (v very much smaller than c) that the Lorentz equations may be replaced by the following equations:

$$x' = x - vt$$

$$y' = y$$

$$t' = t$$

where the primed and unprimed frames represent the frames of Mavis and Stan respectively.

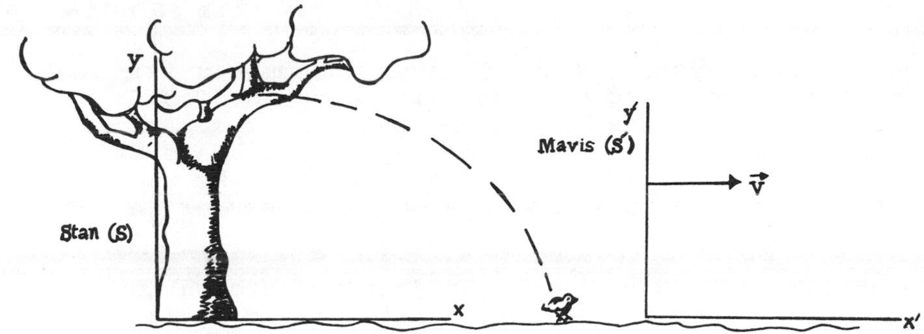

Solution: When the velocities with which we deal approach the speed of light, we can no longer use classical mechanics, and must replace this theory by relativistic mechanics. The purpose of this problem is to show us how the Lorentz transformation (which is part of the relativistic mechanics) reduces to the Galilean transformation (which is part of classical mechanics) when the velocities we are concerned with are small when compared with c.

The Lorentz transformation, relating the space and time coordinates of an event as observed in S' to the space and time coordinates of the same event as observed in S is

$$x' = \frac{x - vt}{\sqrt{1 - v^2/c^2}}$$

$$y' = y \qquad (1)$$

$$z' = z$$

$$t' = \frac{t - xv/c^2}{\sqrt{1 - v^2/c^2}}$$

where v is the relative velocity of S and S'.

The event which we wish to locate in S and S' (see figure) is the landing of the bird. Since S' moves relative to S at a velocity of v = 1 m/s, and the speed of light is 3×10^8 m/s, we find

$$\frac{v}{c} = \frac{1}{3 \times 10^8} = 0.333 \times 10^{-8} \ll 1$$

Hence, we may neglect v^2/c^2 in the equations of (1) because it is negligible when compared with 1. Therefore

$$c' = \frac{x - vt}{\sqrt{1}} = x - vt$$

$$y' = y \qquad (2)$$

$$z' = z$$

$$t' = \frac{t - x\,v/c^2}{\sqrt{1}} = t - \frac{xv}{c^2}$$

Furthermore,

$$\frac{v}{c^2} = \frac{1}{9 \times 10^{16}} = 0.111 \times 10^{-16} < < 1$$

Now x would have to be enormous if xv/c^2 were to be comparable to t. Whence, we may neglect xv/c^2 in the last equation of (2) and

$$t' = t$$

Two inertial systems S and S' have a common x-axis and parallel y-axes, and S' moves with a speed of 0.6c relative to S in the direction of the x-axis. An observer in S sees a rocket moving with a speed of 0.1c in the positive y-direction. What is the speed and direction of the rocket as seen by an observer in the S'-system?

Solution: According to the Lorentz transformation, the coordinates of an event as recorded in S' (x', y', z', t') are related to the coordinates of an event as recorded in S (x, y, z, t) by

$$x' = \frac{x - vt}{\sqrt{1 - (v^2/c^2)}}, \quad y' = y, \; z' = z,$$

$$t' = \frac{t - (vx/c^2)}{\sqrt{1 - (v^2/c^2)}} .$$

Here, v is the relative velocity of the 2 frames of reference.

It follows that the velocity of an object with coordinate x' in frame S' is

$$u'_x = \frac{dx'}{dt'} = \frac{(dx/dt') - v(dt/dt')}{\sqrt{1 - (v^2/c^2)}}$$

$$= \frac{(dx/dt) \times (dt/dt') - v(dt/dt')}{\sqrt{1 - (v^2/c^2)}}$$

But, from the initial equations, we have

$$t = \sqrt{1 - (v^2/c^2)}\,t' + (vx/c^2).$$

$$\frac{dt}{dt'} = \sqrt{1 - \frac{v^2}{c^2}} + \frac{v}{c^2}\frac{dx}{dt'}$$

$$\frac{dt}{dt'} = \sqrt{1 - \frac{v^2}{c^2}} + \frac{v}{c^2}\frac{dx}{dt} \times \frac{dt}{dt'}$$

Since $dx/dt = u_x$, the velocity of the same object relative to S, we have

$$\therefore \frac{dt}{dt'}\left(1 - \frac{vu_x}{c^2}\right) = \sqrt{1 - \frac{v^2}{c^2}}$$

$$\text{or} \quad \frac{dt}{dt'} = \frac{\sqrt{1 - (v^2/c^2)}}{1 - \left(u_x v/c^2\right)}$$

$$u'_x = \frac{[(dx/dt) - v](dt/dt')}{\sqrt{1 - (v^2/c^2)}}$$

$$= \frac{u_x - v}{\sqrt{1 - v^2/c^2)}} \times \frac{\sqrt{1 - (v^2/c^2)}}{1 - (u_x v/c^2)} = \frac{u_x - v}{1 - (u_x v/c^2)} . \quad (1)$$

Similarly,

$$u'_y = \frac{dy'}{dt} \times \frac{dt}{dt'} = \frac{dy}{dt} \times \frac{dt}{dt'}$$

$$= \frac{u_y \sqrt{1 - (v^2/c^2)}}{1 - (u_x v/c^2)} .$$

(2) In this problem, S sees the rocket move in the y direction with speed .1c. Hence, $u_x = 0$, $u_y = 0.1c$, and $v = 0.6c$. Using (1) and (2)

$$\therefore \quad u'_x = - 0.6c, \quad u'_y = 0.1c \times \sqrt{1 - 0.6^2} = 0.08c.$$

To an observer in S', therefore, the rocket appears to have components of velocity of -0.6c in the x-direction and of 0.08c in the y-direction. It thus appears to have a velocity of $\sqrt{0.6^2 + 0.08^2}c = 0.605c$ in a direction making an angle of $\tan^{-1}(0.08/0.60) = \tan^{-1} 0.133$, that is an angle of 7°36′ with the negative direction of the x-axis.

• PROBLEM 951

A rocket has a length L = 600 m measured at rest on the earth. It moves directly away from the earth at constant velocity, and a pulse of radar is sent from earth and reflected back by devices at the nose and tail of the rocket. The reflected signal from the tail is detected on earth 200 sec after emission and the signal from the nose 17.4×10^{-6} sec later. Calculate the distance of the rocket from the earth and the velocity of the rocket with respect to the earth.

<u>Solution:</u> First we will make a non-relativistic calculation. The speed of the pulse is 3×10^8 m/sec (equal to c, the speed of light). If the rocket is a distance R from the earth then the pulse travels 2R and

$$(3 \times 10^8 \text{ m/sec})(200 \text{ sec}) = 2R , \; R = 3 \times 10^{10} \text{ m}$$

To calculate the speed v of the rocket, we note that the pulse from the front end arrived 17.4×10^{-6} sec after that from the back. Thus this pulse was sent into space a distance

$$\tfrac{1}{2}(17.4 \times 10^{-6} \text{ sec})(3 \times 10^8 \text{ m/sec}) = 2.61 \times 10^3 \text{ m}$$

farther. This distance is equal to L + vt where

$$t = \tfrac{1}{2}(17.4 \times 10^{-6} \text{ sec}) = 8.7 \times 10^{-6} \text{ sec}$$

Thus: $$L + vt = 2.61 \times 10^3 \text{ m}$$

$$v = \frac{2.61 \times 10^3 \text{ m} - L}{t} = \frac{2.61 \times 10^3 \text{ m} - 0.6 \times 10^3 \text{ m}}{8.7 \times 10^{-6} \text{ sec}} = 2.31 \times 10^8 \text{m/sec}$$

The factor of $\frac{1}{2}$ arises because we are interested only in the time of the rocket to ground and not in the total time of flight from ground to ground.

According to the above calculation (which we might suspect from the start to be incorrect), the ratio $v/c = 0.77$. Thus it is very probable that relativistic effects will be important. To the observer on the ground the Lorentz length contraction makes the rocket's length appear to be $L\sqrt{1 - \beta^2}$ where $\beta = v/c$. Then the pulse travels a distance $L\sqrt{1-\beta^2} + vt$ farther, which is equal to ct where $t = \frac{1}{2} \times 17.4 \times 10^{-6}$ sec.

Thus

$$L\sqrt{1 - \beta^2} + vt = ct$$

which can be solved to obtain

$$\beta = \frac{(ct/L)^2 - 1}{(ct/L)^2 + 1}$$

$$= 0.9$$

The distance R will be the same as in the previous calculation.

• PROBLEM 952

In a bubble chamber, a pion collides with a proton and three particles are produced, as shown in the Figure. One of the particles is the neutral K^0, which after traveling a distance of about 1×10^{-1} m decays into two pions of opposite charge. If the speed of the K^0 is 2.24×10^8 m/s, determine the rest lifetime.

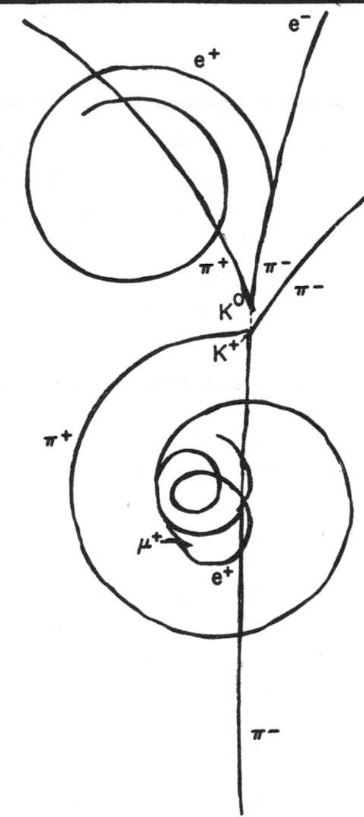

Solution: The Lorentz transformation, of the special theory of relativity, may be used to relate the rest lifetime of the neutral particle, t_0, to the relative lifetime, t, as measured in the laboratory frame of reference. The laboratory lifetime t is given by

$$t = \frac{\text{distance traveled between creation and annihilation, } d}{\text{speed of the particle, } v}$$

$$= \frac{d}{v} = \frac{1 \times 10^{-1}\ \cancel{m}}{2.24 \times 10^{8}\ \cancel{m}/s} = 4.5 \times 10^{-10}\ s$$

Using the relativistic expression for time dilation, the neutral particle's lifetime in its rest frame is

$$t_0 = t\sqrt{1 - \frac{v^2}{c^2}} = 4.5 \times 10^{-10}\sqrt{1 - \frac{5 \times 10^{16}}{9 \times 10^{16}}}\ s$$

$$= 4.5 \times 10^{-10}\sqrt{\frac{4}{9}}\ s = \left(\frac{2}{3}\right)(4.5 \times 10^{-10})s$$

$$= 3.0 \times 10^{-10}\ s$$

• PROBLEM 953

A photon rocket is being propelled through space. The propellant consists of photons. The mass of the rocket is not constant throughout the motion, for it continually loses mass in the form of photons. Use the principles of conservation of momentum and conservation of energy to show that only about 5 per cent of the mass of the photon rocket remains after the rocket has reached a speed of 99.5 per cent of the speed of light.

Solution: Before takeoff the total momentum of the photon-rocket system is zero for the rocket is at rest. Since no external force F acts on the system, then

$$F = 0 = \frac{dP}{dt}$$

where P is the total momentum of the system. Hence P remains constant in time. Consequently, after attaining final speed, the total momentum must still be zero; therefore, the momentum of the photons must equal the final spaceship momentum. (These momentum vectors are oppositely directed to give zero total momentum.) When the rocket has reached its final speed, its rest mass will be a fraction f of the original total rest mass m_0.

The fraction (1 - f) of the original rest mass has been ejected in the form of photons.

total ejected photon momentum = p

$$\text{final rocket momentum} = \frac{(fm_0)v}{\sqrt{1 - v^2/c^2}} = \gamma(fm_0)v \quad \text{where}$$

$$\gamma = \frac{1}{\sqrt{1 - v^2/c^2}}$$ is the relativtistic correction of the rest mass due to the rocket velocity.

Therefore, by conservation of momentum,

$$p = \gamma f m_0 v$$

Since the rocket speed is 99.5 per cent of the speed of light, v may be replaced by c with negligible error.

$$p = \gamma f m_0 c$$

The total mass-energy of the rocket system must remain constant in time, for no energy enters or leaves the closed ejected photons and rocket system. Then

$$\text{total initial energy} = m_0c^2$$

$$\text{final rocket energy} = \gamma(fm_0)c^2$$

$$\text{total ejected photon energy} = pc$$

$$\text{since initial energy} = \text{final energy}$$

$$m_0c^2 = \gamma fm_0c^2 + pc$$

Substituting for p from the previous equation gives

$$m_0c^2 = \gamma fm_0c^2 + \gamma fm_0c^2 = 2\gamma fm_0c^2$$

Solving for f,

$$f = \frac{1}{2\gamma}$$

At a speed of 99.5 per cent c, the value of γ is

$$\frac{1}{\sqrt{1 - \left(\frac{.995\ c}{c}\right)^2}} = 1.0 \times 10^1$$

Therefore, $f = \frac{1}{(2)\left(1 \times 10^1\right)} = 0.05 = 5$ per cent

Therefore, only 5 per cent of the original mass of the rocket remains when the rocket has achieved a speed of 99.5 per cent c.

• PROBLEM 954

In a Van de Graaff accelerator, protons are accelerated through a potential difference of 5×10^6 V. What is the final energy of the protons in electron volts and joules, and what is their mass and their velocity?

Solution: The work needed to move a charge q from position a to position b is

$$W_{ab} = \int_a^b \vec{F}_{app} \cdot d\vec{r}$$

where $\vec{F}_{app}$ is the applied force moving q, and $d\vec{r}$ is an element of the path traversed by the particle in moving from a to b. In an electric field, $\vec{E}$, the force exerted by the field on q is

$$\vec{F} = q\vec{E}$$

But the applied force is equal and opposite to the force exerted by $\vec{E}$ on q, or

$$\vec{F}_{app} = -q\vec{E}$$

Hence, $W_{ab} = -q \int_a^b \vec{E} \cdot d\vec{r} = q \left(- \int_a^b \vec{E} \cdot d\vec{r} \right)$

By definition,

$$V_b - V_a = - \int_a^b \vec{E} \cdot d\vec{r}$$

where V_a is the potential at point a, and similarly for V_b. Then

$$W_{ab} = q(V_b - V_a) = q\,\Delta V$$

The energy gained by accelerating a particle through a potential difference ΔV is the work done on it, or W_{ab}.

A proton carries an elementary positive charge. The energy acquired in traveling through a potential difference of 5 MV is, assuming the proton starts at rest,

$$W_{ab} = q\Delta V = e\Delta V = (1.6 \times 10^{-19}\ C)(5 \times 10^{6}\ V)$$

$$W_{ab} = 8 \times 10^{-13}\ J$$

To determine the mass at this energy, use the equation $E = mc^2$.

$$\therefore \quad m = \frac{E}{c^2} = \frac{8 \times 10^{-13} J}{(3 \times 10^{8})^2\ m^2 \cdot s^{-2}} = 0.89 \times 10^{29}\ kg.$$

This is the mass equivalent of the energy acquired. The total mass the particle now possesses is obtained by adding this mass to the rest mass m_0. That is,

$$M = m + m_0 = (0.89 \times 10^{-29} + 1.672 \times 10^{-27}) kg$$

$$= 1.681 \times 10^{-27}\ kg$$

Also, $$M = \frac{m_0}{\sqrt{1 - v^2/c^2}}$$

$$1 - v^2/c^2 = m_0^2/M^2$$

$$1 - m_0^2/M^2 = v^2/c^2$$

$$\frac{v}{c} = \sqrt{1 - \left(\frac{m_0}{M}\right)^2} = \sqrt{1 - \left(\frac{1.672}{1.681}\right)^2} = .1033$$

$$\therefore \quad v = .1033 \times 3 \times 10^{8}\ m \cdot s^{-1} = 3.10 \times 10^{7}\ m \cdot s^{-1}.$$

• PROBLEM 955

Calculate the magnitude of the gravitational red shift for a photon traveling from the sun to the earth.

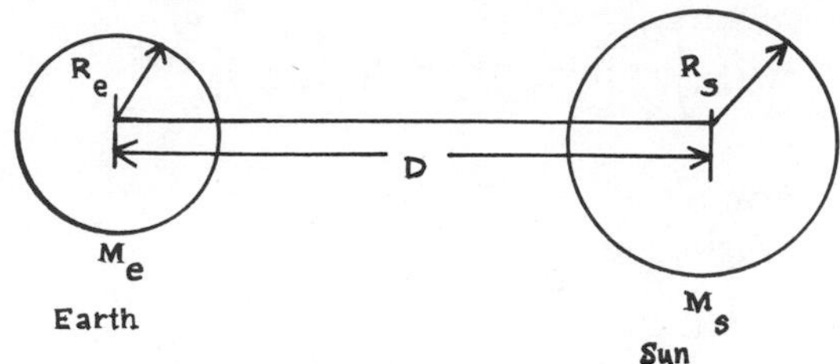

Solution: Because of Einstein's Mass-Energy Relation, any object having energy E has an equivalent mass

$$m = \frac{E}{c^2}$$

where c is the speed of light. If the "object" is a photon, $E = h\nu$ and the equivalent mass is

$$m = \frac{h\nu}{c^2} \tag{1}$$

where h is Planck's constant.

Now, we may ask, what happens if a photon is in a gravitational field? In traveling between 2 points in this field the potential energy of the photon changes. Hence, so must its total energy, E. We may write

$$E' = E + (\emptyset' - \emptyset) \tag{2}$$

where $\emptyset' - \emptyset$ is the change in potential energy of the photon, and E' is its new energy as a result of moving in the gravitational field. Rewriting (2)

$$E' - E = \emptyset' - \emptyset$$

or

$$h\nu' - h\nu = \emptyset' - \emptyset$$

whence,

$$h(\nu' - \nu) = \emptyset' - \emptyset$$

Hence, we expect the photon to undergo a frequency shift of

$$\nu' - \nu = \frac{1}{h}(\emptyset' - \emptyset) \tag{3}$$

as a result of a change in the potential energy of the photon.

If the photon travels from the surface of the sun to the surface of the earth, the primed variables will refer to the surface of the earth. Similarly, the unprimed variables will refer to the sun's surface. In this case, the fractional change in frequency of the photon is

$$\frac{\nu' - \nu}{\nu} = \frac{\emptyset' - \emptyset}{h\nu} \tag{4}$$

Now, (see figure)

$$\emptyset' = \frac{-GM_e m'}{R_e} - \frac{GM_s m'}{D} \tag{5}$$

and

$$\emptyset = \frac{-GM_s m}{R_s} - \frac{GM_e m}{D}$$

where $G = 6.67 \times 10^{-11} \frac{N \cdot m^2}{kg^2}$. From (1)

$$m' = \frac{h\nu'}{c^2} \quad \text{and} \quad m = \frac{h\nu}{c^2} \tag{6}$$

Substituting (6) in (5)

$$\emptyset' = \frac{-GM_e h\nu'}{c^2 R_e} - \frac{GM_s h\nu'}{c^2 D} \qquad \emptyset = \frac{-GM_s h\nu}{c^2 R_s} - \frac{GM_e h\nu}{c^2 D}$$

Rewriting these equations

$$\phi' = \frac{-Gh\nu'}{c^2}\left(\frac{M_e}{R_e} + \frac{M_s}{D}\right)$$

$$\phi = \frac{-Gh\nu}{c^2}\left(\frac{M_s}{R_s} + \frac{M_e}{D}\right)$$

and

$$\frac{\phi' - \phi}{h\nu} = \frac{-G\nu'}{c^2\nu}\left(\frac{M_e}{R_e} + \frac{M_s}{D}\right) + \frac{G}{c^2}\left(\frac{M_s}{R_s} + \frac{M_e}{D}\right)$$

But

$$\frac{\nu' - \nu}{\nu} = \frac{\phi' - \phi}{h\nu}$$

and

$$\frac{\nu' - \nu}{\nu} = \frac{-G\nu'}{c^2\nu}\left(\frac{M_e}{R_e} + \frac{M_s}{D}\right) + \frac{G}{c^2}\left(\frac{M_s}{R_s} + \frac{M_e}{D}\right)$$

or

$$\frac{\nu'}{\nu} - 1 + \frac{G\nu'}{c^2\nu}\left(\frac{M_e}{R_e} + \frac{M_s}{D}\right) = \frac{G}{c^2}\left(\frac{M_s}{R_s} + \frac{M_e}{D}\right)$$

$$\frac{\nu'}{\nu}\left\{1 + \frac{G}{c^2}\left(\frac{M_e}{R_e} + \frac{M_s}{D}\right)\right\} = \frac{G}{c^2}\left(\frac{M_s}{R_s} + \frac{M_e}{D}\right) + 1$$

$$\frac{\nu'}{\nu} = \frac{\frac{G}{c^2}\left(\frac{M_s}{R_s} + \frac{M_e}{D}\right) + 1}{\frac{G}{c^2}\left(\frac{M_e}{R_e} + \frac{M_s}{D}\right) + 1}$$

Hence

$$\frac{\nu'}{\nu} = \frac{G(M_s/R_s + M_e/D) + c^2}{G(M_e/R_e + M_s/D) + c^2} \qquad (7)$$

Before solving for ν'/ν, we may make some approximations in (7). First, the data needed are

$M_s = 1.99 \times 10^{30}$kg $\qquad R_e = 6.37 \times 10^6$m

$M_e = 5.98 \times 10^{24}$kg $\qquad R_s = 6.96 \times 10^8$m

$D = 1.49 \times 10^{11}$m

Now, note that

$$\frac{M_s}{R_s} \gg \frac{M_e}{D}$$

and may be neglected in (7). Furthermore,

$$G\, M_e/R_e + M_s/D \ll c^2$$

and may also be neglected in (7), whence

$$\frac{\nu'}{\nu} \approx \frac{G(M_s/R_s) + c^2}{c^2} = 1 + \frac{G}{c^2}\left(\frac{M_s}{R_s}\right)$$

$$\frac{\nu'}{\nu} \approx 1 + \frac{\left(6.67 \times 10^{-11}\ \mathrm{N{\cdot}m^2/kg^2}\right)\left(1.99 \times 10^{30}\ \mathrm{kg}\right)}{\left(9 \times 10^{16}\ \mathrm{m^2/s^2}\right)\left(6.96 \times 10^8\ \mathrm{m}\right)}$$

$$\frac{\nu'}{\nu} \approx 1 + \frac{1.32733 \times 10^{20}}{6.264 \times 10^{25}}$$

$$\frac{\nu'}{\nu} \approx 1.0000021 \tag{8}$$

Hence the fractional change in the frequency of a photon traveling from the sun to the earth is

$$\frac{\nu' - \nu}{\nu} = \frac{1.0000021\ \nu - \nu}{\nu} = .0000021$$

CHAPTER 33

QUANTUM MECHANICS

• PROBLEM 956

Astronomers have found that many stellar objects contain hydrogen atoms that emit photons. Find the wavelength of this radiation and express the value in centimeters (the conventional unit used by astronomers to measure radio photon spectra) if the approximate value for the frequency of the emmitted photons is 1.42×10^9 Hz.

Solution: The wavelength λ of the photon and the frequency f are related in the following manner:

$$\lambda = \frac{c}{f} \quad \text{where } c \text{ is the speed of light. Hence,}$$

$$\lambda = \frac{3 \times 10^8 \text{ m/s}}{1.42 \times 10^9 \text{Hz}} = 2.1 \times 10^{-1} \text{ m}$$

Now 1 m is equivalent to 10^2 centimeters (cm); therefore,

$$\lambda = 2.1 \times 10^{-1} \cancel{\text{m}} \ 10^2 \text{ cm}/\cancel{\text{m}} = 21 \text{ cm}$$

• PROBLEM 957

A 1-gram mass falls through a height $H = 1$ cm. If all of the energy acquired in the fall were converted to yellow light $\left(\lambda = 6 \times 10^{-5} \text{ cm}\right)$, how many photons would be emitted?

Solution: The energy acquired in the fall is just the potential energy:

$$\begin{aligned} PE &= mhH \\ &= (1 \text{ g}) \times \left(980 \text{ cm/sec}^2\right) \times (1 \text{ cm}) \\ &= 980 \text{ ergs} \end{aligned}$$

The energy of each yellow photon is

$$\begin{aligned} \varepsilon &= h\nu = \frac{hc}{\lambda} \\ &= \frac{\left(6.6 \times 10^{-27} \text{erg-sec}\right) \times \left(3 \times 10^{10} \text{cm/sec}\right)}{6 \times 10^{-5} \text{ cm}} \\ &= 3 \times 10^{-12} \text{ ergs/photon} \end{aligned}$$

which represents one photon having a total energy of 3×10^{-12} ergs. Since n photons have a total energy of 980 ergs, we may set up the following proportion:

$$\frac{n \text{ photons}}{1 \text{ photon}} = \frac{980 \text{ erg}}{3 \times 10^{-12} \text{erg}}$$

From which we have $\quad n = 3 \times 10^{14}$ photons.

• PROBLEM 958

What is the least radiation frequency ν, capable of positron-electron pair production?

Solution: The process in which a photon disappears and an electron-positron pair appears, is known as pair production. The energy of the photon should at least be large enough to provide for the rest masses of the electron and proton. Therefore

$$E_{photon} = m_{electron}c^2 + m_{positron}c^2$$

$$h\nu = 2m_e c^2$$

where ν is the photon frequency. Hence

$$\nu = \frac{2m_e c^2}{h} = \frac{2 \times \left(9.11 \times 10^{-31}\ \text{kg}\right) \times \left(3 \times 10^8 \text{m/s}\right)^2}{6.63 \times 10^{-34}\ \text{J·S}}$$

$$= 2.47 \times 10^{20} \frac{1}{\text{sec}} .$$

• PROBLEM 959

According to the free electron gas theory the average kinetic energy, E, of the free electrons in a metal has been shown to be $\frac{3}{5} E_F$ where E_F is the Fermi energy of the metal. Use this information to estimate the average speed of the valence electrons in copper. (The Fermi energy of copper is 7 eV).

Solution: At temperature T = 0 (absolute zero), the electrons have zero kinetic energy, therefore they will have the smallest possible energies at that temperature. However, the exlusion principle states that no two electrons can be in the same quantum state. Therefore, even at T = 0, the electrons in general must have lowest energies which are different from each other and from zero. The highest of these available "lowest energies" is called the Fermi energy. For a piece of copper metal the average energy is

$$E = \left(\frac{3}{5}\right)(7\ \text{eV}) = 4.2\ \text{eV}$$

Since 1 eV = 1.6×10^{-19} J, the energy may be expressed in joules:

$$E = (4.2\ \cancel{\text{eV}})\left(1.6 \times 10^{-19}\text{J}/\cancel{\text{eV}}\right)$$

$$= 6.7 \times 10^{-19}\ \text{J}$$

The kinetic energy may be written nonrelativistically as

$$E = \frac{1}{2} mv^2$$

The average speed v of a free electron is found by solving this expression for v;

$$v^2 = \frac{2E}{m} = \frac{(2)\left(6.7 \times 10^{-19}\text{J}\right)}{9.11 \times 10^{-31}\ \text{kg}} = 1.47 \times 10^{12}\ \text{m}^2/\text{s}^2$$

or

$$v = 1.21 \times 10^6\ \text{m/s}$$

• PROBLEM 960

What is the wavelength of a 10-eV electron?

Solution: For an electron of this low energy we can neglect the change of electron mass

$$\left(= \frac{m_{rest}}{\sqrt{1 - \frac{v^2}{c^2}}} \right)$$

with velocity. Since kinetic energy $KE = \frac{1}{2}mv^2$ and momentum $p = mv$, we have, because

$$v = \sqrt{\frac{2(KE)}{m}}$$

$p = \sqrt{2m\ KE}$. The de Broglie wave theory of matter tells us that every particle has wave-like characteristics. The electron, then, has a wavelength λ associated with it. It is given by the de Broglie relation,

$$\lambda = \frac{h}{p} = \frac{h}{\sqrt{2m\ KE}}$$

$$= \frac{6.62 \times 10^{-27}\ \text{erg-sec}}{\sqrt{2 \times \left(9.11 \times 10^{-28} g\right) \times (10\ eV) \times \left(1.60 \times 10^{-12} erg/eV\right)}}$$

$$= 3.86 \times 10^{-8}\ cm$$

$$= 3.86\ \text{Å} \quad \text{where} \quad 1\text{Å} = 10^{-8}\ cm.$$

(The unit of energy was converted from electron volts to ergs, because the CGS System is being used.) A photon with this same wavelength would have an energy $\epsilon = h\nu$ but $\nu = \frac{c}{\lambda}$ for a photon. Therefore $\epsilon = \frac{hc}{\lambda}$

$$= \frac{\left(6.62 \times 10^{-27} \text{erg-sec}\right) \times \left(3 \times 10^{10} cm/sec\right)}{\left(3.86 \times 10^{-8} cm\right) \times \left(1.60 \times 10^{-12} erg/eV\right)}$$

$$= 3.2\ keV$$

Such an energetic photon is an X-ray.

• PROBLEM 961

An electron jumps from the orbit for which n = 3 to the orbit for which n = 2, thereby emitting some visible, red light. What is the magnitude of this quantum of energy?

Solution: In the hydrogen atom, the energy of the atom with its electron in quantum level n is

$$E = \frac{2.18 \times 10^{-18}\ \text{joule}}{n^2}$$

The energy of the hydrogen atom with its electron in the n = 2 energy level is

$$E_2 = \frac{2.18 \times 10^{-18}\ \text{joule}}{2^2}$$

The energy of the hydrogen atom with its electron in the n = 3 energy level is

$$E_3 = \frac{2.18 \times 10^{-18}\ \text{joule}}{3^2}$$

Then the magnitude of the quantum of energy is

$$E_2 - E_3 = 2.18 \times 10^{-18} \text{ joule} \times \left(\frac{1}{2^2} - \frac{1}{3^2}\right)$$

$$= 3.03 \times 10^{-19} \text{ joule.}$$

• PROBLEM 962

A small amount of arsenic is present in a germanium crystal. If the energy E of the fifth electron may be represented approximately by the relationship

$$E = \frac{-1 \times 10^{-2} \text{ eV}}{n^2}$$

how much energy is required to free the electron? Does thermal vibration of the ions provide sufficient energy to free the arsenic's fifth electron? At room temperature the thermal energy is 0.04 eV.

Solution: Notice that the relationship

$$E = \frac{-1 \times 10^{-2} \text{ eV}}{n^2}$$

has the same form as the hydrogen-energy equation giving the energy of the nth orbit:

$$E_n = \frac{-13.6 \text{ eV}}{n^2}$$

According to this equation, one has to supply 13.6 eV to free the electron from the ground level (n = 1), and less energy to free it from the other levels. Similarly, the energy needed to raise the arsenic electron to the conduction band where the electron is practically free, is

$$E = 1 \times 10^{-2} \text{ eV.}$$

The average thermal energy of the silicon ions vibrating in the crystal at room temperature is 0.04 eV, so sufficient energy could be transferred during a collision to free the fifth electron of an arsenic atom and allow it to migrate through the crystal.

• PROBLEM 963

When ultraviolet light of frequency 1.3×10^{15} sec^{-1} is shined on a metal, photoelectrons are ejected with a maximum energy of 1.8 electron volts. Calculate the work function of the metal in ergs and electron volts. What is the threshold frequency of this metal?

Solution: This problem is an example of the photoelectric effect. We want to relate the work function of a metal to the energy of the incident radiation. (The work function is the amount of energy needed to release an electron from the attraction of the rest of the metal, and thereby pull it out of the metal.) Let us examine the reaction occurring.

A photon of energy hυ (the ultraviolet radiation) collides with an electron of the metal, and, in the process, gives up all of its energy. If hυ is large enough, the electron will travel through the metal and be released with kinetic energy $\frac{1}{2}mv^2$, where m and v are the electron mass and velocity, respectively. In leaving the metal, the electron loses energy due to collisions with atoms of the metal. The electron also loses energy, equal in amount to the work function, in order to overcome the attraction of the metal and escape. If we examine only those electrons which lie close to the surface of the metal, we observe that they do not go through any collisions and hence cannot lose energy by this means. These surface electrons lose less energy than the interior electrons and therefore will have a maximum amount of kinetic energy when they leave the metal. Using the principle of conservation of energy, we obtain

$$h\upsilon = \frac{1}{2} m\, v^2_{max} + \phi \qquad (1)$$

where ϕ is the work function of the metal. (Note that this relation is true only for surface electrons.) Solving (1) for ϕ, we obtain

$$\phi = h\upsilon - \frac{1}{2} mv^2_{max} \qquad (2)$$

The energy of a photon of the ultraviolet light is

$$h\upsilon = 6.625 \times 10^{-27} \times 1.3 \times 10^{15} \text{erg}$$

$$= 8.61 \times 10^{-12} \text{ erg}$$

Since 1 electron volt = 1.60×10^{-12} erg, the maximum kinetic energy of the photoelectrons is

$$\frac{1}{2} mv^2_{max} = 1.8 \times 1.6 \times 10^{-12} \text{erg}$$

$$= 2.88 \times 10^{-12} \text{ erg}$$

From equation 2, the work function is

$$\phi = h\upsilon - \frac{1}{2} mv^2_{max}$$

$$= 8.61 \times 10^{-12} - 2.88 \times 10^{-12} \text{ erg}$$

$$= 5.73 \times 10^{-12} \text{ erg}$$

Since 1 erg = $.625 \times 10^{12}$ eV

$$\phi = \left(5.73 \times 10^{-12} \text{ erg}\right)\left[.625 \times 10^{12} \frac{\text{eV}}{\text{erg}}\right]$$

$$\phi = 3.58 \text{ eV}$$

The threshold frequency is the smallest frequency of indecent radiation for which the electrons will be released from the metal with no kinetic energy. Setting

$\frac{1}{2} mv^2_{max} = 0$ in equation (1), we find that the threshold frequency, υ_o, is

$$\upsilon_o = \frac{\phi}{h} \tag{3}$$

Using the value of ϕ calculated in the first part of the problem,

$$\upsilon_o = \frac{5.73 \times 10^{-12} \text{ erg}}{6.625 \times 10^{-27} \text{ erg·sec}}$$

or $\upsilon_o = 8.65 \times 10^{14} \text{ sec}^{-1}$

This frequency is in the ultraviolet, and just beyond the blue end of the visible spectrum.

• PROBLEM 964

It is desired to move a small, 50 kg, space vehicle by a lamp which emits 100 watts of blue light (λ = 4700 Å). If the vehicle is in free space what will be its acceleration?

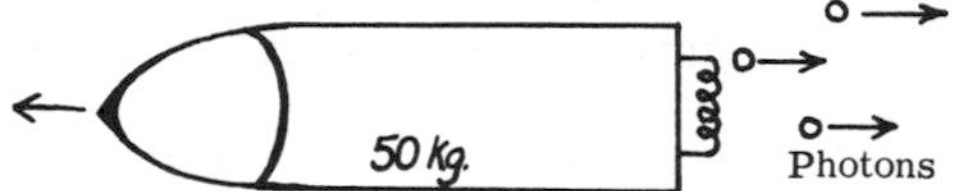

Solution: According to quantum theory, light may be viewed as having wave-like characteristics as well as particle characteristics. In this problem, it is the particle nature of light which determines the behavior of the space vehicle. Since the emitted light carries away momentum and because the latter is conserved, the rocket will be propelled to the left in the figure.

We will suppose that N photons/sec are emitted, with each photon energy hf. Then the power of the lamp is

$$p = \frac{\text{(energy of one photon)(\# of photons)}}{\text{time}}$$

$$p = Nhf$$

By definition, $f = \frac{c}{\lambda}$,

Hence

$$p = \frac{Nhc}{\lambda}$$

Thus

$$N = \frac{p\lambda}{hc}$$

$$= \frac{100 \text{ watt} \times 4.70 \times 10^{-7} \text{ m}}{6.63 \times 10^{-34} \text{ j-sec} \times 3 \times 10^{8} \text{ m/sec}}$$

$$= 2.4 \times 10^{20}$$

Each photon will have momentum, by the de Broglie relations

$$p = \frac{h}{\lambda} = \frac{6.63 \times 10^{-34} \text{ J.s}}{4700 \text{ Å}}$$

$$= \frac{6.63 \times 10^{-34} \text{ J·s}}{4.7 \times 10^{-7} \text{ m}}$$

$$= 1.4 \times 10^{-27} \text{ N-sec}$$

The total force on the vehicle will be, by Newton's second law,

$$F = \frac{d(np)}{dt}$$

Where n is the number of photons emitted and p is the momentum of each photon. Since p is constant, we then have,

$$F = p\frac{dn}{dt}$$

= pN for N is just the number of photons emitted per unit time.

$$F = 1.4 \times 10^{-27} \text{ N-sec} \quad 2.4 \times 10^{20} \text{ sec}^{-1}$$
$$= 3.4 \times 10^{-7} \text{N}$$

Thus the acceleration has the very small value

$$a = \frac{F}{m} = \frac{3.4 \times 10^{-7} \text{ N}}{50 \text{ Kg}} = 6.8 \times 10^{-9} \text{ m/sec}^2$$

• PROBLEM 965

Calculate the energy, in ergs and eV, of the photon which has just sufficient energy to disintegrate a deuteron. What are its frequency and wavelength?

Solution: We can find the minimum photon energy needed to disintegrate the deuteron by assuming that the products of the photon-deuteron collision (a proton and neutron) are at rest. Hence, the conservation of total relativistic energy yields

$$h\nu + M_D c^2 = \left(m_p + m_n\right) c^2 \qquad (1)$$

where h is Planck's constant, ν is the photon's frequency, and c is the speed of light. Note that the initial energy (left side of (1)) is that of the incident photon, plus the rest mass energy of the target deuteron. The final energy (right side of (1)) is the rest mass energy of the reaction products.

$$h\nu = \left(m_p + m_n - M_D\right) c^2$$

Since

$$m_p \approx m_n = 1.6747 \times 10^{-27} \text{ kg}$$

$$M_D = 3.3441 \times 10^{-27} \text{ kg}$$

$$h\nu = \left[(3.3494 - 3.3441) \times 10^{-27} \text{ kg}\right] \times \left(9 \times 10^{16} \text{ m}^2/\text{s}^2\right)$$

$$h\nu = 0.0053 \times 9 \times 10^{-11} \text{ Joules}$$

$$h\nu = 4.77 \times 10^{-13} \text{ Joules} \qquad (2)$$

But $\quad 1 \text{ Joule} = 6.242 \times 10^{18} \text{ eV}$

$$h\nu = (4.77 \times 10^{-13} \text{ J})(6.242 \times 10^{18} \text{ J/eV})$$

$$h\nu = 2.977 \times 10^{6} \text{ eV}$$

From (2), we obtain

$$\nu = \frac{4.77 \times 10^{-13} \text{ J}}{6.63 \times 10^{-34} \text{ J}\cdot\text{s}} = 7.2 \times 10^{20} \text{ s}^{-1}$$

Because the wavelength of the photon is

$$\lambda = \frac{c}{\nu}$$

we find

$$\lambda = \frac{3 \times 10^{8} \text{ m/s}}{7.2 \times 10^{20} \text{ s}^{-1}} = 4.2 \times 10^{-13} \text{ m}$$

Note that the above analysis gives only a lower bound on $h\nu$. The reason for this can be seen by examining the figure. In order to conserve momentum, the reaction products must be in motion, contrary to what we assumed in equation (1). Hence, in reality, $h\nu$ is greater than the value we calculated, since some of the photon's energy goes into the kinetic energy of the reaction products.

• PROBLEM 966

What is the de Broglie wavelength of an electron with a kinetic energy of 1 eV?

Solution: When calculating the de Broglie wavelength, it is important to know whether or not to use relativistic formulas in order to calculate the quantities appearing in the de Broglie formula. One way of deciding this is to realize that, when the velocity v is very small compared with c, (and, hence, the problem is non-relativistic) the kinetic energy is small when compared to the rest mass energy, m_0c^2. The rest mass energy of an electron is 0.512×10^6 eV which is large compared with 1 eV. We need not use relativistic formulas in the present example.

In the formula for the de Broglie wavelength,

$$\lambda = \frac{h}{mv} \qquad (1)$$

it is permissible to insert the rest mass, m_0, for m,

$$m \simeq m_0 = 9.11 \times 10^{-28} \text{ gram.}$$

The kinetic energy is

$$\frac{1}{2}m_0v^2 = 1 \text{ eV.}$$

Because 1 eV = 1.6×10^{-12} erg

$$\frac{1}{2}m_0 v^2 = 1.6 \times 10^{-12} \text{ erg.}$$

Therefore

$$v = \sqrt{\frac{2 \times 1.6 \times 10^{-12} \text{ erg}}{m_0}}$$

$$= \sqrt{\frac{2 \times 1.6 \times 10^{-12} \text{ erg}}{9.11 \times 10^{-28} \text{ g}}}$$

$$= 5.92 \times 10^{7} \text{ cm/sec.}$$

Notice that this is, in fact, very much less than the velocity of light (3×10^{10} cm/sec).

Inserting these values of m and v into equation (1),

$$\lambda = \frac{6.625 \times 10^{-27} \text{ erg sec}}{(9.11 \times 10^{-28} \times 5.92 \times 10^{7})\text{g} \cdot \text{cm/sec}}$$

$$= 1.23 \times 10^{-7} \text{ cm.}$$

This is about ten times larger than the diameter of an atom.

• PROBLEM 967

Calculate the wavelength of a car whose mass is 2×10^3 kg and whose speed is 30 m/s. Determine whether the quantum aspects of particle motion will be observable.

Solution: The de Broglie wavelength of the auto, λ_{auto}, is given by

$$\lambda_{auto} = \frac{h}{mv} = \frac{6.6 \times 10^{-34} \text{ J s}}{\left(2 \times 10^3 \text{ kg}\right)\left(3 \times 10^1 \text{ m/s}\right)} = 1.1 \times 10^{-38} \text{ m}$$

Note that because the speed of the car is much less than the speed of light, this calculation is clearly non-relativistic. This number is very small. Since the dimensions of all man-sized objects with which the automobile interacts are very much larger than 1.1×10^{-38} m, we do not expect to observe wave phenomena (i.e., diffraction , interference) for cars , and classical mechanics gives a very satisfactory description of the car's motion. This is true for the motion of most man-sized objects: the quantum features of man-sized or larger objects are usually unimportant and are difficult to observe.

• PROBLEM 968

Determine the phase velocity of the de Broglie waves associated with a neutron which has an energy of 25 eV.

Solution: If the neutron of mass m has energy 25 eV =

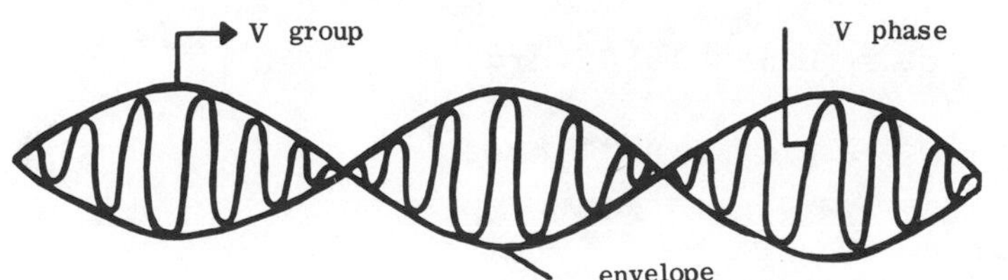

$25 \times 1.062 \times 10^{-19}$ J = 4.00×10^{-18} J, then its speed is given by the relation

$$\tfrac{1}{2} mv^2 = 4.00 \times 10^{-18} \text{ J} \qquad \text{or}$$

$$v = \sqrt{\frac{8.00 \times 10^{-18} \text{ J}}{1.67 \times 10^{-27} \text{ kg}}} = 6.92 \times 10^4 \text{ m}\cdot\text{s}^{-1}.$$

The phase velocity of the associated de Broglie waves is then

$$v_p = \frac{c^2}{v} = \frac{(3.00 \times 10^8)^2 \text{m}^2\cdot\text{s}^{-2}}{6.92 \times 10^4 \text{ m}\cdot\text{s}^{-1}} = 1.30 \times 10^{12} \text{ m}\cdot\text{s}^{-1}.$$

The difference between the phase and group velocities can be seen in the figure. When sinusoidal waves of different frequency (or wavelength) are combined, they appear as in the figure, with their amplitude modulated. Clearly, the frequency of variation of the amplitude of this resultant wave is less than the frequency of variation of the wave enclosed by the amplitude envelope. Similarly, the velocity of the envelope (v_{group}) is different from the velocity of the enclosed wave (v_{phase}). However, the 2 are related by

$$v_{phase} = \frac{c^2}{v_{group}}$$

where c is the speed of light in the case of de Broglie waves. Since the envelope locates the approximate position (due to the uncertainty principle) of the particle, the group velocity of the wave must represent the actual velocity of the particle, or the particle's wave would not be able to keep up with the particle.

• PROBLEM 969

Find the radius of the smallest Bohr orbit for the Hydrogen atom.

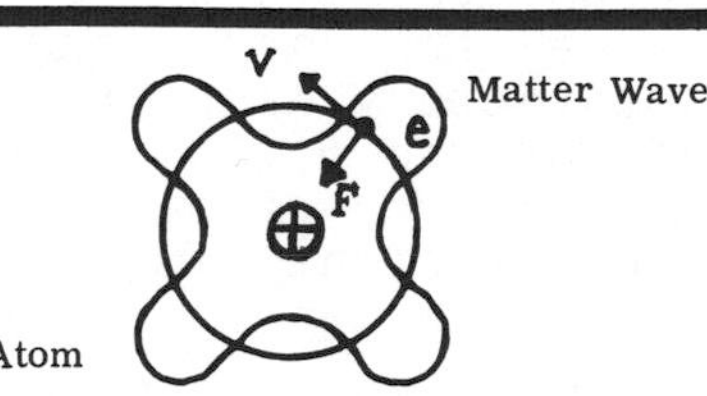

Solution: The Bohr model of the hydrogen atom consists of a single electron of charge -e revolving in a circular orbit about a single proton of charge +e. The electrostatic force of attraction between electron and proton provides the centripetal force that retains the electron in its orbit (see the figure).

Bohr's model assumes that the angular momentum of each orbit is restricted to integral multiples of Planck's constant divided by 2π, $L_n = n \frac{h}{2\pi}$. This can be seen by considering the wave nature of the electron. In order to have a stable electronic orbit, the matter wave of the electron must be stationary around the orbit, as shown in the figure. Therefore, the orbit is an integral multiple of the wavelength (de Broglie wavelength) $\lambda = h/mv$,

$$2\pi r_n = n\lambda$$

or

$$r_n = n \frac{h}{2\pi mv}$$

where v is the orbital velocity of the electron. This equation can also be written as

$$r_n = \frac{L_n}{mv} .$$

The electrostatic force on the electron as it moves in the nth circular orbit, can be written as

$$F = \frac{mv^2}{r_n} = k \frac{e^2}{r_n^2} ,$$

or

$$mv^2 r_n = ke^2 .$$

This is the centripetal force needed to keep the electron in its circular orbit. Bohr's postulate for the quantization of the orbital angular momentum is

$$L_n = mvr_n = n \frac{h}{2\pi} .$$

Squaring both sides, we have

$$m^2 v^2 r_n^2 = n^2 \frac{h^2}{4\pi^2} .$$

Now, we form the ratio

$$\frac{m^2 v^2 r_n^2}{mv^2 r_n} = n^2 \frac{h^2}{4\pi^2 ke^2}$$

we get

$$mr_n = n^2 \frac{h^2}{4\pi^2 ke^2}$$

$$r_n = \frac{h^2}{4\pi^2 ke^2 m} n^2$$

The smallest orbit will have a radius

$$r_1 = \frac{h^2}{4\pi^2 ke^2 m}$$

When the numerical values are substituted, we find for the first Bohr radius

$$r_1 = \frac{\left(6.63 \times 10^{-34} \text{J-sec}\right)^2}{4\pi^2 \times \left(9 \times 10^9 \text{m/farad}\right) \times \left(1.6 \times 10^{-19} \text{coul}\right)^2 \times \left(9.11 \times 10^{-31} \text{kg}\right)}$$

$$= 5.29 \times 10^{-11} \text{ m} .$$

In Bohr's theory, the electron may revolve only in some one of a number of specified orbits.

• PROBLEM 970

Calculate the binding energy of the hydrogen atom in its ground state.

Solution: The potential energy of the electron in the nth Bohr orbit is

$$V_n = -k\frac{e^2}{r_n}$$

The kinetic energy can be obtained as a function of r_n by using Newton's 2nd law. The electrostatic force between the electron and the nucleus causes the centripetal acceleration. Therefore

$$F = ma = \frac{mv^2}{r_n} = \frac{ke^2}{r_n^2}$$

where v is the velocity of the electron. The kinetic energy is

$$T_n = \tfrac{1}{2}mv^2 = \tfrac{1}{2}k\frac{e^2}{r_n}$$

For a circular orbit the kinetic energy is therefore equal to half of the magnitude of the potential energy. The total energy (binding energy) becomes

$$E_n = T_n + V_n = -\tfrac{1}{2}V_n = -\tfrac{1}{2}k\frac{e^2}{r_n}\ .$$

For the first orbit (n = 1),

$$r_1 = \frac{h^2}{4\pi^2 kme^2}\ .$$

If we use the CGS unit system $k = 1$. The binding energy for the ground state then becomes

$$E_1 = -\frac{4\pi^2 k^2 me^4}{2h^2} = -\frac{me^4}{2h^2}$$

$$= -\frac{(9.1\times 10^{-28}\text{g})\times(4.80\times 10^{-10}\text{statC})^4}{2\times(1.05\times 10^{-27}\text{erg-sec})^2}$$

$$= -2.18\times 10^{-11}\text{erg}\times\frac{1}{1.60\times 10^{-12}\text{erg/eV}}$$

$$= -13.6\ \text{eV}$$

This (negative) energy is the total energy of the state, and so, the binding energy (that energy that must be supplied to raise the total energy to zero and thereby release the electron) is 13.6 eV.

• PROBLEM 971

At the position $x_0 = 1$ unit on a screen, the wave function for an electron beam has the value +1 unit, and in an interval Δx and around $x_0 = 1$ there are observed 100 light flashes per minute. What is the intensity of flashes at $x_0 = 2$, 3, and 4 units where ψ has the values +4, +2, and -2 units, respectively?

Solution: In this problem, one can imagine that we are sending photons into an electron cloud, and recording photon-electron collisions (light flashes) in order to find the intensity of ψ at various points. $|\psi(x_0)|^2$ represents the probability density for the electron's wave function and, the probability of finding the electron in an interval Δx about x_0 is $|\psi(x_0)|^2\,\Delta x$. But the intensity of light flashing at x_0 is proportional to $|\psi(x_0)|^2\Delta x$.

This is due to the fact that a light flash, as was said above, corresponds to a collision between a photon and an electron. The photon rebounds and reaches the observer. The number of flashes per unit time at a point therefore, indicates the probability of finding an electron at the point.
Introducing a constant of proportionality A, we can write this relation as

$$I(x_0) = A\left|\psi(x_0)\right|^2 \Delta x$$

Therefore,

$$I(x_0 = 1) = A\left|\psi(x_0 = 1)\right|^2 \Delta x$$
$$= A\left| + 1\right|^2 \Delta x$$
$$= A\Delta x$$
$$= 100 \text{ flashes/min}$$

so that

$$A\Delta x = 100 \text{ flashes/min}$$

Then

$$I(x_0 = 2) = A\left| + 4\right|^2 \Delta x$$
$$= 16A\Delta x$$
$$= 1600 \text{ flashes/min}$$
$$I(x_0 = 3) = A\left|+2\right|^2 \Delta x$$
$$= 4A\Delta x$$
$$= 400 \text{ flashes/min}$$
$$I(x_0 = 4) = A\left|-2\right| \Delta x$$
$$= 4A\Delta x$$
$$= 400 \text{ flashes/min}$$

Notice that even though $\psi(x_0)$ differs in sign for the last two cases, the intensity is the same because the intensity is proportional to the square of the wave function.

• PROBLEM 972

A grain of sand has a mass of 10^{-5} gram. Through what height must it fall from rest in order to have a kinetic energy equal to the energy of a quantum of visible light with a frequency of $5 \times 10^{14} \text{sec}^{-1}$?

Solution: The energy of the quantum is given by the product of its frequency, ν, and Planck's constant h.

$$\varepsilon = h\nu$$
$$= 6.625 \times 10^{-27} \times 5 \times 10^{14}$$
$$= 3.31 \times 10^{-12} \text{erg}$$

When the grain of sand falls through a height H from rest, its final kinetic energy, $\frac{1}{2}mv^2$, is equal to its decrease in gravitational potential energy, mg H.

$$\frac{1}{2}mv^2 = mg\ H$$

Therefore mg H = $h\nu$

$$H = \frac{h\nu}{mg}$$

$$= \frac{3.31 \times 10^{-12}}{10^{-5} \times 980}$$

$$= 3.38 \times 10^{-10} \text{cm}$$

The grain of sand would have to fall through a height of only 3.38×10^{-10}cm. The diameter of an atom is about 10^{-8}cm.

• PROBLEM 973

What will be the maximum kinetic energy of the photoelectrons ejected from magnesium (for which the work function $\varphi = 3.7$ eV) when irradiated by ultraviolet light of frequency 1.5×10^{15} sec^{-1} ?

Solution: The energy of a photon with frequency 1.5×10^{15} sec^{-1} is

$$\epsilon = h\nu = \left(6.6 \times 10^{-27} \text{ erg-sec}\right) \times \left(1.5 \times 10^{15} \text{ sec}^{-1}\right)$$

$$= 9.9 \times 10^{-2} \text{ erg} \times \frac{1\text{eV}}{1.6\times10^{-12}\text{erg}}$$

$$= 6.2 \text{ eV}$$

The maximum kinetic energy of a photoelectron is obtained from whatever energy is left over after the collision of a photon and surface electron has occurred. Since the electron loses energy equal in amount to φ while leaving the metal, we may write

$$KE = h\nu - \varphi$$

$$= 6.2 \text{ eV} - 3.7 \text{ eV}$$

$$= 2.5 \text{ eV}$$

• PROBLEM 974

What is the energy of a photon of blue light whose frequency is 7×10^{14} Hz and the energy of a photon for FM electromagnetic radiation if the frequency is 1×10^{8} Hz?

Solution: We shall use an approximate value for h of 6.6×10^{-34} J s. The energy of a light quantum(photon) is given by

$$E = hf$$

where f is the frequency of the light. Therefore, we have

$$\text{blue light } E = hf = \left(6.6 \times 10^{-34} \text{ Js}\right)\left(7 \times 10^{14} \text{ Hz}\right)$$

$$= 4.6 \times 10^{-19} \text{ J}$$

$$\text{FM waves } E = hf = \left(6.6 \times 10^{-34} \text{ Js}\right)\left(1 \times 10^{8} \text{ Hz}\right)$$

$$= 6.6 \times 10^{-26} \text{ J}$$

Notice that the higher the frequency of the electromagnetic radiation, the greater the energy of the photon.

Silver, atomic weight 107.9 and density 10.5 gm/cm^3, has one free electron per atom. Calculate the Fermi energy of the electrons.

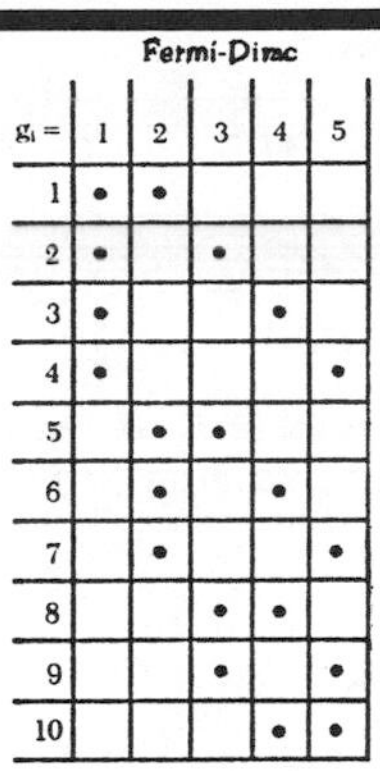

Fermi-Dirac

$g_i =$	1	2	3	4	5
1	•	•			
2	•		•		
3	•			•	
4	•				•
5		•	•		
6		•		•	
7		•			•
8			•	•	
9			•		•
10				•	•

Solution: The Fermi energy is given by

$$\varepsilon_F = \frac{h^2}{8m}\left(\frac{3N}{\pi V}\right)^{2/3} \qquad (1)$$

where V is the molar volume of silver, and N is the number of free electrons in 1 mole of silver.

Since $\quad \text{density} = \dfrac{\text{mass}}{\text{volume}}$

$$\text{density} = \frac{\text{molar mass (M)}}{\text{molar volume (V)}}$$

Hence,

$$V = \frac{M}{\text{density}}$$

But M is the mass of an element in atomic mass units. Therefore

$$V = \frac{107.9 \text{ amu}}{10.5 \text{ g/cm}^3}$$

$$= \frac{107.9 \text{ g/mole}}{10.5 \text{ g/cm}^3}$$

$$= 10.26 \text{ cm}^3\text{/mole}$$

$$= 1.026 \times 10^{-5} \text{ m}^3\text{/mole.}$$

In order to find N, note that each silver atom contributes one electron, (that is, its free or valence electron). Since there are Avogadro's number, (6.02×10^{23}) of particles in a mole of a substance, the mole of silver will contain 6.02×10^{23} free electrons. These electrons are distributed into energy states according to Fermi-Dirac statistics (in other words, each energy state can contain only one particle). The energy levels are filled by placing the electrons first into the lowest energy levels, and then progressively filling the higher levels. The highest energy level into which the last electron is placed is called the Fermi energy. Substituting the values of N and V into (1) and using the given data,

$$\varepsilon_F = \frac{(6.63\times10^{-34}\text{J}\cdot\text{s})^2}{(8)(9.11\times10^{-31}\text{kg})}\left[\frac{3\times6.03\times10^{23}\ \text{elec/mole}}{\pi\times1.026\times10^{-5}\ \text{m}^3\text{/mole}}\right]^{2/3}$$

$$= 8.85 \times 10^{-19}\ \text{Joules}$$

Since $1\ \text{eV} = 1.6 \times 10^{-19}\ \text{J}$

$$\varepsilon_F = \frac{8.85 \times 10^{-19}\ \text{J}}{1.6 \times 10^{-19}\ \text{J/eV}} = 5.54\ \text{eV}$$

We could interpret this as a maximum kinetic energy of the electrons. Then the maximum velocity would be

$$\tfrac{1}{2}mv^2 = 8.85 \times 10^{-19}\ \text{J}$$

$$v^2 = \frac{2 \times 8.85 \times 10^{-19}\ \text{J}}{9.11 \times 10^{-31}\ \text{kg}}$$

$$= 1.94 \times 10^{12}\ \text{m}^2/\text{sec}^2$$

$$v = 1.4 \times 10^{6}\ \text{m/sec}$$

$$= 0.005\ c$$

where c = speed of light.

• PROBLEM 976

In a photoelectric effect experiment it is found that for a certain metal surface the kinetic energy of an electron ejected by blue light of wavelength 4.1×10^{-7} m is 3.2 10^{-19} J. (a) What is the work function of the electrons in the metal? (b) What is the longest wavelength of light that will eject electrons from this surface?

Solution: (a) Light energy is composed of quanta or photons of energy hf. When photons strike the surface of a metal, they transmit this energy completely to the electrons in the metal. The work function E_W is the minimum energy an electron must acquire if it is to leave the metal's surface. The maximum energy of the electrons leaving the surface is carried by the surface electrons and, by conservation of energy is hf - E_W. Non-surface electrons have less than this amount because of energy losses as they cross the surface. The energy the electrons have after they leave the metal is in the form of kinetic energy. Therefore,

$$K = hf - E_W$$

To find the frequency of the photon, we use,

$$f = \frac{c}{\lambda} = \frac{3 \times 10^{8}\ \text{m/s}}{4.1 \times 10^{-7}\ \text{m}} = 7.3 \times 10^{14}\ \text{Hz}$$

Substituting into the first equation,

$$K = hf - E_W$$

$$3.2 \times 10^{-19} J = \left(6.6 \times 10^{-34} J\ s\right)\left(7.3 \times 10^{14} Hz\right) - E_W$$

$$E_W = 4.8 \times 10^{-19} J - 3.2 \times 10^{-19} J =$$

$$1.6 \times 10^{-19}\ J$$

(b) The limiting case occurs when the electron kinetic energy is zero. Therefore we set K = 0 to obtain the limiting frequency.

$$hf - E_W = 0$$

$$f = \frac{E_W}{h} = \frac{1.6 \times 10^{-19} \not{J}}{6.6 \times 10^{-34} \not{J}\ s} = 2.4 \times 10^{14} Hz$$

This corresponds to a wavelength λ given by

$$\lambda = \frac{c}{f} = \frac{3 \times 10^8\ m/s}{2.4 \times 10^{14}\ Hz} = 1.25 \times 10^{-6}\ m$$

• PROBLEM 977

The photoelectric work functions for several metals are listed below. Calculate the threshold wavelengths for each metal. Which metals will not emit photoelectrons when illuminated with visible light?

	W-(Joules)
Cs	3.2×10^{-19}
Cu	6.4×10^{-19}
K	3.6×10^{-19}
Zn	5.8×10^{-19}

Solution: When light with a frequency above some definite level (called the threshold frequency) illuminates certain metals, it is observed that electrons are emitted. The energy of an incident photon is entirely given up to one electron of the metal. If this is an interior electron, it will travel towards the surface of the metal and, in the process, loose energy due to collisions with atoms of the metal. In addition, the electrons will loose energy because they must overcome the attractive force of the atoms of the metal in order to escape from the surface. (The energy needed to overcome this attractive force is called the metal's work function, W). Electrons near the surface of the metal, however, don't experience the collisions described above, and they can't lose energy due to this cause. As a result, these surface electrons will be emitted with a higher kinetic energy than the interior electrons. Hence, using the principle of conservation of energy, we may write, for surface electrons,

$$\tfrac{1}{2} mv^2_{max} + W = h\upsilon,$$

where $\frac{1}{2}mv^2_{max}$ is the kinetic energy of these electrons. At the threshold frequency, υ_0, the emitted electrons will have no kinetic energy. Therefore,

$$h\upsilon_0 = 0 + W$$

or $$\upsilon_0 = \frac{W}{h}$$

The threshold wavelength λ_0 is $\lambda_0\upsilon_0 = c$, thus

$$\lambda_0 = \frac{hc}{W}$$

$$hc = (6.63 \times 10^{-34}\ J\cdot s)(3 \times 10^8\ m/s)$$

$$= 1.99 \times 10^{-25}\ J\text{-}m$$

	λ_0 (meters)	λ_0 (Å)
Cs	6.2×10^{-7}	6200
Cu	3.1×10^{-7}	3100
K	5.5×10^{-7}	5500
Zn	3.4×10^{-7}	3400

The calculated values of λ_0 are shown in the table. To convert to Angstrom units (Å), we note that 1Å = 10^{-10} m. Hence, dividing each value of λ_0 (in units of meters) by 10^{-10} m will yield λ_0 in units of Å.

Since the range of the visible spectrum is 4,000 Å - 7,600 Å, we note that Cu and Zn will not emit photoelectrons if illuminated by visible light.

• PROBLEM 978

When silver is irradiated with ultraviolet light of wavelength 1000 Å, a potential of 7.7 volts is required to retard completely the photoelectrons. What is the work function of silver?

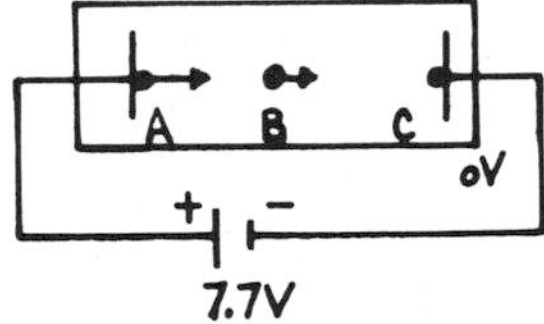

Solution: First, the energy of a 1000-Å photon is

$$E = hv = \frac{hc}{\lambda}$$

$$= \frac{(6.6\times10^{-27}\text{erg-sec})\times(3\times10^{10}\ \text{cm/sec})}{(1.0\times10^{-5}\ \text{cm})\times(1.6\times10^{-12}\ \text{erg/eV})}$$

$$= 12.4\ eV$$

Note that if 7.7 eV stops all photoelectrons, it will

stop the surface photoelectrons also. Hence we may use the photoelectric effect equation,

$$\phi = h\upsilon - \tfrac{1}{2} mv^2_{max} \qquad (1)$$

The electron looses kinetic energy and gains potential energy as it moves through the retarding potential (similar to the conversion of kinetic energy to gravitational potential energy when an object is thrown up from the ground). At plate A, the electron has only kinetic energy. At point B, the electron has both kinetic energy and potential energy. At plate C, the electron has only potential energy, because we are told that a potential of 7.7 volts will completely retard the motion of the photoelectrons. Hence, by the principle of conservation of energy, we relate the energy of the photoelectrons at A and C, or

$$\tfrac{1}{2}mv^2_{max} = \text{P.E. @ C.}$$

But, by the definition of potential energy, (W), we have

$$V_c - V_a = \frac{W_{ac}}{q}$$

where $V_c - V_a$ is the potential difference of the plates, and q is the charge transported between A and C (a photoelectron, in our case). Hence

$$\tfrac{1}{2} mv^2_{max} = q(V_c - V_a)$$

Substituting this in (1), we obtain

$$\phi = h\upsilon - e(V_c - V_a) \qquad (2)$$

Putting the given data in (2),

$$\phi = 1.24 \text{ eV} - (-1.6 \times 10^{-19} \text{ C})(0 - 7.7\text{V})$$

where we have used the fact that $e = -1.6 \times 10^{-19}$C. Because 1.6×10^{-19}J = 1 eV,

$$\phi = 12.4 \text{ eV} - 7.7 \text{ eV} = 4.7 \text{ eV}$$

(Note that we have used the fact that the energy of an electron that is completely stopped by a potential of 7.7 volts is just 7.7 electron volts.)

• PROBLEM 979

There are 2N electrons in a one dimensional infinite square potential well of size L as shown in the figure. What is the energy of the last filled state (the Fermi energy) at T = 0°K. The exclusion principle forbids the occupation of the same energy level by more than two electrons.

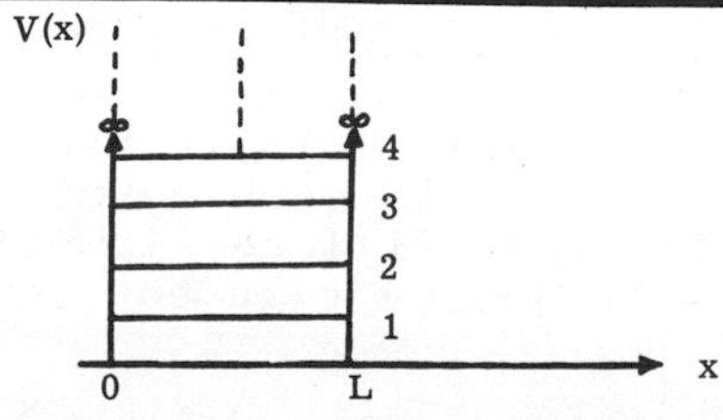

Solution: We can find the momenta of the electrons in the well from the Schroedinger equation. If $\psi(x)$ is the wave function of the electron in the well, then it must satisfy the equation

$$\left[-\frac{\hbar^2}{2\,m}\frac{d^2}{dx^2}+V(x)\right]\psi(x) = E\,\psi(x) \tag{1}$$

where E is the energy of the electron. $\psi(x)$ is non-zero only between $x = 0$ and $x = L$, since the electron cannot escape from an infinitely large potential well. The solution of (1) can be obtained if we write it as

$$\frac{d^2\psi}{dx^2}+\frac{2\,m}{\hbar^2}E\,\psi = 0 \quad \text{for } 0 < x < L. \tag{2}$$

the solution of (2) is

$$\psi(x) = A\cos kx + B\sin kx$$

where $k = \sqrt{\dfrac{2mE}{\hbar^2}}$. Now, we utilize the condition that $\psi(x)$ vanishes at the boundries of the potential.

$$\psi(x = 0) = \psi(x = L) = 0.$$

This gives

$$\psi(0) = A = 0$$

and $\psi(L) = A\cos kL + B\sin kL$

$$= B\sin kL = 0$$

The last equation shows that

$$\sin kL = \sin n\pi = 0, \quad n = 1, 2, \ldots .$$

Therefore the allowed values of k are such that

$$kL = n\pi$$

$$k_n = \frac{n\pi}{L}.$$

The corresponding energy values are

$$E_n^2 = \frac{\hbar^2 k^2}{2m} = \frac{h^2}{(4\pi^2)2m}\,\frac{n^2\pi^2}{L^2}$$

$$= \frac{h^2n^2}{8mL^2}$$

(Here we made use of the definition $\hbar = h/2\pi$).

The energy levels are shown in the figure. We can put only 2 electrons in each level, therefore at $T = 0°K$, 2N electrons fill the lowest N levels, starting from $n = 1$. Notice that the level $n = 0$, which corresponds to zero energy is not allowed on the basis of the uncertainty relation. Since

$$\Delta x \, \Delta p \gtrsim h,$$

for $\Delta x = L$, the momentum of the electron cannot be strictly zero, but has a spread of

$$\Delta p \gtrsim \frac{h}{L} .$$

This corresponds to a non-zero energy even for the lowest level.

The energy of the highest level is

$$E_F = \frac{N^2 h^2}{8mL^2} = \frac{h^2}{8m}\left(\frac{N}{L}\right)^2 .$$

We see that the Fermi energy is a function of the number of electrons per unit length, N/L.

• PROBLEM 980

A 1-gram block rests on a frictionless surface and we measure the position of the block to a precision of 0.1 mm. What velocity have we imparted to the block by the act of measuring its position?

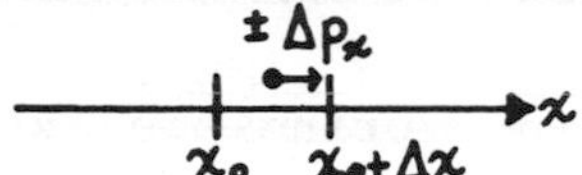

Solution: If we try to determine the position of a particle at a point x_0 along the x axis as shown in the figure we find that our measurement of the position x_0 cannot be made as precise as required (assuming that it is at rest). As we try to confine the particle to a more exact position, we become less certain about whether it really is at rest at that position. This is a consequence of quantum mechanics and is known as the Heisenberg uncertainty principle. If the uncertainty involved in the measurement of position is Δx, then the anticipated uncertainty in the momentum of the particle will be such that

$$\Delta x \, \Delta p_x \approx h$$

where h is Planck's constant. Since $p_x = mv_x$, we have

$$\Delta x \, m\Delta v_x \simeq h$$

or

$$\Delta v_x \approx \frac{h}{m \, \Delta x}$$

$$= \frac{6.6 \times 10^{-27} \text{erg-sec}}{(1 \text{ g}) \times \left(10^{-2} \text{cm}\right)}$$

$$= 6.6 \times 10^{-25} \text{ cm/sec}$$

This velocity is so small that we must consider the block to be still "at rest". The implications of the uncertainty principle for macroscopic objects are unimportant, but for microscopic objects they are crucial. That there is any uncertainty at all in the measurement arises from the fact that we can see the block only by virtue of the scattering of photons from the block and this process imparts momentum to the block.

• **PROBLEM 981**

The energy of an electron in a certain atom is approximately 1×10^{-18} J. How long would it take to measure the energy to a precision of 1 per cent?

Solution: The energy uncertainty is $(.01)(1 \times 10^{-18}\ J) = 1 \times 10^{-20}$ J. This means that the measurement of the energy of the system will yield a value $1 \times 10^{-18} \pm 1 \times 10^{-20}$ J. One form of the Uncertainty Principle relates the lack of certainty as to what the energy of a sistem is (ΔE), to the length of time needed to measure the energy with this degree of accuracy (Δt).

$$\Delta E\ \Delta t = \frac{h}{4\pi}$$

where h is Planks constant. We are given $\Delta E = 1 \times 10^{-20}$ J (i.e. the measured value of energy in the system is $E \pm \Delta E$). Then

$$\Delta t \cong \frac{h}{(\Delta E)(4\pi)} = \frac{6.6 \times 10^{-34}\ \not{J}\ s}{(1 \times 10^{-20}\not{J})(4\pi)} = 5.3 \times 10^{-15}\ s$$

• **PROBLEM 982**

Find the minimum energy of a simple harmonic oscillator using the uncertainty principle $\Delta x \Delta p \geq \hbar$.

Solution: Consider a particle of mass m on a spring of force-constant k. The kinetic and potential energies, respectively, are,

$$K = \frac{1}{2} mv^2 = \frac{p^2}{2m}$$

$$U = \frac{1}{2} kx^2 = \frac{1}{2} m\omega^2 x^2$$

where $p = mv$ and $\omega^2 = \frac{k}{m}$. The total energy is constant (conservation of energy) and is therefore equal to its average value.

$$E = \langle E \rangle = \frac{\langle p^2 \rangle}{2m} + \frac{1}{2} m\omega^2 \langle x^2 \rangle \qquad (1)$$

where $\langle\ \rangle$ indicates the time average. As a result of symmetry with respect to the equilibrium point, $\langle p \rangle$ and $\langle x \rangle$ are zero. The uncertainty in x and p are defined as,

$$(\Delta x)^2 = \langle (x - \langle x \rangle)^2 \rangle = \langle x^2 \rangle - 2\langle x \rangle\langle x \rangle + \langle x \rangle^2$$

$$= \langle x^2 \rangle - \langle x \rangle^2 = \langle x^2 \rangle - 0 = \langle x^2 \rangle$$

and

$$(\Delta p)^2 = \langle (p - \langle p \rangle)^2 \rangle = \langle p^2 \rangle - 2\langle p \rangle \langle p \rangle + \langle p \rangle^2$$

$$= \langle p^2 \rangle - \langle p \rangle^2 = \langle p^2 \rangle - 0 = \langle p^2 \rangle$$

Therefore (1) can be written as,

$$E = \frac{1}{2m}(\Delta p)^2 + \frac{1}{2} m\omega^2 (\Delta x)^2 \qquad (2)$$

Using the uncertainty relation

$$\Delta p \, \Delta x \geq \hbar$$

or

$$(\Delta p)^2 \geq \frac{\hbar^2}{(\Delta x)^2}$$

the total energy (2), becomes,

$$E - \frac{1}{2} m\omega^2 (\Delta X)^2 = \frac{1}{2m}(\Delta p)^2 \geq \frac{\hbar^2}{2m(\Delta X)^2}$$

or

$$E \geq \frac{\hbar^2}{2m} \frac{1}{(\Delta X)^2} + \frac{1}{2} m\omega^2 (\Delta x)^2$$

The value of Δx for which ΔE is a minimum is given by the condition,

$$\frac{dE}{d(\Delta x)} = 0$$

Hence,

$$-2 \frac{\hbar^2}{2m}(\Delta x)^{-3} + 2 \frac{1}{2} m\omega^2 \Delta x = 0$$

$$(\Delta x)^4 = \frac{\hbar^2}{m^2\omega^2}$$

$$(\Delta x)^2 = \frac{\hbar}{m\omega}$$

$$E_{min} = \frac{\hbar^2}{2m} \frac{m\omega}{\hbar} + \frac{m\omega^2}{2} \frac{\hbar}{m\omega}$$

$$= \hbar\omega$$

• PROBLEM 983

An atom emits a photon of green light $\lambda = 5200$ Å in $\tau = 2 \times 10^{-10}$ sec. Estimate the spread of wavelengths in the photon.

Solution: The Heisenberg uncertainty relationship for energy and time is

$$\Delta E \, \Delta t \gtrsim \hbar \qquad (1)$$

where ΔE is the uncertainty in the energy of the system we are observing, and Δt is the time interval over which we observe the system. Also, $\hbar$ is Planck's constant divided by 2π.

The energy of a photon is given by

$$E = h\nu \tag{2}$$

where ν is the frequency of the photon. But

$$c = \nu\lambda \tag{3}$$

where c and λ are the speed and wavelength of light, respectively. From (3) and (2)

$$E = \frac{hc}{\lambda}$$

Taking the derivative of E with respect to λ,

$$\frac{dE}{d\lambda} = \frac{-hc}{\lambda^2} \tag{4}$$

Hence

$$\Delta E \approx \frac{-hc}{\lambda^2}\,\Delta\lambda \tag{5}$$

Using (5) in (1)

$$\frac{-hc}{\lambda^2}\,\Delta\lambda\,\Delta t \gtrsim \hbar$$

$$\Delta\lambda \gtrsim \frac{\hbar\lambda^2}{-hc\Delta t}$$

$$\Delta\lambda \gtrsim \frac{\lambda^2}{-2\pi c\Delta t} \tag{6}$$

Therefore, using the given data,

$$\Delta\lambda \gtrsim \frac{(5200\ \text{Å})^2}{(-2)(3.14)\left(3 \times 10^{8}\text{m/s}\right)\left(2 \times 10^{-10}\text{s}\right)}$$

Since $1\ \text{Å} = 10^{-10}\text{m}$

$$\Delta\lambda \gtrsim -\frac{\left(5.2 \times 10^{-7}\text{m}\right)^2}{\left(37.68 \times 10^{-2}\text{m}\right)}$$

$$\Delta\lambda \gtrsim -.717 \times 10^{-12}\text{m}$$

$$\Delta\lambda \gtrsim -7.17 \times 10^{-13}\text{m} \tag{7}$$

Hence, the spread in wavelength is at least 7.17×10^{-13}m. (We may neglect the minus sign in (7), because, looking at (6), it only indicates that as Δt increases, $\Delta\lambda$ decreases).

• PROBLEM 984

If an atom remains in an excited state for 10^{-8} sec, what is the uncertainty in the energy of that state?

Solution: To solve this we use the Heisenberg uncertainty principle:

$\Delta E\Delta t \geq h$, where h is Planck's constant.

$$\Delta E \geq \frac{h}{\Delta t} = \frac{6.6 \times 10^{-27}\ \text{erg-sec}}{10^{-8}\ \text{sec}} = 6.6 \times 10^{-19}\ \text{ergs}$$

This is the limit of accuracy with which the energy of such an excited atom can ever be measured. It is called the energy width of the excited state.

• PROBLEM 985

Use the uncertainty principle to estimate the kinetic energy of a neutron in a nucleus of radius

$$R = 2 \times 10^{-13} \text{cm} .$$

Solution: We write the uncertainty principle in the form

$$\Delta p \Delta x = h$$

Then

$$\Delta x \cong 2R$$

for the neutron can be found anywhere in the nucleus. The Δx given expresses this lack of certainty as to where in the nucleus it can be found. As a result of the uncertainty principle, the neutron can acquire a momentum

$$p = \Delta p$$

$$= \frac{h}{2R}$$

The kinetic energy, $T = \frac{1}{2}mv^2 = \frac{1}{2}\frac{(mv)^2}{2m} = \frac{p^2}{2m} = \frac{h^2}{8mR^2}$

$$T = \frac{\left(6.63 \times 10^{-27} \text{erg-sec}\right)^2}{8\left(1.67 \times 10^{-24} \text{gm}\right)\left(2 \times 10^{-13} \text{cm}\right)^2} = 8.22 \times 10^{-5} \frac{\text{erg}^2\text{-sec}^2}{\text{gm-cm}^2}$$

$$= 8.22 \times 10^{-5} \frac{\text{erg}^2}{\frac{\text{gm-cm}}{\text{sec}^2}\text{-cm}}$$

$$= 8.22 \times 10^{-5} \frac{\text{erg}^2}{\text{dyne-cm}} = 8.22 \times 10^{-5} \text{erg}$$

• **PROBLEM 986**

A car of mass 1×10^3 kg is traveling at a speed of 10 m/s. At a certain instant of time we measure its position with a precision of 1×10^{-6} m. What is the theoretical limit in precision for measuring the speed of the car?

Solution: The uncertainty principle will be used to find the limit of precision of one variable when the precision of a complementary variable is given. If Δx is the uncertainty (i.e., the limit of precision) in the position of a particle, and if $\Delta p = m\Delta v$ is the uncertainty of the momentum of the particle, then,

$$\Delta x \Delta p = \Delta x m \Delta v \cong \frac{h}{4\pi}$$

where h is Planck's constant. Substitution of the given values for m, and Δx in the equation gives

$$\Delta v = \frac{h}{(\Delta x) 4\pi m} = \frac{6.6 \times 10^{-34} \text{ J s}}{\left(1 \times 10^{-6} \text{ m}\right)(4\pi)\left(1 \times 10^{3} \text{ kg}\right)} = 5.3 \times 10^{-32} \text{m/s}$$

This is a very small uncertainty in the speed of the car and could never be detected by available measurement techniques.

• **PROBLEM 987**

The density of diamond is 3.5 gm/cm^3. What is the order of magnitude of the average velocity and average energy of a carbon atom in diamond at absolute zero?

Solution: Density is defined as

$$\varphi = M/V$$

where M is the mass in a volume V. Solving for M

$$M = \varphi V$$

The number of carbon atoms, n, in this mass is M divided by the atomic mass of carbon

$$n = \frac{M}{(12 \text{ amu})} = \frac{\varphi V}{(12 \text{ amu})}$$

Hence the volume occupied by 1 carbon atom is

$$\frac{V}{n} = \frac{(12 \text{ amu})}{\varphi}$$

$$\frac{V}{n} = \frac{(12 \text{ amu})\left(1.66 \times 10^{-27} \text{ kg/amu}\right)}{\left(3.5 \text{ kg/m}^3\right)}$$

$$\frac{V}{n} = \frac{19.8 \times 10^{-27} \text{ m}^3}{3.5}$$

$$\frac{V}{n} = 5.7 \times 10^{-27} \text{ m}^3$$

Assuming that each carbon atom occupies a cubical volume, the length of one side of this cube, ℓ, will be such that

$$\ell^3 = 5.7 \times 10^{-27} \text{ m}^3$$

$$\ell = 1.8 \times 10^{-10} \text{ m}$$

The mass of a carbon atom, m, is

$$m = (12 \text{ amu})\left(1.66 \times 10^{-27} \text{ kg/amu}\right)$$

$$m \approx 2 \times 10^{-26} \text{ kg}$$

We may now use Heisenberg's uncertainty relationship to find the average velocity of the carbon atom. Since the atom is assumed to be in a cubical volume of length ℓ, the uncertainty in its position is

$$\Delta x = \ell$$

Hence, using the uncertainty relationship (where Δp is the uncertainty in momentum and $\hbar$ is Planck's constant divided by 2π)

$$\Delta p \, \Delta x \gtrsim \hbar$$

$$\Delta p \gtrsim \frac{\hbar}{\ell} = \frac{6.63 \times 10^{-34} \text{ J}\cdot\text{s}}{(2\pi)\left(1.8 \times 10^{-10} \text{ m}\right)}$$

$$\Delta p \gtrsim \frac{6.63 \times 10^{-34} \text{ N}\cdot\text{m}\cdot\text{s}}{11.3 \times 10^{-10} \text{ m}}$$

$$\Delta p \gtrsim .586 \times 10^{-24} \text{ N}\cdot\text{s}$$

$$\Delta p \gtrsim 5.86 \times 10^{-25} \text{ N}\cdot\text{s}$$

The minimum uncertainty in p is then

$$\Delta p_{min} = 5.86 \times 10^{-25} \text{ N}\cdot\text{s}$$

But $\Delta p_{min} = m\Delta v_{min}$, since m is constant. Hence

$$\Delta v_{min} = \frac{\Delta p_{min}}{m} = \frac{5.86 \times 10^{-25} \text{ N}\cdot\text{s}}{2 \times 10^{-26} \text{ kg}}$$

$$\Delta v_{min} = 2.93 \times 10^1 \text{ m/s}$$

$$\Delta v_{min} = 29.3 \text{ m/s}$$

This quantity gives us an approximate value for the velocity of the carbon atom. The average energy is then

$$\begin{aligned} E &= \tfrac{1}{2}mv^2 \\ &= (\tfrac{1}{2})\left(2 \times 10^{-26}\text{kg}\right)(29.3 \text{ m/s})^2 \\ &= \left(10^{-26} \text{ kg}\right)\left(858.5 \text{ m}^2/\text{s}^2\right) \\ &= 8.59 \times 10^{-24} \text{ Joules} \end{aligned}$$

The zero point energy is the least energy a system can have and occurs at absolute zero. It is

$$E_0 = \tfrac{1}{2}hf$$

and

$$f = \frac{2E_0}{h} .$$

Assuming that the magnitude of E_0 is the E calculated above,

$$f = \frac{(2)\left(8.59 \times 10^{-24} \text{ Joules}\right)}{\left(6.63 \times 10^{-34} \text{ Joules-sec}\right)}$$

$$f = \left(\frac{17.18 \times 10^{-24}}{6.63 \times 10^{-34}}\right) s^{-1}$$

$$f = 2.6 \times 10^{10} \text{ s}^{-1}$$

• PROBLEM 988

It was once thought that a neutron is made up of an electron and proton held together by Coulomb attraction. Assume the neutron radius is 10^{-15} m. (a) According to the uncertainty principle, find Δp for such an electron. (b) The lowest average momentum such an electron could have would be $\tfrac{1}{2}\Delta p$. What would be the corresponding energy? (c) What is the electrostatic potential energy of an electron 10^{-13} cm from a proton? (d) From the calculations in (b) and (c) does it appear likely that a neutron could be made up of an electron and a proton?

Solution: (a) The uncertainty principle states that

$\Delta p \Delta x \cong \frac{h}{4\pi}$, where h is Planck's constant, Δp is the uncertainty of the momentum of a particle, and Δx is the uncertainty in the position of the particle. If we assume that the electron can be found anywhere within the neutron, then Δx will be of the order of the neutron radius 10^{-15} m. p can then be found using the uncertainty principle.

$$\Delta p = \frac{h}{4\pi\ \Delta x} = \frac{6.63 \times 10^{-34} \text{ joule-sec}}{4\pi \quad 10^{-15} \text{ m}} = 5.28 \times 10^{-20} \text{ kg-m/sec}$$

(b) We must find a relation between energy E and momentum p. Since

$$E = mc^2 = \left(\frac{m_0}{\sqrt{1 - \frac{v^2}{c^2}}}\right)c^2$$

where m_0 is the rest mass of the electron, and v its speed, we have, upon squaring both sides of the equation,

$$E^2\left(1 - \frac{v^2}{c^2}\right) = \left(m_0\ c^2\right)^2$$

or

$$E^2 = \frac{E^2\ v^2}{c^2} + \left(m_0\ c^2\right)^2$$

$$= \frac{E^2}{c^4}c^2v^2 + \left(m_0\ c^2\right)^2$$

$$= \left(\frac{m^2\ c^4}{c^4}\right)c^2\ v^2 + \left(m_0\ c^2\right)^2$$

$$E^2 = p^2\ c^2 + \left(m_0\ c^2\right)^2. \qquad (1)$$

Here, we used the definition of momentum as $p = mv$. We have $m_0 = 9.11 \times 10^{-31}$ kg, $c = 3 \times 10^8$ m/sec and $p = \frac{\Delta p}{2} = \frac{5.28 \times 10^{-20}}{2}\ \frac{\text{km}}{\text{sec}} = 2.64 \times 10^{-20}\ \frac{\text{km}}{\text{sec}}$. Upon substitution into (1), the result becomes

$$E = \sqrt{\left(2.64 \times 10^{-20}\ \frac{\text{k-m}}{\text{sec}}\right)^2\left(3 \times 10^8\ \frac{\text{m}}{\text{sec}}\right)^2 + \left(9.11 \times 10^{-31}\ \text{kg}\right)^2\left(3 \times 10^8\ \frac{\text{m}}{\text{sec}}\right)^4} = 7.46 \times 10^{-12}$$

Since $1\ \text{eV} = 1.6 \times 10^{-19}$ J

$$= 7.46 \times 10^{-12}\ \text{J} \times \frac{1\ \text{eV}}{1.60 \times 10^{-19}\ \text{J}}$$

$$= 4.67 \times 10^7\ \text{eV}.$$

(c) By the definition of V

$$V = \frac{1}{4\pi\varepsilon_0}\ \frac{(e)(e)}{r} = \frac{\left(9.0 \times 10^9\ \frac{\text{N - m}}{\text{coul}^2}\right)\left(1.60 \times 10^{-19}\ \text{coul}\right)^2}{10^{-13}\ \text{cm}\ \frac{1\text{m}}{10^2\ \text{cm}}}$$

$$= 2.30 \times 10^{-13}\ \text{J} = 2.30 \times 10^{-13}\ \text{J} \times \frac{1\ \text{eV}}{1.60 \times 10^{-19}\ \text{J}}$$

$$= 1.44 \times 10^6\ \text{eV}.$$

(d) No. The energy of the electron is much greater than the energy available to bind the electron to the proton to form the neutron.

• PROBLEM 989

Suppose that the speed of an electron is 1×10^6 m/s and the measurement precision involves an uncertainty in speed of 1 per cent. How precisely can the position of the electron be simultaneously determined?

Solution: The uncertainty in speed is

$$\Delta v = (.01)(1 \times 10^6 \text{ m/s}) = 1 \times 10^4 \text{ m/s}$$

This means that a measurement of the velocity of the electron will yield a value $1 \times 10^6 \pm 1 \times 10^4$ m/s. The Uncertainty Principle relates the lack of knowledge as to where a particle is located (Δx), to the lack of knowledge as to what the momentum of the particle is (Δp), when both the position and momentum of the particle are measured at the same time. The relation is

$$\Delta p \Delta x = m \Delta v \Delta x \cong \frac{h}{4\pi}$$

where m is the mass of the particle, and h is Planck's constant. Since the mass of the electron is 9.1×10^{-31} kg, then

$$\Delta x = \frac{h}{(\Delta v) 4\pi m}$$

$$= \frac{6.6 \times 10^{-34} \text{ J s}}{(1 \times 10^4 \text{ m/s})(4)(3.14)(9.1 \times 10^{-31} \text{ kg})}$$

$$= 5.8 \times 10^{-9} \text{ m}$$

This uncertainty in position is at least 100 million times larger than the size of the electron itself. Therefore, the uncertainty principle imposes significant limitations on measurement in the atom-sized world.

• PROBLEM 990

A mass of 5 kg hangs on a spring which has a spring constant of 2×10^3 newtons/m. (a) Calculate the minimum energy of the system. (b) By optical methods the position of the mass can be determined to within 10^{-7} m. What is the uncertainty in the velocity of the mass?

Solution: (a) The natural frequency of the vibrating mass is given by

$$\omega = \sqrt{\frac{k}{m}}$$

$$= \sqrt{\frac{2 \times 10^3 \text{ nt/m}}{5 \text{ kg}}} = 20 \text{ sec}^{-1}$$

The zero point energy is the residual energy the vibrating particle has at absolute zero. It is given by

$$E = \tfrac{1}{2} hf$$

$$= \frac{1}{4\pi} \times (6.63 \times 10^{-34} \times 20) \text{J·s·s}^{-1}$$

$$= 1.05 \times 10^{-32} \text{ J}$$

(b) If we equate this to the maximum kinetic energy the vibrating particle has (when the elastic potential energy of the particle is zero) then

$$E = \frac{1}{2} mv^2$$

or

$$v^2 = \frac{2 \times 1.05 \times 10^{-32} \text{ J}}{5 \text{ kg}}$$

$$v = 2.0 \times 10^{-17} \text{ m/sec}$$

If the uncertainty in the position is $\Delta x = 10^{-7}$ m, then, according to the uncertainty principle,

$$\Delta x \Delta p = \frac{h}{2\pi}$$

$$\Delta p = \frac{h}{2\pi \Delta x}$$

where $\Delta p = m\Delta v$ is the uncertainty in the momentum of the particle. Therefore the uncertainty in the velocity is

$$\Delta v = \frac{h}{2\pi m \Delta x}$$

$$= \frac{6.63 \times 10^{-34} \text{ J·sec}}{2\pi \times 5 \times 10^{-7} \text{ m·kg}}$$

$$= 2.1 \times 10^{-28} \text{ m/sec}$$

This uncertainty is less than the zero point velocity. Suppose that we attempt to measure the velocity by measuring the time required for the mass to move through $x = 2 \times 10^{-7}$ m. That is,

$$t = \frac{x}{v} = \frac{2 \times 10^{-7} \text{ m}}{2 \times 10^{-17} \text{ sec}} = 10^{10} \text{ sec(about 300 years)}$$

Such a measurment is liable to be interrupted before it is completed.

• PROBLEM 991

Taking the wave properties of the electron into account, find the connection between the errors Δp_x and Δx when measuring the momentum and coordinates of an electron, if Δx is determined by the width d of the slit through which the electron beam passes (Figure below).

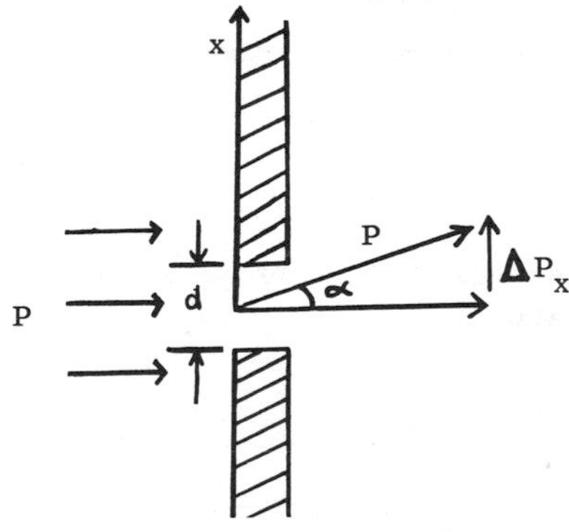

Solution: As the electron is passing through the slit, we lose sight of it. Therefore its position at the slit has an x-axis uncertainty

$$\Delta x = d.$$

As a result of it, the momentum of the electron after it passes through the slit can have an x-component

$$\Delta p_x = p \sin \alpha \ .$$

In order to observe the wave characteristics of the electron, we should be able to display its diffraction pattern. Therefore, the slit should have a size consistent with the single slit condition for observing the first fringes of the diffraction pattern

$$\sin \alpha \gtrsim \frac{\lambda}{d}$$

where λ is the wave length (de Broglie wave length) of the electron.

$$\lambda = \frac{h}{p} \ .$$

Now we calculate $\Delta x \, \Delta p_x$, to obtain the uncertainty relation for the electron;

$$\Delta x \, \Delta p_x \simeq dp \sin \alpha$$

$$\gtrsim dp \frac{\lambda}{d} = dp \frac{h}{pd}$$

$$\gtrsim h \ .$$

• PROBLEM 992

A camera photographs a 120-W sodium lamp 100 m away, the film being exposed for 1/100s. The aperture of the camera has a diameter of 4cm. How many photons enter the camera during the exposure? The wavelength of sodium light is 5893 Å, and all the energy of the lamp is assumed to be emitted as light.

Solution: The energy possessed by one photon of sodium light is $E = hf$, where h is Planck's constant and f is the photon frequency. But $c = \lambda f$ where λ is the wavelength of light and c is the speed of light. Therefore,

$$hf = h \frac{c}{\lambda} = 6.625 \times 10^{-34} \text{J·s} \times \frac{2.998 \times 10^8 \text{m·s}^{-1}}{5893 \times 10^{-10} \text{ m}} = 3.37 \times 10^{-19} \text{ J.}$$

The lamp consumes 120 J of energy per second. Therefore the number of photons emitted per second is

$$n = \frac{120 \text{ J·s}^{-1}}{3.37 \times 10^{-19} \text{J}} = 3.55 \times 10^{20} \text{ s}^{-1} \ .$$

These photons are emitted in all directions and 100 m from the lamp are distributed evenly over a spherical surface of that radius. The number N entering the aperture of the camera per second is thus n multiplied by the fraction of this surface occupied by the aperture. That is,

$$N = n\left(\frac{\pi r^2}{4\pi R^2}\right)$$

where R is the distance from the lens to the lamp, and r is the aperture radius. Then

$$N = 3.55 \times 10^{20} \text{s}^{-1} \times \frac{\pi \times (0.02)^2 \text{m}^2}{4\pi \times (100)^2 \text{m}^2} = 3.55 \times 10^{12} \text{ s}^{-1} \ .$$

Thus in 1/100 s the number of photons entering the camera is 3.55×10^{10}.

• PROBLEM 993

Use the uncertainty principle to show that the rest mass of a photon is zero.

Solution: Let us assume the photon rest mass m_γ is not zero. The Heisenberg uncertainty principle is $p_x \Delta x \geq \frac{h}{4\pi}$ where p_x is the x component of the photon momentum. Hence,

$$m_\gamma v \Delta x \geq \frac{h}{4\pi}.$$

But, for a photon, v = c and

$$m_\gamma \geq \frac{h}{4\pi (\Delta x) c}.$$

Coulomb's law for the force between two charged particles is

$$F = \frac{kq_1 q_2}{d^2}$$

and this force is exerted over arbitrarily large values of d. Consider 2 charges separated by a distance equal to the diameter of the Milky Way galaxy (1×10^{21} m). According to the exchange picture, the electric force between the charged particles is achieved by the exchange of virtual (unobservable) photons between two electrically charged particles. Any measurements made to detect the virtual photon's presence would require measurement precisions exceeding those permitted by the uncertainty principle. The uncertainty in the position of these photons is then the distance over which they are exchanged, (in this instance 1×10^{21} m) for we know that the photons must be somewhere between the 2 charges. Thus

$$m = \frac{h}{4\pi (\Delta x) c} = \frac{6.6 \times 10^{-34} \text{ J s}}{(4)(3.14)\left(1 \times 10^{21} \text{ m}\right)\left(3 \times 10^{8} \text{ m/s}\right)}$$

$$= 1.8 \times 10^{-64} \text{ kg}.$$

This mass is very much smaller than the mass of any other particle and for all practical purposes is zero. The diameter of the Milky Way does not have to be used, however, because according to Coulomb's law, force still exists for even larger distances d. The force only vanishes as d tends toward infinity, but if the distance becomes very large, so does the uncertainty in the position of the photon; hence the photon mass must be precisely zero.

• PROBLEM 994

Find the number of ways that two identical particles $\left(n_i = 2\right)$ can be distributed in five states $\left(g_i = 5\right)$ according to (a) Bose-Einstein and (b) Fermi-Dirac statistics.

Solution: (a) Bose statistics determine the number of distinct ways of placing n_i identical particles in g_i states, where the number of particles in a state is not restricted. Consider the system under consideration to be a linear array of $\left(n_i + g_i - 1\right)$ holes into which

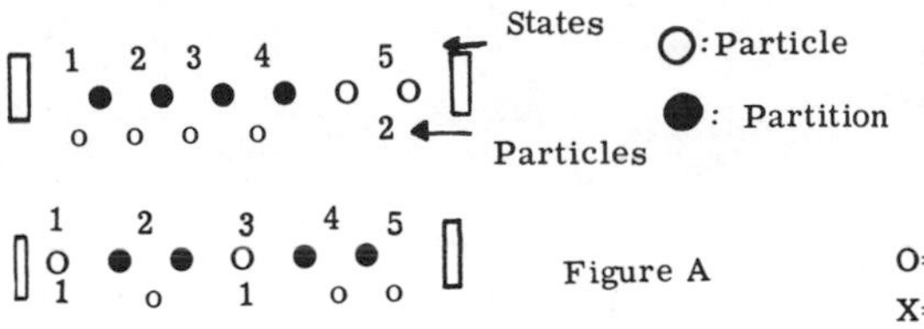

1 2 3 4 5 States O: Particle ●: Partition 2 Particles

1 2 3 4 5

Figure A

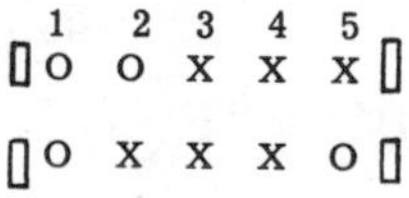

1 2 3 4 5

O O X X X

O X X X O

O=Particle X=Empty State

Figure B

either particles or partitions that separate the states can be inserted. Note that there are $(g_i - 1)$ such partitions to separate the entire cell into g_i states. The remaining n_i holes which are separated into groups by these partitions, represent the distribution of the particles among the various states (see Fig. a).

The number of distinct permutations of n_i particles and $(g_i - 1)$ partitions over $(n_i + g_i - 1)$ holes is the same as the number of distinct arrangements of n_i particles among the g_i states. Now, the number of permutations of $(n_i + g_i - 1)$ distinguishable objects is $(n_i + g_i - 1)!$. But, n_i particles and $(g_i - 1)$ partitions actually are indistinguishable and we must divide the above number by the number of permutations of n_i particles and by the number of permutations of $(g_i - 1)$ partitions. The result gives the number of distinct arrangements.

$$N_{BE} = \frac{(n_i + g_i - 1)!}{n!\,(g_i - 1)!}$$

Substituting the numerical values,

$$N_{BE} = \frac{6!}{2!\;4!} = 15$$

Two possible distributions are shown in Fig. a.

(b) In Fermi statistics a quantum state can contain only one particle. As before, we first find the number of ways of distributing n_i in distinguishable particles over g_i states. The first particle can be put in any of the g_i states, and for each choice of a state, the second particle can be put in any of the $(g_i - 1)$ remaining states, and so on. The last particle will have $(g_i - n_i + 1)$ possible states to choose from. The total number of configurations is

$$g_i(g_i - 1) \;\cdots\; (g_i - n_i + 1) = \frac{g_i!}{(g_i - n_i)!}$$

However, the actual indistinguishability of the particles requires that we divide out the number of identical configurations from this number. n_i particles give rise to $n_i!$ permutations of the particles among themselves. Thus, we have

$$N_{FD} = \frac{g_i!}{n_i\left(g_i - n_i\right)!}$$

$$= \frac{5!}{2!\ 3!} = 10$$

Two possible distributions are shown in Fig. b.

• PROBLEM 995

In an experiment involving the gravitational red shift, two identical nuclei are placed at different heights in a tower. The nuclei each emit gamma rays. The difference in height of the two nuclei is 2.2×10^3 cm. What is the fractional difference in the frequency of the γ-rays?

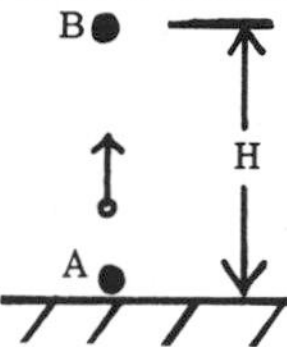

Solution: Consider a photon emitted by nucleus A located at the lower gravitational potential. Its energy upon emission is

$$E_1 = hf_0$$

where h is Plank's constant and f_0 is the frequency associated with the photon. As the photon rises, it gains potential energy. The law of conservation of energy demands that the total energy of the photon remain constant in time. The frequency of the photon must then decrease to offset the increase in potential energy to maintain the total energy constant. After travelling a height H, its energy is

$$E_2 = hf + mgH$$

m is the mass equivalent of its energy which is given by Einstein's mass-energy relationship

$$m = \frac{hf}{c^2}$$

To satisfy the conservation of energy, we must have

$$E_1 = E_2$$

$$hf_0 = hf + \frac{hfgH}{c^2}$$

or $$\frac{f_0}{f} = 1 + \frac{gH}{c^2}$$

$$= 1 + \frac{980\ \text{cm/sec}^2 \times 2.2 \times 10^3\ \text{cm}}{\left(3 \times 10^{10}\ \text{cm/sec}\right)^2}$$

$$= 1 + 2.3 \times 10^{-15}$$

The frequencies differ by 2.3 parts in 10^{15}. This minute change in frequency is termed the gravitational red shift (for the frequency decreases and shifts towards the red part of the spectrum as the light leaves the Earth).

• PROBLEM 996

A collimated beam of silver atoms emerges from a furnace at $1500^\circ K$, passes through a circular hole, and falls on a screen 1m away. Assume that all the atoms travel with the same speed. What size hole is likely to give the smallest spot size on the screen? The mass of a silver atom is 1.8×10^{-25}kg. (See figure).

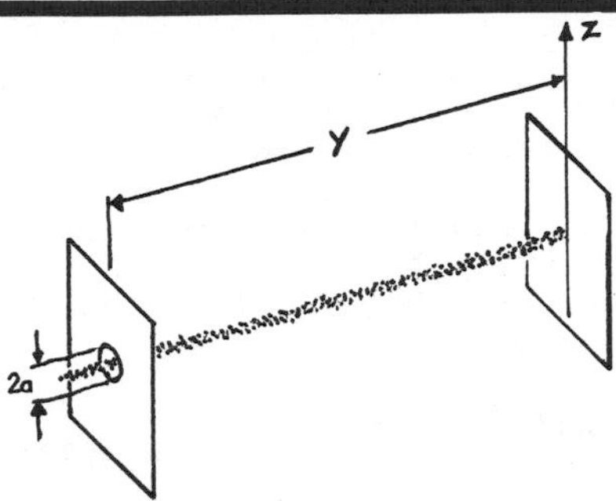

Solution: If the hole has a radius a, the uncertainty in the z-coordinate of an atom passing through the hole is 2a. Thus

$$\Delta z = 2a .$$

But if p_z is the momentum of the atom in the z-direction, then, at the hole, the Heisenberg Uncertainty Relationship yields

$$\Delta p_z \quad \Delta z \approx h$$

where Δp_z is the uncertainty in the z momentum. But

$$\Delta p_z = m\Delta v_z$$

where Δv_z is the uncertainty in the z velocity of the silver atoms. Hence

$$m\Delta v_z \approx \frac{h}{2a} \quad \text{or} \quad \Delta v_z \approx \frac{h}{2am} .$$

Thus the atoms have an uncertainty in velocity in the z-direction of the order of h/2am. But the velocity in the z-direction is classically zero. Hence, the atoms, by quantum-mechanical arguments, have velocities around the value h/2am in the z-direction.

In the y-direction the atoms have a velocity which is assumed for simplicity to be the same for all atoms. The average kinetic energy possessed by an atom at temperature T is 3/2 kT, where k is Boltzmann's constant and T is given in degrees Kelvin. Thus the silver atoms of mass m have velocities v_y given by

$$v_y = \sqrt{3kT/m} .$$

They traverse the distance y in time t. Since no force acts on the silver atoms in the y direction

$$y = v_y t$$

or

$$t = y/v_y$$

In the same time the maximum distance achieved in the z-direction due to the z-velocity of the atoms is, similarly,

$$a = \Delta v_z \times t = \frac{y\Delta v_z}{v_y} = \frac{hy}{2am}\sqrt{\frac{m}{3kT}} = \frac{hy}{2a}\sqrt{\frac{1}{3mkT}} = \frac{6.6 \times 10^{-34} \text{J}\cdot\text{s} \times 1 \text{ m}}{2a} \times$$

$$\sqrt{\frac{1}{3 \times 1.8 \times 10^{-25} \text{kg} \times 1.38 \times 10^{-23} \text{J}\cdot\text{K deg}^{-1} \times 1500 \text{ K deg}}}$$

$$= \frac{3.12}{a} \times 10^{-12} \text{ m}^2 .$$

Thus the largest possible distance from the axis at which a silver atom can strike the screen is found by observing the trajectory of the atom at the top of the hole. The furthest it will travel from the center of the hole is

$$r = a + z = a + (3.12/a) \times 10^{-12} \text{m}^2 .$$

$$\frac{dr}{da} = 1 - \frac{3.12}{a^2} \times 10^{-12} \text{ m}^2 ,$$

and for a minimum of r this quantity must be zero . It can be verified that this is a minimum by a second differentiation. Thus the radius of the hole which gives the smallest spot on the screen is that for which

$$\frac{3.12}{a^2} \times 10^{-12} \text{ m}^2 = 1 \quad \text{or} \quad a = 1.77 \times 10^{-6} \text{ m}.$$

In classical physics the spot size would be decreased indefinitely by reducing the size of the hole. Because of the wave nature of the electron, quantum mechanics does not supply the same answer. After a certain point, diminishing the size of the hole increases the size of the spot because of diffraction effects produced by the hole on the silver atoms. A minimum size of spot therefore results for a finite hole size.

• PROBLEM 997

Doubly charged α-particles of energy 7.33 MeV are emitted from one isotope of thorium. What is the distance of closest approach of such an α-particle to a gold nucleus? The mass of the α-particle is 6.69 X 10^{-27} kg, and the atomic number of gold is 79.

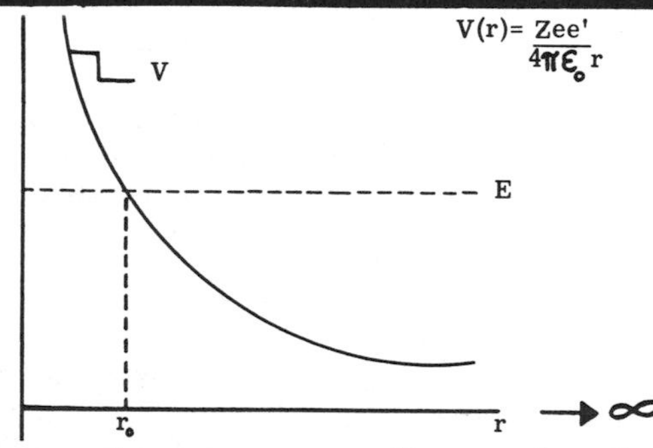

Solution: The figure shows an energy diagram for the α-particle gold nucleus interaction. Initially, we assume the α-particle to be emitted from the thorium sample with a kinetic energy T_0. Since the thorium and gold nucleus are separated by an effectively infinite distance, the α-particle gold nucleus system has no initial potential energy (V=0). Hence, the initial energy of the system is totally kinetic and

$$E_0 = T_0 = 7.33 \text{ MeV} .$$

Since energy is conserved, this is the value of E for all time t. Looking at the diagram, we see that for a given E, the closest the α-particle can come to the gold nucleus is r_0 (distance of closest approach). This is true because, classically, the particle cannot penetrate the potential barrier to the left of r_0, for, if it did, it would have a negative kinetic energy. This can be seen by noting that, at any time, the energy of the system can be written

$$E = T + V$$

or

$$T = E - V .$$

If $V > E$, as it is for values of $r < r_0$, then $T < 0$. Note that, at r_0, we may write

$$V(r_0) = E$$

or

$$\frac{Zee'}{4\pi\varepsilon_0 r_0} = 7.33 \text{ MeV}$$

where Ze is the charge of the gold nucleus, and e' is the charge of the α-particle. Since

$$1 \text{ eV} = 1.602 \times 10^{-13} \text{ J}$$

$$\frac{Zee'}{4\pi\varepsilon_0 r_0} = 7.33 \times 1.602 \times 10^{-13} \text{ J} = 11.743\ 10^{-13} \text{ J}$$

Hence,

$$r_0 = \frac{Zee'}{4\pi\varepsilon_0(11.743 \times 10^{-13} J)}$$

$$= \frac{79 \times 1.602 \times 10^{-19} C \times 2 \times 1.602 \times 10^{-19} C}{4\pi \times 8.85 \times 10^{-12} C^2 \cdot N^{-1} \cdot m^{-2} \times 11.743 \times 10^{-13} J}$$

$$= 3.102 \times 10^{-14} \text{ m.}$$

• PROBLEM 998

Consider a system of N particles each of which can exist in only two energy levels + ε and - ε.If the probability of occupying an energy level at temperature T is given by

$$P_E = e^{-E/KT}$$

where E is the energy of the level, and K is Boltzmann's constant, calculate the internal energy of the system.

Solution: The ratio of the number of particles in levels $E_1 = \varepsilon$ and $E_2 = -\varepsilon$ is given by

$$\frac{N_1}{N_2} = \frac{P_1}{P_2} = \frac{e^{-E_1/KT}}{e^{-E_2/KT}}$$

$$= \frac{e^{-\varepsilon/KT}}{e^{\varepsilon/KT}} = e^{-2\varepsilon/KT} \qquad (1)$$

The total number of particles, N, in the system is constant though each particle can make transitions from one level to the other. Substituting the result

$$N = N_1 + N_2$$

in (1), we get

$$\frac{N - N_2}{N_2} = e^{-2\varepsilon/KT}$$

$$\frac{N}{N_2} = 1 + e^{-2\varepsilon/KT}$$

giving $$\frac{N_2}{N} = \frac{1}{1 + e^{-2\varepsilon/KT}} = \frac{e^{2\varepsilon/KT}}{1 + e^{2\varepsilon/KT}} .$$

where we multiplied both the numerator and the denominator by $e^{2\varepsilon/KT}$ for the last step.

Similarly, for N_1/N, we have

$$\frac{N_1}{N} = \frac{N_1}{N_2}\frac{N_2}{N} = e^{-2\varepsilon/KT}\frac{e^{2\varepsilon/KT}}{1 + e^{2\varepsilon/KT}}$$

$$= \frac{1}{1 + e^{2\varepsilon/KT}}$$

The internal energy of the system is given by the sum of the energies of the particles in each level,

$$U = N_1E_1 + N_2E_2 = N_1\varepsilon + N_2(-\varepsilon)$$

$$= \varepsilon(N_1 - N_2) = \varepsilon N\ (N_1/N - N_2/N)$$

$$= \varepsilon N\ \frac{1 - e^{2\varepsilon/KT}}{1 + e^{2\varepsilon/KT}}$$

$$= \varepsilon N\ \frac{e^{-\varepsilon/KT} - e^{\varepsilon/KT}}{e^{\varepsilon/KT} + e^{-\varepsilon/KT}}$$

$$= \varepsilon N \tanh\ (-\varepsilon/KT) = -\varepsilon N \tanh\ (\varepsilon/KT)$$

As $T \to 0$, $\tanh\ (\varepsilon/KT) \to 1$, and we have

$$U_{(T \to 0)} = -\varepsilon N$$

This result shows that all the particles occupy the lower level at $T = 0^\circ K$. As $T \to \infty$, $\tanh\ (\varepsilon/KT) \to 0$ and

$$U_{(T \to \infty)} = 0$$

which shows that both levels are occupied with equal probability at $T \to \infty^\circ K$, i.e. $N_1 \simeq N_2$.

• PROBLEM 999

A molecule has no net charge, but its charge distribution may be equivalent to two charges $\pm$ q separated by a small distance a. Then the molecule is said to be a polar molecule, and to have a dipole moment $\mu = qa$.

In an electric field E such molecules, originally of random orientation, will tend to align themselves either parallel or antiparallel to the field. If parallel the potential energy of the molecule is $-\mu E$, if antiparallel $+\mu E$. Calculate (a) the ratio of the number of molecules in each energy level to the total number, (b) the average energy per molecule of a system of HCl molecules, if the dipole moment of HCl, μ, is 3.44×10^{-30} coul-m, and the gas is put into a uniform electric field $E = 1.5 \times 10^{7}$ V/m, at T = 350 K°.

Solution: (a) We have a two energy level problem. The number of molecules with energies $+\mu E$ and $-\mu E$ respectively are

$$\frac{N_1}{N} = \frac{1}{1 + e^{2E/KT}}$$

$$\frac{N_2}{N} = \frac{e^{2E/KT}}{1 + e^{2E/KT}}$$

where K is the Boltzmann constant.

$$\frac{\mu E}{KT} = \frac{(3.44 \times 10^{-30} \text{ coul.m})(1.5 \times 10^{7} \text{ V/m})}{(1.38 \times 10^{-33} \text{ J/K°})(350 \text{ K°})}$$

$$= 1.07 \times 10^{-2}$$

Since $\mu E/KT << 1$, we use the Taylor Series approximation for $e^{\mu E/KT}$

$$e^{\mu E/KT} \simeq 1 + \frac{\mu E}{KT}$$

Thus

$$\frac{N_1}{N} \simeq \frac{1}{2 + 2\frac{\mu E}{KT}} = \frac{1}{2 + 0.0214} = 0.495$$

$$\frac{N_2}{N} \simeq \frac{1 + \frac{2\mu E}{KT}}{2 + 2\frac{\mu E}{KT}} = \frac{1 + 0.0214}{2 + 0.0214} = 0.505$$

(b) If U is the internal energy of the gas, the average energy per unit molecule is given as

$$\bar{E} = \frac{U}{N} = \frac{-\mu E N \tanh \frac{\mu E}{KT}}{N}$$

$$= -\mu E \tanh \frac{\mu E}{KT}$$

For $\frac{\mu E}{KT} << 1$, we can use the approximation

$$\tanh \frac{\mu E}{KT} \simeq \frac{\mu E}{KT}$$

Therefore $\bar{E} \simeq - \mu E \cdot \frac{\mu E}{KT}$

$$\simeq - \left(3.44 \times 10^{-30} \text{ coul.m}\right)\left(1.5 \times 10^{7} \text{ V/m}\right) \times 1.07 \times 10^{-2}$$

$$\simeq - 5.5 \times 10^{-25} \text{ J.}$$

• PROBLEM 1000

Suppose that an electron bounces back and forth along the x axis in a box of length 10^{-10} m. (a) What is its lowest energy level? (b) What wavelength of radiation would be emitted if the electron changed from the n = 2 to the n = 1 state?

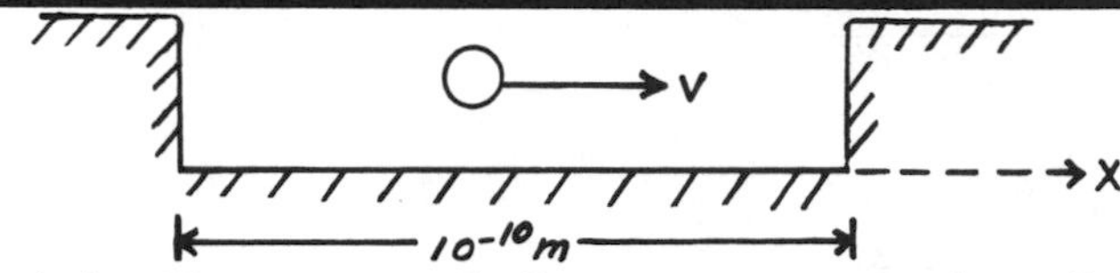

Solution: (a) No external forces act on the electron except when it hits the walls and is reflected elastically. Therefore, it experiences no loss of energy and its momentum while it travels between the walls is constant in magnitude. Wilson and Sommerfeld stated a general rule prescribing the quantization of a system which undergoes periodic motion. This rule is

$$\oint p_q dq = nh \tag{1}$$

where p_q is the momentum associated with the periodic coordinate q. (In our case, the x position of the particle is varying periodically. Hence, q = x.). Also, n is an integer, h is Planck's constant, and the integral in (1) is evaluated over 1 period of the variable q. (For this example, we evaluate (1) over 1 period of x).

If we consider the electron to be at the left wall at the beginning of its cycle, then

$$\oint p_x dx = \int_0^L mv dx + \int_L^0 (-mv) dx$$

$$= 2mvL. \tag{2}$$

Note that the integral is split into 2 parts because the momentum changes direction in 1 cycle of motion. Using (2) in (1)

$$2mvL = nh$$

or

$$p = mv = \frac{nh}{2L}. \tag{3}$$

Assuming the electron to be nonrelativistic, its energy is

$$E = \frac{1}{2}mv^2 = \frac{p^2}{2m} = \frac{n^2h^2}{8mL^2} .$$

The lowest energy level occurs in the n = 1 state.

$$E_1 = \frac{h^2}{8mL^2} = \frac{\left(6.625 \times 10^{-34}\right)^2}{8\left(9.11 \times 10^{-31}\right) \times 10^{-20}} \text{joule}$$

$$= 6.02 \times 10^{-18} \text{ joule.}$$

Because 1 joule = 6.24×10^{18} eV

$$E_1 = \left(6.02 \times 10^{-18} \text{ joule}\right)\left(6.24 \times 10^{18} \frac{\text{eV}}{\text{joule}}\right)$$

$$E_1 = 37.5 \text{ eV}$$

where ν is the photon frequency.

(b) The energy of the photon is

$$h\nu = E_2 - E_1 = \frac{h^2}{8mL^2}\left(2^2 - 1^2\right)$$

$$h\nu = \frac{\left(6.625 \times 10^{-34} \text{ J} \cdot \text{s}\right)^2}{(8)\left(9.11 \times 10^{-31} \text{ kg}\right)\left(10^{-20} \text{ m}^2\right)}(4 - 1)$$

$$= 18.1 \times 10^{-18} \text{ joule.}$$

Since 1 joule = 6.24×10^{18} eV

$$h\nu = \left(18.1 \times 10^{-18} \text{ joule}\right)\left(6.24 \times 10^{18} \frac{\text{eV}}{\text{joule}}\right)$$

$$h\nu = 113 \text{ eV}$$

$$= 18.1 \times 10^{-18} \text{ joule.}$$

From $c = \nu\lambda$, the wavelength λ is

$$\lambda = \frac{hc}{E} = \frac{6.625 \times 10^{-34}\left(3.0 \times 10^8\right)}{18.1 \times 10^{-18}} \text{m}$$

$$= 1.10 \times 10^{-8} \text{ m} = 110 \text{ A.}$$

• PROBLEM 1001

When the wavelength of the incident light exceeds 6500 Å, the emission of photoelectrons from a surface ceases. The surface is irradiated with light of wavelength 3900 Å. What will be the maximum energy, in electron volts, of the electrons emitted from the surface?

Solution: Einstein's photoelectric equation relates

the energy of the incident quanta to the maximum energy of the emitted electrons (= W) by the relation

$$hf = h\frac{c}{\lambda} = W + W_0 = W + hf_0 = W + h\frac{c}{\lambda_0},$$

where W_0 is the work function of the surface and λ_0 the cut-off wavelength. Hence the maximum energy of the emitted photoelectrons in the problem is

$$W = hc\left(\frac{1}{\lambda} - \frac{1}{\lambda_0}\right) = 6.6 \times 10^{-34}\ \text{J} \cdot \text{s} \times$$

$$3.0 \times 10^{8}\ \text{m} \cdot \text{s}^{-1}\left(\frac{1}{3.9 \times 10^{-7}\ \text{m}} - \frac{1}{6.5 \times 10^{-7}\ \text{m}}\right)$$

$$= 19.8 \times 10^{-19}\left(\frac{1}{3.9} - \frac{1}{6.5}\right)\ \text{J}$$

$$= \frac{19.8 \times 10^{-19}\ \text{J}}{1.6 \times 10^{-19}\text{J/eV}} \times \left(\frac{6.3 - 3.9}{3.9 \times 6.5}\right)$$

$$= \frac{19.8 \times 10^{-19}}{1.6 \times 10^{-19}} \times \frac{2.6}{3.9 \times 6.5}\ \text{eV} = 1.27\ \text{eV}.$$

• PROBLEM 1002

Radioastronomy studies indicate that the clouds of matter between stars consist not only of simple atoms but include molecules that may contain several atoms. From a region of space labeled Sgr B by astronomers, photons are observed with a frequency of 1.158×10^{11}Hz. Determine the rotational constant B tor this microwave radiation if the transition is known to be from the j = 1 state to the ground state (j = 0).

Solution: The rotational energy of a particle in terms of its angular momentum L is

$$E = \frac{L^2}{2MR^2} = BL^2$$

where B is a constant. The quantum mechanical expression for L^2 is $j(j + 1)\hbar$, where $\hbar = \frac{h}{2\pi}$ and j takes on positive integral values. The letter j also classifies the possible rotational energy states of mass M. The energy of the upper state must therefore be

$$E_U = Bj(j + 1)\hbar = B1(1 + 1)\hbar = 2B\hbar$$

while the energy of the lower state is

$$E_L = B0(0 + 1)\hbar = 0.$$

The energy difference between these two states must equal the photon energy hf (conservation of energy):

$$hf = E_U - E_L$$

where f is the frequency of the observed radiation .Hence

$$2B \frac{h}{2\pi} = hf$$

$$B = \pi \times 1.158 \times 10^{11} \text{ Hz.}$$

$$= 3.636 \times 10^{11} \text{ Hz.}$$

• PROBLEM 1003

Compute the wavelength of the electron matter waves in a Davisson-Germer apparatus if the electron velocity is 4.43×10^6 m/s.

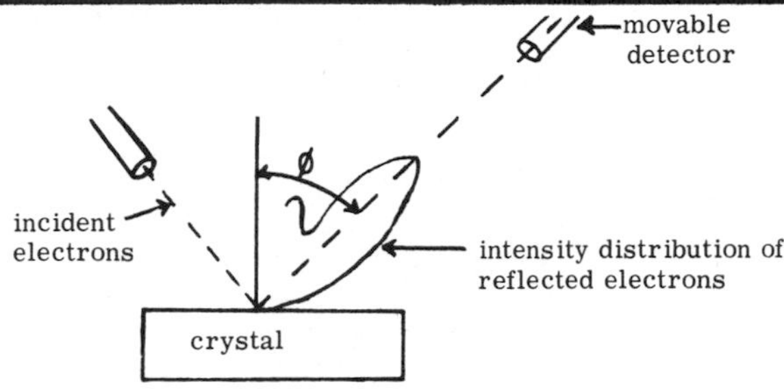

Davisson-Germer Apparatus

Solution: According to the de Broglie wave theory of matter, every particle has wave-like characteristics. To every particle there is associated a wave with wavelength given by:

$$\lambda = \frac{h}{P} = \frac{h}{mV} .$$

For an electron $\left(\text{of mass } 9.1 \times 10^{-31} \text{ kg.}\right)$ and velocity 4.43×10^6 m/s we then have

$$\lambda = \frac{6.6 \times 10^{-34} \text{Js}}{\left(9.1 \times 10^{-31} \text{ kg}\right)\left(4.43 \times 10^6 \text{ m/s}\right)} = 1.64 \times 10^{-10} \text{ m}$$

The wavelength for a "matter wave" is now called the particles's de Broglie wavelength. The Davisson-Germer apparatus is used to exhibit the interference effects of the electron "matter wave."

• PROBLEM 1004

A beam of electrons of kinetic energy $T = 5$ MeV impinges on a single slit of width 1 micron $\left(10^{-6} \text{ m}\right)$, causing a diffraction pattern (see figure). Calculate the width of the central maximum at a plane 3 in behind the plane of the slit.

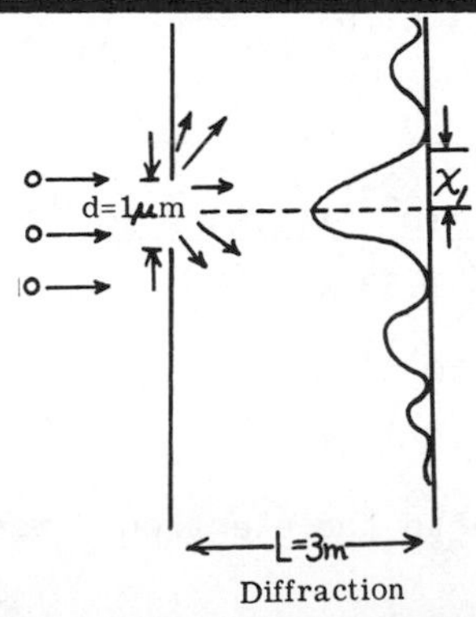

Diffraction

Solution: According to the de Broglie wave theory of matter every particle has wave-like characteristics. Electrons then should display diffraction effects when passing through a narrow slit, as do light waves. The wavelength associated with the moving electron is the de Broglie wavelength

$$\lambda = \frac{h}{p} \qquad (1)$$

where p is the momentum of the electron and h is Planck's constant.

The p appearing in (1) is the relativistic momentum of the electron. This quantity is related to the energy E of the electron by

$$E^2 = p^2c^2 + m_0^2 c^4$$

where m_0 is the rest mass of the electron. The energy E is equal to the kinetic energy of the electron, T, plus the rest energy, m_0c^2.

$$E = T + m_0c^2$$

Hence,

$$\left(T + m_0c^2\right) = p^2c^2 + m_0c^4$$

$$T^2 + 2m_0c^2T = p^2c^2$$

Therefore

$$p^2 = \frac{T^2 + 2m_0c^2T}{c^2}$$

$$p = \frac{\sqrt{T\left(T+2m_0c^2\right)}}{c}$$

Now, $m_0c^2 = \left(9.31 \times 10^{-31}\ K_g\right)\left(9 \times 10^{16}\ m^2/s^2\right)$

$$= 83.79 \times 10^{-15}\ \text{Joules}$$

because 1 Joule = 6.24×10^{18} eV

$$m_0c^2 = .5 \times 10^6\ \text{eV}$$

Hence,

$$p = \frac{\sqrt{\left(5\times10^6\ \text{eV}\right)\left(5\times10^6\ \text{eV} + 1 \times 10^6\ \text{eV}\right)}}{3 \times 10^8\ \text{m/s}}$$

$$p = \frac{\sqrt{30.0 \times 10^{12}\ \text{eV}^2}}{3 \times 10^8\ \text{m/s}}$$

$$p = \frac{5.48 \times 10^6\ \text{eV}}{3 \times 10^8\ \text{m/s}}$$

$$p = 1.83 \times 10^{-2}\ \frac{\text{eV}\cdot\text{s}}{\text{m}}$$

whence,

$$\lambda = \frac{h}{p} = \frac{6.63 \times 10^{-34}\ \text{J}\cdot\text{s}}{1.83 \times 10^{-2}\ \frac{\text{eV}\cdot\text{s}}{\text{m}}}$$

since 1 Joule = 6.24×10^{18} eV

$$\lambda = \frac{\left(6.63 \times 10^{-34}\right)\left(6.24 \times 10^{18}\right)\ \text{m}}{\left(1.83 \times 10^{-2}\right)}$$

$$= 22.6 \times 10^{-14}\ \text{m}$$

$$= 2.26 \times 10^{-13}\ \text{m}$$

The diffraction pattern due to the electron waves may be treated as if it were caused by the diffraction of light waves. We may then use the formula for the maxima produced by diffracting light rays to analyze the maxima produced by electron waves.

With respect to the diffraction pattern (see the figure), we have $d = 10^{-6}$ m and L = 3 m.

$$x_1 = \frac{\lambda L}{d} = \frac{2.26 \times 10^{-13} \text{ m} \times 3 \text{ m}}{10^{-6} \text{ m}} = 6.8 \times 10^{-7} \text{ m}$$

The width of the central maximum will be $2x_1 = 1.4 \times 10^{-6}$ m, which would be difficult to observe.

If the electron beam were of lower energy, 50,000 eV for example, the central maximum would have a width of 3.2×10^{-6} m (0.0032 mm), which is more easily measured.

• PROBLEM 1005

Find the first five energy eigenvalues for a hydrogen atom. (An equation in which an operation on a function gives a constant times the function is called an eigenvalue equation. The function is called an eigenfunction of the operator and the constant is called an eigenvalue. The Schroëdinger equation has eigenfunctions which are the possible spatial portions of the wave functions and eigenvalues which are the possible values of the energies involved.)

<u>Solution:</u> Quantum mechanics extends classical mechanics into microscopic phenomena by taking quantum considerations into account. Schröedinger developed a wave equation describing both the wave and matter aspects of matter. To find the energy values of the eigenstates of hydrogen, consider the Schroedinger equation expressed in spherical coordinates.

$$\psi(r,\theta,\phi) = R(r)y(\theta,\phi).$$

In general, the total energy of the hydrogen electron is due to its angular momentum (rotation with radius r), its linear momentum along the variable radius r, and its potential energy due only to its distance r from the nucleus. The Schroëdinger equation for the radial part R(r) of the wavefunction can be obtained at once as follows. The angular momentum equals L = mvr. The rotational energy of the particle at radius r is

$$\frac{1}{2}mv^2 = \frac{1}{2}m\left(\frac{L}{mr}\right)^2 = \frac{L^2}{2mr^2}.$$

Rotational energy, the angular motion of the particle, is related to the $y(\theta,\phi)$ part of the wavefunction. The angular momentum of the electron in a stable state around the nucleus (energy eigenstate) is quantized as

$$L^2 = \ell(\ell + 1)\hbar^2 \qquad \ell = 0,1,2,\ldots$$

where $\hbar$ is Planck's constant divided by 2π.

As far as the radial motion along r is concerned, the contribution of the rotational motion to the total energy of the particle, $\frac{L(L+1)\hbar^2}{2mr^2}$, depends only on the radial position

r. Potential energy can be viewed as any energy which depends on a distance r and reduces to zero at infinite distance. This permits us to consider the energy due to rotation as a form of potential energy. Hence, the one-dimensional radial motion takes place in an effective potential (important since it is expressed in terms of only one variable r).

$$U(r) = \frac{L(L+1)\hbar^2}{2m_e r^2} + V(r) \tag{1}$$

where V(r) is the electrostatic potential.

The radial part of the Schroedinger equation is given by

$$-\frac{\hbar^2}{2m_e}\frac{1}{r^2}\frac{d}{dr}\left(r^2 R'\right) + U(r)R(r) = ER(r) \tag{2}$$

where E is the total energy (eigenvalue) corresponding to an orbit (eigenstate) of radius r and $R' = \frac{dR(r)}{dr}$. For the lowest energy states, let ℓ equal zero. Also, for an electron a distance r from a nucleus of charge Ze, the potential energy is

$$V(r) = \frac{-KZe^2}{r} = \frac{-Ke^2}{r} \tag{3}$$

where K is the Coulomb constant and Z = 1 for hydrogen. We therefore have

$$\frac{-\hbar^2}{2m_e}\frac{1}{r^2}\frac{d}{dr}\left(r^2R'\right) - \frac{Ke^2}{r}R = ER. \tag{4}$$

Let $$\lambda^2 = \frac{-2m_eE}{\hbar^2}. \tag{5}$$

We assume λ^2 is positive since the energy E must be negative if the electron is bound to the nucleus. Multiplying (4) by λ^2/E we have

$$\frac{1}{r^2}\frac{d}{dr}\left(r^2R'\right) + \frac{2m_eKe^2}{\hbar^2}\frac{R}{r} = \lambda^2R. \tag{6}$$

A solution of Eq. (6) has to approach zero as r approaches ∞ since the energy is zero at infinite distance. Rewriting the equation,

$$R'' + \left(\frac{2R}{r} + \frac{2m_eKe^2}{\hbar^2}\frac{R}{r}\right) = \lambda^2R. \tag{7}$$

For large r, the terms in parentheses are insignificant and we have

$$R'' = \lambda^2R \tag{8}$$

which is satisfied by

$$R \simeq e^{-\lambda r} \tag{9}$$

which goes to zero when r, the distance of the electron from the nucleus, is infinite. This solution will be true for all r if the terms in parentheses in (7) cancel each other. To find the value of λ which makes this true, we set these terms equal to zero.

$$\frac{2R'}{r} + \frac{2m_e Ke^2}{\hbar^2}\frac{R}{r} = 0.$$

We know that $R' = -\lambda e^{-\lambda r} = -\lambda R$. Therefore we have

$$\frac{-2\lambda R}{r} + \frac{2m_e Ke^2}{\hbar^2}\frac{R}{r} = 0 \tag{10}$$

$$\text{and } \lambda = \frac{m_e Ke^2}{\hbar^2} = \frac{1}{0.529 \text{ A}} \tag{11}$$

since $\hbar^2/m_e Ke^2 \simeq 0.529$ A is the Bohr radius. Therefore this value of λ corresponds to the ground energy level (n = 1). This minimum energy is found from (5)

$$E_1 = \frac{-\hbar^2\lambda^2}{2m_e} = -13.6 \text{ eV}.$$

The energy eigenvalues corresponding to the eigenfunctions involved in the well-behaved solutions to the radial equation (1) are

$$E_n = \frac{E_1}{n^2} \tag{12}$$

where n is the quantum number. Therefore

$$E_1 = -13.6 \text{ eV}$$

$$E_2 = \frac{-13.6 \text{ eV}}{(2)^2} = -3.4 \text{ eV}$$

$$E_3 = \frac{-13.6 \text{ eV}}{(3)^2} = -1.51 \text{ eV}$$

$$E_4 = \frac{-13.6 \text{ eV}}{(4)^2} = -0.85 \text{ eV}$$

$$E_5 = \frac{-13.6 \text{ eV}}{(5)^2} = -0.54 \text{ eV}.$$

• PROBLEM 1006

The radiation from an x-ray tube operated at 50 kV is diffracted by a cubic KCl crystal of molecular mass 74.6 and density $1.99 \times 10^3 \text{kg·m}^{-3}$. Calculate (a) the short-wavelength limit of the spectrum from the tube, and (b) the glancing angle for first-order reflection from the principal planes of the crystal for that wavelength.

Solution: (a) When an electron passes through a potential difference V, it acquires energy eV. If all this energy is used in producing one quantum of x-radiation, then hf = eV or f = eV/h, where f is the photon frequency. Since $\lambda = c/f$, where c is the speed of light and λ is the photon wavelength

$$\lambda = \frac{c}{f} = \frac{ch}{eV} .$$

The electron may have lost some of its acquired energy before producing the quantum of radiation. The f-value calculated above is thus the maximum possible frequency of the x-radiation emitted and λ the corresponding short-wavelength limit of the emitted spectrum. The value is

$$\lambda = \frac{3.0 \times 10^{8} m \cdot s^{-1} \times 6.6 \times 10^{-34} J \cdot s}{1.6 \times 10^{-19} C \times 5 \times 10^{4} V} = 0.248 \text{ Å}.$$

(b) In order to apply Bragg's law, we must find the separation of the principal planes of the KCl crystal. We know that the atomic mass of KCl is equal to the sum of the atomic masses of K(35.1) and Cl(39.1). Its value is then 74.6 amu. Since 1 amu is the gram mass of 1 mole of a substance, 1 mole of KCl has a mass of 74.6 g or 74.6×10^{-3} kg. If the density of KCl is 1.99×10^{3} kg/m^{3}, 1 mole of KCl has a volume

$$V = \frac{74.6 \times 10^{-3} \text{ kg}}{1.99 \times 10^{3} \text{ kg/m}^{3}} = 3.75 \times 10^{-5} \text{ m}^{3}$$

Since there are 6×10^{23} molecules in 1 mole, the volume v occupied by 1 molecule is

$$v = \frac{V}{6 \times 10^{23}} = \frac{3.75 \times 10^{-5} \text{ m}^{3}}{6 \times 10^{23}}$$

$$v = 6.25 \times 10^{-29} \text{ m}^{3} .$$

Each molecule of KCl is composed of 2 atoms. The volume, v' per atom is then

$$v' = \frac{v}{2} = 3.13 \times 10^{-29} \text{ m}^{3} .$$

If we assume each atom to be centered in a cube of side d, then

$$v' = d^{3} = 3.13 \times 10^{-29} \text{ m}^{3}$$

or

$$d = 3.150 \times 10^{-10} \text{ m}$$

Thus the linear separation of atoms, i.e., the separation of the principal planes, is

$$d = 3.150 \times 10^{-10} \text{ m} = 3.150 \text{ Å}.$$

Bragg's law relates the glancing angle to d by the equation $2d \sin \theta = m\lambda$, where m is the order number. Giving λ the value calculated above, we obtain

$$\sin \theta = \frac{m\lambda}{2d} = \frac{(1)(0.248 \text{ Å})}{(2)(3.150 \text{ Å})} = 0.0394.$$

$$\theta = 2.25^{\circ} .$$

• PROBLEM 1007

A careful analysis shows that the energy of the photon in gamma radiation is slightly less than the difference between the energy of the two nuclear states. In the decay, the gamma-ray photon has momentum, which must be balanced by a recoiling nucleus. Therefore, the nucleus acquires a small portion of the available transition energy. Find what fraction of the transition energy is acquired by the $^{43}_{19}K$ nucleus in the emission of a 0.22-MeV gamma photon. Assume that the nucleus was originally at rest.

M γ M

$P_{initial} = 0$ E_2, P_2 E_1, P_1

γ emission

Solution: The momenta and the total energies of the particles before and after the decay are shown in the figure. The rest mass, M, of the potassium nucleus is 7.1×10^{-26} kg. The energy of the photon, E_2 in MKS units is

$$E_2 = (2.2 \times 10^5 \text{ eV})(1.6 \times 10^{-19} \text{ J/eV})$$

$$= 3.5 \times 10^{-14} \text{ J}$$

The momentum of the photon is given by

$$p_2 = \frac{E_2}{c} = \frac{3.5 \times 10^{-14} \text{ J}}{3 \times 10^8 \text{ m/s}} = 1.17 \times 10^{-22} \text{ kg m/s}$$

The nucleus was initially at rest (see fig.) Therefore, the total momentum of the products after γ - emission must be zero, as a result of the conservation of total momentum.

$$\vec{p}_1 + \vec{p}_2 = \vec{p}_{initial} = 0$$

or $$p_1 = p_2$$

The recoil of the nucleus can be treated non-relativistically since we don't expect it to acquire a large velocity because of its large mass. If the mass of the nucleus is M, and its recoil velocity is v, its momentum will be

$$p_1 = Mv.$$

Equating the momenta of the photon and the nucleus after the γ-emission, we get

$$mv = p_2$$

or $$v = \frac{p_2}{m}$$

$$= \frac{1.17 \times 10^{-22} \text{ kg m/s}}{7.1 \times 10^{-26} \text{ kg}} = 1.6 \times 10^3 \text{ m/s}$$

The kinetic energy of the nucleus is

$$K = \tfrac{1}{2} mv^2 = (\tfrac{1}{2})(7.1 \times 10^{-26} \text{ kg})(1.6 \times 10^3 \text{ m/s})^2$$

$$= 9.1 \times 10^{-20} \text{ J}$$

which corresponds to an energy of 0.6 eV. The fraction f of energy acquired by the nucleus is

$$f = \frac{\text{energy of the nucleus}}{\text{total energy}}$$

$$= \frac{K}{K + E_2} \simeq \frac{K}{E_2}$$

Since $E_2 >> K$

$$= \frac{6 \times 10^{-1}\ \text{eV}}{2.2 \times 10^5\ \text{eV}} = 2.7 \times 10^{-6}$$

• PROBLEM 1008

Starting from Planck's radiation law, show that one can obtain Wien's displacement law, $\lambda_{max} T$ = constant. It is known that this constant is equal to 2.891×10^6 nm · K deg. Obtain the value of Planck's constant, given that Boltzmann's constant is 1.380×10^{-23} J · K deg^{-1}.

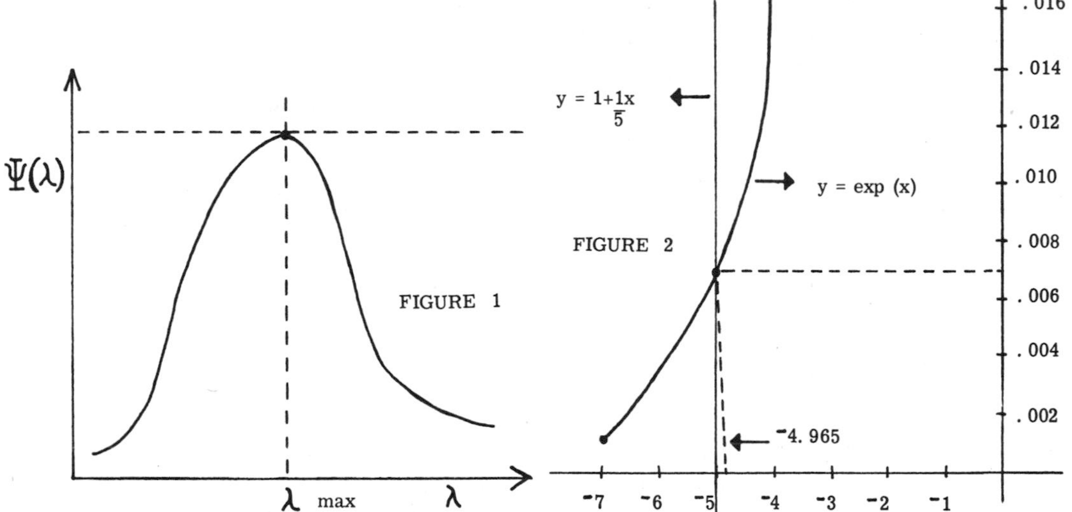

Solution: As shown in the figure, the λ_{max} appearing in Wien's displacement law is the value of λ at which $\psi(\lambda)$ is a maximum. In order to show that Wien's Law follows from Planck's radiation law, we calculate the values of λ for which $\psi(\lambda)$ is a maximum. This will yield the value of λ_{max} as a function T.

Planck's radiation law connects the monochromatic energy density in an isothermal blackbody enclosure with the wavelength and absolute temperature T

$$\psi = \frac{8\pi ch\lambda^{-5}}{\exp(ch/\lambda kT) - 1} .$$

where h is Planck's constant, and k is Boltzmann's constant. Thus

$$\frac{d\psi}{d\lambda} = -\frac{40\pi ch\lambda^{-6}}{\exp(ch/\lambda kT) - 1}$$

$$- \frac{8\pi ch\lambda^{-5} \times [-(ch/kT\lambda^2)\exp(ch/\lambda kT)]}{[\exp(ch/\lambda kT) - 1]^2}$$

$$= \frac{8\pi ch\lambda^{-6}}{\exp(ch/\lambda kT) - 1}\left[-5 + \frac{(ch/\lambda kT)\exp(ch/\lambda kT)}{\exp(ch/\lambda kT) - 1}\right].$$

For maxima or minima of ψ, $d\psi/d\lambda$ must be zero. The term outside the bracket becomes zero for either $\lambda = 0$ or $\lambda = \infty$. Both of these are minima, as can be verified by differentiating again. When the expression inside the bracket becomes zero, we have a maximum, and for this

$$\frac{(ch/\lambda_{max}kT)\exp(ch/\lambda_{max}kT)}{\exp(ch/\lambda_{max}kT) - 1} = 5$$

$$(ch/\lambda_{max}kT)\ \exp(ch/\lambda_{max}kT) = 5\left(\exp(ch/\lambda_{max}kT) - 1\right)$$

$$\exp(ch/\lambda_{max}kT)\left(5 - ch/\lambda_{max}kT\right) = 5$$

or $\exp(-\ ch/\lambda_{max}kT) = 1 - ch/5\lambda_{max}kT$ (1)

This is a transcendental equation, which must be solved graphically. Letting

$$x = -\ ch/\lambda_{max}kT$$

equation (1) becomes

$$\exp(x) = 1 + \frac{x}{5} \tag{2}$$

In order to find x, we draw a graph of $y = \exp(x)$, and another graph $y = 1 + x/5$. The intersection points of these 2 graphs are the values of x which satisfy (2). From figure (2), we obtain

$$x = -\ 4.965$$

as the solution set of (2).

Thus for a maximum of the radiation curve,

$$\exp(-\ ch/\lambda_{max}kT) = 1 - ch/5\lambda_{max}kT$$

and this implies that $ch/\lambda_{max}kT = 4.965$.

$$\lambda_{max}\ T = \frac{ch}{4.965\ k} = \text{const},$$

which is Wien's displacement law.

Experimentally, $\lambda_{max}\ T = 2.891 \times 10^{-3}$ m $\cdot$K deg.

Solving for h

$$h = \frac{(4.965\ k)(\lambda_{max}T)}{c}$$

$$h = \frac{4.965\ k \times 2.891 \times 10^{-3}\ m \cdot K\ deg}{c}$$

$$= \frac{4.965 \times 1.380 \times 10^{-23}\ J \cdot K\ deg^{-1} \times 2.891 \times 10^{-3}\ m \cdot K\ deg}{2.998 \times 10^{8}\ m \cdot s^{-1}}$$

$$= 6.607 \times 10^{-34}\ J \cdot s.$$

• PROBLEM 1009

Electrons of energies 10.20 eV, 12.09 eV, and 13.06 eV colliding with a hydrogen atom, can cause radiation to be emitted from the latter. Calculate in each case the principal quantum number of the orbit to which the electron in the hydrogen atom is raised and the wavelength of the radiation emitted if it drops back to the ground state.

Solution: Bohr theory relates the wavelength of the radiation emitted by a hydrogen atom to the principal quantum numbers of the energy levels involved by the equation

$$\frac{1}{\lambda} = R\left(\frac{1}{n_1^2} - \frac{1}{n_2^2}\right) \qquad \text{or } f = \frac{c}{\lambda} = Rc\left(\frac{1}{n_1^2} - \frac{1}{n_2^2}\right),$$

where c is the speed of light, f is the frequency of the radiation and R is the Rydberg constant.

The energy of the quantum of radiation emitted is

$$E = hf = Rch\left(\frac{1}{n_1^2} - \frac{1}{n_2^2}\right).$$

(Here, h is Planck's constant.)

This is the energy emitted in the form of a quantum of radiation when the electron drops from the orbit characterized by the quantum number n_2 to that characterized by the quantum number n_1. If the electron is raised from the orbit with quantum number n_1 to the orbit with quantum number n_2, it must absorb an equal amount of energy.

Before being struck by an electron, a hydrogen atom will be in the ground state with $n_1 = 1$. It is, in any case, true that if n_1 had a value higher than 1, then E, the absorbed energy, could not be greater than 3.40 eV, the limiting energy for $n_1 = 2$. Thus, if E has the values 10.20 eV, 12.09 eV, and 13.06 eV, the atom absorbing these energies from the incoming electrons, then

$$E = Rch\left(\frac{1}{n_1^2} - \frac{1}{n_2^2}\right).$$

$$E = (1.097 \times 10^7\ m^{-1})(2.997 \times 10^8\ m \cdot s^{-1})$$

$$(6.625 \times 10^{-34}\ J \cdot s)\left(\frac{1}{n_1^2} - \frac{1}{n_1^2}\right)$$

$$E = 2.178 \times 10^{-18} \left(\frac{1}{n_1^2} - \frac{1}{n_2^2}\right) \quad J$$

Since the given energies are calculated in terms of electron volts, we transform 2.178×10^{-18} J into eV noting that

$$1\ J = 6.242 \times 10^{18}\ eV$$

whence $E = (2.178 \times 10^{-18}\ J)(6.242 \times 10^{18}\ eV/J) \times \left(\frac{1}{n_1^2} - \frac{1}{n_2^2}\right)$

$$E = (13.60\ eV)\left(\frac{1}{n_1^2} - \frac{1}{n_2^2}\right)$$

Assuming that $n_1 = 1$, and using the given data, we obtain

$$\left(1 - \frac{1}{n_2^2}\right) = \frac{10.20}{13.60} = \frac{3}{4} \qquad \text{or } n_2 = 2$$

$$\left(1 - \frac{1}{n_2^2}\right) = \frac{12.09}{13.60} = \frac{8}{9} \qquad \text{or } n_2 = 3$$

$$\left(1 - \frac{1}{n_2^2}\right) = \frac{13.06}{13.60} = \frac{24}{25} \qquad \text{or } n_2 = 5$$

We interpret these results to mean that an incident electron, of energy 10.20 eV, will cause the hydrogen atom electron to jump from $n = 1$ to $n = 2$, and similarly for the other 2 cases.

In dropping back to the ground state, the wavelength emitted in the three cases will be given from the original equation quoted. Thus

$$\frac{1}{\lambda} = R\left(1 - \frac{1}{n_2^2}\right)$$

$$\frac{1}{\lambda} = R\left(1 - \frac{1}{4}\right) = \frac{3R}{4} \qquad \text{or} \qquad \lambda = \frac{4}{3R}$$

$$\frac{1}{\lambda} = R\left(1 - \frac{1}{9}\right) = \frac{8R}{9} \qquad \text{or} \qquad \lambda = \frac{9}{8R}$$

$$\frac{1}{\lambda} = R\left(1 - \frac{1}{25}\right) = \frac{24R}{25} \qquad \text{or} \qquad \lambda = \frac{25}{24R}$$

whence

$$\lambda = \frac{4}{3 \times 1.097 \times 10^7\ m^{-1}} = 121.57 \times 10^{-9}\ m$$

$$\lambda = \frac{9}{8 \times 1.097 \times 10^7\ m^{-1}} = 102.57 \times 10^{-9}\ m$$

$$\lambda = \frac{25}{24 \times 1.097 \times 10^7 \text{ m}^{-1}} = 94.97 \times 10^{-9} \text{ m}$$

• PROBLEM 1010

Show that Wien's law and the Rayleigh-Jeans law are special cases of the Planck radiation formula.

Solution: The monochromatic energy density within an isothermal blackbody enclosure is given by Planck's relation

$$\Psi = \frac{8\pi ch\lambda^{-5}}{\exp(ch/\lambda kT) - 1} \tag{1}$$

where λ is the wavelength of the radiation, h is the Planck's constant, and T is the absolute temperature of the blackbody. The Rayleigh-Jeans law was found to conform to experimental data for low frequencies (or large wavelengths). Making the approximation in (1) that λ is very large, then $ch/\lambda kT$ is small and $\exp(ch/\lambda kT)$ can be replaced by the first two terms in the expansion of that function in terms of powers of its exponent. Subsequent terms in the expansion will be so small as to be negligible. Hence

$$\exp\left(\frac{ch}{\lambda kT}\right) - 1 \approx 1 + \frac{ch}{\lambda kT} - 1 = \frac{ch}{\lambda kT} .$$

$$\Psi \approx 8\pi ch\lambda^{-5} \times \frac{\lambda kT}{ch} = 8\pi kT\lambda^{-4},$$

which is the Rayleigh-Jeans law.

Wien's Law diverges from the experimental data in the realm of large wavelengths. Hence, in the limit of small wavelengths, (1) should approach Wien's Law.

For small λ, $ch/\lambda kT$ is large, and $\exp(ch/\lambda kT) >> 1$. Hence,

$$\exp(ch/\lambda kT) - 1 \approx \exp(ch/\lambda kT).$$

Therefore, (1) becomes

$$\Psi = \frac{8\pi ch\lambda^{-5}}{\exp(ch/\lambda kT)}$$

which is of the form of Wien's Law

$$\Psi = \frac{c_1}{\lambda^5} \frac{1}{e^{c_2/\lambda T}}$$

with $c_1 = 8\pi ch$, $c_2 = ch/k$.

• PROBLEM 1011

Show that the energy eigenvalues E_n, of a particle moving between impenetrable walls is given by the relationship

$$E_n = \frac{h^2}{8mL^2} n^2$$

where h is Planck's constant, m the particle mass, L the distance between the walls, and n = 1, 2, 3, ...

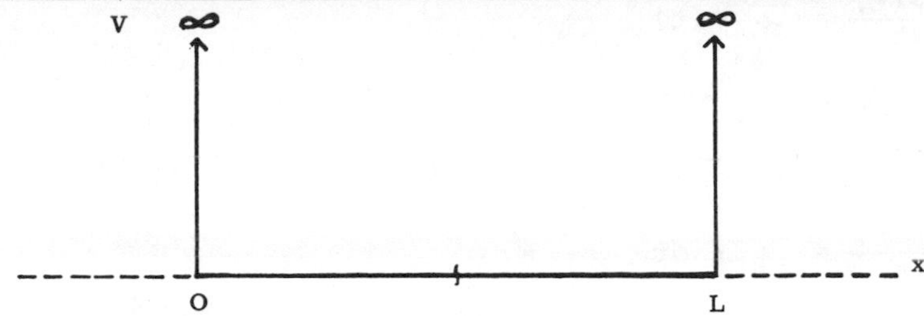

Solution: In order to find the energy eigenvalues, we must, in general, solve Schroedinger's Equation. Since our problem is one dimensional, this equation reduces to

$$\frac{-\hbar^2}{2m} \frac{\partial^2 \Psi}{\partial x^2} + V\Psi = i\hbar \frac{\partial \Psi}{\partial t} \qquad (1)$$

where m is the mass of the particle we are studying $i = \sqrt{-1}$, $\hbar$ is Planck's constant over 2π, and V is the potential that m is subject to. Ψ is the wave function which describes the motion of the particle and it is generally a function of x and t. In order to solve (1), we use the method of separation of variables, and express Ψ as the product of 2 functions, one with only a time dependence, and the other with only a spatial dependence. Hence,

$$\Psi = \psi(x)\ \phi(t) \qquad (2)$$

Substituting (2) in (1)

$$\frac{-\hbar^2}{2m} \frac{\partial^2}{\partial x^2}\left[\psi(x)\ \phi(t)\right] + V\ \psi(x)\ \phi(t)$$

$$= i\hbar \frac{\partial}{\partial t}\left[\psi(x)\ \phi(t)\right]$$

$$\frac{-\hbar^2}{2m}\phi(t)\frac{d^2\ \psi(x)}{dx^2} + V\ \phi(t)\ \psi(x) = i\hbar\ \psi(x)\frac{d\ \phi(t)}{dt}$$

Dividing both sides by $\Psi = \psi(x)\ \phi(t)$

$$\frac{-\hbar^2}{2m}\frac{1}{\psi(x)}\frac{d^2\ \psi(x)}{dx^2} + V = i\hbar\frac{1}{\phi(t)}\frac{d\ \phi(t)}{dt} \qquad (3)$$

Note that if v is a function of x alone, the left side of (3) is also a function of x alone, and the right side is a function only of t. The only way a function of x can equal a function of y is if both functions equal the same constant K. Hence, we separate (3) into

$$\frac{-\hbar^2}{2m}\frac{1}{\psi(x)}\frac{d^2\ \psi(x)}{dx^2} + V = K \qquad (4)$$

$$i\hbar\frac{1}{\phi(t)}\frac{d\ \phi(t)}{dt} = K \qquad (5)$$

Remember that this is true only if V is time independent. We first solve the differential equation in (5). Rewriting this equation

$$\frac{d\,\phi(t)}{dt} = \frac{K}{i\hbar}\,\phi(t)$$

or $$\frac{d\,\phi(t)}{\phi(t)} = \frac{K}{i\hbar}\,dt$$

$$\int \frac{d\,\phi(t)}{\phi(t)} = \frac{K}{i\hbar}\int dt$$

$$\ln\phi(t) = \frac{K}{i\hbar}\,t + C$$

where C is a constant. Taking the exponential of both sides

$$\phi(t) = e^{\left(\frac{Kt}{i\hbar} + C\right)} = e^{C}\,e^{k\,t/i\hbar} \tag{6}$$

But e^C is a new constant. Letting

$$e^C = A$$

we may write (6) as

$$\phi(t) = A\,c^{kt/i\hbar} = A\,e^{-\,i\,k\,t/\hbar} \tag{7}$$

Equation (7) may be written in terms of sines and cosines since

$$e^{-\,ix} = \cos x - i\sin x$$

Hence, $\phi(t) = A\left[\cos Kt/\hbar - i\sin Kt/\hbar\right]$

and $\phi(t)$ is an oscillatory function of time with frequency $\omega_0 = K/\hbar$. The energy of particle is

$$E = h\nu$$

and $$\omega = \frac{2\pi E}{h} = \frac{E}{\hbar}$$

But the only physical interpretation ω_0 can have is that it is the particle's frequency. Hence

$$\omega = \omega_0$$

or $$\frac{E}{\hbar} = \frac{K}{\hbar}$$

and $$E = K. \tag{8}$$

Putting (8) in (5)

$$\frac{i\hbar}{\phi(t)}\;\frac{d\,\phi(t)}{dt} = E$$

or $$i\hbar\,\frac{d}{dt}\,\phi(t) = E\,\phi(t) \tag{9}$$

Equation (9) is an eigenvalue equation, since an operator ($i\hbar\, d/dt$) acts on a function $(\phi(t))$ and gives back the function multiplied by a constant (E). The constant E, is called the eigenvalue of $\phi(t)$.

Now that we have found K, we may rewrite (4) as

$$\frac{-\hbar^2}{2m}\,\frac{1}{\psi(x)}\,\frac{d^2\,\psi(x)}{dx^2} + V = E$$

or $$\frac{-\hbar^2}{2m}\,\frac{1}{\psi(x)}\,\frac{d^2\,\psi(x)}{dx^2} = E - V$$

$$\frac{+\hbar^2}{2m}\,\frac{d^2\,\psi(x)}{dx^2} = (V - E)\,\psi(x) \qquad (10)$$

The real problem is to solve (10) for the given V. A particle moving between impenetrable walls is a picturesque way of describing a particle in an infinite potential well. (See figure.) We may describe this V by

$$V = \begin{cases} \infty, & x \le 0 \\ 0, & 0 \le x \le L \\ \infty, & x \ge L \end{cases}$$

Hence, within the well, V = 0 and (10) becomes

$$\frac{d^2\psi(x)}{dx^2} + \frac{2mE}{\hbar^2}\,\psi(x) = 0$$

This is the equation of simple harmonic motion, and has the general solution

$$\psi(x) = B\cos\left(\frac{\sqrt{2mE}}{\hbar}\right)x + C\sin\left(\frac{\sqrt{2mE}}{\hbar}\right)x \qquad (11)$$

In order to "taper" (11) to the problem at hand, note that

$$\psi(0) = 0$$
$$\psi(L) = 0 \qquad (12)$$

since, if the potential is infinite at these points, we cannot expect to find the particle there. Using (12) in (11)

$$\psi(0) = B = 0$$

$$\psi(L) = B\cos\left(\frac{\sqrt{2mE}}{\hbar}\right)L + C\sin\left(\frac{\sqrt{2mE}}{\hbar}\right)L = 0$$

Hence $$C\sin\left(\frac{\sqrt{2mE}}{\hbar}\right)L = 0$$

C cannot be 0, otherwise $\psi(x) = 0$ for all x, and this is a trivial solution. Therefore, it must be that

$$\sin\left(\frac{\sqrt{2mE}}{\hbar}\right) L = 0$$

or $$\frac{L\sqrt{2mE}}{\hbar} = n\pi \qquad n = 1, 2, \ldots \qquad (13)$$

Note that if n = 0 in (13), this implies that E = 0, always. Again, (11) would be a trivial solution for this case, since B = 0. Hence,

$$E = \frac{n^2 \pi^2 \hbar^2}{L^2 \, 2m} = \frac{n^2 h^2}{8mL^2} \qquad n = 1, 2, \ldots$$

These are the energy eigenvalues of a particle in an infinite square well.

• PROBLEM 1012

Use the quantum aspect of light to derive the formula for the Doppler effect. Assume that the light source moves with a nonrelativistic velocity with respect to the observer.

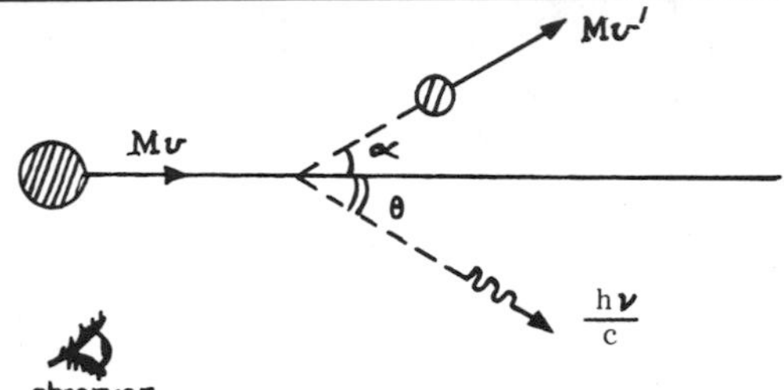

Solution: Let M be the mass of the source and $\vec{v}$ its velocity. In order to emit photons, the atoms of the source must initially be in excited states. If the internal energy of the excited source is E, the total energy of the source before emission is

$$E_t = \frac{1}{2} Mv^2 + E.$$

When a photon is emitted, the internal energy changes by an amount $h\nu_0$ where ν_0 is the frequency of the photon observed by the source. The source suffers a recoil as a result of emission and acquires a new velocity v'. By the law of conservation of energy,

$$\frac{1}{2} Mv^2 + E = \frac{1}{2} Mv'^2 + E' + h\nu \qquad (1)$$

where ν is the frequency of the photon as measured by the observer.

From the figure, we write the conservation of the momentum in directions parallel and perpendicular to $\bar{v}$ as

$$Mv = Mv' \cos\alpha + \frac{h\nu}{c} \cos\theta. \qquad (2)$$

$$0 = Mv' \sin\alpha + \frac{h\nu}{c} \sin\theta. \qquad (3)$$

Since $E' = E - h\nu_0$, (1) can be written as

$$Mv^2 = Mv'^2 + 2h(\nu - \nu_0). \tag{4}$$

Rewriting (2) and (3) as

$$Mv' \cos \alpha = Mv - \frac{h\nu}{c} \cos \theta$$

$$Mv' \sin \alpha = \frac{h\nu}{c} \sin \theta$$

and squaring both sides

$$M^2 v'^2 \cos^2 \alpha = M^2 v^2 + \frac{h^2 \nu^2}{c^2} \quad \cos^2 \theta - 2Mv \frac{h\nu}{c} \cos \theta$$

$$M^2 v'^2 \sin^2 \alpha = \frac{h^2 \nu^2}{c^2} \sin^2 \theta$$

and adding the two, we get

$$M^2 v'^2 = M^2 v^2 + \frac{h^2 \nu^2}{c^2} - 2Mv \frac{h\nu}{c} \cos \theta. \tag{5}$$

Here we made use of the trigonometric identity $\cos^2 \theta +$ $+ \sin^2 \theta = 1$. Combining (4) and (5), we have

$$M^2 v'^2 = M^2 v^2 - 2hM(\nu - \nu_0) = M^2 v^2 + \frac{h^2 \nu^2}{c^2} - 2Mv \frac{h\nu}{c} \cos \theta$$

or $$2hM(\nu - \nu_0) - 2Mv \frac{h\nu}{c} \cos \theta + \frac{h^2 \nu^2}{c^2} = 0.$$

If the mass M is sufficiently large, we may neglect the last term in the preceding equation,

$$2hM(\nu - \nu_0) = 2Mv \frac{h\nu}{c} \cos \theta$$

giving $$\nu = \frac{\nu_0}{1 - \frac{v}{c} \cos \theta} .$$

Therefore, the frequency of the emitted light gets smaller as the source moves faster with respect to the observer.

CHAPTER 34

RADIATION

• PROBLEM 1013

A sample of a radioactive material contains one million radioactive nuclei. The half-life is 20 sec. How many nuclei remain after 10 sec?

Solution: We will employ 2 methods of solution. One will be very physical, and the other will be more mathematical. Suppose that after every 10 sec period, a fraction f of the number of nuclei present at the beginning of the period remains at the end of the period.

Then, at time t = 0 sec there are 10^6 nuclei. At time t = 10 sec there are 10^6 f nuclei. At the end of the next 10 sec a fraction f of these remain. Therefore, at time t = 20 sec there are $10^6 f^2$ nuclei. But 20 sec is the half-life, during which half the nuclei disintegrate.

Therefore

$$f^2 = \frac{1}{2}$$

$$f = 0.707.$$

The number of nuclei remaining after 10 sec is $10^6 \times 0.707$ or 707,000.

Now, we set up a differential equation describing the process of radioactive decay. It is observed that the rate of decay of nuclei is proportional to the number of nuclei present, or

$$\frac{dN}{dt} = -\lambda N \qquad (1)$$

where the minus sign indicates that the number of nuclei is decreasing with time. We may write (1) as

$$\frac{dN}{N} = -\lambda dt.$$

Integrating both sides of this equation,

$$\ln N = -\lambda t + c.$$

Taking the exponential of both sides:

$$N = e^{-\lambda t + c} = e^{-\lambda t} e^c.$$

Because e^c is only a constant, we replace it by A

$$N(t) = Ae^{-\lambda t} \tag{2}$$

Assume that at t = 0, we have N_0 nuclei. Then

$$N(t = 0) = Ae^{\circ} = A = N_0$$

$$N_0 = A.$$

Therefore, from (2),

$$N(t) = N_0 e^{-\lambda t}. \tag{3}$$

We also know that after 20 sec, we have $\frac{1}{2}$ the original number of nuclei, $N_0/2$. Hence

$$N(20\text{ sec}) = N_0 e^{-(20\text{ sec})\lambda} = \frac{N_0}{2}$$

or $$e = {}^{-(20\text{ sec})\lambda} = \frac{1}{2}$$

$$2 = e^{(20\text{ sec})\lambda}.$$

Taking the logarithm of both sides,

$$\ln 2 = (20\text{ sec})\lambda.$$

Therefore

$$\lambda = \left(\frac{1}{20\text{ sec}}\right)\ln 2.$$

Substituting this in (3), we obtain

$$N(t) = N_0 e^{-\left[\left(\frac{1}{20\text{ sec}}\right)\ln 2\right]t}$$

Hence, after 10 sec, assuming $N_0 = 10^6$ nuclei,

$$N(10\text{ sec}) = (10^6\text{ nuclei})e^{-\left[\left(\frac{1}{20\text{ sec}}\right)\ln 2\right]10\text{ sec}}$$

$$N(10\text{ sec}) = (10^6\text{ nuclei})e^{-\frac{1}{2}\ln 2}$$

$$N(10\text{ sec}) = (10^6\text{ nuclei})e^{\ln 2^{-\frac{1}{2}}}$$

But $$e^{\ln x} = x.$$ Then

$$N(10\text{ sec}) = \left(10^6\text{ nuclei}\right)\left(2^{-\frac{1}{2}}\right)$$

$$N(10\text{ sec}) = \frac{\left(10^6\text{ nuclei}\right)}{\sqrt{2}} = 0.707 \times 10^6\text{ nuclei}.$$

• PROBLEM 1014

The half-life of radon is 3.80 days. After how many days will only one-sixteenth of a radon sample remain?

Solution. A half-life of 3.80 days means that every 3.80 days, half the amount of radon present decays. Since one-sixteenth is a power of one-half, this problem can be solved by counting . After 3.80 days, one-half the original sample remains. In the next 3.80 days, one-half of this decays so that after 7.60 days one-fourth the original amount remains. After 11.4 days, one-eighth the original amount remains, and after four half-lives (15.2 days), one-sixteenth the original amount remains.

As an alternate solution, the formula for decaying matter can be used.

$$\frac{N}{N_0} = e^{-\lambda t_{(1/2)}}$$

λ is an experimental constant which can be determined from the half life. Therefore, for $\frac{N}{N_0} = \frac{1}{2}$,

$$\ln \frac{N}{N_0} = -\lambda t_{(1/2)}$$

$$\lambda = \frac{\ln \frac{N_0}{N}}{t_{(1/2)}} = \frac{\ln 2}{t_{(1/2)}} = \frac{0.693}{3.80 \text{ days}} = 0.182/\text{day}.$$

We want $N/N_0 = 1/16 = e^{-\lambda t} = e^{-0.182t}$.

$$-0.182t = \ln 1/16 = -2.77$$

$$t = 15.2 \text{ days}.$$

• PROBLEM 1015

A solution containing radiophosphorus, P^{32}, which is a β-emitter with a half-life of 14 days, surrounds a Geiger counter which records 10^3 counts per minute. If the same experiment is performed 28 days later, what counting rate will be obtained?

Solution: The number of radioactive atoms still present after time t is given by the radioactive decay formula

$$N = N_0 e^{-\lambda t} \qquad (1)$$

The number of atoms present after one half-life (τ) of P^{32} is, by definition, $N_0/2$, whence

$$N(\tau) = N_0 e^{-\lambda\tau} = \frac{N_0}{2}$$

or

$$e^{\lambda\tau} = 2$$

Taking the logarithm of both sides of this equation

$$\lambda\tau = \ell n\ 2$$

or

$$\lambda = \frac{1}{T} \ln 2 \tag{2}$$

Using (2) in (1)

$$N = N_0 e^{-\left(\frac{t}{T} \ln 2\right)}$$

Hence, the decay rate is

$$\frac{dN}{dt} = \left(-\frac{1}{T} \ln 2\right) N_0 e^{-\left(\frac{t}{T} \ln 2\right)} \tag{3}$$

At $t = 0$,

$$\left(\frac{dN}{dt}\right)_{t=0} = \left(-\frac{1}{T} \ln 2\right) N_0 \tag{4}$$

Rewriting (3) using (4)

$$\frac{dN}{dt} = \left(\frac{dN}{dt}\right)_{t=0} e^{\left(-\frac{t}{T} \ln 2\right)} \tag{5}$$

At the beginning of the 28 days, the decay rate is

$$\left(\frac{dN}{dt}\right)_{t=0} = 10^3 \text{ counts/min.}$$

At $t = 28$ days,

$$\frac{dN}{dt} = (10^3 \text{ counts/min})\left(e^{-\left(\frac{28 \text{ days}}{14 \text{ days}}\right) \ln 2}\right)$$

$$\frac{dN}{dt} = (10^3 \text{ counts/min})\left(e^{-2 \ln 2}\right)$$

$$\frac{dN}{dt} = (10^3 \text{ counts/min})\left(e^{\ln 2^{-2}}\right)$$

But

$$e^{\ln x} = x \text{ , whence}$$

$$\frac{dN}{dt} = (10^3 \text{ counts/min})(2^{-2})$$

$$\frac{dN}{dt} = 250 \text{ counts/min.}$$

Note that the time involved is two half-lives. Thus the final counting rate will be $(\frac{1}{2})^2 = \frac{1}{4}$ of the initial counting rate.

• PROBLEM 1016

How much energy is required to break up a C^{12} nucleus into three α particles?

Solution: This reaction is

$$C^{12} \rightarrow He^4 + Be^8$$

$$Be^8 \rightarrow 2He^4$$

Energy is required since the mass of the three α particles is greater than the mass of the C^{12} nucleus.

This is so because the C^{12} nucleus can be considered to be a system of bound α particles, and work must be done (energy must be added) to break up a bound system into its constituent parts. The additional mass of the products comes from energy-mass conversion. To find the additional energy required, calculate the change in mass. By definition, the atomic mass of C^{12} is 12 AMU (exactly). And,

$$3 \times m(He^4) = 3 \times (4.002\ 603 \text{ AMU}) = 12.007\ 809 \text{ AMU}$$

Therefore, the energy required is

$$\varepsilon = \left[3 \times m(He^4) - m(C^{12})\right] \times c^2$$

$$= (12.007\ 809\ AMU - 12\ AMU) \times c^2$$

$$= (0.007\ 809\ AMU) \times (931.481\ MeV/AMU)$$

$$= 7.274\ MeV.$$

• PROBLEM 1017

The gold leaves of the machine in the figure periodically diverge and then collapse. Describe how this perpetual-motion machine operates and explain why it is not a perpetual-motion machine.

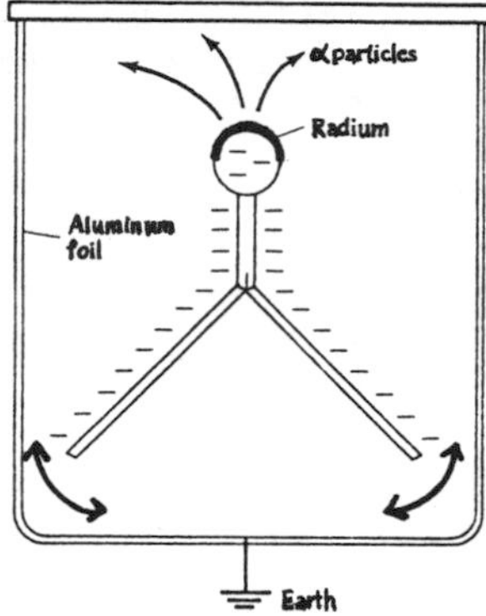

Solution: Radium atoms are radioactive and have a half-life of 1,622 years. For radium

$$^{226}_{88}Ra \longrightarrow {}^{222}_{86}Rn + {}^{4}_{2}He \tag{1}$$

The alpha particle (the ^4_2He nucleus) with 2 quanta of positive charge, is ejected with a kinetic energy of 4.77 MeV and escapes from the surface of the metal. Therefore, if a piece of radium is placed on an electroscope stem, the electroscope becomes negatively charged. This is due to the fact that only a part of the radium atom is emitted as an alpha particle. The number of electrons around the radium nucleus remains the same. Thus, for each alpha particle that escapes 2 quanta of negative charge are left on the electroscope mount and gold leaves. As radium atoms decay, the leaves slowly diverge due to the mutual repulsion of the negative charge on the two foil strips. At the instant they touch the grounded metal surface of the container, the negative charge migrates from the leaves. The gravitational forces cause the leaves to collapse to their original position. The leaves immediately begin to diverge again, repeating the cycle over and over until there are no more radium nuclei present. Since the half-life of radium is 1,622 years, the machine would "run" for many years without any apparent slowing down. From today's perspective, though, we see that the energy source is derived from the nuclear energy released in the nuclear reaction described in (1). This energy is converted to mechanical motion of the gold leaves. Therefore, the device is not a perpetual-motion machine.

A sample of gold is exposed to a beam of neutrons, and the reaction $Au^{197} + n = Au^{198} + \gamma$ absorbs 10^6 neutrons per second. Au^{198} emits β-particles and has a half-life of 2.70 days. How many atoms of Au^{198} are present after 2 days of continuous irradiation?

Solution: At any instant during the irradiation, the increase in the number of Au^{198} atoms in unit time will be the number being produced less the number disintegrating. Thus, if λ is the decay constant for the β decay,

$$dN/dt = 10^6\ s^{-1} - \lambda N.$$

This follows because the reaction occurs once for every neutron (n) absorbed. If 10^6 neutrons are absorbed per second, 10^6 Au^{198} atoms (as well as 10^6 γ ray photons) are produced per second.

$$\frac{dN}{10^6\ s^{-1} - \lambda N} = dt \qquad \int_0^N \frac{dN}{10^6\ s^{-1} - \lambda N} = \int_0^t dt \tag{1}$$

there being no atoms of Au^{198} present at time t = 0 when the irradiation starts.

Letting

$$u = 10^6\ s^{-1} - \lambda N$$

$$du = -\lambda\ dN$$

Since $u = 10^6\ s^{-1}$ when N = 0, and $u = 10^6\ s^{-1} - \lambda N$ when N = N, (1) becomes

$$-\frac{1}{\lambda}\int_{10^6\ s^{-1}}^{10^6\ s^{-1} - \lambda N} \frac{du}{u} = \int_0^t dt$$

or $$-\frac{1}{\lambda}\ \ln(u)\Big|_{10^6\ s^{-1}}^{10^6\ s^{-1} - \lambda N} = t$$

$$-\frac{1}{\lambda}\ \ln\left[\frac{10^6\ s^{-1} - \lambda N}{10^6\ s^{-1}}\right] = t$$

$$\ln\left[1 - \frac{\lambda N}{10^6\ s^{-1}}\right] = -\lambda t$$

and $$1 - \frac{\lambda N}{10^6\ s^{-1}} = \exp(-\lambda t)$$

$$N = \frac{10^6\ s^{-1}}{\lambda}[1 - \exp(-\lambda t)] \tag{2}$$

Note that in general, the equation of radioactive decay is

$$N = N_0 \, e^{-\lambda t}$$

if N_0 is the original number of atoms which are decaying. After one half life (τ), $N_0/2$ atoms are left and

$$N(\tau) = \frac{N_0}{2} = N_0 \, e^{-\lambda\tau}$$

or $\quad 2 = e^{\lambda\tau}$

Hence $\lambda\tau = \ln 2$ and $\lambda = \frac{1}{\tau} \ln 2$. Using this fact in (2)

$$N = \frac{(10^6 \text{ s}^{-1})(\tau)}{\ln 2}\left[1 - \exp\left(-\frac{(\ln 2)t}{\tau}\right)\right]$$

where τ is the half-life period of the β-activity. After 2 days,

$$N = \frac{(10^6 \text{ s}^{-1})(2.7 \text{ days})}{(.6932)}\left[1 - \exp\left(-\frac{(\ln 2)(2 \text{ days})}{(2.7 \text{ days})}\right)\right]$$

Since $\quad$ 1 day = 86,400 secs

$$N = \frac{(10^6)(86{,}400)}{(.6932)}\left[1 - \exp\left(-\frac{2}{2.7}\ln 2\right)\right]$$

$$N = 1.35 \times 10^{11} \text{ atoms.}$$

• PROBLEM 1019

What is the height of the Coulomb barrier for an α particle and a Pb^{206} nucleus? Use nuclear radius $R \cong 1.4 \, A^{1/3} \times 10^{-13}$cm where A is the mass number.

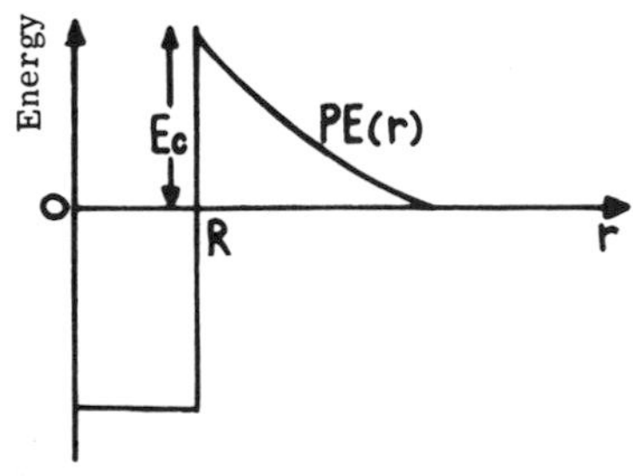

Potential Well as a Function of Radius

Solution: Within the nucleus there is an attractive nuclear force which is short range. This force is much larger than the repulsive Coulomb force between the protons, but it is effective only within the nuclear radius R. Therefore α particles within a nucleus are in a potential well consisting of a nuclear potential (negative since the force is attractive) for radius $r < R$ and a Coulomb potential (positive since the force is repulsive) for $r > R$. This is shown in the diagram. For the alpha particle to escape the nucleus, it must acquire an energy greater than the Coulomb potential barrier ε_c. The maximum repulsion between two nuclei occur when they are just touching. If they were any closer, the nuclear force would overcome the Coulomb repulsion force and the nuclei would attract and fall into each other. The maximum Coulomb potential ε_c occurs when the nuclei repulsion is at a maximum. Therefore, the Coulomb barrier ε_c is just the electrostatic potential energy between the two nuclei when the distance between their centers is equal to the sum of their radii (that is, when they are just in "contact").

$$R_{Pb} \cong 1.4 \times (206)^{1/3} \times 10^{-13}\text{cm} \qquad R_\alpha \cong 1.4 \times (4)^{1/3} \times 10^{-13}\text{ cm}$$

$$\cong 1.4 \times 5.91 \times 10^{-13}\text{cm} \qquad \cong 1.4 \times 1.59 \times 10^{-13}\text{cm}$$

$$\cong 8.2 \times 10^{-13}\text{ cm} \qquad \cong 2.2 \times 10^{-13}\text{ cm}$$

Electrostatic potential energy is

$$PE = \frac{q_1 q_2}{r}$$

where q_1 and q_2 are the charges and r the distance between them. The charge on each of the nuclei is equal to the number of protons Z they contain, multiplied by the charge e on a proton. Therefore

$$\varepsilon_c = \frac{(Ze)_{Pb} \times (Ze)_\alpha}{R_{Pb} + R_\alpha}$$

$$\cong \frac{82e \times 2e}{(8.2 \times 10^{-13}\text{ cm}) + (2.2 \times 10^{-13}\text{ cm})}$$

$$\cong \frac{164e^2}{10.4 \times 10^{-13}\text{ cm}}$$

Now, the square of the electronic charge can be expressed as $e^2 = 1.44 \times 10^{-13}$ MeV-cm. Thus,

$$\varepsilon_c \cong \frac{164 \times (1.44 \times 10^{-13}\text{ MeV-cm})}{10.4 \times 10^{-13}\text{ cm}} \cong 22.7\text{ MeV}$$

This energy is large compared to the kinetic energy of α particles emitted from radioactive nuclei.

• PROBLEM 1020

A hospital receives and puts into storage a batch of 100 mCi of radioiodine which has a half-life of 8 days. For how long can the batch be kept in storage and still provide a therapeutic dose of 12 mCi·hr?

Solution: The decay of a radioactive sample is governed by the relation

$$N = N_0 \, e^{-\lambda t}$$

where λ is the decay constant, N_0 is the initial number of atoms in the sample, and N is the number of atoms remaining after time t. Hence, the number of atoms, N', which have decayed is

$$N' = N_0 - N = N_0\left(1 - e^{-\lambda t}\right)$$

The activity I of the sample is defined as the number of decays per unit time, or

$$I = \frac{dN'}{dt} = \lambda N_0 \, e^{-\lambda t} = \lambda N$$

Defining the initial activity I_0 as

$$I_0 = \lambda N_0$$

we may write

$$I = I_0 \, e^{-\lambda t}$$

A "dose" D of the radioactive substance represents a certain number of decays of the parent element. A dose administered from time t to time t' has the value

$$D = I_0 \int_t^{t'} e^{-\lambda t} \, dt.$$

If the radioelement may be left in an implant for a long period, t' can be made to tend to infinity. This will give us the maximum value of D.

$$D_{max} = \lim_{t' \to \infty} I_0 \int_t^{t'} e^{-\lambda t} \, dt$$

Let $\quad u = -\lambda t \qquad\qquad du = -\lambda \, dt$

or $\quad t = -u/\lambda \qquad\qquad dt = -du/\lambda$

Then, when t = t, $u = -\lambda t$, and when t = t', $u = -\lambda t'$. Therefore

$$D_{max} = \lim_{t' \to \infty} I_0 \int_{-\lambda t}^{-\lambda t'} e^u \, (-du/\lambda)$$

$$D_{max} = -\lim_{t' \to \infty} \frac{I_0}{\lambda} \int_{-\lambda t}^{-\lambda t'} e^u \, du$$

$$D_{max} = - \lim_{t' \to \infty} \frac{I_0}{\lambda} \left[e^u \right]_{-\lambda t}^{-\lambda t'}$$

$$D_{max} = - \lim_{t' \to \infty} \frac{I_0}{\lambda} \left[e^{-\lambda t'} - e^{-\lambda t} \right]$$

$$D_{max} = \frac{I_0}{\lambda} e^{-\lambda t}$$

Since $\lambda = \frac{\ln 2}{\tau}$

$$D_{max} = \frac{I_0 \tau}{\ln 2} e^{-\lambda t}$$

where τ is the half-life of radioiodine. Thus, if $D_{max} = 12$ mCi·hr,

$$12 \text{ mCi·hr} = \frac{100 \text{ mCi} \times 8 \times 24 \text{ hr}}{0.6932} e^{-\lambda t}.$$

$e^{-\lambda t} = 4.327 \times 10^{-4}$, or $\exp\left(-\frac{t \ln 2}{\tau}\right) = 4.327 \times 10^{-4}$.

Solving for t

$$-\frac{t \ln 2}{\tau} = \ln\left(4.327 \times 10^{-4}\right)$$

or $$t = \frac{-\tau}{\ln 2} \ln\left(4.327 \times 10^{-4}\right)$$

$$t = \frac{\tau \log[1/(4.327 \times 10^{-4})]}{\log 2}$$

$$= \frac{8 \times 3.3638}{0.3010} \text{ days} = 89.4 \text{ days}.$$

The batch may thus be kept in storage for 89.4 days.

• PROBLEM 1021

A neutron decays into an electron, a proton and an antineutrino. Calculate the kinetic energy shared by the electron and the antineutrino.

Solution: The neutrino and antineutrino are particles which have a negligibly small and possibly zero mass. They can carry energy and momentum, and presumably travel with the speed of light. The neutrino is different from the photon in that the photon has spin $\hbar$ and the neutrino spin $\hbar/2$.

We will make the calculation in atomic mass units.

(a.m.u.) Since

$$1 \text{ kg} = 6.024 \times 10^{26} \text{ amu}$$

$$m_p = 1.67 \times 10^{-27} \text{ kg}$$

$$= (1.67 \times 10^{-27} \text{ kg})\left(6.024 \times 10^{26} \frac{\text{amu}}{\text{kg}}\right)$$

$$= 1.007593 \text{ amu}$$

Similarly,

$$m_n = 1.008982 \text{ amu}$$

$$m_e = 0.000549 \text{ amu}$$

where m_p, m_n, m_e are the masses of the proton, neutron and electron, respectively.

The reaction occurring is

$$n^0 \rightarrow e^{-1} + p^{+1} + \bar{\gamma}^0$$

where n^0, e^{-1}, p^{+1} and $\bar{\gamma}^0$ are the symbols for a neutron, electron, proton and antineutrino, respectively. Since we want to calculate the kinetic energy shared by the electron and antineutrino, we apply the principle of conservation of relativistic energy and obtain

$$m_n c^2 = m_e c^2 + m_p c^2 + m_{\bar{\gamma}^0} c^2 + T_e + T_p + T_{\bar{\gamma}^0}$$

where T_e, T_p and $T_{\bar{\gamma}^0}$ are the kinetic energies of the electron, proton and antineutrino respectively, and $m_n c^2$, $m_e c^2$, $m_p c^2$, $m_{\bar{\gamma}^0} c^2$ are the rest energies of the neutron, electron, proton and neutrino. But

$m_{\bar{\gamma}^0} = 0$. Also, the proton remains at rest after the decay, and, therefore, $T_p = 0$. Hence,

$$\left(m_n - m_e - m_p\right) c^2 = T_e + T_{\bar{\gamma}^0} = T$$

Using the previous mass calculations

$$T = (.000840 \text{ amu})(9 \times 10^{16} \text{ m}^2/\text{s}^2)$$

$$= (.000840 \text{ amu})(1.66 \times 10^{-17} \text{ kg/amu})(9 \times 10^{16} \text{ m}^2/\text{s}^2)$$

$$= 1.26 \times 10^{-13} \text{ Joules}$$

Since 1 Joule $= 6.24 \times 10^{18}$ eV

$$T = 7.86 \times 10^5 \text{ eV}$$

and this is shared by the electron and antineutrino.

• PROBLEM 1022

What is the expression that corresponds to the case of positron decay?

Solution: For a particular mass number A, only one element with this mass number is stable. If an atom of a different element has this mass number, it will decay into the stable atom. A nucleus that has less protons than the stable nucleus has less charge than the stable one. It therefore undergoes β^- decay. This results in the formation of a proton which increases the charge of the atom and the ratio of Z (proton) to A.

$$n \rightarrow p + e^- + \bar{\nu}_e$$

If the nucleus has an excess of protons, it converts them to neutrons in a process known as β^+ or positron decay.

$$p \rightarrow n + e^+ + \nu_e$$

In the above processes the electron (or positron) and the neutrino ν_e created are immediately ejected from the nucleus.

The positron decay of a nucleus (Z, A) forms the nucleus (Z - 1, A). Originally, we have a nucleus plus Z atomic electrons with a total (that is, atomic) mass m (Z,A). In the decay process, a positron is emitted and a nucleus with atomic number Z - 1 is formed. Since the nuclear charge has decreased by one unit, one of the original Z atomic electrons is superfluous and is shed. Therefore, the final system consists of a nucleus (Z - 1, A) plus Z - 1 atomic electrons, together with the emitted positron and the excess electron. The total mass of the final system is $m(Z - 1,A) + m(\beta^+) + m(e^-)$, or $m(Z - 1,A) + 2m$ since a neutrino has no mass. Hence, the total available energy for positron decay is found from the amount of mass converted to energy.

$$\begin{aligned} \varepsilon_{\beta+} &= \left\{m(Z,A) - \left[m(Z - 1,A) + 2m_e\right]\right\} \times c^2 \\ &= \left[m(Z,A) - m(Z - 1,A)\right] \times c^2 - 2m_e c^2 \\ &= \Delta m \times c^2 - 2m_e c^2 \end{aligned}$$

and the maximum positron kinetic energy is $2m_e c^2$ = 1.02 MeV less than the mass-energy difference between the parent and daughter atoms.

• PROBLEM 1023

What is the available energy for the α decay of Po^{210}?

Solution: Some unstable nuclei, especially those with mass numbers above 200, spontaneously emit helium nuclei (α particles). Emission of an α particle by a nucleus decreases the original nuclear charge particles

Z (protons) by two and decreases the original mass number A (protons plus neutrons) by four.

$$N_Z^A \rightarrow N_{Z-2}^{A-4} + He_2^4$$

If N_Z^A has a greater mass than the combined mass of N_{Z-2}^{A-4} and He_2^4 then it is unstable and can decay by the emission of an α particle. The available energy for the α-decay process is given by the mass available for mass-energy conversion.

Alpha-particle emission from Po^{210} leaves Pb^{206}. Therefore, the pertinent masses are:

$m(Po^{210}) = 209.98287$ AMU

$$m(Pb^{206}) = 205.97447 \text{ AMU}$$
$$m(He^4) = 4.00260 \text{ AMU}$$
$$m(Pb^{206}) + m(He^4) = 209.97707 \text{ AMU}$$

The available energy ε_a is:

$$\varepsilon_a = \left[m(Po^{210}) - m(Pb^{206}) - m(He^4)\right] \times c^2$$

$$\varepsilon_a = (209.98287 \text{ AMU} - 209.97707 \text{ AMU}) \times c^2$$

$$= (0.00580 \text{ AMU}) \times (931.481 \text{ MeV/AMU})$$

$$= 5.40 \text{ MeV}$$

Actually, this decay energy is shared by the α particle and the Pb^{206} nucleus (because the linear momenta of the two fragments must be equal and opposite). Consequently, the α particle emitted by Po^{210} has a kinetic energy of 5.30 MeV and the recoil Pb^{206} nucleus has a kinetic energy of 0.10 MeV.

• PROBLEM 1024

A uranium nucleus under certain conditions will spontaneously emit an alpha particle, which consists of two protons and two neutrons. If the nucleus was initially at rest and the speed of the emitted alpha particle is 2×10^7 m/s, what is the "recoil" speed of the nucleus? The nuclear mass is 3.9×10^{-25} kg and the alpha-particle mass is 6.7×10^{-27} kg.

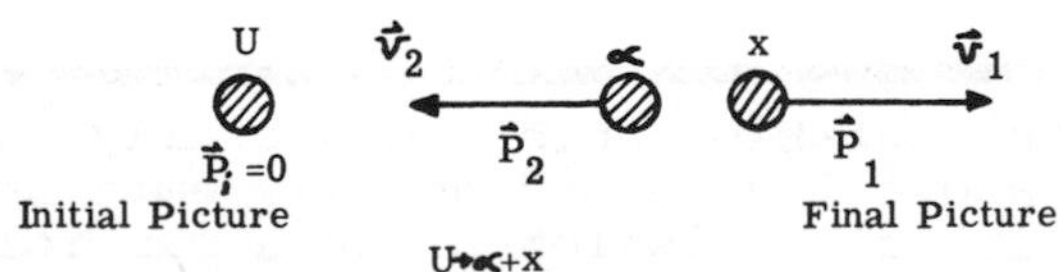

Solution: The "nuclear" force responsible for the particle emission is not explained, but this information is not needed if it is recognized that the total momentum of the system is zero. The mass of the recoiling nucleus $m_1 = 3.9 \times 10^{-25}$ kg; the mass of the alpha particle $m_2 = 6.7 \times 10^{-27}$ kg; and the velocity of the alpha particle $v_2 = 2 \times 10^7$ m/s are the known observables.

As shown in the figure, the momentum of the initial state is zero, since the uranium atom is initially at rest. Therefore, the vectorial sum of the momenta of the fragments in the final state is also zero. (We are viewing the α-decay of the uranium atom from the center of mass frame of the motion.)

The speed of fragment x is expected to be smaller than that of the α-particle since x is more massive than α. Both speeds are therefore non-relativistic and we are allowed to use the non-relativistic formulae. From the conservation of momentum, we have

$$\vec{P}_f = \vec{P}_i = 0$$

$$\vec{P}_1 + \vec{P}_2 = 0$$

or

$$m_2\vec{v}_2 + m_1\vec{v}_1 = 0$$

Therefore

$$\vec{v}_1 = -\frac{m_2}{m_1}\vec{v}_2 .$$

We see that $\vec{v}_1$ and $\vec{v}_2$ have opposite directions. The magnitude of $\vec{v}_1$ is

$$v_1 = \frac{m_2 v_2}{m_1} = \frac{(6.7 \times 10^{-27}\ \text{kg})(2 \times 10^7\ \text{m/s})}{3.9 \times 10^{-25}\ \text{kg}} = 3.4 \times 10^5\ \text{m/s}$$

After emission, the alpha particle and nucleus move apart as free particles according to Newton's first law because the force causing the separation quickly becomes negligible.

• PROBLEM 1025

If the "average" alpha particle speed is 1.3×10^7 m/s within the nucleus of $^{238}_{92}U$, how many collisions will the particle make with the barrier each second? Also determine how many years are required before the average alpha particle escapes from the uranium nucleus. One year is approximately 3.1×10^7s. Only one out of 10^{38} collisions with the barrier results in the escape of an alpha particle.

Solution: As a result of the very strong nuclear attraction, an α particle in the nucleus is like a particle in a deep well. The attractive barrier that confines the α particle to the nucleus is actually a "potential well," as shown in the figure. As long as the particle doesn't have sufficient kinetic energy, according to classical physics it can not get out of this potential well. However, quantum physics states that even if the particle is not ener-

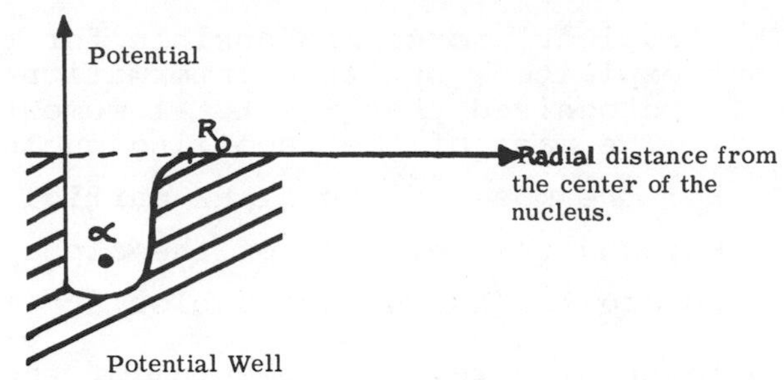

getic enough, there is a finite probability of escape from the well. In fact, it was quantum physics that explained the radioactive emission of certain particles from nuclei, in which tremendous nuclear forces bind the nuclear matter together.

We can assume that the diameter, $2R_0$, of the nucleus is representative of the distance L the particle travels between collisions with the walls of the well. Therefore, the distance L is

$$L = 2R_0 = (2)\left(9 \times 10^{-15}\ \text{m}\right) = 1.8 \times 10^{-14}\ \text{m}$$

The number of times the alpha particle encounters the barrier each second, N, can be calculated since we know the average speed of the particle between collisions. If a distance of L meters must be traversed to make one collision, then the total number of collisions taking place in one second is

$$N = \frac{\bar{v}}{L} = \frac{1.3 \times 10^{7}\ \cancel{\text{m}}/\text{s}}{1.8 \times 10^{-14}\ \cancel{\text{m}}} = 7.2 \times 10^{20}\ \text{collisions/s}$$

We are told that 10^{38} collisions must occur on the average before an alpha particle tunnels through the barrier. The time t required for an α particle to escape is

$$t = \frac{1 \times 10^{38}\ \text{collisions}}{7.2 \times 10^{20}\ \text{collisions/s}} = 1.4 \times 10^{17}\ \text{s}$$

The average time for escape, t, may be written as

$$t = \frac{1.4 \times 10^{17}\ \cancel{\text{s}}}{3.1 \times 10^{7}\ \cancel{\text{s}}/\text{year}} = 4.5 \times 10^{9}\ \text{years.}$$

• PROBLEM 1026

B^{10} is bombarded with neutrons, and α particles are observed to be emitted. What is the residual nucleus?

Solution: Only α particles (helium nuclei) are observed to be emitted in the reaction. The reaction can be described as follows:

$${}^{10}_{5}\text{B} + {}^{1}_{0}\text{n} \rightarrow {}^{A}_{Z}(\text{X}) + {}^{4}_{2}\text{He}$$

where the superscript gives the mass number A. It is the total number of protons and neutrons in that nucleus. In a nuclear reaction the total nucleon number and the total charge is conserved, therefore the mass number A of the unknown nucleus must be such that

$$10 + 1 = A + 4.$$

Hence $A = 7$.

The subscripts refer to the atomic numbers, total number of protons in each nucleus. Since the above reaction involves protons and neutrons only, the protons carry the total charge. The conservation of total electric charge in that case reduces to the conservation of the total number of protons. Therefore,

$$5 + 0 = Z + 2$$

or

$$Z = 3.$$

The nucleus with $A = 7$, $Z = 3$ is ${}^{7}_{3}Li$.

• PROBLEM 1027

The maximum permissible dosage for scientific workers using γ-radiation is 6.25 milliroentgens per hour. What is the safe working distance from a 20-Ci source of cobalt-60 which has a dose rate of 27 roentgens (R) per hour at a distance of 1m? If the source is used in a lead container which reduces the γ-radiation emitted to 1%, how much closer can the scientists work?

Solution: The radiation from the source is emitted uniformly in all directions. Hence at any distance r the radiation is passing through an area $4\pi r^2$. The intensity of radiation per unit volume thus decreases as r increases according to an inverse-square-power law. The diminution of the intensity of the γ-radiation due to absorption in the air may be neglected in comparison with this inverse-square-law effect. Hence if r is the safe working distance,

$$\frac{I(r)}{I(r_0)} = \frac{r_0^2}{r^2}$$

where $I(r)$ is the intensity at a distance r from the source, and $I(r_0)$ is the value of the intensity at r_0 . Hence

$$r^2 = \frac{I(r_0)r_0^2}{I(r)}$$

$$r = r_0\sqrt{\frac{I(r_0)}{I(r)}}$$

But we know that when $r_0 = 1m$, $I(r_0)$ is 27 roentgens/hr. Hence, if $I = 6.25$ milliroentgens/hr at r,

$$r = (1m)\sqrt{\frac{27 \text{ r/hr}}{6.25 \times 10^{-3} \text{ r/hr}}}$$

or

$$r = \sqrt{\frac{27 \times 10^3}{6.25}} \times 1m = 65.7 \text{ m}.$$

If the lead container cuts the radiation to 1% of its former value, then by the same arguments, the new safe working distance r_1 is given by

$$r_1 = r_0\sqrt{\frac{I(r_0)}{I(r)}}$$

Note that only $(I r_0)$ is changed. $I(r_0)$ is now 27×10^{-2} roentgens/hr, and

$$r_1 = (1m)\sqrt{\frac{.27 \times 10^3}{6.25}} = 6.57 \text{ m}$$

• PROBLEM 1028

The dirt floor of the Shanidar Cave in the northern part of Iraq has been examined. Below the layer of soil that contained arrowheads and bone awls was a layer of soil that yielded flint tools and pieces of charcoal. When the charcoal was examined it was discovered that in 1 kg of carbon, approximately 9.4×10^2 carbon-14 nuclei decayed each second. It is known that in 1 kg of carbon from living material, 1.5×10^4 disintegrations of carbon-14 occur each second. Use these data to calculate when people of the stone age culture occupied the cave.

Solution: The number of nuclei of a radioactive substance at time t, is given by

$$N(t) = N_0 e^{-\lambda t}$$

where N_0 is the number of nuclei at $t = 0$, and λ is the decay rate per nucleus. The half-life, T, is defined as the time required for the exponential factor to equal ½;

$$T = \frac{1}{\lambda} \ln 2$$

Therefore, we can also write (1) as

$$N(t) = N_0 e^{-t/T \ln 2}$$

$$= N_0 e^{\ln (\frac{1}{2}) t/T}$$

$$= N_0 (\tfrac{1}{2})^{t/T}$$

Initially, there were $N_0 = 1.5 \times 10^4$ radioactive carbon atoms decaying per second in a kg. of carbon, when carbon was part of a living material. The measured number of disintegrations per 1 kg. of carbon is found to be $N = 9.4 \times 10^2$ per second. From (2)

$$9.4 \times 10^2 = 1.5 \times 10^4 \times (\tfrac{1}{2})^{t/T}$$

or $$(\tfrac{1}{2})^{t/T} = \frac{9.4 \times 10^2}{1.5 \times 10^4} \simeq \frac{1}{16}$$

Since $(\frac{1}{2})^4 = \frac{1}{16}$, we have

$$t = 4\ T.$$

The half-life of carbon-14 is 5730 years. Therefore the tree was burned

$$t = 4 \times (5730 \text{ years}) = 2.3 \times 10^4 \text{ years ago.}$$

• PROBLEM 1029

The mass absorption coefficients for the K_α and K_β radiations of silver are $13.6\ cm^2 \cdot g^{-1}$ and $58.0\ cm^2 \cdot g^{-1}$ when palladium is used as an absorber. What thickness of palladium foil of density $11.4\ g \cdot cm^{-3}$ reduces the intensity of the K_α radiation to one-tenth of its incident value? What is then the percentage reduction in the intensity of the K_β radiation?

Solution: The relation which describes the absorption of x-radiation is $I = I_0 e^{-\mu z}$.

Solving for z (which locates a point inside the absorber)

$$\ell n \frac{I}{I_0} = -\mu z$$

or

$$z = -\frac{1}{\mu} \ell n \frac{I}{I_0}$$

$$z = \frac{1}{\mu} \ln \frac{I_0}{I} = \frac{1}{\mu_m p} \ln \frac{I_0}{I} ,$$

where μ is the linear absorption coefficient, μ_m the mass absorption coefficient, p the density of the absorber and I_0 the intensity of the incident radiation. If the K_α radiation is to be reduced to one-tenth of its incident value, the thickness required is

$$z = \frac{1}{13.6 \text{ cm}^2 \cdot \text{g}^{-1} \times 11.4 \text{g} \cdot \text{cm}^{-3}} \ell n\, 10 = 1.49 \times 10^{-2} \text{cm.}$$

For the K_β radiation with this thickness of absorber,

$$\frac{I}{I_0} = \exp\left(-58.0 \text{cm}^2 \cdot \text{g}^{-1} \times 11.4 \text{g} \cdot \text{cm}^{-3} \times 1.49 \times 10^{-2} \text{cm}\right)$$

$$= \exp(-9.85) = 5.28 \times 10^{-5} .$$

Hence,

$$\frac{I_0 - I}{I_0} \times 100 = \left(1 - \frac{I}{I_0}\right) \times 100 = \left(1 - 5.28 \times 10^{-5}\right) \times 100$$

$$\frac{I_0 - I}{I_0} \times 100 = 99.995\%$$

which is the percentage reduction in the intensity of the K_β radiation.

• PROBLEM 1030

A thickness of 48 cm of Al^{27} reduces the intensity of γ-rays from ThC'' to 1% of its original value. The density of aluminum is 2.65 $g \cdot cm^{-3}$. What is the mass absorption coefficient involved and the atomic cross section for this process?

Solution: The relation involving intensity I and linear absorption coefficient μ is $I = I_0 e^{-\mu z}$, where I_0 is the incident intensity of the radiation. Solving for μ ,

$$\ell n \frac{I}{I_0} = -\mu x$$

$$\mu = -\frac{1}{x} \ell n \frac{I}{I_0}$$

or

$$\mu = \frac{1}{x} \ell n \frac{I_0}{I}$$

Knowing that $I(48 \text{ cm}) = 1\% \, I_0 = .01 \, I_0$,

$$\mu = \frac{1}{48 \text{ cm}} \ell n \frac{I_0}{.01 \, I_0} = \frac{1}{48 \text{ cm}} \ell n\, 100$$

$$\mu = \frac{4.605}{48 \text{ cm}} = .0959 \text{ cm}^{-1}$$

But, if μ_m is the mass absorption coefficient and p the density of Al^{27}, then $\mu = \mu_m p$ or

$$\mu_m = \frac{\mu}{p} = \frac{0.0959 \text{ cm}^{-1}}{2.65 \text{ g}\cdot\text{cm}^{-3}} = 0.0362 \text{ cm}^2\cdot\text{g}^{-1} .$$

A volume of aluminum obtained by taking 1 cm^2 of the surface area and a length of 48 cm perpendicular to this removes 99% of the photons from a γ-ray beam incident at right angles on the surface area. This volume is 48 cm^3 and has a mass of 2.65 $g\cdot cm^{-3} \times 48\ cm^3$. The number of moles in this mass is thus $(2.65 \times 48g)/27\ g\cdot mole^{-1}$ (where 27g is the mass of 1 mole of Al^{27}.), and thus contains $[(2.65 \times 48/27 \text{ mole} \times 6.02 \times 10^{23} \text{ mole}^{-1}]$ atoms, bringing in Avogadro's number.

If each atom for this purpose has an effective area σ (effective in the sense that this is the available target area that the atom provides for an incident γ-ray), σ is the atomic cross-section for the process, and the projected area of all atoms on the surface must make up 99% of the surface area. This follows because 99% of the incident γ radiation is scattered by the Al^{27} atoms.

$$\frac{2.65 \times 48 \times 6.02 \times 10^{23}}{27} \sigma = \frac{99}{100} \times 1 \text{ cm}^2 .$$

$$\sigma = \frac{27 \times 99}{2.65 \times 48 \times 6.02 \times 10^{25}} \text{cm}^2 = 0.349 \times 10^{24} \text{cm}^2$$

• PROBLEM 1031

When a uranium nucleus $^{235}_{92}U$ captures a neutron, fission occurs. If one of the fission fragments formed is the krypton nucleus $^{95}_{36}Kr$, identify what nuclei are formed as the krypton decays to the stable nucleus $^{95}_{42}Mo$ by a succession of β-decays.

Solution: When a nucleus of atomic number Z and atomic weight A decays into another nucleus by emitting an electron, the atomic weight of the new nucleus has the same A but its atomic number is Z + 1,

$$^{A}_{Z}X \rightarrow {}^{A}_{Z+1}Y + e^- + \overline{\nu}_e . \qquad (1)$$

Nucleus X has charge +Ze, where e is the unit charge. The charge of Y is + (Z + 1)e and that of the electron is - e. The neutrino (ν_e) is a chargeless particle.

Therefore the total charge of the decay products is

$$+ (Z + 1)e + (- e) + 0 = + Ze$$

This is equal to the charge of the initial particle, due to the law of conservation of charge.

By using the decay equation (1) and the periodic table, we find the following intermediate decays for the transition

$^{95}_{36}Kr \rightarrow ^{95}_{42}Mo.$

$^{95}_{36}Kr \rightarrow ^{95}_{37}Rb + e^- + \bar{\nu}_e$ Rb-rubidium

$^{95}_{37}Rb \rightarrow ^{95}_{38}Sr + e^- + \bar{\nu}_e$ Sr-strontium

$^{95}_{38}Sr \rightarrow ^{95}_{39}Y + e^- + \bar{\nu}_e$ Y -yittrium

$^{95}_{39}Y \rightarrow ^{95}_{40}Zr + e^- + \bar{\nu}_e$ Zr-zirconium

$^{95}_{40}Zr \rightarrow ^{95}_{41}Nb + e^- + \bar{\nu}_e$ Nb-niobium

$^{95}_{41}Nb \rightarrow ^{95}_{42}Mo + e^- + \bar{\nu}_e$ Mo-molydenum

• PROBLEM 1032

There are $N_0 = 10^{25}$ uranium-238 nuclei in a sample. (a) What is the number of uranium nuclei remaining in the sample after 10^8 years if the decay rate per nucleus, λ, is 5×10^{-18} sec^{-1} ? (b) What is the half-life of uranium?

Solution:

(a) It is known that each nuclear disintegration takes place independently of any of the others. The radioactive decay rate therefore involves only the instantaneous number N(t) of the decaying nuclei present;

$$\frac{dN(t)}{dt} = - \lambda N(t) \tag{1}$$

where the constant of proportionality λ, is known as the decay rate per nucleus.

The solution of (1) is known to be

$$N(t) = N_0 e^{-\lambda t} \tag{2}$$

where N_0 is the number of nuclei at $t = 0$.

There are approximately 3.1×10^7 sec in one year, therefore 10^8 years equals $(10^8 \text{ years}) \times (3.1\times 10^7 \text{ sec/year}) = 3.1 \times 10^{15}$ sec. The number of uranium atoms remaining at the end of this period is

$$N = 10^{25} \times e^{-(5 \times 10^{-18} sec^{-1}) \times (3.1 \times 10^{15} sec)}$$

$$= 10^{25} \times e^{-0.0155} = 10^{25} \times 0.984 = 9.84 \times 10^{24}$$

which is practically the original number.

(b) The half-life, T, is defined as the time after which the number of radioactive nuclei has decreased to half its original value. From equation (2)

$$\tfrac{1}{2} N_0 = N_0 e^{-\lambda T}, \quad \text{or} \quad \tfrac{1}{2} = e^{-\lambda T}$$

giving $\ln \tfrac{1}{2} = - \ln 2 = - \lambda T$,

$$T = \frac{\ln 2}{\lambda} = \frac{0.7}{5 \times 10^{-18}\ \text{sec}^{-1}} = 1.4 \times 10^{17}\ \text{sec.}$$

$$= \frac{1.4 \times 10^{17}\ \text{sec}}{3.1 \times 10^{7}\ \text{sec/year}} = 4.5 \times 10^{9}\ \text{years.}$$

• **PROBLEM 1033**

If a rock sample is found to contain approximately 1 polonium atom ${}^{214}_{84}Po$ for every 8.7×10^{20} uranium nuclei ${}^{238}_{92}U$, what is the half-life of polonium.

Solution: Each decaying uranium atom produces one polonium nucleus along the decay chain. Let N_u denote the number of uranium atoms decaying slowly (the half-life of ${}^{238}U$ is $T_U = 4.5 \times 10^{9}$ years), and N_p that of its decay product polonium. The rate of change of N_p consists of two parts. One of these is the rate of incrase of Po-nuclei as a result of the decay of U-atoms;

$$\left(\frac{dN_p}{dt}\right)_1 = - \frac{dN_u}{dt} = \lambda_U N_u \ .$$

where λ_u is the decay rate of uranium per nucleus. The enormousness of the ratio of U-atoms to Po-nuclei shows that the decay rate of polonium is much greater than that of uranium. Since uranium decays very slowly, we may regard the rate dN_u/dt as substantially constant over a long period of time.

The number of the Po-nuclei decreases as a result of the decay of Po. This decay rate is given by

$$\left(\frac{dN_p}{dt}\right)_2 = - \lambda_p N_p$$

where λ_p is the decay constant of polonium. The total rate of change of the polonium nuclei is

$$\frac{dN_p}{dt} = \left(\frac{dN_p}{dt}\right)_1 + \left(\frac{dN_p}{dt}\right)_2 = \lambda_u N_U - \lambda_p N_p$$

$$\text{or} \quad \cong \text{constant} - \lambda_p N_p \qquad (1)$$

For times sufficiently larger than the life-time of polonium, the rate of change of the polonium population, due to uranium decay, will be negligible, and the rate of change of the polonium population is dominated by the fast decay of polonium. This can also be seen from the solution of (1). Let us write (1) as

$$\frac{dN_p}{dt} = -\lambda_p \left(N_p - \frac{\lambda_U N_u}{\lambda_p} \right) .$$

If we define $N' = N_p - \frac{\lambda_U N_u}{\lambda_p}$, then

$$\frac{dN'}{dt} = \frac{d}{dt}\left(N_p - \text{constant}\right) = \frac{dN_p}{dt}$$

or $$\frac{dN'}{dt} = -\lambda_p N' .$$

This is the same as the decay equation for a radioactive material. Its solution, therefore is

$$N'(t) = N'_{t=0}\, e^{-\lambda_p t}$$

or $$N_p(t) - \frac{\lambda_U N_u}{\lambda_p} = \left(N_p - \frac{\lambda_U N_u}{\lambda_p} \right)_{t=0} e^{-\lambda_p t} .$$

Because of its very slow decay, N_u is approximately the initial number of uranium atoms. Since there are no polonium atoms initially, $N_p = 0$ at $t = 0$. We have

$$N_p(t) \simeq \frac{\lambda_U N_u}{\lambda_p} \left(1 - e^{-\lambda pt}\right).$$

When t is large, i.e., $t\lambda_p >> 1$, $e^{-\lambda pt}$ becomes negligible;

$$N_p \simeq \frac{\lambda_U N_u}{\lambda_p} . \qquad (2)$$

The half-life is defined as

$$T = \frac{1}{\lambda} \ln 2,$$

therefore the half-life of polonium from equation (2) is

$$T_p = \frac{1}{\lambda_p} \ln 2 \simeq \frac{N_p}{N_u} \frac{\ln 2}{\lambda_U} = \frac{N_p}{N_u} T_U$$

$$= \frac{1 \text{ nucleus}}{8.7 \times 10^{20} \text{ nuclei}} \times \left(4.5 \times 10^9 \text{ years}\right)$$

$$= 5 \times 10^{-12} \text{ year}$$

$$= \left(5 \times 10^{-12} \text{ year}\right) \times \left(3.1 \times 10^7 \text{ sec/year}\right)$$

$$= 1.6 \times 10^{-4} \text{ sec.}$$

CHAPTER 35

X-RAYS

• PROBLEM 1034

It is desired to produce penetrating x-rays of wavelengths about 0.20 A. What is the minimum voltage at which the x-ray tube can be operated?

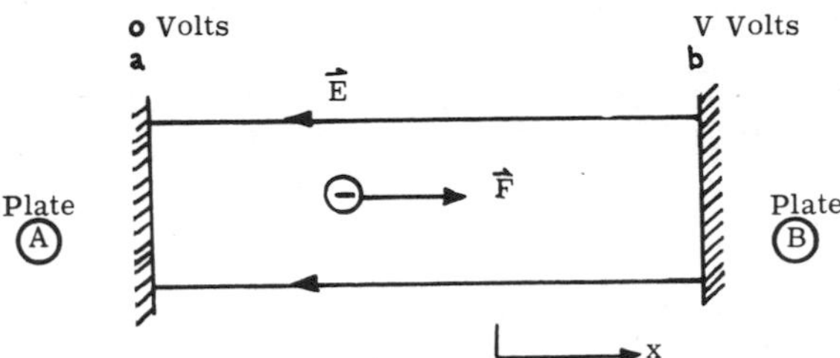

Solution: An x-ray tube accelerates electrons through a potential difference. In order to see how this occurs, let us refer to the figure. The net force on an electron emitted from plate A is, by definition of electric field

$$\vec{F} = e\vec{E}$$

where e is the signed charge of an electron, and $\vec{E}$ is the electric field intensity. Hence, the work done by this force (since it is the resultant force on the electron) is equal to the change in kinetic energy of the electron

$$\frac{1}{2}m_e v_b^2 - \frac{1}{2}m_e v_a^2 = \int_a^b \vec{F} \cdot d\vec{r}.$$

Assuming that the initial velocity, v_a, of the electron is zero,

$$\frac{1}{2}m_e v_b^2 = \int_a^b e\vec{E} \cdot d\vec{r}$$

$$\frac{1}{2}m_e v_b^2 = e\int_a^b \vec{E} \cdot d\vec{r}$$

Replacing the signed number e by $-|e|$ (since $e < 0$), we may write

$$\frac{1}{2}m_e v_b^2 = -|e|\int_a^b \vec{E} \cdot d\vec{r} = |e|\left(V_b - V_a\right)$$

Hence

$$\frac{1}{2}m_e v_b^2 = |e|(V_b - V_a).$$

Assuming that $V_a = 0$ volts

$$\frac{1}{2}m_e v_b^2 = |e|V_b.$$

If all the energy of the electron when it reaches point b is changed into the energy of an x-ray photon, we obtain

$$\frac{1}{2}m_e v_b^2 = |e|V_b = h\nu.$$

Hence $$V_{bmin} = \frac{h\nu}{|e|}.$$

V_b is the minimum voltage needed to produce x-rays of frequency ν. (Only those electrons which give up all their energy to the x-ray photons will produce x-rays).

$$V_{bmin} = \frac{h\nu}{|e|}$$

But $$\nu = \frac{c}{\lambda}$$

where c = speed of light and λ is the x-ray wavelength.

$$V_{bmin} = \frac{hc}{|e|\lambda}$$

$$V_{bmin} = \frac{6.63 \times 10^{-34} \text{ joule-sec} \quad 3.0 \times 10^{8} \text{ m/sec}}{1.60 \times 10^{-19} \text{ coul} \quad 0.20 \times 10^{-10} \text{m}} = 6\bar{2},000 \text{volts}$$

• PROBLEM 1035

Estimate the minimum voltage needed to excite K radiation from an x-ray tube with a tungsten target, and calculate the wavelength of the K_α line.

Solution: Moseley found experimentally that the x-ray line spectrum varies in a regular way from element to element, unlike the irregular variations of optical spectra. This regular variation occurs because characteristic x-rays are due to transitions involving the innermost electrons of the atom. Because of the shielding of the other electrons the inner electron energies do not depend on the complex interactions of the outer electrons, which are responsible for the complicated optical spectra. Also, the inner electrons are shielded from the interatomic forces responsible for the binding of the atoms in solids, According to the Bohr model of the atom, the energy of an electron in the first orbit is proportional to the square of the nuclear charge. Mosely therefore, reasoned that the energy, and thus the frequency, of a characteristic x-ray photon should vary as the square of the atomic number of the element. He plotted the square root of the frequency of particular x-ray lines versus the atomic number Z of the element.He found that his curves could be described by the general equation, $f = A^2 \quad (Z - b)^2$

Where f is the frequency of the x-ray and A and b are constants for each line. One family of lines, called the K-series, has b=1. If the bombarding electron in an x-ray tube knocks an electron from the n=1 inner orbit of a target atom out of the atom, photons are emitted corresponding to transitions of other electrons to the vacancy in the n=1 orbit. The lowest frequency line corresponds to the lowest energy transition, from n=2 to n=1. This line is called the K_α line. Bohr's relation for the frequency of a photon emitted from a one electron atom is,

$$f = Z^2 \frac{2\pi^2 m e^4}{(4\pi E_o)^2 h^3} \left[\frac{1}{n_2^2} - \frac{1}{n_1^2}\right] \qquad (2)$$

The energy E of a photon is given by hf. Using Z - 1 in place of Z in eq (2) so as to fit the form of Moseley's equation (1) for the K-series, we find,

$$E = hf = \frac{2\pi^2 m e^4}{(4\pi E_o)^2 h^2} \left[\frac{1}{n_2^2} - \frac{1}{n_1^2}\right] (z-1)^2 \qquad (3)$$

For K radiation to occur, an electron must be knocked from the $n_1 = 1$ orbit to infinity $(n_2 = \infty)$. This is the minimum energy that must be transmitted to the atom for K radiation and is,

$$E_{ionization} = \frac{2\pi^2 me^4}{(4\pi E_o)^2 h^2} (Z - 1)^2 \left(\frac{1}{\infty} - 1\right)$$

$$= 2.18 \text{ X } 10^{-18} \ (Z - 1)^2 \text{ joules}$$

$$= 13.6 \text{ ev } (Z - 1)^2$$

For tungsten, Z = 74, and the energy input required is $(13.6 \text{ ev}) (73)^2 = 72{,}800$ ev. So the anode must be at least 72,800 volts above the cathode potential. The first line in the K series of tungsten has a wavelength given by E = hf. But $f\lambda_{K\alpha} = c$ and

$$E = hf = \frac{hc}{\lambda_{K\alpha}} = 13.6 \text{ ev } (Z - 1)^2 \left(\frac{1}{1^2} - \frac{1}{2^2}\right)$$

$$\lambda_{K\alpha} = \frac{6.625 \times 10^{-34} \text{ joule-sec } (3.0 \times 10^8 \text{ m/sec})}{(13.6 \times 1.60 \times 10^{-19} \text{ joule}) (73)^2 (1 - 1/4)}$$

$$= 0.21 \times 10^{-10} \text{ m} = 0.21 \text{ A}$$

• PROBLEM 1036

An x-ray tube with a copper target is found to be emitting lines other than those due to copper. The K_α line of copper is known to have a wavelength of 1.5405 Å, and the other two K_α lines observed have wavelengths of 0.7092 Å and 1.6578 Å. Identify the impurities.

Solution: According to Moseley's equation for K_α radiation,

$$\frac{1}{\lambda} = R(Z - 1)^2\left(\frac{1}{1^2} - \frac{1}{1^2}\right) .$$

Thus, if λ is the wavelength of CuK_α radiation and λ_1 and λ_2 the wavelengths of the two unknown K_α radiations, then

$$\frac{\lambda_1}{\lambda} = \frac{(Z - 1)^2}{(Z_1 - 1)^2} = \frac{0.7092 \text{ Å}}{1.5405 \text{ Å}} .$$

But for copper $Z = 29$. Therefore

$$Z_1 - 1 = 28\sqrt{1.5405/0.7092} = 41.$$

$Z_1 = 42$, and we know that the impurity is molybdenum. Similarly,

$$Z_2 - 1 = 28\sqrt{1.5405/1.6578} = 27.$$

$Z_2 = 28$, and we know that the impurity is nickel.

• PROBLEM 1037

In an experiment, x-rays of frequency f are scattered by the electrons in a block of paraffin. It is found that the x-rays scattered at an angle of less than 90°, have a wavelength f', greater than f. Interpret this result in terms of a collision of a photon with an electron.

Solution: The collision is shown in the diagram. The photon is scattered through an angle θ, and the electron through an angle φ. The momentum of the photon is given by the de Broglie relationship.

$$p = \frac{h}{\lambda} = \frac{hf}{c} \quad \text{using} \quad \lambda f = c$$

As in all collision problems, the law of conservation of momentum may be applied to this collision. The momentum of the photon-electron system, then must remain constant throughout the collision. Since momentum is a vector quantity, (having both direction and magnitude) we must resolve the momenta of the electron and photon into x and y components. Conservation of momentum can then be applied as follows:

$$\frac{hf}{c} = \frac{hf'}{c}\cos\theta + mv\cos\varphi \text{ (x component)} \qquad (1)$$

$$\frac{hf'}{c}\sin\theta = mv\sin\varphi \quad \text{(y component)} \tag{2}$$

The law of conservation of energy can also be applied to the collision analysis because the collision is elastic. The total energy of the electron-photon system must then remain constant throughout the collision. Or

$$hf + m_0c^2 = hf' + mc^2 \tag{3}$$

where m_0 is the rest mass of the electron. And m is the new relativistic mass $\left(= \frac{m_0}{\sqrt{1 - \frac{v^2}{c^2}}}\right)$.

It incorporates the kinetic energy the electron has, after the collision.

The angle φ can be eliminated by squaring (1) and (2) and adding. Then

$$\left(\frac{hf}{c} - \frac{hf'}{c}\cos\theta\right)^2 = m^2\nu^2\cos^2\varphi$$

$$\frac{h^2f'^2}{c^2}\sin^2\theta = m^2\nu^2\sin^2\varphi$$

$$\frac{h^2}{c^2}\left(f^2 + f'^2 - 2ff'\cos\theta\right) = m^2\nu^2\left(\cos^2\varphi + \sin^2\varphi\right)$$

or

$$h^2\left(f^2 + f'^2 - 2ff'\cos\theta\right) = m^2\nu^2c^2 \tag{4}$$

for $\cos^2\varphi + \sin^2\varphi = 1$

Next the energy equation is squared to obtain

$$\left[h(f - f') + m_0c^2\right]^2 = m^2c^4 \tag{5}$$

Consider now the quantity

$$m^2c^4 - m^2\nu^2c^2 = c^2m^2\left(c^2 - \nu^2\right) \tag{6}$$

We know that

$$m^2 = \frac{m_0^2}{1 = \nu^2/c^2}$$

Thus

$$m^2\left(c^2 - \nu^2\right) = m_0^2c^2$$

and (6) simplifies to $m_0^2c^4$. Therefore by subtracting (4) from (5) we obtain

$$\left[h(f - f') + m_0c^2\right]^2 - h^2\left(f^2 + f'^2 - 2ff'\cos\theta\right) = m^2c^2\left(c^2 - \nu^2\right) = m_0^2c^4 .$$

Simplifying this equation gives the result

$$2hm_0c^2(f - f') - 2h^2ff'(1 - \cos\theta) = 0$$

or

$$1 - \cos\theta = \frac{m_0^2c^2}{h}\,\frac{f - f'}{ff'} \tag{7}$$

Using the relationship $\lambda f = c$, equation (7) is reduced to

$$1 - \cos\theta = \frac{m_0c}{h}(\lambda' - \lambda) \tag{8}$$

This process of scattering of photons is known as the Compton effect, and is a clear indication of an instance in which a wave motion behaves like a particle. Notice that the change in wavelength depends only on the angle of scattering θ and is independent of the wavelength itself. The quantity

$$\lambda_0 = \frac{h}{m_0 c} = 0.0242\text{Å}$$

is known as the Compton wavelength.

• PROBLEM 1038

(a) Establish the numerical relationship between the minimum V frequency ν_m in sec^{-1} of an emitted x-ray and the voltage V applied to an x-ray tube.
(b) What is the minimum voltage which must be applied to the x-ray tube to produce x-rays of wavelength 10^{-8} cm?

Solution. (a) The minimum potential required to boost the speed of the electron between the plates of an x-ray tube, to a value sufficient to excite the target atoms on the screen, is determined by the wavelength of the emitted photons (x-rays). The kinetic energy of the electron should therefore be at least as large as the energy of the outgoing photon.

The electron, when moving between the plates, acquires the kinetic energy

$$KE = eV$$

where V is the voltage across the tuve.

$$KE = V(\text{volts}) \times 1.60 \times 10^{-19} \text{ joule}$$

$$= 1.60 \times 10^{-12} \text{ V erg.}$$

(This could also have been obtained directly from the knowledge that 1 eV is 1.60×10^{-12} erg.) Therefore, the minimum energy of an electron being equivalent to its minimum frequency multiplied by Planck's constant h, we find

$$E = h\nu_m = 1.60 \times 10^{-12} V$$

$$\nu_m = \frac{1.60 \times 10^{-12} s^{-1}}{6.625 \times 10^{-27}}$$

$$\nu_m = 2.41 \times 10^{14} s^{-1}.$$

This is the required relationship between ν_m and V.

(b) A wavelength, λ, of 10^{-8} cm corresponds to a frequency

$$\nu = \frac{c}{\lambda}$$

$$= \frac{3 \times 10^{10}}{10^{-8}} sec^{-1}$$

$$= 3 \times 10^{18}\ \text{sec}^{-1}.$$

In order to produce this frequency, the voltage across the tube must be at least

$$V_{min} = \frac{\nu}{2.41 \times 10^{14} V\cdot s}$$

$$= \frac{3 \times 10^{18}}{2.41 \times 10^{14}} V$$

$$= 12{,}500 \text{ volts.}$$

• **PROBLEM 1039**

At a temperature of 18° C a beam of diffracted monochromatic x-rays is observed at an angle of 150.8° to the incident beam after being diffracted by a crystal with cubic structure. At a temperature of 318°C the corresponding beam makes an angle of 141.6° with the incident beam. What is the mean coefficient of linear expansion of the crystal in the given temperature range?

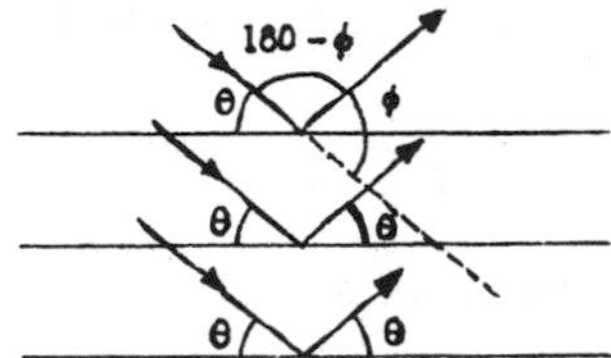

Solution: If a beam of monochromatic x-rays is deviated by an angle ϕ after diffraction from a set of crystal planes, it is seen from the diagram that, if θ is the glancing angle of the x-rays on this set of planes,

$$2\theta + (180 - \phi) = 180° \qquad \text{or} \qquad \theta = \frac{\phi}{2}.$$

When the temperature is 18°C, the appropriate interplanar spacing is d, and the glancing angle for diffraction from this set of planes is 150.8°/2 = 75.4°.

Bragg's Law is

$$m\lambda = d \sin \theta$$

where m is the order number, d is the interplanar spacing, λ is the x-ray wavelength and θ is the angle the incident x-ray beam makes with the atomic plane from which it is reflected (see figure). Thus $2d \sin 75.4° = m\lambda$.

When the temperature is 318°C, the interplanar spacing has increased to d', and the glancing angle has dropped to 141.6°/2 = 70.8°. Thus $2d' \sin 70.8° = m\lambda$, the wavelength and order of diffraction being unchanged. Hence,

$$\frac{d'}{d} = \frac{\sin 75.4°}{\sin 70.8°} = 1.024.$$

But d' = d(1 + α × 300 C deg), where α is the mean coefficient of linear expansion at right angles to the set of planes considered. Since the crystal is cubic, the coefficient of linear expansion is the same in all directions.

$$\therefore \quad 1 + 300 \text{ C deg} \times \alpha = 1.024.$$

$$\therefore \quad \alpha = \frac{0.024}{300 \text{ C deg}} = 8.3 \times 10^{-5} \text{ per C deg.}$$

• PROBLEM 1040

A 100-keV X ray is Compton scattered through an angle of 90°. What is the energy of the X ray after scattering?

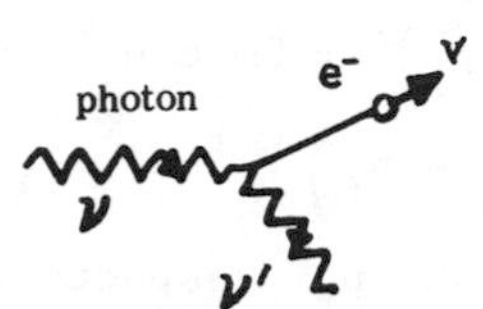

Fig. 1. Compton Effect

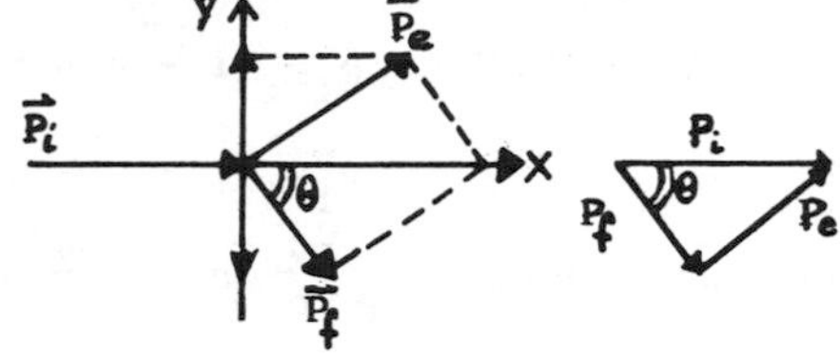

Fig. 2

Solution: When X-rays pass through a crystal, some of the X-rays knock electrons out of the crystal. The scattering of electromagnetic waves (light, X-rays, etc.) by the electrons in solids can be considered to be a collision between a photon of energy $h\nu$ and an electron (Fig. 1). The electron absorbs some of the energy of the incident photon and the scattered photon therefore has less energy and thus a lower frequency ν'. The collision is elastic, hence total energy as well as total momentum is conserved during the collision (Fig. 2). Hence,

$$E_i^{ph} + E_i^{el} = E_f^{ph} + E_f^{el}$$

$$\vec{p}_i^{\,ph} = \vec{p}_f^{\,ph} + \vec{p}_f^{\,el} .$$

The expressions for energies and momenta are

$$p_i = \frac{h\nu}{c} , \ p_f = \frac{h\nu'}{c} ; \quad p_e = \frac{m_e v}{\sqrt{1-\beta^2}}$$

$$E_i^{ph} = p_i c , \ E_f^{ph} = p_f c ; \quad E_i^{el} = m_e c^2 , \ E_f^{el} = \frac{m_e c^2}{\sqrt{1-\beta^2}}$$

where m_e is the rest mass of the electron, $\beta = \frac{v}{c}$. Conservation of momentum is shown schematically in Fig. 2. Using the law of cosines for the triangle in the figure,

$$p_e^2 = p_i^2 + p_f^2 - 2p_i p_f \cos\theta ;$$

adding and subtracting the quantity $2p_i p_f$ on the right hand side, we have

$$p_e^2 = (p_i - p_f)^2 + 2p_i p_f (1 - \cos\theta).$$

The expression for the electron energy is modified to eliminate β from the expression for convenience;

$$\left(E_f^{el}\right)^2 = \frac{m_e^2 c^4}{1 - \beta^2}$$

or

$$\left(E_f^{el}\right)^2 - m_e^2 c^4 = \frac{m_e^2 c^4 \beta^2}{1 - \beta^2} = \left(\frac{m_e v}{\sqrt{1-\beta^2}}\right)^2 c^2$$

therefore $$\left(E_f^{el}\right)^2 = m_e^2c^4 + p_e^2c^2 .$$

From conservation of energy

$$p_ic + m_ec^2 = p_fc + \sqrt{m_e^2c^4 + p_e^2c^2}$$

or

$$\sqrt{m_e^2c^4 + p_e^2c^2} = \left(p_i - p_f\right)c + m_ec^2 .$$

Squaring both sides, we obtain another expression for p_e^2 ;

$$p_e^2 = \left(p_i - p_f\right)^2 + 2m_ec\left(p_i - p_f\right) .$$

Equating the two expressions we obtained for p_e^2 ;

$$\left(p_i - p_f\right)^2 + 2p_ip_f(1 - \cos\theta) = \left(p_i - p_f\right)^2 + 2m_ec\left(p_i - p_f\right)$$

or

$$p_ip_f(1 - \cos\theta) = m_ec\left(p_i - p_f\right) .$$

Now, we substitute $\frac{h\nu}{c}$ and $\frac{h\nu'}{c}$ for p_i and p_f respectively;

$$\nu\nu'(1 - \cos\theta) = \frac{m_ec^2}{h}(\nu - \nu') ,$$

and divide both sides by $\nu\nu'$ to obtain Compton's equation

$$\frac{1}{h\nu'} = \frac{1}{h\nu} + \frac{1}{m_ec^2}(1 - \cos\theta)$$

Using the values $m_ec^2 = 511$ keV and $\cos 90^\circ = 0$, we find

$$\frac{1}{h\nu'} = \frac{1}{100\text{ keV}} + \frac{1}{511\text{ keV}}$$

or

$$h\nu' = \frac{(100\text{ keV}) \times (511\text{ keV})}{(100\text{ keV}) + (511\text{ keV})} = \frac{51100}{611}\text{ keV} = 84\text{ keV}$$

The electron, of course, carries off the remainder of the incident energy:

$$KE = 100\text{ keV} - 84\text{ keV} = 16\text{ keV}$$

• PROBLEM 1041

X-radiation of wavelength 0.8560 Å is scattered from a carbon target. Calculate the change in wavelength produced for radiation scattered at 90°, and the energy and direction of the corresponding recoil electrons. (See figure).

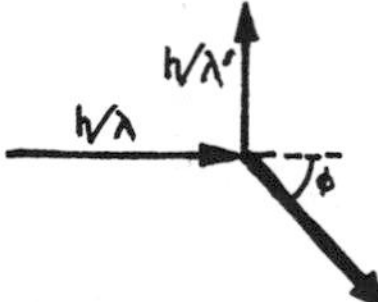

Solution: In a Compton collision, an x-ray is incident on an unbound (free) target electron, and a collision takes place. After the collision, the electron is scattered, but it is observed that the scattered x-ray has a wavelength, λ', which is different than the wavelength, λ, of the incident x-ray. (Because of the observed particulate behavior of the x-rays, this experiment gave further support to the photon theory of light). The resulting change in wavelength is given by the formula

$$\lambda' - \lambda = 2\frac{h}{mc}\sin^2\frac{\theta}{2} ,$$

where θ is the angle of scatter, m is the electron rest mass, c is the speed of light and h is Planck's constant. If θ is 90°,

$$\lambda' - \lambda = \frac{h}{mc} = \frac{6.625 \times 10^{-34} \text{ J·s}}{9.108 \times 10^{-31}\text{kg} \times 2.998 \times 10^{8}\text{m·s}^{-1}}$$

$$= 0.0242 \text{ Å}.$$

The energy given to the electron is therefore equal to the loss of energy of the photon.

$$E = h\frac{c}{\lambda} - h\frac{c}{\lambda'} = 6.625 \times 10^{34}\text{J·s} \times 2.998 \times 10^{8}\text{m·s}^{-1} \times \left(\frac{10^{10}}{0.8560\text{m}} - \frac{10^{10}}{0.8802\text{m}}\right)$$

$$= 6.377 \times 10^{-17} \text{ J}.$$

In order that momentum may be conserved in the collision (see figure), the electron must have a momentum in the initial direction of h/λ and a momentum of h/λ' at right angles to this. The tangent of the angle ϕ at which the electron is scattered is the ratio of the latter momentum to the former, since these momenta are equal to the components of the electron's momentum in the two mutually perpendicular directions. Hence

$$\tan \phi = \frac{h/\lambda'}{h/\lambda} = \frac{\lambda}{\lambda'} = \frac{0.8560 \text{ Å}}{0.8802 \text{ Å}} = 0.9725.$$

$$\phi = 44^\circ 12' .$$

CHAPTER 36

NUCLEAR ENERGY/REACTIONS

• PROBLEM 1042

What is the binding energy of the lithium nucleus?

Solution: The binding energy is the energy released when a nucleus is formed; it is what holds the nucleus together. We would have to add this energy again in order to break up the nucleus. The source of this energy, released when the nucleus was destroyed, is in the form of a mass loss in the nucleons. Therefore, by comparing the "standard" mass of all the nucleus, (protons and neutrons) and the actual mass of the nucleus, we can calculate the mass defect - the amount of mass converted into energy in the formation of the atom. Einstein's theory tells us that mass and energy are equivalent. Since there are 931 Mev (energy) per 1 amu (mass) we can claulate the energy released in the destruction of the nucleus.

In the isotope Li_3^7 there are 3 protons and 4 neutrons (7-3). So

$$z = 3, \quad A = 7, \; M = 7.01822$$

where z is the atomic number, A the mass number, and M the atomic mass of Lithium.

Therefore, mass defect

$= [3(1.00814) + 4(1.00898) - 7.01822]$

$= [(3.02442 + 4.03592) - 7.01822]$ amu

$= [7.06034 - 7.01822]$

$= 0.04212$ amu

Converting mass to energy:binding energy in Mev

$= 931 \times$ mass defect

$= 931 \times 0.04212$ in amu

$= 39.2$ Mev

• PROBLEM 1043

What is the total binding energy and the binding energy per nucleon of the nucleus of $_{24}Cr^{52}$ which has a mass of 51.95699 amu?

Solution: The nucleus of $_{24}Cr^{52}$ is made up of 24 protons and 52 - 24 = 28 neutrons. The combined mass of the particles making up the Cr nucleus is thus

$$\Sigma m = 24 \times 1.00819 + 28 \times 1.00893 = 52.4460 \text{ amu, where}$$

we used the facts that the mass of a proton is 1.00819 amu, and that the neutron mass is 1.00893 amu. The mass defect or the difference in the mass of the constituent particles of $_{24}Cr^{52}$ and an atom of $_{24}C^{52}$, is 52.44660 - 51.95699 = 0.48961 amu. The binding energy is, from Einstein's mass-energy relation,

$$E = (\text{mass defect})\ c^2$$

$$E = (.48961 \text{ amu})\left(9 \times 10^{16} m^2/s^2\right)$$

Since

$$1 \text{ amu} = 1.67 \times 10^{-27} \text{ kg}$$

$$E = (.48961 \text{ amu})\left(1.67 \times 10^{-27} \text{ amu/kg}\right)\left(9 \times 10^{16} \text{ m}^2/s^2\right)$$

$$E = 7.36 \times 10^{-11} \text{ Joules}$$

But

$$1 \text{ eV} = 1.602 \times 10^{-19} \text{ Joules}$$

and

$$E = \frac{\left(7.36 \times 10^{-11} \text{ Joules}\right)}{\left(1.602 \times 10^{-19} \text{ Joules/eV}\right)} = 4.6 \times 10^{8} \text{ eV}$$

The binding energy per nucleon is thus

$$\frac{4.6 \times 10^{8} \text{ eV}}{52} = 8.9 \times 10^{6} \text{ eV}.$$

• PROBLEM 1044

A nucleus of mass M emits a γ ray of energy $\vec{E}_\gamma$. The nucleus was initially at rest. What is its recoil energy after the emission?

Solution: From momentum conservation we have

$$0 = p_\gamma + p_{nuc}$$

In addition we know that $E = h\upsilon = hc/\lambda$ and by the deBroglie relation $p = h/\lambda$. Therefore we have $E = pc$ and $p_\gamma = E_\gamma/c$. Hence,

$$\left|p_{nuc}\right| = \frac{E_\gamma}{c}.$$

The recoil energy is given by

$$K_{nuc} = \tfrac{1}{2} Mv^2 = \frac{M^2v^2}{2M} = \frac{(Mv)^2}{2M} = \frac{p_{nuc}^2}{2M} = \frac{E_\gamma^2}{2Mc^2}$$

The last equality involves substituting E_γ/c for p_{nuc}. We have assumed that the recoil velocity may be treated as nonrelativistic.

• PROBLEM 1045

If one atom of hydrogen (mass 1.673×10^{-27} kilogram) unites with one atom of lithium (mass 11.648×10^{-27} kilogram) to form two helium atoms (mass 6.646×10^{-27} kilogram each), how much kinetic energy in joules is released in this nuclear reaction? How many atoms of hydrogen would have to be transformed to generate 9.8 joules (9.8 joules of work are done when 1 kilogram of mass is raised 1 meter)?

Solution: The energy released in this reaction manifests itself as a loss of mass in the final product. This means that there must be a difference between the mass of the reactants and products, and this mass difference appears as energy.

The mass of the products, one atom of hydrogen and one atom of lithium, is equal to the mass of two helium atoms plus the mass difference.

$$1 \text{ hydrogen atom} + 1 \text{ lithium atom}$$

$$= 2 \text{ helium atoms} + \Delta M$$

$$1.673 \times 10^{-27} \text{ kg} + 11.648 \times 10^{-27} \text{ kg}$$

$$= 2\left(6.646 \times 10^{-27}\right) \text{kg} + \Delta M$$

Whence

$$\Delta M = 0.029 \times 10^{-27} \text{ kg}$$

From Einstein's relation $\Delta E = \Delta Mc^2$ we find

$$\Delta E = 0.029 \times 10^{-27} \text{ kg} \times \left(3 \times 10^8 \text{ m/sec}\right)^2$$

$$= 0.26 \times 10^{-9} \text{ joules}$$

The number of hydrogen atoms required for 9.8 joules is

$$N = \frac{9.8 \text{ joules}}{0.26 \times 10^{-9} \text{ joules}}$$

$$= 38 \times 10^9 \text{ atoms approximately.}$$

• PROBLEM 1046

The masses of ${}_1H^1$ and ${}_2He^4$ atoms are 1.00813 amu and 4.00386 amu, respectively. How much hydrogen must be converted to helium in the sun per second if the solar constant is 1.35 $kW\cdot m^{-2}$ and the earth is 1.5×10^8 km from the sun?

Solution: The energy falling on a 1-m^2 area at the distance of the earth from the sun, in 1 second, is 1.35×10^3 J. The total energy radiated from the sun is thus

$$E = \left(1.35 \times 10^3 \text{ J}\cdot\text{s}^{-1}\right)4\pi r^2$$

where $4\pi r^2$ is the area of a sphere centered at the sun, with radius r equal to the separation distance of the earth and sun.

$$E = 1.35 \times 10^3 \text{ J}\cdot\text{m}^{-2} \times 4\pi \times 1.5^2 \times 10^{22} \text{ m}^2$$

$$= 3.82 \times 10^{26} \text{ J.}$$

If four atoms of hydrogen combine to give one atom of helium, energy is released. This follows because the rest mass energy of 4 hydrogen atoms is greater than that of 1 helium atom. From Einstein's mass-energy relation, this excess rest mass energy must be released as energy every time $4\,{}_1H^1$ atoms combine to form 1 ${}_2He^4$ atom. The energy released is then

$$E' = \left((4 \times 1.00813 - 4.00386)\,\text{amu}\right)c^2$$

But 1 amu = 1.66×10^{-27}kg, whence

$$E' = \left((4.03252 - 4.00386)\,\text{amu}\right)\left(1.66 \times 10^{-27}\text{kg/amu}\right) \times \left(9 \times 10^{16}\ \text{m}^2/\text{s}^2\right)$$

$$E' = (.02866)\left(14.94 \times 10^{-11}\ \text{J}\right)$$

$$E' = 4.27 \times 10^{-12}\ \text{J}$$

Hence, for every 4 ${}_1H^1$ atoms used, an amount of energy equal to E' is released.

The number of hydrogen atoms converted per second to produce the energy radiated by the sun is thus $n = 4 \times (E/E')$, and the mass of hydrogen converted per second is

$$M = n \times (\text{mass of 1 } {}_1H^1 \text{ atom})$$

Noting that 1 ${}_1H^1$ atom has a mass

$$m = 1.00813\ \text{amu}$$

we find $$M = n \times m = \frac{4\,E\,m}{E'}$$

$$M = \frac{(4)(3.82 \times 10^{26}\ \text{J})(1.00813\ \text{amu})}{(4.27 \times 10^{-12}\ \text{J})}$$

Using the fact that

$$1\ \text{amu} = 1.66 \times 10^{-27}\ \text{kg}$$

$$M = \frac{(4)(3.82 \times 10^{26}\ \text{J})(1.00813\ \text{amu})(1.66 \times 10^{-27}\ \text{kg/amu})}{(4.27 \times 10^{-12}\text{J})}$$

$$M = 5.99 \times 10^{11}\ \text{kg}$$

• PROBLEM 1047

How much energy is released in the fission of 1 kg of U^{235}?

Solution. Fission can be induced by adding energy to the nucleus in the form of the binding energy of a captured neutron. A typical fission reaction involving U^{235} is

$$U^{235} + n \rightarrow Ba^{139} + Kr^{95} + 2n.$$

Though the total number of protons and neutrons remains the same, the mass diminishes. The missing mass, arising from neutrons decaying into protons and electrons, is converted into energy.

The amount of mass-energy that is converted to kinetic energy in the fission process is approximately 200 MeV per nucleus. (This is only about 0.1 percent of the total mass-energy of a uranium nucleus; the other 99.9 percent remains in the masses of the neutrons and protons and is therefore not available for conversion into kinetic energy.) In 1 kg of U^{235}, there are approximately 2.5×10^{24} atoms. Therefore, the total energy release is

$$\begin{aligned} \varepsilon &= (200 \text{ MeV}) \times \left(2.5 \times 10^{24}\right) \\ &= 5.0 \times 10^{26} \text{ MeV} \\ &= \left(5.0 \times 10^{26} \text{ MeV}\right) \times \left(1.6 \times 10^{-6} \text{ ergs/MeV}\right) \\ &= 8.0 \times 10^{20} \text{ ergs.} \end{aligned}$$

We can convert this into another popular unit by noting that the explosion of 1 ton of TNT releases approximately 4.1×10^{16} ergs. Thus, the fission of 1 kg of U^{235} releases an amount of energy

$$\varepsilon = \frac{8.0 \times 10^{20} \text{ ergs}}{4.1 \times 10^{16} \text{ ergs/ton TNT}} \cong 20 \text{ kilotons TNT.}$$

This is approximately the size of the original atomic bomb of 1945.

• PROBLEM 1048

How much energy would be released if deuterium could be made to form helium in a fusion reaction?

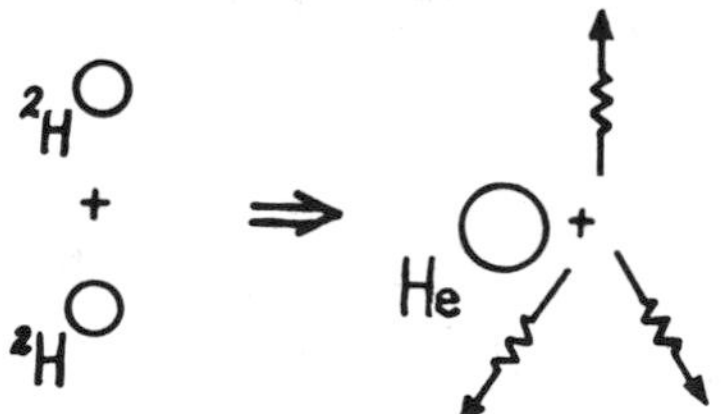

Solution: The difference in the mass of the helium nucleus, and the two deuterium nuclei, is the mass defect, Δm.

$$m_{He} - 2m_{2H} = \Delta m$$

Noting that 1 atomic mass unit (a.m.u.) equals 1.66×10^{-27} kg, we may express all masses in terms of a.m.u.'s.

$$m_{2H} = 2.01419 \text{ amu}$$

$$m_{He} = 4.00278 \text{ amu}$$

Thus

$$\Delta m = 0.0256 \text{ amu.}$$

This mass loss resulting from the fusion of the two deuterium nuclei into a helium nucleus, is converted into energy and released during the fusion process.

$$E = \Delta mc^2 = (.0256 \text{ amu}) \times \left(3 \times 10^8 \frac{\text{meter}}{\text{sec}}\right)^2$$

$$= (.0256 \text{ amu})\left(1.66 \times 10^{-27}\frac{\text{kg}}{\text{amu}}\right)\left(9 \times 10^{16} \frac{m^2}{s^2}\right)$$

(The unit of Δm was changed to kilograms to be compatible with the MKS system being used.) Hence

$$E = \Delta mc^2 = .383 \times 10^{-11} \text{ Joules}$$

• PROBLEM 1049

Calculate the minimum photon energy (in electron volts) required to create a real electron-positron pair. Express all numbers to four significant figures.

Solution: The rest mass-energy E of an electron or positron is

$$E = m_e c^2 = \left(9.110 \times 10^{-31}\text{kg}\right)\left(2.998 \times 10^8 \text{m/s}\right)^2 = 8.188 \times 10^{-14}\text{J}$$

If the created pair of particles possess no kinetic energy, then by the conservation of energy, the photon energy E_γ must be equal to the sum of the rest mass-energies of the two particles:

$$E_\gamma = 2E = 1.638 \times 10^{-13}\text{J}$$

Since $1 \text{ eV} = 1.602 \times 10^{-19}\text{J}$, the required energy may be written

$$E_\gamma = \frac{1.638 \times 10^{-13}\cancel{\text{J}}}{1.602 \times 10^{-19}\cancel{\text{J}}/\text{eV}} = 1.022 \times 10^6\text{eV}$$

This energy is the minimum or threshold energy required for creation of the electron-positron pair. Photons with this much energy are from the x-ray or gamma-ray region of the electromagnetic spectrum.

Note however, that although we have satisfied the conservation of energy in our analysis, we have not satisfied the conservation of momentum. The photon has an initial momentum, but the electron and positron have no final momentum, since we have required them to be at rest. Hence, the energy of the incoming photon must be greater than 1.022×10^6eV, since, in any practical experiment, some agent must carry away momentum (and energy) at the end of the reaction. This is why pair production cannot occur in a vacuum.

• PROBLEM 1050

The two protons in a helium nucleus are separated by about 2×10^{-15} m. Calculate the electrostatic potential energy and thus estimate the fractional change in the mass of helium.

Solution: The electrostatic potential energy of a system of two charges separated in space by a distance R is

$$V = K\frac{q_1 q_2}{R}$$, where K is a constant having the value $9 \times 10^9 \frac{N\cdot m^2}{c^2}$.

For two protons separated by 2×10^{-15} m, the potential energy is

$$V = \frac{\left(9 \times 10^9 \frac{N\cdot m^2}{c^2}\right)(1.6\times 10^{-19}\ c)^2}{(2 \times 10^{-15}\ m)}$$

$$V = 1.15 \times 10^{-13}\ \text{Joules}$$

By $E = mc^2$, this energy is equivalent to a mass

$$\Delta m = \frac{1.15 \times 10^{-13}\ J}{9 \times 10^{16}\ \frac{m^2}{s^2}}$$

$$\Delta m = 1.28 \times 10^{-30}\ kg$$

Δm represents a mass increase of the helium atom due to electrostatic potential energy.

In calculating the mass of a helium atom, we may neglect the mass of the electrons, because they have a small mass when compared with the nuclear components of the atom (protons and neutrons). Hence, the mass of the helium atom is approximately equal to the mass of the helium nucleus.

The helium nucleus consists of two protons and two neutrons of total mass

$$m = (2 \times 1.672 \times 10^{-27} + 2 \times 1.675 \times 10^{-27})\text{kg}$$

$$= 6.69 \times 10^{-27}\ kg$$

The fractional change in mass of the helium nucleus is

$$\frac{\Delta m}{m} = \frac{1.28 \times 10^{-30}}{6.69 \times 10^{-27}} = 1.9 \times 10^{-4}.$$

• PROBLEM 1051

Find the Q value for the disintegration $_{60}Nd^{144} \rightarrow {}_2He^4 + {}_{58}Ce^{140}$.

Solution: Q represents the amount of energy released as a result of the conversion of mass to energy. To find the amount of mass converted, find the difference in the amount of mass of the reactants and the products.

From the tables of isotope masses, in atomic mass units,

$_2He^4$	= 4.00387	$_{60}Nd^{144}$	= 143.95556
$_{58}Ce^{140}$	= 139.94977	Products	= 143.95364
	143.95364	Δm	= 0.00192

The atomic mass unit is $\frac{1}{12}$ of the mass of a C^{12} atom and is equal to 1.66×10^{-27} kg. To find Δm in kg, it has to be multiplied by one amu.

$$Q = \Delta mc^2 = 2.87 \times 10^{-18} \text{ joule}$$

$$= (0.00192 \text{ amu}) \times \left(1.66 \times 10^{-27} \text{ kg/amu}\right) \times \left(3.0 \times 10^8 \text{ m/sec}\right)^2.$$

Since very small energies are involved, when dealing with atoms, energies are expressed in electron volts. Converting joules to MeV,

$$Q = \frac{2.87 \times 10^{-16} \text{ joule}}{1.6 \times 10^{-16} \text{ joule/eV}} = 1.79 \text{ eV}.$$

• PROBLEM 1052

If a nuclear reactor is designed to deliver 1 MW. of heat energy continuously, how many fission events must occur each second to sustain this power level? How much uranium-235 would be consumed each year?

Solution: It is known that the amount of energy released per fission event is about 200 MeV. In joules, this energy becomes

$$E = \left(2.0 \times 10^8 \text{ eV}\right) \times \left(1.6 \times 10^{-19} \text{ J/eV}\right) = 3.2 \times 10^{-11} \text{ J}.$$

The total number, n, of nuclei undergoing fission each second to produce 1 MW = 10^6 W of power is

$$n = \frac{\text{Power}}{\text{Energy per fission}} = \frac{1.0 \times 10^6 \text{ J/sec}}{3.2 \times 10^{-11} \text{ J/nuclei}}$$

$$= 3.1 \times 10^{16} \text{ nuclei/sec}.$$

Since

$$1 \text{ year} = 365 \text{ days/year} \times 24 \text{ hrs/day} \times 60 \text{ min/hr} \times 60 \text{ sec/min}$$

$$\simeq 3.1 \times 10^7 \text{ sec.},$$

the total number N of uranium-235 atoms consumed in one year is

$$N = \left(3.1 \times 10^7 \text{ sec/year}\right) \times \left(3.1 \times 10^{16} \text{ nuclei/sec}\right)$$

$$= 9.6 \times 10^{23} \text{ nuclei/year}.$$

The mass m of one uranium-235 atom is approximately

$$m = \left(2.35 \times 10^2 \text{ nucleons}\right) \times (\text{average mass of one nucleon})$$

$$= \left(2.35 \times 10^2 \text{ nucleons}\right) \times \left(1.67 \times 10^{-27} \text{ kg/nucleon}\right)$$

$$= 3.92 \times 10^{-25} \text{ kg.}$$

The total mass M of uranium fuel consumed in one year is

$$M = mn = \left(3.92 \times 10^{-25} \text{ kg/atom}\right) \times \left(9.6 \times 10^{23} \text{ atoms/year}\right)$$

$$= 3.8 \times 10^{-1} \text{ kg/year.}$$

• PROBLEM 1053

Consider the decay of the positively charged pion, π^+. Pion → muon + neutrino. The energy equivalent of the mass of the pion is about 140 MeV, and the muon and neutrino produced in the decay have rest masses corresponding to energies of 106 MeV and zero, respectively. How much kinetic energy is available to the particles created in the decay?

Solution: The difference of the energy equivalents of the masses of the pion and its decay products is

$$140 \text{ MeV} - 106 \text{ MeV} = 34 \text{ MeV.}$$

Let us consider the frame of reference in which the pion was at rest. The total energy of the system is given by the energy equivalent of the pion mass. After the decay, the total mass of the decay products is less than the pion mass. The principle of conservation of energy requires this mass difference to be transformed into another form of energy, hence the two daughter particles (muon and neutrino) share it as kinetic energy.

• PROBLEM 1054

At a particular time, N_0 atoms of a radioactive substance with a disintegration constant λ_1 are separated chemically from all other members of the radioactive series. At what time thereafter is the number of radioactive atoms of the daughter product, with disintegration constant λ_2, a maximum?

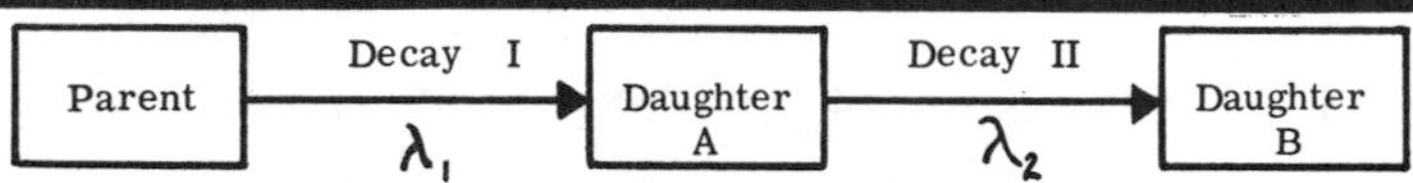

Solution: The figure shows the situation described. At $t = 0$, we isolate N_0 atoms of a radioactive material. This is the parent substance. As time progresses the parent undergoes decay I, and becomes daughter product A. Similarly, daughter A decays into daughter B. Our problem is to find out at what time the number of atoms of daughter A is a maximum.

Let us first look at decay I. It is observed experimentally that the rate of decay of any radioactive element is proportional to the number of atoms available for decay at a particular time t. Hence,

$$\frac{dN(t)}{dt} \propto N(t)$$

This can be written as an equation if we insert a constant of proportionality, λ. In the case of radioactive decay, λ is called the disintegration constant. Hence,

$$\frac{dN(t)}{dt} = -\lambda N(t)$$

where the minus sign indicates that the number of radioactive atoms of the parent element, N(t), is decreasing with time. Applying this equation to the decay of the parent to daughter product A, we obtain

$$\frac{dN_1(t)}{dt} = -\lambda_1 N_1(t) \qquad (1)$$

where λ_1 is the disintegration constant for decay I, and $N_1(t)$ is the number of parent atoms at any time t. Now, daughter product A gains radioactive atoms from decay process I, but also loses atoms due to its own decay. Hence, the time rate of change of atoms of daughter product A is given by

$$\frac{dN_2(t)}{dt} = -\frac{dN_1(t)}{dt} - \lambda_2 N_2(t) \qquad (2)$$

where λ_2 is the disintegration constant for decay II, and $N_2(t)$ is the number of atoms of daughter A at time t. (Note that we use $-dN_1(t)/dt$ in (2) because the number of atoms gained by daughter A from decay I is greater than zero, but $dN_1(t)/dt < 0$, from (1).) Using (1) in (2)

$$\frac{dN_2(t)}{dt} = \lambda_1 N_1(t) - \lambda_2 N_2(t) \qquad (3)$$

Solving the differential equation in (1) will give us $N_1(t)$

$$\frac{dN_1(t)}{N_1(t)} = -\lambda_1 \, dt$$

or $$\int_{N_0}^{N_1(t)} \frac{dN_1(t)}{N_1(t)} = -\lambda_1 \int_0^t dt$$

where we assume that

$$N_1(t) = N_0 \qquad \text{at } t = 0$$

$$N_1(t) = N_1(t) \qquad \text{at } t = t.$$

Then $$\ell_n N_1(t) \Big|_{N_0}^{N_1(t)} = -\lambda_1 t$$

and $\ell_n \frac{N_1(t)}{N_0} = -\lambda_1 t$

Taking the expotential of both sides of this equation, we obtain

$$N_1(t) = N_0 e^{-\lambda_1 t} \qquad (4)$$

Inserting (4) in (3)

$$\frac{dN_2(t)}{dt} = \lambda_1 N_0 e^{-\lambda_1 t} - \lambda_2 N_2(t)$$

or $\frac{dN_2(t)}{dt} + \lambda_2 N_2(t) = \lambda_1 N_0 e^{-\lambda_1 t}$

Multiplying both sides by $e^{\lambda_2 t}$

$$e^{\lambda_2 t} \frac{dN_2(t)}{dt} + \lambda_2 e^{\lambda_2 t} N_2(t) = \lambda_1 N_0 e^{(\lambda_2 - \lambda_1)t}$$

or $\frac{d}{dt} \left[e^{\lambda_2 t} N_2(t)\right] = \lambda_1 N_0 e^{(\lambda_2 - \lambda_1)t}$

Solving this differential equation

$$d \left[e^{\lambda_2 t} N_2(t)\right] = \lambda_1 N_0 e^{(\lambda_2 - \lambda_1)t} dt$$

and $\int d \left[e^{\lambda_2 t} N_2(t)\right] = \lambda_1 N_0 \int e^{(\lambda_2 - \lambda_1)t} dt$

$$e^{\lambda_2 t} N_2(t) = \frac{\lambda_1 N_0}{\lambda_2 - \lambda_1} \int e^{(\lambda_2 - \lambda_1)t} (\lambda_2 - \lambda_1) dt$$

$$e^{\lambda_2 t} N_2(t) = \frac{\lambda_1 N_0}{\lambda_2 - \lambda_1} e^{(\lambda_2 - \lambda_1)t} + C \qquad (5)$$

where C is a constant of integration. Noting that, at t = 0, there are no daughter atoms of type A, we can write

$$N_2(0) = 0$$

and $N_2(0) = \frac{\lambda_1 N_0}{\lambda_2 - \lambda_1} + C = 0$

Hence, $C = -\frac{\lambda_1 N_0}{\lambda_2 - \lambda_1} \qquad (6)$

Inserting (6) in (5)

$$e^{\lambda_2 t} N_2(t) = \frac{\lambda_1 N_0}{\lambda_2 - \lambda_1} \left[e^{(\lambda_2 - \lambda_1)t} - 1\right]$$

Solving for $N_2(t)$

$$N_2(t) = \frac{\lambda_1 N_0}{\lambda_2 - \lambda_1}\left(e^{-\lambda_1 t} - e^{-\lambda_2 t}\right)$$

This gives us the number of daughter atoms of type A as a function of time . This is a maximum when

$$\frac{dN_2(t)}{dt} = 0$$

Then $$\frac{dN_2(t)}{dt} = \frac{\lambda_1 N_0}{\lambda_2 - \lambda_1}\left(-\lambda_1 e^{-\lambda_1 t} + \lambda_2 e^{-\lambda_2 t}\right) = 0$$

This equation is zero when

$$\lambda_1 e^{-\lambda_1 t} = \lambda_2 e^{-\lambda_2 t}$$

or $$\frac{\lambda_1}{\lambda_2} = e^{-(\lambda_2 - \lambda_1)t}$$

Solving for t

$$\ell_n \frac{\lambda_1}{\lambda_2} = -(\lambda_2 - \lambda_1)t = (\lambda_1 - \lambda_2)t$$

or $$t = \frac{1}{\lambda_1 - \lambda_2}\ \ell_n \frac{\lambda_1}{\lambda_2} \qquad (7)$$

Hence, $N_2(t)$ is a maximum at the time given by (7).

• PROBLEM 1055

Analyze the reaction where two neutral pions are created from the annihilation of a neutron-antineutron pair. Assume that the neutron and its twin were initially at rest (see figure).

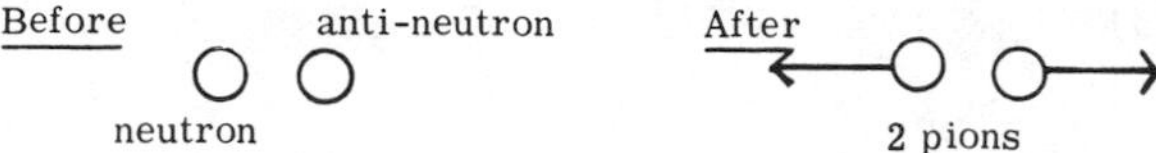

Solution: We wish to analyze the annihilation of a neutron-antineutron pair. We may relate the energies and momenta of the products of the annihilation to the energies and momenta of the neutron-antineutron pair by the laws of conservation of energy and momentun.

Initially, the neutron and antineutron are at rest, and therefore, have only rest energy. Furthermore, the neutron and antineutron have equal masses, and

$$2m_n c^2 = E_{\pi_1} + E_{\pi_2} \qquad (1)$$

where "n", "π_1", "π_2" refer to the neutron and 2 pions respectively.

Applying conservation of momentum,

$$0 = \vec{p}_{\pi_1} + \vec{p}_{\pi_2}\ , \qquad (2)$$

since the neutron and antineutron are initially at rest. But, relativistically,

$$\vec{p} = \frac{m_0\vec{v}}{\sqrt{1 - v^2/c^2}}$$

where $\vec{v}$ is the velocity of the particle whose momentum we wish to measure, and m_0 is its rest mass. By (2)

$$\frac{m_{0\pi_1}\vec{v}_1}{\sqrt{1 - v_1^2/c^2}} = \frac{-m_{0\pi_2}\vec{v}_2}{\sqrt{1 - v_2^2/c^2}} \tag{3}$$

But $m_{0\pi_1} = m_{0\pi_2}$, and

$$\frac{\vec{v}_1}{\sqrt{1 - v_1^2/c^2}} = \frac{-\vec{v}_2}{\sqrt{1 - v_2^2/c^2}} \tag{4}$$

Taking the dot product of each side of (4) with itself, we have (since $\vec{v} \cdot \vec{v} = (v)(v) \cos 0^\circ = v^2$)

$$\frac{v_1^2}{\left(1 - v_1^2/c^2\right)} = \frac{v_2^2}{\left(1 - v_2^2/c^2\right)}$$

$$v_1^2 = \frac{v_2^2\left(1 - v_1^2/c^2\right)}{\left(1 - v_2^2/c^2\right)}$$

$$v_1^2\left(1 - v_2^2/c^2\right) = v_2^2\left(1 - v_1^2/c^2\right)$$

$$v_1^2\left(c^2 - v_2^2\right) = v_2^2\left(c^2 - v_1^2\right)$$

$$v_1^2c^2 - v_1^2v_2^2 = v_2^2c^2 - v_1^2v_2^2$$

$$v_1^2c^2 = v_2^2c^2$$

$$v_1^2 = v_2^2 \tag{5}$$

Therefore, the magnitudes of $\vec{v}_1$ and $\vec{v}_2$ have the same value, say v. Using (2) and (3)

$$0 = \frac{m_{0\pi_1}\vec{v}}{\sqrt{1 - v^2/c^2}} + \frac{m_{0\pi_2}\vec{v}}{\sqrt{1 - v^2/c^2}} \tag{6}$$

Hence the momenta of the 2 pions are equal and opposite. From (1), we may calculate the kinetic energies of π_1 (T_{π_1}) and π_2 (T_{π_2}). Noting that the energy of any particle equals the sum of its rest energy and kinetic energy, we may write

$$E = m_0c^2 + T\ .$$

With (1)

$$2m_nc^2 = m_{\pi_1}c^2 + T_{\pi_1} + m_{\pi_2}c^2 + T_{\pi_2}$$

But $m_{\pi_1} = m_{\pi_2}$ and

$$2m_n c^2 - 2m_\pi c^2 = T_{\pi_1} + T_{\pi_2} \tag{7}$$

The mass-energy of the two neutrons is

$$E_n = 2m_n c^2 = (2)\left(1.67 \times 10^{-27}\text{kg}\right)\left(3 \times 10^8 \text{m/s}\right)^2 = 3 \times 10^{-10}\text{J}$$

The rest mass-energy of the two neutral pions is

$$E_\pi = 2m_\pi c^2 = (2)\left(2.4 \times 10^{-28}\text{kg}\right)\left(3 \times 10^8 \text{m/s}\right)^2 = 4.3 \times 10^{-11}\text{J}$$

Therefore

$$T_{\pi_1} + T_{\pi_2} = 3 \times 10^{-10}\text{J} - 0.43 \times 10^{-10}\text{J}$$

$$T_{\pi_1} + T_{\pi_2} = 2.57 \times 10^{-10}\text{J} \tag{8}$$

To find how this energy is divided among the pions, note that

$$E = \frac{m_0 c^2}{\sqrt{1 - v^2/c^2}}$$

where v is the velocity of the particle whose energy we wish to measure. Hence

$$E_{\pi_1} = \frac{m_{0\pi_1} c^2}{\sqrt{1 - v_1^2/c^2}}$$

$$E_{\pi_2} = \frac{m_{0\pi_2} c^2}{\sqrt{1 - v_2^2/c^2}}$$

But $v_1 = v_2$, and $m_{\pi_1} = m_{\pi_2}$. Whence

$$E_{\pi_1} = E_{\pi_2}$$

or

$$m_{\pi_1} c^2 + T_{\pi_1} = m_{\pi_2} c^2 + T_{\pi_2}$$

and

$$T_{\pi_1} = T_{\pi_2} .$$

Using (8),

$$T_{\pi_1} = T_{\pi_2} = 1.29 \times 10^{-10}\text{J} .$$

• PROBLEM 1056

In the reaction ${}_5B^{11} + {}_2He^4 \rightarrow {}_7N^{14} + {}_0n^1$, the masses of the boron and nitrogen atoms and the α-particle are 11.01280 amu, 14.00752 amu, and 4.00387 amu, respectively. If the incident α-particle had 5.250 MeV of kinetic energy and the resultant neutron and nitrogen atom had energies of 3.260 MeV and 2.139 MeV, respectively, what is the mass of the neutron?

Solution: We may apply the principle of conservation of total energy to this reaction. The total energy of the reactants is the sum of their rest mass energies (given by Einstein's mass-energy relation,

$E_{rest} = mc^2$) and their kinetic energies. Hence,

$$E_{react} = m_B c^2 + m_\alpha c^2 + T_\alpha \tag{1}$$

where B and α stand for the boron and α particle respectively. m stands for rest mass, and T for kinetic energy. (Note that the boron is initially at rest). Similarly, the total energy of the products is

$$E_{prod} = m_N c^2 + m_n c^2 + T_N + T_n \tag{2}$$

where N and n stand for the nitrogen and neutron, respectively. Then, equating (1) and (2) by the principle of conservation of total energy

$$m_B c^2 + m_\alpha c^2 + T_\alpha = m_N c^2 + m_n c^2 + T_N + T_n$$

Solving for m_n

$$\frac{\left(m_B + m_\alpha - m_N\right)c^2 + \left(T_\alpha - T_N - T_n\right)}{c^2} = m_n$$

$$m_n = (m_B + m_\alpha - m_N) + \frac{\left(T_\alpha - T_N - T_n\right)}{c^2}$$

Substituting the given data

$$m_n = (11.01280 + 4.00387 - 14.00752) \text{ amu} + (5.250 - 2.139 - 3.260) \frac{\text{MeV}}{c^2} \tag{3}$$

Now,

$$1 \text{ MeV} = 10^6 \text{ eV} = \left(10^6\right)\left(1.602 \times 10^{-19} \text{ J/eV}\right)$$

$$1 \text{ MeV} = 1.602 \times 10^{-13} \text{ J}$$

and

$$\frac{1 \text{ MeV}}{c^2} = \frac{1.602 \times 10^{-13} \text{ J}}{9 \times 10^{16} \text{ m}^2/\text{s}^2} = 1.78 \times 10^{-30} \text{ kg}$$

Since 1 kg = 6.024×10^{26} amu

$$\frac{1 \text{ MeV}}{c^2} = \left(1.78 \times 10^{-30} \text{ kg}\right)\left(6.024 \times 10^{26} \frac{\text{amu}}{\text{kg}}\right)$$

$$\frac{1 \text{ MeV}}{c^2} = 1.072272 \times 10^{-3} \text{ amu}$$

Then, (3) becomes

$$m_n = 1.00915 \text{ amu} - \left(.149)(1.072272 \times 10^{-3} \text{ amu}\right)$$

$$m_n = 1.00899 \text{ amu}$$

• PROBLEM 1057

Calculate the mass of the light isotope of helium from the following reaction, which has a Q-value of 3.945 MeV:

$${}_3Li^6 + {}_1H^1 = {}_2He^4 + {}_2He^3.$$

The masses in amu of ${}_1H^1$, ${}_2He^4$, and ${}_3Li^6$ are 1.00813, 4.00386, and 6.01692, respectively.

Solution: In the reaction 3.945 MeV of energy is released. By Einstein's mass energy relation

$$E = mc^2,$$

this energy is equivalent to a mass whose value is:

$$m = \frac{E}{c^2} = \frac{3.945 \times 10^6 \text{ eV}}{9 \times 10^{16} \text{ m}^2/\text{s}^2}$$

Since $\quad 1 \text{ eV} = 1.6 \times 10^{-19}$ Joules

$$m = \frac{(3.945 \times 10^6 \text{ eV})(1.6 \times 10^{-19} \text{ Joules/eV})}{9 \times 10^{16} \text{ m}^2/\text{s}^2}$$

$$m = 7.013 \times 10^{-30} \text{ kg}$$

Converting this to atomic mass units by noting that

$$1 \text{ kg} = 6.024 \times 10^{26} \text{ amu}$$

we obtain

$$m = (7.013 \times 10^{-30} \text{ kg})(6.024 \times 10^{26} \text{ amu/kg})$$

$$m = 4.23 \times 10^{-3} \text{ amu}$$

$$m = .00423 \text{ amu}$$

This must be the difference in mass between reactants and products, or

$$m = m_{react.} - m_{prod.} \qquad (1)$$

The sum of the masses of the initial particles is

$$m_{react.} = 1.00813 + 6.01692 = 7.02505 \text{ amu} \qquad (2)$$

But

$$m_{prod.} = m_\alpha + m_{He} \qquad (3)$$

Using (3) in (1)

$$m = m_{react.} - m_\alpha - m_{He}$$

Hence, $\quad m_{He} = m_{react.} - m_\alpha - m$

Using (2)

$$m_{He} = 7.02505 \text{ amu} - 4.00386 \text{ amu} - .00423 \text{ amu}$$

$$m_{He} = 3.01696 \text{ amu}$$

This must be the mass of an atom of the light isotope of helium.

• PROBLEM 1058

A deuterium atom moving with kinetic energy of 0.81×10^{-13} J collides with a similar atom at rest. A nuclear inelastic reaction takes place and a neutron is observed to be emitted at right angles to the original direction of motion. Determine its kinetic energy, given that the other product of the reaction is an atom of the light isotope of helium and that the rest masses of a neutron, a deuterium atom, and a light helium atom are 1.6747, 3.3441, and 5.0076, respectively, in units of 10^{-27} kg.

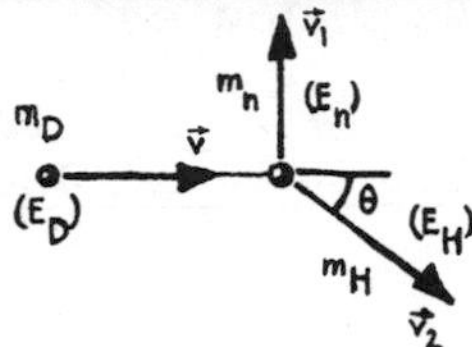

Solution: Before doing this problem, we must see if it is necessary to use relativistic considerations. The total relativistic energy of a particle is the sum of its rest mass energy and its relativistic kinetic energy, or

$$E = m_0c^2 + T$$

where m_0 is the particle's rest mass. Hence,

$$T = E - m_0c^2$$

But $$E = m_0c^2/\sqrt{1 - v^2/c^2}$$

where v is the particle's velocity. Therefore,

$$T = m_0c^2\left(\frac{1}{\sqrt{1 - v^2/c^2}} - 1\right)$$

Solving for v/c,

$$\frac{T}{m_0c^2} + 1 = \frac{1}{\sqrt{1 - v^2/c^2}}$$

$$1 - v^2/c^2 = \left(\frac{m_0c^2}{T + m_0c^2}\right)^2$$

$$\frac{v}{c} = \sqrt{1 - \left(\frac{m_0c^2}{T + m_0c^2}\right)^2}$$

For the incident deuterium atom,

$$\frac{v}{c} = \sqrt{1 - \left(\frac{(3.3441 \times 10^{-27}\text{ kg} \times 9 \times 10^{16}\text{ m}^2/\text{s}^2)}{.81 \times 10^{-13}\text{ J} + (3.3441 \times 10^{-27}\text{ kg}\times 9\times 10^{16}\text{m}^2/\text{s}^2)}\right)^2}$$

or $\frac{v}{c} = 5.382 \times 10^{-4}$

Since this is very small, the problem is extremely non-relativistic. We now proceed with a classical analysis of the collision.

Looking at the figure, we may write the following 2 equations from the principle of conservation of momentum.

$$m_D v = m_H v_2 \cos\theta \qquad (1)$$

$$m_n v_1 = m_H v_2 \sin\theta \qquad (2)$$

Since the collision is inelastic, we must account for the fact that energy, Q, is gained or lost in the reaction. Hence, the principle of conservation of energy yields

$$\tfrac{1}{2} m_D v^2 + Q = \tfrac{1}{2} m_n v_1^2 + \tfrac{1}{2} m_H v_2^2 \qquad (3)$$

If $Q > 0$, energy is released in the reaction, and is absorbed as kinetic energy by the reaction products. Now we solve for v_1 in terms of Q.

First, square (1) and (2), then add

$$m_D^2 v^2 = m_H^2 v_2^2 \cos^2\theta$$

$$+ \quad m_n^2 v_1^2 = m_H^2 v_2^2 \sin^2\theta$$

$$m_D^2 v^2 + m_n^2 v_1^2 = m_H^2 v_2^2$$

or $$m_H v_2^2 = \frac{m_D^2 v^2 + m_n^2 v_1^2}{m_H} \qquad (4)$$

From (3) $$m_H v_2^2 = 2Q + m_D v^2 - m_n v_1^2 \qquad (5)$$

Combining (4) and (5)

$$2Q + m_D v^2 - m_n v_1^2 = \frac{m_D^2 v^2 + m_n^2 v_1^2}{m_H}$$

or $$2Qm_H + m_D m_H v^2 - m_n m_H v_1^2 = m_D^2 v^2 + m_n^2 v_1^2$$

$$\left(m_n^2 + m_n m_H\right) v_1^2 = 2Qm_H + \left(m_D m_H - m_D^2\right) v^2$$

Finally, $$v_1^2 = \frac{2Q\, m_H + m_D\left(m_H - m_D\right)v^2}{m_n\left(m_n + m_H\right)}$$

and $$\tfrac{1}{2} m_n v_1^2 = \frac{Q\, m_H + \tfrac{1}{2} m_D v^2 \left(m_H - m_D\right)}{\left(m_n + m_H\right)} \qquad (6)$$

This is the neutron kinetic energy.

Now, note that in (6), we have an unknown variable, namely, Q.

But, we can obtain Q by noting that the only

mechanism which can be responsible for Q is a difference in mass between the products and reactants of the collision. This follows from Einstein's mass-energy relation, since a mass difference Δm is equivalent to an energy

$$E = (\Delta m)c^2 \tag{7}$$

Now, the mass entering the reaction is the sum of the masses of the incident and target deuterons, or

$$2\ m_D \tag{8}$$

The sum of the masses of the products is

$$m_n + m_H$$

Hence, $\Delta m = m_n + m_H - 2\ m_D$

$$\Delta m = [1.6747 + 5.0076 - 2(3.3441)] \times 10^{-27}\ kg$$

$$\Delta m = 59 \times 10^{-31}\ kg$$

Now, $Q = E = (59 \times 10^{-31}\ kg)(9 \times 10^{16}\ m^2/s^2)$

$$Q = 5.31 \times 10^{-13}\ J \tag{9}$$

Inserting (9) and the given data in (6), we obtain

$$\tfrac{1}{2}\ m_n v_1^2 =$$

$$\frac{(5.31\times10^{-13}J)(5.0076\times10^{-27}kg)+(.81\times10^{-13}J)(5.0076-3.3441)\times10^{-27}Kg)}{\left[(1.6747 + 5.0076) \times 10^{-27}\ kg\right]}$$

$$= \frac{26.5904 \times 10^{-40} + 1.3474 \times 10^{-40}}{6.6823 \times 10^{-27}}\ J$$

$$= 4.1809 \times 10^{-13}\ J$$

• PROBLEM 1059

Given the rest masses of the various particles and nuclei involved in the fission

$${}_0n^1 + {}_{92}U^{235} \rightarrow {}_{56}Ba^{141} + {}_{36}Kr^{92} + 3\,{}_0n^1\ ,$$

calculate the energy released in ergs and electron volts.

Solution: The nuclear masses will be quoted in atomic mass units or u. The atomic mass unit is 1/12 of the mass of a ${}_6C^{12}$ atom. The reaction is

$${}_0n^1 + {}_{92}U^{235} \rightarrow {}_{56}Ba^{141} + {}_{36}Kr^{92} + 3\,{}_0n^1$$

The masses of the reacting particles are

Mass of neutron, ${}_0n^1$ = 1.0087 u

Mass of ${}_{92}U^{235}$ = <u>235.0439 u</u>

Combined mass of reactants = 236.0526 u

The masses of the products are

Mass of $_{56}Ba^{141}$ = 140.9139 u

Mass of $_{36}Kr^{92}$ = 91.8973 u

Mass of three neutrons, $3\,_0n^1$ = 3.0261 u

Combined mass of products = 235.8373 u

The mass of the reactants is greater than the mass of the products by 0.2153 u. Hence, if all this mass is converted to energy, we have, by Einstein's mass energy relation, an equivalent amount of energy of

$$E = mc^2 = (0.2153\ u)c^2$$

But, 1u. = 1.66×10^{-24}gm

$$E = (0.2153\ u)\left(1.66 \times 10^{-24}\text{gm/u}\right)\left(9 \times 10^{20}\text{cm}^2/\text{s}^2\right)$$

$$= 3.27 \times 10^{-4}\text{erg}$$

But $1\ \text{erg} = \dfrac{1}{1.6 \times 10^{-12}}\ \text{eV}$ and

$$E = \frac{3.21 \times 10^{-4}\text{erg}}{1.6 \times 10^{-12}\text{erg/eV}}$$

$$= 2.01 \times 10^8\ \text{eV} \qquad (1)$$

The energy released in the fission of one uranium 235 nucleus is 201 MeV. Conventional fuels and conventional explosives release their energy by means of chemical reactions. The energy liberated in a chemical reaction is due to a readjustment of the behavior of electrons in atoms and molecules. A good idea of its order of magnitude may be obtained by comparing the E calculated above with the energy needed to remove an electron from a hydrogen atom(the ionization energy of hydrogen).

Ionization energy of hydrogen = 2.18×10^{-11}erg

$$= \frac{2.18 \times 10^{-11}}{1.60 \times 10^{-12}}\ \text{eV}$$

$$= 13.6\ \text{eV} \qquad (2)$$

Comparing equations (1) and (2) we see that the fission of one nucleus of uranium 235 releases about ten million times as much energy as a chemical reaction between one or two atoms. One pound of uranium releases as much energy as several thousand tons of a conventional fuel.

• PROBLEM 1060

When lithium is bombarded by 10-MeV deuterons, neutrons are observed to emerge at right angles to the direction of the incident beam. Calculate the energy of these neutrons and the energy and angle of recoil of the associated beryllium atom. Relevant masses in amu are: $_0n^1$ = 1.00893, $_3Li^7$ = 7.01784, $_1H^2$ = 2.01472, and $_4Be^8$ = 8.00776.

Solution: Since the deuteron's kinetic energy is much smaller than its rest mass energy (≈ 1876 MeV), the collision is non-relativistic. The equation governing the reaction is

$$_3Li^7 + {_1H^2} = {_0n^1} + {_4Be^8}\ .$$

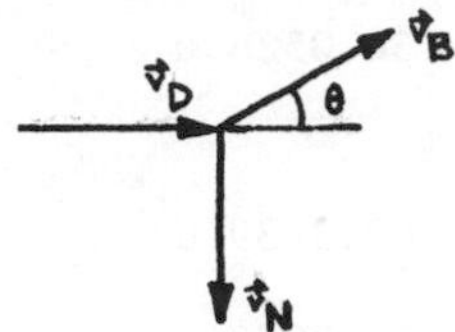

The sum of the masses of the initial atoms is 9.03256 amu, and of the final atoms 9.01669 amu. The difference in mass, 0.01587 amu, appears, by Einstein's mass-energy relation, as

$$E = (.01587\ \text{amu})c^2$$

amount of kinetic energy. Hence,

$$E = (.01587\ \text{amu})\left(1.66 \times 10^{-27}\text{kg}\right)\left(9 \times 10^{16}\ \text{m}^2/\text{s}^2\right)$$

$$E = 14.77\ \text{MeV}$$

Since total energy (that is, rest mass energy plus kinetic energy) is conserved in the reaction, the final products have a combined kinetic energy of

$$(10 + 14.77)\text{MeV} = 24.77\ \text{MeV}\ .$$

When we remember that the momentum of a particle p is related to its kinetic energy E by the relation $p = \sqrt{2mE}$, then the principle of conservation of momentum, applied in the initial direction and at right angles to it, gives the following equations, in self-explanatory notation: (see figure)

$$\sqrt{2m_D E_D} = \sqrt{2m_B E_B}\ \cos\theta \qquad (1)$$

and

$$\sqrt{2m_N E_N} = \sqrt{2m_B E_B}\ \sin\theta \qquad (2)$$

$$2m_D E_D + 2m_N E_N = 2m_B E_B \qquad (3)$$

It was also shown above that

$$E_N + E_B = 24.77\ \text{MeV}. \qquad (4)$$

Solving (4) for E_N

$$E_N = 24.77\ \text{MeV} - E_B \qquad (5)$$

Using (5) in (3)

$$2m_D E_D + 2m_N(24.77\ \text{MeV}) - 2m_N E_B = 2m_B E_B$$

Solving for E_B

$$E_B\left(m_B + m_N\right) = m_D E_D + m_N(24.77\ \text{MeV})$$

or

$$E_B = \frac{m_D E_D + m_N(24.77\ \text{MeV})}{m_B + m_N}$$

whence

$$E_B = \frac{(2.01472\ \text{amu})(10\ \text{MeV}) + (1.00893\ \text{amu})(24.77\ \text{MeV})}{8.00776\ \text{amu} + 1.00893\ \text{amu}}$$

$$E_B = \frac{45.13840\ \text{amu} \cdot \text{MeV}}{9.01669\ \text{amu}} = 5.01\ \text{MeV}$$

Using this in (5)

$$E_n = 24.77\ \text{MeV} - 5.01\ \text{MeV} = 19.76\ \text{MeV}$$

Further, we obtain for the angle of recoil (using (1) and (4)

$$\tan\theta = \sqrt{\frac{m_N E_N}{m_D E_C}} = \sqrt{\frac{(1.00893\text{ amu})(19.76\text{ MeV})}{(2.01472\text{ amu})(10\text{ MeV})}}$$

$$= \sqrt{.9895} = .9948$$

Hence, $\theta \approx 44^\circ 50'$.

• PROBLEM 1061

Verify that the fusion of four protons releases approximately 25 MeV for the proton-proton fusion cycle.

Solution: The fusion of two hydrogen atoms produces one deuterium atom

$$^1_1H + {}^1_1H \rightarrow {}^2_1H + e^+ + \nu_e. \qquad (1)$$

The fusion of deuterium with hydrogen produces the helium atom

$$^1_1H + {}^2_1H \rightarrow {}^3_2He + \gamma. \qquad (2)$$

Finally, the fusion of helium with helium gives

$$^3_2He + {}^3_2He \rightarrow {}^4_2He + {}^1_1H + {}^1_1H. \qquad (3)$$

The chain of events (1), (2) and (3) is known as the proton-proton cycle, which is one of the schemes offered to describe the conversion of hydrogen into helium in stars.

If we multiply equations (1) and (2) by two and sum the resulting equations and (3), we get

$$2{}^1_1H + 2{}^1_1H \longrightarrow 2{}^2_1H + 2e^+ + 2\nu_e$$

$$2{}^1_1H + 2{}^2_1H \longrightarrow 2{}^3_2He + 2\gamma$$

$$^3_2He + {}^3_2He \longrightarrow {}^4_2He + {}^1_1H + {}^1_1H$$

$$6{}^1_1H + 2{}^2_1H + 2{}^3_2He \longrightarrow 2{}^1_1H + 2{}^2_1H + 2{}^3_2He + {}^4_2He + 2e^+ + 2\nu_e + 2\gamma$$

or $4{}^1_1H \longrightarrow {}^4_2He + 2e^+ + 2\nu_e + 2\gamma$

Before the reaction the total nuclear mass is:

$$4 \times (\text{Atomic mass of hydrogen}) = 4 \times 1.0073\text{ amu}$$
$$= 4.0292\text{ amu}$$

After reaction the total mass is

Atomic mass of ^4He + 2 x (mass of positron)

$$= (4.0015 + 2 \times 0.0011)\text{ amu} = 4.0026\text{ amu}$$

The energy released in the fusion reaction is equivalent to the difference in mass:

$$4.0292 - 4.0026 = 0.0266\text{ amu}$$

$$= \left(931\ \frac{\text{MeV}}{\text{amu}}\right)(0.0266\text{ amu}) = 25\text{ MeV}.$$

CHAPTER 37

SPECIAL ADVANCED PROBLEMS AND APPLICATIONS

BASIC KINETICS AND KINEMATICS

• PROBLEM 1062

In the two pulley systems shown in Fig. 1a, determine the velocity and acceleration of block 3 when blocks 1 and 2 have the velocities and acceleration shown.

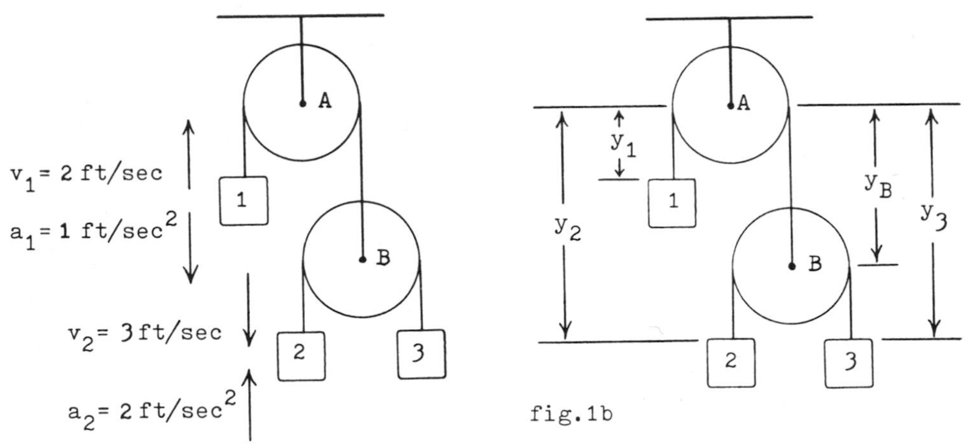

fig.1a

fig.1b

Solution: Figure 1b defines the positions relative to the fixed pulley A needed to solve solve this problem.

The lengths of the cord are assumed to be constant and the section of cord over the pulleys to remain constant, thus yielding the following constraint equations

$$y_1 + y_B = K_1, \tag{a}$$

$$(y_2 - y_B) + (y_3 - y_B) = K_2,$$

or $$y_2 + y_3 - 2y_B = K_2. \tag{b}$$

Differentiating each equation (a) and (b) twice yields:

$$\dot{y}_1 + \dot{y}_B = 0 \tag{c}$$

$$\ddot{y}_1 + \ddot{y}_B = 0 \quad \text{(d)}$$

$$\dot{y}_2 + \dot{y}_3 - 2\dot{y}_B = 0 \quad \text{(e)}$$

$$\ddot{y}_2 + \ddot{y}_3 - 2\ddot{y}_B = 0 \quad \text{(f)}$$

These equations lead directly to the desired solutions upon substitution of the information from Figure 1a. If it is supposed that down is positive, then

$$v_1 = \dot{y}_1 = -2 \text{ ft/sec}, \qquad v_2 = \dot{y}_2 = 3 \text{ ft/sec},$$

(g)

$$a_1 = \ddot{y}_1 = 1 \text{ ft/sec}^2, \qquad a_2 = \ddot{y}_2 = -2 \text{ ft/sec}^2.$$

First solve (c) and (d) to find the motion of pulley B.

$$-2 \text{ ft/sec} + \dot{y}_B = 0$$

$$\dot{y}_B = 2 \text{ ft/sec} \quad \text{(h)}$$

$$1 \text{ ft/sec}^2 + \ddot{y}_B = 0$$

$$\ddot{y}_B = -1 \text{ ft/sec}^2. \quad \text{(i)}$$

Now using (g), (h) and (i) in equations (e) and (f), it is possible to obtain the desired results:

$$3 \text{ ft/sec} + \dot{y}_3 - 2\,(2 \text{ ft/sec}) = 0$$

$$\dot{y}_3 = 1 \text{ ft/sec}$$

$$-2 \text{ ft/sec}^2 + \ddot{y}_3 - 2\,(-1 \text{ ft/sec}^2) = 0$$

$$\ddot{y}_3 = 0$$

Thus, block 3 is moving down with a constant velocity

$$v_3 = 1 \text{ ft/sec}.$$

• PROBLEM 1063

A braking device in a rifle is designed to reduce recoil. It consists of a piston attached to the barrel. The piston moves in a cylinder filled with oil. When the shot is fired the barrel and the piston recoil at an initial velocity V_0. The oil under pressure passes through tiny holes in the piston causing the piston and the barrel to decelerate at a rate proportional to their velocity $a = -kv$. Express (a) v in terms of t, (b) x in terms of t, (c) v in terms of x. Draw the corresponding motion curves.

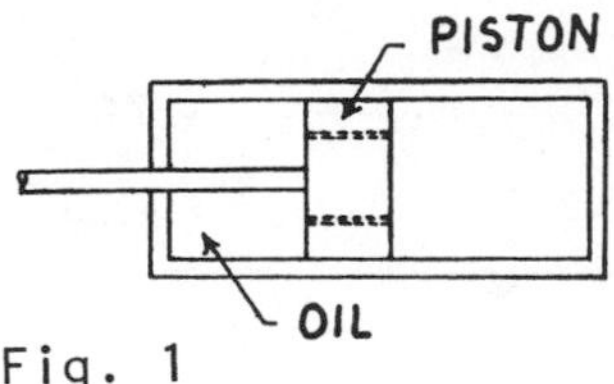

Fig. 1

Solution: (a) The basic definition of acceleration is

$$a = \frac{dv}{dt} \quad . \tag{a}$$

Substituting the expression given for the acceleration yields

$$- kv = \frac{dv}{dt} \quad . \tag{b}$$

Rearranging to separate variables yields

$$- k\, dt = \frac{dv}{v} \quad . \tag{c}$$

Now it is possible to integrate equation (c) to get

$$- k \int_0^t dt = \int_{v_0}^{v} \frac{dv}{v}$$

$$- kt = \ln \frac{v}{v_0} \quad . \tag{d}$$

If antilogs of equation (d) are taken, we arrive at the desired form

$$v = v_0\, e^{-kt} \tag{e}$$

This curve is shown in Figure 2.

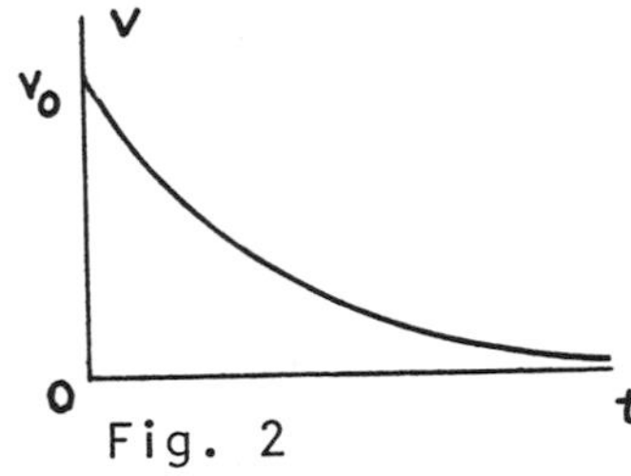

Fig. 2

(b) Again, starting with a basic definition, this time for v, we have

$$v = \frac{dx}{dt} \tag{f}$$

Substitution of the expression (e) into (f) yields

$$v_0\, e^{-kt} = \frac{dx}{dt} \quad ,$$

$$v_0 e^{-kt} dt = dx. \tag{g}$$

Integrating (g)

$$v_0 \int_0^t e^{-kt} dt = \int_0^x dx ,$$

$$-\frac{v_0}{k} e^{-kt} \Big|_0^t = x,$$

$$-\frac{v_0}{k} (e^{-kt} - e^0) = x,$$

$$x = \frac{v_0}{k} (1 - e^{-kt}). \tag{h}$$

This curve is shown in Figure 3.

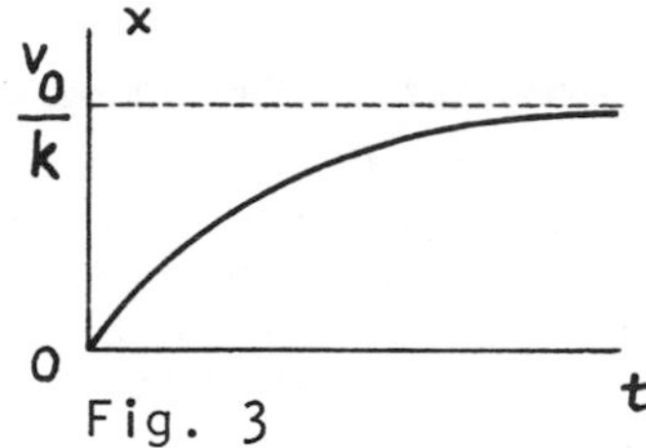

Fig. 3

(c) Part c may be done in two ways:

Using the chain rule for differentials, equation (a) may be rewritten

$$a = \frac{dv}{dt} = \frac{dx}{dt}\frac{dv}{dx} = v\frac{dv}{dx} . \tag{i}$$

Substituting $a = -kv$ in equation (i), we get

$$-kv = v\frac{dv}{dx}$$

or
$$\frac{dv}{dx} = -k,$$

$$dv = -k\, dx.$$

Integrating to solve yields

$$v - v_0 = -kx$$

or
$$v = v_0 - kx.$$

As an alternate method, equations (e) and (h) can be combined. From (e) we know

$$e^{-kt} = \frac{v}{v_0} .$$

Substituting for the exponential in (h) yields

$$x = \frac{v_0}{k}\left(1 - \frac{v}{v_0}\right)$$

or $kx = v_0 - v$

or $v = v_0 - kx.$

This curve is illustrated in Figure 4.

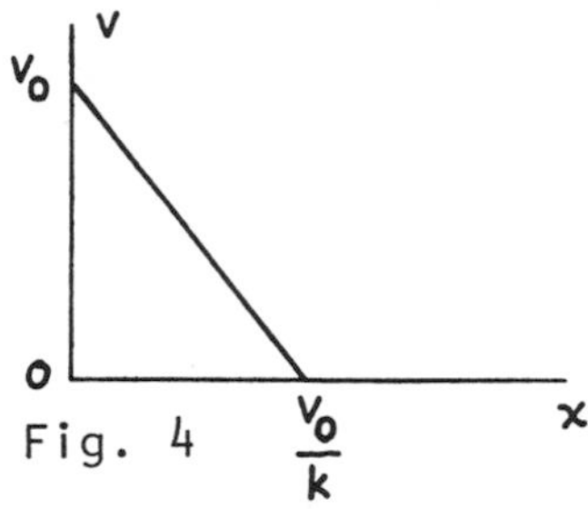

Fig. 4

• PROBLEM 1064

Two blocks, A and B, are attached by a cord wrapped around a frictionless, massless pulley, C. The coefficient of friction between each block and the horizontal platform is 0.3. Block A weighs 10 lb, block B weighs 20 lb. If the platform rotates about the vertical axis shown, determine the angular speed at which the blocks start to slide radially.

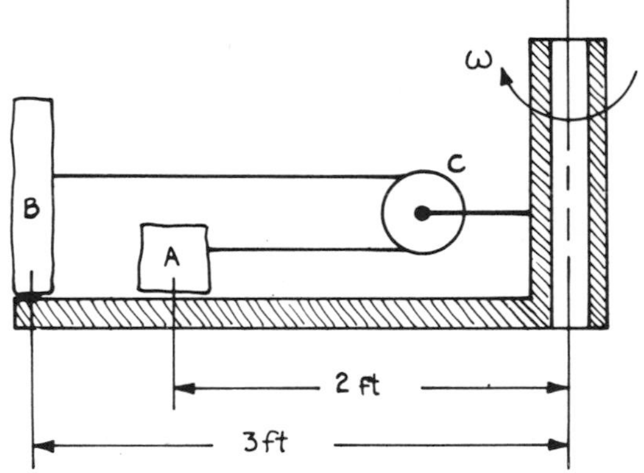

Solution: The two blocks will start sliding radially when the centrifugal force on B is sufficient to overcome (a) the force of friction between block B and the table and (b) the tension in the cord which is equal to the centrifugal force on block A plus the force of friction between block A and the table. Using the formula for centrifugal force:

$$F_C = \frac{m\ v^2}{r} = \frac{W\ v^2}{gr} = \frac{W\,\omega^2\,r^2}{gr} = \frac{W\ \omega^2\ r}{g}$$

and for friction: $F_f = \mu\ W$,

where W is the weight of a block, ω is the angular velocity, r the radius, g = 32 ft/sec ^{2}, the acceleration due to gravity, and μ the coefficient of static friction, we can write the desired equation as:

$$\frac{W_B\ \omega^2\ r_B}{g} = \mu\ W_B + \mu\ W_A + \frac{W_A\,\omega^2\,r_A}{g}$$

where the subscripts A and B refer to the two blocks.

$$\frac{W_B\ \omega^2\ r_B}{g} - \frac{W_A\ \omega^2\ r_A}{g} = \mu\ \left(W_A + W_B\right)$$

$$\frac{\omega^2\left(W_B\ r_B - W_A\ r_A\right)}{g} = \mu\ \left(W_A + W_B\right)$$

$$\omega^2 = \frac{\mu\ g\ \left(W_A + W_B\right)}{W_B\ r_B - W_A\ r_A}$$

$$\omega = \sqrt{\frac{\mu\ g\left(W_A + W_B\right)}{W_B\ r_B - W_A\ r_A}}\ .$$

Substituting the numerical values, yields

$$\omega = \sqrt{\frac{.3\ \times\ 32\ (10\ +\ 20)}{20\ \times\ 3\ -\ 10\ \times\ 2}} = \sqrt{7.2} \doteq 2.68 \text{ radians/sec.}$$

ENERGY METHODS

• PROBLEM 1065

A slender homogeneous bar, shown in Figure 1, is 4 ft long and weighs 1.2 lb. A spring is attached to it as shown, 3 ft from the lower end which is hinged. When the bar is in a vertical position the spring is compressed 0.12 ft. The bar is released from rest. What should the spring constant be if the bar comes to rest when it just reaches the horizontal position, Figure 2?

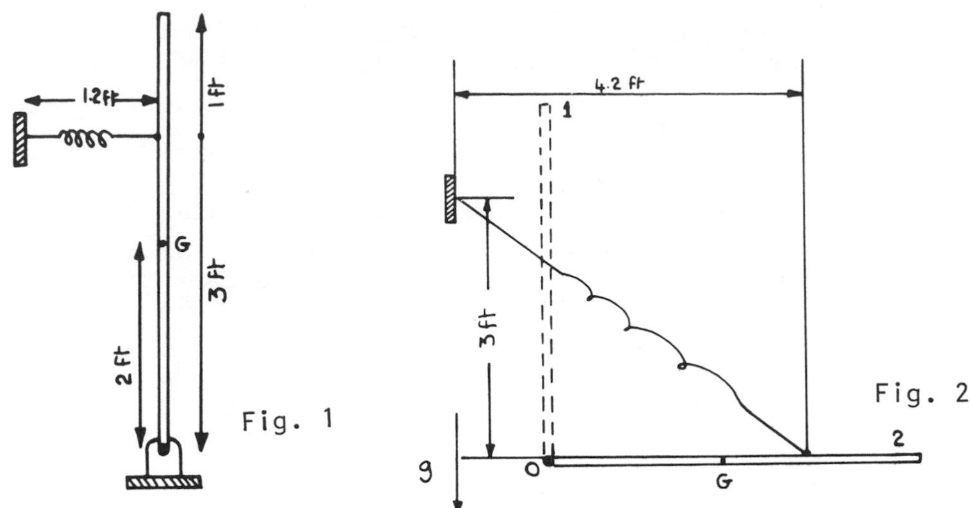

Solution: The system is conservative since only spring and gravity forces are acting, and if the hinge is assumed to be frictionless. We therefore use the principle of conservation of mechanical energy, i.e.,

$$(KE)_1 + (PE)_1 = (KE)_2 + (PE)_2$$

(Bar in vertical position, 1) (Bar in horizontal position, 2.)

Further, since the bar is at rest in both positions, the above equation reduces to

$$(PE)_1 = (PE)_2 \qquad (1)$$

The potential energy of the system is the sum of that of the spring and the gravitational potential energy. Potential energy of a spring is $\frac{1}{2}K\delta^2$ where K is the spring constant and δ its extension or compression. In position 1, $\delta_1 = 0.12$ ft. Thus the free length of the spring is 1.2 + 0.12 = 1.32 ft. In position 2, the length of the spring is $(4.2^2 + 3^2)^{1/2} = 5.16$ ft. Thus $\delta_2 = 5.16 - 1.32 = 3.84$ ft. The gravitational potential energy of a mass m is mgh where h is the height of its center of gravity above the datum. Let us assume the datum to be the horizontal plane passing through the hinge at O. Thus the total potential energies in the two positions are:

$$(PE)_1 = \frac{1}{2} K (0.12)^2 + (1.2)(2)$$
$$= 0.0072 K + 2.4 \text{ ft-lb}$$

$$(PE)_2 = \frac{1}{2} K (3.84)^2 + (1.2)(0)$$
$$= 7.378 K \text{ ft-lb.}$$

Substituting these values into equation (1) yields

$$0.0072 K + 2.4 = 7.378 K$$

or $$K = 0.3256 \text{ lb/ft.}$$

Note that this is not the equilibrium position. The bar will oscillate. The bottom position will be an amplitude extreme, where the bar is momentarily at rest. To consider the equilibrium position we need to use force equilibrium.

• PROBLEM 1066

A child of mass m sits in a swing of negligible mass suspended by a rope of length ℓ. Assume that the dimensions of the child are negligible compared with ℓ. His father pulls the child back until the rope makes an angle of one radian with the vertical, then pushes with a force F = mg along the arc of the circle, releasing at the vertical.

a) How high up will the swing go?

b) How long did the father push?

Compare this with the time needed for the swing to reach the vertical position with no push.

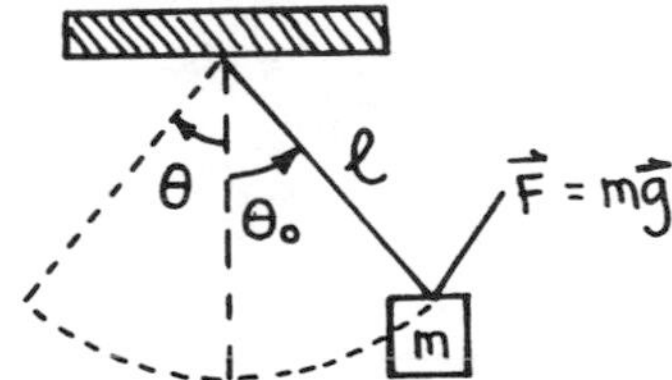

Solution: The father does work in pushing the swing. The work done increases the total energy of the swing and child as the swing moves from its initial position, θ_0 = 1 radian, to the vertical position where the father stops pushing. From that point on, total energy of the swing and child remains constant.

Work done by the father is found from

$$W = \int \vec{F} \cdot d\vec{r} = \int F\, dr \cos\theta \tag{1}$$

where r is the distance along the path.

$$W = \int_0^{\ell\theta_0} mg \cos(0°)\, dr = mg\ell\theta_0 \,. \tag{2}$$

(a) Now we can use conservation of energy to find how high the swing goes. (Let the potential of the swing and child be O at the vertical position where the father lets go.)

$$(\text{PE at } \theta_0) + W = \text{PE at } \theta = E_{total} = \text{constant} \quad (3)$$

$$mg(\ell - \ell\cos\theta_0) + mg\ell\theta_0 = mg(\ell - \ell\cos\theta)$$

$$mg\ell\ (1 - \cos\theta_0 + \theta_0) = mg\ell\ (1 - \cos\theta)$$

$$1 - 0.54 + 1 = 1 - \cos\theta$$

$$\cos\theta = 0.46$$

$$\theta = 63° \text{ above the horizon.}$$

b) We need to find the tangential acceleration of the velocity of the swing at the bottom of its arc, which can be found by a second application of the conservation of energy principle as follows:

$$PE_{\text{at }\theta} + W = KE_{\text{at bottom}} = E_{\text{total}} \tag{4}$$

$$mg\ell\ (1 - \cos\theta) + mg\ell\theta_0 = \frac{1}{2}\ mv^2$$

$$mg\ell\ (1.46) + mg\ell = \frac{1}{2}\ mv^2$$

$$v^2 = 2\ g\ell\ (2.46) = 4.92\ g\ell \tag{5}$$

Application of Newton's Law allows us to find the tangential acceleration, a_T.

$$\Sigma F_T = ma_T$$

$$mg + mg\sin\theta_0 = ma_T \tag{6}$$

But $mg\sin\theta_0$, the component of gravity in the tangential direction, does not stay constant. It gets smaller as the angle decreases. Thus, the tangential acceleration is not constant. We can obtain an approximate solution by integrating the gravity force between O and θ_0, and using that equivalent force.

$$\int_0^{\theta_0} mg\sin\theta\ d\theta = -\ mg\cos\theta\Big|_0^{\theta_0 = 1\text{ rad}}$$

$$= [-\ 0.54 + 1]\ mg$$

$$= 0.46\ mg \tag{7}$$

Substituting this value for $mg\sin\theta_0$ in Equation (6) yields

$$mg + 0.46\ mg = ma_T$$

$$a_T = 1.46\ g.$$

Now to find how long the father pushed write

$$a_T = \frac{dv}{dt} = 1.46\ g$$

$$\int_0^V dV = 1.46\, g \int_0^t dt$$

$$t = \frac{v}{1.46\, g}.$$

Using the value of v from Equation (5) yields

$$t = \frac{\sqrt{4.92\, g\ell}}{1.46\, g}$$

$$t = 3.37 \sqrt{\frac{\ell}{g}}\ .$$

The force decelerating the child will be the gravity force. This force will be of the magnitude given in equation (7). Writing F = ma,

$$0.46\, mg = ma$$

$$a = 0.46\, g.$$

The time will again be given by

$$t = \frac{v}{a} = \frac{v}{0.46\, g}. \qquad (8)$$

If there is no push, conservation of energy yields a velocity of $\sqrt{2\, g\ell\,(1 - \cos\theta_0)}$. Substituting this in equation (8) yields

$$t = \frac{\sqrt{2\, g\ell\,(0.46)}}{0.46\, g}$$

$$t = 2.09 \sqrt{\frac{\ell}{g}}.$$

ANGULAR MOMENTUM

• PROBLEM 1067

A particle of mass m is released from rest at point a in Fig. 1 falling parallel to the (vertical) y-axis. (a) Find the torque acting on m at any time t, with respect to origin O. (b) Find the angular momentum of m at any time t, with respect to this same origin. (c) Show that the relation $\tau = dl/dt$ yeilds a correct result when applied to this problem.

Solution: (a) The torque is given by $\tau = \mathbf{r} \times \mathbf{F}$, its magnitude being given by

$$\tau = rF \sin\theta.$$

$r \sin\theta = b$ and $F = mg$ so that

$$\tau = mgb = \text{a constant.}$$

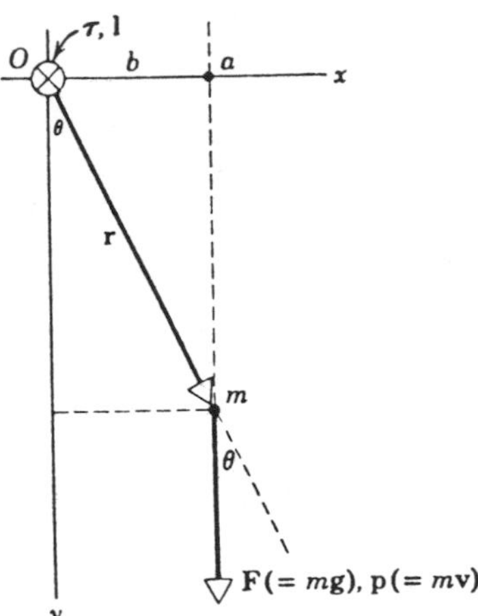

Figure 1

Note that the torque is simply the product of the force (mg) times the moment arm (b). The right-hand rule shows that τ is directed perpendicularly into the figure.

(b) The angular momentum is given by $\mathbf{l} = \mathbf{r} \times \mathbf{p}$, its magnitude being given by

$$l = rp \sin\theta.$$

$r \sin\theta = b$ and $p = mv = m(gt)$ so that

$$l = mgbt.$$

The right- hand rule shows that $\mathbf{l}$ is directed perpendicularly into the figure, which means that $\mathbf{l}$ and τ are parallel vectors. The vector $\mathbf{l}$ changes with time in magnitude only, its direction always remaining the same in this case.

(c) Since $d\mathbf{l}$, the change in $\mathbf{l}$, and τ are parallel, we can replace the vector relation $\tau = d\mathbf{l}/dt$ by the scalar relation

$$\tau = dl/dt.$$

Using the expression for τ and l from (a) and (b) above

$$mgb = \frac{d}{dt}(mgbt) = mgb,$$

Which is an identity. Thus the relation $\tau = dl/dt$ yields correct results in this case. Canceling the constant b out of the first two terms above substituting for gt the equivalent quantity v,

$$mg = \frac{d}{dt}(mv).$$

Since mg = F and mv = p, this is the familiar result F = dp/dt. Thus, relations such as $\tau = d\mathbf{l}/dt$, though often vastly useful, are not new basic postulates of classical mechanics but are rather the reformulation of the Newtonian laws for rotational motion.

Note that the values of τ and l depend on choice of origin, that is, on b. In particular, if b = 0, then $\tau = 0$ and l = 0.

• PROBLEM 1068

Show that the angular momentum of a particle about a point 0 will be equal to zero if any one of the following conditions applies

(a) $\vec{P} = 0$

(b) the particle is at point 0

(c) $\vec{P}$ is parallel (or anti-parallel) to $\vec{r}$

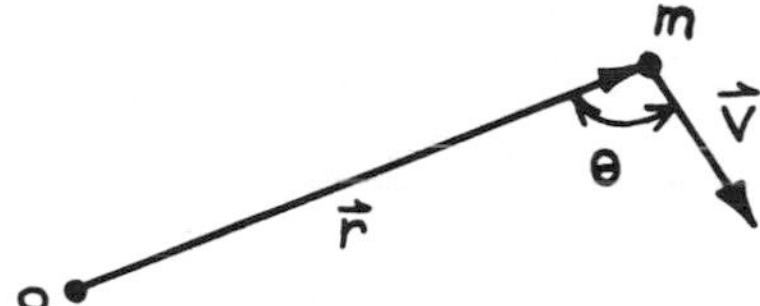

Solution: In general, for a particle of mass m and velocity $\vec{v} = (v_1\,\hat{i} + v_2\,\hat{j} + v_3\,\hat{k})$ located a distance r from point 0, $\vec{r} = (r_1\,\hat{i} + r_2\,\hat{j} + r_3\,\hat{k})$; angular momentum $\vec{L} = \vec{r} \times m\,\vec{v}$.

In scalar form, this equation becomes $L = r\,m\,v\,\sin\theta$ where θ is the angle between $\vec{r}$ and $\vec{v}$.

a) $\vec{P} = m\,\vec{v}$. If $\vec{P} = 0$ then m v must be 0.

$L = r\,(0)\,\sin\theta$

$L = 0$

b) If the particle is located at point 0 then $\vec{r} = 0$ and r = 0.

$(0)\,(m\,v)\,\sin\theta = 0$

$L = 0$

c) If $\vec{P}$ is parallel or anti-parallel to $\vec{r}$ then $\vec{v}$ is parallel or anti-parallel to $\vec{r}$ since $\vec{P}$ has the same direction as $\vec{v}$ because m is a scalar. If $\vec{v}$ is parallel or anti-parallel to $\vec{r}$ then $\theta = 0°$ or $180°$. In either case, $\sin\theta = 0$.

$$r\,m\,v\,(0) = 0$$

$$L = 0$$

• PROBLEM 1069

> In Figure 1, a small object of mass m is attached to a light string which passes through a hollow tube. The tube is held by one hand and the string by the other. The object is set into rotation in a circle of radius r_1 with a speed v_1. The string is then pulled down, shortening the radius of the path to r_2. Find the new linear speed v_2 and the new angular speed ω_2 of the object in terms of the initial values v_1 and ω_1 and the two radii.

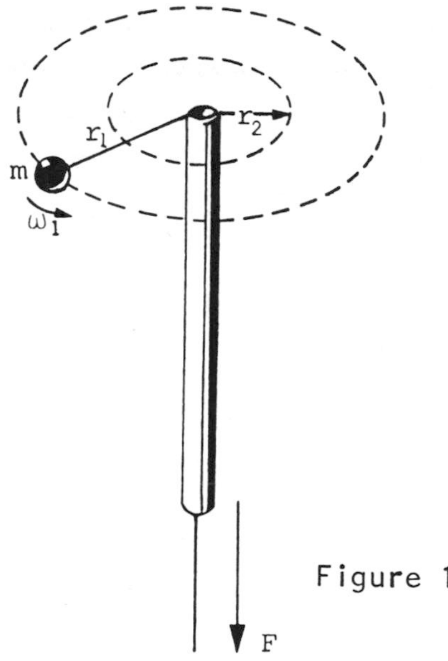

Figure 1

Solution: The downward pull on the string is transmitted as a radial force on the object. Such a force exerts a zero torque on the object about the center of rotation. Since no torque acts on the object about its axis of rotation, its angular momentum in that direction is constant. Hence

initial angular momentum = final angular momentum,

$$mv_1r_1 = mv_2r_2,$$

and

$$v_2 = v_1\left(\frac{r_1}{r_2}\right) .$$

Since $r_1 > r_2$, the object speeds up on being pulled in.

In terms of angular speed, since v_1 equals $\omega_1 r_1$ and v_2 equals $\omega_2 r_2$,

$$mr_1^{\,2}\omega_1 = mr_2^{\,2}\omega_2$$

and

$$\omega_2 = \left(\frac{r_1}{r_2}\right)^2 \omega_1 ,$$

so that there is an even greater increase in angular speed over the initial value.

• PROBLEM 1070

A particle of mass m is attached to the end of a string and moves in a circle of radius r on a frictionless horizontal table. The string passes through a frictionless hole in the table and, initially, the other end is fixed.

a) If the string is pulled so that the radius of the circular orbit decreases, how does the angular velocity change if it is ω_o when $r = r_o$?

b) What work is done when the particle is pulled slowly in from a radius r_o to a radius $r_o/2$?

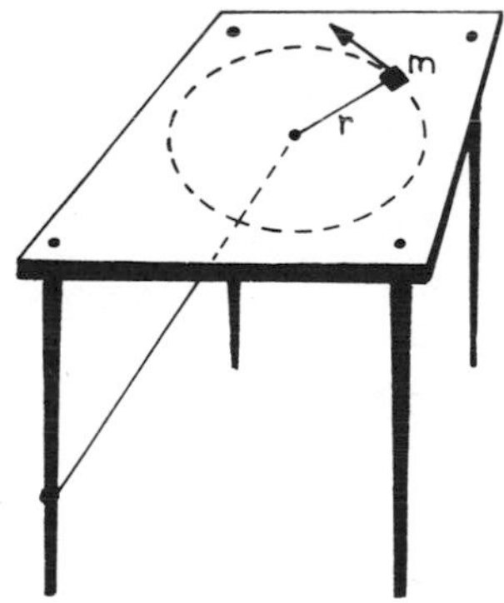

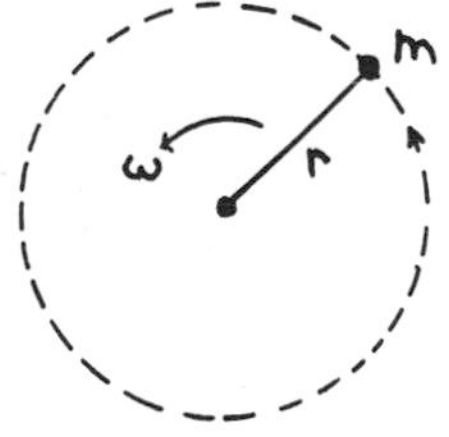

Fig. 1

Solution: a) In this problem, no external torques act on the particle, therefore, angular momentum is conserved. Angular momentum, L, equals $\vec{r} \times m\vec{v}$ and, for this problem, $L = mr^2\omega$ since the motion is circular and $r\vec{\omega} = \vec{v}$.

If the strings length is altered from r_o to r, the angular rotation changes from ω_o to ω.

However, $L = L_o$ (angular momentum is conserved) and it follows that $mr^2\omega = mr_o^2\omega_o$.

Rearranging the above expression and dividing by m yields

$$\omega = \frac{r_o^2\,\omega_o}{r^2} = \left(\frac{r_o}{r}\right)^2 \omega_o .$$

b) The work done shortening the string is equal to the integral of the tension in the string times an infinitesimal distance integrated over the total length change. Mathematically, this is written as

$$W = \int_{r_o}^{r_o/2} T \cdot dr$$

where W is work and T is tension.

The tension in the string is merely the centripetal force in this problem.

$$T = \frac{mv^2}{r} = mr\omega^2$$

Integrating, $\quad W = \int_{r_o}^{r_o/2} mr\omega^2 dr.$

Using the expression for ω from part a),

$$W = \int_{r_o}^{r_o/2} mr \left[\left(\frac{r_o}{r}\right)^2 \omega_o\right]^2 dr$$

$$W = mr_o^4\,\omega_o^2 \int_{r_o}^{r_o/2} \frac{dr}{r^3}\, dr$$

$$W = mr_o^4\omega_o^2 \left[-\frac{1}{2}\left(\frac{1}{r^2}\right)\right]_{r_o}^{r_o/2}$$

$$W = mr_o^4\omega_o^2 \left[\left(-\frac{1}{2}\right)\left\{\left(\frac{2}{r_o}\right)^2 - \left(\frac{1}{r_o}\right)^2\right\}\right]$$

$$W = mr_o^4\omega_o^2 \left(-\frac{3}{2}\right) r_o^{-2}$$

$$W = -\frac{3}{2}\, mr_o^2\omega_o^2$$

The negative sign indicates that the work is done on the particle, which is as it should be.

• PROBLEM 1071

A small ball swings in a horizontal circle at the end of a cord of length ℓ_1 which forms an angle θ_1 with the vertical. The cord is slowly shortened by pulling it through a hole in its support until the free length is ℓ_2 and the ball is moving at an angle θ_2 from the vertical. a) Derive a relation between ℓ_1, ℓ_2, θ_1, and θ_2. b) If ℓ_1 = 600 mm, θ_1 = 30° and, after shortening, θ_2 = 60°, determine ℓ_2.

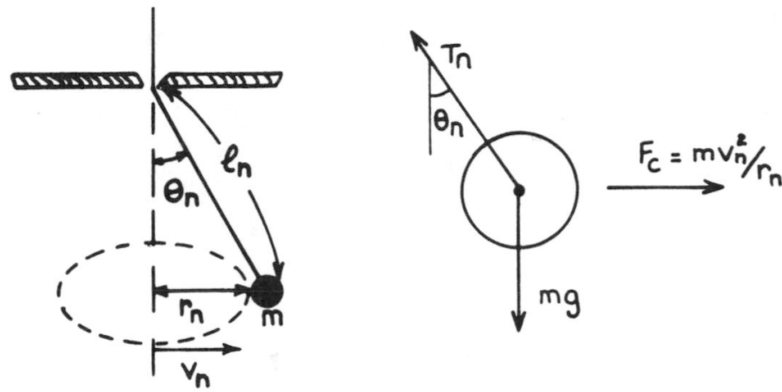

Solution: In the system shown, ℓ_n is the cord length, θ_n is the cone angle cut out by the cord as it revolves, r_n is the distance from the mass to the axis of rotation, and v_n is the velocity of the mass.

To find the relationship between ℓ_1, ℓ_2, θ_1 and θ_2 when the cord is shortened from ℓ_1 to ℓ_2, one should first analyze a free body diagram of the particle.

Since the particle is in a circular motion, the inward component of T must supply the centripetal force, $m\, v_n^2/r_n$.

$$T_n \sin \theta_n = \frac{m\, v_n^2}{r_n} \qquad (1)$$

Also, the vertical component of T must balance the weight.

$$T_n \cos \theta_n = m\, g \qquad (2)$$

Dividing (1) by (2) yields:

$$\text{Tan } \theta_n = \frac{m\, v_n^2}{m\, g\, r_n} = \frac{v_n^2}{g\, r_n} \qquad (3)$$

One more relationship is needed to solve the problem. Since no external torques act on the system, angular momentum L is conserved.

$$L_1 = L_2$$

$$m\, r_1\, v_1 = m\, r_2\, v_2$$

$$r_1\, v_1 = r_2\, v_2. \qquad (4)$$

If one rearranges (3),

$$g\, r_n^{\,3} \tan\theta_n = r_n^{\,2}\, v_n^{\,2}. \qquad (5)$$

From (4), it follows that $(r_1\, v_1)^2 = (r_2\, v_2)^2$. (6)

Combining (5) and (6), $g\, r_1^{\,3} \tan\theta_1 = g\, r_2^{\,3} \tan\theta_2$. (7)

Finally, from geometry, $r_n = \ell_n \sin\theta_n$ (8)

Using this relation in (7) and dividing both sides by g produces the desired result.

$$(\ell_1 \sin\theta_1)^3 \tan\theta_1 = (\ell_2 \sin\theta_2)^3 \tan\theta_2.$$

In this problem, $\ell_1 = .6\text{m}$, $\theta_1 = 30°$, $\theta_2 = 60°$

Solving for ℓ_2 yields

$$\ell_2 = \sqrt[3]{\frac{(\ell_1 \sin\theta_1)^3 \tan\theta_1}{\sin\theta_2^{\,3} \tan\theta_2}}$$

$$\ell_2 = \frac{\ell_1 \sin\theta_1}{\sin\theta_2} \sqrt[3]{\frac{\tan\theta_1}{\tan\theta_2}},$$

and substituting in the numbers yields

$$\ell_2 = \frac{.6\text{ m } (\sin 30°)}{\sin 60°} \sqrt[3]{\frac{\tan 30°}{\tan 60°}}$$

$$= \frac{.6\text{ m } (.5)}{(.87)} \sqrt[3]{\frac{.58}{1.73}}$$

$$= .24\text{ m}.$$

• **PROBLEM** 1072

The pendulum in figure 1 consists of a homogeneous prismatic bar of mass m and length ℓ, which hangs at rest on its frictionless suspension O. A spherical pellet of mass m travels with a horizontal velocity v_1 and strikes it in the middle. Immediately after the impact, the pellet moves with velocity v_2 to the right and the pendulum begins to rotate about O with initial angular velocity ω. Solve for v_2 and ω in terms of v_1 for the cases in which the collision is: 1.) completely elastic, and 2.) completely inelastic.

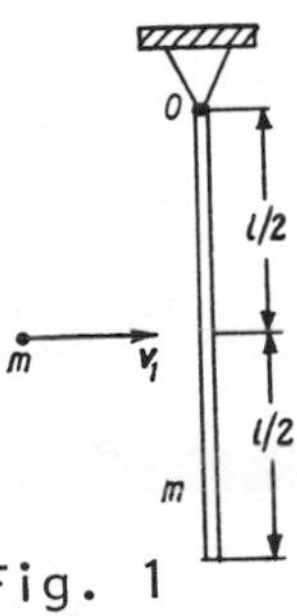

Fig. 1

Solution: Since not only the normal force, but also the reaction at O, becomes large during the impact, the principle of impulsive forces is useless for the determination of v_2 and ω. However, here we can apply the principle of impulsive moments about O.

The angular momentum about O of the system of two bodies before the impulse originates from the pellet alone. It is normal to the plane of motion and has the magnitude

$$H_{O1} = m \frac{\ell}{2} v_1 . \tag{1}$$

The total angular momentum immediately after the impulse has the same direction and the magnitude

$$H_{O2} = m \frac{\ell}{2} v_2 + \frac{m\ell^2}{3} \omega . \tag{2}$$

The second term in equation (2) is the angular momentum of the bar, $I\omega$, where I is the moment of inertia of the bar about O, which is equal to $m\ell^2/3$.

Since no external forces that have a static moment about O become large during the impulse, we have $H_{O1} = H_{O2}$, or substituting the values from (1) and (2),

$$m \frac{\ell}{2} v_2 + \frac{m\ell^2}{3} \omega = m \frac{\ell}{2} v_1 . \tag{3}$$

If the impulse is elastic the kinetic energy of the system is conserved. Thus we have

$$\frac{m}{2} v_2^2 + \frac{1}{2} \frac{m\ell^2}{3} \omega^2 = \frac{m}{2} v_1^2 . \tag{4}$$

Hence, by (3) and (4) we have the following equations for the determination of v_2 and ω:

$$v_2 + \frac{2}{3} \ell \omega = v_1 , \qquad v_2^2 + \frac{1}{3} \ell^2 \omega^2 = v_1^2 .$$

In addition, we have the requirement that $(\ell/2)\omega \geq v_2$. The solution yields

$$\omega = \frac{12}{7}\frac{v_1}{\ell} \text{ and } v_2 = -\frac{1}{7} v_1 .$$

Thus, both bodies move after the impulse, and in such a way that the speed of the pellet relative to the pendulum if $v_2' = \ell/2\omega - v_2 = v_1$ to the left. The velocity of the pellet relative to the pendulum is reversed.

If the pellet remains imbedded in the pendulum, the impulse is completely inelastic. Then, instead of (4), we have the condition

$$v_2 = \frac{\ell}{2}\omega . \qquad (5)$$

and, from (3) and (4) it follows that

$$\omega = \frac{6}{7}\frac{v_1}{\ell} \text{ and } v_2 = \frac{3}{7} v_1 .$$

• PROBLEM 1073

A gyroscope consists of a uniform circular disk of mass M = 1 kg and radius R = 0.2 m. The disk spins with an angular velocity $\omega = 400 \text{ sec}^{-1}$. The gyroscope precesses with the axes making an angle of 30° with the horizontal. The gyroscope wheel is attached to its axis at a point a distance $\ell = 0.3$ m from the pivot which supports the whole structure. What is the precessional angular velocity?

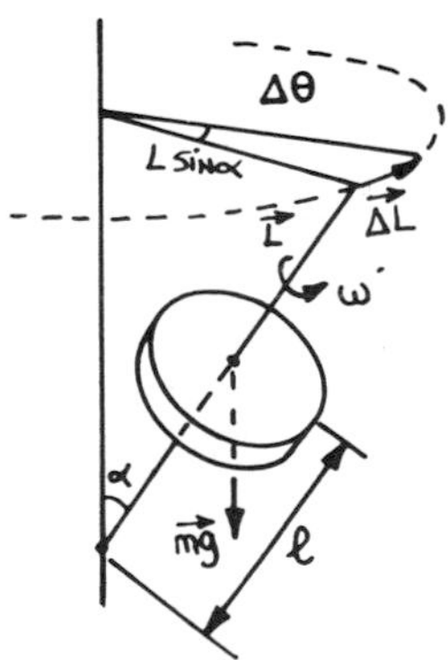

Solution: First, establish the general formula for regular precession. Refer to the figure. $|L| = I\omega$ for a symmetric object spinning around its symmetry axis. The torque τ from the weight is $mg\ell \sin\alpha$; this is directed perpendicular to the plane containing $\vec{L}$ and the vertical axis, according to the rule for a vector cross product. In a time Δt the torque effects a change $\Delta L = \tau\Delta t = mg\ell \sin\alpha\Delta t$ in the angular momentum, also perpendicular to $\vec{L}$. Thus, after Δt, the angular momentum will have changed its direction; the horizontal component will have moved by an angle $\Delta\theta = \Omega\Delta t$. ($\Omega$ is the precessional angular velocity.) There is no change in the magnitude of $\vec{L}$ since its increment $\Delta\vec{L}$

is perpendicular. Comparing the arc length to radius in the circle described by the tip of $\vec{L}$, the result is $\Delta\theta = \Delta L/(L \sin \alpha)$; $L \sin \alpha$ is the radius of this circle. Thus, $\Omega = \Delta\theta/\Delta t = (1/L \sin \alpha)(\Delta L/\Delta t)$. Substituting the above expressions for L and ΔL gives

$$\Omega = 1/(I\omega \sin \alpha)(mg\ell \sin \alpha\Delta t/\Delta t) = mg\ell/(I\omega).$$

For the uniform disk we have $I = \frac{1}{2}mR^2$, so $\Omega = 2g\ell/(R^2\omega)$.

Use $g = 9.8\ m/s^2$, $R = 0.2\ m$, $\omega = 400\ s^{-1}$, $\ell = 0.3\ m$. All these are mks units. Then,

$$\Omega = 2 \cdot 9.8 \cdot 0.3/[(0.2)^2 \cdot 400] \sim 0.368\ s^{-1}.$$

Note that the precessional angular velocity does not depend on the mass of the disk nor on the angle that its axes makes with the horizontal.

• PROBLEM 1074

The rate of steady precession $\dot{\phi}$ of the cone shown about the vertical is observed to be 20 rpm. Knowing that r = 100 mm and h = 200 mm, determine the rate of spin $\dot{\psi}$ of the cone about its axis of symmetry if $\beta = 135°$.

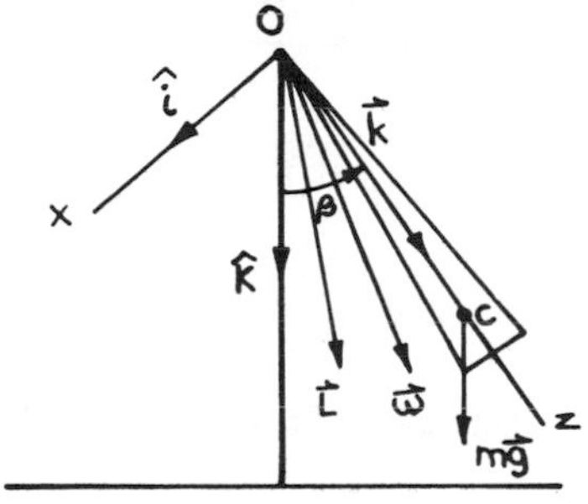

Fig. 1

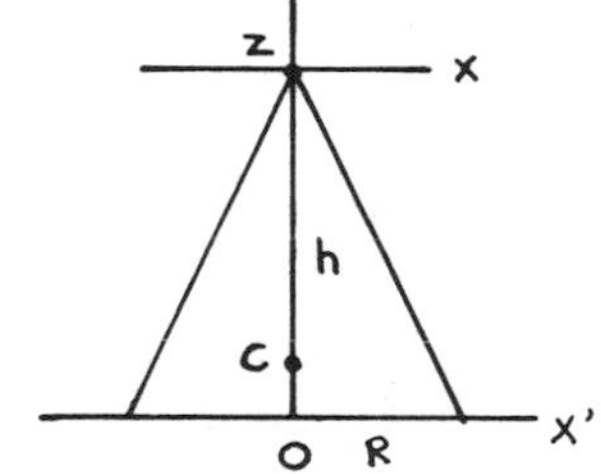

Fig. 2

Solution: Choose a coordinate system $\hat{i}, \hat{j}, \hat{k}$ which is fixed in the cone with $\hat{k}$ along the axis of symmetry. $\hat{K}$ is a unit vector fixed in space along the vertical. The cone has radius r, height h, and its center of mass is located a distance $\vec{a} = a\hat{k}$ from 0 on the symmetry axis. The cone precesses about the vertical with a constant angular velocity $p = \dot{\phi}$. The spin about the symmetry axis is $s = \dot{\psi}$.

From figure 1, $\hat{K} = \sin \beta\hat{i} + \cos \beta\hat{k}$. The angular momentum vector lies in the x, z plane.

$$\vec{\omega} = \omega_1\hat{i} + s\hat{k}.$$

The center of mass, C, rotates about $\vec{\omega}$ with a velocity

$$\vec{v}_c = \vec{\omega} \times \vec{a} = (\omega_1\hat{i} + s\hat{k}) \times a\hat{k} = -a\omega_1\hat{j}.$$

In the fixed system, C rotates around the vertical with velocity

$$\vec{v}_c = p\hat{k} \times \vec{a} = (p \sin \beta\hat{i} + p \cos \beta\hat{k}) \times a\hat{k}$$

$$= -ap \sin \beta\hat{j}.$$

Since both velocities are for the same point, a comparison gives

$$\omega_1 = p \sin \beta.$$

The only force acting on the top is the weight $\vec{W} = mg\hat{k}$. It produces a torque, τ, about 0 of

$$\vec{\tau} = \vec{a} \times \vec{W} = a\hat{k} \times mg\hat{k} = a\hat{k} \times mg(\sin \beta\hat{i} + \cos \beta\hat{k})$$

$$= amg \sin \beta\hat{j}. \qquad (1)$$

The angular momentum is given by

$$\vec{L} = I_x\omega_1\hat{i} + I_z s\hat{k}.$$

$\vec{L}$ also lies in the x, z plane and rotates with it about the vertical. From Newton's Second Law $\vec{\tau} = \frac{d\vec{L}}{dt}$; the rate of change of a fixed vector in a rotating coordinate system is $\frac{d\vec{A}}{dt} = \vec{\Omega} \times \vec{A}$. In this case

$$\vec{\tau} = p\hat{k} \times \vec{L} = p(\sin \beta\hat{i} + \cos \beta\hat{k}) \times (I_x\omega_1\hat{i} + I_z s\hat{k})$$

$$= (p^2 I_x \cos \beta \sin \beta - pI_z s \sin \beta)\hat{j}.$$

Comparing this with equation (1) and substituting in $\omega_1 = p \sin \beta$ gives

$$amg \sin \beta = p^2 I_x \cos \beta \sin \beta - psI_z \sin \beta.$$

Solving for the spin gives

$$s = \frac{pI_x \cos \beta}{I_z} - \frac{amg}{pI_z}. \qquad (2)$$

Next, determine the moments of inertia. For the right circular cone shown in Figure 2 the center of mass is at $\vec{z} = h/4$ and the moments of inertia are

$$I_z = \frac{3}{10}mR^2 \quad \text{and} \quad I_{x'} = \frac{m}{20}(3R^2 + 2h^2).$$

For this problem we need I_x, the moment of inertia about the x-axis through the vertex. To obtain this use the parallel axis Theorem, $I_0 = I_c + mr^2$ where r is the perpendicular distance between the parallel lines through 0 and C.

$$I_C = I_{x'} - mr_1^2 = I_{x'} - m\frac{h^2}{16}$$

$$I_x = I_C + mr_2^2 = I_C + \frac{9}{16}mh^2 = I_{x'} - \frac{1}{16}mh^2 + \frac{9}{16}mh^2$$

$$= I_{x'} + \frac{1}{2}mh^2 = \frac{3}{20}mR^2 + \frac{1}{10}mh^2 + \frac{1}{2}mh^2 = \frac{3}{20}m(R^2 + 4h^2).$$

So, $$I_x/I_z = \frac{3/20m(R^2 + 4h^2)}{3/10\ mR^2} = \frac{1}{2}\left[1 + 4\left(\frac{h}{R}\right)^2\right].$$

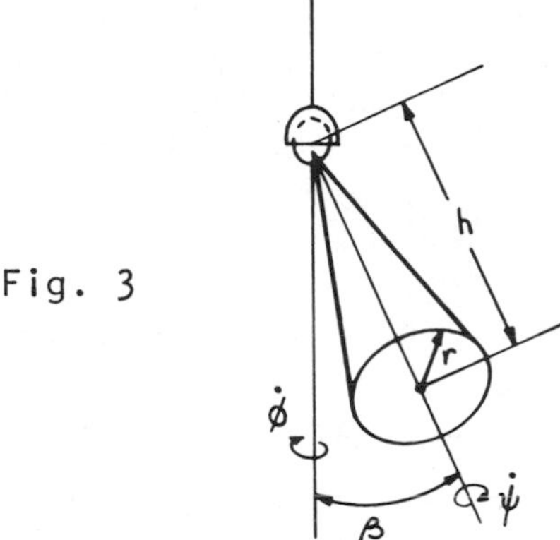

Fig. 3

For this problem p = 20 rpm=0.33rad/sec, R = 10 cm, h = 20 cm, β = 135° and $a = h - \frac{1}{4}h = \frac{3}{4}h = 15$ cm. Substitution of these values into equation (2) gives

$$s = \frac{\pi}{2}\left[1 + 4\left(\frac{20}{10}\right)^2\right] \cos 135° - \frac{15\ \text{cm}\ \ 980\ \text{cm/sec}^2}{\pi\ \text{rad/sec}\ \frac{3}{10}\ (10\ \text{cm})^2}$$

$$= -18.88\ \text{rad/sec} - 155.97\ \text{rad/sec}$$

$$= -174.85\ \text{rad/sec} = -1670\ \text{rpm}.$$

This is the angular velocity of the cone about its symmetry axis. The negative sign means $\vec{s}$ points in the negative $\hat{k}$ direction.

• PROBLEM 1075

A spinning target in a shooting gallery is dynamically equivalent to two thin disks of equal mass, m, connected by a light bar. The radius of the disks is a = 400 mm and the bar has a length 2a = 800 mm. The target is initially rotating about its' axis of symmetry with a rate ω_0 = 40 rpm. A bullet of mass $m_0 = m/100$ and traveling with a velocity v_0 = 100 m/s relative to the target, hits the target and is embedded in point C. Determine (a) the angular velocity of the target immediately after collision, (b) the precession of the ensuing motion, (c) the rates of precession and spin of the ensuing motion.

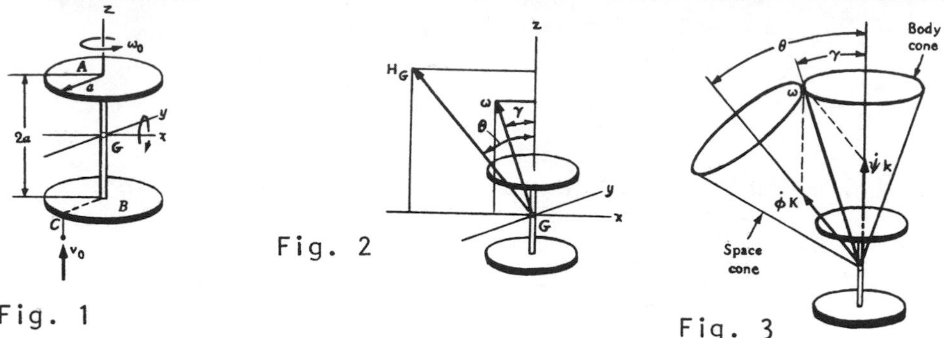

Fig. 1 Fig. 2 Fig. 3

Solution: We need the principal axes of the target to solve this problem. With the simplifying assumption that the bullet does not change the principal axes, note that the x,y,z axes shown are the principal axes.

$$I = I_z = \frac{1}{2}ma^2.$$

Find $I' = I_x = I_y$ by use of the parallel-axis theorem. The moment of inertia of the disk with respect to an axis through it, parallel to the x or y axis in the figure, is $\frac{1}{4}mr^2$. Since the mass of each disk is $(\frac{1}{2}m)$ and the distance from the parallel axis to the axis in the figure is a, the moment of inertia of one disk is

$$I' = I_x = I_y = \frac{1}{4}(\frac{1}{2}m)a^2 + (\frac{1}{2}m)a^2.$$

Due to symmetry, it is possible to multiply by two to find the Moment of Inertia of the total system.

$$I' = I_x = I_y = 2\left[\frac{1}{4}(\frac{1}{2}m)a^2 + (\frac{1}{2}m)a^2\right] = \frac{5}{4}ma^2$$

The total angular momentum of the target-bullet system is conserved during collision and remains constant during the ensuing motion. Taking moments about the coordinate origin G yields

$$\vec{H}_G = -a\hat{j} \times m_0 v_0 \hat{k} + I\omega_0 \hat{k}$$

$$\vec{H}_G = -m_0 v_0 a\hat{i} + I\omega_0 \hat{k}. \tag{1}$$

Now determine the angular velocity after impact by invoking the conservation of H_G. Using

$$\vec{H} = K_x\omega_x\hat{i} + I_y\omega_y\hat{j} + I_z\omega_z\hat{k},$$

the result is

$$-m_0 v_0 a = I'\omega_x = \frac{5}{4} ma^2 \omega_x$$

$$\omega_x = \frac{4}{5}\frac{m_0 v_0}{ma};$$

$$0 = I'\omega_y\ ,\ \omega_y = 0;$$

$$I\omega_0 = I\omega_z$$

$$\omega_z = \omega_0.$$

$$\vec{\omega} = -\frac{4}{5}\frac{m_0 v_0}{ma}\hat{i} + \omega_0 \hat{k}. \qquad (2)$$

While this equation is correct it is not very helpful since the body axes x,y,z are moving in space in an unknown way. For the target considered,

$$\omega_0 = 40 \text{ rpm} = 4.19 \text{ rad/sec}, \quad m_0/m = 1/100\ ,$$

$$a = 0.400 \text{ m}, \quad v_0 = 100 \text{ m/sec};$$

we find $\omega_x = -2$ rad/sec, $\omega_y = 0$, $\omega_z = 4.19$ rad/sec.

This gives

$$\omega = \sqrt{\omega_x^2 + \omega_z^2} = 4.64 \text{ rad/sec} = 44.3 \text{ rpm}$$

with angle $\gamma = \arctan \dfrac{-\omega_x}{\omega_z} = 25.5°$ to the z-axis. (Figure 2).

The angle θ shown in fig. 2 is between the precession axis and the z-axis. (H_G is fixed in space; the target wobbles around it.)

$$\theta = \arctan\left(\frac{m_0 v_0 a}{I\omega_0}\right) = \arctan\left(\frac{2m_0 v_0}{ma\omega_0}\right)$$

$$\theta = 50.0°.$$

Figure 3 shows $\vec{\omega}$, the space and body cones and $\dot{\phi}$ and $\dot{\psi}$ which, added vectorially, must equal ω. Using the law of sines,

$$\left|\frac{\omega}{\sin(\pi-\theta)}\right| = \left|\frac{\dot{\phi}}{\sin\gamma}\right| = \left|\frac{\dot{\psi}}{\sin(\theta-\gamma)}\right|;$$

$$\frac{\omega}{\sin\theta} = \frac{\dot{\phi}}{\sin\gamma} = \frac{\dot{\psi}}{\sin(\theta-\gamma)}\ .$$

This gives

$$\dot{\phi} = 24.9 \text{ rpm}\ ,\ \dot{\psi} = 24.0 \text{ rpm}.$$

A spacecraft, with a mass m = 2000kg, rotates with an angular velocity of $\omega = (0.05 \text{ rad/s})\hat{i} + (0.15 \text{ rad/s})\hat{j}$. Two small jets, located at points A and B, are turned on in a direction parallel to the z-axis. Each jet has a thrust of 25N. The radii of gyration of the spacecraft are $k_x = k_z = 1.5$m and $k_y = 1.75$m. Determine the required time of operation for each jet, so that the angular velocity of the spacecraft reduces to zero.

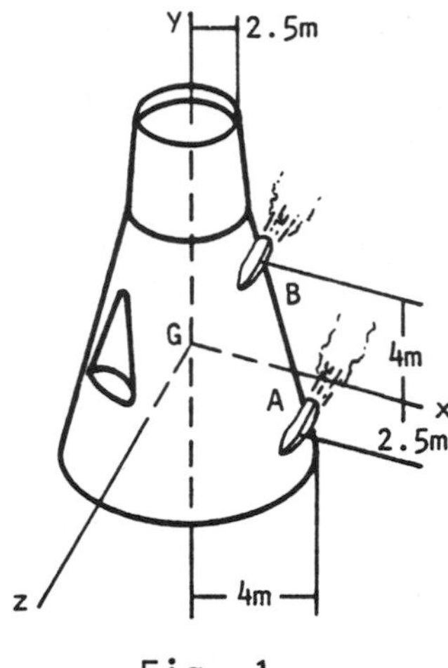

Fig. 1

Solution: Choose a coordinate system fixed in the body such that the rockets at A and B lie in the x, y plane and the origin is at the center of mass. The positions of A and B are $\vec{r}_1$ and $\vec{r}_2$ respectively. Qualitatively, what happens is both the rockets oppose the original motion about the y axis but B will increase the original motion about the x-axis while A will oppose it. Thus, A will have to be fired longer in order to compensate for the increase about the x-axis due to B. The torque, $\vec{\tau}$, produced by A and B is

$$\vec{\tau}_B = \vec{r}_1 \times \vec{F}_1 = y_1F_1\vec{i} - x_1F_1\vec{y}$$

(1)

$$\vec{\tau}_A = \vec{r}_2 \times \vec{F}_2 = -y_2F_2\vec{i} - x_2F_2\vec{j}.$$

From Newton's Second Law, $\vec{\tau} = I\vec{\alpha}$ where I is the moment of inertia and $\vec{\alpha}$ is the angular acceleration. In components this becomes

$$\vec{\tau} = I_x\alpha_x\vec{i} + I_y\alpha_y\vec{j} + I_z\alpha_z\vec{k} \tag{2}$$

where I_x, I_y and I_z are the moments of inertia about the x, y, z axes. Comparing equations (2) and (3) gives

$$\alpha_x^A = \frac{d\omega_x^A}{dt} = -\frac{y_2F_2}{I_x} = -C_1 \ ; \quad \frac{d\omega_y^A}{dt} = -\frac{x_2F_2}{I_y} = -C_2; ; \quad \frac{d\omega_z^A}{dt} = 0$$

$$\frac{d\omega_x^B}{dt} = \frac{y_1F_1}{I_x} = C_3 \ ; \quad \frac{d\omega_y^B}{dt} = -\frac{x_1F_1}{I_y} = -C_4 \ ; \quad \frac{d\omega_z^B}{dt} = 0. \tag{3}$$

These equations can be integrated directly to give

$$\Delta\omega_x^A = -C_1t_A \ ; \quad \Delta\omega_y^A = -C_2t_A \ ; \quad \omega_z^A = \text{constant}$$

$$\Delta\omega_x^B = C_3t_B \ ; \quad \Delta\omega_y^B = -C_4t_B \ ; \quad \omega_z^B = \text{constant} \tag{4}$$

where $\Delta\omega = \omega(t) - \omega(0)$ is the change in angular velocity about each axis due to firing the rockets.

Since initially $\vec{\omega} = 0.2$ rad/sec $\vec{i} + 0.1$ rad/sec $\vec{j}$; $\omega_z(0) = 0$, the constants in equation (4) must also be zero. Since we want the final angular velocity to be zero, the sum of the initial angular momentum plus the additional increments about each axis must be zero. So,

$$\omega_{x0} + \Delta\omega_x^A + \Delta\omega_x^B = 0$$

$$\omega_{y0} + \omega_y^A + \Delta\omega_y^B = 0.$$

Substitution from equation (3) gives

$$C_1t_A - C_3t_B = \omega_{x0}$$

$$C_2t_A + C_4t_B = \omega_{y0}$$

These are two simultaneous equations in the unknowns t_A and t_B. From the theory of equations, the solutions are

$$t_A = \frac{1}{\Delta}\begin{vmatrix} \omega_{x0} & -C_3 \\ \omega_{y0} & C_4 \end{vmatrix} = \frac{1}{\Delta}(C_4\omega_{x0} + C_3\omega_{y0})$$

$$t_B = \frac{1}{\Delta}\begin{vmatrix} C_1 & \omega_{x0} \\ C_2 & \omega_{y0} \end{vmatrix} = \frac{1}{\Delta}(C_1\omega_{y0} - C_2\omega_{x0}) \tag{5}$$

where

$$\Delta = \begin{vmatrix} C_1 & -C_3 \\ C_2 & C_4 \end{vmatrix} = C_1C_4 + C_2C_3.$$

For this problem $x_1 = 2.5$ m, $y_1 = 4$ m, $x_2 = 4$ m, $y_2 = 2.5$ m

$m = 2 \times 10^3$ kg, $F_1 = F_2 = 25$ n, $k_x = k_z = 1.5$ m and $k_y = 1.75$ m.

From equation (3) the C values are

$$C_1 = y_2F_2/I_x = \frac{2.5 \text{ m} \quad 25 \text{ n}}{2 \times 10^3 \text{kg}(1.5\text{m})^2} = 0.0139 \frac{\text{rad}}{\text{sec}^2}$$

$$C_2 = x_2F_2/I_y = \frac{4 \text{ m} \quad 25 \text{ n}}{2 \times 10^3 \text{kg}(1.75\text{m})^2} = 0.0163 \frac{\text{rad}}{\text{sec}^2}$$

$$C_3 = y_1F_1/I_x = \frac{4 \text{ m} \quad 25 \text{ n}}{2 \times 10^3 \text{kg}(1.5\text{m})^2} = 0.0222 \frac{\text{rad}}{\text{sec}^2}$$

$$C_4 = x_1F_1/I_y = \frac{2.5 \text{ m} \quad 25 \text{ n}}{2 \times 10^3 \text{kg}(1.75\text{m})^2} = 0.0102 \frac{\text{rad}}{\text{sec}^2}$$

$$\Delta = C_1C_4 + C_2C_3 = 0.000503 \text{ rad/s}^4.$$

Substitution in eq. (5) gives the times

$$t_A = \frac{C_4\omega_{x0} + C_3\omega_{y0}}{\Delta} = \frac{0.0102 \times 0.05 + 0.0222 \times 0.15}{0.000503}$$

$$= 7.634 \text{ sec.}$$

$$t_B = \frac{C_1\omega_{y0} - C_2\omega_{x0}}{\Delta} = \frac{0.0139 \times 0.15 - 0.0163 \times 0.05}{0.000503}$$

$$= 2.525 \text{ sec.}$$

Thus, it is necessary to fire A approximately three times as long as B in order to stop the capsule's rotation. This agrees with our initial qualitative remarks regarding the motion.

ELECTROMAGNETICS

• PROBLEM 1077

A copper strip 2.0cm wide and 1.0mm thick is placed in a magnetic field with B = 1.5T, as in Figure 1. If a current of 200 A is set up in the strip, what Hall potential difference appears across the strip?

Solution: The Hall electric field is given by

$$E_H = \frac{jB}{ne};$$

but

$$E_H = \frac{V_{xy}}{d}, \quad j = \frac{i}{A} = \frac{i}{dh}, \quad \text{and} \quad n = \frac{dN_0}{M},$$

where h is the thickness of the strip. Combining these equations gives

$$V_{xy} = \frac{iB}{neh} = \frac{(200\ \text{A})(1.5\ \text{T})}{(8.4 \times 10^{28}/\text{m}^3)(1.6 \times 10^{-19}\text{C})(1.0 \times 10^{-3}\text{m})}$$

$$= 2.2 \times 10^{-5}\text{V} = 22\mu\text{V}.$$

(a) (b)

Figure 1

These potential differences, though quite measurable, are not large.

• PROBLEM 1078

In Figure 1 assume that B = 2.0 T, l = 10cm, and v = 1.0m/s. Calculate (a) the induced electric field observed by S' and (b) the emf induced in the loop.

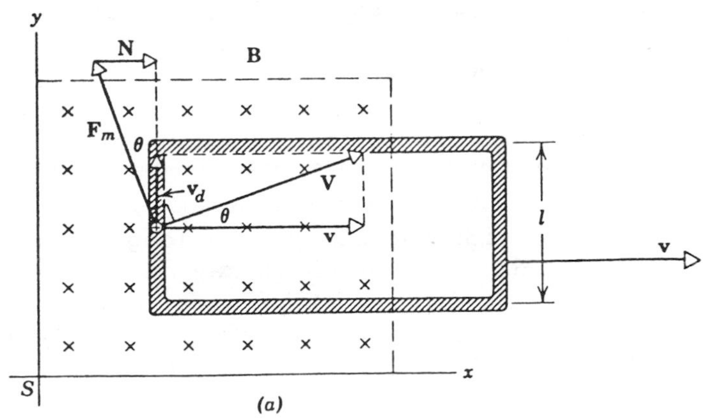

(a)

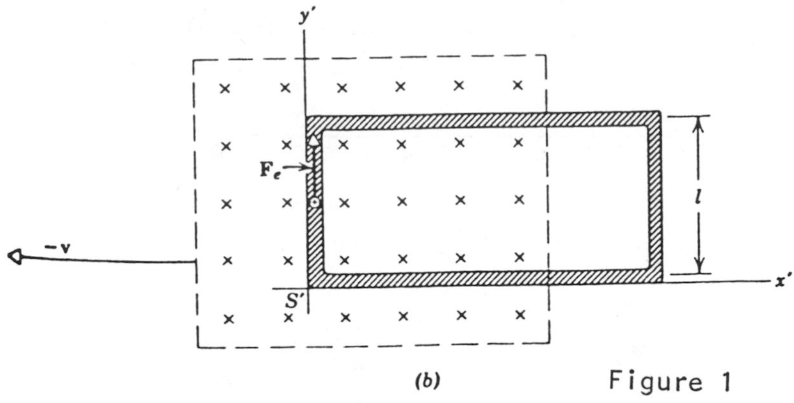

Figure 1

Solution: (a) The electric field, which is apparent only to observer S', is associated with the moving magnet and is given in magnitude by

$$E = vB = (1.0 \text{ m/s})(2.0 \text{ T}) = 2.0 \text{ V/m}.$$

(b) Observer S would calculate the induced (motional) emf from

$$\mathcal{E} = Blv = (2.0 \text{ T})(1.0 \times 10^{-1}\text{m})(1.0 \text{ m/s}) = 0.20 \text{ V}.$$

Observer S' would not regard the emf as motional and would use the relationship

$$\mathcal{E} = El = (2.0 \text{ V/m})(1.0 \times 10^{-1}\text{m}) = 0.20 \text{ V}.$$

As must be the case, both observers agree as to the numerical value of the emf.

• PROBLEM 1079

Figure 1 shows a flat strip of copper of width a and negligible thickness carrying a current i. Find the magnetic field B at point P, at a distance R from the center of the strip, at right angles to the strip.

Solution: Subdivide the strip into long infinitesimal filaments of width dx, each of which may be treated as a wire carrying a current di given by i(dx/a). The field contribution dB at point P in Fig. 1 is given, for the element shown, by the differential formula for a long cylindrical wire, which is

$$dB = \frac{\mu_0}{2\pi}\frac{di}{r} = \frac{\mu_0}{2\pi}\frac{i(dx/a)}{R \sec\theta}\ .$$

Note that the vector dB is at right angles to the line marked r.

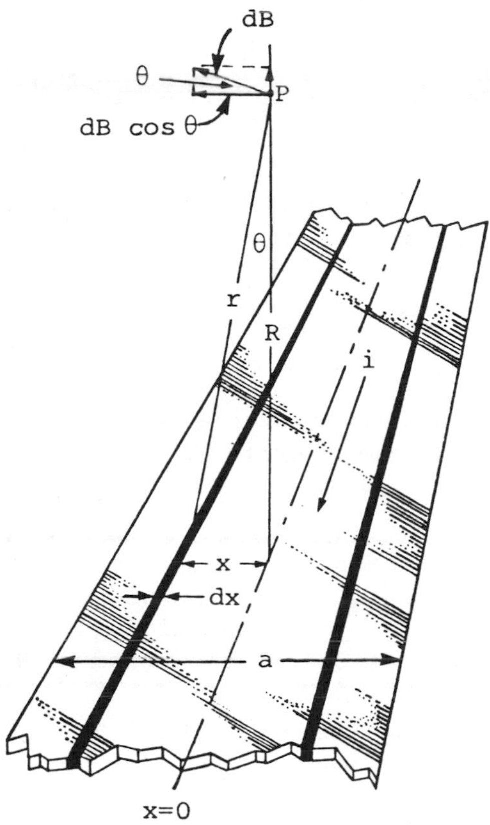

Figure 1

Only the horizontal component of dB, dB cos θ, is effective, the vertical component being canceled by the contribution associated with a symmetrically located filament on the other side of the orgin. Thus B at point P is given by the (scalar) integral

$$B = \int dB \cos\theta = \int \frac{\mu_0 i(dx/a)}{2\pi R \sec\theta}\cos\theta$$

$$= \frac{\mu_0 i}{2\pi aR}\int\frac{dx}{\sec^2\theta}\ .$$

The variables x and θ are not independent, being related by

$$x = R \tan\theta$$

or

$$dx = R \sec^2\theta\ d\theta.$$

Bearing in mind that the limits on θ are $\pm\tan^{-1}(a/2R)$ and eliminating dx from this expression for B,

$$B = \frac{\mu_0 i}{2\pi a R} \int \frac{R \sec^2\theta \, d\theta}{\sec^2\theta}$$

$$= \frac{\mu_0 i}{2\pi a} \int_{-\tan^{-1} a/2R}^{+\tan^{-1} a/2R} d\theta = \frac{\mu_0 i}{\pi a} \tan^{-1} \frac{a}{2R} \ .$$

At points far from the strip, a/2R is a small angle, for which $\tan^{-1}\alpha \cong \alpha$. Thus, as an approximate result,

$$B \cong \frac{\mu_0 i}{\pi a}\left(\frac{a}{2R}\right) = \frac{\mu_0}{2\pi} \frac{i}{R} \ .$$

This result is expected because at distant points the strip cannot be distinguished from a cylindrical wire.

• PROBLEM 1080

What must be the width a of a rectangular guide such that the energy of electromagnetic radiation whose free-space wavelength is 3.0cm travels down the guide (a) at 95% of the speed of light? (b) At 50% of the speed of light?

Solution: The group speed is given by:

$$v_{gr} = 0.95c = c\sqrt{1 - \left(\frac{\lambda}{2a}\right)^2} \ .$$

Solving for a yields a = 4.8cm; repeating for $v_{gr} = 0.50c$ yeilds a = 1.7cm.

If $\lambda = 2a$, then $v_{gr} = 0$ and energy cannot travel down the guide. For the radiation considered in this example $\lambda = 3.0$cm, so that the guide must have a width a of at least ½ x 3.0cm = 1.5cm if it is to transmit this wave. The guide whose width we calculated in (a) above can transmit radiations whose free-space wavelength is 2 x 4.8cm = 9.6cm or less.

• PROBLEM 1081

An observer is at a distance r from a point light source whose power output is P_0. Calculate the magnitudes of the electric and the magnetic fields. Assume that the source is monochromatic, that it radiates uniformly in all directions, and that at distant points it behaves like the traveling plane wave of Figure 1.

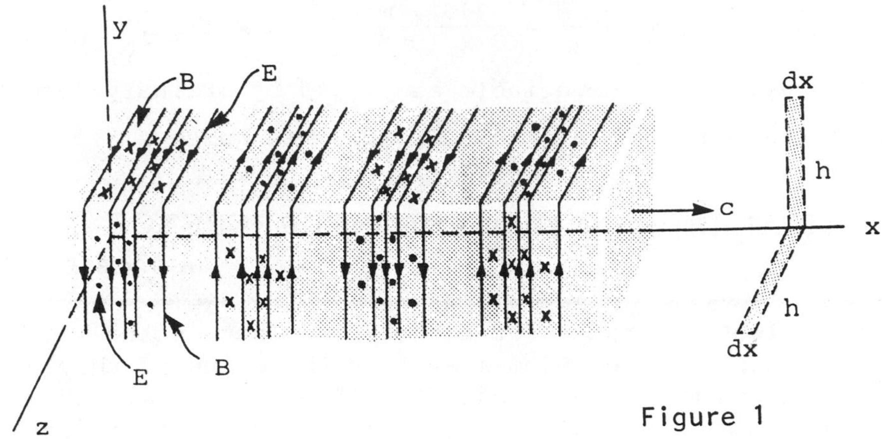

Figure 1

Solution: The power that passes through a sphere of radius r is $(\bar{S})(4\pi r^2)$, where $\bar{S}$ is the average value of the Poynting vector at the surface of the sphere. This power must equal P_0, or

$$P_0 = \bar{S}4\pi r^2.$$

From the definition of S

$$\bar{S} = \overline{\left(\frac{1}{\mu_0} EB\right)} .$$

Using the relation E = cB to eliminate B leads to

$$\bar{S} = \frac{1}{\mu_0 c} \overline{E^2}.$$

The average value of E^2 over one cycle is $\frac{1}{2}E_m^2$, since E varies sinusoidally. This leads to

$$P_0 = \left(\frac{E_m^2}{2\mu_0 c}\right)(4\pi r^2),$$

or

$$E_m = \frac{1}{r}\sqrt{\frac{P_0\mu_0 c}{2\pi}} .$$

For $P_0 = 10^3$W and r = 1.0m this yields

$$E_m = \frac{1}{(1.0\text{m})} \sqrt{\frac{(10^3\text{W})(4\pi \times 10^{-7}\text{Wb/A}\cdot\text{m})(3 \times 10^8\text{m/s}}{2\pi}}$$

$$= 240 \text{ V/m}.$$

The relationship $E_m = cB_m$ leads to

$$B_m = \frac{E_m}{c} = \frac{240 \text{ V/m}}{3 \times 10^8 \text{ m/s}} = 8 \times 10^{-7}\text{T}.$$

Note that E_m is appreciable as judged by ordinary laboratory standards but that B_m (= 0.008 gauss) is quite small.

OPTICAL DIFFRACTION AND INTERFERENCE

• PROBLEM 1082

In double-slit Fraunhofer diffraction what is the fringe spacing on a screen 50cm away from the slits if they are illuminated with blue light (λ = 480nm = 4800 Å), if d = 0.10mm, and if the slit width a = 0.02mm? What is the linear distance from the central maximum to the first minimum of the fringe envelope?

Solution: The intensity pattern is given by $I_\theta = I_m(\cos\beta)^2 (\frac{\sin\alpha}{\alpha})^2$, the fringe spacing being determined by the interference factor $\cos^2\beta$. The position of the first minimum of the fringe enevelope is given by

$$\Delta y = \frac{\lambda D}{d},$$

where D is the distance of the screen from the slits. Substituting yields

$$\Delta y = \frac{(480 \times 10^{-9}\text{m})(50 \times 10^{-2}\text{m})}{0.10 \times 10^{-3}\text{m}} = 2.4 \times 10^{-3}\text{m} = 2.4\text{mm}.$$

The distance to the first minimum of the envelope is determined by the diffraction factor $(\sin\alpha/\alpha)^2$ in

$I_\theta = I_m(\cos\beta)^2 \left(\frac{\sin\alpha}{\alpha}\right)^2$. The first minimum in this factor occurs for $\alpha = \pi$.

The angle is given by:

$$\alpha = \frac{\pi a}{\lambda}\sin\theta$$

$$\sin\theta = \frac{\alpha\lambda}{\pi a} = \frac{\lambda}{a} = \frac{480 \times 10^{-9}\text{m}}{0.02 \times 10^{-3}\text{m}} = 0.024.$$

This is so small that it is assumed that $\theta \cong \sin\theta \cong \tan\theta$, or

$$y = D\tan\theta \cong D\sin\theta = (50\text{cm})(0.024) = 1.2\text{cm}.$$

There are about ten fringes in the central peak of the fringe envelope.

• PROBLEM 1083

How many fringes are formed per millimeter if light beams of wavelength 632.8 nm intersect at an angle of 5°?

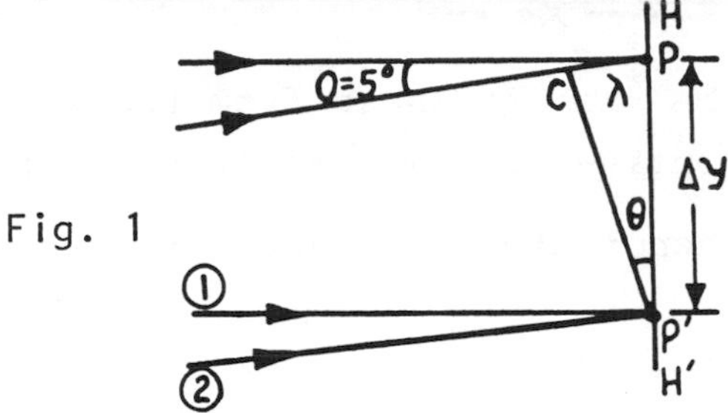

Fig. 1

Solution: Figure 1 shows the two monochromatic beams of the same wavelength and inclined to each other at an angle θ. These two beams interfere on the photographic plate HH', producing bright and dark lines. Since the beam (1) is seen to be in constant phase across the surface of the hologram plane, the interference pattern, or fringes, will be separated by an amount Δy, whenever the path difference between the two beams is one wavelength

From the triangle CPP',

$$\sin\theta = \frac{CP}{PP'} = \frac{\lambda}{\Delta y} .$$

Therefore,

$$\Delta y = \frac{\lambda}{\sin\theta} .$$

Hence the number of fringes per mm is equal to

$$\frac{1}{\Delta y\,(\text{mm})} = \frac{\sin\theta}{\lambda\,(\text{mm})}$$

$$= \frac{\sin 5^\circ}{6.328 \times 10^{-4}}$$

$$= 138\,(\text{mm})^{-1}$$

• PROBLEM 1084

Two glass plates are nearly in contact and make a small angle θ with each other. Show that the fringes produced by interference in the air film have a spacing equal to λ/2θ if the light is incident normally and has wavelength λ.

Solution: Let θ be the angle between the two glass plates

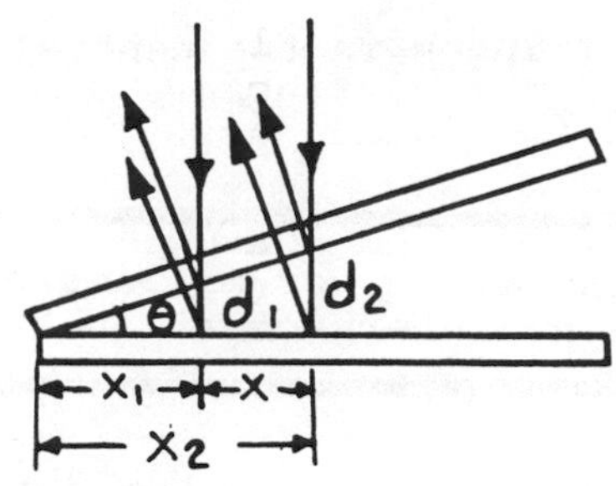

and let x_1 and x_2 be the distances from the edge of the wedge of two consecutive fringes, as shown in the figure.

If d_1 and d_2 denote the air gaps for these two fringes, then

$$2d_1 = n\lambda \tag{1}$$

and

$$2d_2 = (n+1)\lambda \tag{2}$$

where λ is the wavelength and n is an integer. Subtracting (1) from (2)

$$2(d_2 - d_1) = \lambda \,. \tag{3}$$

From the figure, $\tan\theta = \dfrac{d_1}{x_1} = \dfrac{d_2}{x_2}$. Assuming θ to be very small, the approximation $\tan\theta \simeq \theta$ can be made. Therefore,

$$d_2 - d_1 = \theta(x_2 - x_1)$$

$$= \theta x \tag{4}$$

where

$$x = (x_2 - x_1)$$

Substituting for $d_2 - d_1$ into equation (3),

$$2\theta x = \lambda$$

Then,

$$x = \frac{\lambda}{2\theta} \,.$$

• PROBLEM 1085

Monochromatic light of wavelength 400mμ from a distant point source falls on an opaque plate in which there is a small circular opening. As a screen is moved toward the plate from a large distance away, the Fresnel diffraction pattern on the screen first has a dark center when the distance from plate to screen is 160cm. Find the diameter of the central disk in the diffraction pattern if a lens of focal length 160cm is placed just to the right of the circular opening.

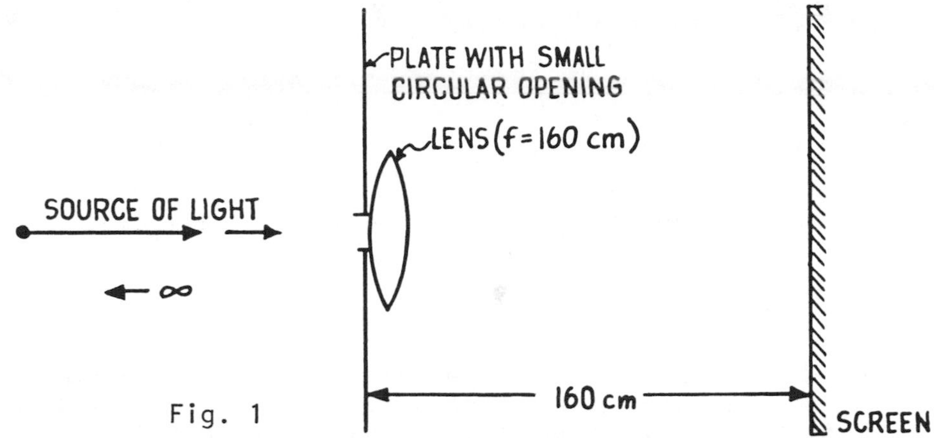

Fig. 1

Solution: We have a circular aperture illuminated by coherent light from a source infinitely distant from the aperture. This implies that all points on the aperture are in phase with all other points. We now place a screen an infinite distance from the aperture and slowly move it towards the aperture observing the center spot of the screen. At some distance the path length from the light at the circumference of the aperture will be just one wavelength out of phase with light from the center of the aperture, which can be represented algebraically as $R_1 = R_o + \lambda$ in figure (2). We have learned from our study of diffraction that this is just the condition for destructive interference. Now if we move the screen closer to the aperture, the center of the screen will have a bright spot when the path difference between a circumferential ray and a central ray is $3\lambda/2$ and dark when there is a 2λ path difference, etc. Each of the path differences defines the edges of Fresnel zones.

CIRCUMFERENTIAL RAY, R_1

r

RADIUS OF PATTERN ON THE SCREEN

CENTRAL RAY, R_0

Fig. 2

Looking at figure (2) for our problem when R_o is 160cm, r will just be the outer radius of the second Fresnel zone. From figure (2),

$$R_1^2 = R_o^2 + r^2 \qquad (1)$$

and $R_1 = R_o + \lambda$ because there is destructive interference at $R_o = 160$cm. (2)

Substituting for R_1 in equation (1) yields

$$R_o^2 + 2\lambda R_o + \lambda^2 = R_o^2 + r^2$$

The R_o^2 terms cancel, and so,

$$r^2 = 2\lambda R_o + \lambda^2$$

or

$$r = \sqrt{\lambda^2 + 2\lambda R_o}$$

$$= \left[(400x10^{-9}m)^2 + 2 \times 400 \times 10^{-9}m \times 1.6m\right]^{1/2}$$

$$= 1.13 \times 10^{-3}m, \tag{3}$$

which is the radius of the aperture. If we now place a 160cm focal length lens on the screen side of the aperture, the lens will convert an infinite distance on the screen side to a point 160cm from the aperture (as in figure (1)). Stating it another way, the screen at 160cm from the aperture with a 160cm focal length lens will produce a Fraunhofer diffraction pattern of the source. Now from any standard optics text Fraunhofer diffraction of a circular aperture is

$$\frac{d/2}{\ell} = \frac{1.22\lambda}{2r} \tag{4}$$

where d is the diameter of the central disk; ℓ is the distance from the aperture; λ is the wavelength of the light used and r is the radius of the aperture. Now solving for the diameter of the central disk we have

$$d = \frac{\ell \times 1.22 \times \lambda}{r}$$

where $\ell = 1.6m$, $\lambda = 400x10^{-9}m$, and $r = 1.13x10^{-3}m$.

Hence $$d = \frac{1.6m \times 1.22 \times 400 \times 10^{-9}m}{1.13 \times 10^{-3}m} = 6.91 \times 10^{-4}m.$$

• **PROBLEM** 1086

A Young's experiment is set up with the following characteristics: Monochromatic source ($\lambda = 0.55\mu$), slit separation d = 3.3 mm, distance from slits to screen D = 3m (see figure).

1) Calculate the fringe spacing.

2) Place a sheet of glass with plane parallel faces and thickness e = 0.01 mm in front of slit F_1.

a) Determine the direction of the displacement of the fringes and the formula giving the relationship for their displacement.

b) Knowing that the fringes are displaced by 4.73 ± .01 mm find the index of refraction of the glass and its error.

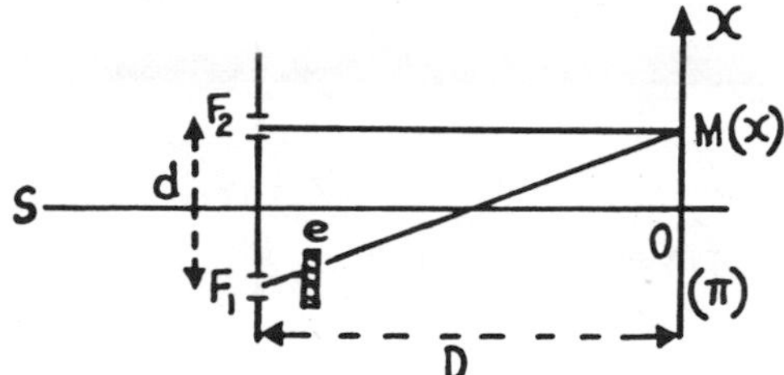

Solution: Here we need to concentrate on the interference between two slits. From a standard optics text we find that the intensity of the interference pattern on N slits is,

$$I = \frac{I_o}{N^2} \frac{\sin^2 N\delta}{\sin^2 \delta} \tag{1}$$

where I_o is the initial intensity; I is the intensity at the screen; N is the number of slits; and δ is given by,

$$\delta = \frac{\pi d}{\lambda} \sin \theta \tag{2}$$

where λ is the wavelength of coherent monochromatic light from the source; d is the slit separation, and θ is the angle between the normal to the slit system and the point on the screen. For small angles, $\sin\theta = x/D$ where x is the distance from the center of the screen to a point at which we wish to measure the intensity and D is the distance from slits to screen.

Substituting into equation (2) gives the result

$$\delta = \frac{\pi d}{\lambda} \frac{x}{D} \tag{3}$$

For two slits N = 2. Substituting this into equation (1) we realize we can expand the $\sin^2 2\delta$ term because,

$$\sin 2\delta = 2 \sin\delta \cos\delta \ . \tag{4}$$

Squaring both sides results in,

$$\sin^2 2\delta = 4 \sin^2\delta \cos^2\delta \ . \tag{5}$$

Substituting this into equation (1) and cancelling terms,

$$I = I_o \cos^2\delta \ . \tag{6}$$

The fringe spacing i is the distance between two maxima or two minima. We therefore let $i = x_2 - x_1$ and $\delta = \pi$. Applying equation (3),

$$\pi = \frac{\pi d i}{\lambda D} \quad . \tag{7}$$

Solving for i,

$$i = \frac{\lambda D}{d} \quad . \tag{8}$$

Substituting the given values for λ, D, and d into equation (8),

$$i = \frac{(.55 \times 10^{-6})(3)}{3.3 \cdot 10^{-3}} = 5 \times 10^{-4} m \quad . \tag{9}$$

Now we insert a sheet of glass of thickness 0.01 mm and index of refraction n in front of one of the slits. The light of this slit will now travel a different optical distance to a position x on the screen. Initially before the glass plate was inserted in front of the slit, the path difference was,

$$\delta_1 = F_1M - F_2M = x \frac{\lambda}{i} \quad . \tag{10}$$

The glass plate will add an additional path difference (n - 1)e so the new path difference is,

$$\delta = x \frac{\lambda}{i} + (n-1)e \tag{11}$$

so, the new δ for a maximum will be pλ (p being an integer) or,

$$p\lambda = x \frac{\lambda}{i} + (n-1)e \quad . \tag{12}$$

Solving for x,

$$x = \frac{i}{\lambda}\left[p\lambda - (n-1)e\right] \tag{13}$$

so the shift in fringes will be the change in x:

$$\Delta x = - \frac{i}{\lambda} (n-1)e \quad . \tag{14}$$

To measure the index of refraction we solve for n:

$$n = 1 - \frac{\lambda}{i} \frac{\Delta x}{e} \quad . \tag{15}$$

So we do the measurement as follows. Observe the fringe system with no glass plate, record the positions x of the maxima, then insert the glass plate, record the new positions of the maxima and determine the shift Δx of the maxima. In our problem $\Delta x = -4.73$ mm, substituting values into equation (15),

$$n = 1 - \frac{0.55 \times 10^{-3}}{0.5} \frac{(-4.73)}{10^{-2}} = 1.5203 \ . \qquad (16)$$

To determine the error in n we want to look at the relationship $d(\Delta x)/\Delta x$. Differentiating equation (15) we have

$$dn = -\frac{\lambda}{ie} d(\Delta x) \ . \qquad (17)$$

Solving equation (14) for $-\frac{\lambda}{ie}$,

$$-\frac{\lambda}{ie} = \frac{n-1}{\Delta x} \ . \qquad (18)$$

Substituting for $-\frac{\lambda}{ie}$ in equation (17),

$$dn = (n-1) \frac{d(\Delta x)}{\Delta x} \ .$$

Substituting values

$$dn = 0.5 \quad \frac{2 \times 10^{-2}}{4.73} = 2 \times 10^{-3},$$

so $n = 1.520 \pm 0.002$.

• PROBLEM 1087

Calculate, approximately, the relative intensities of the secondary maxima in the single-slit Fraunhofer diffraction pattern.

Solution: The secondery maxima lie approximately halfway between the minima and are found from

$$\alpha \cong (m + \tfrac{1}{2})\pi \qquad m = 1,2,3,\ldots.$$

Substituting into the formula for intensity in single-slit diffraction yields

$$I_\theta = I_m \left[\frac{\sin(m + \frac{1}{2})\pi}{(m + \frac{1}{2})\pi} \right]^2 ,$$

which reduces to

$$\frac{I_\theta}{I_m} = \frac{1}{(m + \frac{1}{2})^2 \pi^2} \ .$$

This yields, for m = 1,2,3,..., I_θ/I_m = 0.045, 0.016, 0.0083, etc. The successive maxima decrease rapidly in intensity.

DOPPLER EFFECT

• PROBLEM 1088

A laser emits a monochromatic light beam, of wavelength λ, which falls normally on a mirror moving at velocity V. What is the beat frequency between the incident and reflected light?

Solution: When a source of light is in motion relative to an observer or vice versa, the light waves exhibit a change in frequency as seen by that observer. This phenomenon is known as the Doppler effect, and the Doppler shift for light is given as

$$\nu_{observed} = \nu\sqrt{\frac{c \pm v}{c \mp v}} \tag{1}$$

where ν is the frequency of the light in an inertial frame of reference, v is the speed of the source relative to the observer, and c is the speed of light. In this problem v is the speed of the mirror. Let us choose the mirror to be moving away from the laser, so that it absorbs the light as if it were an observer moving away at speed v; it then re-emits the light as if it were a source moving away at speed v. In both cases the source and observer are separating from one another, so the frequency decreases. To get $\nu_{observed} < \nu$, we need the lower signs in equation (1).

Now, when the mirror absorbs the light, we have

$$\nu_{absorbed} = \nu\sqrt{\frac{c - v}{c + v}} \tag{2}$$

Similarly, when it re-emits the light, the frequency shift is given by

$$\nu_{emitted} = \nu_{absorbed}\sqrt{\frac{c - v}{c + v}} = \nu\left(\frac{c - v}{c + v}\right) . \tag{3}$$

The beat frequency is the difference in frequencies between the incident and reflected light:

$$\nu_{beat} = \nu - \nu_{emitted}$$

$$\nu_{beat} = \nu - \nu\left(\frac{c - v}{c + v}\right)$$

$$= \nu\left[1 - \frac{c - v}{c + v}\right]$$

$$= \nu\left[\frac{2v}{c + v}\right]$$

$$\nu_{beat} = \frac{c}{\lambda}\left[\frac{2v}{c + v}\right]$$

when $v \ll c$, then $c + v \cong c$. In this case $\nu_{beat} \cong \frac{2v}{\lambda}$.

• PROBLEM 1089

The Milky Way galaxy rotates once in 200 million years, and our sun is located about 30,000 light years from the galactic center. As a result, the earth is moving through space relative to the other galaxies. What is the observed Doppler shift in Å of the hydrogen line of 6563 Å for light coming from other galaxies? Consider two cases: a) The line of observation is in the direction of the earth's motion; b) The line of observation is perpendicular to the direction of the earth's motion. Ignore other causes of observed Doppler effects.

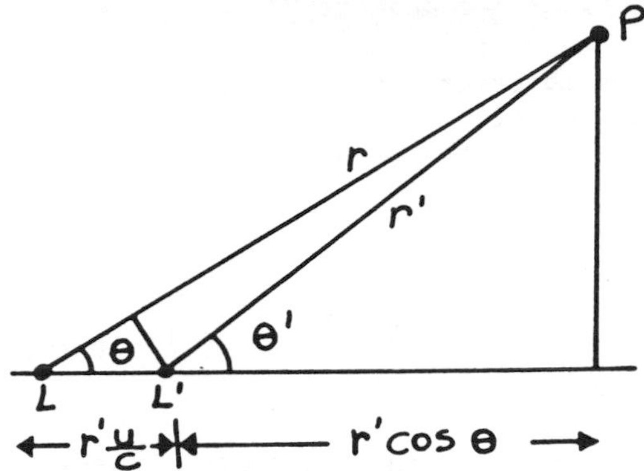

Solution: The relativistic Doppler shift is given by the expression

$$\nu' = \nu\sqrt{\frac{1 - u/c}{1 + u/c}}$$

Multiplying both the numerator and denominator by the factor $\sqrt{1 - u/c}$, one obtains the expression

$$\nu' = \nu \sqrt{\frac{1 - u/c}{1 - (u/c)^2}}$$

where ν' is the observed frequency of light of frequency ν in the frame of reference of the source; u is the relative source-observer velocity, and c is the speed of light.

For case (a), the light is travelling parallel to the earth's motion, and u is given by $u = R\Omega$, with R = 30,000 light-years, and

$$\Omega = \frac{2\pi}{200(10^6)} \text{ rad/year.}$$

Thus,

$$u = \frac{30,000(2\pi)}{200(10^6)} \text{ light-years (rad/year)}$$

$= 9.425(10^{-4})c$ (where c represents the speed of light) or

$$\left(\frac{u}{c}\right) = 9.425(10^{-4}).$$

Now since $u \ll c$, $\nu' \simeq \nu\{1 - (u/c)\}$, or, since $\nu' = c/\lambda'$ and $\nu = c/\lambda$ (λ = the wavelength of light),

$$\frac{1}{\lambda'} \simeq \frac{1}{\lambda}\{1 - (u/c)\}, \text{ with } \lambda = 6563\text{Å} .$$

Thus, $\lambda' = 6569.2$ Å, or $\Delta\lambda = \lambda' - \lambda = 6.2$ Å.

b) Where the line of observation is perpendicular to the direction of the earth's motion, the observed frequency shift, which is purely a relativistic effect, is called the transverse Doppler effect. The frequency shift is given by the expression

$$\nu = \nu'[1 - (u/c)^2]^{\frac{1}{2}}.$$

The derivation of this effect is indicated in the figure. The generalized Doppler shift is given by

$$\nu = \nu' \frac{1 + (u/c)\cos\theta'}{\sqrt{1 - (u/c)^2}}$$

where, as indicated, the observer (on the earth) is located at point P at rest in the unprimed coordinate system, and the source of light is at rest in the primed system. For transverse observation,

$$\theta = \frac{\pi}{2},$$

$$\cos\theta' = -\frac{u}{c}$$

Thus,

$$\nu = \nu' \frac{1 - (u/c)^2}{\sqrt{1 - (u/c)^2}} = \nu'[1 - (u/c)^2]^{\frac{1}{2}}$$

or

$$\frac{1}{\lambda} = \frac{1}{\lambda'}[1 - (u/c)^2]^{\frac{1}{2}}, \text{ with } (u/c) = 9.425(10^{-4}).$$

Thus, $\lambda = 6563.003$ Å, or $\Delta\lambda = 0.003$ Å.

TRAVELING AND STANDING WAVES

• PROBLEM 1090

(a) The maximum pressure variation P that the ear can tolerate in loud sounds is about 28 N/m^2 (=28 Pa). Normal atmospheric pressure is about 100,000 Pa. Find the corresponding maximum displacement for a sound wave in air having a frequency of 1000 Hz.
(b) In the faintest sound that can be heard at 1000 Hz the pressure amplitude is about 2.0×10^{-5} Pa. Find the corresponding displacement amplitude.

Solution: (a) The pressure amplitude is given by:

$$y_m = \frac{P}{k\rho_0 v^2}.$$

The speed of sound in air is, v = 331 m/s so that

$$k = \frac{2\pi}{\lambda} = \frac{2\pi\nu}{v} = \frac{2\pi \times 10^3}{331} m^{-1} = 19 m^{-1}.$$

The density of air ρ_0 is 1.22 kg/m^3. Hence, for P = 28 Pa

$$y_m = \frac{28}{(19)(1.22)(331)^2} m = 1.1 \times 10^{-5} m.$$

The displacement amplitudes for the loudest sounds are about 10^{-5}m, a very small value.

(b) From $y_m = P/k\rho_0 v^2$, using these values for k, v, and ρ_0, with $P = 2.0 \times 10^{-5}$ N/m^2,

$$y_m \cong 8 \times 10^{-12} m \cong 10^{-11} m.$$

• PROBLEM 1091

A transverse sinusoidal wave is generated at one end of a long horizontal string by a bar which moves the end up and down through a distance of 0.50cm. The motion is continuous and is repeated regularly 120 times per second.

(a) If the string has a linear density of 0.25kg/m and is kept under tension of 90 N, find the speed, amplitude, frequency, and wavelength of the wave motion.

(b) Assuming the wave moves in the +x-direction and that, at t=0, the end of the string described by x=0 is in its equilibrium position y=0, write the equation of the wave.

(c) As this wave passes along the string, each particle of the string moves up and down at right angles to the direction of the wave motion. Find the velocity and acceleration of a particle 2.0 ft. from the end.

Solution: (a) The end moves 0.25cm away from the equilibrium position, first above it, then below it; therefore, the amplitude y_m is 0.25cm.

The entire motion is repeated 120 times each second so that the frequency is 120 vibrations per second, or 120 Hz.

The wave speed is given by $v = \sqrt{F/\mu}$. But F = 90 N and μ = 0.25kg/m, so that

$$v = \sqrt{\frac{90 \text{ N}}{0.25 \text{kg/m}}} = 19 \text{m/s}.$$

The wavelength is given by $\lambda = v/\nu$, so that

$$\lambda = \frac{19 \text{ m/s}}{120 \text{ vib/s}} = 16 \text{cm}.$$

(b) The general expression for a transverse sinusoidal wave moving in the +x-direction is

$$y = y_m \sin(kx - \omega t - \phi).$$

Requiring that y = 0 for the conditions x = 0 and t = 0 yeilds

$$0 = y_m \sin(-\phi),$$

which means that the phase constant ϕ may be taken to be zero. Hence for this wave

$$y = y_m \sin(kx - \omega t),$$

and with the values just found,

$$y_m = 0.25\text{cm},$$

$$\lambda = 16\text{cm} \quad \text{or} \quad k = \frac{2\pi}{\lambda} = \frac{2\pi}{16\text{cm}} = 0.39\text{cm}^{-1},$$

$$v = 19\text{m/s} = 1900\text{cm/s} \text{ or } \omega = vk = (1900\text{cm/s})(0.39\text{cm}^{-1})$$
$$= 740\text{s}^{-1} = 740\text{Hz},$$

the equation for the wave is

$$y = 0.25 \sin(0.39x - 740t)$$

where x and y are in centimeters and t is in seconds.

(c) The general form of this wave is

$$y = y_m \sin(kx - \omega t) = y_m \sin k(x - vt).$$

The v in this equation is the constant horizontal velocity of the wavetrain. It is not the velocity of a particle in the string through which this wave moves; this particle velocity is neither horizontal nor constant. Each particle moves vertically, that is, in the y-direction. In order to determine the particle velocity designated by the symbol u, concentrate on a particle at a particular position x-that is, x is now a constant in this equation-and see how the particle displacement y changes with time. With x constant

$$u = \frac{\partial y}{\partial t} = -y_m \omega \cos(kx - \omega t),$$

in which the partial derivative $\partial y/\partial t$ shows that although in general y is a function of both x and t, assume that x remains constant so that t becomes the only variable. The acceleration a of the particle at this (constant) value of x is

$$a = \frac{\partial^2 y}{\partial t^2} = \frac{\partial u}{\partial t} = -y_m \omega^2 \sin(kx - \omega t) = -\omega^2 y.$$

For a particle at x = 62cm with

$$y_m = 0.25\text{cm}, \quad k = 0.39\text{cm}^{-1}, \quad \omega = 740\ \text{s}^{-1},$$

$$u = -y_m v \cos(kx - \omega t)$$

or $u = -0.25(740)\cos\left[(0.39)(62) - 740)t\right] = -185 \cos(24 - 740t)$

and $$a = -\omega^2 y$$

or $a = -(740)^2 0.25 \sin\left[(0.39)(62) - (740)t\right] = -13.7\times10^4 \sin(24 - 740t)$

where t is expressed in seconds u in cm/s and a in cm/s^2.

POLARIZATION

• PROBLEM 1092

Describe the polarization state of the following waves:

1) $\vec{E}_T = \hat{\imath}\, E_\circ \sin[2\pi(z/\lambda - vt)]$

$\quad + \hat{\jmath}\, E_\circ \cos[2\pi(z/\lambda - vt)]$.

2) $\vec{E}_T = \hat{\imath}\, E_\circ \sin[2\pi(z/\lambda + vt)]$

$\quad + \hat{\jmath}\, E_\circ \sin[2\pi(z/\lambda + vt - 1/8)]$.

3) $\vec{E}_T = \hat{\imath}\, E_\circ \sin[2\pi(z/\lambda - vt)]$

$\quad - \hat{\jmath}\, E_\circ \sin[2\pi(z/\lambda - vt)]$.

Solution: 1) The two components of $\vec{E}_T$ are

$$E_x = E_\circ \sin\left[2\pi\left(\frac{z}{\lambda} - vt\right)\right], \qquad E_y = E_\circ \cos\left[2\pi\left(\frac{z}{\lambda} - vt\right)\right].$$

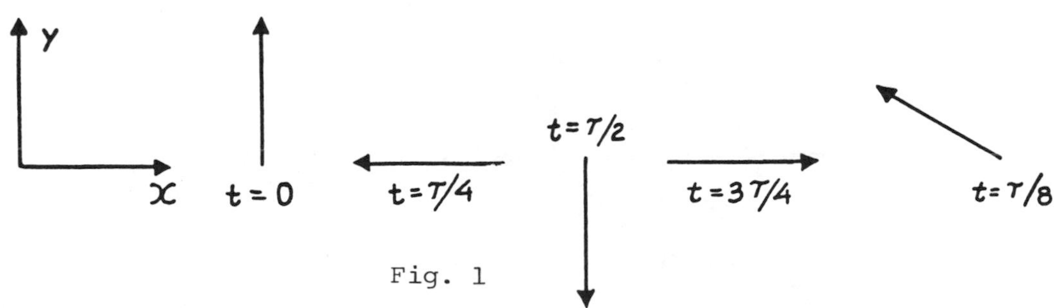

Fig. 1

These are actual components of a real vector, not phasors, so we want to construct the resultant at various times and also some convenient place like z = 0.

t	0	$\tau/4$	$\tau/2$	$3\tau/4$	$\tau/8$ $(\tau = \frac{1}{v})$
E_x	0	$-E_\circ$	0	$E_\circ$	$-E_\circ/\sqrt{2}$
E_y	$E_\circ$	0	$-E_\circ$	0	$+E_\circ/\sqrt{2}$

The resultant vector is simply a vector of length E, rotating counterclockwise. The polarization is circular.

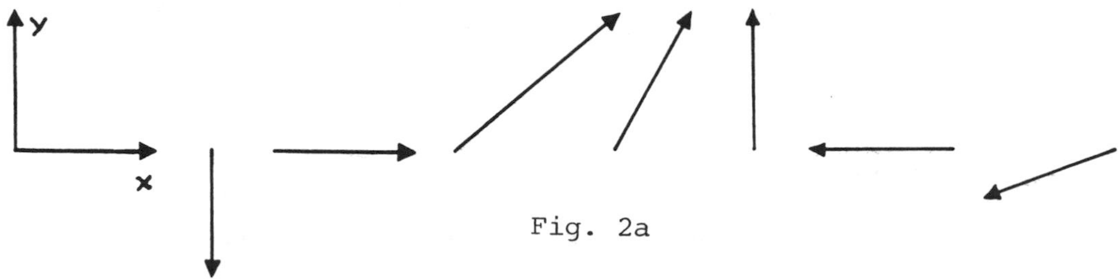

Fig. 2a

2) The components of the given vector are

$$E_x = E_\circ \sin \left[2\pi\left(\frac{z}{\lambda} + vt\right)\right]$$

$$E_y = E_\circ \sin \left[2\pi\left(\frac{z}{\lambda} + vt - \frac{1}{8}\right)\right]$$

Again we consider the point z = 0 and follow the resultant as time progresses.

t	0	$\tau/8$	$2\tau/8$	$3\tau/8$	$4\tau/8$	$5\tau/8$	$6\tau/8$
E_x	0	$+E_\circ \sin \frac{\pi}{4}$	$E_\circ$	$E_\circ \sin \frac{\pi}{4}$	0	$-E_\circ \sin \frac{\pi}{4}$	$-E_\circ$
E_y	$-E_\circ \sin \frac{\pi}{4}$	0	$+E_\circ \sin \frac{\pi}{4}$	$E_\circ$	$E_\circ \sin \frac{\pi}{4}$	0	$-E_\circ \sin \frac{\pi}{4}$

The locus of the end of $E_{\text{Resultant}}$ is an ellipse at 45 degrees to the axes, as shown in figure 2b.

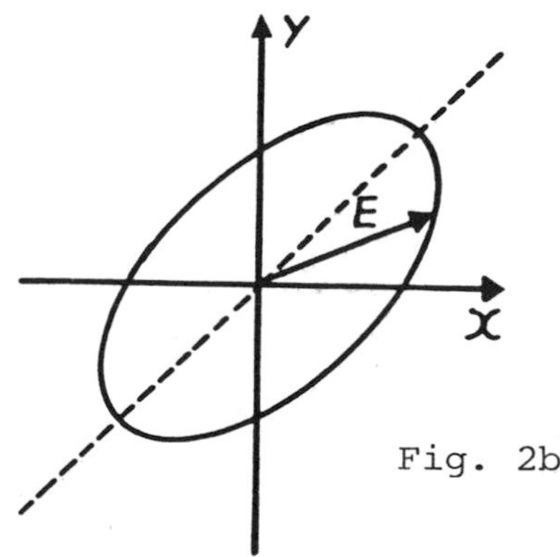

Fig. 2b

To find the semi-major axis, look at the time when $E_x = E_y$: this is halfway between t = 0 and t = τ/8: t = τ/16.

Hence

$$E_x = E_\circ \sin\left(\frac{\pi}{8}\right), \quad E_y = E_\circ \sin\left(\frac{-\pi}{8}\right) :$$

$$E_R = E_\circ \sin\left(\frac{\pi}{8}\right)\sqrt{2} = 0.542E_\circ$$

To find the semi-minor axis, which is τ/4 later, t = τ/16 + τ/4 = 5τ/16. So we have:

$$E_x = E_\circ \sin\left(\frac{5\pi}{8}\right), \quad E_y = E_\circ \sin\left(\frac{3\pi}{8}\right),$$

$$E_R = E_\circ \sin\left(\frac{3\pi}{8}\right)\sqrt{2} = 1.31E_o .$$

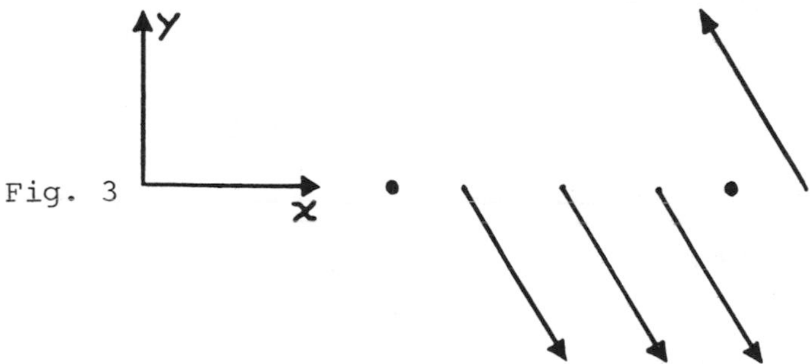

Fig. 3

3) The components of $\vec{E}_T$ are

$$E_x = E_\circ \sin\left[2\pi\left(\frac{x}{\lambda} - vt\right)\right] .$$

$$E_y = -E_\circ \sin\left[2\pi\left(\frac{z}{\lambda} - vt\right)\right] .$$

As before, z = 0 is most convenient point.

t	0	τ/8	τ/4	3τ/8	4τ/8	5τ/8
E_x	0	$E_\circ \sin\frac{\pi}{4}$	$E_\circ$	$+E_\circ \sin\frac{\pi}{4}$	0	$-E_\circ \sin\frac{\pi}{4}$
E_y	0	$-E_\circ \sin\frac{\pi}{4}$	$-E_\circ$	$-E_\circ \sin\frac{\pi}{4}$	0	$E_\circ \sin\frac{\pi}{4}$

Thus the polarization is linear, along a line at 45 degrees to the axes. It has amplitude $E_\circ/\sqrt{2}$.

1) Two linearly polarized waves are in phase, but have different amplitudes. At x = 0

$$\vec{E}_1 = \hat{\imath}\, A_1 \cos 2\pi\nu t + \hat{\jmath}\, B_1 \cos 2\pi\nu t,$$

$$\vec{E}_2 = \hat{\imath}\, A_2 \cos 2\pi\nu t + \hat{\jmath}\, B_2 \cos 2\pi\nu t.$$

Show that $\vec{E}_T = \vec{E}_1 + \vec{E}_2$ is also linearly polarized, and find its polarization direction.

2) Two circularly polarized waves (a right and a left) can be added to form a linearly polarized wave: At x = 0,

$$\vec{E}_1 = \hat{\imath}\, E_\circ \cos 2\pi\nu t + \hat{\jmath}\, E_\circ \sin 2\pi\nu t,$$

$$\vec{E}_2 = \hat{\imath}\, E_\circ \cos (2\pi\nu t + \alpha) - \hat{\jmath}\, E_\circ \sin (2\pi\nu t + \alpha).$$

Show that $\vec{E}_T$ is linearly polarized, and find its polarization direction.

3) An elliptically polarized wave is written (at z = 0) as

$$\vec{E}_T = \hat{\imath}\, A \sin 2\pi\nu t + \hat{\jmath}\, B \cos 2\pi\nu t.$$

Show that this can be decomposed into a linearly and a circularly polarized wave.

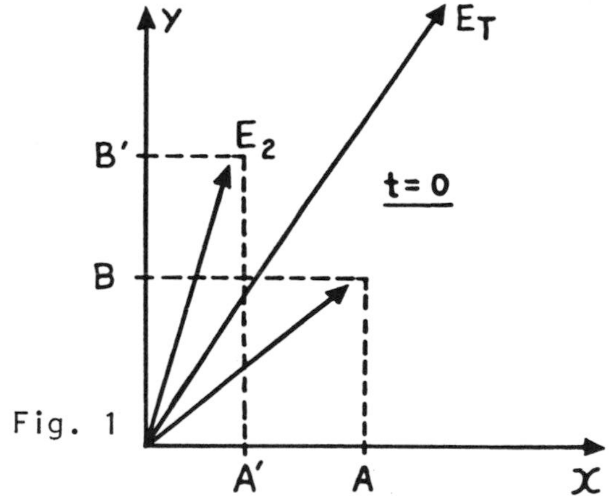

Fig. 1

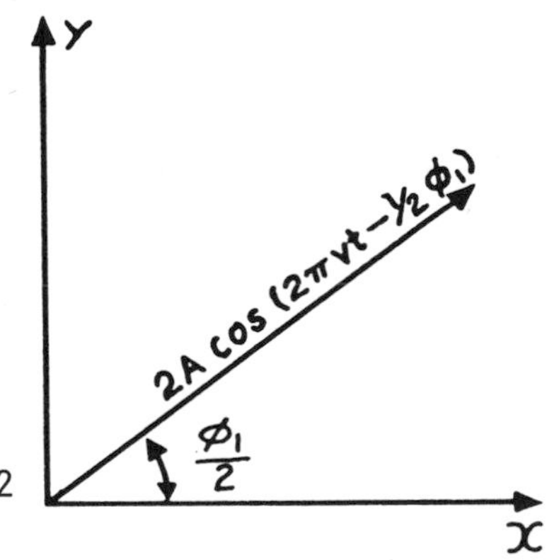

Fig. 2

Solution: 1) $E_1 = (\hat{\imath}A_1 + \hat{\jmath}B_1) \cos 2\pi\nu t,$

$$E_2 = (\hat{\imath}A_2 + \hat{\jmath}B_2) \cos 2\pi\nu t.$$

Now, add the components of E_1 and E_2 together to find the expression for E_T. Then, $E_T = \{\hat{\imath}(A_1 + A_2) + \hat{\jmath}(B_1 + B_2)\} \cos 2\pi\nu t$.

The point here is that the quantity in { } just specifies a vector, and the time variation is the same for all parts of it. So the vector lies along a line and changes size, but not direction. Therefore, $\bar{E}_T$ is linearly polarized. In the case of circular polarization, this is not true, since the x and y components vary differently in time, one being large when the other is small.

2) Left: $E_1 = \hat{i}E_\circ \cos 2\pi\nu t + \hat{j}E_\circ \sin 2\pi\nu t$,

Right: $E_2 = \hat{i}E_\circ \cos(2\pi\nu t + \alpha) - \hat{j}E_\circ \sin(2\pi\nu t + \alpha)$.

$$E_T = \hat{i}E_\circ\{\cos 2\pi\nu t + \cos(2\pi\nu t + \alpha)\} + \hat{j}E_\circ\{\sin 2\pi\nu t - \sin(2\pi\nu t + \alpha)\}$$

$$\cos(2\pi\nu t + \alpha) = \cos(2\pi\nu t + \tfrac{\alpha}{2} + \tfrac{\alpha}{2})$$

Using one of the double angle formulas, we find

$$\cos(2\pi\nu t + \alpha) = \cos(2\pi\nu t + \tfrac{\alpha}{2}) \cos\tfrac{\alpha}{2} - \sin(2\pi\nu t + \tfrac{\alpha}{2}) \sin\tfrac{\alpha}{2}$$

$$= \cos(2\pi\nu t + \tfrac{\alpha}{2}) \cos\tfrac{\alpha}{2} - (\sin 2\pi\nu t \cos\tfrac{\alpha}{2} + \cos 2\pi\nu t \sin\tfrac{\alpha}{2}) \sin\tfrac{\alpha}{2}$$

where we have made use of the formula

$$\sin(x + y) = \sin x \cos y + \cos x \sin y.$$

Then, $\cos(2\pi\nu t + \alpha)$

$$= \cos(2\pi\nu t + \tfrac{\alpha}{2}) \cos\tfrac{\alpha}{2} - \sin 2\pi\nu t \cos\tfrac{\alpha}{2} \sin\tfrac{\alpha}{2} - \cos 2\pi\nu t \sin^2\tfrac{\alpha}{2}.$$

Therefore, $\cos 2\pi\nu t + \cos(2\pi\nu t + \alpha)$

$$= \cos 2\pi\nu t + \cos(2\pi\nu t + \tfrac{\alpha}{2}) \cos\tfrac{\alpha}{2} - \sin 2\pi\nu t \cos\tfrac{\alpha}{2} \sin\tfrac{\alpha}{2}$$

$$- \cos 2\pi\nu t \sin^2\tfrac{\alpha}{2}.$$

Substituting $1 - \cos^2\frac{\alpha}{2}$ for $\sin^2\frac{\alpha}{2}$ in the preceding expression yields the following result:

$$\cos(2\pi\nu t) + \cos(2\pi\nu t + \alpha) = \cos(2\pi\nu t) + \cos(2\pi\nu t + \tfrac{\alpha}{2}) \cos\tfrac{\alpha}{2}$$

$$- \sin(2\pi\nu t) \cos\tfrac{\alpha}{2} \sin\tfrac{\alpha}{2} + \cos(2\pi\nu t) \cos^2\tfrac{\alpha}{2} - \cos(2\pi\nu t).$$

The $\cos(2\pi\nu t)$ terms cancel one another, and so,

$\cos(2\pi\nu t) + \cos(2\pi\nu t + \alpha)$

$$= \cos(2\pi\nu t + \tfrac{\alpha}{2}) \cos\tfrac{\alpha}{2} + \cos\tfrac{\alpha}{2} \Big[\cos(2\pi\nu t) \cos\tfrac{\alpha}{2}$$

$$- \sin(2\pi\nu t) \sin\tfrac{\alpha}{2}\Big].$$

By applying the double angle formula $\cos(x + y) = \cos x \cos y - \sin x \sin y$, we have the result that $\cos(2\pi\nu t) + \cos(2\pi\nu t + \alpha)$ $= 2\cos(2\pi\nu t + \frac{\alpha}{2}) \cos\frac{\alpha}{2}$. Similarly, $\sin(2\pi\nu t) - \sin(2\pi\nu t + \alpha)$ $= 2\sin\frac{\alpha}{2} \cos(2\pi\nu t + \frac{\alpha}{2})$.

Therefore,

$$E_T = 2\hat{\imath}E_o \cos\left(2\pi\nu t + \frac{\alpha}{2}\right) \cos\frac{\alpha}{2} + 2\hat{\jmath}E_o \sin\frac{\alpha}{2} \cos\left(2\pi\nu t + \frac{\alpha}{2}\right)$$

$$= 2E_o\left(\hat{\imath}\cos\frac{\alpha}{2} + \hat{\jmath}\sin\frac{\alpha}{2}\right)\cos\left(2\pi\nu t + \frac{\alpha}{2}\right).$$

Since the two components are in phase, we can add them in a vector diagram: E_T is a vector of magnitude $2A\cos\{2\pi\nu t - (\phi_1/2)\}$ at an angle of $\phi_{1/2}$ to the y axis.

Notice that we can see some easy limiting cases in the first two lines: If $\alpha = 0$ the y components cancel out, while the x components add to $E_T = \hat{\imath}2E_0 \cos(2\pi\nu t)$ ($\alpha = 2\pi$ just multiplies everything by -1). If $\alpha = \pi/2$, we get $E_T =$

$$2E_o\left(\hat{\imath}\cos\frac{\pi}{4} + \hat{\jmath}\sin\frac{\pi}{4}\right)\cos\left(2\pi\nu t + \frac{\pi}{4}\right)$$

$$= \sqrt{2}E_o(\hat{\imath} + \hat{\jmath})\left(\cos 2\pi\nu t \cos\frac{\pi}{4} - \sin 2\pi\nu t \sin\frac{\pi}{4}\right)$$

$$= E_o(\hat{\imath} + \hat{\jmath})(\cos 2\pi\nu t - \sin 2\pi\nu t)$$

linearly polarized at 45 degrees.

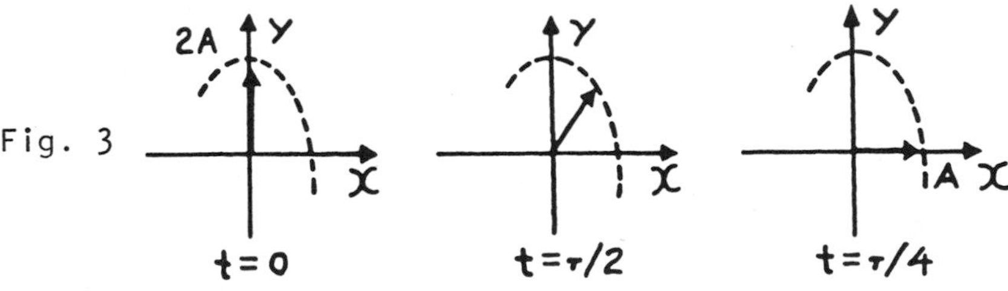

Fig. 3

3) $E = \hat{\imath}A\sin 2\pi\nu t + \hat{\jmath}B\cos 2\pi\nu t.$

First take out a circularly polarized part:

$E_o = \hat{\imath}A\sin 2\pi\nu t + \hat{\jmath}A\cos 2\pi\nu t.$

What is left is $E_{lin} = \hat{\jmath}(B - A)\cos 2\pi\nu t$, a linearly polarized wave. To show that the original wave is elliptically polarized, draw the vector at various times, as shown in the figure.

RESISTIVE CIRCUITS

• PROBLEM 1094

In the circuit shown in Fig. 1, find v_1 and the voltage v across both sources if i_s is given as 12A.

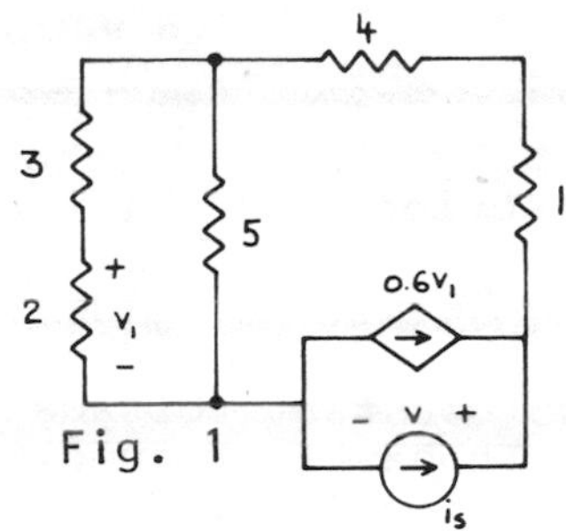

Fig. 1

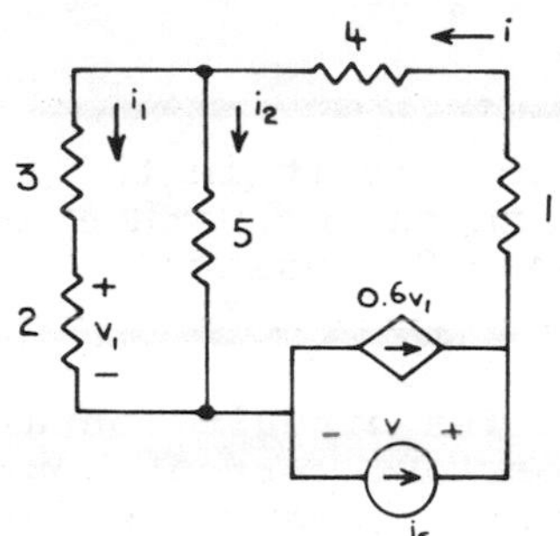

Fig. 2

Solution: In Fig. 2 observe that

$$i = i_s + 0.6v_1 = i_1 + i_2.$$

Since i_1 and i_2 both flow through a branch with the same equivalent resistances, they must be equal. Thus we have

$$i = i_s + 0.6v_1 = 2i_1 = 2i_2.$$

We can write $v_1 = i_1 R$ where $R = 2\text{-}\Omega$. Since $i = 2i_1$ we have

$$i_1 = \tfrac{1}{2}i = \tfrac{1}{2}(i_s + 0.6\ v_1)$$

$$v_1 = i_1 R = \tfrac{1}{2}(i_s + 0.6v_1)R$$

Substituting 2-Ω of R and 12A for i_s, solve for v_1

$$v_1 = \tfrac{1}{2}(12 + 0.6v_1)\ 2$$

$$v_1 = 12 + 0.6v_1$$

$$0.4\ v_1 = 12$$

giving $$v_1 = \frac{12}{0.4} = 30V.$$

v is found by calculating i and the equivalent resistance R_{eq} across the terminals of the two sources.

From Fig. 3 we find $v = R_{eq}\ i = 7.5(30) = 225V.$

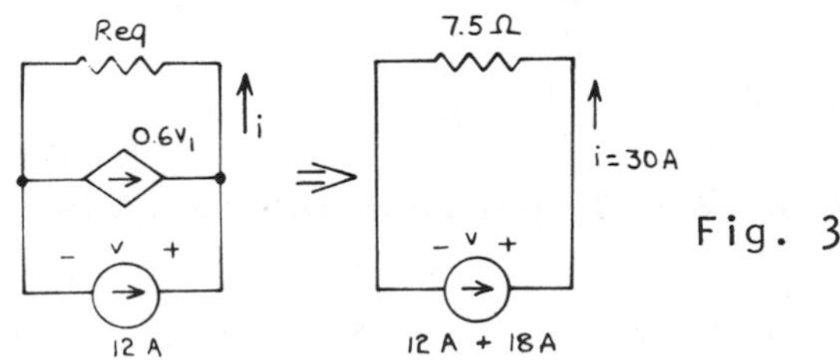

Fig. 3

• PROBLEM 1095

Analyze the circuit in the figure below using Kirchoff's Rules. Find the magnitude and direction of I_2, the current in the upper 2Ω resistor.

Solution: The circuit contains two constant voltage sources and two constant current sources. It has four junctions where three or more wires join, labelled A, B, C, and D, as shown. To begin, we label the unknown currents I, I_1, I_2, I_3, and I_4, as indicated in the figure.

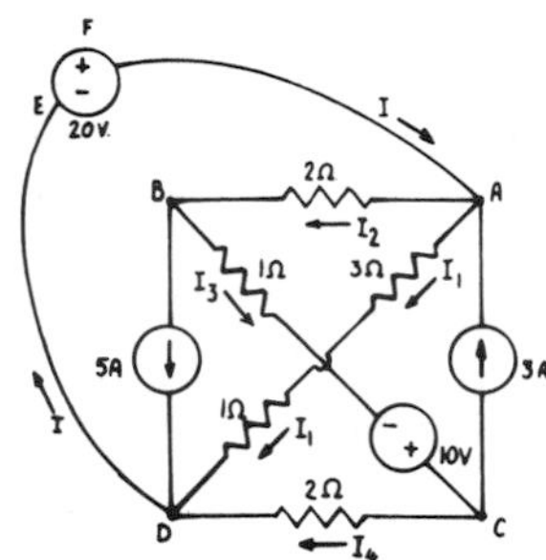

This problem has five unknowns (the five unknown currents) and, therefore, requires five independent equations. Three independent equations are obtained by applying Kirchoff's Current Sum rule at any three of the four junctions. For convenience, we ignore units and choose junctions A, B, and C:

$$\text{at A, } I + 3 = I_2 + 5; \tag{1}$$

$$\text{at B, } \quad I_2 = I_3 + 5; \tag{2}$$

$$\text{at C, } \quad I_3 = I_4 + 3. \tag{3}$$

The two additional independent equations required for the solution are obtained by applying Kirchoff's Voltage Sum rule about closed loops in the circuit. As it is difficult to represent the potential drops across the constant current sources, we choose the loops ADEF and ABCDEF:

$$\text{loop ADEF, } 20 = 3I_1 + I_1, \tag{4}$$

$$\text{loop ABCDEF, } 20 = 2I_2 + I_3 - 10 + 2I_4. \tag{5}$$

From (4), by inspection, $I_1 = 5$ amperes. Multiplying (2) by minus two gives

$$-2I_2 + 2I_3 = -10,$$

and, rewriting (5),

$$2I_2 + I_3 + 2I_4 = 30.$$

The sum of these two equations is

$$3I_3 + 2I_4 = 20. \qquad (6)$$

Multiplying (3) by two gives

$$2I_3 - 2I_4 = 6$$

which, when summed with (6), results in

$$5I_3 = 26$$

or, $I_3 = 26/5$ amperes. Substituting this result back into (6) gives

$$3(26/5) + 2I_4 - 20,$$

or $I_4 - 11/5$ amperes.

The remaining two currents are found by substituting these results, first into (2) and then into (1):

$$I_2 = (26/5) + 5,$$

$$I = I_2 + 2.$$

Therefore, the current in the upper 2Ω resistor has the magnitude $I_2 = 51/5$ amperes, and flows in the direction of the arrow shown in the figure. The total current flowing in the circuit is $I = 61/5$ ampere.

BASIC CIRCUIT ANALYSIS

• PROBLEM 1096

In the resistive ladder network of Fig. 1, deduce the relationship between v_4 and v_0, between i_4 and v_0, and between i_0 and v_0.

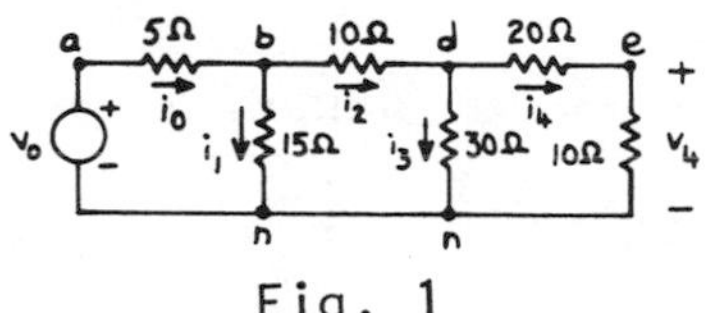

Fig. 1

Solution: By using the nodes and current directions indicated in Fig. 1,

$$i_4 = \frac{1}{10} v_4 \qquad \text{(from Ohm's Law.)}$$

Since, $v_d = v_{de} + v_4$ and $v_{de} = 20\ i_4 = 20 \left(\frac{1}{10} v_4\right) = 2\ v_4$,

then $v_d = 2\ v_4 + v_4 = 3\ v_4$.

The current i_3 through the 30 Ω resistance is

$$\frac{v_d}{30} = \frac{3\ v_4}{30} = \frac{v_4}{10}$$

Summing the current at node d yields

$$i_2 = i_3 + i_4 = \frac{v_4}{10} + \frac{1}{10} v_4 = \frac{v_4}{5}$$

Since, $v_b = v_{bd} + v_d$ and $v_{bd} = 10 i_2 = 2\ v_4$, then

$$v_b = 2\ v_4 + 3\ v_4 = 5\ v_4$$

The current i_1 through the 15Ω resistor is

$$\frac{v_b}{15} = \frac{5\ v_4}{15} = \frac{v_4}{3}$$

Summing the currents at node b gives

$$i_0 = i_1 + i_2 = \frac{v_4}{3} + \frac{v_4}{5} = \frac{8}{15} v_4$$

Since $v_0 = v_{ab} + v_b$ where $v_{ab} = 5 i_0 = 5 \left(\frac{8}{15} v_4\right) = \frac{8}{3} v_4$,
gives, $v_0 = \frac{8}{3} v_4 + 5\ v_4 = \frac{23}{3} v_4$ the relationship between v_4 and v_0.

Since we have already found

$$i_4 = \frac{1}{10} v_4 \ ; \qquad v_4 = 10 i_4 \text{ gives}$$

$v_0 = \frac{23}{3} v_4 = \frac{230}{3} i_4$ the second required relationship.

Finally, $i_0 = \frac{8}{15} v_4$ which gives

$$v_0 = \frac{24}{3} v_4 = \frac{23}{3} \frac{15}{8} i_0 = \frac{115}{8} i_0$$

which is also a required result.

• PROBLEM 1097

In the circuit shown in Fig. 1, $v_1 = 3e^{-2\times10^4 t}$ V. Find: (a) v_2; (b) v_3; (c) v_4.

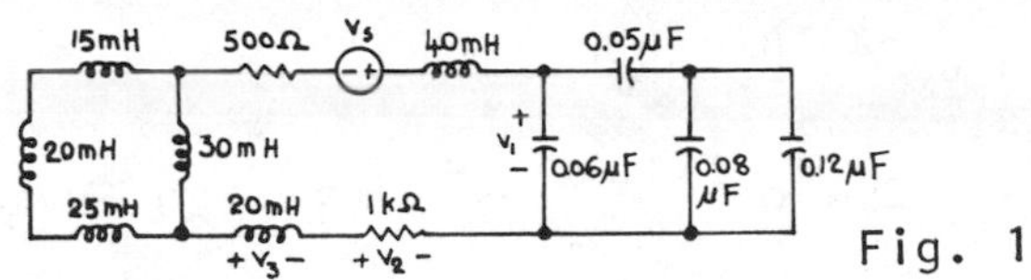

Fig. 1

Solution: Combining the inductors on the left and the capacitors on the right, forms a single loop circuit shown in Fig. 2.

The current can be found through the .1μF capacitor, hence the current through the loop by use of

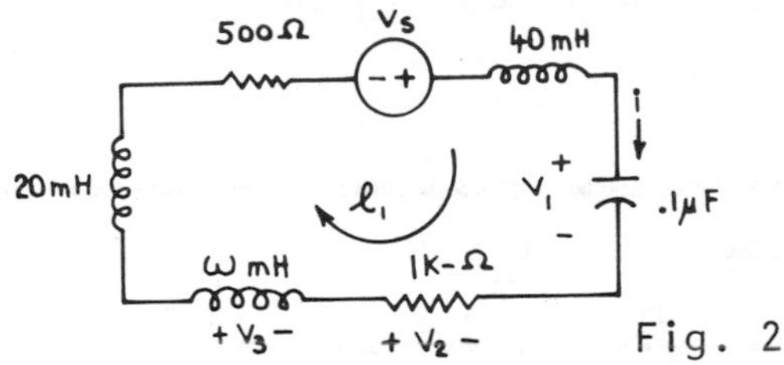

Fig. 2

$$i = C\frac{dv_1}{dt} \quad \text{is}$$

$$i = C\frac{d\left[3e^{-2\times10^4 t}\right]}{dt}$$

$$i = 0.1 \times 10^{-6}\ (-\ 2 \times 10^4)(3)\ e^{-\ 2 \times 10^4 t}$$

$$i = -\ 6\ e^{-\ 2 \times 10^4 t}\ \text{mA.}$$

Find $v_2 = iR$

$$v_2 = iR = -\left[-\ 6\ (1k)\ e^{-2\times10^4 t}\right] = 6e^{-2\times10^4 t}\ \text{V}$$

Also find $v_3 = L\dfrac{di}{dt}$

$$v_3 = -\left[(.02)\ \frac{d\left[-\ 6e^{-2\times10^4 t}\ \text{mA}\right]}{dt}\right] = -\ 2.4e^{-2\times10^4 t}\ \text{V}$$

v_s can be found by summing the voltages around the loop ℓ_1 in Fig. 2.

$$v_s = 40 \text{ mH} \frac{di}{dt} + v_1 - v_2 - v_3 + 20 \text{ mH} \frac{di}{dt} + 500\, i$$

Note that

$$v_1 = 3e^{-2\times10^4 t}$$

$$v_2 = 6e^{-2\times10^4 t}$$

$$v_3 = -\,2.4\, e^{-2\times10^4 t} \;; \quad -\,v_3 = 20 \text{ mH} \frac{di}{dt}$$

$$-\,\frac{v_2}{2} = 500i = -\,3e^{-2\times10^4 t}$$

$$-\,(2\, v_3) = 40 \text{ mH} \frac{di}{dt} = 4.8\, e^{-2\times10^4 t}$$

thus, $v_s = [4.8 + 3 - 6 - (-\,2.4) + 2.4 - 3]e^{-2\times10^4 t}$

$$v_s = 3.6e^{-2\times10^4 t} \quad .$$

• PROBLEM 1098

Find v_x in the circuit shown in Fig. 1 by: (a) nodal analysis; (b) mesh analysis; (c) beginning on the right side of the circuit and alternating source transformations and source and resistance combinations until only a single loop circuit remains.

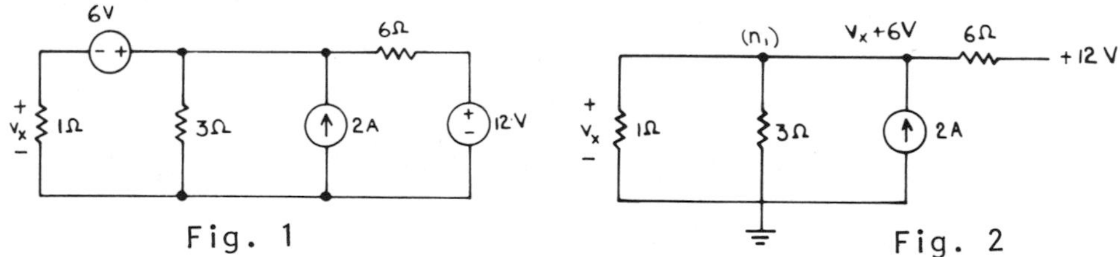

Solution: (a) Remove the 6-V and the 12-V source from Fig. 1 and re-draw a new circuit as shown in Fig. 2.

By setting the voltage at node n:$v_x + 6$, a single KCL equation can be derived and solved for v_x directly.

Thus, for node n_1,

$$2 = (v_x + 6)\,\frac{1}{3} + ([v_x + 6]) - 12)\,\frac{1}{6} + \frac{v_x}{1}$$

$$2 = \frac{v_x}{3} + 2 + \frac{v_x}{6} + 1 - 2 + v_x$$

$$1 = \frac{9v_x}{6}$$

$$v_x = \frac{2}{3} \text{ V.}$$

(b) Write three KVL equations for the three loops shown in Fig. 3.

However, there is a current source in the circuit. Thus, the analysis must be modified. One standard procedure is to remove the current source leaving an open circuit in its place, writing down the reduced-number of loop equations and, by relating the current source to the currents, pick up the extra equations necessary. This yields for $\ell_1 - \ell_2$:

$$12 + 6i_2 - 3(i_1 + i_3) = 0$$

for ℓ_3

$$6 - 3\,(i_1 + i_3) - 1i_3 = 0$$

and $\quad i_1 + i_2 = 2$

Fig. 3

Substituting i_1 from the current equation into the voltage equations gives us

$$6 + 9i_2 - 3i_3 = 0$$

$$0 + 3i_2 - 4i_3 = 0.$$

By direct substitution of $i_3 = 3/4\ i_2$ into the first equation results in $i_2 = -\,8/9$ which then gives $i_3 = -\,2/3$. This means $i_3 = 2/3$ A flowing down the 1Ω resistor

Substituting i_1 from the current equation into the voltage equations gives us

$$6 + 9i_2 - 3i_3 = 0$$

$$0 + 3i_2 - 4i_3 = 0.$$

By direct substitution of $i_3 = 3/4\ i_2$ into the first equation results in $i_2 = -\,8/9$ which then gives $i_3 = -\,2/3$. This means $i_3 = 2/3$ A flowing down the 1Ω resistor giving us $v_x = 2/3$ V with the polarity as indicated in Figure 3.

(c) The 12-V source and the 6-Ω resistor in the circuit of Fig. 1 can be transformed into a current source and a parallel resistor as shown in Fig. 4.

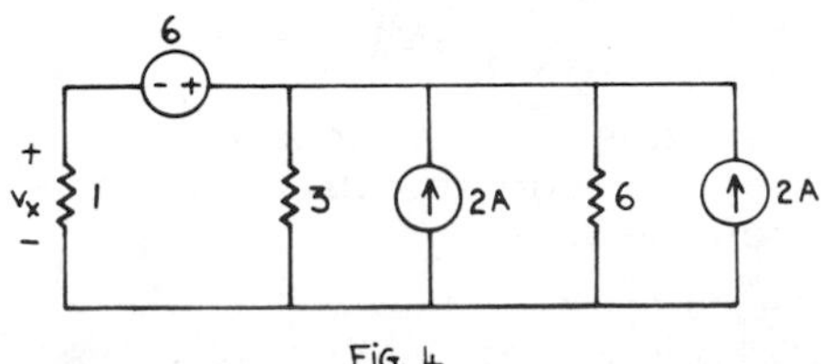

FIG. 4

The 3-Ω and 6-Ω resistors are combined. The expression

$$\frac{1}{R_T} = \frac{1}{R_1} + \frac{1}{R_2}$$

gives us that the resulting resistance is 2Ω. The two 2-A sources add to form a single 4-A source and the resulting practical current source can be transformed into a voltage source and series resistor. The circuit shown in Fig. 5 is the resulting single loop circuit.

Writing a KVL equation around the loop shown

$$8 - 6 = i(2 + 1)$$

we have $i = \frac{8-6}{2+1} = \frac{2}{3}$ A

giving $v_x = (1)\frac{2}{3} = \frac{2}{3}$ V.

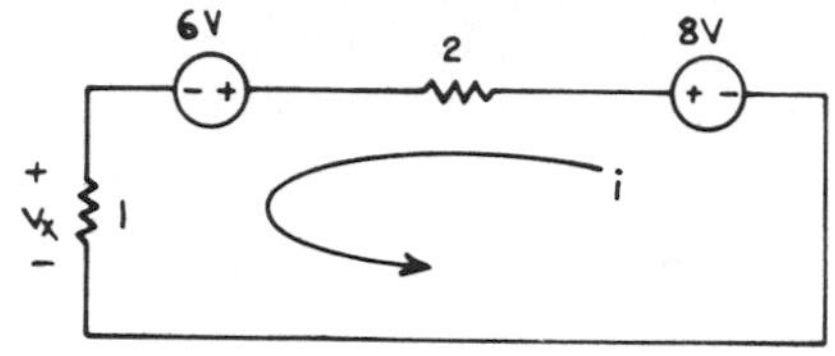

FIG. 5

RL AND RC CIRCUITS

• PROBLEM 1099

For the circuit shown in Fig. 1, find: (a) i_L; (b) v_L.

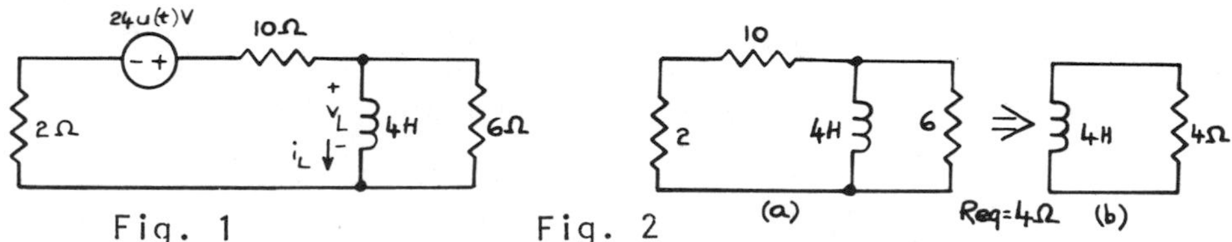

Fig. 1 Fig. 2

Solution: We can determine the complete response $i_L(t)$ by finding the sum of the natural and forced responses.

In the circuit of Fig. 1, the natural response would be the response which occurs when the 24-V source is "off" or short-circuited.

The natural response for the circuit in Fig. 2(b) is, therefore,

$$i_n = A\,e^{-t}$$

The forced response is the response that would occur at t = ∞. Fig. 3 shows the circuit for t = ∞, with the inductor short circuited.

$$i_f = i_L(\infty) = \frac{24\ V}{12\ \Omega} = 2A$$

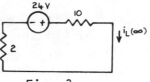

Fig. 3

The complete response becomes

$$i_L(t) = i_n + i_f = Ae^{-t} + 2,$$

since the current through an inductor cannot change instantaneously and $i(0^-) = 0$. Thus,

$$i(0^+) = 0$$

$$i_L(0^+) = A + 2 = 0$$

giving, $A = -2$

$$i_L(t) = 2(1 - e^{-t})\ u(t)\ A.$$

Find the voltage v_L in the same way.

$$v_L = v_n + v_f$$

We already know that $v_f = v_L(\infty) = 0$ so that

$$v_L = v_n + 0 = V_0\ e^{-t}.$$

V_0 is the initial voltage across the inductor. We can find this voltage by observing that at $t = 0^+$, $i_L = 0$ so that the voltage across the 6-Ω resistor is equal to $v_L(0^+)$. Since all the current in the loop flows through the 6-Ω resistor

$$v_L(0^+) = \frac{24}{6 + 2 + 10}(6) = 8V$$

thus $v_L(t) = 8\ e^{-t}\ u(t)\ V.$

• PROBLEM 1100

For the circuit of Fig. 1, let $i_s = 2u(t)$ A and find; (a) i_L; (b) i_1.

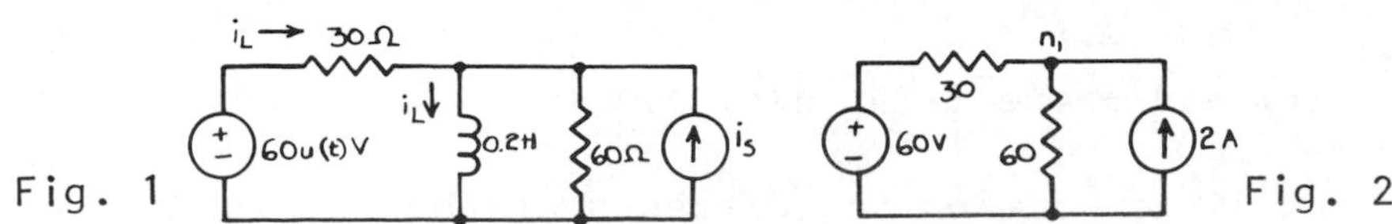

Fig. 1 Fig. 2

Solution: Since both sources turn "on" at $t = 0$, $i_L(0) = 0$, by finding the voltage across the 60-Ω resistor at $t = 0^+$, we find the voltage across the inductor. Writing a KCL equation for node n_1 in Fig. 2 gives $v_L(0^+)$.

$$2 = \frac{v_L - 60}{30} + \frac{v_L}{60}$$

$$\left(\frac{1}{30} + \frac{1}{60}\right) v_L = 2 + \frac{60}{30}$$

$$v_L(0^+) = \frac{4}{\left(\frac{1}{30} + \frac{1}{60}\right)} = \frac{4}{.05} = 80V$$

The RL circuit which gives the natural response of the circuit in Fig. 1 is shown in Fig. 3.

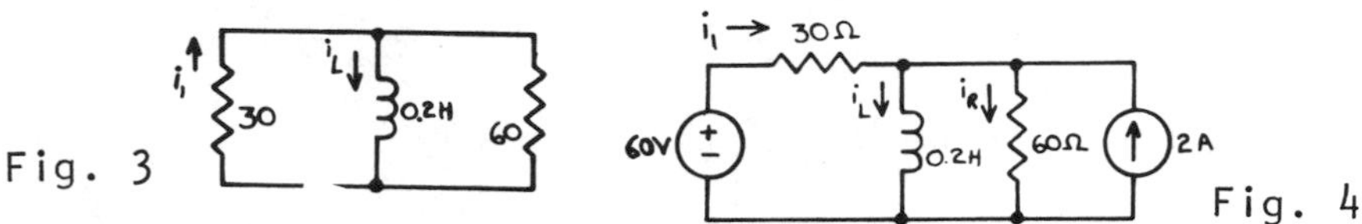

Fig. 3 Fig. 4

$$R_{eq} = 30//60 = \frac{30(60)}{30 + 60} = 20\ \Omega$$

We can now write

$$v_L(t) = 80\ e^{-\frac{20}{0.2}t} = 80\ e^{-100t}\ u(t)\ V.$$

Substituting $v_L(t)$ into the following equation gives $i_L(t)$

$$i_L(t) = i_0 + \frac{1}{L}\int_0^t v_L(T)dT$$

$$i_0 = 0,$$

$$i_L(t) = \frac{1}{0.2}\int_0^t 80\ e^{-100T}\ dT$$

$$i_L(t) = \frac{80}{0.2}\left(\frac{1}{-100}\right)[e^{-100T}]_0^t$$

$$i_L(t) = -4\ (e^{-100t} - 1)A.$$

$$i_L(t) = 4 - 4\ e^{-100t}\ u(t)\ A.$$

Find i_1 by summing the currents at node n_1 in Fig. 4.

$$2 + i_1 = i_L + i_R$$

$$i_R = \frac{v_L}{60} = \frac{80}{60} e^{-100t} = \frac{4}{3} e^{-100t}$$

$$2 + i_1 = 4 - 4e^{-100t} + \frac{4}{3} e^{-100t}$$

$$i_1 = -2 + 4 - 4e^{-100t} + \frac{4}{3} e^{-100t}$$

$$i_1(t) = 2 - \frac{8}{3} e^{-100t} u(t) \text{ A.}$$

• PROBLEM 1101

For the network of fig. 1

(a) Choose i(t) as the unknown of the circuit and write a first-order differential equation in i(t).

(b) Give the homogeneous solution to the equation obtained in (a).

(c) Give the particular solution to the equation obtained in (a).

(d) Write down the total solution of the equation obtained in (a) and determine the unknown constant using the initial condition.

(e) Sketch the plot of i(t) versus t.

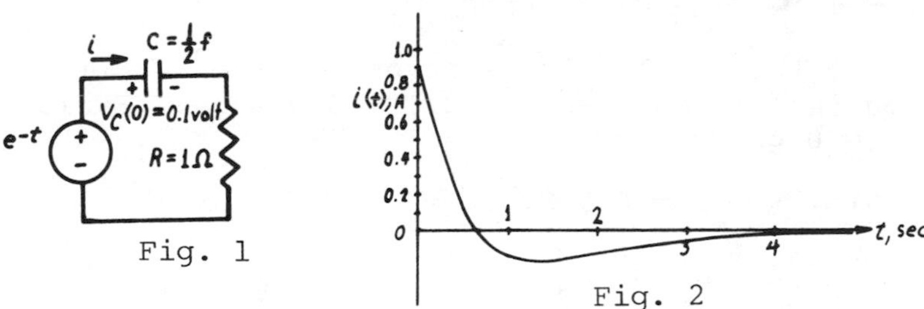

Fig. 1

Fig. 2

Solution: (a) In general, for a series RC circuit,

$$\frac{1}{C}\int i(t)\, dt + Ri(t) = v(t).$$

For this problem we have

$$2\int i\, dt + i = e^{-t}.$$

A differential equation is obtained by differentiating the above equation with respect to t. Thus

$$2i + \frac{di}{dt} = -e^{-t}.$$

(b) The homogeneous equation is

$$2i + \frac{di}{dt} = 0.$$

Assume a solution of the form $i = e^{mt}$.

Substituting this into the differential equation gives the characteristic equation,

$$2 + m = 0$$

whose solution is $m = 2$. Hence

$$i_h = Ke^{-2t} \text{ A.}$$

(c) The particular solution is found by assuming a current of the same form as the driving function. $i = ae^{-t}$. Substituting this into the differential equation gives

$$2ae^{-t} - ae^{-t} = -e^{-t}.$$

Solving for a

$$2a - a = -1$$

or

$$a = -1.$$

The particular solution is

$$i_p = -e^{-t} \text{ A.}$$

(d) The total solution is

$$i = i_h + i_p = Ke^{-2t} - e^{-t}.$$

At $t = 0$ the total voltage across R is $e^{-0} - 0.1 = 0.9$ volts. The current through R is $0.9/1 = 0.9$ amps. Evaluating i for $t = 0$ gives

$$i(0) = K - 1 = 0.9 \text{ A.}$$

Solving for K we get $K = 1.9$.

The final solution is

$$i(t) = 1.9e^{-2t} - e^{-t}\text{A.}$$

(e) A plot of i(t) is shown in fig. 2.

• **PROBLEM** 1102

With reference to the circuit shown in Fig. 1, let $v_s = 30u(t)$ V and determine: (a) $v_c(t)$; (b) $v_1(t)$.

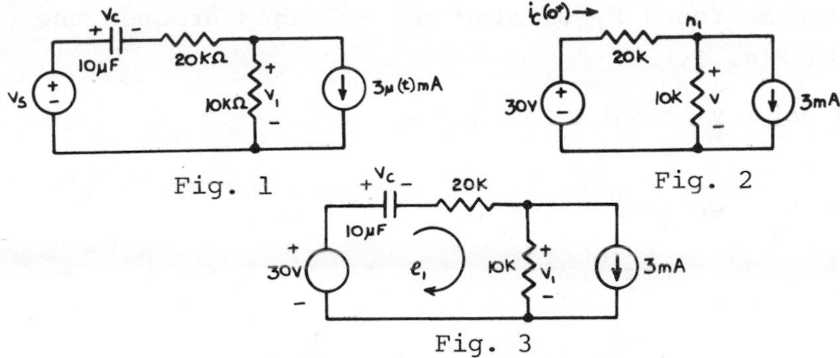

Fig. 3

Solution: (a) Since all sources are "dead" for $t < 0$, $v_c(0^+) = 0$. Replacing the capacitor with a **short circuit** yields the circuit for $t = 0^+$ in Fig. 2.

Writing a KCL equation for node n_1

$$- 3 \text{ mA} = \frac{v - 30}{20k} + \frac{v}{10k}$$

gives the initial conditions

$$v = \frac{- 3 \text{ mA} + \frac{3}{2} \text{ mA}}{\left(\frac{1}{20k} + \frac{1}{10k}\right)} = - 10 \text{ V}$$

$$i_c(0^+) = - \frac{v - 30}{20k} = - \frac{- 10 - 30}{20k} = 2 \text{ mA}.$$

One can use

$$v_c(t) = V_0 + \frac{1}{C} \int_{t_0}^{t} i(T)\, dT$$

given $i(t) = 2\, e^{-\frac{t}{R_{eq} C}}$ mA,

$R_{eq} = 30\text{k}\Omega$, and $T = 0.3$ s, to find the capacitor voltage.

Hence, $$v_c(t) = 0 + \frac{1}{10 \times 10^{-6}} \int_0^t 2 \times 10^{-3}\, e^{-\frac{T}{0.3}}\, dT$$

$$v_c(t) = \frac{2 \times 10^{-3}}{10 \times 10^{-6}} (- 0.3) \left[e^{-\frac{T}{0.3}} \right]_0^t$$

$$v_c(t) = - 60 \left(e^{-\frac{t}{0.3}} - 1 \right) u(t) \text{ V}.$$

v_1 can be found by summing the voltages around the loop ℓ_1 in Fig. 3.

$$30 = v_C + v_2 + v_1$$

$$30 = 60 - 60\, e^{-\frac{t}{0.3}} + i_C(t)(20k) + v_1$$

$$i_C(t) = 2\, e^{-\frac{t}{0.3}} \text{ mA}$$

$$v_1 = 30 - 60 + 60\, e^{-\frac{t}{0.3}} - 40\, e^{-\frac{t}{0.3}}$$

$$v_1 = \left[-30 + 20\, e^{-\frac{t}{0.3}} \right] u(t) \text{ V}$$

Note that $v(0) = [-30 + 20]\text{V} = -10\text{V}$, corresponds to the initial condition found earlier.

INDEX

Numbers on this page refer to <u>PROBLEM NUMBERS,</u> not page numbers

Absolute zero, 987
Acceleration, 58-60, 72, 88-131, 164-5, 217, 334, 621, 964
  angular acceleration, 73, 155, 172, 184-209, 249
  average, 63, 69, 71, 77
  centripetal, 146, 147, 153, 159, 164, 165, 215, 711
  constant, 70, 74, 83, 89, 128, 206, 273, 317
  graph, 67
  gravitational, 78, 80, 90, 140-3, 162, 264, 367, 369
  instantaneous, 71
  linear, 101
  moon, 94
  radial, 155, 156, 162
  rotational, 130
  uniform, 64, 77, 87
Accelerator, 626
Accelerator, Van de Graaff, 954
Accelerometer, 109
Action and reaction, 174
Acoustics, 839
Adiabatic, 501
  expansion, 522
  process, 527
Aerodynamics, 434
Alpha, 580
  decay, 1017, 1024, 1025
  particle, 335, 711, 997, 1026
  particle emission, 1023
Alternating, 769
AMA, 289, 290
Ammeter, 655, 670, 683, 796
Ampere's law, 705, 743, 745
Ampere's circuital law, 734
Amplitude, 362, 370, 381, 807
Amplitude of vibration, 379
Anemometer, 758
Annihilation, 1055
Anode, 794
Antineutrino, 1021
Antinode, 837, 839
Archimede's principle, 393-407, 428, 429, 639, 817
Area of a parallelogram, 4
Atomic cross section, 1030
Atoms, 919
  copper, 913
  deuterium, 1058
  hydrogen, 970, 1009
  number of, 913
  radium, 1017
Atwood's machine, 115, 119
Average values, 982
Avogadro's number, 490, 493, 496, 508

Bacon, F. T., 794
Banked, 166
Banking angle, 166
Barometers, 416, 453, 519
Battery, 648
  Bacon, 794
  car, 789
Beam, 34, 35
Beam intensity, 626
Beats, 832
Beat note, 831
Bernoulli, 430-4
  principle, 437
  theorem, 427
Berillium, 335
Beta:
  decay, 1022, 1031
  emitter, 1015
  particle emission, 1018
Betatron, 760
Biot-Savart law, 706, 712, 740, 742
Body problem, 279
Body, rigid, 196, 344
Bohr:
  atom, 339
  magneton, 710
  model, 583, 910, 924, 969, 1035
  theory, 969
Boltzman constant, 277, 1008
Boltzman distribution, 998, 999
Boyle's law, 412, 419, 508, 512, 513, 515
Bragg's law, 1006, 1039
Breakdown, 557
Brewster angle, 812
Btu, 459, 460
Bulk modulus, 355, 357, 501

Numbers on this page refer to PROBLEM NUMBERS, not page numbers

Buoyancy, 396, 401, 639, 817
Buoyant effect of air, 405

Calibrated, 655
Calorie, 461, 463
Calorific value of coal, 657
Calorimeter, 476, 481, 482, 484
Capacitance, 606, 608, 689, 695, 777
    equivalent, 687, 688
    in parallel, 694
    parallel plate, 633
Capacitor, 606, 658, 687-94, 763-4, 769
    discharge of, 690
    in parallel, 687, 689
    in series, 687, 689
    parallel plate, 610-17, 638, 694
Capillaries, 426
Capillary tube, 412, 422
Carbon-14 nuclei, 1028
Carnot cycle, 533, 535
Carnot refrigerator, 535
Carnot's theorem, 529
Cathode-ray tube, 779
Cavendish balance, 138
Celsius and Fahrenheit scales, 439
Celsius Kelvin scale, 443
Centigrade scale, 440
Centripetal, 176
Change length of a day, 341
Charge, 559, 562, 564, 584, 652, 693
    bound, 618
    conservation of, 680, 691, 1031
    distribution, 564, 595
    free, 618
    in magnetic field, 709
    induction of, 551
    infinite sheet, 566
    oscillating, 809
    plate, 566
Charle's law, 504
Circuit, 668, 768, 769
    AC, 766
    LC, 772
    LR, 697
    Magnetic, 734
    Parallel, 667
    Tuning, 778
    RC, 692, 695
    Resistive, 682
Circular, 338
Circular wire loop, 755
Cloud chamber, 522
Rotating coils, 756
Toroidal coil, 705
Collision, 275, 296, 299, 301-32, 472, 938
    cylinder, 493
    elastic, 305, 310, 315
    inelastic, 317, 326, 329
    particles in, 332

Component method, 11
Compressibility, 355, 356
Compression, 38
Compton, 1040
    collision, 1041
    effect, 1037, 1040
    wavelength, 1037
Conduction, 549
    heat, 537
Conductivity-thermal, 538, 540-5
Conductor-spherical, 592
Consumption, rate of, 132
Contact angle, 422, 424
Continuity, equation of, 433-5
Continuity, law of, 437
Contour, 760
Conversion formula, 440, 441
Correction of rest mass, 953
Cost, 650
Coulomb, 552, 576-87, 596-7, 699, 721, 993
    attraction, 988
    barrier, 1019
    force, 598
Critical angle, 859-62, 869
Crystal structure, 913
Current, 643-6, 652-6, 668-84, 696, 773, 789-94
    alternating, 659, 762, 771
    induced, 736, 750
    peak, 798
    time dependent, 761
Curvature, center of, 846
Curvature, radius of, 165, 854
Cyclotron, 713, 715-17

Numbers on this page refer to PROBLEM NUMBERS, not page numbers

Damping factor, 380
Davisson-Germer apparatus, 1003
DC motor, 698
DC source, 768
de Broglie, 964, 1044
theory of matter, 960
wavelength, 921, 960, 966, 967, 991, 1004
waves, 968, 1003
Debye equation, 469
Decay, 1014, 1047, 1053
constant, 1020
radioactive, 1013, 1015, 1018, 1020, 1033, 1054
rate, 1032
Deceleration, 142
Deflection, 631
full-scale, 655, 670
maximum, 671
Degree of freedom, 534
Density, 32, 135, 140, 150, 393-404, 414-5, 817, 918, 987
atomic, 919
electromagnetic energy, 810
liquid, 392
relative, 401, 413
water, 512
Deuterium, 1048
Deuteron, 965, 1060
Deviation, 909
Dew point, 520
Dielectric, 613-618
coefficient, 617, 693
constant, 588
strength, 557, 613
Differential equations, 378, 1011, 1013
Differential hoist, 292
Diffraction, 901, 906, 1004
Diffraction grating, 905, 907
Diffraction pattern, 902, 903
Diode, 659
Dipole, 594
Dipole moment, 594, 999
Disintegration, 1054
Disintegration constant, 1054
Displacement, 5, 66-8, 370, 381
displacement current, 633, 638, 574
displacement ratio, 261
displacement-time curve, 65
displacement law-Wien's, 1008
Distance, 12, 16, 56, 71, 131
average, 488, 493
nearest approach of, 926, 997
Doppler effect, 832, 840, 841, 842, 1012
Dot product, 324
Double slit, 892
Dynamics, 96-218

Earth's rotation, 341
Earth satellite, 147
Echo, 826
Echo-sonar, 868
Efficiency, 261, 289-295, 529-38, 548, 657, 774-6, 789, 790, 795
carnot engine, 530
heat engine, 533
thermal, 530
Effort, 289-92
Eigenfunctions, 1005, 1011
Einstein's mass-energy relation, 955, 1043, 1045, 1046, 1057, 1058, 1060
Einstein postulates, 931
Elastic, 828
Elastic spring, 222
Elasticity, 818
Electric field, 550-660, 719
Electric and magnetic fields, 719
Electric field, definition of, 760
Electric field intensity, 550, 594, 599, 607, 610, 630, 735
Electric field strength, 560
Electron, 625, 960, 961
collision frequency, 916
conduction, 632
drift of, 637
valence, 637
Electron-positron pair, 1049
Electron transition, 922
Electron volt, 262, 616, 619
Electron volt-joule conversion, 760
Electroplating, 634, 635
Electroscope, 1017
Electrostatic, 550-618
Elevator, 125, 127
Elongation, 347

Numbers on this page refer to PROBLEM NUMBERS, not page numbers

Emf, 680, 698, 754, 756, 795
back, 746
counter, 787
definition of, 760
induced, 741, 748-755, 761, 798
self induced, 739
Emission, 1044
Emissivity, 547
Energy, 219-279, 527-536, 780-798, 1042-1061
average, 379, 987
binding, 603, 962, 970, 1042, 1043
conservation of, 234, 315, 327, 377, 473, 479, 773, 1056
electrical, 690, 785, 786
electron, 1038
equipartition, theorem of, 534
Fermi, 959, 975
fractional loss, 308
gravitational, 276, 277
heat, 270, 464, 467, 473, 479, 485, 525
internal energy, 531, 532, 534
kinetic energy, 225-277, 294-336, 946-7, 1044-1060
kinetic and potential, 270, 362, 388
maximum transfer in collision, 310
quantum of, 961
radiated, 546
recoil, 1044
relativistic, 946, 965, 1058, 1060
rest mass, 929, 946, 966, 1056, 1060
rotational, 191, 206, 248, 250
thermal, 548
threshold, 604, 962, 1049
total, 235, 279, 362
zero point, 987, 990
Energy density, 564
Energy dissipated, 561, 698
Energy eigenvalues, 1011
Energy level, 924, 999, 1000, 1002
Energy-mass, 1016
Energy quantization, 974
Energy stored in capacitor, 612, 691
Engine, 294
reversible, 529, 536
heat, 530, 533
Entropy, 523, 524, 525, 526, 536
Equilibrant, 37
Equilibrium, 22-55, 119, 266, 287, 349, 398, 587
Equilibrium of forces, 708
Equilibrium-rotational, 42, 50
Equilibrium-translational, 50
Equipartition, 500
Error, percentage, 655
Euler equations, 344, 345
Exchange picture, 993
Excited state, 984
Expansion, 508
expansion, coefficients of, 449, 455
expansion due to temperature, 445
expansion-linear, 446-457
expansion of air, 509
expansion of gases, 503, 516
expansion-thermal, 448-456
Explosion, 325
External, 326

Fahrenheit, 440, 441
Fahrenheit and Celsius temperature scales, 442
Faraday's law, 736, 748-761
Fermat's principle, 845
Field, 584, 592
Field, induction of, 754
Field intensity, 588
Field strength, 570
Film-thin, 890
Fission, 1031, 1047, 1052
Flow of incompressible fluids in pipes, 436
Fluid flow, 431, 435
Fluid statics, 410
Fluid, viscous, 429
Flux, 750, 752, 754
density, 638, 700, 722, 738
intensity of, 575
luminous, 887, 888
magnetic, 703, 734, 741, 751, 755, 756, 759, 760, 761
magnetic lines of, 700
photon, 992

radiant, 887
Flywheel, 250, 346
Focal length, 829, 846-53, 872-85
Focal point, 829, 846
Force, 22-55, 96-218, 296-343, 408-427, 576-618
average, 269, 318, 320
balancing of components, 27
buoyant, 398, 403, 404, 406, 425, 639
centripetal, 144-5, 158-175, 242-5, 711-720
constant, 361
Coriolis, 196, 216
electric, 627
electromotive, 558, 751, 757, 761
electrostatic, 576, 578, 596-8, 604, 609, 639, 993
electrostatic and gravitation-al, 629
external forces, 39, 265, 324
fictitious, 213, 214, 215
frictional, 46-55, 113, 202, 258, 270, 282, 284, 287, 290
gravitational, 79, 81, 101, 117, 137, 144-51, 264, 389, 593, 597
magnetic, 707, 714, 721-31
magnetomotive force, 732, 734
normal, 202, 258, 268, 282
nuclear, 604, 1019
on a charge, 584
on a wire, 724-5, 729-30, 738
on an electron, 607
on current carrying wires, 723
reaction, 104
restoring, 361, 367, 369
resultant, 99, 112, 131, 173, 577
retarding, 114
variable, 266
viscous retarding force, 639
Force-time diagram, 316
Forces, intermolecular, 498
Forces, vector addition of, 117
Frame of reference:
accelerated, 211, 385
inertial, 162, 218
noninertial, 213, 214, 215
Fraunhofer diffraction, 901, 902, 904
Free-body diagram, 44, 125
Free fall, 56-83, 137, 264, 272
Free fall equation, 211
Freezing, 487
Frequency, 362, 370, 383, 809-35, 890, 956
angular, 362, 370, 379, 381, 807
beat, 839
natural, 379, 990
of oscillation, 365, 375, 382
oscillator, 717
of revolution of an electron, 924
resonance, 778
threshold, 963
vibrational of molecules, 391
wave, 800
Friction, 46-55, 100, 104, 120, 128, 167, 209, 268, 317, 470
coefficient, 52, 100
equilibrium with, 274
kinetic, 54, 55, 121, 123
rolling, 282
sliding, 50, 51, 53, 243, 258, 284
starting, 46
static, 47, 48, 121, 167, 195, 387
static and kinetic friction, 49
Frictionless, 208, 265
Fringes, 891, 897
Fringes-interference, 895
Fundamental, 839
Fundamental note, 815, 817

Galilean transformation, 336, 937, 949
Galvanometer, 660, 670, 671
Gamma-radiation, 1007, 1027, 1044
intensity of, 1027, 1030
Gas, 458, 506, 523
at constant volume, 534
diatomic, 534
electron, 959
equation, 419, 517, 532
expansion, 517
ideal, 493-518, 522, 528, 532, 534

universal constant of, 505
Gas law, 417, 490, 519, 520, 532
Gas molecule, diameter of, 498
Gas thermometer, 521
Gauge pressure, 494, 507, 514
Gauss's law, 554, 555, 559, 563, 567, 571, 574, 575, 613-5
Gaussian surface, 554, 555, 614
Geiger counter, 1015
Generator, 795
Germanium crystal, 962
Glancing angle, 1039
Gradient, potential, 606, 607, 559
Gradient, pressure, 397
Grating formula, 905, 907
Gravitation, 389
gravitation, universal law of, 135, 143, 153, 279
Gravitational attraction, 139, 596, 599, 602
Gravitational fields, 141, 251, 337
Gravitational red shift, 955, 995
Gravity, 149, 272
Gravity, center of, 33
Gyrofrequency, 718
Gyroscope, 346

Half life, 692, 1013, 1014, 1015, 1018, 1032
Half-wave plate, 811
Harmonic, 839
Harmonic, simple, 382
Harmonics, 817
Heat, 254, 461, 471, 478, 532, 534, 536, 647
capacities, 480, 482
condition of, 541
conducted, 537
flow of, 481, 541
latent, 470, 538
law of, 549
quantity of, 523
rate of transfer, 543
Heat of fusion, 473, 474, 475
Heat of melting, 472
Heat of vaporization, 531
Helium, 502, 1050
Helmholtz, 706
Hoist, 293
Hooke's law, 267, 361, 366, 367, 375, 379, 380, 391
Horsepower, 281, 285, 294
Huygen's principle, 891, 903
Hydraulic press, 356, 420, 421
Hydrodynamics, 437
Hydrogen, 597
Hydrogen atom, 583, 712, 924
Hydrogen fuel cell, 794
Hydrogen spectrum, 922
Hydrostatics, 437, 512

Illuminance, 888, 889
Illumination, 886
IMA, 290
Image, 847, 878, 882
distance, 873
real, 876, 881, 885
virtual, 847, 849, 850, 853, 873, 874, 876, 881, 884
Impedance, 747, 764-778
Impulse, 203, 303, 309, 316, 319, 320
Incidence, angle of, 844, 861
Incline, 44, 243, 271, 288
Inclined plane, 246, 289, 290
Incompressible liquid, 433
Induced, 551
Induced electric field, 759
Inductance, 696, 697, 737, 767, 771
Inductance-mutual, 749
Inductance-self, 739, 744, 746
Induction, 756
Induction-electromagnetic, 758
Induction-magnetic, 706, 717, 730, 734-745
Inductor, 765, 768, 770, 771
Inelastic, 309, 321, 332
Inertia, 818
Inertia-rotational, 152, 190, 247, 248, 340
Inertial coefficients, 180
Insulating material, 545
Integral-definite, 74
Integral-line, 760
Intensity, 836, 971, 1029
electric, 556, 565-575, 590, 606, 614, 618, 639
field, 756
luminous, 887, 888, 889

Numbers on this page refer to PROBLEM NUMBERS, not page numbers

magnetic, 733
radiation, 666
Interfere, 901
Interference, 836, 890, 892, 893, 894, 897, 906
constructive, 890, 896
destructive, 890, 896, 898, 900
double slit, 891, 893, 894, 906
pattern, 895, 896
single slit, 903
Interferometer, 897
Irreversible, 529
Isothermal, 509
Isovolumic process, 534

K radiation, 1035
K-alpha line, 1035
K-alpha radiation, 1036
Kelvin degrees, 494
Kelvin temperatures, 504
Kilowatt-hour, 654
Kinematics, 56-95, 102, 107, 113, 128, 148, 240, 377, 621
angular, 73, 172, 192
equations, 71, 75, 95, 142, 206, 630
equations for constant acceleration, 92, 93, 116, 143, 217, 274
rotational, 179, 184
Kinetic theory, 495, 500, 534
Kirchhoff, 784
current law, 674, 678, 686
node equation, 676
voltage law, 674, 686, 696
Kundt's tube, 838

Lattice, 913
Length contraction, 931
Lens, 878, 880, 881, 882, 884, 909
concave, 874, 880, 884
converging, 875, 876, 885
convex, 872, 878, 880
divergent, 884
eye, 879
objective, 879
Lens formula, 882, 883
Lenz's law, 736, 750, 751
Lift, 434
Light, 855
Light, velocity of, 855, 858, 890, 933, 935, 949
Line of action, 50
Line of charge, 565
Linear absorption coefficient, 1029, 1030
Linear differential equation, 696
Linear expansion, 453, 454
Linear expansion, coefficient of, 899, 1039
Linear expansivity, 445
Linear molecules, length of, 925
Lorentz contraction, 928, 937, 951
Lorentz equations, 949
Lorentz transformation, 937, 945, 950, 952
Loudspeaker, 788

MA, 289
Mach number, 827, 842
Magnet, 699
bar, 702
Magnetic field, 701-756
Magnetic field of a long wire, 703
Magnetic flux density, 757
Magnetic lines of force, 723
Magnetic moment, 660, 699, 710
Magnetic pole, 699, 702, 721
Magnification, 853, 873, 876, 877, 878, 881, 883, 885
Magnifying power, 877
Magnitude, 15, 17
Magnitude and phase of the impedance, 777, 779
Magnitude of vectors, 3
Mass, 814, 915, 917, 1051
absorption coefficients, 1029, 1030
atomic, 911, 1016
atomic unit, 917, 923, 1051
center of, 32, 180, 182, 203, 279, 332, 415
density of, 206, 919
distributed, 202
earth, 139
electron, 920
equivalent, 954, 955

Numbers on this page refer to <u>PROBLEM NUMBERS</u>, not page numbers

fractional change in, 923
fractional change in helium, 1050
reduced, 279, 391
relativistic, 930, 943
spectrometer, 640, 714
variable, 333
Mass-energy, 923
Mass-energy conversion, 934, 936, 1023
Mass-energy equivalence, 942
Mass-energy relation, 717, 932, 954, 1047
Maximum, central, 1004, 904
Maxwellian distribution, 496
Mean free path, 492, 493, 508
Mean free time, 493
Mean specific heat capacity, 469
Measurement precision, 989
Mechanical advantage, 291, 421
actual, 291
imaginary, 291
Mechanical equivalent of heat, 462, 463, 484
Melting, 396, 472
Mercury column, 416
Microphone, 788
Microscope, 877
compound, 881
Millikan oil drop experiment, 610, 611, 639
Minimum, 900, 901, 902
Minimum size of planet for retaining oxygen, 499
Mirror, 844, 854
concave, 846, 847, 850, 851, 852, 853
convex, 848
plane, 843
spherical, 829
Mirror formula, 854
Molar heat capacity at constant pressure, 534
Molar specific heat, 534
Molecular weight, 507, 923
Molecules, 490
polar, 999
size of, 488
stable, 391
Moment, 33-45, 130, 168, 195, 204
Moment arms, 28
Moment of inertia, 130, 177-82, 192-210, 232, 250, 341-5
Momentum, 296-343, 432, 964, 988, 1041
angular, 187, 189, 192, 194, 196, 197, 199, 210, 338-343, 344, 346, 373, 924, 926
change in, 303, 319
conservation of, 296-343, 1024, 1044, 1049, 1055, 1058, 1060
linear momentum, 308, 322
photon, 953
total momentum, conservation of, 1007
transverse momentum, 299
Moseley, 1035
equation, 1036
Motion, 57, 269, 338, 382
accelerated, 59
angular simple harmonic, 387
circular, 144, 154, 159, 160, 175, 358
damped harmonic, 386
equation of, 345, 807
free fall, 89
harmonic, 367, 368, 369, 379
in electric field, 622
linear, 64
of charge, 622
orbital, 169
pendulum, 239
periodic, 1000
perpetual, 1017
projectile, 90, 91, 93, 95, 134
rotational, 193, 208, 244, 343
simple harmonic, 360, 361, 370, 377, 378, 381, 384, 385, 1011
translational, 208
uniform circular, 157, 158, 161, 163, 164
Motor, 787
Motor, electric, 785
Motor, starter, 789

Neutron, 988
Neutron-antineutron pair, 1055
Neutron decays, 1021
Neutron, mass of, 1056

Numbers on this page refer to PROBLEM NUMBERS, not page numbers

Newton's laws, 22
Newton's first law, 26, 111, 119
Newton's law of cooling, 539
Newton's law of universal gravitation, 138, 143, 149, 389, 596
Newton's second law, 96-218, 279, 379, 389, 398, 403, 406, 432, 597, 630, 711
analogue of, 196
rigid body analog of, 130, 202, 249
system of variable mass, 132
Newton's third law, 26, 51, 104, 107, 126, 127, 406, 432, 470, 576
Newton's rings, 896, 899
Nitrogen, 335
Nodes, 834, 837-9
Nuclear radius, 1019
Nucleus, 918

Object, 882
Object distance, 873
Objective, 877
Ohm's law, 556, 644-9, 669-81, 767, 776, 784, 792
Ohm's law, magnetic analogue of, 734
Oil drop, 639
Optical center, 878, 880
Optical length, 858
Optical path difference, 898
Orbit, 961
circular, 144, 170, 175
Oscillation, 403
small, 363, 378
Oscillator, harmonic, 365, 375, 383, 388-91, 982
Oscilloscope, 607
Overtones, 839

Parallel-axis theorem, 130, 182, 359
Parallel connection, 651, 674, 677, 694
Parallelogram method, 11
Path difference, 900
Peak value, 779
Pendulum, 241, 368, 369, 457
ballistic, 326, 327, 331
compound, 385
conical, 171
ideal, 372
physical, 359
simple, 239, 364, 371
tension, 376
Performance, coefficient of, 535
Period, 145, 147, 358-78, 383-8
natural, 367
small oscillation, 372
vibration, 361
Permeability, 700, 703, 733, 750, 808
constant of, 740
relative, 733, 734
Permittivity, 618, 808
of free space, 694
relative, 618
Perpendicular-axes theorem, 182
Phase, 766, 897
Phase angle, 769
Phase change, 473, 890, 898, 900
Phase difference, 901, 903
Phase opposition, 777
Phase shift, 768, 772, 836
Photoelectric effect, 963, 973, 976, 977, 978
Photoelectric equation, 1001
Photoelectrons, 973, 978, 1001
Photometer, 889
Photon, 337, 604, 955-7, 964, 974, 976, 983, 992, 995, 1007, 1049
Photoneutron effect, 604
Pions, 1055
Planck's constant, 914, 983, 987, 1008
Planck's radiation law, 1008, 1010
Plane-inclined, 54, 105, 117, 120, 123, 230
Plane grating, 908
Plane-polarized light, 811
Plane wave, 903
Poiseuille's law, 436
Polarity, 648
Polarization, 812
Pole, 699
Polonium, 1033
Position, 89
Positive-ray parabolas, 735
Positron decay, 1022
Potential, 207, 553, 557, 562, 582,

586, 614, 656, 675, 773, 791, 1011
Potential difference, 556, 582, 605, 616, 620, 625, 673, 687, 752
Potential of a sphere, 562
Potential energy, 207-224, 327-9, 391, 578, 595, 955
Coulomb's law, 603
electrostatic, 988, 1019, 1050
gravitational, 222, 243, 260, 972, 326
gravitational and electrostatic, 600
spring's, 243
Power, 273, 280-8, 312, 478, 548, 651, 677, 772, 780-3, 932, 964
Power, average, 796, 798
Power, electrical, 657, 784, 789, 790
Power, mechanical, 281, 287, 789
Power factor, 796
Power of a heater, 483
Poynting vector, 810
Precess, 346
Precision, 981
Pressure, 408-35, 488-516
absolute, 413
air, 510
atmospheric, 416, 519
constant-pressure process, 528
definition of, 395, 511
hydrostatic, 412
partial, 417
Principal axis, 344, 880
Principal focus, 880
Prism, 870, 871, 909
Process, 509
Projectile, 92
Projection, angle of, 91
Proper lifetime, 945
1-MeV proton, 709
Proton-proton fusion cycle, 1061
Pulley, 115, 291
Pulley, small frictionless, 118
Pyknometer, 392
Pythagorean theorem, 91

Q, 380
Q-value, 1057
Quantization, 1000
Quantum, 623, 960
of man-sized or larger objects, 967
of particle motion, 967
Quantum mechanics, 1005
Quantum number, 1009
principal, 924
Quantum statistics, 994

Radiation, 549, 666, 1013-1033
Radiation, electromagnetic, 809
Radiator, ideal, 547

Radio star, 900
Radio telescope, 900
Radio waves, 778
Radioactive, 1017, 1028, 1054
Radioactive material, 1013
Radioactivity, 1013, 1017
Radius of gyration, 133, 181, 191, 248, 249
Radius, turning, 165
Range, 90, 92
Ray diagrams, 844, 846, 872
Rayleigh-Jeans law, 1010
Reactance, 764, 765, 767, 768, 769, 771, 777, 779
Reactance, capacitive, 763
Reactance, inductive, 737, 747
Reaction:
chemical, 323
fusion, 1048
nuclear, 1026, 1045
nuclear inelastic, 1058
thermonuclear, 936
Reactor, nuclear, 1052
Recoil, 304, 313, 330
Reference, accelerated, 129
Reflection, 843-854
angle of, 844
law of, 845, 870
specular, 845
total internal, 859
Refraction, 855-869
angle of, 861, 864, 870
Refractive index, 855-7, 859, 862-3, 865, 867, 869, 871, 896, 898

Numbers on this page refer to PROBLEM NUMBERS, not page numbers

Refracting surface, spherical, 866
Relative humidity, 520
Relativistic, 631, 928-955
- equation for relative velocity, 941
- expression for the kinetic energy, 947
- mechanics, 949
- particle, 938
- velocity addition, 940
- velocity transformation, 948, 950

Relativity, 930, 935, 939, 955, 966, 1004
- Galilean, 217
- special, 929, 931, 937, 940, 943, 945

Relaxation time, 632
Reluctance, 732, 734
Resistance, 641-686, 696, 767, 771
- coefficient of, 665
- equivalent, 676, 681, 684, 686
- external, 674
- internal, 648, 674
- parallel, 676
- series, 675

Resistivity, 641-686
Resistor, see Resistance
Resistor, shunt, 670
Resolution, angular, 895
Resonance, 777, 837
Rest mass, 942
Rest mass of photon, 993
Resultant, 11, 15, 19, 37
Right hand rule, 703, 727, 736
Rocket, 333
Rolling, pure, 203
Rolls, 199, 208, 232
Rolling without slipping, 201, 204, 209
Root mean square (RMS), 776, 779, 796, 798, 762
- speed, 496

Rotation, 184, 209, 210
- dynamics, 204
- instantaneous, 201
- period of, 145, 146

Rowland ring, 732, 733
Rutherford scattering, 927
Rydberg constant, 1009

Satellite, 144
Scalar product, 3
Schroedinger equation, 979, 1005
Screw jack, 261
Separation of variables, 1011
Series, 677, 767
Series, Balmer, 922
Series connection, 651, 674
Shear modulus, 351
Sines, law of, 23
Slipping, 195, 202, 203, 205, 207, 208
Slit-thin, 901
Snell's law, 812, 856, 857, 862, 864, 865, 867, 869, 871
Solar constant, 547, 810, 1046
Solar energy, 548
Solenoid, 743, 749, 759
Solenoid switch, 697
Solid angle, 887
Sound, 823, 824, 826, 830, 833
Sound, speed of, 823, 825-8, 841
Source, AC, 768
Specific gravity, 394, 401, 413, 414
Specific heat, 471, 473, 475, 477, 479, 480, 482-4, 486, 501, 522, 525, 526, 539, 654
Specific heat capacity, 466, 478
Spectrum, 905, 907
Spectrum, visible, 908
Speed, 19, 56, 57, 86
- angular, 250
- average, 61, 62, 77, 493
- most probable, 496
- of electromagnetic wave, 808
- relative, 941
- R. m. s., 491, 495
- rotational, 186, 191
- terminal, 621

Sphere, 568
Spring, 124, 220, 222, 362, 365, 375, 378
Spring constant, 220, 267
Statics, 24, 25, 31, 34, 35
Stefan's law, 547, 549, 666
Stoke's law, 429, 639
STP, 508
Strain, 348, 349, 352, 353, 449
Strain-tensile, 347
Stress, 348, 352, 353, 449
- longitudinal, 347

Numbers on this page refer to PROBLEM NUMBERS, not page numbers

shearing, 351
Supercooled water, 487
Superposition, 804
Surface tension, 422-6,
Susceptibility, 618
Symmetrical top, 344
Symmetry, 570
Synchrocyclotron, 943
Synchronization of clocks, 933
Systems, 217
center of mass, 332
closed, 752
rotated coordinate, 3

external, 39, 344, 345
Torricelli's theorem, 430
Torsional constant, 660
Trajectory, 218, 627
Transformer, 773-6
Transistor amplifier, 788
Transition, 924
Transmission cables, 793
Transmission line, 773
Transverse deflecting field, 630
Transverse electric field, 631
Triple point of water, 444
Tunnelling through barrier, 1025
Turntable, 188

Tackle, 45
Tank, 778
Telescope, 879
Temperature, 419, 440, 441, 444, 448, 459, 466-8, 475, 480, 494, 507, 537, 548
absolute, 504, 505
coefficient of resistance, 663, 685
dependence of resistance, 664
of sun's surface, 547
Tension, 24-6, 38, 115, 118, 120, 125, 157, 244, 817, 818, 820
string, 813, 814, 816
Thermal conductivity, coefficient of, 537
Thermal expansion, coefficient of, 448
Thermodynamic isobaric process, 534
Thermodynamics, first law of, 534
Thermodynamics, second law of, 531
Thermometer, 444
Thermometric property, 521
Thomson's apparatus, 735
J. J. Thomson's experiment, 719
Thrust, 281
Time average, 388
Time constant, 692
Time dilation, 944, 945, 952
Toroid, 744
Torques, 28-45, 184-197, 344-6, 660, 731

Uncertainty, 984, 989
in position, 986
of momentum, 986
Uncertainty principle, 980-90, 993, 996
Uniform, 57
Uranium, 1031, 1033
Uranium-238, 1032
Uranium nuclei, 1032

Van der waals equation of state, 498
Vaporization, 483
Variation of mass with velocity, 939
Vector, 1, 3, 13, 15, 16, 17, 18, 19
displacement, 7, 10
resultant, 7
unit, 3
Vector addition, 1, 2, 8, 9, 23, 768, 769, 772
Vector diagram, 85
Vector product, 3
Vector subtraction, 12
Velocities, addition of, 14, 20, 21, 84-6, 940
Velocities, group, 968
Velocity, 13-21, 56-95, 225-251, 296-343
angular, 144, 154-6, 172, 184, 192, 195, 198, 200, 203, 205, 206, 208, 218, 248, 345, 358
average, 59, 65, 68, 82, 83,

490, 987
change in, 69
drift, 636, 637
escape, 151, 251, 499
exhaust, 132
in a string, 821
instantaneous, 68, 69
of gas molecules, 499
of sound, 501, 837, 838
of waves, 835
phase, 968
relative, 14, 212
resultant, 17, 18
square of average, 497
terminal, 639, 429, 114
Velocity-time curve, 66, 77
Venturi meter, 437
Vibrations, longitudinal, 815
Vibrations, simple harmonic, 811
Virial theorem, 277
Viscosity, 436, 639
Viscous medium, 114
Voltage, 560, 643, 645, 777
instantaneous, 766, 779
terminal, 674
Voltmeter, 670, 671, 679, 683, 776, 779, 796
Voltmeter, AC, 779
Volume, 356, 419, 447, 494, 498, 504, 508, 509
Volume expansion, 453
Volumetric expansion coefficient, 447, 451-2, 456

Water-displaced, 402
Wattmeter, 796
Wave equation, 1005
Wave function, 971, 1011
probability, 971
Wave motion, 799, 1037
power and intensity in, 803
Wave number, 807
Wave pulse, 806
Wave speed, 807
Wavelength, 799-842, 890, 956, 960, 967, 1009
cut-off, 1001
radiation, 1000
sound, 833
spread of, 983
Waves, 800, 807, 842
compression, 802, 803
electromagnetic, 810
longitudinal, 819
matter, 1003
oscillating, 801
plane, 810, 903
radio, 809
resultant, 807
simple, 807
sound, 822, 825, 833
spherical, 836
standing, 804, 815, 834, 838
transverse, 805, 819
Waves, in a wire, 819
Weight, 135, 580
apparent, 146
atomic, 912
density, 355
Well-infinite square potential, 979
Wheatstone bridge, 685
Wien's law, 1010
Wilson and Sommerfeld, 1000
Wire, straight, 701
Wires, vibrating, 820
Work, 252-279, 280-295, 534, 536, 553, 561, 600, 604, 625, 647, 650, 752
by a gas, 511, 532
external, 265, 531
internal, 265
total, 528
Work-energy theorem, 191, 274, 329, 331, 366, 437, 625
Work function, 963, 973, 976, 978, 1001
photoelectric, 977
Work input, 289
Work output, 289

X-radiation, 1041
X-ray, 1006, 1034, 1037, 1038, 1040
X-ray diffraction, 1006
X-ray line spectrum, 1035
X-ray tube, 1034
X-rays, diffracted monochromatic, 1039

Young experiment, 891, 895
Young's modulus, 347-9, 352, 353, 382, 407, 449, 802, 815, 819, 828